Merry Christmas,
H. B!

Love,
Susan

1991

Also by Robert M. Parker, Jr.

BURGUNDY: A Comprehensive Guide to the Producers,
Appellations, and Wines

THE WINES OF THE RHÔNE VALLEY
AND PROVENCE

PARKER'S WINE BUYER'S GUIDE

BORDEAUX (First Edition): The Definitive Guide for
the Wines Produced Since 1961

BORDEAUX

A COMPREHENSIVE GUIDE TO THE WINES PRODUCED FROM 1961–1990

ROBERT M. PARKER, JR.

Drawings by
CHRISTOPHER WORMELL

Maps by
JEANYEE WONG

Simon & Schuster
New York London Toronto
Sydney Tokyo Singapore

SIMON & SCHUSTER
Simon & Schuster Building
Rockefeller Center
1230 Avenue of the Americas
New York, New York 10020

Designed by Levavi & Levavi, Inc.
Manufactured in the United States of America

1   3   5   7   9   10   8   6   4   2

Library of Congress Cataloging in Publication Data
Parker, Robert M.
Bordeaux: A comprehensive guide to the wines produced from 1961–1990/by
Robert M. Parker, Jr.; drawings by Christopher Wormell; maps by
Jeanyee Wong.
p.   cm.
Includes bibliographical references and index.
1. Wine and wine making—France—Bordelais.   I. Title.
TP553.P36   1991
641.2'2'094471—dc20
91-23731
CIP
ISBN: 0-671-67460-9

To those wine producers who consider quality,
individuality, character, risk, and sincerity
of action to be of paramount importance.

ACKNOWLEDGMENTS

I would like to acknowledge the following people.

Jean-Michel Arcaute, Jim Arsenault, Anthony Barton, Eva Barton, Bruce Bassin, Ruth Bassin, Jean-Claude Berrouet, Michel Bettane, Bill Blatch, Jean-Eugène Borie, Monique Borie, Gail Bradney, Christopher Cannan, Dick Carretta, Bob Cline, Kerri Conan, Geoffrey Connor, Kristin Costello, Jane Crawford, Jean Delmas, Sherwood Deutsch, Michael Dresser, Stanley Dry, Paul Evans, Bob Fiore, Joel Fleischman, Michael Franklin, Eric Fournier, Jean-Paul Gardère, Sita Garros, Steve Gilbertson, Bernard Godec, Michael Goldstein, Dan Green, Philip Guyonnet-Duperat, Josué Harari, Alexandra Harding, Brenda Hayes, Karen Holden, Tom Hurst, Jean-Paul Jauffret, Nathaniel Johnston, Archie Johnston, Denis Johnston, Ed Jonna, Allen Krasner, Carole Lalli, Bob Lescher, Susan Lescher, Eliot Mackey, Eve Metz, Frank Metz, Jay Miller, Sidney Moore, Kishin Moorjani, Jean-Pierre Moueix, Christian Moueix, Jean-François Moueix, Jean-Jacques Moueix, Mitchell Nathanson, Jill Norman, Les Oenarchs—Bordeaux Chapter, Les Oenarchs—Baltimore Chapter, Daniel Oliveros, Bob Orenstein, Yves Pardes, Maia and Pat Parker, Joan Passman, Georges Pauli, Allen Peacock, Frank Polk, Bruno Prats, Nicholas De Rabaudy, Martha Reddington, Dominique Renard, Dr. Alain Raynaud, Michel Rolland, Dany Rolland, Tom Ryder, Ed Sands, Bob Schindler, Jay Schweitzer, Abdulah Simon, Ernie Singer, Elliott Staren, Daniel Vergely, Jean-Claude Vrinat, Karen Weinstock, Joseph Weinstock, and Jeanyee Wong.

CONTENTS

THE RED AND WHITE WINES OF GRAVES   474

POMEROL   557

1: USING THIS BOOK

There can be no question that the romance, if not downright mysticism, of opening a bottle of Bordeaux from a famous château has a grip and allure that are hard to resist. Writers for years have written glowing accounts of Bordeaux wines, sometimes giving them more respect and exalted status than they have deserved. How often has that fine bottle of Bordeaux from what was allegedly an excellent vintage turned out to be diluted, barely palatable, or even repugnant? How often has a wine from a famous château let you and your friends down when tasted? On the other hand, how often has a vintage written off by the critics provided some of your most enjoyable bottles of Bordeaux? And how often have you tasted a great Bordeaux wine, only to learn that the name of the château is uncelebrated?

This book is about just such matters. It is a wine consumer's guide to Bordeaux. Who is making Bordeaux's best and worst wines? What has a

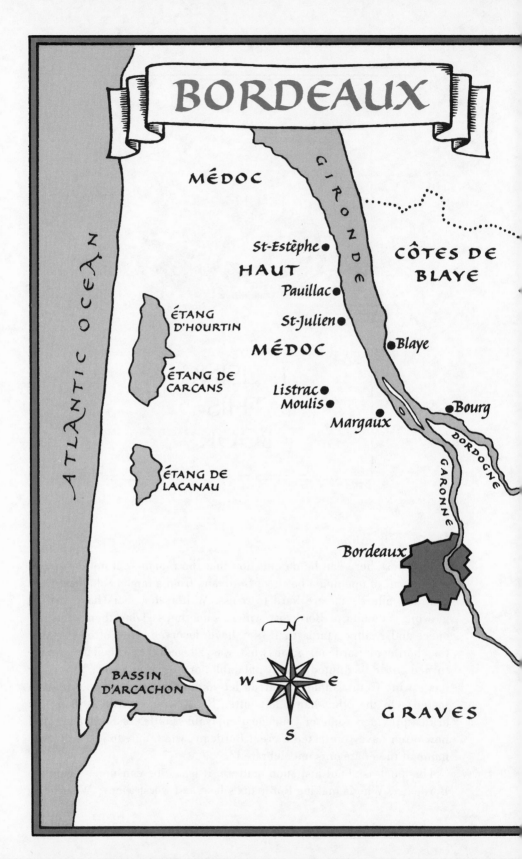

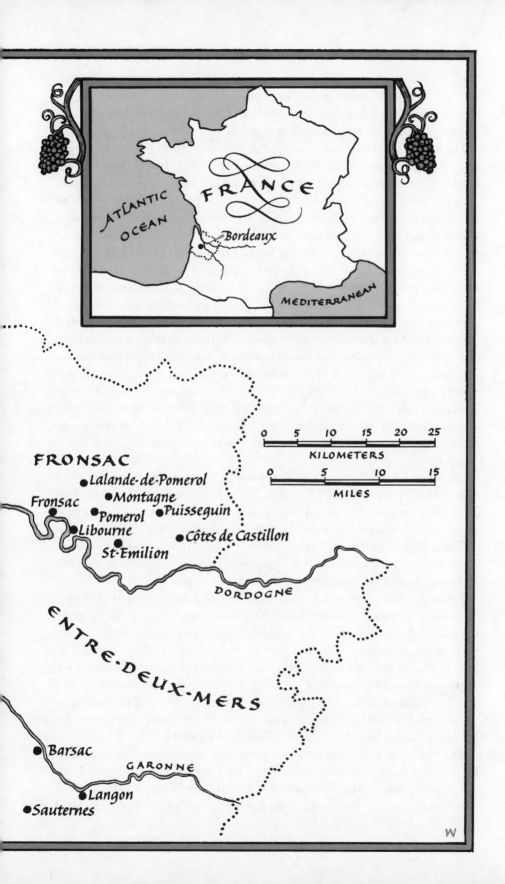

ATLANTIC
OCEAN

FRANCE

Bordeaux

MEDITERRANEAN

FRONSAC

Lalande-de-Pomerol

Montagne

Fronsac

Pomerol

Puisseguin

Libourne

Côtes de Castillon

St-Emilion

DORDOGNE

ENTRE-DEUX-MERS

Barsac

GARONNE

Langon

Sauternes

0   5   10   15   20   25
KILOMETERS

0   5   10   15
MILES

W

specific château's track record been over the last 20–30 years? Which châteaux are overrated and overpriced and, of course, which are underrated and underpriced? These issues are discussed in detail.

The evaluations that are contained in this work are the result of extensive tastings conducted in Bordeaux and in America. I have been visiting Bordeaux every year since 1970, and since 1978 I have gone to Bordeaux as a professional at least twice a year to conduct barrel tastings of the young wines, as well as to do comparative tastings of different wines and vintages that have been bottled and released for sale. Since 1970, I have tasted most of the wines in the top years a half dozen or more times.

It is patently unfair to an estate to issue a final judgment about a wine after only tasting it one time. Consequently, when I do tastings of young Bordeaux, I try to taste them as many times as possible to get a clear, concise picture of the wine's quality and potential. I have often equated the tasting of an infant, unbottled wine with that of taking a photograph of a long-distance runner at the beginning of a race. One look or tasting of such a wine is only a split-second glimpse of an object that is constantly changing and moving. To effectively evaluate the performance and quality in a given vintage, one must look at the wine time after time during its 16–24 month prebottling evolution, and then evaluate it numerous times after bottling to see if the quality or expected potential is still present.

Obviously, some wines as well as general vintages are much easier to assess than others. The 1978, 1982, 1985, 1986, and 1989 Bordeaux all displayed various degrees of excellence at the top estates when first tasted in late March following the vintage. However, my first look at the 1979s in March 1980, and 1981s in March 1982, offered fewer clues as to what these wines were likely to become. Three months later, in June 1980 and June 1982, respectively, the direction and quality level of the 1979s and 1981s were much more apparent and easy to chart. For certain, tasting young wine requires total concentration and an extreme dedication to tasting the wine as many times as possible in its youth, both at the individual châteaux and in comparative tastings against its peers. This is the only valid method by which to obtain an accurate look at the quality and potential of the wine. For this reason, I visit Bordeaux at least twice a year, spending over a month in the region each year visiting all the major châteaux in all of the principal appellations of the Médoc, Graves, Sauternes, St.-Emilion, and Pomerol.

The châteaux visits and interviews with the winemakers are extremely important in accumulating the critical data about the growing season, the harvest dates, and vinification of the château's wines. Most of the winemakers at the Bordeaux châteaux are remarkably straightforward and honest in their answers, whereas owners will go to great lengths to glorify the wine they have produced.

In addition to doing extensive visits to the specific Bordeaux châteaux in all appellations of Bordeaux in good, poor, and great vintages, I insist on comparative tastings of cask samples of these new vintages. For these tastings I call many of Bordeaux's leading *négociants* to set up what most consumers would call massive comparative day-long tastings of 60–100 wines. In groups of 10–15 wines at a time, an entire vintage, from major classified growths to minor Crus Bourgeois, can be reviewed several times over a course of two weeks of extensive tastings. Such tastings corroborate or refute the quality I have found to exist when I have visited the specific château. Because I do these types of broad, all-inclusive tastings at least three times before the young Bordeaux wine is bottled, I am able to obtain numerous looks at the infant wine at 6, 9, and 18 months of age, which usually give a very clear picture of the wines' quality.

Despite the fact that young Bordeaux wines are constantly changing during their evolution and aging process in the barrel, the great wines of a given vintage are usually apparent. It has also been my experience that some wines that ultimately turn out to be good or very good may be unimpressive or just dumb when tasted in their youth from the cask. But the true superstars of a great vintage are sensational, whether they are 6 months or 20 months old.

When I taste young Bordeaux from the cask, I prefer to judge the wine after the final blend or *assemblage* has been completed. At this stage, the new wine has had only negligible aging in oak casks. For me, it is essential to look at a wine at this infant stage (normally in late March and early April following the vintage) because most wines can be judged without the influence of oak, which can mask fruit and impart additional tannin and aromas to the wine. What one sees at this stage is a naked wine that can be evaluated on the basis of its richness and ripeness of fruit, depth, concentration, body, acidity, and natural tannin content, unobscured by evidence of oak aging.

The most important component I look for in a young Bordeaux is fruit. Great vintages, characterized by ample amounts of sunshine and warmth, result in grapes that are fully mature, and that produce rich, ripe, deeply fruity wines. If the fruit is missing, or unripe and green, the wine can never be great. In contrast, grapes that are allowed to stay on the vine too long in hot, humid weather become overripe and taste pruny and sometimes raisiny, and are also deficient in acidity. They too have little future. Recent vintages that, in their youth, throughout all appellations of Bordeaux, have been marked by the greatest ripeness, richness, and purity of fruit are 1982, 1985, 1986, and 1989, all high-quality vintages for Bordeaux. Vintages that exhibited the least fruit and an annoying vegetal character have been 1974, 1977, and 1984, poor to mediocre vintages.

In early summer or fall following the vintage, I return to Bordeaux to get another extensive look at the wines. At this time the wines have settled down completely, but are also marked by the scent of new oak barrels. The intense grapey character of their youth has begun to peel away, as the wines have now had at least 3–4 months of cask aging. If extensive tastings in March or April give a clear overall view of the vintage's level of quality, comprehensive tastings in June and again the second March following the vintage are almost always conclusive evidence of where the vintage stands in relation to other Bordeaux vintages, and how specific wines relate in quality to each other.

With regard to vintages of Bordeaux in the bottle, I prefer to taste these wines in what is called a "blind tasting." A blind tasting can be either "single blind" or "double blind." This does not mean one is actually blindfolded and served the wines, but rather that in a single-blind tasting, the taster knows the wines are from Bordeaux, but does not know the identities of the châteaux or the vintages. In a double-blind tasting, the taster knows nothing other than that several wines from anywhere in the world, in any order, from any vintage, are about to be served.

For bottled Bordeaux, I prefer to conduct all my Bordeaux tastings under single-blind conditions. I do not know the identity of the wine, but since I prefer to taste in peer groups, I always taste wines from the same vintage. Additionally, I never mix Bordeaux with non-Bordeaux wines, simply because whether it be California or Australia Cabernet Sauvignons, the wines are distinctly different, and while comparative tastings of Bordeaux versus California may be fun and make interesting reading, the results are never very reliable or especially meaningful to the wine consumer who desires the most accurate information. Remember that whether one employs a 100-point rating system or a 20-point rating system the objectives and aims of professional wine evaluations are the same—to assess the quality of the wine vis-à-vis its peers and to determine its relative value and importance in the international commercial world of wine.

When evaluating wines professionally, it goes without saying that proper glasses and the correct serving temperature of the wine must be prerequisites to any objective and meaningful tasting. The best generally available glass for critical tasting is that approved by the International Standards Organization. Called the ISO glass, it is tulip shaped and has been designed specifically for tasting. As for the temperature, 60–65 degrees Fahrenheit is best for evaluating both red and white wines. Too warm a temperature and the bouquet becomes diffuse and the taste flat. Too cold a temperature and there is no discernible bouquet and the flavors are completely locked in by the overly chilling effect on the wine.

When I examine a wine critically, there is both a visual and physical examination. Against a white background, the wine is first given a visual exam for brilliance, richness, and intensity of color. A young Bordeaux wine that is light in color, hazy or cloudy (or both) has serious problems. For Bordeaux red wines, color is extremely important. Virtually all the great Bordeaux vintages have shared a very deep, rich, dark ruby color when young, whereas the poorer vintages often have weaker, less rich-looking colors because of poor weather and rain. Certainly, in 1961, 1970, 1982, 1983, 1985, 1986, and 1989 the general color of the red wines of Bordeaux has been very dark. In 1978 and 1975, it was dark but generally not so deep in color as the aforementioned vintages. In 1973, 1974, 1980, and 1984 the color was rather light.

In looking at an older wine, the rim of the wine next to the glass should be examined for amber, orange, rust, and brown colors. These are signs of maturity and are normal. When they appear in a good vintage of a wine under 6 or 7 years old something is awry. For example, young wines that have been sloppily made and exposed to unclean barrels or air will mature at an accelerated rate and take on the look of old wines when in fact they are still relatively young by Bordeaux standards.

In addition to looking at the color of the wines, I examine the "legs" of the wine. The legs are the tears or residue of the wine that run down the inside of the glass. Rich Bordeaux vintages tend to have "good legs" because the grapes are rich in glycerol and alcohol, giving the wine a viscosity that causes this "tearing" effect. Examples of Bordeaux vintages that produced wines with good to excellent legs would be 1989, 1986, 1985, 1983, 1982, 1970, and 1961.

After the visual examination is completed, the actual physical examination of the wine takes place. The physical exam is composed of two parts, the wine's smell, which depends on the olfactory sense, and the wine's taste, the gustatory sense, which is tested on the palate. After swirling a wine, the nose must be placed into the glass (not the wine) to smell the aromas that issue from the wine. This is an extremely critical step because the aroma and odor of the wine will tell the examiner the ripeness and richness of the underlying fruit, the state of maturity, and whether there is anything unclean or suspicious about the wine. The smell of a wine, young or old, will tell a great deal about the wine's quality, and no responsible professional taster understates the significance of a wine's odors and aromas, often called the nose or bouquet.

Emile Peynaud, in his classic book on wine tasting, *Le Goût du Vin* (Bordas, 1983), states that there are nine principal categories of wine aromas. They are:

1. animal odors: smells of game, beef, venison
2. balsamic odors: smells of pine trees, resin, vanilla
3. woody odors: smells of new wood of oak barrels
4. chemical odors: smells of acetone, mercaptan, yeasts, hydrogen sulfide, acidity, and fermentation
5. spicy odors: smells of pepper, cloves, cinnamon, nutmeg, ginger, truffles, anise, mint
6. empyreumatic odors: smells of *crème brûlée*, smoke, toast, leather, coffee
7. floral odors: smells of violets, roses, lilacs, jasmine
8. fruity odors: smells of blackcurrants, raspberries, cherries, plums, apricots, peaches, figs
9. vegetal odors: smells of herbs, tea, mushrooms, vegetables

The presence or absence of some or all of these aromas, their intensity, their complexity, their persistence, all serve to create the bouquet or nose of a wine that can be said to be distinguished, complete, and interesting, or flawed and simple.

Once the wine's aroma or bouquet has been examined thoroughly, the wine is tasted, sloshed, or chewed around on the palate while also inhaled to release the wine's aromas. The weight, richness, depth, balance, and length of a wine are apparent from the tactile impression the wine leaves on the palate. Sweetness is experienced on the tip of the tongue, saltiness just behind the tongue's tip, acidity on the sides, and bitterness at the back. Most professional tasters will spit the wine out, although some wine is swallowed in the process.

The finish or length of a wine, its ability to give off aromas and flavors even though it is no longer on the palate, is the major difference between a good young wine and a great young wine. When the flavor and the aroma of the wine seem to last and last on the palate, it is usually a great, rich wine that has just been tasted. The great wines and great vintages are always characterized by a purity, opulence, richness, depth, and ripeness of the fruit from which the wines are made. When the wines have both sufficient tannin and acidity, the balance is struck. It is these qualities that separate many a great 1989, 1986, 1983, 1982, 1970, or 1961 Bordeaux from a good 1981, 1978, 1975, or 1966 Bordeaux.

TASTING NOTES AND RATINGS

All of my tastings were done in peer-group, single-blind conditions when possible (meaning that the same type of wines were tasted against each other and the producers' names were not known), in my tasting room, in the cellars of the producers, or in the offices of major Bordeaux *négociants*. The ratings reflect an independent, critical look at the wines. Neither price nor the reputation of the producer/grower affect the rating in any manner. I spend three months of every year tasting in vineyards. During the other nine months of the year, six and sometimes seven-day work weeks are devoted solely to tasting and writing. I do not participate in wine judgings or trade tastings for many reasons, but principal among these are the following: (1) I prefer to taste from an entire bottle of wine, (2) I find it essential to have properly sized and cleaned professional tasting glasses, (3) the temperature of the wine must be correct, and (4) I alone will determine the time allocated to the number of wines to be critiqued.

THE RATING SYSTEM
96–100   Extraordinary
90–95   Outstanding
80–89   Above average to very good
70–79   Average
50–69   Below average to poor

The numerical rating given is a guide to what I think of the wine vis-à-vis its peer group. Certainly, wines rated above 85 are very good to excellent, and any wine rated 90 or above will be outstanding for its particular type. While some have suggested that scoring is not well suited to a beverage that has been romantically extolled for centuries, wine is similar to other consumer products. There are specific standards of quality that full-time wine professionals recognize, and there are benchmark wines against which all others can be judged. I know of no one with three or four different glasses of wine in front of him or her, regardless of how good or bad the wines might be, who cannot say "I prefer this one to that one." Scoring wines is simply taking a professional's opinion and applying some sort of numerical system to it on a consistent basis. Scoring permits rapid communication of information to expert and novice alike.

The rating system I employ in my wine journal, *The Wine Advocate*, is the one I have utilized in this book. It is a 50–100 point scale, the most repugnant of all wines meriting 50 since that is the starting point of the scale, and the most glorious gustatory experience commanding 100. I prefer my system to the once widely quoted 20-point scale called the Davis Scale—of the University of California at Davis—because it permits much more flexibility in scoring. It is also easier to understand because the numbers correspond to the American grading system, and avoid the compression of scores from which the Davis Scale suffers. It is not without problems, however, because readers will often wonder what the difference is between an 86 and 87, both very good wines. The only answer I can give is a simple one: when tasted side by side, I thought the 87-point wine slightly better than the 86-point wine.

The score given for a specific wine reflects the quality of the wine at its best. As I mentioned earlier, I often tell people that evaluating a wine and assigning a score to a beverage that will change and evolve in many cases for up to 10 or more years is analagous to taking a photograph of a marathon runner. Much can be ascertained but like a picture of a moving object, the wine will also evolve and change. I retry wines from obviously badly corked or defective bottles, since a wine from such a single bad bottle does not indicate an entirely spoiled batch. Many of the wines reviewed here I have tasted many times, and the score represents a cumulative average of the wine's performance in tastings to date. Scores do not tell the entire story about a wine. The written commentary that accompanies the ratings is often a better source of information regarding the wine's style and personality, the relative quality level vis-à-vis its peers, the relative value, and its aging potential than any score could ever indicate.

Here then is a general guide to interpreting the numerical ratings:

A score of 90–100 is equivalent to an A and is given only for an outstanding or special effort. Wines in this category are the very best produced for their type and, like a three-star Michelin restaurant, merit the trouble to find and try. There is a big difference between a 90 and a 99, but both are top marks. As you will note throughout the text, there are few wines that actually make it into this top category simply because there just are not many truly great wines.

A score of 80–89 is equivalent to a B in school and such a wine, particularly in the 85–89 range, is very, very good; many of the wines that fall into this range often are great values as well. I would not hesitate to have any of these wines in my own personal collection.

A score of 70–79 represents a C, or an average mark, but obviously 79 is a much more desirable score than 70. Wines that receive scores between 75 and 79 are generally pleasant, straightforward wines that simply lack complexity, character, or depth. If inexpensive, they may be ideal for uncritical quaffing. Below 70 is a D or an F, depending on where you went to school; for wine, too, it is a sign of an imbalanced, flawed, or terribly dull or diluted wine that will be of little interest to the knowledgeable wine consumer.

In terms of awarding points, my scoring system gives every wine a base of 50 points. The wine's general color and appearance merit up to 5 points. Since most wines today are well made, thanks to modern technology and the increased use of professional oenologists, they tend to receive at least 4, often 5 points. The aroma and bouquet merit up to 15 points, depending on the intensity level and extract of the aroma and bouquet as well as the cleanliness of the wine. The flavor and finish merit up to 20 points, and again, intensity of flavor, balance, cleanliness, and depth and length on the palate are all important considerations when giving out points. Finally, the overall quality level or potential for further evolution and improvement—aging—merits up to 10 points.

Scores are important to let the reader gauge a professional critic's overall qualitative placement of a wine vis-à-vis its peers. However, it is also vital to consider the description of the wine's style, personality, and potential. No scoring system is perfectly objective, but a system that provides for flexibility in scores, if applied without prejudice, can quantify different levels of wine quality and provide the reader with a professional's judgment. However, there can never be any substitute for your own palate nor any better education than tasting the wine yourself.

ANTICIPATED MATURITY— WHAT IS IT?

Because of the number of inquiries I receive regarding when a given Bordeaux wine has reached a point in its evolution that it is said to be ready to drink, I have provided an estimated range of years over which the châteaux's wines should be consumed for the specific vintage. I call this time frame the "anticipated maturity." Before one takes my suggestions too literally, let me share with you the following points.

1. If you like the way a wine tastes when young, do not hesitate to enjoy it in spite of what the guidelines may say. There can never be any substitute for your own palate.
2. I have had to make several assumptions, the primary ones being that the wine was purchased in a healthy state, and you are cellaring the wine in a cool, humid, odor- and vibration-free environment that does not exceed 65 degrees Fahrenheit in the summer.
3. The estimates are an educated guess based on how the wine normally ages, its quality, balance, and the general depth of the vintage in question.
4. The estimates are conservative. I have assumed a maturity based on my own palate, which tends to prefer a wine more fresh and exuberant over one that has begun to fade, but one that may still be quite delicious and complex.

Consequently, if you have cool, ideal cellars, the beginning year in the estimated range of maturity may err in favor of drinking the wine on the young side. I presume most readers would prefer, given a choice, to open a bottle too early rather than too late. This philosophy has governed my projected maturity period for each wine.

EXAMPLES

Now.　Totally mature; immediate drinking is suggested within several years of the "last tasted" date.

Now–may be in decline.　Based on the age of the wine and knowledge of the château and the specific vintage, this designation is utilized where a fully mature wine discussed in the 1985 edition of *Bordeaux* has not been recently retasted and is believed to have passed its apogee and begun its decline.

Now–probably in serious decline.　Based on the age of the wine and knowledge of the château and the specific vintage, this designation is utilized when a wine in the 1985 edition of *Bordeaux* was at the end of its plateau of maturity and, while not recently retasted, is believed to be well past its plateau of maturity.

Now–1997.　The wine has entered its plateau of maturity where it should be expected to remain until 1997, at which time it may begin to slowly decline. The "now" dates from the time of the last tasted note.

1992–2010.　This is the estimated range of years during which I believe the wine will be in its plateau period—the years over which it will be at its best for drinking. Please keep in mind that Bordeaux wines from top vintages tend to decline slowly (just the opposite of Burgundy) and that a wine from an excellent vintage may take another 10–15 years to lose its fruit and freshness after the last year in the stated plateau period.

ABOUT THE BOOK'S ORGANIZATION

This book has been divided into the major geographical regions of Bordeaux. Within each region, the famous châteaux and many minor châteaux deserving recognition are reviewed. The emphasis, for obvious reasons, is on the major Bordeaux estates that are widely available and highly promoted in this country. The quality of these wines over the period 1961–1989 is examined closely. For lesser-known châteaux, the selection process has been based on two factors, quality and recognition. High-quality, lesser-known estates are reviewed, as well as those estates that have gotten distribution into the export markets, regardless of their quality. I have made every effort over the last 20 years to discover and learn about the underpublicized châteaux in Bordeaux. Because older vintages of these wines are virtually impossible to find, plus the fact that the majority of the Crus Bourgeois wines must be drunk within 5–7 years of the vintage, the focus for most of these lesser-known Crus Bourgeois wines is on what they have accomplished in the period 1982–1990. I feel the châteaux that are reviewed are the best of these lesser-known estates, but to err is human, and it would be foolish for both you and me to believe that there is not some little estate making exquisite wine that I have omitted altogether.

At the beginning of each chapter on the Bordeaux appellations is my classification of the wines from that appellation. This analysis is based on their overall quality vis-à-vis each other. This is not a book that will shroud quality differences behind skillfully worded euphemisms. Within each appellation the châteaux are reviewed in alphabetical order. For those who love lists, my overall classification of the top 153 wine-producing estates of Bordeaux may be found beginning on page 116.

With respect to the specific vintages covered, tasting emphasis has generally been given to only the good vintages. Vintages such as 1977, 1972, 1968, 1965, and 1963 are generally not reviewed because they were very poor years, and few Bordeaux châteaux made acceptable quality wine in those years. Furthermore, such vintages are not commercially available. As for the actual tasting notes, the "anticipated maturity" refers to the time period at which I believe the wine will be at its apogee. This is the time period during which the wine will be fully mature and should ideally be drunk. These estimates as to anticipated maturity are conservative and are based upon the assumption that the wine has been purchased in a sound, healthy condition, and has been kept in a vibration-free, dark, odor-free, relatively cool (below 65 degrees Fahrenheit) storage area. For the wine-tasting terms I employ, and for the proper methods of cellaring Bordeaux wines, see Chapter 7, "A User's Guide to Bordeaux" and Chapter 9, "A Glossary of Wine Terms."

ONE FURTHER CAVEAT

When a book such as this is revised, difficult decisions must be made regarding the retention of tasting notes on wines that have not been reevaluated in the seven years that have lapsed since I wrote the first edition. As readers will discover, most of the best wines in top vintages have been retasted since the first edition and the changes in text and ratings, where warranted, have been made. Because a serious tasting note is the professional's photograph of a wine during its life, and moreover, since all the tasting notes in this book are dated, I have opted to leave those original tasting critiques in the book as part of the history of that property's record of wine quality.

2: SOME REFLECTIONS SINCE THE FIRST EDITION OF *BORDEAUX*

THE DECADE OF THE CENTURY

"The decade of the century." I first saw that expression in the column of the *Baltimore Sun*'s fine wine critic, Michael Dresser. He wrote, "the decade of the eighties had produced more great wines in Bordeaux than in all of the prior seven decades combined." At first that statement astonished me, but upon reflection, I have come to realize that it was accurate. A few weeks later, in fact, I noticed that the cover page of France's best wine publication, *La Revue du Vin de France,* promoted an article called "La Décennie du Siècle," or The Decade of the Century.

Wine consumers have been so bombarded from both the trade and the wine press with copious quantities of information about the extraordinary quality of the vintages of the decade that it has become easy to take such unprecedented success for granted. Yet Bordeaux is truly enjoying a golden age that appears to be unparalleled in its history. During the most recent decade, the eighties, 1982 may be the vintage of reference, but 1989 is not far behind, and 1985 and 1986 have numerous supporters. There are even strong arguments for specific 1983s. The decade produced no truly disappointing years. Both 1980 and 1984 are perceived as bad years, but in reality, they are simply acceptable rather than dazzling vintages. Additionally, 1987 suffers from a poor reputation. However, one taste of the best wines reveals that this is not only an adequate vintage, but a tasty, surprisingly useful one that has been unjustly maligned.

When has Bordeaux ever had such success in the past? In the seventies, 1972, 1974, and 1977 were terrible years, and even the two years that were believed to be great, 1970 and 1975, have proven notoriously inconsistent despite some noteworthy successes. The decade of the sixties was a difficult period for the Bordelais. Nearly half of that decade's vintages—1963, 1965, 1968, and 1969—produced many frightfully undrinkable wines.

More ancient decades also cannot compare favorably with the extraordinary success of the eighties. In the fifties, 1951, 1954, and 1956 rank among the worst vintages Bordeaux has ever endured. Of course many know of the great success Bordeaux enjoyed in 1945, 1947, 1949, and even 1948, but even allowing for that extraordinary quartet, what about the rest of the decade? It is largely remembered only for a devastating war. It was nearby Cognac and Armagnac, not Bordeaux that enjoyed good vintages in 1943 and 1944. The decade of the thirties is understandably scorned by Bordeaux enthusiasts. No great vintage emerged from this decade. Yes, 1934 and 1937 had a handful of early supporters, but time in the bottle proved unkind to those two years. Nothing truly dazzling emerged from what must be the most dismal decade for quality red Bordeaux wines this century.

If there is a decade that may have rivaled the eighties as a legitimate "decade of the century," it is the "roaring twenties." Although most of the wines are now passé—having gone to their graves many years ago—Bordeaux old-timers speak with respect and adulation about the opulent, gloriously rich, fragrant 1921s and the even more supple, round, generously endowed 1929s. The latter vintage still enjoys a mystique and magical quality unequaled by any modern-day year. Was it the real "vintage of the century" as so many octogenarian wine connoisseurs claim?

In their prime, between the mid-thirties and mid-sixties, the 1929s were prized for their silky textures, opulence of superripe fruit, and heady, alcoholic, velvety finishes.

The only contemporary vintage comparable to 1929 may be 1982, and to a lesser extent, 1989. Most of the 1929s began their decline a good 20–25 years ago. From the twenties, only the 1928s remain drinkable today. Too tannic and massive to be enjoyed in their first 30 or 40 years of life, the 1928s blossomed in the seventies and are still magnificent wines today. The years 1924 and 1926 were both good, but a tasting held in Bordeaux in 1991 of all the first-growths from those two vintages resulted in point scores primarily in the 60s and 70s. These wines came from cold private Bordeaux cellars.

The second decade of the 1900s fared poorly, as did the first. However, the century started off with 1900, a vintage that in many ways (if you believe the ever-decreasing numbers of octogenarians in Bordeaux) most closely resembled the 1929 and 1982 vintages.

Bordeaux has just enjoyed its most remarkable decade of this century and the results are private cellars that are full of high-quality wine. Those wine enthusiasts who have followed the eighties closely and who have had the discretionary income to afford the best wines are set for life.

SOME FACES THAT HAVE INFLUENCED AND CHANGED BORDEAUX FOR THE BETTER

A number of individuals have stood out in the eighties for the profound quality of the wines they make, for the high standards they have encouraged, and for the positive influence they have had on their peers.

On Bordeaux's right bank, particularly in the appellations of Pomerol, St.-Emilion, Fronsac, and Canon-Fronsac, the Libourne oenologist Michel Rolland is single-handedly responsible for the renaissance in quality at so many estates. Rolland is also the proprietor of Bon Pasteur in Pomerol and Fontenil in Fronsac, as well as a handful of other small estates in Lalande-de-Pomerol and St.-Emilion. His philosophy is as unwavering as it is clear. He believes in very late harvesting and extended macerations. Those who have followed him have witnessed the resurrection of their moribund estates to quality levels that challenge the best wines in their appellations.

Rolland's philosophy is at odds with the prevailing oenological opinion aimed at producing technically correct wines. He eschews safety and the general lack of risk taking. As he sees it, his mission is to produce wines that either excite or dazzle. Among the oenologists of his region, Rolland alone has led the charge to harvest the grapes as late as possible, risking the fall rains, yet picking fruit with an element of *sur-maturité* that gives the wines a splendid, concentrated character, richer, more complete bouquets, and intense flavors. He has advocated both crop thinning as well as bleeding the tanks of excess juice to increase the wine's concentration in such high-yield years as 1985, 1986, 1989, and 1990.

Moreover, Rolland is the only Bordeaux oenologist who has advised his clients (if they can, and if they are willing to accept the risks involved) to bottle their wines later than normal without any fining or filtration. This runs counter to accepted oenological doctrine that counsels earlier and earlier bottling, as well as filtering wines immediately after malolactic fermentation—so they are showy and tasty for early arriving journalists. These same technocrats adamantly insist that their clients vigorously fine and filter so no deposit will form in the bottle for at least 7–8 years. Rolland has stepped back and said that it is quality that matters the most, not commercial necessity. Bordeaux, in Rolland's opinion, built its reputation on individualistic, high-quality wines, and yet it is this characteristic that so many of today's wines lack. Too many wines are compromised in order to produce a more commercially viable product and Rolland will have none of this. For that reason, he stands as a ray of hope in a region increasingly dominated by commercially oriented, high-tech oenologists.

Rolland is not the only oenologist to have revolutionized winemaking and brought the quality (at least of the estates he represents) to higher and higher levels. The mayor of St.-Julien is a middle-aged, exuberant, handsome gentleman by the name of Georges Pauli. He is also the oenologist and technical director of all the estates of the Domaines Cordier —a prestigious group of châteaux that includes many famous estates, the most renowned of which are Gruaud-Larose, Talbot, Cantemerle, Lafaurie-Peyraguey, and Clos des Jacobins. He has been with the Cordier firm for almost his entire career, and has had sole responsibility for the winemaking since 1978. A great believer in late harvesting and minimal processing (much like Rolland), Pauli has raised the level of all of the Cordier wines to impeccably high standards. Now in 1991, Gruaud-Larose and Talbot routinely produce wines that rival the quality of the first-growths. Cantemerle is producing its most interesting wines since the early fifties, and the famous Sauternes estate of Lafaurie-Peyraguey is now turning out decadently rich wines that rank just below the level of that appellation's superstar, Yquem. Even the lesser-known estates in the Cordier stable have benefitted immensely from the vast talent of Georges Pauli. For that reason, consumers the world over now regard the Cordier wines as having the greatest price/quality ratio of any establishment in Bordeaux.

Another influential oenologist is Denis Dubourdieu, the proprietor of several estates, including Clos Floridene in Graves and Reynon in the Premières Côtes de Bordeaux. His enormous legacy is the dramatic increase in the quality of Bordeaux's dry white wines, which has primarily occurred since the mid-eighties.

Based on the results of his research at the Institute of Oenology in Bordeaux, Denis Dubourdieu began by utilizing new oak barrels to ferment his white wines and promoting his philosophy called *"macération pelliculaire,"* or extended skin contact with the fermenting wines. Dubourdieu realized long ago that the flavor and aromatic complexity of wines came from the grape skin. It was his decision to begin skin contact with the white wines and utilize more new oak that revolutionized the moribund Bordeaux white wine–making industry. Even top Graves estates benefitted immensely from his counsel. It was Dubourdieu who encouraged Château de Fieuzal to develop his methods. The results, beginning in 1985, were a succession of superb white wines. When Dubourdieu's techniques began to be employed at other Graves estates, such as La Tour-Martillac and Carbonnieux, the quality of their wines also soared.

The generic white wines of Bordeaux have never been more enjoyable to drink. Dozens of châteaux that practice the *"la méthode* Dubourdieu" are making tasty, crisp, satisfying and complete dry white wines that generally sell at modest prices. The old days of insipid, tasteless, technically correct but uninteresting dry white wines from Bordeaux have ended. Denis Dubourdieu is the man who profoundly changed white winemaking in this region.

While oenologists such as Rolland, Pauli, and Dubourdieu have set impeccably high standards by breaking away from oenological norms, there are a handful of proprietors of unheralded estates who have, because of their single-minded obsession with quality, proven that the consuming public does consider the wine's quality and character of greater importance than its official pedigree.

Since the early eighties, Bordeaux connoisseurs have been aware of the extraordinary increase in quality of a number of estates that are not part of the famous 1855 classification. The following gentlemen have taken their estates (the names of which were largely unknown a decade ago) to the forefront of quality. In Margaux is Jean-Luc Vonderheyden, the winemaker at Château Monbrison, who is turning out a wine that is vastly superior to many of the appellation's classified growths. In St.-Estèphe it is Henri Duboscq, who runs Château Haut-Marbuzet, with great enthusiasm. In the Haut-Médoc the man is Jean Gautreau, whose passion is producing classic, long-lived red wines from his beloved Château Sociando-Mallet. Along the hillsides outside the village of St.-Emilion there is François Mitjavile, who is fashioning a wine at his Château Le Tertre-Roteboeuf that resembles the old, great vintages of Pétrus. All of these men have proven that superb quality is recognized and rewarded. Their wines are among the most sought after in the world and are often on stricter allocation and are more difficult to find than many more prestigious names.

These gentlemen share many of the same principles that have made oenologists such as Rolland , Pauli, and Dubourdieu so successful. They harvest late, they obtain yields that are often half the size of their more famous neighbors, and finally, they abhor the food-processing mentality of so many estates. The bottom line for Vonderheyden, Duboscq, Gautreau, and Mitjavile is that their wines must not only faithfully express their *terroir* and their vintage of origin, but they must give pleasure.

The conservative, artisanal, minimal-interference winemaking philosophies of those people I have mentioned have nothing in common with another gentleman. Jean-Michel Cazes, proprietor of Château Lynch-Bages in Pauillac and Les-Ormes-de-Pez in St.-Estèphe, as well as the administrator of a number of properties owned by the huge insurance conglomerate, AXA, has already greatly shaped the last half of the decade of the eighties. I predict his influence will impact significantly on many wines produced during the decade of the nineties. These properties include Pichon-Longueville-Baron, Cantenac-Brown, and Petit-Village, to single out the most prominent. What makes Cazes so influential is that he applies nothing less than blatantly commercial principles to the making and marketing of wine. Yet he succeeds in producing irrefutably delicious, even decadent, full-bodied, opulently styled wines that please both the masses and the experienced connoisseur. He has done this by having some of the highest yields at his Médoc properties. However, through scientific winemaking and liberal use of techniques, such as *saigner* (bleeding the tanks) and numerous filtrations designed to sculpture and process the wine to a soft, evolved, drinkable state long before most of its peers, he has garnered accolade after accolade from much of the world's wine press. The results have been soaring sales, with more and more of his Médoc neighbors enviously watching the huge success Jean-Michel Cazes has enjoyed. His critics—and they are numerous—continue to argue that the weakness of all these "winemaking gimmicks and shortcuts" will become increasingly apparent as the "Cazized" wines age. As much as I disagree (intellectually) with the Cazes approach, the wines he produces consistently impress me. Will they hold up? Only time will tell. For now, Jean-Michel Cazes has profoundly changed the style of Bordeaux by breaking away from traditional techniques to produce some of the most compelling wines in Bordeaux.

THE REVOLUTION
OF THE BARREL

There is no doubt that new oak barrels are in fashion, not only in Bordeaux, but throughout France, Western Europe, California, South America, and Australia. The word has gotten out that a cellar full of new oak casks signifies a commitment to quality, success, and wealth. The increased percentage of new oak used by many châteaux (the first-growths routinely use 100%, most other classified growths somewhere between 30–70%) has significantly enhanced the cleanliness and stability of many wines. The old, oxidized, musty, damp-basement aromas from dirty, unsanitary, old barrels are largely a thing of the past, replaced by the seductive, sweet, toasty, vanillin scents of new oak. In years where the wines are low in acid, rich, ripe, and generously endowed, new oak provides much needed support, definition and structure to the wine. This was certainly the case in the superripe, hot, dry years of 1982 and 1989.

But with Bordeaux's remarkable financial success and willingness to invest in enormous quantities of new barrels, there is a danger—the excessive use of new oak. The intrinsic character of both the vintage and the vineyard can be masked by too much of a good thing. It has become à la mode to employ as much new oak as possible, and the forceful, oaky aromas now take the upper hand in many of the less well-endowed Bordeaux wines. I have noticed this lamentable trend not only in lighter-weight years such as 1987, but even in riper, richer years such as 1989 and 1990. I agree that the smell of new oak exclusively is preferable to a musty aroma, but many Bordeaux châteaux do not produce wines that are rich and concentrated enough to stand up to the high percentage of new oak barrels utilized. The results are vulgar wines.

Nevertheless, the use of new oak will continue, and as long as the wines can support a healthy dosage of it, they will benefit immensely from the fact that new oak barrels are much more hygienic than older barrels.

THE PROLIFERATION OF SECOND LABELS

Secondary wines with secondary labels are not a recent development. Léoville-Las Cases first made a second wine (Clos du Marquis) in 1904, and in 1908 Châteaux Margaux produced its first Le Pavillon Rouge du Château Margaux.

Yet a decade ago, about the only second labels most Bordeaux wine enthusiasts encountered were those from Latour (Les Forts de Latour), Margaux (Le Pavillon Rouge du Château Margaux), and perhaps that of Lafite-Rothschild (Moulin-des-Carruades). Today, virtually every classified growth, as well as many Crus Bourgeois and numerous estates in Pomerol and St.-Emilion have second labels for those batches of wine deemed not sufficiently rich, concentrated, or complete enough to go into their top wine, or "grand vin." This has been one of the major developments of the eighties, fostered no doubt by the enormous crop sizes in most of the vintages. A handful of cynics have claimed it is largely done to keep prices high, but such charges are nonsense. The result has generally been far higher quality for the château's best wine. It allows a château to declassify the production from young vines, from vines that overproduce, and from parcels harvested too soon or too late, into a second, or perhaps even a third wine that still has some of the quality and character of the château's grand vin.

The gentleman who encouraged most châteaux to develop second wines was the famed oenologist, Professor Emile Peynaud. A comparison between the second wines listed in this edition and in the 1985 edition of *Bordeaux* will reveal that the number of second wines has increased more than tenfold. Some properties, such as Léoville-Las Cases, have even begun to utilize a third label for wines deemed not good enough for the second label!

Of course all this complicates buying decisions for consumers. The wine trade has exacerbated matters by seizing on the opportunity to advertise wine that "tastes like the grand vin" for one-half to one-third the price. In most cases, there is little truth to such proclamations. I find that most second wines have only a vague resemblance to their more esteemed siblings. Most are the product of throwing everything that would normally have been discarded into another label for commercial purposes. Some second wines, such as those of the first-growths, particularly Les Forts de Latour and Bahans-Haut-Brion, are indeed excellent, occasionally outstanding (taste the 1982 Les Forts de Latour or 1989 Bahans-Haut-Brion), and can even resemble the style and character of the grand vin. But the words *caveat emptor* should be etched strongly in the minds of consumers who routinely purchase the second labels of Bordeaux châteaux thinking they are getting something reminiscent of the property's top wine.

THE RENAISSANCE OF BARSAC AND SAUTERNES

Perhaps the most unlikely event in Bordeaux during the last five years has been the extraordinary success enjoyed by the Barsac/Sauternes producers. In 1985, the region was in an economic and emotional depression. The horrible decade of the sixties with four disastrous vintages— 1963, 1964, 1965, and 1968—had precluded investments in new barrels, as well as other viticultural and technical improvements. There was little reason for optimism during the seventies, a pitiful decade where only three vintages—1971, 1975, and 1976—turned out well. By 1980, the future looked to be so unpromising that many producers, struggling financially to keep their estates viable, considered selling their domaines.

While the early eighties continued to batter producers' spirits, the fine, abundant crop of 1983 lifted hopes, only to be crushed again with the disappointing 1984 vintage and mediocre 1985 harvest.

But in 1986 the renaissance began. The vintage was superb, the finest since 1967. It was followed by a 1988 vintage that many European producers are calling the greatest since 1937, another top-flight, powerful year in 1989, and a promising 1990. This good fortune, thanks to Mother Nature, was accompanied by significantly increased interest displayed by the world wine press, as well as a trend (at least in fashion-conscious European circles) toward serving these decadently rich, sweet wines as apéritifs.

The combination of a succession of high-quality crops and increased worldwide demand for these nectars has resulted in a much-needed infusion of capital into the region. That money has been invested in new barrels and better equipment. The quality of these sweet wines soared in proportion to the uplifted spirits of its producers. Many of the perennial underachievers, such as Rabaud-Promis and La Tour Blanche, are now making some of the greatest wines of the appellation. The longtime stars, such as Climens, Suduiraut, Coutet, and of course, the great Yquem, continue to master the fine art of making sweet wine with complexity, power, and balance.

Moreover, many producers have developed a certain esprit de corps bolstered by their new enthusiasm, sounder financial well-being, and the success their wines are enjoying in the international marketplace. Quality, which is at an all-time high, is even carrying over to the obscure sweet white wine–making appellations across the river in Loupiac and Sainte-Croix-du-Mont.

Part of the success the Barsac/Sauternes wines have witnessed over the last five years can be attributed to a remarkable lady, Madame Sita Garros, who was hired to do promotion and publicity for the producers. Many public relations people often make the mistake of simply hyping their clients' wines, but Sita Garros set out to inform, educate, and make all of the wines of Barsac/Sauternes available to the wine press for tasting any time and any place. The result has been a sympathetic and hospitable press that has been willing to share with its readers the positive news emerging from this bucolic region.

THE MATURE HARVEST

A number of better Bordeaux tasters often express dismay, perhaps even shock, at how soft the tannin is and how low the acidity is in so many recent Bordeaux vintages. The reason for the soft tannins is easy to explain. Bordeaux producers, more than any other, have mastered the ability to pick grapes that are not just analytically mature, but are also physiologically mature. This has not been an easy task to learn. The old 100-day rule, where the grapes were picked 100 days after the flowering, has been largely abandoned in favor of as late a harvest as possible, with most of the best properties looking for a certain element of *sur maturité*, recognizing that while the grape itself may be analytically ripe, the grape skin may still not be mature. Grapes harvested too soon produce wines that possess green, astringent tannin, making them less attractive for early drinking.

Certainly during the decade of the eighties, the late harvest has been immensely assisted by the climate, which has provided a bevy of unbelievably hot, dry years. Even those vintages somewhat tainted by rain—1981, 1987, and 1988—were relatively hot, dry years. In the classic hot years—1982, 1983, 1985, 1986, and 1989—the average time between the flowering and the harvest date was 110–117 days. The later harvest, when taken into consideration with modern-day, gentle wine presses that avoid crushing the grape seeds and thereby extracting harshness, and the fact that more and more producers completely destem, has resulted in wines that still possess tannin levels that remain as high as in older vintages. Yet the wines taste softer and riper, and can deceptively appear ready to drink. When analyzed, tannin levels, alcohol levels, and extract levels for the top vintages of the eighties do not differ significantly from such monumental vintages as 1959 and 1961.

There are four components that foster longevity. In order of importance, they are tannin, alcohol, acidity, and extract. High levels of only one of these components—acidity—makes a wine unpleasant to drink young. The Bordelais, primarily their two most revered oenologists, Emile Peynaud and Pascal Ribéreau-Gayon, were the first to realize that by lowering acidity (by virtue of a late harvest), while maintaining high levels of tannin, alcohol, and extract, Bordeaux could produce wines that could be drunk younger, yet would age well for 20–30 years, perhaps longer.

It becomes immediately apparent in a vertical tasting of almost any wine from a major château that vintages of the eighties taste softer, richer in fruit, and more supple than vintages in the seventies, sixties, and fifties. In fact, if the tasting is held with the identity of the vintages kept secret from the tasters, I have noticed time and time again that people find the tannins and the wines from decades before 1980 to be tougher, and the wines seemingly more structured.

Does this mean that the softer, lusher, more richly fruity style of the eighties is a new trend in Bordeaux and that these wines will not last as long? I do not think so. Much of the hard tannins found in vintages of the fifties, sixties, and seventies were the results of different winemaking techniques. Bordeaux winemakers harvested their grapes earlier, often did not destem (it is the stems that impart a greener, more astringent taste as well as bitterness), generally used less Merlot in their blends, and had vineyards that were much younger—particularly after the devastating 1956 freeze that killed so many vines, not only in Pomerol and St.-Emilion, but also in the Graves and Médoc. During the decade of the eighties, the trend toward total destemming, the tendency to harvest 10–17 days later than in prior decades, the advent of new wine presses, and the fact that the average age of most of the vineyards is now 25–30 years, have resulted in fruit that exhibits superb maturity. This, along with the extraordinary string of long, hot, dry summers during the decade of the eighties, has resulted in wines lower in acidity, with riper fruit, and softer, more supple textures.

The argument that the later harvest produces wines that are defectively low in acidity is also without merit. All of the top vintages in the decade of the eighties—1982, 1983, 1985, 1986, and 1989—have been relatively low in acidity because the grapes were fully mature. Virtually every great Bordeaux vintage this century—1900, 1928, 1929, 1945, 1947, 1949, 1953, 1959, 1961, and more recently, 1982 and 1989—have been characterized by low acidity. In fact, one is well advised to remember what the famous Bordeaux oenologist, Emile Peynaud, said in his treatise called, *Le Goût du Vin*, that "the first attribute of a great red wine is to be low in acidity."

This low acidity argument (an obsession with so many new-world technocrats) is a myth regarding the quality or aging potential of a given vintage—at least for red wine. Because so many viticultural regions of the new world produce overripe fruit that must be acidified for balance, there has been a natural preoccupation with a wine's acid level or pH. In Europe's finest viticultural regions, low acidity is usually synonymous with a very high-quality year. One suspects if the same critics had had a chance to taste the 1900s, 1929s, 1947s, 1949s, 1953s, 1959s, or 1961s when they were 2–3 years old, they would have found them surprisingly soft and forward. Virtually all of the *régisseurs* and *maîtres de chais* who are old enough to know claim these vintages all possessed early charm and drinkability. That is one of the singular signs of a great young Bordeaux vintage. The prerequisite that Bordeaux has to taste nasty and raw, and be undrinkable young, to be great old is a fallacy. This has never been the case and it is time to put this absurd notion to rest.

The ideal physiological maturation date for picking grapes in Bordeaux is not easy to discern. Vignerons struggled in the excessively hot, dry years of 1989 and 1990 deciding the optimum time to harvest. Many harvested too early because the oenologists, as a general rule, counseled picking early when the grapes, rather than the grape skins, were fully mature. In both 1989 and 1990 many producers picked their Cabernet Sauvignon too early. Of course there is always the danger of waiting too late. For that reason, many estates that are in an enviable financial position to afford large picking teams have begun to employ more and more harvesters. One of the untold stories about the great success Mouton-Rothschild has enjoyed since the 1982 vintage is that they have increased their number of pickers threefold from the number used during the seventies. They are now able to harvest the entire vineyard in 2–3 days. This allows them to wait for the perfect moment of maturity and then quickly attack the vineyard, picking it as rapidly as possible. Prior to 1981, it often took Mouton-Rothschild 10–21 days to complete the harvest.

Because of the pressure to harvest at the optimum moment, many estates have begun to employ mechanical harvesters because they are less costly and more efficient. Mechanical harvesting machines can work twenty-four hours a day, seven days a week. However, most of the top estates continue to use people rather than machines. There is the fear that the machines, which tend to operate best only on young vines, and are not nearly as selective as an individual can be—often picking up leaves, and even rusted metal from the wiring that holds the vines in place—will never be able to achieve the success of a well-trained group of harvesters. Two of the leading oenology professors, Emile Peynaud and Michel Rolland, have vociferously condemned the use of mechanical harvesters. But more and more major châteaux employ machines, recognizing the considerable cost savings and added flexibility they offer.

COMPETITION AND THE INFORMED MARKETPLACE

Amidst all the attention given to new wine presses, new and better grape clones, and adventurous winemaking techniques—such as cryo-extraction (increasingly used in Barsac/Sauternes) and reverse osmosis (used by several prominent Médoc estates)—a simple fact has been overlooked: the proprietors of most Bordeaux châteaux have become keenly competitive with each other.

Until the eighties it was nearly always possible for a renowned Bordeaux château to sell wine on the basis of its standing or so-called reputation in one of the many hierarchies of quality. As auction prices have long suggested, the fact that some of Bordeaux's greatest estates—Lafite-Rothschild between 1961 and 1974, Margaux between 1963 and 1977, Ausone between 1960 and 1975, Mouton-Rothschild between 1972 and 1981, and Haut-Brion between 1966 and 1970—made mediocre wines was ignored by seemingly intelligent and informed buyers. Today's well-informed consumer is not going to make egregious mistakes and the châteaux realize it.

Remarkably, many of today's superstars have been making great wine only for the last 3–4 years. For example, consider such great St.-Emilions as L'Angélus, Troplong-Mondot, Le Tertre-Roteboeuf, Larmande, Grand-Mayne, and the two famous Premiers Grands Crus Classés, Trottevieille and La Gaffelière. Ten years ago, no informed buyer would have even considered buying those wines. In fact, one can go to any of the major appellations and point to once-moribund estates that have dramatically increased the quality of their wines, in most cases in response to competition from neighbors and the fact that today the marketplace is so congested with so many high-quality wines that only wines of true class, individuality, and character have a chance. Competition has never been keener, and the wine consumer has been the beneficiary. While some famous names continue to perform below their official classification, never in the history of Bordeaux have so many estates been making so much fine wine.

ASCERTAINING MATURITY

Most Americans fret entirely too much over the notion that there is a perfect moment to drink a bottle of wine. There is none. Most modern-day vintages can be drunk when released and the top examples held for 20–30 years. The evolution of Bordeaux in the bottle is extremely slow. During the aging process the color lightens and begins to take on an orange/brownish hue. This will happen faster with Merlot-based wines that are lower in acidity. It also occurs in years of great ripeness, such as 1982, 1983, 1985, and 1989.

The key to maturity is the bouquet. When the bouquet begins to exhibit more than just rich aromas of red and black fruits, herbs, and new oak, and takes on nuances of tobacco, cedar, spices, coffee, mocha, and wet forest-like aromas, the wine has evolved from an adolescent state to a more mature stage of its life. What is so remarkable about a Bordeaux wine is that even when fully mature, if well kept, it can last 15–20, sometimes 30 or more years at its apogee before beginning to decline. A very general rule of thumb that may be useful is espoused by a number of my colleagues in France and England. They claim that a wine that requires 10 years to reach full maturity should easily hold at that plateau of maturity for the same amount of time, 10 years. It will take an additional ten years for the wine to collapse. This is a conservative estimate, but it does make sense and can be easily applied, at least for the top estates that make the most concentrated and complete wines.

Of course, when a wine is mature is a matter of conjecture, as well as personal taste. As a general rule, the French prefer their Bordeaux in its grapey youth, the English are fond of the very aged, soft taste that takes decades to occur. The important thing for consumers to remember is that there is no one magical moment. My experience suggests that even the lightest, softest Bordeaux vintages (1967, 1976, 1987) will last 10–15 years; the most concentrated and richest vintages (1982, 1986, 1989) will last 25–35 years. As I have already stated, I do not subscribe to the theory that the vintages of the eighties will mature more quickly simply because their tannins are softer, their acids lower, and the wines made from riper fruit.

PRODUCTION YIELDS

During the fifties and sixties, a yield of 40 hectoliters per hectare would have been considered enormous. Yet not only have such yields been attained during the decade of the eighties, they have been exceeded in nearly every vintage, culminating in 1989 and 1990 with an average production of 65 hectoliters per hectare (equivalent to 3.7 tons per acre). In fact, the production in 1990 would have been higher had not the French government intervened to restrict the yields and to compel producers to declassify excess production.

The yields are even more remarkable given the fact that almost all of the major estates are now routinely practicing a crop thinning (called *vendange verte* or *éclaircissage* by the French). This procedure, which involves cutting off up to 50% of the unripe grape bunches in July, is still a controversial one. Most of the authorities believe this technique is far more advantageous than harvesting a huge crop and then bleeding the tanks *(saigner)* of excess juice to increase the proportion of solids to the remaining must. What is now happening because of the high yields is that top serious properties are both crop thinning and doing a *saigner*, trying to increase the concentration of their wines.

Most Bordeaux producers remain incredibly sensitive about their remarkable yields during the eighties and have charged that the wine press has been unduly critical, even cynical. Moreover, they claim that higher yields are not achieved because greedy growers are pushing grape production to the maximum. They argue the abundant crops are the result of healthier clones, the advent of modern sprays that prevent the dreaded *pourriture*, odium, and mildew (diseases that destroyed 30–80% of the volume for certain vintages of the fifties, sixties, and seventies), as well as the fact that the young vineyards, many of which were replanted completely after the killer freeze of 1956, are now fully mature and producing at a maximum.

However, when higher yields result in wines that taste diluted and lack a mid-palate and length, questions must be posed or raised. There is no doubt that more and more fine wines are being produced in Bordeaux than ever before, but at the same time, the excessive yields are a legitimate cause for concern. Is it really possible to make great wines today from yields that are six times what they were in 1961 or 1959?

NO DEPOSIT–
NO RETURN

Most serious wine drinkers know that one of the healthiest signs in a fine bottle of Bordeaux is sediment, the fine particles, sometimes crystal-like, that precipitate and fall to the bottom of the bottle of wine. What these dust-like particles signify is that the wine is a natural wine that has not been stripped or eviscerated of its flavor and aging potential by excessive fining or filtration. Yet more and more Bordeaux wine producers are cleaning up their wines and excessively fining and filtering them—sometimes to death. Why?

Traditional logic has been that restaurants, ignorant consumers, as well as the wine trade, particularly importers, wholesalers, and retailers, do not want to deal with wine that has dropped a sediment because they do not have the time to explain this to naïve consumers. Their unpersuasive arguments include: (1) people think sediment is bad, (2) restaurants don't want to take the time to buy decanters, (3) restaurants don't want to train their staffs to decant, and (4) restaurants don't want to take the precaution of carrying the bottle to the table gently to prevent the sediment from becoming dislodged and making the wine cloudy.

And what about the objectives of an oenologist, which clash directly with those of wine lovers? The oenologist's principal goal is stability and safety. Consequently, they often argue vigorously that intense fining and filtration are needed, particularly for the richest, densest, thickest wines because it is those wines that will throw more sediment (just check your bottles of 1959, 1961, 1970, and 1982 Bordeaux and you will see considerably more sediment forming in these rich, highly extracted vintages than lighter-weight years such as 1981, 1979, or 1967). I remember tasting a fabulous 1989 St.-Emilion in April 1991, just before it was to be bottled. The wine was a true treasure, but the proprietor stated that his oenologist said it needed to be fined several times and filtered at least 2–3 times because the wine was too rich and thick, and would throw such heavy sediment, presenting "commercial problems." Fine wines should reflect both the vintage character and their *terroir* to the fullest extent possible. Why go to the trouble of taking all the risks necessary to make great wine and then excessively fine and filter it, stripping it of the character that took so much effort to produce?

Most serious Bordeaux châteaux continue to only lightly filter their wine, but there has been a trend, because of the tendency to bottle Bordeaux earlier and earlier, to not only filter the wine after the malolactic fermentation, but fine and filter it again prior to bottling. I know of no serious Bordeaux estate that sterile filters their wine through German-made micropore filter machines as do so many California producers. Nevertheless, why not put in the bottle what one tastes from the barrel? It is not a surprise that most of the greatest winemakers in the world refuse, if possible, to filter their otherwise stable, biologically sound wines. All agree that if a wine is allowed to settle naturally in barrel or tank and not rushed into the bottle, excessive fining or filtration is not necessary. All agree that filtration extracts significant flavor material from the wine. Even the lightest fining and filtration removes some of the wine's aromatic and flavor potential. The need for more consumer education, the irresponsibility of the wine trade that encourages these procedures, combined with the growing obsession for perfectly clear, sediment-free bottles of wine has caused many great wines to be excessively fined and filtered, and in essence, be destroyed. How many times has the trade said to their producers in Bordeaux, "give me a bottle with no deposit and there will be no problems with its being returned"? A natural, unprocessed, minimally fined, unfiltered wine is alive, and if it is exposed to poor storage conditions, or hot temperatures, it will often become fizzy, popping its cork, and become undrinkable.

And is not this the real problem? Much of the wine trade prefers to buy, ship, stock, and sell denuded, stabilized, compromised, eviscerated wines because they will not accept responsibility for the proper shipping and storage of minimally processed, living wines.

It is time to hold irresponsible importers, wholesalers, retailers, and restaurateurs accountable for wine that is abused and damaged by poor storage conditions. I have seen too many bottles of fine wine that are ruined by excessive exposure to heat. The problem is rampant carelessness and a cavalier ignorance of the fundamentals of good wine storage. And of course, it is the consumer who suffers. Wine, especially handcrafted, fine wine is a fragile, living beverage. If it has not been overly processed, pasteurized, or excessively fined or filtered, several days of storage at temperatures of 80 degrees or above will cause a loss of bouquet and a lack of focus in its flavors. Several weeks at these temperatures will give it baked, hollow, astringent flavors, and several months will render it lifeless.

Thousands of bottles and cases of damaged or dead Bordeaux wine are bought each year by unsuspecting wine consumers. Pity the poor consumer who lays a lifeless, baked wine away in his cellar for 5, 10, or 15 years, expecting something magical to emerge from the bottle, only to find that it died from abusive treatment early in its life. Wine importers who fail to ship their wines during the cooler seasons of spring and fall when the temperatures are less extreme are at fault. Wine importers who ship their wines during the summer and fail to use temperature-controlled containers (called reefers), which add anywhere from 4–25 cents to the cost of a bottle of wine, are irresponsible. How many times does one read in wine advertisements that the newest vintage of Bordeaux is to arrive in the United States during the hottest months—June, July, and August? It happens almost every year. And what are the results? Why do the châteaux proprietors and the *négociants,* the very people who produce, broker, sell, and arrange shipment of these wines, permit this to happen year after year?

The problem extends not only to importers, but also to wholesalers, retailers, and restaurants that store their fine wine in warehouses or non-air-conditioned rooms with temperatures over 65 degrees. These people should be singled out, blacklisted, and boycotted. They care little that expensive bottles of wine that are damaged or dead are sold and found wanting by the wine consumer, not because the grower or producer made bad wine, but because the wine was destroyed during shipping or storage. It sickens me to see and taste so many damaged bottles of wine. Wineries and wine brokers who fail to accept responsibility for wine after it has been sold are as guilty as importers, wholesalers, retailers, and restaurants. The end result is that the winery receives complaints about the quality of its wine and begins to overly process the wine, often pasteurizing and sterile filtering it, thereby killing the wine's personality and flavor long before it leaves the winery.

Fortunately, a lot of poorly treated wine can be spotted by visual examination, such as pushed-out corks, dried residue of tears of wine on the outside of the bottle, stained labels, and low fills in young vintages.

In short, the liquor and beer dinosaurs who have controlled the wine business for so long, and who care little about how wine is handled, as well as those wineries and wine brokers who claim no responsibility for the wine after it is sold, should be exposed for what they are.

WHY BORDEAUX
COSTS WHAT IT
DOES

Consumers in every state are confronted with an array of Bordeaux wine prices that must be terribly confusing given the enormous price differences between shops—even within the same city. What I have done in the following chart is take the official price in French francs (the current exchange rate is 5.7 francs to the dollar) for which 19 of the most respected Bordeaux châteaux sold their wines. I have done this for all of the vintages from 1982 through 1989. Of course, what we pay in dollars depends on not only the fluctuating value of our currency, but also on the number of stops the wine has to make before the retailer sells it to the consumer. In many states the wine must pass through a system that involves the Bordeaux courtier's margin (2%), the Bordeaux broker's profit margin (usually 5–10%), the importer's profit margin (usually 20–40%), and the wholesaler's healthy 20–50% markup. Finally the wine arrives to the retailer, who usually takes anywhere from 20–60% markup. No wonder Bordeaux, as well as other imported wines, is so expensive. Now you know why a case of 1989 Haut-Brion, sold by the château last year for $484 (based on 5.7 francs per dollar), was offered to American consumers for $850–$1000!

The chart (see page 45) reveals rather convincingly that these 19 famous estates, by and large, have been astonishingly conservative with respect to their price increases. In particular, the first-growths have increased their prices over a 7-year span by only 35%. Moreover, considering the opening prices for the 1990 first-growths, which are down by 15–20%, then the overall percentage increase since 1982 is even more conservative. The markups are amazingly modest, particularly when compared to some of the leading California Cabernet producers, such as Heitz, Dunn, Stag's Leap, and Spottswoode, whose prices have doubled, or increased by more than 100% since they released their 1982s. In fact, the highest price increases are not from the first-growths, but from Léoville-Las Cases (93% increase in price between 1982 and 1989), Pichon Lalande (86% increase between 1982 and 1989), Canon (a whopping 127% increase between 1982 and 1989), and Lynch-Bages (109% increase in price between 1982 and 1989).

THE COST IN FRENCH FRANCS OF 19 BORDEAUX WINES FROM 1982–1989, AND THE PERCENTAGE OF INCREASE IN THE PRICE OF THE WINES DURING THAT PERIOD

(per bottle opening price)

	82	83	84	85	86	87	88	89	% INC. 82–89
LATOUR	170	170	180	210	180	130	182	230	35%
LAFITE-ROTHSCHILD	170	170	170	200	180	128	182	230	35%
MOUTON-ROTHSCHILD	170	170	170	200	180	130	180	230	35%
MARGAUX	170	170	170	200	180	130	180	230	35%
HAUT-BRION	170	170	170	220	180	126	180	225	32%
AUSONE	190	195	—	250	225	150	225	275	45%
CHEVAL BLANC	170	170	180	225	180	130	180	230	35%
LEOVILLE-LAS CASES	70	90	110	140	110	86	115	135	93%
DUCRU-BEAUCAILLOU	70	90	110	110	95	70	100	125	78%
BEYCHEVELLE	60	70	92	92	78	62	78	95	58%
BRANAIRE-DUCRU	38	52	65	70	65	47	60	67	76%
LEOVILLE-BARTON	45	50	55	62	57	45	57	68	51%
PICHON-LALANDE	67	85	100	110	95	70	100	125	86%
GRAND-PUY-LACOSTE	42	48	60	75	65	45	68	75	78%
FIGEAC	95	100	110	110	100	70	110	125	31%
CANON	55	65	—	100	90	68	100	125	127%
LA CONSEILLANTE	85	125	140	180	125	82	125	175	105%
L'EVANGILE	110	150	145	195	150	82	125	180	63%
LYNCH-BAGES	55	60	85	85	78	55	83	115	109%

The media and wine trade often aim their barbed pens at the Bordelais, blaming them for spiraling prices. Yet as this chart poignantly demonstrates, they are the least guilty parties in the chain of distribution. In most cases their price increases are significantly less than the profit margins taken by those firms involved in selling Bordeaux after it is released by the château. This is one reason why those retailers/firms in the United States that are able to direct import often have much more competitive pricing than those that go through the quadruple-tiered system.

Consider the following. The top vineyards in Bordeaux are fully planted and their production is finite. The yearly production of a Lafite-Rothschild, a Pétrus, or a Léoville-Las Cases (which of course varies depending on weather conditions) is unlikely to be significantly different one hundred years from now. When one considers that these wines are in demand the world over, I, for one, am surprised that Bordeaux prices are not even higher. Perhaps there are fewer connoisseurs of fine wine than we have all been led to believe!

Star Ratings for Appellations
*****—An outstanding vintage
****—A very good to excellent vintage
***—An above-average to good vintage
**—An average-quality vintage
*—A poor vintage
No stars (0)—An appallingly bad vintage

3: A SUMMARY OF BORDEAUX VINTAGES: 1945–1990

This chapter is a general assessment and profile of the Bordeaux vintages 1945 through 1990. While the top wines for each acceptable vintage are itemized, it should be remembered that the perception of a vintage should be regarded as a general view of that particular viticultural region. In mediocre and poor vintages, good wines can often be made by skillful vintners who are willing to make a careful selection of only the best grapes and *cuvées* of finished wine. In good, even great years, thin, diluted, characterless wines can be made by incompetent and greedy producers. For wine consumers, a vintage summary is important as a general guide to the level of potential excellence that could have been attained in a particular year by a conscientious grower or producer of wine.

1990—A Quick Study
(9-12-90) *

St.-Estèphe *****   Graves Red **

Pauillac ***   Graves White ****

St.-Julien ***   Pomerol ***

Margaux ***   St.-Emilion *****

Médoc/Haut-Médoc Crus Bourgeois ****   Barsac/Sauternes ***

Size: Enormous; along with 1986 and 1989 the largest crop ever harvested
   in Bordeaux.

Important information: The hottest year since 1947 and the sunniest year
   since 1949 caused extraordinary stress in some of the best vineyards in the Graves and Médoc. Consequently, the heavier soils
   from such appellations as St.-Estèphe, the limestone hillsides and
   plateau areas of St.-Emilion, as well as the Fronsacs excelled.

Maturity status: Exceptionally low-acid wines (far below acid levels in
   1985, 1982, and even 1989); but high tannins suggest early drinkability with the most complete wines (a minority) having 15–20 or
   more years of longevity.

Price: Opening future prices were down 15–20% below 1989.

   Most of the great Bordeaux vintages of this century are the result of
relatively hot, dry years. For that reason alone, 1990 should elicit considerable attention. The most revealing fact about the 1990 vintage is that
it is the second-hottest vintage of the century, barely surpassed by 1947.
It is also the second-sunniest vintage, eclipsed only by 1949 in the post–
World War II era. The amount of sunshine and the extraordinarily hot
summers Bordeaux has enjoyed during the eighties are frequently attributed to the so-called "greenhouse effect" and consequent global warm-
ing about which such ominous warnings have been issued by the
scientific community. Yet consider the Bordeaux weather for the period
between 1945–1949. Amazingly, that era was even more torrid than
1989–1990. (One wonders if there was concern then about the glaciers of
the north and south poles melting.)
   The weather of 1990 was auspicious because of its potential to produce
great wines, but weather is only one part of the equation. The summer
months of July and August were the driest since 1961, and August was
the hottest since 1928, the year records were first kept. September (the
month that most producers claim "makes the quality") was not, weather-
wise, a particularly exceptional month. The year 1990 was the second-

---

* Dates in parentheses denote actual day on which the Bordeaux harvest began, according
to the French Ministry of Agriculture.

wettest year among the great hot-year vintages, surpassed only by 1989. As in 1989, the rain fell at periods that should give rise for concern. For example, on September 15 a particularly violent series of thunderstorms swept across Bordeaux, inundating much of the Graves region. On September 22–23 there was modest rainfall over the entire region. On October 7 and October 15 light showers were reported throughout the region. Most producers have been quick to state that the rain in September was beneficial. They argue that the Cabernet Sauvignon grapes were still too small and their skins too thick. Many Cabernet vines had shut down and the grapes refused to mature because of the excessive heat and drought. The rain, the producers suggest, promoted further ripening and alleviated the blocked state of maturity. This is an appealing argument that has some merit, but unfortunately, too many châteaux panicked and harvested too soon after these rain storms. This is confirmed when the wines are tasted.

When tasting the wines from 1990, the most striking characteristic is their roasted quality, no doubt the result of the extremely, perhaps excessively hot summer. The September rains may have partially alleviated the stress from which those vineyards planted with Cabernet in the lighter, better-drained soils were suffering, but they also swelled many of the grape bunches and no doubt contributed to another prolifically abundant crop size.

There is no doubt that the great vintages have all been relatively hot, dry years. But was 1990 too torrid? Were the yields so high that in spite of the exceptional weather there were just too many grapes to make profound wines? The weather in 1990 put even more stress on the Bordeaux vineyards than the heat and drought of 1989. One of the keys to understanding this vintage is that the best wines of 1990 have often emerged from those vineyards planted on the heavier, less well-drained, less desirable vineyard soils. For example, in my tasting notes, heavier soils from such appellations as St.-Estèphe, Fronsac, and the hillside and plateau vineyards of St.-Emilion produced richer, more concentrated, and more complete wines than many of the top vineyards planted on the fine, well-drained, gravel-based soils of Margaux and the Graves.

The crop size was enormous in 1990, approximately equivalent to the quantity of wine produced in 1989. In reality, more wine was actually made, but because the French authorities intervened and required significant declassifications, the actual declared limit matches 1989, which means that for both vintages the production is 30% more than in 1982. Officially, however, many châteaux made even stricter selections in 1990 than in 1989 and the actual quantity of wine declared by many producers under the grand vin label is less than in 1989.

Across almost every appellation, the overall impression one gets of the dry red wines is that of extremely low acidity (as low and in some cases even lower than in 1989), high tannins (in most cases higher than in 1989), but an overall impression of softness and forward, precocious, extremely ripe, sometimes roasted flavors. Because the tannins are so soft (as in 1982, 1985, and 1989), it is very likely that these wines will provide considerable enjoyment when they are young.

The second consecutive year of great heat, sunshine, and drought apparently caused even more stress for those vineyards planted in light, gravelly soil than in 1989. Many proprietors in the Graves and Margaux regions suggested that they were almost forced to harvest their Cabernet too soon because it was drying up on the vine. This, combined with extremely high yields, no doubt explains why the Graves and Margaux appellations, much as in 1989 and 1982 (two other hot, dry years), were less successful.

Some surprising strengths in this vintage include all four of the Médoc first-growths. Astoundingly, it can be safely said that they have made slightly richer, fuller, more complete wines in 1990 than in 1989. Else-where in the Médoc, particularly in St.-Julien and Pauillac, a bevy of relatively soft, round, forward, fruity wines with high alcohol, high, soft tannin, and extremely low acidity have been made. In essence, one might call them a synthesis in style between a top 1985 and a top 1976. The strongest left-bank appellation in 1990 is St.-Estèphe. Sensational in quality, many wines are every bit as good as their 1989 counterparts.

On the right-bank, Pomerol enjoyed a far less successful vintage than in 1989, but the properties sitting on the St.-Emilion border, such as L'Evangile, La Conseillante, and Bon Pasteur, all managed to produce wines that will be among the top wines of the vintage. In the case of L'Evangile and Bon Pasteur, their 1990s are probably superior to their 1989s.

St.-Emilion, never a consistent appellation, has produced perhaps its most homogeneous and greatest vintage of the last ten years for all three sectors of the appellation—the plateau, the vineyards at the foot of the hillsides, and the vineyards on sandy, gravelly soil. It is interesting to note that both Cheval Blanc and Figeac made better 1990s than 1989s, and yet they possess the same type of soil base that gave considerable problems to the Cabernet producers in the Médoc—one of the mysteries of the vintage.

The year 1990 is a forward, charming vintage, with very few wines (except, of course, the first-growths) that can be said to have aging poten-tial beyond 10–15 years. Nevertheless, the irony is that the St.-Emilions, normally the most inconsistent wines of Bordeaux, will probably prove, along with the St.-Estèphes, to be the longest-lived wines in this vintage, with 15–20 or more years of longevity. Otherwise, most wines, much like the 1989s, will be delicious young.

The dry white wines of Graves, as well as generic white Bordeaux, have enjoyed an excellent, perhaps even an outstanding vintage that is superior to 1989. Poor judgment in picking the 1989s too soon was not repeated with the 1990s, which have more richness and depth than most 1989s.

As for the sweet white wines of the Barsac/Sauternes region, this vintage will be historic in the sense that most of the white wine producers finished their harvest before the red wine producers, something that has not happened since 1949. However, despite considerable power and a sweet, very sugary style, only a handful of these wines displayed much complexity or focus. While they are being talked up because of their impressive statistical credentials, sunshine and high sugar readings alone do not make for great Barsacs and Sauternes. Botrytis and acidity are of fundamental importance. The 1990s look to me to be inferior to the profound sweet wines produced in Barsac and Sauternes in 1986, 1988, as well as 1989.

The Best Wines

Note: These recommendations are based on numerous barrel tastings of the wines at both the châteaux and at comparative tastings in spring 1991.

St.-Estèphe:	Cos d'Estournel, Cos Labory, Montrose
Pauillac:	Lafite-Rothschild, Latour, Mouton-Rothschild
St.-Julien:	Ducru-Beaucaillou, Léoville-Las Cases
Margaux:	Margaux, Rausan-Ségla
Médoc/Haut-Médoc/ Moulis/Listrac/ Crus Bourgeois:	Lanessan, La Tour St.-Bonnet, Moulin-Rouge, Sociando-Mallet, Tour Haut-Caussan, Tour du Haut-Moulin
Graves Red:	Haut-Brion, La Mission-Haut-Brion, Pape-Clément
Graves White:	Domaine de Chevalier, Clos Floridene, de Fieuzal, La Tour-Martillac
Pomerol:	Bon Pasteur, Clinet, La Conseillante, L'Evangile, La Fleur de Gay, Lafleur, Petit-Village, Pétrus, Le Pin, Trotanoy, Vieux-Château-Certan

Fronsac/Canon
Fronsac: Canon-de-Brem, de Carles, Cassagne-Haut-
Canon-La-Truffière, Fontenil, Pez-Labrie, La
Vieille-Cure
St.-Emilion: L'Angélus, L'Arrosée, Ausone, Beauséjour,
Canon, Cheval Blanc, Figeac, Pavie, Le Tertre-
Roteboeuf
Barsac/Sauternes: Climens, Raymond-Lafon, Rieussec, Suduiraut,
La Tour Blanche

1989—A Quick Study
(8-31-89)

St.-Estèphe ****   Graves Red ***
Pauillac *****   Graves White **
St.-Julien ****   Pomerol *****
Margaux ***   St.-Emilion ****
Médoc/Haut-Médoc Crus Bourgeois ****   Barsac/Sauternes ****

Size: Mammoth; along with 1990 and 1986, the largest declared crop in
the history of Bordeaux.

Important information: Excessively hyped vintage by virtually everyone
but the Bordeaux proprietors. American, French, even English
writers were all set to declare it the vintage of the century until
serious tasters began to question the extract levels, phenomenally
low acid levels, and the puzzling quality of some wines. However,
plenty of rich, dramatic, fleshy wines have been produced that
should age reasonably well.

Maturity status: High tannins and extremely low acidity, much like 1990,
suggest early drinkability, with only the most concentrated wines
capable of lasting 20–30 or more years.

Price: The most expensive opening prices of any vintage. Nearly two
years after the vintage, the market has not pushed prices up as it
did with the last vintage (1982) that received great praise, and as
the wines arrive in the bottle, most 1989s can be purchased within
20% of their opening price.

The general news media, primarily ABC television and *The New York
Times*, first carried the news that several châteaux began their harvest
during the last days of August, making 1989 the earliest vintage since
1893. An early harvest generally signifies a torrid growing season and
below-average rainfall—almost always evidence that a top-notch vintage
is achievable. In his annual *Vintage and Market Report*, Peter Sichel
reported that between 1893 and 1989 only 1947, 1949, 1970, and 1982

were years with a similar weather pattern, but none of these years were as hot as 1989.

Perhaps the most revealing and critical decision (at least from a qualitative perspective) was the choice of picking dates. Never has Bordeaux enjoyed such a vast span of time (August 28–October 15) over which to complete the harvest. Some châteaux, most notably Haut-Brion and the Christian Moueix–managed properties in Pomerol and St.-Emilion, harvested during the first week of September. Other estates waited and did not finish their harvesting until mid-October. During the second week of September, one major problem developed. Much of the Cabernet Sauvignon, while analytically mature and having enough sugar to potentially produce wines with 13% alcohol, was actually not ripe physiologically. Many châteaux, never having experienced such growing conditions, became indecisive. Far too many deferred to their oenologists, who saw technically mature grapes that were quickly losing acidity. The oenologists, never ones to take risks, advised immediate picking. As more than one proprietor and *négociant* said, by harvesting the Cabernet too early, a number of châteaux lost their chance to produce one of the greatest wines of a lifetime. This, plus the enormously large crop size, probably explains the good yet uninspired performance of so many wines from the Graves and Margaux appellations.

There was clearly no problem with the early-picked Merlot as much of it came in between 13.5% and a whopping 15% alcohol level—unprecedented in Bordeaux. Those properties who crop-thinned—Pétrus, La Fleur Pétrus, and Haut-Brion—had yields of 45–55 hectoliters per hectare, and super concentration. Those who did not crop-thin had yields as preposterously high as 80 hectoliters per hectare.

Contrary to the reports of a totally "dry harvest," there were rain showers on the 10th, 13th, 18th, and 22nd of September that did little damage unless the property panicked and harvested the day after the rain. Some of the lighter-styled wines may very well be the result of jittery châteaux owners who unwisely picked after the showers.

The overall production was, once again, staggeringly high.

While the enormous hype from spectators outside of Bordeaux bordered on irresponsible, the Bordelais had a far more conservative view of the 1989 vintage. Consider the following. England's Hungerford Wine Company, run with great flair by Nicholas Davies, sent out a questionnaire to 200 of the major Bordeaux proprietors. Their comments were fascinating. When asked to compare the 1989 vintage with another vintage, the most popular comparison (25% of those polled) was with 1982). Fourteen percent compared it to 1985, 10% to 1986, 8% to 1988, 7% to 1961, and 6% to 1947. Only Peter Sichel, the president of Bordeaux's prestigious Union des Grands Crus (who appears far too young to remember) compared it to 1893. In this same intriguing survey, the proprietors, when asked for a general qualitative assessment, responded in the following manner. Sixty-four percent rated it excellent, 17% rated it very good, 4% said it was the vintage of the century, and 10% rated it superb (meaning, I suppose, better than excellent, but not vintage-of-the-century material). The other 5% were unsure of what they had produced.

In general, the wines are the most alcoholic Bordeaux I have ever tasted, ranging from 12.8% to over 14.5% for many Pomerols. Acidities are extremely low and tannin levels surprisingly high. Consequently, in looking at the structural profile of the 1989s, one sees wines 1% to 2% higher in alcohol than the 1982s or 1961s; with much lower acidity levels than the 1982s, 1961s, and 1959s, yet high tannin levels. Fortunately, the tannins are generally ripe and soft, à la 1982, rather than dry and astringent as in 1988. This gives the wines a big, rich fleshy feel in the mouth similar to the 1982s. The top 1989s have very high glycerin levels, but are they as concentrated as the finest 1982s and 1986s? In Margaux the answer is a resounding "no" as this is clearly the least-favored appellation, much as it was in 1982. In Graves, except for Haut-Brion, La Mission-Haut-Brion, Haut-Bailly, and de Fieuzal, the wines are relatively light and undistinguished. In St.-Emilion, the 1982s are more consistent as well as more deeply concentrated. Some marvelously rich, enormously fruity, fat wines were made in St.-Emilion in 1989, but there is wide irregularity in quality. However, in the northern Médoc, primarily St.-Julien, Pauillac, and St.-Estèphe, as well as in Pomerol, many exciting, full-bodied, very alcoholic, and tannic wines have been made. The best of these seem to combine the splendidly rich, opulent, fleshy texture of the finest 1982s with the power and tannin of the 1986s.

However, the softness of the tannins, very high pHs (3.7–4.0 is the norm in this vintage), and low acidity, characteristics that caused a number of American critics to malign and erroneously dismiss the 1982s, is even more evident in the 1989s. Furthermore, the 1989s were made from much higher yields (20%–40% more wine per acre) than the 1982s. This has caused more than one *négociant* to suggest, in a pejorative sense, that the best 1989 red Bordeaux have more in common with Côte-Rôtie or California than classic claret. Such statements are pure nonsense. The best of these wines are powerful, authoritative examples of their types; they do not taste like Côte-Rôtie or California Cabernet. However, because these wines are so individualistic as well as forward, I expect the vintage, much like 1982, to be controversial.

As with the 1982s, this is a vintage that will probably be enjoyable to drink over a broad span of years. Despite the high tannin levels, the low acidities combined with the high glycerine and alcohol levels give the wines a fascinatingly fleshy, full-bodied texture. While there is considerable variation in quality, the finest 1989s from Pomerol, St.-Julien, Pauillac, and St.-Estèphe will, in specific cases, rival some of the greatest wines in 1982 and 1986. Because of that, I believe readers who desire to drink these wines will have to purchase them as futures.

The Best Wines

St.-Estèphe:	Cos d'Estournel, Haut-Marbuzet, Meyney, Montrose
Pauillac:	Clerc-Milon, Grand-Puy-Lacoste, Lafite-Rothschild, Lynch-Bages, Mouton-Rothschild, Pichon-Longueville Baron, Pichon-Longueville–Comtesse de Lalande
St.-Julien:	Beychevelle, Branaire-Ducru, Ducru-Beaucaillou, Léoville-Barton, Léoville-Las Cases, Talbot
Margaux:	Cantemerle, Margaux, Monbrison, Palmer, Rausan-Ségla
Médoc/Haut-Médoc/ Moulis/Listrac/ Crus Bourgeois:	Beaumont, Le Boscq, Chasse-Spleen, Gressier Grand-Poujeaux, Lanessan, Maucaillou, Moulin-Rouge, Potensac, Poujeaux, Sociando-Mallet, La Tour de By, Tour Haut-Caussan, Tour du Haut-Moulin, La Tour St.-Bonnet, Vieux-Robin
Graves Red:	Bahans-Haut-Brion, Haut-Bailly, Haut-Brion, La Mission-Haut-Brion
Graves White:	Clos Floridene, Haut-Brion, Laville-Haut-Brion
Pomerol:	Bon Pasteur, Clinet, La Conseillante, Domaine de L'Eglise, L'Evangile, Lafleure, Lafleur de Gay, La Fleur Pétrus, Le Gay, Gombaude-Guillot, Les Pensées de Lafleur, Pétrus, Le Pin, Trotanoy, Vieux-Château-Certan
Fronsac/Canon Fronsac:	Canon, Canon-de-Brem, Canon-Moueix, Cassagne-Haut-Canon-La-Truffière, Dalem, La Dauphine, Fontenil, Mazeris, Moulin-Haut-Laroque, Moulin-Pey-Labrie
St.-Emilion:	L'Angélus, Ausone, Cheval Blanc, La Dominique, La Gaffelière, Grand-Mayne, Magdelaine, Pavie-Macquin, Soutard, Le Tertre-Roteboeuf, Trottevieille

Barsac/Sauternes: Climens, Coutet, Coutet-Cuvée Madame, Doisy-
                    Védrines, Guiraud, Lafaurie-Peyraguey, Rabaud-
                    Promis, Raymond-Lafon, Rieussec, Suduiraut,
                    Suduiraut-Cuvée Madame, La Tour Blanche

1988—A Quick Study
(9-20-88)

St.-Estèphe ***   Graves Red ****
Pauillac ***   Graves White ***
St.-Julien ***   Pomerol ****
Margaux ***   St.-Emilion ***
Médoc/Haut-Médoc Crus Bourgeois **   Barsac/Sauternes *****

Size: A large crop equivalent in size to 1982, meaning 30% less wine than
    was produced in 1989 and 1990.

Important information: Fearing a repeat of the rains that destroyed the
    potential for a great year in 1987, many producers once again pulled
    the trigger on their harvesting teams too soon. Unfortunately, co-
    pious quantities of Médoc Cabernet Sauvignon were picked too
    early.

Maturity status: Because of good acid levels and relatively high, more
    astringent tannins, there is no denying the potential of the 1988s to
    last for 20 or 30 years. How many of these wines will retain enough
    fruit to stand up to the tannin remains to be seen.

Price: Prices range 20–40% below the 1989s, so the best wines offer
    considerable value.

The year 1988 is a good but rarely thrilling vintage of red wines, and
one of the greatest vintages of this century for the sweet wines of Barsac
and Sauternes.

The problem with the red wines is that there is a lack of superstar
performances on the part of the top châteaux. This will no doubt ensure
that 1988 will always be regarded as a good rather than excellent year.
While the 1988 crop size was large, it was exceeded in size by the two
vintages that followed it, 1989 and 1990. The average yield in 1988 was
between 45–50 hectoliters per hectare, which was approximately equivalent to the quantity of wine produced in 1982. The wines tend to be well
colored, extremely tannic, and firmly structured, but also too often they
exhibit a slight lack of depth, and finish short, with noticeably green,
astringent tannins.

These characteristics are especially evident in the Médoc where it was
all too apparent that many châteaux, apprehensive about the onset of rot
and further rain (as in 1987) panicked and harvested their Cabernet

Sauvignon too early. Consequently, they brought in Cabernet that often achieved only 8–9% sugar readings. Those properties that waited (too few indeed) made the best wines.

In Pomerol and St.-Emilion the Merlot was harvested under ripe conditions, but because of the severe drought in 1988 the skins of the grapes were thicker and the resulting wines were surprisingly tannic and hard.

In St.-Emilion many properties reported bringing in Cabernet Franc at full maturity and obtaining sugar levels that were reportedly higher than ever before. However, despite such optimistic reports much of the Cabernet Franc tasted fluid and diluted in quality. Therefore, St.-Emilion, despite reports of a very successful harvest, exhibits great irregularity in quality.

The appellation of Graves probably produced the best red wines of Bordeaux in 1988.

While there is no doubt that the richer, more dramatic, fleshier 1989s have taken much of the public's attention away from the 1988s, an objective look at the 1988 vintage will reveal some surprisingly strong performances in appellations such as Margaux, Pomerol, Graves, and in properties in the northern Médoc that eliminated their early-picked Cabernet Sauvignon, or harvested much later. The year 1988 is not a particularly good one for the Crus Bourgeois because many harvested too soon. The lower prices they receive for their wines do not permit the Crus Bourgeois producers to make the strict selection that is necessary in years such as 1988.

The one appellation that did have a superstar vintage was Barsac and Sauternes. With a harvest that lasted until the end of November and textbook weather conditions for the formation of the noble rot, *Botrytis cinerea*, 1988 is already considered by European authorities to be the finest vintage since 1937. Almost across the board, including the smaller estates, the wines have an intense smell of honey, coconut, oranges, and other tropical fruits. It is a remarkably rich vintage with wines of extraordinary levels of botrytis, great concentration of flavor; yet the rich, unctuous, opulent textures are balanced beautifully by zesty, crisp acidity. It is this latter component that makes these wines so special and the reason why they have an edge over the 1989s.

One must also remember that the 1988 Bordeaux vintage offers wines that, in general, are priced 25–40% below the same wines in 1989. It is a vintage where the best wines will be ready to drink in 4–5 years, but will last for up to 15–25 years. For the sweet wines of Barsac/Sauternes, 30–40 more years of aging potential is not unrealistic.

The Best Wines

St.-Estèphe: Calon-Ségur, Haut-Marbuzet, Meyney, Phélan-Ségur

Pauillac: Clerc-Milon, Lafite-Rothschild, Latour, Lynch-Bages, Mouton-Rothschild, Pichon-Longueville Baron, Pichon-Longueville–Comtesse de Lalande

St.-Julien: Gruaud-Larose, Léoville-Barton, Léoville-Las Cases, Talbot

Margaux: Monbrison, Rausan-Ségla

Médoc/Haut-Médoc/
Moulis/Listrac/
Crus Bourgeois: Fourcas-Loubaney, Gressier Grand-Poujeaux, Poujeaux, Sociando-Mallet, Tour du Haut-Moulin

Graves Red: Les Carmes Haut-Brion, Domaine de Chevalier, Haut-Bailly, Haut-Brion, La Louvière, La Mission-Haut-Brion, Pape-Clément

Graves White: Domaine de Chevalier, Clos Floridene, Couhins-Lurton, de Fieuzal, Laville-Haut-Brion, La Louvière, La Tour-Martillac

Pomerol: Bon Pasteur, Certan de May, Clinet, L'Eglise-Clinet, La Fleur de Gay, Gombaude-Guillot-Cuvée Speciale, Lafleur, Petit-Village, Pétrus, Le Pin, Vieux-Château-Certan

St.-Emilion: L'Angélus, Ausone, Canon-la-Gaffelière, Clos des Jacobins, Larmande, Le Tertre-Roteboeuf, Troplong-Mondot

Barsac/Sauternes: d'Arche, Broustet, Climens, Coutet, Coutet-Cuvée Madame, Doisy-Daëne, Doisy-Dubroca, Guiraud, Lafaurie-Peyraguey, Lamothe-Guignard, Rabaud-Promis, Rayne-Vigneau, Rieussec, Sigalas Rabaud, Suduiraut, La Tour Blanche

1987—A Quick Study
(10-3-87)

St.-Estèphe **	Graves Red ***
Pauillac **	Graves White ****
St.-Julien **	Pomerol ***
Margaux **	St.-Emilion **
Médoc/Haut-Médoc Crus Bourgeois *	Barsac/Sauternes *

Size: A moderately sized crop that looks almost tiny in the scheme of the gigantic yields during the decade of the eighties.

Important information: The most underrated vintage of the decade of the
    eighties, producing a surprising number of ripe, round, tasty wines,
    particularly from Pomerol, Graves, and the most seriously run es-
    tates in the northern Médoc.
Maturity status: The best examples are deliciously drinkable and should
    be consumed between 1991 and 1998.
Price: Low prices are the rule rather than the exception for this attrac-
    tive, undervalued vintage.

More than one Bordelais has said that if the rain had not arrived during
the first two weeks of October 1987 ravaging the quality of the unharvested Cabernet Sauvignon and Petit Verdot, then 1987—not 1989 or
1982—would be the most extraordinary vintage of the decade of the
eighties. Wasn't it true that August and September had been the hottest
two months in Bordeaux since 1976? But, the rain did fall, plenty of it,
and it dashed the hopes for a top vintage. Yet much of the Merlot was
primarily harvested before the rain. The early-picked Cabernet Sauvignon was adequate, but that picked after the rains began was in very
poor condition. Thanks in part to the two gigantic-sized crops of 1985
and 1986, both record years at the time, most Bordeaux châteaux had
full cellars, and were mentally prepared to eliminate the vats of watery
Cabernet Sauvignon harvested in the rains that fell for 14 straight days
in October. The results for the top estates are wines that are light to
medium bodied, ripe, fruity, round, even fat, with low tannins, low acidity, and lush, captivating, charming personalities.

While there is a tendency to look at 1987 as a poor year and to compare
it with such other recent uninspiring vintages as 1977, 1980, and 1984,
the truth is that the wines could not be more different. In the 1977, 1980,
and 1984 vintages, the problem was immaturity because of cold, wet
weather leading up to the harvest. In 1987, the problem was not a lack
of maturity, as the Merlot and Cabernet were ripe. In 1987, the rains
diluted fully mature, ripe grapes.

The year 1987 is the most underrated vintage of the decade for those
estates where a strict selection was made and/or the Merlot was harvested in sound condition. The wines are deliciously fruity, forward,
clean, fat, and soft, without any degree of rot. Prices remain a bargain
even though the quantities produced were relatively small. This is a
vintage that I search out on restaurant wine lists. I have bought a number
of the wines for my cellar because I regard 1987, much like 1976, as a
very soft, forward vintage that produced wines for drinking in their first
decade of life.

The Best Wines

St.-Estèphe: Cos d'Estournel

Pauillac: Lafite-Rothschild, Latour, Mouton-Rothschild, Pichon-Longueville Baron, Pichon-Longueville–Comtesse de Lalande

St.-Julien: Gruaud-Larose, Léoville-Barton, Léoville-Las Cases, Talbot

Margaux: d'Angludet, Margaux, Palmer

Médoc/Haut-Médoc/
Moulis/Listrac/
Crus Bourgeois: None

Graves Red: Bahans-Haut-Brion, Domaine de Chevalier, Haut-Brion, La Mission-Haut-Brion, Pape-Clément

Graves White: Domaine de Chevalier, Couhins-Lurton, de Fieuzal, Laville-Haut-Brion, La Tour-Martillac

Pomerol: Certan de May, Clinet, La Conseillante, L'Evangile, La Fleur de Gay, Petit-Village, Pétrus, Le Pin

St.-Emilion: Ausone, Cheval Blanc, Clos des Jacobins, Clos Saint-Martin, Grand-Mayne, Magdelaine, Le Tertre-Roteboeuf, Trottevieille

Barsac/Sauternes: Coutet, Lafaurie-Peyraguey

1986—A Quick Study
(9-23-86)

St.-Estèphe ****	Graves Red ***
Pauillac *****	Graves White **
St.-Julien *****	Pomerol ***
Margaux ****	St.-Emilion ***
Médoc/Haut-Médoc Crus Bourgeois ***	Barsac/Sauternes *****

Size: Colossal; along with 1989 and 1990 one of the three largest crops ever produced in Bordeaux.

Important information: An irrefutably great year for the Cabernet Sauvignon grape in the northern Médoc, St.-Julien, Pauillac, and St.-Estèphe. The top 1986s beg for 10–15 more years of cellaring, and one wonders how many purchasers of these wines will lose their patience before the wines have reached full maturity.

Maturity status: The wines from the Crus Bourgeois, Graves, and the right bank can be drunk now, but the impeccably structured Médocs need at least 10–15 more years.

Price: Still realistic except for a handful of the superstar wines as the marketplace remains saturated with fine 1986s, as well as other good vintages. For the top wines, expect this vintage to begin to soar in price when the wines are about 10–12 years of age.

The year 1986 is without doubt a great vintage for the northern Médoc, particularly for St.-Julien, Pauillac, and St.-Estèphe, where many châteaux produced wines that are their deepest and most concentrated since 1982, and with 20–30 plus years of longevity. Yet it should be made very clear to readers that unlike the great vintage of 1982, or very good vintages of 1983 and 1985, the 1986s are not flattering wines to drink young. Most of the top wines of the Médoc will require a minimum of a decade of cellaring to shed their tannins, which are the highest ever measured for a Bordeaux vintage. If you are not prepared to wait for the 1986s to mature, this is not a vintage that makes sense to buy. If you can defer your gratification, then many wines will prove to be the most exhilarating Bordeaux wines produced since 1982.

Why did 1986 turn out to be such an exceptional year for many Médocs, as well as Graves wines, and produce Cabernet Sauvignon grapes of uncommon richness and power? The weather during the summer of 1986 was very dry and hot. In fact, by the beginning of September, Bordeaux was in the midst of a severe drought that began to threaten the final maturity process of the grapes. Rain did come, first on September 14 and 15, which enhanced the maturity process and mitigated the drought conditions. This rain was welcome, but on September 23, a ferocious, quick-moving storm thrashed the city of Bordeaux, the Graves region, and the major right bank appellations of Pomerol and St.-Emilion.

The curious aspect of this major storm, which caused widespread flooding in Bordeaux, was that it barely sideswiped the northern Médoc appellations of St.-Julien, Pauillac, and St.-Estéphe. Those pickers who started their harvest around the end of September found bloated Merlot grapes and unripe Cabernets. Consequently, the top wines of 1986 came from those châteaux that (1) did most of their harvesting after October 5, or (2) eliminated from their final blend the early picked Merlot, as well as the Cabernet Franc and Cabernet Sauvignon harvested between September 23 and October 4. After September 23 there were an extraordinary 23 days of hot, windy, sunny weather that turned the vintage into an exceptional one for those who delayed picking. It is, therefore, no surprise that the late-harvested Cabernet Sauvignon in the northern Médoc that was picked after October 6, but primarily between October 9 and 16, produced wines of extraordinary intensity and depth. To no one's suprise, Château Margaux and Château Mouton-Rothschild, which produced the vintage's two greatest wines, took in the great majority of their Cabernet Sauvignon between October 11 and 16.

In Pomerol and St.-Emilion, those châteaux that harvested soon after the September 23 deluge got predictably much less intense wines. Those that waited (i.e., Vieux-Château-Certan, Lafleur, Le Pin) made much more concentrated, complete wines. As in most vintages, the harvest date in 1986 was critical, and without question the late pickers made the finest wines. Perhaps the most perplexing paradox to emerge from the 1986 vintage is the generally high quality of the Graves wines, particularly in spite of the fact that this area was ravaged by the September 23 rainstorm. The answer in part may be that the top Graves châteaux eliminated more Merlot from the final blend than usual, therefore producing wines with a much higher percentage of Cabernet Sauvignon.

Lastly, the size of the 1986 crop established another record, as the harvest exceeded the bumper crop of 1985 by 15%, and was 30% larger than the 1982 harvest. This overall production figure, equaled in both 1989 and 1990, is somewhat deceiving, as most of the classified Médoc châteaux made significantly less wine in 1986 than in 1985. It is for that reason, as well as the super maturity and tannin levels of the Cabernet Sauvignon grape, that most Médocs are noticeably more concentrated, more powerful, and more tannic in 1986 than they were in 1985.

All things considered, 1986 offers numerous exciting, as well as exhilarating wines of profound depth and exceptional potential for longevity. Yet I continue to ask myself, how many readers are willing to defer their gratification until the turn of the century when these wines will be ready to drink?

The Best Wines

St.-Estèphe: Cos d'Estournel, Montrose

Pauillac: Clerc-Milon, Grand-Puy-Lacoste, Haut-Bages-Libéral, Lafite-Rothschild, Latour, Lynch-Bages, Mouton-Rothschild, Pichon-Longueville Baron, Pichon-Longueville–Comtesse de Lalande

St.-Julien: Beychevelle, Ducru-Beaucaillou, Gruaud-Larose, Lagrange, Léoville-Barton, Léoville-Las Cases, Talbot

Margaux: Margaux, Palmer, Rausan-Ségla

Médoc/Haut Médoc/Moulis/Listrac/Crus Bourgeois: Chasse-Spleen, Fourcas-Loubaney, Gressier Grand-Poujeaux, Lanessan, Maucaillou, Poujeaux, Sociando-Mallet

Graves Red: Domaine de Chevalier, Haut-Brion, La Mission-
Haut-Brion, Pape-Clément
Graves White: None
Pomerol: Certan de May, Clinet, L'Eglise-Clinet, La Fleur
de Gay, Lafleur, Pétrus, Le Pin, Vieux-Château-
Certan
St.-Emilion: L'Arrosée, Canon, Cheval Blanc, Figeac, Pavie,
Le Tertre-Roteboeuf
Barsac/Sauternes: Climens, Coutet-Cuvée Madame, de Fargues,
Guiraud, Lafaurie-Peyraguey, Raymond-Lafon,
Rieussec, Yquem

1985—A Quick Study
(9-29-85)

St.-Estèphe ***	Graves Red ****
Pauillac ****	Graves White ****
St.-Julien ****	Pomerol ****
Margaux ***	St.-Emilion ***
Médoc/Haut-Médoc Crus Bourgeois ***	Barsac/Sauternes **

Size: A very large crop (a record at the time) that was subsequently
surpassed by harvest sizes in 1986, 1989, and 1990.

Important information: The top Médocs may turn out to represent clones
of the gorgeously seductive, charming 1953 vintage. Most of the top
wines are suprisingly well developed, displaying fine richness, a
round, feminine character, and exceptional aromatic purity and
complexity.

Maturity status: Seemingly drinkable from their release, the 1985s continue to develop quickly, yet should last in the top cases for 20–25
years. The top Crus Bourgeois are delicious and should be consumed before the mid-nineties.

Price: Released at outrageously high prices, the 1985s have not appreciated in value to the extent of other top vintages. Prices in 1991 now
look more attractive, particularly in view of the delicious drinking
these wines now offer.

Any vintage, whether in Bordeaux or elsewhere, is shaped by the
weather pattern. The 1985 Bordeaux vintage was conceived in a period
of apprehension. January 1985 was the coldest since 1956. (I was there
on January 16 when the temperature hit a record low 14.5 degrees Centigrade.) However, fear of damage to the vineyard was greatly exaggerated by the Bordelais. One wonders about the sincerity of such fears and

whether they were designed to push up prices for the 1983s and create some demand for the overpriced 1984s. In any event, the spring and early summer were normal, if somewhat more rainy and cooler than usual in April, May, and June. July was slightly hotter and wetter than normal, August was colder than normal but extremely dry. The September weather set a meteorological record—it was the sunniest, hottest, and driest September ever measured. The three most recent top vintages —1961, 1982, and 1989—could not claim such phenomenal weather conditions in September.

The harvest commenced at the end of September and three things became very apparent in that period between September 23 and September 30. First, the Merlot was fully mature and excellent in quality. Second, the Cabernet Sauvignon grapes were not as ripe as expected, and barely reached 11% natural alcohol. Third, the enormous size of the crop caught everyone off guard. The drought of August and September had overly stressed the many Cabernet vineyards planted in gravelly soil, and actually retarded the ripening process. The smart growers stopped picking Cabernet, risking foul weather, but hoping for higher sugar levels. The less adventurous settled for good rather than very good Cabernet Sauvignon. The pickers who waited and picked their Cabernet Sauvignon in mid-October clearly made the best wines as the weather held up throughout the month of October. Because of the drought, there was little botrytis in the Barsac and Sauternes regions. Those wines have turned out to be monolithic, straightforward, and fruity, but in general, lacking complexity and depth.

In general, 1985 is an immensely seductive and attractive vintage that has produced numerous well-balanced, rich, very perfumed yet tender wines. The 1985s are destined to be consumed over the next 15 years while waiting for the tannins of the 1986s to melt away and for richer, fuller, more massive wines from vintages such as 1982 and 1989 to reach full maturity. The year 1985 was a year of great sunshine, heat, and drought, so much so that many of the vineyards planted on lighter, more gravelly soil were stressed.

In the Médoc, 1985 produced an enormous crop. Where the châteaux made a strict selection, the results are undeniably charming, round, precocious, opulent wines with low acidity, and an overall elegant, almost feminine quality. The tannins are soft and mellow.

Interestingly, in the Médoc it is one of those years, much like 1989, where the so-called super seconds, such as Cos d'Estournel, Lynch-Bages, Léoville-Las Cases, Ducru-Beaucaillou, Pichon-Longueville–Comtesse de Lalande, and Léoville-Barton, made wines that rival and in some cases even surpass the more illustrious first-growths. In many vintages (1986 for example) the first-growths soar qualitatively above the rest. That is not the case in 1985.

In the best-case scenario, the top 1985s may well evolve along the lines of the beautiful, charming 1953 vintage.

Most of the Médoc growers, who were glowing in their opinion of the 1985s, called the vintage a blend in style between 1982 and 1983. Others compared the 1985s to the 1976s. Both of these positions seem far off the mark. The 1985s are certainly lighter, without nearly the texture, weight, or concentration of the finest 1982s or 1986s, but at the same time most 1985s are far richer and fuller than the 1976s.

On Bordeaux's right bank, in Pomerol and St.-Emilion, the Merlot was brought in at excellent maturity levels, although many châteaux had a tendency to pick too soon (i.e., Pétrus and Trotanoy). While the vintage is not another 1982 or 1989, it certainly is a fine year in Pomerol. It is less consistent in St.-Emilion because too many producers harvested their Cabernet before it was physiologically fully mature. Interestingly, many of the Libourneais producers compared 1985 stylistically to 1971.

The vintage, which is one of seductive appeal, was priced almost too high when first released. The wines have not appreciated to the extent that many deserve and now look more reasonably priced than at any time in the past.

The Best Wines

St.-Estèphe:	Cos d'Estournel, Haut-Marbuzet
Pauillac:	Lafite-Rothschild, Lynch-Bages, Mouton-Rothschild, Pichon-Longueville–Comtesse de Lalande
St.-Julien:	Ducru-Beaucaillou, Gruaud-Larose, Léoville-Barton, Léoville-Las Cases, Talbot
Margaux:	d'Angludet, Lascombes, Margaux, Palmer, Rausan-Ségla
Graves Red:	Haut-Brion, La Mission-Haut-Brion
Graves White:	Domaine de Chevalier, Haut-Brion, Laville-Haut-Brion
Pomerol:	Certan de May, La Conseillante, L'Eglise-Clinet, L'Evangile, Lafleur, Le Pin, Pétrus
St.-Emilion:	Canon, Cheval Blanc, de Ferrand, Soutard, Le Tertre-Roteboeuf
Barsac/Sauternes:	Yquem

1984—A Quick Study
(10-5-84)

St.-Estèphe*　　　　　　　　　　　　　　Graves Red**
Pauillac**　　　　　　　　　　　　　　　　Graves White*
St.-Julien**　　　　　　　　　　　　　　　Pomerol**
Margaux*　　　　　　　　　　　　　　　　　St.-Emilion*
Médoc/Haut-Médoc Crus Bourgeois*　　　Barsac/Sauternes*

Size: A small- to medium-sized crop of primarily Cabernet-based wine.

Important information: The least attractive current vintage for drinking today, the 1984s, because of the failure of the Merlot crop, are essentially Cabernet-based wines that remain well colored, but compact, stern, and forbiddingly backward and tannic. The best examples may prove surprisingly good, but they need at least another 5–7 years.

Maturity status: Will they be worth the wait?

Price: Virtually any 1984 can be had for a song as most retailers who bought this vintage are stuck with the wines.

The wine press is a curious thing to behold. Many wine writers, most of whom should have known better, maliciously condemned the 1984 vintage as a wash-out during the summer, a good 2 months before the harvest began. Then when the wines were released, the same critics were urging buyers to "purchase these lovely miracle" wines. As usual, the truth lies somewhere in between.

After three abundant vintages, 1981, 1982, and 1983, the climatic conditions during the summer and autumn of 1984 hardly caused euphoria among the Bordelais. First, the vegetative cycle began rapidly, thanks to a magnificently hot, sunny April. However, that was followed by a relatively cool and wet May, which created havoc in the flowering of the quick-to-bud Merlot grape. The result was that much of the 1984 Merlot crop was destroyed long before the summer weather actually arrived. The terrible late spring and early summer conditions made headlines in much of the world's press, which began to paint the vintage as an impending disaster. However, July was dry and hot, and by the end of August, some overly enthusiastic producers were talking about the potential for superripe, tiny quantities of Cabernet Sauvignon. There were even several reporters who were calling 1984 similar to the 1961 vintage. Their intentions could only be considered sinister as 1984 could never be justly compared to 1961.

Following the relatively decent beginning in September, the period between September 21 and October 4 was one of unexpected weather difficulties climaxed by the first cyclone (named Hortense) ever to hit the area, tearing roofs off buildings and giving nervous jitters to winemakers. However, after October 4 the weather cleared up and producers began to harvest their Cabernet Sauvignon. Those who waited picked relatively ripe Cabernet in good condition, although the Cabernet's skin was somewhat thick and the acid levels extremely high, particularly by the standards of more recent vintages.

The problem that existed early on with the 1984s and that continues to present difficulties today is that the wines lack an important percentage of Merlot to counterbalance their narrow, compact, high-acid character. Consequently, there is a lack of fat and charm, but the wines are deep in color, as they are made from Cabernet Sauvignon.

Unquestionably the late pickers made the best wines and most of the top wines have emerged from the Médoc and Graves. They will be longer lived, but probably less enjoyable than the wines from the other difficult vintage of that decade, 1980.

In St.-Emilion and Pomerol, the vintage, if not quite the unqualified disaster painted by the wine press, is, nevertheless, disappointing. Many top properties—Ausone, Canon, Magdelaine, Belair, La Dominique, Couvent-des-Jacobins, and Tertre-Daugay—declassified their entire crop. It was the first vintage since 1968 or 1972 where many of these estates made no wine under their label. Even at Pétrus only 800 cases were made, as opposed to the 4,500 cases produced in both 1985 and 1986.

Seven years after the vintage, the top 1984s remain relatively narrowly constructed, tightly knit wines still displaying a healthy color, but lacking ampleness and charm. Whether they will ever develop any charm is debatable, but there is no doubt that the best examples of the 1984 vintage will keep for some time to come.

The Best Wines

St.-Estèphe: Cos d'Estournel
Pauillac: Latour, Lynch-Bages, Mouton-Rothschild, Pichon-Longueville–Comtesse de Lalande
St.-Julien: Gruaud-Larose, Léoville-Las Cases
Margaux: Margaux
Graves Red: Domaine de Chevalier, Haut-Brion, La Mission-Haut-Brion
Graves White: None
Pomerol: Pétrus, Trotanoy
St.-Emilion: Figeac
Barsac/Sauternes: Yquem

1983—A Quick Study
(9-26-83)

St.-Estèphe **   Graves Red ****
Pauillac ***   Graves White ****
St.-Julien ***   Pomerol ***
Margaux *****   St.-Emilion ****
Médoc/Haut-Médoc Crus Bourgeois **   Barsac/Sauternes ****

Size: A large crop, with overall production slightly inferior to 1982, but in the Médoc, most properties produced more wine than they did in 1982.

Important information: Bordeaux, as well as all of France, suffered from an atypically tropical heat and humidity attack during the month of August. This caused considerable overripening, as well as the advent of rot in certain *terroirs*, particularly in St.-Estèphe, Pauillac, Pomerol, and the sandier plateau sections of St.-Emilion.

Maturity status: At first the vintage was called more classic (or typical) than 1982, with greater aging potential. Eight years later, the 1983s are far more evolved and closer to maturity than the 1982s. In fact, this is a vintage that is approaching full maturity at an accelerated pace.

Price: Prices for the top 1983s remain reasonable because virtually everyone who admires great claret bought heavily in 1982. The only exceptions are the 1983 Margauxs, which are irrefutably superior to their 1982 counterparts.

The year 1983 was one of the most bizarre growing seasons in recent years. The flowering in June went well for the third straight year, ensuring a large crop. The weather in July was so torrid that it turned out to be the hottest July on record. August was extremely hot, rainy, and humid, and as a result, many vineyards began to have significant problems with mildew and rot. It was essential to spray almost weekly in August of 1983 to protect the vineyards. Those properties that did not spray diligently had serious problems with mildew-infected grapes. By the end of August, a dreadful month climatically, many pessimistic producers were apprehensively talking about a disastrous vintage like 1968 or 1965. September brought dry weather, plenty of heat, and no excessive rain. October provided exceptional weather as well, so the grapes harvested late were able to attain maximum ripeness under sunny, dry skies. Not since 1961 had the entire Bordeaux crop, white grapes and red grapes, been harvested in completely dry, fair weather.

The successes that have emerged from 1983 are first and foremost from the appellation of Margaux, which enjoyed its greatest vintage of the decade. In fact, this perennial underachieving appellation produced many top wines, with magnificent efforts from Margaux, Palmer, and Rausan-Ségla (the vintage of resurrection for this famous name), as well as d'Issan and Brane-Cantenac. These wines remain some of the best-kept secrets of the decade.

The other appellations had numerous difficulties, and the wines have not matured as evenly or as gracefully as some prognosticators had suggested. The northern Médoc, particularly the St.-Estèphes, are disappointing. The Pauillacs range from relatively light, overly oaky, roasted wines that are hollow in the middle, to some exceptional successes, most notably from Pichon-Longueville–Comtesse de Lalande, Mouton-Rothschild, and Lafite-Rothschild.

The St.-Juliens will not be remembered for their greatness, with the exception of a superb Léoville-Poyferré. In 1983 Léoville-Poyferré is amazingly as good as the other two Léovilles, Léoville-Las Cases and Léoville-Barton. During the eighties, there is not another vintage where such a statement could be made. The Cordier siblings, Gruaud-Larose and Talbot, made good wines, but overall, 1983 is not a memorable year for St.-Julien.

In Graves, the irregularity continues, with wonderful wines from those Graves châteaux in the Pessac-Léognan area (Haut-Brion, La Mission-Haut-Brion, Haut-Bailly, Domaine de Chevalier, and de Fieuzal), but with disappointments elsewhere in the appellation.

On the right bank, in Pomerol and St.-Emilion, inconsistency is again the rule of thumb. Most of the hillside vineyards in St.-Emilion performed well, but the vintage was mixed on the plateau and in the sandier soils, although Cheval Blanc made one of its greatest wines of the decade. In Pomerol, it is hard to say who made the best wine, but the house of Jean-Pierre Moueix did not fare well in this vintage. Other top properties, such as La Conseillante, L'Evangile, Lafleur, Certan de May, and Le Pin, all made wines that are not far off the quality of their great 1982s.

Even the top wines continue to mature at an accelerated pace and are far more developed from both an aromatic and palate perspective than their 1982 peers.

The Best Wines

St.-Estèphe: None

Pauillac: Lafite-Rothschild, Mouton-Rothschild, Pichon-Longueville–Comtesse de Lalande

St.-Julien: Gruaud-Larose, Léoville-Las Cases, Léoville-Poyferré, Talbot

Margaux: d'Angludet, Brane-Cantenac, Cantemerle
(southern Médoc), d'Issan, Margaux, Palmer,
Prieuré-Lichine, Rausan-Ségla

Médoc/Haut Médoc/
Moulis/Listrac/
Crus Bourgeois: None

Graves Red: Domaine de Chevalier, Haut-Bailly, Haut-Brion,
La Louvière, La Mission-Haut-Brion

Graves White: Domaine de Chevalier, Laville-Haut-Brion

Pomerol: Certan de May, L'Evangile, Lafleur, Pétrus, Le
Pin

St.-Emilion: L'Arrosée, Ausone, Belair, Canon, Cheval Blanc,
Figeac, Larmande

Barsac/Sauternes: Climens, Doisy-Daëne, de Fargues, Guiraud,
Lafaurie-Peyraguey, Raymond-Lafon, Rieussec,
Yquem

1982—A Quick Study
(9-13-82)

St.-Estèphe *****   Graves Red ***
Pauillac *****   Graves White **
St.-Julien *****   Pomerol *****
Margaux ***   St.-Emilion *****
Médoc/Haut-Médoc Crus Bourgeois ****   Barsac/Sauternes ***

Size: An extremely abundant crop, which at the time was a record year,
but has since been equalled in size by 1988, and surpassed in
volume by 1985, 1986, 1989, and 1990.

Important information: The most concentrated and potentially complex
and profound wines since 1961 were produced in virtually every
appellation except for Graves and Margaux.

Maturity Status: Most Crus Bourgeois should have been drunk by 1990
and the lesser wines in St.-Emilion, Pomerol, Graves, and Margaux
are close to full maturity. For the bigger-styled Pomerols, St.-Emi-
lions, and the northern Médocs—St.-Julien, Pauillac, and St.-Es-
tèphe—the wines are evolving at a glacial pace. They have lost
much of their baby fat and have gone into a much more tightly knit,
massive yet much more structured, tannic state.

Price: No modern-day Bordeaux vintage since 1961 has accelerated as
much in price and yet continues, even in recessionary times, to
appreciate in value. Prices are now so frightfully high consumers
who did not purchase these wines as futures can only look back
with envy at those who bought the 1982s when they were first

offered as futures at what now appear to be bargain-basement prices. Who can remember a great vintage being sold at opening prices of: Pichon-Lalande ($110), Léoville-Las Cases ($160), Ducru-Beaucaillou ($150), Pétrus ($600), Cheval Blanc ($550), Margaux ($550), Certan de May ($180), La Lagune ($75), Grand-Puy-Lacoste ($85), Cos d'Estournel ($145), and Canon ($105)? These were the average prices for which the 1982s were sold during the spring, summer, and fall of 1983!

France's most respected wine publication, *Revue Du Vin De France*, and Europe's most skilled and authoritative wine commentator, Michel Bettane, were the first to announce that the 1982 vintage was one of exceptional richness, ripeness, and concentration. Bettane called 1982 the greatest Bordeaux vintage since 1929.

When I issued my report on the 1982 vintage in the April 1983 *Wine Advocate*, I remember feeling that I had never tasted richer, more concentrated, more promising wines than the 1982s. Nine years later, despite some wonderfully successful years such as 1985, 1986, 1989, and 1990, 1982 remains the modern-day point of reference for the greatness Bordeaux can achieve.

The finest wines of the vintage have emerged from the northern Médoc appellations of St.-Julien, Pauillac, and St.-Estèphe, as well as Pomerol and St.-Emilion. They have hardly changed since their early days in barrel, and while displaying a degree of richness, opulence, and intensity I have rarely seen, as they approach their tenth birthdays, most remain relatively unevolved and backward wines.

The wines from other appellations have matured much more quickly, particularly those from Graves, Margaux, and the lighter, lesser wines from Pomerol, St.-Emilion, and the Crus Bourgeois.

Today, no one could intelligently deny the greatness of the 1982 vintage. However, in 1983 this vintage was received among America's wine press with a great deal of skepticism. There was no shortage of outcries about these wines' lack of acidity and "California" style after the vintage's conception. It was suggested by some writers that 1981 and 1979 were "finer vintages," and that the 1982s, "fully mature," should have been "consumed by 1990." Curiously, these writers fail to include specific tasting notes. Of course, wine tasting is subjective, but such statements are nonsense, and it is impossible to justify such criticism of this vintage, particularly in view of how well the top 1982s taste in 1991, and how rich as well as slowly the first-growths, super seconds, and big wines of the northern Médoc, Pomerol and St.-Emilion are evolving. Even in Bordeaux the 1982s are now placed on a pedestal and spoken of in the

same terms as 1961, 1949, 1945, and 1929. Moreover, the marketplace
and auction rooms, perhaps the only true measure of a vintage's value,
continue to push prices for the top 1982s to stratospheric levels. Pierre
Coste, one of Bordeaux's most astute tasters and writers, and someone
who also feels 1982 is the greatest Bordeaux vintage since 1929, contends
that the consistent criticism of the 1982s by certain Americans has nothing to do with the vintage's quality. Could it be that these writers, having
failed to inform their readers of the vintage's greatness, could only protect their standing by criticizing it and/or trying to instill doubt about the
merits of having purchased it? *In vino veritas* becomes *in vino politique.*

The reason why so many 1982s were so remarkable was because of the
outstanding weather conditions. The flowering occurred in hot, sunny,
dry, ideal June weather that served to ensure a large crop. July was
extremely hot and August slightly cooler than normal. By the beginning
of September the Bordeaux producers were expecting a large crop of
excellent quality. However, a September burst of intense heat that lasted
for nearly 3 weeks sent the grape sugars soaring, and what was considered originally to be a very good to excellent vintage was transformed
into a great vintage for every appellation except Margaux and the Graves,
whose very thin, light, gravelly soils suffered during the torrid September
heat. For the first time many producers had to vinify their wines under
unusually hot conditions. Many lessons were learned that were employed
again in subsequent hot vinification years such as 1985, 1989, and 1990.
Rumors of disasters from overheated or stuck fermentations proved to
be without validity, as were reports that rain showers near the end of the
harvest caught some properties with Cabernet Sauvignon still on the
vine.

When analyzed, the 1982s are the most concentrated, high-extract
wines since 1961, with acid levels that while low, are no lower than in
years of exceptional ripeness such as 1949, 1953, 1959, 1961, and, surprisingly, 1975. Though some skeptics pointed to the low acidity, many
of those same skeptics fell in love with the 1985s, 1989s, and 1990s, all
Bordeaux vintages that produced wines with significantly lower acids and
higher pH's than the 1982s. Tannin levels were extremely high, but
subsequent vintages, particularly 1986, 1988, 1989, and 1990, produced
wines with even higher tannin levels than the 1982s.

Recent tastings of the 1982s continue to suggest that the top wines of
the northern Médoc need another 10–15 years of cellaring. Most of the
best wines seem largely unevolved since their early days in cask. They
have fully recovered from the bottling and display the extraordinary expansive, rich, glycerin- and extract-laden palates that should serve these
wines well over the next 15–20 years. If the 1982 vintage remains sen-

sational for the majority of St.-Emilions, Pomerols, St.-Juliens, Pauillacs, and St.-Estèphes, the weakness of the vintage becomes
increasingly more apparent with the Margaux and Graves wines. Only
Château Margaux seems to have survived the problems of overproduction, loosely knit, flabby Cabernet Sauvignon wines from which so many
other Margaux properties suffered. The same can be said for the Graves,
which are light and disjointed when compared to the lovely 1983s Graves
produced. Only La Mission-Haut-Brion and Haut-Brion produced better
1982s than 1983s.

On the negative side are the prices one must now pay for a top wine
from the 1982 vintage. Is this a reason why the vintage still receives
cheap shots from a handful of American writers? Those who bought them
as futures made the wine buys of the century. But those who did not and
still want to drink the wines of this vintage are faced with the prospect
of paying prices that are often higher than what one would pay for a fine
1970 claret. That may make no sense, but for today's generation of wine
enthusiasts 1982 is what 1945, 1947, and 1949 were for an earlier generation of wine lovers.

Lastly, the sweet wines of Barsac and Sauternes in 1982, while maligned originally for their lack of botrytis and richness, are not that bad.
In fact, Yquem and the Cuvée Madame of Château Suduiraut are two
remarkably powerful, rich wines that can stand up to the best of the
1983s, 1986s, and 1988s.

The Best Wines

St.-Estèphe:	Calon-Ségur, Cos d'Estournel, Haut-Marbuzet, Montrose
Pauillac:	Les Forts de Latour, Grand-Puy-Lacoste, Haut-Batailley, Lafite-Rothschild, Latour, Lynch-Bages, Mouton-Rothschild, Pichon-Longueville Baron, Pichon-Longueville–Comtesse de Lalande
St.-Julien:	Beychevelle, Branaire-Ducru, Ducru-Beaucaillou, Gruaud-Larose, Léoville-Barton, Léoville-Las Cases, Léoville-Poyferré, Talbot
Margaux:	Margaux, La Lagune (southern Médec)
Médoc/Haut Médoc/ Moulis/Listrac/ Crus Bourgeois:	Tour Haut-Caussan, Maucaillou, Potensac, Poujeaux, Sociando-Mallet, La Tour St.-Bonnet
Graves Red:	Haut-Brion, La Mission-Haut-Brion, La Tour-Haut-Brion

Graves White: None
Pomerol: Bon Pasteur, Certan de May, La Conseillante, L'Enclos, L'Evangile, Le Gay, Lafleur, Latour à Pomerol, Petit-Village, Pétrus, Le Pin, Trotanoy, Vieux-Château-Certan
St.-Emilion: L'Arrosée, Ausone, Canon, Cheval Blanc, La Dominique, Figeac, Pavie
Barsac/Sauternes: Raymond-Lafon, Suduiraut-Cuvée Madame, Yquem

1981—A Quick Study
(9-28-81)

St.-Estèphe**	Graves Red**
Pauillac***	Graves White**
St.-Julien***	Pomerol***
Margaux**	St.-Emilion**
Médoc/Haut-Médoc Crus Bourgeois*	Barsac/Sauternes*

Size: The moderately large crop that in retrospect now looks modest.

Important information: The first vintage in a succession of hot, dry years that would continue nearly uninterrupted through 1990. The year 1981 would have been a top vintage had the rain not fallen immediately prior to the harvest.

Maturity status: Most 1981s are close to full maturity, yet the best examples are capable of lasting for at least another decade.

Price: A largely ignored and overlooked vintage, 1981 remains underpriced and a reasonably good value.

This vintage has been labeled more "classic" than either 1983 or 1982. What classic means to those who call 1981 a classic vintage is that this year is a typically good Bordeaux vintage of medium-weight, well-balanced, graceful wines. Despite a dozen or so excellent wines, 1981 is in reality only a good vintage, surpassed in quality by both 1982 and 1983, and also by 1978 and 1979.

The year 1981 could have been an outstanding vintage had it not been for the heavy rains that fell just as the harvest was about to start. There was a dilution of the intensity of flavor in the grapes as heavy rains drenched the vineyards between October 1 and 5, and again between October 9 and 15. Until then, the summer had been perfect. The flowering occurred under excellent conditions; July was cool, but August and September hot and dry. One can only speculate, that had it not rained,

1981 might well have also turned out to be one of the greatest vintages in the post–World War II era.

The year 1981 did produce a large crop of generally well-colored wines of medium weight and moderate tannin. The dry white wines have turned out well, but should have been consumed by now. Both Barsacs and Sauternes suffered as a result of the rains and no truly compelling wines have emerged from these appellations.

There are a number of successful wines in 1981, particularly from such appellations as Pomerol, St.-Julien, and Pauillac. Ten years after the vintage, the 1981s have generally reached their plateau of maturity, and only the best will keep for another 10–15 years. The wines' shortcomings are their lack of the richness, flesh, and intensity that more recent vintages have possessed. Most red wine producers had to chaptalize significantly because the Cabernets were harvested under 11% natural alcohol, and the Merlot under 12%, no doubt because of the rain.

The Best Wines

St.-Estèphe:	None
Pauillac:	Lafite-Rothschild, Latour, Pichon-Longueville–Comtesse de Lalande
St.-Julien:	Ducru-Beaucaillou, Gruaud-Larose, Léoville-Las Cases, St.-Pierre
Margaux:	Giscours, Margaux
Médoc/Haut-Médoc Crus Bourgeois:	None
Graves Red:	La Mission-Haut-Brion
Graves White:	None
Pomerol:	Certan de May, La Conseillante, Pétrus, Le Pin, Vieux-Château-Certan
St.-Emilion:	Cheval Blanc
Barsac/Sauternes:	Climens, de Fargues, Yquem

1980—A Quick Study
(10-14-80)

St.-Estèphe*	Graves Red**
Pauillac**	Graves White*
St.-Julien**	Pomerol**
Margaux**	St.-Emilion*
Médoc/Haut-Médoc Crus Bourgeois*	Barsac/Sauternes****

Size: A moderately sized crop was harvested.

Important information: Nothing very noteworthy can be said about this
   mediocre vintage.

Maturity status: With the exception of Château Margaux and Pétrus,
   virtually every 1980 should be consumed over the next several
   years.

Price: Low.

For a decade that became known as the golden age of Bordeaux, or
the decade of the century, the eighties certainly did not begin in an
auspicious fashion. The summer of 1980 was cool and wet, the flowering
was unexciting because of a disappointing June, and by early September
the producers were looking at a return of the two most dreadful vintages
of the last 30 years, 1963 and 1968. However, modern-day antirot sprays
did a great deal to protect the grapes from the dreaded *pourriture*. For
that reason, the growers were able to delay their harvest until the
weather began to improve at the end of September. The weather in early
October was favorable until rains began in the middle of the month, just
as many producers began to harvest. The results have been light, diluted,
frequently disappointing wines that have an unmistakable vegetal and
herbaceous taste and are often marred by excessive acidity as well as
tannin. Those producers who made a strict selection and who picked
exceptionally late, such as the Mentzelopoulos family at Château Margaux (the wine of the vintage), made softer, rounder, more interesting
wines that began to drink well in the late eighties and should continue to
drink well until the turn of the century. However, the number of properties that could be said to have made wines of good quality are few.

As always in wet, cool years, those vineyards planted on lighter, gravelly, well-drained soils, such as some of the Margaux and Graves properties, tend to get better maturity and ripeness. Not surprisingly, the top
successes generally come from these areas, although several Pauillacs,
because of a very strict selection, also have turned out well.

As disappointing as the 1980 vintage was for the red wine producers,
it was an excellent year for the producers of Barsac and Sauternes. The
ripening and harvesting continued into late November, generally under
ideal conditions. This permitted some rich, intense, high-class Barsac
and Sauternes to be produced. Unfortunately, their commercial viability
suffered from the reputation of the red wine vintage. Anyone who comes
across a bottle of 1980 Climens, Yquem, or Raymond-Lafon will immediately realize that this is an astonishingly good year.

The Best Wines

St.-Estèphe: None
Pauillac: Latour, Pichon-Longueville–Comtesse de Lalande
St.-Julien: Talbot
Margaux: Margaux
Médoc/Haut-Médoc/ Moulis/Listrac/ Crus Bourgeois: None
Graves Red: Domaine de Chevalier, La Mission-Haut-Brion
Graves White: None
Pomerol: Certan de May, Pétrus
St.-Emilion: Cheval Blanc
Barsac/Sauternes: Climens, de Fargues, Raymond-Lafon, Yquem

1979—A Quick Study
(10-3-79)

St.-Estèphe **   Graves Red ****
Pauillac ***   Graves White **
St.-Julien ***   Pomerol ***
Margaux ****   St.-Emilion **
Médoc/Haut-Médoc Crus Bourgeois **   Barsac/Sauternes *

Size: A huge crop that established a record at that time.

Important information: In the last 2 decades this is one of the only cool years that turned out to be a reasonably good vintage.

Maturity status: Contrary to earlier reports, the 1979s have matured very slowly, largely because the wines have relatively hard tannins and good acidity, two characteristics that most of the top vintages during the decade of the eighties have not possessed.

Price: Because of the lack of demand, and the vintage's average-to-good reputation, prices remain low except for a handful of the limited production, glamour wines of Pomerol.

The year 1979 has become the forgotten vintage in Bordeaux. A record-setting crop that produced relatively healthy, medium-bodied wines that displayed firm tannins and good acidity closed out the decade of the seventies. Over the next decade this vintage was rarely mentioned in the wine press. No doubt most of the wines were consumed long before they reached their respective apogees. Considered inferior to 1978 when conceived, the 1979 vintage will prove superior—at least in terms of aging potential. Yet aging potential alone is hardly sufficient to evaluate a vintage, and many 1979s remain relatively skinny, malnourished, lean, compact wines that naïve commentators have called classic rather than thin.

Despite the inconsistency from appellation to appellation, a number of strikingly good, surprisingly flavorful, rich wines have emerged from appellations such as Margaux, Graves, and Pomerol.

With few exceptions, there is no hurry to drink the top 1979s since their relatively high acid levels (compared to more recent hot year vintages) and good tannin levels, as well as sturdy framework should ensure that the top 1979s age well for at least another 10–15 years.

This was not a good vintage for the dry white wines or sweet white wines of Barsac and Sauternes. The dry whites did not achieve full maturity and there was never enough botrytis for the Barsac and Sauternes to give the wines that honeyed complexity that is fundamental to their success.

Prices for 1979s, where they can still be found, are the lowest of any good recent Bordeaux vintage, reflecting the general lack of excitement for most 1979s.

The Best Wines

St.-Estèphe:	Cos d'Estournel
Pauillac:	Lafite-Rothschild, Latour, Pichon-Longueville– Comtesse de Lalande
St.-Julien:	Gruaud-Larose, Léoville-Las Cases
Margaux:	Giscours, Margaux, Palmer, du Tertre
Graves Red:	Les Carmes Haut-Brion, Domaine de Chevalier, Haut-Bailly, Haut-Brion, La Mission-Haut-Brion
Pomerol:	Certan de May, L'Enclos, L'Evangile, Lafleur, Pétrus
St.-Emilion:	Ausone
Barsac/Sauternes:	None

1978—A Quick Study
(10-7-78)

St.-Estèphe **	Graves Red *****
Pauillac ***	Graves White ****
St.-Julien ****	Pomerol **
Margaux ****	St.-Emilion ***
Médoc/Haut-Médoc Crus Bourgeois **	Barsac/Sauternes **

Size: A moderately sized crop was harvested.

Important information: The year Harry Waugh, England's gentlemanly wine commentator, dubbed, "the miracle year."

Maturity status: Most wines are fully mature.
Price: High.

The year 1978 turned out to be an outstanding vintage for the red wines of Graves and a good vintage for the red wines from the Médoc, Pomerol, and St.-Emilion. There was a lack of botrytis for the sweet white wines of Barsac and Sauternes and the results were monolithic, straightforward wines of no great character. The dry white Graves, much like the red wines of that appellation, turned out exceedingly well.

The weather profile for 1978 was hardly encouraging. The spring was cold and wet, and poor weather continued to plague the region through June, July, and early August, causing many growers to begin thinking of such dreadful years as 1963, 1965, 1968, and 1977. However, in mid-August a huge anticyclone, high-pressure system settled over southwestern France and northern Spain and for the next nine weeks the weather was sunny, hot, and dry, except for an occasional light rain shower that had negligible effects.

Because the grapes were so behind in their maturation (contrast that scenario with the more recent advanced maturity years such as 1989 and 1990), the harvest began extremely late on October 7. It continued under excellent weather conditions, which seemed, as Harry Waugh put it, miraculous, in view of the miserable weather throughout much of the spring and summer.

The general view of this vintage is that it is a very good to excellent year. The two best appellations are Graves and Margaux, which have the lighter, better drained soils that support cooler weather years. In fact, Graves (except for the disappointing Pape-Clément) probably enjoyed its greatest vintage after 1961. The wines, which at first appeared intensely fruity, deeply colored, moderately tannic, and medium bodied, have aged much faster than the higher acid, more firmly tannic 1979s, which were the product of an even cooler, drier year. Most 1978s had reached full maturity twelve years after the vintage and some commentators were expressing their disappointment that the wines were not better than they had believed.

The problem is that, much like in 1979, 1981, and 1988, there is a shortage of truly superstar wines. There are a number of very good wines, but the lack of excitement in the majority of wines has tempered the postvintage enthusiasm. Moreover, the lesser wines in 1978 have an annoyingly vegetal, herbaceous taste because those vineyards not planted on the best soils never fully ripened despite the impressively hot, dry, *"fin de saison."* Another important consideration is that the selection process, so much a fundamental principle in the decade of the '80s, was employed less during the seventies as many properties simply bottled everything under the grand vin label. In talking with proprietors today, many feel that 1978 could have lived up to its early promise had a stricter selection been in effect when the wines were made.

This was a very difficult vintage for properties in the Barsac/Sauternes region because very little botrytis formed due to the hot, dry autumn. The wines, much like the 1979s, are chunky, full of glycerin and sugar, but lack grip, focus, and complexity.

The Best Wines

St.-Estèphe: None

Pauillac: Les Forts de Latour, Grand-Puy-Lacoste, Latour, Pichon-Longueville–Comtesse de Lalande

St.-Julien: Ducru-Beaucaillou, Gruaud-Larose, Léoville-Las Cases, Talbot

Margaux: Giscours, La Lagune (southern Médoc), Margaux, Palmer, Prieuré-Lichine, du Tertre

Médoc/Haut-Médoc/ Moulis/Listrac/ Crus Bourgeois: None

Graves Red: Les Carmes Haut-Brion, Domaine de Chevalier, Haut-Bailly, Haut-Brion, La Mission-Haut-Brion, La Tour-Haut-Brion

Graves White: Domaine de Chevalier, Haut-Brion, Laville-Haut-Brion

Pomerol: Lafleur

St.-Emilion: L'Arrosée, Cheval Blanc

Barsac/Sauternes: None

1977—A Quick Study
(10-3-77)

St.-Estèphe *	Graves Red *
Pauillac *	Graves White *
St.-Julien *	Pomerol 0
Margaux *	St.-Emilion 0
Médoc/Haut-Médoc Crus Bourgeois *	Barsac/Sauternes *

Size: A small crop was produced.

Important information: A dreadful vintage, clearly the worst of the decade; it remains, in a pejorative sense, unequaled since.

Maturity status: The wines, even the handful that were drinkable, should have been consumed by the mid-eighties.

Price: Despite distress sale prices, there are no values to be found.

This is the worst vintage for Bordeaux during the decade of the seventies. Even the two mediocre years of the eighties, 1980 and 1984, are far superior to 1977. Much of the Merlot crop was devastated by a late spring frost. The summer was cold and wet. When warm, dry weather finally arrived just prior to the harvest, there was just too little time left to save the vintage. The harvest resulted in grapes that were both analytically and physiologically immature and far from ripe.

The wines, which were relatively acidic and overtly herbaceous to the point of being vegetal, should have been consumed years ago. Some of the more successful wines included a decent Figeac, Giscours, Gruaud-Larose, Pichon Lalande, Latour, and the three Graves estates of Haut-Brion, La Mission-Haut-Brion, and Domaine de Chevalier. However, I have never been able to recommend any of these wines. They have no value from either a monetary or pleasure standpoint.

1976—A Quick Study
(9-13-76)

St.-Estèphe ***	Graves Red *
Pauillac ***	Graves White ***
St.-Julien ***	Pomerol ***
Margaux **	St.-Emilion ***
Médoc/Haut-Médoc Crus Bourgeois *	Barsac/Sauternes ****

Size: A huge crop, the second largest of the decade, was harvested.

Important information: This hot, drought-like vintage could have proved to be the vintage of the decade had it not been for preharvest rains.

Maturity status: The 1976s tasted fully mature and delicious when released in 1979. Yet the best examples continue to offer delightful, sometimes even sumptuous drinking. It is one of a handful of vintages where the wines have never closed up and been unappealing.

Price: The 1976s have always been reasonably priced because they have never received accolades from the wine pundits.

A very highly publicized vintage, 1976 has never quite lived up to its reputation. All the ingredients were present for a superb vintage. The harvest date of September 13 was the earliest harvest since 1945. The weather during the summer had been torridly hot, with the average temperatures for the months of June through September only exceeded by the hot summers of 1949 and 1947. However, with many vignerons predicting a "vintage of the century," very heavy rains fell between September 11 and 15, bloating the grapes.

The crop that was harvested was large, the grapes were ripe, and while the wines had good tannin levels, the acidity levels were low and their pH's dangerously high. The top wines of 1976 have offered wonderfully soft, supple, deliciously fruity drinking since they were released in 1979. I had fully expected that these wines would have to be consumed before the end of the decade of the eighties. However, the top 1976s appear to have stayed at their peak of maturity without fading or losing their fruit. I wish I had bought more of this vintage given how delicious the best wines have been over such an extended period of time. They will not make "old bones," and one must be very careful with the weaker 1976s, which have lacked intensity and depth from the beginning. These wines were extremely fragile and have increasingly taken on a brown cast to their color as well as losing their fruit. Nevertheless, the top wines continue to offer delicious drinking and persuasive evidence that even in a relatively diluted, extremely soft-styled vintage, with dangerously low acid levels, Bordeaux wines, where well stored, can easily last 15 or more years.

The 1976 vintage was at its strongest in the northern Médoc appellations of St.-Julien, Pauillac, and St.-Estèphe, weakest in Graves and Margaux, and mixed in the Libournais appellations of Pomerol and St.-Emilion.

For those who admire decadently rich, honeyed, sweet wines, this is one of the two best vintages of the seventies, given the abundant quantities of botrytis that formed in the vineyards and the lavish richness and opulent style of the wines of Barsac/Sauternes.

The Best Wines

St.-Estèphe:	Cos d'Estournel, Montrose
Pauillac:	Haut-Bages-Libéral, Lafite-Rothschild, Pichon-Longueville–Comtesse de Lalande
St.-Julien:	Beychevelle, Branaire-Ducru, Ducru-Beaucaillou, Léoville-Las Cases, Talbot
Margaux:	Giscours, La Lagune (southern Médoc)
Médoc/Haut Médoc/ Moulis/Listrac/ Crus Bourgeois:	Sociando-Mallet
Graves Red:	Haut-Brion
Graves White:	Domaine de Chevalier, Laville-Haut-Brion
Pomerol:	Pétrus
St.-Emilion:	Ausone, Cheval Blanc, Figeac
Barsac/Sauternes:	Climens, Coutet, de Fargues, Guiraud, Rieussec, Suduiraut, Yquem

1975—A Quick Study
(9-22-75)

St.-Estèphe **   Graves Red **
Pauillac ****   Graves White ***
St.-Julien ****   Pomerol *****
Margaux **   St.-Emilion ***
Médoc/Haut-Médoc Crus Bourgeois ***   Barsac/Sauternes ****

Size: After the abundant vintages of 1973 and 1974, 1975 was a moderately sized crop.

Important information: After three consecutive poor-to-mediocre years,
the Bordelais were ready to praise to the heavens the 1975 vintage.

Maturity status: The slowest-evolving vintage in the last thirty years.

Price: Trade and consumer uneasiness concerning the falling reputation
of this vintage, as well as the style of even the top wines that remain
hard, closed, and nearly impenetrable, make this an attractively
priced year for those with patience.

Is this the year of the great deception, or the year where some irrefutably classic wines were produced? Along with 1964 and 1983, this is
perhaps the most tricky vintage with which to come to grips. There are
some undeniably great wines in the 1975 vintage, but the overall quality
level is distressingly uneven, and the number of failures is too numerous
to ignore.

Because of the three previous large crops and the international financial crisis brought on by high oil prices, the producers, knowing that
their 1972, 1973, and 1974 vintages were already backed up in the marketplace, pruned their vineyards to guard against a large crop. The
weather cooperated; July, August, and September were all hot months.
However, in August and September several large thunderstorms dumped
enormous quantities of rain on the area. It was localized, and most of it
did little damage except to frazzle the nerves of winemakers. However,
several hailstorms did ravage the central Médoc communes, particularly
Moulis, Lamarque, and Arcins, and some isolated hailstorms damaged
the southern Léognan-Pessac region.

The harvest began during the third week of September and continued
under generally good weather conditions through mid-October. Immediately after the harvest, the producers were talking of a top-notch vintage,
perhaps the best since 1961. So what happened?

Looking back after having had numerous opportunities to taste and
discuss the style of this vintage with many proprietors and winemakers,
it is apparent that the majority of growers should have harvested their

Cabernet Sauvignon later. Many feel it was picked too soon, and the fact that at that time many were not totally destemming only served to exacerbate the relatively hard, astringent tannins in the 1975s.

This is one of the first vintages I tasted (although on a much more limited basis) from cask, visiting Bordeaux as a tourist rather than a professional. In 1975, many of the young wines exhibited great color, intensely ripe, fragrant noses, and immense potential. Other wines appeared to have an excess of tannin. The wines immediately closed up 2–3 years after bottling, and in most cases still remain stubbornly hard and backward. There are a number of badly made, excessively tannic wines where the fruit has already dried out and the color has become brown. Many of them were aged in old oak barrels (new oak was not nearly as prevalent as it is now), and the sanitary conditions in many cellars were less than ideal. However, even allowing for these variations, I have always been struck by the tremendous difference in the quality of wines in this vintage. To this day the wide swings in quality remain far greater than in any other recent year. For example, how could La Mission-Haut-Brion, Pétrus, L'Evangile, and Lafleur produce such profoundly great wines yet many of their neighbors fail completely? This remains one of the vintage's mysteries.

This is a vintage for true Bordeaux connoisseurs who have the patience to wait the wines out. The top examples, which usually come from Pomerol, St.-Julien, and Pauillac (the extraordinary success of La Mission-Haut-Brion and La Tour-Haut-Brion, and to a lesser extent, Haut-Brion, is an exception to the sad level of quality in Graves), are wines that have still not reached their apogees. Could the great 1975s turn out to resemble wines from a vintage such as 1928 that took 30-plus years to reach full maturity? The great successes of this vintage are capable of lasting and lasting because they have the richness and concentration of ripe fruit to balance out their tannins. However, there are many wines that are too dry, too astringent, or too tannic to develop gracefully.

I purchased this vintage as futures, and I remember thinking I secured great deals on the first-growths at $350 a case. But I have invested in 15 years of patience, and the wait for the top wines will be at least another 10 years. Waiting 25 years for a wine to mature can painfully push one's discipline to the limit. This is the vintage for delayed gratification.

The Best Wines
St.-Estèphe: Haut-Marbuzet, Meyney, Montrose
Pauillac: Lafite-Rothschild, Latour, Mouton-Rothschild, Pichon-Longueville–Comtesse de Lalande
St.-Julien: Branaire-Ducru, Gloria, Gruaud-Larose, Léoville-Barton, Léoville-Las Cases

Margaux: Giscours, Palmer
Médoc/Haut-Médoc/
Moulis/Listrac/
Crus Bourgeois: Greysac, Sociando-Mallet, La Tour St.-Bonnet
Graves Red: Haut-Brion, La Mission-Haut-Brion, Pape-
Clément, La Tour-Haut-Brion
Pomerol: L'Enclos, L'Evangile, La Fleur Pétrus, Le Gay,
Lafleur, Nenin, Pétrus, Trotanoy, Vieux-Château-
Certan
St.-Emilion: Cheval Blanc, Figeac, Magdelaine, Soutard
Barsac/Sauternes: Climens, Coutet, de Fargues, Raymond-Lafon,
Rieussec, Yquem

1974—A Quick Study
(9-20-74)

St.-Estèphe *	Graves Red **
Pauillac *	Graves White *
St.-Julien *	Pomerol **
Margaux *	St.-Emilion *
Médoc/Haut-Médoc Crus Bourgeois *	Barsac/Sauternes *

Size: An enormous crop was harvested.

Important information: Should you still have stocks of the '74s, it is best
to consume them over the next several years, or donate them to
charity.

Maturity status: A handful of the top wines of the vintage are still alive
and well, but aging them any further will prove fruitless.

Price: These wines were always inexpensive and I can never imagine
them fetching a decent price unless you find someone in need of
this year to celebrate a birthday.

As a result of a good flowering and a dry, sunny May and June, the
crop size was large in 1974. The weather from mid-August through October was cold, windy, and rainy. Despite the persistent soggy conditions, the appellation of choice in 1974 turned out to be Graves. While
most 1974s remain hard, tannic, hollow wines lacking ripeness, flesh,
and character, a number of the Graves estates did produce surprisingly
spicy, interesting wines. Though somewhat compact and attenuated,
they are still enjoyable to drink sixteen years after the vintage. The two
stars are La Mission-Haut-Brion and Domaine de Chevalier, followed by
Latour in Pauillac and Trotanoy in Pomerol. Should you have remaining
stocks of these wines in your cellar, it would be foolish to push your luck.

In spite of their well-preserved status, my instincts suggest drinking them soon.

The vintage was equally bad in the Barsac/Sauternes region. I have never seen a bottle to taste.

It is debatable as to which was the worst vintage during the decade of the seventies—1972, 1974, or 1977.

1973—A Quick Study
(9-20-73)

St.-Estèphe **	Graves Red *
Pauillac *	Graves White **
St.-Julien **	Pomerol **
Margaux *	St.-Emilion *
Médoc/Haut-Médoc Crus Bourgeois *	Barsac/Sauternes *

Size: Enormous; one of the largest crops of the seventies.

Important information: A sadly rain-bloated, swollen crop of grapes in poor-to-mediocre condition was harvested.

Maturity status: The odds are stacked against finding a 1973 that is still in good condition, at least from a regular-size bottle.

Price: Distressed sale prices, even for those born in this year.

In the mid-'70s, the best 1973s had some value as agreeably light, round, soft, somewhat diluted yet pleasant Bordeaux wines. With the exception of Domaine de Chevalier, Pétrus and the great sweet classic, Yquem, all of the 1973s have faded into oblivion.

So often the Bordelais are on the verge of a top-notch vintage when the rains arrive. The rains that came during the harvest bloated what would have been a healthy, enormous grape crop. Modern-day sprays and techniques such as *saigner* were inadequately utilized in the early '70s, and the result in 1973 was a group of wines that lacked color, extract, acidity, and backbone. The wines were totally drinkable when released in 1976. By the beginning of the '80s, they were in complete decline, save Pétrus.

The Best Wines *

St.-Estèphe: de Pez
Pauillac: Latour
St.-Julien: Ducru-Beaucaillou
Margaux: None

* This list is for informational purposes only as I suspect all of the above wines, with the possible exception of Pétrus, are in serious decline unless found in larger-format bottlings that have been perfectly stored.

Médoc/Haut-Médoc/
   Moulis/Listrac/
    Crus Bourgeois: None
    Graves Red: Domaine de Chevalier, La Tour-Haut-Brion
   Graves White: None
     Pomerol: Pétrus
    St.-Emilion: None
Barsac/Sauternes: Yquem

1972—A Quick Study
(10-7-72)

St.-Estèphe 0	Graves Red *
Pauillac 0	Graves White 0
St.-Julien 0	Pomerol 0
Margaux *	St.-Emilion *
Médoc/Haut-Médoc Crus Bourgeois 0	Barsac/Sauternes 0

Size: A moderately sized crop was harvested.
Important information: The worst vintage of the decade.
Maturity status: Most wines have long been over the hill.
Price: Extremely low.

The weather pattern of 1972 was one of unusually cool, cloudy summer months with an abnormally rainy month of August. While September brought dry, warm weather, it was too late to save the crop. The 1972 wines turned out to be the worst of the decade—acidic, green, raw, and vegetal tasting. The high acidity did manage to keep many of them alive for 10–15 years, but their deficiencies in fruit, charm, and flavor concentration were far too great for even age to overcome.

As in any poor vintage, some châteaux managed to produce decent wines, with the well-drained soils of Margaux and Graves turning out slightly better wines than elsewhere.

There are no longer any wines from 1972 that would be of any interest to consumers.

The Best Wines *
    St.-Estèphe: None
     Pauillac: Latour
    St.-Julien: Branaire-Ducru, Léoville-Las Cases
    Margaux: Giscours, Rausan-Ségla

* This list is for informational purposes only as I suspect all of the above wines are in serious decline unless found in larger-format bottlings that have been perfectly stored.

Médoc/Haut-Médoc/
   Moulis/Listrac/
     Crus Bourgeois: None
      Graves Red: La Mission-Haut-Brion, La Tour-Haut-Brion
     Graves White: None
       Pomerol: Trotanoy
     St.-Emilion: Cheval Blanc, Figeac
 Barsac/Sauternes: Climens

1971—A Quick Study
(9-25-71)

St.-Estèphe **   Graves Red ***
Pauillac ***   Graves White **
St.-Julien ***   Pomerol ****
Margaux ***   St.-Emilion ***
Médoc/Haut-Médoc Crus Bourgeois **   Barsac/Sauternes ****

Size: Small to moderate crop size.

Important information: A good to very good, stylish vintage with the strongest efforts emerging from Pomerol and the sweet wines of Barsac/Sauternes.

Maturity status: Every 1971 has been fully mature for nearly a decade, with the best *cuvées* capable of lasting another decade.

Price: The small crop size kept prices high, but most 1971s, compared to other good vintages of the last thirty years, are slightly undervalued.

Unlike 1970, 1971 was a small vintage because of a poor flowering in June that caused a significant reduction in the Merlot crop. By the end of the harvest, the crop size was a good 40% less than the huge crop of 1970.

Early reports of the vintage have proven to be overly enthusiastic. Some experts (particularly Bordeaux's Peter Sichel), relying on the small production yields when compared to 1970, even claimed that the vintage was better than 1970. This has proved to be totally false. Certainly the 1971s were forward and delicious, as were the 1970s when first released, but unlike the 1970s, the 1971s lacked the great depth of color, concentration, and tannic backbone. The vintage was mixed in the Médoc, but it was a fine year for Pomerol, St.-Emilion, and Graves.

Buying 1971s now could prove dangerous unless the wines have been exceptionally well stored. Twenty years after the vintage there are a handful of wines that have just reached full maturity—Pétrus, Latour, Trotanoy, La Mission-Haut-Brion. Well-stored examples of these wines will continue to drink well for at least another 10–15 years. Elsewhere, storage is everything. This could be a vintage at which to take a serious look provided one can find reasonably priced, well-preserved bottles.

The sweet wines of Barsac and Sauternes were successful and are in full maturity. The best of them have at least 1–2 decades of aging potential and will certainly outlive all of the red wines produced in 1971.

The Best Wines

St.-Estèphe: Montrose
Pauillac: Latour, Mouton-Rothschild
St.-Julien: Beychevelle, Gloria, Gruaud-Larose, Talbot
Margaux: Palmer
Médoc/Haut-Médoc/
Moulis/Listrac/
Crus Bourgeois: None
Graves Red: Haut-Brion, La Mission-Haut-Brion, La Tour-Haut-Brion
Graves White: None
Pomerol: Petit-Village, Pétrus, Trotanoy
St.-Emilion: Cheval Blanc, La Dominique
Barsac/Sauternes: Climens, Coutet, de Fargues, Yquem

1970—A Quick Study
(9-27-70)

St.-Estèphe ****	Graves Red ****
Pauillac *****	Graves White ***
St.-Julien *****	Pomerol ****
Margaux ***	St.-Emilion ***
Médoc/Haut-Médoc Crus Bourgeois ***	Barsac/Sauternes ***

Size: An enormous crop that was a record setter at the time.

Important information: The first modern-day abundant crop that combined high quality with large quantity.

Maturity status: Initially, the 1970s were called precocious and early maturing. Most of the big 1970s have aged very slowly and are now in full maturity, with only a handful of exceptions. The smaller wines, Crus Bourgeois, and lighter-weight Pomerols and St.-Emilions should have been drunk by 1980.

Price: Expensive, no doubt because this is the most popular vintage between 1961 and 1982.

Between the two great vintages 1961 and 1982, 1970 has proved to be the best year, producing wines that were attractively rich, and full of charm and complexity. They have aged more gracefully than many of the austere 1966s and seem fuller, richer, more evenly balanced and consistent than the hard, tannic, large-framed but often hollow and tough 1975s. The year 1970 proved to be the first modern-day vintage that combined high production with impeccable quality. Moreover, it was a splendidly uniform and consistent vintage throughout Bordeaux, with every appellation able to claim its share of top-quality wines.

The weather conditions during the summer and early fall were perfect. There was no hail, no weeks of drenching downpours, no frost, and no spirit-crushing inundation at harvest time. It was one of those rare vintages where everything went well and the Bordelais harvested one of the largest and healthiest crops they had ever seen.

The year 1970 was the first vintage that I tasted out of cask, visiting a number of châteaux with my wife as tourists on my way to the cheap beaches of Spain and north Africa during summer vacations in 1971 and 1972. Even from their early days I remember the wines exhibiting great color, an intense richness of fruit, fragrant, ripe perfume, full body, and plenty of tannin. However, it seems inevitable that when wines taste well young, certain writers falsely assume they will not last. Terry Robards, then the wine reporter for *The New York Times*, even went so far as to call the wines the product of a "nouvelle" vinification, claiming many of them would not last until 1980. It is an irony that almost all of Bordeaux's greatest vintages—1900, 1929, 1947, 1949, 1953, 1961, and most recently, 1982, and perhaps 1989—have all been produced from superripe grapes where the wines tasted extremely well when young, causing a certain degree of controversy with respect to their perceived aging potential. Keeping in mind that even lightweight Bordeaux vintages such as 1976 can last up to 15 or more years when well stored, it is not surprising that most top 1970s, 21 years after the vintage, are just reaching their plateau of maturity. Certain wines, for example, Latour, Pétrus, Gruaud-Larose, Mouton-Rothschild, and Montrose, are still not close to maturity.

Perhaps the most phenomenal characteristic of the 1970s is the overall balance and consistency of the wines. I long ago consumed all my Cru Bourgeois and smaller-scaled wines, as it was the first vintage where buying from lesser appellations paid off handsomely.

As for the sweet wines, they have had to take a back seat to the 1971s because there was less botrytis. Although the wines are impressively big and full, they lack the complexity, delicacy, and finesse of the best 1971s.

In conclusion, 1970 will no doubt continue to sell at high prices for decades to come, because this is the most consistently excellent, and in some cases outstanding vintage between 1961 and 1982.

The Best Wines

St.-Estèphe: Cos d'Estournel, Haut-Marbuzet, Lafon-Rochet, Montrose, Les-Ormes-de-Pez, de Pez

Pauillac: Grand-Puy-Lacoste, Haut-Batailley, Latour, Lynch-Bages, Mouton-Rothschild, Pichon-Longueville–Comtesse de Lalande

St.-Julien: Ducru-Beaucaillou, Gloria, Gruaud-Larose, Léoville-Barton, St.-Pierre

Margaux: Giscours, Lascombes, Palmer

Médoc/Haut-Médoc/
Moulis/Listrac/
Crus Bourgeois: Sociando-Mallet

Graves Red: Domaine de Chevalier, de Fieuzal, Haut-Bailly, La Mission-Haut-Brion, La Tour-Haut-Brion

Graves White: Domaine de Chevalier, Laville-Haut-Brion

Pomerol: La Conseillante, La Fleur Pétrus, Lafleur, Latour à Pomerol, Pétrus, Trotanoy

St.-Emilion: L'Arrosée, Cheval Blanc, La Dominique, Figeac, Magdelaine

Barsac/Sauternes: Yquem

1969—A Quick Study
(10-6-69)

St.-Estèphe 0   Graves Red *
Pauillac 0   Graves White 0
St.-Julien 0   Pomerol *
Margaux 0   St.-Emilion 0
Médoc/Haut-Médoc Crus Bourgeois 0   Barsac/Sauternes *

Size: Small.

Important information: My candidate for the most undesirable wines produced in Bordeaux in the last 30 years.

Maturity status: I never tasted a 1969, except for Pétrus, that could have been said to have had any richness or fruit. I have not seen any of these wines except for Pétrus for a number of years, but they must be unpalatable.

Price: Amazingly, the vintage was offered at a relatively high price, but almost all the wines except for a handful of the big names are totally worthless.

Whenever Bordeaux has suffered through a disastrous vintage (like that of 1968) there has always been a tendency to lavish false praise on the following year. No doubt Bordeaux, after their horrible experience in

1968, badly wanted a fine vintage in 1969, but despite some overly optimistic proclamations by some leading Bordeaux experts at the time of the vintage, 1969 has turned out to be one of the least attractive vintages for Bordeaux wines in the last two decades.

The crop was small, and while the summer was sufficiently hot and dry to ensure a decent maturity, torrential September rains dashed everyone's hopes for a good vintage, except some investors who irrationally moved in to buy these insipid, nasty, acidic, sharp wines. Consequently, the 1969s, along with being extremely unattractive wines, were quite expensive when they first appeared on the market.

I can honestly say I have never tasted a red wine in 1969 I did not dislike. The only exception would be a relatively decent bottle of Pétrus (rated in the upper seventies) that I had twenty years after the vintage. Most wines are harsh and hollow, with no flesh, fruit, or charm, and it is hard to imagine that any of these wines are today any more palatable than they were during the seventies.

In the Barsac and Sauternes region, a few proprietors managed to produce acceptable wines, particularly d'Arche.

1968—A Quick Study
(9-20-68)

St.-Estèphe 0	Graves Red*
Pauillac 0	Graves White 0
St.-Julien 0	Pomerol 0
Margaux 0	St.-Emilion 0
Médoc/Haut-Médoc Crus Bourgeois 0	Barsac/Sauternes 0

Size: A small, disastrous crop in terms of both quality and quantity.

Important information: A great year for California Cabernet Sauvignon, but not for Bordeaux.

Maturity status: All of these wines must be passé.

Price: Another worthless vintage.

The year 1968 was another of the very poor vintages the Bordelais had to suffer through in the sixties. The culprit, as usual, was heavy rain (it was the wettest year since 1951) that bloated the grapes. However, there have been some 1968s that I found much better than anything produced in 1969, a vintage with a "better" (I am not sure that is the right word to use) reputation.

At one time wines such as Figeac, Gruaud-Larose, Cantemerle, La Mission-Haut-Brion, Haut-Brion, and Latour were palatable. Should anyone run across these wines today, the rule of caveat emptor would seemingly be applicable, as I doubt that any of them would have much left to enjoy.

1967—A Quick Study
(9-25-67)

St.-Estèphe **	Graves Red ***
Pauillac **	Graves White **
St.-Julien **	Pomerol ***
Margaux **	St.-Emilion ***
Médoc/Haut-Médoc Crus Bourgeois *	Barsac/Sauternes ****

Size: An abundant crop was harvested.

Important information: A Graves, Pomerol, St.-Emilion year that favored the early harvested Merlot.

Maturity status: Most 1967s were drinkable when released in 1970 and should have been consumed by 1980. The top wines, where well stored, will keep for another few years but are unlikely to improve.

Price: Moderate.

The year 1967 was a large, useful vintage in the sense that it produced an abundant quantity of round, quick-maturing wines. Most should have been drunk before 1980, but a handful of wines continue to display remarkable staying power and are still in the full bloom of their maturity. This is a vintage that clearly favored Pomerol, and to a lesser extent Graves. Holding onto these wines any longer seems foolish, but I have no doubt that some of the biggest wines, such as Latour, Pétrus, Trotanoy, and perhaps even Palmer, will last until the turn of the century. Should one find any of the top wines listed below in a large-format bottle (magnums, double magnums, etc.) at a reasonable price, my advice would be to take the gamble.

As unexciting as most red wines turned out in 1967, the sweet wines of Barsac and Sauternes were rich and honeyed, with gobs of botrytis present. However, readers must remember that only a handful of estates were truly up to the challenge of making great wines during this very depressed period for the wine production of Barsac/Sauternes.

The Best Wines

St.-Estèphe:	Calon-Ségur, Montrose
Pauillac:	Latour
St.-Julien:	None
Margaux:	Giscours, La Lagune (southern Médoc), Palmer
Médoc/Haut-Médoc/ Moulis/Listrac/ Crus Bourgeois:	None

         Graves Red: Haut-Brion, La Mission-Haut-Brion
       Graves White: None
           Pomerol: Pétrus, Trotanoy, La Violette
         St.-Emilion: Cheval Blanc, Magdelaine, Pavie
   Barsac/Sauternes: Suduiraut, Yquem

1966—A Quick Study
(9-26-66)

St.-Estèphe***   Graves Red****
Pauillac***   Graves White***
St.-Julien***   Pomerol***
Margaux***   St.-Emilion**
Médoc/Haut-Médoc Crus Bourgeois**   Barsac/Sauternes**

Size: An abundant crop was harvested.

Important information: The most overrated "top" vintage of the last 25
    years.

Maturity status: The best wines are in their prime, but most wines are
    losing their fruit before their tannins.

Price: Expensive and overpriced.

While the majority opinion is that 1966 is the best vintage of the decade
after 1961, I would certainly argue that for Graves, Pomerol, and St.-
Emilion, 1964 is clearly the second-best vintage of the decade. And I am
beginning to think that even 1962, that grossly underrated vintage, is, on
overall merit, a better year than 1966. Conceived in somewhat the same
spirit as 1975 (overhyped after several unexciting years, particularly in
the Médoc), 1966 never developed as well as many of its proponents
would have liked. The wines, now 25 years of age, for the most part have
remained austere, lean, unyielding, tannic wines that are losing their
fruit before their tannin melts away. Some notable exceptions do exist.
Who could deny the exceptional wine made at Latour (the wine of the
vintage) or the great Palmer?

All the disappointments that emerged from this vintage were unexpected in view of the early reports that the wines were relatively precocious, charming, and early maturing. If the vintage is not as consistent
as first believed, there are an adequate number of medium-weight, classically styled wines. However, they are all overpriced as this vintage has
always been fashionable and it has had no shortage of supporters, particularly from the English wine-writing community.

The sweet wines of Barsac and Sauternes are also mediocre. Favorable
conditions for the development of the noble rot, *Botrytis cinerea,* never
occurred.

The climatic conditions that shaped this vintage started with a slow flowering in June, intermittently hot and cold weather in July and August, and a dry and sunny September. The crop size was large, and the vintage was harvested under sound weather conditions.

I would be skeptical about buying most 1966s except for one of the unqualified successes of the vintage.

The Best Wines

St.-Estèphe:	None
Pauillac:	Grand-Puy-Lacoste, Latour, Mouton-Rothschild, Pichon-Longueville–Comtesse de Lalande
St.-Julien:	Branaire-Ducru, Ducru-Beaucaillou, Gruaud-Larose, Léoville-Las Cases
Margaux:	Lascombes, Palmer
Médoc/Haut-Médoc/ Moulis/Listrac/ Crus Bourgeois:	None
Graves Red:	Haut-Brion, La Mission-Haut-Brion, Pape-Clément
Pomerol:	Lafleur, Trotanoy
St.-Emilion:	Canon
Barsac/Sauternes:	None

1965—A Quick Study
(10-2-65)

St.-Estèphe 0	Graves Red 0
Pauillac 0	Graves White 0
St.-Julien 0	Pomerol 0
Margaux 0	St.-Emilion 0
Médoc/Haut-Médoc Crus Bourgeois 0	Barsac/Sauternes 0

Size: A tiny vintage.

Important information: The quintessential vintage of rot and rain.

Maturity status: The wines tasted terrible from the start and must be totally reprehensible today.

Price: Worthless.

The vintage of rot and rain. I have had little experience tasting the 1965s. It is considered by most experts to be one of the worst vintages in the post–World War II era. A wet summer was bad enough, but the undoing of this vintage was an incredibly wet and humid September that caused rot to voraciously devour the vineyards. Antirot sprays had not yet been developed. It should be obvious that these wines are to be avoided.

1964—A Quick Study
(9-22-64)

St.-Estèphe ***   Graves Red *****
Pauillac *   Graves White ***
St.-Julien *   Pomerol *****
Margaux **   St.-Emilion ****
Médoc/Haut-Médoc Crus Bourgeois *   Barsac/Sauternes *

Size: A large crop was harvested.

Important information: The classic examples of a vintage where the early picked Merlot and Cabernet Franc produced great wine, and the late-harvested Cabernet Sauvignon, particularly in the Médoc, was inundated. The results included numerous big name failures in the Médoc.

Maturity status: The Médocs are past their prime, but the larger-scaled wines of Graves, Pomerol, and St.-Emilion can last for another 10–15 years.

Price: Smart Bordeaux enthusiasts have always recognized the greatness of this vintage in Graves, Pomerol, and St.-Emilion, and consequently prices have remained high. Nevertheless, compared to such glamour years as 1959 and 1961, the top right bank and Graves 1964s are not only underrated, but in some cases underpriced as well.

One of the most intriguing vintages of Bordeaux, 1964 produced a number of splendid, generally underrated and underpriced wines in Pomerol, St.-Emilion, and Graves where many proprietors had the good fortune to have harvested their crops before the rainy deluge began on October 8. Because of this downpour, which caught many Médoc châteaux with unharvested vineyards, 1964 has never been regarded as a top Bordeaux vintage. While the vintage can be notoriously bad for some of the properties of the Médoc and the late-harvesting Barsac and Sauternes estates, it is excellent to outstanding for the three appellations of Pomerol, St.-Emilion, and Graves.

The summer had been so hot and dry that the French minister of agriculture announced at the beginning of September that the "vintage of the century was about to commence." Since the Merlot grape ripens first, the harvest began in the areas where it is planted in abundance. St.-Emilion and Pomerol harvested at the end of September and finished their picking before the inundation began on October 8. Most of the Graves properties had also finished harvesting. When the rains came, most of the Médoc estates had just begun to harvest their Cabernet Sauvignon and were unable to successfully complete the harvest because of torrential rainfall. It was a Médoc vintage noted for some extraordinary and famous failures. Pity the buyer who purchased Lafite-Rothschild, Mouton-Rothschild, Lynch-Bages, Calon-Ségur, or Margaux! Yet not everyone made disappointing wine. Montrose in St.-Estèphe and Latour in Pauillac made the two greatest wines of the Médoc.

Because of the very damaging reports about the rainfall, many wine enthusiasts approached the 1964 vintage with a great deal of apprehension.

The top wines from Graves, St.-Emilion, and Pomerol are exceptionally rich, full-bodied, opulent, and concentrated wines with high alcohol, an opaque color, super length, and unbridled power. Amazingly, they are far richer, more interesting and complete wines than the 1966s, and in many cases, compete with the finest wines of the 1961 vintage. Because of low acidity, all of the wines reached full maturity by the mid-eighties. The best examples exhibit no sign of decline and can easily last for another 10–15 or more years.

The Best Wines

St.-Estèphe:	Montrose
Pauillac:	Latour
St.-Julien:	Gruaud-Larose
Margaux:	None
Médoc/Haut-Médoc/ Moulis/Listrac/ Crus Bourgeois:	None
Graves Red:	Domaine de Chevalier, Haut-Bailly, Haut-Brion, La Mission-Haut-Brion
Pomerol:	La Conseillante, La Fleur Pétrus, Lafleur, Pétrus, Trotanoy, Vieux-Château-Certan
St.-Emilion:	L'Arrosée, Cheval Blanc, Figeac, Soutard
Barsac/Sauternes:	None

1963—A Quick Study
(10-7-63)

St.-Estèphe 0	Graves Red 0
Pauillac 0	Graves White 0
St.-Julien 0	Pomerol 0
Margaux 0	St.-Emilion 0
Médoc/Haut-Médoc Crus Bourgeois 0	Barsac/Sauternes 0

Size: A small to moderate-sized crop was harvested.

Important information: A dreadfully poor year that rivals 1965 for the feebleness of its wines.

Maturity status: The wines must now be awful.
Price: Worthless.

The Bordelais have never been able to decide whether 1963 or 1965 was the worst vintage of the sixties. Rain and rot, as in 1965, were the ruination of this vintage. I have not seen a bottle of 1963 for over twenty years.

1962—A Quick Study
(10-1-62)

St.-Estèphe ****	Graves Red ***
Pauillac ****	Graves White ****
St.-Julien ****	Pomerol ***
Margaux ***	St.-Emilion ***
Médoc/Haut-Médoc Crus Bourgeois ***	Barsac/Sauternes ****

Size: An abundant crop size, in fact, one of the largest of the decade of the sixties.

Important information: A terribly underrated vintage that had the misfortune of following one of the greatest vintages of the century.

Maturity status: The Bordeaux old-timers claim the 1962s drank beautifully by the late sixties, and continued to fill out and display considerable character, fruit, and charm in the seventies. As the decade of the nineties begins, the top 1962s are still lovely, rich, round wines full of finesse and elegance.

Price: Undervalued, particularly when one considers the prices of its predecessor, 1961, and the overpriced 1966s.

Coming after the great vintage of 1961, it was not totally unexpected that 1962 would be underestimated. This vintage appears to be the most undervalued year for Bordeaux in the post–World War II era. Elegant, supple, very fruity, round, and charming wines that were neither too tannic nor too massive were produced in virtually every appellation. Because of their precociousness, many assumed the wines would not last, but they have kept longer than anyone would have ever imagined. Most 1962s do require consumption, but they continue to surprise me, and well-preserved examples of the vintage can easily be kept through the turn of the century.

The weather was acceptable but not stunning. There was a good flowering because of a sunny, dry May, a relatively hot summer with some impressive thunderstorms, and a good, as the French say, *fin de saison*, with a hot, sunny September. The harvest was not rain free, but the inundations that could have created serious problems never occurred.

Not only was the vintage very successful in most appellations, but it was a top year for the dry white wines of Graves as well as the sweet nectars from Barsac/Sauternes.

The Best Wines

St.-Estèphe:	Cos d'Estournel, Montrose
Pauillac:	Batailley, Lafite-Rothschild, Latour, Lynch-Bages, Mouton-Rothschild, Pichon-Longueville–Comtesse de Lalande
St.-Julien:	Ducru-Beaucaillou, Gruaud-Larose
Margaux:	Margaux, Palmer
Médoc/Haut-Médoc/Moulis/Listrac/Crus Bourgeois:	None
Graves Red:	Haut-Brion, Pape-Clément
Graves White:	Domaine de Chevalier, Laville-Haut-Brion
Pomerol:	Lafleur, Pétrus, Trotanoy, La Violette
St.-Emilion:	Magdelaine
Barsac/Sauternes:	Yquem

1961—A Quick Study
(9-22-61)

St.-Estèphe *****
Pauillac *****
St.-Julien *****
Margaux *****
Médoc/Haut-Médoc Crus Bourgeois ***

Graves Red *****
Graves White ***
Pomerol *****
St.-Emilion ***
Barsac/Sauternes **

Size: An exceptionally tiny crop was produced: in fact, this is the last vintage where a miniscule crop resulted in high quality.

Important information: One of the legendary vintages of the century.

Maturity status: The wines, drinkable young, have, with only a handful of exceptions, reached maturity and are all at their apogee in 1991. Most of the best examples will keep for at least another 10–15 years.

Price: The tiny quantities plus exceptional quality have made the 1961s the most dearly priced, mature vintage of great Bordeaux in the marketplace. Moreover, prices will only increase, given the microscopic qualities that remain—an auctioneer's dream vintage.

The year 1961 is one of eight great vintages produced in the post–World War II era. The others—1945, 1947, 1949, 1953, 1959, 1982, and 1989—all have their proponents, but none is as revered as 1961. The wines have always been prized for their sensational concentration and magnificent penetrating bouquets of superripe fruit and rich, deep, sumptuous flavors. Delicious when young, these wines, which have all reached full maturity except for a handful of the most intensely concentrated examples, are marvelous to drink. However, I see no problem in holding the best-stored bottles for at least another 10 years.

The weather pattern was nearly perfect in 1961, with spring frosts reducing the crop size and then sunny, hot weather throughout the summer and the harvest, resulting in splendid maturity lavels. The small harvest guaranteed high prices for these wines, and today's prices for 1961s make them the equivalent of liquid gold.

The vintage was excellent throughout all appellations of Bordeaux except for the Barsac/Sauternes. This region benefitted greatly from the vintage's reputation, but a tasting of the 1961 sweet wines will reveal that even Yquem is mediocre. The incredibly dry weather conditions resulted in very little botrytis, and the results are large-scaled, but essentially monolithic sweet wines that have never merited the interest they have enjoyed. The only other appellation that did not appear to be up to the overall level of quality was St.-Emilion, where many vineyards had still not fully recovered from the killer freeze of 1956.

In tasting the 1961s, the only two vintages that are somewhat similar in richness and style are 1959 and 1982. The 1959s tend to be lower in acidity, but have actually aged more slowly than the 1961s, whereas the 1982s would appear to have the same physical profile of the 1961s, but less tannin.

The Best Wines

St.-Estèphe:	Cos d'Estournel, Haut-Marbuzet, Montrose
Pauillac:	Latour, Lynch-Bages, Mouton-Rothschild, Pichon-Longueville–Comtesse de Lalande, Pontet-Canet
St.-Julien:	Beychevelle, Ducru-Beaucaillou, Gruaud-Larose, Léoville-Barton
Margaux:	Malescot St.-Exupéry, Margaux, Palmer
Médoc/Haut-Médoc/ Moulis/Listrac/ Crus Bourgeois:	None
Graves Red:	Haut-Bailly, Haut-Brion, La Mission-Haut-Brion, La Tour-Haut-Brion, Pape-Clément
Graves White:	Domaine de Chevalier, Laville-Haut-Brion
Pomerol:	Latour à Pomerol, Pétrus, Trotanoy
St.-Emilion:	L'Arrosée, Canon, Cheval Blanc, Figeac, Magdelaine
Barsac/Sauternes:	None

1960—A Quick Study
(9-9-60)

St.-Estèphe **   Graves Red **
Pauillac **   Graves White *
St.-Julien **   Pomerol *
Margaux *   St.-Emilion *
Médoc/Haut-Médoc Crus Bourgeois 0   Barsac/Sauternes *

Size: A copious crop was harvested.

Important information: The two rainy months of August and September were this vintage's undoing.

Maturity status: Most 1960s should have been consumed within their first 10–15 years of life.

Price: Low.

I remember drinking several delicious magnums of 1960 Latour, as well as having found good examples of 1960 Montrose, La Mission-Haut-Brion, and Gruaud-Larose in Bordeaux. However, the last 1960 I consumed, a magnum of Latour, was drunk over 15 years ago. I would guess that even that wine, which was the most concentrated wine of the vintage according to the Bordeaux cognoscenti, is now in decline.

1959—A Quick Study
(9-20-59)

St.-Estèphe *****   Graves Red *****
Pauillac *****   Graves White ****
St.-Julien ****   Pomerol ***
Margaux ****   St.-Emilion **
Médoc/Haut-Médoc Crus Bourgeois ***   Barsac/Sauternes *****

Size: Average.

Important information: The first of the modern-day years to be designated "vintage of the century."

Maturity status: The wines, maligned in their early years for having low acidity and lacking backbone (reminiscent of the 1982s), have aged more slowly than the more highly touted 1961s. In fact, comparisons between the top wines of the two vintages often reveal the 1959s to be less evolved, with deeper color, and more richness and aging potential.

Price: Never inexpensive, the 1959s have become increasingly more expensive as serious connoisseurs have begun to realize that this vintage not only rivals 1961, but in specific cases, surpasses it.

This is an irrefutably great vintage that inexplicably was criticized at its inception, no doubt because of all the hype and praise it received from its conception. The wines, which are especially strong in the northern Médoc and Graves, and less so on the right bank (Pomerol and St.-Emilion were still recovering from the devastating deep freeze of 1956), are among the most massive and richest wines ever made in Bordeaux. In fact, the two modern-day vintages that are frequently compared to 1959 are the 1982 and 1989. Those comparisons may have merit.

The 1959s have evolved at a glacial pace, and are often in better condition (especially the first-growths Lafite-Rothschild and Mouton-Rothschild) than their 1961 counterparts, which are even more highly touted. The wines do display the effects of having been made in a classic, hot, dry year, with just enough rain to keep the vineyards from being stressed. They are full bodied, extremely alcoholic and opulent, with high degrees of tannin and extract. Their colors have remained impressively opaque and dark, and display less brown and orange than the 1961s. If there is one nagging doubt about many of the 1959s, it is whether they will ever develop the sensational perfume and fragrance that is so much a part of the greatest Bordeaux vintages. Perhaps the great heat during the summer of 1959 did compromise this aspect of the wines, but it is still too soon to know.

The Best Wines

St.-Estèphe:	Cos d'Estournel, Montrose, Les-Ormes-de-Pez
Pauillac:	Lafite-Rothschild, Latour, Lynch-Bages, Mouton-Rothschild, Pichon-Longueville Baron
St.-Julien:	Ducru-Beaucaillou, Langoa-Barton, Léoville-Barton, Léoville-Las Cases
Margaux:	Lascombes, Malescot St.-Exupéry, Margaux, Palmer
Graves Red:	Haut-Brion, La Mission-Haut-Brion, Pape-Clément, La Tour-Haut-Brion
Pomerol:	L'Evangile, Lafleur, Latour à Pomerol, Pétrus, Trotanoy, Vieux-Château-Certan
St.-Emilion:	Cheval Blanc, Figeac
Barsac/Sauternes:	Climens, Suduiraut, Yquem

1958—A Quick Study
(10-7-58)

St.-Estèphe *	Graves Red ***
Pauillac *	Graves White **
St.-Julien *	Pomerol *
Margaux *	St.-Emilion **
Médoc/Haut-Médoc Crus Bourgeois *	Barsac/Sauternes *

Size: A small crop was harvested.

Important information: An unfairly maligned vintage.

Maturity status: The wines are now fading badly. The best examples almost always emerge from the Graves appellation.

Price: Inexpensive.

I have less than two dozen tasting notes of 1958s, but several that do stand out are all from the Graves appellation. Haut-Brion, La Mission-Haut-Brion, and Pape-Clément all made very good wines. They probably would have provided excellent drinking if consumed during the sixties or early seventies. I most recently had the 1958 Haut-Brion in April 1991. It was still a relatively tasty, round, soft, fleshy, tobacco- and mineral-scented and flavored wine, but one could see that it would have been much better if it had been consumed 10–15 years ago. Even richer was the 1958 La Mission-Haut-Brion, which should still be excellent if well-preserved bottles can be found.

1957—A Quick Study
(10-4-57)

St.-Estèphe**	Graves Red***
Pauillac***	Graves White**
St.-Julien**	Pomerol*
Margaux*	St.-Emilion*
Médoc/Haut-Médoc Crus Bourgeois*	Barsac/Sauternes***

Size: A small crop.

Important information: A brutally cold, wet summer.

Maturity status: Because the summer was so cool, the red wines were extremely high in acidity, which has helped them stand the test of time. Where well-kept examples of 1957 can be found, this could be a vintage to purchase, provided the price is right.

Price: The wines should be realistically and inexpensively priced given the fact that 1957 does not enjoy a good reputation.

For a vintage that has never been received very favorably, I have been surprised by how many respectable and enjoyable wines I have tasted, particularly from Pauillac and Graves. In fact, I would be pleased to serve my most finicky friends the 1957 La Mission-Haut-Brion or 1957 Haut-Brion. And I would certainly be pleased to drink the 1957 Lafite-Rothschild. I had two excellent bottles of Lafite in the early eighties, but have not seen the wine since.

It was an extremely difficult year weather-wise, with very wet periods from April through August that delayed the harvest until early October.

The wines had good acidity, and in the better-drained soils there was surprising ripeness given the lack of sunshine and excessive moisture. The 1957 Bordeaux, much like their Burgundy counterparts, have held up relatively well given the high acid and green tannins these wines have always possessed.

1956—A Quick Study
(10-14-56)

St.-Estèphe 0	Graves Red 0
Pauillac 0	Graves White 0
St.-Julien 0	Pomerol 0
Margaux 0	St.-Emilion 0
Médoc/Haut-Médoc Crus Bourgeois 0	Barsac/Sauternes 0

Size: Miniscule quantities of pathetically weak wine were produced.

Important information: The coldest winter in Bordeaux since 1709 did unprecedented damage to the vineyards, particularly those in Pomerol and St.-Emilion.

Maturity status: I have not seen a 1956 in over 15 years, and only have a total of five notes on wines from this vintage.

Price: A worthless vintage produced worthless wines.

The year 1956 stands out as the worst vintage in modern-day Bordeaux, even surpassing such unspeakably bad years as 1963, 1965, 1968, 1969, and 1972. The winter and unbelievably cold months of February and March killed many of the vines in Pomerol and St.-Emilion, and retarded the budding of those in the Médoc. The harvest was late, the crop was small, and the wines were virtually undrinkable.

1955—A Quick Study
(9-21-55)

St.-Estèphe ****	Graves Red ****
Pauillac ***	Graves White ***
St.-Julien ***	Pomerol ***
Margaux ***	St.-Emilion ****
Médoc/Haut-Médoc Crus Bourgeois **	Barsac/Sauternes ****

Size: A large, healthy crop was harvested.

Important information: For a vintage that is now almost forty years old, this tends to be an underrated, undervalued year, although it is not comparable to 1953 or 1959. Yet the wines have generally held up and are firmer and more solidly made than the once-glorious 1953s.

Maturity status: After a long period of sleep, the top wines appear to finally be fully mature. They exhibit no signs of decline.

Price: Undervalued, except for La Mission-Haut-Brion, the wine of the vintage, if not the decade.

For the most part, the 1955s have always come across as relatively stern, slightly tough-textured, yet impressively deep, full wines with fine color, and excellent aging potential. What they lack, as a general rule, is fat, charm, and opulence.

The weather conditions were generally ideal, with hot, sunny days in June, July, and August. Although some rain fell in September, its effect was positive rather than negative.

For whatever reason, the relatively large 1955 crop has never generated the excitement that other vintages in the fifties, such as 1953 and 1959, elicited. Perhaps it was the lack of many superstar wines that kept enthusiasm muted. Among more recent years, could 1988 be a rerun of 1955?

The Best Wines

St.-Estèphe: Calon-Ségur, Cos d'Estournel, Montrose, Les-Ormes-de-Pez

Pauillac: Latour, Lynch-Bages, Mouton-Rothschild

St.-Julien: Léoville-Las Cases, Talbot

Margaux: Palmer

Graves Red: Haut-Brion, La Mission-Haut-Brion, Pape-Clément

Pomerol: L'Evangile, Lafleur, Latour à Pomerol, Pétrus, Vieux-Château-Certan

St.-Emilion: Cheval Blanc, La Dominique, Soutard

Barsac/Sauternes: Yquem

1954—A Quick Study
(10-10-54)

St.-Estèphe 0

Pauillac *

St.-Julien *

Margaux 0

Médoc/Haut-Médoc Crus Bourgeois 0

Graves Red *

Graves White 0

Pomerol 0

St.-Emilion 0

Barsac/Sauternes 0

Size: A small crop was harvested.

Important information: A terrible late-harvest vintage conducted under appalling weather conditions.

Maturity status: It is hard to believe anything from this vintage would still be worth drinking.

Price: The wines have no value.

The year 1954 was a miserable vintage throughout France, but especially in Bordeaux where the producers continued to wait for full maturity after an exceptionally cool, wet August. While the weather did improve in September, the skies opened toward the end of the month and for nearly four weeks one low-pressure system after another passed through the area, dumping enormous quantities of water that served to destroy any chance for a moderately successful vintage.

It is highly unlikely any wine from this vintage could still be drinkable today.

1953—A Quick Study
(9-28-53)

St.-Estèphe *****	Graves Red ****
Pauillac *****	Graves White ***
St.-Julien *****	Pomerol ***
Margaux ****	St.-Emilion ***
Médoc/Haut-Médoc Crus Bourgeois ***	Barsac/Sauternes ***

Size: An average-sized crop was harvested.

Important information: One of the most seductive and hedonistic Bordeaux vintages ever produced.

Maturity status: According to Bordeaux old-timers, the wines were absolutely delicious during the fifties, even more glorious in the sixties, and sublime during the seventies. Charm, roundness, fragrance, and a velvety texture were the hallmarks of this vintage, which now must be approached with some degree of caution unless the wines have been impeccably stored and/or the wines are available in larger-format bottlings.

Price: No vintage with such appeal will ever sell at a reasonable price. Consequently, the 1953s remain luxury-priced wines.

The year 1953 must be the only Bordeaux vintage where it is impossible to find a dissenting voice about the quality of the wines. Bordeaux old-timers and some of our senior wine commentators (particularly Edmund Penning-Rowsell and Michael Broadbent) talk of 1953 with adulation. Apparently the vintage never went through an unflattering stage. They were delicious from cask, and even more so from bottle. For that reason, much of the vintage was consumed before its tenth birthday. Those who waited have seen the wines develop even greater character during the sixties and seventies. Many wines, especially on this side of the Atlantic, began displaying signs of age (brown color, dried-out fruit flavors) during the eighties. In Bordeaux, when a château pulls out a 1953 they are usually in mint condition, and they are some of the most beautifully sumptuous, rich, charming clarets anyone could ever desire. A more modern-day reference point for 1953 may be the very best 1985s, perhaps even some of the lighter 1982s, although my instincts tell me the 1982s are more alcoholic, richer, fuller, heavier wines.

If you have the discretionary income necessary to buy this highly prized vintage, prudence should dictate that the wines be from cold cellars, and/or in larger-format bottles.

The Best Wines

St.-Estèphe: Calon-Ségur, Cos d'Estournel, Montrose
Pauillac: Grand-Puy-Lacoste, Lafite-Rothschild, Lynch-Bages, Mouton-Rothschild
St.-Julien: Beychevelle, Ducru-Beaucaillou, Gruaud-Larose, Langoa-Barton, Léoville-Barton, Léoville-Las Cases, Talbot
Margaux: Cantemerle (southern Médoc), Margaux, Palmer
Graves Red: Haut-Brion, La Mission-Haut-Brion
Pomerol: La Conseillante
St.-Emilion: Cheval Blanc, Figeac, Magdelaine, Pavie
Barsac/Sauternes: Climens, Yquem

1952—A Quick Study
(9-17-52)

St.-Estèphe **	Graves Red ***
Pauillac ***	Graves White ***
St.-Julien ***	Pomerol ****
Margaux **	St.-Emilion ***
Médoc/Haut-Médoc Crus Bourgeois **	Barsac/Sauternes **

Size: A small crop was harvested.

Important information: The 1952 vintage was at its best in Pomerol, which largely completed its harvest prior to the rains.

Maturity status: Most wines have always tasted hard, too astringent, and lacking fat, charm, and ripeness. The best bottles could provide surprises.

Price: Expensive, but well-chosen Pomerols may represent relative values.

An excellent spring and summer of relatively hot, dry weather with just enough rain was spoiled by stormy, unstable, cold weather before and during the harvest. Much of the Merlot and some of the Cabernet Franc in Pomerol and St.-Emilion was harvested before the weather turned foul, and consequently, the best wines tended to come from these appellations. The Graves can also be successful because of the superb drainage of the soil in that appellation, particularly in the Pessac/Léognan area. The Médocs have always tended to be relatively hard and disappointing, even the first-growths.

The Best Wines

St.-Estèphe:	Calon-Ségur, Montrose
Pauillac:	Latour, Lynch-Bages
St.-Julien:	None
Margaux:	Margaux, Palmer
Graves Red:	Haut-Brion, La Mission-Haut-Brion, Pape-Clément
Pomerol:	La Fleur Pétrus, Lafleur, Pétrus, Trotanoy
St.-Emilion:	Cheval Blanc, Magdelaine
Barsac/Sauternes:	None

1951—A Quick Study
(10-9-51)

St.-Estèphe 0	Graves Red 0
Pauillac 0	Graves White 0
St.-Julien 0	Pomerol 0
Margaux 0	St.-Emilion 0
Médoc/Haut-Médoc Crus Bourgeois 0	Barsac/Sauternes 0

Size: A tiny crop was harvested.

Important information: Even today, 1951 is considered one of the all-time worst vintages for dry white, dry red, and sweet wines from Bordeaux.

Maturity status: Undrinkable young, Undrinkable old.

Price: Another worthless vintage.

Frightfully bad weather in the spring, summer, and both before and during the harvest (rain and unseasonably cold temperatures) was the complete undoing of this vintage, which has the ignominious pleasure of having one of the worst reputations of any vintage in the post–World War II era.

1950—A Quick Study
(9-17-50)

St.-Estèphe **	Graves Red ***
Pauillac ***	Graves White ***
St.-Julien ***	Pomerol *****
Margaux ***	St.-Emilion ****
Médoc/Haut-Médoc Crus Bourgeois *	Barsac/Sauternes ****

Size: An abundant crop was harvested.

Important information: Many of the Pomerols are great, yet they have been totally ignored by the chroniclers of the Bordeaux region.

Maturity status: Most Médocs and Graves are now in decline. The top heavyweight Pomerols can be splendid with years of life still left.

Price: The quality of the Pomerols has remained largely a secret and the wines are, consequently, undervalued.

The year 1950 is another example where the Médoc formed the general impression of the Bordeaux vintage. This relatively abundant year was the result of good flowering, a hot, dry summer, and a difficult early September complicated by large amounts of rain.

The Médocs, all of which are in decline, were soft, forward, medium-bodied wines that probably had a kinship to more recent vintages such as 1971 and 1981. The Graves were slightly better, but even they are probably passé. The two best appellations were St.-Emilion, which produced a number of rich, full, intense wines that aged quickly, and Pomerol, which had its fourth superb vintage in succession—unprecedented in the history of that area. The wines are unbelievably rich, unctuous, and concentrated, and in many cases are capable of rivaling the greatest Pomerols of such more highly renowned vintages as 1947 and 1949.

The other appellation that prospered in 1950 was Barsac/Sauternes. Fanciers of these wines still claim 1950 is one of the greatest of the post–World War II vintages for sweet wines.

The Best Wines

St.-Estèphe:	None
Pauillac:	Latour
St.-Julien:	None
Margaux:	Margaux
Médoc/Haut-Médoc/ Moulis/Listrac/ Crus Bourgeois:	None
Graves Red:	Haut-Brion, La Mission-Haut-Brion
Pomerol:	L'Evangile, La Fleur Pétrus, Le Gay, Lafleur, Pétrus, Vieux-Château-Certan
St.-Emilion:	Cheval Blanc, Figeac, Soutard
Barsac/Sauternes:	Climens, Coutet, Suduiraut, Yquem

1949—A Quick Study
(9-27-49)

St.-Estèphe *****   Graves Red *****
Pauillac *****   Graves White ***
St.-Julien *****   Pomerol ****
Margaux ****   St.-Emilion ****
Médoc/Haut-Médoc Crus Bourgeois ***   Barsac/Sauternes *****

Size: A small crop was harvested.

Important information: The driest and sunniest vintage since 1893, and
    rivaled (weather-wise not qualitatively) in more recent years only
    by 1990.

Maturity status: The best wines are still in full blossom, displaying re-
    markable richness and concentration.

Price: Frightfully expensive.

Among the four extraordinary vintages of the late forties—1945, 1947,
1948, and 1949—this has always been my favorite. The wines, slightly
less massive and alcoholic than the 1947s, also appear to possess greater
balance, harmony, and fruit than the 1945s and more complexity than
the 1948s. In short, the top wines are magnificent. The year 1949 is
certainly one of the most exceptional vintages of this century. Only the
right-bank wines (except for Cheval Blanc) appear inferior to the quality
of their 1947s. In the Médoc and Graves it is a terrific vintage, with
nearly everyone making wines of astounding ripeness, richness, opulence, power, and length.

The vintage was marked by the extraordinary heat and sunny conditions that Bordeaux enjoyed throughout the summer. Those consumers
who have been worried that 1989 and 1990 were too hot to make great
wine only need to look at the weather statistics for 1949. It was one of
the two hottest vintages (the other being 1947) since 1893, as well as the
sunniest vintage since 1893. It was not a totally dry harvest, but the
amount of rainfall was virtually identical to that in a year such as 1982.
Some of the rain fell before the harvest, which, given the dry, parched
condition of the soil, was actually beneficial.

Even the sweet wines of Barsac and Sauternes were exciting. Buying
1949s today will cost an arm and a leg as these are among the most
expensive and sought-after wines of the twentieth century.

The Best Wines

St.-Estèphe: Calon-Ségur, Cos d'Estournel
Pauillac: Grand-Puy-Lacoste, Latour, Mouton-Rothschild

St.-Julien: Gruaud-Larose, Léoville-Barton, Talbot
Margaux: Palmer
Graves Red: Haut-Brion, La Mission-Haut-Brion, Pape-Clément
Pomerol: La Conseillante, L'Evangile, Lafleur, Pétrus, Trotanoy, Vieux-Château-Certan
St.-Emilion: Cheval Blanc
Barsac/Sauternes: Climens, Coutet, Yquem

1948—A Quick Study
(9-22-48)

St.-Estèphe ***   Graves Red ****
Pauillac ****   Graves White ***
St.-Julien ****   Pomerol ***
Margaux ****   St.-Emilion ***
Médoc/Haut-Médoc Crus Bourgeois ***   Barsac/Sauternes **

Size: An average to below-average crop size was harvested.

Important information: A largely ignored, but good-to-excellent vintage overshadowed by both its predecessor and successor.

Maturity status: The hard and backward characteristics of these wines have served them well during their evolution. Most of the larger, more concentrated 1948s are still attractive wines.

Price: Undervalued given their age and quality.

When Bordeaux has three top vintages in a row it is often the case that one is totally forgotten, and that has certainly proven correct with respect to 1948. It was a very good year that had the misfortune to fall between two legendary vintages.

Because of a difficult flowering due to wet, windy, cool weather in June, the crop size was smaller than in 1947 and 1949. However, July and August were fine months weather-wise, with September exceptionally warm and dry.

Despite the high quality of the wines, they never caught on with claret enthusiasts. And who can fault the wine buyers? The 1947s were more flashy, opulent, alcoholic, and fuller bodied, and the 1949s more precocious and richer than the harder, tougher, more tannic, and unforthcoming 1948s.

In 1991, this is a vintage that in many cases has matured more gracefully than the massive 1947s. The top wines tend to still be in excellent condition. Prices remain reasonable, if only in comparison to what one has to pay for 1947 and 1949.

The Best Wines

St.-Estèphe: Cos d'Estournel

Pauillac: Grand-Puy-Lacoste, Latour, Lynch-Bages, Mouton-Rothschild

St.-Julien: Langoa-Barton, Léoville-Barton (the wine of the Médoc)

Margaux: Cantemerle (southern Médoc), Margaux, Palmer

Graves Red: Haut-Brion, La Mission-Haut-Brion, Pape-Clément

Pomerol: Pétrus

St.-Emilion: Cheval Blanc

Barsac/Sauternes: None

1947–A Quick Study
(9-15-47)

St.-Estèphe ****   Graves Red ****

Pauillac ****   Graves White ***

St.-Julien ****   Pomerol *****

Margaux ***   St.-Emilion *****

Médoc/Haut-Médoc Crus Bourgeois *   Barsac/Sauternes ***

Size: An abundant crop was harvested.

Important information: A year of extraordinary extremes in quality with some of the most port-like, concentrated wines ever produced in Bordeaux. This is also a vintage of unexpected failures (i.e., Lafite-Rothschild).

Maturity status: Except for the most concentrated and powerful Pomerols and St.-Emilions, this is a vintage that requires immediate consumption as many wines have gone over the top and are now exhibiting excessive volatile acidity and dried-out fruit.

Price: Preposterously high given the fact that this was another "vintage of the century."

This quintessentially hot-year vintage produced many wines that are among the most enormously concentrated, port-like, intense wines I have ever tasted. Most of the real heavyweights in this vintage have emerged from Pomerol and St.-Emilion. In the Médoc, it was a vintage of remarkable irregularity. Properties such as Calon-Ségur, Mouton-Rothschild, and Margaux made great wines, but certain top growths, such as Lafite-Rothschild and Latour, as well as super seconds such as Léoville-Barton, produced wines with excessive acidity.

The top wines are something to behold if only because of their excessively rich, sweet style that comes closest, in modern-day terms, to 1982. Yet I know of no 1982 that has the level of extract and intensity of the greatest 1947s.

The reasons for such intensity were the exceptionally hot months of July and August, which were followed (much like in 1982) by a torridly hot, almost tropical heat wave in mid-September just as the harvest began. Those properties that were unable to control the temperatures of hot grapes had stuck fermentations, residual sugar in the wines, and in many cases, levels of volatile acidity that would horrify modern-day oenologists. Those who were able to master the tricky vinification made the richest, most opulent red wines Bordeaux has produced during the twentieth century.

The Best Wines

St.-Estèphe:	Calon-Ségur
Pauillac:	Grand-Puy-Lacoste, Mouton-Rothschild
St.-Julien:	Ducru-Beaucaillou, Léoville-Las Cases
Margaux:	Margaux
Graves Red:	Haut-Brion, La Mission-Haut-Brion, La Tour-Haut-Brion
Pomerol:	La Conseillante, L'Enclos, L'Evangile, La Fleur Pétrus, Lafleur, Latour à Pomerol, Nenin, Pétrus, Rouget, Vieux-Château-Certan
St.-Emilion:	Canon, Cheval Blanc, Figeac, La Gaffelière-Naudes
Barsac/Sauternes:	Climens, Suduiraut

1946—A Quick Study
(9-30-46)

St.-Estèphe **	Graves Red *
Pauillac **	Graves White 0
St.-Julien **	Pomerol 0
Margaux *	St.-Emilion 0
Médoc/Haut-Médoc Crus Bourgeois 0	Barsac/Sauternes 0

Size: A small crop was harvested.

Important information: The only year in the post–World War II era where the Bordeaux vineyards were invaded by locusts.

Maturity status: The wines must certainly be over the hill.

Price: Except for the rare bottle of Mouton-Rothschild (needed by billionaires to complete their collections), most of these wines have little value.

A fine, hot summer, particularly in July and August, was spoiled by an unusually wet, windy, cold September that delayed the harvest and caused rampant rot in the vineyards. The 1946s are rarely seen in the marketplace. I have only eleven tasting notes for the entire vintage.

I do not know of any top wines, although Edmund Penning-Rowsell claims the 1946 Latour was excellent. I have never seen a bottle.

1945—A Quick Study
(9-13-45)

St.-Estèphe ****	Graves Red *****
Pauillac *****	Graves White *****
St.-Julien *****	Pomerol *****
Margaux ****	St.-Emilion *****
Médoc/Haut-Médoc Crus Bourgeois ****	Barsac/Sauternes *****

Size: A tiny crop was harvested.

Important information: The most acclaimed vintage of the century.

Maturity status: Certain wines from this vintage (only those that have been stored impeccably) are still not fully mature.

Price: The most expensive clarets of the century.

No vintage in the post–World War II era, not even 1989, 1982, 1961, 1959, or 1953, enjoys the reputation that the 1945 vintage does. The celebration of the end of an appallingly destructive war, combined with the fact that the weather was remarkable, produced one of the smallest, most concentrated crops of grapes ever seen. In the late eighties, I have been fortunate to have had the first-growths on two separate occasions, and there seems to be no doubt that this is indeed a remarkable vintage that has taken almost 45 years to reach its peak. The great wines, and they are numerous, could well last for another 20–30 years, making a mockery of most of the more recent great vintages that must be consumed within 25–30 years of the vintage.

The vintage is not without critics, some of whom have said that the wines are excessively tannic and many are drying out. There are wines that match these descriptions, but if one judges a vintage on the performance of the top properties, such as the first-growths, super seconds, and leading domaines in Pomerol and St.-Emilion, 1945 remains in a class by itself.

The reason for the tiny crop was the notoriously frigid spell during the month of May *(la gelée noire)* that was followed by a summer of exceptional heat and drought. An early harvest began on September 13, the same day that the harvest began in both 1976 and 1982.

The Best Wines

St.-Estèphe: Calon-Ségur, Montrose, Les-Ormes-de-Pez

Pauillac: Latour, Mouton-Rothschild, Pichon-Longueville–Comtesse de Lalande, Pontet-Canet

St.-Julien: Gruaud-Larose, Léoville-Barton, Talbot

Margaux: Margaux, Palmer

Graves Red: Haut-Brion, La Mission-Haut-Brion, La Tour-Haut-Brion

Graves White: Laville-Haut-Brion

Pomerol: La Fleur Pétrus, Gazin, Latour à Pomerol, Pétrus, Rouget, Trotanoy, Vieux-Château-Certan

St.-Emilion: Canon, Cheval Blanc, Figeac, La Gaffelière-Naudes, Larcis-Ducasse, Magdelaine

Barsac/Sauternes: Suduiraut, Yquem

4: EVALUATING
THE WINES
OF BORDEAUX

ST.-ESTÈPHE

Of all the wines produced in the Haut-Médoc, those of St.-Estèphe have the reputation of being the slowest to mature, and the toughest, most tannic wines. While this generalization may have been true 20 or 30 years ago, the wines now being made in St.-Estèphe reveal an increasing reliance on the softer, fleshier Merlot grape, as well as a vinification aimed at producing more supple, earlier-maturing wines.

St.-Estèphe, which has 2,821 acres under vine, is the least prestigious of the four well-known Haut-Médoc appellations including Margaux,

Pauillac, and St.-Julien. In the 1855 classification, only five wines were considered outstanding enough to be ranked. However, from a consumer's perspective, the commune of St.-Estèphe has numerous Cru Bourgeois châteaux that are currently making wine as good as many classified growths. Several of these Cru Bourgeois estates are producing better wine than two of the five classified growths in St.-Estèphe. In any reclassification of St.-Estèphe, Cos Labory would be hard pressed to keep its standing, whereas top-notch, lesser-known estates making excellent wine, such as de Pez, Haut-Marbuzet, Meyney, and Les-Ormes-de-Pez, would certainly merit serious consideration for elevation into the ranks of the classified growths.

Even with the growers of St.-Estèphe consciously trying to make a more supple style of wine, the wines of this region generally remain among the most backward and unyielding wines produced in Bordeaux. Of course, the soil is less gravelly in St.-Estèphe and also has a higher clay content. Consequently, the drainage is slower. The resulting wines are relatively higher in acidity and lower in pH, and their textures chunkier and more burly than, for example, wines made from vineyards planted in light, gravelly soil.

At present, virtually everyone agrees that Cos d'Estournel is making this commune's finest wine, particularly since the early eighties. Coincidentally, it is also the first château one sees when crossing over the Pauillac boundary into St.-Estèphe. The eccentric pagoda-styled château sits on a ridge overlooking Pauillac's famous Lafite-Rothschild. Several recent vintages, particularly the 1986, 1985, and 1982, would even suggest that Cos d'Estournel has first-growth aspirations. Cos d'Estournel's wine represents a brilliant combination of modern technology and respect for tradition. It is a wine supple enough to drink by age 5 or 6, but made to age and improve for as many as 10–20 years.

The chief rival to Cos d'Estournel is Montrose. Montrose is hidden on one of St.-Estèphe's tiny back roads, closer to the Gironde River. Until the mid-1970s, Montrose made one of Bordeaux's biggest, deepest, and slowest-maturing wines. Many Bordelais compared it to Latour because of its weight and richness. Since then, Montrose has curiously lightened its style and shown an increasing reliance on more Merlot in the final blend. Whereas older vintages of Montrose needed a good 15–20 years to shed their cloak of tannin, the more recent vintages of this wine have been drinking well within 5–6 years. It is too early to say whether the profound 1989 and 1990 Montrose represent a return to the style that made Montrose the most heralded wine of the appellation during much of this century.

Potentially as good as any St.-Estèphe, as well as just about any

ST·ESTÈPHE

● CHÂTEAU ——— ROAD

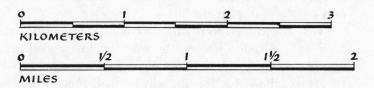

0   1   2   3
KILOMETERS

0   1/2   1   1½   2
MILES

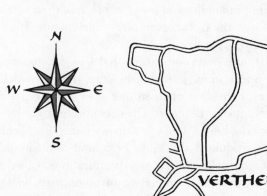

VERTHEUIL

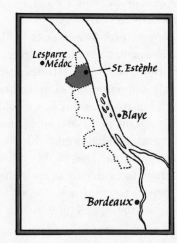

Lesparre
●Médoc   St. Estèphe

●Blaye

Bordeaux●

Cissac
CISSAC-MÉDOC

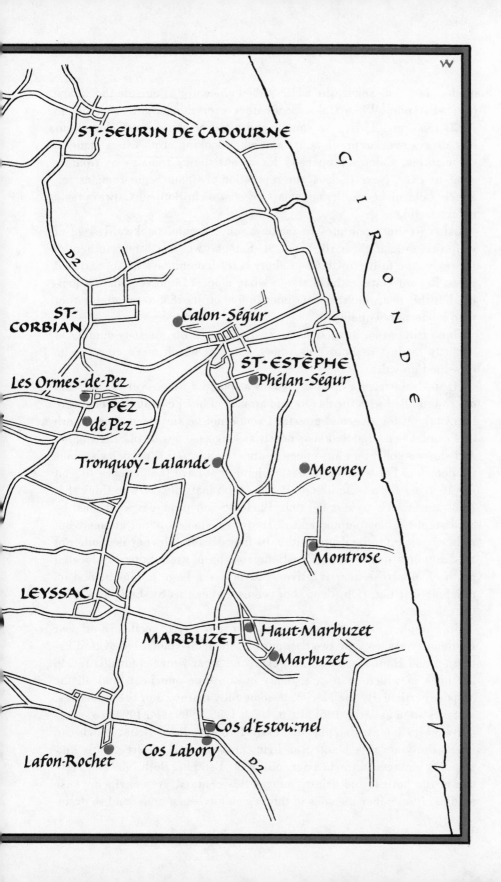

W

ST-SEURIN DE CADOURNE

D2

ST-
CORBIAN

Calon-Ségur

ST-ESTÈPHE
Phélan-Ségur

Les Ormes-de-Pez

PEZ
de Pez

Tronquoy-Lalande

Meyney

G
I
R
O
N
D
E

Montrose

LEYSSAC

MARBUZET Haut-Marbuzet
Marbuzet

Cos d'Estournel
Cos Labory
Lafon-Rochet D2

Médoc, is Calon-Ségur, the white-walled château just outside the village of St.-Estèphe. When Calon-Ségur does everything right, as it did in 1982, 1953, and 1947, one cannot find a better wine. But Calon-Ségur has always been unpredictable, and when looking at its wines made in the eighties, Calon's propensity for inconsistency remains as troublesome as ever. Nevertheless, the reputation of Calon-Ségur remains relatively untarnished, although smart *négociants* in Bordeaux always taste before buying.

Lafon-Rochet continues to make a solid, tannic, backward style of wine that fanciers of hard, tough St.-Estèphe wines will find authentic. However, the fifth-growth Cos Labory is this commune's most overrated wine. Recent vintages have shown some modest improvements in quality, but this is a wine that continues to live off its 1855 reputation rather than modern-day quality.

One of the great attractions of St.-Estèphe is the glorious number of expertly made Cru Bourgeois wines, some of which merit elevation to classified growths.

Haut-Marbuzet, for openers, makes a splendid wine, overtly spicy and oaky, and filled with the flavors and aromas of blackcurrants. If one were to mistake it for a second-growth, I would not be surprised. The superb de Pez makes a wine that lasts nearly as long as any wine of St.-Estèphe, and shrewd collectors have been beating a path to this property's wines for decades. For wine enthusiasts who do not have the patience to wait the 10 years for a wine like de Pez to reach maturity, or who think that Haut-Marbuzet's style is too rich, Phélan-Ségur produces what must be St.-Estèphe's most supple and richly fruity wine. It is not an ager, but rather is meant to be drunk within its first decade. Meyney is another of St.-Estèphe's outstanding Cru Bourgeois properties. Superbly located north of Montrose near the river, Meyney is a large producer, and its reliability for big, rich, deep, fine wines makes this St.-Estèphe a wine to seek out.

St.-Estèphes are not wines to look for and buy in mediocre or poor Bordeaux vintages. The two best performers in off-vintages are Cos d'Estournel and Haut-Marbuzet. However, the great vintages for this region are ones in which there are plenty of sunshine and heat, and all the grapes, particularly the Merlot, become fully mature. For these reasons, vintages such as 1959, 1961, 1970, 1982, 1986, 1989, and 1990 are superlative years for St.-Estèphe. Excessively hot and dry years, which can stress the vineyards planted on light, gravelly soil, are frequently outstanding vintages in the heavier soils of St.-Estèphe. Both 1989 and 1990, two of the hottest and driest vintages this century, are convincing case studies. Remember the soils of this region are less porous, and so drainage is not as good as in other Médoc appellations. Vintages where there was abundant rain are frequently less successful in St.-Estèphe than in nearby St.-Julien or Margaux. For example, 1987, 1983, 1980, 1977, and 1974 were more successful in other Médoc appellations. An important factor for the success of the vintage in St.-Estèphe is a healthy, very ripe Merlot crop, which will help to cut the normally higher-than-average acidity and tannins of St.-Estèphe's wines. The years 1989, 1982, 1976, and 1970 were all years that favored the Merlot grape, and as a consequence, St.-Estèphe produced numerous outstanding wines.

St.-Estèphes, as the least glamorous wines of the famous Médoc, offer excellent wine values. This applies not only to the famous classified growths, but also to the appellation's excellent array of Cru Bourgeois wines.

A CONSUMER'S CLASSIFICATION OF THE CHÂTEAUX OF ST.-ESTÈPHE

OUTSTANDING
Cos d'Estournel

EXCELLENT
Calon-Ségur
Haut-Marbuzet
Montrose

VERY GOOD
Chambert-Marbuzet
Lafon-Rochet
Meyney
Les-Ormes-de-Pez
de Pez
Phélan-Ségur

GOOD
Coutelin-Merville
Laffitte-Carcasset
Lavillotte
Lilian Ladouys
Petit Bocq
Tronquoy-Lalande

Andron-Blanquet, Beau-Site, Beauséjour, Le Boscq, Capbern-
Gasqueton, Cave Cooperative Marquis de St.-Estèphe, La
Commanderie, Cos Labory, Le Crock, Houissant, MacCarthy,
Marbuzet, Les Pradines

ANDRON-BLANQUET (Cru Bourgeois Exceptionnel) AVERAGE

Production: 7,000 cases	Grape varieties:
	Merlot—35%
	Cabernet Sauvignon—30%
	Cabernet Franc—30%
	Petit Verdot—5%
Secondary label: St.-Roch	
Vineyard size: 39.5 acres	Proprietor: Bernard Audoy
Time spent in barrels: 14–16 months	Average age of vines: 25 years
Evaluation of present classification: An inconsistent wine that should be downgraded to a Cru Bourgeois	
Plateau of maturity: 3–8 years following the vintage	

Andron-Blanquet should produce better wine. The vineyard, which is
close to those of Lafite-Rothschild in neighboring Pauillac and the famous Cos d'Estournel in St.-Estèphe, is located on a plateau of gravelly
soil that is considered to be slightly warmer than other micro-climates in
St.-Estèphe. However, the use of machine harvesters to pick much of
the crop is not an indication that the highest quality is sought. The wine
is vinified properly, with a relatively long maceration period, yet Andron-
Blanquet consistently tastes diluted, and lacks concentration, character,
and charm. The institution of a second wine at the request of the oenologist and proprietor, Bernard Audoy, may help explain why the 1989 is
the best recent vintage.

VINTAGES

1989—This perennial underachiever appears unable to muster the nec-
· essary motivation to produce high-quality wine. The 1989 is sur-
82 prisingly light, but intensely fruity in a straightforward, jammy,
medium-bodied style. It should be drunk within its first 5–7 years
of life. Anticipated maturity: Now–1996. Last tasted, 4/91.

1988—The 1988 is light and lacking the charming fruitiness of the 1989.
· It finishes short and is too acidic. Anticipated maturity: Now–
74 1995. Last tasted, 4/91.

1986—Despite reports of renewed commitment to improving the quality
  ·   here, this estate continues to represent one of the most notorious
74   underachievers in the St.-Estèphe firmament. The 1986 is surprisingly light for the vintage, with medium to dark ruby color,
some ripeness and length, but the overriding impression is one of
hard tannins that are excessive for the amount of fruit. Anticipated maturity: 1992–1996. Last tasted, 11/89.

1985—The 1985 is a shallow, somewhat thin, and watery wine that is
  ·   medium bodied, and has a light, innocuous fragrance of diluted
67   fruit, and a ready-to-drink texture. It should be drunk over the next
3–5 years. Anticipated maturity: Now–1994. Last tasted, 10/88.

BEAU-SITE (Cru Bourgeois Exceptionnel)   AVERAGE

Production: 18,000 cases	Grape varieties: Cabernet Sauvignon—70% Merlot—30%
Secondary label: none	
Vineyard size: 67 acres	Proprietor: Emile Castéja
Time spent in barrels: 12–14 months	Average age of vines: 25 years
Evaluation of present classification: The quality equivalent of a good Cru Bourgeois	
Plateau of maturity: 3–10 years following the vintage	

The lovely, well-situated Château Beau-Site (meaning the beautiful place) was acquired by the well-known Bordelais family of Emile Castéja in 1955. The main part of the vineyard is situated on a plateau overlooking the Gironde River near the village of St.-Corbian. Beau-Site should be an excellent wine, but its performance in the sixties and seventies was spotty. Did the high percentage of Cabernet Sauvignon result in a wine that was too often tannic and tough? Whatever the reason, hiring the famous oenologist, Pascal Ribereau-Gayon, and the decisions to harvest later and to utilize one-third new oak casks have all produced increasingly more supple and popular wines in the eighties. Nevertheless, this is still a fickle St.-Estèphe, with an abundance of tannin, although now the tannins are riper and smoother.

The wines of Beau-Site are distributed exclusively through the *négociant* firm of Borie-Manoux.

VINTAGES

1989—This is probably the best wine produced at Beau-Site since their
· 1982. Deep ruby/purple in color, with a moderately intense bou-
85 quet of superripe cassis fruit, minerals, and spicy oak, this medium-bodied, moderately tannic, concentrated wine has more
power and opulence than most vintages of Beau-Site. Drinkable
young, it should age gracefully for up to a decade. Anticipated
maturity: 1993–2000. Last tasted, 4/91.

1988—Medium dark ruby, with a tight but emerging bouquet of herbs,
· oak, and red fruits, this lean, austere, medium-bodied St.-Es-
77 tèphe has abundant astringent tannins to resolve. There is some
ripe fruit lurking in the wine, but the overall impression is one of
toughness and a backward, somewhat compact style. Anticipated
maturity: 1992–1997. Last tasted, 4/91.

1986—This Cru Bourgeois tends to produce rather firm, austere wines
· that are usually well made but need 2–3 years in the bottle to
79 round out. The 1986 is medium ruby-colored, with a tight yet
spicy bouquet of herbaceous, currancy fruit. It is medium bodied,
tannic, and firm. Anticipated maturity: Now–1996. Last tasted,
3/89.

BEAUSÉJOUR (Cru Bourgeois)   AVERAGE

Production: 7,500 cases	Grape varieties:
	Cabernet Sauvignon—50%
	Merlot—40%
	Malbec—5%
	Petit Verdot—5%
Secondary label: none	
Vineyard size: 37 acres	Proprietor: Jacques Brossard
Time spent in barrels: 12–14 months	Average age of vines: 25 years
Evaluation of present classification: Should be maintained	
Plateau of maturity: 3–8 years following the vintage	

I rarely see this wine, which is primarily sold in Germany, Belgium, and
Switzerland; however, those vintages that I have tasted have been relatively coarse wines that lack charm and finesse. Interestingly, the property has been in the same family for nearly three centuries. The current
proprietor, Jacques Brossard, claims his wines need at least 8–10 years
of bottle age to prove their merit.

LE BOSCQ (Cru Bourgeois Supérieur)   AVERAGE

Production: 6,500 cases	Grape varieties: Merlot—50% Cabernet Sauvignon—30% Cabernet Franc—10% Petit Verdot—10%
Secondary label: none	
Vineyard size: 37 acres	Proprietor: Philippe Durand
Time spent in barrels: 18 months	Average age of vines: 30 years
Evaluation of present classification: Should be maintained	
Plateau of maturity: 3–8 years following the vintage	

The vineyard of Le Boscq is located at the very northern end of the appellation of St.-Estèphe, with a good view of the Gironde River. It has extremely gravelly, clay soil, and the wine is vinified in stainless-steel vats and aged in small oak casks for 18 months. Given the high percentage of Merlot it is not surprising that the wine is soft and fruity. In years where there is a tendency toward overripeness, Le Boscq can be disjointed and flabby. Nevertheless, in good vintages, such as 1982 and 1989, this wine provides reasonably priced, fine drinking in its first decade of life.

CALON-SÉGUR (Third-Growth)   EXCELLENT

Production: 20,000 cases	Grape varieties: Cabernet Sauvignon—65% Merlot—25% Cabernet Franc—10%
Secondary label: Marquis de Ségur	
Vineyard size: 123.5 acres	Proprietors: The Capbern- Gasqueton and Peyrelongue families
Time spent in barrels: 24–26 months	Average age of vines: 35 years
Evaluation of present classification: Should be maintained	
Plateau of maturity: 8–30 years following the vintage	

Situated on a bed of sandy gravel and iron-enriched limestone in the northernmost reaches of the commune of St.-Estèphe is Calon-Ségur, the most northerly classified growth. Like its nearby neighbor, Château Montrose, there is a live-in owner, the bushy-eyebrowed and burly Philippe Capbern-Gasqueton. The white château of Calon-Ségur dominates the landscape, with two towers and their unusually rounded roofs. Surrounding the château is a stone wall, or clos, which, while common in Burgundy, is unusual in Bordeaux.

The history of Calon-Ségur dates back to Roman times when the commune of St.-Estèphe was known as "de Calones." Notoriety as a wine-producing estate is no doubt enhanced by the famous eighteenth-century quotation attributed to the Marquis de Ségur, who surprised friends with his statement, "I make my wine at Lafite and Latour, but my heart is in Calon." His emotional attachment to Calon has been immortalized with a heart on Calon's label.

For much of the twentieth century, Calon-Ségur did almost everything right, often producing wines that were every bit as good as the first-growths. There were extraordinary efforts in 1926, 1928, and 1929, and in the dismal decade of the thirties a fine 1934 was produced. In the late forties and early fifties, few properties in Bordeaux could match the stunning successes that Calon-Ségur enjoyed in 1945, 1947, 1948, 1949, and 1953. Following 1953, there was not another truly profound wine produced at Calon-Ségur until 1982. They were not bad, but even the top years during the sixties and seventies tended to turn out wines that were slightly oxidized, with tired fruit and sometimes an excessive, musty, old-wood flavor, as well as excessive, astringent tannins. The feeling by knowledgeable insiders in Bordeaux was that the bringing up of the wine in the cellars—the so-called *élevage*—was suspect, and that the wines were bottled too late and the racking and cleanliness of the old barrels was often handled in a casual, if not indifferent, manner.

Since 1982, Calon-Ségur has regained much of the original form, turning out fine wines in 1985, 1986, 1988, 1989, and 1990. Nevertheless, this great historic estate has been surpassed in the hierarchy of quality by Cos d'Estournel. Of course, Monsieur Gasqueton would argue that of all the St.-Estèphes, Calon-Ségur remains the most faithful to the traditional style of long-lived wines that are slow to evolve and blossom. In that sense, he is correct, and traditionalists would be well advised to consider the recent efforts of this beautifully situated, historically significant estate that is the last (geographically speaking) of the classified growths in the famed 1855 classification.

VINTAGES

1989—This property has turned in a distinguished effort in 1989. It has
an impressive deep ruby color, a sweet, chewy, dense texture,
88 full body, plenty of alcohol, and gobs of soft tannins. Quite precocious, it will have a life span of at least 15 years. It reminded
me of a downsized version of the 1982. Anticipated maturity:
1996–2010. Last tasted, 4/91.

1988—The 1988 Calon-Ségur outshines the 1989. Deeply colored, superbly balanced, rich and full bodied, it appears to be a worthy
91 candidate for 20–25 years of longevity. It is a classic example of
this château's wine. I should also note that it is surprisingly powerful for the vintage. It gets my nod as the finest Calon-Ségur
since the 1982. Anticipated maturity: 1998–2020. Last tasted,
4/91.

1987—Light to medium ruby, with a washed-out, herbal, woody, faintly
fruity bouquet, this soft, medium-bodied wine should be drunk
75 over the next 5–6 years. Anticipated maturity: Now–1996. Last
tasted, 6/90.

1986—This wine may turn out to merit a rating several points higher
than the score shown. Calon-Ségur possesses a deep ruby color,
89 with a tight, yet ripe, blackcurrant bouquet backed up with subtle
scents of herb, cedar, and sweet oak. On the palate, the wine is
the richest wine made at this estate since the 1982, as it is full
bodied with excellent, perhaps even outstanding, depth and
length. Curiously, in this vintage Calon-Ségur used an inordi-
nately high percentage of Cabernet Sauvignon (90% Cabernet
Sauvignon, 10% Merlot). Normally the percentage of Merlot is
significantly higher. Anticipated maturity: 1997–2015. Last tasted,
9/90.

1985—The 1985 was bottled very late (January 1988), which I feel was a
mistake, although the wine is ripe and fruity. With a little more
86 depth, the 1985 Calon-Ségur could have been special. Anticipated
maturity: Now–2000. Last tasted, 12/89.

1984—The 1984 needs several years to round out, but it is a medium-
bodied, light, relatively soft wine with some aromas of new oak
75 and decent balance. The color suggests a 1973. Anticipated maturity: Now–1992. Last tasted, 9/88.

1983—When I first tasted this wine in spring 1984, it was surprisingly
soft, with grapey flavors, a hot, alcoholic finish, a rather fragile
82 framework. Later in the year, it was ripe and flavorful, but low in
acidity, and again, alcoholic. In style, color, and texture, it reminded me of a 1976. Fully mature and loosely structured, this

wine should be drunk up. Anticipated maturity: Now–1996. Last tasted, 2/88.

1982—The best vintage of Calon-Ségur since 1947? Gasqueton continues
·   to think so, in spite of the fact that the wine remains stubbornly
92   backward and nearly impenetrable. This massive wine has a dark ruby color, with an opulent, intense, exotic, rich fruitiness, full body, significant tannins, and a hard, tough-textured finish. Now tasting more backward than I ever imagined it would, the 1982 Calon-Ségur is a classic wine that evidences the great potential this estate possesses. Anticipated maturity: 1998–2015. Last tasted, 5/91.

1981—Rather light, but nevertheless charming, elegant, fruity, and
·   clearly marked by new wood, the 1981 Calon-Ségur reflects both
83   the inconsistency of this famous estate and the 1981 vintage. Soft on the palate, it can be drunk now. Anticipated maturity: Now– 1995. Last tasted, 5/88.

1979—An elegant, charming, somewhat straightforward style of wine,
·   with good, soft, supple fruit, light tannin, medium ruby color, and
80   a pronounced ripe Merlot character. Anticipated maturity: Now– 1993. Last tasted, 10/84.

1978—A distinctly mediocre effort, with medium ruby color, a pleasing,
·   yet one-dimensional, ripe, leafy, spicy, Merlot aroma, average
78   flavor intensity, and a short, simple finish. Some tannin is pres- ent, but this wine requires immediate consumption. Anticipated maturity: Now. Last tasted, 3/88.

1976—Once a pleasant, supple, deliciously fruity wine, the 1976 has
·   begun to lose its fruit and commence its decline. Medium garnet
78   in color with brown at the edge, this wine has a well-developed bouquet of hickory wood, ripe fruit, and spice. The soft flavors are marked by low acidity and an astringent dryness in the finish. Drink immediately. Anticipated maturity: Now. Last tasted, 7/87.

1975—While the color exhibits some surprising brown at the edge, this
·   is certainly a mature and enjoyable 1975 St.-Estèphe. It is fully
87   mature, with rich, expansive, generously endowed flavors, excel- lent concentration, and fine depth that is missing in some other well-regarded vintages of Calon-Ségur. It is one of the more pre- cocious and flattering 1975s. Drink it over the next 5 years. Antic- ipated maturity: Now–1997. Last tasted, 2/88.

1974—Somewhat typical of this vintage, Calon-Ségur produced a shal-
·   low, though pleasingly colored wine with just enough fruit to make
69   it palatable. It is still holding together, no doubt because of its high acidity. Caveat emptor. Last tasted, 2/86.

1973—In its prime in 1976–1978, this was one of the more pleasant 1973
· Bordeaux wines. While not tasted recently, it would be most
65 shocking if the wine had much fruit left to it. Last tasted, 9/77.

1971—Fading badly, as evidenced by the brown color, the 1971 Calon-
· Ségur has a decaying mushroom aroma, soft, barely alive flavors,
65 and an acidic finish. My notes reveal I enjoyed a good bottle in
1977, but time has not been kind to this vintage of Calon-Ségur.
Last tasted, 10/80.

1970—Another convincing piece of evidence that Calon-Ségur's reputa-
· tion for producing long-lived wine is hardly justified by its perfor-
80 mance in the sixties and seventies. Fully mature in 1978, with an
attractive, charming, moderately intense bouquet of ripe Merlot
fruit and spicy oak, this garnet-colored, slightly brownish wine
has soft, supple fruit, medium body, and little tannin remaining.
Anticipated maturity: Now–may be in decline. Last tasted, 1/81.

1967—Calon-Ségur made one of the best 1967s, which for several years
· outperformed its more heralded older sibling, the 1966. Rich,
84 soft, supple, and deeply fruity, the wine had a voluptuous texture.
The bouquet offered ripe fruit and good cedary scents. The fruit
has now begun to fade so immediate consumption is advised.
Anticipated maturity: Now–may be in decline. Last tasted,
10/80.

1966—This wine continues to hold on to life but it is living dangerously.
· It has a lovely, full-intensity bouquet of cedar wood and ripe fruit.
87 Very satisfying on the palate, with good concentration and length,
this is arguably the best Calon-Ségur of the sixties. Anticipated
maturity: Now–1994. Last tasted, 1/87.

1964—Lacking fruit and coarsely textured, with a damp earthy, musty
· aroma, and modest flavors and proportions, this wine is still hold-
75 ing together, but seems to hold little promise for the future. Anticipated maturity: Now–probably in serious decline. Last tasted,
6/78.

1962—My first tasting experience, early in the seventies, found the 1962
· Calon-Ségur to be especially light, lacking richness and fat, and
76 to be browning at the edge. Tasted again, in Bordeaux, in the late
eighties revealed a wine that was still alive but light and uninteresting. Anticipated maturity: Now. Last tasted, 1/87.

1961—A good, solid wine, but given the vintage and the overall quality
· of its two most famous neighbors, Montrose and Cos d'Estournel,
83 the 1961 Calon-Ségur is a disappointment. The color lacks the
great depth and richness of this vintage, and this wine seems
much less concentrated and rich than others. In 1987, the wine

was fit to drink, but living dangerously with high acidity poking
its head through the moderate levels of extract. It remains a mediocre effort, particularly for a 1961. Anticipated maturity: Now–
1994. Last tasted, 6/87.

OLDER VINTAGES

Lamentably, the greatest vintages of Calon-Ségur, except for the 1982
and 1988, have been the 1928 (rated 94 and absolutely fabulous in October 1988), 1945 (rated as highly as 92), 1947 (worthy of a 94 rating at its
peak in 1985, but now beginning to fade), 1949 (rated 95 in January 1989),
and 1953 (a 92, but beginning to dry out when last tasted in March 1988).

CAPBERN-GASQUETON (Grand Bourgeois Exceptionnel)

AVERAGE

Production: 11,000 cases	Grape varieties: Cabernet Sauvignon—70% Cabernet Franc—20% Merlot—10%
Secondary label: Le Grand Village Capbern	
Vineyard size: 86.5 acres	Proprietor: The Capbern-Gasqueton family
Time spent in barrels: 12–18 months	Average age of vines: 30 years
Evaluation of present classification: Should be maintained	
Plateau of maturity: 5–10 years following the vintage	

While this is a Cru Bourgeois, it has been rumored that Capbern benefits
from those vats produced at Calon-Ségur that are not deemed suitable
for that estate's grand vin. The wine, which is matured entirely in old,
small casks, has a tendency to be hard and lacking in flavor dimension
and character. The best recent vintages have been the 1982, 1988, and
1989.

CAVE COOPERATIVE MARQUIS DE ST.-ESTÈPHE

Reputed to be the finest and most modernly equipped cooperative in the Médoc, this conglomerate of over two-hundred producers (controlling 926 acres of vineyards) turns out an enormous quantity of wine that is sold not only under the name of the cooperative, Marquis de St.-Estèphe, but also under the name of the estate. Some of the small, but reputable estates that have their wines produced and bottled at the cooperative include Les Pradines, l'Hôpital, Le Roc, and, what is probably the finest estate the cooperative can boast, Château Faget. The latter property, a tiny domain of 10 acres owned by Maurice Lagarde, consistently turns out wines that are rich, full bodied, and reasonably priced. Visitors to the cooperative should specifically request a tasting of this particular *cuvée*. Most of the wines of the cooperative are aged only in vats, and rarely have the benefit of new oak casks; therefore, they should be drunk in their first 5–6 years of life.

CHAMBERT-MARBUZET (Cru Bourgeois)   VERY GOOD

Production: 4,000 cases	Grape varieties: Cabernet Sauvignon—70% Merlot—30%
Secondary label: MacCarthy	
Vineyard size: 20 acres	Proprietor: Henri Duboscq
Time spent in barrels: 16 months	Average age of vines: 30 years
Evaluation of present classification: The quality equivalent of a fifth-growth	
Plateau of maturity: 2–8 years following the vintage	

The talented and flamboyant Henri Duboscq, proprietor of the more well-known Château Haut-Marbuzet in St.-Estèphe, is also the owner of this small estate located near the village of Marbuzet. It was acquired by the Duboscq family in 1962. Like Haut-Marbuzet, the vinification consists of a relatively high fermentation temperature, a long *cuvaison*, the bringing up of the wine in at least 50% new oak casks, and the avoidance of any type of filtration at the time of bottling. The wines of Chambert-Marbuzet have exhibited luscious rich fruit, married with abundant, sometimes lavish quantities of toasty new oak. They are easy to understand and drink. If Chambert-Marbuzet is to be criticized at all, it would be because at times the wine can be entirely too obvious, and the potential to age beyond a decade is suspect. Nevertheless, the quality is high, and the wine enjoys increasing popularity.

VINTAGES

1989— The 1989 Chambert-Marbuzet exhibits plenty of toasty new oak,
· an exotic bouquet of black fruits and spices, is exuberantly fruity,
86 very soft, medium bodied, and finishes with a whopping blow of
alcohol and tannin. It is flashy, but lacking some substance in the
mid-palate. Drink it over the next 7–8 years. Anticipated maturity: Now–1995. Last tasted, 4/91.

1988— Abnormally light, fragrant, and evolved, the 1988 is surprisingly
· shy and subdued for a wine from this estate. It should be drunk
83 over the near term, within 2–4 years of the vintage. Anticipated
maturity: Now–1993. Last tasted, 4/91.

1987— Green, herbal, washed-out fruit flavors are followed by a medium-
· bodied wine with soft tannins that lacks concentration. It should
74 be drunk up. Anticipated maturity: Now–may be in decline. Last
tasted, 3/90.

1986— In all my cask tastings the 1986 was an impressive wine, with
· deep ruby/black color, super depth, richness, full body, stunning
87 length, and enough tannin to insure a positive evolution for 5–6
years. Muscular and brawny, it is marked by the toasty vanilla of
100% new oak barrels. The wine is excellent, but much lighter
than I had thought it to be when tasted from cask. It is a sleeper
of the vintage. Anticipated maturity: Now–1997. Last tasted,
4/90.

1985— The rating of the 1985 may be conservative, as I thought it to be
· a slightly better wine in cask prior to bottling. It is a deep, pow-
86 erful wine packed with jammy fruit, an overt spicy oakiness, medium to full body, and soft texture. Anticipated maturity: Now–
1993. Last tasted, 3/89.

LA COMMANDERIE (Cru Bourgeois)   AVERAGE

Production: 7,000 cases	Grape varieties: Cabernet Sauvignon—60% Merlot—30% Cabernet Franc—10%
Secondary label: none	
Vineyard size: 50 acres	Proprietor: Gabriel Meffre
Time spent in barrels: 10–14 months in barrels and vats	Average age of vines: 25 years
Evaluation of present classification: Should be maintained	
Plateau of maturity: 4–8 years following the vintage	

This property, which sits on well-drained, gravelly and clay soils, is owned by Gabriel Meffre, the proprietor of the Cru Bourgeois Château du Glana in St.-Julien. The wine is made in a modern, commercial style, emphasizing supple, easygoing fruit and smooth, light tannins, and is ready to drink when bottled. It could be more complex, but it is certainly clean and understandable to the masses.

COS D'ESTOURNEL (Second-Growth)   OUTSTANDING

Production: 28,000–32,000 cases	Grape varieties:
	Cabernet Sauvignon—60%
	Merlot—40%
Secondary label: Marbuzet	
Vineyard size: 160.5 acres	Proprietor: The Prats family
Time spent in barrels: 18 months	Average age of vines: 35 years
Evaluation of present classification: Since 1982, the quality	
equivalent of a first-growth	
Plateau of maturity: 8–30 years following the vintage	

Under the inspired direction of Bruno Prats, Cos d'Estournel (pronounced, surprisingly, with a sounded oss in *Cos*) has risen to the top of its class in St.-Estèphe. Since 1982, the wines have gone from one strength to another, and in most vintages, Cos d'Estournel can be expected to produce one of the best wines of the Médoc. This oriental-looking château, sitting on a ridge immediately north of the Pauillac border and its famous neighbor Lafite-Rothschild, is distinguished by the high percentage of Merlot used in the blend—40%—and the elevated use of new oak casks—100% in 1986, 75% in other top years. This proportion of Merlot is among the highest used in the Haut-Médoc, and also accounts for the fleshy, richly textured character so noticeable in recent vintages of Cos d'Estournel. Bruno Prats, the manager and owner, belongs to the avant-garde of new wine technology. This is one of the few major Bordeaux estates to be adamantly in favor of filtration of wine, both before cask aging and bottling. However, Prats may be having second thoughts, as he decided to eliminate the second filtration prior to the bottling of the 1989. The results speak for themselves—Cos d'Estournel, after having to play runner-up to Montrose in the fifties and sixties, has emerged in the eighties as the leader in St.-Estèphe.

VINTAGES

1989—While the 1989 Cos d'Estournel will, in all likelihood, prove to be
·   an outstanding wine, I would have to rate it behind the quality of
90   the château's splendid 1982, 1985, 1986, and 1990. It is a medium-

bodied, rich, concentrated wine displaying an impressive color, and a nose of superripe black fruits, toasty oak, and licorice. In the mouth, the wine tastes like a blend of the 1985 and 1982, although it is neither so elegant as the 1985 nor so powerful and opulent as the 1982. The finish is long, alcoholic, and lush. There is every possibility that this wine may turn out to be as good as the château's memorable 1953. Anticipated maturity: 1992–2008. Last tasted, 4/91.

1988—The 1988 has an intriguing bouquet of exotic spices and black
·   fruits, but it is savagely tannic, austere, and difficult to penetrate.
86   It should outlive the 1989, but I remain concerned about its over-
all balance and future ability to provide charm and pleasure. Anticipated maturity: 1997–2012. Last tasted, 4/91.

1987—This wine is fully ready to drink, displaying a plummy, toasty,
·   weedy bouquet, light to medium body, some soft, fleshy fruit, low
83   acidity, and soft tannins in the finish. It should be consumed over
the next 7–8 years. Anticipated maturity: Now–1996. Last tasted, 3/91.

1986—The 1986 Cos d'Estournel from Bruno Prats is made from a blend
·   of 68% Cabernet Sauvignon, 30% Merlot, and 2% Cabernet
95   Franc. It is a very highly extracted wine, with a black/ruby color
and plenty of toasty, smoky notes in the bouquet that suggest ripe plums and licorice. On the palate, it is a massive, huge, ripe, extremely concentrated wine, with sensational depth and richness. It has a great deal more power, weight, and tannin than the more opulent, and perhaps more charming 1985. Additionally, this is one of the few vintages where proprietor Prats utilized 100% new oak. Anticipated maturity: 1995–2015. Last tasted, 1/91.

1985—The 1985, a 60% Cabernet Sauvignon, 40% Merlot wine, also
·   aged in 100% new oak, is cast from the same mold as the 1982
95   and 1953 vintages of this wine. It is forward, with a fabulously
scented bouquet of toasty new oak and concentrated red fruit. On the palate, it is very rich, lush, long, full bodied, and in spite of its youthful appeal, should age beautifully for 12–18 years. It is a wonderful marriage of power and elegance. Anticipated maturity: Now–2009. Last tasted, 4/91.

1984—From the first time tasted, the 1984 has been a star of this modest
·   vintage. Sufficiently ruby in color with a moderately intense,
84   spicy, tarry, oaky, cassis-scented bouquet, this medium-bodied
wine has good concentration, soft-yet-firm tannins, and tart acidity. Anticipated maturity: Now–1996. Last tasted, 10/88.

1983—At first glimpse in March 1984, this Cos d'Estournel was raw,
·   tannic, angular, and unyielding, although it had good color and
85   weight on the palate. Later in the year the wine was showing more
      richness and fruit, but still decidedly tannic in a hard, lean way.
      Recent tastings have established that this wine is maturing
      quickly, taking on an advanced color. Never the picture of bal-
      ance, this slightly clumsy effort should be drunk over the next
      4–6 years. It is somewhat of a disappointment for the vintage.
      Anticipated maturity: Now–1995. Last tasted, 4/90.

1982—A monumental wine that has exhibited gobs of explosive black-
·   currant fruit from the very first cask samples tasted at the château
97   in March 1983. Unctuous, massive, rich, full bodied, and loaded
      with extract and tannin, this remains one of the greatest Cos
      d'Estournels I have ever tasted. In 1990, the wine was still youth-
      ful and firm, with huge reserves of fruit. Anticipated maturity:
      1995–2015. Last tasted, 12/90.

1981—Deep ruby color, with a spicy, rich, briary, tightly knit bouquet,
·   this wine is deeper and more promising than the 1983, but rela-
83   tively light, compact, and lean. This restrained wine should be at
      its best if drunk over the next 5–7 years. Anticipated maturity:
      Now–1995. Last tasted, 5/90.

1980—Unquestionably a success for the vintage, though obviously not a
·   great wine, the 1980 Cos d'Estournel has medium ruby color, an
83   interesting, slightly spicy and herbaceous aroma, and well above
      average, fruity flavors for the vintage. Anticipated maturity:
      Now–may be in decline. Last tasted, 10/84.

1979—The best of the 1979 St.-Estèphes, Cos d'Estournel has a dark
·   ruby color, with a developing bouquet of ripe cherries, cassis, and
86   some vanillin, oaky scents. Full, yet corpulent for the vintage,
      with surprising weight and depth, this wine has aged slowly and
      still needs another 2–3 years of bottle age to be fully mature.
      Anticipated maturity: 1993–2000. Last tasted, 11/89.

1978—Very highly regarded by the château, I have found the 1978 to be
·   very good, but not as graceful or as well balanced as the 1979. It
85   is dark ruby with a moderately intense bouquet of herbs, black
      cherries, spice, oak, and leather. On the palate, the wine is me-
      dium to full bodied, with a dusty tannic texture. Anticipated ma-
      turity: Now–2005. Last tasted, 1/88.

1976—One of the better 1976s, Cos d'Estournel somehow succeeded in
·   avoiding the feebleness and fragile character of many of the wines
86   from this early maturing vintage. Now fully mature, but in no
      danger of collapse, this wine has a complex bouquet of red berry

fruit, spices, and toasty oak. Supple, with good fruit, this soft, round, elegant wine should be drunk over the next 5 years. Anticipated maturity: Now–1994. Last tasted, 2/90.

1975—I had higher hopes for the 1975 Cos d'Estournel in the early
·   stages, but like an increasing number of wines from this vintage
77   it appears incapable of living up to its potential. The color is
     medium ruby. The wine is still harshly tannic and angular, and
     while full bodied, it lacks charm and fruit. It can handle another
     5–6 years of cellaring, although I have begun to lose hope that it
     will ever provide great pleasure or charm. Anticipated maturity:
     Now–2005. Last tasted, 9/90.

1974—Adequate color, but this stalky, unripe wine still tastes green and
·   hollow. Anticipated maturity: Now–probably in serious decline.
67   Last tasted, 10/81.

1973—Eleven years ago the fruit had already faded and the sure signs of
·   approaching senility—a brownish, pale color—were apparent. It
65   is now over the hill. Last tasted, 10/80.

1971—From a vintage that was very irregular in quality, the 1971 Cos
·   d'Estournel is now fully mature. Medium to dark ruby, with an
84   orange-brownish edge, this wine has a silky, rather seductive
     quality with good, supple fruit. It should be consumed immedi-
     ately. Anticipated maturity: Now–1994. Last tasted, 1/87.

1970—Still youthfully dark ruby with a reticent, yet promising plummy
·   bouquet, a concentrated deep, rich, weighty feel on the palate,
87   and plenty of mouth-puckering tannin still present, the 1970 re-
     mains an impressive, yet backward, somewhat coarse and rustic
     wine. Why, at 20 years of age, is it not more complex? Anticipated
     maturity: Now–2010. Last tasted, 7/90.

1967—Now beginning to fade badly, this wine was at its prime from 1976
·   to 1978, but never had impressive depth or concentration. Antic-
73   ipated maturity: Now–probably in serious decline. Last tasted,
     9/79.

1966—A very good 1966, yet not top flight, the Cos d'Estournel is me-
·   dium to dark ruby, with some browning. It has very good concen-
85   tration, in the somewhat lean, austere character of the vintage,
     and plenty of tannin in the finish. Although it does not yet seem
     to be mature, I would drink it over the near term before the fruit
     begins to fade. Anticipated maturity: Now. Last tasted, 10/84.

1964—Because of the heavy rains in this year, wine was rather a hit or
·   miss proposition with most Médoc châteaux. If the grapes were
72   picked early, then the château probably made good wine, but if
     they were harvested following the storms, the grapes were diluted
     by heavy rains and the results predictable. This wine—raw, un-

generous, yet surprisingly well colored—lacks fruit and complexity, and is not likely to improve any further. Anticipated maturity: Now—probably in serious decline. Last tasted, 10/78.

1962—This is a typical St.-Estèphe in the sense that wines from this commune are generally described as being hard and unyielding.
·
86   Nevertheless, all the components are there, the dark ruby color, the very good concentration and weight, and the moderate tannin. Anticipated maturity: Now. Last tasted, 12/83.

1961—Typically dark and densely pigmented with no sign of browning at the edge, this big, intense, concentrated, still tannic wine has
·
92   at least a decade of life left in it. The fragrant bouquet offers up scents of cedar, oriental spices, and fruitcake. It is very rich, deep, and long on the palate, with masses of ripe black fruits. An opulent beauty! Anticipated maturity: Now–2000. Last tasted, 1/91.

OLDER VINTAGES

The finest old vintages of Cos d'Estournel that I have been privileged to taste include an excellent 1959 (rated 92, and more youthful than the 1961 when tasted in November 1989), a superb, voluptuous, graceful, decadently fruity, soft 1953 (drunk from magnum in June 1989 and rated 95), disappointing bottles of 1947 (others claim it to be fabulous) and 1945, but a profound magnum of 1928 (rated 97) drunk at the château with Monsieur Prats in March 1988.

COS LABORY (Fifth-Growth)   AVERAGE

Production: 7,000 cases	Grape varieties: Cabernet Sauvignon—40% Merlot—30% Cabernet Franc—25% Petit Verdot—5%
Secondary label: none	
Vineyard size: 37 acres	Proprietor: The Audoy family
Time spent in barrels: 12–16 months	Average age of vines: 25 years
Evaluation of present classification: Should be downgraded to a Cru Bourgeois, although the high quality of both the 1989 and 1990 should be noted	
Plateau of maturity: 5–12 years following the vintage	

One of the most disappointing wines of all the classified growths, Cos Labory is another prominent, even blatant example of the need for a more relevant classification than the 1855 Classification of the Wines of

the Gironde. Ranked a fifth-growth in 1855, the wine would have a difficult time obtaining Cru Bourgeois status in any new hierarchy. The
owners, the Audoy family, produce a fruity, bland, light, often feebly
colored wine that lacks bouquet, flavor, concentration, and length. The
wine is exposed to a cool vinification that minimizes flavor and color
extraction, and is filtered twice, once prior to barrel aging and again
prior to bottling. (Filtration can strip a wine if performed excessively.)
There would appear to be little excuse for such indifferent practices as
the vineyard is beautifully placed, adjacent to both that of Cos d'Estournel and Lafite-Rothschild.

The price for this low quality is high—no doubt because of Cos Labory's fifth-growth status. However, there are numerous Crus Bourgeois
in St.-Estèphe that make much better and more interesting wine than
Cos Labory. From a consumer's perspective, this is a wine to approach
with a great deal of caution. The brilliant 1989 and 1990, I hope, offer
reassuring evidence that quality is on the move upward.

VINTAGES

1989—The 1989 is undeniably the finest example of Cos Labory I have
·   ever tasted. I should note that the 1990, tasted from cask, looked
89   to be just as dazzling! Black/ruby in color, with a huge bouquet of
       cassis, this formidable 1989 has layers of extract, a very high
       tannin level, and a hefty level of alcohol. Does this vintage signal
       the beginning of a renaissance of Cos Labory? Anticipated matu-
       rity: 1995–2015. Last tasted, 4/91.

1988—The 1988 Cos Labory is a pleasant, well-colored, tannic, medium-
·   bodied wine, with fine overall balance and good length. It should
84   provide decent rather than inspired drinking. Anticipated matu-
       rity: 1992–2000. Last tasted, 3/90.

1986—The 1986 Cos Labory is light, but does exhibit a pleasant as well
·   as charming berry fruitiness married with an attractive subtle
79   oakiness. It seems to reveal some of the vast size of the 1986 crop,
       particularly the lightness of the Merlot that was apparent in some
       vineyards in that vintage. Anticipated maturity: Now–1996. Last
       tasted, 11/89.

1985—Cos Labory performed well in 1985, producing a soft, oaky, ripe
·   wine, with medium body, good concentration, and attractive
85   length—surprisingly competent. Anticipated maturity: Now–
       1998. Last tasted, 6/89.

1983—The 1983 is disturbingly light, innocuous, simple, and plain. A
·   respectable *vin de table*, but hardly a wine of classified-growth
70   quality. Anticipated maturity: Now–probably in serious decline.
       Last tasted, 6/84.

1982—In the context of the vintage, a rather mediocre wine, but in the
·   context of Cos Labory's performance record, a solid, amply en-
75   dowed wine, with good concentration, very good color, and mod-
       erate tannins. Anticipated maturity: Now–1997. Last tasted,
       1/88.

1979—Medium ruby, with a shallow, faint, fruity aroma, this medium-
·   bodied wine has a light intensity, dull fruitiness, simple flavors,
65   and little tannins. Anticipated maturity: Now–probably in serious
       decline. Last tasted, 9/84.

1978—Fully mature, with a burnt, stemmy, leafy aroma, this light- to
·   medium-weight wine has diluted fruit flavors, and light to moder-
67   ate tannins. A very mediocre wine. Last tasted, 5/83.

1976—Faded, damp cellar aromas offer too little ripe fruit and too much
·   wet earthy components for a good Bordeaux wine. Light to me-
55   dium ruby color now shows ample evidence of age as the brown
       color sets in. Anticipated maturity: Now–Probably in serious de-
       cline. Last tasted, 2/80.

1975—A tannic, angular wine, with no charm, little fruit in evidence,
·   and a severe, hard, tannic bite to it. Anticipated maturity: Now–
64   1995. Last tasted, 12/81.

1971—Poor winemaking and perhaps overcropping as well have ac-
·   counted for a very mediocre, thin, green, nasty wine that shows
52   the ugliest side of Bordeaux. Last tasted, 4/78.

1970—An acceptable wine that provided decent, if hardly inspired,
·   drinking in the late seventies, this medium ruby wine exhibited a
70   simple, yet straightforward fruitiness, some pleasing spicy,
       cherry components, and light to medium body. Anticipated ma-
       turity: Now–probably in serious decline. Last tasted, 2/80.

COUTELIN-MERVILLE (Grand Bourgeois)   GOOD

Production: 7,000 cases	Grape varieties:
	Merlot—35%
	Cabernet Franc—35%
	Cabernet Sauvignon—20%
	Malbec—5%
	Petit Verdot—5%
Secondary label: none	
Vineyard size: 37 acres	Proprietor: Guy Estager
Time spent in barrels: 16–22 months	Average age of vines: 25 years
Evaluation of present classification: Should be maintained	
Plateau of maturity: 8–15 or more years following the vintage	

I wish I knew the wines of this moderately sized estate better. Those vintages I have tasted—1986, 1982, 1975, and 1970—all represented intensely concentrated, powerful, highly tannic, yet interesting old-style, well-made wines. The proprietor, Guy Estager, from France's Corrèze region (much like the family of Jean-Pierre Moueix in Libourne), marches to the beat of a different drummer in St.-Estèphe, as his blend of grapes suggests he is a great proponent of Cabernet Franc. Perhaps this explains why their wines have a compelling fragrance, but it does not explain their aging potential, power, and muscle. Low yields of under 40 hectoliters per hectare account for that. All things considered, this is a wine that Estager claims needs at least 15–20 years in the top vintages to reach maturity! He would appear to be right. This could well be a property to look at more seriously.

LE CROCK (Cru Bourgeois Exceptionnel) AVERAGE

Production: 16,000 cases	Grape varieties: Cabernet Sauvignon—68% Merlot—32%
Secondary label: none	
Vineyard size: 79 acres	Proprietor: The Cuvelier family
Time spent in barrels: 20–24 months	Average age of vines: 30 years
Evaluation of present classification: The quality equivalent of a Cru Bourgeois	
Plateau of maturity: 5–12 years following the vintage	

This attractive, two-story château, located south of the village of St.-Estèphe, has been owned by the Cuvelier family since 1903. While the superbly situated château—which sits on a hill overlooking a lake usually inhabited by numerous swans—is a site even the most jaded photographer could hardly ignore, the wines have rarely been exciting. The high percentage of Merlot used would seemingly insure plenty of flesh and suppleness, but my experience with the wines of Le Crock indicates they are entirely too tannic, tough-textured, and often give the impression of being severe and excessively austere.

There is nothing to criticize about the attention given by the Cuvelier family to the vineyard and the modern vinification, which is overseen by the famed oenologist, Professor Emile Peynaud. Nevertheless, the wines of Le Crock generally seem to lack fruit, although they are certainly full-bodied, dense wines capable of lasting 10–12 years.

VINTAGES

1989—Historically, this property turns out hard, lean, frequently charm-
· less wines. However, the 1989 has more fruit than usual, good
83 ruby color, a blackberry fruitiness, medium body, low acidity, but
high tannins. It lacks complexity, but should offer serviceable
drinking over the next 5–6 years. Anticipated maturity: Now–
1996. Last tasted, 4/91.

1988—The 1988 Le Crock is similar in quality to the 1989, but is totally
· different in style. Leaner, smaller-scaled, and neither so tannic
82 nor so alcoholic, it should be drunk over the next 5–6 years.
Anticipated maturity: Now–1996. Last tasted, 11/90.

1986—I have consistently found the 1986 Le Crock to lack richness, and
· simply taste too hard and astringent for the amount of fruit that it
74 seemingly possesses. Anticipated maturity: 1992–1997. Last
tasted, 4/90.

1985—The 1985 has medium body, moderately deep flavors, and some
· hard astringence in the finish—too much press wine in the blend?
73 Overall, it is an uninspired winemaking effort. Anticipated maturity: Now. Last tasted, 3/89.

HAUT-MARBUZET (Grand Bourgeois Exceptionnel)

EXCELLENT

Production: 20,000 cases	Grape varieties: Merlot—50% Cabernet Sauvignon—40% Cabernet Franc—10%
Secondary label: Tour-de-Marbuzet	
Vineyard size: 98.8 acres	Proprietor: Henri Duboscq
Time spent in barrels: 18 months	Average age of vines: 30 years
Evaluation of present classification: Should be upgraded to a third-growth	
Plateau of maturity: 3–15 years following the vintage	

Haut-Marbuzet is one of the oldest estates in St.-Estèphe, but fame can
be traced only to 1952, when it was purchased by the father of the current
proprietor, Henri Duboscq. The vineyard is beautifully situated facing
the Gironde River, on a gradual slope of gravelly soil intermixed with
calcareous clay. Duboscq, a flamboyant personality who tends to describe his wines by making analogies to prominent female movie stars,

has created one of the most immensely popular wines of Bordeaux, particularly in France, Belgium, Holland, and England, where the great majority of Haut-Marbuzet is sold. He believes in late harvesting, thereby bringing in grapes that are nearly bursting with ripeness, macerating them for at least three weeks, and then aging the entire crop for 18 months in 100% new oak barrels. Indeed his methods result in an intense, opulent, and lavish fruitiness, with a rich, spicy, exotic bouquet. To the wine enthusiast, Haut-Marbuzet produces one of the most obvious yet sexiest wines of the entire Bordeaux region.

Some Duboscq critics have charged that his winemaking style borders on vulgarity, but he would argue that the new oak simply adds a charm and unctuous quality to the traditional muscular, tough texture that emerges from so many wines made in St.-Estèphe. Other critics have suggested that Haut-Marbuzet fails to age gracefully. While the wine is usually delicious when released, my tastings of old vintages back through 1961 have generally indicated that Haut-Marbuzet is best when drunk within the first 10–15 years of life.

Despite the criticisms, no one argues with the success proprietor Duboscq has enjoyed. He produces a Bordeaux that behaves more like a decadent Burgundy or Rhône.

VINTAGES

1989—While Haut-Marbuzet's 1989 is not "vintage of the century" ma-
·   terial, it does display an intense, smoky, curranty bouquet, lush,
89   creamy, broad flavors, excellent ripeness, plenty of alcohol, and
       6–10 years of drinking potential. It is reminiscent of a downsized
       version of the magnificent 1982. Anticipated maturity: 1992–2002.
       Last tasted, 4/91.

1988—The 1988 is less dramatic than the 1989, but is still a flashy,
·   seductive, full-bodied, amply endowed, as well as generously
89   oaked wine. The tannins are slightly more aggressive than fans of
       this property's wines usually expect. Nevertheless, the wine ex-
       hibits plenty of extract and size. Anticipated maturity: Now–
       2000. Last tasted, 3/91.

1987—Surprisingly fragrant (aromas of smoky oak and herbs dominate),
·   this soft, medium-bodied, heady wine is not concentrated, but is
82   still tasty and pleasant. Anticipated maturity: Now–1993. Last
       tasted, 4/90.

1986—The 1986 has continued to improve since I first tasted it in cask.
·   The deep ruby/purple color, enormous bouquet of smoky oak,
90   exotic spices, and plummy fruit of the 1986 suggest that it can be

drunk immediately, but the tannins in the finish indicate this wine will be even more stunning with several years of cellaring. An interesting, unique, and satisfying wine! Anticipated maturity: 1992–2003. Last tasted, 2/90.

1985—The 1985 Haut-Marbuzet has the fleshpot personality that makes this wine so sexy and appealing. A big, toasty, plum-scented bouquet offers generous amounts of fruit. On the palate, the wine is supple, spicy, rich, and immensely tasty. It is a delight to drink now, but should keep 6–9 years. Anticipated maturity: Now–1997. Last tasted, 5/90.

· 88

1984—The 1984 Haut-Marbuzet has tons of oaky aromas in the bouquet, a soft, supple fruitiness, and decent length. However, the fruit is beginning to dry out and immediate consumption is advised. Anticipated maturity: Now. Last tasted, 3/88.

· 78

1983—Extremely dense with an almost port-like, dark ruby color, ripe, rich, plummy nose, fat, intense, viscous flavor, and moderate tannin, this generous wine is drinking beautifully, but will keep for another 5–6 years. Anticipated maturity: Now–1996. Last tasted, 1/85.

· 88

1982—A ravishing, luscious wine that seems to suggest a decadently rich Pomerol rather than a stiff, tannic St.-Estèphe. Very intensely flavored with a gorgeous, perfumed bouquet of chocolatey, cedary, ripe, blackcurrant fruit and toasty oak, the 1982 Haut-Marbuzet seems to have produced the perfect marriage of exotic, spicy, vanillin, oak, and opulently rich fruit. The high tannin content suggests cellaring of at least another decade is possible, but why defer your gratification? The 1982 and the 1961 are the finest Haut-Marbuzets I have ever drunk. Anticipated maturity: Now–2000. Last tasted, 11/90.

· 93

1981—Another intriguing wine, the 1981 Haut-Marbuzet is very deeply colored, with a ripe, plummy, spicy, oaky bouquet, full bodied, with plenty of concentration and a soft, alcoholic finish. Anticipated maturity: Now–1994. Last tasted, 10/88.

· 85

OLDER VINTAGES

Fully mature, very good vintages for Haut-Marbuzet include 1978 (rated 87) and 1979 (rated 86), both excellent wines. The 1975 (rated 90 in March 1989) is outstanding, as is the 1970 and 1961 (both rated 90), the latter two wines drunk with enormous pleasure from magnum in 1988. None of these vintages, save for the 1975, is likely to improve with further cellaring.

HOUISSANT (Cru Bourgeois Supérieur)   AVERAGE

Production: 11,000 cases	Grape varieties: Cabernet Sauvignon—70% Merlot—30%
Secondary label: none	
Vineyard size: 50 acres	Proprietor: Jean Ardouin
Time spent in barrels: The wine is aged only in vats	Average age of vines: 15 years
Evaluation of present classification: Should be downgraded to a Cru Bourgeois	
Plateau of maturity: 3–8 years following the vintage	

The half-dozen or so vintages of Houissant I have tasted have never made a favorable impression. The wine tends to be diluted, not always fresh and focused, and tastes as if the crop size is pushed to the maximum.

LAFFITTE-CARCASSET (Cru Bourgeois)   GOOD

Production: 8,500 cases	Grape varieties: Cabernet Sauvignon—74% Merlot—25% Petit Verdot—1%
Secondary label: Château La Vicomtesse	
Vineyard size: 50 acres	Proprietor: Vicomte Philippe de Padirac
Time spent in barrels: 12–18 months	Average age of vines: 35 years
Evaluation of present classification: Should be maintained	
Plateau of maturity: 5–8 years following the vintage	

This is not a wine that I know well, but those vintages I have tasted— 1988, 1986, 1985, and 1982—seem to belong to the elegant, finesse-school of winemaking. Somewhat light, but still tasty and harmonious, with none of the tough-textured, often excessive tannin many St.-Estèphes reveal, the wines from Laffitte-Carcasset seem to be at their best within 7–8 years of the vintage. The vineyard is well located on high ground in the very northern part of the St.-Estèphe appellation.

LAFON-ROCHET (Fourth-Growth)   VERY GOOD

Production: 12,000–14,000 cases	Grape varieties: Cabernet Sauvignon—80% Merlot—20%
Secondary label: Le Numero 2 de Lafon-Rochet	
Vineyard size: 111 acres	Proprietor: The Tesseron family
Time spent in barrels: 18–24 months	Average age of vines: 30 years
Evaluation of present classification: Should be maintained	
Plateau of maturity: 8–20 years following the vintage	

While ranked a fourth-growth in the 1855 classification, most observers today argue that the superbly situated vineyard of Lafon-Rochet (adjacent to both that of Lafite-Rothschild and Cos d'Estournel) should routinely produce wine with more character and flavor than it habitually does. The current owners, the Tesserons, purchased the property in 1959 and began a gradual but significant program to restore the vineyards and the run-down château. Today the château has been totally renovated, and the new cellars are housed in a bright, cream-colored one-story château with a two-story cave in its middle. The decision to plant a high percentage of Cabernet Sauvignon in the relatively heavy, clay-dominated soils of St.-Estèphe has been considered by some to be a major error, and the reason why Lafon-Rochet often tastes tannic, austere, and excessively dry and lean. However, since 1982, a combination of intelligent, quality-oriented decisions, such as (1) to destem, (2) to harvest slightly later, (3) to increase the percentage of new oak, and (4) to make a second wine from weaker vats, have resulted in more impressive first wines, culminating with a brilliant effort in 1989.

While Lafon-Rochet produced numerous disappointing wines (given the château's pedigree) during the decade of the seventies, the efforts made in the eighties clearly support its position in the 1855 classification.

VINTAGES

1989—   The 1989 Lafon-Rochet may ultimately eclipse the tannic,
·   brawny, age-worthy 1986. Certainly it will have more charm and
89   appeal in youth than the 1986. Dark ruby, with an intense bouquet
     of overripe cassis, this chewy, well-endowed, full-bodied wine is

reminiscent of the excellent 1970. Opulent as well as tannic, it may justify an outstanding rating in a decade. Anticipated maturity: 1996–2015. Last tasted, 4/91.

1988— The 1988 is not as alcoholic as the 1989, has medium body, good
· ripe fruit, and commendable harmony. Surprisingly concentrated
87 for the vintage, this excellent dark ruby-colored wine should age nicely for 5–15 years. Anticipated maturity: 1995–2010. Last tasted, 11/90.

1987— Medium ruby, with a herbaceous, peppery, spicy bouquet, this
· medium-bodied, angular wine lacks depth, ripeness, and charm.
71 Its future is doubtful. Anticipated maturity: Now–1992. Last tasted, 5/90.

1986— On numerous occasions this wine seemed forbiddingly tannic
· from cask and virtually impossible to evaluate, but it has turned
88 out to be one of the best wines made at this estate since the glorious 1970. Deep ruby/purple, with a full-intensity, smoky, spicy, rich, curranty bouquet, this full-bodied, powerful, tannic wine will handsomely repay those who have the patience to cellar it for at least a decade. Anticipated maturity: 1998–2015. Last tasted, 2/90.

1985— The 1985 Lafon-Rochet is fleshy, chewy, has good color, firm
· tannins and medium body, yet lamentably, is one-dimensional.
83 Perhaps more character will emerge with additional bottle age. Anticipated maturity: Now–1999. Last tasted, 4/89.

1984— Medium ruby with a compact, straightforward bouquet of spicy
· oak and berry fruit, the 1984 is light bodied, and beginning to
77 shed tannins as well as its fruit. It should be drunk up. Anticipated maturity: Now. Last tasted, 3/88.

1983— In early tastings against the other top St.-Estèphes, Lafon-Rochet
· rivaled Cos d'Estournel. Rich, full bodied, deeply concentrated
86 and loaded with fruit, this moderately tannic, dark-colored wine displays excellent potential for extended aging. For the vintage, it is a meritorious effort. Anticipated maturity: 1992–2005. Last tasted, 1/88.

1982— This is not a great 1982, particularly in the context of the vintage.
· Very dark, with the characteristic ripe, intense, plummy aroma
85 of the 1982 vintage in evidence, this wine is surprisingly lush and fat, even for the year. The wine still possesses a healthy lashing of tannin, and has firmed up considerably in the late eighties, revealing greater weight and structure than I initially believed. Anticipated maturity: 1994–2008. Last tasted, 1/89.

1980—Adequate color, particularly in view of the vintage, however, the
   ·   good 1980s have more charm and supple fatness than this wine,
  70   which has an annoying vegetal character to it. Drink up. Antici-
        pated maturity: Now–may be in decline. Last tasted, 11/84.

1979—A successful wine was made by Lafon-Rochet in 1979. Dark ruby,
   ·   with a pronounced aroma of new oak and black cherries, this wine
  85   has plenty of stuffing, and is a more successful wine than the
        château's 1978. The wine has been stubborn to shed its tannin.
        Will the fruit fade before enough of the tannin melts away? It
        could be even more charming. Anticipated maturity: 1992–1999.
        Last tasted, 6/89.

1978—This is a supple, straightforward, fruity wine that could use more
   ·   stuffing and character. Moderately dark in color, with an easy-
  82   going supple texture, pleasant, soft, fruity flavors, and a short
        finish, it should be drunk over the next 5–6 years. Anticipated
        maturity: Now–1995. Last tasted, 6/89.

1976—In this vintage, Lafon-Rochet produced a light, rather fragile wine
   ·   that has been fully mature since 1980. Medium ruby, with some
  74   brown at the edges, as well as diffuse and diluted flavors. Antici-
        pated maturity: Now–probably in serious decline. Last tasted,
        7/81.

1975—The 1975 Lafon-Rochet is a big, surprisingly deeply colored,
   ·   chunky wine that continues to exhibit the harsh, tannic, angular
  82   character possessed by many 1975s. Despite the color and inten-
        sity, it exhibits little complexity or direction. While large-scaled,
        the wine is clumsy and too one-dimensional. Anticipated matu-
        rity: Now–2000. Last tasted, 4/88.

1973—Now pale, with a damp, faded, musty aroma, dissipated fruit
   ·   flavors, and a washed-out, short finish, the 1973 Lafon-Rochet is
  64   best forgotten. Last tasted, 10/82.

1971—Light bodied, yet somewhat charming and fruity in 1978, this wine
   ·   was fully mature then, and one can only imagine that 13 more
  76   years of bottle age has seriously eroded any appeal it might have
        had. Last tasted, 6/78.

1970—The 1970 is the best Lafon-Rochet made in the seventies. Still
   ·   youthfully rich, with a deep ruby color exhibiting only a slight
  87   amber edge, this intensely concentrated, deep, full-bodied wine
        has oodles of blackcurrant fruit, a heavy overlay of chalky tannin,
        and at least another decade of life. It is a rich, intense wine, but
        I wonder when the tannins will melt away. Anticipated maturity:
        Now–2000. Last tasted, 5/90.

1966—Certainly an old-style Lafon-Rochet, the 1966 remains a dusty,
·   tannic, briary wine, with fading fruit, significant browning at the
69   edges, yet gobs of tannin still in evidence. Beginning to dry out
       and take on a hollow, astringent character, this wine is in serious
       decline. Last tasted, 6/87.

1961—Still rich and concentrated, with plenty of astringent tannins, this
·   spicy, ripe, full-bodied and full-flavored wine has plenty of ex-
85   tract, and a dusty, chalky finish. It is a good rather than superb
       1961 that can be drunk now, or held for another 5–10 years. The
       tannins may ultimately prove excessive for the wine's fruit, so
       current drinking is recommended. Anticipated maturity: Now–
       1996. Last tasted, 11/88.

LAVILLOTTE (Cru Bourgeois)   GOOD

Production: 7,000 cases	Grape varieties: Cabernet Sauvignon—75% Merlot—25%
Secondary label: none	
Vineyard size: 29.6 acres	
Time spent in barrels: 16–20 months	Proprietor: Jacques Pedro Average age of vines: 20 years
Evaluation of present classification: Should be upgraded to a Cru Bourgeois Exceptionnel or fifth-growth	
Plateau of maturity: 8–15 years following the vintage	

This estate makes a terribly underrated wine that appears on the verge
of being discovered by a greater and greater number of merchants and
consumers. At the time proprietor Jacques Pedro purchased Lavillotte
in 1962 it was in deplorable condition. Pedro comes from a family of
French viticulturists who had lived in Algeria until it was granted inde-
pendence from France. His philosophy combines a mixture of modern
technology and healthy respect for tradition. This contrast is evident: his
vineyards are harvested by machine, but the *cuvaison* is at least three
weeks long; the wine is aged in two-year-old barrels purchased from
Château Latour and fined with egg whites, but is never filtered. The
results, based on vintages such as 1982, 1985, 1986, and 1989—the only
vintages I have tasted—are surprisingly concentrated, intense, full-bodied wines, with a great deal of fragrance, complexity, and richness. Each
of the aforementioned vintages will easily mature gracefully for over a
decade. This would appear to be one of the best, yet least well-known
sources for fine wine from St.-Estèphe.

LILIAN LADOUYS (Cru Bourgeois)   GOOD

Production: 7,000 cases	Grape varieties: Cabernet Sauvignon—60% Merlot—40%
Secondary label: under consideration	
Vineyard size: 50 acres	Proprietor: Lilian and Christian Thiéblot
Time spent in barrels: 16–20 months	Average age of vines: 32 years
Evaluation of present classification: This resurrected property has only produced two vintages, 1989 and 1990, but hopes are high	
Plateau of maturity: 5–15 years following the vintage	

This small vineyard, recently resurrected by Christian and Lilian Thié-blot (until 1989 the wine was vinified and sold by a large cooperative), has the advantage of both serious financial and human commitment to excellence. The vineyard, which has vines between the ages of 25 and 45 years, is near those of such renowned Bordeaux superstars as Cos d'Estournel and Lafite-Rothschild. Both the 1989 and 1990 were surprisingly rich, intensely concentrated, full-bodied, chewy wines exhibiting high class and character. The wine will be marketed exclusively by the huge Bordeaux *négociant* firm of Dourthe. While two vintages do not make a star, most observers feel this up and coming St.-Estèphe estate will be a name to reckon with during the '90s.

MacCARTHY (Cru Grand Bourgeois)   AVERAGE

Production: 3,500 cases	Grape varieties: Cabernet Sauvignon—65% Merlot—35%
Secondary label: none	
Vineyard size: 17.2 acres	Proprietor: Henri Duboscq
Time spent in barrels: 12–15 months; the wine is aged primarily in vats	Average age of vines: 25 years
Evaluation of present classification: Should be maintained	
Plateau of maturity: 3–8 years following the vintage	

The name obviously comes from one of the many Irish families that descended on Bordeaux in the eighteenth century. This tiny vineyard's wines are rarely seen, but those few vintages I have tasted were unmemorable. The wines are casually made, and the results would appear to be indifferent. Since 1989, the vineyards and château have been owned by Henri Duboscq and the property absorbed by his Chambert-Marbuzet. MacCarthy is now the name of that estate's second wine.

MARBUZET (Cru Grand Bourgeois Exceptionnel)   AVERAGE

Production: 10,000–15,000 cases	Grape varieties: Cabernet Sauvignon—60% Merlot—40%
Secondary label: none	
Vineyard size: 17.2 acres	Proprietor: Bruno Prats
Time spent in barrels: 14–16 months	Average age of vines: 8 years
Evaluation of present classification: This is the secondary label of Cos d'Estournel, which blends vats of its wines not considered fine enough with the production from this estate	
Plateau of maturity: 2–8 years following the vintage	

If I had to pick one of the most beautiful and romantically situated properties in the Médoc, it would be this gloriously situated château with its superb terrace and wonderful gardens. In fact, the château, which faces the Gironde River, has a remarkable resemblance to the White House in Washington, D.C.

This is a tiny domain, but the production has soared since the mid-1980s because the rejected vats of wine made at Château Cos d'Estournel are blended with the tiny production of Marbuzet. Proprietor Bruno Prats believes this wine should be smooth, supple, and ideal for drinking in its first 7–8 years of life. The only vintage that has been imbued with a great deal of tannin is the 1986. As second wines go, it is a competent, reasonably priced effort.

VINTAGES

1989—The 1989 Marbuzet is an ideal second wine—richly fruity, supple,
  ·   fragrant, and perfect for drinking over the next 5–7 years. Antic-
 85   ipated maturity: Now–1997. Last tasted, 4/91.

1988—The 1988 Marbuzet is excessively tannic, hard, lean, and green.
  ·   It may hold up in the bottle, but I doubt if it will ever provide
 75   much pleasure. Anticipated maturity: Now–1994. Last tasted,
         4/90.

1986—The 1986 is a serious wine, with plenty of power, tannin, and
  ·   depth. For consumers looking for a good value from Bordeaux
 85   that can be cellared for up to a decade, the very good 1986 Mar-

buzet offers quality that will satisfy both the palate and the purse. Anticipated maturity: Now–2000. Last tasted, 4/89.

1985— The 1985 Marbuzet is a deeply colored, juicy, intensely fruity
·   wine that offers excellent ripeness, good body, and plenty of
85   charm. Drink it over the next 5–6 years. Anticipated maturity: Now–1994. Last tasted, 4/89.

MEYNEY (Grand Bourgeois Exceptionnel)   VERY GOOD

Production: 30,000 cases	Grape varieties:
	Cabernet Sauvignon—70%
	Merlot—24%
	Cabernet Franc—4%
	Petit Verdot—2%
Secondary label: Prieuré de Meyney	
Vineyard size: 126 acres	Proprietor: Domaines Cordier
Time spent in barrels: 16 months	Average age of vines: 40 years
Evaluation of present classification: Should be upgraded to a third-growth	
Plateau of maturity: 8–25 years following the vintage	

Meyney, the large vineyard of over 126 acres immediately north of Montrose, with a splendid view of the Gironde River, has made notably flavorful, robust wines that offer considerable value to the shrewd consumer looking for quality rather than prestige. The wines have been remarkably consistent, and since 1975 have rivaled many of the Médoc's classified growths. The wine is fairly big styled, with good fruit and excellent aging potential of 20–25 years. Some observers have even commented that Meyney's distinctive perfume of licorice, prunes, and truffles is caused by a geological abberation; much of the Meyney vineyard sits on an outcropping of iron-enriched blue clay that has never been found elsewhere in the Médoc. Ironically, such soils also exist in Pomerol, particularly underlying the famed vineyard of Château Pétrus. For visitors to St.-Estèphe, Meyney also merits attention, because this is one of the few old ecclesiastical buildings in the Médoc, and has been well preserved by its owners, the Cordier firm.

Fortunately for consumers, the wines of Meyney continue to be grossly underpriced. Vinification and upbringing are controlled by one of Bordeaux's greatest oenologists, Georges Pauli, who also happens to be the mayor of St.-Julien. That, combined with its fabulous location in St.-Estèphe, translates into stunningly rich, individualistic wines that rival the best of not only St.-Estèphe, but of the Médoc.

VINTAGES

1989 —The 1989 Meyney may turn out to be the finest Meyney ever
· produced. The astonishing opaque, black/ruby color, a bouquet
92 of minerals and damson plums, the alcoholic, massive flavors and
mouth-coating tannins all combine to create a sensory overload.
Slightly reminiscent of the 1982 but even more massive and more
structured, the 1989 will prove uncommonly long-lived as well as
profoundly flavored. A tour de force! Anticipated maturity: 1995–
2025. Last tasted, 4/91.

1988 —If you lack patience, you will want no part of the 1988. More
· brutally tannic than the 1989, yet packed with fruit, the 1988 will
88 need at least a decade of cellaring. It recalls the wonderful 1975
Meyney that is just now beginning to drink well. Anticipated maturity: 1998–2015. Last tasted, 4/91.

1987 —For the vintage, this is a success. Medium deep ruby, with a fra-
· grant, spicy, herbaceous, plummy bouquet, this soft yet moder-
82 ately tannic, flavorful wine will make ideal drinking over the next
5–7 years. Anticipated maturity: Now–1997. Last tasted, 5/90.

1986 —The 1986 Meyney is a very impressive wine, and should prove to
· be one of the longest-lived Meyneys. Sensational from its early
91 days in cask, it remains a huge, powerful, black/purple-colored
wine with enormous extract as well as fabulous depth and richness. This wine does not have the precocious appeal of the more
supple and charming 1985, but if one has the patience to wait for
it to mature, it will last 25–30 years. For a Cru Bourgeois, it
competes with many of the finest 1986s made in Bordeaux. It is,
irrefutably, one of the top sleepers of the vintage. Anticipated
maturity: 1995–2015. Last tasted, 10/90.

1985 —The 1985 is a surprisingly rich, ripe, supple, and even voluptuous
· wine for such a young Meyney—normally a stubbornly slow wine
88 to evolve. A crushed blackcurrant bouquet, elegantly wrought
flavors, and excellent length all combine to make this one of the
finest bargains and wines of the vintage. Anticipated maturity:
Now–2005. Last tasted, 12/89.

1984 —The 1984 will keep for another 10–12 years; it has a deep ruby
· color, excellent depth, medium to full body, and plenty of berry
84 fruit. Anticipated maturity: Now–1996. Last tasted, 6/87.

1983 —Meyney was successful in 1983. The wine is very dense, with a
· ripe, roasted, blackcurrant aroma, unctuous, thick, rich flavors,
85 average acidity, and moderate tannins. A fat, fleshy, concentrated, rustic wine, it is capable of evolving for another 10 years.
Anticipated maturity: Now–2000. Last tasted, 9/88.

1982—The 1982 is probably not as extraordinary as the 1986, but it is a
· massive, powerful, concentrated, unctuously textured wine burst-
90 ing with tarry, truffle, licorice, and plum-scented fruit. In the last
several years it has taken on more structure than when it was
released, and there is now less jamminess. This big, muscular,
brawny, alcoholic wine should reach full maturity in 2–3 years,
and continue to evolve for at least 10–15 years. Among recent
vintages, the 1982 most resembles the 1989. Anticipated maturity: 1993–2010. Last tasted, 10/90.

1981—Another example of Meyney's forte—chunky, densely flavored,
· powerful wines that have plenty of color, authority, and weight.
85 This vintage lacks complexity and elegance, but compensates
with oodles of ripe blackcurrant fruit. Anticipated maturity:
Now–2000. Last tasted, 1/88.

1979—Undoubtedly a good wine for this prolific, yet underrated vintage,
· the 1979 Meyney has dark ruby color, a rather simple grapey,
81 spicy, stemmy aroma, moderately full body, and light tannins.
Anticipated maturity: Now–1995. Last tasted, 3/88.

1978—A textbook Meyney—dark colored, chunky, fruity, loaded with
· flavors of herbs, blackcurrants, and plums—this wine has plenty
84 of extract, mouth-gripping tannins, and another 10 years of life.
A good Meyney. Anticipated maturity: Now–2000. Last tasted,
4/87.

1976—A mediocre effort, this wine is palatable and good for uncritical
· quaffing, but it is now in decline, and destined for senility if not
74 consumed immediately. Anticipated maturity: Now–probably in
serious decline. Last tasted, 8/79.

1975—Undoubtedly this is the best Meyney of the seventies. The 1975
· continues to develop stunningly in the bottle. Dark ruby with just
90 a trace of amber, and with a powerful, rich bouquet of cedar,
plums, and licorice, as well as deep, ripe, fruity flavors, this full-
bodied wine has reached its plateau of maturity. It is not only a
superlative effort from Meyney, but it is also the finest wine of
the St.-Estèphe appellation in 1975. Anticipated maturity: Now–
2010. Last tasted, 9/90.

1971—Still drinking nicely, the 1971 Meyney is dark ruby in color,
· chunky, "foursquare" as the English say, without much complex-
80 ity, but offering a good robust mouthful of claret. Anticipated
maturity: Now–1994. Last tasted, 9/79.

1970—Fully mature, this dark ruby-colored wine has a trace of orange/
· brown at the edge. It is a full-bodied, firm, austere wine with a
83 dry, slightly astringent finish. However, I would have liked to

have found more fruit. It should last another 8–10 years. Anticipated maturity: Now–1999. Last tasted, 10/89.

OLDER VINTAGES

In 1978, Cordier's superb oenologist, Georges Pauli, began to exercise
his talents with the making of Meyney. Previously, the wine had a tendency to turn out overly tannic and astringent. Vintages of the sixties,
particularly 1966, 1962, and 1961, are good wines, but not comparable to
the great Meyneys of 1982, 1986, and 1989. The finest old Meyney I have
tasted is the 1959 (rated 86 and drunk most recently in 1987).

MONTROSE (Second-Growth)   EXCELLENT

Production: 27,000 cases	Grape varieties: Cabernet Sauvignon—65% Merlot—25% Cabernet Franc—10%
Secondary label: La Dame de Montrose	
Vineyard size: 168 acres	Proprietor: Jean-Louis Charmolue
Time spent in barrels: 22–24 months	Average age of vines: 25 years
Evaluation of present classification: Should be maintained	
Plateau of maturity: 3–25 years following the vintage for top vintages after 1970; prior to 1971, 15–35 years following the vintage	

One of the Médoc's best-situated vineyards and one of the commune's
most impeccably clean and well-kept cellars, Montrose was for years
associated with huge, dense, powerful wines that needed several decades
of cellaring to be soothing enough to drink. For example, Jean Paul
Jauffret, the head of Bordeaux's CIVB, served me the 1908 Montrose in
1982, blind, to see if I could guess its age. The wine had plenty left in it
and tasted like it was at least 30 years younger.

The owner, the affable Jean-Louis Charmolue, had obviously lightened
the style of Montrose in response to his perception that dense, excruciatingly tannic wines are no longer popular with consumers. The change in
style is particularly noticeable with the vintages of the late seventies and
early eighties, as more Merlot has been introduced into the blend at the
expense of Cabernet Sauvignon and Petit Verdot. Montrose fans were
not amused by the "nouveau" style. Since 1986, Montrose appears to be
returning to a more forceful, muscular style, reminiscent of pre-1975
vintages. Certainly the 1989 and 1990 vintages for Montrose produced

true blockbuster wines not seen from this property since 1959. Anyone who has had the pleasure of drinking some of Montrose's greatest vintages—1953, 1959, 1961, 1964, and 1970—can no doubt attest to the fact that Montrose produced a bevy of massive wines that reveal a style not unlike the pre-1983 Latours, only more angular and aggressive. The wines of Montrose were especially strong in the period 1953–1971 when they were usually the best wines produced in St.-Estèphe. Since then, the quality has been surpassed by rival Cos d'Estournel.

Visitors to St.-Estèphe will find the modest château of Montrose situated on the high ground with a magnificent view of the Gironde River. The property, owned by the Charmolue family since 1896, does make a worthy visit, given the splendid *cuverie*, with its old, huge, open oak vats and striking new barrel cellar. Like many of its neighbors, Château Montrose has a new state-of-the-art tasting room and reception area.

VINTAGES

1989—Montrose produced a 1989 that not only rivals, but surpasses the
·   brilliant 1986. It actually has the potential to be the best Montrose
92   since the colossal 1959. Dark ruby/purple, with an intense aroma
        of crushed raspberries and minerals, the 1989 has a full-bodied,
        highly extracted feel on the palate, plus gobs of soft tannins, low
        acidity, and high alcohol in a long finish. It is more concentrated
        than the 1982 but less tannic than the 1986. Anticipated maturity:
        1996–2010. Last tasted, 4/91.

1988—Consistently unimpressive, the 1988 Montrose is light, probably
·   too tannic, and lacks richness and depth as well as a finish. High
83   yields and too early a harvest date have left their mark on the
        1988. Anticipated maturity: 1992–2000. Last tasted, 11/90.

1986—The Montrose vintages from 1978 through 1985 (with the excep-
·   tion of the 1982) displayed an alarming lightness and wimpish
91   character that was very un-Montrose-like. That *nouveau* style
        came to a resounding halt with this vintage, which produced a
        vast, immense, brawny Montrose, with gobs of fruit, a boatload
        of tannin, and enough muscle and depth to remind the league of
        classic Montrose fans of great vintages such as 1970, 1964, 1959,
        and 1953. This deep, full-bodied, chewy wine should last for at
        least 30 years, but enthusiasts must defer their gratification for
        another 8 or 9 years. Anticipated maturity: 1997–2025. Last
        tasted, 3/90.

1985—The 1985 Montrose has an elevated amount of Merlot (40%), and
·   therefore tastes surprisingly soft, elegant, and ready to drink. It
85   is a far cry from the behemoth wines fashioned at this estate in
        the fifties and sixties, and continues the lighter, commercial style

that this estate began to develop in the late seventies. Anticipated maturity: Now–2000. Last tasted, 12/89.

1984—Medium ruby with a light-intensity fragrance of soft, oaky, berry
　·　　fruit, the 1984 makes a clean, adequate impression on the palate
　77　but falls off in the finish. A lighter-styled, picnic Montrose. Antic-
　　　ipated maturity: Now–1994. Last tasted, 6/88.

1983—Not nearly as big or as tannic as one might expect, the 1983
　·　　Montrose has adequate tannin, a decent ruby color, a spicy,
　83　plummy nose, medium body, and an astringent finish. Anticipated
　　　maturity: 1992–2000. Last tasted, 11/88.

1982—This was the finest wine made at Montrose following the glorious
　·　　1970, but it has been subsequently eclipsed by both the 1986 and
　89　1989. Very dark ruby, with a rich, intense aroma of spicy oak and
　　　ripe fruit, this full-bodied wine has a deep, rich, unctuous texture,
　　　plenty of round, yet noticeable tannins, and a long, supple finish.
　　　In the late eighties it took on more weight and structure. Antici-
　　　pated maturity: 1992–2008. Last tasted, 1/89.

1981—Montrose produced an elegant, understated, shy, medium-weight
　·　　wine in 1981. This streamlined version of Montrose is fully ma-
　84　ture, but seems to lack the necessary concentration and richness
　　　to last very long. I find it excessively austere. Anticipated matu-
　　　rity: Now–2000. Last tasted, 12/90.

1980—Lean, tannic, with a light ruby color, I doubt if this wine will ever
　·　　be more than an expensive quaffing wine. It is a dubious 1980.
　72　Anticipated maturity: Now–probably in decline. Last tasted,
　　　2/84.

1979—This is a good wine, but a disappointing effort for Montrose. Me-
　·　　dium ruby-colored, with a light-intensity bouquet of cherry fruit
　82　intermingled with spicy oak, this austere, dry wine is astringent
　　　in the finish because of aggressive tannins. Anticipated maturity:
　　　Now–1996. Last tasted, 3/88.

1978—Similar to the 1979, although deeper in color, this restrained,
　·　　tannic wine displays good ripe fruit, a stylish, medium-weight
　84　texture, yet lacks character, complexity, and richness. This vin-
　　　tage marked the beginning of the new lighter-styled Montrose.
　　　How will it age? Anticipated maturity: Now–1996. Last tasted,
　　　9/88.

1976—Undoubtedly one of the successes from this vintage and destined
　·　　to be one of the longest-lived wines of 1976, Montrose continues
　86　to exhibit a dark ruby color, a spicy, vanillin oakiness, and a
　　　generous, deep, blackcurrant fruitiness. While many 1976s have
　　　turned brown and begun to dry out, losing their fruit, Montrose

remains young, impressive, and promising. Anticipated maturity: Now–1998. Last tasted, 3/89.

1975— The 1975 Montrose still tastes hard, backward, and tannic, but it
· does exhibit a fine deep color, a ripe, weighty, full-bodied texture,
87 and a concentrated albeit tough finish. This wine needs an additional 4–5 years of cellaring. Still it's impressive, rather than enjoyable. Anticipated maturity: 1995–2015. Last tasted, 12/90.

1974— Not a bad effort in what has turned out to be a below-average
· quality year for Bordeaux. The 1974 Montrose is lean and sinewy,
72 but it still exhibits good color, some attractive fruit, oak, and earthy scents in the bouquet, and an acidic finish. Anticipated maturity: Now–probably in decline. Last tasted, 6/85.

1973— Between 1976–1979 this was a pleasant effort in a year that pro-
· duced far too many diluted, thin wines. Now it has lost the fruit
65 and only the oak, alcohol, and tannin remain. The wine is only of academic interest. Last tasted, 8/86.

1971— At peak, the 1971 Montrose is attractive, with an enthralling
· leathery, cedary, ripe, fragrant, fruity bouquet, supple, moder-
86 ately rich flavors, and medium body. It is still charming and surprisingly well endowed for a 1971. Owners of this wine should make plans to drink it up. Anticipated maturity: Now–1996. Last tasted, 2/87.

1970— Undeniably the greatest Montrose since 1961, this massive, inky
· giant has exceptional concentration to go along with its hard tan-
94 nins. At 20 years of age, it has clearly resisted change. Still an infant, this enormously concentrated, huge wine should be cellared until 2000 or beyond. In size, weight, and life expectancy, it is not unlike the 1970 Latour. For those with both patience and youth, it is an outstanding wine. Anticipated maturity: 2000–2020. Last tasted, 8/90.

1967— A surprisingly good wine for the vintage, Montrose was at its best
· between 1975 and 1979. Now in decline as the fruit recedes, and
82 the dusty tannins and oak become more dominant, this medium ruby-colored wine still has good body and enough interest in the bouquet to hold many people's attention. Drink up. Anticipated maturity: Now–1994. Last tasted, 10/81.

1966— The 1966 is still dark ruby with a peppery, very spice, yet tight,
· relatively closed bouquet. The 1966 Montrose is austere and
86 tough on the palate, with good fruit and firm, rough tannins. Comparatively, it is not as massive or as rich as the 1970, 1964, or 1961, but is still backward and austere. Will the fruit hold up to the tannins? Anticipated maturity: Now–2005. Last tasted, 1/90.

1964—The 1964 Montrose was one of only a handful of Médocs harvested
·   prior to the rains, so the wine exhibits unexpected depth, rich-
92   ness, and vigor. Richer and more intense than the 1966, with a
        far darker, more opaque color, this huge, old-style, ripe wine
        offers a substantial mouthful of rich, unctuous claret. Amazingly,
        it still tastes less than a decade old. It is a great success for the
        vintage, and may prove to be the longest-lived wine of the Médoc.
        An extraordinary success! Anticipated maturity: 1994–2020. Last
        tasted, 2/90.
1962—The 1962 Montrose was at its peak in 1985. Dark ruby with a
·   complex bouquet of ripe, cedary, black cherry aromas, this lovely
88   wine is surprisingly rich and deep on the palate, and supple and
        long in the finish. Delicious now. Anticipated maturity: Now–
        1993. Last tasted, 5/82.
1961—A stunning wine from a superb vintage, the 1961 Montrose is still
·   in need of another 10 years of cellaring. The deep, opaque dark
95   ruby color, the huge bouquet of ripe cassis fruit and mineral
        scents, the full-bodied, dense, compelling richness and length,
        plus gobs of tannin, all point to a monumental bottle of wine for
        drinking during the first 20–30 years of the next century. Antici-
        pated maturity: 2000–2030. Last tasted, 12/89.

OLDER VINTAGES

The 1959 (consistently rated between 94 and 96) is a great wine that
rivals the quality of the 1961. It is still fascinatingly youthful. The contrast between the 1953 (rated 93) and 1955 (rated 90) is dramatic. The
former is sweet, round, even voluptuous, the latter powerful, hard, and
similar to the 1964 and 1970. Among the vintages of the late forties, I
have found the 1945 to be mediocre and the 1947 disjointed, slightly
volatile and attenuated.

LES-ORMES-DE-PEZ (Grand Bourgeois)   VERY GOOD

Production: 14,000 cases	Grape varieties: Cabernet Sauvignon—55% Merlot—35% Cabernet Franc—10%
Secondary label: none Vineyard size: 74 acres	Proprietors: André and Jean- Michel Cazes
Time spent in barrels: 14–18 months	Average age of vines: 25–30 years
Evaluation of present classification: Should be upgraded to a fifth- growth	
Plateau of maturity: 5–12 years following the vintage	

Les-Ormes-de-Pez is one of Bordeaux's most popular wines, due in large part to the wine's generously flavored, plump, sometimes sweet and fat personality. Don't discount the extensive promotional efforts of the owner, Jean-Michel Cazes, either. The wine rarely disappoints. The color of Les-Ormes-de-Pez tends to be quite dark, and since 1975, the flavors increasingly supple and designed for easy comprehension by the masses. However, the wine can age for 7–12 years. Older vintages from the forties and fifties, made in a more massive, dense style, can often represent outstanding values, because the wine has been impeccably made for decades. Les-Ormes-de-Pez is a wine that consumers, looking for high quality at modest prices, should always give serious consideration.

VINTAGES

1989—The most opulent and intense Les-Ormes-de-Pez, since the 1982, the 1989 is full bodied and endowed with a great deal of soft
86   tannins. It should provide robust drinking for at least a decade. Anticipated maturity: Now–2000. Last tasted, 11/90.

1988—The 1988 is, curiously, similar to the 1989, but it does not have quite the weight or jammy fruit of the 1989. For the vintage, it is
85   surprisingly forward and should drink well for up to a decade. Anticipated maturity: Now–1996. Last tasted, 11/90.

1987—Soft, weedy, diluted fruit does little to make a favorable impression. In the mouth, the wine is loosely knit and overtly commer-
77   cial. It requires prompt drinking. Anticipated maturity: Now–1993. Last tasted, 3/90.

1986—No doubt because of the vintage, 1986 has produced one of the more tannic and intense wines from Les-Ormes-de-Pez since
86   their exceptional 1970. This ripe, deep, chewy wine has plenty of

fat and fruit to balance out the aggressive tannins, and should keep for several decades, although it will probably be drinkable after another 3–4 years. Anticipated maturity: 1992–2005. Last tasted, 3/89.

1985— The 1985 has turned out to be an agreeable, soft, fruity wine
·   without a great deal of depth, but with a pleasant fruitiness and
83   immediate accessibility. Anticipated maturity: Now–1993. Last tasted, 1/90.

1984— Light to medium ruby with soft, round, shallow flavors that con-
·   vey the taste of weeds and cassis, the 1984 should be drunk up.
82   Anticipated maturity: Now–1993. Last tasted, 12/88.

1983— Very deeply colored, with a fat, ripe, round, richly fruity charac-
·   ter, this full-bodied, well-made wine has good, silky, but substan-
84   tial tannins, and low acidity. Anticipated maturity: Now–1995. Last tasted, 5/88.

1982— A top-flight effort from Les-Ormes-de-Pez, this is a very concen-
·   trated wine with a penetrating bouquet of ripe blackcurrant fruit
87   and spicy oak. Thick, dense, powerful, fruity flavors are sup- ported by soft but significant tannins. Reminiscent of the gor- geous wine made by Les-Ormes-de-Pez in 1970 only softer and ultimately shorter lived, this wine should be drunk over the next 5–6 years. Anticipated maturity: Now–1996. Last tasted, 11/89.

1981— This is a straightforward style of wine, which is not up to the
·   excellent quality of the 1982, or very good 1983, but is still robust
78   and fruity, with a generous texture and a pleasing, rounded, soft finish. Anticipated maturity: Now–1993. Last tasted, 1/83.

1979— A mediocre effort from Les-Ormes-de-Pez, this wine is light in
·   color, with a fully mature, fruity bouquet, some damp, oaky aro-
75   mas, and a soft, rather lean finish. Anticipated maturity: Now– probably in decline. Last tasted, 6/84.

1978— A very good wine that exhibits deep, blackcurrant, ripe fruit, a
·   medium- to full-bodied feel on the palate, and good solid tannins.
85   The bouquet is beginning to reveal complex cedary, spicy scents. The tannins are melting away. It is a husky, fleshy wine that should age well for 10–12 years. Anticipated maturity: Now– 1994. Last tasted, 3/88.

1976— Moderately intense jammy fruit suggests an overripe character on
·   the palate. The wine is soft, with low acidity, and a diluted, thin
72   finish. Drink up! Anticipated maturity: Now–probably in serious decline. Last tasted, 5/82.

1975— Successful for the vintage, and better than several of the more
·   expensive "classified growths," the 1975 Les-Ormes-de-Pez is
84   rich and full bodied, with a leathery, ripe, fruity bouquet. Dusty,

spicy, generally ripe flavors with some astringent tannins are still evident. It should be drunk over the next 4–6 years. Anticipated maturity: Now–1996. Last tasted, 11/88.

1971—Somewhat light and already fading when first tasted in 1977, this
· wine has consistently exhibited a harsh, biting acidity and lack of
65 fruit. Caveat emptor. Last tasted, 6/85.

1970—Les-Ormes-de-Pez is a massive, intense, ripe, rich wine, with an
· uncanny resemblance to the 1970 Lynch-Bages (coincidentally
88 owned and produced by the same family). This robust, somewhat coarse, fleshy, enormously constructed wine has tremendous extract, gobs of tannin, and an opaque, dark ruby color. What it lacks in finesse it makes up for in strength and richness. It continues to evolve at a snail's pace. Anticipated maturity: Now–2005. Last tasted, 11/90.

OLDER VINTAGES

During the mid-1980s, I had the opportunity to drink the 1947, 1953, 1955, 1959, and 1961, all plucked off the wine lists of several Bordeaux restaurants, particularly the renowned St. James. All of them were still in fine condition, massive, robust, nearly coarse wines that represented the old style of Bordeaux winemaking. I have no doubt that well-stored examples of this château's wines from the forties, fifties, and sixties could represent fine values today.

PETIT BOCQ (Cru Bourgeois)   GOOD

Production: 1,000 cases	Grape varieties: Merlot—80% Cabernet Sauvignon—20%
Secondary label: none	
Vineyard size: 5 acres	Proprietors: Francis and Modeste Soquet
Time spent in barrels: 14–16 months	Average age of vines: 25 years
Evaluation of present classification: Should be upgraded to a Grand Bourgeois Exceptionnel or fifth-growth	
Plateau of maturity: 3–12 years following the vintage	

Unfortunately, this distinctive wine with the highest percentage of Merlot on any property in St.-Estèphe has never, to my knowledge, been seen in the export markets. Proprietor Souquet, who has spent his life working in a winemaking family, fashions one of St.-Estèphe's most hedonistic wines. The 1982, 1985, and 1989 were bursting with unctuous black fruits, were explosively rich and full, causing me to wonder why this property has not gained more recognition from Bordeaux wine enthusiasts. While the high percentage of Merlot suggests that Petit Bocq will not age well, the 1982, last tasted in 1989, was still in remarkable condition and had at least another decade of life to it. This is clearly a property worth representation in the world's export markets, although the quantities of wine available will no doubt be miniscule.

DE PEZ (Cru Bourgeois Supérieur)   VERY GOOD

Production: 12,000 to 14,000 cases	Grape varieties: Cabernet Sauvignon—70% Merlot—15% Cabernet Franc—15%
Secondary label: none	
Vineyard size: 62 acres	Proprietor: Robert Dousson
Time spent in barrels: 16 months	Average age of vines: 25 years
Evaluation of present classification: Should be upgraded to a fifth-growth	
Plateau of maturity: 8–18 years following the vintage	

It is difficult to miss Château de Pez and the twin towers as one passes through the one-horse village of Pez. For decades, this estate has made a muscular yet excellent, sometimes tough-textured wine that is capable of lasting for up to two decades. If the wine of de Pez is to be criticized at all, it is for rarely attaining an exceptional rating. Reliable and solid as it may be, de Pez seems incapable of hitting the heights that other notable Crus Bourgeois, particularly Haut-Marbuzet, Meyney, and since the late eighties, Phélan-Ségur, routinely achieve. I have often wondered whether an increased percentage of Merlot (perhaps 25–40%) in the blend might not give the unduly restrained, frequently lean de Pez more flesh and character.

The current proprietor, Robert Dousson, can actually say he has spent his entire life at de Pez: he was born there in 1929. A hands-on proprietor, always at the property, he believes strongly in unmanipulated, unfiltered wines. Additionally, the longevity of his wines and their popularity in England and northern Europe has never gone to his head. The prices for de Pez remain among the most reasonable in the Médoc.

VINTAGES

1989—By the standards of de Pez, the 1989 is atypical, although the fans
·   of this property will probably be at odds with my opinion. Opu-
87   lently rich and more precocious and direct than usual, the 1989
de Pez has layers of cassis fruit intertwined with scents of Provençal herbs and toasty oak. Surprisingly fleshy for de Pez, with
low acidity, this full-bodied effort will drink well young, but
boasts the requisite depth and balance to last for 12–15 years.
Anticipated maturity: 1994–2005. Last tasted, 4/91.

1988—This is a more typical effort from de Pez, with a reserved and
·   polite bouquet of moderately ripe blackcurrants, minerals, and
84   wood. In the mouth, the wine is medium bodied, slightly astringent, austere, and restrained. It lacks flesh and appears compact,
but it is, nevertheless, stylish and well made. Anticipated maturity: 1992–2000. Last tasted, 4/91.

1986—I have my reservations about this vintage of de Pez only because
·   it has been so forbiddingly impenetrable and tannic. Tasted sev-
82   eral times after bottling, the wine has an impressive dark ruby
color, but the nose is completely locked in, and on the palate, the
wine is abrasively coarse, revealing none of the flesh, charm, or
concentration one expects to find even in the youngest claret.
Nevertheless, it is hard to believe that this property has not made
at least a good wine, but patience is most definitely required.
Anticipated maturity: 1996–2005. Last tasted, 3/90.

1985—This charming, elegant wine avoids the hard, tough tannin often
·   found in the wines of this vintage. Deep ruby, with a moderately
86   intense, enthralling bouquet of spicy oak and cassis, this medium-
to full-bodied, surprisingly precocious-tasting de Pez drinks well,
yet should last for at least another 10–12 years. Anticipated maturity: Now–2001. Last tasted, 11/89.

1983—As well made as many of the more highly regarded 1983s, de Pez
·   has a dark color and dense, rich, ripe fruity flavors, a significant
85   tannin content, and a spicy, moderately tannic finish. Traditionally made, it will require another 4–5 years of cellaring. Anticipated maturity: 1993–2005. Last tasted, 1/88.

1982—Much rounder and fruitier than the 1983, the 1982 is very dark
·   ruby with an intense cassis bouquet, round, generously endowed,
86   luscious flavors, high but velvety tannins, and a fine, heady finish.
Anticipated maturity: Now–2003. Last tasted, 1/89.

1981—This is the least successful de Pez in the trio of fine claret vintages
·   —1981, 1982, and 1983. A medium-weight wine, the 1981 is aus-
77   tere and unyielding, but has good fruit and a firm, tannic, lean

structure. This wine has remained tight and unevolved, but I fear the fruit is beginning to dry out. Anticipated maturity: Now–1995. Last tasted, 6/87.

1979—Medium to dark ruby color, with an evolved bouquet of spice and
· herbaceous, blackcurrant scents, this medium-bodied wine has
83 good fruit, moderate tannins, and a dry, slightly astringent, moderately long finish. Anticipated maturity: Now–1993. Last tasted,
7/86.

1978—A success for de Pez, the 1978, which has more Merlot than usual
· because of flowering problems with the 1978 Cabernet crop, is a
85 rich, supple, deep, fruity wine with plenty of extract and tannin.
Medium to full bodied, it has developed fully, but shows no signs
of decline. Anticipated maturity: Now–2000. Last tasted, 11/88.

1976—From its birth, the 1976 de Pez displayed excellent winemaking
· and a strict selection of only the best barrels in this copious vin-
84 tage. Darker colored than most 1976 Bordeaux, with a ripe, rich,
fruity aroma and soft, underlying tannins, this wine has been fully
mature since the early eighties. It is a top-notch effort for the
vintage. Anticipated maturity: Now–1993. Last tasted, 10/87.

1975—This wine remains brutally tannic and nearly undrinkable. While
· it exhibited excellent concentration and fruit from the cask, it has
78 been dormant and closed during its life in the bottle. Will the fruit
outlast the tannin? Increasingly, the answer appears to be a resounding no. No doubt the 1975 de Pez will continue to age for
10, perhaps 15, years, but will it ever be enjoyable? Anticipated
maturity: Now–2005. Last tasted, 11/90.

1973—Now faded, the 1973 was (until 1980) one of the most enjoyable
· wines of what turned out to be a terribly weak, diluted vintage of
76 frail, watery wines. Not so for the de Pez, which exhibited a
lovely, charming, moderately intense, berry fruitiness, and soft,
supple flavor. In large formats—such as magnums—this wine
may still be vibrant. Anticipated maturity: Now–probably in serious decline. Last tasted, 3/85.

1970—De Pez produced a classic in 1970. Still surprisingly fresh and
· focused, this wine has a dark ruby/garnet color and a spicy, rich,
86 blackcurrant aroma intertwined with scents of leather. Typically
firm, with plenty of muscle and underlying depth, this tannic,
austere wine should continue to age for 10–15 years. Anticipated
maturity: Now–2005. Last tasted, 8/89.

PHÉLAN-SÉGUR (Grand Bourgeois Exceptionnel) VERY GOOD

Production: 25,000–28,000 cases	Grape varieties:
	Cabernet Sauvignon—55%
	Merlot—30%
	Cabernet Franc—15%
Secondary label: Franck Phélan	
Vineyard size: 135.8 acres	Proprietor: Xavier Gardinier
Time spent in barrels: 13–15 months	Average age of vines: 22 years

Evaluation of present classification: Should be maintained, although it should be noted that the quality since 1986 merits comparison with Médoc's best fourth- and fifth-growths.

Plateau of maturity: Since 1986, 5–14 years following the vintage

After a terribly troubled beginning in the decade of the eighties, this property was sold by the Delon family to Xavier Gardinier in 1985. The new proprietor was forced to recall four vintages (1982, 1983, 1984, and 1985) because a foul chemical stench had developed in many of the bottles. A lawsuit was instituted by the château against a prominent manufacturer of herbicides, alleging that it was the use of these chemicals that caused the off aroma. However, Phélan-Ségur is now in firmly committed, competent hands. The beautiful estate, which has been recently cleaned and refurbished by the new owners, has the potential to produce one of the finest wines of St.-Estèphe, because the vineyard borders both those of Montrose and Calon-Ségur. The progress made by the new owners was especially evident with excellent wines produced in the latter vintages of the eighties. However, vintages prior to 1985, particularly those in the late seventies and early eighties, are suspect.

VINTAGES

1989—A strict selection, the use of 40% new oak, and an extended maceration have produced a rich, full-bodied 1989 that offers both
88   power and finesse. Deep ruby/purple, with gobs of red and black fruits in its aroma, this concentrated, impressively structured wine will prove to be a crowd pleaser. It is the finest Phélan-Ségur I have ever tasted. Anticipated maturity: 1995–2003. Last tasted, 4/91.

1988—The 1988 Phélan-Ségur is lighter than the 1989, but is still a
87   textbook example of a St.-Estèphe. A toasty, blackcurrant-scented bouquet is followed by a medium-bodied wine with fine balance and length. It has less aging potential than the 1989. Anticipated maturity: Now–1997. Last tasted, 4/91.

1987—A light, weedy bouquet precedes stern, one-dimensional, tannic
 ·   flavors that lack flesh and charm. I see no future for this wine.
71   Anticipated maturity: Now. Last tasted, 6/89.

1986—The 1986 Phélan-Ségur is the first respectable effort by the new
 ·   regime. Medium dark ruby, with a tight-but-emerging bouquet of
82   weedy cassis fruit, this medium-bodied, tannic, yet concentrated
        wine lacks only flesh and complexity. Anticipated maturity: Now–
        1998. Last tasted, 3/89.

1983—In three separate tastings from cask samples, the wine tasted
 ·   flawed. Judgment reserved. Last tasted, 3/85. (Note: This wine as
 ?   well as the 1984 and 1985 were subsequently recalled from the
        marketplace by the new owners because of a suspicious chemical
        aroma.)

1982—Overproduction seems to have given this wine, which has dark
 ·   ruby color, less weight and richness than many of its peers. Soft,
78   forward, and a trifle diffuse, but big, grapey, and supple, yet
        slightly unstructured, this wine seems to be a candidate for rapid
        maturation. Last tasted, 10/84. (Note: This vintage was also re-
        called by the new owners, who claimed the wine had developed a
        chemical stench in the late eighties.)

1981—Rather shallow, light, with a stemmy bouquet, the 1981 Phélan-
 ·   Ségur has just enough fruit to cover the wine's framework. Light
74   tannins and some ominous browning at the edge mandates con-
        sumption. Anticipated maturity: Now–may be in decline. Last
        tasted, 9/84.

1979—Medium ruby in color with a charming, ripe, berry bouquet that
 ·   shows full maturity. Soft Merlot flavors dominate this easy-to-
75   drink, pleasant, one-dimensional wine. Anticipated maturity:
        Now–1993. Last tasted, 6/81.

1978—Straightforward grapey flavors and a simple personality have
 ·   given way to reveal some attractive, light-intensity, spicy, ripe,
74   cherry aromas. However, this medium-bodied wine finishes short,
        and lacks weight and grip. Anticipated maturity: Now. Last
        tasted, 10/82.

1976—Fully mature by 1980, this wine was pleasant, soft, fruity, and
 ·   easy to drink. The wine has lost the medium ruby color, replaced
75   by a dull brownish cast. Drink now, if ever. Anticipated maturity:
        Now–probably in serious decline. Last tasted, 10/80.

1975—The 1975 was one of the best wines made during the seventies by
 ·   Phélan-Ségur. This wine shows good fruit intensity, weight, rich-
84   ness, and direction, which have been missing in more recent
        vintages of Phélan-Ségur. Fully mature, with a moderately in-

tense, cedary, ripe, fruity bouquet, this is an attractively flavored wine. Anticipated maturity: Now–1992. Last tasted, 12/87.

LES PRADINES (Unclassified) AVERAGE

Production: 4,000 cases	Grape varieties: Cabernet Sauvignon—60% Merlot—35% Cabernet Franc—5%
Secondary label: none	
Vineyard size: 20 acres	Proprietor: Jean Gradit
Time spent in barrels: 12 months, primarily in vats	Average age of vines: 25 years
Evaluation of present classification: The quality equivalent of a Cru Bourgeois	
Plateau of maturity: 3–7 years following the vintage	

Produced and bottled by St.-Estèphe's Cave Cooperative, these straight-forward, tough-textured wines are typical of the appellation, but too frequently lack charm and fruit. However, the wines are fairly priced.

TRONQUOY-LALANDE (Grand Bourgeois) GOOD

Production: 7,500 cases	Grape varieties: Cabernet Sauvignon—50% Merlot—50%
Secondary label: none	
Vineyard size: 42 acres	Proprietor: Arlette Castéja
Time spent in barrels: 12 months in both barrels and tanks	Average age of vines: 25 years
Evaluation of present classification: Should be maintained	
Plateau of maturity: Since 1982, 5–10 years after the vintage; previously, the wine was very slow to evolve	

Tronquoy-Lalande is an historic property with a fine twin-towered châ-teau on the premises. The wine was highly regarded a century ago, but has lost popularity because of the superlative quality of other St.-Estèphe Crus Bourgeois, such as Meyney, Haut-Marbuzet, Les-Ormes-de-Pez, and more recently, Phélan-Ségur. I have followed every wine since the late seventies, and they lack consistency from vintage to vintage. At best, it is a very dark, huge, clumsy sort of wine, with an earthy, distinctive character. The wine is distributed exclusively by the Bordeaux firm of Dourthe. The finest recent vintage is the black-colored, dense, super-ripe 1989.

PAUILLAC

There is no more famous appellation of the Haut-Médoc and Bordeaux than Pauillac. While the commune of Margaux has a more lyrical and romantic name, as well as a famous first-growth château of the same title, it is Pauillac's vineyards that lay claim to three of the Médoc's four first-growths. Yes, the fabled, fabulously expensive Pauillac trio of Lafite-Rothschild, Mouton-Rothschild, and Latour all reside here, and they are formidably backed up by a bevy of wines, some brilliant, some terribly overrated, and some seriously overlooked or forgotten. Eighteen wines from Pauillac were included in the original 1855 classification, and today only two or three estates would have trouble holding on to their position should an independent study of the quality of the wines be done.

The textbook Pauillac would tend to have a rich, full-bodied texture, a distinctive bouquet of blackcurrants and cedary scents, and excellent aging potential. Since virtually all of the permitted vineyard acreage (2,566 acres) is controlled by the eighteen classified growths, there are fewer Cru Bourgeois wines in Pauillac than in a commune such as St.-Estèphe. However, one is likely to encounter a wide diversity in the Pauillac styles. Among the three famous first-growths, for example, the wines could not be more different. Granted, their soils all share the gravelly composition that reflects the sun's heat and affords excellent drainage. However, Lafite-Rothschild's vineyard—tucked in a northern part of Pauillac right on the St.-Estèphe border—has a limestone base, resulting in wines that are Pauillac's most aromatically complex and subtly flavored. Lafite's bouquet has of course the telltale Pauillac "cedarwood" aroma, although Lafite rarely matches Mouton-Rothschild for sheer opulence and power, or Latour for consistency. Of the other, non-first-growth Pauillacs, the lighter, aromatic Lafite style, albeit on a lower level, is best exemplified by the silky, light Haut-Batailley.

Mouton-Rothschild sits on a gravel ridge above the Médoc's largest town, Pauillac. In addition to the gravelly soil, Mouton has more sandstone in the soil base and uses an abnormally high percentage of Cabernet Sauvignon in making the wine. When everything works out right, these factors can produce the most decadently rich, fleshy, and exotic wine of not only Pauillac, but of the entire Médoc. In many ways, the wine of Mouton personified the flamboyant, bold owner, the Baron Philippe de Rothschild, who died in 1988. Mouton, of course, is not the only Pauillac made in a big, rich, opulent style. Several kilometers south, on another slightly elevated ridge called the Bages plateau, Lynch-Bages makes a wine that can be splendidly deep and concentrated, clearly earning its reputation as the "poor man's Mouton."

Latour is Pauillac's other first-growth, and this grand old estate, British owned yet French managed, has few if any peers when it comes to consistency from one vintage to the next. For most of this century (until 1983, that is), Latour, along with Montrose in St.-Estèphe, has been the slowest to mature and longest-lived wine made in Bordeaux. The vineyard's location in southern Pauillac—next to St.-Julien—would seemingly suggest a more supple style of wine, but up until the early eighties, when that style of Latour surprisingly emerged, Latour's wine had been as backward and as tannic as any. The soil at Latour is almost pure fine gravel that affords superb drainage, better than that enjoyed by Lafite-Rothschild or Mouton-Rothschild. That in itself may help explain why in rainy vintages such as 1960, 1968, 1969, 1972, and 1974 Latour easily outdistanced the other Pauillac first-growths. Latour is simply Latour, and in Pauillac, there are no "look-alikes" in style or character.

There are several other Pauillacs that have distinctive styles, making generalizations about the wine of this commune difficult. Perhaps the most interesting wine of this group is Pichon-Longueville–Comtesse de Lalande (called Pichon Lalande by most). Pichon Lalande sits adjacent to Latour, near the St.-Julien border. Unlike Latour, Pichon does indeed produce a St.-Julien-styled Pauillac—silky, graceful, supple, suave, and drinkable at a relatively young age. However, it would be foolish to assume that this precocious-tasting wine does not age well—it does. The property has always made great wine, but over the last several decades theirs has been every bit as good as the other Pauillac first-growths, and certainly more consistent from vintage to vintage than Lafite-Rothschild and Mouton-Rothschild.

Grand-Puy-Lacoste never seems to receive the publicity that the other top Pauillacs do. For years this property, which sits well back from the Gironde River, was the joy of Bordeaux's leading gourmet (and from some accounts, gourmand as well), Raymond Dupin. Monsieur Dupin has died, but his reputation for holding lavish dinner parties remains unchallenged by anyone in Bordeaux today. Now the property, the wine cellars, and the winemaking philosophy are in the capable sure hands of Jean-Eugène Borie and his son, Xavier Borie. Their first vintage was a lovely 1978. You can be sure this is a property to watch, with a style unlike anything else I've described. It is a true Pauillac—cleaner, more

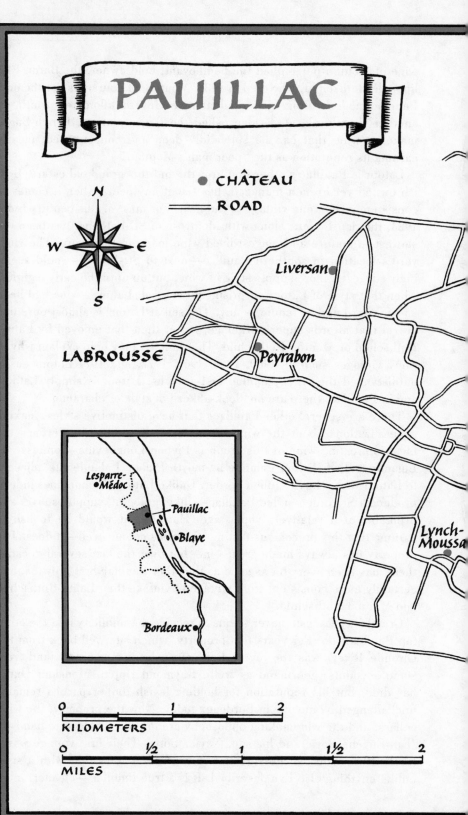

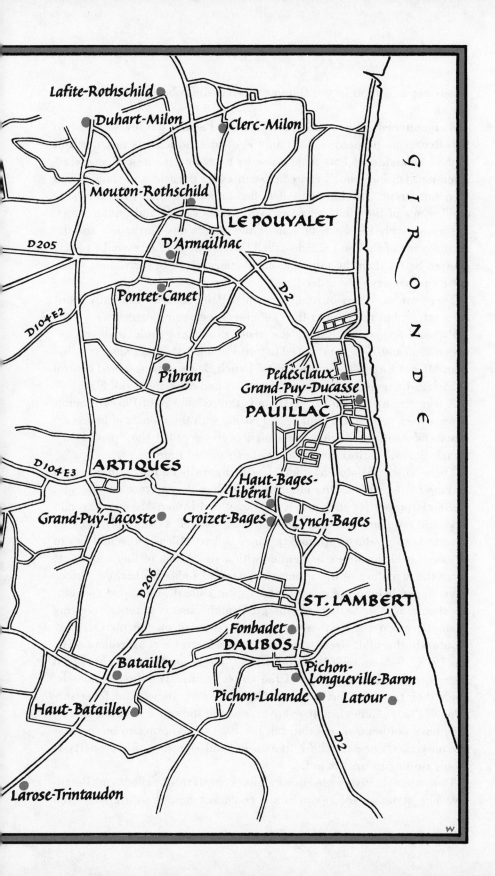

Lafite-Rothschild

Duhart-Milon

Clerc-Milon

Mouton-Rothschild

LE POUYALET

D205

D'Armailhac

D104E2

Pontet-Canet

Pibran

Pedesclaux
Grand-Puy-Ducasse

D2

PAUILLAC

D104E3   ARTIQUES

Haut-Bages-
Libéral

Grand-Puy-Lacoste   Croizet-Bages   Lynch-Bages

D206

ST. LAMBERT

Fonbadet

DAUBOS

Batailley

Pichon-
Longueville-Baron

Haut-Batailley

Pichon-Lalande   Latour

D2

Larose-Trintaudon

GIRONDE

W

consistent now than in the Dupin era—but still robust, tannic, and flavorful.

As mentioned earlier, unlike St.-Estèphe, Pauillac has few well-known Cru Bourgeois properties. Certainly Fonbadet, which sits just north of Pichon Lalande and Latour, is a worthy entry into the new Médoc classification. Obscure small châteaux such as La Bécasse and Gaudin also merit attention. The best non-classified-growth Pauillacs are the "second" wines of the famous first-growth estates Latour and Lafite, which are respectively Les Forts de Latour and Moulin des Carruades, and the second wine of Pichon Lalande called Reserve de la Comtesse. Les Forts is often better than the rank-and-file Pauillacs, and Reserve de la Comtesse can be very good indeed.

There are a cluster of other classified Pauillacs that generally merit their rating, but rarely offer the excitement their price suggests.

Pichon-Longueville Baron, the most prominent underachiever between 1960 and 1985, has soared in terms of quality since 1986. Now that Jean-Michel Cazes, the proprietor of Lynch-Bages, has assumed control at Pichon-Longueville Baron, expectations and excitement run high.

A less renowned Pauillac château is the reliable Haut-Bages-Libéral. Always dark ruby, fat, chunky, and oozing with the aromas of blackcurrants and cedarwood, this wine might well be called the "poor man's Lynch-Bages," as it is always a very fairly priced wine.

There are a half-dozen other classified-growth Pauillacs that are all making better wine as the nineties begin than they were a decade ago. Certainly properties such as Pontet-Canet and Duhart-Milon-Rothschild have the requisite financial underpinning, as well as superbly situated vineyards to produce top quality wine. Duhart-Milon-Rothschild began to assert itself in the early eighties with a succession of fine wines that carry the signature of the winemaking staff of Lafite-Rothschild. Prices have lagged behind the quality increases at Duhart-Milon, and consumers should use that to their advantage. Pontet-Canet is a more interesting example, given the vast estate superbly situated on the plateau near Mouton-Rothschild. Great wines can be produced here, as evidenced by the 1929, 1945, and 1961. Unfortunately, the property had a checkered history under the ownership of the Cruse family. The Tesserons, who made their fame and fortune in the Cognac region, are working feverishly to push Pontet-Canet into the elite category of the super seconds. So far, they have not been successful, but the 1989 should prove to be the best Pontet-Canet since the 1961. It is a hopeful sign that this property is finally turning things around.

Two other relatively obscure Pauillacs are Haut-Batailley and Batailley. The styles of these two wines could not be more different, even though they share adjacent vineyards. Haut-Batailley has more of a St.-Julien personality than even Pichon-Longueville–Comtesse de Lalande. It is soft, forward, and, in the top vintages, an enthrallingly elegant, graceful, easy to drink wine. On the other hand, Batailley is the antithesis of Haut-Batailley. It consistently produces a chunky, muscular, hard, stubbornly backward style of wine that could be underrated when tasted young. In fact, I have made that mistake many times. Batailley often needs a good 10–15 years to reveal its class. It is by no means a super second, but one of the most reasonably priced—and now one of the best made—Pauillacs for the price.

There are also the two properties owned by the late Baron Philippe de Rothschild. Both Clerc-Milon, which has enjoyed a renaissance since 1985, and Mouton-Baronne-Philippe, which seems to have been neglected until 1989, are wines that remain reasonably priced. They are made in a supple (critics would say commercial), forward style that many admire. Between the two, Clerc-Milon appears at the moment to be the more interesting and flavorful wine.

More than any other Médoc appellation, Pauillac, because of the concentration of the three first-growths and some prominent super seconds, tends to establish the overall reputation for a particular vintage in the Médoc. Some would even argue that how goes Pauillac, so goes the public's view of the vintage for Bordeaux. Although nothing so general can be viewed in black-and-white terms, there is no doubt that the quality of winemaking in Pauillac is significantly better in 1991 than a decade before.

However, Pauillac, even with the better draining soils, still needs hot, relatively dry years to achieve greatness. The eighties may have represented the golden age for all of Bordeaux, but no appellation profited more than Pauillac. After a good vintage in 1981, 1982 was spectacular —the best overall vintage for the appellation since 1961; 1983 was a good if uneven year, largely because of high yields; and 1984, like most of Bordeaux, proved mediocre. The 1985 is overrated, but certainly very good, while 1986 has proven to be a profoundly great vintage, rivaling 1982 and likely to outlive the 1982s. The 1987 was underrated, 1988 very good, 1989 uneven—but at least very good to exceptional, and 1990 a terrific year for the first-growths. Of course, in Pauillac more than in any other region except for Margaux, a healthy crop of Cabernet Sauvignon grapes dictates a good vintage. Most estates have at least two-thirds of their vineyards planted with Cabernet, so if that grape fails to ripen, the entire appellation will no doubt have problems.

A CONSUMER'S CLASSIFICATION
OF THE CHATEAUX OF PAUILLAC

OUTSTANDING

Lafite-Rothschild
Latour
Mouton-Rothschild
Pichon-Longueville–Comtesse de Lalande

EXCELLENT

Grand-Puy-Lacoste
Lynch-Bages
Pichon-Longueville Baron

VERY GOOD

Duhart-Milon-Rothschild
Les Forts de Latour
Haut-Batailley
Pontet-Canet

GOOD

Batailley
La Bécasse
Clerc-Milon
Fonbadet
Gaudin
Grand-Puy-Ducasse
Haut-Bages-Libéral
D'Armailhac (known as Mouton-Baronne-Philippe
between 1956 and 1989)

OTHER NOTABLE PAUILLAC PROPERTIES

Bellegrave, Bernadotte, Colombier-Monpelou, La Couronne,
Croizet-Bages, La Fleur Milon, Haut-Bages-Monpelou,
Lynch-Moussas, Moulin des Carruades, Pedesclaux, Peyrabon,
Pibran, Plantey, La Rose Pauillac

BATAILLEY (Fifth-Growth) GOOD

Production: 23,000 cases	Grape varieties:
	Cabernet Sauvignon—70%
	Merlot—20%
	Cabernet Franc—9%
	Petit Verdot—1%
Secondary label: none	
Vineyard size: 128.4 acres	Proprietor: Emile Castéja
Time spent in barrels: 18 months	Age of vines: 30 years
Evaluation of present classification: Should be maintained	
Plateau of maturity: 10–25 years following the vintage	

Batailley, an attractive château sitting in a small clearing surrounded by large trees, is located well inland from the Gironde River. The vineyards, which were all part of the 1855 classification, are situated between those of Haut-Batailley to the south and Grand-Puy-Lacoste to the north. England's David Peppercorn has frequently made the point (and I would agree completely) that because the *négociant* firm of Borie-Manoux controls the distribution of Batailley, and because the wines are not freely traded or available for tasting in the normal commercial circles of Bordeaux, there has been a tendency to ignore this estate. This has resulted in a wine that is undervalued.

The property has been run since 1961 by Emile Castéja, who continues to turn out relatively old-style, solid, well-colored, somewhat rustic Pauillac that can be difficult to assess at a young age. I have frequently commented that while the wine can handle significant cellaring, it rarely excites or inspires, but is essentially reliable and fairly priced. Although I stand by those comments, I have begun to believe that I have underrated several of the vintages. Wine enthusiasts who have patience no doubt admire Batailley's reputation for longevity, as well as its reasonable prices. Given the increased efforts to improve the quality that began in the late eighties, it is unlikely that Batailley can remain the lowest-priced classified-growth Pauillac.

VINTAGES

1989—When first tasted I thought the 1989 to be the finest Batailley in over three decades. Now it has gone into a hard, tannic, tough
90 stage that suggests a great deal of patience will be necessary. The ruby/purple color is sound, and the bouquet of toasty, smoky oak,

chocolate, and superripe cassis is followed by a medium-bodied, rich, nicely extracted wine with gobs of rough tannins and relatively good acidity for a 1989. This is a large-scaled, traditionally styled wine that will need at least a decade of bottle age. Anticipated maturity: 2000–2018. Last tasted, 4/91.

1988—Typically stern, tough, closed, and difficult to penetrate, the 1988
  ·   displays a dark ruby color, a reticent bouquet of minerals, black-
 85   currants, and oak, medium body, and an elevated tannin level.
      Anticipated maturity: 1997–2008. Last tasted, 4/90.

1986—The 1986's rating may turn out to be conservative as this wine
  ·   tends to show better after 10–12 years in the bottle than it does
 86   when young. Made from 70% Cabernet Sauvignon, 20% Merlot,
      and the balance Petit Verdot and Cabernet Franc, and 1986 is full
      bodied, deep ruby/purple in color, but extremely hard and tannic.
      However, it appears to have the depth and concentration of fruit
      necessary to outlast the tannins. Anticipated maturity: 2000–
      2015. Last tasted, 4/90.

1985—Not surprisingly, the 1985 Batailley has the ripeness of the vintage
  ·   well displayed, but also carries the Batailley firmness and tannic
 86   toughness as personality traits. It is well made, reserved, and
      stylish. Anticipated maturity: 1993–2005. Last tasted, 4/90.

1984—The 1984 Batailley is light, with moderately intense berry fruit,
  ·   an underlying vegetal character, low acidity, but a soft palate
 82   impression. Anticipated maturity: Now–1993. Last tasted, 3/88.

1982—Soft, relatively fat, fruity flavors lack the great concentration of
  ·   the very best 1982s, but nevertheless offer juicy blackcurrants
 87   nicely mixed with a pleasing vanillin oakiness. Moderate tannins
      have become much more noticeable in the late eighties, suggest-
      ing greater aging potential than I initially believed. Anticipated
      maturity: 1995–2010. Last tasted, 1/90.

1980—Light, thin, and lacking fruit, this shallow, short-tasting wine is
  ·   clearly not one of the better efforts from this mediocre vintage.
 67   Anticipated maturity: Now–may be in decline. Last tasted, 3/83.

1979—Good, dark ruby color, with a ripe, but emerging bouquet of cassis
  ·   fruit, oak, and earthy scents. The aggressively hard tannins in the
 83   1979 have begun to melt away, revealing a spicy, compact, aus-
      tere wine that will age well, but never elicit much excitement.
      Anticipated maturity: Now–2000. Last tasted, 3/89.

1978—A solid, durable wine, the 1978 Batailley is quite attractive, with
  ·   an exotic, moderately intense bouquet of cassis, anise, and spicy
 84   components. Full bodied, with surprisingly soft, supple fruit,
      round, ripe tannins, and good length, this is a very good effort

from Batailley. Anticipated maturity: Now–2000. Last tasted, 2/84.

1976—A straightforward sort of wine, which is fully mature, this medium
  ·   ruby-colored wine has a spicy, plump, fruity bouquet, medium
 81   body, attractive, gentle, almost polite flavors, and a rather short,
        yet soft finish. Anticipated maturity: Now–1993. Last tasted, 4/84.

1975—An unusual, yet enjoyable wine, the 1975 Batailley has a full-
  ·   blown bouquet of ripe, chocolatey fruit, a sweet, ripe palate
 83   impression, and an astringent, tannic finish. The wine appears at
        odds with itself, given the ripe, sweet, round flavors suggesting
        maturity, and hard tannin dictating future aging. In 1990, the wine
        remained stubbornly hard and tough textured, giving rise to
        doubts about the fruit holding up. Anticipated maturity: Now–
        2000. Last tasted, 3/90.

1971—An aroma highly suggestive of freshly brewed tea and ripe tanger-
  ·   ines suggests overripeness. On the palate, the wine is diffuse,
 73   lacking direction, and is somewhat watery and uninteresting. This
        is a curious and unappealing rendition of Batailley. Anticipated
        maturity: Now–probably in serious decline. Last tasted, 2/79.

1970—In many respects, this wine typifies Batailley and the style of wine
  ·   so often produced there—dark ruby, with a bouquet that offers
 82   ripe fruit, some mild oaky notes, but not much complexity. On
        the palate, the wine is chunky and fleshy, with good concentra-
        tion, firm tannins, and a monolithic personality. Anticipated ma-
        turity: Now–1996. Last tasted, 6/87.

1966—The 1966 Batailley is now entering its mature period. The bouquet
  ·   offers modest, ripe blackcurrant aromas. The flavors are plump
 82   and solid, but the wine, which is satisfying, still leaves the taster
        desiring more substance, fruit, and charm. Anticipated maturity:
        Now. Last tasted, 3/84.

1964—Batailley turned out one of the northern Médoc's most successful
  ·   wines in 1964. Rich, full bodied, and now fully mature, with an
 87   enthralling cedary, spicy, plum-like bouquet, this large-scaled
        Batailley is displaying some amber at the edge, but exhibits won-
        derful fruit and length. Anticipated maturity: Now–2000. Last
        tasted, 5/90.

1962—Batailley's 1962 has been disappointing when tasted stateside, yet
  ·   several bottles opened at the château in 1988 were gloriously
 87   perfumed, supple, fleshy, and totally mature. None contained the
        austere, sometimes rude tannins Batailley can possess. Antici-
        pated maturity: Now–1994. Last tasted, 3/88.

1961—In this great vintage, I have found Batailley to be a nice, compact,
·   fruity wine, with good color, a robust, dusty texture on the palate,
84   but not the best example of what the 1961 vintage was all about.
        Anticipated maturity: Now–may be in decline. Last tasted, 3/79.

LA BÉCASSE (Unclassified)   GOOD

Production: 2,500 cases	Grape varieties: Cabernet Sauvignon–60% Cabernet Franc–20% Merlot–20%
Secondary label: none	
Vineyard size: 12.5 acres	Proprietor: Georges Fonteneau
Time spent in barrels: 18–22 months	Average age of vines: 50 years
Evaluation of present classification: Should be upgraded to a Cru Bourgeois Exceptionnel, perhaps even a fifth-growth	
Plateau of maturity: 5–15 years following the vintage	

I owe a great deal of thanks to Bernard Ginestet, who first told me about
this Pauillac gem that has previously been known only to a fiercely loyal
group of insiders who buy the production. This group includes several of
the greatest restaurants in France (such as Lucas Carton and La Tour
d'Argent). The wine appears to have excellent concentration and aging
potential based on the 1982 and 1986 that I tasted for the first time in
1990. This is a property that clearly deserves more attention.

BELLEGRAVE (Cru Bourgeois Supérieur)   AVERAGE

Production: 1,500 cases	Grape varieties: Cabernet Sauvignon–80% Merlot–15% Petit Verdot–5%
Secondary label: none	
Vineyard size: 7.5 acres	Proprietor: Henry J. Van der Voort
Time spent in barrels: 14–18 months	Average age of vines: 18 years
Evaluation of present classification: The quality equivalent of a Cru Bourgeois	
Plateau of maturity: 3–10 years following the vintage	

The tiny production of this property, owned by the San Francisco–based Van der Voort family, who also import wines from France under the name Bercut-Vandervoort, is rarely seen. The vineyard and winemaking are both in good hands as they are looked after by Pierre Peyronie, the owner of the nearby Château Fonbadet. The few vintages I have tasted of Belle-grave have been competent, straightforward examples of a Pauillac.

BERNADOTTE (Cru Bourgeois Supérieur)   AVERAGE

Production: 1,600 cases	Grape varieties: Cabernet Sauvignon–53% Merlot–40% Cabernet Franc–5% Petit Verdot–2%
Secondary label: none Vineyard size: 7.5 acres	Proprietor: The Eklund family of Switzerland
Time spent in barrels: 12–18 months	Average age of vines: 20 years
Evaluation of present classification: The quality equivalent of a Cru Bourgeois	
Plateau of maturity: 2–7 years following the vintage	

The first vintage of Bernadotte to be estate-bottled was the 1983, and having tasted not only that vintage, but each vintage since, I have been unimpressed by the light, somewhat diluted, one-dimensional, and indif-ferent style of the wines. The property does have the distinction of being Swiss owned.

CLERC-MILON (Fifth-Growth)   GOOD

Production: 10,000 cases	Grape varieties: Cabernet Sauvignon–70% Merlot–20% Cabernet Franc–10%
Secondary label: none Vineyard size: 69 acres	Proprietor: The Rothschild family
Time spent in barrels: 18–22 months	Average age of vines: 38 years
Evaluation of present classification: Should be maintained, although it should be noted that since 1985, the quality has improved	
Plateau of maturity: 5–14 years following the vintage	

Another of the Baron Philippe Rothschild estates, Clerc-Milon was acquired in 1970. While there is no château, the vineyard is brilliantly placed next to both Mouton-Rothschild and Lafite-Rothschild, immediately adjacent to the huge oil refinery that dominates the tranquil town of Pauillac. Until 1985, the wine produced was frequently light and undistinguished. Recent vintages have displayed a lush fruity quality, as well as greater depth and flavor dimension. In comparison with the Baron's other estate-bottled wines, Clerc-Milon is the most forward and easiest to appreciate when young. Given the quality of the 1986 and 1989 vintages, the wine is currently undervalued.

VINTAGES

1989—The 1989 Clerc-Milon is a wonderfully hedonistic wine. Deep
  ·   ruby, with an intense, roasted, smoky bouquet of plums and cur-
  90   rants, this full-bodied wine is packed with fruit, is chewy and
        opulent as well as very soft and alcoholic. In spite of the preco-
        cious impression, the tannin levels are high, similar in fact to the
        1986. For the first time in my experience, the difference between
        Clerc-Milon and Mouton-Rothschild is negligible. A great value.
        Anticipated maturity: 1993–2010. Last tasted, 4/91.

1988—The 1988 is deep in color, with a moderately intense bouquet of
  ·   herbs, smoke, and blackcurrants. The hardness it revealed when
  89   it was young has melted away, and at present, a rich, creamy
        texture offers up considerable roasted fruit flavors complemented
        by lavish amounts of oak. This is a crowd-pleasing style of Pauil-
        lac for drinking over the next decade. Anticipated maturity: Now–
        2001. Last tasted, 4/91.

1987—Soft-yet-ripe aromas of currants, smoky oak, and herbs can be
  ·   coaxed from the glass. In the mouth, the wine is ready to
  76   drink—light, but round and correct. Anticipated maturity: Now–
        1992. Last tasted, 12/89.

1986—The 1986 is among the greatest Clerc-Milon in my memory, and
  ·   continues to represent one of the better values of the 1986 vin-
  90   tage. Dark ruby/purple with a super bouquet of sweet, toasty new
        oak, plums, blackcurrants, licorice, and cedar, on the palate, the
        wine is very concentrated, rich and powerful, yet atypically soft
        and fleshy for a 1986. While this wine should age well for another
        two decades, it can be drunk much earlier than many of the 1986
        Pauillacs. It is a sleeper of the vintage. Anticipated maturity:
        1992–2006. Last tasted, 1/91.

1985—The 1985 is a gorgeous wine, deep colored with a complex bou-
  ·   quet of blackcurrants, minerals, and smoky oak. On the palate,
  89   this wine is rich, full bodied, powerful, and surprisingly struc-

tured and long for a 1985. It is one of the surprises of the vintage. Anticipated maturity: Now–2000. Last tasted, 9/89.

1984—Beginning to exhibit some orange and amber color, this oaky,
·   herbaceous Clerc-Milon has adequate ripeness, medium body,
78   high acidity, and a lashing of tannin. It should be drunk up. Anticipated maturity: Now–1993. Last tasted, 11/88.

1983—This is a pleasant, lightweight wine that offers a ripe fruity, oaky
·   bouquet, yet quickly falls away on the palate. A medium-bodied
79   wine, it has matured very rapidly. Anticipated maturity: Now– 1992. Last tasted, 1/90.

1982—The 1982 Clerc-Milon is a charming, forward, ripe, fruity wine
·   with an open-knit, lovely bouquet of ripe berry fruit, and oaky,
84   vanillin scents. Medium to full bodied, with soft, light tannins, this wine is ready to drink. Anticipated maturity: Now–1995. Last tasted, 1/90.

1981—The 1981 exhibits good, dark color, medium body, a classy, com-
·   plex cedary, oaky, ripe blackcurrant bouquet, some acidity in the
82   finish, and a compact personality. Anticipated maturity: Now– 1995. Last tasted, 3/87.

COLOMBIER-MONPELOU (Cru Grand Bourgeois)   AVERAGE

Production: 8,000 cases	Grape varieties:
	Cabernet Sauvignon–70%
	Merlot–20%
	Cabernet Franc–5%
	Petit Verdot–5%
Secondary label: Grand Canyon	
Vineyard size: 34.6 acres	Proprietor: Bernard Jugla
Time spent in barrels: 19–22 months	Average age of vines: 39 years
Evaluation of present classification: Should be maintained	
Plateau of maturity: 3–8 years following the vintage	

This property, purchased by proprietor Bernard Jugla in 1970, consists of one contiguous vineyard well-situated on the high plateau above the village of Pauillac. Given the high percentage of Cabernet Sauvignon and the fact that the average age of the vines is an impressive 39 years, one would expect a great deal more concentration and intensity. Certainly, the vinification and *élevage* are completely traditional, as the wine is kept in oak casks for 19–22 months, and bottled with minimal clarification. The problem is that most of the wines I have tasted from Colombier- Monpelou are light, lacking concentration and distinction. Nevertheless, there is a considerable market for the wines of this château, as France's famed Savour Club remains one of their principal buyers, as well as a number of European countries.

VINTAGES

1989 —In 1990 the 1989 Colombier-Monpelou exhibited meager flavors
· and a light, washed-out character. This year, the wine tastes
78 better, although it is clearly made in a fruity, soft, forward style. Anticipated maturity: Now–1996. Last tasted, 4/91.

1988 —The 1988 possessed a very oaky nose, but not enough depth or
· body to warrant interest. Anticipated maturity: Now–1993. Last
78 tasted, 4/91.

1986 —While the 1986 Colombier-Monpelou does not compete with the
· classified growths of Pauillac, it is an attractive, well-colored,
80 ripe, fruity, medium- to full-bodied wine that will easily repay if kept for 7–10 years. Anticipated maturity: Now–1995. Last tasted, 11/90.

1985 —I have never been particularly impressed with this wine, al-
· though, to its credit, it is usually reasonably priced. The 1985 is a
74 decent, soft, undistinguished claret. Anticipated maturity: Now– 1992. Last tasted, 3/88.

LA COURONNE (Cru Bourgeois Exceptionnel)   AVERAGE

Production: 2,200 cases	Grape varieties: Cabernet Sauvignon–70% Merlot–30%
Secondary label: none	
Vineyard size: 10 acres	Proprietor: The family of Jean-Eugène Borie
Time spent in barrels: 12–16 months	Average age of vines: 25 years
Evaluation of present classification: The quality equivalent of a Cru Bourgeois	
Plateau of maturity: 4–10 years following the vintage	

This small vineyard, created in 1879, is located inland, and is run by Xavier Borie, the son of Jean-Eugène Borie, and also the proprietor of Grand-Puy-Lacoste. For whatever reason, the Bories' magic winemaking touch that is evident at their other properties has not worked at La Couronne. The wine tends to be one-dimensional and simple. I have tasted virtually all of the vintages in the eighties and there is not one that I would serve enthusiastically to friends.

CROIZET-BAGES (Fifth-Growth)   AVERAGE

Production: 9,500 cases	Grape varieties:
	Cabernet Sauvignon—40%
	Cabernet Franc—30%
	Merlot—30%
Secondary label: Enclos de Moncabon	
Vineyard size: 54.3 acres	Proprietor: Madame L. Quié
Time spent in barrels: 12–18 months	Average age of vines: 30 years

Evaluation of present classification: Should be downgraded to a
  Grand Bourgeois
Plateau of maturity: 5–12 years following the vintage

Croizet-Bages is owned and managed by the Quié family that also owns the well-known Margaux estate, Rauzan-Gassies, and the reliable Cru Bourgeois, Bel-Orme-Tronquoy-de-Lalande. I have always found Croizet-Bages to be one of the lightest and quickest-maturing Pauillacs. The wine has been a consistent underachiever for no valid reason. The vineyard is ideally located on the Bages plateau, the vines are old, and the vinification is traditional. Excessive crop yields and indifferent cellar treatment may in part explain the disappointing results. Never terribly deep or spectacular, Croizet-Bages is a sound, gentle, soft, fruity wine, which is generally fully mature within 4–5 years.

VINTAGES

1989—Unfortunately, insipidness is the rule at this property. How any-
·   one could produce such a light, overtly herbaceous, innocuous
73   wine in 1989 escapes logic. Croizet-Bages excelled in doing just
     that. Anticipated maturity: Now–1997. Last tasted, 4/91.

1988—The 1988 is marginally better than the 1989, straightforward,
·   pleasant, soft, but shallow. Life is too short to drink Croizet-
74   Bages. Anticipated maturity: Now–1995. Last tasted, 4/91.

1987—Overtly vegetal, thin, and compact, this undistinguished wine
·   should be drunk up. Anticipated maturity: Now–1993. Last
69   tasted, 11/89.

1986—The 1986 is soft and fruity with some tannin, but is essentially
·   one-dimensional and undistinguished, particularly in view of its
76   reputation. Anticipated maturity: Now–1993. Last tasted, 3/89.

1985—The 1985 is soft, one-dimensional, and no better than most ge-
·   neric Bordeaux red wines. Anticipated maturity: Now–1993. Last
73   tasted, 3/88.

1984—This is a light, watery, disappointing wine from one of the few
·   Pauillac estates that continues to ignore quality. Anticipated ma-
70   turity: Now–1992. Last tasted, 3/87.

1983—From the cask, this wine was light, innocuous, dull, and bland.
·   While some fruit was present, the color and weight suggested a
68   wine that was overcropped and diluted. Drink up. Anticipated
     maturity: Now–may be in decline. Last tasted, 3/84.

1982—For whatever reason, this wine lacks the richness and character
·   that one usually expects from a 1982. Medium ruby, with a very
75   developed, spicy, ripe cherry, earthy bouquet, soft, rather flabby
     flavors, and a short, rather clumsy finish, the 1982 Croizet-Bages
     is acceptable, but given the vintage, not what it should be. Drink
     it up. Anticipated maturity: Now–1993. Last tasted, 1/85.

1981—Disappointingly light, already fully mature, the 1981 Croizet-
·   Bages should be drunk up before it fades into oblivion. Antici-
72   pated maturity: Now–probably in serious decline. Last tasted,
     6/84.

DUHART-MILON-ROTHSCHILD (Fourth-Growth) VERY GOOD

Production: 15,000–20,000 cases	Grape varieties: Cabernet Sauvignon—70% Merlot—25% Cabernet Franc—5%
Secondary label: Moulin de Duhart	
Vineyard size: 111 acres	Proprietor: Domaines de Rothschild
Time spent in barrels: 22–24 months	Average age of vines: 18 years
Evaluation of present classification: Since 1982, should be upgraded to a third-growth	
Plateau of maturity: 8–25 years following the vintage	

The "other" Pauillac château owned by the Rothschilds of Lafite-Rothschild fame, Duhart-Milon-Rothschild was purchased in 1962. The poorly
maintained vineyards were totally replanted during the mid- and late
sixties. Because the vineyard is still young, particularly for a classified
growth, the wines of the late sixties and seventies have not lived up to
the expectations of wine enthusiasts who assume the Rothschild name is
synonymous with excellence. The quality began to improve in 1978, and
since 1982, Duhart's wines have been excellent, and occasionally outstanding.

This is one of the few famous Médoc properties that does not have a château. The wine is made in a large, modern, aesthetically dreadful warehouse on the backstreets of Pauillac.

VINTAGES

1989—The 1989 has an intense bouquet of creamy blackcurrant fruit and
·   exotic spices. There is even a touch of the famous Pauillac "lead-
88   pencil" smell. Medium bodied, rich, and alcoholic, this volup-
        tuous-styled wine has all the components necessary to seduce
        tasters for the next 8–12 years. It is not so big a wine as I had
        originally thought, having shed much of its fat in the last year.
        Qualitatively, it is behind the 1982 and 1988. Anticipated matu-
        rity: 1992–2008. Last tasted, 4/91.

1988—The 1988 Duhart-Milon is superior to the 1989. A compelling bou-
·   quet of ripe fruit, spices, cedar, and herbs roars from the glass.
91   It is rich, full bodied, admirably concentrated and long, with
        plenty of tannin. Meticulous winemaking has enabled this estate
        to avoid the astringent taste of so many 1988 Médocs. This is a
        star of the vintage. Anticipated maturity: 1995–2010. Last tasted,
        4/91.

1987—A surprisingly mature, attractive bouquet of herbs, cedar, and
·   black fruits suggest a richer wine than what actually exists. In the
81   mouth, the wine is round, but soft and short. Drink it over the
        next 4–5 years. Anticipated maturity: Now–1993. Last tasted,
        11/89.

1986—I have to give very good marks to the 1986, which has excellent
·   depth, plenty of richness, a lot of spicy oak, as well as a classy
87   bouquet of herbaceous blackcurrants, cedar, and spicy, toasty
        oak. It has a good deal of tannin in the finish, but I just would like
        to see a bit more stuffing and complexity. Anticipated maturity:
        1995–2008. Last tasted, 3/90.

1985—The 1985 Duhart is a fine, medium-bodied wine that is showing
·   slightly less intensity from the bottle than from cask. Medium
86   deep ruby, with an open-knit, spicy oak, curranty bouquet, ele-
        gant and stylish, the 1985 could use more depth, but for drinking
        over the next decade, it is a fine choice. Anticipated maturity:
        Now–2000. Last tasted, 2/89.

1984—Moderately colored, with little bouquet, the 1984 has compact,
·   narrow flavors, a spicy, tightly knit texture, and moderate tannins
74   in the austere, slightly acidic finish. Anticipated maturity: Now–
        1994. Last tasted, 10/88.

1983 — The 1983 Duhart has excellent color, a solid, firm structure, yet a
·   quickly developing, expansive, ripe fruity, cassis-dominated bou-
86   quet, round, admirably concentrated flavors, and some tannins in
the finish. This is a very good, rich, medium- to full-bodied Duhart. Anticipated maturity: 1992–2005. Last tasted, 6/89.

1982 — The 1982 Duhart-Milon has turned out to be the best wine I have
·   ever tasted from this well-known but generally underachieving
92   Pauillac estate. In numerous tastings of 1982s, it has proved to be
an immense, rich, tannic, and backward wine with extraordinary
concentration, but a great deal of potential finesse and elegance.
For those who were lucky enough to buy it at the early low prices
asked for in the 1982 Bordeaux futures, this wine has turned out
to be quite stunning, with the potential to last for another 15–20
years. Anticipated maturity: 1995–2015. Last tasted, 1/89.

1981 — All of the Lafite domains were successful in 1981. Quite backward
·   in development, this deep ruby colored wine has an attractive
84   bouquet that suggests crushed blackcurrants, fresh leather, and
new oak. Relatively big, quite tannic, concentrated, astringent,
and dry in the finish, this backward, somewhat dull wine begs for
time. However, does the wine have enough fruit to outlast the
tannins? Anticipated maturity: 1992–2005. Last tasted, 1/85.

1979 — Quite an elegant wine, the 1979 Duhart-Milon has good, dark ruby
·   color, with a moderately intense, complex, cedary bouquet, me-
83   dium body, restrained power and richness, but good balance and
harmony. The precocious development of the bouquet and amber
color at the edges suggests early maturity. Anticipated maturity:
Now–1996. Last tasted, 7/86.

1978 — A medium-bodied wine with a well-developed, ripe fruity, spicy,
·   toasty, iron-scented bouquet, and soft, savory, round flavors, the
84   1978 Duhart-Milon is the first wine in a succession of vintages
that began to correctly reflect the style and character of the famous sibling, Lafite-Rothschild. The 1978 Duhart-Milon is fully
mature. Anticipated maturity: Now. Last tasted, 3/88.

1976 — Ruby garnet, with a fully developed, moderately intense, cedary,
·   vanillin, fragrant bouquet, this forward-styled wine has soft,
84   round, attractive flavors, light tannins, low acidity, and a casual
resemblance to Lafite, particularly in the bouquet. Its forward
charms and up-front fruit have served it well, but additional cellaring would be hazardous. Drink up. Anticipated maturity: Now.
Last tasted, 4/90.

1975 — A disappointment given the vintage, the 1975 Duhart-Milon has a
·   big, herbal, almost minty aroma, a spicy, vegetal fruitiness, and
75   a sweet burnt quality that suggests over-chaptalization. Fully ma-

ture, but disjointed and unique in style. Anticipated maturity: Now—may be in decline. Last tasted, 5/84.

1974—A poor, watery wine. Very disappointing. Last tasted, 1/78.

·
62

1970—In this vintage that produced such wonderfully balanced, richly
·   fruity wines, Duhart-Milon has made a wine with an attractive,
70   earthy, spicy, oaky bouquet, but it lacks fruit, and finishes short, with excessive acidity. It remains tart, astringent, and generally unpleasant. Anticipated maturity: Now. Last tasted, 10/88.

1966—The 1966 has a dusty texture with dry, slightly acidic flavors, yet
·   perplexingly, an attractive, cedary, ripe fruity bouquet that prom-
75   ises much more than the meager flavors deliver. Anticipated maturity: Now—may be in decline. Last tasted, 11/79.

LA FLEUR MILON (Cru Grand Bourgeois)   AVERAGE

Production: 6,000 cases	Grape varieties: Cabernet Sauvignon—70% Merlot—30%
Secondary label: none	
Vineyard size: 31.6 acres	Proprietor: André Gimenez
Time spent in barrels: 22–24 months	Average age of vines: 30 years
Evaluation of present classification: The quality equivalent of a Cru Bourgeois	
Plateau of maturity: 5–12 years following the vintage	

I rarely see the wines from this producer, but the vineyard, which consists of a number of small parcels, is located on the high plateau north of the town of Pauillac, near both Mouton-Rothschild and Lafite-Rothschild. Those vintages I have tasted—1983, 1985, and 1986—were slightly vegetal, coarse, and lacking charm and flesh.

FONBADET (Cru Bourgeois Supérieur)　　　　　　GOOD

Production: 8,500 cases	Grape varieties:
	Cabernet Sauvignon—60%
	Merlot—19%
	Cabernet Franc—15%
	Malbec—3%
	Petit Verdot—3%
Secondary labels: multiple names, notably, Tour du Roc-Milon and two tiny estates owned by Peyronie, Haut-Pauillac and Padernac	
Vineyard size: 37 acres	Proprietor: Pierre Peyronie
Time spent in barrels: 15–18 months	Average age of vines: 50 years
Evaluation of present classification: Should be upgraded to a fifth-growth	
Plateau of maturity: 5–15 years following the vintage	

Should any reclassification of the wines of the Médoc be done, Fonbadet would have to be elevated to the rank of fifth-growth. This is an expertly vinified wine that can, in vintages such as 1990, 1986, 1982, and 1978, surpass several of the classified growths of Pauillac. In style, it is always darkly colored, with a very rich, blackcurrant bouquet, an intense concentration of flavor, and full body. I find it reminiscent of the style of the two fifth-growth Pauillacs, Lynch-Bages and Haut-Bages-Libéral. The secrets are extremely old vines (more than 50 years of age), tiny yields (usually under 35 hectoliters per hectare), and the brilliant location of the vineyard near both Pichon-Longueville Baron and Pichon-Longueville–Comtesse de Lalande.

VINTAGES

1989—The 1989 is surprisingly light, soft, alcoholic, and will no doubt
·　　be short-lived because of its low acidity. There is plenty of fruit
83　　but the overall effect is of a flabby, unstructured wine. Antici-
　　　pated maturity: 1992–1998. Last tasted, 4/91.

1988—The 1988 tastes tart, lean, and anorexic. Lack of fruit is cause for
·　　concern. Anticipated maturity: Now–1996. Last tasted, 4/91.
75

1986—The 1986 Fonbadet is certainly the best wine made at this poten-
·　　tially excellent vineyard since the 1982. There is abundant chewy
86　　fruit, noticeable muscle and tannin, and impressive length. The

wine should come into its own by the early nineties, but last 10–
12 years thereafter. Given the extract levels this wine can possess, an elevated use of new oak casks at this property might
prove beneficial. Anticipated maturity: Now–2003. Last tasted,
4/89.

1985—The 1985 has a good deep ruby color and an attractive berry
  ·   perfume, but its chunky flavors reveal little complexity. Antici-
 80   pated maturity: Now–1996. Last tasted, 10/88.

1984—Surprisingly alcoholic, with adequate fruit, full body, and an old-
  ·   fashioned, rustic feel to it, the 1984 is rough and disjointed. An-
 72   ticipated maturity: Now–1992. Last tasted, 3/88.

1983—This looks to be a top-notch effort from Fonbadet. Nearly as dark
  ·   as the opaque 1982, but less concentrated, this rich, medium-
 85   bodied, moderately tannic wine offers a generous mouthful of
         cedary, cassis-flavored fruit. Anticipated maturity: Now–1996.
         Last tasted, 3/89.

1982—The ripe, rich, blackberry aromas surge from the glass; this gor-
  ·   geous wine is very deep, concentrated, and well structured. On
 87   the palate, the wine is full bodied, moderately tannic, opulently
         fruity, and long. A sleeper of the vintage. Anticipated maturity:
         Now–2000. Last tasted, 1/89.

1981—The 1981 is richly fruity, darkly colored, more precocious, and
  ·   will mature earlier than either the 1982 or 1983. It is a wine that
 84   is charming, well-balanced, and satisfying. Anticipated maturity:
         Now–may be in decline. Last tasted, 2/84.

1978—A textbook Pauillac, the 1978 Fonbadet has a well-developed bou-
  ·   quet of cedar, ripe plums and currants, and well-balanced, deeply
 86   fruity flavors. Quite impressive. Anticipated maturity: Now–may
         be in decline. Last tasted, 2/84.

LES FORTS DE LATOUR* (Unclassified)   VERY GOOD

Evaluation: The quality equivalent of a fourth-growth

The staff at Latour have always maintained that the "second" wine of
Latour was equivalent in quality terms to a "second-growth" in the 1855
classification. In fact, they claim that blind tastings of Forts de Latour
are held at Latour against the wines produced by the second-growths. If
Forts de Latour does not do extremely well, then a decision must be

* Because Les Forts de Latour is widely regarded as the finest of all the "second wines,"
  and in tastings, frequently rated above more famous Pauillacs, its stature is such that it
  merits separate coverage.

made whether to declassify it as regional Pauillac. In specific vintages, for example, 1978 and 1982, I would agree with their assessment, but in more objective terms, the wine is comparable to a fourth-growth in quality, which still establishes this wine as the finest "second" wine produced in Bordeaux.

The wine, which is vinified exactly the same way as Latour, comes from three vineyards called Petit Batailley, Comtesse de Lalande, and Les Forts de Latour. Additionally, selected lots of Latour (often from young vines) not considered quite "grand" enough, are also blended with the wine from the aforementioned vineyards. The character of Forts de Latour is astonishingly similar to Latour itself, only lighter and quicker to mature. Les Forts de Latour is certainly the finest of the second labels or *marques* produced by the well-known châteaux in Bordeaux. It is not inexpensive, but given its similarity to the great Latour at half the price, it merits consideration. To Latour's credit, the wine is only released when the château deems it close to maturity.

VINTAGES

1989—This should turn out to be the finest Forts de Latour since the
·   glorious 1982. When tasted in 1991, it was round, generously
87   endowed, surprisingly supple (even for the second wine of La-
       tour), low in acidity, with a long, fleshy, heady finish. It will no
       doubt be released early by the château, given its precocious style.
       Anticipated maturity: 1993–2004. Last tasted, 4/91.

1988—This medium-bodied, somewhat austere, noticeably oaky and
·   tannic Forts de Latour possesses good aging potential, but lacks
85   charm, complexity, and a bit of concentration. Nevertheless, it is
       an elegant, somewhat restrained wine. Anticipated maturity:
       1993–2002. Last tasted, 4/90.

1987—The delightful 1987 Forts de Latour is, to my taste, a better wine
·   than the 1988. The forward-yet-intriguing bouquet of walnuts,
86   spicy oak, cedar, and herbs is followed by a surprisingly concen-
       trated, generously fruity, medium- to full-bodied wine with excel-
       lent balance and depth. It is a top-notch success for the vintage.
       Anticipated maturity: Now–1997. Last tasted, 4/90.

1986—This wine has consistently exhibited a great deal of oak and pep-
·   pery, mineral-scented blackcurrant fruit in its blossoming nose.
86   In the mouth, it exhibits the tannic ferocity that characterizes
       many 1986s, but is surprisingly lighter than I would have ex-
       pected. A good effort, but it could use more depth and concentra-
       tion, particularly if one compares it with the 1982 or 1989.
       Anticipated maturity: 1993–2005. Last tasted, 4/90.

1985—Latour made one of the lightest wines I have ever tasted from this
·   property in this very good vintage. Not surprisingly, their second
84   wine is also forward. Soft, with only medium body, and a surprisingly short, undistinguished finish, this smooth, lightweight Latour should be drunk over the next 5–6 years. Anticipated
maturity: Now–1996. Last tasted, 4/91.

1984—A weedy, cedary bouquet lacks fruit. In the mouth, the wine is
·   light, has some annoyingly high acidity, and some vague, cur-
80   ranty, cedary fruitiness. The relatively high acidity will keep the
wine alive, but I doubt that it will ever be enjoyable. Anticipated
maturity: Now–1995. Last tasted, 12/89.

1983—Quite soft and fully mature, with a hint of the famed Latour
·   bouquet of minerals, walnuts, and blackcurrants, this medium-
84   bodied, round, moderately concentrated wine should be drunk
over the next 5–7 years. It makes an interesting comparison with
the enormously concentrated, more backward 1982. Anticipated
maturity: Now–1996. Last tasted, 7/90.

1982—This black/purple-colored wine is remarkably close in character
·   to the great 1982 Latour, but sells for one-fourth to one-fifth the
92   price. Splendidly concentrated, with Latour's classic bouquet of
walnuts, blackcurrants, and minerals, this wine has the remarkable, full-bodied opulence of the vintage, soft tannins, and a finish
that one sees only in years of great ripeness, such as 1959, 1961,
1982, and 1989. To date, it is the finest Forts de Latour ever
produced. Anticipated maturity: Now–2005. Last tasted, 5/91.

1981—While this wine lacks muscle, weight, and the compelling concen-
·   tration of the 1982, it is still an elegantly wrought, stylish wine
85   that indeed resembles the grand vin. Medium to deep ruby color,
with an emerging bouquet of wet stones, cassis, and oak, this
medium-bodied, gracefully made Latour is just beginning to drink
well, but should last for another 5–7 years. It is restrained, but
attractive and well-balanced. Anticipated maturity: Now–1995.
Last tasted, 4/88.

1978—Still quite dark with a rich, intense, cassis, oaky nose, ripe, mod-
·   erately tannic, yet supple flavors, and excellent length, this wine
87   is fully mature, but will keep for another decade. After the 1982,
this is my favorite vintage. Anticipated maturity: Now–2000. Last
tasted, 10/89.

1976—Forward, smooth, and showing ripe fruit and less tannin than its
·   big brother, this wine can be drunk now, but is quite ordinary in
76   the total Bordeaux scheme of things. Anticipated maturity: Now.
Last tasted, 10/89.

1975—True to the vintage and to Latour, this wine is tannic, lean, ag-
· gressive, and still in need of bottle age. The color remains im-
85 pressive, the richness and depth appear to be present, but the
tannins refuse to yield. Anticipated maturity: 1992–2000. Last
tasted, 10/89.

1974—Latour made one of the top wines of the vintage, so it is not
· surprising to find Forts de Latour better than many a more-famous
74 classified growth. A trifle austere and lean, but spicy, with good
fruit, a hard, tough personality, yet short, soft finish, this wine
seems to suggest potential for improvement, but the personality
of the entire vintage scares me off. Respectable given the year.
Drink up. Anticipated maturity: Now–may be in decline. Last
tasted, 1/83.

1972—Surprisingly dark colored, with an amber/brownish edge, this
· soft, chunky, somewhat rugged wine offers good chocolatey, her-
74 baceous, stemmy fruit, a good palate impression, and a short
finish. Drink up. Anticipated maturity: Now–may be in serious
decline. Last tasted, 4/80.

1970—This very fine wine is fully mature, and ideally requires consump-
· tion. Very dark ruby, with a smooth, round, ripe blackcurrant and
84 cedar bouquet, savory, full, generous flavors, and a slightly tart,
acidic finish that detracts from an otherwise fine performance in
1970. Drink now. Anticipated maturity: Now–1993. Last tasted,
1/85.

1967—The 1967 was beginning to fade in the eighties. For a number of
· years, this wine could lay claim to giving wine enthusiasts on a
84 budget a good introduction to the style of Latour. Drink up. Anticipated maturity: Now–may be in decline. Last tasted, 3/82.

1966—The 1966 Forts de Latour is a textbook Pauillac, which displays
· near perfectly proportioned scents of blackcurrants, spices,
85 leather, and cedar, ripe-yet-supple flavors, a long fruity texture
and palate impression, and light tannins. It is now at its zenith.
Drink up! Anticipated maturity: Now–may be in decline. Last
tasted, 12/88.

GAUDIN (Unclassified)   GOOD

Production: 5,000 cases	Grape varieties:
	Cabernet Sauvignon—85%
	Merlot—15%
Secondary label: none	
Vineyard size: 25 acres	Proprietor: Pierre Bibian
Time spent in barrels: 24 months	Average age of vines: 30–100 years
Evaluation of present classification: The quality equivalent of a Cru Bourgeois Exceptionnel	
Plateau of maturity: 5–12 years following the vintage	

This is a serious estate, with an excellently situated vineyard near the village of St.-Lambert, between the more famed vineyards of Pichon Lalande and Lynch-Bages. The proprietor, who had his wine vinified by the cooperative of Pauillac until 1968, produces a relatively old-style, traditional Pauillac, with a month's *cuvaison*, the use of a small percentage of new oak casks, and at least 24 months of barrel aging so the wine does not have to be filtered prior to bottling. The three vintages I have tasted, 1982, 1985, and 1986, all had plenty of stuffing, concentration, and fullness, suggesting they were capable of lasting 10–15 more years. This is a relatively unknown estate that merits a closer look.

GRAND-PUY-DUCASSE (Fifth-Growth)   GOOD

Production: 18,000 cases	Grape varieties:
	Cabernet Sauvignon—64%
	Merlot—32%
	Cabernet Franc—4%
Secondary label: Artigues-Arnaud	
Vineyard size: 81.5 acres	Proprietor: J.P.A. de la Beaumelle
Time spent in barrels: 18–22 months	Average age of vines: 20 years
Evaluation of present classification: Should be maintained	
Plateau of maturity: 4–14 years following the vintage	

This fifth-growth Pauillac has been largely ignored by consumers and the wine press. Admittedly, the wine rarely appears in tastings arranged for the wine press because the distribution is controlled exclusively by the *négociant* Mestrezat. Unquestionably, the current prices for vintages of

Grand-Puy-Ducasse are below most other Pauillacs, making it a notable value given the fine quality that now routinely emerges from the modern cellars located not in the middle of a beautiful vineyard, but rather in downtown Pauillac.

Extensive renovations as well as replanting began in 1971, culminating in 1986 with the installation of a new *cuverie* equipped with computerized stainless-steel tanks. The percentage of new oak casks has been increased to 50%. As a consequence, the future looks encouraging for Grand-Puy-Ducasse. With the well-placed vineyard, one parcel adjacent to Mouton-Rothschild and Lafite-Rothschild, another on the gravelly plateau near Batailley, Grand-Puy-Ducasse is a château to which value-conscious consumers should be giving more consideration.

The style of wines here is quite fruity and supple rather than tannic, hard, and backward. Most vintages of Grand-Puy-Ducasse are drinkable within 5 years of the vintage, yet exhibit the potential to last for 10–15 years.

VINTAGES

1989—The 1989 is forward, with a cedary, ripe, moderately intense bou-
·   quet. Not a blockbuster, but spicy and delicious, with abundant
87   quantities of chocolate and cassis-flavored fruit. This may be the
       finest wine from this property in decades. Excellent value. Antic-
       ipated maturity: Now–2002. Last tasted, 4/91.

1988—The 1988 Grand-Puy-Ducasse is a lighter-weight version of the
·   1989, less alcoholic, but more tannic and compact. Nevertheless,
85   it has fine fruit and attractive ripeness. Anticipated maturity:
       Now–1996. Last tasted, 4/91.

1986—I would like to have seen a bit more depth and excitement in the
·   1986, but it is a pretty, charming, medium-bodied, atypically
85   lighter-styled Pauillac for the vintage. Drinkable now, it will cer-
       tainly last another 7–8 years. Anticipated maturity: Now–1995.
       Last tasted, 11/90.

1985—The 1985 Grand-Puy-Ducasse is a textbook Pauillac, not a block-
·   buster in any manner, but a cedary, spicy, fragrant wine with fine
86   depth, a supple texture, some fatness and flesh, as well as a
       smooth, graceful finish. Anticipated maturity: Now–1997. Last
       tasted, 11/90.

1984—The style of Grand-Puy-Ducasse consistently offers a soft, supple,
·   engaging fruitiness and medium body. The 1984 is a pleasing,
81   round, well-made wine for drinking over the next 3–5 years. An-
       ticipated maturity: Now. Last tasted, 10/88.

1979—The 1979 is medium to dark ruby, with a spicy, ripe, fruity bou-
   ·   quet, and attractively silky, soft flavors that show noticeable ma-
   82   turity. This is a charming, quite fruity wine with medium body.
         Anticipated maturity: Now. Last tasted, 7/86.

1978—Good solid color, a ripe blackcurrant, somewhat herbaceous bou-
   ·   quet, and round, generous flavors characterize the 1978 Grand-
   82   Puy-Ducasse. Quite precocious for the vintage, and showing very
         well at present, this is a wine to drink over the next 6–7 years.
         Anticipated maturity: Now–may be in decline. Last tasted, 5/84.

1976—Rather mature, with a loosely knit, jammy, somewhat overripe
   ·   aroma of plummy fruit and spicy oak, this soft, velvety wine lacks
   76   concentration and acidity, but is very round and ready. It is now
         beginning to crack up. Anticipated maturity: Now–probably in
         serious decline. Last tasted, 9/87.

1975—The 1975 is dark ruby in color, with a stalky, vegetal note to an
   ·   otherwise attractive bouquet. Ripe, round, deep fruit has an ag-
   84   gressive, rustic texture to it, and despite the wine's concentration
         and hefty proportions, the overall impression is one of coarseness.
         A good wine that just misses being excellent. Anticipated matu-
         rity: Now–1996. Last tasted, 6/86.

1971—One of my favorite wines from Grand-Puy-Ducasse, this lovely,
   ·   round, charming, effusively fruity wine was fully mature by 1978,
   85   but has continued to remain at that plateau without fading or
         losing its fruit. A complex cedary, ripe fruity bouquet is seductive
         and complex. Soft, round, velvety flavors are satisfyingly rich and
         lengthy. A total success for Grand-Puy-Ducasse. Drink up. Antic-
         ipated maturity: Now–1993. Last tasted, 3/84.

GRAND-PUY-LACOSTE (Fifth-Growth)   EXCELLENT

Production: 13,000–14,000 cases	Grape varieties:
	Cabernet Sauvignon—70%
	Merlot—25%
	Cabernet Franc—5%
Secondary label: Lacoste-Borie	
Vineyard size: 111 acres	Proprietor: The Borie family
Time spent in barrels: 20–22 months	Average age of vines: 35 years
Evaluation of present classification: Should be upgraded to a third-growth, particularly since 1978	
Plateau of maturity: 7–20 years following the vintage	

I never had the pleasure of meeting Raymond Dupin, the late owner of Grand-Puy-Lacoste. Dupin had a monumental reputation as one of Bordeaux's all-time great gourmets. According to some of his acquaintances he was a gourmand as well. Prior to his death in 1980, he sold Grand-Puy-Lacoste in 1978 to the highly talented and respected Jean-Eugène Borie who then installed his son, Xavier, at Grand-Puy-Lacoste. An extensive remodeling program for Grand-Puy's ancient and dilapidated cellars was completed by 1982, just in time to produce the finest wine made to date by Xavier Borie. Borie continues to live at the modernized château with his wife and family. As expected by the cognoscenti of Bordeaux, Grand-Puy-Lacoste has surged to the forefront of leading Pauillacs.

Grand-Puy-Lacoste, which sits far back from the Gironde River on the "Bages" plateau, has enjoyed a solid reputation for big, durable, full-bodied Pauillacs, not unlike its neighbor a kilometer away, Lynch-Bages. However, the wines of the sixties and seventies, like those of Lynch-Bages, showed an unevenness in quality that in retrospect may have been due to the declining health of the owner. For example, highly regarded vintages such as 1961, 1966, and 1975 were less successful at Grand-Puy than its reputation would lead one to expect. Other vintages during this period, particularly the 1976, 1971, 1969, and 1967, were close to complete failures for some unexplained reason, but probably inattentiveness to detail.

However, since 1978 Grand-Puy-Lacoste has been making excellent wines, and no doubt the 1982 will be remembered as one of the greatest wines of this château's long history. In comparison to the Dupin style, the Borie style of Grand-Puy-Lacoste has been to harvest later and thereby produce wines with more of a cassis fruitiness, yet without sacrificing the wine's power and body. The price of Grand-Puy-Lacoste has not kept pace with the quality, remaining modest, even undervalued, particularly in vintages such as 1989, 1986, and 1982.

VINTAGES

1989—While a number of the 1989s resemble their 1982 counterparts, Grand-Puy-Lacoste's 1989 comes closest in identity to their 1986.
89　　I doubt that it is better than either the 1982 or 1986 as it appears to be neither so concentrated as the 1982 nor so powerful as the 1986. However, this is a classic Pauillac. A penetrating bouquet of intense blackcurrants is followed by a tannic, rich, concentrated, big-boned, generously constituted wine that is admirably made. Anticipated maturity: 1994–2010. Last tasted, 4/91.

1988—The 1988 is deep ruby, has a reticent bouquet, an austere, firm,
·   very tannic framework, and medium body. While the wine has
85   noticeable richness and depth, I envision the fruit and tannin
fighting it out for at least 6–7 years, with the high tannins ultimately gaining the upper hand. Anticipated maturity: 1995–2005.
Last tasted, 4/91.

1987—The most pleasurable aspect of this wine is the bouquet of cassis
·   and weedy scents. In the mouth, the wine is hard, tannic, and
76   lacking charm and flesh. Anticipated maturity: Now–1995. Last
tasted, 4/90.

1986—The 1986 appears to be bursting at the seams with cedary, black-
·   currant fruit, nicely supported by toasty new oak. Except for the
90   1982, it is the best wine from Grand-Puy-Lacoste in the last 25
years. It has a deep, rich, blackcurrant bouquet, powerful, intense flavors of red fruits, licorice, and new oak, and finishes long
and deep on the palate with a solid lashing of tannin. Anticipated
maturity: 1995–2010. Last tasted, 1/90.

1985—The 1985 is a big, juicy, beefy, rich, supple Pauillac oozing with
·   aromas of blackcurrants and new oak. Seductive and full bodied,
88   with excellent ripeness, this lusty, smooth-textured wine is drinking well now. Anticipated maturity: Now–1998. Last tasted, 3/90.

1984—Not very appealing, the 1984 Grand-Puy-Lacoste is tannic, aus-
·   tere, severe, and lacking in fruit and flesh. Anticipated maturity:
75   Now–1994. Last tasted, 10/88.

1983—Open knit, ripe, with a dark ruby color and a rich, weedy, black-
·   currant aroma, this rapidly evolving wine exhibits good concen-
86   tration, a round, gentle texture, and a fine finish. It has reached
full maturity. Anticipated maturity: Now–1995. Last tasted, 3/89.

1982—This is a stupendous Grand-Puy-Lacoste, with the remarkable
·   richness, intensity of fruit, and powerful, long finish that usually
92   characterize a first-growth. Still dark purple, almost opaque, with
a huge aromatic bouquet of superripe cassis, this velvety, concentrated wine displays tremendous fruit extract, but also mouth-
gripping tannins. From its early days of grapey, almost formless
fruitiness, it has gained considerable structure, and now looks
like a candidate for extended aging. Anticipated maturity: 1996–
2015. Last tasted, 4/90.

1981—Light in style for Grand-Puy, the 1981 has more in common with
·   the 1979 than either the substantial 1982 or full-bodied, yet ele-
80   gant 1978. An elegant mixture of ripe berry fruit and spicy oak
overlaid with soft tannins makes this wine very easy to drink now.
Anticipated maturity: Now–1993. Last tasted, 4/90.

1979—Quite precocious, with a surprisingly mature bouquet of ripe
 · berry fruit, cedar, spicy oak, and flowers, medium bodied, with
 83 soft flavors, a gentle, round texture, and pleasant, yet short finish,
   this wine is well-made in a lighter style than usual. Anticipated
   maturity: Now–1996. Last tasted, 3/88.

1978—The first vintage made under the expert management of Jean-
 · Eugène Borie and his son, Xavier, the 1978 remains a classic
 88 Pauillac with fine cellaring potential. Dark ruby garnet with a
   ripe, intense bouquet of cassis, fruit, cedar, and vanillin oakiness,
   this wine is rich, with excellent body and the tannins quickly
   melting away. It can be drunk now or cellared for another decade.
   Anticipated maturity: Now–2002. Last tasted, 4/91.

1976—An acceptable wine for certain, but this Grand-Puy-Lacoste is
 · surprisingly jammy, overripe, with a scent of fresh tea. Soft,
 72 flabby, and loosely knit on the palate, this wine is now fully mature. Drink up! Anticipated maturity: Now. Last tasted, 7/80.

1975—The first few bottles tasted were mediocre wine, lacking weight,
 · richness, and character. One bottle, tasted in London, was soft
 86 and one-dimensional, without the grip and length of many of the
   1975s. Several subsequent tastings revealed a fuller-bodied, rich,
   smoky, cedar-scented wine with fine depth and richness. A late
   bloomer? The wine appears to be very good, but bottle variation
   may be a problem. Anticipated maturity: Now–2000. Last tasted,
   11/88.

1971—Beginning to fall apart, this wine was fully mature by 1977. Quite
 · brown in color, with an oxidized, stale, faded bouquet, it has soft,
 62 dissipated, fruity flavors, and no tannin present. This wine possesses plenty of sharp acidity. Anticipated maturity: Now–probably in serious decline. Last tasted, 7/77.

1970—Extremely inconsistent from bottle to bottle, I have found bottles
 · of the 1970 Grand-Puy-Lacoste that were ripe, deeply colored,
 90 rich on the palate, with oodles of lovely blackcurrant fruitiness,
   but little tannin. Other bottles have displayed an unpleasant barnyard aroma and tannic, acidic, sharp flavors. Two bottles tasted
   in 1988 were excellent, possessing all the characteristics of a
   classic Pauillac. I have come to believe that my bad experiences
   with this wine came from abused (poorly stored) bottles. The wine
   is fully mature with a powerful bouquet of cedar, blackcurrants,
   tar, and herbs. Full bodied, rich, and long, this wine should continue to drink well until the end of the century. It is one of the
   stars of the vintage. Anticipated maturity: Now–2003. Last
   tasted, 12/88.

1967—Premature senility, a problem which seems to have plagued
·   Grand-Puy-Lacoste in the sixties and early seventies, is again the
65   culprit here. Quite brown, with a decaying, leafy aroma, and
         shallow, feeble flavors. Last tasted, 2/83.

1966—A successful wine was produced by Grand-Puy-Lacoste in 1966.
·   Now fully mature, with a moderately intense, smoky, cassis-dom-
84   inated bouquet, soft, savory flavors, and somewhat of a short
         finish, this is an austere wine to enjoy over the next several years
         before it fades. Anticipated maturity: Now–probably in decline.
         Last tasted, 11/84.

1964—Quite successful in this very uneven rain-plagued vintage, the
·   1964 Grand-Puy-Lacoste offers robust, chunky, generous black-
86   currant flavors, a substantial, plump, rustic texture, good length,
         and sizable weight. It is now fully mature, but has the requisite
         depth to last for another 5–7 years. Anticipated maturity: Now–
         1995. Last tasted, 11/88.

1962—Just beginning to fade, this wine has a lovely bouquet of ripe fruit,
·   caramel, and spices with a soft, savory style. It is fruity and lush
82   on the palate, but clearly tails off in the glass. Anticipated matu-
         rity: Now–probably in decline. Last tasted, 9/81.

1961—Certainly not in the top league of 1961s, this moderately dark
·   ruby/garnet wine lacks great concentration, as well as the wealth
85   of fruit and density of color that are the two hallmarks of this
         great vintage. Nevertheless, the wine is very good and now at its
         apogee, with a fine bouquet and ripe, cedary, blackcurrant flavors
         which still have some tannin to lose. Anticipated maturity: Now.
         Last tasted, 9/81.

OLDER VINTAGES

At a dinner party in Bordeaux in 1989, I was astonished by the superb
1947 (I rated it 94) and the 1949 (rated 96). Both wines, from a private
cellar in that city, were remarkably concentrated, rich, expansively flavored wines that demonstrated why Grand-Puy-Lacoste was so highly
regarded in the post–World War II vintages. The 1959, one of my hosts
told me, was just as good, but I have yet to taste a bottle.

HAUT-BAGES-LIBÉRAL (Fifth-Growth)   GOOD

Production: 12,000 cases	Grape varieties: Cabernet Sauvignon—70% Merlot—25% Petit Verdot—5%
Secondary label: none Vineyard size: 61.7 acres	Proprietor: The Merlaut Family Consortium Administrator: Bernadette Villars
Time spent in barrels: 16–18 months	Average age of vines: 24 years

Evaluation of present classification: Should be maintained
Plateau of maturity: 5–15 years following the vintage

This modestly sized château sitting just off Bordeaux's main road of wine, D2, has been making consistently fine undervalued wine since the mid-1970s. Fortunately for consumers, the price has not yet caught up with the château's level of high quality. The vineyard, consisting of three parcels, is superbly situated. The major portion (just over 50%) is adjacent to the main Latour vineyard. Another parcel is next to Pichon Lalande, and a third is further inland near Grand-Puy-Lacoste.

The famous Cruse family of Bordeaux had thoroughly modernized Haut-Bages-Libéral in the seventies, but in 1983 decided to sell the property to the same syndicate that owns and manages two other well-known châteaux, Chasse-Spleen in Moulis and La Gurgue in Margaux. The decision to install the highly talented Bernadette Villars as administrator was hailed as a great coup given her considerable abilities. The vineyard, replanted in the early sixties, is now coming into maturity. No doubt the young vines accounted for the mediocre quality of the wine in the sixties and early seventies. However, in 1975 an excellent wine was produced, and this success has been followed by several recent vintages that have also exhibited high quality, particularly 1985 and 1986. For reasons that are not yet clear, both the 1989 and 1990, while competent wines, were less impressive than I would have anticipated.

Haut-Bages-Libéral produces a strong, ripe, rich, very blackcurranty wine, no doubt as a result of the high percentage of Cabernet Sauvignon.

VINTAGES

1989—The 1989 Haut-Bages-Libéral tasted surprisingly light. It has a
· brilliant ruby/purple color, low acidity, and moderate, soft tan-
84   nins, but finishes short. It is a good effort, but is atypically re-

strained and subdued for a 1989 Pauillac. Did the record-setting crop yields cause the dilution? Anticipated maturity: 1992–1999. Last tasted, 4/91.

1988—The 1988 exhibits some greenness to the tannins, is medium bod-
·   ied, spicy, but light and indifferent. Drink it over the next 5–6
81   years. Anticipated maturity: 1992–1998. Last tasted, 4/91.

1987—Soft, diluted, weedy, and disjointed, the 1987 Haut-Bages-Libéral
·   has a dubious future. Anticipated maturity: Now–1993. Last
72   tasted, 10/89.

1986—The percentage of new oak casks used at Haut-Bages-Libéral was
·   increased and the selection process tightened, and the result in
90   1986 is their finest wine since the 1975, and certainly one of the
       best wines ever made at the property. Dark ruby/purple, with an
       expansive bouquet of plums, sweet toasty oak, and blackcurrants,
       this dense, full-bodied, chewy wine has a suppleness that will
       allow it to be drunk in the early nineties. But it also has the
       balance, richness, and tannin content to age well for at least
       another 20 years. Anticipated maturity: 1993–2015. Last tasted,
       3/90.

1985—The black/ruby-colored 1985 is a rich, dense, full-bodied wine
·   with great color, loads of extract, and a powerful, long, ripe finish.
89   It is one of the stars of the vintage. Anticipated maturity: Now–
       2005. Last tasted, 9/89.

1984—I tasted this wine many times and have terribly inconsistent tast-
·   ing notes covering several plump, fruity, one-dimensional exam-
72   ples to several that tasted overripe, low in acid, and bizarre. From
       a bottle purchased in Bordeaux in 1988, the wine tasted hollow,
       attenuated, and charmless. Anticipated maturity: Now–1993.
       Last tasted, 3/88.

1983—The 1983 is a big, brash, aggressive sort of wine, with intense
·   color, a full-blown bouquet of ripe blackcurrants, deep, full,
85   thick, fruity flavors, and a long, moderately tannic finish. This
       brawny wine has, like many 1983s, matured more quickly than
       expected. Anticipated maturity: Now–1994. Last tasted, 3/89.

1982—This is a very good 1982, with a voluptuous, rich, silky texture,
·   layers of blackcurrant fruit, and some attractive vanillin oaky
87   scents. This fat, densely colored, tannic wine should develop
       quite well over the next decade, despite a noticeable lack of acid-
       ity and a slightly jammy character. Anticipated maturity: Now–
       2003. Last tasted, 5/91.

1981—The 1981 is typical in style for Haut-Bages-Libéral: dark ruby,
·   with a big, spicy, smoky, blackcurrant bouquet, rich, abundant
84   flavors, medium body, and a tannic, slightly astringent finish. For

the vintage, it is a big, chewy mouthful of wine that offers broad crowd appeal. Anticipated maturity: Now–2000. Last tasted, 9/87.

1980—One-dimensional, this wine has a spicy, light intensity, dull bouquet, malnourished flavors, and a short, acidic finish. It needs to
69 be drunk. Anticipated maturity: Now–may be in decline. Last tasted, 11/86.

1979—The 1979 is another full-flavored, robust wine from Haut-Bages-Libéral. Quite dark ruby, with an appealing ripe cassis, spicy
83 bouquet, and a full-bodied, meaty texture, this wine has high acidity and enough tannin to warrant cellaring. Neither refined nor elegant, it is robust, rustic, and straightforward. Anticipated maturity: Now–1997. Last tasted, 2/87.

1978—A solid wine, but given the vintage, it is a bit of a disappointment. Dark ruby, with a stemmy, smoky, somewhat burnt bouquet, the
70 wine is weedy and herbaceous on the palate, with annoyingly high acidity in the finish. The wine's balance is suspect. Anticipated maturity: Now. Last tasted, 6/86.

1976—The 1976 is a notable success in this mixed vintage. Haut-Bages-Libéral is fully mature, yet will hold for another 3–4 years. Dark
84 ruby, with an amber edge, this forceful, spicy, cedary, blackcurrant-scented wine has surprising concentration for the vintage, as well as a juicy, rich, fruity texture. Anticipated maturity: Now–1992. Last tasted, 12/88.

1975—This wine continues to exhibit an impressive dark ruby color, a complex, cedary, ripe fruit, tar-scented bouquet, sweet, rich, in-
89 tense flavors, excellent length, full body, and the potential for another 10–15 years of evolution. The hard tannins of the 1975 vintage are still apparent, but the wine's surprising concentration and extract levels make it one of the better-balanced wines of the vintage. Anticipated maturity: Now–2005. Last tasted, 9/90.

1974—Thin, hollow, and harsh on the palate, this wine lacks fruit and charm. Anticipated maturity: Now–probably in serious decline.
55 Last tasted, 3/79.

1970—Dark ruby, with a spicy, vegetal aroma of celery and cloves, this wine tastes out of balance, with an emerging flavor of herbal tea.
70 Drink up. Anticipated maturity: Now–probably in serious decline. Last tasted, 4/77.

HAUT-BAGES-MONPELOU (Cru Bourgeois)   AVERAGE

Production: 5,000 cases	Grape varieties: Cabernet Sauvignon—75% Merlot—25%
Secondary label: none	
Vineyard size: 25 acres	Proprietor: Emile Castéja
Time spent in barrels: 14–16 months	Average age of vines: 25 years
Evaluation of present classification: Should be maintained	
Plateau of maturity: 2–8 years following the vintage	

This vineyard, located inland near that of Grand-Puy-Lacoste, has been owned by the Castéja family since 1947. The wines, light, fruity, and generally undistinguished, are commercialized exclusively by Mr. Castéja's *négociant* firm, Borie-Manoux.

HAUT-BATAILLEY (Fifth-Growth)   VERY GOOD

Production: 7,500–8,500 cases	Grape varieties: Cabernet Sauvignon—65% Merlot—25% Cabernet Franc—10%
Secondary label: La Tour d'Aspic	
Vineyard size: 49.4 acres	Proprietor: Madame Brest-Borie
Time spent in barrels: 18–20 months	Average age of vines: 28 years
Evaluation of present classification: Should be maintained	
Plateau of maturity: 4–15 years following the vintage	

Haut-Batailley is not one of the better-known estates in Pauillac. The vineyard is managed by the reputable and well-known Jean-Eugène Borie, who lives at Ducru-Beaucaillou in St.-Julien, and also owns Grand-Puy-Lacoste. He oversees this property, which is owned by a cousin. Perhaps the reasons for obscurity within the Pauillac firmament are the modest production, the lack of a château on the estate (the wine is made at Borie's La Couronne estate), and secluded location on the edge of a woods, far away from the Gironde River.

Recent vintages of Haut-Batailley have demonstrated the full potential of the property under the expert winemaking team of Borie and his son. However, the wines of this estate have not always been the model of consistency one would expect. In general, the weakness tends toward lightness and excessive softness in style. Most wines of Haut-Batailley are fully mature long before their first decade ends, an anomaly for a Pauillac. Nevertheless, the last several vintages, particularly the 1989 and 1982, have shown greater concentration and grip than ever before. However, I tend to think of Haut-Batailley as having more of a St.-Julien personality than that of a true Pauillac. That is ironic given the fact that this estate was created in 1942 when it was severed from the original vineyard of Batailley—irrefutably a classic Pauillac in both taste and character.

VINTAGES

1989—The 1989 Haut-Batailley has a gorgeous amount of up-front, satiny
·   fruit, is lush and ripe as well as long. The palate impression is
89   almost one of sweet, jammy fruit because of its superrichness.
        Aging in 50% new oak casks has helped give additional structure.
        This hedonistic wine will warrant drinking over its first decade of
        life. Anticipated maturity: 1992–2002. Last tasted, 4/91.

1988—In comparison to the 1989, the 1988 is a lightweight, lean, closed,
·   hard-edged wine that lacks charm and finesse. The tannin level
83   may prove excessive for the fruit component. Anticipated matu-
        rity: 1993–1998. Last tasted, 4/91.

1987—Far more flattering to taste than the 1988, Haut-Batailley has
·   turned in a respectable performance in 1987. The wine is round,
82   agreeably fruity, spicy, and charming. It should be drunk over
        the next 3–4 years. Anticipated maturity: Now–1994. Last tasted,
        4/90.

1986—After tasting this wine several times out of cask, I had believed
·   that the 1986 Haut-Batailley was one of the finest wines made at
84   this estate in more than a decade. However, three tastings from
        the bottle have revealed a wine that is attractive, but does not
        have the depth or aging potential that I originally thought. It is
        atypically supple and silky for a 1986, with a pleasing currant
        fruitiness married nicely to toasty oak. It is medium bodied, but
        seems to fall off on the palate, revealing a diffuse character.
        Anticipated maturity: Now–1996. Last tasted, 6/90.

1985—The 1985 is a soft, agreeable, elegantly wrought wine that is
·   fruity, medium bodied, and tasty, but likely to be short-lived.
85   Anticipated maturity: Now–1995. Last tasted, 3/89.

1984—Aged aromas of tea are followed by an adequately fruity wine that
·   is light and shallow. The 1984 Haut-Batailley should be drunk up.
74   Anticipated maturity: Now–1993. Last tasted, 6/88.

1983 — An indifferent vintage for Haut-Batailley, the wine exhibits youth-
·   ful, dark ruby color, attractive, fat, soft flavors, moderate tannins,
82   and an unusual dryness on the palate. It has never tasted harmo-
     nious. Anticipated maturity: Now–1995. Last tasted, 3/89.

1982 — The best Haut-Batailley I have tasted. Voluptuous, almost sweet,
·   ripe, rich berry fruit and vanillin oakiness soar from the glass.
90   Quite intense, supple, and profoundly concentrated, this wine
     delivers a stunning display of superripe fruit, with adequate tan-
     nin to give it focus and balance. This is a great Haut-Batailley.
     Anticipated maturity: 1992–2005. Last tasted, 1/90.

1981 — This is one of my favorite Haut-Batailleys between 1971 and 1981.
·   Silky on the palate and quite perfumed, with a pronounced oaky
85   bouquet, this velvety, round, pleasant wine is quite delicious. It
     has matured rapidly. Anticipated maturity: Now–1995. Last
     tasted, 2/88.

1979 — Lacking depth and concentration, this light- to medium-ruby-col-
·   ored wine has a pleasant, round, supple texture, medium body,
76   and a light finish. Anticipated maturity: Now. Last tasted, 3/87.

1978 — A very charming, supple wine that is a delight to drink now, the
·   1978 Haut-Batailley is a straightforward, effusively fruity wine,
82   with a nice touch of spicy oak, light tannins, and a warm, round
     finish. Ready now. Anticipated maturity: Now. Last tasted, 4/84.

1976 — Fully mature with soft, supple, rather modest flavors, low acidity,
·   an amber/ruby color, and a short finish. Drink immediately! An-
74   ticipated maturity: Now–may be in decline. Last tasted, 9/80.

1975 — The astringency of the 1975 vintage has given this wine atypical
·   backbone and firmness, especially for a Haut-Batailley. A dark
81   ruby color with just a trace of amber is followed by a wine that
     has a ripe, plummy, open-knit bouquet dominated by the smell of
     cedar and herbs. Medium bodied, with moderate tannins, ade-
     quate depth and texture, this is a dull 1975. Anticipated maturity:
     Now–1995. Last tasted, 10/88.

1973 — Shallow, watery, and now quite decrepit, this wine was at its
·   meager best in 1978. It is of little interest now. Last tasted, 6/86.
64

1970 — The 1970 is a top-flight effort for Haut-Batailley, and a wine that
·   behaves in personality and character like a true Pauillac, rather
87   than a St.-Julien. Rather rich and full for Haut-Batailley, with a
     good, firm underpinning of tannins still evident, this dark ruby
     wine has a complex bouquet and fine long finish. Anticipated
     maturity: Now–1995. Last tasted, 10/83.

1966—Solid, firm, true in style to the 1966 vintage, Haut-Batailley has
 ·   evolved slowly, and is presently at its apogee. A modest bouquet
84   of spices and blackcurrant fruit is quite attractive. It is medium
      bodied with good, rather than excellent, concentration. The finish
      is solid and a bit tough. Anticipated maturity: Now–1994. Last
      tasted, 4/82.

1962—This moderately fruity wine has soft, round, easygoing flavors, a
 ·   good finish, and a fully developed bouquet. It has been fully ma-
84   ture for over a decade. Drink up! Anticipated maturity: Now–may
      be in decline. Last tasted, 3/83.

1961—In the context of the vintage's great reputation, this wine tastes
 ·   atypical and comparable to the style of the 1962. Soft, ripe, spicy
84   fruit on the nose reveals full maturity. However, the intense ripe-
      ness that exists in so many 1961s is not present in Haut-Batailley.
      Soft, round, plump, fruity flavors are overlaid with oak in this
      medium-bodied wine. Drink up. Anticipated maturity: Now–
      1995. Last tasted, 7/83.

LAFITE-ROTHSCHILD (First-Growth)   OUTSTANDING

Production: 26,000–33,000 cases	Grape varieties:
	Cabernet Sauvignon—70%
	Merlot—20%
	Cabernet Franc—5%
	Petit Verdot—5%
Secondary label: Moulin des Carruades	
Vineyard size: 222 acres	Proprietor: Barons de Rothschild
	Administrator: Eric de Rothschild
Time spent in barrels: 24–30 months	Average age of vines: 40 years
Evaluation of present classification: Should be maintained	
Plateau of maturity: 10–35 or more years following the vintage	

Bordeaux's most famous property and wine, Lafite-Rothschild, with its
elegant, undersized, and understated label has become a name synonymous with wealth, prestige, history, respect, and wines of remarkable
longevity.

While the vintages since 1975 have witnessed the production of a
succession of superlative Lafites, the record of Lafite between 1961 and
1974 was one of surprising mediocrity for a first-growth. It has always

remained a mystery to me why more wine critics did not cry foul after tasting some of the Lafite wines made during this period. The official line from the château has always been that the wines were made in such a light, elegant style that they were overmatched in blind tastings by bigger, more robust wines. Certainly such things do happen, but the mediocrity of Lafite was particularly evidenced by wines from very fine vintages—1966, 1970, 1971—that were surprisingly deficient in color, excessively dry and overly oaked, and abnormally high in acidity. Several vintages—1969, 1971, 1974—were complete failures yet released for high prices under the Lafite name.

The reasons for such occurrences are not likely to ever be revealed by the Rothschild family, but given the great record of successes since 1975, the problems in the sixties and early seventies seem related to the following. The absentee and casually interested owners lived in Paris and casually supervised the goings-on at Lafite. Certainly the management of Lafite since 1975 has been diligent by a concerned and committed Eric de Rothschild. Additionally, the wine at Lafite was kept too long in oak barrels. In the past, the wine often aged a minimum of 32–36 months in oak barrels, whereas now 24–30 months is maximum. This change has undoubtedly caused Lafite to taste fruitier and fresher. Thirdly, the current winemaking staff at Lafite consciously pick the grapes later to obtain greater ripeness and lower acidity in their wines.* Finally, Lafite-Rothschild is being bottled over a shorter period of time. There have been unsubstantiated reports that Lafite often dragged out the bottling operation over as many as 8–12 months. If true, then more-than-acceptable levels of bottle variation would exist.

Regardless of the record of the immediate past, Lafite-Rothschild is now producing great wines, and the turnabout in quality clearly occurred with the magnificent 1975. One could successfully argue that, since 1981, Lafite-Rothschild has produced one of the Médoc's best wines in years such as 1981, 1982, 1983, 1986, 1987, 1988, and 1990.

VINTAGES

1989—Even if the 1989 is not as perfect as the 1982, or as potentially
    ·   long-lived as the 1986 and 1988, it is still a great Lafite. The wine
    92   is forward, with the telltale fragrance of lead pencils, cedar, and
         currancy fruit. Because of a high glycerin and abundant alcohol

* The selection process is undoubtedly more severe than in the past. In the abundant vintages of the late eighties, Lafite routinely eliminated half of their crop. In 1990, a whopping 60% of the harvest was either sold off in bulk or relegated to the second wine.

content, the hot, early harvest has clearly stamped an imprint on Lafite. The wine is almost too easy to taste and appreciate, as it is rich, medium to full bodied, expansive, and more supple and obvious than usual. Speculating when this wine might be in full blossom is no easy chore given its sexy, sensual style. It is somewhere between the 1953 and 1976 in stylistic terms. Anticipated maturity: 1997–2020. Last tasted, 4/91.

1988 — The 1988 Lafite is the wine of the Médoc, as well as a top candi-
· date for the wine of the vintage. Much deeper in color than the
95 1989, the 1988 has the classic Lafite bouquet of cedar, subtle herbs, dried pit fruits, and cassis. Extremely concentrated, with brilliantly focused flavors and huge tannins, this backward yet impressively endowed Lafite-Rothschild will probably never enjoy the publicity of the 1982, 1986, and 1989, but do not be surprised to see it rivaling those wines in 15–20 years. Anticipated maturity: 2000–2035. Last tasted, 4/91.

1987 — I would not be surprised to see this wine fill out with several
· additional years in the bottle, largely because Lafite is a noto-
87 riously bad performer in the first few years after bottling. Out of cask, the 1987 was the most complex wine I tasted from this vintage, but now, the nose seems only a fraction of what it was from cask. The lead-pencil, vanillin-scented, leafy, cedary bouquet is just beginning to emerge. In the mouth, the wine is light, displaying a soft, supple texture, some acidity, but little tannin. It will probably improve, and may ultimately merit a higher score. Anticipated maturity: Now–1999. Last tasted, 10/90.

1986 — The 1986 is vastly superior to the 1985, and it is one of the block-
· busters of the vintage. Lafite's 1986 possesses outstanding rich-
99 ness, a deep color, medium body, a graceful, harmonious texture, and very fine length. In particular, its extraordinary perfume of cedar, chestnuts, minerals, and rich fruit should guarantee that this turns out to be a legendary Lafite. In 15–20 years, it should rival past legends such as the 1959 and 1953. Anticipated maturity: 2000–2030. Last tasted, 5/91.

1985 — The 1985 Lafite should be better, but for followers of fashion, its
· star-studded price will fetch you a moderately intense, cedary,
87 woody, herb-and-leather-scented bouquet, and attractive, very forward and developed flavors displayed in a medium-bodied format. The finish is softly tannic and after a pensive sip, one is likely to ask, Is this all there is? Anticipated maturity: 1995–2008. Last tasted, 3/91.

1984—The personality of Lafite comes through in the 1984 vintage. An
· elegant bouquet of herbaceous, cedary fruit is first class. New
84 oak dominates the palate and some hard tannins exhibit a dryness
at the finish. The 1984 is a light but well-balanced wine. Anticipated maturity: Now–1997. Last tasted, 1/88.

1983—The 1983 has shed its tannic shell, yet I am sure it will still require
· another 8–10 years to mature. A dark-colored wine, with excel-
92 lent concentration, and a surprisingly tough, fleshy texture, it
seems to have more in common with the wines made at Latour.
However, the bouquet of celestial cedar and black fruits intertwined with minerals is classic Lafite. Along with Château Margaux and Palmer, this is one of the three strongest candidates for
wine of the vintage. Anticipated maturity: 1998–2030. Last
tasted, 10/90.

1982—There is probably no great wine of Bordeaux that has provided
· more disappointments to me than Lafite-Rothschild. In such ex-
100 traordinary vintages as 1945, 1947, 1949, 1961, and 1970, this
wine was nowhere near the quality level if should have been. Yet,
when Lafite does everything right, as it did in 1953, 1959, 1975,
1976, 1981, 1982, 1986, 1988, and 1990, their wines are perhaps
as compellingly profound and complex as any wine made in Bordeaux. It is a wine that often needs a good 4–5 years after bottling
to really prove its potential.

In recent tastings of 1982s I attended, the 1982 Lafite-Rothschild was staggering. In one tasting I confused it with the Mouton-Rothschild. Yet, it should be easy to identify because of its
fascinating perfume of cedar, spicy oak, currants, herbs, and
minerals. The 1982 is a good decade away from maturity, and
seems to have all the prerequisites needed to age for 25–35 years.
The wine is now even deeper colored than I remember, displaying
a black/ruby color with absolutely no sign of age, an incredibly
rich, expansive, penetrating bouquet that is truly the sort of stuff
that makes legends. On the palate, the wine is atypically powerful, rich, and concentrated for a Lafite-Rothschild, but is impeccably poised and balanced, with all of the elegance one expects
but so rarely gets from this great property. This is truly a dazzling
wine of monumental proportions. Anticipated maturity: 2000–
2025. Last tasted, 5/91.

1981—Possessing the classic Lafite bouquet, as well as being the most
· interesting and complex wine among the 1981 Médocs, the 1981
93 Lafite is just beginning to open. Ripe blackcurrant fruit intermin-

gled with cedary scents and spices is extremely promising. On
the palate the wine is hard, quite tannic, rich, and full bodied,
with long length and a multidimensional personality. Although
elegant and significantly less weighty than the 1982 or 1986, it has
obviously been vinified to last for decades. Anticipated maturity:
1992–2025. Last tasted, 3/91.

1980—A lightweight, agreeable wine from Lafite, the 1980 has a moder-
·   ately intense aroma of cassis and fresh tobacco, and soft, charm-
83   ing flavors. A success for the vintage. Anticipated maturity: Now–
       1994. Last tasted, 6/87.

1979—Not quite the size of the 1981, but graceful and perhaps more
·   typically Lafite than the 1982 or 1983, this wine has a dark ruby
90   color, a tight but complex bouquet of blackcurrants, spice, and
       vanillin oakiness, medium body, firm tannins, and a long, crisp
       finish. Anticipated maturity: Now–2005. Last tasted, 10/84.

1978—If vintage charts were always correct, this 1978 would be con-
·   sidered far superior to the 1979 Lafite. However, I personally tend
88   to prefer the 1979. Medium ruby with some amber, a pronounced
       ripe, savory, fruity, cedary, slightly herbaceous bouquet, surpris-
       ingly approachable velvety flavors, and a long, supple finish, this
       moderately tannic wine seems to be developing quickly. Antici-
       pated maturity: Now–2005. Last tasted, 6/90.

1976—The 1976 Lafite clearly stands far above the crowd in this vintage.
·   A beautiful bouquet of seductive cedarwood, spices, and ripe fruit
96   precedes a very concentrated, darkly colored wine, with great
       length and texture. Some amber is just beginning to appear at the
       edge. The 1976 may turn out to be the best Lafite of the '70s. It is
       gorgeous to drink at present, but it will keep. Anticipated matu-
       rity: Now–2005. Last tasted, 5/91.

1975—1975 was a watershed vintage for Lafite-Rothschild. Emile Pey-
·   naud, Bordeaux's famed oenologist, oversaw the vinification while
96   Lafite was in search of a new winemaker. The first great Lafite
       since 1959, in weight, power, and style it coincidentally resembles
       the 1959. An intense cedary, ripe, rich, fruity, tobacco-scented
       bouquet seems at times to suggest a great Graves. On the palate,
       the wine explodes with deep fruit, full body, remarkable texture
       and length. It is great wine that tastes less complex, but more
       powerful than the superb 1976. Anticipated maturity: Now–2010.
       Last tasted, 6/91.

1974—It was very difficult to make good wine in 1974, but certainly a
·   first-growth is expected to make a strict selection of its best lots
56   and sell only the best. This wine is browning badly, has a tired,

stale, flat taste, and is inexcusably diluted, and very short and thin on the palate. Quite poor. Last tasted, 11/82.

1973—One of the charming 1973s, this light, somewhat watery, thin wine
· has Lafite's classic perfumed bouquet, short, compact, agreeable
72 flavors, and little tannin. That was in 1980, the last time I tasted it. Anticipated maturity: Now—probably in serious decline. Last tasted, 12/80.

1971—Another disappointment for Lafite, the 1971 has always tasted
· flat, is quite brown in color, with a stewed, slightly dirty, rusty,
60 nondescript bouquet suggesting a poor *élevage* (the French term for bringing up the wine). Now close to its demise, this wine is of no value except to those who care only for labels. Last tasted, 11/82.

1970—Upon graduation from law school, my parents gave me a case of
· this wine. I was simply overjoyed to get it, knowing the chateau's
79 reputation and the excellence of the 1970 vintage. Tastings from my own supply and elsewhere have always left me questioning the wine's lack of intensity and richness. The bouquet is richly perfumed with the scent of cedarwood and ripe fruit, but on the palate, the wine tastes slightly sour, acidic, and looks surprisingly light in color for a 1970. A perplexing wine that with time has seen the bouquet grow more complex and the flavors more shallow and acidic. Subsequent tastings have firmly convinced me that the 1970 Lafite is barely above average. Several bottles opened in April 1990 in Bordeaux with the firm of Nathaniel Johnston confirmed the mediocrity of this wine. Anticipated maturity: Now—1998. Last tasted, 4/90.

1969—The 1969 Lafite has been consistently unusual to smell, with a
· cooked, burnt aroma, short flavors that suggest coffee and herbs,
62 and a hollow framework. This is a poorly made, ungracious wine that is unpalatable. Last tasted, 11/78.

1967—A vintage in which Lafite could certainly have done better. Light
· ruby with browning very much in evidence, this wine in the mid-
72 1970s had a fragrant, spicy, charming bouquet, easygoing, simple fruity flavors, and light tannins. Now it is quite tired with old, faded, fruit flavors. Drink up! Anticipated maturity: Now—probably in serious decline. Last tasted, 12/80.

1966—1966 is a very highly regarded vintage in which the 1966 Lafite is
· a mirror image of the 1970. Highly acclaimed in certain corners,
84 I have the same problems with the 1966 Lafite as I did with the 1970. The bouquet is complex enough, although not particularly deep or intense, but on the palate, the wine is disturbingly light,

a trifle too acidic, and very dry, astringent, and austere in the finish. Furthermore, the color is quite pale when compared with other top 1966s. Certainly good, but hardly a notable success given the vintage's reputation. Where's the fruit? It will hold for 10–15 years, but why wait? Anticipated maturity: Now–2002. Last tasted, 1/89.

1964—Given the overblown praise for the 1961, 1966, and 1970 Lafites,
·   it seems as though the 1964, a wine obviously made after the
80   rains, is a wine that has taken more criticism than it deserves. Not that it is sublime or profound, but it has consistently shown a chunky, fruity character, and a whiff of some of Lafite's fabulous bouquet. Anticipated maturity: Now. Last tasted, 7/82.

1962—This wine has been fully mature for several decades, but it contin-
·   ues to drink well. In fact, two tastings in 1991 were encouraging.
86   The classic Lafite bouquet of lead pencils, tobacco, herbs, cedar, and spices is this wine's greatest attraction. In the mouth, the wine is soft, elegant, somewhat short, but round and gentle. It has been living dangerously for over a decade, so why hold on to it? Anticipated maturity: Now–1996. Last tasted, 5/91.

1961—This wine has a phenomenal reputation. However, I have now
·   tasted the wine on eight separate occasions where I found it to be
84   shockingly light, too acidic, disturbingly austere, and surprisingly ungenerous for a 1961. Moreover, recent tastings have suggested that the wine was clearly drying out. The color is light ruby with a brownish cast. The wine does have the penetrating "cigar box" Lafite bouquet, yet even it seems shy, given the legendary status of this wine. Lacking the weight, concentration, and majesty of the great 1961s, this is a wine about which far too many writers have euphemistically said that it "needed time," was "elegant," or "not properly understood," when they should have used the words overrated and disappointing. In the context of the vintage and the estate of Lafite-Rothschild, it represents an indifferent winemaking effort. Caveat emptor. Anticipated maturity: Now–2000. Last tasted, 12/89.

OLDER VINTAGES

My Lafite scorecard is dotted with far more disappointments than successes. In the fifties, Lafite-Rothschild produced two monumental wines, the 1953 (rated 97 in April 1990 when drunk from magnum) and the 1959 (a 96–98 wine). The former needs drinking up soon; the latter will last for another 20–30 years. The 1950, 1952, and 1955 are uninspir-ing. The 1957, while not great, is nevertheless surprisingly good (twice I have rated it in the 86–88 range). In the forties, the 1947 is disappointing, the 1949 good, but far from profound, and the 1945 excessively astringent and out of balance. Among the ancient vintages, I have very good notes only for one vintage in the thirties (not a good decade for Bordeaux). The 1934 (rated 90), drunk from magnum in 1986, was wonderful.

In April 1991, I had the opportunity to taste (from a friend's cellar in Bordeaux) the 1929, 1928, 1926, and 1924. The wines had been purchased in the thirties and kept in a cold Bordeaux cellar until this tasting. All of them were disappointing with scores of 59 for the 1929 (faded and sickly), 68 for the 1928 (some elegance but attenuated and short as well as the only Lafite ever pasteurized), 67 for the 1926 (hard, dried out), and 69 for the 1924 (slightly more freshness than the 1926).

I had the legendary 1870 at lunch with Eric de Rothschild in November 1990, and it still possessed some fruit but the bouquet most closely resembled a foul sewer and it would not blow off. Eric de Rothschild claimed to have tasted a far superior bottle several weeks earlier. *C'est la vie!* The saying "There are no great wines, only great bottles," was appropriate after my experience with the 1870.

LATOUR (First-Growth)   OUTSTANDING

Production: 20,000 cases	Grape varieties: Cabernet Sauvignon—80% Merlot—10% Cabernet Franc—10%
Secondary label: Les Forts de Latour	
Vineyard size: 148 acres	Proprietor: Allied-Lyons, a British syndicate Administrator: Christian Le Sommer
Time spent in barrels: 20–24 months	Average age of vines: 35 years
Evaluation of present classification: Should be maintained	
Plateau of maturity: Before 1983, 15–40 years following the vintage; since 1983, 10–25 years following the vintage	

Impressively situated on the Pauillac/St.-Julien border, immediately north of the walled vineyard of Léoville-Las Cases, Latour's vineyard can be easily spotted from the road because of the creamy-colored, fortress-like tower. Notably depicted on the wine's label, this formidable tower overlooking the vineyards and the Gironde River remains from the seventeenth century, when it was built on the site of a fifteenth-century fortress used by the English to fend off attacks by pirates.

Latour is one of a handful of major Bordeaux châteaux to be controlled

by foreign interests. Since 1963, Latour has been under English ownership with the French retaining a minority interest in the estate.

The wine produced here has been an impeccable and classic model of
consistent excellence, both in great, mediocre, and poor vintages. For
that reason, many have long considered Latour to be the Médoc's finest
wine. Latour's reputation for making Bordeaux's best wine in mediocre
or in poor vintages—such as 1960, 1972, 1974—has been totally justified,
although in the recent poor Bordeaux vintages—1977, 1980, and 1984—
Latour's wines were surprisingly light and eclipsed in quality by a number of other châteaux. The wine of Latour also has a remarkable record
of being a stubbornly slow-developing wine, requiring a good 20–25 years
of bottle age to shed its considerable tannic clout and reveal its stunning
power, depth, and richness. This style, often referred to by commentators as virile, masculine, and tough, may be undergoing a subtle, yet very
perceptible softening up. This is adamantly denied by the staff at Latour,
but my tastings of recent vintages, particularly those from 1978 onward,
irrefutably suggest a more gentle and accessible style.

While the 1982, and to a lesser extent the 1986, are undeniably great
Latours, on the whole the estate did not have a distinguished decade.
Insiders suggested the tiny *cuverie* was too small to handle the gigantic
crop sizes of 1983, 1985, and 1986. As a consequence, the fermentation
tanks had to be emptied too soon in order to make room for the arriving
grapes. The underground cellars and *cuverie* were subsequently enlarged
—just in time to handle 1989, the largest vintage ever harvested in Bordeaux. However, an objective tasting analysis of the 1979, 1981, 1983,
1985, 1988, and 1989 Latours leaves one with the impression that in these
years, Latour is a significantly lighter, less powerful and concentrated
wine than it was in any decade earlier in this century.

The property's flirtation with a more accessible, lighter style may have
ended if my instincts about the barrel tastings of the 1990 are on target.
In 1990, an ambitious David Orr became the new chairman of the board
and instituted a brutal selection process. The 1990 looks to be a return
to the black/purple-colored, opaque, broad-shouldered, massive style
Latour exhibited in years past.

Even if a more supple, earlier-maturing Latour is now being crafted by
the winemaking staff, the wine of Latour remains one of Bordeaux's most
concentrated, rich, tannic, and full-bodied wines. When mature, it has a
unique bouquet of fresh walnuts and leather, blackcurrants and gravelly,
mineral scents. While comparing the great vintages of the famous first-
growths of Pauillac over the years 1945–1975, it is interesting to note
that regardless of the vintage, Latour will have the darkest color, the
most reticent bouquet, and a restrained, but rich, deep, full-bodied,
muscular character and texture on the palate. Lafite-Rothschild tends to

have the lightest color, and when vinified properly, the finest and most complex bouquet. Yet in Lafite-Rothschild, the surge of complex aromas is often followed by a wine that is sharper, more acidic, and less weighty on the palate. Mouton-Rothschild tends to be darker in color than Lafite, yet lighter than Latour. However, in a great vintage, Mouton-Rothschild is the most silky and decadently opulent of the three wines. Since 1975, the wine of Lafite has taken on greater strength and vigor, and since 1982 Mouton has become significantly richer and fuller, while Latour has become lighter. Consequently, generalizations about the styles of these three great wines are less valid today than they were a mere 5 years ago.

VINTAGES

1989—The 1989 Latour is one of that great estate's more notable efforts, since their monumental 1982. (However, the 1990 will be the vin-
89 tage that announces the "return" of Latour.) Deep ruby/purple, with a penetrating bouquet of cassis, this elegant, medium-bodied, surprisingly approachable wine is bursting with fruit and extract. The finish is admirably long and persistent. The wine has a high tannin count (although lower than the 1990), but the tannins are largely obscured by the wine's fine fruit and depth. For lovers of Latour, this is a shockingly understated wine. Anticipated maturity: 1997–2015. Last tasted, 4/91.

1988—The 1988 is deep in color, has a complex mineral-and-blackcurrant-scented bouquet, medium body, nicely extracted flavors, but
88 ferocious tannins in the finish. Patience will most definitely be required for the 1988, which may prove to be longer lived than the 1989. However, I doubt it will ever offer as much pleasure. Anticipated maturity: 2000–2025. Last tasted, 4/91.

1987—The 1987 Latour was made from 75% Cabernet Sauvignon and 25% Merlot, without any Cabernet Franc or Petit Verdot used in
86 the blend. The wine has a deep ruby color, and a surprisingly backward yet promising bouquet of blackcurrants, spicy oak, and herbs. In the mouth, it is medium bodied, exhibits more power and tannin than many wines in this vintage, and finishes with surprising authority. It is one of the few 1987s that I find not ready to drink. It and Mouton-Rothschild are the only two wines that will actually last more than 15 years. The 1987 is a notable success for Latour, comparable to their 1983 and 1985. Anticipated maturity: 1992–2010. Last tasted, 4/91.

1986—The 1986 Latour has a sensational deep ruby/purple color, a promising bouquet of mineral-scented, blackcurrant fruit inter-
91 mixed with the classic walnut scents that seem to emerge from

Latour's well-placed vineyard. On the palate, the wine is undoubtedly excellent, with medium to full body, very fine concentration, and impressive length. However, there is a certain flatness in the middle palate, and by Latour's standards the wine is not as brawny or as potentially monumental as I would have suspected in a vintage where the Cabernet Sauvignon and other Médoc first-growths excelled. Nevertheless, this wine should easily last 20–25 years, but I do not see it taking a place as one of the many extraordinary wines that have been produced at this property. Anticipated maturity: 1996–2012. Last tasted, 5/91.

1985—Somewhat weak when considered in the context of what Latour
·   is capable of achieving, the 1985 is medium bodied, has a good
87   but not dense ruby color, a moderately intense berry fragrance, and fine depth and length, but is surprisingly light and accessible for the style of this estate. Anticipated maturity: 1992–2008. Last tasted, 5/91.

1984—Curiously, the 1984 tastes nearly as fine as the lightish 1985.
·   Spicy, woodsy, mineral, herbal scents and ripe fruit swell in the
84   glass. It has good length and grip, plus adequate tannin for 5–9 years of further cellaring. Anticipated maturity: Now–1997. Last tasted, 3/89.

1983—As one might expect, the 1983 Latour has a medium color, but
·   tastes flabby and disjointed, and lacks firmness and structure.
87   The use of 100% new oak barrels has provided some needed framework, but this wine is not likely to be one of Latour's greats. The wine is outdistanced by the rival first-growth Pauillacs— Lafite-Rothschild and Mouton-Rothschild. A rather disappointing effort. Anticipated maturity: 1992–2005. Last tasted, 3/89.

1982—This is a big, deep, rich, intense Latour with the 1982 vintage's
·   telltale personality traits—great dark ruby/purple color, a terrific
98   ripe, highly concentrated lushness, and significant tannin content. Early on, the wine did not have the backward toughness usually associated with this château but in 1990, the wine had firmed up considerably and appeared poised for a 30- to 35-year life span. It is undoubtedly one of the two best Latours since the 1961. Anticipated maturity: 1997–2025. Last tasted, 5/91.

1981—The 1981 tastes remarkably velvety and supple for such a young
·   Latour—not that this is a malevolent occurrence—because the ex-
88   cellence, complexity, and richness of the wine are still present. The color is dark ruby, the bouquet offers plenty of ripe cassis and spicy oak, and the flavor is generous, silky, moderately tannic, and long in the finish. This Latour may turn out to be similar to the 1971. Anticipated maturity: 1993–2005. Last tasted, 9/90.

1980—In the mediocre vintages of the fifties, sixties and early seventies,
·   Latour frequently made the best wine in the Médoc. Not so in
83   1980. The wine is clearly well above average for the vintage, but
        lacks weight and richness. Fruity, charming, supple, with a pleas-
        ant fruitiness, it is slightly short on the palate. Anticipated matu-
        rity: Now–1994. Last tasted, 11/84.

1979—From cask samples, the 1979 Latour tasted typically tough, back-
·   ward, and astringent, but now it is surprisingly precocious and
87   forward, although not yet ready to drink. Dark ruby with an in-
        tense bouquet, filled with cassis fruit, some scents of cedarwood
        and vanillin, this medium-bodied Latour has well-balanced, fleshy
        flavors, an underlying supple, smooth texture, and ripe, round
        tannin in the finish. Reminiscent of the 1971 Latour, only lighter.
        Anticipated maturity: 1992–2000. Last tasted, 11/89.

1978—The 1978 is a magnificent Latour, and should turn out to be the
·   second-best wine produced by Latour in the seventies. While it
93   can't match the incredible concentration of the massive 1970, or
        the pure strength of the powerful 1975, it is impeccably balanced
        with oodles of ripe blackcurrant fruit, fat, intensely concentrated
        flavors with a stunningly big bouquet, and a long, deep, very fine
        finish. It is ready to drink. Anticipated maturity: Now–2010. Last
        tasted, 5/91.

1976—I have had my share of arguments with Latour's staff over the
·   relative merits of this wine, which I deem slightly shallow, lacking
83   depth, and, for a Latour, somewhat hollow and angular on the
        palate. Of course, the château thinks differently, but the proof is,
        as always, in the bottle. The wine succeeds for the vintage, but
        this Latour is not likely to get better, only worse as the fruit
        continues to fade and the harsh tannins ascend. Anticipated ma-
        turity: Now–1996. Last tasted, 2/87.

1975—Of the recent vintages of Latour, this is the most backward as it
·   begs for 10–15 or more years of cellaring. Still young, astringent,
92   and very impressive as it approaches is sixteenth birthday, this
        Latour has a splendid blackcurrant aroma, with a whiff of cedar,
        mineral scents, and walnuts. This wine will reward the patient
        collector with greatness at the turn of the century. It is still amaz-
        ingly backward. Anticipated maturity: 2000–2025. Last tasted,
        5/91.

1974—In this mediocre year of rather green, stalky, hollow wines, La-
·   tour produced one of the very best wines of the vintage. Still not
86   fully mature, this dark ruby wine has good fruit, a medium body,
        surprising depth and ripeness for the vintage, and a sinewy,
        tannic finish. It avoids the telltale harshness and fruit deficiency

found in so many 1974s. Anticipated maturity: 1992–2000. Last tasted, 10/90.

1973—A featherweight for Latour, even considering the watery, diluted
   • character of most wines from this vintage, the 1973 Latour still
   78 offers light, charming, somewhat complex drinking as it has held together much better than I would have suspected. Soft, ripe, moderately intense flavors seem dominated by Merlot and exhibit no tannin. This atypical Latour requires immediate drinking. Anticipated maturity: Now. Last tasted, 2/87.

1972—A disastrous vintage for Bordeaux, yet Latour produced a rather
   • big, deeply colored, somewhat disjointed, and clumsy wine, but
   75 one with good fruit, a herbaceous, cedary bouquet, and good flavor concentration. Drink now! Anticipated maturity: Now—may be in decline. Last tasted, 12/83.

1971—Just beginning to enter its plateau of maturity, this graceful wine
   • exudes blackcurrants, cedar, and iron-like scents from its bou-
   91 quet. Dark ruby with just a trace of amber, this wine has very good concentration, a lightly tannic finish, and a fleshy, chewy texture. Medium weight for a Latour, yet remarkably flavorful and concentrated for a 1971, this is the wine of the Médoc as well as a terribly underrated Latour. Anticipated maturity: Now–2008. Last tasted, 5/91.

1970—One of the most massive Latours produced in the post-World War
   • II era, the 1970 is bigger and richer than any Latour in this period
   99 except the 1945, 1959, 1961, and 1982. Extremely full bodied, enormously concentrated, astonishingly slow to develop, impenetrably dark ruby, and yet so, so promising. Dense, powerful, and overpowering on the palate, this huge wine is the wine of the vintage. Anticipated maturity: 1995–2030. Last tasted, 5/91.

1969—In this ungracious vintage Latour produced an acceptable wine of
   • average color and concentration, but lean, angular, and charm-
   74 less. Anticipated maturity: Now—may be in decline. Last tasted, 6/76.

1967—Unquestionably the best wine produced in the Médoc in 1967, the
   • Latour has dark ruby color with some browning at the edges, a
   88 medium- to full-bodied feel, plenty of blackcurrant fruit, and some light, soft tannins still present. Head and shoulders above the other first-growths, this wine has the classic Latour bouquet of black walnuts, blackcurrants, mineral scents, and cedarwood. Anticipated maturity: Now–1997. Last tasted, 1/85.

1966—This is a great wine. Not only is it the finest of all the Médoc first-
   • growths in 1966, it has turned out to be the wine of the vintage.
   95 Very dark ruby color with an amber edge, the wine boasts a top-

notch bouquet of leather, spices, tobacco, and ripe fruit. Quite
concentrated, rich and powerful, it has shed much of its ferocious
tannins and is easily the best wine produced by Latour in the
sixties, omitting of course, the monumental 1961. Anticipated
maturity: Now–2008. Last tasted, 5/91.

1964— In 1964, as in 1966 and 1967, Latour was the best wine in the
·   Médoc. The 1964 is drinking beautifully now, but it should hold
90   for at least another decade. The bouquet is powerful, spicy, and
filled with aromas of minerals, black fruits, and licorice. Rich,
round, supple, generous flavors show excellent concentration.
Soft tannins and a silky, rich, very long finish make this a sumptuous, even opulent Latour. Anticipated maturity: Now–2005.
Last tasted, 5/91.

1962— Latour, once again, produced one of the finest wines of the vin-
·   tage. This hefty, powerful wine has a dense, almost opaque color,
93   significantly less charm and roundness than the 1964, but concentrated, thick, rich flavor that still exhibits surprising tannins. This
is an old-style, heavyweight Latour that can be drunk now or held
for at least two more decades. Some Latour observers claim this
is the last of the thick, highly extracted Latours made prior to the
château's acquisition of stainless-steel vats in 1964. I disagree.
Anticipated maturity: Now–2010. Last tasted, 5/91.

1961— A remarkably viscous, huge, intense wine that is one of the big-
·   gest and richest wines I have ever tasted from Latour. The 1961
100   is port-like, with an almost syrupy character, yet so well balanced
given its herculean proportions. A phenomenal bouquet of English
walnuts, cassis, and cedar inundates the nose. A wine with incredible concentration and length, the 1961 Latour has the potential to last another 50 years. Anticipated maturity: 2000–2050.
Last tasted, 4/90.

OLDER VINTAGES

The fifties were not nearly as successful for Latour as were the sixties.
The 1959 (consistently rated between 94 and 98) is the château's only
heroic effort in that decade. The 1953 is disappointing, particularly in
the context of the year. Both the 1955 and 1952 are more interesting but
far from dazzling. The 1949 is magnificent (when last tasted in March
1989, I gave it a 98). I prefer it to the renowned 1945 (always a bit too
astringent and volatile), and to the terribly inconsistent 1947. The latter
vintage never impressed me until April 1990 when I drank a stunning
bottle in Bordeaux (served blind) with Jean-François Moueix and Dominique Renard. I rated it a 90. Drunk again in May 1991, the 1947 was
very good, slightly volatile with an orange, ice tea-like color.

Among the truly ancient vintages, I found the 1928 incredible in 1988 (a 99 rating), and the famous 1929 (rated 87 in November 1990) becoming volatile and attenuated, but still delicious. The immortal 1870, drunk from a magnum in the late eighties (I rated it 91), was truly spectacular. The wine had such a deep color and rich, intense taste, I could have mistaken it for a 25- to 30-year-old claret. Can these pristine bottles that appear from time to time truly be authentic examples of the vintage?

LYNCH-BAGES (Fifth-Growth)   EXCELLENT

Production: 40,000–45,000 cases	Grape varieties: Cabernet Sauvignon—70% Merlot—15% Cabernet Franc—10% Petit Verdot—5%
Secondary label: Haut-Bages-Averous	
Vineyard size: 187.7 acres	Proprietor: Jean-Michel Cazes
Time spent in barrels: 18–20 months	Average age of vines: 35 years
Evaluation of present classification: Should be upgraded to a second-growth	
Plateau of maturity: 6–25 years following the vintage	

The château itself is located just west of Bordeaux's Route du Vin (D2) as one approaches the dull, commercial town of Pauillac from the south. It is situated on a small ridge that rises above the town and the adjacent Gironde River called, not surprisingly, the Bages plateau. Until recently the kindest thing that could be said about the buildings was that they were utilitarian. However, Lynch-Bages has benefited enormously from a major facelift and renovation. The château now sports a new facade, new cellars exhibiting large stainless-steel tanks, and a state-of-the-art tasting room.

Except for these recent changes, this large estate has remained essentially intact since the sixteenth century. Half the name is taken from the plateau upon which the château and cellars are located, and the rest results from 75 years of ownership (during the seventeenth and eighteenth centuries) by Thomas Lynch, the son of an Irish immigrant whose family ran the property. After Thomas Lynch sold Lynch-Bages it passed through the hands of several wine merchants before being purchased in 1937 by Jean Charles Cazes, the grandfather of the current-day proprietor, Jean-Michel Cazes. In his time, Jean Charles Cazes was already a renowned proprietor and winemaker, having directed the fortunes of one of the leading Cru Bourgeois of St.-Estèphe, Château Les-Ormes-des-Pez. He continued to handle both châteaux until 1966 when his son André, a prominent politician who had been the mayor of Pauillac for nearly two decades, took control. André's reign lasted until 1973, when Jean-Michel Cazes assumed control of both Lynch-Bages and Les-Ormes-des-Pez. Jean-Michel, who spent several years in America, had developed an international perspective of wine as well as business. He made perhaps the smartest decision of his business career in 1976 when he hired the brilliant Daniel Llose as director of Château Lynch-Bages and Les-Ormes-des-Pez.

After the great success Lynch-Bages enjoyed under Jean-Michel's father, André, in the fifties (1952, 1953, 1955, 1957, and 1959 were all among the top wines of that decade) and in the sixties (1961, 1962, and 1966), Jean-Michel's inheritance consisted of a disappointing 1972 still in cask. Even his first vintage, 1973, was largely a washout. This was followed by another disappointing year in 1974, and for Lynch-Bages, less-than-exhilarating wine from the sometimes-troublesome vintage of 1975. Jean-Michel Cazes recognized that the old wooden vats created sanitation problems, and also made it difficult to control the proper fermentation temperature in both cold and hot years. At the same time (the late seventies), Cazes flirted with a newer style, producing several vintages of Lynch-Bages that were lighter and more elegant. Longtime fans and supporters of Lynch-Bages were dismayed. Thankfully, after Jean-Michel Cazes installed twenty-five large stainless-steel vats in 1980, the slump in quality between 1971 and 1979 came to an abrupt end. Lynch-Bages produced a very good 1981 and continued to build on that success with highly successful wines in nearly every vintage since.

The vineyard itself is located midway between Mouton-Rothschild and Lafite-Rothschild to the north, and Latour, Pichon-Longueville–Comtesse de Lalande, and Pichon-Longueville Baron to the south. Despite the enormous amount of modernization and rebuilding that has taken place at Lynch-Bages, the general philosophy of making wine remains quite traditional. Since 1980, as I have mentioned, the vinification has taken place in new steel tanks. After that, the wine is put directly into small French oak casks. The percentage of new casks has increased from 25% in the 1982 vintage to 60% in more recent vintages such as 1988 and 1989. Lynch-Bages spends an average of 18–20 months in these oak casks, is fined with egg whites, and lightly filtered prior to bottling. Now that the vineyards are fully planted, production has soared from an average of 20,000–25,000 cases in the seventies, to an average of nearly

45,000 cases in the abundant years of the eighties. In addition, from 20–30% of the harvest is relegated to the second wine of Lynch-Bages, Haut-Bages-Averous.

In 1990, Cazes began making a dry, rich white Bordeaux from a vineyard in the northern Médoc. The wine, a blend of 40% Semilion, 40% Sauvignon, and 20% Muscadelle, was fermented in new oak and aged in cask for nearly 12 months prior to bottling. The debut vintage was remarkably impressive with a level of quality reminiscent of a top white Graves.

In the famous 1855 Classification of the Wines of Gironde, Lynch-Bages was positioned in the last tier as a fifth-growth. I know of no professional in the field today who would not argue that its present-day quality is more akin to a second-growth. Englishman Oz Clarke light-heartedly argues that those responsible for the 1855 classification must have been essentially Puritans because they "couldn't bear to admit that a wine as openheartedly lovely as Lynch-Bages could really be as important as other less-generous growths."

Just as it is difficult not to enjoy a bottle of Lynch-Bages, so is it difficult not to appreciate the affable, seemingly always open and gregarious Jean-Michel Cazes, the architect behind Lynch-Bages' more recent stratospheric rise to international prominence. The confident Cazes, who, having attended school in America, speaks English like a native, has a global vision, and anyone who talks with him knows he wants his wines to be lusty, open, and direct, yet also reflect the class and character of a top Pauillac. For that reason he always prefers vintages such as 1985 and 1982 to more tannic and severe years such as 1988 and 1986. He is also an untiring ambassador not only for his own wines, but for the wines of the entire Bordeaux region. There rarely seems to be a conference, symposium, or international tasting of Bordeaux where one does not encounter Monsieur Cazes. There is no other producer in Pauillac (with the possible exception of Madame Lencquesaing of Pichon Lalande) who travels so extensively, and who pleads his case so eloquently for these wines.

VINTAGES

1989—I own the 1982, 1983, and 1985 Lynch-Bages, but I have no prob-
·   lem in saying that the 1989 is the finest young Lynch-Bages I have
96   ever tasted. Its opaque, black/purple color suggests a level of
       concentration one rarely sees in a Bordeaux. It will not have the
       round, seductive charm of the 1985, and it is sweeter and richer
       than the 1982. Some might accuse this wine of being too ex-

tracted, too weighty, and too un-claret-like, but that is what the great old Lynch-Bages vintages of 1970, 1961, and 1955 all offered. This is not the wine to drink if you are looking for elegance or something to stimulate intellectual conversation. This is a bruiser, a powermonger that wants to grab all your attention. It is a super wine, probably the finest made at this property since the 1970, which, in a more modern way, it resembles. Anticipated maturity: 1996–2015. Last tasted, 4/91.

1988—Undoubtedly, this is the biggest wine produced in the northern
·   Médoc in 1988. The saturated black/ruby/purple color suggests
90   excellent ripeness and plenty of concentration. The bouquet exhibits roasted black raspberries and currants, as well as an earthy, robust character. In the mouth, the wine is full bodied, rich, and full, with an attractive cedary, herbaceous, black fruit character. This fleshy, broad-shouldered wine characterizes the style of the château, and should prove enormously rewarding to those consumers who have admired the wines of this property. It also avoids the harsh astringency that plagues many 1988s. Anticipated maturity: 1993–2010. Last tasted, 4/91.

1987—The 1987 Lynch-Bages is a densely colored, herbaceous, rich,
·   medium-bodied, soft, supple wine for current drinking. Antici-
82   pated maturity: Now–1995. Last tasted, 11/89.

1986—What remarkable tastings should occur in the twenty-first century
·   between the opulent, seductive 1982 and 1985 and the powerful,
90   brawny, tannic, dense, muscular 1986 and 1989 Lynch-Bages. The results will make interesting reading for decades. At present, I have a strong preference for the 1982 and 1989, but I would not want anyone to shortchange the immense, huge, behemoth 1986, or the seductive, flashy 1985. The 1986 is black/purple in color, and extremely rich and tannic. But are the tannins too prominent and astringent? I doubt that anyone will be capable of answering that question for at least a decade. As for now, this wine is more admirable for remarkable size and weight than for charm and enjoyability. Anticipated maturity: 1998–2020. Last tasted, 4/91.

1985—Once more Lynch-Bages has made one of the top wines of the
·   vintage. The 1985 tastes as if it were a toned-down 1982. Dense
90   ruby/purple in color, with a big, full-intensity bouquet of blackcurrant fruit and smoky oak, this corpulent, rich, intense, brawny wine has gobs of flavor, full body, and should mature nicely for 10–15 more years. It provides delicious drinking today! Anticipated maturity: Now–2005. Last tasted, 1/91.

1984—One of the top successes of the vintage, the 1984 Lynch-Bages,
·   which is nearly 100% Cabernet Sauvignon, is a forceful, fleshy,
84   supple wine with plenty of herbaceous-scented, ripe fruit, a
         round, generous texture, and good length. Anticipated maturity:
         Now–1995. Last tasted, 10/89.

1983—A success for this very good, yet surprisingly inconsistent vintage,
·   the Lynch-Bages 1983 is a full-blown, big, ripe, gutsy Pauillac,
88   with an intense bouquet of ground beef and blackcurrant fruit,
         and deep, rich, briary flavors. Quite full bodied, alcoholic, and
         long, this substantial wine has a heady, alcoholic finish with the
         tannins quickly melting away. Anticipated maturity: Now–2002.
         Last tasted, 3/89.

1982—In its first 6 months of life, I thought the 1982 Lynch-Bages was a
·   very good, yet somewhat flabby, fat example of the 1982 vintage.
93   After 1 year in the cask, the wine deepened, and began to show
         significant tannin content, as well as the structure that was miss-
         ing early in its life. From the bottle, Lynch-Bages is a massive,
         huge, densely colored wine, with an intense bouquet of ripe cassis
         fruit intermingled with scents of hot tar, soy sauce, and vanillin
         oakiness. Viscous, rich, very full and concentrated on the palate,
         with plenty of soft tannins, this big-framed, extroverted, deca-
         dently intense Lynch-Bages is in the same league as the outstand-
         ing 1970 and 1961 wines produced at this château. Anticipated
         maturity: Now–2010. Last tasted, 5/91.

1981—After a period in the late seventies where Lynch-Bages seemed
·   to be taking suppleness in winemaking too far, I detected with
85   the 1981 a partial return to the very rich, robust, ripe, huge ex-
         tract style of the great Lynch-Bages wines like the 1970, 1962,
         and 1961. Certainly the monumental 1982 and excellent 1983 will
         eclipse the 1981 in stature, but this wine is quite good, and the
         best Lynch-Bages since 1975. Very dark ruby, with a strong,
         aggressive bouquet of blackcurrants, cedar, and new oak, this
         ripe wine has surprising density on the palate, with plenty of
         tannin. The 1981 shows lots of gutsy character. Anticipated ma-
         turity: Now–1998. Last tasted, 12/88.

1980—Somewhat variable from bottle to bottle, this lightweight Lynch-
·   Bages has a cedary, fruity, somewhat stalky, herbaceous aroma,
78   light-intensity flavors, and a short, greenish, unripe finish. Antic-
         ipated maturity: Now–may be in decline. Last tasted, 4/87.

1979—Made in a period when Lynch-Bages was flirting with a lighter,
·   more precocious, supple style, this wine is attractive, but atypical
79   for what fans of Lynch-Bages expect. Medium bodied with soft,

crisp, berryish flavors, light tannins, and some pleasing spicy, oaky notes, it is quite drinkable now. Anticipated maturity: Now–1993. Last tasted, 6/88.

1978—Very similar to the 1979 in that this wine is round, fruity, and
·   straightforward in style, with soft, spicy blackcurrant flavors of
82 moderate intensity. Ready to drink now, it should continue to drink well for another 5–6 years. A good, but not particularly noteworthy effort from Lynch-Bages. Anticipated maturity: Now–1994. Last tasted, 1/88.

1976—Fully mature and beginning to lose its fruit, the 1976 Lynch-Bages
·   is still fruity, but diffuse, with no grip or "attack," and displaying
72 disturbing browning at the edge. Owners of this vintage of Lynch-Bages should run, not walk, to the wine cellar, and consume it immediately. Anticipated maturity: Now—may be in decline. Last tasted, 3/86.

1975—This precociously styled Lynch-Bages is chocolatey, with ripe
·   blackcurrant and cedar aromas, dusty, fat, savory flavors, and
79 ripe tannins that are falling away. Interestingly, it lacks the great depth of color of many 1975s, and has increasingly taken on an amber/orange color in the late eighties. I should note that at least one-third of the 1975s I have tasted have been disappointing, raising serious questions about bottle variation. Anticipated maturity: Now–1995. Last tasted, 4/91.

1974—A surprisingly weak effort from Lynch-Bages, this watery, hollow
·   wine fades remarkably fast in the glass, and the shallow, pale
60 colors suggest a wine that was diluted significantly by rain and perhaps overcropping. Anticipated maturity: Now—may be in decline. Last tasted, 2/80.

1973—Disappointing for Lynch-Bages, this light, feeble wine has a
·   washed-out color, a chaptalized bouquet of hot, burnt fruit, and
55 thin, nondescript flavors. It was at its best in 1978. Last tasted, 2/78.

1971—Lynch-Bages was clearly in a slump during this period. A number
·   of very fine, graceful, fruity 1971 Pauillacs were produced, but
58 not here. Now decrepit and very brown, with a musty, faded, dead vegetal bouquet, and short, sharp acidic flavors. A failure for the vintage. Last tasted, 10/79.

1970—The 1970 remains a massive, inky-colored wine with gobs of
·   blackcurrant, cedary, ground beef, leathery flavors and aromas.
95 This huge, ponderous wine is still youthfully powerful, but the ferocious tannins are melting away. Although it lacks finesse and elegance, it offers an immensely enjoyable, robust, generous

mouthful of hedonistic claret that will last for at least another decade. Anticipated maturity: Now–2008. Last tasted, 2/91.

1966—Dark ruby with a slight amber edge, this wine appears to have the requisite concentration and structure, yet for whatever reason the wine tastes dull, lacks complexity and character, and finishes in a one-dimensional, tannic manner. It is capable of aging, but it mysteriously does not sing. Anticipated maturity: Now–2000. Last tasted, 9/90.

·
84

1964—The 1964 Lynch-Bages is a failure, not so much because of faulty winemaking, but as a result of the château's decision to pick late to obtain maximum ripeness in the grapes. Such decisions always run the risk of foul weather, and in 1964, Lynch-Bages was one of the châteaux to get caught badly in the deluge that ensued. Thin, old, watery, and uninteresting. Last tasted, 1/91.

·
55

1962—One of the all-time popular wines of the château, this wine has been drinking beautifully since 1970, and continues to be delightful. It indicates just how long a top-class Bordeaux can remain at its apogee. However, the regular bottle size seems to be losing some of the exuberant, unabashed, gutsy fruitiness. Cedary and blackcurrant aromas still prevail, and this wine still has a wonderful, silky voluptuousness that has made it so pleasurable. Owners are advised to catch the wonderment now, or risk losing its pleasure altogether. Anticipated maturity: Now–1995. Last tasted, 11/89.

·
89

1961—The best Lynch-Bages made during the sixties, its rich, cedary, massive aromas of blackcurrants and leather are still present in plentiful amounts. Not terribly refined, but deep, powerful, concentrated, alcoholic, and extremely long on the palate, this huge wine has been at its apogee since the late seventies, but will hold for another 10 years. Anticipated maturity: Now–2000. Last tasted, 12/89.

·
94

OLDER VINTAGES

Lynch-Bages enjoyed a glorious decade of the fifties, producing superlative wines in 1959 (94 points), 1957 (88 points), 1955 (92 points), 1953 (90 points), and 1952 (91 points). Such consistent brilliance was not again evident until the succession of super performances that began in 1982.

LYNCH-MOUSSAS (Fifth-Growth) AVERAGE

Production: 13,000 cases	Grape varieties: Cabernet Sauvignon—70% Merlot—25% Cabernet Franc—5%
Secondary label: none	
Vineyard size: 61.7 acres	Proprietor: Emile Castéja
Time spent in barrels: 14–16 months	Average age of vines: 17 years
Evaluation of present classification: Should be downgraded to a Cru Bourgeois	
Plateau of maturity: 4–10 years following the vintage	

Lynch-Moussas is owned and controlled by the Castéja family, who operate the well-known Bordeaux *négociant* business, Borie-Manoux. While the wines of the firm of Borie-Manoux have demonstrated considerable improvement in vintages since the early eighties, particularly their famous estates in Pauillac (Château Batailley), in St.-Emilion (Château Trottevieille), and in Pomerol (Domaine d'Eglise), this estate continues to turn out light, often diluted, simple wines that lack character and stature. Even in the best Pauillac vintages such as 1986 and 1989, the wine has been light and deficient in complexity and character. In most vintages, Lynch-Moussas should be consumed within 5–8 years of the vintage.

VINTAGES

1989—The 1989 is pleasant and cleanly made, but uncommonly light and
· soft for such a well-placed vineyard. Anticipated maturity. Now–
79 1996. Last tasted, 5/91.

1988—Light, yet fruity and medium bodied, with good concentration,
· this soft, somewhat one-dimensional wine should be drunk over
81 the next 5–7 years. Anticipated maturity: Now–1995. Last tasted,
4/90.

1986—The 1986 is a stern-yet-light wine, without enough richness and
· fruit to hold up the tannins. Nevertheless, if you like your claret
77 on the leaner, tougher side, you may prefer the 1986 more than I
do. Anticipated maturity: Now–1996. Last tasted, 11/89.

1985—The wines of Lynch-Moussas tend to be light and early maturing,
· and the 1985 displays those characteristics, in addition to being
78 soft, fruity, and one-dimensional. Anticipated maturity: Now–
1994. Last tasted, 4/89.

MOULIN DES CARRUADES* (Unclassified)   AVERAGE

> Evaluation: The quality equivalent of a Médoc Grand Bourgeois
> Exceptionnel

The second wine of Lafite is produced from the youngest sections of the vineyard, as well as from lots of wine not considered of high-enough quality for Lafite. The wine benefits from the same vinification as Lafite and of course the same cellar treatment, except that a smaller percentage of new oak barrels is utilized. Despite the care given the wine, I have never considered Moulin des Carruades to ever be remotely comparable to the quality of the Forts de Latour, the second wine of Château Latour. Nevertheless, it is a correct wine, but the quality level is more akin to a good Cru Bourgeois than a top classified growth. However, the price, because of the association with a name as great as Lafite-Rothschild, is quite high, making Moulin des Carruades a relatively poor wine value.

The finest recent vintages have been 1989 and 1988, followed by 1982 and 1986. The wine should be drunk within its first 10 years of life.

MOUTON-BARONNE-PHILIPPE (D'ARMAILHAC)
(Fifth-Growth)   GOOD

Production: 16,000 cases	Grape varieties: Cabernet Sauvignon—70% Merlot—17% Cabernet Franc—13%
Secondary label: none	
Vineyard size: 126 acres	Proprietor: The family of the late Baron Philippe de Rothschild
Time spent in barrels: 18–22 months	Average age of vines: 40 years
Evaluation of present classification: Should be maintained	
Plateau of maturity: 5–14 years following the vintage	

This remains the least well-known, and to the consuming public the most obscure property of the late Baron Philippe Rothschild's trio of Pauillac estates. The Baron acquired Mouton-Baronne-Philippe in 1933 when it

---

* Recently this second wine was renamed Les Carruades de Lafite.

was known as Mouton d'Armailhacq. In 1956 the name was changed to
Mouton-Baron-Philippe, and in 1975 to Mouton-Baronne-Philippe in tribute to the Baron's wife who died the following year.* The cellars are
adjacent to Mouton-Rothschild, and the winemaking team of Patrick
Léon and Lucien Sionneau that overlooks the renowned Mouton-Rothschild and Clerc-Milon, also attends to the winemaking at Mouton-
Baronne.

Despite the impressive age of the vineyard, the wine has tended to be
relatively light, quick to mature, and easily outdistanced in complexity,
character, and longevity by the two siblings. However, there has been a
noticeable trend to upgrade the quality of the wines. While the quality of
the 1982 is no doubt due to the vintage itself, the higher quality of
Mouton-Baronne-Philippe began in earnest with the fine 1985, and has
been continued since. The 1989 may be the best wine produced at this
property in modern times.

VINTAGES

1989—The château acknowledges that the 1989 vintage of Mouton-
·   Baronne-Philippe is its best wine in over three decades. It has a
87   very forward, creamy richness, gobs of velvety fruit, a heady
         alcohol content, and a fat, lush finish. For those who like their
         claret gushing with fruit, this charming wine will provide much
         pleasure over the next decade. Anticipated maturity: 1992–2000.
         Last tasted, 4/91.

1988—When compared with the 1989, the 1988 is much lighter, more
·   compact, noticeably hard and lean, and has a short finish. Antic-
82   ipated maturity: 1992–1998. Last tasted, 4/91.

1987—Light to medium ruby, with a soft, round, weedy fruitiness, this
·   is a round, somewhat diluted, picnic wine. Anticipated maturity:
77   Now–1996. Last tasted, 10/89.

1986—I found the 1986 Mouton-Baronne-Philippe to be an attractively
·   soft, rich, medium-bodied wine, with a pleasing and charming
86   suppleness, a nice dosage of sweet oak, and a precocious person-
         ality, especially for a wine from this vintage. Anticipated matu-
         rity: 1992–2002. Last tasted, 9/90.

1985—Thanks to the efforts of administrator Philippe Cottin and wine-
·   maker Patrick Léon, the quality level of Mouton-Baronne-Phi-
86   lippe began to rise with this vintage. The 1985 is a creamy-
         textured, fat, lush, lovely wine with a seductive, rich fruitiness,
         precocious personality, and low acidity. It is gorgeous for drinking

* The name, beginning with the 1989 vintage, will once again be D'Armailhac.

over the next decade. Anticipated maturity: Now–2000. Last tasted, 1/89.

1984—The 1984 is a medium ruby with a soft, somewhat diluted, fruity
·   aroma, spicy, short in the finish, but pleasant. Anticipated matu-
75   rity: Now–may be in decline. Last tasted, 10/88.

1983—Amply proportioned, the 1983 Mouton-Baronne-Philippe is less
·   concentrated and richly fruity than the 1982, but still impressively
83   full, well structured, and concentrated. Anticipated maturity:
      Now–2000. Last tasted, 3/89.

1982—While no one should confuse this wine with Mouton-Rothschild's
·   legendary 1982, this wine is commendable. Dark ruby, with a
86   cedary, ripe blackcurrant bouquet of moderate intensity, this
      wine is full bodied, with very good concentration, plenty of dusty,
      yet ripe tannins, and very fine length on the palate. Anticipated
      maturity: 1992–2005. Last tasted, 1/89.

1981—Dark ruby, with a rather closed, tight bouquet of currants and
·   plums, this moderately tannic wine shows good, ripe fruit, me-
83   dium body, and fine length. Lighter than Mouton-Rothschild, but
      the stylistic similarities are present. Anticipated maturity: Now–
      1996. Last tasted, 12/84.

MOUTON-ROTHSCHILD (First-Growth)   OUTSTANDING

Production: 25,000–30,000 cases	Grape varieties: Cabernet Sauvignon—85% Cabernet Franc—7% Merlot—8%
Secondary label: none Vineyard size: 185.2 acres	Proprietor: The family of the late Baron Philippe de Rothschild
Time spent in barrels: 20–24 months	Average age of vines: 45 years
Evaluation of present classification: Should be maintained	
Plateau of maturity: 12–40 years following the vintage	

Mouton-Rothschild is the place and wine that the late Baron Philippe Rothschild singularly created. No doubt his aspirations for Mouton, beginning at the age of 21 when he acquired the estate, were high. However, through the production of an opulently rich and remarkably deep and exotic style of Pauillac, he has been the only person able to effectuate a change in the 1855 classification of the wines of the Médoc. The

Baron died in January 1988, and his daughter is now the spiritual head of this winemaking empire. She continues to receive extraordinary assistance from the talented Mouton team of Philippe Cottin, Patrick Léon, and Lucien Sionneau. Mouton's legendary *maître de chai*, Raoul Blondin, has finally taken his well-deserved retirement, but he can often be spotted in the cellars talking with his successor, Michel Bosq.

In 1973, Mouton-Rothschild was officially classified a "first-growth," which permitted the flamboyant Baron to change his defiant wine labels from *"Premier ne puis, second ne daigne, Mouton suis"* (First I cannot be, second I will not call myself, Mouton I am) to *"Premier je suis, second je fus, Mouton ne change"* (First I am, second I was, Mouton does not change).

There is no question that several of the greatest bottles of Bordeaux I have ever drunk have been Moutons. The 1929, 1945, 1947, 1949, 1953, 1959, 1970, 1982, and 1986 are stunning examples of Mouton at its best. However, I have also experienced too many mediocre vintages of Mouton that are embarrassing for a first-growth to produce, and obviously irritating for a consumer to purchase and taste. Certainly the record in the last two and a half decades is one in which great wines were produced in 1961, 1970, 1982, 1986, 1989, and 1990. The 1980, 1979, 1978, 1977, 1976, 1974, 1973, 1967, and 1964, however, fell well below first-growth standards. This criticism of Mouton seems to have had an effect because Mouton's performance since 1982 has been consistently brilliant.

Why has Mouton-Rothschild been so successful since 1982? There are several reasons. The selection process is undoubtedly more severe than it was during the sixties and seventies. Moreover, the vineyard is harvested later as the château now routinely employs several hundred additional harvesters (up to 600 pickers) to swoop down on the vineyard when the grapes are fully mature. This has allowed Mouton to harvest its 185-acre vineyard in 3 to 5 days since 1982. Previously, it often took 2 to 3 weeks to complete the picking.

The reasons for the commercial success of this wine are numerous. To begin with, the labels of Mouton are collector's items. Since 1945, the Baron Philippe Rothschild has commissioned an artist to do an annual painting, which is depicted on the top of the label. There has been no shortage of masters to appear on the Mouton-Rothschild labels from such Europeans as Miró, Picasso, Chagall, and Cocteau, to the Americans Warhol, Motherwell, and in 1982, John Huston. Secondly, the opulence of Mouton in the great vintages differs significantly in style from the austere elegance of Lafite-Rothschild, and the powerful, tannic, dense, and muscular Latour. Thirdly, the impeccably kept château itself, with its superb wine museum, is the Médoc's (and possibly the entire Bordeaux region's) top tourist attraction. And lastly, there was the Baron himself, who did so much to promote not only his wines, but all the wines of Bordeaux. His daughter, Philippine, appears more than capable of continuing her father's legacy.

VINTAGES

1989—The evolution of this wine will be fascinating to follow. I say this because the wine, while dark ruby/purple in color, is not too opaque. However, if one were to evaluate the bouquet on a 50–100 point scale, it would probably merit a 96 or 97. Perfumed with oriental spices, soy sauce, leather, toasty oak, mocha, and gobs of blackcurrants, the aromas are amazingly developed for such a young wine. In the mouth, however, despite the impressive concentration, the wine appears to lack weight and depth, and the finish is surprisingly unimpressive given the great up-front fragrance. This is undoubtedly an outstanding Mouton, but comparable to the 1985 rather than the compellingly perfect wines produced in 1986 and 1982. It should be drinkable quite early, and I suspect most admirers of the flashy, dramatic style of wine made at Mouton will want to consume it early. Anticipated maturity: 1993–2008. Last tasted, 4/91.

· 92

1988—The 1988 has an aroma of exotic spices, minerals, blackcurrants, and oak. In the mouth, it is a much firmer, tougher, more obviously tannic wine than the 1989. It is a beautifully made 1988 that will last 20–30 years, but the astringency of the tannins is slightly troubling. Patience will be a necessity for the purchasers of this wine. Anticipated maturity: 2000–2030. Last tasted, 4/91.

· 90

1987—This would appear to be a sure bet for the wine of the vintage. Certainly, it is the most complete and backward 1987, with at least 10–15 years of aging potential. The touching dedication from the late Baron Philippe de Rothschild's daughter on the label is almost worth the price of one bottle. Additionally, 1987 was the last vintage of the Baron, and thus will probably fetch a fortune in 40 or 50 years. One of the deepest and most opaque wines of the vintage, with a tight, yet promising bouquet of cedar and blackcurrants, this wine exhibits surprising depth, medium to full body, and plenty of tannin in the finish. Anticipated maturity: 1996–2010. Last tasted, 11/90.

· 88

1986—In 1986, Mouton-Rothschild produced the most profound wine of a great northern Médoc vintage. The opaque black/ruby color is sensational, and may be even denser than that of the 1982. The bouquet of minerals, celestial blackcurrants, smoky new oak, and

· 100

oriental spices seems to explode upward from the glass. On the palate, the wine has incredible concentration, full body, fabulous length, and is . . . well . . . perfect. This is an exemplary effort! Given the 1986 vintage and the sensational ripeness of the late-picked Cabernet Sauvignon, it is not surprising to see what a monument has been constructed at Mouton in 1986. What fun it will be to compare the 1982 and 1986 over the next three to four decades. Anticipated maturity: 1999–2040. Last tasted, 1/91.

1985—This estate compares their 1985 to their 1959, but to me it is more
   ·   akin to their 1962 or 1953. The rich, complex, well-developed
   92   bouquet of oriental spices, toasty oak, herbs, and ripe fruit is wonderful. On the palate, the wine is also very rich, forward, long, and sexy. It is clearly the top first-growth in the Médoc in 1985, but I remain surprised by how evolved and ready to drink this wine is. Anticipated maturity: Now–2008. Last tasted, 5/91.

1984—During the decade of the eighties, Mouton was the hottest first-
   ·   growth in Pauillac. The 1984, which is almost 100% Cabernet
   85   Sauvignon, will be one of the longest-lived wines of this vintage. Full bodied, tannic, concentrated, and rich in extract, this wine should have a surprisingly long life. It is a considerable surprise in a generally poor vintage. Anticipated maturity: 1994–2005. Last tasted, 3/90.

1983—The classic Mouton lead-pencil, cedary nose has begun to
   ·   emerge. Medium dark ruby, this elegant, medium-bodied wine
   90   will never be a great or legendary Mouton. The flavors are ripe and moderately rich. With good depth and some firm tannins to resolve, this offering from Mouton is bigger and richer than the 1981, 1979, or 1978. Austere by the standards of Mouton and the vintage, the 1983 resembles the château's fine 1966. Anticipated maturity: 1992–2015. Last tasted, 10/90.

1982—One of the very greatest young wines I have ever tasted, each
   ·   time I have had an opportunity to evaluate this wine, I have been
  100   apprehensive of finding less than pure perfection. However, on each occasion the brilliance of Mouton is confirmed. The 1982 vintage was a perfect one for Mouton-Rothschild, who employed 600 pickers, and harvested this large vineyard in just 7—versus the normal 21—days. The 1982 Mouton presents a gustatory and olfactory smorgasbord. When tasting it I recall what Michael Broadbent said about the 1945 Mouton: "This is not claret, it is Mouton, a Churchill of a wine." The 1982 is incredibly rich on the palate with an opulence, weight, and concentration that one can only compare to the very greatest Moutons, the 1929 and 1945. In

the late eighties, the wine began to close up, and in 1990 it appeared much more backward than I initially suspected. It remains, however, one of the legends of this century, but it needs at least a decade of cellaring. Anticipated maturity: 2000–2030. Last tasted, 2/91.

1981—This is a good but uninspiring Mouton that I prefer to the 1979,
·   1978, and 1976. It is not nearly as rich and concentrated as the
84   1982, 1975, or 1970, and not as full or tannic as the 1983. This
        wine may turn out to resemble the stylish and delicious 1971.
        Moderately dark ruby color, with an evolving bouquet of leather
        and blackcurrants, this wine has good firm tannins, a lean, stern
        toughness, and an astringent finish. Is there enough fruit? Antic-
        ipated maturity: Now–2005. Last tasted, 5/91.

1980—This is an uninspiring effort from Mouton, notwithstanding the
·   vintage conditions that were unfavorable. Medium ruby color,
74   with a stemmy, stalky, unripe aroma, lean, austere, overly tannic
        flavors, and an astringent finish. Time may help, but I have my
        doubts. Anticipated maturity: Now–1993. Last tasted, 10/83.

1979—The 1979 is a good wine; however, it does not compare favorably
·   with the efforts turned in by the other first-growths in this year.
85   Rather high in acidity, with an austere, tight, hard, closed person-
        ality, on the palate the wine exhibits adequate weight and some
        ripe blackcurrant fruit, but tails off in the finish. The tannins and
        acidity appear too elevated for the wine's fruit. Anticipated ma-
        turity: 1992–2000. Last tasted, 3/89.

1978—Quite tannic and unyielding, but nevertheless exhibiting more
·   richness, concentration, and depth than the 1979, this medium
87   dark ruby wine has developed rapidly. Ripe aromas of herba-
        ceous-scented berry fruit, coffee, tobacco, and vanillin oakiness
        are enthralling. Medium bodied, round, and approaching full ma-
        turity, this surprisingly soft wine should drink nicely for another
        10–18 years. For a first-growth, it should be more concentrated.
        Anticipated maturity: Now–1995. Last tasted, 4/90.

1977—Thin, vegetal, stemmy, and charmless, this medium ruby wine
·   should have been declassified completely rather than sold as a
66   "first-growth" to unsuspecting consumers. Last tasted, 4/81.

1976—Medium to dark ruby with some browning at the edges, this wine
·   is approaching maturity and exhibits an interesting, moderately
85   intense bouquet of ripe plums, spicy oak, and leather. Plenty of
        tannin is still evident, but the overall balance and depth of fruit
        suggest that the tannin will clearly outlive the fruit. It lacks the
        depth and concentration to be great, but for the vintage it is a
        respectable Mouton for drinking over the next decade. I must say

that the wine's evolution has been much slower than I would have suspected. Anticipated maturity: Now–2000. Last tasted, 3/89.

1975 —Still incredibly backward, yet for certain, the 1975 Mouton is loaded with chewy, blackcurrant fruit, a dusty, leathery texture,
·
90   and the hard tannins so typical of this vintage. It is full bodied and weighty on the palate, and the dark ruby color is just beginning to exhibit a hint of amber. The biggest Mouton of the seventies, this stubbornly slow-to-develop wine still requires considerable patience. Let's hope the fruit holds up. Anticipated maturity: 1995–2020. Last tasted, 7/90.

1974 —A below-average effort from Mouton, this wine has the telltale hollowness of the vintage, a stale, flat bouquet, and deficiency in
·
69   rich fruitiness. Anticipated maturity: Now–probably in serious decline. Last tasted, 5/81.

1973 —The year Mouton was officially made a "first-growth" was cele-brated by a beautiful label done by Pablo Picasso. Whether
·
65   judged by an art or wine critic, the label clearly surpasses the wine. Very oaky and woody, with rapidly fading fruit, this is a wine worth having if only for the historic significance of the bottle's label. Anticipated maturity: Now–probably in serious decline. Last tasted, 2/82.

1971 —Extremely enjoyable and mature by 1980, this medium weight Mouton offers charm, elegance, and the classic Mouton "lead
·
86   pencil" bouquet. Moderately powerful and rich, this is a delight-ful Mouton for drinking over the next 2–3 years. Anticipated maturity: Now–1996. Last tasted, 6/82.

1970 —This vintage produced a classic Mouton that continues to develop at a snail's pace. The wine is dark ruby with a tight, closed bou-
·
92   quet that reluctantly yields scents of walnuts, cassis, leather, and, of course, aromas of cedars and herbs. Powerful on the palate with plenty of mouth-puckering tannin present, this wine remains an infant. Curiously, the wine tastes explosively rich and intense when first opened, but within 10–15 minutes, it closes up completely. My gut feeling is that the 1970 Mouton remains at least 10–15 years away from maturity, but its frighteningly backward character is beginning to give me some concerns. I would be remiss in not mentioning that no Mouton I have tasted (I have had the 1970 over two dozen times) has demonstrated as much bottle variation as this vintage. At first, I thought it was bad storage or abusive treatment, but I have begun to believe that the severe bottle variation is attributable to the château. Will this Mouton enjoy a 40- to 60-year life span? Only time will tell. Anticipated maturity: 2000–2030. Last tasted, 10/90.

1967—I tasted one agreeably fruity, fairly simple, medium-weight, and
  ·   fully mature 1967 Mouton in 1974. More recently the wine has
 70   shown itself to be shallow, hollow, and in decline. In the late
        eighties, a musty, mushroomy quality emerged. Drink up! Antic-
        ipated maturity: Now—probably in serious decline. Last tasted,
        1/91.

1966—This is an outstanding Mouton that, while not in the class of the
  ·   1961 or 1982, can clearly be called one of the half-dozen best
 90   Médocs. Like many 1966s, it has remained dry, austere, and
        buttoned-up for longer than most observers would have preferred.
        However, the moderately dark ruby color, the evolving bouquet
        of tobacco, cedar, spices, and mineral-scented Cabernet Sauvi-
        gnon fruit, and rich, yet tightly restrained flavors, as well as the
        long finish, all suggest high quality and another decade of evolu-
        tion. Anticipated maturity: Now–2005. Last tasted, 12/89.

1964—The 1964 Mouton is a notable failure because it was picked late
  ·   in the deluge of rain that wiped out those châteaux that were
 55   waiting for extra ripeness. One wonders why Bordeaux's best
        châteaux do not declassify the entire crop when they produce a
        wine this miserable. A sweet, cooked bouquet is followed by
        equally sweet, disjointed, flabby flavors. Last tasted, 1/91.

1962—Noticeable bottle variation, always a plague when tasting older
  ·   wines, and most likely caused by different storage conditions, has
 90   been the one common characteristic that I find among my 1962
        Mouton tasting notes. The score reflects the well-kept bottles that
        are now fully mature. A huge bouquet of blackcurrant fruit,
        spices, and leather all combine to captivate the olfactory senses.
        Silky, soft, nicely concentrated flavors are supple, round, and
        long. Will the seductive 1985 turn out to be this fine? Anticipated
        maturity: Now–1996. Last tasted, 12/88.

1961—Still remarkably backward for its age, this dark, densely colored
  ·   Mouton has a rich, multidimensional bouquet of cedar, leather,
 92   cinnamon, and ripe fruit. Big, tough, yet increasingly austere on
        the palate, the wine does possess admirable concentration and
        length. There is still plenty of tannin remaining to preserve this
        big wine for another 10 or 20 years, but I am beginning to believe
        the wine is outstanding rather than sublime. Can this wine really
        be still too young to drink? Anticipated maturity: 1992–2020. Last
        tasted, 1/91.

OLDER VINTAGES

Mouton-Rothschild produced two profoundly great wines during the fifties. I prefer the 1959 (rated 99 in 1990) to all of Mouton's more recent vintages except for 1982 and 1986. It is a nearly perfect wine, with enormous extract and 20 more years of evolution. The 1953 (rated 96) is becoming increasingly fragile and holding it any longer may prove risky. Nevertheless, this is the most fragrant, spicy, perfumed Mouton I have ever tasted. Mouton produced a trio of great wines in the late forties. The 1945 (rated 100 on three separate occasions), 1947 (always rated between 92 and 96), and 1949 (consistently above 96) are all mind-boggling. All three wines should continue to drink well for at least another decade. I know of no great Moutons from the thirties, but the 1929 (rated 86 in April 1991) is still drinkable, though only a shadow of what it was. The 1928, 1926, and 1924, all tasted in April 1991, were fading badly. None of them merited a score above the mid-seventies.

PEDESCLAUX (Fifth-Growth)   AVERAGE

Production: 7,500 cases	Grape varieties:
	Cabernet Sauvignon—65%
	Merlot—20%
	Cabernet Franc—10%
	Malbec—5%
Secondary label: none	
Vineyard size: 42 acres	Proprietor: Bernard Jugla
Time spent in barrels: 18–23 months	Average age of vines: 38 years
Evaluation of present classification: Should be downgraded to a Cru Bourgeois	
Plateau of maturity: 3–10 years following the vintage	

Pedesclaux gets my nod as the most obscure classified growth in the 1855 classification of the wines of the Gironde. Much of the wine is sold in Europe, particularly Belgium. I have never been impressed, finding it robust, but straightforward, lacking depth, and, to my taste, having an excess of tannin.

PEYRABON (Cru Bourgeois)   AVERAGE

Production: 2,200 cases	Grape varieties: Cabernet Sauvignon—50% Merlot—27% Cabernet Franc—23%
Secondary label: none	
Vineyard size: 11.5 acres	Proprietor: Jacques Babeau
Time spent in barrels: 12–16 months	Average age of vines: 20 years
Evaluation of present classification: Should be maintained	
Plateau of maturity: 3–8 years following the vintage	

This is an obscure Pauillac with its vineyards situated in the commune of Saint-Sauveur. The wines, particularly the 1982, 1983, 1985, and 1986, are competent if uninspiring.

PIBRAN (Cru Bourgeois)   AVERAGE

Production: 4,500 cases	Grape varieties: Cabernet Sauvignon—60% Merlot—24% Cabernet Franc—10% Petit Verdot—6%
Secondary label: none	
Vineyard size: 20 acres	Proprietor: AXA Insurance Group Administrator: Jean-Michel Cazes
Time spent in barrels: 14–18 months	Average age of vines: 30 years
Evaluation of present classification: The quality equivalent of a Cru Bourgeois Exceptionnel	
Plateau of maturity: 4–12 years following the vintage	

My experience with the wines of Pibran consists of only the 1978, 1981, 1982, 1983, 1985, 1988, 1989, and 1990 vintages, all of which produced competent examples for these vintages. The wine, which is usually well colored, is aged in oak casks, and has a dense, concentrated, moderately tannic style. If it lacks complexity and finesse, it more than compensates for that with its power and muscular personality. Given its moderate price, it provides one with a good introduction to the wines of Pauillac.

Since Jean-Michel Cazes and his winemaker, Daniel Llose, took over responsibility for the making of Pibran, the wine has become more noticeably fruity, plump, and tasty. Both the 1988 and 1989 exhibited a more modern style than previous vintages, and no doubt, because of their fat, fruity style, will have considerable crowd appeal.

PICHON-LONGUEVILLE BARON (Second-Growth)

EXCELLENT

Production: 14,000 cases	Grape varieties: Cabernet Sauvignon—80% Merlot—20%
Secondary label: Les Tourelles de Pichon	
Vineyard size: 76.5 acres	Proprietor: AXA Insurance Group
	Administrator: Jean-Michel Cazes
Time spent in barrels: 18–22 months	Average age of vines: 25 years
Evaluation of present classification: Should be maintained, particularly since 1986	
Plateau of maturity: 8–25 years following the vintage	

This noble-looking château opposite Pichon-Longueville–Comtesse de Lalande and Latour, which made a modest comeback in wine quality in the early eighties, was sold in the late 1980s by its owners—the Bouteiller family—to the insurance conglomerate known as AXA. To the company's credit, they hired Jean-Michel Cazes of Château Lynch-Bages to oversee the vineyard and winemaking. The Cazes touch, which included later picking dates, a stricter selection, the introduction of a second wine, and the utilization of a higher percentage of new oak casks, has made for a dramatic turnaround in quality. As a consequence, Pichon-Longueville Baron now merits its prestigious second-growth status.

The vineyard is superbly situated on gravelly soil with a full southerly exposure. Much of the vineyard is adjacent to that of Château Latour. It has been speculated that the lack of brilliance in many of Pichon Baron's wines in the sixties and seventies was a result of both casual viticultural practices and poor cellar management. I remember passing by the cellars on a torridly hot afternoon in July, only to see the newly bottled vintage stacked up outside the cellars roasting in the relentless sunshine. Under the Cazes team, such recklessness has no doubt stopped.

Rhetoric and public relations efforts aside, the best evidence that Pauillac once again has two great Pichons are the wines that have been produced at Pichon Baron since 1986. This château should prove to be one of the great superstars of the nineties. Great wines emerged from here in 1988 and 1989, yet prices have remained reasonable, a fact that should immediately be put to use by consumers looking for a superb Pauillac at an affordable price. If the 1988 and 1989 are indicative of the style Jean-Michel Cazes has in mind for Pichon Baron, expect a powerful, bold, intensely concentrated wine along the lines of the pre-1983 Latours—high praise indeed!

VINTAGES

1989—The 1989 is this property's finest wine in at least three decades.
· It is one of the most seductive wines of the vintage, with a black/
94 purple color suggesting exceptional extract and superripeness. The aroma reminded me of essence of cassis and plums intertwined with the scent of smoky new oak. Spectacularly rich and ripe, with layer upon layer of compelling extract, this well-balanced, full-bodied wine has the requisite tannin and depth to age well for two to three decades. Anticipated maturity: 1995–2018. Last tasted, 4/91.

1988—The 1988 Pichon Baron promises to be one of the half-dozen
· superstars of the Médoc in that vintage. While it may not rival the
90 1989, the price of 30% less than the 1989 makes it a wine that should appeal to those who want an excellent bargain in a great Pauillac from a good vintage. Surprisingly large scaled for a 1988, it is deep in color, rich, tannic, and medium to full bodied. When mature, it may resemble the successful 1966 (similar texture, weight, and character). Anticipated maturity: 1998–2010. Last tasted, 4/91.

1987—This is a fine wine for the vintage. Rich, long, supple, and fat,
· this tasty, generously endowed Pauillac should drink well for an-
84 other 5–7 years. Anticipated maturity: Now–1996. Last tasted, 11/90.

1986—Forgetting for a moment the 1988 and 1989, the 1986 has turned
· out to be one of the best wines made from this perennial under-
88 achiever in the last 25 years. Deep black/ruby in color, with a fragrant, expansive bouquet of oak and blackcurrants, this brawny, full-bodied, rich wine has plenty of tannin yet, atypically for the vintage, a pleasing suppleness that will permit it to be drunk in the early nineties. Anticipated maturity: 1993–2005. Last tasted, 10/90.

1985—The 1985 Pichon-Longueville Baron is fruity and agreeable, but
·   diffuse, slightly flabby, and unstructured. It is a tasty, but essen-
83   tially one-dimensional wine. Anticipated maturity: Now–1998.
     Last tasted, 10/90.

1983—The 1983 is certainly a better-structured wine than the 1982,
·   but as it has aged, it has, curiously, become less interesting.
85   Dark ruby, with a spicy, cassis-and-herb-scented bouquet, this
     medium-bodied wine still has plenty of tannin, but appears to be
     maturing rapidly. Anticipated maturity: Now–2005. Last tasted,
     3/89.

1982—Early in the lives of both the 1982 and 1983 vintages of Pichon
·   Baron, I had thought the 1983 to be the better-balanced wine. I
88   still have nagging concerns about the overall balance in the 1982,
     but must admit that I appear to have considerably underrated the
     1982. Despite a glaring lack of acidity to give the wine focus and
     definition, there is no doubting the fabulously rich, cedary,
     smoky, curranty bouquet and massive, rich, sweet, expansive
     fruit flavors that combine to make an overwhelming mouthful of
     wine. It seems to get by despite its lack of acidity because of its
     fairly high tannin content, and I was indeed surprised by how well
     the 1982 Pichon Baron showed in recent tastings. My feeling is
     that owners of it should begin to consume it, with a caveat being
     that it should continue to drink well for at least another 6–12
     years, perhaps longer. This wine seems to be much better now
     than it ever was out of cask or in its early days following the
     bottling. Anticipated maturity: Now–2002. Last tasted, 2/91.

1981—The 1981 is overtly oaky, without any great depth or intensity.
·   With average concentration of fruit, and somewhat short in the
83   finish, this Pichon Baron is a charming, agreeable, precociously
     styled wine that is ideal for consumption over the next 5–6 years.
     Anticipated maturity: Now–1993. Last tasted, 2/87.

1980—Thin, vegetal, unripe fruity flavors reveal deficiencies in aroma,
·   flavor, and length. Last tasted, 2/83.
60

1979—For whatever reasons, the 1979 Pichon Baron is gloriously supple
·   and ready to drink. It has ample velvety, blackcurrant fruit, a
84   spicy, tarry, oaky bouquet, and soft, precocious flavors. Antici-
     pated maturity: Now–1994. Last tasted, 3/88.

1978—Fat, plump, jammy, and one-dimensional, the 1978 Pichon Baron
·   lacks grip and backbone, has a loosely knit structure, and a
82   sweet, short finish. It has reached full maturity. Anticipated ma-
     turity: Now–1994. Last tasted, 7/88.

1975 — A very medicinal, unusual nose suggesting burnt coffee is offput-
·   ting. Chaptalized, sweet, unstructured flavors dissipate and fade
64   in the glass. A soft, uncharacteristic, and disjointed 1975. Anticipated maturity: Now—probably in serious decline. Last tasted,
8/90.

1971 — A poor effort from Pichon Baron, this dried-out, hollow wine ex-
·   hibits a washed-out brownish color, an artificial, sugary ripeness
65   of fruit, and a poor, astringent, tannic finish. Quite disappointing.
Anticipated maturity: Now—probably in serious decline. Last
tasted, 9/78.

1970 — Decently colored, but rather light in weight with an astringent,
·   very tannic feel on the palate, this medium-bodied wine does not
73   appear to have the fruit to outdistance the tannin. Only a gambler
would bet on it. Anticipated maturity: Now—1995. Last tasted,
3/86.

1966 — Rather imbalanced and perplexing to taste, the 1966 Pichon
·   Baron has good, dark ruby color, with just a little amber at the
82   edge, a spicy, aggressive, cedary, blackcurrant bouquet intermingled with decaying vegetation smells. Big, fleshy, but disjointed
on the palate, with an excess of tannin, this wine can be drunk
now. No doubt the 1966 will age for another decade or more, but
the wine is coarse and rustic. Anticipated maturity: Now—2000.
Last tasted, 2/87.

1961 — After having some mediocre bottles of this wine, the last several
·   times I tasted it, it performed well. Still dark ruby with an orange
86   edge, the 1961 Pichon Baron has a big, spicy, damp-earth, cedary
bouquet, and rich, fat, substantial flavors that lack the multidi-
mension of the finest 1961s. Anticipated maturity: Now—2000.
Last tasted, 2/88.

OLDER VINTAGES

The finest old vintages of Pichon-Longueville Baron I have tasted included the 1959 (better as well as less evolved than the 1961, and a wine
I have rated between 87 and 90), a fine, dense 1955 (rated 87), and a
robust, fragrant, fully mature 1953 (rated 89). I have only tasted the
following vintages once, but I was disappointed with the 1949, 1947, and
1945.

PICHON-LONGUEVILLE–COMTESSE
DE LALANDE (Second-Growth)

OUTSTANDING

Production: 20,000–25,000 cases	Grape varieties: Cabernet Sauvignon—50% Merlot—35% Cabernet Franc—7% Petit Verdot—8%
Secondary label: Reserve de la Comtesse	
Vineyard size: 150.6 acres	Proprietor: Madame May-Elaine de Lencquesaing
Time spent in barrels: 18–24 months	Average age of vines: 22 years
Evaluation of present classification: Should be upgraded to a first-growth	
Plateau of maturity: 5–20 years following the vintage	

At present, Pichon-Longueville–Comtesse de Lalande (Pichon Lalande) is unquestionably the most popular and, since 1978, the most consistently brilliant wine of Pauillac. In many vintages it rivals and occasionally surpasses the three famous first-growths of this commune. The wines of Pichon Lalande have been very successful since 1961, but there is no question that in the late seventies and early eighties, under the energetic helm of Madame de Lencquesaing, the quality has risen to an extremely high plateau.

The wine is made in an intelligent manner, and is darkly colored, supple, fruity, and smooth enough to be drunk young. It has the distinction, along with Château Palmer in Margaux, to be one of the most famous Médoc estates that utilizes more than 30% Merlot in the blend. Yet Pichon Lalande has the requisite tannin, depth, and richness to age gracefully for 10–20 years. The high proportion of Merlot (35%) no doubt accounts for part of the wine's soft, fleshy characteristic.

The property was once part of a single estate called Pichon-Longueville that was divided in 1850. Madame de Lencquesaing's father, Édouard Miailhe, purchased it in 1924, but it is his daughter who has been responsible for the current fame. Significant investments were made during the eighties. A new *cuvier* was built in 1980, a new barrel-aging cellar and tasting room (with a spectacular vista of neighboring Château Latour) in 1988, and in 1990, the renovations of the château were completed. Madame Lencquesaing resides at the château, which sits across the road from Pichon-Longueville Baron. Its vineyards lie both in Pauillac and St.-Julien, the latter characteristic often given as the reason for Pichon Lalande's supple style.

In addition to Madame de Lencquesaing's remarkable vigor and belief in her wine, it should be noted that few châteaux in the Médoc have a more talented *régisseur* than Jean-Jacques Godin (a protégé of Emile Peynaud, who apprenticed under Michel Delon of Léoville-Las Cases) and *maître de chai*, Francis Lopez. Their contributions to the impeccable quality of Pichon Lalande are significant.

VINTAGES

1989—The 1989 Pichon Lalande looks to be a clone of the phenomenal · 1982. While the alcohol content is higher in the 1989, the wine is 93 black/purple in color, with a bouquet of sweet cassis and plum- like fruit that roars from the glass. In the mouth, the wine is formidably concentrated, expansive, seductive, and generous. The finish must last for up to a minute. The tannin levels are high, but less than in either 1986 or 1988. Anticipated maturity: 1993– 2015. Last tasted, 4/91.

1988—The 1988 has evolved beautifully over the last year, and is one of · the stars of the vintage. Dark ruby, with a full-intensity bouquet 90 of black plums and currants, it is silky smooth and full bodied as well as one of the most highly extracted wines of the vintage. Seductively precocious, it should drink superbly over the next 10–15 years. During Pichon Lalande's marvelous decade of the eighties, only the 1982, 1986, and 1989 are better. Anticipated maturity: 1992–2008. Last tasted, 5/91.

1987—This wine typifies Pichon Lalande with graceful, velvety texture, · rich, cassis-scented and -flavored fruit, medium body, and a sat- 87 iny finish. It is faithful to the style of wine sought by the château. Offering a fragrant, velvety mouthful of wine, it should easily last for another decade. It is one of my favorite wines of the vintage. Anticipated maturity: Now–2000. Last tasted, 5/91.

1986—The 1986 is the most tannic as well as the largest-framed Pichon · Lalande since the 1959 and 1945. Whether it will ultimately 96 eclipse the 1982 remains to be seen, but one will have to wait a good 7–8 years before consuming this sleeping beauty. Dark ruby/ purple, with a tight yet profound bouquet of cedar, blackcurrants, spicy oak, and minerals, this full-bodied, very deeply concen- trated, exceptionally well-balanced wine should prove to be one of the longest-lived Pichon Lalandes in the last 30 years. Antici- pated maturity: 1995–2020. Last tasted, 9/90.

1985— The 1985 Pichon Lalande is an outstanding wine, but I do not
· think it reaches the same level of quality as the 1989, 1986, 1983,
90 1982, or 1978. It has a deep ruby color and a ripe, oaky, curranty
bouquet with a trace of herbaceousness. On the palate, the wine
is rich, elegant, supple, and not unlike the style of either the 1979
or 1981. It is a lovely wine. Anticipated maturity: Now–2002. Last
tasted, 9/90.

1984— The 1984 Pichon Lalande is a highly successful wine for the vin-
· tage. A ripe, toasty, herbaceous, jammy bouquet is followed by a
86 wine that has a creamy texture, sweet, broad, surprisingly ripe
flavors, and a fine finish. Considering the vintage, it is an unbelievable wine. Drink it over the next 5–6 years. Anticipated maturity: Now–1996. Last tasted, 3/89.

1983— One of the great wines of the vintage, Pichon Lalande's 1983 is
· quite exceptional, and better than several of the Pauillac first-
93 growths, most notably Latour. Especially powerful and rich for
Pichon Lalande, this dark ruby wine has an intense bouquet of
cedar, herbs, blackcurrants, violet-scented fruit, vanillin, and
oak, a full-bodied and excellent concentration, good acidity, and
sensational length. It is unquestionably a star of the vintage. Anticipated maturity: Now–2008. Last tasted, 5/91.

1982— If you want to have a tasting of your collection of 1982s, and you
· like to gamble, put your money on the group's favorite being the
99 1982 Pichon Lalande, which seems to get better and better, going
from strength to strength every time I taste it. My first impression
of this wine was that it lacked structure and probably would not
turn out to be as good as the 1981. How wrong I was! I subsequently upgraded my notes not only from barrel tastings, but also
from early tastings after bottling. I know it is hard to believe, but
since then it has gotten even better. The 1986 may ultimately rival
the 1982, but this wine is about as hedonistic and seductive a
bottle of Pauillac as I have ever tasted. The bouquet displays
incredible ripeness, great extract, and a perfume that simply
must be smelled to be believed. The wine is awesome on the
palate, with velvety, rich, concentrated flavors, impeccable balance, and a seductive, precocious charm that the wine seems to
have had since its first days in bottle. All these qualities suggest
that it will only get better over the next 5–10 years. It is tasting
so extraordinarily well now, I would be reckless in not suggesting
to readers who own some to try a bottle. It is magical: there is no
other word for it. Will it get better? I suspect it will, but when a

wine is this thrilling, it should be drunk. Anticipated maturity: Now–2010. Last tasted, 10/90.

1981—The 1981 is a deliciously supple, fat, silky wine that exudes ripe
 ·   flavors of blackcurrants and huge aromas of spicy oak and violets.
89   A lovely, full-bodied wine that is somewhat precociously styled and probably best consumed over the next 12 years. Deep ruby in color, and deliciously fruity, this Pichon Lalande is a top success for the vintage. Anticipated maturity: Now–1998. Last tasted, 4/91.

1980—A lovely, medium-weight wine that has been very well vinified,
 ·   the 1980 Pichon Lalande is delightful for current drinking. The
84   bouquet offers spicy, cedary scents intermingled with copious ripe aromas of blackcurrants. This is a soft, velvety, very nicely concentrated wine from a vintage considered poor to mediocre. Anticipated maturity: Now–1993. Last tasted, 12/88.

1979—Another top success for the vintage, and a worthy challenger to
 ·   the outstanding 1978 that preceded it, the 1979 Pichon Lalande is
92   dark ruby in color, with a ripe, full-intensity, cedary, blackcurrant-scented bouquet that in certain bottles seems dominated by a herbaceous character. Quite velvety, rich, and gentle on the palate, and developing quickly, this round, generous, yet stylish and elegant wine has impeccable balance. Anticipated maturity: Now–1998. Last tasted, 4/91.

1978—More tannic than the 1979 or 1981 Pichon Lalandes, this wine is
 ·   among the deepest and richest wines produced at the château
93   during the seventies. The telltale vanillin, spicy, blackcurrant, cedar scents are present. This medium- to full-bodied wine has a lush, deep, velvety texture, and has fully resolved most of the tannins. Will it outlast the 1979? Anticipated maturity: Now–2005. Last tasted, 9/90.

1976—Lacking the concentration and character of the best years, this
 ·   wine is, nevertheless, highly successful for the vintage. The color
84   is medium ruby, with some brown and amber at the edges. A gentle, suave, interesting, mature bouquet, and soft, round, curranty flavors have provided pleasure since the late seventies. Yet the wine refuses to fade. Still at its peak. Anticipated maturity: Now–1995. Last tasted, 2/88.

1975—In an extensive blind tasting of the 1975 clarets in spring 1984 at
 ·   Sothebys in London, I mistook this wine for a Pauillac first-
92   growth. It is a big-boned, full-bodied Pichon Lalande with more flesh and vigor than usual. A superlative bouquet of cedar, to-

bacco, and ripe plummy fruit is followed by a big wine with deep flavors, long length, and soft tannins that have melted away in the last few years. Anticipated maturity: Now–2005. Last tasted, 1/88.

1974—Now past prime by a good decade, the 1974 Pichon Lalande is
· light ruby/amber in color with a frail, dissipated bouquet, and
67 soft, very faded flavors. Last tasted, 9/80.

1973—Again completely gone, the light ruby, brown-colored wine was at
· its best in 1978, but like so many light, diluted 1973s, it is now
62 thin and empty. Last tasted, 10/80.

1971—The 1971 is an attractive wine, although I have not recently re-
· tasted it. The last note I have (from a magnum) suggested the
81 wine had a mature, spicy, caramel-scented, ripe, complex bou-
quet. Soft, gentle, spicy flavors exhibited good concentration. Quite pleasant, but this wine, I believe, should have been drunk by the mid-1980s. Last tasted, 2/83.

1970—Now fully mature, the 1970 Pichon Lalande is a delight to drink.
· Its bouquet offers ripe, almost exotic, chocolatey, cedary aromas.
90 On the palate, it is big, ripe, rich, and flavorful, with a velvety
texture and satiny finish. Anticipated maturity: Now–2000. Last tasted, 3/88.

1967—The 1967 was best in 1975, when it had some charm, and just
· enough fruit to balance out the acidity and tannins. Not tasted
75 recently, but given the light, frail character, the wine is most
likely to have faded badly. Last tasted, 7/78.

1966—Now ready to drink, this moderately dark ruby-colored wine has
· a rich, toasty, peppery, somewhat minty bouquet, and firm,
88 fleshy, tannic flavors. Medium bodied, with good concentration,
as well as the austerity that marks the vintage, the 1966 Pichon Lalande should be drunk over the next decade. Anticipated ma-turity: Now–2000. Last tasted, 3/88.

1964—A delicious, yet chunky, four square sort of wine, the 1964 Pichon
· Lalande continues to evolve in the bottle. It exhibits an appealing
85 blackcurrant and herb-scented, earthy, spicy, almost Graves-like
bouquet. In the mouth, the wine has soft, nicely endowed, ripe flavors that have reached full maturity. Anticipated maturity: Now–1993. Last tasted, 3/88.

1962—Quite flavorful, elegant, and deliciously charming as so many of
· the 1962s have proven to be, this fully mature wine has a moder-
85 ate- to full-intensity bouquet of ripe, blackcurrant fruit, cedar,
and mineral scents. It is medium weight on the palate with a good

measure of fruit and charm still in evidence. It should continue
to drink delightfully for the near term. Anticipated maturity:
Now–1994. Last tasted, 3/88.

1961—In 1978, I had the 1961 Pichon Lalande from a magnum in which
· it was quite unready, but since then I have had the wine several
95 times from a regular bottle (most recently at the château in March
1988) where it was equally impressive, and approaching its apogee. Dark, almost opaque in color, with a huge, ripe, plummy
bouquet and savory scents of cedar, toffee, and chocolate, the
1961 Pichon Lalande is rich, full bodied, viscous, and deep on the
palate with a luscious, silky finish. Stylistically, it is reminiscent
of the 1982 and 1989. This wine will continue to drink well for
another decade. Anticipated maturity: Now–2000. Last tasted,
3/88.

OLDER VINTAGES

Pichon Lalande has rarely been a star performer in tastings of older
wines, adding evidence to those who claim the greatest wines made at
the property are those being produced today. The finest vintages, for me,
have been the gloriously decadent 1952 and 1953 (both drunk in 1988 and
rated in the high eighties). However, both wines quickly fell apart in the
glass, suggesting that they have begun to decline. The 1959, 1955, 1949,
and 1947 have left me decidedly unmoved, but the 1945 (tasted in January 1989 and rated 96) was worthy of that vintage's reputation. The bottle
I had would have lasted for another decade in a cool cellar.

PLANTEY (Cru Bourgeois)   AVERAGE

Production: 12,000 cases	Grape varieties:
	Cabernet Sauvignon—45%
	Merlot—45%
	Cabernet Franc—10%
Secondary label: none	
Vineyard size: 64 acres	Proprietor Gabriel Meffre
Time spent in barrels: 10–14 months	Average age of vines: 20 years
Evaluation of present classification: Should be maintained	
Plateau of maturity: 3–8 years following the vintage	

This wine has always impressed me as a standard-quality, fruity, supple,
easy-to-drink Pauillac of no great distinction or aging potential. The most
successful recent vintages have been 1982 and 1989.

PONTET-CANET (Fifth-Growth)   VERY GOOD

Production: 25,000–40,000 cases	Grape varieties: Cabernet Sauvignon—68% Merlot—20% Cabernet Franc—12%
Secondary label: Les Hauts de Pontet	
Vineyard size: 185.2 acres	Proprietor: The Tesseron family
Time spent in barrels: 18–24 months	Average age of vines: 27 years
Evaluation of present classification: Should be maintained	
Plateau of maturity: 8–30 years following the vintage	

With the largest production of any classified growth wine of the Médoc, and with the enviable vineyard positioned directly across from Mouton-Rothschild, one would expect the quality and stature of the wines of Pontet-Canet to be exceptionally high. Yet take a close look at the track record of Pontet-Canet over the period 1962–1983. While the wines were sound and competent, they have lacked that special ingredient called excitement. In the last several years a renewed vigor and commitment, as evidenced by the new ownership, has commenced. A totally new vinification cellar was constructed, a secondary label for weaker vats was launched, and a higher percentage of new oak was inaugurated. Yet in spite of this, the vineyards are still harvested by machine, an unwise decision if quality is not to be compromised.

Until 1975, the ubiquitous Cruse firm owned Pontet-Canet and tended to treat the wines as a brand name to be used for promotional purposes, rather than as a distinctive, individual, estate-bottled wine from Pauillac. The wine was not château-bottled until 1972, and for years batches of the wine were sold to the French railways without a vintage date, yet always marketed as Pontet-Canet. In 1975, the Cruse firm was forced to sell Pontet-Canet as a result of a trial that had found the firm negligent in blending and labeling practices. Guy Tesseron, a well-known Cognac merchant, purchased Pontet-Canet and has delegated responsibility for the management of this estate to his son, Alfred. I believe everyone in Bordeaux agrees that Pontet-Canet possesses a vineyard with enormous potential, provided it is carefully managed and exploited. If the initial wines from Guy and Alfred Tesseron lacked the character expected of them, several of the recent vintages, most notably the 1986 and 1989, give strong signs that Pontet-Canet is serious about challenging the elite of Pauillac.

VINTAGES

1989—The 1989 looks to be the finest Pontet-Canet since the heroic
·   1961. The wine has an impressive deep ruby/purple color, a highly
89   scented nose of exceptionally ripe cassis fruit and licorice, full
       body, an excellent mid-palate, and a rich, intense, relatively
       tannic finish. It can fairly be compared with the 1986, yet this
       rendition has more fat and ripeness. It should prove long-lived.
       Anticipated maturity: 1997–2025. Last tasted, 4/91.

1988—The 1988 is an above-average-quality wine. It typifies many of the
·   Médocs in this vintage with its very fine color, but narrowly con-
83   structed personality, high tannins, and a leanness and austerity
       that some will mistakenly call "classic." It should age well for 7–
       15 years, but it will always lack charm and flesh. Anticipated
       maturity: 1997–2008. Last tasted, 11/90.

1987—Pontet-Canet's 1987 is a success in this difficult vintage. An at-
·   tractive spicy, vanillin-scented, and cassis-dominated bouquet is
84   followed by soft, smooth, easy-to-drink flavors. This medium-bod-
       ied wine should be drunk up over the near term. Anticipated
       maturity: Now–1996. Last tasted, 4/90.

1986—The 1986 is dark ruby in color, with an intense bouquet of sweet
·   oak and cedary blackcurrants. This wine has excellent depth and
88   richness, full body, and sensational extraction of fruit. It lingers
       and lingers on the palate, with quite a tannic finish. This wine
       should not be touched before the mid-1990s, and is capable of
       lasting for 15–20 years thereafter. Thirty percent new oak casks
       were used. Along with the 1989, it represents the finest Pontet-
       Canet since 1961. Anticipated maturity: 1996–2012. Last tasted,
       4/90.

1985—An elegant, tasty, stylish wine, the 1985 Pontet-Canet is well
·   colored, with a moderately intense blackcurrant, toasty oak bou-
86   quet. While not nearly as concentrated as the 1986, it should still
       evolve nicely. Anticipated maturity: 1992–2001. Last tasted,
       4/90.

1984—Hard and austere, the 1984's fruit remains buried beneath abun-
·   dant tannins. A dubious 1984. Anticipated maturity: Now–may
74   be in decline. Last tasted, 4/90.

1983—A good vintage for Pontet-Canet, the 1983 is moderately dark
·   ruby in color, with a sweet, ripe blackcurrant fruitiness, and bri-
86   ary, concentrated flavors that linger on the palate. The tannins

have melted away faster than I would have thought. Anticipated maturity: 1992–2003. Last tasted, 4/90.

1982—The vintage's telltale deep ruby, almost purple color is present, · as well as the fabulous ripe aromas of ripe black cherries, spicy 87 oak, and fresh tar. Quite fat and plump on the palate, with a viscous, very ripe character, adequate acidity, and a long, alcoholic, very tannic finish, this is a big, corpulent wine that has put on considerable weight and structure in the late eighties, and now seems poised for a long life. It has the tannin to last for 10–15 years. Anticipated maturity: 1995–2010. Last tasted, 4/90.

1979—The 1979 is an undistinguished Pauillac, with a bland, moderately · intense, blackcurrant aroma, soft, charming, round flavors, me- 80 dium body, and light tannins in the finish. Anticipated maturity: Now. Last tasted, 4/90.

1978—In contrast to the 1979, a much more tannic, reserved wine for · long-term cellaring, the 1978 Pontet-Canet has dark ruby color 82 and a spicy, ripe, yet generally tight and closed bouquet. While certainly a good wine, it seems to be missing length and complex- ity. Anticipated maturity: Now–2000. Last tasted, 4/90.

1976—Not particularly outstanding, the Pontet-Canet, like so many 1976 · Bordeaux, is quite mature, with an amber, brownish color. Me- 75 dium bodied, with good, soft, round, fruity flavors, this wine is slightly deficient in acidity and length, but very agreeable. Antic- ipated maturity: Now–may be in decline. Last tasted, 10/84.

1975—A good, solid, slightly rustic 1975 with a well-developed toasty, · cedary, caramel-and-tobacco-scented bouquet, Pontet-Canet 85 lacks the tremendous grip and size of the best 1975 Pauillacs, but has good fruit, and a firm, long, alcoholic finish. The best Pontet- Canet of the seventies? Anticipated maturity: Now–2000. Last tasted, 4/90.

1971—An ambivalent sort of wine, with both positive and negative attri- · butes, this fully mature, somewhat brownish-colored wine has an 81 interesting, spicy, fruity, complex bouquet, and a savory, satis- fying sweet palate impression. However, sharp acidity in the fin- ish detracts considerably from the overall impression. Drink up. Anticipated maturity: Now–probably in serious decline. Last tasted, 7/82.

1970—Good, dark ruby color still exists. The bouquet of wood and ripe · plums is enjoyable, but lacks complexity. In the mouth, the wine 82 has plump, chunky, fruity flavors of good intensity, but seems to miss the mark when it comes to interest and length. Hopefully, it will get better, but I am unsure. Anticipated maturity: Now–1996. Last tasted, 4/90.

1966 — The 1966 Pontet-Canet is a leaner styled, tight, hard wine that to this day remains firm and closed. It is also beginning to lose its
·
77 fruit. The wine is moderately ruby, with some amber, a restrained, cedary, blackcurrant bouquet, and an austere, astringent finish. Anticipated maturity: Now–1994. Last tasted, 4/90.

1964 — I prefer the 1964 Pontet-Canet to the 1966 simply because of the
·
84 supple, lush fruitiness and straightforward, gustatory pleasure. Browning at the edge, with virtually all of the tannin gone, this wine requires consumption. Anticipated maturity: Now–probably in serious decline. Last tasted, 5/83.

1961 — Pontet-Canet produced a great 1961, although a distressingly high
·
94 incidence of variation as a result of the numerous English bottlings is undoubtedly a problem. The best bottles exhibit rich, deep color, with a full-blown, ripe, deep bouquet of spices and plums, viscous, round, supple flavors, and the sumptuous length that typify this great vintage. Now fully mature, the good examples of this wine will last a decade. Certainly the best Pontet-Canet I have ever tasted. The wine performed splendidly at a vertical tasting at Pontet-Canet in 1990. Anticipated maturity: Now–2005. Last tasted, 4/90.

OLDER VINTAGES

My notes reveal a satisfying 1959 (rated 85), a dull, tough, still-dense, charmless 1955 (rated 76), a magnificent 1945 (rated 93 in April 1990) with a stupendous oriental spice bouquet and smashing concentration. Lastly, the 1929 (rated 90 at the same tasting) had an orange-brownish color, but tasted sweet, opulent, and remarkably deep. Very few of the vintages prior to 1975 were estate-bottled, so buyers should exercise considerable caution.

LA ROSE PAUILLAC   AVERAGE

This cooperative, consisting of 125 vineyard owners who control 272 acres of vineyards in Pauillac, was created in 1932. At present, it is the most successful cooperative in Bordeaux, with 6,000 private clients as well as significant sales to many of Bordeaux's most prestigious *négociants*. The cooperative produces three *cuvées*, the majority of which is labeled La Rose Pauillac. In addition, two domains that vinify their wines at the cooperative, Château Haut-Milon and Château Haut-St.-Lambert, sell their wines under their own label, but it is entirely made and bottled at the cooperative. The cooperative has been using increasing percentages of small oak barrels, with a tiny percentage of them new. I tasted the 1982, 1983, 1985, and 1986 vintages of La Rose Pauillac in 1988 and they exhibited a soft, agreeable, clean, but not particularly distinguished style of wine. These wines should be drunk in their first 5–7 years of life.

ST.-JULIEN

If Pauillac is famous for having the Médoc's largest number of first-growths, and Margaux for being the most widely known appellation, St.-Julien is the Médoc's most underrated commune. The winemaking in St.-Julien—from the lesser-known Cru Bourgeois châteaux such as Terrey-Gros-Cailloux and Lalande Borie, to the three flagship estates of this commune, Léoville-Las Cases, Ducru-Beaucaillou, and Gruaud-Larose —is consistently both distinctive and brilliant. St.-Julien starts where the commune of Pauillac stops, and this is no better demonstrated than where Léoville-Las Cases and Latour meet at the border. Heading south from Pauillac, Léoville-Las Cases is on the right, followed by Léoville-Poyferré on both the left and right, Langoa and Léoville-Barton on the right, Ducru-Beaucaillou on the left, Branaire-Ducru on the right, and Beychevelle on the left. At normal driving speeds, the time necessary to pass all of these illustrious properties is no more than five minutes. Further inland and lacking a view of the Gironde are the two large Cordier properties, Gruaud-Larose and Talbot, as well as Lagrange and St.-Pierre.

There is no commune in the Médoc where the art of winemaking is practiced so highly as in St.-Julien. Consequently, the wine consumer has the odds stacked in his/her favor when purchasing a wine from here, a fact that cannot be said elsewhere in the Médoc. In addition to a bevy of fine wines from the Cru Bourgeois châteaux of St.-Julien, the eleven classified growths are all turning out wonderfully crafted wines, yet all vary greatly in style.

Léoville-Las Cases is the most Pauillac-like of the St.-Juliens for two main reasons. The vineyards sit next to those of Pauillac's famous first-growth, Latour, and owner Michel Delon makes a deeply concentrated,

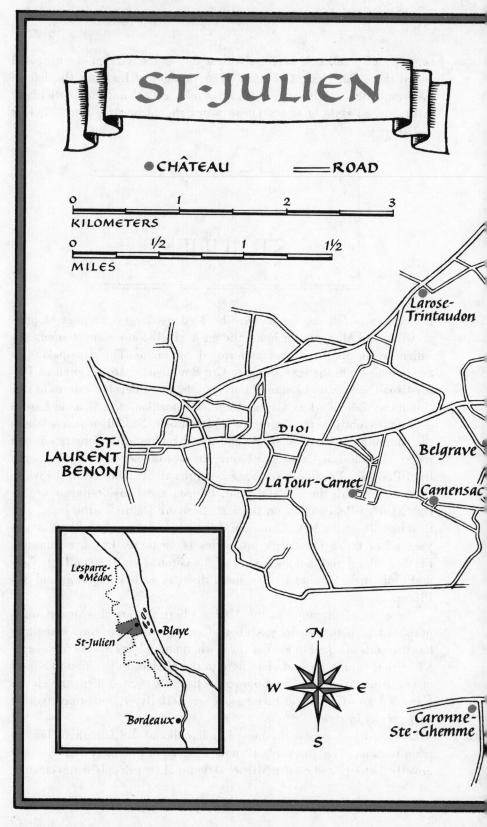

ST·JULIEN

● CHÂTEAU   ═══ROAD

0   1   2   3
KILOMETERS

0   ½   1   1½
MILES

Larose-
Trintaudon

D101

ST-
LAURENT
BENON

Belgrave

La Tour-Carnet

Camensac

Lesparre-
Médoc

Blaye

St-Julien

Bordeaux

Caronne-
Ste-Ghemme

N
W   E
S

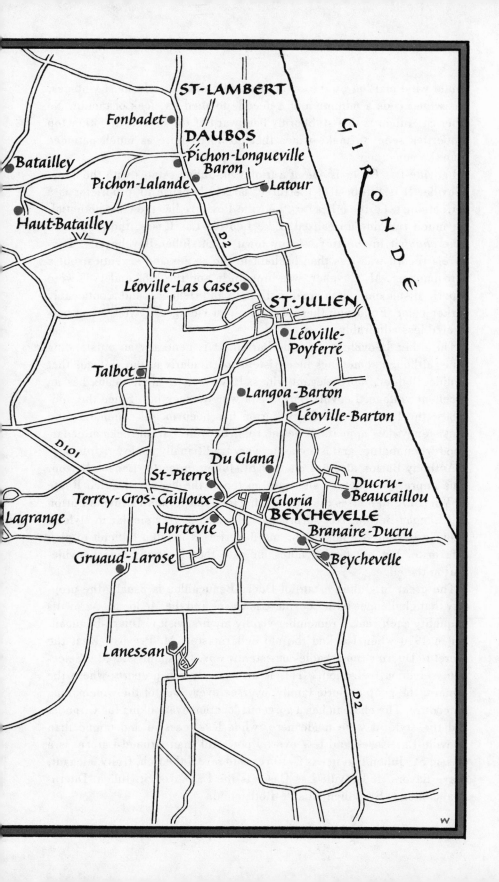

ST-LAMBERT

Fonbadet

DAUBOS

Batailley

Pichon-Longueville
Baron

Pichon-Lalande

Latour

Haut-Batailley

D2

Léoville-Las Cases

ST-JULIEN

Léoville-
Poyferré

Talbot

Langoa-Barton

Léoville-Barton

D101

Du Glana

St-Pierre

Ducru-
Beaucaillou

Terrey-Gros-Cailloux

Gloria

BEYCHEVELLE

Lagrange

Hortevie

Branaire-Ducru

Gruaud-Larose

Beychevelle

Lanessan

D2

GIRONDE

W

tannic wine marked by the scent of vanillin oakiness. In most vintages, this wine needs a minimum of a decade to shed its cloak of tannin. No other St.-Julien is this stubbornly backward at the outset; the other top properties seem to make wines that do not require as much patience from the consumer.

Léoville-Las Cases is one of a trio of St.-Julien estates with the name Léoville. It is the best of the three, largely because its proprietor is a perfectionist. Of the other two, Léoville-Poyferré has the most potential, yet much remains unrealized. Like Léoville-Las Cases, the office and wine *chai* sit in the tiny, sleepy town of St.-Julien-Beychevelle. Poyferré's record was less than brilliant in the sixties and seventies, but a new manager, M. Cuvelier, was brought in and the 1982 and 1983 were superb, displaying much greater strength and richness, and a noticeably darker color. Following these dynamic two vintages, Poyferré has performed less admirably.

The other Léoville is Léoville-Barton. It is generally an outstanding wine, although sometimes inconsistent, particularly in the vintages that produce lighter, more elegant wines. However, when Bordeaux has an excellent vintage, Léoville-Barton is a wine to seek out. Since the mid-1980s, the handsome Anthony Barton has been in full command, and consistency now appears to be the rule. Léoville-Barton reeks of cedarwood when mature and is a classic, very traditionally made St.-Julien.

Anthony Barton also has another St.-Julien property, Langoa-Barton. This impressive château sits right on top of the heavily traveled Route du Vin (D2) and houses the winemaking facilities for both Léoville-Barton and Langoa-Barton. Not surprisingly, Langoa is very similar in style to Léoville-Barton—cedary, rich, and flavorful. It is often difficult to pick a favorite, but my tasting notes indicate that I usually give Léoville-Barton the edge.

The great St.-Julien estate of Ducru-Beaucaillou is usually the property that challenges both Léoville-Las Cases and the Médoc first-growths in quality each year. I remember vividly my first visit to Ducru-Beaucaillou in 1970 when I asked the old cellarmaster, M. Prévost, what the secret to Ducru's remarkable consistency was. He simply stated, "Selection, selection, selection." This is an expertly run property where the owners, the genteel Borie family, oversee every step of the winemaking procedure. The château has a gorgeous location overlooking the Gironde, and the style of wine made here, while less massive and tannic than Léoville-Las Cases and less overtly powerful than Gruaud-Larose, is a classic St.-Julien that needs 8–10 years to reveal the rich, fruity, elegant, suave flavors. If Léoville-Las Cases is the Latour of St.-Julien, Ducru-Beaucaillou is St.-Julien's Lafite-Rothschild.

Within shouting distance of Ducru-Beaucaillou are Branaire-Ducru and Beychevelle, the two most southern St.-Juliens. Beychevelle is widely known, perhaps because tourists love the gardens (the Médoc's most photogenic), and the wine is supple, fruity, light, and quick to mature. While good, even outstanding as in 1982, 1986, and 1989, Beychevelle has always had a better reputation than its performance record would lead one to believe.

Just the opposite is the case with Branaire-Ducru, the rather drab, sullen-looking château across the road from Beychevelle. Despite a slump in quality after 1982, Branaire rebounded strongly with a great effort in 1989. Furthermore, the price for Branaire remains one of the lowest for a wine of such quality. Branaire is a bigger wine than its neighbor, Beychevelle, always darkly colored and usually possessed of an exotic, richly scented bouquet of cedar and chocolate. Branaire will never have the aging potential of the three Léovilles or Ducru-Beaucaillou, but between the ages of 8 and 20, Branaire can be an opulently rich, distinctive style of wine.

Two other great wines of St.-Julien are made at Gruaud-Larose and Talbot, both very large estates owned by the Cordier family. Gruaud-Larose sits back off the river behind Beychevelle and Branaire-Ducru. Gruaud-Larose and stablemate and immediate northern neighbor Talbot produce densely colored, rich, fruity wines. Gruaud is usually superior to Talbot, which has a tendency to sometimes be lean, but the quality of these two wines, while historically quite good, has been brilliant since 1978. Furthermore, because they both produce in excess of 35,000 cases of wine, and the price charged seems remarkably modest, Gruaud-Larose and Talbot immensely satisfy both the purse and the palate. In particular, Gruaud-Larose has performed at what is certainly a first-growth level since 1961, although one hears critics of Gruaud-Larose suggest that it lacks the great complexity and staying power of a true first-growth. Both of these points have proved baseless when the wine is compared in blind tastings against the first-growths.

The remaining two St.-Julien classified growths, Lagrange and St.-Pierre, both have undergone significant personality changes. Lagrange, lowly regarded for decades, has taken on new owners from Japan, and with some expert start-up advice from Michel Delon of Léoville-Las Cases, improvements since 1982 have been remarkable. Since Lagrange's low price reflects years of mediocrity and the trade's lack of confidence in this wine, shrewd Bordeaux enthusiasts might do well to take an interest in this up-and-coming property.

St.-Pierre has always been a terribly underrated property. Until recently it was Belgian-owned and the style of wine it produced was rich in color and extract, full bodied, sometimes a bit rustic, but always satisfyingly fat, robust, and fruity. Now the property and the wine are under the watchful eye of the late Henri Martin's son-in-law, Jean-Louis Triaud, also manager of St.-Julien's most famous Cru Bourgeois, Gloria. The transition to a "Martinized" style of St.-Julien was readily apparent with their first vintage, the 1983, a richly fruity, almost sweet, easy-to-drink, supple wine that has huge popular appeal.

St.-Julien is not without some wonderful Cru Bourgeois properties. In addition to the excellent Gloria, there are the very good Terrey-Gros-Cailloux and Hortevie, both made at the same property; the stylish, elegant Lalande Borie; the rather commercial, sometimes dull, sometimes good du Glana; and a bevy of good *"deuxième"* or second wines from the major châteaux. The best of these is the Clos du Marquis from Léoville-Las Cases.

St.-Julien is a good commune for treasure hunting when Bordeaux has a poor or mediocre vintage. In fact, St.-Julien's soil is similar to the light, gravel-based earth of Margaux, except that it is richer in clay. This affords the wines more body and viscosity. Since most of the major vineyards are close to the Gironde, they tend to have excellent, well-drained, deep beds of gravel soil. In 1984, 1980, and 1977, all difficult years, St.-Julien produced more acceptable wines than elsewhere in Bordeaux. For the moment, the two Cordier estates, Gruaud-Larose and Talbot, as well as Branaire-Ducru, Ducru-Beaucaillou, and Léoville-Las Cases seem to do the best job in the so-called "off-vintages."

In the excellent-to-great vintages, St.-Juliens are quintessential Médocs. The 1989, 1986, 1985, 1982, 1978, 1970, 1961, and 1959 from St.-Julien are the truly great vintages for this appellation, followed by 1988, 1983, 1979, 1976, 1966, and 1962.

A CONSUMER'S CLASSIFICATION OF THE CHÂTEAUX OF ST.-JULIEN

OUTSTANDING
Ducru-Beaucaillou
Gruaud-Larose
Léoville-Las Cases

EXCELLENT
Beychevelle
Branaire-Ducru
Léoville-Barton
Talbot

VERY GOOD
Gloria
Hortevie
Lagrange
Langoa-Barton
Léoville-Poyferré
St.-Pierre

GOOD
Lalande Borie
Terrey-Gros-Cailloux

OTHER NOTABLE ST.-JULIEN PROPERTIES
La Bridane
Glana

BEYCHEVELLE (Fourth-Growth)   EXCELLENT

Production: 30,000 cases	Grape varieties: Cabernet Sauvignon—60% Merlot—28% Cabernet Franc—8% Petit Verdot—4%
Secondary labels: Amiral de Beychevelle and Reserve de L'Amiral	
Vineyard size: 177.8 acres	Proprietor: Sociètè Civile Administrator: Maurice Ruelle
Time spent in barrels: 20 months	Average age of vines: 20 years
Evaluation of present classification: Should be upgraded to a third-growth	
Plateau of maturity: 7–20 years following the vintage	

Tourists visiting Bordeaux are unlikely to miss Château Beychevelle because it is the first major château passed on the D2 road leading north into the commune of St.-Julien. The beautiful flowering gardens that face the road have caused many speeding drivers to stop and take photographs.

The wines of Beychevelle can also be beautifully produced. During the decades of the sixties and seventies, the lack of consistency from vintage to vintage was a problem. Moreover, the wine has been disappointing in mediocre years, such as 1974 and 1987. Even in top years, Beychevelle tastes uncommonly smooth, supple, and drinkable at a young age. This seems to give purists and traditionalists cause for unnecessary concern. Most recent top vintages of Beychevelle, while fully mature by the time they are 10 years old, have the requisite stuffing to age well for 15 or more years. However, this is generally not a property whose wines require laying away for decades.

In the early eighties, the owners began to realize that the ultra-smooth style of Beychevelle was, as the English say, "not making old bones." Since 1982, there has been an increasing reliance on the firmer, more muscular Cabernet Sauvignon in the blend, a lengthening of the all-important *cuvaison* period, the increased usage of new oak, and the introduction of a second label for lighter vats of wine. These techniques have significantly improved the quality of Beychevelle, with great wines produced in 1982, 1986, and 1989. The light, supple, elegant, quick-maturing style of wine made in the sixties and seventies has, since 1982, moved to a firmer constructed, more concentrated type of St.-Julien without, however, sacrificing any of the wine's flattering up-front style and charm.

Beychevelle is one of St.-Julien's most expensive wines, often selling at a price level just below that of Léoville-Las Cases and Ducru-Beaucaillou. The current ownership appears committed to pushing Beychevelle into the elite grouping of wines known as the "super seconds," or those estates that often produce wines of first-growth quality.

VINTAGES

1989—In 1989, Beychevelle produced a compelling wine that rivals the
  ·   1986 and 1982—the two other superstars made at this beautiful
  91   estate during the decade of the eighties. An exquisite bouquet of
        superripe fruit, vanillin, flowers, and licorice precedes a delicious
        array of flavors that swell and expand on the palate. Very rich and
        concentrated, extremely long, with a hefty dose of high—but soft
        —tannins, this wine may well take the prize as the most hedonis-
        tic wine among the 1989 St.-Juliens. Anticipated maturity: 1993–
        2008. Last tasted, 4/91.

1988—Somewhat astringent, a little hollow, with an underripe, green
  ·   streak to the flavors, the 1988 Beychevelle should age well for 10–
  84   12 years, but I doubt if it will ever provide excitement. Was the
        Cabernet Sauvignon harvested too early? Anticipated maturity:
        1994–2002. Last tasted, 4/91.

1987—Light, with a two-dimensional bouquet of vanillin oak and herbs,
  ·   this medium-bodied wine is soft, slightly diluted, yet ideal for
  78   drinking young. Anticipated maturity: Now–1995. Last tasted,
        11/90.

1986—While quite outstanding and deserving to be in any conscien-
·   tiously stocked wine cellar, the 1986 Beychevelle does not quite
92   have the extraordinary concentration and potential for longevity
       that I had thought it would. Nevertheless, this is still one of the
       best Beychevelles in the last 30 years. With its black/ruby color
       and huge bouquet of roasted fruit, this full-bodied, concentrated,
       rich wine should not be drunk before the mid-1990s. Anticipated
       maturity: 1994–2010. Last tasted, 1/91.

1985—The 1985 admirably reflects the character of this charming vin-
·   tage. Deep ruby, low in acidity, ripe, round, fruity, and preco-
87   cious, this medium-bodied, supple wine is very tasty and displays
       the cedary, blackcurrant fruit so common in the wines of St.-
       Julien. Anticipated maturity: Now–1997. Last tasted, 3/90.

1984—The 1984 has turned out well for the vintage. A raspberry-
·   scented, spicy nose is followed by a medium-bodied wine with
79   high acidity and some underlying greenness. Anticipated matu-
       rity: Now–1995. Last tasted, 10/89.

1983—Dark ruby with some amber at the edge, this wine has a ripe,
·   intense, cassis smell. Moderately rich and tannic on the palate,
85   with good depth, the 1983 continues to exhibit an aggressive
       texture, and a long, rough finish. This is a good rather than pro-
       found Beychevelle. Anticipated maturity: Now–2002. Last tasted,
       1/89.

1982—Over recent vintages, Beychevelle has not been a wine I have felt
·   comfortable evaluating early on. The 1982 appeared to lack acid-
92   ity and to be too disjointed to be outstanding, but since it has been
       bottled, the wine has gone from one strength to another. Anyone
       who owns it probably has one of the three best Beychevelles (the
       other candidates are the 1986 and 1989) made in the last 30 years.
       It has a fabulously rich, concentrated, smoky, toasty bouquet
       that suggests not only gobs of rich blackcurrant fruit, but also
       plenty of vanillin-scented new oak. The wine is slightly deficient
       in acidity, but it does not taste disjointed or unstructured, as
       there are wonderfully lush, velvety, rich, full-bodied flavors,
       and plenty of tannin in the finish, which helps give it defini-
       tion. While somewhat precocious, this wine will not be fully
       mature until the early 1990s. Certainly it is capable of lasting
       another 20 years. Anticipated maturity: 1992–2012. Last tasted,
       5/91.

1981—The 1981 is significantly lighter than either the 1982 or 1983.
·   Forward, quite fruity, with a straightforward, oaky, fruity bou-
83   quet, medium bodied, with a healthy color, this is a supple, soft,

charming wine that already provides pleasant drinking. Anticipated maturity: Now–1997. Last tasted, 1/88.

1979—Diffuse and soft in style, this medium-bodied, moderately ruby-
·   colored wine has been drinkable for at least 5–6 years. The fruit
81   is holding nicely, but the wine lacks excitement. Anticipated maturity: Now–may be in decline. Last tasted, 10/83.

1978—Dark ruby/garnet with some amber at the edge, the 1978 Beychev-
·   elle tastes close to maturity. A lovely bouquet of ripe berry fruit,
85·   oak, and spice is followed by a wine that is slightly sweet, soft,
and savory, with some unresolved tannins. It remains a bit
chunky, but is still satisfying and flavorful. Anticipated maturity:
Now–1996. Last tasted, 1/89.

1976—Technically, the 1976 Beychevelle is not the most perfect wine.
·   The acidity is low and the pH high, but statistics aside, this wine
85   has retained its immensely enjoyable, plummy, fat, fruity character. I would have thought it to be in decline now, but this
seductive effort from Beychevelle continues to provide surprising
pleasure. Anticipated maturity: Now–1994. Last tasted, 11/90.

1975—Early in this wine's life, it tasted precocious and forward for the
·   normally tannic, hard wines of the vintage. However, this wine
86   has now firmed up, and it should turn out to be the longest-lived
Beychevelle of the seventies. Dark ruby, with a ripe, spicy,
leather-and-blackcurrant-scented bouquet, this full-bodied,
weighty, muscular Beychevelle is atypically powerful. Whether it
will ever resolve all the tannins remains debatable. Anticipated
maturity: Now–2005. Last tasted, 10/89.

1974—Beychevelle made a good showing in 1974, producing a supple,
·   easygoing, fruity, gentle wine that is now fully mature. Anticipated
77   maturity: Now–probably in serious decline. Last tasted, 3/79.

1973—Now totally faded and dissipated, this light wine should have been
·   drunk by 1980. Last tasted, 2/81.
65

1971—Quite attractive and fully mature, the 1971 Beychevelle, while not
·   classically structured, but rather loosely knit and too soft, never-
83   theless has a savory, spicy, fruity clout, with moderately intense
flavors and light tannin. Anticipated maturity: Now–may be in
decline. Last tasted, 2/83.

1970—Fully mature with a spicy, plum-like bouquet, and some caramel
·   aromas, the 1970 Beychevelle is round, fruity, quite silky and
85   soft, and nicely concentrated. It lacks complexity and the depth
of the best 1970s, but is still quite attractive. Anticipated maturity: Now–1996. Last tasted, 4/88.

1967—In the early and mid-1970s, this wine was attractive, flavorful,
· spicy, with above-average fruity intensity for the vintage. Now,
70 the wine has lost that exuberant fruitiness and begun to fade
badly. Some fruit still remains, but this wine should have been
drunk up prior to 1980. Last tasted, 3/81.

1966—One of my favorite Beychevelles, this wine has constantly shown
· well in tastings of the 1966s. Quite mature, with an expansive,
86 complex, ripe, fruity, spicy, cedary bouquet, and supple, soft,
velvety flavors, this Beychevelle has consistently exhibited good
concentration, as well as the tough, tannic firmness of the 1966
vintage. Although fully mature for over a decade, it displays no
signs of decline. Anticipated maturity: Now–1994. Last tasted,
1/88.

1964—Beginning to crack up ever so slightly, the 1964 Beychevelle still
· has a good measure of chunky fruitiness a rustic, medium- to full-
83 bodied feel on the palate, and a creeping brownish cast to the
color. The bouquet is particularly spicy for Beychevelle. Anticipated maturity: Now–may be in decline. Last tasted, 1/81.

1962—This is another example of a Beychevelle that has not stood the
· test of time. My notes reveal I had a good example in a Bordeaux
74 restaurant in 1970, but more recent tastings have displayed a tired
and fatigued wine, with some fruit and character still remaining,
but most definitely on the slide. Anticipated maturity: Now–probably in serious decline. Last tasted, 7/79.

1961—The 1961 Beychevelle continues to age gracefully, but it is not in
· the top league of 1961s. I have always regarded it as a fruity,
88 concentrated wine that has a voluptuous, expansive, even sweet
taste. The wine has been fully mature for over a decade. Anticipated maturity: Now–1994. Last tasted, 1/88.

OLDER VINTAGES

For unexplainable reasons, Beychevelle does not frequently appear in
my tasting notes of older vintages. The 1959 and 1952, each tasted only
once, were solid, but hardly inspiring. A 1953 (rated 92 in 1987) was
terrific, the second-best Beychevelle I have ever tasted. The finest mature Beychevelle (I have high hopes for the 1982, 1986, and 1989) I have
tasted was the 1928, drunk in March 1988. I rated it in the upper nineties
and found it to have at least a decade of life left.

BRANAIRE-DUCRU (Fourth-Growth)   EXCELLENT

Production: 20,000 cases	Grape varieties: Cabernet Sauvignon—60% Merlot—25% Cabernet Franc—10% Petit Verdot—5%
Secondary label: Duluc	
Vineyard size: 118.5 acres	Proprietor: Société Civile
Time spent in barrels: 18–24 months	Average age of vines: 18 years

Evaluation of present classification: Should be upgraded to a third-growth

Plateau of maturity: 5–15 years following the vintage

I have always found Branaire-Ducru to be curiously underrated, under-valued, and somewhat forgotten whenever Bordeaux enthusiasts discuss their favorite wines. Travelers passing through St.-Julien have no doubt noted the drab beige building directly opposite Beychevelle on the Médoc's main wine road. Several of the recent vintages, particularly 1975, 1976, 1982, and 1989, have been magnificently scented, deep, rich wines that are as good as most of the first-growths in those years, not to mention the other top wines of St.-Julien. However, between 1982 and 1989, the property produced a series of indifferent wines that appeared to reflect overly abundant crop sizes and less than strict selection. The introduction of a new winemaking team, as well as a second label in the late eighties, appear to have been the necessary cures to get Branaire back on track.

The vineyards of Branaire, like those of many Bordeaux châteaux, are spread out in a morsellated fashion throughout the commune of St.-Julien. Branaire is one of the few non-first-growth châteaux to use 75% new oak barrels every year, and in contrast to many châteaux that have decreased the duration of their *cuvaison* to produce a more forward and supple wine, Branaire keeps the skins in contact with the grape juice for a full month.

The wines of Branaire have a distinctive character. For a St.-Julien they are particularly spicy, with an almost exotic aroma of spicy, oaky, vanillin character. On the palate, the wine often has a pronounced, distinctive chocolatey component that makes Branaire relatively easy to spot in blind tastings. This personality trait is especially noticeable in the great vintages of 1975, 1976, 1982, and 1989.

VINTAGES

1989—It appears the slump in quality that began in 1983 at Branaire-
·   Ducru has been resoundingly stopped by a new winemaking team
92   that turned in a superlative effort in 1989. Reminiscent of the
         1982, the 1989 has a forward, expansive bouquet of ripe plums
         and minerals that soars from the glass. In the mouth, the wine is
         pure silk. Luscious to the point of opulence, this full-bodied wine
         is bursting with chocolatey, blackcurrant fruit. Aging in oak casks
         has given it the definition it needed, as well as some tannic firm-
         ness, but this is a lusty Branaire to consume early in its life.
         Anticipated maturity: 1993–2005. Last tasted, 4/91.

1988—In contrast to the 1989 Branaire, the 1988 is light, angular, and
·   pleasant, but one-dimensional. Anticipated maturity: Now–1998.
81   Last tasted, 4/91.

1986—Branaire was in the midst of a slump when the 1986 was con-
·   ceived. The culprit would appear to be overproduction, without a
84   subsequent strict selection process. However, restaurants will
         love the 1986, which offers surprisingly ripe, forward, cedary,
         herbaceous blackcurrant fruit, married nicely with plenty of
         sweet, vanilla-scented, toasty oak. The wine is medium bodied
         and somewhat atypical for the vintage given the suppleness and
         precocious appeal, but it is an attractive, easy-to-like, and easy-
         to-understand wine. Anticipated maturity: Now–1997. Last
         tasted, 3/90.

1985—The 1985 is a spicy, plummy, tasty wine with undeniable appeal
·   because of precocious fruitiness. Once past all the up-front charm
85   and make-up, there is not much depth or tannin. Anticipated
         maturity: Now–1995. Last tasted, 3/81.

1984—The 1984 Branaire has adequate color, but the texture and flavors
·   are not generous. The acidity is high and the finish short and
74   tannic. I doubt if cellaring will add more charm. Anticipated ma-
         turity: Now. Last tasted, 3/88.

1983—Somewhat soft for Branaire, with a medium-weight texture and
·   relatively lush fruit, the 1983 is a moderately tannic, compact
84   wine that is similar to the 1981 Branaire only less elegant and
         charming. Anticipated maturity: Now–1996. Last tasted, 6/84.

1982—I have had the 1982 Branaire-Ducru on eight separate occasions.
·   Once in Bordeaux and four times from my cellar, it was every-
91   thing it should have been—a wonderfully rich, supple, smoky,
         violet-and-blackcurrant-scented wine that was about as concen-
         trated a Branaire as I have ever tasted. It was supple and preco-
         cious, but extremely long, and seemed to grow and expand in the

glass with airing. However, on the other occasions, the wine had a shockingly light to medium ruby color, very little concentration, and a short, somewhat cooked finish. I noted that the disappointing bottles were all from lots of Branaire-Ducru released in the marketplace 1 to 2 years after the initial shipments. Whether the wine suffered because of poor storage or transportation conditions one cannot know, but I saw no sign from the bottles to suggest this. What could possibly account for such significant differences in quality? Anticipated maturity: 1992–2008. Last tasted, 10/90.

1981—Somewhat understated in personality, the 1981 Branaire is quite
  ·   successful, but forward, precociously supple, and fruity. The bou-
 85   quet is already showing expansive, complex, chocolatey, cedary
       components. Anticipated maturity: Now–1998. Last tasted, 11/84.

1980—A pleasant, fruity, soft, round wine without any of the vintage's
  ·   unripe vegetal greenness present, the 1980 Branaire-Ducru is
 78   fully mature. Anticipated maturity: Now–may be in decline. Last
       tasted, 2/83.

1979—Ready to drink as full maturity seems very close, the 1979 Bran-
  ·   aire has a full-intensity, spicy, cedary, ripe blackcurrant bouquet.
 84   On the palate, the wine is soft, supple, with generous silky fruiti-
       ness, light to moderate tannins, and good length and weight. A
       very stylish, round, elegant wine. Anticipated maturity: Now–
       1994. Last tasted, 9/90.

1978—The 1978 is not up to the quality level of the 1979. The wine has
  ·   good color, an attractive, spicy, ripe bouquet, but on the palate it
 80   has a sharpness and angular quality that gives it an attenuated
       feel. Anticipated maturity: Now–1994. Last tasted, 11/88.

1976—This Branaire has been fully mature and delicious to drink since
  ·   its release in 1979. Medium ruby, with some browning at the
 87   edge, the 1976 Branaire has a full-blown, captivating bouquet of
       spicy oak, ripe fruit, caramel, and toffee scents. In the mouth,
       the wine is soft, silky, and admirably concentrated for a 1976. It
       has a round and generous finish. Despite low acidity and overall
       fragility, the wine continues to drink beautifully. However, don't
       push your luck. Drink up. Anticipated maturity: Now–1994. Last
       tasted, 12/89.

1975—This is a great Branaire that rivals both the 1982 and 1989, but it
  ·   will prove considerably longer lived than those two vintages. It
 92   has a full-intensity bouquet of spicy, vanillin oakiness, ripe fruit,
       and cedarwood. In the mouth, the wine is chocolatey, gloriously

concentrated, rich, and spicy, with the once aggressive tannins now melting away. It is a great success for the vintage, and rivaled in St.-Julien only by Léoville-Las Cases and Léoville-Barton. Anticipated maturity: Now–2005. Last tasted, 11/90.

1974—One of the very best St.-Juliens produced in this poor vintage, the
·   1974 Branaire is now fully mature, and quite good. A complex
82 bouquet of spicy oak, flowers, and ripe blackcurrant fruit has the depth of a much better vintage. Medium bodied, with good fruit, and just a trace of brown at the edge, this is a noteworthy success for the vintage. Drink up! Anticipated maturity: Now–may be in decline. Last tasted, 3/80.

1971—A mediocre wine for Branaire, with a diffuse, somewhat watery
·   character, rust/brown color at the edges, and light body and ex-
71 tract. It should have been drunk up by 1980. Last tasted, 10/79.

1970—The 1970 is a dark ruby wine that is now approaching maturity.
·   This Branaire is a plump, somewhat fat wine, with good, chewy
84 fruit, some coarse, dusty tannins, and plenty of oak aromas. Big and powerful rather than elegant, it is a good, but not excellent wine for the château. Anticipated maturity: Now–1993. Last tasted, 2/83.

1966—This has always been a beautiful Branaire. It is now fully mature,
·   but in no danger of falling off for at least another couple of years.
88 The 1966 is dark ruby, with some amber at the edge. It has the telltale big, intense, spicy, blackcurrant, tarry, truffle-scented bouquet, soft, silky, ripe, rich, deep, savory flavors, and a long finish. The flavors appear to have become more sweet and expansive in the late eighties. It is a lovely success from St.-Julien for the 1966 vintage. Anticipated maturity: Now–1994. Last tasted, 2/89.

1964—The 1964 has only been tasted once, and that was in the early
·   seventies. At that time, the wine was chunky and fruity, without
70 much direction or character, and browning prematurely. Probably well past its prime. Last tasted, 4/72.

1962—Branaire usually can be counted on to age extremely well, how-
·   ever, this wine was brown, fading badly, and very sweet and sug-
58 ared when last tasted in 1986. It had little redeeming interest, and I suspect it has completely collapsed by now. Last tasted, 5/86.

1961—This is a very good Branaire, but to my thinking, not as good as
·   the fine 1966, or nearly as successful as the outstanding wines
83 made in 1975, 1982, and 1989. Good, dark ruby color with amber at the edges indicates maturity. On the palate, the wine is full bodied, flavorful, and deep, but the tannin is coarse, and the

dusty texture lacks elegance and finesse. Anticipated maturity: Now–1995. Last tasted, 2/83.

OLDER VINTAGES

Curiously, I have tasted only one vintage of Branaire-Ducru older than the 1961. The 1959 did not distinguish itself when I had it in 1988. Lacking fruit and too alcoholic, it appeared to be cracking up.

LA BRIDANE (Cru Bourgeois)   AVERAGE

Production: 8,500 cases	Grape varieties: Cabernet Sauvignon—55% Merlot—45%
Secondary label: none	
Vineyard size: 42.5 acres	Proprietor: Pierre Saintout
Time spent in barrels: 14–16 months	Average age of vines: 20 years
Evaluation of present classification: Should be maintained	
Plateau of maturity: 5–14 years following the vintage	

This solidly made wine usually has considerable power, weight, and a chunky fruitiness. What it frequently lacks are those elusive qualities called charm and finesse. Nevertheless, the wine keeps well and is usually reasonably priced.

DUCRU-BEAUCAILLOU (Second-Growth)   OUTSTANDING

Production: 16,500 cases	Grape varieties: Cabernet Sauvignon—65% Merlot—25% Cabernet Franc—5% Petit Verdot—5%
Secondary label: La Croix	
Vineyard size: 123.5 acres	Proprietor: Jean-Eugène Borie
Time spent in barrels: 20 months	Average age of vines: 30 years
Evaluation of present classification: Should be upgraded to a first-growth	
Plateau of maturity: 10–30 years following the vintage	

Ducru-Beaucaillou, sitting among an outcropping of trees, with a splendid view of the Gironde River, has one of the great settings in the Médoc. The property belongs to Jean-Eugène Borie. He inherited it from his father, who purchased the estate in 1941. Borie is one of an ever-decreasing number of live-in proprietors. In the last three decades, he has brought the quality of Ducru-Beaucaillou up to a level where vintages such as 1961, 1966, 1970, 1973, 1976, 1978, 1981, 1982, 1983, 1985, 1986, and 1989 can challenge any of the Médoc first-growths. Passion for his wine, an obsessive commitment to quality, remarkable modesty, and numerous trips abroad as ambassador for Bordeaux have made him one of this region's most respected wine personalities.

The wine of Ducru-Beaucaillou is the essence of elegance, symmetry, balance, breed, class, and distinction. It is never one of the most robust, richest, or fruitiest wines of St.-Julien, and by its nature is a stubbornly slow developer. Most of the finest vintages of Ducru-Beaucaillou usually take at least 10 years to reveal their stunning harmony of fruit and power.

Ducru-Beaucaillou is a great wine for a number of reasons. The meticulous attention to detail, the brutal selection process—whereby only the finest grapes and finest barrels of wine are permitted to go into the bottle —and the conservative viticultural practices followed, all play major roles in the success of this wine. Not surprisingly, the great Bordeaux oenologist, Emile Peynaud, has been employed as a consultant since 1953, which, coincidentally, was a great vintage for Ducru.

Ducru-Beaucaillou is one of Bordeaux's most expensive second-growths, reflecting the international demand for the wine and the consistently high quality. Does the St.-Julien vineyard merit "first-growth" status? Many wine enthusiasts, including this writer, would argue that Ducru-Beaucaillou, Léoville-Las Cases, and Gruaud-Larose merit elevation because of their consistently exceptional performance over the last 25 years.

VINTAGES

1989—
·
92
    Ducru-Beaucaillou has made another exceptional wine in 1989 that tastes like a hypothetical blend of their 1986 and 1982. Less powerful and concentrated than the 1982, but not nearly as backward or as tannic as the 1986, the 1989 is one of the Médoc's most elegantly rendered wines. Dark ruby, with a more perfumed, toasty character than usual, this medium-bodied, currant-flavored wine exhibits plenty of depth, low acidity, good tannins, and an

understated yet authoritative style that makes it a benchmark for
its type. Anticipated maturity: 1997–2020. Last tasted, 4/91.

1988—The 1988 is a medium-bodied wine without the depth and inten-
· 　　sity of fruit of the 1989. It has high tannins and good ripeness,
88　　and it is another Médoc that appears to recall the style of the 1966
　　　vintage. Anticipated maturity: 1996–2008. Last tasted, 4/91.

1987—Some attractive ripe fruit can be found in this successful, elegant,
· 　　yet surprisingly tannic and closed Ducru. It should prove to be
83　　one of the longer-lived 1987s. Anticipated maturity: 1992–2000.
　　　Last tasted, 4/91.

1986—Ducru will never have the massiveness of Gruaud-Larose or the
· 　　power and depth of Léoville-Las Cases, but this wine fully justi-
94　　fies the château's reputation as the Lafite-Rothschild of St.-Ju-
　　　lien. It's an interesting wine that often closes up after bottling,
　　　not to open again for 8–10 years. I fully expect the 1986 to do this,
　　　although it has certainly been showing extremely well immedi-
　　　ately after the bottling. The 1986 is a very great wine, more tannic
　　　and hard than the 1982, but as concentrated and deep as that
　　　legendary Ducru. The balance is virtually perfect, but significant
　　　patience will be required waiting for this classic example of
　　　Ducru-Beaucaillou to reach its plateau of maturity. One disturb-
　　　ing note concerning the 1986 Ducru is that I have come across a
　　　surprisingly high percentage of bad bottles that had the smell of
　　　damp cardboard, suggesting defective corks. I have asked the
　　　Borie family about this and they claim to have had no problems
　　　with corks in 1986. Anticipated maturity: 1998–2020. Last tasted,
　　　4/91.

1985—The 1985 does not have the sheer power of either of the Ducrus
· 　　made in 1982 or 1986, yet it has a wonderful, rich, ripe, generous,
91　　curranty fruitiness, medium to full body, a creamy texture backed
　　　by ripe tannins, and a long, balanced, impressive finish. This is
　　　one 1985 that may well turn out to be a clone of this property's
　　　1953—high praise indeed. Anticipated maturity: 1992–2010. Last
　　　tasted, 4/91.

1984—The 1984 is soft, has some attractive, weedy Cabernet Sauvignon
· 　　fruit, but tails off in the mouth. It is light and, I suppose, elegant.
79　　Anticipated maturity: Now–1994. Last tasted, 4/91.

1983—1983 is a good, rather than great, vintage for Borie's Ducru-Beau-
· 　　caillou. The 1983 has a dark ruby color with only a hint of amber,
87　　an expansive bouquet of ripe blackcurrant fruit, minerals, and a
　　　moderate oakiness. Aggressively tannic, rather hard, still youth-
　　　ful and backward, this is a more forceful-styled, medium-bodied

rendition of Ducru-Beaucaillou. It has neither the charm of the 1985 nor the opulence or power of the 1982. Anticipated maturity: 1994–2005. Last tasted, 4/91.

1982—In three recent tastings of the 1982, on one occasion the wine
· seemed dull, dumb, and closed, and virtually impossible to judge.
94 At another tasting, it was quite rich, concentrated, extremely young, and backward, but easy to appreciate as a superb Ducru, as well as the best wine made at this estate since the 1961.* I know this is all confusing, but I think the message is that you do not dare open a bottle of this wine for at least another 5–7 years. It is extremely backward, quite tannic, very full bodied and powerful for a Ducru-Beaucaillou, and nowhere near ready to drink. It is clearly the greatest wine made at the property since the 1961. My crystal ball would suggest that the 1982 Ducru-Beaucaillou should be nearing maturity at the turn of the century. Anticipated maturity: 2000–2020. Last tasted, 4/91.

1981—Another undeniable success for the vintage, the 1981 Ducru-
· Beaucaillou offers deep, dark ruby color, plenty of concentrated,
90 blackcurrant flavors, a deft touch of oak aging, and an expansive, very long finish. This is a beautifully crafted wine that has obviously been vinified with care. Anticipated maturity: 1993–2008. Last tasted, 4/91.

1980—Ducru can often be counted on in off vintages, but the 1980 lacks
· charm and fruit, has good structure, but finishes short and is a bit
74 harsh. Anticipated maturity: Now–1993. Last tasted, 4/91.

1979—Ducru has produced so many exceptional wines in the last several
· decades that when the château does not produce a wine that is
84 among the top dozen or so best wines of the Médoc, I am quite surprised. This offering is a good, but not great Ducru. Medium ruby in color, and noticeably lighter in style than previous efforts, this moderately intense, soft, pleasant wine should evolve quickly. Anticipated maturity: Now–1995. Last tasted, 4/91.

1978—The 1978 is irrefutably one of the finest wines of the vintage.
· Moderately dark ruby (with no signs of amber), with a deep, rich,
90 spicy, multidimensional bouquet of fresh cassis, toasty oak, and subtle earthy scents, and full bodied, with a degree of ripeness and richness that is only evident in the finest wines, the 1978 Ducru has savory flavors, soft tannins, and a long, clean finish. It

* At a vertical tasting at the château in 1991, it was the most impressive wine of the last 20 years.

has just about reached its plateau of maturity. Anticipated maturity: 1992–2010. Last tasted, 4/91.

1977—One of the more attractive 1977s with surprisingly ripe character,
  ·   and not marred by too much acidity or vegetal aromas, the 1977
 78   Ducru will continue to improve. Good solid fruit, yet not complex, this medium-bodied wine has some charming attributes to it. Anticipated maturity: Now–may be in decline. Last tasted, 2/84.

1976—This is a lovely Ducru that retains much of the silky, elegant
  ·   personality of a top-class St.-Julien. However, it does not have
 85   the concentration and richness of the 1982, 1978, 1970, or 1961. Now fully mature, this medium-weight, firm, yet rich, savory, and well-constituted 1976 has plenty of character and elegance. Anticipated maturity: Now–1996. Last tasted, 2/89.

1975—A very traditional, old-style claret with oodles of dusty tannins,
  ·   the 1975 Ducru-Beaucaillou has a hard, muscular, sinewy person-
 85   ality, deep, ripe fruit, and an excessive amount of astringent, aggressive tannins. Recent tastings have revealed more depth of fruit, and while some of the tough tannins have begun to melt away, this is still a hard style of Ducru. Anticipated maturity: Now–2015. Last tasted, 11/90.

1974—A bit hollow, noticeably vegetative, yet spicy and still palatable—
  ·   barely—this is a wine that should be consumed. Anticipated ma-
 70   turity: Now–may be in decline. Last tasted, 3/88.

1973—The 1973 Ducru is certainly one of the best wines of this watery
  ·   vintage. It drank well for 15 years before beginning to fade. Hold-
 79   ing it any longer would be senseless. The 1973 Ducru was fully mature by 1978, but miraculously retained its fruit until 1988. It has just begun to fade. Drink up. Anticipated maturity: Now– probably in serious decline. Last tasted, 12/88.

1971—For whatever reason, the 1971 vintage for Jean-Eugène Borie's
  ·   Ducru-Beaucaillou was not as good as it should have been. Now
 78   fully mature, the bouquet exhibits light intensity, cedary, vanillin aromas. The flavors are satisfying, but the coarse texture and astringent tannins are cause for concern. Anticipated maturity: Now–may be in decline. Last tasted, 10/87.

1970—The 1970 is a great Ducru-Beaucaillou, certainly the best after
  ·   1961 and before 1982. It is also the best of the St.-Juliens, sur-
 91   passing both Léoville-Barton and Gruaud-Larose. The deep, rich color has begun to reveal some amber. On the palate, the wine is intense, with layers of ripe fruit admirably complemented by spicy oak. Richly fruity, this impeccably balanced, generously

endowed, smooth-as-silk Ducru has great length. Anticipated maturity: Now–2000. Last tasted, 1/90.

1967—For Ducru, the 1967 is a rather coarse, bland, obviously chaptal-
·   ized wine, without the graceful fruit and spicy exuberance nor-
74   mally found in wines from this estate. Drink up. Anticipated
maturity: Now–probably in serious decline. Last tasted, 10/78.

1966—A very flavorful wine now in full maturity, the 1966 Ducru-Beau-
·   caillou defines such wine adjectives as elegant, graceful, and
87   well-bred. Medium dark ruby with an amber edge, the bouquet is
spicy, cedary, and subtly herbaceous. Velvety, round, medium-
bodied flavors exhibit good concentration. Drink it over the next
5 years. Anticipated maturity: Now–1996. Last tasted, 11/87.

1964—Solid, rustic, amiable, and pleasantly full and firm, the 1964
·   Ducru-Beaucaillou lacks complexity and character, but offers a
78   mushroom-scented, robust, round mouthful of claret. The fruit is
just beginning to fade. All things considered, this was a success
for a 1964 northern Médoc. Anticipated maturity: Now. Last
tasted, 2/87.

1962—I have inconsistent notes for the 1962 Ducru-Beaucaillou. My
·   early notes suggested the wine was beginning to lose its fruit. Two
85?   tastings in the early eighties revealed a wine with a light to medium
ruby color, a mature, fruity, damp cellar, woody bouquet, and
soft flavors that appeared to be beginning to fade. Two tastings in
the late eighties were much more successful. The wine was
deeper colored, richer, with an attractive cedary aroma and long,
velvety flavors. Will the real 1962 Ducru-Beaucaillou please come
forward? Anticipated maturity: Now–1996. Last tasted, 11/89.

1961—Fully mature, yet continuing to exhibit gobs of rich, lush, expan-
·   sive fruit, this dark ruby wine has amber/orange edges, and pos-
96   sesses an exotic bouquet of ripe fruit, vanillin, caramel, mint, and
cedar. Fat, rich, and loaded with sweet, highly extracted fruit,
this velvety, beautifully crafted wine has a 60–75 second finish.
It is a brilliant wine that should hold up nicely for up to a decade.
Anticipated maturity: Now–2005. Last tasted, 5/91.

OLDER VINTAGES

The greatest old vintages of Ducru-Beaucaillou I have tasted include a
magnificently opulent (rated 93, although slightly volatile) 1947 drunk in
1987, a quintessentially elegant and perfumed 1953 (rated 93 and last
tasted in 1988), and a solid, but well-endowed, yet atypically muscular

1959 (rated 90). Whether it is the condition of the bottles or the vintages I am not sure, but I have unenthusiastic tasting notes for the 1957, 1955, and 1945.

GLANA (Cru Bourgeois Exceptionnel)   AVERAGE

Production: 20,000 cases	Grape varieties: Cabernet Sauvignon—70% Merlot—25% Petit Verdot—5%
Secondary label: none	
Vineyard size: 105 acres	Proprietor: Gabriel Meffre
Time spent in barrels: 18 months in casks and vats	Average age of vines: 20 years
Evaluation of present classification: Should be maintained	
Plateau of maturity: 2–8 years following the vintage	

It has been said that Glana produces a blatantly commercial wine—soft, overtly fruity, and too easy to drink. Yet the prices are reasonable, the wine ripe, cleanly made, and ideal for newcomers to Bordeaux. Some vintages tend to be too jammy—1982, 1985, and 1989, for example—but in tastings people always seem to enjoy this plump St.-Julien. It must be drunk within its first decade of life, preferably before it turns 8 years old.

GLORIA (Unclassified)   VERY GOOD

Production: 20,000 cases	Grape varieties: Cabernet Sauvignon—65% Merlot—25% Cabernet Franc—5% Petit Verdot—5%
Secondary labels: Haut- Beychevelle Gloria and Peymartin	

Vineyard size: 123.5 acres	Proprietor: The family of the
	  late Henri Martin
	Administrator: Jean-Louis
	  Triaud

Time spent in barrels and vats: 16 months	Average age of vines: 20 years
Evaluation of present classification: Should be upgraded to a fourth- growth	
Plateau of maturity: Since 1978, 5–10 years following the vintage; prior to 1978, 5–18 years following the vintage	

Gloria has always been used as an example of why the 1855 classification of the Médoc wines is so outdated. Not included in the original classification, Gloria has made wines (from vineyards purchased from neighboring classified châteaux) over the last two and a half decades that in vintages such as 1961, 1966, 1970, 1971, 1975, 1976, 1982, 1985, 1986, and 1989 are certainly as good as many of the wines produced by many of the classified growths. Shrewd merchants and consumers have long known Gloria's quality, and the wine has been widely merchandised in America and abroad.

The late Henri Martin, Gloria's owner, died in February 1991. He was one of the Médoc's legendary figures. His wines were no doubt made for sheer crowd appeal. They were round, generous, slightly sweet, with wonderful cedary, spicy, almost exaggerated bouquets. Nothing is likely to change under the management of his son-in-law, Jean-Louis Triaud. Interestingly, the wine is primarily matured in large oak *foudres* rather than the more conventional 55-gallon barrels. They perform surprisingly well young, but can age for up to 12–15 years. The Gloria style of the sixties and early seventies changed after the mid-1970s. Gloria vintages from 1978 onward definitely appear to be wines that are lighter, more obviously fruity, and less tannic than those wines that were made previously. Well-made, stylish, delicious wines they continue to be, but there is no question that recent vintages are not made to last as long as the wines made in 1975, 1971, 1970, 1966, and 1961. Nevertheless, this is still a gloriously exuberant, delicious St.-Julien that continues to sell at a price well below its actual quality level.

VINTAGES

1989—The 1989 Gloria is a fat, plump, deliciously agreeable wine with a
·   considerable alcoholic kick in the finish. Opulently fruity, with
86   soft tannins, it will be a fine wine to drink for at least 7–10 years.
     It does remind me of the 1982 at a similar stage of development.
     Anticipated maturity: 1993–2000. Last tasted, 4/91.

1988—The 1988 is unabashedly fruity, less powerful than the 1989, but
·   similarly smooth and easy to understand. No wonder Gloria is
85   called a beginner's Bordeaux. Anticipated maturity: Now–1997.
     Last tasted, 4/91.

1987—Light, soft, intensely herbaceous, this medium-bodied wine
·   should provide near-term drinking. Anticipated maturity: Now–
78   1996. Last tasted, 10/89.

1986—Gloria has graced many tables in America and, of course, the de
·   facto ascendancy of this Cru Bourgeois to the quality of a classi-
86   fied growth was a lifelong ambition of proprietor Henri Martin.
     The 1986 has as much structure as any Gloria in the last 15 years,
     a deep ruby color, and plenty of tannin, but I had to ask myself if
     it really, in fact, had as much fruit as it needed to balance out the
     hard tannins in the wine. This should certainly be a very fine
     Gloria, but it will need at least 5–6 years to soften, unusual for a
     wine from this property. Anticipated maturity: 1994–2002. Last
     tasted, 10/90.

1985—The 1985 displays fine depth and richness. Deep in color, with a
·   weedy, herbaceous, cedary, blackcurrant bouquet, it offers up a
86   rich mouthful of succulent claret. Drink it over the next decade.
     Anticipated maturity: Now–1995. Last tasted, 10/90.

1984—Very light and vegetal to smell, this light- to medium-bodied wine
·   is diffuse and watery. Anticipated maturity: Now–may be in de-
72   cline. Last tasted, 9/89.

1983—A forward, typically spicy, herbaceous-scented, fruity Gloria, the
·   1983 has more noticeable tannin than the 1982, but less rich,
82   glossy fat fruit. Anticipated maturity: Now–1995. Last tasted,
     1/89.

1982—A gloriously fruity, spicy, almost grapey Gloria, the 1982 is
·   charmingly drinkable and has the telltale spicy, cedary bouquet
87   and soft, lightly tannic flavors, as well as the greatest depth, of
     any Gloria since 1970. It is just beginning to develop the nuances
     that suggest a mature wine. Despite being an attractive, deli-

ciously fruity wine, the 1982 Gloria should last longer than I initially believed as it has firmed up considerably in the late eighties. Anticipated maturity: Now–2000. Last tasted, 11/90.

1981— Very similar to the stylish, yet mature 1979 Gloria, this wine
  ·   offers supple, cedary, olive-tinged flavors, medium body, and a
  80   more austere character than the 1979. The Gloria telltale sweetness on the palate is present. Anticipated maturity: Now–1994. Last tasted, 1/88.

1980— Light, slightly vegetal, and lacking the roundness and fruity character, the 1980 is a mediocre wine. Anticipated maturity: Now–probably in serious decline. Last tasted, 3/84.
  ·
  73

1979— Very forward and quite ready to drink, this wine has an attractive
  ·   fruity character, a medium-bodied, nicely ripe, savory, sweet,
  82   lush texture, and little or no tannins present. This wine will hold for a few more years, but other than some further bottle bouquet development, it is ready now. Anticipated maturity: Now–1993. Last tasted, 4/87.

1978— Round, flavorful, fruity, with a bouquet suggestive of herbs and
  ·   cinnamon, this wine is deliciously mature. The sweetness and
  83   fruitiness on the palate are almost burgundian. It should be drunk up. Anticipated maturity: Now. Last tasted, 1/88.

1976— Gloria's huge, plummy, spicy bouquet is enticing. Dark ruby/
  ·   garnet, with plenty of sweet, ripe fruit in evidence, this medium
  84   to full-bodied wine is deep, very fruity, and has been ready to drink since the late seventies. It appears to be in no danger of losing its fruit. Anticipated maturity: Now–1995. Last tasted, 1/88.

1975— The 1975 is an older, more traditional, powerful-styled Gloria than
  ·   the château has produced in more recent vintages. A big, volup-
  88   tuous bouquet of spicy oak, ripe plummy fruit, and chocolate is first rate. In the mouth, the wine is full bodied with an alcoholic, ripe, deep, rich, chewy texture, and a moderately tannic, long finish. It is one of the most impressive Glorias in years. Anticipated maturity: 1992–2002. Last tasted, 10/90.

1973— In the mid-1970s, this wine could be enjoyed for light, fruity,
  ·   simple charms. It has now faded badly. Anticipated maturity:
  72   Now–probably in serious decline. Last tasted, 4/81.

1971— A beautiful wine, the 1971 Gloria has been fully mature since
  ·   1979, but has not lost a thing, although amber, brownish colors
  86   are becoming more apparent. The bouquet is highly perfumed, exhibiting scents of cedar, plums, vanillin spice, and sweet oak.

On the palate, the wine is silky, gentle, and very fruity and sweet. An unquestioned success. I have not tasted this wine since 1984. Anticipated maturity: Now–may be in decline. Last tasted, 10/84.

1970—Another triumphant success for Gloria, the 1970 is richer and
· fuller than the lovely 1971, with longer-term keeping possibilities.
87 Dark ruby color with some amber at the edge, with a fully mature bouquet of sweet fruit, cedar, and a spicy, vanillin oakiness, this wonderful, rich, fruity, medium-bodied wine remains impressive. The finish is gentle and soft. This is a voluptuous, decadently fruity Gloria. Anticipated maturity: Now–1991. Last tasted, 1/88.

GRUAUD-LAROSE (Second-Growth)   OUTSTANDING

Production: 32,000 cases	Grape varieties: Cabernet Sauvignon—64% Merlot—24% Cabernet Franc—9% Petit Verdot—3%
Secondary label: Sarget de Gruaud-Larose	
Vineyard size: 202.5 acres	Proprietor: Domaines Cordier
Time spent in barrels: 18–24 months	Average age of vines: 35 years
Evaluation of present classification: Should be upgraded to a first-growth	
Plateau of maturity: 10–35 years following the vintage	

Gruaud-Larose produces St.-Julien's most massive and backward wine. The production is large and the quality consistently high. Since 1978, Gruaud-Larose has produced wines of first-growth standards, especially in vintages such as 1979, 1982, 1983, 1985, and 1986. Acquired by the Cordier family in 1934, the beautiful château, which sits on the plateau of St.-Julien rather than riverside, is not likely to be seen unless the visitor to the Médoc turns off the main Route du Vin (D2) at the town of St.-Julien-Beychevelle and takes route D101 in a westerly direction. Because the wine is not sold in the volatile marketplace (exclusivities are given in each foreign market), the price for Gruaud-Larose tends to be remarkably modest, especially in view of both its official position in the Bordeaux hierarchy as well as its outstanding quality.

Gruaud-Larose is owned by Domaines Cordier, which also owns the neighboring Château Talbot in St.-Julien, and a bevy of other fine estates · in the Médoc and St.-Emilion. Gruaud-Larose is frequently compared with the neighboring Talbot, since both wines are under the same ownership, and Cordier's highly respected oenologist, Georges Pauli, oversees the vinification and upbringing of the two wines. Certainly the comparison in quality between them over recent vintages makes for a lively topic of conversation. In my opinion, Gruaud-Larose has had the edge in most vintages, especially 1986, 1982, 1981, 1979, 1975, 1974, 1970, 1966, 1962, and 1961. In 1989, 1983, 1980, 1976, and 1971, I think Talbot may have made the better wine of these two St.-Juliens.

Critics of Gruaud-Larose argue that the wine is too chunky, too solid and massive, and often does not fulfill the high expectations given the wine when it is young. I think such arguments can easily be rebuffed. If the wine is to be criticized at all, it is because Gruaud-Larose can be impossibly closed and backward in its youth. Remember that most of the top vintages of the eighties have needed at least a decade of cellaring before reaching maturity.

VINTAGES

1989—The 1989 Gruaud-Larose is another massive, tannic, nearly impenetrable wine. While the château calls it a "1982, only superior," I did not think it to be as concentrated as either the 1982 or the 1986. Medium ruby/purple in color, ferociously tannic, but deep and backward, this vintage of Gruaud may evolve for 20–30 years, but does it have the requisite depth of fruit to balance out the tannins? This wine could well behave similarly to the stubbornly tannic, still charmless 1975. A wine to purchase for your grandchildren? Anticipated maturity: 2000–2025. Last tasted, 4/91.

· 88

1988—The 1988 is probably a 30-year wine. Extremely hard and backward, but concentrated, long, and full bodied, it reminded me of the 1975, only less savage. Let's hope the fruit holds up. Anticipated maturity: 2000–2025. Last tasted, 11/90.

· 89

1987—Typical of most of the Cordier wines in 1987, this is a surprisingly muscular, robust, chunky wine, with plenty of concentrated, weedy, cassis fruit hiding under a veneer of hard tannins. Medium to full bodied, intense, and powerful, this is a wine to consider purchasing by parents who have children born in 1987. Anticipated maturity: 1994–2005. Last tasted, 10/90.

· 84

1986—There seems to be no doubt about the quality of the 1986 Gruaud-Larose, which in 20 years should rival the extraordinary 1982, 1961, 1949, and 1928 made at this vast estate of 202 acres. From the first time I tasted this wine in cask, I have thought it to be among the blockbusters of the vintage. It has a black/purple

· 97

color, mammoth structure, a fabulous wealth of fruit, and a finish
that seems to last several minutes. This is indeed first-growth
quality, but then, when, in the last decade, has a Gruaud-Larose
not matched the quality of the first-growths? Given the enormous
structure, impressive concentration, and massive tannins, one
must wonder when this wine will be ready to drink. That may
preclude a number of consumers from actually deciding to buy it.
For many readers, this is probably a wine to lay down for their
children, rather than for them to realistically consider drinking in
their own lifetimes. Anticipated maturity: 2000–2030. Last
tasted, 4/91.

1985 —Georges Pauli, the brilliant oenologist for Cordier, likens the 1985
·   St.-Juliens to the 1979s, but I have to think this is a conservative
90   comparison. The 1985 Gruaud-Larose has evolved beautifully,
         and now in the bottle, it exhibits a lovely, sweet, fragrant bouquet
         of berry fruit, truffles, and smoky oak. On the palate, the wine is
         fat, long, forward for Gruaud, medium to full bodied, and deep.
         It will drink well young. Anticipated maturity: Now–2003. Last
         tasted, 10/90.

1984 —All the Cordier wines were successful in 1984, but what else is
·   new? The 1984 Gruaud is almost 100% Cabernet. It is a big, virile,
83   rich, tannic, spicy, densely colored, powerful, somewhat hard-
         edged wine that will age for 10 years. Anticipated maturity: Now–
         2000. Last tasted, 10/89.

1983 —An unctuous, rather viscous, deep, plummy wine, with excellent
·   extract of fruit, an opaque, dark ruby color, superb concentration,
90   sound acidity, and plenty of alcohol, the 1983 Gruaud-Larose is a
         big and promising wine, with considerable tannin in the finish.
         Anticipated maturity: 1993–2015. Last tasted, 3/89.

1982 —Since the handsome Georges Pauli took over the reins for making
·   the wines of Cordier in the mid-1970s, the style of the top two
97   wines, Gruaud-Larose and Talbot, has moved toward a massive,
         rich, concentrated, age-worthy style with Talbot being the more
         supple of the two. Gruaud-Larose has clearly become one of the
         richest and longest-lived, as well as most muscular, wines of the
         entire Bordeaux hierarchy. The 1982 was spectacular from cask
         and has continued to perform well from bottle, displaying an awe-
         some richness and mammoth constitution to go along with enough
         tannin and body to suggest that one will probably have to wait at
         least another 10–15 years for this wine to reach maturity. It is one
         of the darkest and most opaque-colored 1982s, and has a huge,
         spicy, blackcurrant, grilled-meat aroma. I cannot see it ready to

drink until the end of this century, and it is certainly capable of lasting 25–30 years into the next. It remains the finest Gruaud-Larose since the 1961. Anticipated maturity: 1997–2020. Last tasted, 5/91.

1981— A top success for the vintage, the 1981 Gruaud-Larose is dark
· ruby, with a full-intensity bouquet of ripe blackcurrants, spicy
88 oak, plums, leather, smoked meat, and violets. This wine is concentrated on the palate, with rich, tannic, lingering flavors. The tannins are melting away and the wine is close to maturity. Anticipated maturity: Now–2005. Last tasted, 10/89.

1980— Unusually variable from bottle to bottle, the 1980 Gruaud-Larose
· can be soft, fruity, spicy, and attractive. It is short in the finish
72 and lean, as well as overtly herbaceous, hard, and acidic. It should be drunk up. Anticipated maturity: Now–1994. Last tasted, 6/87.

1979— This is a typical Gruaud-Larose: dark-colored, ripe, with fat,
· fruity, meaty flavors suggestive of herbs, plums, and black cher-
88 ries. In the mouth, the wine has full body, medium-soft tannins, and a supple, smooth finish. Because of its forward charms, it is undeniably appealing now. Anticipated maturity: Now–1998. Last tasted, 1/91.

1978— In 1978, Gruaud-Larose produced a dark-colored wine with gobs
· of aggressive tannins. Built for long-term cellaring, the 1978
87 Gruaud-Larose has a big, briary, tar-and-herb-scented bouquet, deep, intense, ripe, relatively hard flavors, and a full-bodied, long finish. The 1978 has taken longer to mature than the 1979, and it is slightly inferior in quality. Anticipated maturity: 1992–2005. Last tasted, 10/90.

1976— Not one of the better efforts for Gruaud-Larose, the 1976 lacks
· the rich, soft, silky fruitiness that characterizes the top wines of
73 this irregular vintage. It seems to have an imbalance of tannin, and an annoying acidity in the finish. Drink it up. Anticipated maturity: Now–1993. Last tasted, 2/83.

1975— The 1975 Gruaud-Larose is potentially greater than my score may
· reflect. I continue to have reservations about the high levels of
90 mouth-puckering tannins that exist in this otherwise big, impressive wine. Still opaque in color (with a hint of amber), with a tight, yet rich, promising, cedar-box, chocolatey bouquet, and a deep, weighty, dusty feel on the palate, this wine has exceptional length. At 15 years of age, it remains an impossibly hard, yet promising wine. If only owners have the patience to wait. Anticipated maturity: 1998–2020. Last tasted, 10/90.

1974—Now fully mature, and not likely to hold together for more than a
·   few more years, this off-year Gruaud has surprisingly good color,
76   with a pleasingly mature, moderately intense bouquet of cassis
        and spices, medium body, tart acidity, and a vegetal aspect to its
        fruit. The wine is becoming more attenuated. Anticipated matu-
        rity: Now—may be in decline. Last tasted, 7/87.

1973—Soft and fruity, but fading badly, this wine has held together
·   longer than I would have ever expected. It requires immediate
67   drinking, but offers simple, straightforward, one-dimensional,
        washed-out flavors. Anticipated maturity: Now—probably in seri-
        ous decline. Last tasted, 7/86.

1971—Gruaud-Larose represented a good example of the 1971 vintage.
·   It has been fully mature for over a decade and now reveals the
81   telltale brown color of approaching decline. This vintage of
        Gruaud was fruity, plummy, spicy, soft, and agreeable. It has
        now begun to dry out. Anticipated maturity: Now. Last tasted,
        12/88.

1970—This wine has consistently performed well as it has evolved, yet
·   it is still not quite ready to drink. Dark ruby (some amber is
87   discernible at the edge), Gruaud-Larose's 1970 has a chunky,
        plummy fruitiness and exhibits full body, considerable tannin, a
        chewy, corpulent texture, and a long, dusty finish. Anticipated
        maturity: 1992–2005. Last tasted, 1/89.

1967—At peak in the mid-1970s, this wine was effusively fruity, ripe,
·   round, and sweet. Now the color has taken on a brownish cast,
74   the flavors seem to be at odds with each other, and the wine tastes
        like it is cracking up. Some of my friends claim to have drunk
        much better bottles, so perhaps I have been unlucky. Anticipated
        maturity: Now—may be in decline. Last tasted, 3/89.

1966—A classic vintage for Gruaud-Larose, the 1966 remains surpris-
·   ingly young, relatively unevolved, but austere, with a blackcur-
88   rant, cedary, earthy fruitiness, and firm tannins. The finish is dry,
        but long and still youthful. In style and texture, the 1966 Gruaud-
        Larose resembles a big Pauillac. Will the 1966 Gruaud-Larose
        ever shed its tannic toughness? Anticipated maturity: Now—2015.
        Last tasted, 1/89.

1964—One of only a handful of vintage successes in the Médoc, Gruaud-
·   Larose continues to taste uncommonly fruity, deep, and round.
87   There is no evidence of dilution from the heavy rains that ruined
        many others. This is a succulently textured, generous, perfumed
        wine with medium to full body. The 1964 Gruaud-Larose has been
        fully mature for over a decade without drying out. A sleeper!
        Anticipated maturity: Now—1995. Last tasted, 12/88.

1962—A surprisingly big, darkly colored wine that continues to perform
·   admirably, the 1962 Gruaud-Larose remains concentrated for the
87   vintage, with deep, blackcurranty, cedary, and herbaceous fla-
        vors, full body, and a satiny finish. This intensely fruity wine has
        drunk well and been fully mature for over two decades. It has yet
        to exhibit signs of cracking up—a testament to how long well-
        balanced Bordeaux can last at its apogee. Anticipated maturity:
        Now–2000. Last tasted, 11/89.

1961—To my way of thinking, this is the greatest mature Gruaud-Larose
·   I have ever drunk. This big, powerful, rich, densely concentrated
96   wine remains young, fresh, and vigorous, with a full decade of life
        ahead. It continues to exhibit a dark color, with a wonderfully
        fragrant quality (plums, minerals, tar, cedar, soy sauce, and lico-
        rice), a viscous texture, sensational depth of fruit, and a fabulous,
        albeit alcoholic, finish. This is claret at its most decadent. Antic-
        ipated maturity: Now–2015. Last tasted, 12/89.

OLDER VINTAGES

Undoubtedly, the greatest old Gruaud-Larose I have had the pleasure
to taste was the 1928 (rated 98 in 1988). My other notes reveal tremendous disparity and considerable bottle variation. I have seen many over-
the-hill bottles of the 1947 and 1949, but several 1949s were outstanding
(more recently in 1989, a score of 93 was given). Friends have also
advised me that the 1947 can be wonderful, but I have had no such luck.
The fifties was not a great decade for Gruaud-Larose. The 1953 (rated 90
in 1987) is the pick of this period. Neither the 1955 nor the 1959 has ever
shined from my glass. The 1945 enjoys a great reputation, but the two
bottles I have tasted were dried out, astringent, and nearly undrinkable.

HORTEVIE (Cru Bourgeois)   VERY GOOD

Production: 1,500 cases	Grape varieties:
	Cabernet Sauvignon—65%
	Merlot—35%
Secondary label: none	
Vineyard size: 8.6 acres	Proprietor: Henri Pradère
Time spent in barrels: 14 months;	Average age of vines: 25 years
aged in tank until 1989 when oak	
casks were introduced	
Evaluation of present classification: The quality equivalent of a	
Grand Bourgeois Exceptionnel	
Plateau of maturity: 3–10 years following the vintage	

The tiny production of Hortevie comes from a vineyard of Henri Pradère, who also owns Terrey-Gros-Cailloux. Although both these wines are made by identical methods from the same vineyard, Hortevie is produced from older vines, and is treated as a *tête de cuvée* of Terrey-Gros-Cailloux. Pradère's tendency to pick late has always resulted in rich, concentrated, low-acid wines that begged for some structure from new oak casks. These were finally introduced at Hortevie in the late eighties, although the majority of the production of both Hortevie and Terrey-Gros-Cailloux is still aged in tank until the proprietor deems it ready for bottling. Hortevie is a consistently good St.-Julien and has long represented a fine value. While not long-lived, the top vintages, such as 1982, 1986, and 1989, are capable of aging well for a decade.

VINTAGES

1989—The 1989 is an excellent wine, rich, powerful, concentrated, and
·   alcoholic, with a long, heady finish. It should prove to be this
87   property's finest wine since 1982. Anticipated maturity: 1992–
       2000. Last tasted, 4/91.

1988—The 1988 is typical of the vintage: abrasively tannic, lean, aus-
·   tere, and in need of 2–3 years of cellaring. It is well made, but
85   lighter and less complete than the 1989. Anticipated maturity:
       1992–2000. Last tasted, 4/91.

1986—There are only 1,500–1,800 cases made of this very reliable, rich,
·   full-bodied, chunky, fleshy wine that provides immense satisfac-
87   tion rather than great finesse and complexity. The 1986, deep
       ruby/purple in color, has a plummy, licorice-scented bouquet, fat,
       fleshy flavors, and plenty of solid tannins in the finish. It is a

sleeper of the vintage. Anticipated maturity: Now–1998. Last
tasted, 9/89.

1985—The 1985 Hortevie is deep in color, fat, supple, big, and chunky,
·   with a full-intensity bouquet of road tar and blackberries. It is a
85   meaty, hefty wine, short on finesse, but big on flavor. Anticipated
        maturity: Now–1996. Last tasted, 4/89.

1984—Thin, hard, very tannic, the 1984 Hortevie does not have enough
·   fruit to cover its bones. Last tasted, 4/86.

73

LAGRANGE (Third-Growth)   VERY GOOD

Production: 20,000 cases	Grape varieties: Cabernet Sauvignon—50% Merlot—50%
Secondary label: Les Fiefs de Lagrange	
Vineyard size: 138 acres	Proprietor: The Suntory Company
Time spent in barrels: 18–20 months	Average age of vines: 10–12 years
Evaluation of present classification: Since 1983, should be maintained	
Plateau of maturity: 7–20 years following the vintage	

Prior to 1983, Lagrange (a third-growth) had suffered numerous blows to
its reputation as a result of a pathetic track record of quality in the sixties
and seventies. The well-situated vineyards represent a rare unmorsel-
lated property adjacent to Gruaud-Larose, so there was no reason why
good wine should not have been produced.

The future appears promising. In 1983 the huge Japanese company,
Suntory, purchased Lagrange, and began an extraordinary renovation of
not only the château and the *chais*, but also the vineyards. No expense
has been spared, and such talented people as Michel Delon of Léoville-
Las Cases (who acts as a consultant), Marcel Ducasse, and the property's
young, enthusiastic oenologist, Kenji Suzuta, have begun to make stunning wines in an amazingly short period of time. The decision to launch
a second label, and the interesting blend of grapes that are planted and
now being used for the final wine (50% Merlot and 50% Cabernet Sauvignon) make Lagrange the only St.-Julien—in fact, the only classified
growth—to have such a high percentage of Merlot in the final blend.

Not only has the quality of the wines been upgraded, but Lagrange is now a beautiful château with tranquil gardens and a lake teeming with wildlife.

If vintages from 1985 on reveal any particular style, it is one that favors an impressive depth of flavor welded to plenty of tannin, toasty new oak, and an underlying succulence and fatness that is no doubt due to the high percentage of Merlot. Clearly, the new proprietors seem intent on producing a wine that can age for 20 or more years, yet have appeal when young.

While the world press has applauded the extraordinary turnaround made at Château Margaux by the Mentzelopoulos family, less has been written about the turn of events at Château Lagrange, although in 1990 the *Wall Street Journal*, amazingly, ran a front-page story about this showpiece property. Nevertheless, this wine currently remains considerably underpriced given the quality level of the wines that is now emerging.

VINTAGES

1989—Dark ruby/purple, with an intense, nearly roasted bouquet of cas-
·   sis, herbs, and smoky new oak, this full-bodied, unctuous wine is
89   deeply extracted, tannic, powerful, low in acidity, but undeniably
       impressive! Anticipated maturity: 1995–2010. Last tasted, 4/91.

1988—Dark ruby/purple, with a closed but spicy, reticent bouquet that
·   vaguely suggests cedar, plums, and green olives, this medium-
86   bodied, surprisingly hard and tannic wine will need 4–6 years of
       bottle age to soften. Will the fruit hold up? Anticipated maturity:
       1997–2008. Last tasted, 4/91.

1986—Here is a classic example of a wine that is showing significantly
·   more complexity and richness from the bottle than out of cask,
92   although it was certainly a potentially outstanding wine when
       tasted from the barrel. In a vintage that produced a number of
       enormously structured, rich, concentrated wines, Lagrange is an-
       other of the blockbuster wines that seems capable of lasting 30–
       35 years. Black/ruby in color, with a closed-but-burgeoning bou-
       quet of spicy new oak, black fruits, and flowers, this muscular,
       full-bodied, tannic wine is packed with fruit, and is clearly one of
       the great long-distance runners from this vintage. I admire how
       the significant investment made by the Japanese owners in this
       property has paid off with a thrilling, albeit amazingly backward,
       wine. The finest Lagrange to date! Anticipated maturity: 2000–
       2025. Last tasted, 11/90.

1985
·
89
—Lagrange's recent vintages are powerfully constructed wines made to survive several decades of aging with grace and complexity. The 1985 is deep, rich, long, and, for a 1985, surprisingly backward and tannic. Medium bodied, elegant, and packed with fruit, it is a long-distance runner. Anticipated maturity: 1995–2010. Last tasted, 9/89.

1984
·
82
—Take a lot of yen (remember, a Japanese concern owns this property), persuade a perfectionist such as Michel Delon of Léoville-Las Cases to help consult with respect to the making of the wine, and just like that you have the ingredients for instant stardom. The 1984 is moderately ruby, and tannic, exhibits plenty of new, toasty oak and good fruit, and is a success for this minor vintage. Anticipated maturity: Now–1994. Last tasted, 3/89.

1983
·
86
—Potentially a sleeper of this vintage, Lagrange is deep in color, spicy, and rich, with full-bodied, briary, cassis flavors, good firm tannins, and a long finish. If the wine resembles the style of Léoville-Las Cases, it's not surprising because Michel Delon, the gifted winemaker at Las Cases, oversaw the vinification of Lagrange in 1983. Anticipated maturity: Now–2000. Last tasted, 3/89.

1982
·
85
—This was a successful vintage for Lagrange, as well as the last wine made under the old regime. Perhaps the 1982 is not the equal of the excellent 1983, but it is still an improvement over previous efforts from Lagrange. Dark ruby, with a well-developed bouquet of ripe berry fruit and vanillin oak, the wine is also precocious on the palate, displaying rich, lush, nicely concentrated flavors and full body. Anticipated maturity: 1992–2000. Last tasted, 1/85.

1979
·
78
—The 1979 is a bit too herbaceous and stalky, but once past the rather unimpressive bouquet, the wine shows good ripe fruit, a supple, soft texture, and a spicy finish. It will be ready early. Anticipated maturity: Now–1992. Last tasted, 3/83.

1978
·
80
—Dark ruby in color, with a ripe berry bouquet suggestive of Merlot, the 1978 has generous, straightforward, fruity flavors, light to moderate tannins, medium body, and a pleasant finish. A good, if unexciting, wine. Anticipated maturity: Now–may be in decline. Last tasted, 3/83.

1975
·
70
—The color is dark ruby, yet one is hard pressed to find any fruit behind a wall of abrasive tannins. Very severe and bitter on the palate, with an excess of tannins, this will require a lengthy stay in the cellar just to soften. However, my guess is that the fruit

will never be adequate enough to balance out the harsh qualities of this wine. Anticipated maturity: Now–1998. Last tasted, 4/84.

1973—A total failure—no fruit, no charm, just watery, thin flavors with
·   entirely too much acidity and tannin. Last tasted, 10/79.
50

1971—A little wine, compact, a bit tannic, lean and short in the finish,
·   the 1971 Lagrange is the kind of claret that is an embarrassment
65   to the commune of St.-Julien, as well as Bordeaux. Charmless,
      coarse. Last tasted, 10/78.

1970—The 1970 is the best Lagrange of the seventies, as nothing of this
·   quality level was seen again until 1982 and 1983. Dark ruby, with
84   chunky flavors, good, ripe, blackcurrant fruit, a solid, moderately
      long finish, and potential for further evolution, this is a respect-
      able effort from Lagrange. Anticipated maturity: Now–1994. Last
      tasted, 4/81.

1966—Light, fruity, simple, and one-dimensional, the 1966 Lagrange has
·   been fully mature for a number of years, and seems totally devoid
72   of the complexity, breadth of character, and length one expects
      in a third-growth St.-Julien. Drink up. Anticipated maturity:
      Now–1992. Last tasted, 4/80.

1964—Lagrange's 1964 was pale in color and very stringy and skinny on
·   the palate when I tasted it in 1980 for the first and only time. It is
60   a dubious effort for certain in this mixed, rainy vintage. Antici-
      pated maturity: Now–probably in serious decline. Last tasted,
      3/84.

1962—While the 1962 was reportedly a success for the vintage, my ex-
·   perience in two separate tastings has shown the wine to have
70   adequate color, but too much acidity, a harsh, aggressive finish,
      and little of the rich fruity charm one expects from a St.-Julien.
      Drink up. Anticipated maturity: Now–probably in serious de-
      cline. Last tasted, 2/81.

1961—Produced in a period when the wines of Lagrange were quite
·   mediocre, the 1961 is a surprisingly good effort. Dark ruby with
85   amber at the edge, this is a chunky, flavorful wine, with some
      delicious blackcurrant fruit, a pleasant oaky spiciness, and very
      good suppleness and length on the palate. Anticipated maturity:
      Now–1992. Last tasted, 2/84.

LALANDE BORIE (Bordeaux Supérieur) GOOD

Production: 8,000 cases	Grape varieties:
	Cabernet Sauvignon—65%
	Merlot—25%
	Cabernet Franc—10%
Secondary label: none	
Vineyard size: 44.4 acres	Proprietor: Jean-Eugène Borie
Time spent in barrels: 18–22 months	Average age of vines: 20 years
Evaluation of present classification: Should be maintained	
Plateau of maturity: 5–10 years following the vintage	

This domain is a relatively recent creation. In 1970, Jean-Eugène Borie, the proprietor of Ducru-Beaucaillou, purchased a parcel of 74 acres that had at one time been part of Château Lagrange. Borie planted 18 hectares, or slightly over 44 acres, in 1970, which today remains the size of the vineyard. The cellars and *chai* of the winery are actually located in a building of an ancient cru called St.-Louis du Bosc, which, as a winemaking domain, no longer exists. For a number of years many consumers have thought of Lalande Borie as the second label of Ducru-Beaucaillou, but that misunderstanding should be put to rest.

The early vintages of Lalande Borie tended to be light, owing to the youth of the vines. However, recent vintages, particularly the 1986 and 1989, have begun to express the potential of this well-situated vineyard. This is a property to keep an eye on in the 1990s for consumers looking for good values from St.-Julien.

VINTAGES

1989—The 1989 is a forward, deliciously blackcurrant-scented wine that
·   possesses medium to full body, excellent concentration, and a
86   long, heady, soft finish. Anticipated maturity: 1993–2004. Last
       tasted, 4/91.

1988—This is a good wine, somewhat tough-textured, yet spicy, with an
·   attractive, herbaceous, spicy fruitiness. Once the tannins in the
81   finish begin to melt away, the wine may merit a higher score.
       Anticipated maturity: 1992–2000. Last tasted, 4/91.

1986—With many 1986s, the questions continue to be, When will the
·   tannins be totally resolved? And is the fruit sufficient to balance
85   them out? This deep ruby/purple wine is dense, huge, and backward on the palate, but also has very aggressive tannins, and
       appears a good decade away from maturity. This could turn out

to be one of the sleepers of the vintage, but my reservations about the level of tannins in the wine give me some cause for concern. Anticipated maturity: 1995–2005. Last tasted, 4/89.

1985—The 1985 Lalande Borie is very accessible, soft, fruity, pleasant,
·   medium bodied, and charming. Anticipated maturity: Now–1996.
84   Last tasted, 4/89.

LANGOA-BARTON (Third-Growth)   VERY GOOD

Production: 7,500 cases	Grape varieties:
	Cabernet Sauvignon—70%
	Merlot—20%
	Cabernet Franc—8%
	Petit Verdot—2%
Secondary label: Lady Langoa	
Vineyard size: 49.4 acres	Proprietor: Anthony Barton
Time spent in barrels: 22–24 months	Average age of vines: 25 years
Evaluation of present classification: Should be maintained	
Plateau of maturity: 8–22 years following the vintage	

Langoa-Barton is an impressively large château that sits directly on the well-traveled D2, or Médoc Route du Vin. The wine of the well-known second-growth, Léoville-Barton, is also made in the château's cellars. Both Langoa and Léoville-Barton are the properties of Anthony Barton, an Irishman, whose family has had an interest in the Bordeaux area since 1821.

The late Ronald Barton, and now his handsome nephew, Anthony, have produced top-class wine that critics have called uncompromisingly traditional and classic. Both are St.-Julien wines with a distinctive Pauillac character and personality. Since the wines are made in the same wine cellar, by the same staff, the first question someone always asks is how they differ. In most years, Léoville-Barton edges out Langoa, but often it has been close. Both wines are big, ripe, concentrated, spicy wines that frequently lack the youthful suppleness and commercial upfront fruit of some of their neighbors. Nevertheless, they age extremely well, and when mature, combine the savory, complex, graceful fruitiness of St.-Julien with the cedary toughness and virility of Pauillac.

Neither Léoville nor Langoa-Barton has ever enjoyed the reputation of Léoville-Las Cases and Ducru-Beaucaillou. That may now begin to change since Anthony Barton has full responsibility for the property, taking over when his uncle, Ronald, died in 1986. There is a new *régis-*

seur, Michel Raoul, a stricter selection, and the increased usage (now 50%) of new oak. These moves, plus a hard-headed, refreshingly realistic view that wine is not really sold until the consumer buys a bottle and drinks it, have all combined to make Langoa-Barton and Léoville-Barton grossly underpriced, particularly now that the quality level is close to the "super second" level.

My only criticism of Langoa-Barton and Léoville-Barton is that in some of the lighter Bordeaux vintages such as 1979, 1971, 1974, and 1973, the wines of these two châteaux taste less successful than many of their peers. Whatever the reason, both châteaux have excelled in top vintages such as 1986, 1985, 1982, 1975, 1970, 1961, 1959, and 1953. Langoa-Barton, as well as its sister château, produces wine for the true claret connoisseur.

VINTAGES

1989—The 1989 Langoa-Barton tasted much lighter than the same wine
  ·   from this property's sibling, Léoville-Barton. It is a medium-bod-
86   ied, pretty wine, but much less tannic, powerful, and concen-
       trated than many other St.-Juliens. Well balanced, with a nice
       marriage of oak and red fruits, this wine has surprisingly good
       acidity for the vintage, but not the power of most St.-Juliens.
       Anticipated maturity: 1992–2005. Last tasted, 4/91.

1988—The 1988 has some ripeness in the aroma, but like so many 1988s,
  ·   the promise is not totally fulfilled on the palate. Austere, com-
85   pact, and medium bodied, this wine is pleasant rather than pro-
       found. Anticipated maturity: 1993–2000. Last tasted, 4/91.

1987—A smaller-scaled wine, the 1987 is spicy, has a sense of elegance
  ·   and breeding, medium body, some underlying greenness, but
84   sound, ripe fruit. It is an attractive, delicious wine that is nearly
       as good as the 1988. Anticipated maturity: Now–1995. Last
       tasted, 11/90.

1986—Ever so stubbornly, the 1986 Langoa-Barton is beginning to shed
  ·   some of its enormously hard tannins to reveal a wine that has
87   plenty of depth, full body, a spicy, burly texture, and 20–25 years
       of aging potential. The fruit does appear to be sufficient to hold
       up to the tannins, but again, patience is a required asset in order
       to fully appreciate this wine. Anticipated maturity: 1998–2010.
       Last tasted, 11/90.

1985—The 1985 Langoa-Barton is a stylish wine, deep in color, medium
  ·   bodied, with an elegant bouquet of blackcurrant fruit and spicy
88   oak. It is not a big, rich, blockbuster sort of wine, but rather a

richly fruity, suave, and graceful St.-Julien. Anticipated maturity: 1992–2003. Last tasted, 11/90.

1984—While the 1984 Langoa has good color, a spicy, somewhat closed
·   bouquet, and firm-yet-malnourished flavors, it has turned astrin-
72   gent. It has no hope of further positive evolution. Anticipated
      maturity: Now–1993. Last tasted, 2/90.

1983—From the cask, the 1983 Langoa-Barton was impressively deep in
·   color, full bodied, admirably concentrated, but extremely tannic.
84   However, although it appears to have the fruit to outlast the ag-
      gressive tannins, I feel this is a rustic, somewhat old-style, atten-
      uated wine that comes across a bit clumsily. Anticipated
      maturity: 1995–2005. Last tasted, 3/89.

1982—This is a top-class Langoa-Barton that is turning out better than
·   the excellent 1975. Comparable to the fine 1970, 1959, and 1948
89   yet fruitier, the 1982 has a rich, deep ruby color, an intense ripe,
      blackcurrant bouquet, a big, tough, full-bodied framework, and
      exceptional potential. Very rich, tannic, big, and promising, this
      wine needs time. Anticipated maturity: 1995–2010. Last tasted,
      6/90.

1981—Like many vintages for the Barton-owned pair of Léoville and
·   Langoa, it is often difficult to conclude which is the better wine
82   since they are made and handled identically. The 1981 Langoa is
      medium bodied, with good color, a spicy, moderately fruity bou-
      quet, and solid tannins that are beginning to soften. It is a trifle
      austere. Anticipated maturity: Now–1995. Last tasted, 10/90.

1980—One of the delicious wines of the vintage, the 1980 Langoa should
·   be consumed. This wine is savory and spicy, with soft, round,
81   attractively ripe, fruity, yet monolithic flavors. Anticipated matu-
      rity: Now. Last tasted, 2/88.

1979—While the 1979 is an appealing wine, it lacks concentration, and
·   tastes supple and light for Langoa-Barton. It is medium ruby/
78   garnet, with a forward, supple, spicy bouquet, soft, average-in-
      tensity flavors, and a short finish. Anticipated maturity: Now–
      1993. Last tasted, 2/88.

1976—Very easy to drink, soft, and slightly sweet, with no abrasive
·   tannin present, the 1976 Langoa has been fully mature for at least
79   a decade. Now browning at the edges, this wine should be drunk
      up. Anticipated maturity: Now. Last tasted, 2/88.

1975—An excellent Langoa, the 1975 has an open-knit, full-intensity,
·   seductive bouquet of cedarwood, vanillin spices, and ripe fruit.
88   On the palate, the wine is full bodied and loaded with tannin as
      well as rich fruit. There is fine length. This wine remains a big,

complex St.-Julien that wants to be a Pauillac. Anticipated maturity: Now–2000. Last tasted, 1/90.

1971—This Langoa is an obviously chaptalized wine, which unfortunately is now browning quite a bit. The 1971 Langoa seems to be
•
69   quite flabby and unknit, and finishes rather diffusely. It was fully mature when last tasted. My notes do show a surprisingly rich, flavorful bottle was tasted in 1982, so perhaps some bottle variation exists with this wine. Anticipated maturity: Now–probably in serious decline. Last tasted, 4/83.

1970—A wonderfully successful wine, the 1970 Langoa smells and tastes
•
88   comparable to a top Pauillac. A big, yet restrained bouquet of cedar and blackcurrants is first rate. On the palate, the wine is ripe, weighty, rich, tannic, full bodied, and several years away from its zenith. This is Langoa at its best. Anticipated maturity: Now–2000. Last tasted, 2/88.

1966—Another unquestioned success for Langoa, the 1966, while very
•
87   good, is not up to the 1975 or 1982 quality level. Amber at the edge, with a solid ruby color, the 1966 has a full-intensity, spicy, cedary, rich bouquet, lean, somewhat austere flavors, but a good round, generous finish. Anticipated maturity: Now–1996. Last tasted, 4/85.

1964—The tannin and acid seem to clearly outbalance the fruit in the
•
72   1964 Langoa. Chunky, but a trifle lean and thin on the palate, the wine's attractively spicy, complex bouquet leaves the palate unfulfilled. Others have apprised me that good bottles of this wine do exist. Anticipated maturity: Now–may be in decline. Last tasted, 4/83.

1961—Tasted next to the 1959 at Anthony Barton's extravagant vertical
•
89   tasting at the International Wine Center in New York City, it was hard to pick which wine was the best. The 1959 perhaps was more alcoholic, but the 1961 was filled with a richly scented smell of cedar, oak, vanillin, and ripe fruit. On the palate, the rich, round, sweet, ripe fruitiness of the vintage was capably displayed. Fully mature. Anticipated maturity: Now–may be in decline. Last tasted, 10/82.

OLDER VINTAGES

The 1959 (rated 90) Langoa-Barton has been marvelous on the two occasions I have tasted it. The same could be said for the 1953 (a 90-point wine in 1988), the 1952 (88 and excellent, but tough), and the glorious 1948 (rated 93). I have never seen a bottle of the 1945 or anything older.

LÉOVILLE-BARTON (Second-Growth)   EXCELLENT

Production: 20,000 cases	Grape varieties: Cabernet Sauvignon—70% Merlot—20% Cabernet Franc—8% Petit Verdot—2%
Secondary label: Lady Langoa	
Vineyard size: 99 acres	Proprietor: Anthony Barton
Time spent in barrels: 24 months	Average age of vines: 25 years
Evaluation of present classification: Should be maintained	
Plateau of maturity: 8–25 years following the vintage	

Léoville-Barton is generally acknowledged to have an edge on its sibling, Langoa-Barton. Both properties are owned by Anthony Barton. Unlike other proprietors, Barton uses only a small amount of the supple, fleshy Merlot in the blend (although it has been increased to 20% with plantings in the mid-1980s), whereas the proportion of Cabernet Sauvignon is high not only for the commune of St.-Julien, but for the Médoc in general.

Léoville-Barton is made at Langoa-Barton because there is no château at Léoville. The main vineyard for Léoville-Barton sits immediately behind the town of St.-Julien-Beychevelle, and runs in a westerly direction where it intersects with the large vineyard of Château Talbot.

The inconsistencies of the seventies have been replaced by a consecutive string of successful wines in the eighties. Since 1985, Anthony Barton has refined rather than changed the traditional style of this wine. Among all of the top wines of St.-Julien, it represents the finest value.

VINTAGES

1989—Léoville-Barton's 1989 is an elegantly wrought, admirably concentrated wine that reminds me of a hypothetical blend of the
89   château's 1985 and 1986. It has gobs of tannin, an inner core of
sweet, expansive, curranty fruit, and low acidity. The finish is
moderately long. At this point, I would rank this vintage of Léoville-Barton behind the 1982, 1985, and 1986. Anticipated maturity: 1995–2010. Last tasted, 4/91.

1988—Like many of its neighbors in the Médoc, the 1988 is a hard,
tough, severely styled wine that will last 10–20 years, and my
88   doubts about whether it had sufficient fruit to stand up to the
tannins now appear unwarranted. Patience will most definitely be
needed, but the wine is excellent, with plenty of rich, deep, cur-

ranty fruit. It may well merit a higher rating in 4–5 years. Anticipated maturity: 1997–2012. Last tasted, 4/91.

1987—The 1987 is maturing nicely, exhibiting a moderately sweet, cur-
·   ranty, oaky nose, round, gentle flavors, decent acidity, and a
85   surprisingly long finish. It is an unqualified success for the vin-
       tage! Anticipated maturity: Now–1996. Last tasted, 11/90.

1986—In contrast to the elegant, graceful, finesse-filled 1985 (which may
·   turn out to resemble the classic 1953 in 15 years), the 1986 is a
92   great wine, but so, so backward and tannic. This huge, dense,
       medium- to full-bodied wine exhibits tremendously rich, classic,
       weedy, blackcurrant fruitiness with airing, and boasts the judi-
       cious use of new oak barrels. The tannins are elevated, but
       then this is a seriously concentrated, old-style, intense wine for
       long-term cellaring. I had a few reservations about the cask
       samples I saw, but after tasting the wine several times from
       bottle, I have no reservations. Cellaring of at least a decade is
       warranted—even required. Anticipated maturity: 1999–2020.
       Last tasted, 11/90.

1985—Anthony Barton's 1985 may turn out to be a remake of the châ-
·   teau's splendid 1953. Deep ruby with a complex, complete, and
92   intense bouquet of sweet, superripe, curranty fruit, minerals, and
       new oak, this medium-bodied wine has exceptional balance, fine
       length, gobs of fruit, and soft tannins in the finish. It is already a
       joy to drink. Anticipated maturity: 1992–2007. Last tasted, 4/91.

1984—Deeper on the palate than Langoa-Barton, the 1984 Léoville-Bar-
·   ton has a spicy, richly fruity nose, good body, length, and tannins,
84   and plenty of new toasty oak smells. Anticipated maturity: Now–
       1995. Last tasted, 3/88.

1983—Initially extremely tannic and hard, with a very deep color, plenty
·   of alcohol, and a rich, ripe, weighty fruitiness, this wine has ma-
86   tured much more quickly than I would have expected. It is a good
       but not great wine that needs to be carefully monitored. Antici-
       pated maturity: 1992–2002. Last tasted, 3/89.

1982—The 1982 Léoville-Barton from both cask and early tastings con-
·   sistently looked to be the best wine made by this well-known,
93   historic estate since the glorious 1959. Now, at more than 8 years
       of age, there is no doubt that it is the best Léoville-Barton made
       in the last 30 years. It is very concentrated, extremely backward
       and tannic, and given the massive concentration, power, and
       body, it should not be ready to drink until the late 1990s. I have
       never tasted a more concentrated Léoville-Barton. It has beauti-
       fully balanced oak, acidity, tannin, and ripe, red currant fruit.

The bouquet is starting to emerge, but this wine remains a closed blockbuster example of the vintage. The late Ronald Barton claimed this was the greatest wine he made in his lifetime—what praise! Anticipated maturity: 1995–2010. Last tasted, 9/90.

1981 · 84 —This medium-bodied wine has an attractive spicy, blackcurrant fruitiness, melted tannin, and a decent finish. The 1981 is a good wine, but it lacks excitement and is clearly outdistanced by several other St.-Juliens in this vintage. Anticipated maturity: Now–1996. Last tasted, 2/89.

1980 · 83 —A lovely wine and fine success for the vintage, the 1980 Léoville-Barton has a surprisingly good color, a spicy, caramel-scented, deep bouquet, soft, ripe fruity flavors, moderate tannins, and a good finish. This wine should be drunk up. Anticipated maturity: Now–may be in decline. Last tasted, 10/83.

1979 · 75 —Surprisingly light and precociously fruity, with little grip or backbone, this medium-bodied, moderately fruity wine has charm and a savory, easygoing character, but tastes a bit watery. It requires drinking. Anticipated maturity: Now. Last tasted, 1/88.

1978 · 86 —This is a very attractive Léoville-Barton that seems to be developing at a more accelerated pace than I had initially expected. A lovely, rather full, big bouquet of smoky, berryish, ripe fruit is first class. On the palate, the wine shows a good cedary, spicy, deep fruity constitution, moderate tannins, and a long finish. Just about ready. Anticipated maturity: Now–1995. Last tasted, 1/88.

1977 · 78 —Although a trifle weedy and herbaceous to smell, the 1977 Léoville-Barton is well above average in quality for the vintage with soft, flavorful, fully mature flavors. Anticipated maturity: Now–may be in decline. Last tasted, 10/82.

1976 · 85 —A very successful wine, Léoville-Barton obtained much more fruit and stuffing in its 1976 than did Langoa. Rich, fully mature, with a plummy fruitiness, and fat, lazy finish, this wine's bouquet seems to jump from the glass. Sweet, ripe, velvety fruit caresses the palate. It is a little low in acidity, but delicious for drinking now. Anticipated maturity: Now–1993. Last tasted, 7/87.

1975 · 90 —The 1975 is a large-scaled, traditionally styled wine, with an uncanny resemblance to Pauillac, rather than a more suave, gentle St.-Julien. Quite dark ruby, with some amber at the edge, this full-bodied Léoville has a deep, spicy, long, hefty amount of fruit, melted tannins, a bouquet that develops cedary aromas as it sits in the glass, and excellent length. Patience is no longer required for this outstanding 1975. Anticipated maturity: Now–2000. Last tasted, 11/89.

1971—Now fading badly, and best drunk up immediately, the 1971 Léo-
·   ville-Barton has a sweet, caramel, candy-like nose, soft, shallow
70   flavors that show no tannins, and a watery, weak finish. It will
     only become more astringent. Anticipated maturity: Now—may be
     in decline. Last tasted, 3/85.

1970—It seems that Barton excels in dry, hot years such as 1970. Deep
·   ruby with an amber edge, the wine is rich and full on the palate,
87   with excellent concentration, a full-intensity bouquet of blackcur-
     rants and cedar wood, and moderate tannins. A ripe wine that is
     now ready to drink, this muscular, larger-scaled Léoville should
     continue to age well. Anticipated maturity: Now—2000. Last
     tasted, 6/88.

1966—The 1966 is a good, reliable wine that, in view of the vintage,
·   could perhaps have been better. A moderately intense, spicy,
84   fruity bouquet that exhibits plenty of oak is seductive enough.
     However, the palate impression is that austerity dominates the
     fruit. Fully mature, but capable of holding, this is a good, but
     hardly top-rank 1966. Anticipated maturity: Now—1994. Last
     tasted, 2/87.

1964—Darker in color, richer in flavor, and longer on the palate than the
·   1966, this chunky, fleshy wine shows impressive fruit, soft, yet
86   noticeable tannins, and a ripe, fruity bouquet. Anticipated matu-
     rity: Now—1993. Last tasted, 9/87.

1962—Too angular, dry, and austere, with the fruit beginning to fade
·   and be dominated by the tannins, this medium ruby, moderately
75   intense wine should be consumed. Anticipated maturity: Now—
     may be in decline. Last tasted, 4/83.

1961—Several tastings in the early eighties must have been from less-
·   than-perfect bottles because I was never excited by this wine.
92   Two tastings in the late eighties revealed a terrific wine, splen-
     didly perfumed with cedar, herbs, and sweet black fruits, rich,
     full bodied, and long. Based on the best bottles, this wine is fully
     mature, but is capable of lasting for another decade. Anticipated
     maturity: Now—2000. Last tasted, 11/89.

OLDER VINTAGES

Five old vintages are outstanding, all meriting scores in the nineties—
the 1959 (rated 94 and better than the 1961 when tasted side by side in
1989), 1953 (rated 93 and glorious in 1988), 1949 (rated 94), 1948 (rated
96), and 1945 (rated 98). The last three vintages of exotically rich, opulent, even thick wines were tasted in 1989. In fact, Léoville-Barton appears to have been at the very top of its class between 1945 and 1961,

when it can be persuasively argued that Léoville-Barton was producing far better wines than its rivals, Ducru-Beaucaillou, Léoville-Las Cases, and Léoville-Poyferré. Following 1961, it was not until 1982 that another profoundly great wine was produced.

LÉOVILLE-LAS CASES (Second-Growth)   OUTSTANDING

Production: 25,000 cases	Grape varieties: Cabernet Sauvignon—67% Merlot—17% Cabernet Franc—13% Petit Verdot—3%
Secondary labels: Clos du Marquis and Grand Parc	
Vineyard size: 209 acres	Proprietor: Sociètè Civile Administrator: Michel Delon
Time spent in barrels: 18 months	Average age of vines: 30 years
Evaluation of present classification: Should be upgraded to a first-growth	
Plateau of maturity: 8–30 years following the vintage	

Léoville-Las Cases is unquestionably one of the great names and wines of Bordeaux. Situated next to Latour, Léoville-Las Cases' main vineyard of over 100 acres is the picturesque, enclosed vineyard depicted on the wine's label. The estate is one of Bordeaux's largest, and while the meticulous and passionate commitment to quality may be equaled by several others, it is surpassed by no one. The man responsible is Michel Delon, who succeeded his father, Paul. A bachelor who is as admired as he is scorned, Delon is the perfectionist architect behind the ascendancy of Léoville-Las Cases. His critics, and there are many, claim he plays games when selling his wines, doling out tiny quantities in great vintages, the critics claim, to artificially drive up the price. Yet no one can argue about the splendid quality of his wines, the product of an almost-maniacal obsession to be the best in St.-Julien. Who else would declassify over 50% of their crop in an abundant vintage such as 1986 or an astonishing 67% in 1990? Who else would introduce not only a second wine, but a third wine (Bignarnon) as well? Who else would lavishly install marble floors in the air-conditioned *chais*? Like him or not, Michel Delon, ably assisted by Michel Rolland (not the Libourne oenologist) and Jacques Depoizier, is making one of the greatest wines in the Médoc.

The wines of Léoville-Las Cases have been excellent in the post–World War II era, yet the period from 1975 onward has witnessed the production of a string of successes that have come close to perfection in vintages such as 1975, 1978, 1982, 1985, 1986, 1988, and 1989. In fact, these wines are as profound as most of the Médoc's first-growths in those vintages.

In comparison to Ducru-Beaucaillou, its chief rival in St.-Julien, the wines of Léoville-Las Cases tend to be a shade darker in color, more tannic, larger scaled, more concentrated, and of course built for extended cellaring. They are traditional wines, designed for connoisseurs who must have the patience to wait the 10 to 15 years necessary for them to mature properly. Should a reclassification of Bordeaux's 1855 classification take place, Léoville-Las Cases, like Ducru-Beaucaillou and Gruaud-Larose, would merit and receive serious support for first-growth status.

VINTAGES

1989—Michel Delon is one Bordeaux administrator who is never satisfied
·   with the status quo. Once again he has hit the jackpot with an
95   enthralling 1989 that in weight, texture, and character resembles
      a synthesis of his 1982 and 1986. Delon harvested his Merlot on
      September 5 and 6, producing *cuvées* of Merlot that ranged from
      13% to 14.5% alcohol. His Cabernet was harvested the 24th and
      25th of September. Fifty percent of the crop was relegated to the
      second wine, the Clos du Marquis. Opaque deep ruby/purple (one
      of the thickest wines in color that I saw), this superbly extracted
      wine has an awesome bouquet of black and red fruits nicely inter-
      spersed with scents of vanillin. Staggeringly rich, opulent, long,
      and mouth filling, Las Cases is packed with fruit and is large
      framed, yet astonishingly well balanced. The feel in the mouth
      and the approximately one minute finish make it taste surprisingly
      similar to the perfect 1982. Anticipated maturity: 1996–2020. Last
      tasted, 4/91.

1988—The 1988 is a star of the vintage in the Médoc. The full-intensity
·   bouquet of black cherries and toasty new oak is captivating.
92   Beautifully balanced, medium-bodied, concentrated flavors ex-
      hibit wonderful ripeness and excellent tannins, and flash a déjà
      vu impression of the 1966. The 1988 Léoville-Las Cases avoids
      the harsh, dry, astringent tannins of other 1988s. It is Delon's
      fourth-best wine of the decade, following the 1982, 1989, and
      1986. Anticipated maturity: 1995–2020. Last tasted, 4/91.

1987—The 1987 is deep ruby-colored, with a moderately intense bouquet
·   of cassis and spicy new oak. With no trace of underripeness, or
87   any indication of dilution, this is a rich, medium- to full-bodied

wine that is probably better than the château's 1981, and every
bit as good as their excellent 1976. One of the vintage's best!
Anticipated maturity: Now–2000. Last tasted, 4/91.

1986—Michel Delon, the formidable administrator of Léoville-Las
  ·   Cases, likens his 1986 to his 1966 and 1961. Having had both
 97   those wines, I have to say the 1986 vintage is far superior. Only
        the 1982 is a finer Léoville-Las Cases made in the last 30 years.
        From the dense, virtually opaque, ruby/black/purple color,
        which offers up aromas of intense blackcurrants and black
        cherries, as well as a hefty dose of toasty new oak, this beauti-
        fully crafted, full-bodied wine shows extraordinary extract,
        near-perfect balance, and remarkable length and persistence
        on the palate. With as much tannin as in any recent Léoville-
        Las Cases, this wine is certainly going to need a minimum of
        10–15 years of cellaring. Anticipated maturity: 1998–2030. Last
        tasted, 4/91.

1985—Michel Delon's 1985 Léoville-Las Cases seems to get better and
  ·   better every time I go back to it. It looks to be superior to either
 92   the 1981 or 1983, which says something. Quite deep in color, as
        well as ripe and forward for a Las Cases wine, this medium- to
        full-bodied, concentrated wine will mature quickly, but hold
        nicely. Anticipated maturity: Now–2004. Last tasted, 10/90.

1984—This wine is very similar to the 1981 produced at Las Cases. Spicy
  ·   with the vanillin touch of toasty oak, very good fruit, and medium
 84   to full body, this is a very successful wine for the year. Antici-
        pated maturity: Now–1997. Last tasted, 1/90.

1983—This is unquestionably one of the top wines of the vintage. How-
  ·   ever, interested buyers should keep in mind that this dark ruby,
 90   deep, extremely tannic and raw wine will require 15 or more years
        of cellaring to reach peak. Dark in color, explosively fruity, with
        excellent depth and length, but mouth-shocking tannins, this is
        an infant giant of a wine. Anticipated maturity: 1995–2020. Last
        tasted, 3/90.

1982—The 1982 Léoville-Las Cases is utterly profound. From the very
  ·   first days in cask it looked to be one of the great superstars of our
100   times, and it has only improved in the bottle. I have never tasted
        a more concentrated and rich wine from this estate, and it is just
        now beginning to shed some of the considerable tannin. It needs
        until the turn of the century to reach full maturity. What makes
        this wine so special? To begin with, it has always been character-
        ized by one of the purest and richest bouquets of classic cedary
        aromas and blackcurrant fruit, with toasty vanillin notes. Stun-

ningly well-balanced, concentrated flavors simply linger on the palate for a full minute or more. There is an extra dimension to virtually everything about the 1982 Léoville-Las Cases, and whether it is from a brief whiff or the first taste, one realizes the wine is something quite compelling, as well as rare. I know the proud proprietor, Michel Delon, thinks his 1986 is every bit as good, but for me, the 1982 is simply the finest wine I have ever tasted from this estate. In several tastings I have attended of the 1982s, this was clearly the top wine among a stellar group of St.-Juliens. Anticipated maturity: 2000–2025. Last tasted, 4/91.

1981 —This wine will no doubt live in seclusion given the herculean effort
· turned in by Las Cases in 1982, but make no mistake about it, the
88 1981 is very good. Quite dark ruby, with a spicy, oaky, ripe, berryish bouquet of moderate intensity, this big, tannic, full-bodied, amply endowed wine has outstanding length and concentration. Anticipated maturity: 1992–2005. Last tasted, 10/90.

1980 —A solid, respectable effort for the year, but like many wines from
· this vintage, there is just not enough fruit to cover the bones.
75 Anticipated maturity: Now–may be in decline. Last tasted, 10/84.

1979 —Not dissimilar to the style of the excellent 1978, but slightly less
· concentrated and more supple, the 1979 Las Cases has a spicy,
86 cedary, ripe fruity bouquet, medium body, light tannins, and an attractive texture, balance, and length. Anticipated maturity: Now–2000. Last tasted, 10/90.

1978 —The 1978 is a great Las Cases that appears to have immense
· potential. It certainly is one of the top wines of this very good
92 vintage. Dark ruby with some amber at the edge and an intense cassis, vanillin, spicy, lead-pencil-scented bouquet, the rich, full, deep flavors are still firmly encased behind a wall of tannin. This beautifully crafted wine offers considerable promise, but cellaring is still advised. It is one of my favorite examples of the 1978 vintage. Anticipated maturity: 1994–2015. Last tasted, 10/90.

1976 —The 1976 Las Cases has shed all tannin and exhibits ripe, berryish
· fruit, some subtle, spicy, oaky, vanillin aromas, and a plump,
84 soft, round texture. It is a surprisingly concentrated, yet mature 1976 that is drinking well at present and should continue to do so over the next several years. This is another example of a 1976 that was seemingly fully mature when released in 1979, but despite low acidity and fragile balance, remained at its apogee for over a decade. Drink it up. Anticipated maturity: Now–1994. Last tasted, 10/90.

1975—The 1975 is a classic Léoville-Las Cases that is loaded with poten-
·　　tial, but remains stubbornly backward. Dark ruby, with only a
92　　slight trace of amber, the wine has an emerging bouquet of black
　　　cherries, leather, and spicy oak. Full bodied, thick, and aggres-
　　　sively tannic, yet admirably concentrated and long, the 1975 Las
　　　Cases should prove the longest-lived of all this château's wines
　　　produced in the sixties and seventies. Anticipated maturity:
　　　1995–2020. Last tasted, 10/90.

1974—The color is sound and still youthful looking, but the problem this
·　　wine has is the lack of fruit that results in a short finish and an
70　　empty taste on the palate. Time has helped soften the wine's
　　　astringency, but the fruit continues to fade. Anticipated maturity:
　　　Now—may be in decline. Last tasted, 7/85.

1973—Still drinkable, but clearly losing its freshness and lively, fruity
·　　character, the 1973 Las Cases is light, supple, and pleasant, but
70　　quite one-dimensional, and now beginning to fade. Drink up! An-
　　　ticipated maturity: Now—probably in serious decline. Last tasted,
　　　5/80.

1971—The 1971 is an unbalanced Léoville-Las Cases, exhibiting too
·　　much tannin, a loosely knit structure, and fruity flavors that seem
73　　to dissipate rapidly in the glass. An austere, unyielding wine in
　　　which the tannin clearly has the edge over the fruit. Nevertheless,
　　　there is interest in the bouquet, and the color remains sound.
　　　Anticipated maturity: Now—1994. Last tasted, 10/90.

1970—This wine has always enjoyed a considerable reputation. But the
·　　emperor has no clothes. On each of the seven occasions I have
77　　tasted the 1970 Léoville-Las Cases, I have found it lean, angular,
　　　and light for the vintage. Lacking concentration, austere,
　　　and surprisingly compact for a 1970, this is a disappointing
　　　wine that will only become more attenuated and unpleasant as it
　　　gets older. The last tasting, from a bottle from the château,
　　　confirmed its mediocrity. Anticipated maturity: Now—1995. Last
　　　tasted, 3/90.

1966—A classic Léoville-Las Cases, as well as a textbook St.-Julien, this
·　　dark ruby-colored wine has some amber at the edges, as well as
90　　a rich, full-intensity bouquet of ripe blackcurrants, spices, and
　　　cedar. The wine is perfectly balanced on the palate, with an ex-
　　　cellent fruity intensity, and long, lingering, silky flavors. This is a
　　　fully mature, quintessentially elegant Las Cases and is one of the
　　　great wines of the 1966 vintage. Anticipated maturity: Now—2000.
　　　Last tasted, 12/88.

1964—I never tasted this wine in the early seventies when it was re-
· putedly at its best. Recent examples have been dry, astrin-
71 gent, acidic, and revealing a glaring deficiency in fruit. Anticipated maturity: Now–probably in serious decline. Last tasted,
5/86.

1962—A lovely wine, not quite in the top flight of 1962s, but nevertheless
· charming, round, and gentle, with soft fruit, and a moderately
85 intense, fully developed bouquet. Anticipated maturity: Now.
Last tasted, 1/85.

1961—From such a highly regarded vintage, the 1961 Las Cases has
· consistently proven to be good, but in the context of the vintage,
84 a disappointment. It has a good ruby color with some amber at
the edge, a briary, yet surprisingly one-dimensional, compact
bouquet, and dusty, spicy, coarse flavors. The wine lacks the
depth, concentration, and complexity one expects from a Bordeaux superstar in a great vintage. The dry, austere, tannic, fruitless finish suggests that further aging will only exaggerate the
wine's lack of harmony and richness. Anticipated maturity: Now–
1995. Last tasted, 1/88.

OLDER VINTAGES

The 1959 (rated 86) is superior to the 1961, but not a compelling wine.
Other vintages from the fifties and forties have never lived up to what
one would expect from a super second. The two best older examples
during this period are the 1955 (rated 92 in 1988) and the variable 1947
(rated as high as 90 in 1989).

LÉOVILLE-POYFERRÉ (Second-Growth)   VERY GOOD

Production: 25,000 cases	Grape varieties: Cabernet Sauvignon—66% Merlot—34%
Secondary label: Moulin-Riche	
Vineyard size: 148.2 acres	Proprietor: Didier Cuvelier
Time spent in barrels: 18–22 months	Average age of vines: 30 years
Evaluation of present classification: Should be downgraded to a fourth-growth	
Plateau of maturity: 8–20 years following the vintage	

Talk to just about any knowledgeable Bordelais about the potential of the vineyard of Léoville-Poyferré, and they will unanimously agree that Poyferré has the soil and capacity to produce one of the Médoc's greatest red wines. In fact, some will argue that Léoville-Poyferré has better soil than any of the other second-growth St.-Juliens. But the story of Léoville-Poyferré since 1961 is one of disappointment. Despite modernizations to the cellars, the introduction of a second wine, the elevated use of new oak, and the increasingly watchful eyes of Didier Cuvelier, the wine still does not compete in quality with Léoville-Las Cases, Ducru-Beaucaillou, Léoville-Barton, Gruaud-Larose, and Talbot. Such investments are admirable, but the two finest vintages of the eighties are still the 1982 and 1983. Both years exhibit the depth and richness that this property is capable of attaining. But as the nineties begin, it appears these two wines were not indicative of a new era for Léoville-Poyferré, as many Bordelais had believed. The problem, I think, is that even in the eighties the wine tends to be excessively high in acidity. Does the château harvest too early?

VINTAGES

1989 —If the tannins had not been so forbiddingly high, I would
· have been more supportive of this château's 1989. It should
87 be the finest Léoville-Poyferré since the 1983, but the tannin level is not entirely balanced by the wine's concentration. If the mid-palate fills out, this will be a potentially outstanding wine. Dark ruby, but not as opaque or purple as some 1989s tend to be, this medium-bodied wine looks to be a long-distance runner. Anticipated maturity: 1998–2020. Last tasted, 4/91.

1988 —The 1988 is extremely austere, overburdened with tannin, lean,
· and lacks fruit and charm. It will age well, but will it ever provide
83 much pleasure? Anticipated maturity: 1994–2006. Last tasted, 4/91.

1987 —Thin, weedy, angular, and tough textured, the 1987 is not a suc-
· cess. Anticipated maturity: Now–1992. Last tasted, 11/90.
73

1986 —This is a good rather than dazzling 1986. On close examination,
· the wine is excessively tannic without the fruit to soften and bal-
87 ance the wine's astringency. Moreover, the wine's mid-range palate is somewhat short, no doubt caused by the enormous crop size in the vintage. That criticism aside, what one gets is a wine with great color, a plummy, spicy bouquet, medium to full body, and very good length with considerable tannic clout. Anticipated maturity: 1996–2010. Last tasted, 10/89.

1985— The 1985 Léoville-Poyferré has good color, a soft, round, fruity,
· medium-bodied feel on the palate, a toasty, new oaky bouquet,
85 ripe, melted tannins, and a moderately long finish. Anticipated
maturity: Now–1998. Last tasted, 4/90.

1984— Very tannic and hard, the 1984 Léoville-Poyferré seems to lack
· the requisite amount of fruit for the existing tannin. It is just too
75 severe; perhaps in 2 to 3 years it will open. Anticipated maturity:
Now–1994. Last tasted, 6/88.

1983— Nearly a match for the excellent 1982 made by Léoville-Poyferré,
· the 1983 has been consistently impressive. Deep dark ruby, with
90 a classic bouquet of blackcurrants, plums, and new oak, this wine
reveals very good to excellent concentration of fruit, a seductive
suppleness, and a long finish. Initially, I thought it would require
long-term cellaring, but the wine has evolved at a rapid pace, and
it is delicious for current drinking. A beauty! Anticipated maturity: Now–2003. Last tasted, 4/90.

1982— The 1982 has surprisingly high acidity for the vintage, a tremen-
· dous amount of extract, richness, and body, plenty of mouth-
92 searing tannins, and a deep ruby/purple color. It hardly seems to
have changed since I first tasted it out of cask in March 1983. It
is powerful and rich, and I would agree with France's finest taster
of Bordeaux, Michel Bettane, that it is probably the most sublime
wine made at this estate since the legendary 1928 and 1929. I
would not expect it to be fully mature until the end of the 1990s,
and it should last for at least another decade. Anticipated maturity: 2000–2020. Last tasted, 1/90.

1981— Consistently perplexing to judge, the 1981 Poyferré has adequate
· tannin and acidity, a soft, jammy, mid-range, and a short finish.
83 Surely a good wine with 4–5 years of evolution ahead of it, but
certainly not one of the leading St.-Juliens in 1981. Anticipated
maturity: Now–1993. Last tasted, 12/86.

1979— Medium to dark ruby with an amber edge, this wine has an open-
· knit, ripe, rather port-like bouquet. Soft, flabby flavors have mod-
78 est appeal, but the wine is quite loosely knit and diffuse in the
finish. Anticipated maturity: Now. Last tasted, 5/84.

1978— An easygoing wine, with soft, charming, above-average-intensity
· flavors, medium body, and very light tannins, this is a wine that
80 has obviously been vinified for near-term consumption. Anticipated maturity: Now. Last tasted, 4/82.

1976— Very soft, flabby, almost soupy, fruity flavors show good ripeness,
· but little structure, grip, or balance. A sweet, simple, fruity wine
75 that can be quaffed easily, but it does not deliver "classified

growth" breed or character. Drink up. Anticipated maturity: Now—probably in serious decline. Last tasted, 6/83.

1975—Several outstanding performances of this wine in early tastings of
    •   the 1975s proved to be an unreliable guide to its potential quality.
    ?   Dark ruby, with a spicy, closed, woody bouquet, the 1975 Poy-
ferré has a flavor suggestive of ripe black cherries. There is significant tannin that will require patience to resolve. The wine is
very inconsistent from bottle to bottle, suggesting a sloppy approach to the blending of the different barrels prior to bottling.
Some bottles can be superb, while others merely good. Unfortunately, the latter seem to represent the majority. More recent
tastings continue to reveal puzzling bottle variation. Anticipated
maturity: Now—2000. Last tasted, 11/88.

1971—Fully mature, simple, straightforward, with a bouquet reminis-
    •   cent of cranberry juice, medium bodied, somewhat compact
   75   and lean, this is a pleasant, but hardly inspiring wine. Anticipated maturity: Now—probably in serious decline. Last tasted,
6/79.

1970—Foul barnyard aromas have long beset this wine, which otherwise
    •   shows a good, dark ruby color, ripe, savory fruit, moderate tan-
   65   nins, and a decent finish. I had once hoped that time would cause
dissipation of the stinky smells, but they have only gotten worse.
Last tasted, 10/83.

1966—Given the listless management that Poyferré was under during
    •   this period, it is a wonder that the 1966 turned out as well as it
   83   did. Now fully mature, this medium-bodied, stylish wine has good
blackcurrant fruit, a complex, yet restrained bouquet of cedar
and spices, and a good crisp, clean finish. Anticipated maturity:
Now. Last tasted, 9/84.

1964—Some fruit can be found, but first one's palate must fend off
    •   abnormally high acidity and harsh tannins. It is only memorable
   55   because of the obvious deficiencies. Last tasted, 11/75.

1962—Much of the Léoville-Poyferré vineyard was replanted in 1962,
    •   and while the young, infant vines may have been the reason for
   67   some of the lackluster wines produced in the late sixties and early
seventies, they had nothing to do with the mediocre 1962. Light,
overly acidic, with some redeeming fruit flavors, this light- to
medium-weight wine should be drunk up. Anticipated maturity:
Now—probably in serious decline. Last tasted, 9/77.

1961—The 1961 is very good but not in the top class of wines from this
    •   vintage. Certainly rich, flavorful, and concentrated with fruit, this
   87   wine represents a rather rare phenomenon for Poyferré during a

period of mediocrity. Dark ruby, with an attractive cedary, spicy, mature bouquet, on the palate, the 1961 Léoville-Poyferré is deep, supple, ripe, and long, but fully mature. Anticipated maturity: Now–1993. Last tasted, 3/80.

OLDER VINTAGES

Unfortunately, I have never tasted the legendary 1928 and 1929, but the 1945, 1953, 1955, and 1959, all drunk in the late eighties, were unexciting, generally coarse, and rustic wines.

ST.-PIERRE (Fourth-Growth)   VERY GOOD

Production: 8,000 cases	Grape varieties: Cabernet Sauvignon—70% Merlot—25% Cabernet Franc—5%
Secondary labels: Clos de Uza and St. Louis-le-Bosq	
Vineyard size: 50 acres	Proprietors: The Martin family and Jean-Louis Triaud
Time spent in barrels: 20–22 months	Average age of vines: 30 years
Evaluation of present classification: Should be maintained	
Plateau of maturity: 7–20 years following the vintage	

St.-Pierre is the least known of the classified-growth St.-Julien châteaux. Much of the production of St.-Pierre has traditionally been sold to eagerly awaiting wine enthusiasts in Belgium, no doubt because the former owners, Monsieur Castelein and Madame Castelein-Van den Bussche, were Belgian. In 1982, one of the Médoc's great personalities, Henri Martin, purchased the property.

The vineyards of St.-Pierre are well located right behind the town of St.-Julien-Beychevelle, and a drive past them will reveal a high percentage of old and gnarled vines, always a sign of quality.

The style of wine of St.-Pierre has tended to be rich and full bodied, even thick and coarse in some vintages. Always deeply colored, sometimes opaque, St.-Pierre is a big, rustic, dusty-textured wine. While it can lack the finesse and charm of many St.-Juliens, such as Ducru-Beaucaillou and Léoville-Las Cases, it compensates for that deficiency with its obvious (some would say garish) display of power and muscle.

Recent vintages, particularly those since 1985, have not sacrificed any of the wine's size, but have added a forward, succulent character, and, I believe, more complexity. All in all, the wines of St.-Pierre, when compared with those of the top châteaux of St.-Julien, are vastly underrated. This estate continues to languish in the shadows cast by the glamorous superstars of the St.-Julien appellation. Given the usually realistic price, consumers should put this lack of recognition to good use.

VINTAGES

1989—The 1989 is an excellent wine, reminiscent of the style of many
·　　1982s. Dark ruby/purple, with a smashing aroma of jammy,
89　　superripe blackcurrants and new oak, this full-bodied, opulent
　　　wine offers a luscious, heady mouthful of pleasure. Aging in 75%
　　　new oak casks has given it the necessary framework. This flashy,
　　　very low-acid wine will offer dramatic drinking when young. Anticipated maturity: 1993–2010. Last tasted, 4/91.

1988—The 1988 is one of the fruitier 1988s, a characteristic often missing in many of the compact, somewhat austere wines of the
·
88　　Médoc. Deep ruby, medium bodied, with an attractively long,
　　　well-balanced finish, the 1988, while likely to be overlooked given
　　　this château's effort in 1989, is, nevertheless, a classy wine. Anticipated maturity: 1992–1999. Last tasted, 4/91.

1986—The 1986 has turned out to be outstanding. It is a powerfully
·　　constructed, dark ruby-colored wine, with plenty of muscle and
90　　richness, an intriguing bouquet of exotic spices, sweet toasty oak,
　　　and plummy fruit. On the palate, the wine is very concentrated
　　　and tannic. This brawny, large-scaled wine has an underlying
　　　suppleness that suggests it should be drinkable at an earlier age
　　　than many of the other top 1986 Médocs. Anticipated maturity:
　　　1994–2012. Last tasted, 11/90.

1985—The 1985 St.-Pierre is rich, chewy, fat, and deep, with just the
·　　right amount of new oak. It reminds me of the fine 1981 made
87　　at this property. Anticipated maturity: Now–1998. Last tasted,
　　　11/90.

1984—A lightish, soft, fruity wine, the 1984 should be drunk over the
·　　next 3–4 years for the uncomplicated, yet pleasing, medium-
82　　bodied fruitiness. Anticipated maturity: Now–1993. Last tasted,
　　　10/87.

1983—Surprisingly similar in style to the 1982, fat, succulent, and very
·　　concentrated with a soft, rich, almost jammy concentration, this
87　　full-bodied, robust wine has a seductive lushness and will make
　　　excellent drinking. Anticipated maturity: Now–1998. Last tasted,
　　　3/89.

1982 · 88 —A lovely, supple, ripe, savory, richly fruity wine with medium to full body, a moderately intense bouquet of vanillin oakiness and ripe fruit, the 1982 St.-Pierre seems forward and lush, but exhibits sufficient underlying tannin to develop nicely. Anticipated maturity: Now–2000. Last tasted, 3/89.

1981 · 88 —A top-notch wine, certainly one of the most successful wines of this vintage, the 1981 St.-Pierre is impressively dark ruby and very aromatic, with the scent of ripe berry fruit, cedarwood, and caramel. On the palate, it is quite rich, medium to full bodied, long, lush, and moderately tannic. It is a big, extroverted St.-Julien, with considerable personality. Anticipated maturity: Now–2000. Last tasted, 11/88.

1979 · 85 —A robust, virile wine for a 1979, this St.-Pierre has impressive color, a chunky, satisfying, rich fruity character, some whiffs of cedarwood, and a solid, moderately tannic finish. Not elegant, but nevertheless substantial and flavorful. Anticipated maturity: Now–1995. Last tasted, 11/88.

1975 · 86 —Impressive for sure, but like so many 1975s, one wonders whether it will live up to potential. Still dark in color, with only a slight amber edge, this full-bodied wine has ripe, chocolatey fruit, but also mouth-lashing, high tannins that remain dry and astringent. The 1975 St.-Pierre is a robust, muscular wine that still requires time in the bottle. Anticipated maturity: 1992–2005. Last tasted, 11/89.

1971 · 83 —Ready to drink, this wine is quite spicy, with a plummy, cedary nose that offers high expectations on the palate. The wine is good, but less promising than the fine bouquet suggests. The somewhat coarse, rough flavors are heavy-handed and too aggressive. Anticipated maturity: Now. Last tasted, 6/82.

1970 · 87 —A sleeper of the vintage, the 1970 St.-Pierre is dark ruby, is loaded with spicy, blackcurrant fruit, and has full body, plenty of round, ripe tannins, and substantial length on the palate. Fully mature, but made to last, the 1970 St.-Pierre can rival many of Bordeaux's best estates in 1970. Anticipated maturity: Now–2005. Last tasted, 6/87.

1961 · 87 —This is a fine 1961, with a fully mature, sweet, savory, plummy spiciness, medium to full body, an expansive dark garnet color, and a long, alcoholic finish. Anticipated maturity: Now–1994. Last tasted, 7/85.

TALBOT (Fourth-Growth)　　　　　EXCELLENT

Production: 38,000 cases	Grape varieties: Cabernet Sauvignon—70% Merlot—20% Cabernet Franc—5% Petit Verdot—5%
Secondary label: Connétable de 　Talbot	
Vineyard size: 247 acres	Proprietor: Domaines Cordier
Time spent in barrels: 18–24 　months	Average age of vines: 35 years
Evaluation of present classification: Should be upgraded to a second- 　growth	
Plateau of maturity: 7–25 years following the vintage	

The sibling château of Gruaud-Larose, the famous second-growth, Talbot is also owned by Domaines Cordier. The huge single vineyard of Talbot is situated inland from the Gironde River, well behind the tiny hamlet of St.-Julien-Beychevelle, and just north of Gruaud-Larose.

Talbot is named after the English commander, John Talbot, the Earl of Shrewsbury, who was defeated in battle at Castillon in 1453. The château makes consistently fine, robust, yet fruity, full-bodied wines that would be moved upward should any new reclassification of the wines of the Médoc be done. The wine is vinified in the same manner as Cordier's Gruaud-Larose, but the two wines do not resemble each other except for this enviable record of consistent high quality. Gruaud-Larose always tends to be a fuller-bodied, more tannic and muscular wine. Talbot usually has to take a second seat to Gruaud-Larose in head-to-head competition, but in certain vintages, Talbot can surpass the more prestigious sibling. For example, the 1986, 1985, and 1982 Talbot are almost a match for the brilliant wines of Gruaud-Larose of those years, and in 1989, 1983, 1980, 1976, and 1971, Talbot can be said to have bested Gruaud-Larose.

Talbot is a wine that needs 5–8 years to reveal its class and character, and like Gruaud-Larose tends to be undervalued in the current-day Bordeaux wine market. Of particular significance is the fact that Talbot has been consistently brilliant since the 1975 vintage. The 1977 is the only weak wine produced in this period.

A modest amount of delicious, dry white wine (from 100% Sauvignon) is made at Talbot. Called Caillou Blanc du Château Talbot, it is a deliciously fresh, fragrant white—one of the finest produced in the Médoc. It must, however, be drunk within 2–4 years of the vintage.

VINTAGES

1989—The 1989 Talbot may not be so backward as the 1989 from its
·   sister château, Gruaud-Larose, but it is a fascinating wine that
90 resembles the 1982. However, the 1982 exhibited more weight
   and extract at a similar stage of development. Opaque black/ruby,
   with a huge bouquet of black fruits and spices, this highly extracted, medium- to full-bodied wine is voluptuous on the palate,
   with a fine finish. Lower in acidity than the 1982, but higher in
   tannin than the 1986, the 1989 Talbot promises to drink well in its
   first decade. Anticipated maturity: 1994–2015. Last tasted, 4/91.

1988—The 1988 is dark ruby, with a well-focused personality brimming
·   with spicy, chocolatey, blackcurrant fruit buttressed by good
88 acidity and high tannins. If the tannins fade a little and the fruit
   takes over, this will be an outstanding wine. Anticipated maturity:
   1997–2015. Last tasted, 4/91.

1987—The 1987 Talbot is a surprisingly tannic, tough-textured wine, but
·   has a gorgeous nose of cedar and weedy, earthy blackcurrants.
85 Deep in color, with a good deal of tannin and medium body, this
   is a vintage that will keep for 10–15 years. Anticipated maturity:
   1993–2000. Last tasted, 11/90.

1986—The 1982 Talbot is a marvelous wine, but it's my gut feeling that
·   the 1986 is simply the finest Talbot made at this vast 250-acre
96 estate since the legendary 1945. The fact that there are 40,000
   cases of this wine is good news for the consumer, as there will be
   plenty to go around. The wine, which has been so special since
   the first taste from cask, is classically structured, with a penetrating fragrance of peppery, spicy, weedy blackcurrants and tar,
   an enormous concentration of flavor on the palate, and staggering
   length. The tannins are noticeable, but they are ripe tannins,
   somewhat softer than those found in many of the 1986 Médocs.
   In comparison with stablemate Gruaud-Larose, the Talbot is
   more developed and flattering to taste today. This should prove to
   be an extraordinarily long-lived wine, and, as are virtually all the
   Cordier wines, a marvelous value for your money. Anticipated
   maturity: 1996–2020. Last tasted, 11/90.

1985—The 1985 Talbot is a down-sized version of their 1982, and is now
·   flattering to taste and drink. Very deep in color, with a ripe, rich,
89 berry-like fragrance, this supple, fleshy, medium-bodied wine has
   loads of fruit, a smooth, graceful finish, and excellent balance.
   Anticipated maturity: Now–2000. Last tasted, 4/90.

1984—The Cordiers seem to do well in the so-called "off years" (i.e.,
·   1968 Talbot and 1974 Gruaud-Larose), so it is no surprise to see
82 how good their 1984s are. The 1984 Talbot is 94% Cabernet Sau-

vignon and 6% Merlot. It is quite elegant and stylish with a lovely bouquet of spring flowers and ripe curranty fruit, medium to full body, and good tannins. It needs 2–3 years of aging. Anticipated maturity: Now–1996. Last tasted, 3/88.

1983—Full bodied, with a deep, almost opaque ruby/purple color, a for-
·   ward, cassis-scented aroma, and rich, lush flavors, the 1983 Tal-
91   bot is a large-scaled wine that is drinking surprisingly well. It is one of the great successes of the vintage. Anticipated maturity: Now–2008. Last tasted, 3/89.

1982—The 1982 is showing better now than it was from either cask or
·   early bottle tastings. I am amazed at how rich, powerful, concen-
95   trated, and complex this wine has become. In one recent tasting, the bouquet was more peppery than in another tasting, but in both it was a massive wine with incredibly expansive, sweet, rich fruit on the palate. Although the wine is approachable and drinkable now, it displayed the potential to last and evolve for another 20 years. It is one of the most remarkable Talbots I have ever tasted, and I have to believe that at least for the next 10–12 years it will compete very favorably with the otherworldly 1986 Talbot. Antic-ipated maturity: 1994–2015. Last tasted, 5/91.

1981—Attractive and well made, the 1981 Talbot exhibits surprising
·   elegance and suppleness for this property. Dark ruby, with a
85   moderately intense bouquet of cassis and meaty, leathery, tarry aromas, this medium-bodied wine has good concentration and light tannins. It is drinkable now. Similar in style to the 1979, the 1981 is a shade fruitier and deeper. Anticipated maturity: Now–2000. Last tasted, 4/89.

1980—More successful than Gruaud-Larose in 1980, this wine offers
·   solid, straightforward fruity flavors, none of the vegetal charac-
82   ters found in the worst 1980s, and a solid, round, flavorful finish. Anticipated maturity: Now–may be in decline. Last tasted, 6/83.

1979—A richly fruity Talbot, with a precocious, forward appeal, this
·   medium-bodied wine has a velvety texture, and a soft, round
84   finish. Anticipated maturity: Now. Last tasted, 2/84.

1978—Developing very nicely in the bottle, the 1978 Talbot has a con-
·   centrated, ripe, round, rich, herbaceous-scented, blackcurrant
87   fruitiness, a bouquet suggestive of plums and cedary, toasty oak, a generous texture, and some tannins in the finish. It has just reached its plateau of maturity. Anticipated maturity: Now–2000. Last tasted, 10/90.

1976—The variable 1976 vintage reached its greatest heights in the com-
·   mune of St.-Julien where a number of fine wines were produced.
86   Talbot is one of them. Fully mature, but capable of holding for

several more years, this immensely enjoyable wine has a lovely cedary, spicy, ripe plummy bouquet, soft, round, nicely concentrated flavors, and a velvety, satisfying finish. Anticipated maturity: Now–1994. Last tasted, 11/87.

1975—When young it was not impressive, as it seemed to lack concentration, grip, and character. Despite some good performances in
·
84   the early eighties, the wine now appears angular and tough. Not that darkly colored for a 1975, and now exhibiting some amber, this wine has a well-developed bouquet of spicy, vanillin, blackcurrant fruit, a dusty, tannic, rather weighty texture, and good length. It is much more evolved than its sibling, the 1975 Gruaud-Larose. Anticipated maturity: Now–2000. Last tasted, 11/87.

1971—One of the most stylish and complete wines of the vintage, the
·
86   1971 Talbot is now fully mature, but showing no signs of fading. It has good concentration, a lively, berryish, fruity quality, a deft touch of vanillin oakiness, and medium to full body. Very well structured for a 1971, it is without any brown color or soupy softness that afflicts many of the wines of this vintage. The 1971 Talbot is certainly a successful wine from this vintage. Anticipated maturity: Now–1994. Last tasted, 3/89.

1970—The 1970 Talbot is good, but not up to the quality level expected.
·
78   Too austere, a trifle harsh and unyielding, this wine lacks one of the telltale characteristics of the 1970 vintage—a rich, glossy fruitiness. The bouquet shows Médoc breeding, iron-like mineral scents, oak, and blackcurrants, but the tannin overwhelms the fruit. Time may help, but this wine's balance appears suspect. Anticipated maturity: Now–1993. Last tasted, 11/87.

1967—One of the more attractive wines of the vintage, the 1967 Talbot
·
75   is now cracking up. Short, compact flavors now exhibit little of the rich, fruity, robustness exhibited in the mid-1970s. Anticipated maturity: Now. Last tasted, 1/83.

1966—Age has given this wine some complexity as a result of bottle
·
77   bouquet. However, this vintage did not produce a profound example of Talbot. Hard, austere, lean flavors reveal little evidence that rich, ripe fruit is hidden behind a shield of tannin and acidity. The color is light, the fruit just adequate, the finish short. Anticipated maturity: Now–1993. Last tasted, 9/84.

1964—This is an attractive, if uncomplex, 1964. Talbot is adequately
·
82   fruity, chunky, a trifle hard and coarse in the finish, but overall, a good mouthful of claret. Anticipated maturity: Now–may be in decline. Last tasted, 3/79.

1962—An elegant Talbot, finely etched and reminiscent of the style of
·   the 1971, this medium-bodied, flavorful, fully mature wine is hold-
84   ing up nicely in the bottle. A fragrant, spicy, cedary bouquet is
interesting and shows good fruit. Rather reserved on the palate,
with polite flavors, some unresolved tannins still present, and
above-average length, this is a good, rather than great, Talbot.
Anticipated maturity: Now—may be in decline. Last tasted, 2/83.

1961—One would naturally expect the 1961 Talbot to completely over-
·   whelm the 1962. When tasted side by side, the wines are more
85   similar than not, a trait that is abnormal given the different styles
of these two vintages. The 1961, like the 1962, is a bit austere and
lean, has medium to full body, a rather stern, unyielding texture,
and good, rather than excellent, concentration. The wine lacks
the color and richness of the best 1961s, but is still a good wine.
In the context of the vintage, the 1961 Talbot must be viewed as
a disappointment. Anticipated maturity: Now—may be in decline.
Last tasted, 1/85.

OLDER VINTAGES

The 1953, 1949, and profound 1945 (rated a 94 in 1988) are the finest
old vintages of Talbot I have tasted. The 1949 and 1953 (both 90-point
wines) are not likely to improve and should be drunk up; the extraordinary 1945 can be kept for 10–15 more years!

TERREY-GROS-CAILLOUX (Cru Bourgeois)   GOOD

Production: 8,000 cases	Grape varieties:
	Cabernet Sauvignon—65%
	Merlot—30%
	Petit Verdot—5%
Secondary label: none	
Vineyard size: 37.5 acres	Proprietors: André Fort and
	Henri Pradère
Time spent in barrels: 14 months	Average age of vines: 15 years
in vats and barrels	
Evaluation of present classification: The quality equivalent of a	
Grand Bourgeois Exceptionnel	
Plateau of maturity: 3–7 years following the vintage	

The cellars of this well-run Cru Bourgeois are located just off the famous
D2 in the direction of Gruaud-Larose and Talbot. They house not only
Terrey-Gros-Cailloux, but also the wine of Hortevie. Terrey-Gros-Cail-

loux tends to be a richly fruity, round, occasionally full-bodied wine that offers delicious drinking if consumed within the first 7–8 years. It is not long-lived, but the decision by the proprietors in the late eighties to begin to use some new oak casks to give the wine more definition and structure should prove beneficial to the wine's longevity.

VINTAGES

1989—I would have expected a better performance from this normally
· well-run estate. The 1989 exhibits an attractive ripe fruit, but
85 tastes too one-dimensional and simple to merit higher marks. Perhaps more character will emerge with aging in the new oak casks this property now utilizes. Anticipated maturity: Now–1997. Last tasted, 11/90.

1988—The 1988 tastes surprisingly light, straightforward, and undistin-
· guished. Is this wine going through an unflattering stage? Antici-
80 pated maturity: Now–1993. Last tasted, 11/90.

1986—This husky wine has tremendous richness and intensity of fruit, a
· full-bodied texture, somewhat low acidity, but plenty of length
86 and hedonistic appeal. It is not one of the most classically struc-tured wines in the vintage. Anticipated maturity: Now–1997. Last tasted, 3/90.

1985—This Cru Bourgeois is consistently well made and well known for
· the plump, fleshy, chunky style of St.-Julien that is short on fi-
85 nesse but not flavor. The 1985 is rich, ripe, sweet, low in acidity, meaty, and tasty. Anticipated maturity: Now–1995. Last tasted, 3/89.

1984—Soft, fruity, unsubstantial, and inconsequential, this wine should
· be drunk over the next 2–3 years. Anticipated maturity: Now–
75 may be in decline. Last tasted, 3/88.

MARGAUX AND THE SOUTHERN MÉDOC

Margaux is certainly the largest and most sprawling of all the Médoc's principal wine-producing communes. The 2,847 acres under vine now exceed that of St.-Estèphe. A first-time tourist to Margaux immediately realizes just how spread out the châteaux of Margaux are. Only a few sit directly on Bordeaux's Route du Vin (D2), and these are Dauzac, Prieuré-Lichine, Palmer, and Malescot St.-Exupéry. Château Margaux is just off the main road in the town of Margaux, but the other major châteaux are sprinkled throughout the five principal communes of this appellation: Arsac, Labarde, Cantenac, Margaux, and Soussans.

Margaux has the greatest number of classified-growth châteaux (Crus Classés) in the 1855 classification. A total of twenty-one Margaux châteaux made the grade, which is four more than Pauillac's seventeen châteaux that were included, ten more than St.-Julien's eleven, and sixteen more than St. Estèphe's five châteaux.

From an outsider's view, Margaux thus appears to have the highest number of quality wine producers; however, nothing could be further from the truth. From 1961 to 1982 there are at least a half-dozen estates in Margaux that have a dreadful record of performance, and at least another four or five properties that should be downgraded to fifth-growth status should any revised classification of the wines of the Médoc be done and the five-tiered hierarchy maintained. Since 1983, a number of these estates have improved the quality of their wines, but this remains Bordeaux's leading appellation of underachievers. Even the regal first-growth queen herself, Château Margaux, went through a period of mediocrity that was dramatically reversed when the Mentzelopoulos family purchased Château Margaux in 1977 from the Ginestets, who had inadvertently permitted this grande dame to slip considerably in quality (not price, however) below first-growth quality standards.

Despite the irregularity and lackluster track record of many Margaux châteaux over the last two and a half decades, the fragrant bouquet and seductive charm of a few great Margaux wines are what set these wines apart from a St.-Julien or Pauillac. The bouquet of a fine Margaux is unquestionably more intense and compelling than those found in the wines of St. Julien, Pauillac, and St.-Estèphe. This has been well chronicled in virtually all the writings on Bordeaux wine, but what is not said is that the great wines of Margaux are in real terms limited to Château Margaux, Palmer, and, since 1983, Rausan-Ségla.

No one will argue that properties such as Rauzan-Gassies, Brane-Cantenac, Durfort-Vivens (all second-growths), and Cantenac-Brown and Malescot St.-Exupéry (both third-growths) have great soils, superb vineyards, and immense potential, but except for the recent turnabout in quality for several of these estates, the wines of these estates have been terribly inconsistent and, in far too many vintages, mediocre or poor in quality.

The great diversity of soils and quality level of wines produced in Margaux is challenging for even the most devoted Bordeaux wine enthusiast. Generally, the white-colored soils in Margaux are the lightest and most gravelly of the Médoc, and when one gets down to Ludon where La Lagune is located, a high percentage of sand appears in the soil base.

Since 1977, Château Margaux has made unquestionably the greatest and most powerful wine of this appellation. It is a virile, very concentrated, and densely colored wine.

Château Margaux's chief competitor historically has been Palmer. However, Palmer's style of wine is different. It shares a dark color and deep concentration of flavor with Château Margaux, but it is a more supple, rounder, less tannic wine resulting from a high percentage of Merlot used in the blend. Palmer does have a fabulously complex bouquet that in certain vintages—1961, 1966, 1970, 1983, and 1989 come to mind immediately—is hauntingly perfect.

The newest pretender to the Margaux throne is Rausan-Ségla, a superb vineyard that until 1983 could claim to be this appellation's most notorious underachiever. Today Rausan-Ségla produces riveting wines of great flavor, depth, and complexity, with a purity that is breathtaking.

Another recognizable style of Margaux wine would be typified by those with an intense fragrance, but lighter weight, less concentrated, and less tannin. Certainly Prieuré-Lichine, Lascombes, d'Issan, and Malescot St.-Exupéry all produce wines in this manner.

Prieuré-Lichine, the home of the late Alexis Lichine, tends to produce very stylish, elegant, fragrant wines. The property has generally been much more consistent than many of its more famous neighbors. Certainly Lascombes, a wine that I adore when it is made well, has been like a yo-yo in terms of quality. The reports of a renewed vigor and commitment to higher quality from its corporate owners are apparently true if the wines Lascombes produced since 1982 are any indication.

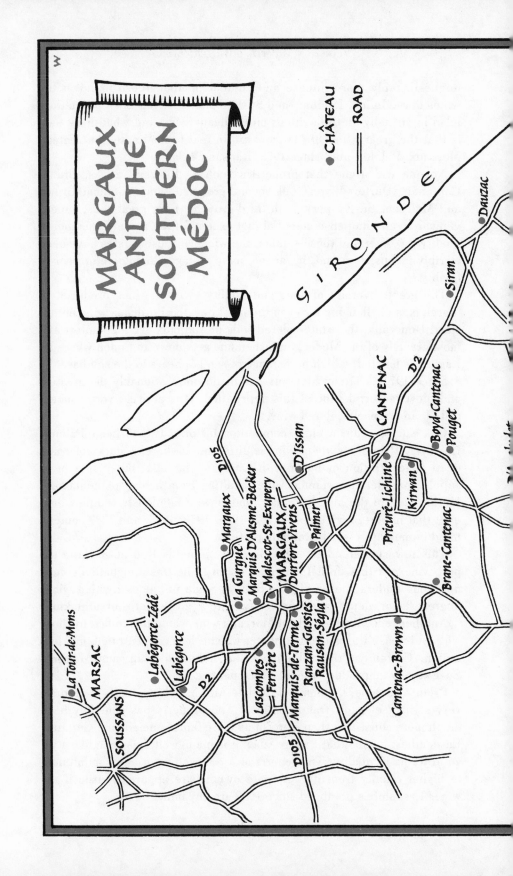

MARGAUX AND THE SOUTHERN MÉDOC

● CHÂTEAU
══ ROAD

GIRONDE

La Tour-de-Mons
MARSAC
Labégorce-Zédé
Labégorce
SOUSSANS
D2

Margaux
D105
Marquis D'Alesme-Becker
Malescot-St-Exupery
La Gurgue
MARGAUX
Durfort-Vivens

Lascombes
Ferrière
Marquis-de-Terme
Rauzan-Gassies
Rausan-Ségla
D105

D'Issan
Palmer

CANTENAC
D2

Prieuré-Lichine
Kirwan
Cantenac-Brown
Brane-Cantenac

Boyd-Cantenac
Pouget

Siran

Dauzac

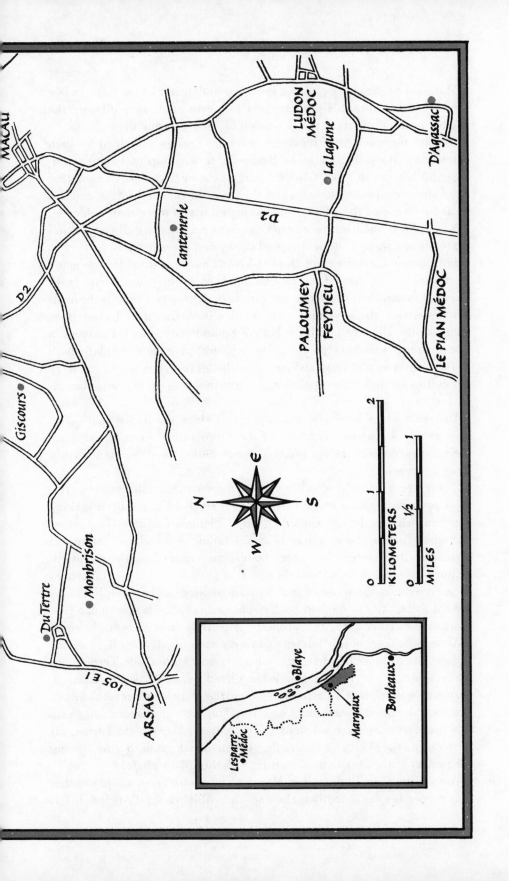

MACAU

LUDON
MÉDOC

D'Agassac

La Lagune

Cantemerle

D2

D2

PALOUMEY

FEYDIEU

LE PIAN MÉDOC

Giscours

N
W E
S

KILOMETERS
0   ½   1   2

MILES
0   1

Du Tertre

Monbrison

D 105 E1

ARSAC

Lesparre-
Médoc

Blaye

Margaux

Bordeaux

Malescot St.-Exupéry enjoys a great reputation and I have tasted a few superb bottles from this property, yet it is overrated, as is d'Issan, the moated castle property that has slipped in quality during the eighties.

Despite the number of mediocre, even poor wines produced by such noteworthy Margaux estates as Brane-Cantenac, Durfort-Vivens, Dauzac, and Kirwan in the 1961–1980 period, the encouraging thing is that all of these properties have halted their nose dives, and in the eighties turned in some of their best winemaking efforts in more than a decade. Yet in spite of their improvements, no one could realistically argue that these estates should not be demoted in any new classification.

Both Brane-Cantenac and Durfort-Vivens have provided far too many unexciting, often flawed wines. As much as I enjoy the company of Lucien Lurton, the proprietor, the wines from these two estates throughout the sixties and seventies were terribly inconsistent and sometimes undrinkable. However, with the help of Emile Peynaud and, I suspect, a more careful selection process, the eighties have been kind to both Brane-Cantenac and Durfort-Vivens, but both properties would still have difficulties holding on to their second-growth status in any new classification.

Dauzac's wines have also made progress since the late seventies, as have those of Kirwan. Yet both of these properties, even allowing for their improvements, rarely produce wines better than the Médoc's top Crus Bourgeois.

There are a handful of other classified-growth Margaux estates. The most promising estate is du Tertre, which since 1978 has been making excellent wine under the capable hand of Philippe Capbern-Gasqueton. Cantenac-Brown, the producer of rustic, tannic, hard wines that appeal to those with nineteenth-century tastes, may move into the twentieth century in terms of its wine style now that Jean-Michel Cazes of Lynch-Bages overlooks the winemaking. Rauzan-Gassies can be good, but leans toward a chunky, full-bodied St.-Estèphe style of wine rather than a true Margaux. Furthermore, the property is terribly inconsistent. Marquis d'Alesme-Becker, hardly known and rarely seen, produces a light wine.

Two other classified châteaux, Giscours and Marquis-de-Terme, can make some of the richest and longest-lived wines of the appellation. Giscours was a proven performer during the sixties and seventies, but seriously declined in the early eighties. The 1989 of Giscours suggests this property may have rebounded. In contrast, Marquis-de-Terme, off form during the sixties and seventies, began to make superb wine, among the richest of the appellation, starting with the 1983 vintage.

Among the Crus Bourgeois in Margaux, most observers would say that four properties consistently make fine wine. Monbrison, d'Angludet, Labégorce-Zédé, and Siran are very good estates making typically elegant, perfumed, aromatic wine. Labégorce-Zédé's wine tends to be the most robust and richest of this quartet, Monbrison the most classic and compelling, Siran the most masculine and tannic, and d'Angludet the most supple and charming.

Lastly, two major properties and classified growths in the south of Margaux both make excellent wine. La Lagune is one of my favorite wines. Brilliantly made, the wine can resemble both a Pomerol and a burgundy, but it is always deliciously rich, round, fruity, and complex. The quality seems to get better with each passing vintage. Cantemerle is the other treasure of the southern Médoc and after an uneven period in the late seventies, Cantemerle has been making superb wine, with the 1983 and 1989 its crowning achievements. Both La Lagune and Cantemerle, no doubt because they are not in the famous Margaux appellation, are considerably undervalued in the scheme of Bordeaux wine pricing.

Vintages for Margaux and southern Margaux can often be vastly different from those for the communes of St.-Julien, Pauillac, and St.-Estèphe, which sit a good distance to the north. This is not a region in which to look for good wines in off-vintages. The thin soil seems to produce thin wines in rainy years, although there are always exceptions. Also, extremely torrid, drought-like summers without adequate rainfall tend to stress those vineyards with high plantations of Cabernet Sauvignon, retarding the ripening process while at the same time roasting the grapes. This explains why 1982, 1989, and 1990 were less successful in Margaux than in the northern Médoc. The finest vintages for Margaux wines have been 1986, 1983, 1979, 1978, 1970, 1966, and 1961.

A CONSUMER'S CLASSIFICATION OF THE CHÂTEAUX OF MARGAUX AND THE SOUTHERN MÉDOC

OUTSTANDING

Margaux
Palmer
Rausan-Ségla (since 1983)

EXCELLENT

La Lagune
Monbrison

VERY GOOD

**d'Angludet, Cantemerle, Giscours, Marquis-de-Terme,
Marsac-Séguineau, Prieuré-Lichine, du Tertre**

GOOD

Brane-Cantenac, Cantenac-Brown, Charmant, Durfort-Vivens, La
Gurgue, Labégorce-Zédé, Larruau, Lascombes,
Malescot St.-Exupéry, Siran

OTHER NOTABLE MARGAUX AND SOUTHERN MÉDOC PROPERTIES
Bel-Air-Marquis d'Aligre, Boyd-Cantenac, Dauzac, Desmirail, Deyrem-
Valentin, Ferrière, d'Issan, Kirwan, Labégorce, Marquis d'Alesme-
Becker, Martinens, Paveil-de-Luze, Pouget, Rauzan-Gassies, Tayac,
La Tour-de-Mons

D'ANGLUDET (Cru Bourgeois Exceptionnel) VERY GOOD

Production: 13,000 cases	Grape varieties:
	Cabernet Sauvignon—60%
	Merlot—30%
	Petit Verdot—7%
	Cabernet Franc—3%
Secondary label: Domaine Baury	
Vineyard size: 79 acres	Proprietor: Peter A. Sichel
Time spent in barrels: 16–18 months	Average age of vines: 18 years
Evaluation of present classification: The quality equivalent of a Médoc fifth-growth	
Plateau of maturity: 6–18 years following the vintage	

Peter A. Sichel, the proprietor of d'Angludet, is a multifaceted individual. He is not only a highly respected Bordeaux wine broker, but also the president of the promotional arm of the Bordeaux wine industry, the Union des Grands Crus. He is a part owner in the famous Margaux estate of Palmer, as well as proprietor of his own château and residence, d'Angludet.

Sichel purchased this property in 1961 when it was in deplorable condition, and has been solely responsible for taking the property, which sits in the southwestern corner of Margaux on what is called the plateau Le Grand Poujeau (shared by three Margaux estates, Giscours, du Tertre, and d'Angludet), from virtual post–World War II obscurity to international prominence. It is irrefutable that the wine made at d'Angludet frequently surpasses some of its more illustrious siblings in the Margaux appellation.

The history of the estate is old, even by Bordeaux standards, and can be traced back to the early fourteenth century. The estate's wines had a good reputation, and appear numerous times in wine references from the sixteenth through the eighteenth centuries, but by the time the famous classification of 1855 was founded, the property was in bad condition—a reason often offered as to why it was excluded from that classification.

The wines of d'Angludet have gone from one strength to another since the early eighties. This coincides with the fact that so much of the vineyard was replanted in the early sixties. Now the vines have a healthy average age of 18 years. While the high percentage of Merlot (30%) gives the wine some of the fatness and suppleness that the famous sibling, Château Palmer, enjoys, d'Angludet can last for 10–20 years. Today, the wine is clearly of classified-growth quality, yet the price has remained extremely modest. Vintages prior to 1978 are generally undistinguished, but since that time there have been some marvelous to excellent wines, including a superb 1983, and excellent wines in both 1986 and 1989.

VINTAGES

1989—The 1989 d'Angludet is probably this property's best wine since
  ·   their excellent 1983. It does not, however, appear to have the
  87   stuffing necessary to surpass that wine. It is fat, plump, intensely
         fruity with a good ruby color, supple texture, high alcohol, and
         soft tannins. Anticipated maturity: 1992–2002. Last tasted, 4/91.

1988—The 1988 is a sinewy, surprisingly light wine, medium bodied, low
  ·   in extract levels and tannins, and exhibiting straightforward,
  81   solid, but unexciting flavors. Anticipated maturity: 1992–1998.
         Last tasted, 4/91.

1987—This is a delicious wine that should be consumed by 1993. It
  ·   exhibits fine ripeness, light to medium body, very soft tannins,
  84   and an easygoing, smooth finish. One can easily detect that the
         Merlot in d'Angludet has given this vintage attractive, charming
         suppleness and an easygoing character. Anticipated maturity:
         Now–1996. Last tasted, 11/90.

1986—Dark ruby, with an attractive oaky, plummy nose, and medium
  ·   body, this is an aggressively tannic d'Angludet that exhibits good
  86   flavor depth, yet needs to be kept for several years before it will
         be ready to drink. Anticipated maturity: 1992–2000. Last tasted,
         11/90.

1985—The 1985 d'Angludet lacks depth and seems to have a slight hole
  ·   in its mid-range. Otherwise, it has good color, a plummy, spicy,
  83   obvious bouquet, soft, medium-bodied flavors, fine ripe berry
         fruit, and light tannins in the finish. Anticipated maturity: Now–
         1996. Last tasted, 11/90.

1983—This is the best d'Angludet I have ever tasted. It offers further
· evidence of just how successful, and better than 1982, the 1983
89 vintage in Margaux can be. Deep ruby/purple colored with some
amber at the edge, this relatively full-bodied, thick, rich, concentrated wine is still young, yet bursting with concentration and
ripeness. Long, with moderate, soft, ripe tannins, this is a d'Angludet for drinking over a 12–15-year period. Anticipated maturity: Now–2003. Last tasted, 11/90.

1982—Soft and loosely knit, the 1982 exhibits some amber at the edge,
· a forward, earthy, cedary, fruitcake sort of bouquet, loosely struc-
84 tured, low acid flavors, and a soft, round finish that is lacking
grip. Anticipated maturity: Now–1995. Last tasted, 11/90.

1981—Medium ruby, with some amber at the edge, the relatively tightly
· knit nose reluctantly gives up aromas of dusty earth, old barrels,
81 and some crisp, curranty fruit. In the mouth, it has the leanness
and compactness that typifies the 1981 vintage. Close to maturity
and well made, this is a lighter-styled, yet pleasant d'Angludet.
Anticipated maturity: Now–1995. Last tasted, 11/90.

1978—Fully mature, with a big, spicy, rich, plummy bouquet, this solidly
· built, relatively fat, intense d'Angludet has shed its tannins and
85 should be consumed. Anticipated maturity: Now–1996. Last
tasted, 11/90.

1975—Unfortunately, I bought a half-dozen bottles of this wine when it
· was released, and it has remained a stubbornly hard, gutsy,
72 coarsely textured wine that has never provided charm. I have only
two bottles left in my cellar and am wondering if the wine will
ever come around. It still has relatively good color, with only a
slight amber at the edge. There is some thickness, but the hard
tannins and astringency obliterate any joy in drinking this dry,
rustic wine. Anticipated maturity: 1992–2000. Last tasted, 11/90.

1970—Some amber at the edge suggests this wine is beginning to fade.
· In the mouth, it exhibits some ripeness and a slight musty, damp,
76 earthy fruitiness. Medium bodied, yet coarse and one-dimensional, this wine should be consumed. Anticipated maturity:
Now–1994. Last tasted, 11/90.

BEL-AIR MARQUIS D'ALIGRE
(Cru Bourgeois Exceptionnel)   AVERAGE

Production: 5,000 cases	Grape varieties: Cabernet Sauvignon—30% Cabernet Franc—20% Merlot—35% Petit Verdot—15%
Secondary label: Bel-Air-Marquis de Pomereu	
Vineyard size: 42 acres	Proprietor: Pierre Boyer
Time spent in barrels: 18–20 months	Average age of vines: 35 years
Evaluation of present classification: Should be maintained	
Plateau of maturity: 4–12 years following the vintage	

I rarely have seen this wine, but it has admirers, particularly in the Benelux countries. My notes do reveal satisfying examples of the 1978 and 1979. To the proprietor's credit, his yields of 35 hectoliters per hectare are very modest and he uses only organic fertilizers.

BOYD-CANTENAC (Third-Growth)   AVERAGE

Production: 8,000 cases	Grape varieties: Cabernet Sauvignon—67% Merlot—20% Cabernet Franc—7% Petit Verdot—6%
Secondary label: none	
Vineyard size: 44.4 acres	Proprietor: The Guillemet family
Time spent in barrels: 24 months	Average age of vines: 30 years
Evaluation of present classification: Should be downgraded to a Cru Bourgeois	
Plateau of maturity: 8–20 years following the vintage	

This is a distressingly inconsistent estate that, unfortunately, no longer merits its rank as a third-growth. It, and the nearby Château Pouget, have been owned by the well-known Guillemet family since the early 1930s. The proprietor lives at Château Pouget since there is no official château at Boyd-Cantenac, and the wines are vinified and cellared in a warehouse adjoining Pouget. It has always been a mystery why these wines are not better. While discussing the overall philosophy with the owner, one is impressed by the relatively low yields and attention to detail evidenced by the staff at Boyd-Cantenac. Nevertheless, for every good vintage of Boyd-Cantenac, there seem to be several where the wine falls well short of expectations. Perhaps a stricter selection, utilization of a second label, and a higher percentage of new oak might result in more consistency in the cellars. I have often found the wine impressive prior to bottling, but a bit coarse and attenuated in tastings afterwards. As a consequence, this wine is never on my purchasing list, and I suspect many strangers to Bordeaux often confuse it with the two better-known, and now better-made, wines with the word *Cantenac* as part of their name, Brane-Cantenac and Cantenac-Brown.

VINTAGES

1989—The 1989 is a thick, unctuous, heavyweight wine, low in acidity,
·   but enormously rich, fruity, and full. It has high alcohol and
86   plenty of tannin, so it should age well, yet be drinkable early.
     Anticipated maturity: 1993–2003. Last tasted, 4/91.

1988—The 1988 has a problem, at least those samples I tasted did. The
·   disturbing nail-polish aroma suggested something was wrong.
?   Otherwise, it is an atypically big, brawny, rustic-styled 1988.
     Judgment reserved. Last tasted, 4/91.

1986—For some reason, Boyd-Cantenac tends to be a hard, sometimes
·   dull wine and the 1986 has these characteristics plus diluted fla-
78   vors, no doubt caused by the excessive vineyard yields, as well as
     a lenient selection process at the château. This medium-bodied,
     rather tannic wine should be consumed early in its life because of
     the lack of extract. Anticipated maturity: Now–1996. Last tasted,
     3/90.

1985—The 1985 Boyd-Cantenac exhibits good ruby color and has a
·   sweet, tasty, plummy fruitiness, medium body, low acidity, and a
83   dull finish. It is good, but not exciting. Anticipated maturity:
     Now–1995. Last tasted, 3/89.

1984—Quite light, thin, and insubstantial, the 1984 is barely acceptable.
·   It should be drunk up. Anticipated maturity: Now–probably in
70   serious decline. Last tasted, 6/87.

1983—In this very good vintage, Boyd-Cantenac has turned in one of its
·   better efforts. Dark ruby in color, with a full-blown, spicy, ripe
87   plummy aroma, rich, full-bodied, concentrated flavors, and
     plenty of tannin, this big, robust Margaux has begun to shed some

of its tannins, but still needs 5 years to reach maturity. Anticipated maturity: 1995–2010. Last tasted, 11/89.

1982—Virtually identical in quality to the 1983 Boyd-Cantenac, but
·   styled differently, the 1982 has a dark ruby color with a trace of
86   amber, a rich, fragrant, ripe black cherry bouquet, unctuous, fat,
       fleshy flavors, full body, and moderate tannins. Anticipated ma-
       turity: 1992–2005. Last tasted, 1/90.

1981—Boyd-Cantenac's 1981 is a lean, compact, attenuated wine that
·   has begun to dry out. The diluted flavors exhibit a vegetal char-
69   acter and uncharacteristic lightness and lack of body. Fading.
       Last tasted, 2/87.

1979—A flavorful, beefy, corpulent wine, with good concentration, a
·   precocious, soft, round personality, and attractively supple yet
84   rustic flavors, the 1979 Boyd-Cantenac is fully mature. Medium
       to full bodied, and displaying no signs of decline, this wine should
       continue to evolve and drink well. Anticipated maturity: Now–
       1996. Last tasted, 12/87.

1978—Not as powerful as the 1982, 1983, and 1975, but bigger and richer
·   than the 1979, this darkly colored wine has plenty of blackcurrant
85   fruit, an earthy, spicy bouquet, and rich, medium- to full-bodied
       flavors backed up nicely by firm, somewhat aggressive tannins.
       Anticipated maturity: Now–2000. Last tasted, 10/82.

1975—The most powerful wine made at Boyd-Cantenac over the last
·   several decades, this broodingly dark-colored wine (a slight or-
86   ange/rust hue is noticeable) remains hard and tight. The spicy,
       mineral-scented, cedary aroma, and big, ripe, mouth-puckering
       tannic flavors make this the largest-scaled Boyd-Cantenac I have
       tasted. However, after 15 years the wine was stubbornly severe
       and unyielding. Anticipated maturity: 1995–2010. Last tasted,
       6/90.

1971—Fully mature, with a damp cellar, earthy, plummy, spicy bouquet,
·   the 1971 Boyd-Cantenac has above-average, soft, round flavors,
82   medium body, some browning at the edge, and a pleasing finish.
       Anticipated maturity: Now–may be in decline. Last tasted, 6/82.

1970—A textbook Boyd-Cantenac, beefy, fat, richly textured, with
·   plenty of blackcurrant fruit, this medium- to full-bodied wine has
83   good extract and a savory richness. Fully mature. Anticipated
       maturity: Now–1994. Last tasted, 11/86.

1966—The 1966 Boyd-Cantenac has begun to fade. The color has taken
·   on a rusty/orange hue at the edge. The nose exhibits some dried-
62   out, decayed vegetation, cedar, and old wood. In the mouth, the
       wine is compact, lean, and finishes with coarse, harsh tannins

that obliterate any charm this medium-bodied wine once possessed. Now past its prime. Last tasted, 5/88.

1961—Only tasted once, but the 1961 Boyd-Cantenac was impressively
·   big, aggressive, ripe, and concentrated, with a rather coarse,
85   dusty texture, gobs of mouth-watering tannin still present, and a
       long, robust finish. This wine lacks finesse, but is robust and
       virile. Anticipated maturity: Now–1995. Last tasted, 11/80.

BRANE-CANTENAC (Second-Growth)   GOOD

Production: 30,000–35,000 cases	Grape varieties:
	Cabernet Sauvignon—70%
	Merlot—15%
	Cabernet Franc—13%
	Petit Verdot—2%
Secondary labels: Château Notton and Domaine de Fontarney	
Vineyard size: 210 acres	Proprietor: Lucien Lurton
Time spent in barrels: 18–20 months	Average age of vines: 25 years

Evaluation of present classification: Should be downgraded to a
  Médoc fifth-growth, although the quality since 1982 has improved
Plateau of maturity: 5–15 years following the vintage

Brane-Cantenac is owned by one of the most famous winemaking families in Bordeaux. Lucien Lurton and his wife live in a modest château whose viticultural history traces back to the early part of the eighteenth century. This property enjoyed an outstanding reputation in the early nineteenth century when the wines were made by the owner who named it, the Baron de Branne. Once the owner of the famous Pauillac estate now called Mouton-Rothschild, Baron de Branne was a highly respected viticulturist whose political connections were so formidable that Brane-Cantenac was rated a second-growth in the 1855 classification despite some skeptics who felt that the vineyards did not produce wines that merited such a high standing. Today, the huge Lurton family, which includes Lucien's brother André—who has considerable holdings in the Graves and Entre-Deux-Mers—and a family of ten children, qualifies as the largest winemaking family of the region.

One of the Médoc's largest properties, Brane-Cantenac's extensive vineyards (just over 200 acres) lie west of the village of Cantenac and well inland from the Gironde River. Because of the property's large production and a very friendly and charming owner, Lucien Lurton, the wines of Brane-Cantenac have enjoyed a large measure of commercial success throughout the world. This has occurred notwithstanding a record of mediocrity that was particularly acute throughout the period 1967–1981. Curiously, most wine writers turned their heads in the other direction rather than point out what were obvious flaws in the makeup of Brane-Cantenac's wines during this era. The most prominent problems with Brane-Cantenac during this slump were the wines' excessive lightness and frequent distressing barnyard aromas. One can only speculate, but such flaws must have been caused by a lack of selection and sloppy, as well as unsanitary, management of the cellars.

However, Brane-Cantenac's inconsistent track record has improved in the eighties. The famous oenologist, Emile Peynaud, was brought in to supervise the vinification and in 1982 and 1983 Brane-Cantenac produced its best wines since 1961.

Even with this renewed level of quality, the wines of Brane-Cantenac are made in a forward, fruity, soft style that makes the wine easily appreciated when young. Recent vintages have been fully mature within 5–6 years after bottling.

VINTAGES

1989—I found the 1989 Brane-Cantenac to be similar to their 1982, only
  ·   higher in alcohol and lower in acidity, with a loosely structured
  86   yet powerful, concentrated, fruity taste. Lots of new oak has given
        the wine much-needed form and focus. Although lacking in finesse, this wine offers a big, succulent mouthful of juicy fruit
        along with a blast of alcohol in the finish. Anticipated maturity:
        1992–2001. Last tasted, 4/91.

1988—The 1988 is weedy, even green, suggesting that the Cabernet
  ·   Sauvignon was harvested too early. Light bodied and lacking con-
  77   centration and class, it is an undistinguished effort. Anticipated
        maturity: Now–1995. Last tasted, 11/90.

1986—The 1986 has wonderful opulence and fatness that is surprising to
  ·   see, particularly in view of the tannic style of many of the 1986
  88   Médocs. However, there is no doubting its ability to age well, as
        it has plenty of tannin. This full-bodied, impressive Brane-Cantenac displays loads of ripeness, and is deep and long on the
        palate, with excellent balance. Along with the 1983, this is one of
        the two best wines produced at the property since the 1961. Anticipated maturity: 1993–2008. Last tasted, 10/90.

1985—The 1985 Brane-Cantenac, made in a succulent, forward, sweet,
· 　　seductive style is oozing with scents of oak and velvety, superripe
87 　　fruit. One might argue that more grip and tannin could be ex-
　　　pected, but the style of the 1985 vintage is well delineated in this
　　　attractive precocious, tasty wine. Anticipated maturity: Now–
　　　1997. Last tasted, 10/90.

1984—Light to medium ruby, very spicy and herbaceous, but fruity, soft,
· 　　and ideal for near-term drinking. Anticipated maturity: Now–
73 　　1993. Last tasted, 11/89.

1983—Forward, seductive, and flavorful, the 1983 Brane-Cantenac has
· 　　a fragrant, plummy, coffee-and-chocolate-scented bouquet, a
89 　　sweet, savory, round texture, light to moderate tannins, and a
　　　long, heady finish. Delicious and generously flavored, this wine
　　　has developed quickly, but should continue to evolve for another
　　　decade. Anticipated maturity: Now–1999. Last tasted, 2/91.

1982—The 1982 is a marvelously rich, deep, fat, intensely perfumed
· 　　wine, with very lovely fruity flavors, plenty of round, ripe tannins,
87 　　and a precocious personality. Medium bodied and opulently
　　　fruity, this wine has drunk well since bottling. Anticipated matu-
　　　rity: Now–1998. Last tasted, 12/89.

1981—This is a charming, soft, fruity, straightforward wine, with me-
· 　　dium body and a clean, undistinguished finish. Anticipated ma-
82 　　turity: Now–1993. Last tasted, 6/87.

1980—Light with an innocuous, faintly fruity aroma, this light-bodied
· 　　wine has shallow, yet clean, fruity flavors, and a short finish.
74 　　Drink up. Anticipated maturity: Now–probably in serious de-
　　　cline. Last tasted, 10/84.

1979—The 1979 is medium ruby, with a herbaceous, slightly dull, now
· 　　washed-out bouquet. Medium bodied and soft, the wine is begin-
75 　　ning to dry out. Anticipated maturity: Now–1994. Last tasted,
　　　6/87.

1978—Made in a period when the wines of Brane-Cantenac were fre-
· 　　quently disappointing, the 1978 is a modest success. Medium
82 　　ruby with a moderately intense, berryish, earthy bouquet, very
　　　soft, round, plump flavors with little acidity or tannin present, this
　　　is one 1978 that is fully mature. Anticipated maturity: Now–1994.
　　　Last tasted, 11/87.

1977—Light, faintly fruity, with shallow, somewhat herbaceous flavors,
· 　　this medium-bodied wine is medium ruby, with some tannin in
67 　　the finish. Drink up. Anticipated maturity: Now–probably in se-
　　　rious decline. Last tasted, 4/81.

1976—Now fading and beginning to exhibit considerable brown at the
·   edges, this loosely knit wine lacks firmness, concentration, and
65   structure. The round, pleasant, soft, somewhat flabby, fruity fla-
       vors have become more unknit with the passage of time, and the
       barnyard dirtiness has become more pronounced. Drink it up.
       Anticipated maturity: Now–probably in serious decline. Last
       tasted, 11/87.

1975—Fully mature, the 1975 Brane-Cantenac has a generous, earthy,
·   spicy, leathery, mushroom-like bouquet, sweet, relatively soft,
83   fruity flavors, medium body, and adequate length. Anticipated
       maturity: Now–1994. Last tasted, 11/87.

1971—Very dirty, barnyard smells predominate. On the palate, the wine
·   is diffuse, frail, very tannic and lean, weakly constituted, and just
62   barely palatable. Avoid. Last tasted, 3/84.

1970—After my first edition of *Bordeaux* I received several letters from
·   readers claiming that my ungenerous review of the 1970 Brane-
85?   Cantenac (I rated it a 65 and called it distressingly poor) was
       inconsistent with their tastings. I was a participant in a Bordeaux
       tasting where the wine was served as part of a horizontal tasting
       of the 1970 vintage. Two of the three bottles were deep ruby
       in color, with a spicy, herbaceous, earthy scent (rather than the
       dirty barnyard smell I described), and medium bodied, with
       a soft, relatively concentrated finish. Another bottle was not
       nearly as good as the other two, but not nearly as bad as the
       1970 Brane-Cantenac I described in the 1985 edition of this
       book. For whatever reason, there does appear to be a great
       deal of bottle variation with this vintage; certainly the good ex-
       amples are wines that merit a score in the mid-eighties, the bad
       bottles are deplorable. Anticipated maturity: Now–1995. Last
       tasted, 3/89.

1967—When it was at its peak in 1975–1976, the 1967 Brane-Cantenac
·   was an adequate wine. However, its charm then was a soft, easy-
70   going fruitiness. It has now faded and the wine tastes hollow and
       austere. Last tasted, 10/80.

1966—Between 1961 and 1982, the 1966 vintage of Brane-Cantenac has
·   always been my favorite. The wine was fully mature by the late
69   seventies, but has begun to tire badly. The once-stylish bouquet
       of cedar and plummy fruit is now a vague, vegetal, musty, old oak
       aroma. There is still some sweet fruit on the palate, but the tannin
       and acidity clearly have the upper hand. This wine should have
       been drunk up years ago. Last tasted, 11/88.

1964—Although not tasted recently, my notes from 1978 indicate that
·   the wine was attractively fat and sweet, surprisingly ripe and
80   fruity, with the tannin no longer evident. Anticipated maturity:
         Now–probably in serious decline. Last tasted, 12/78.
1961—According to some of my friends in Bordeaux, this wine was ex-
·   cellent in the late sixties. When I tasted it in 1979 it was still a
74   good wine, although clearly beginning to dry out. The last bottle
         I tasted displayed relatively high, hard tannins, a medium garnet
         color, and much more herbaceousness in the bouquet than I re-
         member. In the finish, the alcohol and tannins now overwhelm
         the fruit. Anticipated maturity: Now–1994. Last tasted, 11/89.

CANTEMERLE (Fifth-Growth)   VERY GOOD

Production: 20,000 cases	Grape varieties:
	Cabernet Sauvignon—40%
	Merlot—40%
	Cabernet Franc—18%
	Petit Verdot—2%
Secondary label: Villeneuve de Cantemerle	
Vineyard size: 131 acres	Proprietor: Société Assurances Mutuelles du Batiment et Travaux Publics
	Administrator: Jean Cordier
Time spent in barrels: 18 months	Average age of vines: 25 years
Evaluation of present classification: Should be upgraded to a third-growth	
Plateau of maturity: 5–18 years following the vintage	

The lovely château of Cantemerle, sitting amidst a heavily wooded park
just adjacent to the famous D2 (the major route leading from Bordeaux
to the Médoc) has a winemaking history that goes back to the late sixteenth century. For most of the current century the property was owned
by the Dubos family, who did a lot to establish this property's reputation
for gloriously fragrant, elegantly rendered wines. However, financial
problems, along with family quarrels, led to the sale of Cantemerle in
1980 to a syndicate, of which the famous Cordier firm is a part. In the
seventies the property was allowed to deteriorate and the wine suffered
in vintages after 1975. Since the syndicate's acquisition, Cantemerle has
been completely renovated with new cellars, a new winemaking facility,
a state-of-the-art tasting room, and, most importantly, a greater commitment to quality.

Prior to 1980 there was also considerable bottle variation, and in a number of vintages the wines suffered from old barrel smells and a lack of fruit. With Georges Pauli, the oenologist for all the Cordier properties, now overlooking the winemaking, Cantemerle has gone from one strength to another. The 1983 and 1989 are the two best wines made to date under the new management. Quality should only increase, as the vineyard, which has been significantly replanted, comes of age. The style of Cantemerle is a rich, supple fruitiness, and intensely fragrant bouquet. Given the lighter soils of their vineyards and high percentage of Merlot, this will never be a blockbuster wine. Cantemerle at its best always possesses a degree of fragrance and precociousness that give undeniable early appeal. Because of the improvements made during the eighties, this property now deserves a higher ranking than in the 1855 classification.

VINTAGES

1989—I am going to climb out on a limb and predict that the 1989
  ·   Cantemerle is this estate's finest wine since the monumental
92   1953. The Merlot was picked late, September 14, then the harvest
       was stopped to wait for the Cabernet to ripen physiologically. The
       last Cabernet was brought in on October 9. This ruby/purple wine
       has an explosive bouquet of crushed blackberry fruit and violets,
       an opulent, lush texture bolstered by hefty alcohol levels and soft
       tannin. At several tastings of the southern Médocs (principally
       Margaux wines), this was the star of the show. Anticipated maturity: 1994–2010. Last tasted, 4/91.

1988—The 1988 is a success, particularly in view of how severe and
  ·   tough so many Médocs have turned out. It possesses adequate
87   hard, dry tannin, but unlike many Médocs, there is sufficient fruit
       to balance the wine's astringence. This stylish wine is medium
       bodied, elegant, and classy, with a plummy, mineral-and-herb-
       scented bouquet. Anticipated maturity: 1993–2005. Last tasted,
       4/91.

1986—For whatever reason, the 1986 is an uncommonly tannic, rather
  ·   stern and hard-edged Cantemerle that seems at odds with the
82   amount of fruit in this light, delicately styled wine. Perhaps this
       wine will age better than I suspect, but the tannins appear over-
       whelming. Anticipated maturity: 1992–1998. Last tasted, 4/90.

1985—The 1985 is Cantemerle at its most polite, stylish, and under-
  ·   stated. Supple, medium ruby in color, with an open-knit bouquet
85   of raspberries and oak, it tastes more akin to a Volnay than a
       Médoc. Anticipated maturity: Now–1997. Last tasted, 11/90.

1984—The 1984 is a success for the vintage. It is a fruity, medium-
  ·   bodied, gracefully assembled wine that should now be consumed.
 79   Anticipated maturity: Now–1994. Last tasted, 3/89.

1983—The first vintage of Cantemerle to be made in the new cellars, the
  ·   1983 is special, and one of the great wines of this vintage. The
 91   color remains dark ruby/purple and the bouquet explodes from
       the glass with scents of ripe plums, flowers, and oak. On the
       palate, this generous wine is supple, concentrated, extremely
       long in the finish, with soft tannins. This is Cantemerle's lushest
       and ripest style of wine. Anticipated maturity: Now–2005. Last
       tasted, 2/91.

1982—The 1982 is a very good Cantemerle, precociously supple, fat, and
  ·   fruity. Fully mature, it is loaded with lush berry fruit and has a
 85   soft, round texture and generous, elegantly wrought flavors. An-
       ticipated maturity: Now–2000. Last tasted, 1/89.

1981—The 1981 has a ruby color, a pronounced vanillin, oaky compo-
  ·   nent, a ripe cassis, fruity taste, moderate tannin, and a decent
 82   finish. This is a good, yet relatively lean, compact wine. Antici-
       pated maturity: Now–1995. Last tasted, 1/89.

1979—Surprisingly ready to drink, Cantemerle's 1979 is charmingly
  ·   fruity, soft, pleasant, and round, but seems to lack grip and
 82   length. Anticipated maturity: Now–may be in decline. Last
       tasted, 2/83.

1978—Medium dark ruby with some amber at the edge, the 1978 has
  ·   begun to develop a musty, old-barrel aroma that detracts from the
 81   otherwise cedary, spicy, black fruit character. In the mouth,
       there is a sense of fatness. The astringent tannins in the finish
       suggest that perhaps there is not enough fruit for the amount of
       tannin. Anticipated maturity: Now–1994. Last tasted, 8/88.

1976—Unfortunately, the 1976 Cantemerle is in decline, exhibiting a
  ·   brownish color, pale, weak, washed-out flavors that taste cooked
 60   and highly chaptalized. Coming apart at the seams, this is a wine
       to drink up quickly. Last tasted, 4/84.

1975—The 1975 is still remarkably hard, tannic, and tough. Rustic, full
  ·   bodied, and muscular on the palate, the wine exhibits plenty of
 84   concentration, but the astringent, even severe tannins of the 1975
       vintage continue to give rise to doubts about how well this wine is
       evolving. Anticipated maturity: 1993–2005. Last tasted, 1/88.

1971—The 1971 has been fully mature for over a decade. Medium ruby
  ·   with some amber/orange color at the edges, this wine has a light-
 83   intensity, fragrant bouquet suggestive of berry fruit and oak. On
       the palate, the flavors reveal adequate fruit and concentration,

but the acidity is a bit sharp in the finish. Drink up. Anticipated maturity: Now–probably in serious decline. Last tasted, 10/83.

1970—This wine continues to evolve beautifully and has turned out to be
 · one of the sleepers of the vintage. The fragrant bouquet of plums,
87 fruitcake, cedar, and spicy oak is followed by a medium-bodied, concentrated wine with gobs of fruit, excellent length, and overall balance. The wine appears to have just entered the plateau of maturity. This is undoubtedly the best Cantemerle made during the seventies. Anticipated maturity: Now–1997. Last tasted, 2/89.

1967—In the mid-1970s, this was a pleasingly fruity, yet firm wine that
 · had good concentration, a savory, round, plummy character, and
79 an adequate finish. Now in decline, the acidity and tannins have overwhelmed what fruit is left. Last tasted, 1/86.

1966—Like many 1966s, the Cantemerle has been slow to evolve. It is
 · now beginning to lose its fruit rather than to open up and blossom.
84 This medium-weight wine has a stylish, elegant bouquet filled with the scents of truffles and blackcurrant fruit. On the palate, the wine is impressively structured, but a trifle lean, unyielding, and ungenerous. Drink it up. Anticipated maturity: Now–may be in decline. Last tasted, 2/82.

1962—Still gorgeously perfumed after so many years, the 1962 Cante-
 · merle has a lovely, seductive, full-blown bouquet, round, gener-
86 ous, pleasingly fruity, savory flavors, and no tannins present. An elegant, ripe, delicious wine for drinking now. Anticipated maturity: Now–1994. Last tasted, 4/81.

1961—Still superb, in fact even better than when I last tasted it in 1984,
 · the 1961 is impressively opaque dark ruby with only some amber/
92 orange at the edge. The huge bouquet of smoky, earthy, black-currant fruit, spring flowers, leather, and plums is followed by a lush, full-bodied, concentrated wine with that taste of *sur-maturité* (overripeness) that frequently characterizes the great vintages in Bordeaux. Still loaded and in fabulous condition, this unctuous, opulently styled wine should continue to drink well. Anticipated maturity: Now–2000. Last tasted, 1/88.

OLDER VINTAGES

The 1959 (rated 89) is not far off the pace of the glorious 1961. Somewhat lighter, but decadently fruity, expansive, and even sweet in the mouth, this wine was drinking beautifully and displaying no signs of deterioration when tasted in Bordeaux in 1987. The finest Cantemerle I have ever tasted, however, is the 1953 (rated 94). I have had it twice in the last 5 years and it exhibited all the seductive charm one expects from a vintage that apparently drank well when released in the mid-1950s, and where well stored, has continued to delight Bordeaux enthusiasts. Not as deep in color as the 1959 or 1961, yet wonderfully sweet and generous in the mouth, this hauntingly perfumed, classic example of Cantemerle must be the best wine made at the property in the last 40 years; although I have high hopes that the 1983 and 1989 may ultimately turn out to be nearly as good.

CANTENAC-BROWN (Third-Growth)　　　　　　GOOD

Production: 15,000 cases	Grape varieties: Cabernet Sauvignon—75% Merlot—17% Cabernet Franc—8%
Secondary labels: Canuet and Lamartine	
Vineyard size: 79 acres	Proprietor: La Compagnie du Midi Administrators: Jean-Michel Cazes and Daniel Llose
Time spent in barrels: 16–20 months	Average age of vines: 25 years
Evaluation of present classification: Should be downgraded to a fifth-growth	
Plateau of maturity: Prior to 1980, 10–20 years following the vintage; since 1980, 5–15 years following the vintage	

Cantenac-Brown has had a checkered recent history. Sold in 1968 by the famous Bordelais, Jean Lawton, to the Du Vivier family, the property was sold again in 1980 to the huge Cognac house, Remy-Martin. More recently, the property was sold once again to a huge insurance conglomerate that had the intelligence to put Jean-Michel Cazes and his brilliant team of winemakers, led by Daniel Llose, in charge.

The vineyard is not among the best situated in the commune of Cantenac, and has traditionally produced relatively hard, tannic wines that were often too burly and muscular. Under the new management, the direction has been toward wines that are softer and less robust. This is a positive development, particularly in view of the fact that so many vintages of Cantenac-Brown had such an excess of tannin, as well as a dry, charmless character. The sad truth is that many of this estate's wines lost their fruit long before their tannins. More skeptical observers claim the vineyard, which sits on deep, gravelly soil, will never produce wines of great elegance. That remains to be seen.

Visitors to the region are well advised, if for photogenic reasons only, to follow the well-marked road (right before the village of Issan) that passes in front of this exceptional Victorian château with its striking red brick and Tudor decor. It is one of the more impressive edifices in the Médoc, yet stands out as distinctly un-French in appearance, resembling an oversized English manor house more than a French château.

VINTAGES

1989—The 1989 does not appear to have the sheer class and focus of the
  ·   other wines that are being made by Jean Michel Cazes. For those
  86   who like an affable style of wine that is easy to drink, the 1989
        offers generous amounts of soft, easygoing blackcurrant fruit,
        medium body, some hollowness, and a soft finish. It is deceptively
        easy to drink, but essentially unexciting. Anticipated maturity:
        Now–2001. Last tasted, 4/91.

1988—Prior to bottling, the 1988 tasted rich, complex, and concentrated.
  ·   After bottling, the wine has not performed as well. More atten-
  85   uated, with an elevated level of tannin, this spicy, medium-bodied
        wine is well made, but it is not as impressive as I originally
        believed. Anticipated maturity: 1993–2000. Last tasted, 4/91.

1986—The 1986 displays both power and elegance in a medium- to full-
  ·   bodied format. The color is deep ruby, and on the palate, the wine
  85   exhibits classic blackcurrant fruit, with a toasty, spicy oak com-
        ponent. This foursquare, somewhat monolithic wine does not lack
        tannin. Anticipated maturity: 1995–2010. Last tasted, 9/89.

1983—A typical effort from Cantenac-Brown, this dark-colored, ripe,
  ·   robust, rich, full-bodied, coarsely structured wine has good con-
  85   centration and plenty of power, but, as is so often the case with
        this wine, it lacks charm and finesse. Anticipated maturity: 1993–
        2005. Last tasted, 1/89.

1981—Still firm and hard, the 1981 Cantenac-Brown has impressive
  ·   color, a chocolatey, smoky, herbaceous bouquet, dusty, coarse,
  81   tannic flavors, and medium body. The tannin appears to have the
        upper hand. Anticipated maturity: 1992–2000. Last tasted, 9/88.

1978—A light, insipid perfume of diluted red fruits fades quickly. Lack-
  ·   ing concentration and surprisingly light, this indifferent wine
  74   finishes with noticeable acidity and tannin. Disappointing. Antic-
        ipated maturity: Now–1994. Last tasted, 10/88.

1976—Watery berryish aromas intermingle with aromas of herbs and
·   musty oak. Shallow, pale, light bodied, and in the process of
59   collapse, this is a wine to avoid. Last tasted, 1/88.

1975—The 1975 Cantenac-Brown has a complex, oaky, smoky bouquet,
·   with attractive, relatively full, but harshly tannic flavors. Medium
84   bodied, the 1975 is fully mature. It is a good, but unexciting effort
         for the vintage. Anticipated maturity: Now–1995. Last tasted,
         9/87.

1971—A thin, angular, muscular wine that lacks richness and flesh, the
·   1971 Cantenac-Brown tastes hollow and austere, and is best
64   drunk up before the meager fruit dissipates even more. Anticipated
         maturity: Now–probably in serious decline. Last tasted, 12/78.

1970—Dense ruby in color, with a big, blackcurrant, cinnamon, herb,
·   leather, and mineral-scented bouquet, this massive wine has huge
86   tannins which refuse to melt away. At nearly 20 years of age, the
         1970 remains a muscular wine that is impressive only for power
         and toughness. Anticipated maturity: 1995–2010. Last tasted,
         3/88.

1966—A compact, muscular, firm wine, with a dusty, rather coarse tex-
·   ture, some spice and leathery aromas, medium to full body, but
83   deficient in richness and just too acidic and austere. Anticipated
         maturity: Now–may be in decline. Last tasted, 4/80.

CHARMANT (Cru Bourgeois)   GOOD

Production: 1,500 cases	Grape varieties:
	Cabernet Sauvignon—50%
	Merlot—45%
	Petit Verdot—5%
Secondary label: none	
Vineyard size: 12.5 acres	Proprietor: René Renon
Time spent in barrels: 12–20 months	Average age of vines: 70–100 years
Evaluation of present classification: I have never tasted the wine	
Plateau of maturity: Unknown	

I have not had an opportunity to taste this wine, but it is highly prized by
none other than Bernard Ginestet, who knows as much about the appellation of Margaux as any human being. The proprietor, René Renon,
believes in extremely old vines (half of his vineyard is over 100 years of
age, a fact that makes his vineyard the oldest in Margaux in terms of

vine age). Ginestet has told me this is the best Cru Bourgeois in the Médoc—high praise indeed.

DAUZAC (Fifth-Growth)   AVERAGE

Production: 20,000 cases	Grape varieties:
	Cabernet Sauvignon—65%
	Merlot—30%
	Petit Verdot—5%
Secondary label: Laborde	
Vineyard size: 123.5 acres	Proprietor: S.A.F. Chatellier
Time spent in barrels: 16–18 months	Average age of vines: 18 years
Evaluation of present classification: Should be downgraded to a Cru Bourgeois	
Plateau of maturity: 5–12 years following the vintage	

Despite new owners in 1978 who have invested considerable sums of money in the vineyards and winery, the wines of Dauzac remain among the least distinguished of all the Médoc classified growths. Surely, the estate would be demoted should any new classification ever take place.

The impressive new winery is one of the first major classified growths the visitor to the Médoc encounters after passing through Macau on the famous D2 heading north. The improvements made since 1978 by the new owners, the Chatellier family, include the installation of stainless-steel fermentation tanks in 1981, an extensive program of new vineyard plantings, and the increased usage of new oak barrels, now representing 33% of the total cooperage used to age the wine.

VINTAGES

1989—The unstructured, diffuse, shockingly light 1989 has some pleas-
·   ant jammy, berry fruit in evidence, but little else. Dauzac is very
79   soft and low in acidity. Anticipated maturity: Now–1998. Last
       tasted, 4/91.

1988—The 1988 is superior to the 1989, with a deeper color, medium
·   body, and an attractive yet low-key red currant fruitiness en-
83   hanced slightly by the smell and taste of new oak. The wine has
       some hard tannins in the finish that need to melt away. Antici-
       pated maturity: 1993–2000. Last tasted, 4/91.

1986—This wine tastes closed and hard. It is difficult to find sufficient
·   fruit necessary for balance. The finish is short and attenuated.
76   Anticipated maturity: 1992–1998. Last tasted, 3/90.

1985—The 1985 Dauzac is a compact, ruby-colored wine that is tightly
   ·   knit and concentrated. I found little charm, complexity, or sub-
   77   stance. This is not Cru Classé quality. Anticipated maturity:
         Now–1995. Last tasted, 3/89.

1984—This is a chunky, deep ruby–colored wine with obvious oak in the
   ·   bouquet and some mean tannins in the finish. Narrowly focused
   71   flavors inadequately cover the wine's hardness and astringency.
         Several years ago I thought cellaring might be beneficial, but the
         wine appears to be drying out. Last tasted, 3/88.

1983—Given this vintage and the high number of successful wines made,
   ·   particularly in Margaux, Dauzac's 1983 is good, but uninspiring.
   80   Medium ruby, with a spicy, vanillin-scented aroma, rather ripe,
         uncomplex, cherryish flavors, and medium body, the wine is light
         for a 1983 and is maturing rapidly. Anticipated maturity: Now–
         1994. Last tasted, 6/84.

1982—An enjoyable, charming, plump, fruity wine with a good ruby
   ·   color, a spicy, savory fatness on the palate, and soft, ripe tannins
   82   in the finish. It is a good rather than noteworthy effort. Antici-
         pated maturity: Now–1995. Last tasted, 3/87.

1981—The 1981 is an understated and shallow style of wine. Light to
   ·   medium bodied, it exhibits a spicy, oaky component, and moder-
   77   ately intense, cherry-like flavors. Anticipated maturity: Now–
         probably in serious decline. Last tasted, 2/86.

1979—The 1979 is a solid, one-dimensional wine, with a sense of dull-
   ·   ness and blandness pervading its bouquet and flavors. The wine
   75   is dark ruby in color, but austere and simple. Anticipated matu-
         rity: Now–1993. Last tasted, 5/86.

1978—A light, delicate, yet fragrant wine that suffers from lack of con-
   ·   centration and depth, the 1978 Dauzac does offer a pleasantly
   76   fragrant bouquet of fruit and oak, and straightforward, soft fla-
         vors. Anticipated maturity: Now–probably in serious decline.
         Last tasted, 10/83.

1971—The 1971 is a washed-out, diluted, very simple wine that has little
   ·   interest and character left. Light ruby, with dull, acidic, fruity
   55   flavors that seem very meager, the 1971 Dauzac is well past
         prime. Last tasted, 3/80.

1970—Moderate dark garnet, with some brown at the edge, the herba-
   ·   ceous, tea-like, spicy bouquet suggests full maturity. More-
   73   over, it is medium bodied, soft, slightly diluted, and thin in the
         finish. Anticipated maturity: Now–may be in decline. Last tasted,
         6/88.

1966—A lean, austere, tight, compact wine, the 1966 Dauzac has some
·   interesting woodsy, mushroom-like aromas in the bouquet, but it
74   is lacking in concentration, complexity, and character. Anticipated maturity: Now–1994. Last tasted, 6/88.

DESMIRAIL (Third-Growth)   AVERAGE

Production: 4,500 cases	Grape varieties:
	Cabernet Sauvignon—80%
	Merlot—10%
	Cabernet Franc—5%
	Petit Verdot—5%
Secondary label: Château Baudry	
Vineyard size: 44.5 acres	Proprietor: Lucien Lurton
Time spent in barrels: 20 months	Average age of vines: 20 years
Evaluation of present classification: Should be downgraded to a Cru Bourgeois	
Plateau of maturity: 3–12 years following the vintage	

This property, which currently has no attached château, was ranked a
third-growth in the 1855 classification. However, following World War I
most of the property was sold in a piecemeal fashion until little remained.
The original château of Desmirail is now owned by the Zuger family, who
have renamed it Marquis d'Alesme. The proprietor of Brane-Cantenac,
Lucien Lurton, has, over the last several decades, purchased parcels of
vines that originally composed the vineyard of Desmirail. The name was
resurrected in 1980 when the last parcel, a 5-acre plot of the original
vineyard, was acquired from Château Palmer. A *chai* and building that
Lucien Lurton purchased in the village of Cantenac has now become
known as Château Desmirail.

    Based on vintages in the eighties, the wine hardly merits its third-
growth ranking. Qualitatively, it is the equivalent of a good Cru Bourgeois. The vintages 1986, 1985, 1983, and 1982, all tasted relatively round
and forward, with some earthy blackcurrant fruit, soft tannins, and a
style that emphasized suppleness and early drinkability. The best vintage
to date has been the 1983, followed by the 1986. Based on these vintages,
this is a wine to drink in the first decade of life.

DEYREM-VALENTIN (Cru Bourgeois) AVERAGE

Production: 4,500 cases	Grape varieties: Cabernet Sauvignon—45% Merlot—45% Cabernet Franc—5% Petit Verdot—5%
Secondary label: none	
Vineyard size: 25 acres	Proprietor: Jean Sorge
Time spent in barrels: 14–18 months	Average age of vines: 20 years
Evaluation of present classification: Should be maintained	
Plateau of maturity: 4–10 years following the vintage	

I have only seen a handful of the wines of Deyrem-Valentin. The vintages I have tasted, 1978, 1981, 1982, and 1983, had good color, but seemed to be relatively straightforward, compact wines, which were correctly and competently made, but lacked excitement. If they were to be criticized, it would be because the wines were aggressively tannic and severe in style. They must be drunk within their first 5–7 years of life.

DURFORT-VIVENS (Second-Growth) GOOD

Production: 8,000 cases	Grape varieties: Cabernet Sauvignon—82% Cabernet Franc—10% Merlot—8%
Secondary label: Domaine de Curé-Bourse	
Vineyard size: 49.4 acres	Proprietor: Lucien Lurton
Time spent in barrels: 20 months	Average age of vines: 23 years
Evaluation of present classification: Should be downgraded to a Médoc fifth-growth	
Plateau of maturity: 6–18 years following the vintage	

This famous second-growth is owned by Lucien Lurton, also the renowned proprietor of another famed second-growth in Margaux Château Brane-Cantenac. The vineyards of Durfort-Vivens should produce better wine. Perhaps it is unfair to blame Lurton for the miserable track record of Durfort-Vivens between 1961 and 1981. However, the vineyards are now a respectable age and are certainly well placed within the appellation. One wonders if the high percentage of Cabernet Sauvignon (the highest of any southern Médoc) gives the wine less charm and more toughness than is ideal.

Vintages since 1982 have exhibited improvement, but this still looks to be a château where the winemaker and owner could use a wake-up call.

VINTAGES

1989—Early tastings of the 1989 Durfort-Vivens revealed an objection-
·   able lees character in the aroma, suggesting that the wine needed
86   racking. After bottling, the wine has proven to be admirably concentrated, low in acidity, tannic, meaty, and potentially very good. A valid comparison with the fleshy 1982 is not without merit. Anticipated maturity: 1994–2005. Last tasted, 4/91.

1988—The 1988 is astringent and hollow, with a vegetal character sug-
·   gesting that the Cabernet Sauvignon was picked before attaining
74   maturity. It is short, compact, and attenuated. Anticipated maturity: 1993–2000. Last tasted, 4/91.

1986—The 1986 has considerable tannin, as well as an impressive deep
·   ruby color. Yet it does not possess the ripeness, sweetness, or
84   depth of fruit necessary to back up the tannins. It is a good wine, but lower yields could have resulted in something special. Anticipated maturity: 1994–2000. Last tasted, 4/90.

1985—The 1985 Durfort-Vivens has a deep ruby color, and a fragrant,
·   spicy, rich, and intense bouquet of fruit, olives, and oak. On the
87   palate, the wine has a creamy richness, medium to full body, light tannins, but fine length. This is one of the best examples of Durfort I have ever tasted. Anticipated maturity: Now–1998. Last tasted, 4/89.

1984—A commendable 1984 with a spicy, fruity, medium-bodied, soft
·   character, the 1984 Durfort-Vivens will offer easy, uncritical
79   drinking. Anticipated maturity: Now–1993. Last tasted, 3/89.

1983—A well-balanced, admirably constructed, muscular wine, the 1983
·   Durfort is leaner and more austere than many of its Margaux
86   counterparts. It has concentrated, ripe, rich fruitiness, plenty of aggressive tannins, and good length. Anticipated maturity: 1993–2005. Last tasted, 2/91.

1982—The 1982 must be among the most seductive wines this estate has
·   recently made. It boasts a big, lovely, ripe, rich, blackcurrant
87   bouquet, deep, supple, concentrated flavors, a long finish, and

adequate tannin for another 5–8 years of cellaring. The 1982 marked a dramatic turnabout in the quality of this estate's wines. Anticipated maturity: Now–2000. Last tasted, 1/90.

1981—This is a typical pre-1982 Durfort-Vivens. Sinewy, lean, and an-
·   gular, this wine needs additional fruit and flesh to balance out the
74   excessive tannins and acidity. It has remained charmless and now appears to be drying out. Anticipated maturity: Now–1993. Last tasted, 2/87.

1980—The 1980 is thin, herbaceous, watery, and quite unattractive.
·   Time will only make matters worse for this meagerly endowed
64   wine. Last tasted, 6/86.

1978—A solid effort from Durfort, the 1978 has a light-intensity bouquet
·   of herbaceous, raspberry/cherry fruit and spicy oak. I find the
76   wine's flavors austere and still excessively tannic. It is becoming more and more out of balance. Caveat emptor! Last tasted, 6/87.

1976—This is a straightforward, fruity wine, with a chunky texture, and
·   a spicy, woody, rather closed bouquet. Medium bodied, supple,
75   and attractively long and fruity in the finish, it is a rather good effort from Durfort-Vivens. Anticipated maturity: Now–may be in decline. Last tasted, 6/84.

1975—Extremely disappointing in the vintage, the 1975 Durfort-Vivens
·   is quite light in color, disturbingly brown at the edges, and has a
52   very pronounced stinky, barnyard aroma. Furthermore, it tastes surprisingly diluted, feeble, and thin on the palate. A miserable effort. Last tasted, 6/84.

1974—The 1974 Durfort-Vivens is a poor wine even taking into consid-
·   eration the mediocrity of the vintage. Harshly tannic, virtually
50   devoid of fruit, this hollow wine has no fruit, no charm, and no future. Last tasted, 3/84.

1973—As bad as the 1974, but totally different in style. Watery, hollow,
·   thin, and barely resembling a wine, this unbelievably shallow,
50   brown-colored wine has lost any fruit it may have once possessed. Last tasted, 10/79.

1971—The 1971 is an attractive wine that is still holding a plummy,
·   spicy, moderately endowed, rich fruitiness. This medium-bodied
75   wine is fully mature, but showing no signs of falling apart. Antic- ipated maturity: Now–probably in serious decline. Last tasted, 3/84.

1970—A tough, angular, rustic sort of wine, the 1970 is medium to full
·   bodied, quite tannic, and has good color, but seems to lack sup-
74   pleness and the rich, glossy fruitiness so prevalent in this vintage.

Anticipated maturity: Now–may be in decline. Last tasted, 11/79.

1966—Austere, tight, hard, and unyielding with good grip and harsh
·   tannins still very much in evidence, this severe style of wine lacks
70   both finesse and charm. Anticipated maturity: Now–may be in
        decline. Last tasted, 10/78.

1962—High acidity, thin, tart, short flavors, and a harsh finish make this
·   a very unattractive wine that is likely to get only more out of
62   balance as the fruit continues to fade. Last tasted, 10/78.

FERRIÈRE (Third-Growth)   AVERAGE

Production: 3,000 cases	Grape varieties: Cabernet Sauvignon—47% Merlot—33% Petit Verdot—12% Cabernet Franc—8%
Secondary label: none	
Vineyard size: 12 acres	Administrator: A syndicate owned by the English group Bass Charrington
Time spent in barrels: 15–21 months	Average age of vines: 15 years
Evaluation of present classification: The quality equivalent of a Cru Bourgeois	
Plateau of maturity: 5–10 years following the vintage	

The wine from this tiny property, which is made by the staff at Château Lascombes (the actual property is still owned by Madame André Durand-Feuillerat), is among one of the most obscure wines made in the Médoc and is primarily sold in France. It does not deserve its reputation as a third-growth and is rarely as good as many of the top Crus Bourgeois. Nevertheless, if judged by vintages such as 1982, 1983, 1985, and 1986, this wine is a soft, round, fruity wine of little distinction. Some observers have suggested that it has, in fact, become the second wine of Lascombes, but officially that is not the case. Lascombes' second wine is called Château Segonnes.

GISCOURS (Third-Growth) VERY GOOD

Production: 30,000 cases	Grape varieties: Cabernet Sauvignon—70% Merlot—25% Cabernet Franc—3% Petit Verdot—2%
Secondary label: Cantelaude	
Vineyard size: 173 acres	Proprietor: The Tari family
Time spent in barrels: 18–24 months	Average age of vines: 30 years
Evaluation of present classification: Should be maintained	
Plateau of maturity: 6–20 years following the vintage	

Giscours is a vast estate of over 600 acres (less than a third are under vine) in the most southern portion of the Margaux commune known as Labarde. The estate, once in deplorable condition, was rescued in 1952 by the Tari family, and has experienced a resurgence in quality and prestige. Pierre Tari began to assume more control in 1970 and has become one of the leading spokespersons for Bordeaux. Until the late eighties, he was president of Bordeaux's Union des Grands Crus, an association of châteaux banded together for one common cause: to promote the virtues of Bordeaux wines. Pierre Tari's passion for promotion may have gone too far as the quality of Giscours, which soared in the seventies, slumped following the 1981 vintage. However, it appears again to have rebounded.

The decline in quality in Giscours did not go unnoticed by the firm of Gilbey-Loudenne, who controlled the international exclusivity for the sale of wines produced at Giscours. Because of the difficulties Giscours experienced following 1981, the exclusivity was terminated, and now the wine is sold on the free market.

The imposing château of Giscours is one of the largest of the Médoc, and well worth a visit. It is set in a beautiful park with many ancient trees. The style of wine produced has been excellent in the last two decades. Except for the slump in quality during much of the eighties (the wine tasted too overtly commercial, flabby, and soft), Giscours has been characterized by a deep, often opaque color, gobs of concentration, and a muscular and rich construction with plenty of tannin. Furthermore, Giscours' record in "off" vintages such as 1980, 1974, 1973, and 1972 is far superior to most other renowned Bordeaux châteaux. Part of the reason for that may be the apparatus used at Giscours, which, in years when the grapes are not ripe, heats the incoming grapes to 60 degrees centigrade for 30–60 seconds in order to extract color and fruit. While this procedure has been scoffed at by other proprietors, Giscours' record in less than great years has been admirable. In 1990 Giscours became one of the first Médoc properties to use new equipment that removed excess water from the grapes by the process of osmosis.

Those who drink Giscours regularly prize it for its dark color, intense, chewy, robust richness, and full body. Despite the power and flesh, as well as considerable tannin, it has not had a good track record for evolving gracefully past age 15. Perhaps that will change when top vintages such as 1975 and 1978 reach full maturity.

At present, Pierre Tari has relinquished control of running Giscours to his daughter, Madame Nicole Heeter-Tari, who appears capable of bringing Giscours into the top rung of third-growths in the Bordeaux hierarchy. I would be remiss in not adding that the price of Giscours has remained more reasonable than many of its peers.

VINTAGES

1989—The 1989 Giscours is the first reassuringly fine wine made at this
· 　　property since the 1981. It exhibits a black/ruby color, and a big,
87　　forceful bouquet of overripe plums and licorice. In the mouth, the
　　　wine has the telltale succulent character of the vintage, a chewy
　　　texture, excellent concentration, high alcohol, low acidity, and a
　　　very long, opulent finish. It should prove seductive and heady to
　　　nearly everyone. Anticipated maturity: 1993–2008. Last tasted,
　　　4/91.

1988—The 1988 is a clumsy, excessively overripe wine with an aroma of
· 　　peach and apricot jam. Loosely structured, sweet, and formless,
75　　its tannins are not adequate enough to give it any grip or preci-
　　　sion. Anticipated maturity: Now–1996. Last tasted, 4/91.

1986—Cask samples of the 1986 Giscours consistently tasted awkward
· 　　and disjointed, and after three bottle tastings, I remain worried
74　　about this wine's potential. There is plenty of ripe fruit, but
　　　the pervading impression is one of raisiny overripeness rather
　　　than balance. Aromas of peaches, apricots, and prunes are
　　　followed by a wine that displays abundant spicy new oak,
　　　extremely low acidity, and a loosely knit, alcoholic, com-
　　　mercial character. Given the immense production of Giscours,
　　　one wonders if there should have been a stricter selection.
　　　Disappointing. Anticipated maturity: Now–1995. Last tasted,
　　　1/91.

1985—During much of the eighties, most of the structure of Giscours
·   was sacrificed in favor of a lighter, fruitier, ready-to-drink wine.
84   This is especially evident with the 1985 and 1986 vintages. The
      1985 is light, fruity, agreeable, and charming, but lacks grip and
      length. It will be short-lived. Anticipated maturity: Now–1995.
      Last tasted, 1/90.

1984—Giscours always manages to come out on top in off years—re-
·   member how good their 1980 turned out to be? The 1984 is round,
83   very fruity, fat, and for lack of a better work—just tasty. Antici-
      pated maturity: Now–1993. Last tasted, 11/88.

1983—Giscours was not as successful as many other Margaux châteaux
·   in this vintage. Medium ruby with a soft, fruity, silky texture,
86   light tannins, and medium body, the 1983 Giscours will evolve
      quickly as the acidity is low, the pH high, and the wine lacking
      tannin and great depth. Anticipated maturity: Now–1996. Last
      tasted, 11/88.

1982—A precociously styled wine for the vintage, the 1982 Giscours
·   is dark ruby with some amber, with a very ripe, rich, berryish
86   bouquet, and full bodied, with fat, loosely knit, deep flavors.
      The wine has considerable amounts of alcohol, and a lush, silky
      finish. Flavorful, but unstructured, the 1982 Giscours has
      developed quickly. Anticipated maturity: Now–2000. Last tasted,
      12/90.

1981—The 1981 Giscours is a charming wine with a supple, graceful
·   fruitiness, a rich, spicy, berry fruit bouquet, lush, deep flavors,
86   light to moderate tannins, and a long finish. This wine has drunk
·   well since its release and can be expected to age well. Anticipated
      maturity: Now–1996. Last tasted, 8/88.

1980—This was an outstanding success for this mediocre vintage. It had
·   sweet, ripe fruit, but has now begun to dry out. Originally one of
79   the best wines of the vintage, it should have been consumed by
      1988. Last tasted, 12/88.

1979—Beautifully full, voluptuous aromas of ripe plums and vanillin
·   oak, and floral fragrances jump from the glass. On the palate, this
88   wine has very good concentration, medium to full body, and mod-
      erate, round, ripe tannins. The 1979 Giscours is a noteworthy
      success for the vintage. Anticipated maturity: Now–2003. Last
      tasted, 12/88.

1978—A big, broodingly dark ruby–colored wine, with an exuberant
·   bouquet of ripe blackcurrants, truffles, and wood, this tannic,
90   chunky, fleshy, full-bodied Giscours has impressive extract and
      concentration. The wine has evolved slowly and is essentially

unchanged since I first tasted it. Anticipated maturity: 1992–2005. Last tasted, 5/91.

1977—Giscours has a habit of excelling in Bordeaux's off years, but
· nothing special was made in 1977. It is medium ruby, with dry,
70 vegetal, lean, skinny flavors, and enough tannin in the finish to outlast the fruit by a decade. Last tasted, 6/82.

1976—Always one of my favorite 1976s, Giscours produced a deeply
· colored, plump, quite round, and generously fruity wine, with
81 medium to full body and a lush texture. The wine has been fully mature for over a decade, yet when last tasted from a magnum, it was still delicious and plump. Drink up. Anticipated maturity: Now. Last tasted, 5/87.

1975—The best Giscours in the last two decades, the 1975 remains a
· young and powerful, rich wine that is loaded with potential. Still
91 dark ruby with no amber, this wine has a deep, full, tight bouquet of blackcurrant fruit and spicy, tarry scents. Full bodied, tannic, but possessed with layers of fruit, this remains a wine for the patient. I originally thought this wine would be fully mature by 1990, but like so many of the top 1975s, it has evolved at a snail's pace. I am betting on the fruit holding up. Anticipated maturity: 1992–2010. Last tasted, 11/89.

1974—Attractive for the vintage, the 1974 Giscours had a medium ruby
· color, a fragrant, spicy, fruity bouquet, and soft, moderately in-
78 tense flavors. Anticipated maturity: Now–probably in serious decline. Last tasted, 2/81.

1973—At its prime in 1976–1979, this was one of the top wines of this
· watery, light vintage. Now in serious decline, the wine has lost its
72 charming, soft berry fruitiness and straightforward, easygoing style. Last tasted, 4/86.

1971—An impressively dark-colored wine for the vintage, the 1971 Gis-
· cours is rather robust and chunky, but lacking in polish and fi-
84 nesse. It makes a big palate impression with its dusty, ripe, substantial fruit and weight, but it finishes coarsely. This is a brawny, oafish example of Giscours that is unlikely to ever come into harmony. Anticipated maturity: Now–1993. Last tasted, 1/87.

1970—A big, dark ruby, dense, rich, fat wine, with oodles of ripe fruit,
· and a good lashing of tannin, the 1970 Giscours is fully mature,
87 very concentrated, with a big framework and gutsy, meaty, leathery texture. Although lacking finesse, it offers a muscular, rich mouthful of wine. Anticipated maturity: Now–2000. Last tasted, 11/89.

1967—Now fading and past its prime, the 1967 Giscours was quite rich,
·   savory, and flavorful in the period between 1975 and 1979. How-
84? ever, the fruit is now beginning to drop off, the acidity is emerging
from the wine's structure, and the color is taking on more and
more brown. Anticipated maturity: Now—probably in serious decline. Last tasted, 6/84.

1966—Since the last time I tasted this wine in 1984 it has nearly col-
·   lapsed. The dark ruby/amber at the edge has changed to medium
74   ruby with plenty of rust. The wine's nose has begun to dry out,
displaying old barrel and herbaceous, musty, fruit flavors. In the
mouth, the wine is high in acidity and tannins, and has lost nearly
all of its fruit. This was once a wonderfully supple, big, tasty,
corpulent wine, but it has now gone into serious decline. Last
tasted, 1/91.

1962—Like the 1966 and 1967, this wine is past its prime. However, the
·   bouquet still exhibits spicy, floral-scented, ripe fruit. In the
80   mouth, the wine lacks the plump, rich fruity character of other
Giscours, and tails off in the finish. Anticipated maturity: Now—
probably in serious decline. Last tasted, 1/81.

1961—This wine has held up nicely despite having been fully mature for
·   well over 15 years. The color has lightened into a medium dusty
87   ruby, but the rich, full, earthy, superripe, curranty bouquet is still
lively and penetrating. In the mouth, the wine has the foursquare,
beefy, chunky character that often characterizes Giscours, a certain tarry, slightly oxidized character, but finishes with plenty of
richness and a heady alcohol content. This wine requires immediate consumption. Last tasted, 1/91.

LA GURGUE (Unclassified) GOOD

Production: 6,000 cases	Grape varieties: Cabernet Sauvignon—70% Merlot—25% Petit Verdot—5%
Secondary label: none	
Vineyard size: 31 acres	Proprietor: Bernadette Villars
Time spent in barrels: 12–18 months	Average age of vines: 30 years

Evaluation of present classification: The quality equivalent of a Médoc fifth-growth, particularly since 1983

Plateau of maturity: 5–12 years following the vintage

With its well-placed vineyard, just to the west of Château Margaux, this Cru Bourgeois has made considerable strides in quality since it changed ownership in 1978, when it was sold to Bernard Taillan and Chantovent. The person largely responsible for the increased quality of the wines is Madame Bernadette Villars, who also makes the wines at Chasse-Spleen in Moulis and Haut-Bages-Libéral in Pauillac.

In top vintages, La Gurgue is a wonderfully supple, deeply colored, rich, smoothly textured wine that is not meant to make old bones. Although for drinking in its first 10–12 years, it is rewarding. The price is also attractive.

VINTAGES

1989—Bernadette Villars has fashioned a lovely 1989 at La Gurgue that
·   is bursting with ripe plums and blackcurrants. Impressively rich,
86   heady, and alcoholic, this velvety wine already provides delicious drinking. Anticipated maturity: 1992–1997. Last tasted, 4/91.

1988—Early tastings from cask were unimpressive, but following bot-
·   tling, the wine came to life. Moderately deep ruby, with an im-
87   pressive bouquet of spring flowers, blackcurrants, and licorice, this medium-bodied, surprisingly soft and intense 1988 already provides excellent drinking. Fortunately, the wine avoids the relatively hard tannins that so frequently typify this vintage. Anticipated maturity: Now–1997. Last tasted, 4/91.

1986—The 1986 La Gurgue may ultimately surpass the outstanding 1983
·   made here. Quite deep, with a stunning bouquet of black fruits
88   and spicy oak, it is voluptuous and deep on the palate, with a nice supple richness that I did not detect when I saw the wine out of cask. This lovely wine can be drunk much younger than many of

the top Médocs, and is certainly one of the sleepers of the vintage. Anticipated maturity: 1992–1999. Last tasted, 8/89.

1985—The 1985 has gobs of blackcurrant fruit and is deep, velvety, lush,
·   medium to full bodied, and intensely concentrated. Anticipated
86   maturity: Now–1995. Last tasted, 4/88.

1984—Light, soft, and relatively attractive when first released, the 1984
·   has deteriorated since and is now taking on a hollow, coarse,
73   empty character lacking fruit. It should have been consumed by
        now as its future is dubious. Last tasted, 3/88.

1983—Now beginning to tire ever so slightly, the 1983 La Gurgue is still
·   an impeccably made, round, generously endowed, spicy, richly
85   fruity Margaux that qualitatively surpasses many of the classified
        growths. To age it any longer would push one's luck, so immedi-
        ate consumption is advised. Anticipated maturity: Now. Last
        tasted, 4/89.

D'ISSAN (Third-Growth)   AVERAGE

Production: 10,000–12,000 cases	Grape varieties: Cabernet Sauvignon—75% Merlot—25%
Secondary label: Candel	
Vineyard size: 79 acres	Proprietor: Madame Emmanuel Cruse Administrator: Lionel Cruse
Time spent in barrels: 18 months	Average age of vines: 20 years
Evaluation of present classification: Should be downgraded to at least a fifth-growth	
Plateau of maturity: 5–15 years following the vintage	

The seventeenth-century Château d'Issan is one of the most strikingly beautiful estates in the Médoc. It is surrounded by a moat and has a Sleeping Beauty castle ambience. Since 1945 d'Issan has been owned by the famous Cruse family of Bordeaux who exclusively controlled the marketing of this wine through their *négociant* business. Now the wine is freely sold to all *négociants* in Bordeaux. Undoubtedly the quality has improved, but I have had too many bad experiences with tasting excellent, sometimes even outstanding cask samples only to find the wine significantly lighter and less interesting when bottled. Either the cask samples were not representative of the wine (a rarity in Bordeaux), or the wine was entirely too processed and excessively fined and filtered prior to bottling.

When good (the 1900 is considered one of the greatest wines ever made in Bordeaux), d'Issan is prized for its soft, fleshy, yet delicate character, and immense perfume. Finding a d'Issan today with such characteristics is no easy task. The best recent vintage has been the 1983, which was glorious from cask and remains better than some of the lighter, somewhat diluted efforts of the late eighties.

Most vintages of d'Issan can be drunk at an extremely early age, yet have the ability to last. At present, the property does not merit its status as a third-growth and objectively should be downgraded to either a fifth-growth or Cru Bourgeois.

VINTAGES

1989—D'Issan is normally a light, delicate wine, so it is foolish to expect
· a powerful or blockbuster wine. Even so, lightness has its limits.
83 The 1989 provides a fruity, straightforward, smooth, agreeable glass of wine, but there are Bordeaux Supérieurs that offer the same characteristics. It is ripe, but low in acidity. Anticipated maturity: Now–1997. Last tasted, 4/91.

1988—The staff must have been asleep at the controls when the 1988
· was made. Light, sinewy, lacking fruit and depth, this medium-
75 bodied wine has too much acidity and tannin. Caveat emptor! Last tasted, 4/91.

1986—This wine has performed poorly after bottling, making me wonder
· if it is going through an awkward stage. It appears to be a diluted,
78 light, overcropped wine that displays neither the fragrance nor the complexity one expects from a third-growth. It is forward, soft, and ready to drink. Anticipated maturity: Now–1994. Last tasted, 3/90.

1985—The 1985 d'Issan is a charmer, and is undeniably already appeal-
· ing to drink. Medium ruby in color, it has a floral and berry-
87 scented bouquet interwoven with the scents of toasty oak. Soft, fruity flavors display excellent ripeness and silky tannins. Antici-pated maturity: Now–1997. Last tasted, 3/90.

1984—Soft, weedy, light, and ready to drink, the 1984 d'Issan has a
· medium ruby color, and finishes abruptly with some noticeable
72 tannins. Anticipated maturity: Now–1993. Last tasted, 6/88.

1983—The most impressive recent d'Issan, the 1983 has an exotic, rich,
· spicy, plummy bouquet and soft, cherry, lush, fruity flavors. Low
88 in acidity, this precocious, seductive, round wine is fully mature. Anticipated maturity: Now–2000. Last tasted, 2/91.

1982—Moderately dark ruby in color with an expansive, rich, spicy,
· earthy bouquet, this relatively unstructured 1982 has reached full
85 maturity. The wine displays a smooth black cherry fruit, a supple richness, and light tannins. There is an absence of grip. Antici-pated maturity: Now–1997. Last tasted, 1/90.

1981—This wine is in danger of becoming more attenuated and losing so
· much fruit that the charm and light-bodied appeal will disappear.
82 Nevertheless, there is still enough ripe berry and plummy fruit,
but the wine does appear to be ever so slightly drying out in the
finish. Anticipated maturity: Now–1994. Last tasted, 3/89.

1979—This wine has developed considerably over the last 4–5 years and
· now has an amber edge to its medium ruby color. The slightly
78 herbaceous, moderately intense, oaky, berryish nose is pleasant,
but not complex. In the mouth, the wine is light to medium bodied, with some elegance, but it finishes short and a bit hard.
Anticipated maturity: Now. Last tasted, 3/89.

1978—Along with the 1983, this is probably my favorite d'Issan in the
· last 20 years. It exhibits a medium dark ruby color with only some
86 amber at the edge. The floral, intensely ripe, spicy aroma is followed by a relatively rich, medium- to full-bodied, concentrated
wine with excellent depth and as much length as one is likely to
ever find in a d'Issan. The tannins have nearly melted away, and
the wine is close to reaching full maturity. Anticipated maturity:
Now–1999. Last tasted, 3/89.

1976—I had several very mature, somewhat fading examples of this wine
· in the early eighties, but when I tasted it in a Bordeaux restaurant
76 in 1988, it seemed much better. It was quite ripe and there was
some browning to the color, but there was that super-mature,
heady fruitiness of the best 1976s, plenty of alcohol, and a soft,
lush finish. Perhaps there is considerable bottle variation, but my
last experience with this wine was pleasant. Anticipated maturity:
Now–1995. Last tasted, 3/88.

1975—One of the few classified growths that can be drunk now, the 1975
· d'Issan has a good, dark ruby color, a spicy, chewy, muscular
82 texture, good ripeness of fruit, and medium body, but tastes
somewhat dull. Anticipated maturity: Now–probably in serious
decline. Last tasted, 5/84.

1970—This wine has always been relatively tight and unforthcoming, yet
· it continues to show no signs of drying out or fading. It is a solidly
79 built, tightly knit, muscular d'Issan with good color, a dusty,
almost coarse fruitiness, and some rough tannins in the finish. I
had expected this wine to display greater evolution by now, but it
seems to be suspended in time. My question has always been
whether the fruit would outlast the tannins, and I am beginning
to think it will not. Anticipated maturity: Now–2000. Last tasted,
3/89.

KIRWAN (Third-Growth)

Production: 8,000–12,000 cases	Grape varieties:
	Cabernet Sauvignon—40%
	Merlot—30%
	Cabernet Franc—20%
	Petit Verdot—10%
Secondary label: none	
Vineyard size: 76.6 acres	Proprietor: Schröder & Schÿler
Time spent in barrels: 20 months	Average age of vines: 20 years
Evaluation of present classification: Should be downgraded to a Médoc fifth-growth	
Plateau of maturity: 5–14 years following the vintage	

Kirwan is another Margaux estate that would have a hard time holding its position in Bordeaux's 1855 classification should a reclassification take place. Like many other Margaux classified growths, Kirwan has not had a very distinguished track record. I have been a continual critic of Kirwan's wines, because I have consistently found them too light, dull, and bland to justify the lofty classification and price tag. However, an extensive rehabilitation program was begun in 1967 (the first vintage to be estate-bottled) and vintages since 1978 have exhibited slightly more promise.

Nevertheless, even allowing for the improvements that have been made, this wine remains relatively compact, a lighter-styled Margaux that rarely provides the fragrance or flavor depth one expects from a classified growth. Given the owner's obvious financial commitment, it is difficult to understand why this wine is not better. Perhaps the surprisingly high percentage of Cabernet Franc and Petit Verdot are partly to blame. I also suspect the selection process is not as strict as required to produce the highest quality.

VINTAGES

1989—Kirwan's wines have improved during the eighties, so I was dis-
· appointed that the 1989 did not excite me more. Elegant, charm-
83 ing, and soft, but lacking some intensity and character, it
represents a good short-term claret. Anticipated maturity: Now–
1999. Last tasted, 4/91.

1988—The 1988 is shallow, but cleanly made and vaguely fruity, with
· some hard tannins in the finish. Anticipated maturity: 1993–1997.
79 Last tasted, 4/91.

1986—Given the low percentage of Cabernet Sauvignon (40%), 1986 is
·   not the type of vintage in which Kirwan would have been expected
85   to excel. Much more powerful, intense, and tannic than the
        stylish, elegant 1985 produced here, the 1986 is a rich, intense,
        full-bodied wine with plenty of tannin. It should prove to be the
        longest-lived Kirwan in decades. Anticipated maturity: Now–
        1995. Last tasted, 3/89.

1985—The 1985 is one of the better examples of Kirwan I have tasted. It
·   has very fine color and a moderately intense bouquet of blackcur-
85   rants and new oak. Firm and elegant, with well-delineated flavors,
        this medium-bodied wine should age nicely. Anticipated matu-
        rity: Now–1997. Last tasted, 3/89.

1984—The 1984 has a touch of green, vegetal character to its nose, but
·   is clean, medium bodied, and fully mature. Anticipated maturity:
76   Now–1993. Last tasted, 3/88.

1983—The finest Kirwan produced in recent memory, the 1983 continues
·   to exhibit a dark ruby color, as well as a moderately intense, rich,
87   oaky, curranty aroma. Still youthfully tannic, with aggressively
        rich, plummy, fruity flavors and good length, the 1983 Kirwan
        should have a relatively long evolution. Anticipated maturity:
        1992–2000. Last tasted, 3/89.

1982—A rather loosely knit wine with very good color, jammy, grapey
·   fruit, low acidity, and a lush, supple texture, this medium- to full-
84   bodied wine has a precocious personality, a charming fruitiness,
        and will evolve rapidly. Anticipated maturity: Now–1995. Last
        tasted, 3/89.

1981—This vintage of Kirwan has been better received by others. I have
·   found the wine to be soundly colored but chunky, one-dimen-
75   sional, and bland. It is burdened with excessive tannin and acid-
        ity. Anticipated maturity: Now–1993. Last tasted, 3/89.

1980—Light and thin, but solid and adequate, this ruby-colored wine has
·   held up better than I thought it would. Anticipated maturity:
72   Now–may be in decline. Last tasted, 3/89.

1979—An unspectacular, but overall solid effort from Kirwan, this dark
·   ruby wine has a moderately intense, herbaceous, fruity, oaky
83   aroma, straightforward cherryish flavors, medium body, good
        acidity, and light tannins. Anticipated maturity: Now–1994. Last
        tasted, 4/84.

1978—Beginning to exhibit some browning at its edges, this wine has an
·   overripe quality, but pleasing fat, supple fruitiness and medium
80   body. It needs to be drunk up. Anticipated maturity: Now–1993.
        Last tasted, 3/89.

1976—In total collapse, the 1976 has a brown/rusty color, washed-out,
·   vegetal fruit flavors, and excessive alcohol in the finish. Last
58   tasted, 3/89.

1975—Medium ruby, with a tight, yet emerging bouquet of dusty, cedary
·   fruit, this wine is severe and austere, with high acidity and tannin.
71   It appears incapable of blossoming, and I suspect the fruit will
       continue to fade. Anticipated maturity: Now–1993. Last tasted,
       3/89.

1971—In full decline, the 1971 brownish-colored Kirwan is a light,
·   weedy-scented wine that has lost its fruit and offers no depth or
62   complexity. Last tasted, 3/89.

1970—The 1970 has more stuffing than the 1971, but tastes light and
·   meagerly endowed for a 1970. Now fully mature, the wine has a
75   spicy, berrylike bouquet, medium body, and average concentra-
       tion. Anticipated maturity: Now–probably in serious decline.
       Last tasted, 2/82.

LABÉGORCE (Cru Bourgeois)   AVERAGE

Production: 12,000 cases	Grape varieties: Cabernet Sauvignon—55% Merlot—40% Cabernet Franc—5%
Secondary label: none	
Vineyard size: 71.6 acres	Proprietor: Hubert Perrodo
Time spent in barrels: 12–14 months	Average age of vines: 20 years
Evaluation of present classification: Should be maintained	
Plateau of maturity: 3–8 years following the vintage	

Jean-Robert Condom took responsibility for the management of this
property in 1978. After significant investments, encouraged by the huge
négociant, Dourthe (who controls much of the worldwide distribution of
Labégorce), this has become a consistently well-made Cru Bourgeois in
the appellation of Margaux. While it may lack the fragrance and suppleness of an excellent Margaux Cru Bourgeois such as La Gurgue, or the
pure power and aging potential of a Monbrison, the wine has character
and is fairly priced. In late 1989, the estate was sold to Hubert Perrodo.
    Although many knowledgeable consumers are impressed with the
wine's delicacy, Labégorce seems to me to have more of a St.-Estèphe

style without the fragrance found in many Margaux. It is often as good as many of the Margaux classified growths as well as considerably less expensive. The best recent vintage has been 1983, followed by 1989 and 1986. Top years or Labégorce should be consumed within 8 years of the vintage.

LABÉGORCE-ZÉDÉ (Cru Bourgeois)　　　　　　GOOD

Production: 10,500 cases	Grape varieties: Cabernet Sauvignon—50% Merlot—35% Cabernet Franc—10% Petit Verdot—5%
Secondary label: Château de l'Amiral	
Vineyard size: 64.22 acres	Proprietor: G.F.A. Labégorce-Zédé Administrator: Luc Thienpont
Time spent in barrels: 14–20 months	Average age of vines: 25 years
Evaluation of present classification: Should be maintained, although certain vintages are as good as a Médoc fifth-growth	
Plateau of maturity: 6–12 years following the vintage	

The Belgian Thienpont family owns and manages Labégorce-Zédé, and like the wine of their famous Pomerol estate of Vieux-Château-Certan, this is traditionally made. Since 1979, when young Luc Thienpont took over, the quality increased. Labégorce-Zédé, with a plain, drab farmhouse and vineyards in both the communes of Soussans and Margaux, usually requires 5–6 years to reach maturity, but can retain fruit and harmony for 5–10 more years in top vintages such as 1983 and 1989. I personally prefer the wines of Labégorce-Zédé to Labégorce, given the extra measure of perfume and richness often found in the former.

VINTAGES

1989—The 1989 is the finest wine I have tasted from this well-run Cru
·　　Bourgeois. Dark in color (nearly black), with an intense aroma of
87　　plums and licorice, this full-bodied, large-scaled wine has layers
　　　of fruit, very high tannins, as well as an impressively long finish.
　　　The proprietor's decision to use 35% new oak in 1989 will add
　　　additional complexity. This should prove to be one of the Cru

Bourgeois stars. Anticipated maturity: 1992–2005. Last tasted, 4/91.

1988—The 1988 lacks substance and length. Like many 1988 Médocs, it
 ·   possesses a slightly hollow, underripe character. Anticipated ma-
78   turity: 1992–1996. Last tasted, 4/91.

1986—This wine displays a moderately intense, flowery, currant-scented
 ·   bouquet, medium body, attractive fruitiness, and moderate tan-
84   nins in the finish. It is not of the same quality as the 1985 or 1983,
        but it is certainly a stylish, medium-weight 1986. Anticipated ma-
        turity: 1992–1997. Last tasted, 4/91.

1985—The 1985 is an elegantly perfumed wine of medium body, with
 ·   ripe fruit, excellent balance, and soft tannins in its finish. Antici-
85   pated maturity: Now–1996. Last tasted, 3/89.

1984—The 1984 has decent color, some herbaceous, spicy fruit, a touch
 ·   of new oak, and a short finish. Anticipated maturity: Now. Last
76   tasted, 11/87.

1983—This wine has reached its plateau of maturity and exhibits a rich,
 ·   vanillin, floral, licorice, curranty-scented bouquet and full-bod-
86   ied, fleshy, almost fat flavors, with a soft, smooth, silky finish. It
        is a textbook as well as seductive Margaux. Anticipated maturity:
        Now–1994. Last tasted, 11/89.

LA LAGUNE (Third-Growth)   EXCELLENT

Production: 25,000 cases	Grape varieties: Cabernet Sauvignon—55% Merlot—20% Cabernet Franc—20% Petit Verdot—5%
Secondary label: Ludon-Pomiès-Agassac	
Vineyard size: 136 acres	Proprietor: The Ayala Champagne firm
Time spent in barrels: 18–22 months	Average age of vines: 31 years
Evaluation of present classification: Should be upgraded to a Médoc second-growth	
Plateau of maturity: 7–20 years following the vintage	

La Lagune is one of Bordeaux's shining success stories. In the 1950s, the property was so run-down that numerous potential buyers, including the late Alexis Lichine, scoffed at the herculean task of replanting the vineyards and rebuilding the winery to re-establish La Lagune as a truly representative member of Bordeaux's elite group of 1855 Cru Classè châteaux.

In 1958, George Brunet, an entrepreneur, acquired the property and totally replanted the vineyard and constructed what today remains one of the most sophisticated wineries in the Médoc. Brunet did not stay long enough to reap the accolades from his massive investment in the property; he moved to Provence where he built one of that area's best wineries, Château Vignelaure. He sold La Lagune in 1962 to the Ayala Champagne firm, which has continued to renovate and manage La Lagune with the same fervor and passion. Their most revolutionary concept (which has remained uncopied) was the construction of a series of pipelines from the vats to the barrel aging cellars for transporting the wine without any exposure to air.

La Lagune is the very first classified growth encountered on the famous D2 road to the Médoc from Bordeaux. It is less than ten miles from the city. The vineyard is set on very light, gravel-like, sandy soils not unlike those of the Graves appellation south of Bordeaux. La Lagune was also the first château to position a woman, the late Jeanne Boyrie, as manager of the estate in 1964. In the chauvinist world of Bordeaux, this was a revolutionary development. While she was never able to penetrate the inner circle of the male-dominated wine society, no one took lightly her stern, formidable, meticulous personality, as she was undoubtedly one of the most conscientious and competent managers in all of Bordeaux. Following her mother's death in November 1986, Jeanne Boyrie's daughter, Caroline Desvergnes, assumed the responsibilities for running this property.

The style of wine produced at La Lagune has been described as both Pomerol-like and Graves-like. One notable connoisseur has called it "very burgundian." All three of these descriptions have merit. It can be a rich, fleshy, solid wine, with sometimes an overpowering bouquet of vanillin oak (it is one of the only non-first-growths to use 100% new oak barrels in nearly every vintage) and black cherries. The wine of La Lagune is usually fully mature by the tenth year of life, but will certainly keep 15 or 20 years. The quality and strength of La Lagune have improved significantly since 1966. As the vineyard has gotten older La Lagune has continued to emerge as one of the great—and surprisingly reasonably priced—wines of the Médoc. They have been particularly strong since 1976, so cost-conscious consumers should certainly make themselves aware of this impeccably made wine that, of all the top Bordeaux classified growths, is irrefutably the region's greatest value.

VINTAGES

1989—The hedonistic, rich, opulent, velvet-textured 1989 is reminiscent
·   of the 1982 La Lagune, except it is less tannic and concentrated.
90   Moderately dark ruby in color, with a big, intense bouquet of ripe
plums and toasty oak, it is richly concentrated, with an abundance of fruit, medium to full body, and soft tannins. This is a
sensual and alluring style of Bordeaux. Anticipated maturity:
1992–2008. Last tasted, 4/91.

1988—The 1988 has a streak of herbaceousness, and tart, aggressive
·   tannins that appear to have the upper hand in the wine's balance.
84   Medium bodied, spicy, and straightforward, the 1988 lacks
the flesh and chewy opulence of top vintages of La Lagune. Is
there enough fruit? Anticipated maturity: 1993–2002. Last tasted,
4/91.

1987—Fully mature, ripe, surprisingly round and charming, this me-
·   dium-bodied wine requires drinking. Anticipated maturity: Now–
82   1993. Last tasted, 12/89.

1986—The brawny 1986 La Lagune displays a marriage of smoky, toasty
·   oak and gobs of plum-like fruit that is marvelous. A larger-scaled
90   wine than usual, the 1986 will turn out to be the most tannic, long-
lived La Lagune in three decades. Anticipated maturity: 1994–
2010. Last tasted, 12/89.

1985—The 1985 is soft, ripe, fleshy, and aromatic. Medium bodied,
·   gentle, and open knit, this is a lush, smoothly textured wine.
87   Anticipated maturity: Now–2003. Last tasted, 12/89.

1984—Less attractive now than from the cask, the 1984 is medium ruby,
·   very oaky (too woody?), tough and stern on the palate, with more
74   tannin than fruit. I would not gamble on this wine. Last tasted,
12/89.

1983—Following the monumental wine produced at La Lagune in 1982,
·   it is easy to overlook the 1983, which is a very good, rather than
87   great, wine. The late Madame Boyrie compared it to the 1981, but
with more substance and vigor. I agree. It is dark ruby, with a
full-bodied texture, rich plummy fruit, and moderate tannins
present. It is just beginning to open up. Anticipated maturity:
1993–2000. Last tasted, 12/89.

1982—As close to a perfect La Lagune as one can hope to find, this dark
·   ruby-colored wine has a sensational aroma of roasted nuts, ripe
93   black cherries, and vanillin oak that gushes from the glass. Quite
full bodied on the palate, with significant tannin present, this wine
fills the mouth with incredibly rich cassis fruit. A powerful, rich,
concentrated finish lasts and lasts. This is a fantastic La Lagune,

with a 25-year evolution ahead of it. It is maturing very slowly. Anticipated maturity: 1994–2010. Last tasted, 1/91.

1981 —Bottle variation at first seemed a problem, but recent tastings of
·   this wine have been consistent. A medium-bodied, spicy,
83   plummy, cherryish-flavored wine, with good extract, an appealing
          texture, and pleasant finish. It could use more flavor dimension
          and depth as the wine is compact. Anticipated maturity: Now–
          1998. Last tasted, 12/89.

1979 —The 1979 La Lagune is still youthful, but it is opening up and
·   revealing an oaky, ripe plummy fruitiness, a moderately intense,
84   spicy, vanillin aroma, and a clean, somewhat lean, dry finish.
          This is a satisfying, but unexciting La Lagune. Anticipated ma-
          turity: Now–1996. Last tasted, 12/89.

1978 —The 1978 La Lagune remains deep in color, with no sign of ma-
·   turity. The expansive bouquet suggests roasted nuts, plums, and
88   fresh new oak. On the palate, the wine is tannic, but lush and
          silky, with oodles of fruit present. It has been slow to evolve,
          and at its age, still tastes young and vigorous. Anticipated matu-
          rity: 1994–2005. Last tasted, 12/89.

1977 —Stalky and light, yet soft, fruity, and one-dimensional, the 1977
·   La Lagune is best consumed over the next 2–3 years. Anticipated
72   maturity: Now–probably in serious decline. Last tasted, 1/82.

1976 —In a vintage that produced numerous frail, diluted, fragile wines,
·   the 1976 La Lagune is a firmly made, concentrated, successful
88   wine. Now fully mature, this medium to dark ruby wine, with only
          a trace of amber at the edge, has a full-blown bouquet of vanillin
          oak, grilled nuts, and ripe plums. On the palate, it has an elegant,
          stylish texture, medium to full body, expansive, sweet, lush fruit,
          and a heady, but silky finish. Oh, how I wish I had bought more
          of this wine! Anticipated maturity: Now–1995. Last tasted, 12/89.

1975 —The 1975 La Lagune is a chunky specimen, with plenty of deep,
·   ripe fruit, a firm tannic underpinning, and a long, dusty-yet-youth-
85   ful finish. It is an atypically big and backward wine for La Lagune.
          Will the fruit outlast the tannin? I am beginning to have my
          doubts. Anticipated maturity: 1994–2005. Last tasted, 12/89.

1971 —Fully mature, with an open-knit, aromatic, complex bouquet of
·   cedarwood and ripe fruit, this medium-bodied wine is silky, lush,
85   and seductively round and fruity. Anticipated maturity: Now–
          may be in decline. Last tasted, 3/82.

1970 —Still surprisingly firm, but, I believe, fully mature, the 1970 La
·   Lagune has dark ruby color, a big, plummy, woodsy, and mush-
87   room-like bouquet, full-bodied, deep, concentrated, berryish fruit

flavors, good tannins, and a long finish. This is a fine La Lagune that falls just short of being outstanding. Anticipated maturity: Now–2000. Last tasted, 1/91 (from a magnum).

1967—One of the best 1967s, at its apogee by 1976, this wine has a soft,
· round, burgundian character, quite a complex bouquet of truffles,
83 caramel, and raspberry fruit, and little tannin. Anticipated maturity: Now–probably in serious decline. Last tasted, 1/80.

1966—Fully mature, the 1966 is supple and fleshy, with an attractive
· plummy fruitiness, medium body, and a soft, easy finish. Antici-
84 pated maturity: Now–probably in serious decline. Last tasted, 4/78.

1962—Tasted only once, the 1962 La Lagune was browning badly, and
· was quite soft on the palate, with dissipated, washed-out, fruity
55 flavors. It seemed to be clearly coming apart at the seams. Pass it by. Last tasted, 8/78.

1961—An unusual wine, very peppery and Rhône-like, with an odd me-
· dicinal nose, disjointed flavors, and a hot, alcoholic finish. A
60 strange style of La Lagune made ostensibly from very young vines. Last tasted, 10/77.

LARRUAU (Cru Bourgeois) GOOD

Production: 1,000 cases	Grape varieties: Cabernet Sauvignon—66% Merlot—34%
Secondary label: none	
Vineyard size: 7.5 acres	Proprietor: Bernard Château
Time spent in barrels: 18 months	Average age of vines: 15 years
Evaluation of present classification: Should be upgraded to a Médoc fifth-growth	
Plateau of maturity: 5–12 years following the vintage	

One of my personal goals is to taste more wines from Bernard Château, the young proprietor and winemaker of Château Larruau. He produces intensely concentrated wine, if the 1983 and 1986 are typical of the wines this tiny estate turns out. The property is also highly regarded by Margaux's most knowledgeable observer, Bernard Ginestet, who ranks Larruau as highly as such classified growths as Lascombes, Giscours, and Durfort-Vivens.

LASCOMBES (Second-Growth) GOOD

Production: 35,000–40,000 cases	Grape varieties: Cabernet Sauvignon—63% Merlot–33% Petit Verdot–3% Cabernet Franc–1%
Secondary labels: Segonnes and La Gombaude	
Vineyard size: 232.2 acres	Proprietor: Bass Charrington
Time spent in barrels: 18 months	Average age of vines: 18 years
Evaluation of present classification: Should be downgraded to a fourth-growth	
Plateau of maturity: 6–20 years following the vintage	

Lascombes is one of the largest estates in the Médoc. The vineyards are not contiguous, but consist of more than 40 separate plots of vines spread throughout the Margaux appellation. Because of this, the harvest at Lascombes can be one of the most difficult to manage, and may, in part, help explain why the wines can be inconsistent.

Lascombes' onetime popularity was no doubt a result of the herculean efforts made by the late Alexis Lichine, who owned the property between 1951 and 1971. He oversaw a thorough renovation of the wine cellars, as well as an aggressive plan of vineyard acquisition from surrounding properties. Because of Lichine's commitment to high-quality wines, a succession of very good vintages of wine from Lascombes resulted.

Since 1971, when Lichine sold Lascombes to the English firm of Bass Charrington, the quality and consistency of Lascombes noticeably dropped. However, most vintages from 1982 onward reflect a more serious commitment to quality wine.

The château itself is one of the more hospitable of the region, with an ivy-colored facade, extraordinary state-of-the-art swimming pool, and gorgeously manicured gardens. The owners, the Bass Charrington group, have a reputation in Bordeaux for throwing lavish parties at Château Lascombes. One such party held in the mid-1980s became rather raucous, with the dancing girls from the famous Parisian saloon called the Crazy Horse actually disrobing and taking dips in the pool.

As I have indicated, the quality of the wines since 1982 has improved. Most vintages of Lascombes have been relatively concentrated and robust, and while not fetching top marks, are reliably good.

The property also produces an excellent dry rosé sold as Chevalier de

Lascombes. This wine is one of the best rosés of Bordeaux. It is a shame there is not a greater market for fine, inexpensive rosés.

VINTAGES

1989—Lascombes' 1989 has an aroma of roasted peanuts, something I
·   have frequently found in Grenache-based Châteauneuf du Papes.
85   A muscular, tannic wine, it has a powerful, rich, alcoholic finish.
      I would not be surprised to see this exuberantly styled wine turn
      out much better than my projected rating. Anticipated maturity:
      1993–2002. Last tasted, 4/91.

1988—The 1988 may be superior to the 1989. It is deep ruby/purple, with
·   a moderately intense bouquet of cedar, plums, and currants. In
86   the mouth, it is medium to full bodied, well balanced, and not
      excessively tannic as many 1988 Médocs tend to be. Anticipated
      maturity: 1994–2002. Last tasted, 4/91.

1986—I liked the 1985 Lascombes better than the 1986, which, for what-
·   ever reason, displays some dilution in the mid-range, probably
83   due to the record-breaking size of the Bordeaux crop in 1986. I
      also suspect the tannins are too elevated for the amount of depth
      the wine possesses. Nevertheless, this is a tasty but uncomplex
      wine. Anticipated maturity: 1992–2000. Last tasted, 11/89.

1985—The 1985, while lacking some grip and structure, is very repre-
·   sentative of the vintage. Ripe, round, fruity, and medium bodied,
86   this lush, aromatic wine already drinks well. Anticipated matu-
      rity: Now–1998. Last tasted, 2/90.

1984—Light to medium ruby, the 1984 Lascombes has an attractive soft,
·   herbaceous, berry-like fruitiness, medium body, some toasty oak,
79   light tannins, and should be drunk up. Anticipated maturity:
      Now–1995. Last tasted, 3/89.

1983—Medium to dark ruby in color, with a rich, spicy, berry-like aroma
·   of some intensity, this fat, concentrated, smoothly textured wine
87   has reached maturity. It appears to be one of the best wines made
      at the property in over a decade. Anticipated maturity: Now–
      2000. Last tasted, 3/89.

1982—In 1982, Lascombes emerged from a prolonged period of medi-
·   ocrity. Moderately dark ruby, with a fragrant, rich, ripe, intense
87   bouquet of vanillin oak and ripe fruit, on the palate, this wine is
      plump, richly fruity, medium bodied, and has a long finish. The
      soft tannins are quickly melting away. Anticipated maturity:
      Now–2000. Last tasted, 3/89.

1981—The 1981 has a light to medium ruby/orange color, with a simple,
·   somewhat herbaceous aroma, modest, meagerly endowed flavors,
72   and a short finish. The wine is losing its fruit and becoming more
       attenuated. Anticipated maturity: Now–may be in decline. Last
       tasted, 3/89.

1980—Green and vegetal with an annoyingly high acidity level and shal-
·   low, diffuse, washed-out flavors. Ignore. Last tasted, 8/83.
60

1979—While the commune of Margaux seemed to have produced a num-
·   ber of fine wines in 1979 (like those from Margaux, Palmer, and
76   Giscours), Lascombes has consistently tasted light and diluted.
       Moderately concentrated fruit, plenty of oak, and increasingly
       noticeable tannin and acidity all suggest trouble ahead. Antici-
       pated maturity: Now–1992. Last tasted, 3/89.

1978—Surprisingly green (even vegetal), lean, and acidic without any of
·   the plump, round, generous, ripe, rich fruit that is one of the
76   landmarks of this vintage, the 1978 Lascombes lacks depth and
       richness, and seems quite mediocre given the high quality of the
       vintage. Anticipated maturity: Now–may be in decline. Last
       tasted, 3/89.

1977—Extremely thin, stalky, and vegetal, this nasty little wine has very
·   little to like. Last tasted, 1/82.
60

1976—Disappointingly light and diffuse, with overly ripe, washed-out
·   flavors, this low-acid wine is fading badly. Last tasted, 3/89.
62

1975—Early on, this wine was consistently inconsistent. It has now set-
·   tled down and appears to be a big, ripe, rich, full-bodied, in-
86   tensely flavored, but essentially one-dimensional wine. It is very
       spicy, with a Pauillac-like, minty, gingery bouquet, and robust
       flavors. Anticipated maturity: Now–2001. Last tasted, 3/89.

1971—In the mid- to late 1970s, this was one of my favorite vintages of
·   Lascombes. It has begun to tire badly, taking on a brown/rust
80   color and losing some of its supple, intense fruitiness. This
       elegantly wrought wine still retains some vestiges of its com-
       plex, spicy, earthy, ripe plummy bouquet and soft, rich, yet
       fading, flavors. Anticipated maturity: Now–1994. Last tasted,
       3/89.

1970—A fine example of Lascombes—darkly colored, ripe, full bodied,
·   richly fruity, and fleshy—the 1970 is now fully mature, but has
87   the concentration of fruit and structure to hold for 4–6 more
       years. It is a spicy, fragrant, and altogether satisfying mouthful

of amply endowed wine. Anticipated maturity: Now–1996. Last tasted, 6/88.

1966—A top-notch effort from Lascombes, the 1966 is better than the
· 1970, certainly more complete and charming than the 1975, and
88 has proven longer lived than either the 1982 or 1983 will be—I think. Dark ruby with an amber edge, this wine has very good richness and length to go along with its voluptuous, seductive bouquet. It has been fully mature for over a decade, but continues to exhibit high class. It is one of my favorite 1966s. Anticipated maturity: Now–1995. Last tasted, 3/89.

1962—A beautiful wine, fragrant, spicy, with a certain fat sweetness to
· its taste, this textbook Margaux has a big, intense bouquet and
87 wonderfully silky, lush flavors. It has been fully mature since 1976. Anticipated maturity: Now–may be in decline. Last tasted, 11/81.

1961—A substantial Lascombes, but lacking complexity and the great
· depth associated with this vintage, the 1961 Lascombes is dark
85 in color with an amber edge. It possesses a smoky, earthy, ripe bouquet, a touch of raw acidity in the finish, and a good, but unspectacular finish. Fully mature, the wine requires consumption. Anticipated maturity: Now–may be in decline. Last tasted, 10/79.

OLDER VINTAGES

I have no tasting notes on Lascombes from the thirties, forties, or early fifties, but I have two superb notes on the 1959 Lascombes (rated 90), which I have rated higher than any of the aforementioned Lascombes vintages. In 1988, from magnum, this wine had a huge mocha, cedary, plummy bouquet, full-bodied, remarkably intense, concentrated flavors (that seemed much younger and less evolved than the 1961), as well as a heady, cedary, spicy finish. It was a large-scaled, classic Margaux that is the finest Lascombes I have tasted.

MALESCOT ST.-EXUPÉRY (Third-Growth)　　　GOOD

Production: 17,000 cases	Grape varieties: Cabernet Sauvignon—50% Merlot—35% Cabernet Franc—10% Petit Verdot—5%
Secondary labels: de Loyac and 　Domaine du Balardin	
Vineyard size: 84 acres	Proprietor: Roger Zuger
Time spent in barrels: 18 months	Average age of vines: 35 years
Evaluation of present classification: Should be downgraded to a fifth-growth	
Plateau of maturity: 4–15 years following the vintage	

Malescot St.-Exupéry sits right in the town of Margaux, a few blocks north of Château Palmer on Bordeaux's main Route du Vin (D2). Malescot has long enjoyed a very favorable reputation, particularly for long-lived, traditionally made, firmly styled wines.

The Zuger family, the proprietors since 1955, claims that the style of Malescot will not be changed so as to be more supple and drinkable when released. However, it seems to me that recent vintages, particularly those in the seventies and eighties, are not nearly as tannic nor as hard as the wines of the sixties. The well-placed vineyards (some of them adjacent to those of Château Margaux) now tend to produce a lighter-styled wine that frequently suggests indifferent winemaking. A bit more energy, vision, and ambition from the owners could work wonders at this property. Malescot, like a number of other Margaux châteaux, is a perennial underachiever, and the result is a wine that is not nearly as good as its lofty position in Bordeaux's 1855 classification would suggest. Perhaps the saddest fact is that as much as I adore claret, except for the 1959 and 1961, there has not been a vintage of Malescot I would purchase.

VINTAGES

1989—The 1989 displays the big, ripe, heady bouquet typical of so many
　·　　wines of this vintage. It is ripe, richly fruity, and expansive on the
　86　palate, with some generous alcohol in the finish. If it gains some
　　　structure and grip, my rating will seem stingy. This may turn out
　　　to be one of the best Malescots in years. Anticipated maturity:
　　　1993–2002. Last tasted, 4/91.

1988—The 1988 is more classic, with a stylish mix of oak and blackcur-
· rants in its bouquet. This elegantly wrought wine is medium bod-
84 ied, austere, yet backed up with sufficient fruit to age well.
Anticipated maturity: 1993–2005. Last tasted, 4/91.

1986—I found the 1986 Malescot to be herbaceous and cedary, but too
· light, and displaying the dilution caused by the enormous crop
82 size. Perhaps a stricter selection would have resulted in a wine
with both finesse and flavor. Anticipated maturity: 1992–2001.
Last tasted, 3/89.

1985—A dominating smell of leafy vegetation and new oak obscures any
· evidence of ripe fruit that this medium-bodied, compact wine may
74 have. Some of my knowledgeable friends in Bordeaux have a high
opinion of this vintage of Malescot, but I have yet to taste a
persuasive example. Anticipated maturity: Now–1997. Last
tasted, 3/89.

1984—Very light, soft, fruity flavors characterize this elegant, yet fragile
· wine. Its meager charms will be fleeting. Anticipated maturity:
76 Now–1992. Last tasted, 11/89.

1983—The 1983 Malescot has a moderately dark ruby color, a ripe ber-
· ryish bouquet, hard, very astringent tannins, medium body, and
83 a severe, compact finish. The wine is tough textured and difficult
to penetrate, as well as alcoholic. The question remains, will the
fruit outlast the tannins? Anticipated maturity: 1995–2003. Last
tasted, 3/89.

1982—Rather atypical for Malescot, the 1982 is round and fruity, yet not
· as deep or as profound as some of the other wines from this
85 vintage. Medium ruby in color with a wild berry-like bouquet, and
medium to full body, this is a very good Malescot. It needs several
more years to shed the tannins. Anticipated maturity: 1992–2000.
Last tasted, 10/89.

1981—The 1981 is a lean, tight, unyielding wine that may develop better
· than I anticipate. However, the wine seems to be deficient in fruit,
78 although the color is sound and the bouquet hints at an underlying
ripeness. Anticipated maturity: Now–2000. Last tasted, 11/84.

1979—Soft, ripe-fruit, oaky aromas are charming and appealing on the
· palate. This offering from Malescot is medium bodied, oaky, sur-
83 prisingly soft and accessible, but well balanced in a lighter style.
Anticipated maturity: Now–1993. Last tasted, 10/89.

1978—Ripe blackcurrant fruit and plenty of spicy vanillin oak dominate
· the bouquet of this medium-bodied, increasingly attenuated,
78 harder-styled wine. The oak is apparent, and the wine appears to

be losing its charm and fruit. It tastes awkward and out of balance. Anticipated maturity: Now–1995. Last tasted, 6/88.

1976— A sound, fruity, straightforward 1976, with a ripe berry-like fruitiness, medium body, a soft, round texture, and a short, yet adequate finish. Fully mature for nearly a decade, the 1976 Malescot should be drunk. Anticipated maturity: Now–may be in decline. Last tasted, 11/87.

• 78

1975— Beginning to take on a pronounced brownish color, this medium-bodied wine has a dusty, spicy, herb-scented bouquet that exhibits little fruit. Now becoming attenuated, the 1975 has lost what charm it once possessed. Its future evolution is likely to be difficult. Anticipated maturity: Now–1993. Last tasted, 2/90.

• 76

1970— This remains a coarse, somewhat old style of wine, with plenty of punch and power, a dusty, rough texture, and a bouquet that suggests minerals, cedar, and licorice. It still tastes austere and tough, yet the color is deep. It could use more fat and generosity. Anticipated maturity: Now–2000. Last tasted, 1/88.

• 82

1967— The color is still surprisingly deep for a 1967, but the fruit is now drying out, and the tannins and acidity are becoming quite overbearing. At one time a good wine from this mixed sort of vintage, but other than this wine's pleasant, spicy bouquet, it lacks real substance and depth to be interesting. Last tasted, 11/79.

• 75

1966— Light and insubstantial in 1984, since then it has continued to dry out, displaying tea, old-barrel, and barnyard-like aromas and flavors. The finish is marred by excessive acidity. Over the hill! Last tasted, 4/88.

• 67

1964— The 1964 Malescot has an uncomplicated style, but given the number of failures in the Médoc in 1964, it is a satisfactory wine. Chunky and darkly colored with a briary, spicy, cedary bouquet, tough, yet substantial flavors, and a coarse finish, this is a gutsy-styled wine. Anticipated maturity: Now–probably in serious decline. Last tasted, 10/78.

• 82

1961— Sampled twice since 1983, this is the best Malescot I have ever tasted. The rich, deep, blackcurrant, spicy, cedary bouquet and long, fat, tannic, concentrated flavors are explosive. It is amazing how remarkably young this large-scaled wine tastes. It can still evolve for another 10–15 years. Even by the standards of the vintage, Malescot has turned in an outstanding effort. Remarkably, no recent vintage of Malescot even remotely resembles this wine. Anticipated maturity: Now–2005. Last tasted, 1/91.

• 92

OLDER VINTAGES

Several older vintages of Malescot I have tasted suggest that the con-centration this wine lacks today was never at issue in the fifties, or in several vintages of the sixties. The 1953 (rated 85) was a bit tired when I tasted it in 1988, but I could see that at one time it had been an excellent wine. The 1959 (rated 90) comes close to rivaling the superb 1961. It has the huge, full-bodied, muscular style of the vintage, a roasted nut and curranty nose, as well as plenty of concentration in an almost overwhelm-ing style. It was amazingly fresh and vigorous when drunk in 1988.

MARGAUX (First-Growth) OUTSTANDING

Production: 30,000–35,000 cases	Grape varieties: Cabernet Sauvignon—75% Merlot—20% Cabernet Franc—5%
Secondary label: Pavillon Rouge du Château Margaux	
Vineyard size: 210 acres	Proprietor: The Mentzelopoulos family
Time spent in barrels: 22–28 months	Average age of vines: 30 years
Evaluation of present classification: Should be maintained	
Plateau of maturity: 9–30 or more years following the vintage	

After a distressing period of mediocrity in the sixties and seventies, when far too many wines lacking richness, concentration, and character were produced under the inadequately financed administration of Pierre and Bernard Ginestet (the international oil crisis and wine market crash of 1973 and 1974 proved their undoing), Margaux was sold in 1977 to André and Laura Mentzelopoulos. Lavish amounts of money were immediately spent on the vineyards and the winemaking facilities. Emile Peynaud was retained as a consultant to oversee the vinification of the wine. Apprehensive observers expected the passing of several vintages before the new financial and spiritual commitments to excellence would be exhibited in the wines of Margaux. It took just one vintage, 1978, for the world to see just how great Margaux could be.

Unfortunately, André Mentzelopoulos died before he could see the full transformation of a struggling first-growth into a brilliantly consistent wine of stunning grace, richness, and complexity. His elegant wife Laura and more recently his savvy, street-smart daughter Corinne run the show. They are surrounded by the considerable talent of the winemaking-team of Paul Pontallier, *maître de chai* Jean Grangerou, and consulting oenologist Emile Peynaud. The immediate acclaim for the 1978 Margaux has been followed by a succession of other brilliantly executed wines, so stunning, so rich and balanced that it is not unfair to suggest that during the eighties there was no better wine made in all of Bordeaux than that of Margaux.

The style of the rejuvenated wine at Margaux is one of opulent richness, a deep, multidimensional bouquet with a fragrance of ripe blackcurrants, spicy vanillin oakiness, and violets. The wine is now considerably fuller in color, richness, body, and tannin than the wines made under the pre-1977 Ginestet regime.

Margaux also makes nearly 4,000 cases of dry white wine. Pavillon Blanc du Château Margaux is produced entirely from a 22-acre vineyard planted exclusively with Sauvignon Blanc. It is fermented in new oak barrels, and bottled after 6–7 months aging in cask. Trivia buffs will want to know that it is made at the small building, called Château Abel-Laurent, several hundred yards up the road from the magnificent château of Margaux. While it is the Médoc's finest white wine—crisp, fruity, subtly herbaceous, and oaky—it is expensive.

VINTAGES

1989—Given all the vital technical statistics concerning Margaux's 1989,
  ·   I would have thought it would be a blockbuster in the mold of the
  90   otherworldly 1982. It is not. It has the same alcohol content
        (12.8%) and same pH (3.8), but more tannin. There is not nearly
        the concentration of fruit exhibited by the 1982. This is surprising
        because the Merlot vineyards were pruned back by 50% in July
        to avoid overcropping. The Merlot was harvested September 9
        and the Cabernet Sauvignon between September 18 and September 25. Several *négociants* felt the château picked the Merlot too
        late and the Cabernet too early. However, this wine will undoubt-
        edly turn out to be an outstanding Margaux, better than the 1981,
        1984, and 1987, but far behind the compelling trio of wines made
        in 1982, 1983, and 1986. I also believe it to be inferior to the
        property's superb 1990, which may turn out to be a clone of the
        legendary 1953. Deep ruby in color (rather than the usual black/
        purple), with a moderately intense bouquet of cassis, oak, and
        spring flowers, this precocious, flattering wine has a medium- to
        full-bodied texture, excellent concentration, and an expansive,
        long, moderately tannic finish. It is reminiscent of the 1985, but
        lighter and more alcoholic. Anticipated maturity: 1995–2010. Last
        tasted, 4/91.

1988—The 1988 has a classic bouquet of violets and blackcurrants inter-
　　　twined with the vanillin scents of new oak. Medium bodied, con-
88　　centrated, but extremely hard and tannic, this elegantly wrought,
　　　yet surprisingly tough-textured wine should outlive the 1989. But
　　　will it ever provide as much pleasure? Anticipated maturity:
　　　2000–2015. Last tasted, 4/91.

1987—While this is undoubtedly a success for the vintage, among the
　　　first-growths I have a strong preference for Mouton-Rothschild,
86　　Lafite-Rothschild, and Haut-Brion. The 1987 Margaux exhibits a
　　　much more herbal note than one normally finds, but there is good
　　　richness, as well as a solid texture, suggesting concentration and
　　　depth. The wine is a bit narrow and compact in the finish, which
　　　leads me to believe that it will continue to evolve and open up. It
　　　should turn out to be nearly as good as the other so-called "off"
　　　years of Margaux during this decade, 1984 and 1980. Anticipated
　　　maturity: 1992–2000. Last tasted, 1/91.

1986—The 1986 Margaux, if not as opulent, precocious, and perfumed
　　　as the exotic 1982, nor as classically proportioned as the 1983, is
98　　certainly the most powerful, tannic, and muscular Margaux made
　　　in decades, if not this entire century. One wonders if the 1928 or
　　　1945 had as much power and depth as the 1986? The black/ruby/
　　　purple color is astonishing in its depth, suggesting a wine of ex-
　　　traordinary richness and ripeness. The nose offers up aromas of
　　　smoky, toasty new oak, black fruits such as plums and currants,
　　　as well as a few flowers. On the palate, the wine is mammoth,
　　　with extraordinary extract, yet perfect balance, and a finish that
　　　simply has to be experienced to be believed. It may indeed merit
　　　a perfect score in about 25–30 years, and stands along with the
　　　1986 Mouton-Rothschild and 1986 Lafite-Rothschild as one of the
　　　three most extraordinary wines of this vintage. Anticipated ma-
　　　turity: 2000–2050. Last tasted, 4/91.

1985—The 1985 Margaux is not in the same league with the 1982, 1983,
　　　or 1986, but it is a lovely, seductive, medium-bodied wine
90　　that has a gorgeous bouquet of toasty new oak, berry fruit, and
　　　violets. On the palate, it is not that concentrated when com-
　　　pared to the '82, '83, or '86, but the balance is superb, and
　　　this wine will hopefully evolve along the lines of the château's
　　　famous 1953. It is remarkably approachable and enjoyable to
　　　drink, and for the next decade will provide considerably more
　　　pleasure than the more ballyhooed and backward trio of 1986,
　　　1983, and 1982. Anticipated maturity: Now–2005. Last tasted,
　　　4/91.

1984—One of the best wines of the vintage, the 1984 Margaux is rich in
·   color and extract, and has an attractive perfume of violets, black-
87   currant fruit, toasty oak, herbs, and licorice. Long, deep, and
     concentrated, for the vintage it is comparable to the property's
     1980. Anticipated maturity: Now–2000. Last tasted, 1/91.

1983—The 1983 Margaux is one of the best wines of the vintage. The
·   Cabernet Sauvignon grapes achieved perfect maturity in 1983,
96   and the result is an astonishingly rich, concentrated, atypically
     powerful and tannic Margaux. The color is dark ruby, the aromas
     exude ripe cassis fruit, violets, and vanillin oakiness, and the fla-
     vors are extremely deep and long on the palate wth a clean, incred-
     ibly long finish. This will certainly be a monumental wine, but it
     remains stubbornly backward and at least a decade away from
     maturity. Anticipated maturity: 2000–2030. Last tasted, 5/91.

1982—I am constantly asked which vintage of Margaux is my favorite
·   since the Mentzelopoulos family took over the winemaking of this
99   property in 1977. Of course, their record has been one of remark-
     able and consistent brilliance, but everyone is entitled to certain
     favorites. While I would rate the 1986 very high because of its
     extraordinary potential for longevity, for pure pleasure, I prefer
     the 1982. I have tasted the 1982 over two-dozen times, and it is
     an extraordinary Margaux. Perhaps it is a bit atypical, but then it
     is the only vintage in the last 91 years to have a spooky resem-
     blance, in terms of the harvest dates, quantity of wine produced,
     and style, to one of the most legendary wines in Bordeaux's his-
     tory, the 1900 Margaux. Apparently, that wine also drank ex-
     tremely well when young.

Certainly the 1982 has a magnificent bouquet of creamy, toasty,
smoky oak and ripe berries in addition to an exotic, almost oriental spice character to the perfume that gives it great individuality. In the mouth, the wine is fabulously concentrated, rich, and
extremely soft, but at the same time very tannic, although the
tannins are supple, even silky. The wine has a finish that must
last for several minutes, and in comparison to the 1983, there is
no doubt that the 1982 is more flattering to taste, and seemingly
more concentrated, opulent, and exotic. However, classicists may
well prefer the structure, austerity, power, and backwardness of
the fabulous 1983. Comparing the two wines is a lot of fun, but
perhaps the only real conclusion that can be drawn is that the
1982 is much more developed, and for the next 20 years will
probably be the wine that provides the greatest degree of plea-

sure. After that, the 1983, and certainly the 1986, should prove to be its equal. Anticipated maturity: 1995–2025. Last tasted, 5/91.

1981— In weight and texture, the 1981 Margaux is closest in style to the
·   1979. It is an outstanding wine, even in the company of the mon-
90   umental wines of 1982, 1983, and 1986, although it does not have the power and weight of these vintages. The bouquet of the 1981 Margaux suggests ripe cassis fruit, spicy vanillin oakiness, and violets. On the palate, the wine is concentrated, tannic, and extremely long. It is just beginning to open and evolve. Anticipated maturity: 1993–2010. Last tasted, 1/91.

1980— Margaux, along with Pétrus, is unquestionably one of the best two
·   wines produced in the 1980 vintage. A wine of uncommon power,
88   concentration, richness, and beauty, the 1980 Margaux has a ruby color, fine extract, and a surprisingly long, supple palate. Medium bodied and still moderately tannic, this wine should continue to drink well for at least a decade. Anticipated maturity: Now–2000. Last tasted, 1/91.

1979— Like the 1980, the 1983, and possibly the 1981, the 1979 Margaux
·   is one of the finest wines of the vintage. Dark ruby with a deeply
93   scented bouquet of spicy, vanillin oak, ripe blackcurrant fruit, and the telltale haunting violet aromas, this wine has a smooth, richly fruity texture and super length. This medium- to full-bodied wine has reached its plateau of maturity. Among the recent top vintages of Margaux, this is probably the most charming. Anticipated maturity: Now–2005. Last tasted, 1/91.

1978— Developing in the bottle as expected, the 1978 Margaux is fuller
·   bodied and more powerful than the 1979, but less charming and
94   fruity. It has a gorgeous, seductive bouquet of ripe fruit and spicy oak, as well as tarry, truffle aromas. A wonderful harmony of oak, fruit, acidity, and tannin, and a finish that just lingers and lingers, all combine to make this a truly great wine. One of the superstars of the vintage, it is close to maturity. Anticipated maturity: 1992–2015. Last tasted, 1/91.

1977— Fully mature, the 1977 Margaux is soft and has a herbaceous,
·   blackcurrant fruitiness, no hollowness or bitterness, and a soft,
78   supple, pleasant, yet undistinguished finish. Anticipated maturity: Now–may be in decline. Last tasted, 4/81.

1976— A pre-Mentzelopoulos wine for certain, the 1976 is light, a trifle
·   jammy and fruity, but straightforward in style and terribly uncom-
70   plex. Anticipated maturity: Now–probably in serious decline. Last tasted, 2/82.

1975—Given the vintage and the excellent must weights measured at
·　　 Margaux, one would have expected this wine to be outstanding.
68　　 It is not even attractively fruity. Quite a disappointment, the 1975
　　　 Margaux is extremely lean and acidic, with shallow flavors, a
　　　 washed-out color, and, quite truthfully, not much concentration
　　　 to it. Anticipated maturity: Now—probably in serious decline.
　　　 Last tasted, 4/84.

1973—Now in complete decline, this light-brownish, ruby wine had some
·　　 light-intensity fruit and charm in 1978, but when last sampled it
55　　 was decrepit and bland. Last tasted, 3/80.

1971—Another mediocre wine produced during the Ginestet reign, the
·　　 1971 is best consumed immediately for what little fruit it has
70　　 remaining. Light ruby, browning badly at the edges, the simple,
　　　 light, fruity bouquet and diluted flavors are hardly inspirational,
　　　 and definitely not what one expects from one of Bordeaux's fabu-
　　　 lously expensive first-growths. Last tasted, 1/91.

1970—The 1970 is better than the 1971 or 1975, but certainly exceeded
·　　 in quality by most of the classified growths of the Médoc, not to
76　　 mention a good number of Crus Bourgeois. From a great vintage
　　　 this is certainly the type of wine to foster consumer ill-will toward
　　　 expensive, presumably "great" first-growth Bordeaux. Compact,
　　　 austere, lacking fruit and richness, this wine has adequate color
　　　 and tannins, but not much flesh to cover the bones. Time may
　　　 help, but then again, it may not. Anticipated maturity: Now—may
　　　 be in decline. Last tasted, 9/83.

1967—Light, charming, and fruity in 1974, beginning to thin out and
·　　 drop its fruit in 1978, and in total disarray in 1991, the 1967
67　　 Margaux is now way past its prime. Last tasted, 1/91.

1966—This has always been one of the best examples of Margaux during
·　　 its period of mediocrity. Too light for a wine of first-growth stan-
83　　 dards, it has continued to exhibit some of the fabulous fragrance
　　　 for which Margaux is famous. Soft, round, fruity flavors are
　　　 suggestive of herbs, cedar, mushrooms, plums, and caramel.
　　　 Fully mature, this wine should be drunk up. Anticipated maturity:
　　　 Now—1994. Last tasted, 1/91.

1964—The 1964 Margaux is a chunky specimen, with good color, but a
·　　 rather dumb, old grapey aroma, a fleshy, tannic texture, but quite
78　　 curiously, no real resemblance to a wine from Margaux. Perplex-
　　　 ing, but drinkable. Anticipated maturity: Now—probably in seri-
　　　 ous decline. Last tasted, 9/77.

1962—This wine should be enjoyed now for the gorgeous, fully mature,
  ·   and quickly evaporating bouquet. It is beginning to decline for
 85   sure, but the full, intensely cedary, fruity bouquet has merits.
          The flavors are soft, and I detect some acidity beginning to poke
          its ugly head through. Drink up! Anticipated maturity: Now–
          1994. Last tasted, 1/91.
1961—The 1961 is a top-flight wine and unquestionably the last great
  ·   Margaux until the Mentzelopoulos era began its remarkable string
 93   of great Margaux in 1978. An intense bouquet filled with the
          scents of ripe plums, flowers, toasted walnuts, and oak is divine.
          This expansive wine is silky, rich, very generously flavored, long,
          and full bodied on the palate. Fully mature, but there is little
          chance of this wine falling apart for at least another decade. I
          have high hopes that the 1982, 1983, and 1986 will ultimately
          surpass this vintage of Margaux. Anticipated maturity: Now–
          1996. Last tasted, 4/91.

OLDER VINTAGES

In 1988 in Paris, I had the opportunity to taste some of Margaux's
magnificent old vintages. The wine of the tasting was the 1900 (a perfect
100), which, if the château's records are correct, had almost identical
technical statistics as the more recent 1982. The wine apparently drank
well young, yet at 88 years of age exhibited no signs of cracking up. It
was sumptuous, expansive, and truly mind blowing. The other great
wines in that tasting were the 1928 (97), 1945 (94), and of course, the
spectacular and legendary 1953 (96). Unless they have magnums or larger
formats, owners of the 1953 should be drinking this wine as it seems near
the brink of decline. But it is still a majestically perfumed, extremely
soft, velvety wine that is, to my mind, the quintessential expression of
Margaux. The 1928 remains amazingly youthful, and I pity those who
purchased this wine during the thirties in the hope that it would reach its
peak during their lifetimes. The extremely powerful and tannic 1945
remains an impressive wine, although it is not among my favorite vintages. There is no rush to drink it.

In 1989, I had a chance to taste the 1947 on two occasions and the
1949 once. I was surprised at just how good the 1947 (rated 92) is because
I had never been that impressed with most of the wines from the Médoc
in that vintage. Among the first-growths in 1947, it is superior to Lafite
and Latour, and just behind the great Mouton. Quite perfumed, rich,
and full bodied, the 1947 Margaux is capable of another decade of evo-

lution. Moreover, there is none of the volatile acidity or harshness that often creeps into many of the Médocs from that year. The 1949 was disappointing, but perhaps it was the bottle I had.

In April 1991, I had the 1926, 1928, and 1929 vintages of Margaux from a private collection in Bordeaux. The 1929 was fading badly, the 1926 spicy, coarse, and unappealing, but the 1928 was once again magnificent. It is an immortal claret.

MARQUIS D'ALESME-BECKER (Third-Growth)　　　AVERAGE

Production: 5,000 cases	Grape varieties:
	Merlot—40%
	Cabernet Sauvignon—30%
	Cabernet Franc—20%
	Petit Verdot—10%
Secondary label: none	
Vineyard size: 22.2 acres	Proprietor: Jean-Claude Zuger
Time spent in barrels: 12 months	Average age of vines: 25 years
Evaluation of present classification: Should be downgraded to a	
Médoc Grand Bourgeois Exceptionnel	
Plateau of maturity: 4–10 years following the vintage	

This small vineyard produces one of the most obscure wines in the famous classification of 1855. The château itself is a beautiful Victorian mansion sitting opposite the mayor's office in the village of Margaux. It has, since 1979, been run by Jean-Claude Zuger, the brother of Roger Zuger, the proprietor of the better-known nearby Margaux château of Malescot St.-Exupéry. So little is known about this wine in the export markets because virtually all the production is sold directly to private customers in France, Switzerland, and Belgium. On the occasions I have had to taste the wine, I have been surprised, given the high percentage of Merlot employed at this property, that the wine is not fuller and more plump. In fact, looking at the actual winemaking process, the maceration period is relatively long, and Zuger claims that the wine is not filtered prior to bottling. Why it does not have more extract and flavor remains a mystery. Nevertheless, Marquis d'Alesme-Becker does have admirers. There is probably no keener observer of the Bordeaux wine scene than Bernard Ginestet, and he is clearly a fan of this property's wines.

Jean-Claude Zuger has invested significantly in upgrading the cellars and vineyards since 1979. But I am yet to be persuaded that this wine merits its reputation in the 1855 classification.

VINTAGES

1988—Medium ruby, with a one-dimensional, curranty, plummy bou-
•   quet, this relatively light, medium-bodied, monolithic Margaux
80   should be consumed over the next 5–7 years. Where is the famed
       Margaux fragrance and velvety, enthralling texture? Anticipated
       maturity: Now–1998. Last tasted, 1/91.

1986—Medium ruby, with a spicy, slightly herbaceous, relatively non-
•   descript bouquet, this medium-bodied, moderately tannic wine
78   lacks charm, as well as fat and concentration. It appears to be
       the product of indifferent winemaking. Anticipated maturity:
       Now–1998. Last tasted, 1/91.

1985—Moderately dark ruby, with an attractive, yet light-intensity bou-
•   quet of blackcurrants, spring flowers, and spicy oak. In the
83   mouth, the wine is soft, medium bodied, and charming. Its rela-
       tively short finish suggests early consumption. Anticipated matu-
       rity: Now–1994. Last tasted, 1/91.

1983—Medium ruby with some amber at the edge, this spicy, medium-
•   bodied wine has a curranty, slightly weedy bouquet, followed by
83   flavors that are solid yet uninspiring and somewhat dominated by
       acidity and tannin in the finish. Anticipated maturity: Now–1995.
       Last tasted, 1/91.

1982—The 1982 is solid and reliable, with an advanced, medium ruby
•   color, a moderately intense blackberry, oaky bouquet, and soft,
81   loosely knit flavors. It requires drinking. Anticipated maturity:
       Now–1993. Last tasted, 4/91.

1979—Ruby with some amber at the edge, the 1979 has a ripe curranty
•   bouquet intermingled with the scents of tar, oak, and herbs. This
78   medium-bodied wine is beginning to reveal some astringent tan-
       nins in the finish, and may be drying out. Drink up. Anticipated
       maturity: Now–may be in decline. Last tasted, 1/91.

1978—A solid effort, the 1978 has an old woodsy aroma, a faint perfume
•   of berry fruit, a round, charming, forward fruitiness, and a some-
80   what short finish. Anticipated maturity: Now–may be in decline.
       Last tasted, 6/84.

1975—The 1975 is an average-quality wine, but somewhat bland and
•   simple. Straightforward fruity flavors, some spicy oak aromas,
77   and a rather hard, sharp finish offer little excitement. Anticipated
       maturity: Now–may be in decline. Last tasted, 5/84.

MARQUIS-DE-TERME (Fourth-Growth)   VERY GOOD

Production: 12,000 cases	Grape varieties: Cabernet Sauvignon—45% Merlot—35% Cabernet Franc—15% Petit Verdot—5%
Secondary label: Domaine des Gondats	
Vineyard size: 86 acres	Proprietor: The Sénéclauze family
Time spent in barrels: 18–24 months	Average age of vines: 28 years
Evaluation of present classification: Should be maintained, possibly elevated based on the quality since 1983	
Plateau of maturity: 7–20 years following the vintage	

One of the least known and—until several years ago—one of the most disappointing classified growths of Margaux, Marquis-de-Terme has had an infusion of much-needed money to modernize the cellars and put the wine in 50% new wood. The owners have also instituted a stricter selection policy with the introduction of a secondary wine.

The quality since 1983 has improved significantly. If the recent vintages since are indicative of the new style, claret enthusiasts should anticipate a deeply colored, more forceful style of Margaux that perhaps most resembles that of Giscours.

VINTAGES

1989—The 1989 is a very good wine, dark ruby, medium to full bodied,
·   fleshy, and chewy, with low acidity and high alcohol. It should
86   develop quickly. Anticipated maturity: 1992–2004. Last tasted,
       4/91.

1988—The 1988 does not have the high glycerin and spongy texture of
·   the 1989, but offers a medium-bodied, elegant, moderately rich
85   glass of claret. Anticipated maturity: 1993–2002. Last tasted,
       4/91.

1986—Consistently impressive from its early days, the 1986 exhibits a
·   nearly black color, enormous richness and depth, sensational ex-
90?   tract, and an extremely long finish. However, prospective pur-
       chasers should be aware that on four occasions I have had bottles
       that were flawed by a smell of damp cardboard, which, in my
       opinion, suggests a problem with the corks. The wine is excep-

tional, and clearly the finest made at this property in decades, but I wonder how much of the production has been affected by whatever is causing the off odor and taste. Anticipated maturity: 1996–2015. Last tasted, 1/91.

1985—The 1985 displays a great concentration of fruit, full body, a super
·   finish, and considerable aging potential. It has turned out to be
88   one of the best Margaux's of 1985. Anticipated maturity: 1992–
         2003. Last tasted, 3/89.

1984—Rather tannic and hard for a 1984, this wine could use 2–3 years
·   of bottle age to open up. Medium to dark ruby, spicy yet tight,
79   the flavors and impression in the mouth are of narrowness. Antic-
         ipated maturity: Now–1994. Last tasted, 10/88.

1983—This is a classic Bordeaux, with a deep ruby color, an emerging
·   bouquet of vanilla, coffee, and black currants, rich, highly ex-
88   tracted fruit, medium body, and a long, moderately tannic finish.
         Anticipated maturity: 1993–2007. Last tasted, 1/91.

1979—Given the château's reputation for producing rather tough,
·   brawny wines, I would have expected this wine to be more back-
82   ward and tannic. Not so. Fragrant, earthy, berry-like aromas
         jump from the glass. Precocious, fruity, and soft, this medium-
         bodied wine should be drunk up. Anticipated maturity: Now–
         1993. Last tasted, 4/84.

1978—This is a rather unimpressive wine from a vintage that was gen-
·   erally excellent for the wines of the Médoc. Dirty, musty, unclean
50   aromas suggest an unkempt wine cellar. On the palate, the wine
         is thin, tastes of mold, and is quite unattractive. A flawed effort.
         Last tasted, 6/83.

1971—Pungent, earthy, smoky aromas intermingle with ripe blackcur-
·   rant scents to provide a rather exotic bouquet. On the palate, the
80   wine is fully mature, soft, much lighter than one would expect
         from the bouquet, and ready to drink. Anticipated maturity:
         Now–probably in serious decline. Last tasted, 2/80.

1970—Very backward, almost opaque ruby in color, with a rich, deep,
·   intense bouquet of spicy oak, smoky fruit, and earthy scents.
84   Dense, powerful, and tannic, and perhaps too robust for its own
         good, this full-bodied wine should age well for another 10–12
         years. Anticipated maturity: Now–may be in decline. Last tasted,
         4/82.

MARSAC-SÉGUINEAU (Cru Bourgeois)　　　　　　VERY GOOD

Production: 3,500 cases	Grape varieties: Merlot—60% Cabernet Sauvignon—28% Cabernet Franc—12%
Secondary label: Gravières-de- 　Marsac	
Vineyard size: 25 acres	Proprietor: Société Civile Administrator: Jean-Pierre 　Angliviel de la Beaudelle
Time spent in barrels: 16–18 　months	Average age of vines: 25 years
Evaluation of present classification: An up and coming estate that is 　now one of the best of the Margaux Cru Bourgeois	
Plateau of maturity: 5–15 years following the vintage	

In the last year, I have had a chance to taste a half-dozen vintages of Marsac-Séguineau, which is controlled by the *négociant* Mestrezat. With a relatively high percentage of Merlot in the blend, the wine is darkly colored, tannic, surprisingly intense, and rich. The two most recent top vintages include a first-class 1990, and a very smooth, large-scaled 1989. This property requires further investigation by consumers looking for excellent wines from the underachieving appellation of Margaux. The entire 25 acre vineyard is located in the commune of Soussans.

MARTINENS (Cru Bourgeois)　　　　　　AVERAGE

Production: 7,500 cases	Grape varieties: Merlot—40% Cabernet Sauvignon—30% Petit Verdot—20% Cabernet Franc—10%
Secondary label: none	
Vineyard size: 75 acres	Proprietors: Simone Dulos and 　Jean-Pierre Seynat-Dulos
Time spent in barrels: 12–18 　months	Average age of vines: 18 years
Evaluation of present classification: Should be maintained	
Plateau of maturity: 3–10 years following the vintage	

I have tasted this wine infrequently, and have never tried an old vintage. Recent years, such as 1989, 1988, 1986, and 1985, have all been abrasively hard, tough-textured wines lacking charm, fruit, and depth. The exceptionally high percentage of Petit Verdot (which rarely ripens except in years such as 1982 and 1989) may account for this wine's stern personality.

MONBRISON (Cru Bourgeois)   EXCELLENT

Production: 5,500 cases	Grape varieties: Merlot—35% Cabernet Sauvignon—30% Cabernet Franc—30% Petit Verdot—5%
Secondary label: Cordat	
Vineyard size: 35 acres	Proprietor: Elizabeth Davis Administrator: Jean-Luc Vonderheyden
Time spent in barrels: 18–22 months	Average age of vines: 20 years
Evaluation of present classification: Should be upgraded to a Médoc third-growth, perhaps higher	
Plateau of maturity: 5–15 years following the vintage	

Which vineyard in the appellation of Margaux has the lowest yields per hectare? No, it is not Château Margaux, nor is it one of the area's plentiful classified growths. It is the Cru Bourgeois, Château Monbrison. This 35-acre estate, acquired by Robert Meacham-Davis in 1921, is now owned by his daughter. Fortunately, one of her sons, Jean-Luc Vonderheyden, is one of the most dedicated wine producers in the Médoc. His extraordinary discipline in keeping production to no more than 35–40 hectoliters per hectare should be emulated by some of his more-famous, perhaps more-greedy, neighbors. By harvesting late and breaking the budget to buy new oak barrels, this superb winemaker has taken Monbrison and made it into one of the shining new stars in the Bordeaux firmament. Some observers, most notably France's Michel Bettane (probably Europe's finest and most outspoken wine critic), suggested in 1990 that if a realistic classification of the Margaux appellation was done, not on the potential of the vineyards, but on the quality of the wines, the top three would be Château Margaux, Rausan-Ségla, and Monbrison!

This is one of those properties where the price can only go up, but it will still never have quite the cache of a classified growth, even though the quality since 1983 has easily been the equivalent of most third- and fourth-growths, and in vintages such as 1988 and 1989, Monbrison is close to a third-growth in quality. Bravo!

VINTAGES

1989—The black/purple-colored 1989 is fabulous. It reveals none of the
·   problems that many Margaux châteaux encountered in 1989.
89   While extremely tannic and backward, it has good acidity, stu-
       pendous concentration and length, as well as the potential to age
       for 20 or more years. Anticipated maturity: 1994–2010. Last
       tasted, 4/91.

1988—The 1988 is indeed a special wine. Black/ruby in color, but not as
·   opaque as the 1989, this highly extracted, rich, concentrated wine
90   surpasses most of the classified growths of Margaux in quality.
       The use of 60% new oak commendably supports the wine's rich-
       ness and size. While the 1989 is a bigger wine, more alcoholic,
       more tannic, and more concentrated, I do believe the 1988 is
       equivalent, but differently styled. Anticipated maturity: 1994–
       2005. Last tasted, 4/91.

1986—The 1986 is a powerful, rich wine, with a great deal of spicy, new
·   oak, aromas of plums and licorice, full body, plenty of extract and
87   flavor depth, and a deep ruby/purple color. There is enough tan-
       nin to suggest extended cellaring is possible. Anticipated matu-
       rity: 1992–2003. Last tasted, 4/91.

1985—The 1985 is rich and full, but nicely balances deep fruit with an
·   elegant bouquet of spicy oak and berries. On the palate, the wine
86   is soft, creamy, and tasty. Anticipated maturity: Now–1996. Last
       tasted, 11/89.

1984—A sleeper of the vintage? Rather amazingly good color for the
·   year, the intense, ripe, herbaceous, blackcurrant bouquet is fol-
86   lowed by a smooth, velvety, concentrated wine with heaps of
       fruit, medium body, and an aftertaste. Anticipated maturity:
       Now–1994. Last tasted, 3/88.

1983—The 1983 Monbrison is the first in a series of very good to out-
·   standing wines from this estate. The wine has shed much of the
86   tannin and now reveals an open-knit, spicy, toasty, curranty nose,
       soft, nearly fat, round flavors, and ample body and alcohol in its
       moderate length. Anticipated maturity: Now–1995. Last tasted,
       3/90.

PALMER (Third-Growth)

Production: 13,000 cases	Grape varieties: Cabernet Sauvignon—55% Merlot—40% Cabernet Franc—5%
Secondary label: Réserve du Général	
Vineyard size: 111 acres	Proprietors: Mahler-Besse, Peter A. Sichel, and Bertrand Bouteiller
Time spent in barrels: 18–24 months	Average age of vines: 35 years
Evaluation of present classification: Should be upgraded to a Médoc first-growth	
Plateau of maturity: 5–25 years following the vintage	

The impressive turreted château of Palmer is majestically situated adjacent to Bordeaux's Route du Vin (D2), in the middle of the tiny village of Issan. It is a worthy spot to stop for a photograph. More important to wine enthusiasts is the fact that the château also produces one of Bordeaux's greatest wines.

The château takes its name from an English general who served under Wellington and arrived in Bordeaux with his army in 1814. He subsequently purchased the property, which was then called Château de Gascq, and began an extensive program of land acquisition and vineyard planting. In less than two decades the property became known as Château Palmer. Sadly, Charles Palmer, who did so much to create this estate, saw his fortune dissipate, became bankrupt, and had been forced out of Château Palmer by a bank foreclosure at the time of his death in 1836. The property has, since 1939, been owned by a syndicate involving Peter A. Sichel, the Mahler-Besse family, and four other participants, the most notable of whom is Bertrand Bouteiller, who manages the day-to-day affairs of Palmer.

Palmer can often be every bit as profound as any of the first-growths. In vintages such as 1961, 1966, 1967, 1970, 1975, 1983, and 1989 it can be better than many of them. While Palmer is officially a third-growth, the wine sells at a price level between the first- and second-growths, no doubt reflecting the high respect Bordeaux merchants, foreign importers, and consumers throughout the world have for this wine.

Palmer is still a traditionally made wine and the enviable track record of success is no doubt attributable to a number of factors. There is the dedication of the Chardon family, who has been making the wine and caring for the vineyard for over a century. Additionally, the *cépage* (blend of grapes) at Palmer is unique in that a very high percentage of Merlot (40%) is used to make the wine. This high proportion of Merlot no doubt accounts for Palmer's Pomerol-like richness, suppleness, and generous, fleshy character. However, its compelling fragrance is quintessentially Margaux. Thirdly, Palmer has one of the longest maceration periods (20–28 days), wherein the grape skins stay in contact with the grape juice. This explains the richness of color, excellent extract, and abundant tannins that are found in most vintages of Palmer. Finally, this is one of only a handful of Médoc properties that remain adamantly against the filtration of their wine.

Palmer consistently made the best wine of the Margaux appellation between 1961 and 1977, but the resurgence of Château Margaux in 1978, which has now taken the place at the top of the Margaux hierarchy, has —for the moment—left Palmer in the runner-up spot, although Palmer's 1989 is clearly superior to that of Margaux.

The style of Palmer's wine is one characterized by a sensational fragrance and bouquet. I have always felt that Palmer's great vintages (1961, 1966, 1970, 1983, and 1989) can often be identified in blind tastings by smell alone. The bouquet has the forward fruity richness of a great Pomerol, but the complexity and character of a Margaux. The wine's texture is rich, often supple and lush, but always deeply fruity and concentrated.

VINTAGES

1989—Palmer has done a magnificent job with their 1989. Viewed last
·   year, it was a wine of immense seduction, but it has, as Palmer
96   so often does, put on considerable weight and now also reveals
        wonderful structure. The expansive, rich, fat texture owes its
        opulence to the high percentage of Merlot used by this property.
        Opaque deep ruby/purple, this full-bodied, satiny wine has considerable alcoholic clout, is low in acidity, but splendidly concentrated and abundantly full of velvety tannins. It will be fascinating
        to see if this wine ultimately rivals the great Palmers made in
        1983, 1970, 1966, and 1961. This is a thrilling 1989! Anticipated
        maturity: 1993–2012. Last tasted, 4/91.

1988—The 1988 offers a promising bouquet of ripe plums, has dense,
·   rich, concentrated fruit, and medium body, but I was surprised
86   by the relatively short finish. Nevertheless, this is one of the best
        wines of the Margaux appellation in 1988. Anticipated maturity:
        1994–2006. Last tasted, 4/91.

1987—The 1987 Palmer is a star of the vintage in the Margaux appella-
· tion. It is a splendidly ripe, nearly opulent wine, exhibiting a great
86 deal of toasty new oak, low acidity, excellent color, and medium
body. No doubt the high percentage of Merlot used by Palmer
worked to their advantage in this charming, deliciously fruity
wine. Anticipated maturity: Now–1999. Last tasted, 11/90.

1986—The 1986 has much more depth than the lighter, softer 1985, and
· has the most tannin and structure of any Palmer since 1975. Its
89 deep ruby/purple color offers up a soft, plummy bouquet, followed
by a concentrated, fleshy wine that has excellent length, and very
good aging potential. Anticipated maturity: 1993–2010. Last
tasted, 3/90.

1985—The 1985 Palmer is a good wine, but it displays a little dilution in
· its mid-range. Deep in color, with a moderately attractive bouquet
87 of jammy fruit and oak, this is a stylish wine with a good finish,
yet it lacks the depth and grip necessary to be considered outstanding. Anticipated maturity: Now–2001. Last tasted, 11/90.

1984—This is a good, solid wine, well colored, with a plummy bouquet.
· On the palate, it lacks weight and finishes short, but there is
82 ripeness to the fruit, a seductive charm, and a precocious appeal.
Anticipated maturity: Now–1995. Last tasted, 4/90.

1983—This superb wine is shaping up as not only one of the two or three
· best wines of the vintage, but the best Palmer since the glorious
97 1961 and 1966. Dark ruby/purple, with a stupendously intense
bouquet of cedar, flowers, licorice, jammy plums, leather, and
spices, this full-bodied, exceptionally concentrated Palmer has
layer upon layer of fruit, as well as a long finish. The tannins are
high, but soft. The wine can be drunk now, although it ideally
needs another 3–4 years of cellaring. This is a magnificent Palmer! Anticipated maturity: 1994–2010. Last tasted, 5/91.

1982—This wine has generally received higher ratings from other tas-
· ters, but I still find it loosely knit, lacking grip, and not as concen-
87 trated or focused as I would expect. It is a delicious, forward
wine, with a lot of fat, blackcurrant, coffee, and fruit flavors,
some spicy new oak, and a heady, loosely knit finish. There is no
doubting the precociousness and suppleness, but I would opt for
drinking it over the next decade. Anticipated maturity: Now–
2000. Last tasted, 6/90.

1981—This is a relatively light, almost indifferent style of Palmer, lack-
· ing depth, and coming across as straightforward, with a simple
81 plummy fruitiness intermingled with scents and flavors of herbs,
oak, and cedar. It is medium bodied and austere for a Palmer.
Anticipated maturity: Now–1995. Last tasted, 6/90.

1980—Light, fruity, and straightforward, the 1980 Palmer is ready to
  ·   drink and should be appreciated for its simple charms. One might
  72   call it a picnic Palmer. Anticipated maturity: Now—probably in
       serious decline. Last tasted, 2/84.

1979—Palmer's 1979 is one of the stars of the vintage, although it has
  ·   been stubbornly slow to evolve. Still dark ruby, with no signs of
  91   aging, the once opulent bouquet is more restrained, but still ex-
       hibits flashy blackcurrant, cedar, licorice, and floral aromas. In
       the mouth, the wine is medium bodied, with excellent concentra-
       tion, some firm tannins, good acidity, and a long, exceptionally
       well delineated finish. It will be interesting to see how much
       additional opulence this wine develops once the tannins have
       melted away. It still needs several more years to reach peak.
       Anticipated maturity: 1993–2005. Last tasted, 6/90.

1978—Dark ruby, with some slight amber at the edge, the 1978 Palmer
  ·   has developed more quickly than the 1979, yet, in my opinion, it
  91   has not reached its plateau of maturity. With breathing, the en-
       thralling bouquet of cedar, truffles, and curranty fruit also offers
       up aromas of pepper and herbs. In the mouth, the wine is medium
       to full bodied, with excellent concentration, moderate tannin, and
       a spicy finish. I had thought this wine would be fully mature by
       now, but there are still some noticeable tannins that need to melt
       away. Anticipated maturity: 1992–2005. Last tasted, 3/91.

1977—Rather thin, ungenerous, and too vegetal and herbaceous, the
  ·   1977 Palmer is medium bodied, somewhat fruity, lightly tannic,
  70   and shows no harsh or bitter qualities. Anticipated maturity:
       Now—probably in serious decline. Last tasted, 4/81.

1976—A deliciously supple, fruity, plump 1976 with a smooth, soft na-
  ·   ture and little tannins, this Palmer is fully mature and has ade-
  83   quate fruit. Unlike many frail, somewhat diluted wines of this
       vintage. Anticipated maturity: Now—may be in decline. Last
       tasted, 8/84.

1975—Over a period of several years, I have had this wine nearly a dozen
  ·   times. In the most interesting tasting, when it was served from an
  91   Imperial, the wine was more evolved than any of the regular-sized
       bottles I tasted. The opposite should be true if you believe that
       larger formats age more slowly. I tend to think they do, but I have
       often heard that the custom-made corks that are required for the
       largest bottles, such as the Jeroboams and Imperials, are often
       loosely fitted, permitting oxygen to get into the wine. In any event,
       this is a superb Palmer, as well as one of the top wines of the
       vintage. It is nearly ready to drink, exhibiting a magnificent bou-

quet of expansive, superripe cassis fruit, cedar, violets, truffles, and oak. In the mouth, the wine is medium to full bodied, rich, with only a trace of the rough tannins so prevalent in many wines of this vintage, and has a heady, lush finish. This is turning out to be one of the best 1975s made in the Médoc. Anticipated maturity: 1993–2008. Last tasted, 5/91.

1974—In this poor vintage, Palmer produced a very mediocre wine with
·   brownish color, a stringy, lean, weak, bland character, and little
64   fruit in evidence. Last tasted, 2/78.

1971—While certainly not in the same class as the 1979, 1975, 1970, and
·   1966, Palmer's reputation for quality and finesse is hardly in dan-
86   ger as a result of this effort. Fully mature, with a good dark ruby
      color, the highly touted Palmer bouquet of berries, flowers, and cassis is readily perceptible. A silky, lush wine, it has been at its peak for over a decade. Anticipated maturity: Now–1994. Last tasted, 12/88.

1970—At age 20 this extraordinary Palmer is just beginning to reach its
·   plateau of maturity. The color is still deep, dark ruby, with only a
95   hint of amber. The spectacular bouquet offers up an exotic con-
      coction of cedar, oriental spices, vanillin oak, and gobs of super-ripe black fruits. In the mouth, the wine has exceptional precision to its medium-bodied, intensely concentrated flavors. The finish is fabulous, and must last for at least one minute. This is a great Palmer that, with another 3–5 years of cellaring, may reach the heights of the nearly perfect 1966 and 1961. Anticipated maturity: Now–2010. Last tasted, 12/90.

1967—The 1967 Palmer reached its zenith several years ago,but seems
·   to be holding ground without losing any of the marvelous per-
86   fumed bouquet and soft, spicy, attractive, medium-weight flavors.
      A very charming, complex wine, it should be drunk up. Antici-pated maturity: Now–1993. Last tasted, 6/84.

1966—This wine continues to be one of the greatest examples of Palmer
·   I have ever tasted. It is almost atypical for the 1966 vintage, which
96   produced so many austere, angular wines. Not only rich and full,
      it is also delicate and loaded with complexity and finesse. This wine gets my nod as one of the best of the vintage, rivaled only by Latour and Lafleur. The haunting bouquet is similar to that already found in the 1961, and those that—with more cellaring—will undoubtedly develop in the 1970 and 1983. It has a plummy, mulberry-like fruitiness, exotic spices, licorice, and a hint of truf-fles. Medium bodied, with a velvety richness, it has a long, ripe, lush finish, and enough grip and focus to continue to drink well

for another decade. Anticipated maturity: Now–2000. Last tasted, 6/91.

1964— A straightforward, somewhat awkward wine with none of Pal-
·   mer's best qualities—the great bouquet, the fleshy texture, and
75   the generous, plummy fruitiness—apparent in this medium-
        bodied, coarsely made wine. Anticipated maturity: Now–proba-
        bly in serious decline. Last tasted, 2/78.

1962— Thanks to several generous subscribers, I was able to taste this
·   wine twice since my original review in *Bordeaux*, where I clearly
89   underrated it. In both bottles the wine exhibited full maturity and
        had a super bouquet, with that Palmer fragrance that is so pene-
        trating and enveloping. In the mouth, the wine is all velvet, with
        soft, medium-bodied flavors, and a moderately long, silky finish.
        This wine should clearly be drunk up, but I suspect it has been at
        its plateau of full maturity since the late seventies. Anticipated
        maturity: Now–1995. Last tasted, 6/90.

1961— I have always felt fortunate to have a friend who bought cases of
·   this wine when it was available for a song. I have also been for-
96   tunate to have had this wine on two or three occasions nearly
        every year of the last decade. I have seen it reach its peak in the
        mid-1980s, and then be somewhat unpredictable over the next 3–
        4 years. The best bottles are still profoundly superb, with a degree
        of richness and opulence that one only sees in great vintages such
        as 1982 and 1961. In fact, the last bottle I had is as stunning a
        1961 Palmer as ever. I rated it 98. However, most bottles seem to
        fall in the 94–96 category and the wine should probably be con-
        sumed before the turn of the century. Never anything less than
        superb, the bouquet is extraordinarily full of black fruits, spices,
        oak, minerals, cedar, and coffee. In the mouth, the wine has that
        compelling multidimensional richness and expansive, sweet,
        powerful finish. It is a magnificent wine, and everything its repu-
        tation suggests. Anticipated maturity: Now–2000. Last tasted,
        12/90.

OLDER VINTAGES

The four great older Palmers I have had a chance to taste were all drunk in the last several years. The 1959 (rated 93) is not far off the quality of the 1961. It is a denser, more structured wine and seems actually less evolved than the 1961. Whether it ever fully develops the incredible fragrance and sweetness of the 1961 remains to be seen, but it is a full-bodied, rich, concentrated, deeply colored, muscular Palmer. While I never had a great bottle of either the 1955 or 1953, in Bordeaux in March 1990, I tasted a 1949 (93) that was fully developed and had an incredibly hedonistic, opulent, texture. I would not push my luck by holding on to it much longer, but if this bottle was typical of the 1949 Palmer, it is a superb wine. In April 1991, I finally tasted the legendary 1945 (rated 97). The wine had none of the harsh, astringent tannins that plague many wines in the vintage. It was splendidly fat, rich with an opulent texture and remarkable vigor and youthfulness. Peter Sichel told me the wine has drunk well since the early fifties! The other great Palmer I had an opportunity to taste was the 1928 (96). This wine, from a vintage that has taken a good 30–40 years to shed its tannin, was still amazingly youthful and structured, as well as a powerful, rich, dazzling bottle of wine. It gave every sign of being capable of lasting for another two decades. Pity the poor consumers who purchased the 1928 when it was released, thinking it would be ready to drink in their lifetime!

PAVEIL-DE-LUZE (Cru Bourgeois)   AVERAGE

Production: 10,000 cases	Grape varieties: Cabernet Sauvignon—70% Merlot—30%
Secondary label: de la Coste Vineyard size: 60 acres Time spent in barrels: 12–15 months	Proprietor: G.F.A. du Château Average age of vines: 20 years
Evaluation of present classification: Should be maintained	
Plateau of maturity: 3–9 years following the vintage	

I have always found the wines of this estate to be bland and undistinguished. Recent tastings from vintages in the late eighties suggest nothing has changed. The Baron Geoffroy de Luze and his three children administer this charming property that has been in the de Luze family for over a century.

POUGET (Fourth-Growth)   AVERAGE

Production: 4,500 cases	Grape varieties: Cabernet Sauvignon—66% Merlot—30% Petit Verdot—4%
Secondary label: none	
Vineyard size: 24.7 acres	Proprietor: Pierre Guillemet
Time spent in barrels: 22–24 months	Average age of vines: 40 years
Evaluation of present classification: Should be downgraded to a fifth-growth	
Plateau of maturity: 5–15 years following the vintage	

Pouget is owned and managed by Pierre Guillemet, the proprietor of Boyd-Cantenac, a much more sizable and better-known Margaux estate. Pouget's wines are vinified in exactly the same way as Boyd-Cantenac. Therefore, it is not surprising that the style of Pouget is sturdy and robust, deeply colored, somewhat coarse, but concentrated.

VINTAGES

1989—Fat, chunky, and beefy, the 1989 lacks complexity, but does offer
·   a generous mouthful of wine. Low acidity, soft tannins, and very
85   high alcohol suggest that this wine should be drunk early. Antici-
        pated maturity: Now–1997. Last tasted, 11/90.

1988—The 1988 Pouget is more compact, less concentrated, and tastes
·   too one-dimensional to elicit much enthusiasm. Anticipated ma-
84   turity: Now–1996. Last tasted, 11/90.

1986—Deep in color, with a dull, indifferent bouquet, this medium-bod-
·   ied wine has plenty of tannin, adequate depth, but little charm or
75   complexity. Anticipated maturity: 1992–1998. Last tasted, 3/90.

1978—A rather perplexing wine, the 1978 Pouget has a very deep, richly
·   pigmented color. On the palate, the wine offers little of the deep,
74   rich fruit implied by the color, but rather has very woody, hard,
        tough flavors that seem unusually severe and backward. I suspect
        the fruit will fade before the tannins. Anticipated maturity: Now–
        1994. Last tasted, 3/88.

1975—The intriguing bouquet of ripe blackcurrant fruit, spicy oak, and
·   mineral scents is top notch. In the mouth, the wine is typically
84   1975, very tannic, severe, hard, and remarkably backward. The
        color is dark and a good concentration of fruit is present, but one

must wait a very long time for this wine to mature. Anticipated maturity: 1992–2000. Last tasted, 5/84.

1974 —A surprisingly good wine for this vintage, the 1974 Pouget has
· good fruit, a chunky texture, some hard tannins to lose, but a
79 healthy ruby color, a good, spicy, curranty bouquet, and an adequate, yet firm finish. Drink up. Anticipated maturity: Now–probably in serious decline. Last tasted, 1/81.

1971 —A lightweight, less-tannic, less-intense version of the 1970, the
· 1971 Pouget is mature, velvety, still holding its fruit, and very
84 attractive, as well as being well made. Anticipated maturity:
Now–probably in serious decline. Last tasted, 2/81.

1970 —A big, rich, solidly constructed, deep, flavorful, somewhat force-
· ful wine, the 1970 Pouget has still not reached its maturity pla-
83 teau. Lacking finesse in favor of power and robustness, this is a
gutsy, rustic-styled Margaux. Anticipated maturity: Now–1993.
Last tasted, 3/83.

PRIEURÉ-LICHINE (Fourth-Growth) VERY GOOD

Production: 23,000–30,000 cases	Grape varieties:
	Cabernet Sauvignon—44%
	Merlot—44%
	Cabernet Franc—6%
	Petit Verdot—6%
Secondary label: Clairefont	
Vineyard size: 148.2 acres	Proprietor: Sacha Lichine
Time spent in barrels: 16–18 months	Average age of vines: 33 years
Evaluation of present classification: Should be maintained	
Plateau of maturity: 5–15 years following the vintage	

The only major château in the Médoc open to tourists seven days a week every week of the year, Prieuré-Lichine was the beloved home of Alexis Lichine, the world-famous wine writer, wine authority, and promoter of the wines of Bordeaux who died in June 1989. Lichine purchased Prieuré in 1951 and began an extensive program of improvements that included tripling the vineyard area. I have always thought that harvest time here must be an incredibly complex operation because Prieuré-Lichine's vineyard is among the most morsellated in the Médoc, with in excess of several dozen parcels spread throughout the vast appellation of Margaux.

The wine of Prieuré tends to be made in a modern, yet intelligent style. It is supple, quick to mature, but has enough tannin and, in good vintages, substance to age well for 8–12 years. The price has always been reasonable.

Since the death of his father, the young Sacha Lichine has taken over the running of this lovely ivy-covered, onetime Benedictine priory. The young Lichine has indicated that he will be producing a wine with more concentration, body, and potential longevity and his intentions appear confirmed with the 1989 vintage. This change is probably in response to a number of critics who have argued that many vintages of Prieuré-Lichine were somewhat light for the reputation of this classified growth. To accomplish his objectives, Lichine has increased the percentage of Merlot in the vineyards, and in 1990 hired the famed oenologist Michel Rolland.

VINTAGES

1989—The 1989 Prieuré-Lichine is one of the richest and fullest wines
·   this property has made in the last three decades. Substantial in
88   size, with gobs of ripe currant fruit, full body, soft, plentiful tan-
         nins, and a heady alcohol degree, this velvety wine should prove
         charming early in its life, but easily last for 15 or more years.
         Sacha Lichine employed 60% new oak in 1989, which he believes
         is essential to support the rich fruit. Anticipated maturity: 1993–
         2005. Last tasted, 4/91.

1988—The 1988 is a light- to medium-bodied wine that is perfumed and
·   well balanced. It avoids the overly tannic character of many 1988
86   Médocs. Medium dark ruby, it has an attractive bouquet of wood,
         currants, herbs, and minerals. Anticipated maturity: Now–2003.
         Last tasted, 4/91.

1986—The thirty-fifth vintage of Alexis Lichine's beloved château should
·   ultimately turn out to be one of the best wines he produced. In
88   fact, the fragrance and elegance may, in 5 to 6 years, entitle it to
         an even better rating. With the exception of the 1989, it is the
         most concentrated Prieuré made in the eighties, and one would
         have to go back to the lovely 1978 or 1971 to find a Prieuré with
         such class and grace. Medium to dark ruby in color, with a very
         seductive, moderately intense bouquet of plummy fruit and
         sweet, toasty oak, this surprisingly supple, yet still structured
         wine has good length and aging potential. Anticipated maturity:
         1992–2005. Last tasted, 11/90.

1985—The lightish, somewhat shallow 1985, while charming and fruity,
·   lacks grip and depth, particularly for a classified growth. Antici-
84   pated maturity: Now–1995. Last tasted, 11/90.

1984—Excessively light, with an aroma of faded tea bags, this soft,
·   shallow wine is now in complete decline. Last tasted, 2/89.
67

1983—Dark ruby, with a moderately intense aroma of ripe blackcur-
·   rants, herbs, cedar, and oak, this is a full-bodied, fleshy, yet
87   supple Prieuré with a long, rich, softly tannic finish. Anticipated
       maturity: Now–2005. Last tasted, 4/90.

1982—More austere and slightly less concentrated than the 1983, the
·   1982 Prieuré has a fragrant, ripe plum-scented bouquet, some
85   spicy oak, and a moderately intense blackcurrant aroma. On the
       palate, the wine is forwardly rich, less concentrated than I had
       hoped when tasted from cask, and is medium bodied, with a
       spicy, slightly tannic finish. Anticipated maturity: 1992–2000.
       Last tasted, 4/90.

1981—Light but attractively fruity and pleasant when young, this wine
·   has continued to lose fruit and taken on a lean, rather light-bodied
75   and underendowed personality. It is also beginning to lose charm
       and the shallow flavors suggest that immediate drinking is war-
       ranted. Anticipated maturity: Now–may be in decline. Last
       tasted, 3/89.

1980—A light ruby-colored wine with very shallow, light-intensity flavors
·   that suggest strawberries, the 1980 Prieuré is soft and one-dimen-
70   sional. Anticipated maturity: Now–probably in serious decline.
       Last tasted, 6/84.

1979—Prieuré tastes particularly light in this vintage. Nevertheless, the
·   wine is medium bodied with soft, pleasant flavors. However, it
80   finishes short. Anticipated maturity: Now–probably in serious de-
       cline. Last tasted, 6/84.

1978—One of the best efforts from Prieuré-Lichine, the 1978 is fully
·   mature and exhibits a ripe, rather rich, fruity, oaky bouquet, with
86   meaty and leathery flavors, good concentration, melted tannins,
       and a long, satisfying finish. Anticipated maturity: Now–1996.
       Last tasted, 6/91.

1977—An acceptable level of quality was reached by Prieuré in this
·   vintage. The wine has medium ruby color, the slight vegetal
73   aroma that is commonplace in the 1977 vintage, and is deficient
       in rich, fleshy fruit. Anticipated maturity: Now–probably in seri-
       ous decline. Last tasted: 4/83.

1976—This wine tasted rather unknit when young, but with age it has
·   pulled itself together (unlike many 1976s), and displays a good,
82   ripe cedary, fruity, spicy bouquet, and soft, fat, nicely concen-
       trated flavors. Anticipated maturity: Now–may be in decline.
       Last tasted, 11/84.

1975 —A typical 1975, tough, hard, and backward, the Prieuré has a
  ·   leathery, ripe fragrance. Full bodied and astringent with hard,
  83   tannic flavors, this wine is just beginning to show signs of shed-
         ding its tannins and revealing some ripe, fleshy fruit. Anticipated
         maturity: Now–1998. Last tasted, 11/84.

1971 —One of the most enjoyable Prieuré-Lichines, the 1971 has for the
  ·   last several years provided immensely satisfying drinking. Fully
  86   mature and possibly just beginning its decline, the 1971 is very
         perfumed and aromatic, with a bouquet redolent of spices, berry
         fruit, and oak. On the palate, it is soft, supple, and so, so velvety.
         Anticipated maturity: Now–1993. Last tasted, 10/89.

1970 —A delightfully fat, fruity, concentrated, velvety Margaux, with
  ·   soft, lush berryish, plummy flavors, some spicy oak, and light
  86   tannins. Fully mature, but still capable of another 4–5 years of
         cellaring, this well-made, elegant wine is quite attractive. Antici-
         pated maturity: Now–1996. Last tasted, 10/89.

1967 —Not tasted since 1980, the 1967 Prieuré-Lichine was a noteworthy
  ·   success in a year when many more famous properties made wine
  84   not nearly as good as Prieuré. Quite aromatic and plummy with a
         ripe, fruity richness. Anticipated maturity: Now–probably in se-
         rious decline. Last tasted, 1/80.

1966 —The 1966 Prieuré is a restrained, elegant, somewhat austere wine
  ·   with a moderately intense, spicy, berryish, ripe fruity bouquet.
  85   On the palate, it exhibits less of the 1966 leanness and reserved
         character, but rather soft, rich fruit, medium body, and a good
         finish. Anticipated maturity: Now–probably in serious decline.
         Last tasted, 12/80.

RAUSAN-SÉGLA (Second-Growth)   OUTSTANDING

Production: 15,000 cases	Grape varieties: Cabernet Sauvignon—66% Merlot—28% Cabernet Franc—4% Petit Verdot—2%
Secondary label: Lamouroux Vineyard size: 107 acres	Proprietor: Walker Family Trust
Time spent in barrels: 20 months	Average age of vines: 25 years
Evaluation of present classification: Should be maintained, but only since 1983	
Plateau of maturity: 7–22 years following the vintage	

Rausan-Ségla can trace its history back to 1661 when the vineyard was created by Pierre des Mesures de Rauzan, who at the time was also the owner of the vineyards that now make up Pichon-Longueville–Comtesse de Lalande and Pichon-Longueville Baron. In 1855, Rausan-Ségla was considered Bordeaux's best wine after the quartet of Premiers Grands Crus, Lafite-Rothschild, Latour, Margaux, Haut-Brion, and the top-ranked second-growth, Mouton-Rothschild. In 1973, Mouton-Rothschild was elevated and now Rausan-Ségla sits at the head of the class of the remaining fourteen second-growths. This position hardly seemed justified by the wines produced during the decades of the sixties and seventies, but the indifferent quality changed dramatically with the 1983 vintage.

Looking back, there appear to be a number of valid reasons for the disappointing wines prior to 1983. First, many of the vintages were marred by a musty, damp, almost barnyard-like aroma that is believed to have come from a bacterial infection in the old wooden vats used to ferment the wine. These were replaced in the eighties with stainless steel. Secondly, there was major replanting after the killer frost of 1956 by then-owner, Monsieur de Meslon. The replanting was largely of prolific clones of Merlot. Many of the wines made in the sixties and seventies no doubt reflected not only the young vines, but also a badly chosen clone. These plantings have been grubbed up in favor of more Cabernet Sauvignon and higher-quality Merlot. Lastly, the fact that Rausan-Ségla was sold exclusively through Eschenauer—one of Bordeaux's famous *négociants*—resulted in the wine's exclusion from the comparative tastings that are common for wines sold on the open market. Obviously, the incentive to improve quality is far greater when the wine is sold on the open market rather than through exclusive arrangements.

Since 1983, the improvements have been remarkable. In that year, Jacques Théo, formerly the head of Alexis Lichine & Company, took over the running of Rausan-Ségla. Additionally, Monsieur Pruzeau replaced the ailing Monsieur Joyeaux as *maître de chai*. The construction of a new *chai* and improvements to the winemaking facility—including the addition of the stainless-steel vats—an increased percentage of new oak, and Theo's severe selections ensuring that only the best of the crop appears in the wine have resulted in a succession of brilliant wines from Rausan-Ségla. The quality of the recent wines puts this estate clearly in the elite group of Bordeaux super seconds. Since 1983, Rausan-Ségla has done only one thing wrong. Jacques Théo irritated many of his Bordeaux peers by declaring the 1987 Bordeaux vintage disappointing. Rausan-Ségla became the first significant Médoc classified growth in decades to not produce a wine for a specific vintage—the 1987.

For the near term, this is a splendid wine worth laying in, as prices have not yet caught up with the new level of quality at this famous old estate. Whether the change in ownership in late 1989 and the discharge of Jacques Théo will negatively influence quality remains to be seen.

VINTAGES

1989—Based on its performances in 1983, 1985, 1986, 1988, and 1989,
·   Rausan-Ségla now rivals Palmer as the second-best-made wine of
90   the Margaux appellation. Quality has soared, in large part be-
     cause of the brutal selection process that ensures only the best
     juice from the vineyard's oldest vines gets into the final blend.
     The 1989 is a seductive, jammy, concentrated wine offering a
     huge bouquet of blackberries and raspberries. Voluptuous on the
     palate, with layer upon layer of fruit and extract, this silky tex-
     tured, flamboyantly styled wine should provide terrific drinking
     when young. Anticipated maturity: 1993–2012. Last tasted, 4/91.

1988—The 1988 is probably superior to the 1989. It may ultimately rival
·   the great 1986. Black/ruby in color, intensely concentrated, full
93   bodied, and tannic, it should prove to be the second-best Rausan-
     Ségla of this decade. What I especially admire about this wine is
     the wonderful purity of raspberry fruit. This is what the French
     call a classic *vin de garde*. Anticipated maturity: 1997–2012. Last
     tasted, 4/91.

1986—In 1986, less than 50% of the crop went into the *grand vin*. The
·   result is a sublime wine, splendidly dark ruby in color, with a
96   super bouquet, plenty of power and richness, and an intriguing
     complexity. Its great fragrance, extraordinary depth and length,
     and medium to full body should make believers out of many of
     those who doubt that Rausan-Ségla has returned to form. It has
     turned out to be one of the top wines of the vintage. Anticipated
     maturity: 1993–2005. Last tasted, 5/91.

1985—The 1985 is richly fruity, supple, and precocious. If it lacks struc-
·   ture and aging potential, there is little doubt that it offers deli-
87   cious near-term drinking in a medium-bodied, elegant, smooth as
     silk style. Anticipated maturity: Now–1997. Last tasted, 11/90.

1984—With good color, and a fresh, spicy, herbaceous-scented bouquet,
·   the 1984 Rausan-Ségla starts off well, but seems to drop off in the
75   mouth. One bottle tasted seemed much richer. Anticipated ma-
     turity: Now–1995. Last tasted, 3/90.

1983—This is the best vintage of Rausan-Ségla in decades. Deeply pig-
·   mented, with a rich, spicy, fragrant bouquet, and aromas and
90   flavors of blackcurrants, licorice, and spicy oak. On the palate,
     the wine is full bodied and concentrated, with excellent length.

Much of the tannin has melted away revealing an opulent, intense wine of great complexity and charm. Nevertheless, this wine can still benefit from cellaring. This is the vintage that announced the renaissance of Rausan-Ségla. Anticipated maturity: Now–2008. Last tasted, 11/90.

1982—Softer and fatter than the 1983, but not so classically propor-
·   tioned, the 1982 Rausan-Ségla is dark ruby with some amber, has
86   a ripe blackcurrant, oaky, fragrant bouquet, medium to full body, and a lush, soft finish. Anticipated maturity: Now–1995. Last tasted, 1/89.

1981—This mediocre wine is light, fruity, round, and one-dimensional.
·   Hardly a wine representative of its official Bordeaux pedigree,
65   this meager Rausan-Ségla should be drunk up. Anticipated maturity: Now–probably in serious decline. Last tasted, 6/84.

1980—The very thin, watery flavors, with a vegetal aroma, as well as
·   little depth or length all combine to make this a very undistin-
60   guished effort. Last tasted, 3/83.

1979—Quite light, round and fruity, the 1979 Rausan-Ségla resembles a
·   simple Bordeaux Supérieur. Drink up. Anticipated maturity:
72   Now–probably in serious decline. Last tasted, 4/84.

1978—True to form for many of the wines that Rausan-Ségla produced
·   in the seventies, the 1978 is fruity, round, and slightly charming,
74   but devoid of flavor interest and complexity. Anticipated maturity: Now–probably in serious decline. Last tasted, 10/82.

1977—Intensely vegetal and thin, the 1977 Rausan-Ségla is a failure.
·   Last tasted, 11/81.
50

1976—A leafy, weedy-scented wine, with light-intensity flavors, light to
·   medium ruby/garnet color, and an awkward, unbalanced feel on
60   the palate, this wine lacks richness and seems very sloppily vinified. Last tasted, 4/80.

1975—Very light in color, with a suspicious brownish cast to the color,
·   the 1975 Rausan-Ségla has a burnt, cooked-fruit aroma, shallow,
55   very tannic and astringent flavors, and a short, nasty finish. This is a pitiful effort in such a fine vintage. Last tasted, 5/84.

1972—Ironically, in this disastrous vintage, Rausan-Ségla made one of
·   the more successful wines. Surprisingly dark, yet now showing a
75   brownish-orange cast, the chunky, one-dimensional wine has good fruit and medium body. Anticipated maturity: Now–probably in serious decline. Last tasted, 7/82.

1971—Medium to light ruby, with some noticeable brown in the color,
·   this wine, which was made during a dreadful period for Rausan-
76   Ségla, still has some life to it. The herbaceous, cedary bouquet

tends to fade quickly in the glass, but there is still enough fruit and ripeness in the wine to provide some degree of charm and pleasure. However, don't push your luck as this wine is quite fragile and near collapse. Last tasted, 1/88.

1970—I am not sure this wine is ever going to open up and blossom. At
·   age 21 it is still quite dark and opaque in color, with only a slight
82   hint of amber at the edge. It is admirably big and full bodied, but rustic and coarsely textured, with entirely too much tannin in its finish. Perhaps I have consistently misread it, but having consumed three-fourths of the case I purchased, I have never gotten the pleasure from this wine that I expected. I guess the lesson is to always beware of those wines that taste hard and tannic when young. This one may still come around, but I doubt it. Anticipated maturity: Now–2000. Last tasted, 1/91.

1966—Similar in style to the 1970, only more austere and not quite as
·   concentrated, the 1966 has a ripe plummy, oaky fragrance of
84   moderate intensity, and graceful, yet still tough and firm flavors. Drinkable now, this fully mature wine will hold for 1 to 2 more years. Anticipated maturity: Now–1993. Last tasted, 4/79.

1962—This is an uncharacteristic wine for the 1962 vintage that pro-
·   duced so many elegant, charming, round, fruity wines. Hard,
75   lean, and austere, without much richness or charm, this wine's fruit has no chance of ever outdistancing the considerable tannins that are still present. Anticipated maturity: Now–probably in serious decline. Last tasted, 2/78.

1961—Not a noteworthy 1961, Rausan-Ségla is a ripe, fruity, somewhat
·   awkward and disjointed wine. While the wine tastes jammy, dif-
81   fuse, and finishes flat, it nevertheless has appeal, as well as plenty of concentration and power. Anticipated maturity: Now–may be in decline. Last tasted, 9/79.

RAUZAN-GASSIES (Second-Growth)   AVERAGE

Production: 11,000 cases	Grape varieties:
	Cabernet Sauvignon—40%
	Merlot—39%
	Cabernet Franc—20%
	Petit Verdot—1%
Secondary label: Enclos de Moncabon	
Vineyard size: 62 acres	Proprietor: The Quié family
Time spent in barrels: 17–22 months	Average age of vines: 30 years
Evaluation of present classification: Should be downgraded to a Cru Bourgeois	
Plateau of maturity: 8–20 years following the vintage	

Historically, Rauzan-Gassies was part of Rausan-Ségla until the French Revolution of 1789. Since 1943 it has belonged to the Quié family. In style, Rauzan-Gassies tends toward heaviness and corpulence for a Margaux, without the fragrance or finesse normally associated with the better wines of this commune. However, it can make fairly concentrated, powerful wines. In most vintages, the wines of Rauzan-Gassies have reached maturity surprisingly fast for a classified growth, usually within 7–8 years of the vintage. Reports continue to emanate from Bordeaux that the quality at Rauzan-Gassies is on the upswing. My tasting notes suggest that such pronouncements are excessively optimistic. The owners, who are gracious and kind people, appear to lack the willpower and ambition to produce wines of classified-growth quality. What a shame!

VINTAGES

1989—Bitter, attenuated, and frightfully tannic, the 1989 Rauzan-Gassies has consistently performed poorly in my tastings. Judgment
· reserved. Last tasted, 4/91.
?

1988—The 1988 is disappointing. Harsh tannins obliterate the fruit, and
· the overall impression created is one of hollowness, with only a
66 skeleton of acidity, wood, and tannin. Caveat emptor! Last tasted, 4/91.

1984—Quite disappointing, the 1984 is a shallow, light, insipid wine with
· no future. Last tasted, 3/89.
67

1983—Not complex, although this fat, grapey, tannic, and astringent
· wine exhibits surprising power and presence in the mouth. Four-
86 square and chunky, the 1983 is typical of Rauzan-Gassies. It

tasted like an old-style, robust St.-Estèphe. Anticipated maturity: 1993–2000. Last tasted, 11/88.

1982—Fat, plummy, velvety, and precocious, with low acidity, this for-
•   ward, tasty, but loosely knit wine is charmingly fruity and
85   straightforward. Anticipated maturity: Now–1995. Last tasted, 11/88.

1981—Surprisingly diffuse, flabby, and lacking depth, richness, and
•   structure, the 1981 is a disappointment. Anticipated maturity:
74   Now–may be in decline. Last tasted, 6/84.

1979—A corpulent, straightforward, plausible wine, with good dark ruby
•   color, a ripe black cherry, oaky bouquet of moderate intensity,
82   and soft, round, somewhat jammy flavors. Anticipated maturity: Now–1992. Last tasted, 4/83.

1978—I had several decent tasting notes on this wine in the early
•   eighties, but when tasted twice recently, the wine appeared out
72   of balance, with a light to medium ruby color, some dusty red fruit aromas, but high acidity, as well as a lack of body and depth. All of this causes me great concern over the wine's future. Antic- ipated maturity: Now–1993. Last tasted, 5/89.

1976—Diluted flavors and a lack of structure and grip have resulted in a
•   wine that tastes shallow, simple, and uninteresting. It is browning
72   badly at the rim. Anticipated maturity: Now–probably in serious decline. Last tasted, 4/83.

1975—A sleeper in this vintage, the 1975 Rauzan-Gassies may well be
•   the best wine produced in the Margaux appellation after Palmer
86   and Giscours. It has excellent dark ruby color, a deep, rich, oaky, blackcurrant-fragrant bouquet, a chewy, full-bodied, very con- centrated feel on the palate, and a tannic, long finish. Anticipated maturity: Now–2000. Last tasted, 5/84.

1970—The 1970 is a simple, one-dimensional, somewhat dull wine that
•   has adequate color, a compact bouquet of fruit and wood, and
78   soft, average, concentrated flavors. Anticipated maturity: Now– probably in serious decline. Last tasted, 4/83.

1966—Still quite lively, crisp, richly fruity, and full on the palate, the
•   1966 Rauzan-Gassies has a spicy, mushroom-like aroma, robust,
81   rather aggressive flavors, and a rather hard, coarse finish. It is an interesting, rather rustic-styled wine. Anticipated maturity: Now–probably in serious decline. Last tasted, 4/83.

1961—Certainly not to be passed by if one should come your way, the
•   Rauzan-Gassies is, however, less successful in this vintage than
85   many of its second-growth peers. Dark ruby, with significant browning at the edges, the wine has an open-knit, fully mature,

spicy, oaky, plummy, toffee-scented bouquet, moderately rich, soft, fruity flavors, and a supple, velvety finish. It is very attractive, but lighter in style than most 1961s. Anticipated maturity: Now–1994. Last tasted, 4/83.

SIRAN (Cru Bourgeois)   GOOD

Production: 12,000 cases	Grape varieties:
	Cabernet Sauvignon—50%
	Merlot—25%
	Petit Verdot—15%
	Cabernet Franc—10%
Secondary labels: Bellegarde and St.-Jacques	
Vineyard size: 86 acres	Proprietor: William Alain B. Miailhe
Time spent in barrels: 18–20 months	Average age of vines: 38 years
Evaluation of present classification: The quality equivalent of a Médoc fifth-growth	
Plateau of maturity: 5–15 years following the vintage	

This outstanding property in Labarde in the southern part of the Margaux appellation is making consistently delicious, fragrant, deeply colored wines that are frequently on a quality level with a Médoc fifth-growth.

The estate is owned and managed by William Alain B. Miailhe, a meticulous grower, who produces in an average year 12,000 cases of rich, flavorful, polished wine that admirably reflects the Margaux appellation. The wine is also distinguished by a Mouton-Rothschild–like label that boasts a different artist's painting each year.

Siran's wine usually needs 5 to 6 years of bottle age to mature properly, and recent vintages have all been quite successful, even the light, mediocre vintage of 1980 where Siran outperformed virtually all of its Margaux peers save Margaux and Giscours. Above all, this is a wine that repays the patient consumer because of its ability to support extended cellaring. The long maceration period (15–25 days) and elevated percentage of the tannic Petit Verdot in the blend give the wine at least 15 years of aging potential in top vintages.

If a new classification of the wines of the Médoc were ever done, Siran would surely be given significant consideration for inclusion as a fifth-growth.

VINTAGES

1989 —Siran remains an underrated (not underpriced, however) wine
that frequently outperforms many of the Margaux appellation's
85   more prestigious wines. The 1989 is a graceful, medium-bodied
wine displaying the vintage's soft, silky texture, plenty of alcohol,
low acidity, and aging potential of 4–8 years. Anticipated maturity: 1992–2000. Last tasted, 4/91.

1988 —The 1988 appears to be better than the 1989. Deep ruby in color,
with a spicy, blackcurrant-scented bouquet, it is a full-bodied
86   wine with more depth and structure. Anticipated maturity: 1992–
2005. Last tasted, 4/91.

1986 —With deep, dark ruby/purple color, plenty of body, as well as
mouth-searing tannins in the finish, the 1986 Siran competently
88   displays the personality characteristics of the vintage. Between
the fragrant, tarry, spicy, curranty bouquet and the hard finish is
plenty of depth and fruit. However, one must defer gratification
for at least 7–8 years before drinking the 1986 Siran. Anticipated
maturity: 1996–2010. Last tasted, 11/90.

1985 —The 1985 Siran is surprisingly powerful for the vintage, rich in
fruit, elegant, long, and aromatic. It will age well. Anticipated
86   maturity: Now–2000. Last tasted, 3/90.

1984 —One of the better wines from this appellation in 1984, the 1984
Siran has good color, an abundance of ripe, sweet fruit, a spicy,
80   moderately intense bouquet, and medium body. It is very well
made. Anticipated maturity: Now–1993. Last tasted, 3/88.

1983 —Approaching full maturity, the 1983 Siran has a smoky licorice-
and-blackcurrant-scented bouquet, rich, expansive flavors that
86   offer more muscle and power than finesse, and a good finish.
Anticipated maturity: Now–1996. Last tasted, 3/88.

TAYAC (Cru Bourgeois) AVERAGE

Production: 16,000 cases	Grape varieties: Cabernet Sauvignon—70% Merlot—25% Petit Verdot—5%
Secondary label: none	
Vineyard size: 84 acres	Proprietor: A. Favin
Time spent in barrels: 14–18 months	Average age of vines: 20 years
Evaluation of present classification: Should be maintained	
Plateau of maturity: 3–10 years following the vintage	

This is a large Cru Bourgeois with most of the vineyards in the commune of Soussans. Based on the half-dozen or so vintages I have tasted, the wine is correctly made, but straightforward and lacking the fragrance and length that the best wines of the Margaux appellation possess. Perhaps a stricter selection and more elevated use of new oak might add to the wine's character and complexity. The best recent vintage of Tayac has been the 1986. It should age gracefully for at least a decade.

DU TERTRE (Fifth-Growth) VERY GOOD

Production: 18,000–20,000 cases	Grape varieties: Cabernet Sauvignon—80% Merlot—15% Petit Verdot—5%
Secondary label: none	
Vineyard size: 123.5 acres	Proprietor: Philippe Capbern-Gasqueton
Time spent in barrels: 24 months	Average age of vines: 30 years
Evaluation of present classification: Should be maintained, although the quality since 1978 may justify elevation to a fourth-growth	
Plateau of maturity: 6–15 years following the vintage	

Du Tertre, located on one of the highest plateaus in the Margaux appellation, was acquired in 1961 by Philippe Capbern-Gasqueton, the proprietor of the famous St.-Estèphe estate, Calon-Ségur. The property was in deplorable condition, and Gasqueton and his investors began an extensive plan to rebuild the château and replant the vineyard. Until 12 years ago, it was extremely easy to forget the wines of this property. The sandy-colored, plain-yet-elegant, two-story château is located in one of the most obscure areas of the Médoc (less than a kilometer from Arsac, near the appellation's top overachiever, Monbrison).

The vineyard is unusual because it is one contiguous parcel and not morsellated as so many Bordeaux château vineyards are. At first glance, it is visually reminiscent of Domaine de Chevalier. In contrast to the relatively high percentage of Merlot planted at Calon-Ségur in St.-Estèphe, Gasqueton has chosen to utilize primarily Cabernet Sauvignon at du Tertre, taking advantage of the gravelly, sandstone soil that dominates his vineyard. The wine, since 1978, has been characterized by relatively deep color, a good bit of power and richness in the top vintages, but perhaps a lack of finesse and that extra-special fragrance that can make a Margaux so enthralling. Nevertheless, the wine continues to sell at a modest price, making it one of the most undervalued of the classified growths of Bordeaux.

As good as this wine now is, I would be curious to see if it could even be improved with the use of a slightly higher percentage of new oak and Merlot.

VINTAGES

1989—The 1989 du Tertre is a charming, soft, medium-bodied wine that
·   lacks concentration and structure. It is evolved, very perfumed
86   (jammy blackcurrants), low in acidity, and ideal for drinking during its first 6–8 years. Anticipated maturity: Now–1998. Last tasted, 4/91.

1988—The 1988 is a good example for the vintage. Medium deep ruby,
·   with a curranty, smoky, oak-dominated nose, this wine has a
87   striking resemblance to this château's excellent 1979. It will drink beautifully young, but also keep well. Anticipated maturity: 1992–2003. Last tasted, 4/91.

1987—This is another good example of how charming this vintage can
·   be. Medium ruby, with an attractively projected bouquet of cur-
83   rants, spicy new oak, and even a scent of spring flowers, in the mouth the wine is round, soft, with surprising fat, low acid, and a gentle finish. Of course it is critical that the wine be consumed over the next 5–6 years. Anticipated maturity: Now–1995. Last tasted, 11/90.

1986—The spicy, ripe, mineral and curranty bouquet is followed by a
·   wine with medium body and good grip. Approachable now, and
86   evolving more rapidly than I would have thought possible several years ago, this elegantly wrought wine remains bargain priced for the vintage. Anticipated maturity: 1993–2005. Last tasted, 3/90.

1985—I have tasted the 1985 du Tertre nine times, five times from cask
  ·   and four times from the bottle. While I have never seen a wine
 87   behave so differently, the two most recent tastings have revealed
        positive results. The last two examples (both tasted in France)
        exhibited a nice deep ruby/purple color with no signs of age and
        a forward, earthy (truffles?), curranty bouquet that was enticing.
        In the mouth, the wine possessed plenty of fat, ripe, supple black-
        berry and curranty flavors, wth just enough soft tannins and acid-
        ity to give the wine grip and focus. This is a luscious, very forward
        style of du Tertre. Anticipated maturity: Now–1998. Last tasted,
        11/90.

1984—This is a moderately successful 1984 with an oaky and herbaceous
  ·   nose. The wine has some depth, but the supple fruit is beginning
 74   to fade, revealing acidic, dry, astringent tannins in the finish.
        Drink it up. Anticipated maturity: Now–1994. Last tasted, 2/89.

1983—Medium to deep ruby, with an intensely spicy, slightly herbaceous
  ·   nose, du Tertre's 1983 is rich and ripe, with medium-bodied fla-
 86   vors that exhibit good concentration and moderate tannins that
        are beginning to melt away. This is a very good, rather than
        exceptional, wine from the 1983 vintage. Anticipated maturity:
        1992–2001. Last tasted, 11/90.

1982—A wonderful, fragrant bouquet of violets, damp earth, cedarwood,
  ·   blackcurrants, and white chocolate jumps from the glass. On the
 87   palate, the wine is lush, medium bodied, and concentrated, with
        ripe fruity flavors. Like most Margauxs of this vintage, it has
        reached its plateau of maturity. Anticipated maturity: Now–1999.
        Last tasted, 1/90.

1981—Medium ruby in color, with a moderately intense, spicy, per-
  ·   fumed bouquet, the 1981 du Tertre is much leaner than the fat,
 83   generously flavored 1982 or excellent 1979. It still possesses some
        tannin, and while pleasant, lacks weight and finishes short. Antic-
        ipated maturity: Now–1994. Last tasted, 7/88.

1979—This has always been one of the sleepers of the vintage. The 1979
  ·   du Tertre continues to exhibit a marvelous tarry, rich, deep,
 89   berry-scented bouquet, fat, supple, very concentrated, fruity fla-
        vors, medium body, and fine length. Enough tannin remains for
        5–7 more years of evolution. This is a bargain-priced wine to look
        for at the auctions. Anticipated maturity: Now–1998. Last tasted,
        1/91.

1978—This wine has reached full maturity and exhibits a surprisingly
  ·   earthy, almost rustic bouquet filled with aromas of chestnuts,
 85   plummy fruit, and old, yet clean barrel smells. In the mouth, the

wine is round, slightly herbaceous, but generously endowed and soft, with a smooth, heady finish. A touch of earthiness on the nose and in the flavors lowers the score. Anticipated maturity: Now–1995. Last tasted, 1/91.

1976—Now beginning to take on a brownish hue, this medium-bodied, spicy, loosely structured wine is quickly cracking up, and should
78 be consumed immediately. Anticipated maturity: Now–1992. Last tasted, 11/87.

1975—This wine has begun to lose fruit, and the relatively hard, astringent tannins now seem to have the upper hand, resulting in a wine
73 that tastes hollow and a bit coarse and tough textured. It has grown increasingly out of balance since I last tasted it. The depth of fruit it once possessed is now dissipated into a wine that exhibits too much acidity and tannin. Last tasted, 9/88.

1970—Medium ruby, with some orange at the edge, this relatively herbaceous, weedy-scented wine has a robust, earthy fruitiness, full
68 body, but excessive tannins and a dried-out, coarse texture. It is out of balance. Last tasted, 11/84.

LA TOUR-DE-MONS (Cru Bourgeois)   AVERAGE

Production: 10,000 cases	Grape varieties: Cabernet Sauvignon—45% Merlot—40% Cabernet Franc—10% Petit Verdot—5%
Secondary label: none	
Vineyard size: 74 acres	Proprietor: The Clauzel- Binaud family Administrator: Bertrand Clauzel
Time spent in barrels: 18 months	Average age of vines: 25 years
Evaluation of present classification: Should be maintained	
Plateau of maturity: 5–14 years following the vintage	

This famous old estate, still run by the Clauzel-Binaud family (who at one time also controlled Château Cantemerle), is only a Cru Bourgeois, but some of its vintages, the 1949 and 1953 for example, are legendary. They have been rated among the best wines of those years. Like Cantemerle, however, the property was allowed to deteriorate in the late seventies and is only now beginning to regain its form. The vineyard, which is in the Margaux commune of Soussans, has an extremely ancient history, with origins tracing back to the late thirteenth century. All of the optimistic talk about the resurgence of La Tour-de-Mons has not been reflected in my tasting notes. Certainly the wines are good, but nothing has emerged during the eighties that would merit an upgrading of this property to classified-growth status as some observers have suggested.

THE LESSER APPELLATIONS: MÉDOC, HAUT-MÉDOC, LISTRAC, AND MOULIS

There are hundreds of châteaux in the vast Médoc that produce notable wines of quality, character, and interest. They frequently offer astonishing wine values in good vintages, and sensationally great values in excellent vintage years. A few of these estates make wine as good as (and in a few instances better than) many of the famous classified growths. However, most of these properties make solid, reliable wines, which if never spectacularly exciting, are nevertheless sound and satisfying. In the very good to great vintages of Bordeaux—1961, 1970, 1975, 1982, 1985, 1986, 1989, and 1990—the wines from the best of these properties especially deserve seeking out.

No other wine regions of Bordeaux have made as much progress as the Crus Bourgeois of the Médoc, Haut-Médoc, Listrac, and Moulis during the eighties. To enjoy Bordeaux on a regular basis, knowledge of the best estates of these appellations is essential.

The Médoc appellation refers to a vast area that now encompasses more than 7,200 acres of vineyards. The appellation name has caused some confusion because the entire region north of the city of Bordeaux, bordered on the west by the Atlantic Ocean and to the east by the Gironde River, is geographically called "the Médoc." However, in terms of the Médoc appellation, the area corresponds to the very northern part of the Bordeaux viticultural area that has long been called the Bas-Médoc. Most of the wines entitled to the Médoc appellation come from the seven communes of Bégadan, St.-Yzans, Prignac, Ordonnac, St.-Christoly, Blaignan, and St.-Germain d'Esteuil.

Making any generalizations about the wines of the Médoc appellation is impossible because of the huge variation in quality. However, in this remote, backwater region of Bordeaux, there has been a noticeable trend in the last several decades to plant more Merlot in the region's heavier, thicker, less porous soils. This has meant the wines possess more up-front charm and more fruit, as well as popular appeal. There also have been several classifications of the wines themselves, but for the purpose of this chapter, I have called everything a "Cru Bourgeois" because the classifications—observed objectively—appear to be political creations rather than any valid attempt to classify the châteaux by their commitment to quality.

The Haut-Médoc appellation also consists of just over 7,200 acres of vineyards. It is a massive area, stretching from the industrial suburb north of Bordeaux called Blanquefort, north to where the Bas-Médoc begins. This region, which skirts around the Médoc appellation, produces wines from fifteen communes, the most famous of which are Saint-Seurin, St.-Laurent, Cussac, St.-Sauveur, Cissac, and Vertheuil. Many producers in the Haut-Médoc make wines that surpass some of the classified growths, and as in the Médoc, the quality of many of the Crus Bourgeois has improved immensely during this last decade.

Listrac is another obscure appellation of Bordeaux. It, like neighboring Moulis, sits well inland and covers just over 1,450 acres of vines. The wines justifiably have a reputation for being tough textured, dry, and astringent, with little charm and fruit. These characteristics have undermined the success of Listrac wines in export markets, but increasingly during the eighties this issue has been addressed by the proprietors. Today the wines are less rugged and tough than in the past, but they are still relatively tannic wines that could use more charm.

Moulis is, for me, the best of the lesser-known Bordeaux appellations. Perhaps this is because so many talented proprietors extract the highest quality possible from this small appellation of just over 1,250 acres. The wines from Moulis are among the longest lived of Bordeaux. In top vintages they are strikingly rich, full bodied, and powerful. There is a bevy of great châteaux in Moulis, including the likes of Chasse-Spleen, Gressier Grand-Poujeaux, Maucaillou, and Poujeaux. Many of the wines of Moulis can rival, at least in terms of longevity, the finest classified growths.

I have organized this chapter by listing the properties in alphabetical order. For those estates that I believe are making wines of classified-growth quality, specific tasting notes are provided. The best vintages of the other estates are mentioned, but tasting notes are not given.

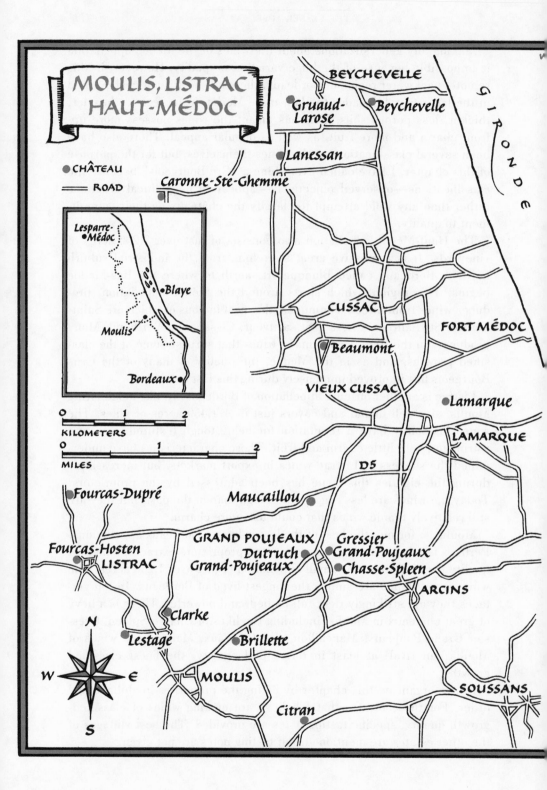

MOULIS, LISTRAC
HAUT-MÉDOC

● CHÂTEAU
━━ ROAD

BEYCHEVELLE

● Gruaud-
  Larose

● Beychevelle

● Lanessan

Caronne-Ste-Ghemme

Lesparre-
● Médoc

● Blaye

Moulis

Bordeaux ●

0   1   2
KILOMETERS

0   1   2
MILES

CUSSAC

● Beaumont

VIEUX CUSSAC

FORT MÉDOC

● Lamarque

LAMARQUE

D5

● Fourcas-Dupré

● Maucaillou

GRAND POUJEAUX
        Dutruch
Grand-Poujeaux

Gressier
● Grand-Poujeaux

● Chasse-Spleen

Fourcas-Hosten
LISTRAC

ARCINS

● Clarke

● Lestage

● Brillette

MOULIS

SOUSSANS

● Citran

N
W   E
S

GIRONDE

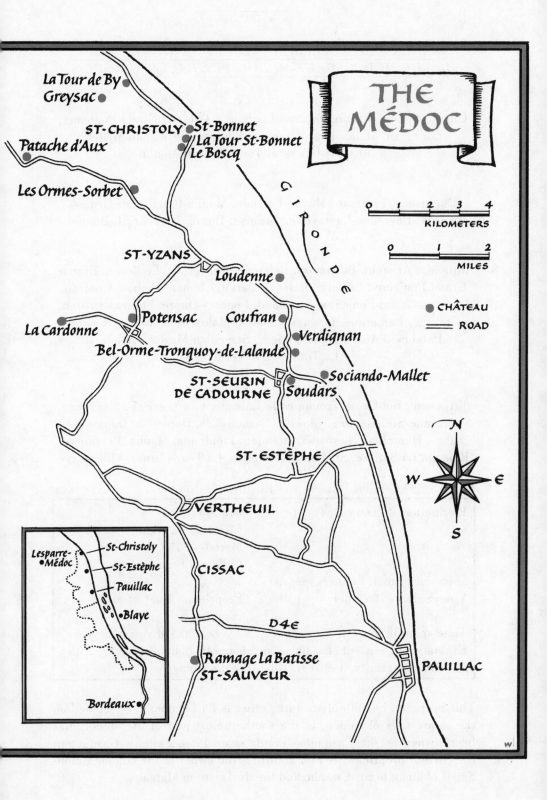

THE
MÉDOC

La Tour de By
Greysac

ST-CHRISTOLY •St-Bonnet
La Tour St-Bonnet
Patache d'Aux Le Boscq

Les Ormes-Sorbet

GIRONDE

0 1 2 3 4
KILOMETERS

0   1   2
MILES

ST-YZANS

Loudenne

La Cardonne Potensac   Coufran   ● CHÂTEAU
                                      ROAD
                        Verdignan
Bel-Orme-Tronquoy-de-Lalande
                            Sociando-Mallet
ST-SEURIN
DE CADOURNE Soudars

N

ST-ESTÈPHE

W   E

VERTHEUIL
S

St-Christoly
Lesparre-
•Médoc   St-Estèphe

CISSAC

Pauillac

•Blaye

D4E

Ramage La Batisse   PAUILLAC
ST-SAUVEUR

Bordeaux •

W

A CONSUMER'S CLASSIFICATION OF THE CHÂTEAUX
OF THE MÉDOC, HAUT-MÉDOC, LISTRAC, AND MOULIS

EXCELLENT

Chasse-Spleen, Citran, Fourcas-Loubaney, Gressier Grand-Poujeaux,
Lanessan, Maucaillou, Potensac, Poujeaux, Sociando-Mallet,
Tour Haut-Caussan, Tour du Haut-Moulin

VERY GOOD

Ducluzeau, Liversan, Mayne-Lalande, Moulin-Rouge, Les Ormes-
Sorbet, Peyredon-Lagravette, Saransot-Dupré, La Tour St.-Bonnet

GOOD

Anthonic, Arnauld, Beaumont, Belgrave, Bellegrave, Le Boscq, Branas-
Grand Poujeaux, Brillette, Cissac, Clarke, Clément-Pichon, Coufran,
Dutruch-Grand-Poujeaux, Fonréaud, Fourcas-Dupré, Fourcas-Hosten,
Greysac, Lamarque, Lestage, Magnol, Malescasse, Moulin A Vent,
Patache d'Aux, Plagnac, Ségur, Semeillan-Mazeau, Soudars,
La Tour de By, Verdignan

OTHER NOTABLE PROPERTIES

d'Agassac, Bel-Orme-Tronquoy-de-Lalande, Camensac, La Cardonne,
Caronne-Ste.-Gemme, Clos des Demoiselles, Duplessis, Duplessis-
Fabre, Hanteillan, Larose-Trintaudon, Loudenne, Moulis, Peyrabon,
Ramage La Batisse, St.-Bonnet, Sénéjac, La Tour-Carnet, Villegeorge

D'AGASSAC (Cru Bourgeois) Ludon-Médoc   AVERAGE

Production: 10,000 cases	Grape varieties:
	Cabernet Sauvignon—60%
	Merlot—30%
	Cabernet Franc—10%
Secondary label: Pomiès-Agassac	
Vineyard size: 86.5 acres	Proprietor: The Gasqueton family
Time spent in barrels: 12 months	Average age of vines: 25 years
Evaluation of present classification: Should be maintained	
Plateau of maturity: 4–9 years following the vintage	

This property, one of only two (the other is La Lagune) to be located on
the sandy soils of Ludon, in the southernmost part of the Médoc, has
been owned by the Gasqueton family since 1960. Philippe Gasqueton,
the current proprietor, is well known as the owner of the famous Calon-
Ségur château in St.-Estèphe and the du Tertre in Margaux.

The wines of d'Agassac have had a track record of inconsistency despite relatively low yields and a conservative and traditional vinification. The wine is robust, frequently lacking charm and fruit. No new oak is used, and perhaps that is an issue that should be addressed. This is a wine to drink within the first decade of life. The best recent vintages have been an excellent 1982, which is now beginning to tire, and a fat, ripe 1985. I found the 1983, 1986, and 1988 indifferent winemaking efforts.

Visitors to the region are well advised to make a detour and go inland from the famous D2 to visit d'Agassac, as it represents a superb example of a medieval fortified castle. The edifice, accessible via multiple tours, is one of the most impressive in the Bordeaux region.

ANTHONIC (Cru Bourgeois) Moulis GOOD

Production: 8,500 cases	Grape varieties:
	Cabernet Sauvignon—65%
	Merlot—30%
	Petit Verdot—5%
Secondary label: none	
Vineyard size: 40 acres	Proprietor: Pierre Cordonnier
Time spent in barrels: 16 months	Average age of vines: 15 years
Evaluation of present classification: An up-and-coming property that should be watched	
Plateau of maturity: 3–10 years following the vintage	

I had the occasion to taste the 1976, 1988, 1989, and 1990 vintages in spring, 1991, and was duly impressed by the stylish, elegant character of these wines. The vineyard is still young, but it is well placed near the more famous Château Clarke. Proprietor Cordonnier utilizes stainless-steel tanks and 30% new oak each year.

ARNAULD (Cru Bourgeois) Haut-Médoc GOOD

Production: 9,000 cases	Grape varieties:
	Merlot—50%
	Cabernet Sauvignon—40%
	Cabernet Franc—10%
Secondary label: none	
Vineyard size: 42 acres	Proprietor: The Theil-Roggy family
Time spent in barrels: 18 months	Average age of vines: 20 years
Evaluation of present classification: Should be maintained	
Plateau of maturity: 3–8 years following the vintage	

North on the famous D2, just past the village of Arcins, is Château Arnauld. This property is owned by the Theil-Roggy family, who long ago established the reputation of Château Poujeaux in nearby Moulis for one of the most distinctive wines of the Médoc.

The wine produced at Arnauld is less structured, no doubt reflecting the elevated percentage of Merlot (50%) used in the blend. Consequently, Arnauld, for all the attractive, rich fruit, is a wine to be drunk in its first 7–8 years of life. It has been well made since the early eighties, with the 1982, 1983, 1985, 1988, and 1989 all supple, exceptionally fruity, and with good color, yet limited long-term aging potential. Prices, however, remain reasonable for this tasty wine.

BEAUMONT (Cru Bourgeois) Haut-Médoc   GOOD

Production: 35,000–40,000 cases	Grape varieties:
	Cabernet Sauvignon—56%
	Merlot—36%
	Cabernet Franc—7%
	Petit Verdot—1%
Secondary label: Moulin-d'Arvigny	
Vineyard size: 216 acres	Proprietor: The insurance
	companies G.M.F. and
	M.A.I.F.
	Administrator: M. Paradivin
Time spent in barrels: 12–16 months	Average age of vines: 17 years
Evaluation of present classification: Should be maintained	
Plateau of maturity: 5–9 years following the vintage	

This large estate had a checkered history until it was acquired by two insurance companies in 1986. The progression in quality since then has been significant, and this is now one of the more interesting, best made, and reasonably priced Crus Bourgeois in the Médoc. The new proprietors' goal has been to produce a supple and amply endowed wine with a great deal of up-front fruit intelligently married with toasty vanillin aromas from a small percentage of new oak barrels. The 1986 was the best Beaumont in the last 20 years. It has been followed by a good 1988 and an excellent 1989. Recent vintages taste as if the percentage of Merlot is considerably higher than the 36% the property claims. This is a wine to seek out for the cunningly made, yet extremely attractive, crowd-pleasing style. The château itself is also noteworthy and worth visiting. An old fortified tower as well as an impressive twin-turreted facade dominate the landscape around the village of Cussac-Fort-Médoc.

BEL-ORME-TRONQUOY-DE-LALANDE
(Cru Bourgeois) Haut-Médoc AVERAGE

Production: 9,000 cases	Grape varieties:
	Cabernet Sauvignon—60%
	Cabernet Franc—20%
	Merlot—20%
Secondary label: Clos du Cardinal	
Vineyard size: 64.2 acres	Proprietor: Paul Quié
Time spent in barrels: 12–16 months	Average age of vines: 35 years
Evaluation of present classification: Should be maintained	
Plateau of maturity: 5–10 years following the vintage	

I remember a profound 1945 Bel-Orme-Tronquoy-de-Lalande drunk on New Year's Day, 1985. I also have good notes on the 1982, and more recently, an opulent, chewy, full-bodied 1989. But generally, my experience with this property, located in the very northern part of the Médoc near the village of Saint-Seurin-de-Cadourne, has been uninspiring.

In the eighties, the ancient style of winemaking, which combined immense power and excruciatingly painful tannin levels, gave way to a high-tech, supple style that often resulted in wines that lacked concentration and character. Perhaps the mechanical harvesters used to bring in the crop here since the mid-1980s coupled with the multiple filtrations this wine must endure result in compromises in this château's potential.

BELGRAVE (Fifth-Growth) Haut-Médoc GOOD

Production: 25,000 cases	Grape varieties:
	Cabernet Sauvignon—60%
	Merlot—35%
	Petit Verdot—5%
Secondary label: none	
Vineyard size: 136 acres	Proprietor: The firm of Dourthe
Time spent in barrels: 20–24 months	Average age of vines: 15 years
Evaluation of present classification: Should be downgraded to a Cru Bourgeois, although quality has improved since 1985	
Plateau of maturity: 5–12 years following the vintage	

When the huge firm of Dourthe (or C.V.B.G. as it is known in Bordeaux) acquired this property in 1980, it was one of the Médoc's most-neglected estates. The owners made significant investments and the property is now a showpiece château that also provides lodging for Dourthe's best clients. Emile Peynaud is the consulting oenologist, and there have been major replantings of the vineyard to lower the exceptionally high percentage of Merlot and increase the percentage of Cabernet Sauvignon.

There was little noticeable improvement in the wines, however, until the mid-1980s when Patrick Atteret—the son-in-law of Jean-Paul Jauffret, the head of Dourthe—was brought in to manage the property. At that time, Michel Rolland, the famed Libourne oenologist, was also hired to provide counseling for the winemaking. Since that time, Belgrave has taken on more color, depth, and ripeness. The 1986 was a classically made wine, with excellent richness, medium to full body, and good mid-term aging potential. The 1988 was successful, but, like so many Médocs, aggressively tannic. The 1989 looks generously endowed, super-ripe, and soft, a forward wine that should be consumed within its first decade.

I still wonder whether or not Belgrave will improve to the point where it again can be considered the qualitative equivalent of a fifth-growth.

BELLEGRAVE (Cru Bourgeois) Listrac   GOOD

Production: 4,000 cases	Grape varieties:
	Cabernet Sauvignon—65%
	Merlot—25%
	Cabernet Franc—5%
	Petit Verdot—5%
Secondary label: none	
Vineyard size: 34.6 acres	Proprietors: Jean-Louis Declercq and Henri Petre
Time spent in barrels: 14–20 months	Average age of vines: 25 years

Evaluation of present classification: Should be maintained, but certainly the 1988 and 1989 were the quality equivalents of a classified growth

Plateau of maturity: 4–12 years following the vintage

Since 1988 two Belgians, Jean-Louis Declercq and Henri Petre, have continued to upgrade this relatively obscure Listrac to one of the best wines of the appellation. They harvest by hand, vinify in a traditional manner with an extremely long 20- to 30-day *cuvaison*, and utilize 50% new oak.

These changes, as well as employing the incredibly talented, brilliant maestro behind the wines at Pichon Lalande—Monsieur Godin—to oversee the upbringing of the wine, have resulted in a series of striking wines. It started with the 1983 and has been followed by an excellent 1985 and 1986, and brilliant wines in 1988, 1989, and 1990. This is a property clearly making wines far above its official pedigree that merits discovery by lovers of Bordeaux looking for wines of both quality and value.

LE BOSCQ (Cru Bourgeois) Médoc   GOOD

Production: 11,000 cases	Grape varieties: Cabernet Sauvignon—70% Merlot—20% Cabernet Franc—10%
Secondary label: none	
Vineyard size: 52 acres	Proprietor: Claude Lapalu
Time spent in barrels: 20 months	Average age of vines: 10 years
Evaluation of present classification: Should be maintained	
Plateau of maturity: 3–7 years following the vintage	

This is a reliable Cru Bourgeois made from a vineyard sandwiched between the two excellent Cru Bourgeois vineyards of La Tour de By and La Tour St.-Bonnet near the village of St.-Christoly. The estate is managed by Claude Lapalu, who also owns the more-famous Patache d'Aux. The style sought at Le Boscq is one of unbridled, up-front, in-your-face fruit and suppleness. Consequently, this is a wine to drink in its first 3–7 years. The vineyard is harvested by mechanical machines, and the vinification and upbringing of the wine are designed to put a wine in the bottle that is immediately drinkable.

The best recent vintages include a delicious 1989, a disappointing 1988, a good 1986, and a fine 1985 and 1982. The latter two vintages require immediate consumption.

BRANAS-GRAND POUJEAUX (Cru Bourgeois) Moulis   GOOD

Production: 4,000 cases	Grape varieties: Cabernet Sauvignon—60% Merlot—35% Petit Verdot—5%
Secondary label: none	
Vineyard size: 14.8 acres	Proprietor: Jacques de Pourquéry
Time spent in barrels: 22–24 months	Average age of vines: 25 years
Evaluation of present classification: Should be maintained	
Plateau of maturity: 6–15 years following the vintage	

This is one of the smallest and least known of the Moulis properties. However, in the vintages I have tasted during the 1980s the wines have exhibited a great deal of full-bodied flavor concentration, and the potential for 10–20 years of longevity. I wish I knew older vintages better, because there is no doubt that the 1985, 1986, and 1989 were enormously promising wines in their youth. A small percentage of new oak is used, and the yields, which rarely exceed 40 hectoliters per hectare, are among the lowest in the middle Médoc.

BRILLETTE (Cru Bourgeois) Moulis   GOOD

Production: 15,000 cases	Grape varieties: Cabernet Sauvignon—50% Merlot—40% Cabernet Franc—5% Petit Verdot—5%
Secondary label: none	
Vineyard size: 79 acres	Proprietor: Monique Berthault
Time spent in barrels: 24 months	Average age of vines: 25 years
Evaluation of present classification: Should be maintained	
Plateau of maturity: 7–10 years following the vintage	

Just about one kilometer north of the town of Moulin-en-Médoc is the vast, 374-acre estate of Brillette, which has only 79 acres under vine, and produces approximately 15,000 cases. The wines of Brillette are not yet well known, but the quality of winemaking is high, and the wines are made in a spicy, oaky, rich fruity style that appeals to many tasters.

Brillette's vineyard, which remains relatively young—with the great majority of it planted in the sixties and seventies—is one entire parcel located on gravelly, sandy soil. Since the early eighties the grapes have been harvested by machine. One-third new oak is used each year, which no doubt gives the wine a telltale smoky, toasty character. The late Raymond Berthault did not live to see how his many improvements ultimately brought the quality level of Brillette up to the level of the best Crus Bourgeois. In fact, vintages such as 1982, 1986, and 1989 could easily pass for a classified growth. Raymond's wife, Monique, has directed the winemaking at the château since her husband's death in 1981.

This is a wine for those who admire a hefty dose of oak in their wines. It is best drunk within a decade of the vintage.

CAMENSAC (Fifth-Growth) Haut-Médoc   AVERAGE

Production: 26,000 cases	Grape varieties:
	Cabernet Sauvignon—60%
	Merlot—20%
	Cabernet Franc—20%
Secondary label: none	
Vineyard size: 118.5 acres	Proprietor: The Forner family
Time spent in barrels: 14–18 months	Average age of vines: 20 years
Evaluation of present classification: Should be downgraded to a Cru Bourgeois	
Plateau of maturity: 5–14 years following the vintage	

Camensac is among the least known of the 1855 classified growths. No doubt its location well inland and west of St.-Julien in the commune of St.-Laurent explains in part the relative obscurity. In addition, the record of mediocrity, unchanged until the seventies, certainly added to a general lack of interest. However, things have changed for the better at Camensac.

The individuals responsible for the revival of Camensac are the Forner brothers, who purchased this estate in 1965 and set about the expensive task of replanting the vineyards and renovating the *chai* and winemaking facilities. The Forners are best known for the modern-styled wines made at their winery called Marqués de Cáceres located in the Rioja region of Spain.

With the help of the omnipresent Bordeaux oenologist, Emile Peynaud, Camensac's wines have lightened up in style, and emphasize more suppleness and fruit. Even though Camensac is now making better wines, they are not representative of fifth-growth quality. They do have a certain St.-Julien-like personality, with good fruit, medium body, and enough tannin to warrant a decade of cellaring in good vintages. However, I noticed in my tastings during the late eighties that many bottles have a damp cardboard-like smell, as if there is a continual problem with the corks. I do not think the problem is the corks, but rather that the Forners's choice of oak barrels tends to give the wine this corky-like character I find off-putting. Nevertheless, behind what I see as a flaw in the wine's bouquet are wines that have good concentration and a straightforward, foursquare style. They are abundantly oaky, but the type of oak used is a problem.

LA CARDONNE (Cru Bourgeois) Médoc AVERAGE

Production: 42,000 cases	Grape varieties: Merlot—58% Cabernet Sauvignon—35% Cabernet Franc—7%
Secondary label: none	
Vineyard size: 240 acres	Proprietor: Domaines Rothschild
Time spent in barrels: None; aged entirely in vats	Average age of vines: 18 years
Evaluation of present classification: Should be maintained	
Plateau of maturity: 3–6 years following the vintage	

Immense optimism sprang forth in 1973 when the Rothschild family (owners of such famed Pauillacs as Lafite-Rothschild and Duhart-Milon) acquired this property in Blaignan. It is a huge enterprise, and the wine is made in a relatively light, indifferent, yet commercially correct style. I have always maintained that the enormous yields and heavy reliance on filtration rob this wine of much concentration and character. It is a wine that must be drunk within 5–6 years of the vintage. Given the level of quality, it is overpriced, but I did think the fine 1990 was the best wine I have yet tasted from this estate.

CARONNE-STE.-GEMME
(Cru Bourgeois) Haut-Médoc AVERAGE

Production: 22,000 cases	Grape varieties: Merlot—65% Cabernet Sauvignon—30% Cabernet Franc—5%
Secondary label: Labat	
Vineyard size: 111 acres	Proprietor: The Nony-Borie family
Time spent in barrels: 15 months	Average age of vines: 30 years
Evaluation of present classification: Should be maintained	
Plateau of maturity: 4–8 years following the vintage	

This estate in St.-Laurent receives little publicity. For both tourists and writers who desire to visit, the property is virtually impossible to find on the back roads of the Médoc. Moreover, the wine is hardly an inspiring gustatory pleasure. My limited experience with this label has found the wine to be generally dark in color, with surprisingly little bouquet, a solid, rather rustic, almost coarse taste, and an excess of tannin. In vintages such as 1975, 1978, and 1981 it was austere and tannic. Since the early eighties, the wine has become increasingly supple as new plantings of Merlot have come of age. The best vintage of Caronne-Ste.-Gemme that I have tasted is the 1982, followed by the 1986. Both are powerful, big, richly fruity wines. This could be a Cru Bourgeois on the rebound.

CHASSE-SPLEEN (Cru Bourgeois) Moulis EXCELLENT

Production: 25,000 cases	Grape varieties: Cabernet Sauvignon—60% Merlot—35% Petit Verdot—3% Cabernet Franc—2%
Secondary label: l'Ermitage de Chasse-Spleen	
Vineyard size: 160.5 acres	Proprietor: A syndicate with the majority partner being the Société Bernard Taillan Administrator: Bernadette Villars
Time spent in barrels: 18–26 months	Average age of vines: 35 years
Evaluation of present classification: Should be upgraded to a Médoc third-growth	
Plateau of maturity: 5–18 years following the vintage	

An outstanding property, Chasse-Spleen has consistently produced fine wine that for the last three decades has often been as good as a third-growth. Even in poor and mediocre vintages, the wine is characterized by a very pronounced, deep ruby color, a bouquet of plummy ripeness, and rich, round, substantial flavors.

The great vintages for Chasse-Spleen, in which the wine can compare favorably to top Médoc classified growths, are 1966, 1970, 1975, 1978, 1985, 1986, and 1989.

Chasse-Spleen was owned by the Lahary family until 1976 when it was purchased by a syndicate whose controlling interest was the Société

Bernard Taillan. The director of the Société, Jacques Merlaut, had the good sense to install his daughter, Bernadette Villars, as the manager. The results have been increasingly inspired wines, with absolutely top-class wines in the late eighties. The vineyard, consisting of 4 parcels, sits on primarily deep, gravelly soil, and boasts many old vines; their average age is an impressive 35 years. This is a property that still adheres to very traditional practices. It is one of only a handful in the Médoc that does not filter either after the malolactic fermentation or before bottling. In fact, the only compromise toward modern-day technology is that part of the crop gets harvested by machine. Improvements under Bernadette Villars are obvious with the introduction of a second wine, the increased usage of 50% new oak casks for aging, and the impeccable attention to every detail. Prices have jumped as the world has begun to discover that Chasse-Spleen was undervalued.

VINTAGES

1989—Make no mistake about it, the 1989 Chasse-Spleen is the finest
· wine this property has produced since their great 1949. This is
92 one rare example where the wonderful performance of a property
in 1985 and 1986 is surpassed by the 1989. This is a spectacularly
rich, powerful, authoritative example of the vintage that can compete with—and even surpass—many of the most-famous names.
The architect of this wine is the immensely talented Bernadette
Villars, who has produced what she considers the finest wine of
her distinguished career. Layer upon layer of concentrated blackcurrant fruit is wrapped in a frame of toasty new oak and decent
acidity. But what is so impressive about this vintage of Chasse-
Spleen is that the explosive finish just goes on and on, lasting
nearly one minute. An awesome wine! Anticipated maturity:
1996–2015. Last tasted, 4/91.

1988—Chasse-Spleen made an excellent 1988. It displays an abundantly
· intense, smoky, blackcurrant bouquet, chewy, intense, full-bod-
87 ied flavors, and a surprisingly long, spicy, tannic finish. It is more
traditionally structured than the 1989, but has nowhere near the
size or potential complexity. Anticipated maturity: 1993–2006.
Last tasted, 4/91.

1986—The black/ruby/purple color of the 1986 suggests a wine of re-
· markable richness and depth. And that is exactly what one gets.
90 The huge bouquet of cassis fruit is nicely backed up by a whiff of
toasty, smoky oak. On the palate, the wine has sensational extract, full body, and massive texture; it should last for at least 15–

20 years. I have rarely been more impressed by a young vintage of Chasse-Spleen than I have been with the 1986. Anticipated maturity: 1996–2010. Last tasted, 11/90.

1985 — The 1985 Chasse-Spleen is fabulously deep in color, with a full-intensity, scented bouquet of spicy new oak, rich curranty fruit, and plums. In the mouth, the wine is very concentrated, long, big framed, but impeccably balanced with quite a finish. Anticipated maturity: 1992–2005. Last tasted, 11/90.

·
90

1984 — One of the better wines from this vintage, the 1984 has good color, an attractive, ripe sweetness to its fruit, medium body, and a velvety texture. Anticipated maturity: Now–1994. Last tasted, 3/88.

·
81

1983 — Still deep ruby in color, with some amber creeping in at the edges, this forward, round, generously endowed Chasse-Spleen has shed most of its tannins and offers a deliciously plump, fleshy mouthful of satisfying claret. I am surprised how quickly it has aged, but there is good depth, and the wine offers charm as well as complexity. Anticipated maturity: Now–1995. Last tasted, 12/89.

·
86

1982 — This wine has not developed nearly as well as I would have hoped. In fact, I would rate the 1985, 1986, and 1989 as significantly richer, more concentrated wines. There is no doubting the 1982 is a good Chasse-Spleen, but it has never quite fulfilled its early promise. Still relatively deep ruby in color, with a spicy, cedary, backward bouquet, the wine reveals the telltale fatness, and fleshy, chunky character of the vintage, but lacks the opulence and aromatic complexity so many of the top 1982s possess. Anticipated maturity: 1992–2001. Last tasted, 1/91.

·
86

1981 — Medium ruby, with an almost dusty, spicy, cedary nose, this austerely styled Chasse-Spleen lacks the richness and concentration to ever be profound. It is medium bodied, a bit dry and tannic in the finish, but pleasant in a straightforward, foursquare way. Anticipated maturity: Now–1995. Last tasted, 11/88.

·
79

1979 — Fully mature and drinking well, the 1979 exhibits an herbaceous, cassis-scented bouquet, medium-bodied flavors, good concentration, and a soft finish with some acidity. Anticipated maturity: Now–1993. Last tasted, 2/88.

·
83

1978 — This was a successful vintage for Chasse-Spleen, and the wine has just now reached full maturity. Much more opaque and deeper colored than the 1979, with a mushroomy, meaty, curranty bouquet, this full-bodied, powerful, muscular Chasse-Spleen still has some tannins to lose, but was immensely enjoyable to drink. Anticipated maturity: Now–2000. Last tasted, 3/89.

·
85

1976—Fully mature and beginning to take on considerable amber at the
· edge, this spicy, soupy-textured Chasse-Spleen should be con-
76 sumed over the next 3–4 years. I detect the fruit beginning to
fade and the alcohol becoming more noticeable. Quite soft and
still perfumed, but beginning, I believe, to decline. Anticipated
maturity: Now—may be in decline. Last tasted, 3/88.

1975—This has always been one of the top wines of an inconsistent
· vintage. Still dense, even opaque, dark ruby with only a slight
90 amber edge, the bouquet of the 1975 reluctantly blossoms in the
glass to reveal scents of grilled nuts, minerals, licorice, and superripe blackcurrants. In the mouth, it is full bodied and powerful, but the tannins, unlike in many 1975s, are noticeable, but not
astringent or green. Just about ready to drink, this wine should
easily last for another 10–20 years. Anticipated maturity: 1992–
2010. Last tasted, 6/88.

OLDER VINTAGES

Anyone lucky enough to run across a bottle of the 1970 Chasse-Spleen
(rated 90 in 1990) should snatch it up. This is a superb wine that after 20
years is still youthful and capable of lasting another 10–15 years. Full
bodied, ripe, and closer in style to the 1975 than any of the more recent
vintages, this is a wine of true classified-growth quality. The price should
also be reasonable. Among the vintages in the sixties, I have good notes
on the 1966 (rated 86), but it has been over a decade since I last tasted
the wine. I have rarely seen any wines from the fifties, but the 1953 is
highly regarded. I was fortunate to buy a case of the 1949 Chasse-Spleen
that had been bottled in England. Every bottle was superb, one of the
few times when buying an older vintage at a reasonable price paid immense dividends. I have high hopes the 1989, 1986, and 1975 will reach
the heights of the 1949. For me, it is the most monumental Chasse-
Spleen I have ever tasted, and could have easily been confused with a
first-growth from that vintage. I consistently rated it between 92 and 95.

CISSAC (Cru Bourgeois) Haut-Médoc   GOOD

Production: 25,000 cases	Grape varieties:
	Cabernet Sauvignon—75%
	Merlot—20%
	Petit Verdot—5%
Secondary label: Abiet	
Vineyard size: 74 acres	Proprietor: The Vialard family
Time spent in barrels: 18 months	Average age of vines: 25 years
Evaluation of present classification: Should be maintained	
Plateau of maturity: 7–10 years following the vintage	

The proprietor of Cissac, Louis Vialard, is one of Bordeaux's most dedicated proprietors. Consequently, his beloved Château Cissac produces one of the best Bourgeois wines of the central Médoc.

Located just north of the town of Cissac, this property produces approximately 20,000 cases of very traditional, full-bodied, tannic, interesting, darkly colored wine. Normally unyielding and reserved when young, Cissac begins to show its true character at around age 6, and can easily age and improve in the bottle for 10 to 15 years in vintages such as 1975, 1985, and 1986.

The wine of Cissac is especially popular in England, and seems to have a growing following among American connoisseurs who have the patience to wait for its slow (for a Cru Bourgeois) but sure evolution.

In looking at the recent vintages, the 1971, 1973, and 1976 are all fully mature, but not quite up to the high standards set by Vialard for Cissac. However, the 1970 is very good and now drinking nicely. The 1975 remains stubbornly backward and youthful, but loaded with potential, as well as oodles of blackcurrant fruit. The 1978 is equally successful, but differently styled, more supple, fruity, and precocious. The 1979 is good, but not exciting, the 1981 is austere, and too lean. The trio of 1982, 1985, and 1986 are all rich, full bodied, powerful, and the most promising Cissacs since the 1975.

Cissac is one of the best-made bourgeois wines, and merits considerable attention from Bordeaux enthusiasts.

CITRAN (Cru Bourgeois) Haut-Médoc EXCELLENT

Production: 42,000 cases	Grape varieties: Merlot—60% Cabernet Sauvignon—40%
Secondary label: Villeranque Vineyard size: 210 acres	Proprietor: Fujimoto—a Japanese syndicate
Time spent in barrels: 18 months	Average age of vines: 20 years
Evaluation of present classification: Since 1987 the wine is the quality equivalent of a Médoc fifth-growth; vintages before 1986 should be approached with considerable caution	
Plateau of maturity: 6–10 years following the vintage	

In the few short years since the acquisition of Citran by a Japanese syndicate, the quality has soared. Until then, Citran was one of the Crus Bourgeois's most notorious underachievers. The renovation of the cellars, the commitment of the new director, Jean-Michel Fernandez, an increased percentage of new oak, a stricter selection process (and subsequent second wine), and excellent advice from the famed Professor Peynaud have resulted in glorious wines in both 1988 and 1989. If there is any criticism, it would be that the property continues to harvest entirely by machine, and that the elevated use of new oak, which gives the wine such a dramatic, smoky, even charred character, is so flamboyant, dramatic, and obvious, that those who admire claret for delicacy and subtlety might be put off by such boldness.

Nevertheless, the new vintages, such as 1988 and 1989, should age well for up to a decade, and are considerably more interesting and pleasurable than anything Citran previously produced. It should also be noted that prices have edged up to take into account the new designer bottle with its striking label that has replaced the old, traditional, somber Château Citran package.

VINTAGES

1989—The 1989 has a smoky, roasted bouquet, with massively rich, blackberry flavors just barely balanced by enough acidity. Opu-
88 lent and supple, with a long, heady, alcoholic finish concealing considerable tannins, this sensual and hedonistic wine will provide excellent early drinking. Anticipated maturity: Now–2000. Last tasted, 4/91.

1988—Starting with the 1988 vintage, Citran has established itself as one of the stars among the Crus Bourgeois. Dark ruby/purple, with a
87 smoky, roasted bouquet of cassis and lavish amounts of new oak, this cunningly made, ripe, overtly commercial wine will prove to be a crowd pleaser because of its direct, forward, plump character. Anticipated maturity: Now–1996. Last tasted, 6/91.

CLARKE (Cru Bourgeois) Listrac   GOOD

Production: 32,000 cases	Grape varieties: Cabernet Sauvignon—45% Merlot—45% Cabernet Franc—8% Petit Verdot—2%
Secondary label: Haut-Médoc-Baron Edmond de Rothschild	
Vineyard size: 259 acres	Proprietor: Baron Edmond de Rothschild
Time spent in barrels: 12 months, plus 8 months in vats	Average age of vines: 5–12 years
Evaluation of present classification: Should be maintained	
Plateau of maturity: 3–7 years following the vintage	

One of the most remarkable and newsworthy recent developments in the Médoc has been the complete restoration and rejuvenation of the old vineyard of Château Clarke. The property boasts a history dating to 1750, and it took the considerable resources of a wealthy member of the famous Rothschild family—Baron Edmond de Rothschild—to accomplish the resurrection. In 1973 work began, and in the following 5 years the area under vine increased dramatically to 259 acres, large enough to have the potential to produce over 30,000 cases of wine. The first wines released, a 1978 and 1979, were given a great deal of hoopla from the wine press, but in actuality they were light, medium-bodied examples that clearly tasted like the product of a young vineyard. However, the commitment to high quality, the financial resources, and the management are all present, so as the vineyard matures, Château Clarke should become one of the best wines made in Listrac.

A vertical tasting I did in 1989 of all the Clarke vintages demonstrated that the early vintages, made from very young vines, have fallen apart. This includes the 1978, 1979, 1980, and 1981. Whether due to the excellent raw materials of the vintage or a denser style, I found the 1982 still rich and fruity, but in need of drinking. The 1983 was light, compact, and angular. I was not impressed with the relatively diluted 1985. However, since 1986 Clarke has taken on more character and concentration. I wonder if yields of 60–70 hectoliters per hectare and mechanical harvesting, as well as the young age of the vines, are not robbing this wine of potential richness.

Château Clarke also produces a delicious dry rosé and a kosher *cuvée* (made according to strict Jewish requirement) of its red wine.

CLÉMENT-PICHON (Cru Bourgeois) Haut-Médoc   GOOD

Production: 10,000 cases	Grape varieties:
	Cabernet Sauvignon—70%
	Merlot—30%
Secondary label: none	
Vineyard size: 57 acres	Proprietor: Clément Fayat
Time spent in barrels: 14–20 months	Average age of vines: 10 years
Evaluation of present classification: Should be maintained	
Plateau of maturity: 3–7 years following the vintage	

This beautiful château, located just to the north of Bordeaux near the sprawling industrial suburb of Parempuyre, is owned by one of the most driven proprietors of the region, Clément Fayat, an industrialist who also has been responsible for the renaissance of the famed St.-Emilion vineyard, La Dominique. Fayat totally renovated the château, which formerly was known as Château de Parempuyre, and originally renamed it Château Pichon. However, that caused legal problems with Madame de Lencquesaing, who felt the name could be confused with her Château Pichon-Longueville–Comtesse de Lalande. The name was then changed to Château Clément-Pichon.

The huge baroque and gothic château was constructed at the end of the nineteenth century and is now inhabited by the Fayat family, who purchased this domain in 1976. They totally replanted the vineyards, which, consequently, are extremely young. The Fayats were shrewd enough to ask their oenologist at La Dominique, the famed Libournais, Michel Rolland, to look after the winemaking at Clément-Pichon. He has performed miracles with a vineyard so young. No doubt Rolland realized the limitations of making a true *vin de garde* and to date has emphasized wines with an up-front, exceptionally fruity, supple style that are meant to be consumed young.

The best vintage so far has been the 1989. It is a gloriously sweet, ripe, expansive wine with good extract and character, but it must be drunk before the mid-1990s. This is a property to keep an eye on in the future.

CLOS DES DEMOISELLES (Cru Bourgeois) Listrac   AVERAGE

Production: 2,000 cases	Grape varieties: Cabernet Sauvignon—60% Merlot—35% Petit Verdot—5%
Secondary label: none Vineyard size: 9.9 acres	Proprietor: Jacques de Pourquéry
Time spent in barrels: 16–20 months	Average age of vines: 16 years
Evaluation of present classification: Should be maintained	
Plateau of maturity: 3–8 years following the vintage	

The wines I have tasted from Clos des Demoiselles during the eighties have been extremely tannic and hard, without sufficient fruit, charm, or balance. The vineyard is still relatively young, and there is no doubt that this well-placed vineyard could produce more interesting wines. The high percentage of new oak used is perhaps too much for the meagerly concentrated wine.

COUFRAN (Cru Bourgeois) Haut-Médoc   GOOD

Production: 35,000 cases	Grape varieties: Merlot—85% Cabernet Sauvignon—15%
Secondary label: La Rose Marechale	
Vineyard size: 158 acres	Proprietors: Jean and Eric Miailhe
Time spent in barrels: 20–24 months	Average age of vines: 35 years
Evaluation of present classification: Should be maintained	
Plateau of maturity: 3–12 years following the vintage	

The large vineyard of Coufran is situated three miles north of the boundary of St.-Estèphe, contiguous to Route D2 after passing through the village of St.-Seurin-de-Cadourne. The property has been in the Miailhe family since 1924 and is now run by Eric Miailhe, the son of Jean, who is a major figure in the promotion of the Crus Bourgeois of Bordeaux.

The most distinctive aspect of Coufran is the high percentage of Merlot used in the blend, which the proprietors have decided succeeds well in the heavier, thicker soils common to this part of the Médoc. This has led some people to rashly conclude that the wine is drinkable upon release. I have not found that to be the case. In top vintages, Coufran is often supple and fruity in cask, but can go into a dumb, tannic stage in the bottle. The wine is a good Médoc, but the yields are extremely high, and again, one wonders whether the property's use of machine harvesters has any effect on the ultimate quality.

Coufran's record in the eighties has been somewhat spotty. The best vintages, 1982, 1986, and 1989, all have the potential for at least 10 years of evolution. I was unimpressed with the lean 1988 and straightforward 1985. The feeling in Bordeaux is that as the young Eric Miailhe takes more and more control of the winemaking, there will be a greater emphasis on intensity and structure.

DUCLUZEAU (Cru Bourgeois) Listrac VERY GOOD

Production: 2,000 cases	Grape varieties: Merlot—90% Cabernet Sauvignon—10%
Secondary label: none Vineyard size: 10 acres	Proprietor: Madame Jean- Eugène Borie
Time spent in barrels: 6 months in small casks and another 6–10 months in *cuves*	Average age of vines: 32 years
Evaluation of present classification: A high-quality Listrac that in certain vintages can compete favorably with some classified growths	
Plateau of maturity: 3–10 years following the vintage	

This property, owned by Monique Borie, the wife of the proprietor of Ducru-Beaucaillou, Haut-Batailley, and Grand-Puy-Lacoste, has, to my knowledge, the highest percentage of Merlot of any wine of the Médoc. The result is an extremely supple yet deliciously round, seductive wine with a great deal of charm and elegance. This wine has been estate-bottled since 1976. Under the management of the Borie team, along with consulting oenologist Emile Peynaud, the estate produces one of the best, yet least well-known wines of the Médoc. The 1982 was glorious. It was followed by a good 1983, a supple, fragrant, seductive 1985, a good 1986, and another lush, amply endowed wine in 1989. Unfortunately, most of this wine is sold in Europe through the *négociant* Pierre Coste in Langon.

DUPLESSIS (Cru Bourgeois) Moulis AVERAGE

Production: 6,000 cases	Grape varieties: Merlot—38% Cabernet Sauvignon—36% Cabernet Franc—15% Malbec—9% Petit Verdot—2%
Secondary label: none Vineyard size: 50 acres	
Time spent in barrels: 18 months	Proprietor: Lucien Lurton Average age of vines: 25 years
Evaluation of present classification: Should be maintained	
Plateau of maturity: 4–10 years following the vintage	

This property, sometimes called Duplèssis-Hauchecorne (after one of the former owners), now belongs to the ubiquitous family of Lucien Lurton. The wine is typical of an older-styled Moulis—coarse, robust, and lacking charm and fruit. The aging of the wine in old oak casks tends to give it a musty, old barrel smell. To date, this wine has been a disappointment. Given the talented team that includes *maître de chai* François Clauzel and oenologist Jacques Boissenot, the proprietor should be able to extract higher quality. For whatever reason, someone at Duplessis seems to be asleep at the wheel.

DUPLESSIS-FABRE (Cru Bourgeois) Moulis   AVERAGE

Production: 8,000 cases	Grape varieties: Cabernet Sauvignon—42% Merlot—42% Cabernet Franc—6% Petit Verdot—6% Malbec—4%
Secondary label: Laborde- Canterane	
Vineyard size: 44 acres	Proprietor: The Pagés family
Time spent in barrels: 18 months	Average age of vines: 20 years
Evaluation of present classification: Should be maintained	
Plateau of maturity: 5–10 years following the vintage	

This property was acquired by the late Guy Pagés in 1974. He began an extensive program of resurrecting and renovating the cellars, as well as replanting the vineyard. The Pagés family is better known for their very fine Listrac estate Fourcas-Dupré. This wine has yet to exhibit the same level of quality as Fourcas-Dupré. Perhaps the vineyard has not reached full maturity, although it is well placed near Brillette on clay and gravelly soils. The wine is aged in two-year-old barrels purchased from the famous first-growths Lafite-Rothschild and Margaux.

Vintages in the eighties have been characterized by a relatively tough texture, and lack charm and finesse. They are big, brawny, and dense. I have reservations about vintages such as 1983, 1985, and 1988 as to whether the fruit can stand up to all the tannin and body.

DUTRUCH-GRAND-POUJEAUX
(Cru Bourgeois) Moulis

GOOD

Production: 12,000 cases	Grape varieties: Cabernet Sauvignon—40% Merlot—30% Cabernet Franc—20% Petit Verdot—10%
Secondary label: La Gravière- Grand-Poujeaux	
Vineyard size: 62.5 acres	Proprietor: François Cordonnier
Time spent in barrels: 18–24 months	Average age of vines: 25 years
Evaluation of present classification: Should be maintained, although certain vintages can compete favorably with a Médoc fifth-growth	
Plateau of maturity: 6–12 years following the vintage	

Dutruch-Grand-Poujeaux, like so many wines of Moulis, often lacks a great deal of charm when it is young. Unlike some neighbors, this is one wine that can have the requisite concentration and depth to stand up to the tannin. After 5–7 years' time, I have often been pleased by just how well this wine turns out. Part of the reason for the excellent concentration is not only the respectable age of the vines, but the fact that much of this vineyard is planted by the ancient system of 10,000 vines per hectare, as opposed to the more conventional 6,600 vines per hectare. This, of course, is believed to create more stress, resulting in more concentrated grapes.

Top recent vintages have included a fine 1979, superb 1982, and top-notch wines made in 1985 and 1986. All of these will require at least 5–7 years to reach their plateau of maturity, where they can be expected to remain for another 5–10 years.

This is an underrated, impressively run property that merits more attention.

FONRÉAUD (Cru Bourgeois) Listrac GOOD

Production: 25,000 cases	Grape varieties:
	Cabernet Sauvignon—40%
	Merlot—40%
	Cabernet Franc—18%
	Petit Verdot—2%
Secondary label: Fontaine-Royale	
Vineyard size: 89 acres	Proprietor: The Chanfreau family
Time spent in barrels: 6 months in casks and 6 months in *cuves*	Average age of vines: 20 years
Evaluation of present classification: Should be maintained	
Plateau of maturity: 5–7 years following the vintage	

This impressively symmetrical white château, with a dominating center turret and spire, sits on the left-hand side of Route D1 as one leaves the tiny village of Bouqueyran in the direction of Lesparre. Since 1982 the property has been owned by the Chanfreau family, who also control the nearby Château Lestage.

The style emphasized is one of soft, fruity, immediately drinkable wines that are limited to 6–7 years of aging ability. The high percentage of Merlot, as well as the owner's decision to age the wine for 6 months in oak casks and 6 months in *cuves*, results in a soft, round wine with immediate appeal. The best recent vintages have been the 1982, 1983, 1985, and 1989.

FOURCAS-DUPRÉ (Cru Bourgeois) Listrac GOOD

Production: 25,000 cases	Grape varieties:
	Cabernet Sauvignon—50%
	Merlot—38%
	Cabernet Franc—10%
	Petit Verdot—2%
Secondary label: Bellevue-Laffont	
Vineyard size: 104 acres	Proprietor: The Pagés family
Time spent in barrels: 18 months	Average age of vines: 25 years
Evaluation of present classification: One of the best of the Cru Bourgeois properties; should be maintained	
Plateau of maturity: 5–10 years following the vintage	

Until his death in 1985, Guy Pagés was responsible for elevating the quality of the wines of Fourcas-Dupré. I purchased and cellared, with great satisfaction, the 1975 and 1978, and have been impressed more recently with the 1982, 1983, and 1986. However, since the 1986, the wine has been less impressive, with a disappointing 1988 and 1989. I hope recent vintages do not reflect a drop in quality, as this has been one of the most consistent properties in Listrac since the early seventies.

The vineyard of Fourcas-Dupré is located on primarily gravelly soil, and the current proprietor, Patrice Pagés, approaches winemaking in a traditional manner. Over three-fourths of the vineyard is harvested by hand, and the rest picked by machine. Twenty-five percent new oak is used, and at its best, the wine is wonderfully perfumed and ripe, with a surprising elegance and suppleness.

FOURCAS-HOSTEN (Cru Bourgeois) Listrac   GOOD

Production: 20,000 cases	Grape varieties: Cabernet Sauvignon—50% Merlot—40% Cabernet Franc—10%
Secondary label: none	
Vineyard size: 105 acres	Proprietor: A syndicate involving Peter A. Sichel, De Rivoyre, Schiller, and individual Danes and Americans
Time spent in barrels: 14–18 months	Average age of vines: 20 years
Evaluation of present classification: This is a fine Cru Bourgeois that comes close in the top vintages to the quality of a Médoc fifth-growth	
Plateau of maturity: 5–9 years following the vintage	

At present, Fourcas-Hosten is a leading vineyard of Listrac. The commune and town sit along the major highway, D1, that traverses the central portion of the Médoc. In 1971, Fourcas-Hosten was sold to a syndicate, dominated by American investors. At that time an extensive plan of renovation in both the vineyard and wine cellars was instituted.

The style of wine of Fourcas-Hosten has changed with the new ownership. The old Fourcas-Hosten wines tended to be hard, tannic, robust, coarse wines, with impressive color and body, but often excessive tannins. The best of the old-style Fourcas-Hosten is the 1970, a big, rich, generously flavored wine that is now approaching maturity. Starting with the light vintage of 1973, the wines took on a pronounced suppleness and fruitiness, with less abrasive tannins in evidence. The 1975 was a fine example of the new-style Fourcas-Hosten, possessing rich, deep, black-currant fruit and aging potential of 10 to 20 years. The 1978 is very drinkable now, soft and flavorful, as is the lighter, more delicate 1979. After 1975, the best vintages are the 1982, 1985, 1986, and 1988.

FOURCAS-LOUBANEY (Cru Bourgeois) Listrac   EXCELLENT

Production: 1,800 cases	Grape varieties:
	Cabernet Sauvignon—60%
	Merlot—40%
Secondary label: none	
Vineyard size: 10 acres	Proprietor: Michel Hostens
Time spent in barrels: 18–24 months	Average age of vines: 38 years
Evaluation of present classification: The quality equivalent of a Médoc fifth-growth	
Plateau of maturity: 5–12 years following the vintage	

This is one of the very best wines, if not the finest wine, of the Listrac appellation. Unfortunately, the tiny production is rarely seen except by a small group of avid Bordeaux aficionados. Proprietor Michel Hostens believes in extremely small yields of no more than 45 hectoliters per hectare. Additionally, his vineyard is among the oldest in Listrac. The use of at least 50% new oak and minimal clarification techniques usually result in a surprisingly concentrated, rich wine that avoids the hard tannins and rustic feel of so many Listracs.

Although I have not tasted a fully mature vintage of Fourcas-Louba-ney, the four vintages I have tasted have been so impressive that this wine would merit inclusion in any revised classification of the wines of Bordeaux as a fifth-growth.

Fourcas-Loubaney is actually made at Michel Hostens's other Listrac château, Moulin de la Borde, which does not quite approach the quality level of Fourcas-Loubaney.

VINTAGES

1989—Soft and forward, with excellent color and a big, plummy, oaky
·   nose, this wine lacks the concentration and grip of the other vin-
85   tages I have tasted of Fourcas-Loubaney, but it still offers a gen-
         erous, amply endowed mouthful of wine. Drink it over the next 5–
         7 years. Anticipated maturity: Now–1998. Last tasted, 4/91.

1988—I have been greatly impressed with the quality of this estate's
· wine in 1985, 1986, and 1988. Black/ruby in color, with a full-
88 intensity bouquet of superpure blackcurrants, herbs, and toasty
new oak, this wine is splendidly concentrated for a 1988 and has
excellent balance and a very long finish. It is a sleeper of the
vintage. Anticipated maturity: 1993–2005. Last tasted, 4/91.

1986—The 1986 is one of the great sleepers of the vintage. Still splen-
· didly dark ruby/purple in color, with a blossoming bouquet of
89 toasty new oak, cassis, licorice, and some floral aromas, this full-
bodied, impeccably balanced, admirably concentrated wine has
loads of extract (no doubt from low yields and old vines), and a
long, intense finish. Oh, how I wish I had bought more of this
wine! Anticipated maturity: 1992–2006. Last tasted, 1/91.

1985—Just reaching its plateau of maturity, the 1985 Fourcas-Loubaney
· has a very intense bouquet of blackcurrants, subtle herbs, and
87 new oak. In the mouth, the wine is supple, expansive, and exhibits fine depth and length. It should be drunk over the next 5–6
years. Anticipated maturity: Now–1996. Last tasted, 1/91.

GRESSIER GRAND-POUJEAUX
(Cru Bourgeois) Moulis

EXCELLENT

Production: 8,500 cases	Grape varieties: Cabernet Sauvignon—55% Merlot—35% Cabernet Franc—10%
Secondary label: none	
Vineyard size: 44 acres	Proprietor: The family of Bernard de Saint-Affrique
Time spent in barrels: 20–24 months	Average age of vines: 27 years
Evaluation of present classification: The quality equivalent of a Médoc fifth-growth	
Plateau of maturity: 7–20 years following the vintage.	

This is a fascinating property to examine. The estate has been in the
same family since it was purchased by Monsieur Gressier in 1724. The
domain has a long track record of making wines that can last for 20 to 30
or more years, and it has not hesitated to declassify certain vintages such
as 1963, 1965, and 1977 that were not up to its standards. The vineyard,
which sits on some of the best gravelly soil of Moulis, has several parcels
of extremely old vines where the production rarely exceeds 15 hectoliters

per hectare. Additionally, a conservative pruning philosophy results in yields that are often much lower than many of the more renowned classified growths. The wine, vinified in old oak fermentation tanks and aged in small casks, can be almost impossible to taste young, but I have become a believer in just how well this wine can last based on a tasting of the 1966, 1970 (a superb wine that I rated 90), and 1975. More recently, terrific wines were made in 1982, 1985, 1986, and 1989.

The château still boasts a cellar with vintages from the twenties. This is no doubt meant to bolster the image that this is the longest-lived wine of Moulis.

VINTAGES

1989—A dark, opaque, ruby/purple color suggests a serious level of
· extract and intensity. The bouquet remains tight, but with swirl-
88 ing, delivers aromas of tar, spices, coffee, and blackcurrants. In the mouth, the wine is packed with fruit and has high levels of glycerin, outstanding concentration, and plenty of tannin in the finish. While the acidity is low, the tannins are high. My guess is that this wine needs another 8–10 years of cellaring. Anticipated maturity: 1999–2015. Last tasted, 4/91.

1986—The 1986 Gressier Grand-Poujeaux is black/ruby/purple in color,
· with a reticent, but blossoming bouquet of minerals, licorice, and
89 blackcurrants. On the palate, the wine displays the judicious use of new oak barrels, outstanding richness and length, and a long, powerful, tannic finish. This is definitely a wine to lay away in your cellar for a minimum of 7–8 years. It could turn out to be one of the sleepers of the vintage. Anticipated maturity: 1997–2020. Last tasted, 4/90.

1985—The 1985, a sleeper of the vintage, is a black/ruby-colored wine
· that is loaded with extract and has a tremendous tannic clout, a
87 long, rich finish, full body, and 10–15 years of further evolution. This is a brilliant old-style wine that should be bought only by those who have patience and a fine, cool cellar. Anticipated maturity: 1996–2010. Last tasted, 3/89.

1984—Quite a serious wine for a 1984, this dark-colored, ripe, rich,
· tannic, medium- to full-bodied wine has plenty of extract, and will
84 reward those who try it. Anticipated maturity: Now–1994. Last tasted, 3/87.

1982—The bouquet is beginning to display signs of maturity. The big,
· almost roasted chestnut, leather, mineral, and blackcurrant bou-
89 quet precedes a powerful, muscular, exceptionally concentrated

wine that almost overpowers the palate, but is impressive for its size, strength, and depth. This wine is not for the shy. Anticipated maturity: 1992–2010. Last tasted, 3/88.

1979— Still remarkably young and backward, this dark ruby-colored,
· herbaceous, peppery, and currant-scented wine is medium bod-
86 ied, with surprisingly strong acidity, and moderate tannins. It lacks the great depth this wine can achieve in top years, and is a more streamlined and civilized rendition of Gressier Grand-Pou-jeaux. Nevertheless, it is still not ready to drink. Anticipated maturity: 1992–2001. Last tasted, 3/88.

1970— A spectacular bouquet of roasted nuts, minerals, tar, licorice, and
· black fruits is clearly of classified-growth quality. In the mouth,
90 the wine displays an almost sumptuous richness, some moderate tannins in the finish, and great concentration and length. This wine has shed much of its hardness and is delicious to drink. It exhibits no signs of losing its fruit. In style and character it is reminiscent of the 1970 Lynch-Bages! Anticipated maturity: Now–2005. Last tasted, 3/88.

GREYSAC (Cru Bourgeois) Médoc   GOOD

Production: 22,000 cases	Grape varieties: Cabernet Sauvignon—50% Merlot—35% Cabernet Franc—10% Petit Verdot—5%
Secondary label: none Vineyard size: 74 acres	Proprietor: The Domaines Codem
Time spent in barrels: 18 months	Average age of vines: 25 years
Evaluation of present classification: Should be maintained	
Plateau of maturity: 5–12 years following the vintage	

In recent years, Greysac has become one of the most popular bourgeois wines in the United States. High quality, and the dynamic personality and marketing ability of the now-deceased, gregarious proprietor— Baron François de Gunzburg—were totally responsible for this wine's acceptance by Americans (who are normally so classification conscious when it comes to Bordeaux wines).

The style of wine at Greysac is one that I have always found very elegant, smooth, and medium bodied, with a complex bouquet filled with currant fruit, and a true, mineral, soil-like aroma. Never an aggressive or overly tannic wine, Greysac is usually fully mature by its sixth or seventh year, and keeps well for up to 12 years.

There have been some splendid successes at Greysac in the seventies. The 1975, while still not fully mature, is my favorite wine from this estate. Rich, full bodied, complex, and powerful, it is an excellent example of a Cru Bourgeois wine. The 1976 is drinking beautifully now. Round, sweet, and ripe, yet well balanced, it is better than many classified growths in this vintage. The 1978 is also ready to drink and should be drunk up. Supple, ripe, and soft, it is very tasty. The 1979 is an elegant, complex, richly flavored, medium-weight wine.

For whatever reasons (perhaps the failing health of the late Baron?), the vintages of the early eighties—1981, 1982, and 1983—tasted less successful than vintages in the seventies. The 1982 was the best of this trio. Yet the quality of Greysac in the late eighties has rebounded with fine efforts in 1986 and 1989. For a wine of its stature, Greysac remains one of the very best wine values among the Crus Bourgeois.

HANTEILLAN (Cru Bourgeois) Haut-Médoc   AVERAGE

Production: 35,000 cases	Grape varieties: Cabernet Sauvignon—48% Merlot—42% Cabernet Franc—6% Petit Verdot—4%
Secondary label: Tour du Vatican	Proprietor: SARL du Hanteillan
Vineyard size: 210 acres	Administrator: Catherine Blasco
Time spent in barrels: 12–18 months	Average age of vines: 18 years
Evaluation of present classification: Should be maintained	
Plateau of maturity: 4–8 years following the vintage	

This is a highly promoted Cru Bourgeois that I have always found to be lacking in fruit and charm. It is classically made with a high-tech *cuvier* designed to produce wines of quality. Nevertheless, the wine comes across as relatively tannic, austere, and compact. I thought I detected more charm and finesse with both the 1989 and 1990. There is a second wine for *cuvées* deemed not acceptable for Hanteillan. The winemaking techniques include a traditional vinification, with a maceration of 20 days, the use of 15% new oak barrels, and only one filtration. The only negative is that the vineyard is harvested by machine. But that alone should not account for the leanness of so many Hanteillan vintages. The best mature wine I have tasted from this estate was the quaffable, straightforward 1985. Run with considerable dedication by Catherine Blasco, the resulting wines from this property may finally begin to live up to their publicity.

LAMARQUE (Cru Bourgeois) Haut-Médoc   GOOD

Production: 25,000 cases	Grape varieties: Cabernet Sauvignon—46% Merlot—25% Cabernet Franc—24% Petit Verdot—5%
Secondary labels: Cap de Haut and Reserve des Marquis d'Evry	
Vineyard size: 123.5 acres	Proprietor: S. C. Gromand d'Evry
Time spent in barrels: 10 months in small casks and 8 months in vats	Average age of vines: 20 years
Evaluation of present classification: Should be maintained	
Plateau of maturity: 4–7 years following the vintage	

One of the outstanding medieval fortress castles in the Bordeaux region, Lamarque, named after the town of the same name, sits just off the main Route du Vin (D2) of the Médoc directly on the road to the ferry boat that traverses the Gironde to Blaye.

Lamarque is a typically good, middle-weight, central Médoc wine. It seems to have a touch of the St.-Julien elegance mixed with round, supple, soft, ripe fruity flavors. The owners, the Gromand family, make the wine with great care. The best of the older vintages included the luscious, rich 1970, powerful, tannic 1975, and supple 1978, all wines that are now in decline, as Lamarque should be consumed within 7–8 years of the vintage.

Lamarque's track record in the eighties began disappointingly with relatively light, fluid wines in 1981, 1982, and 1983. However, the property rebounded strongly with a good 1986 and 1988, and a 1989 that promises to be the best Lamarque made since the powerful 1975. Prices remain among the more reasonable for a Cru Bourgeois.

LANESSAN (Cru Bourgeois) Haut-Médoc   EXCELLENT

Production: 17,000 cases	Grape varieties: Cabernet Sauvignon—75% Merlot—20% Cabernet Franc—5%
Secondary label: Domaine de Sainte-Gemme	
Vineyard size: 99 acres	Proprietor: The Bouteiller family
Time spent in barrels: 24 months	Average age of vines: 20 years
Evaluation of present classification: Inconsistent, but at its best Lanessan is the quality equivalent of a Médoc fifth-growth	
Plateau of maturity: 7–18 years following the vintage	

Lanessan can be one of the outstanding wines of the Haut-Médoc appellation. The wine could probably be given serious consideration for fifth-growth status should any reclassification of the wines of the Médoc take place.

Lanessan, which is located in Cussac immediately south of the commune of St.-Julien, opposite the big vineyard of Gruaud-Larose, makes intensely flavored wines, with deep color, a robust, large-scaled frame, and chewy texture. If they can be criticized for lacking finesse, they more than compensate for that weakness with rich, gutsy, blackcurrant flavors.

The 99 acres, which are being augmented each year with new plantings, produce in excess of 17,000 cases of wine. The property is owned and managed by the Bouteiller family.

Lanessan ages extremely well, as attested by a delightful, but tired 1920 I shared with a friend in 1983. Of more recent vintages, the top successes include the 1970, 1975, 1978, 1982, 1986, 1988, 1989, and 1990. The wines are powerful, individualized wines that are somewhat similar in style and character to the fifth-growth Pauillac, Lynch-Bages.

I have noted above that Lanessan can be inconsistent. Part of the spottiness of Lanessan's performance (the only criticism one could possibly make) is probably because of the château's insistence on using old barrels for aging the wine. Perhaps a small percentage of new barrels each year might prove beneficial for such a robust wine. For visitors to the region, this lovely château, which has been owned by the same family since 1890, is now a museum displaying numerous carriages and an assortment of harnesses. It is open to the public.

VINTAGES

1989—Lanessan's 1989 is very herbaceous. It is diffuse and muddled,
·   but fat, richly fruity, and soft. However, the wine has begun to
86?   pull itself together and exhibit more intensity and character. An-
        ticipated maturity: Now–2000. Last tasted, 4/91.

1988—The 1988 is a splendidly full, rich, highly concentrated wine,
·   surpassing many of the classified growths in this vintage. Much
86   more concentrated than the 1989, with a complex bouquet of
        cedar and blackcurrants intertwined with subtle scents of new
        oak, in the mouth, this plump, highly concentrated, full-bodied
        wine should drink beautifully for 10–15 years. The 1988 is un-
        doubtedly a sleeper of the vintage. Anticipated maturity: 1992–
        2008. Last tasted, 4/91.

1987—Somewhat herbaceous and lean, the 1987 Lanessan has an open-
·   knit bouquet, and soft, round flavors exhibiting a greenness that
74   is indicative of unripe Cabernet Sauvignon. Anticipated maturity:
        Now–1994. Last tasted, 4/90.

1986—This is probably the best Lanessan made in two decades. Still
·   deep ruby/purple in color, with an emerging but reticent bouquet
88   of herbs, leather, grilled meats, and blackcurrants, this full-bod-
        ied, tannic, powerful Lanessan should be sought out by consum-
        ers who like their clarets well defined, tannic, and impressively
        structured. Anticipated maturity: 1993–2010. Last tasted, 3/90.

1985—Smoky, earthy, and ripe blackberry notes soar from the glass. On
·   the palate, the 1985 Lanessan exhibits plenty of depth, lower
87   acidity, and softer tannins than normal, but still offers a forceful,
        meaty mouthful of wine lacking a bit of finesse and charm. It
        compensates for these shortcomings with robustness and ripe-
        ness. Anticipated maturity: 1992–2003. Last tasted, 3/89.

1984—A spicy, slightly vegetal bouquet is followed by a wine that is
·   slightly sweet, rather disjointed, but adequate for drinking over
76   the next 3–4 years. Anticipated maturity: Now–1993. Last tasted,
        4/89.

1982—Given the low acidity and a fat, loosely knit structure, this is not
·   a typical example of Lanessan. However, there is no denying the
86   forward, generously endowed personality, gobs of earthy, black-
        currant fruit, and soft, luscious finish. Anticipated maturity:
        Now–1994. Last tasted, 1/90.

OLDER VINTAGES

It has been more than 5 years since I tasted the outstanding 1970, or
the promising 1975. My bet is that they are still drinking well in 1991.

LAROSE-TRINTAUDON
(Cru Bourgeois) Haut-Médoc   AVERAGE

Production:85,000–90,000 cases	Grape varieties: Cabernet Sauvignon—60% Merlot—20% Cabernet Franc—20%
Secondary labels: Larose-Perganson, Larose-Mascard, and Larose-Sieujean	
Vineyard size: 424 acres	Proprietor: A corporate ownership administered by Elysée Forner
Time spent in barrels: 15–18 months	Average age of vines: 14 years
Evaluation of present classification: Should be maintained	
Plateau of maturity: 4–7 years following the vintage	

The largest vineyard in the Médoc has for years produced a straightforward, supple, correct wine of no great distinction. However, I have noticed that vintages since the mid-1980s have often been characterized by a slight corky smell, suggesting a different type of oak is being employed at Larose-Trintaudon. The result is a cardboard-like aroma that one can both smell and taste. I have been told that this dissipates in time, but since this is a wine to be drunk in its first 5–8 years of life, I am a bit skeptical. This wine has generally represented good value, but since 1985 I have frequently been disappointed.

LESTAGE (Cru Bourgeois) Listrac   GOOD

Production: 21,000 cases	Grape varieties: Merlot—55% Cabernet Sauvignon—41% Petit Verdot—4%
Secondary label: Caroline	
Vineyard size: 118 acres	Proprietor: The Chanfreau family
Time spent in barrels: 14–16 months in vats and barrels	Average age of vines: 20 years
Evaluation of present classification: Should be maintained	
Plateau of maturity: 3–8 years following the vintage	

I have fond memories of many vintages of Lestage, largely because I had few preconceived notions about this wine. They are supple, straightforward, richly fruity efforts, cleanly made and tasty. Until 1985 the entire production was aged in large vats, but in 1985 the proprietor began employing small oak barrels. That decision has resulted in wines with more structure and character. This is never a profound wine, and there is a tendency to produce too much wine per hectare, but this large vineyard in Listrac, with a charming three-story, nineteenth century château, easily fulfills the needs of consumers looking for wines that offer immediate drinkability at a fair price.

The best recent vintages have included the 1982 (now tiring), 1983 (it should be consumed immediately), and a promising 1989 (for drinking over the next 4–5 years).

LIVERSAN (Cru Bourgeois) Haut-Médoc   VERY GOOD

Production: 20,000 cases	Grape varieties:
	Cabernet Sauvignon—49%
	Merlot—38%
	Cabernet Franc—10%
	Petit Verdot—3%
Secondary label: Fonpiqueyre	
Vineyard size: 98.8 acres	Proprietor: Prince Guy de Polignac
Time spent in barrels: 18 months	Average age of vines: 25 years
Evaluation of present classification: Should be maintained, but vintages since the mid-1980s are extremely close in quality to a Médoc fifth-growth	
Plateau of maturity: 4–10 years following the vintage	

Many Bordeaux observers have long considered the excellently placed vineyard of Liversan, which sits between the city of Pauillac and the hamlet of St.-Sauveur, to have the potential to produce wines of classified-growth quality. However, it was not until 1983, when the property was purchased by the Polignac family (previously the largest shareholders of the Pommery champagne firm), that the quality of Liversan began to soar. The construction of a new winery, increased use of new oak barrels (33% each year), and conservative yields that average just under 40 hectoliters per hectare have resulted in a series of excellent wines that sit at the top of the Cru Bourgeois hierarchy. One could even argue that in years such as 1985, 1988, and 1989, Liversan is as good as if not better than, many of the classified growths.

The style produced at Liversan aims for wines with a deep color, fine extract, soft tannins, as well as grip, concentration, and length. The owners attribute the quality of Liversan to the extremely dense plantations of 8,000 vines per hectare, which is 2,000 more vines per hectare than in most Bordeaux vineyards. This dense plantation causes the roots to push deeper into the earth seeking nutrients, and therefore producing wines with greater character and depth.

LOUDENNE (Cru Bourgeois) Médoc   AVERAGE

Production: 19,000 cases	Grape varieties: Cabernet Sauvignon—48% Merlot—41% Cabernet Franc—8% Petit Verdot—3%
Secondary label: none	
Vineyard size: 101 acres for red wine	Proprietor: W. & A. Gilbey, Ltd.
Time spent in barrels: 18–24 months	Average age of vines: 20 years
Evaluation of present classification: Should be maintained	
Plateau of maturity: 3–6 years following the vintage	

The lovely pink Château Loudenne has been owned by the firm of W. & A. Gilbey since 1875. The vineyard, planted on sandy, stony soils, is located at the very northern end of the Médoc, near St.-Yzans. While I have enjoyed the fruity, straightforward white wine, made from a blend of 50% Sauvignon and 50% Semillon, I find the red wine extremely light. Although it is correctly made, it lacks complexity, richness, and staying power. Drink it in the first 3–5 years of life, except in vintages such as 1975 and 1982 when it can last for nearly a decade.

Given the attention to detail exhibited at Loudenne, I have often wondered whether or not this area of the Médoc is capable of producing wines of staying power. However, perhaps Loudenne, with its high-tech red wine winemaking process—where the wine is filtered via the kieselguhr system prior to going into barrel, and then sterile filtered (rare for a Bordeaux château) at bottling—produces wines that are more stripped than they need to be.

Loudenne is also a prominent producer of a crisp, light, dry white wine. The production averages 5,000 cases per year.

MAGNOL (Cru Bourgeois) Haut-Médoc GOOD

Production: 7,000 cases	Grape varieties: Cabernet Sauvignon—66% Merlot—34%
Secondary label: none	
Vineyard size: 42 acres	Proprietor: Barton & Guestier
Time spent in barrels: 18–20 months	Average age of vines: 15 years
Evaluation of present classification: Should be maintained	
Plateau of maturity: 3–5 years following the vintage	

I have been impressed with the soft, fruity, easy-to-like, and easy-to-drink wines of Château Magnol, a property owned by the huge firm of Barton & Guestier. The vineyard is located just north of the city of Bordeaux, east of the sprawling suburb of Blanquefort. The wine is extremely well made in a modern, commercial style, and there is no doubting its seductive, forward charms. Magnol is not a wine to lay away in your cellar; it should be drunk early. The best recent vintages have been the excellent 1985, 1986, and promising 1989.

MALESCASSE (Cru Bourgeois) Haut-Médoc GOOD

Production: 16,000 cases	Grape varieties: Cabernet Sauvignon—70% Merlot—20% Cabernet Franc—10%
Secondary label: none	
Vineyard size: 79 acres	Proprietor: The Tesseron family
Time spent in barrels: 16 months	Average age of vines: 19 years
Evaluation of present classification: Should be maintained	
Plateau of maturity: 4–7 years following the vintage	

Malescasse is a well-situated vineyard located just to the north of the village of Arcins and south of Lamarque. The vineyard was extensively replanted in the early seventies, and the vines are now reaching maturity. The responsibility for the direction of Malescasse rests with Alfred Tesseron, who also looks over his family's more important châteaux, Pontet-Canet and Lafon-Rochet.

This is a seriously run Cru Bourgeois and since the early eighties, the wines have been richly fruity, medium bodied, and ideal for drinking between the ages of 3 and 8. The best vintages to date have been the

1985 and 1986. I was less impressed with the 1988 and the relatively jammy, diluted 1989. Prices for Malescasse tend to be high, in part because one of the Médoc's most famous families owns this estate.

MAUCAILLOU (Cru Bourgeois) Moulis — EXCELLENT

Production: 25,000 cases	Grape varieties: Cabernet Sauvignon—58% Merlot—35% Petit Verdot—7%
Secondary labels: Cap de Haut and Franc-Caillou (this wine appears without a vintage or Moulis appellation)	
Vineyard size: 136 acres	Proprietor: The Dourthe family Administrator: Philippe Dourthe
Time spent in barrels: 24 months	Average age of vines: 19 years
Evaluation of present classification: Easily the equivalent of a fourth- or fifth-growth	
Plateau of maturity: 4–12 years following the vintage	

Maucaillou has consistently represented one of the best wine values in the Médoc. The wine is impeccably made by the robust and exuberant Philippe Dourthe. There is little to criticize at this estate. Maucaillou is a deeply colored wine, with a splendid ripe concentration of fruit, good body, soft tannins, and enough grip and extract to mature gracefully over a 10- to 12-year period. Vintages in the eighties have all been notable successes except for the 1984 and 1987. The 1982 is generous, the 1983 perhaps every bit as good, but more elegant and fragrant, the 1985 round and full bodied, and the 1986 the best Maucaillou made in the previous 20 years. Both the 1988 and superb 1989 promise to provide rich, fleshy, velvety-textured drinking over the next decade. Since the early eighties the wines have been aged in 60% new oak casks with the remainder in two-year-old casks purchased from prominent classified-growth châteaux.

It is not easy to make wines so rich and fat that they can be drunk young while maintaining their ability to age for up to a decade. Maucaillou has clearly succeeded in taming the soil of Moulis, which can render hard, tannic wine. They have produced exceptionally elegant, highly satisfying wines that are among only a handful of underpriced Bordeaux.

For the adventurous travelers who enjoy the back roads of the Médoc, I highly recommend a visit to Château Maucaillou where there is an attractive winemaking museum. In addition, visitors have the opportunity to taste the new wine.

VINTAGES

1989—Excellent efforts were put forth by Maucaillou in both the 1988
· and 1989 vintages. The 1989 has a generous level of gorgeous
88 black raspberry fruit in its bouquet, followed by wonderfully rich, fleshy, highly extracted fruit flavors and a velvety texture, and it is pure seduction and finesse in the finish. Anticipated maturity: Now–2001. Last tasted, 4/91.

1988—The 1988 does not offer the pure hedonism of the 1989, but it is
· an extremely attractive, plump, elegant, richly fruity, medium-
86 bodied wine, the type of wine I search out on restaurant wine lists when trying to find something of high quality at a reasonable price. Anticipated maturity: Now–1998. Last tasted, 4/91.

1986—The 1986 should prove to be slightly better than the 1985, as it is
· a deeper, fuller, and richer wine with a bit more tannin. The black
86 cherry fruit is complemented nicely by some toasty oak. Anticipated maturity: Now–1998. Last tasted, 11/90.

1985—Of all the wines of Moulis, this one displays the most elegance
· and style, although it will never have the power and depth of a
85 Chasse-Spleen or Poujeaux. The 1985 is a stylish, rich, graceful wine with medium to full body, a perfumed, aromatic character, and long finish. Anticipated maturity: Now–1998. Last tasted, 4/91.

MAYNE-LALANDE (Cru Bourgeois) Listrac   VERY GOOD

Production: 6,500 cases	Grape varieties:
	Cabernet Sauvignon—50%
	Merlot—49%
	Petit Verdot—1%
Secondary label: none	
Vineyard size: 32 acres	Proprietor: Bernard Lartigue
Time spent in barrels: 18–22 months	Average age of vines: 25 years
Evaluation of present classification: One of the least-known but best wines of Listrac, this château, in vintages such as 1982, 1985, 1986, and 1989, can compete favorably with a Médoc fifth-growth	
Plateau of maturity: 5–15 years following the vintage	

This little-known Listrac property may emerge during the nineties as one of the stars of the appellation. I had the opportunity to taste most of the

vintages of the eighties, and I was especially impressed by the richness
and intensity of the 1982, the finesse of the 1983, the power and surprising concentration of the 1985, and the potential for 15–20 years of longevity in the 1986. While the 1988 was slightly lean, the 1989 looks to be
one of the best wines this property has made.

The key to their success at this estate is low yields and the dedication
of proprietor Bernard Lartigue. For now, this wine remains known only
to insiders and some of Bordeaux's most innovative restaurateurs, such
as Jean-Pierre Xiradakis, who sells this wine at his well-known restaurant, La Tupina. The price has yet to take off, and therefore Mayne-
Lalande appears to be undervalued at present.

MOULIN-ROUGE (Cru Bourgeois) Haut-Médoc   VERY GOOD

Production: 8,500 cases	Grape varieties:
	Cabernet Sauvignon—50%
	Merlot—40%
	Cabernet Franc—5%
	Petit Verdot—5%
Secondary label: none	
Vineyard size: 37 acres	Proprietor: Veyries-Pelon
Time spent in barrels: 18 months	Average age of vines: 25 years
Evaluation of present classification: Should be maintained, but this is one of the better Crus Bourgeois	
Plateau of maturity: 5–10 years following the vintage	

Moulin-Rouge is one of my favorite Crus Bourgeois. The highly morsellated vineyard (there must be at least 6 separate parcels) is located north
of the village of Cussac-Fort Médoc, just south of the appellation of St.-
Julien. Not surprisingly, the wine often has the character of a good St.-
Julien. It is always deep in color, and in the eighties has been rich, fleshy,
full bodied, and somewhat reminiscent of such wines as Hortevie and
Terrey-Gros-Cailloux. Of course, Moulin-Rouge is significantly less expensive since it is entitled to only the Haut-Médoc appellation.

The only criticism that can be leveled against Moulin-Rouge is for
extremely high yields of 65–75 hectoliters per hectare, but this is a
property where the high yields do not seem to have a negative effect on
the wine's concentration. This is one of the more solid, chunky, fleshy
Crus Bourgeois, and while it may not have great finesse, it does offer
considerable richness, muscle, and character. The best recent vintages
include a nearly outstanding 1989, and very good wines in 1988, 1986,
and 1985.

MOULIN À VENT (Cru Bourgeois) Moulis   GOOD

Production: 10,000 cases	Grape varieties: Cabernet Sauvignon—65% Merlot—30% Petit Verdot—5%
Secondary label: Moulin de Saint-Vincent	
Vineyard size: 62 acres	Proprietor: The Hessel family
Time spent in barrels: 18 months	Average age of vines: 20 years
Evaluation of present classification: Should be maintained	
Plateau of maturity: 5–10 years following the vintage	

This property continues to produce an older style of Moulis—dense, tannic, and requiring several years in the bottle to soften and evolve. The decision in 1981 to begin filtering has softened the tannins. The property uses a significant amount of press wine, resulting in a dark-colored, forceful, powerful style of Moulis that seems to be best when the grapes are fully ripe, as in vintages such as 1982, 1985, and 1989. I also liked the 1986, but I found the 1988 disappointing.

Overall, this is a property that has made considerable improvement in the quality of its wines since 1977 when the young Dominique Hessel began to manage the estate's winemaking.

MOULIS (Cru Bourgeois) Moulis   AVERAGE

Production: 4,500 cases	Grape varieties: Cabernet Sauvignon—60% Merlot—40%
Secondary label: none	
Vineyard size: 30 acres	Proprietor: Jacques Darricarrère
Time spent in barrels: 20–30 months	Average age of vines: 20 years
Evaluation of present classification: Should be maintained	
Plateau of maturity: 4–7 years following the vintage	

The only vintage of Moulis that has impressed me was the 1982. The other good vintages from Moulis in the eighties have been deep in color, but compact, relatively austere, straightforward wines without the complexity and charm one expects. Nevertheless, this is a well-situated vineyard, and the approach to the wine's vinification is traditional.

LES ORMES-SORBET (Cru Bourgeois) Médoc   VERY GOOD

Production: 12,500 cases	Grape varieties:
	Cabernet Sauvignon—65%
	Merlot—35%
Secondary label: De Couques	
Vineyard size: 50 acres	Proprietor: Jean Boivert
Time spent in barrels: 18 months	Average age of vines: 30 years
Evaluation of present classification: Should be maintained, but since 1982 this has been one of the best Crus Bourgeois	
Plateau of maturity: 6–12 years following the vintage	

The current proprietor, Jean Boivert (who took over this estate in 1970), has, since the mid-1980s, produced one of the best wines in the northern Médoc. Boivert is the eighth generation of his family to run this vineyard near the sleepy village of Coequèques since 1730. The dense planting, and Jean Boivert's decision in the seventies to increase the percentage of Cabernet Sauvignon have paid off with an excellent string of good vintages since 1982. The wine spends 18 months in oak casks, of which one-third are new, and there is minimal filtration done at bottling. The style that has emerged at Les Ormes-Sorbet is one of deep color, a pronounced toasty vanillin oakiness from excellent Tronçais barrels. They are wines that have the potential for a decade of longevity.

The best recent vintages include: the sumptuous 1982, which is fully mature; a lighter, but still tasty 1983; a delicious, intensely concentrated wine of classified-growth quality in 1985; another impeccably made wine in 1986; and an oaky, smoky, fat, and concentrated 1989. This is an up-and-coming domain in the northern Médoc.

PATACHE D'AUX (Cru Bourgeois) Médoc   GOOD

Production: 23,000 cases	Grape varieties:
	Cabernet Sauvignon—70%
	Merlot—20%
	Cabernet Franc—10%
Secondary label: none	
Vineyard size: 93.8 acres	Proprietor: Claude Lapalu
Time spent in barrels: 15–16 months	Average age of vines: 20 years
Evaluation of present classification: Should be maintained	
Plateau of maturity: 5–8 years following the vintage	

Patache d'Aux produces wines that have an almost California-like herbaceous, juicy, blackcurrant fruitiness, supple texture, and easy drinkability. In years where the Cabernet does not attain full ripeness, the wine has a tendency to be intensely herbaceous, even bordering on vegetal. However, in ripe vintages, such as 1982, 1986, and 1989, this can be an immensely impressive Cru Bourgeois for drinking in the first 7–8 years of its life. It is often jammy and opulent, and rarely elegant, but for those consumers looking for a well-made, reasonably priced Cru Bourgeois that does not require deferred gratification, this is a worthy choice. Proprietor Claude Lapalu is also the owner and is responsible for the winemaking at Château Le Boscq.

PEYRABON (Cru Bourgeois) Haut-Médoc   AVERAGE

Production: 25,000 cases	Grape varieties: Cabernet Sauvignon—50% Merlot—27% Cabernet Franc—23%
Secondary label: Lapiey	
Vineyard size: 131 acres	Proprietor: Jacques Babeau
Time spent in barrels: 18–24 months	Average age of vines: 20 years
Evaluation of present classification: Should be maintained; an average-quality Cru Bourgeois	
Plateau of maturity: 3–5 years following the vintage	

Because of this wine's wide availability, I would like to have something positive to say about it. The wine—which is made from a large vineyard near St.-Sauveur, sandwiched between Ramage la Batisse and Liversan —is a straightforward, indifferently made, soft wine of lesser character. Despite the reasonable price, I have never considered this wine to represent good value.

PEYREDON-LAGRAVETTE
(Cru Bourgeois) Listrac   VERY GOOD

Production: 3,000 cases	Grape varieties: Cabernet Sauvignon—65% Merlot—30% Malbec—5%
Secondary label: none	
Vineyard size: 17.3 acres	Proprietor: Paul Hostein
Time spent in barrels: 20 months	Average age of vines: 25 years

Evaluation of present classification: This is one of the better wines of
   Listrac, close in quality to a Médoc fifth-growth.
Plateau of maturity: 6–15 years following the vintage

This excellent Listrac is not well known, but if tastings I have done of
vintages such as 1981, 1982, 1983, 1986, and 1989 are any indication,
this may be one of the best-kept secrets of Listrac. The tiny vineyard sits
to the east of most of the other Listrac properties, adjacent to the appellation of Moulis. Two of the best Moulis vineyards, Chasse-Spleen and
Maucaillou, are closer to Peyredon-Lagravette than most of the other
Listrac vineyards. The wine is very traditionally made with an extremely
long *cuvaison* of 25 days and no filtration. The results are an intensely
concentrated, full-bodied, ripe, impressively built wine for drinking over
10–15 years.

The property itself is quite old, tracing its origin to 1546. The current
proprietor, Paul Hostein, eschews the mechanical harvesters so frequently employed in this part of the Médoc, as well as all of the anti-
botrytis treatments that have become à la mode among the properties to
fight mold and rot. Hostein prefers to use an organic method of winemaking. Additionally, his dense vineyard plantations of 9,000 vines per
hectare give him 50% more vines per hectare than in most Bordeaux
vineyards.

I have yet to taste a wine from Peyredon-Lagravette that has been fully
mature, so this would appear to be one of the longer-lived Listracs, with
a character more closely associated with Moulis than Listrac. More attention needs to be paid to Château Peyredon-Lagravette during the
nineties.

PLAGNAC (Cru Bourgeois) Médoc   GOOD

Production: 16,000 cases	Grape varieties:
	Cabernet Sauvignon—70%
	Merlot—30%
Secondary label: none	
Vineyard size: 67 acres	Proprietor: Domaines Cordier
Time spent in barrels: None, the	Average age of vines: 15 years
wine is aged in large *foudres*	
Evaluation of present classification: A well-made Cru Bourgeois	
representing excellent value	
Plateau of maturity: 2–6 years following the vintage	

Looking for a reasonably priced, soft, fruity, easy-to-drink, straightforward Bordeaux? This wine, managed and looked after by the exceptionally talented oenologist for all the Cordier properties, Georges Pauli, is the type of Bordeaux that pleases the crowd, and satisfies both the palate and purse. It is not meant to last, but to provide charm and immediate drinkability. Drink this wine within its first 5–6 years of life. Plagnac's best recent vintages include the 1986 and 1989.

POTENSAC (Cru Bourgeois) Médoc   EXCELLENT

Production: 20,000 cases	Grape varieties:
	Cabernet Sauvignon—60%
	Merlot—25%
	Cabernet Franc—15%
Secondary labels: Gallais-Bellevue,	
Lassalle, and Goudy-la-Cardonne	
Vineyard size: 99 acres	Proprietor: Michel Delon
Time spent in barrels: 20 months	Average age of vines: 25–30
	years
Evaluation of present classification: Should be upgraded to a Médoc	
fifth-growth	
Plateau of maturity: 4–12 years following the vintage	

Since the mid-1970s, Potensac, under the inspired and strong leadership of Michel Delon (also the proprietor of the famed Léoville-Las Cases in St.-Julien), has been making wines that are clearly of classified-growth quality. This large vineyard, situated near St.-Yzans, produces wines so far above the level of quality found in this region of the Médoc that they are a tribute to the efforts of Delon and his *maître de chai*, Michel Rolland.

The wine, which sees at least 20–25% new oak casks, has a rich, cassis and berry-like character, excellent structure, a wonderful purity and balance that is characteristic of Delon's wines, and surprising aging potential. This area of the northern Médoc is rarely capable of producing wines of this quality, but Delon consistently manages to do that at Potensac.

Delon also owns another group of other vineyards that make up the secondary labels for Potensac. A few years ago Potensac was somewhat of an insiders' wine, but that is no longer the case. Nevertheless, this is such a high-quality wine that any serious Bordeaux enthusiast would be making a mistake if he or she did not try it.

VINTAGES

1989—In time, the 1989 Potensac should rival both the 1986 and 1982 as
·   the best wine produced at this Cru Bourgeois property during the
87   decade of the eighties. It is a big, intense, alcoholic wine with
       exceptional ripeness, full body, and a long, chewy, fleshy finish.
       Anticipated maturity: Now–1999. Last tasted, 4/91.

1988—The 1988 manifests an attractive ripeness in the nose, but in the
·   mouth, it lacks the depth and generosity of the 1989. There is
84   some pleasant new oak in evidence, but the short finish suggests
       this wine should be consumed early. Anticipated maturity: Now–
       1995. Last tasted, 4/91.

1986—Potensac made an excellent wine in 1986. In fact, in a blind
·   tasting, the wine could easily be confused with a classified
87   growth. Deep ruby/purple in color, with an elegant, complex
       bouquet of herbs, minerals, spicy oak, and blackcurrants, this
       medium-bodied wine displays rich, well-focused fruit, plenty of
       tannin in the finish, but an overall harmony and complexity that
       is rare in a Cru Bourgeois. Anticipated maturity: 1992–2000. Last
       tasted, 11/90.

1985—The 1985 is a lovely, elegant, supple wine imbued with a good
·   measure of blackcurrant fruit, a deft touch of spicy oak, medium
85   body, and fine length. Anticipated maturity: Now–1996. Last
       tasted, 3/90.

1984—Cleanly made and correct, the 1984 Potensac lacks the fruit and
·   depth to merit higher marks. Several years of cellaring may bring
77   forth more character. Anticipated maturity: Now–1993. Last
       tasted, 3/88.

1983—Beginning to exhibit some amber at the edge, this spicy, cedary,
　·　　surprisingly herbaceous-scented Potensac has good body and an
　84　attractive ripeness, but has reached its plateau of maturity. It is
　　　a good, rather than inspirational, Potensac. Anticipated maturity:
　　　Now–1993. Last tasted, 3/88.
1982—This is undoubtedly the best Potensac I have ever tasted. It re-
　·　　mains to be seen whether the 1986, or ultimately the 1989 will
　87　surpass this gloriously opulent, rich, full-bodied wine. At age 8,
　　　the 1982 Potensac displays no signs of decline. Still relatively
　　　opaque dark ruby, with only a slight hint of amber, this oaky,
　　　cassis-scented wine is round, amply endowed, and finishes with
　　　some soft tannins and noticeable extract and alcohol. The best
　　　Potensac ever made? Anticipated maturity: Now–1996. Last
　　　tasted, 3/90.

POUJEAUX (Cru Bourgeois) Moulis　　　　　EXCELLENT

Production: 22,000 cases	Grape varieties:
	Cabernet Sauvignon—40%
	Merlot—36%
	Cabernet Franc—12%
	Petit Verdot—12%
Secondary label: La Salle de Poujeaux	
Vineyard size: 123.5 acres	Proprietor: The Theil family
Time spent in barrels: 18 months	Average age of vines: 25–30 years
Evaluation of present classification: Should be upgraded to a fifth-growth	
Plateau of maturity: 6–20 years following the vintage	

While there is a considerable rivalry between Poujeaux, Chasse-Spleen, and Maucaillou, most observers agree that year in and year out, these are the three best wines of Moulis. Poujeaux is one of the oldest estates, dating back to 1544 when the vineyards and surrounding area were called La Salle de Poujeaux. The property is now run by the Theil brothers, whose family acquired Poujeaux in 1920.

Poujeaux's style is typical of the wines of Moulis. It is dark ruby in color, tannic, sometimes astringent and hard when young, and therefore usually needs a minimum of 6 to 8 years to soften and mature. It is a slower-developing wine than neighbor Chasse-Spleen, yet has the potential to be one of the longest lived. A splendid bottle of 1928 served to me in 1985 and again in 1988 proved just how magnificent, as well as age-worthy, Poujeaux can be. In the last few years Chasse-Spleen has eclipsed Poujeaux in quality, not because of any problems at Poujeaux, but because of the enormous efforts made at Chasse-Spleen. Nevertheless, Poujeaux is clearly a wine that deserves to be ranked as a fifth-growth in any new classification of the Bordeaux hierarchy.

VINTAGES

1989—Although Poujeaux is one of the bright shining stars of Moulis, I did not feel their 1989 was as splendid as their 1982, 1985, and
86   1986. Even the diminutive Theil brothers are candid in saying the 1982 is the best wine produced here during the eighties. Nevertheless, the 1989 is an excellent wine, exhibiting a moderately intense bouquet of toasty new oak, spicy, blackcurrant fruit, medium to full body, and attractive ripeness and heady alcohol in the finish. It will not be so long-lived as either the 1986 or 1982. Anticipated maturity: 1993–2003. Last tasted, 4/91.

1988—The 1988 rivals the 1989. Although less alcoholic and fleshy, it does display a classic curranty bouquet, a deft touch of toasty
86   new oak, medium body, good acidity, and attractive tannins in the finish. Anticipated maturity: 1994–2005. Last tasted, 4/91.

1987—This is a surprisingly strong effort, particularly for a so-called "off year." Fully mature, this soft, round, charming wine is as smooth
84   as silk. Anticipated maturity: Now–1994. Last tasted, 4/91.

1986—Only time will reveal whether the 1986 Poujeaux is better than the excellent 1982. With deep dark ruby color, a moderately in-
89   tense bouquet of weedy blackcurrants, tobacco, and smoky oak, it is quite enticing. On the palate, the wine is very powerful, rich, full bodied, and capable of lasting at least 15–20 years. Anticipated maturity: 1993–2008. Last tasted, 4/91.

1985—The 1985 Poujeaux is a lush, rich, full-bodied wine with soft tannins in the finish. It has matured quickly for a Poujeaux, and can
86   presently be drunk with great pleasure. Anticipated maturity: Now–1997. Last tasted, 4/91.

1984—The 1984 Poujeaux has adequate ripeness, a moderately intense, spicy, herbaceous, and oaky nose, some fruit and depth, as well
76   as a decent finish. Anticipated maturity: Now–1993. Last tasted, 4/91.

1983—Now fully mature, the 1983 still has a deep ruby color, an intense floral, pure blackcurrant bouquet, soft, medium-bodied flavors,
86   and light tannins in its heady finish. Anticipated maturity: Now–2000. Last tasted, 4/91.

1982—This is the most powerful and concentrated Poujeaux I have
·   tasted in the last decade. Still dark ruby, with only some slight
90   amber at the edge, the 1982 has a cedary, almost grilled nut,
      smoky, cassis-scented bouquet, powerful, full-bodied, concen-
      trated flavors, and a long finish wherein the tannins are just begin-
      ning to melt. While drinkable now, it is still not fully mature.
      Anticipated maturity: 1992–2006. Last tasted, 4/91.

RAMAGE LA BATISSE
(Cru Bourgeois) Haut-Médoc   AVERAGE

Production: 22,000 cases	Grape varieties: Cabernet Sauvignon—64% Merlot—34% Petit Verdot—2%
Secondary labels: Tourteran and Dutellier	
Vineyard size: 133 acres	Proprietor: The Monnoyeur family
Time spent in barrels: 14–16 months	Average age of vines: 20 years
Evaluation of present classification: Should be maintained; an average-quality Cru Bourgeois	
Plateau of maturity: 5–8 years following the vintage	

The vineyards of Ramage La Batisse are located in St. Sauveur, a small
wine-producing region situated inland and west from the small town of
Pauillac. The vineyard has been completely replanted since 1961 and
production has reached 22,000 cases. The wines from the late seventies,
particularly the 1978 and 1979, were quite impressive—supple, oaky,
richly fruity wines of style and character. Even the 1980 was a notable
success in a mediocre vintage. However, since then, the wines of Ramage La Batisse have been inexplicably unimpressive. Even in top years
such as 1982, 1983, 1985, and 1986, they have been excessively tannic,
lean, and austere, with an oakiness that tended to obliterate the wine's
fruit and charm.

This property is well placed, and has the potential to turn out top
wines, as it did in the seventies, but the recent string of indifferent
winemaking efforts makes one wonder what is going on here. Most vintages of Ramage La Batisse are best drunk between 5–10 years of age.

ST.-BONNET (Cru Bourgeois) Médoc   AVERAGE

Production: 22,000 cases	Grape varieties: Cabernet Sauvignon—50% Merlot—50%
Secondary label: none	
Vineyard size: 111 acres	Proprietor: Michel Solivères
Time spent in barrels: 12–14 months; two-thirds of the crop is aged in large vats and one-third in barrels	Average age of vines: 20 years
Evaluation of present classification: Should be maintained; an average-quality Cru Bourgeois	
Plateau of maturity: 3–8 years following the vintage	

I had some excellent wines from this property in the late seventies and early eighties, but I began to detect a serious degree of mustiness and aroma of old barrels in a number of the wines made after 1982. That has become an increasing problem that has had a negative effect on the wine in the bottle. A shame, for at its best St.-Bonnet can be a deliciously round, medium-bodied, supple Bordeaux with a lot of up-front fruit and charm. It was never meant to make old bones.

SARANSOT-DUPRÉ (Cru Bourgeois) Listrac   VERY GOOD

Production: 5,000 cases	Grape varieties: Merlot—60% Cabernet Sauvignon—40%
Secondary label: none, although nearly 1,000 cases of generic Bordeaux white wine are produced	
Vineyard size: 19.6 acres	Proprietor: Yves Raymond
Time spent in barrels: 15–20 months	Average age of vines: 20 years
Evaluation of present classification: An extremely well-made Listrac that in some vintages comes very close to rivaling a Médoc fifth-growth	
Plateau of maturity: 6–15 years following the vintage	

The high percentage of Merlot ensures that in ripe vintages, such as 1982, 1985, 1986, and 1989, this wine has a degree of opulence and fullness not often found in Listrac wines. The wine is usually dark ruby in color, with a bouquet redolent of black fruits, such as plums, as well as licorice and flowers. The best recent vintage is the 1982. When I drank it in 1989, it was still a young, generally unevolved wine. The 1985 resembles the 1982, although it is slightly less ripe and concentrated. There is also a very fine, powerful, more structured 1986, and a thick, rich, intense 1989.

Given the high extraction, ripeness, and intensity of the wines made at Saransot-Dupré, an elevated use of new oak could be beneficial. This is a wine that needs 4–5 years to reach its plateau of maturity, but can last for 12–15 years. To date, this château remains an undiscovered, up-and-coming star of Listrac.

Nearly 1,000 cases of delicious, dry white wine, made from 5 acres of Semillon and Muscadelle, is produced at Saransot-Dupré. I have never seen a bottle outside of France, but it is a delicious Bordeaux Blanc.

SÉGUR (Cru Bourgeois) Haut-Médoc   GOOD

Production: 14,000 cases	Grape varieties: Merlot—45% Cabernet Sauvignon—35% Cabernet Franc—15% Petit Verdot—5%
Secondary label: Ségur-Fillon Vineyard size: 86 acres	Proprietor: Jean-Pierre Grazioli
Time spent in barrels: 4 months in barrels and 12 months in vats	Average age of vines: 15 years
Evaluation of present classification: A solidly reliable, at times quite good Cru Bourgeois	
Plateau of maturity: 4–7 years following the vintage	

Since the mid-1980s, Ségur has become one of the more reliable Cru Bourgeois wines. It can be a soft, deliciously fruity, attractive, ready-to-drink wine that is best in ripe years such as 1985, 1986, 1988, and 1989. In 1985, the proprietor launched a tiny quantity of a special *cuvée* aged in 100% new oak. It is a successful wine, although the quantities produced were tiny.

SEMEILLAN-MAZEAU (Cru Bourgeois) Listrac   GOOD

Production: 1,500 cases

Grape varieties:
Cabernet Sauvignon—50%
Merlot—50%

Secondary label: none
Vineyard size: 29.6 acres   Proprietor: A Société Civile
Time spent in barrels: 20 months   Average age of vines: 20 years
Evaluation of present classification: Should be maintained, but it is
  one of the better Listrac wines
Plateau of maturity: 5–15 years following the vintage

I have had limited experience with the wines of Semeillan-Mazeau, but vintages since 1985 have exhibited a rich, highly extracted, old style of wine with a great deal of power and tannin. My guess is that most of the wines from top vintages can last for 10–15 years. This is another up-and-coming Listrac vineyard that should be watched. Interestingly, the high-quality *négociant* firm of Nathaniel Johnston assumed the exclusivity for distribution of this wine several years ago. That in itself suggests this could be a name to watch in the nineties.

SÉNÉJAC (Cru Bourgeois) Haut-Médoc   AVERAGE

Production: 8,500 cases

Grape varieties:
Cabernet Sauvignon—47%
Cabernet Franc—25%
Merlot—23%
Petit Verdot—3%
Malbec—2%

Secondary label: Domaine de
  l'Artigue
Vineyard size: 50 acres   Proprietor: Charles de Guigné
Time spent in barrels: 12 months   Average age of vines: 20 years
Evaluation of present classification: Should be maintained
Plateau of maturity: 4–6 years following the vintage

Sénéjac is located in the very southern part of the Médoc, west of the town of Parempuyre, and just south of the village of Arsac. The vineyard sits on very light, sandy, gravelly soil, and produces a soft, fruity red wine that is meant to be drunk young. Interestingly, a New Zealander, Jenny Bailey, is the young *maître de chai* at the property. There is a high percentage of Cabernet Franc employed, giving the wine its characteristically spicy, herbaceous bouquet. Since 1985, I have found the wines to be significantly better than preceding vintages. The 1985, for which the château employed 60% new oak barrels, 1986, and 1989 all exhibited considerable charm, concentration, and character.

There is also a tiny quantity of white wine (400 cases), called Blanc de Sénéjac. It is made from Semillon, fermented in 20% new oak casks, and then blended with wine fermented in stainless-steel tanks.

SOCIANDO-MALLET
(Cru Bourgeois) Haut-Médoc   EXCELLENT

Production: 15,000 cases	Grape varieties: Cabernet Sauvignon—60% Merlot—25% Cabernet Franc—10% Petit Verdot—5%
Secondary label: Lartigue-de-Brochon	
Vineyard size: 74 acres	Proprietor: Jean Gautreau
Time spent in barrels: 14–16 months	Average age of vines: 20 years
Evaluation of present classification: The quality equivalent of a Médoc fourth-growth	
Plateau of maturity: 8–25 years following the vintage	

Located in St.-Seurin-de-Cadourne, Sociando-Mallet is making uncompromising wines of extremely high quality that are meant to age gracefully for 10 to 25 years. The vineyards are superbly situated overlooking the Gironde, and the style of wine produced by the meticulous owner—Jean Gautreau, who purchased this run-down property in 1969—is inky black ruby in color, extremely concentrated, full bodied, and loaded with mouth-puckering tannin. Some observers have even claimed that Sociando-Mallet has the greatest potential for longevity of any wine in the Médoc. The keys to the quality of Sociando-Mallet are numerous. First there is the superb vineyard, with excellent exposure and well-drained, gravelly soil, a high density of vines per hectare (8,000), as well as manual-harvesting techniques. A high fermentation temperature of 32–33 degrees centigrade, a three-week or longer maceration period, the use of 50% new oak, and minimal fining and filtration is further evidence of the château's high standards.

The result of all this is irrefutable. Sociando-Mallet is easily the equal of many of the classified growths, and its surging reputation among France's wine connoisseurs has already assured that much of it is purchased within that country. It has become a particular favorite of some of France's greatest temples of cuisine, for example, the top Paris restaurants of Taillevent and Robuchon.

VINTAGES

1989—Sociando-Mallet's 1989 does not compare with their spectacular
·   1982, 1986, or 1990, but it is still one of the best wines made at
88   this property in the last 10 years. A dark ruby/purple color with
        an aroma of wonderfully pure blackcurrants, licorice, and toasty
        new oak is followed by a wine with highly concentrated flavors,
        moderately high tannins, and a long finish. Typical of the property, this wine has the requisite components and depth to last for
        up to 20 years. As I have said many times over the last decade,
        there are few properties in Bordeaux making wines that will last
        as long as Sociando-Mallet's. In style, the 1989 represents a synthesis of the 1982 and 1986, but it is not nearly so concentrated
        as the 1982 or 1990, nor as potentially long-lived as the 1986.
        Anticipated maturity: 1995–2010. Last tasted, 4/91.

1988—The 1988 is medium bodied, somewhat lighter than one might
·   expect from this property, but still concentrated and spicy, with
87   a true sense of balance, and a long finish. It lacks the strength
        and highly extracted flavors seen in the top vintages, but it should
        last for 12–15 years. Anticipated maturity: 1993–2008. Last
        tasted, 4/91.

1986—Jean Gautreau's 1986 is a blockbuster of a wine. Enormously rich
·   and full bodied, with awesome power, it is a classic Médoc with
90   its extraordinary depth, and well-focused bouquet of minerals,
        blackcurrants, violets, and spicy oak. It is an exquisite wine, but
        not for everybody. Do not expect to begin drinking this wine until
        after 2000. Anticipated maturity: 2005–2040. Last tasted, 1/91.

1985—The 1985 Sociando-Mallet is typically dense ruby/purple and has
·   a rich, blackcurrant, classically Médoc bouquet, full body, and
90   sensational concentration and balance. Anticipated maturity:
        1995–2015. Last tasted, 4/91.

1984—One of the darkest 1984s in color, Sociando-Mallet has loads of
·   fruit, body, and tannin, as well as a life expectancy of 10–12
84   years. It is amazingly rich and powerful for a 1984. Anticipated
        maturity: Now–1998. Last tasted, 11/88.

1983—At one time I had high hopes for this wine, but the fruit does not
· seem nearly as ripe or as concentrated as it once was. Still me-
85 dium to dark ruby, with a spicy, mineral-like bouquet that lacks
intensity and ripeness, on the palate, the wine is medium to full
bodied, exhibits good rather than great concentration, and has a
somewhat sinewy, muscular texture, and a good, long finish with
moderate tannins. Anticipated maturity: 1992–2001. Last tasted,
1/90.

1982—Still amazingly opaque, dark ruby/purple, with a moderately in-
· tense bouquet of pure blackcurrants, minerals, licorice, and spicy
92 oak, the 1982 does not display any signs of being close to maturity. The power, richness, and sensational concentration could
easily be confused with a top second-growth. Long, powerful, and
very rich, this tannic (fortunately they are soft tannins) effort is a
winemaking tour de force, as well as an extraordinary example of
what heights the best Crus Bourgeois are capable of reaching.
Anticipated maturity: 1996–2012. Last tasted, 1/91.

1981—The 1981 is a relatively compact, down-sized Sociando-Mallet,
· with medium body, good concentration, but less tannin, and a
83 more supple, lower-acid personality than one normally expects
from this property. It has now reached its plateau of maturity, but
this is not a wine that will decline rapidly. Anticipated maturity:
Now–2000. Last tasted, 3/89.

1979—Approaching full maturity, the 1979 is somewhat similar in tex-
· ture, weight, and extract levels to the 1981. However, the 1979
80 seems a bit more marked by new oak, and has a more aggressive
and less impressive finish. Anticipated maturity: Now–1998. Last
tasted, 3/89.

1978—This is a beautiful wine that has matured much more slowly than
· many other 1978 Médocs. Dark ruby, with no signs of age, the
87 big, cedar, mineral-and-cassis-scented bouquet is intense and enthralling. Medium bodied, concentrated, exhibiting excellent
ripeness with none of the herbaceous aromas that often mark the
less ripe wines of this vintage, this wine's finish is harmonious
and moderately tannic. Anticipated maturity: 1992–2003. Last
tasted, 3/90.

1976—This may well turn out to be one of the three or four best wines of
· the vintage. The two best 1976s have consistently been Lafite-
88 Rothschild and Ausone, but neither of those wines is as backward
or as concentrated as Sociando-Mallet's 1976. Still opaque dark
ruby, with an intense, almost explosive bouquet of black fruits
and spices, this rich, full-bodied, opulently styled Sociando-Mallet comes closest in texture, ripeness, and headiness to the 1982,

but does not quite have the depth or tannins of that vintage. A superb success for the vintage, the 1976 displays none of the precocious, forward, quick-to-mature qualities of most Médocs, nor any of the dilution caused by the preharvest rains. Bravo! Anticipated maturity: Now–2002. Last tasted, 3/88.

1975— Still impossibly backward and closed, the dark ruby/purple–col-
·   ored 1975 Sociando-Mallet is among the most powerful, concen-
90   trated wine I have ever tasted from this property. One may question whether the tannins are too excessive for the fruit, but I do not think that is the case with this massively concentrated, intense, exceptionally well-made wine. It should prove to have an almost timeless quality, and I believe it is one of the few Crus Bourgeois that has the potential to last for 50 years. The finish is so loaded with fruit and tannin that I am persuaded this wine will be absolutely superb when it is fully ready to drink. Anticipated maturity: 1996–2025. Last tasted, 12/90.

1973— Most 1973 clarets had one foot in the grave by the late seventies,
·   and were senile by the mid-1980s. Not the 1973 Sociando Mallet.
86   It is undoubtedly the most concentrated, most structured, and now most interesting wine of the vintage. Drinkable when rela- tively young, but still amazingly rich and deep in color, yet ripe and supple, this is another example of the dedication of proprietor Jean Gautreau. Anticipated maturity: Now–1997. Last tasted, 3/88.

1970— Just now reaching its plateau of maturity, the 1970 Sociando-
·   Mallet has a moderately intense bouquet of minerals, licorice,
87   cedar, herbs, and blackcurrants. Medium bodied and concen- trated, with tannins that have now melted away, this luscious, complex wine has a long finish, and provides immediate satisfac- tion. Anticipated maturity: Now–1999. Last tasted, 3/88.

SOUDARS (Cru Bourgeois) Haut-Médoc   GOOD

Production: 10,000 cases	Grape varieties: Cabernet Sauvignon—55% Merlot—45%
Secondary label: none Vineyard size: 37 acres Time spent in barrels: 20–22 months	Proprietor: Eric Miailhe Average age of vines: 14 years
Evaluation of present classification: An increasingly well-made, tasty, supple Cru Bourgeois	
Plateau of maturity: 3–6 years following the vintage	

The high percentage of Merlot used at Soudars results in a wine that is relatively fat, round, fruity, and easy to drink. Vintages since the early eighties have been impeccably made by young Eric Miailhe. This is not a wine to lay away for more than 5–6 years, but for drinking in its youth, Soudars has a great deal to offer at a reasonable price.

LA TOUR DE BY (Cru Bourgeois) Médoc   GOOD

Production: 40,000 cases	Grape varieties: Cabernet Sauvignon—70% Merlot—26% Cabernet Franc—4%
Secondary labels: Moulin de la Roque and LaRoque de By	
Vineyard size: 170 acres	Proprietor: A partnership of Lapalu, Cailloux, and Pagés
Time spent in barrels: 18 months	Average age of vines: 30 years
Evaluation of present classification: A well-known and consistently good Cru Bourgeois	
Plateau of maturity: 5–10 years following the vintage	

This is one of the best-known Crus Bourgeois for a number of reasons. One is that the vast estate of 170 acres produces nearly 40,000 cases of wine. The property was purchased in 1965 by well-known Médoc vineyard owners, Messeurs Cailloux, Lapalu, and Pagés and they have built new cellars that hold nearly 1,400 aging barrels. Given the huge production and yields of 55–70 hectoliters per hectare, one might think this wine would lack stuffing, but there is always a relatively severe selection process, as well as two secondary labels where weaker vats and wine from younger vines are relegated.

La Tour de By produces well-colored, richly fruity, solid wines that only lack complexity and intensity in the bouquet. The high percentage of Cabernet Sauvignon gives the wines their deep color and firm tannic background. I do not remember tasting a badly made La Tour de By since the mid-1970s, but the top successes have included a round, opulent 1982, a lighter, now fully mature and beginning-to-fade 1983, a fat, delicious 1985, a structured, tannic, powerful 1986 (perhaps the best wine I have ever tasted from La Tour de By), a light 1988, and a very good 1989.

LA TOUR-CARNET (Fourth-Growth) Haut-Médoc AVERAGE

Production: 15,000 cases	Grape varieties: Cabernet Sauvignon—66% Merlot—33% Petit Verdot—1%
Secondary label: none	
Vineyard size: 76.6 acres	Proprietor: A Société Civile
Time spent in barrels: 20 months	Average age of vines: 25 years
Evaluation of present classification: Should be downgraded to a Cru Bourgeois	
Plateau of maturity: 5–12 years following the vintage	

La Tour-Carnet is located in St.-Laurent, and despite its inclusion in the 1855 classification, it has remained largely anonymous. This beautiful property has been restored completely, and boasts a moated medieval castle. The wine suffered considerably from, I suspect, extensive replanting in the sixties. Certainly the 1970, 1971, and 1976 proved to be thin, bland, uninteresting wines that were hardly worthy of the estate's classification. The 1975 is good, rather than special, the 1978 and 1979 are slightly herbaceous and stalky, but more recent vintages, particularly the 1982, 1983, and 1989, are promising. Yet based on this property's performance to date, it does not merit a fourth-growth classification, as the quality of the wine is no better than a Cru Bourgeois.

TOUR HAUT-CAUSSAN (Cru Bourgeois) Médoc EXCELLENT

Production: 6,000 cases	Grape varieties: Cabernet Sauvignon—60% Merlot—40%
Secondary label: La Landotte	
Vineyard size: 42 acres	Proprietor: Philippe Courrian
Time spent in barrels: 18–24 months	Average age of vines: 26 years
Evaluation of present classification: A very good, occasionally excellent Cru Bourgeois that in certain vintages—1982, 1988, 1989, and 1990—can compete favorably with a Médoc fifth-growth	
Plateau of maturity: 6–15 years following the vintage	

Philippe Courrian is the most recent proprietor from this family that has run this excellent Cru Bourgeois since 1877. Not surprisingly, the property takes its name not only from a beautiful windmill situated in the midst of the vineyards, but also from the nearest village, Caussan. The vineyard is located near the more famous properties of Potensac and La Cardonne. Everything about the winemaking is extremely traditional. The extremely low yields of 40–50 hectoliters per hectare, the manual harvesting in an area where most vineyards are picked by machine, the declassifying of inferior lots to a second wine, and the policy against filtration, all typify an estate dedicated to high quality. As Mr. Courrian has said many times, "Why filter? My wine does not contain anything bad." Twenty percent of the casks are new each year, which the proprietor feels is adequate to preserve the character of the vineyard without resulting in an overly oaky wine.

VINTAGES

1989—The 1989 is a more dramatic, alcoholic wine than the 1988, dis-
·　　playing an abundant quantity of new oak in its nose, a robust,
88　　low-acid taste, and enough tannin to support a decade's worth of
　　　aging. It is a surprisingly big, forceful wine that will reward those
　　　shrewd enough to buy it. Anticipated maturity: 1992–2000. Last
　　　tasted, 4/91.

1988—The 1988 is much more evolved, with an elegant, cedary, spicy,
·　　curranty bouquet, medium-bodied, stylish, well-balanced flavors,
86　　and soft tannins. Nevertheless, it has the depth and overall equi-
　　　librium to last 4–7 years. Anticipated maturity: Now–1996. Last
　　　tasted, 4/91.

1986—Still tightly knit, but promisingly deep in color, with a spicy,
·　　cedary, mineral-scented bouquet, this full-bodied, concentrated,
86　　impeccably made wine needs another 2–3 years to shed its tan-
　　　nins, but should provide rewarding drinking. Anticipated matu-
　　　rity: 1993–2002. Last tasted, 11/90.

1985—The 1985 is softer and not quite so opaque as the 1986. Its gener-
·　　ous bouquet offers up aromas of flowers, black fruits, spicy new
85　　oak, and cedar. Velvety textured, full bodied, and admirably con-
　　　centrated, this wine can be drunk now. Anticipated maturity:
　　　Now–1997. Last tasted, 3/90.

1982—This wine is now fully mature, and is the best I have tasted from
·　　Tour Haut-Caussan. The big, ripe, robust nose faithfully reveals
88　　the superripeness attained in 1982. Heady, velvety, flamboyant
　　　flavors that are present in a full-bodied format are attractive and
　　　long. Most of the tannins seem to have fallen away to reveal a big,
　　　juicy, succulent mouthful of Cru Bourgeois. Anticipated maturity:
　　　Now–1995. Last tasted, 3/90.

TOUR DU HAUT-MOULIN
(Cru Bourgeois) Haut-Médoc   EXCELLENT

Production: 20,000 cases	Grape varieties: Cabernet Sauvignon—55% Merlot—40% Petit Verdot—5%
Secondary label: none	
Vineyard size: 84 acres	Proprietor: Laurent Poitou
Time spent in barrels: 18 months	Average age of vines: 25 years

Evaluation of present classification: An excellent Cru Bourgeois that
  can be favorably compared to a Médoc fifth-growth in years such as
  1990, 1989, 1988, 1986, and 1985
Plateau of maturity: 5–14 years following the vintage

The vineyards of this excellent Cru Bourgeois, located near Cussac, are
situated just to the north of Château Lamarque. There is no doubt that
proprietor Laurent Poitou produces one of the most concentrated and
intensely flavored wines among the Crus Bourgeois. He is not averse to
letting the fermentation temperature reach a dangerously high 34–35
degrees centigrade, and he favors a long *cuvaison* of nearly one month.
Additionally, the conservative yields of 45 hectoliters per hectare in a
densely planted vineyard of 10,000 vines per hectare no doubt account
for the impressively dark ruby/purple color of these wines in top years,
as well as their admirable depth and concentration. This is clearly one
of the top Crus Bourgeois. In fact, in a blind tasting, it would embarrass
many classified growths.

VINTAGES

1989—The 1989 is low in acidity, opulent, and alcoholic, yet highly ex-
·   tracted, flamboyant, and dramatic. The rich, full flavors marry
88   well with the new oak. Anticipated maturity: Now–1996. Last
     tasted, 4/91.

1988—The 1988 is a large-sized wine with good definition and aggressive
·   tannins. The wine has gobs of blackcurrant fruit, and a long,
87   impressive finish. Anticipated maturity: Now–1998. Last tasted,
     4/91.

1986—The proprietor considers the 1986 one of the finest wines he has
·   ever made. Dark ruby/purple, with a tight, but emerging bouquet
87   of spicy, herbaceous, blackcurrant fruit, this medium- to full-
     bodied wine is stuffed to the brim with fruit, but still has some

dusty tannins to shed. It needs several more years in the cellar. Anticipated maturity: 1993–2001. Last tasted, 3/90.

1985—This is an easily understood and satisfying wine to drink. It has
  ·   not yet begun to exhibit any signs of reaching full maturity. Still
  86   deep ruby in color, but round, smooth, and velvety textured, this
        immensely fruity yet straightforward style of Tour du Haut-
        Moulin will display greater complexity with another year or two
        of cellaring. Anticipated maturity: 1992–2000. Last tasted, 3/90.

LA TOUR ST.-BONNET (Cru Bourgeois) Médoc   VERY GOOD

Production: 18,000 cases	Grape varieties: Cabernet Sauvignon—45% Merlot—45% Malbec—5% Petit Verdot—5%
Secondary label: La Fuie-St. Bonnet	
Vineyard size: 99 acres	Proprietor: The Pierre Lafon family
Time spent in barrels: 18 months in large *foudres*	Average age of vines: 25 years
Evaluation of present classification: A very good Crus Bourgeois that is frequently as good as a Médoc fifth-growth	
Plateau of maturity: 6–14 years following the vintage	

La Tour St.-Bonnet has always been one of my favorite Cru Bourgeois. The first vintage I tasted, and subsequently purchased, was the 1975. I drank the last bottle several years ago, and even at age 13, it displayed no signs of decline. The vineyard of nearly 100 acres is well situated on a gravelly ridge adjacent to the Gironde River, near the village of St.-Christoly.

This is not a commercially made, supple, ready-to-drink Cru Bourgeois, but, rather, a deeply colored, firm, tannic, full-bodied wine with surprising concentration. Most vintages need at least 3–4 years to shed their tannins, and in top years, such as 1975, 1982 (the finest La Tour St.-Bonnet I have ever tasted), 1985, 1986, 1988, and 1989, they need 10 years or longer. The vineyard is machine harvested, and yields of 40–50 hectoliters per hectare are conservative by today's standards. Interestingly, the wine is not aged in small oak casks, but in larger oak *foudres*. The proprietor, the Lafon family, feels this preserves the wine's intensity and rich, concentrated fruit extract.

This is a classic Cru Bourgeois that comes very close to rivaling some of the Médoc's fifth-growths. It deserves to be better known in America.

VERDIGNAN (Cru Bourgeois) Haut-Médoc — GOOD

Production: 25,000 cases	Grape varieties: Cabernet Sauvignon—55% Merlot—40% Cabernet Franc—5%
Secondary label: Plantey de la Croix	
Vineyard size: 123.5 acres	Proprietor: Eric Miailhe
Time spent in barrels: 12–24 months	Average age of vines: 22 years
Evaluation of present classification: An easy-going, amply endowed, fruity Cru Bourgeois that merits its present standing	
Plateau of maturity: 4–8 years following the vintage	

Verdignan, another one of the Miailhe family's solidly run Cru Bourgeois properties, has its château and vineyards located near the northern Médoc village of St.-Seurin-de-Cadourne. A wine I have consistently enjoyed, it is ripe, supple, and richly fruity, and possesses a straightforward yet powerful blackcurrant aroma. Made in a style designed for early drinking, it is best drunk between 4–8 years of age. Since the early eighties, the wine has taken on more concentration and character. The vineyard is machine harvested, and averages 50–65 hectoliters per hectare. The price for Verdignan has remained reasonable, no doubt due to the significant production.

VILLEGEORGE
(Cru Bourgeois) Haut-Médoc — AVERAGE

Production: 5,000 cases	Grape varieties: Merlot—60% Cabernet Sauvignon—30% Cabernet Franc—10%
Secondary label: none	
Vineyard size: 27 acres	Proprietor: Lucien Lurton
Time spent in barrels: 10–16 months	Average age of vines: 25 years
Evaluation of present classification: Should be maintained; an average-quality Cru Bourgeois	
Plateau of maturity: 3–6 years following the vintage	

In 1973 the omnipresent Lucien Lurton added this small property to his collection of Bordeaux châteaux. The wine is loosely knit, soft, pleasantly fruity, straightforward, and uninspiring. Perhaps the high yields and significant percentage of Merlot, which is planted in very gravelly soil, are the reasons this wine is relatively light and one-dimensional. The best recent vintage has been the 1986, which should be drunk within 10 years of the vintage.

THE RED AND WHITE WINES OF GRAVES

History of wine production in Bordeaux recorded that it was the wines of Graves that were the first Bordeaux wines to be made and exported. Barrels of Graves wine were shipped to England during the English reign over this region of France between 1152 and 1453. Even the Americans, led by the multitalented Thomas Jefferson in 1785, seemed to think that the wines of Graves were among the best wines made in Bordeaux.

Times have changed, and no wine-producing region in Bordeaux has lost more ground, literally and figuratively, than the region of Graves.

The region Graves, which gets its name from the gravelly soil—vestige of Ice Age glaciers—is totally different from the other wine regions of Bordeaux. It begins in what most tourists would think is still the city of Bordeaux, but what is actually the congested southern suburbs known as Talence and Pessac, two high-rise, modern, heavily populated centers of middle-class Bordelais and University of Bordeaux students. The major vineyards in this area happen to be the best of the Graves region, but since the last century they have had to fight off both urban sprawl and blight. A visit to these vineyards will offer a noisy contrast to the tranquil, quiet pastoral settings of the vineyards in the Médoc, Pomerol, and St.-Emilion. The vineyards in this northern sector of Graves now carry the appellation of Pessac-Léognan.

Heading south from Talence and Pessac for the better part of twenty kilometers are the widely scattered vineyards of Graves. The region, once past the commercial suburb of Gradignan, does become pastoral and rural, with vineyards intermingled with pine forests and small farms.

The two southern areas of Graves that produce the best wine are Léognan and Martillac, two small bucolic towns, that seem much further away from the bustling city of Bordeaux than they actually are. These wines too carry the appellation name of Pessac-Léognan.

The entire Graves region produces and is famous for both red and white wines. In 1991, 5,463 acres were planted with red wine–producing grapes, and 4,100 acres with white wine varietals. The top white wines of this region are rare and expensive, and in a few cases, capable of rivaling the finest white wines produced in France. They are produced from two basic grape varieties, the Sauvignon Blanc and Semillon. However, the greatest wines of Graves are the reds. Graves's most famous estate, the American-owned Château Haut-Brion in the northern suburb of Pessac was the first great wine of Bordeaux to get international recognition. It was referred to in 1663 by the English author Samuel Pepys, and between 1785 and 1789 by America's pre-eminent Francophile, Thomas Jefferson. The international acclaim for the wines of Haut-Brion no doubt was the reason why this property was the only non-Gironde to be included in the 1855 Classification of the Wines of the Gironde. Along with Haut-Brion, the other great red wines produced in Graves are Haut-Brion's cross-street rival, La Mission-Haut-Brion, and the great estate in the southern Léognan region, the curiously named Domaine de Chevalier.

There are other fine Graves wines, most notably Pape-Clément and Les Carmes Haut-Brion in Pessac, La Tour-Haut-Brion in Talence, and Haut-Bailly, La Louvière, and de Fieuzal near Léognan, but the overall level of quality winemaking, looked at from a consumer's perspective, is not as high as in such Médoc communes as St.-Julien, Pauillac, and St.-Estèphe.

The wines of Graves, like the Médoc, have their own quality classification. It, too, falsely serves as a quality guide to unsuspecting wine enthusiasts. The first classification occurred in 1953, and the most recent classification in 1959. The 1959 classification (see page 926) listed thirteen châteaux producing red wine with Haut-Brion appearing first, and the remaining twelve listed alphabetically. For the white wine producers (often the same châteaux), there were nine châteaux listed in alphabetical order, with Haut-Brion's miniscule production of white wine excluded at the château's insistence. In 1987, the northern part of the Graves viticultural region was given its own appellation, called Pessac-Léognan, and includes most of the winemaking estates included in the official classifications.

As for the great red wines of Graves, their personality traits are individualistic and unique, and not difficult to decipher when tasted blind in

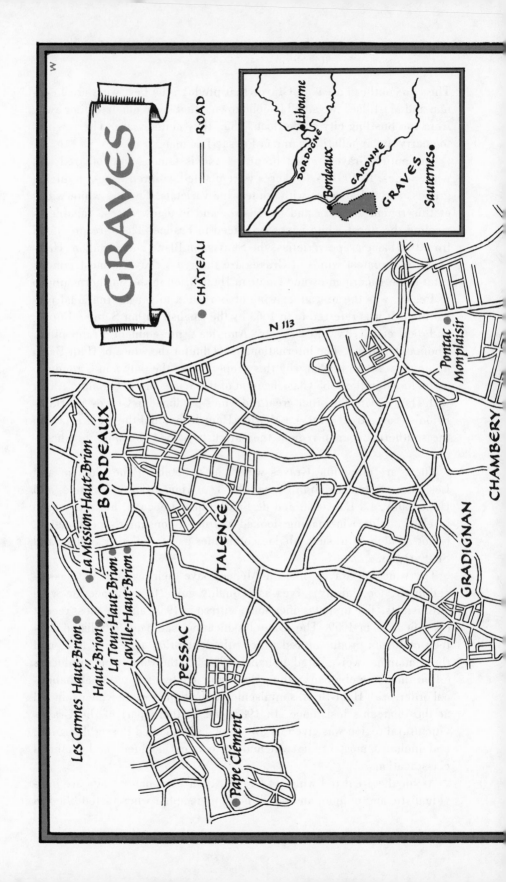

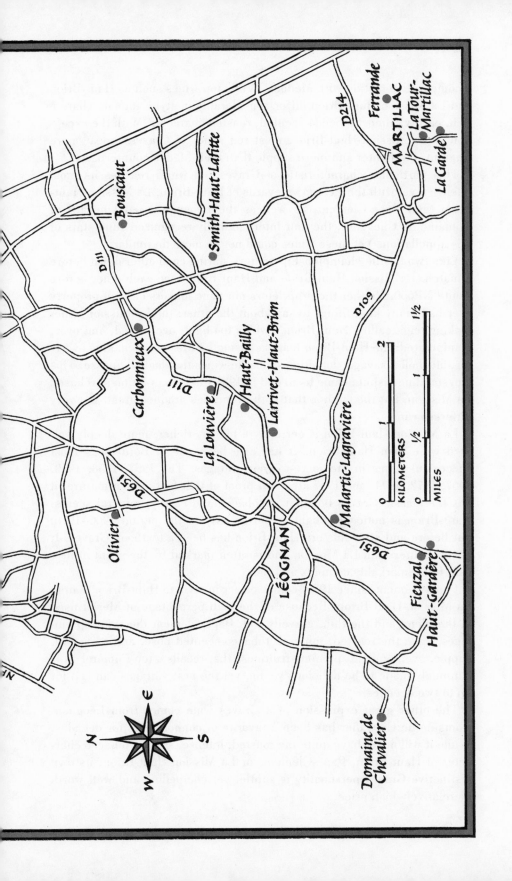

a comparative tasting with Médocs. While top wines such as Haut-Brion
and La Mission-Haut-Brion differ considerably in style, they do share a
rich, earthy, almost tobacco-scented, roasted character. With the exception of La Mission-Haut-Brion, most red wines of Graves appear more
fragrant, but lighter and more supple than their Médoc counterparts.

This particular characteristic of Graves red wines reaches its most
intense level with the Pessac vineyards of Haut-Brion, La Mission-Haut-
Brion, and Pape-Clément, as well as the Léognan-based vineyard of
Domaine de Chevalier, the four internationally recognized superstars of
this appellation. Yet these wines could not be more dissimilar.

Like two hostile championship fighters staring each other down before
a match, La Mission-Haut-Brion and Haut-Brion face each other across
Route NP650. Neither the proprietors nor wine makers of each property
ever had many kind things to say about the other: the La Mission winemaking team calling Haut-Brion's wines too light, overpriced, and over-
manipulated; the Haut-Brion team accusing La Mission of making overly
big, alcoholic, savage, sometimes volatile wines that lacked finesse. This
longstanding dispute came to an end in 1983 when Haut-Brion purchased
La Mission, but the truth is that both properties produce great, but very
different wine.

La Mission-Haut-Brion is certainly a bigger, richer, more deeply colored wine than Haut-Brion. It has also been one of Bordeaux's most
successful wines in mediocre-to-poor vintages. The 1957, 1958, 1960,
1967, 1972, 1974, and 1977 are vivid proof of that fact. When mature, it
has the classic Graves bouquet of tobacco and earthy, mineral scents.
Haut-Brion is noticeably lighter, particularly in the period 1966–1976,
but before and after this era Haut-Brion has been a textbook Graves. It
is still lighter than La Mission and is often marked by the scent of new
oak, but remarkably complex and rich.

Pape-Clément, since 1986, comes closer in style to Haut-Brion than to
La Mission-Haut-Brion. Because of the high percentage of Merlot used
in the blend and the thin, gravelly soil, Pape-Clément does, in top vintages, have the roasted, mineral, tobacco-scented nose, and a smooth,
supple, even opulent, plummy fruitiness that recalls a top Pomerol. It is
cunningly made to be delicious young, yet the best vintages can last for
up to two decades.

The other great expression of a Graves wine comes from Léognan.
Domaine de Chevalier has been a favorite of connoisseurs for decades.
While it will never have quite the roasted, intense, smoky, tobacco character of Haut-Brion, Pape-Clément, or La Mission-Haut-Brion, its own
distinctive Graves personality is subtle, yet compelling and well worth
its relatively high price.

No other Graves wine from Pessac, Talence, or Léognan comes close to matching these four great wines except occasionally Les Carmes Haut-Brion, Bahans-Haut-Brion (the second wine of Haut-Brion), or La Tour-Haut-Brion prior to 1983.

Once away from the annoyingly noisy, traffic-cluttered roads of Pessac and Talence, the Graves region takes on more charm. This is the southern Graves and the wines are less earthy, less smoky and tobacco-scented than the Graves from Pessac and Talence. They are also lighter. Léognan is the center for the best southern Graves. The tiny Domaine de Chevalier, a relatively obscure vineyard hidden by thick forests, performs splendidly well, making miniscule quantities of outstanding white Graves and moderate quantities of the aforementioned smooth, very flavorful, rich, creamy, and complex red wine.

Nearby is Haut-Bailly. Haut-Bailly produces an intensely fruity Graves wine that is usually ready to drink within 5–7 years of the vintage. Some of this château's wines can be long-lived, but this is one wine for which patience is not required. De Fieuzal has made significant strides in quality during the eighties. The white wine has been among the most splendid examples of the appellation since 1985, and the red wine has also taken on more depth, size, and complexity. At present, de Fieuzal may be the most undervalued wine of the entire appellation.

There are of course numerous other Graves wines, yet most of the other classified growths making red wine tend to produce light, rather one-dimensional wines that can be satisfying but will rarely offer much excitement. The reds of Malartic-Lagravière and Smith-Haut-Lafitte would fit this mold nicely. Carbonnieux is more interesting and to my taste has the potential to be higher-quality wine, if only the ownership would aspire to more lofty goals.

Graves is one region to investigate when Bordeaux has a mediocre or poor vintage. The drainage is excellent and in years like 1987, 1974, 1964, and 1958, when the wines of the Médoc were generally diluted and disappointing, properties like La Mission-Haut-Brion, Domaine de Chevalier, and Haut-Brion produced excellent wines from healthy, fully mature grapes. On the other hand, exceptionally hot, drought-like years that often result in superb wines in the northern Médoc, St.-Emilion, and Pomerol tend to severely stress the vineyards of Graves, causing a blockage in the grapes' maturity process. Most recently, particularly hot years such as 1982, 1989, and 1990 were less successful in Graves than elsewhere for this very reason. Recent outstanding vintages for Graves have been 1988 (better than 1990 and 1989 for most properties), 1987 (a sleeper year), 1985, 1983 (better than 1982), 1978 (a sensational vintage), 1971, 1970, 1964, and 1961.

There are numerous properties in Graves, many of them not even classified, that have been making significant qualitative progress, and are, if anything, undervalued. Excellent producers such as La Louvière, Picque-Caillou, Larrivet-Haut-Brion, Clos Floridene, Haut-Gardère, and de France will be names to take seriously during the nineties.

A CONSUMER'S CLASSIFICATION OF THE RED AND WHITE WINE PRODUCING CHÂTEAUX OF GRAVES

OUTSTANDING
Haut-Brion
Laville-Haut-Brion (white only)
La Mission-Haut-Brion

EXCELLENT
Les Carmes Haut-Brion
Domaine de Chevalier
de Fieuzal
Pape-Clément (since 1985)

VERY GOOD
Clos Floridene (white only)
Couhins-Lurton (white only)
Haut-Bailly
La Louvière

GOOD
d'Archambeau, Baret, Carbonnieux, Chantegrive, Cheret-Pitres, Cruzeau, Ferrande, de France, Haut-Gardère, Picque-Caillou, Pontac-Monplaisir, Rahoul, Rochemorin, La Tour-Haut-Brion, La Tour-Martillac

OTHER NOTABLE GRAVES PROPERTIES
Bardins, Bouscaut, Cabannieux, La Garde, La Grave, Haut-Bergey, l'Hospital, Larrivet-Haut-Brion, Malartic-Lagravière, Olivier, Piron, Smith-Haut-Lafitte

D'ARCHAMBEAU (Unclassified) Graves GOOD

Production: 5,000 cases red; 6,000 cases white	Grape varieties: Red: Merlot—50% Cabernet Sauvignon—40% Cabernet Franc—10% White: Semillon—70% Muscadelle—20% Sauvignon—10%
Secondary label: Mourlet	
Vineyard size: 17.29 acres	Proprietor: Jean-Philippe Dubourdieu
Time spent in barrels: 12–15 months	Average age of vines: 20 years
Evaluation of present classification: Equivalent to a well-made Cru Bourgeois	
Plateau of maturity: red: 2–5 years following the vintage; white: 2–5 years following the vintage	

I have only seen a few vintages of d'Archambeau's red wine. They were soft, somewhat commercial in orientation, but round and tasty.

The pride and joy of this small property in the commune of Cérons is the white wine, which comes from a gravelly, clay-like soil, and is made under the auspices of the great white winemaking family of Dubourdieu. This means cold fermentation and the famed *macération pelliculaire* (prolonged skin contact with the fermenting juice). The results are wines that are remarkably fresh and fragrant, with a honeyed, creamy texture, and a long, vividly fruity, generous finish. Consumers should search out recent vintages of this white Graves for drinking in their first 5 years of life.

Prices for d'Archambeau remain reasonable.

BARDINS (Unclassified) Pessac-Léognan AVERAGE

Production: 4,200 cases red; 100 cases white	Grape varieties: Red: Cabernet Franc—52% Merlot—32% Malbec—11% Cabernet Sauvignon—5% White: Semillon—34% Sauvignon—33% Muscadelle—33%
Secondary label: none	
Vineyard size: 17.3 acres	Proprietor: Christian de Bernardy de Sigoyer
Time spent in barrels: 12–15 months	Average age of vines: 25 years
Evaluation of present classification: The quality equivalent of a Médoc Cru Bourgeois	
Plateau of maturity: red: 3–7 years following the vintage; white: 2–4 years following the vintage	

I have only seen a handful of vintages from this tiny property in the commune of Cadaujac, situated adjacently to the more renowned Château Bouscaut. The proprietor has settled on an interesting percentage of grapes, with the very high percentage of Cabernet Franc for the red wines giving them a soft, spicy, herbaceous scent, and the extraordinarily high percentage of Muscadelle for the white wines making them richly fruity, soft, and ideal for drinking young. The best recent vintages have been the 1985, which is now tiring, followed by the 1988.

BARET (Unclassified) Pessac-Léognan   GOOD

Production: 4,000 cases red; 2,900 cases white	Grape varieties: Red: Cabernet Sauvignon—72% Merlot—25% Cabernet Franc—3% White: Semillon—65% Sauvignon—32% Muscadelle—3%
Secondary label: none	
Vineyard size: 17.3 acres	Proprietor: The Ballande family Administrator: The firm of Borie-Manoux
Time spent in barrels: 15–18 months	Average age of vines: 15 years

Evaluation of present classification: The red wine has improved immensely since 1985; the white wine has come of age since 1987; this is increasingly one of the better-made, but lesser-known Graves wines

Plateau of maturity: red: 4–10 years following the vintage; white: 2–5 years following the vintage

Significant changes have been made at Baret since 1981 when Philippe Castéja, one of the principals in the famous *négociant* firm of Borie-Manoux, assumed responsibility. The property, located just outside of Bordeaux in the commune of Villenave d'Ornon, is now making very good wines that deserve to be better known.

The red wine has become deeper, more fruity, and a great deal more interesting and more pleasurable to drink than in the vintages of the sixties and seventies, when they were often coarse and hard. The white wines have soared in quality since 1987, with the addition of some barrel fermentation, extended lees contact, and a cooler fermentation. The results have been some excellent white wines that come close to rivaling all but the very best Graves.

The best recent vintages for the red wine have been 1985, 1988, and 1989. The best recent vintages for the white wine are 1987, 1988, and 1989. This is an up-and-coming property that merits serious consideration.

BOUSCAUT (Cru Classé) Pessac-Léognan

Production: 15,000 cases red; 7,000 cases white	Grape varieties: Red: Merlot—50% Cabernet Sauvignon—35% Cabernet Franc—15% White: Semillon—60% Sauvignon—40%

Secondary label: Valoux

Vineyard size: 111 acres — Proprietor: Lucien Lurton

Time spent in barrels: 20 months — Average age of vines: 35 years

Evaluation of present classification: One of the classic underachievers of the Graves appellation; it no longer merits its status as a Cru Classé

Plateau of maturity: red: 4–12 years following the vintage; white: 2–6 years following the vintage

It was widely believed that after the American syndicate sold Bouscaut in 1980 to the well-known Bordeaux château owner, Lucien Lurton, that the quality at Bouscaut would improve. It has not. This property, among all of the classified growths of Graves, remains content to turn out mediocre white and red wines. The eighteenth-century château, with a lovely pool, was restored completely in the 1960s and is one of the most attractive in the region. Tasting the wines leaves the impression that there is a lack of a selection process. Some claim the high percentage of Merlot in the red wine (from young vines) has been detrimental to the wine's quality. I do not agree with that; I simply think Bouscaut produces too much wine without a severe enough selection to put the best under the château's name.

VINTAGES

Red Wines

1989—The 1989 is similar to the 1988—light, medium bodied, and cor-
   ·   rect—but it has more alcohol, extremely high tannins that appear
   83   excessive for its concentration, and a great deal of oak. Antici-
         pated maturity: Now–1998. Last tasted, 4/91.

1988—The 1988 is a spicy, well-made, medium-bodied wine that is ideal
   ·   for drinking early in its life. Anticipated maturity: Now–1996.
   83   Last tasted, 11/90.

1986—This wine does not display much depth or complexity. It would
·   appear to be the product of an enormous crop size, as the soft,
75   rather thin flavors fade quickly on the palate. Anticipated matu-
     rity: Now–1995. Last tasted, 3/90.

1983—This is an extremely supple, fleshy, medium-weight Graves, with
·   plenty of style and charm. Fortunately, it lacks the abrasive tan-
84   nin so common in many wines of this vintage. Quite spicy on the
     nose, and nicely colored, this wine will be an early maturing 1983.
     Anticipated maturity: Now–1996. Last tasted, 3/88.

1982—The best Bouscaut in two decades, the 1982 is medium dark, with
·   a vividly rich, ripe berry aroma, fat, lush, concentrated flavors,
85   plenty of tannins in the long finish, and good aging potential of 10
     to 12 years. This is a big–styled, impressive Bouscaut. Antici-
     pated maturity: 1992–2000. Last tasted, 1/85.

1981—The 1981 has a light-intensity, spicy, rather reserved bouquet
·   followed by flavors that are quite unyielding, hard, and austere.
74   Is there enough fruit to outlast the abrasive tannins? Probably
     not. Anticipated maturity: Now–1996. Last tasted, 6/84.

1980—Not terribly different from the 1981, only lighter in color and
·   body, the 1980 Bouscaut is an acceptable, but quite one-dimen-
72   sional wine. Anticipated maturity: Now–probably in serious de-
     cline. Last tasted, 2/83.

1978—An average-quality Bouscaut, with a light-intensity, spicy, oaky
·   aroma and modest, fruity, berryish flavors, this wine has a mod-
78   erately tannic, firm finish. Anticipated maturity: Now–probably
     in serious decline. Last tasted, 12/82.

1975—Very closed, unyielding, and painfully tannic and harsh on the
·   palate, the 1975 Bouscaut has above-average color and good
75   weight, but I see no possibility that the fruit can outlive the tan-
     nin. Anticipated maturity: Now–1996. Last tasted, 5/84.

1970—Hard and severe when young, this wine has not developed any
·   richness or character, but remained sternly tannic, woody, and
72   ungenerous, with little charm or fruit. Last tasted, 2/80.

White Wines

1989—Dull, sterile, nearly nonexistent aromas are followed by thin,
·   stripped, high-strung flavors that lack charm, flesh, and charac-
71   ter. Anticipated maturity: Now–1992. Last tasted, 4/91.

1988—This is an uninspired effort at turning out high-quality white
·   wine. An innocuous, light-bodied, eviscerated wine, the 1988
72   Bouscaut should be drunk over the next 2–3 years. Last tasted,
     11/90.

CABANNIEUX (Unclassified) Graves AVERAGE

Production: 7,000 cases red; 4,000 cases white	Grape varieties: Red: Merlot—65% Cabernet Sauvignon—25% Cabernet Franc—10% White: Semillon—80% Sauvignon—20%
Secondary label: none Vineyard size: 52 acres	Proprietor: The Barrière-Dudignac family
Time spent in barrels: 12–18 months	Average age of vines: 15 years

Evaluation of present classification: An average-quality Graves that is the equivalent of a Médoc Cru Bourgeois

Plateau of maturity: red: 2–8 years following the vintage; white: 2–4 years following the vintage

I may have been too conservative in my overall qualitative judgment of this wine because I have tasted some very mineral-scented, smoky red wines from this small estate. The vineyard is well placed near the village of Portets on high ground with exceptional drainage, and the proprietors believe in the use of a small amount of new oak for the red wine.

The white wine is made by utilizing very cold fermentation temperatures and can be, as in 1988, a supple, immensely fruity, soft style of white Graves.

The best red wine vintages have been the 1985 and 1988. I was disappointed with the 1986.

CARBONNIEUX (Cru Classé) Pessac-Leógnan GOOD

Production: 20,000 cases red; 18,000 cases white	Grape varieties: Red: Cabernet Sauvignon—60% Merlot—30% Cabernet Franc—7% Malbec—2% Petit Verdot—1% White: Sauvignon—65% Semillon—34% Muscadelle—1%
Secondary label: La Tour-Léognan	
Vineyard size: 185.25 acres	Proprietor: Tony Perrin
Time spent in barrels: 15–18 months	Average age of vines: 17 years
Evaluation of present classification: Since 1985 there has been significant progress with both the white and red wines, and the property now merits its Cru Classé status	
Plateau of maturity: red: 3–10 years following the vintage; white: 3–12 years following the vintage	

Carbonnieux, one of the largest estates of Graves, had, until the mid-1980s, fit into the pattern of many of the winemaking estates of the Pessac-Léognan area—the white wines were frequently delicious, but the red wines innocuously light and bland. Since the mid-1980s that has changed for the better, with the white wine taking on even higher quality aspirations and the red wine becoming tasty, elegant, supple, and well made.

The property is not only of historic significance, but is among the most scenic of the region. The history of the vineyards can be traced to the thirteenth century, but the modern era of Carbonnieux began in 1956 when Marc Perrin acquired the estate. His son, Tony, now oversees the winemaking. In the mid-1980s, Tony Perrin hired the famed Denis Dubourdieu, to give the whites even more fragrance and concentration. Additionally, the reds have taken on greater depth and intensity.

Most vintages of Carbonnieux, both the red and white wine, should be drunk in their first 7–8 years. Some of the white wine vintages have a remarkable potential to last for up to two decades.

VINTAGES

Red Wines

1989—The 1989 is straightforward, pleasant, oaky, medium bodied, and
 ·   tannic. It is a serviceable, middle-weight wine, but not distin-
83   guished. Anticipated maturity: 1992–2000. Last tasted, 4/91.

1988—The more well-endowed 1988 displays greater flavor precision,
 ·   more charm, medium body, and good length. It is not a big wine,
85   but stylish, flavorful, and graceful. Anticipated maturity: Now–
        1997. Last tasted, 11/90.

1986—The 1986 is impressive for its suave, graceful, cherry fruitiness,
 ·   generous use of toasty new oak, and soft flavors with some ripe
85   tannins in the finish. Anticipated maturity: Now–1996. Last
        tasted, 3/90.

1985—The 1985 has sweet, soft, expansive flavors of cherries and toasty
 ·   oak that made me think of a Premier Cru Beaune, not a Graves.
85   Anticipated maturity: Now–1994. Last tasted, 3/89.

1984—Very pale ruby in color, the 1984 Carbonnieux has a faint perfume
 ·   of berry fruit. On the palate, it is soft, totally mature, fruity, and
79   altogether pleasant—an ideal picnic wine. Anticipated maturity:
        Now–may be in decline. Last tasted, 3/88.

1983—The 1983 is an attractive, plump, spicy, juicy wine, with an ele-
 ·   gant cherry fruitiness, soft, savory texture, light tannins, and a
85   supple finish. Anticipated maturity: Now–may be in decline. Last
        tasted, 1/88.

1982—The 1982 Carbonnieux has a trifle more punch than the 1983,
 ·   better color, and more concentration than the 1981. Still, in the
83   company of other 1982s it tastes too soft, fruity, and surprisingly
        mature. It is a lightweight, yet charming wine. Anticipated ma-
        turity: Now–1994. Last tasted, 1/90.

1981—A light ruby-colored wine, the 1981 Carbonnieux is quite one-
 ·   dimensional, with spicy, soft, jammy fruit, a light-intensity bou-
73   quet, and a weak finish. Anticipated maturity: Now–probably in
        serious decline. Last tasted, 11/84.

1979—This narrowly constructed, compact, austere wine still has me-
 ·   dium ruby color with no sign of age, but there is little bouquet,
71   and the dry, astringent tastes raise serious concerns about the
        evolution of this wine. It is medium bodied and spicy, but lacks
        charm, fat, and fruit. Anticipated maturity: Now–may be in de-
        cline. Last tasted, 2/87.

1978—Made during a period when Carbonnieux was not renowned for
 ·   its red wines, the 1978 has turned out to be a light, delicate, fruity
79   Graves with some herbaceous, earthy notes in the bouquet, and

soft, round, medium-bodied flavors. Anticipated maturity: Now–1994. Last tasted, 3/86.

White Wines

1989—The 1989 has an attractive, smoky, oaky bouquet, some scents of
·   honey and herbs, and soft, agreeable, round, fruity flavors. The
85   low acidity suggests the wine should be drunk early on. Antici-
    pated maturity: Now–1993. Last tasted, 4/91.

1988—The rich, spicy, melon-and-herb-scented bouquet intertwined
·   with aromas of oak is enthralling. On the palate, the wine exhibits
87   good richness, medium body, ripe fruit, adequate acidity, and a
    lush, medium-bodied finish. Anticipated maturity: Now–1998.
    Last tasted, 4/91.

1987—Light, but cleanly made, fresh, with a fragrant herb-, fig-, and
·   melon-scented bouquet, this light- to medium-bodied wine has
82   good fruit, and a crisp, delightful finish. Anticipated maturity:
    Now–1997. Last tasted, 11/90.

LES CARMES HAUT-BRION
(Unclassified) Pessac-Leógnan   EXCELLENT

Production: 1,500 cases red	Grape varieties: Merlot—60% Cabernet Sauvignon—20% Cabernet Franc—20%
Secondary label: none Vineyard size: 8.5 acres	Proprietor: The Chantecaille family
Time spent in barrels: 20–24 months	Average age of vines: 25 years
Evaluation of present classification: Should be upgraded to a Graves Cru Classé	
Plateau of maturity: 6–20 years following the vintage	

In the early seventies, I had the good fortune to walk into a wine shop that was discounting magnums of the 1959 Les Carmes Haut-Brion. I knew nothing about the wine, but I took a chance and bought two magnums. Both proved to be spectacular, and every effort I made to find the wine thereafter was futile. Little did I know then that this tiny jewel of a vineyard, situated on a gravelly knoll in the Bordeaux suburb of Pessac, near the famed Haut-Brion and La Mission-Haut-Brion, is the most-obscure and least-known top-quality red wine of Graves.

The vineyard is named for the group of friars, called Les Carmes, who owned this vineyard between 1584 and 1789. During the French Revolution, the religious order was divested of ownership.

Les Carmes Haut-Brion is a rich, full wine, no doubt because the old Merlot vines benefit from the gravelly and clay soil in which they are planted. A traditional approach to winemaking results in wines that are classic expressions of Graves, deeply colored, intense, and complex. Unfortunately, most of the wine from Les Carmes Haut-Brion is sold by Monsieur Chantecaille through his *négociant* business in Bordeaux to European markets. Since so little wine is made, the chances of finding any in America are remote.

Friends of mine in Bordeaux tell me the quality has even gotten better since 1987, although my tasting notes have always been enthusiastic. This is a wine that comes closest to expressing the quality of Haut-Brion and La Mission-Haut-Brion, not surprisingly, as the vineyards and *terroir* are essentially the same. This small, consistently top-notch performer in Pessac is worth searching out.

VINTAGES

1989—The smoky, tobacco, mineral-like bouquet of the 1989 is enticing.
·   The palate reveals a ripe, roasted, open-knit fruitiness with a
86   finish that is alcoholic and soft. Anticipated maturity: Now–1997.
      Last tasted, 4/91.

1988—The 1988 has a deeper color than, and a rich bouquet similar to,
·   the 1989, but is more concentrated, tannic, and structured. It is
88   an attractive textbook Graves with the characteristic cigar-box,
      mineral-scented aromas and flavors. A sleeper of the vintage!
      Anticipated maturity: Now–1999. Last tasted, 4/91.

1987—In a blind tasting of Graves I participated in, in Bordeaux, I
·   thought the 1987 Les Carmes Haut-Brion was a Haut-Brion. Its in-
86   tense, smoky, ripe, curranty nose is powerful and soars from the
      glass. In the mouth, the wine is rich and very soft, with an opulent
      finish. Anticipated maturity: Now–1994. Last tasted, 3/90.

1986—This is a fleshy, full-bodied wine with an impressive deep ruby
·   color. The high tannins should permit the wine to age well for at
88   least 12–15 years. The bouquet has a sweet, plummy fruitiness,
      with a very pronounced mineral, tobacco character. Medium bodied, with good richness, this wine could well merit a higher score once the tannins soften. Anticipated maturity: 1993–2005. Last tasted, 3/90.

1985—The 1985 is an admirably constituted wine and deep in color, with
·   the unmistakable mineral, tobacco-scented bouquet so typical of
87   the top wines of this appellation. It is supple, smooth, and easy to

appreciate for the delicious, intense fruit and fine length. Anticipated maturity: Now–2000. Last tasted, 3/89.

CHANTEGRIVE (Unclassified) Graves — GOOD

Production: 15,500 cases red; 16,500 cases white	Grape varieties: Red: Cabernet Sauvignon—50% Merlot—40% Cabernet Franc—10% White: Semillon—60% Sauvignon—30% Muscadelle—10%
Secondary labels: Bon Dieu des Vignes, Mayne-Leveque, and Mayne-d'Anice	
Vineyard size: 148 acres	Proprietors: Henri and Françoise Leveque
Time spent in barrels: 12–18 months	Average age of vines: 20 years
Evaluation of present classification: The quality equivalent of a good Médoc Cru Bourgeois	
Plateau of maturity: red: 3–7 years following the vintage; white: 2–4 years following the vintage	

When I am eating at a Bordeaux restaurant, the red and white wines I most frequently search out for value and quality are those made at the attractive Château Chantegrive, located just north of the village of Podensac, adjacent to Route Nationale 113. While proprietor Henri Leveque can trace his family's wine heritage back to 1753, he alone resurrected this property from obscure standing in 1962 to one that is now recognized for high-quality red and white wines that represent excellent quality/price rapport.

The entire vinifications of both the red and white wines take place in spotless stainless-steel tanks. This is one cellar where everything from barrel cellar to fermentation rooms are temperature and humidity controlled—a rarity in Bordeaux. In the mid-1980s a luxury *cuvée* of Leveque's white Graves, the Chantegrive-Cuvée Caroline, was introduced. It is as good as some of the more renowned Crus Classés. Neither the white nor the red wine is meant to be long-lived, but rather to be drunk in the first 5–7 years of life. A strong argument can even be made for drinking the white wines before they reach the age of 5. Nevertheless, the wines are consistently well made, even in lighter-weight vintages, and are textbook examples of their appellation.

The best recent vintages for the red wines have included virtually every year since 1982. Even the 1984 was a success at Chantegrive, producing a spicy, tobacco-scented wine. My favorites remain the 1985, 1986, and 1988.

Among the white wines, those still deserving interest include two Chantegrive-Cuvée Carolines, an excellent 1988 and a very good 1989.

Frugal consumers looking for wines that satisfy both the palate and purse should seek out this consistent overachiever in the southern Graves region.

CHERET-PITRES (Unclassified) Graves   GOOD

Production: 7,500 cases red	Grape varieties:
	Cabernet Sauvignon—50%
	Merlot—50%
Secondary label: none	
Vineyard size: 29.6 acres	Proprietor: Jean Boulanger
Time spent in barrels: 15–20 months	Average age of vines: 35 years
Evaluation of present classification: Easily the equivalent of a good Médoc Cru Bourgeois	
Plateau of maturity: 3–8 years following the vintage	

I have frequently been satisfied by the smoky, tobacco, richly fruity character of the wines of Cheret-Pitres. I have enthusiastic tasting notes of the 1975, 1978, 1982, and 1985. It is not a well-known wine, but because of that it is often a super value. The vineyard is located in the commune of Portets, and no doubt the old vines and high percentage of Merlot give this wine its characteristic fatness and suppleness. No white wine is made at this property.

DOMAINE DE CHEVALIER
(Cru Classé) Pessac-Léognan   EXCELLENT

Production: 5,000 cases red; 800 cases white	Grape varieties: Red: Cabernet Sauvignon—65% Merlot—30% Cabernet Franc—5% White: Sauvignon—70% Semillon—30%
Secondary label: none	
Vineyard size: 44 acres	Proprietor: Lucien Bernard et Cie Administrators: Claude Ricard and Olivier Bernard
Time spent in barrels: red: 24 months; white: 18 months	Average age of vines: 20 years

Evaluation of present classification: The quality equivalent of a Médoc second-growth

Plateau of maturity: red: 5–20 years following the vintage; white: 6–30 years following the vintage

The tiny estate of Domaine de Chevalier, tucked away in the midst of a forest on the southwest outskirts of Léognan, is a true connoisseur's wine. The production is tiny and the wines are among the most highly sought of Graves, but most important, the quality is impeccably high.

Domaine de Chevalier's fame is no doubt due to the aristocratic Claude Ricard, who inherited the property in 1942, but because of family squabbles had to sell the estate in 1983 to the large Bernard distilling company. Despite rumors that wine quality might be sacrificed because of the accountant-dominated mentality of a large corporation, that has not been the case. Claude Ricard was retained to run the property and to train his young apprentice—Olivier Bernard—in the aspects of making two of the most profound wines of the Graves appellation.

The red wines of Domaine de Chevalier do not resemble the intense, rich, earthy style of Graves, best exemplified by Haut-Brion and La Mission-Haut-Brion. The Domaine de Chevalier wines possess a subtle, mineral, earthy aspect, but are much lighter in body and tend to be more Médoc-like in style than the Graves wines from Pessac and Talence. Since the new owners acquired the property, every vintage since 1983 has suggested there has been an intentional effort to produce a bigger, more structured and powerful wine. Yet the underlying charm and finesse of the red Domaine de Chevalier remain the telltale personality traits of this wine.

The white Domaine de Chevalier is the only wine I know of in the Bordeaux region that spends over a year and a half in new oak casks. The production is tiny, and the wine, while fabulous when drunk from cask, usually closes up after bottling, not to blossom for 5–10 or more years. Yet, it has the distinction of actually taking longer to mature, and aging even more gracefully than the superb red wine.

Anyone who visits the southern Graves region will have a difficult time finding Domaine de Chevalier. I became impossibly lost on my first trip to the property in the late seventies. The one-story, modest, cream-colored château, surrounded on three sides by a pine forest, can be found by taking D109 east from Léognan in the direction of Cestas. In less than a kilometer, turn left at the first small road. About 1,500 feet down this road is a small sign on the right indicating the entrance to the vineyard of Domaine de Chevalier.

The soil of this relatively small vineyard has a gravel bed, but also contains clay and iron. Two problems encountered here are that spring frosts and frequent hail can severely damage the crop. No other major château of the Bordeaux region has suffered from these two natural calamities as much as Domaine de Chevalier.

Domaine de Chevalier is an expensive wine, fetching prices similar to those of a Médoc second-growth. However, the quality justifies the price and Domaine de Chevalier truly merits its lofty reputation.

VINTAGES

Red Wines

1989—Domaine de Chevalier has called its 1989 comparable to the 1970,
· 1961, and 1945. If this is true, I have underestimated it. I found
88 it to be a densely concentrated, tannic, medium-bodied, rich, and stylish wine, but at this stage, it appears behind the quality of the 1988, 1986, 1983, 1978, and 1970, not ahead of them. Anticipated maturity: 1996–2015. Last tasted, 4/91.

1988—Domaine de Chevalier produced one of the finest wines of this
· vintage. Dark ruby, with an unevolved but generous bouquet of
90 smoky new oak, cassis, and flowers, this fleshy, generously en-dowed wine is the finest effort from this property since the 1983 and 1986. Powerful, yet also elegant, this is a gorgeously made wine. Anticipated maturity: 1994–2008. Last tasted, 4/91.

1987—This domain consistently does fine work in off years, and the 1987
· boasts an intense, vanilla-scented, toasty, oaky bouquet, ripe
86 raspberry and blackcurrant flavors, medium body, surprising con-

centration, and ample, soft tannins in the finish. Drinkable now. Anticipated maturity: Now–1998. Last tasted, 3/90.

1986—From the bouquet of ripe mineral-and-tobacco-scented fruit,
· which seems to swell in the glass, this medium-bodied, relatively
90 oaky yet deep, profound wine lasts and lasts on the palate. It is one of the most concentrated and richest of any Domaine de Chevalier in the last two decades. There are plenty of tannins in the finish, but they are soft rather than astringent. Anticipated maturity: 1994–2015. Last tasted, 3/90.

1985—The 1985 has the sweet, ripe, rich fruit that is the hallmark of this
· vintage, but also more tannin than many Graves from this vintage.
86 For a 1985, it will be slow to mature, yet it does not have the concentration one usually expects of wines from this property. Anticipated maturity: 1993–2005. Last tasted, 3/90.

1984—The 1984 Domaine de Chevalier contains an unusually high
· amount of Cabernet Sauvignon (90%). It is well marked by toasty
85 new oak, but there are also plenty of ripe fruit, moderate tannins, and fine depth to this wine. This is one of the few stars of the vintage. Anticipated maturity: 1992–1997. Last tasted, 3/89.

1983—It is amazing how a wine that was relatively tannic and hard in
· youth has seen its tannins melt away so quickly. This is now a
90 classic example of Domaine de Chevalier at its best, and it is drinking beautifully. I would never have expected this wonderful wine to mature so quickly. Dark ruby with an intense bouquet of licorice, smoke, blackcurrants, and spices, this medium-bodied, opulently textured, fleshy wine is bursting with fruit and ripeness, and the tannins have fallen away. Luscious and seductive, I would opt for drinking this beauty over the next decade. Anticipated maturity: Now–2001. Last tasted, 11/90.

1982—Hail badly damaged the crop at Domaine de Chevalier in 1982.
· Yet I remember tasting some very fine wines from cask; also,
67 some bottles tasted at the château displayed a rich and powerful wine early in its life. However, recent tastings continue to reveal a weedy, thin, peppery wine, with a dill pickle aroma, decent flavor concentration, but hard, astringent tannins, and an appalling lack of concentration and depth. I have had readers tell me that they have had wonderful examples of this wine, but the bottles I have tasted have been disappointingly hollow and astringent. Anticipated maturity: 1992–2000. Last tasted, 1/91.

1981—The 1981 Domaine de Chevalier is well made, but lacks flavor
· dimension, depth, and charm. A medium-bodied wine, it has a
83 pronounced vanillin oakiness, aggressive tannins, ruby color, and

a lean finish. Will it ever blossom and provide real pleasure? Anticipated maturity: Now–2000. Last tasted, 3/89.

1980—A notable success in this mediocre vintage, Domaine de Chevalier
·   has made a deeply fruity, spicy, open-knit wine, with a bouquet
84   dominated by the scent of new vanillin oakiness. Medium bodied, with surprising concentration and light tannins, this supple, classy wine is ideal for drinking over the next 5–6 years. Anticipated maturity: Now–1994. Last tasted, 10/84.

1979—Very agreeable and drinkable from the time it was bottled, the
·   1979 Domaine de Chevalier is a charmingly supple, fruity, me-
85   dium-bodied wine that refuses to fall apart. A fragrant bouquet of ripe berry fruit and cedar is alluring. On the palate, the wine is supple, medium bodied, oaky, round, and long. Anticipated maturity: Now–1993. Last tasted, 12/89.

1978—Along with the 1970, this is a personal favorite. It is dark ruby in
·   color, with an explosively rich, blackcurrant, spicy, cedary bou-
92   quet, medium to full body, a lush, ripe, fruity texture, and a long, moderately tannic finish. The 1978 Domaine de Chevalier is an exquisite wine, and one of the superstars of the 1978 vintage. Anticipated maturity: Now–2005. Last tasted, 1/91.

1977—One of the better 1977 wines, the Domaine de Chevalier is soft
·   and fruity, with moderately intense, medium-bodied flavors that
76   exhibit a pleasant berry fruitiness. Anticipated maturity: Now– probably in serious decline. Last tasted, 3/81.

1976—An open, spicy, rather earthy, ripe, almost-burnt bouquet is fol-
·   lowed on the palate by a wine that is fully mature, soft, less
78   concentrated than normal, but fruity. Anticipated maturity: Now– may be in decline. Last tasted, 4/87.

1975—We all make mistakes, and a serious one I made was purchasing
·   this wine before I tasted it. The 1975 has consistently proven to
68   be disappointing. Hail, much like in 1982, was again the undoing of the 1975 Domaine de Chevalier. The wine still has an impressive dark ruby, youthful-looking color, but in the mouth, it is hollow and extremely astringent, with mouth-searing tannins, and a hard, nasty finish. Perhaps this wine will exhibit more charm and fruit with aging, but I am increasingly skeptical. Anticipated maturity: Now–2000? Last tasted, 12/90.

1974—This is a flavorful, supple, fruity 1974, without any of the harsh-
·   ness or hollowness that afflicts so many wines from this vintage.
76   Drinkable now, the tannins and overall balance may keep this wine from declining for another 3–4 years. Anticipated maturity: Now–probably in serious decline. Last tasted, 6/80.

1973—I had this wine for the first and only time in 1990, and it was a
· revelation. Most 1973s were in serious decline by the end of that
87 decade, but this wine, drunk with a friend in Bordeaux, was still
a deep ruby color, with only a slight amber edge. The explosively
intense bouquet of plums, smoky vanillin oak, and minerals was
delightful. In the mouth, it was pure velvet, with sweet, expansive, ripe fruit, and a long, heady, alcoholic finish. Can this really
be a 1973? The best wine made on the left bank of Bordeaux in
1973! Anticipated maturity: Now–1995. Last tasted, 4/90.

1971—Quite disappointing, this decrepit, prematurely senile wine has a
· very brown color, hot, almost cooked flavors, and a lean, short
67 finish. It is now past its prime. Last tasted, 3/81.

1970—The 1970 is a wonderfully rich, fragrant, exquisitely scented wine,
· with ripe fruit interlaced with aromas of roasted nuts and vanillin
89 oak. On the palate, the wine is soft, quite mature, very supple,
generously fruity, and ready to drink. It is a top-notch effort from
Domaine de Chevalier. Drink it over the next 5 years. Note: A
magnum drunk in 1990 was even better than this (I scored it 91),
so larger formats of this wine may offer the potential for drinking
over the next decade. Anticipated maturity: Now–1995. Last
tasted, 2/90.

1966—Still tenuously holding on to its fruity component, the 1966 is
· beginning to show a great deal of brown in its color, and tastes a
84 trifle dried out. However, it still retains an elegant, aged, savory
richness and spiciness that gives it plenty of appeal. Anticipated
maturity: Now–may be in decline. Last tasted, 8/82.

1964—When I wrote about this wine in the first edition of this book, I
· gave it an adequate review. Two bottles tasted since were signifi-
90 cantly better. Both exhibited dark ruby color, with some amber/
orange at the rim. Both had bouquets that displayed a roasted,
rich, intensely concentrated character, indicative of a hot vintage.
In the mouth, the wine was extremely full bodied and alcoholic
for a Domaine de Chevalier, but rich, full, intense, and velvety.
Clearly I underrated this wine. While not as superb as the 1964
La Mission-Haut-Brion, the 1964 Domaine de Chevalier is still a
gorgeously fragrant, hedonistic wine with gobs of plump, fat flavors. Anticipated maturity: Now–1995. Last tasted, 11/89.

1961—Not unlike the 1964, the 1961 has better color, but a coarser
· texture, and enough signs to indicate that it was in its prime in
86 the early seventies. The complex, aged bouquet of roasted fruit
and nuts is classy, but on the palate, the wine does not deliver
the expected richness and depth that characterize this vintage. A

bottle tasted in 1989 had more fruit, yet still did not impress me to the extent I would have thought given the vintage. Nevertheless, this is a very good rather than great Domaine de Chevalier. Anticipated maturity: Now–1995. Last tasted, 11/89.

OLDER VINTAGES

The two vintages I tasted of Domaine de Chevalier from the fifties both proved to be excellent wines. The 1959 (rated 89 in 1988) was a fuller, richer, more muscular and tannic wine than the 1961. It will easily last through the end of the century. Fully mature and exceptionally seductive in a 1970 or 1978 sort of style was the gloriously fragrant, voluptuous, and hedonistic 1953 (rated 92 in 1989). Holding on to this wine would be pushing one's luck, so owners should consume it immediately.

White Wines

1989—This wine does not have the concentration of the 1988, and given
·   my high expectations, I am disappointed by the showings to date.
86   There is plenty of intense vanillin oakiness in the bouquet, as well as some faint scents of minerals, herbs, and underripe apricots. However, the wine is medium bodied, and lacks concentration and depth. Anticipated maturity: 1992–1998. Last tasted, 4/91.

1988—The 1988 is a classic Domaine de Chevalier. It exhibits a superb
·   precision, has a perfumed, oaky, mineral-like quality, an austere
90   palate, and an underlying profound richness and exceptional length. It is not a joy to drink now, but it should blossom in 7–8 years and last for 15 or more years. Anticipated maturity: 1997–2005. Last tasted, 4/91.

1987—1987 is a terribly underrated vintage for white Graves. This wine
·   has more depth, ripeness, and complexity than either the 1989 or
88   1986, the two vintages that most casual observers would think to be superior. Pale straw in color, with a more evolved, honeyed, herb-, mineral-, and orange-scented bouquet, this medium-bodied, surprisingly soft, forward Domaine de Chevalier has excellent depth, moderate acidity, and an oaky, alcoholic finish. Anticipated maturity: 1992–2003. Last tasted, 11/90.

1986—Pale straw in color, with a decidedly oaky, ungenerous bouquet,
·   the 1986 is steely, tightly knit, extremely austere, and difficult to
85   appreciate or assess. If it develops more concentration and charm it could merit a higher score, but my notes have been consistent since I first tasted it from barrel. Anticipated maturity: Now–2000. Last tasted, 3/90.

1985—This should turn out to be an extraordinary vintage for Domaine
· de Chevalier. By the standards of this white Graves, it is sump-
93 tuous. While more closed now than when I tasted it from barrel,
the wine still cannot hide an exceptional degree of ripeness and
richness. Full bodied, with good acidity, this brilliantly rendered,
honeyed, fig-, melon-, and mineral-scented and -flavored wine
should provide extraordinary drinking if one has the patience to
wait it out. Anticipated maturity: 1995–2010. Last tasted, 12/90.

1983—Domaine de Chevalier made the best white wine of the appellation
· in this vintage, as well as one of the great successes of the
93 eighties. Impossibly closed when I last tasted it, the 1983 still
reveals that profound mineral, honeyed bouquet, rich, intense,
mouth-filling flavors that are exceptionally well knit, and a long,
explosively rich finish. Nevertheless, the wine has budged
little since its bottling, and gives every indication of being one
of the longest-lived white Domaine de Chevaliers of the last
several decades. Anticipated maturity: 1997–2015. Last tasted,
1/91.

1982—This is a more meaty, fleshy, and obvious example of a white
· Domaine de Chevalier. It lacks the structure and precision, as
87 well as the great depth and haunting complexity, of the 1983, but
it offers plenty of toasty vanillin oak, a big, fat, fleshy texture,
and loads of alcohol and wood in the finish. Anticipated maturity:
Now–2003. Last tasted, 3/90.

1981—Once past a surprisingly strong scent of sulphur, the 1981 displays
· narrowly constructed mineral, melon, and herb-like flavors, me-
82 dium body, high acidity, and plenty of wood, but not the generosity or overall balance and complexity of a typical Domaine de
Chevalier. Anticipated maturity: 1992–2005. Last tasted, 3/88.

1979—This is an example of just how slowly the white Domaine de
· Chevalier matures. Most purchasers, I am sure, have consumed
88 this wine, but it is just beginning to open up and blossom. The
rich aromas of melons, herbs, and oak gently ascend from the
glass. In the mouth, this medium-bodied wine has excellent richness, a persistence on the palate, and a long, crisp finish. Anticipated maturity: Now–2000. Last tasted, 3/89.

1976—One of the more advanced colors for a 14-year-old Domaine de
· Chevalier, this vintage produced a medium gold–colored wine,
88 with a relatively direct, open-knit, honeyed nose, a great deal of
body and glycerin in the mouth, and a long, alcoholic, fat finish. I
find this wine delicious, but atypical for Domaine de Chevalier.
Anticipated maturity: Now–2000. Last tasted, 12/90.

1975—I wish I knew this vintage better, but this wine tastes extremely
  ·   subdued and surprisingly light, and lacks generosity, complexity,
  84   and length. Have I caught it in an ungenerous, closed stage of
       development? Anticipated maturity: Now–1996. Last tasted,
       12/90.

1971—Having had this wine several times, I am now convinced that it is
  ·   a mediocre effort from Domaine de Chevalier. Straightforward,
  73   almost generic scents of no great distinction are followed by a
       medium-bodied, compact, one-dimensional wine that tastes
       nearly sterile. Anticipated maturity: Now–1995. Last tasted,
       12/90.

1970—This is a spectacular vintage for the white wine of Domaine de
  ·   Chevalier. Medium golden in color, with a huge, flamboyant bou-
  93   quet of spices, honeyed fruit, beer nuts, and figs, in the mouth
       the wine is full bodied, rich, luscious, even opulent, with a dra-
       matically long, heady finish. With all of its concentration and
       flamboyance, what makes this so special is super acidity, which
       gives this wine delineation and precision. Anticipated maturity:
       Now–2005. Last tasted, 12/90.

1966—A classy bouquet of minerals and herbs is immediately apparent.
  ·   In the mouth, the wine is medium bodied and still fresh and lively,
  88   with excellent generosity, and a delicate, elegant personality.
       This is a lighter, but interesting and enthralling Domaine de
       Chevalier. Anticipated maturity: Now–1995. Last tasted, 3/86.

1962—The spectacularly fresh, yet huge bouquet of spring flowers, mel-
  ·   ons, herbs, and minerals is hard to beat. Full bodied, exception-
  93   ally rich, creamy textured, yet impeccably balanced, this
       splendidly ripe Domaine de Chevalier has reached full maturity,
       but displays no signs of age in either its color or freshness of fruit.
       It is quite a tour de force in white wine making. Bravo! Antici-
       pated maturity: Now–2000. Last tasted, 3/87.

CLOS FLORIDENE (Unclassified) Graves   VERY GOOD

Production: 1,000 cases red; 1,500 cases white	Grape varieties: Red: Cabernet Sauvignon—80% Merlot—20% White: Semillon—80% Muscadelle—20%
Secondary label: none	
Vineyard size: 15 acres	Proprietor: Denis Dubourdieu
Time spent in barrels: 6–9 months	Average age of vines: 15 years
Evaluation of present classification: The quality equivalent of a white Graves Cru Classé	
Plateau of maturity: 2–5 years following the vintage for the white wine	

This small domain is owned by the white wine making guru of Bordeaux, Denis Dubourdieu. He has long been given credit, and justifiably so, for revolutionizing white wine making in the Bordeaux region with his technique called *macération pelliculaire*. This process permits a period of contact between the skins of the grapes and the juice at a relatively low temperature. This is done because of Dubourdieu's belief, now confirmed by other authorities, that it is the components in the grape's skin that give the wine its aromatic complexity and richness of fruit. Dubourdieu's blend of grapes is also interesting. He utilizes 80% Semillon and 20% Muscadelle, totally ignoring Sauvignon. His belief is that the Muscadelle provides the extraordinary fragrance found in his wines, and the Semillon the body and intensity.

One taste of the wonderful wines he made in 1985, 1987, 1988, 1989, and 1990 reveals that Clos Floridene is a superb white Graves, nearly matching the quality of such legends as Laville-Haut-Brion, Haut-Brion-Blanc, and Domaine de Chevalier. The price remains a relative steal, although Dubourdieu's talents have been recognized throughout Europe and Great Britain; Clos Floridene has indeed been discovered. This is a terribly underestimated, excellent wine that deserves to be a classified growth in the Graves firmament. A modest quantity of good, smooth, red wine is made but it doesn't share the dazzling qualities of the white wine.

COUHINS-LURTON (Unclassified) Pessac-Léognan VERY GOOD

Production: 2,000 cases white	Grape varieties: Sauvignon—100%
Secondary label: Cantebau	
Vineyard size: 15 acres	Proprietor: André Lurton
Time spent in barrels: 10 months	Average age of vines: 15 years
Evaluation of present classification: The quality equivalent of a Cru Classé in the white Graves classification	
Plateau of maturity: 3–8 years following the vintage	

André Lurton, another member of the ubiquitous Lurton family, runs this small gem of a property with great enthusiasm. The result is perhaps the best white Graves made purely from Sauvignon Blanc. Fermented in new oak and aged for nearly 10 months prior to bottling, this is a consistently superb white Graves of surprising complexity, richness, and length. I would not age it past 7–8 years, but that reflects my personal predilection for drinking these wines relatively young and fresh. The price of Couhins-Lurton has not yet caught up to the quality, and enthusiasts of white Graves should be seeking out this difficult-to-find but impeccably made wine.

CRUZEAU (Unclassified) Pessac-Léognan   GOOD

Production: 17,000 cases red; 5,000 cases white	Grape varieties: Red: Cabernet Sauvignon—60% Merlot—40% White: Sauvignon—90% Semillon—10%
Secondary label: none	
Vineyard size: 125 acres	Proprietor: André Lurton
Time spent in barrels: 12 months	Average age of vines: 10 years
Evaluation of present classification: Now equivalent to a good Cru Bourgeois; should improve as the vines get older	
Plateau of maturity: red: 5–8 years following the vintage; white: 2–6 years following the vintage	

André Lurton, who has created quite a viticultural empire for himself in the Graves region, purchased this property in 1973 and began extensive replanting in 1979. The new vineyard is young by Bordeaux standards, but the wine has already begun to show promising potential. Using machine harvesters for the red wine, and producing a creamy textured, open-knit, richly fruity, smoky-scented red Graves, have proven beneficial for attracting buyers looking for immediate gratification.

The white wine, made from grapes that are hand harvested and vinified, and brought up in stainless steel with no exposure to oak, has an almost California-like style, with a great deal of fruit. However, the wine must be drunk within its first several years of life.

Prices for the wines of Cruzeau are remarkably fair, and therein lies much of this wine's appeal.

FERRANDE (Unclassified) Graves   GOOD

Production: 18,000 cases red; 4,500 cases white	Grape varieties: Red: Merlot—34% Cabernet Sauvignon—33% Cabernet Franc—33% White: Semillon—60% Sauvignon—35% Muscadelle—5%
Secondary label: Lognac Vineyard size: 109 acres	Proprietor: The Delnaud family
Time spent in barrels: 15–18 months	Average age of vines: 28 years
Evaluation of present classification: The quality equivalent of a good Cru Bourgeois	
Plateau of maturity: red: 3–10 years following the vintage; white: 2–7 years following the vintage	

This is a consistently reliable, if uninspiring, estate in the commune of Castres. The property has been under the ownership of the Delnaud family since 1954. I have found both the red and white wines of Ferrande to be among the most earthy of the Graves region. In tastings I have noticed that this characteristic can either be admired or disliked intensely.

The white wines have improved a great deal in the last decade and now have much more charm and fruit in evidence. Previously the white wine had a tendency to be not only aggressively earthy, but also extremely austere and angular. The wines are priced fairly and age fairly well, particularly the reds.

The best recent vintages for the red wines have been 1978, 1982, and 1985.

DE FIEUZAL (Cru Classé) Pessac-Léognan   EXCELLENT

Production: 16,500 cases red; 2,500 cases white	Grape varieties: Red: Cabernet Sauvignon—60% Merlot—30% Cabernet Franc—5% Petit Verdot—4% Malbec—1% White: Sauvignon—60% Semillon—40%
Secondary label: L'Abeille de Fieuzal	Proprietor: SA Château de Fieuzal
Vineyard size: 81.5 acres	Administrator: Gérard Gribelin
Time spent in barrels: 18–20 months	Average age of vines: 35 years
Evaluation of present classification: Now the quality equivalent of a Médoc second- or third-growth; since 1985, the white wine has been stunning, and is now capable of rivaling the best of the appellation	
Plateau of maturity: red: 5–20 years following the vintage; white: 4–10 years following the vintage	

De Fieuzal has always been one of the more obscure Graves, which is surprising given the fact that it is a relatively old property and is well recognized by the inhabitants of the region. The cellars are located in the rolling countryside adjacent to D651 on the outskirts of Léognan in the direction of Saucats. De Fieuzal's obscurity appears to have ended abruptly during the mid-1980s, when the wines became noticeably richer and more complex. This is not to say that older vintages were not well made. Many of them were, but they certainly did not have the dazzling character that more recent years have possessed.

Much of the credit for de Fieuzal's rise in quality must go to the enthusiastic administrator, Gérard Gribelin, who took over the running of the property in 1974. In 1977 stainless-steel, temperature-controlled fermentation tanks were installed, and there has been an increasing tendency in the eighties to prolong the maceration period and use more new oak. The great breakthrough for the white wine of de Fieuzal came in 1985 when the property made the first of what was to be a series of stunning white Graves. Gribelin recognizes that his technical director and winemaker, Monsieur DuPouy, has contributed greatly to the restoration of de Fieuzal's reputation. DuPouy is, by any standard of measurement, a perfectionist, and has shown remarkable talent and flexibility in supervising the winemaking at de Fieuzal. Amazingly, the high quality has not been accompanied by soaring prices, as de Fieuzal represents one of the best quality/price ratios in the entire Graves region.

VINTAGES

Red Wines

1989—De Fieuzal's winemaker, the enthusiastic Monsieur DuPouy, harvested his Merlot on September 11 and 12, but found that his Cabernet was not physiologically mature until October 5. He also
· 90 was one of the few Graves producers to cut off grape bunches in July. The result is a fabulously concentrated black/purple–colored 1989 that is the most powerful and large-scaled wine among the Graves. It is a true blockbuster, with layer upon layer of smoky, intensely concentrated, pure blackcurrant fruit, medium to full body, gobs of tannin, and a finish that must last nearly a minute. Anticipated maturity: 1994–2010. Last tasted, 4/91.

1988—The 1988 comes close to rivaling the 1989. It has some alcohol, but is a highly extracted, nearly purple colored wine with an
· 88 excellent nose of sweet currant fruit, medium body, and a compact, very tannic finish. The wine has closed up since its bottling and appears to need considerably more time. Anticipated maturity: 1996–2010. Last tasted, 4/91.

1987—One of the darkest colored wines, de Fieuzal's 1987 is surprisingly robust, richly fruity, and a fuller-bodied, more muscular wine
· 86 than the other top 1987s. There is low acidity, some soft tannins, and surprising alcohol and power in the finish. Although the wine is drinkable, it does not seem to have changed much from when I tasted it from cask. Anticipated maturity: 1992–2000. Last tasted, 3/90.

1986—Powerful and tannic for a de Fieuzal, the 1986 has very deep color, and plenty of depth and power in the finish. It has the
· 87 potential to be the longest-lived de Fieuzal since the 1970. Anticipated maturity: 1994–2008. Last tasted, 1/90.

1985—The 1985 is an elegantly wrought, fruity, deeply colored, medium-bodied wine that has a generous, plump texture, and smooth,
· 86 concentrated flavors. It is more open knit and accessible than the 1986. Anticipated maturity: Now–2003. Last tasted, 1/90.

1984—Surprisingly dark ruby in color, the 1984 de Fieuzal is a chunky,
·   solidly constructed wine with good depth and length. In need of
85   2–3 years of cellaring, it reveals a strong, well-structured,
       Cabernet-dominated personality. It is an unqualified success
       for the vintage. Anticipated maturity: 1992–2000. Last tasted,
       3/89.

1983—The elegant, spicy, richly fruity nose is followed by a wine with
·   good, firm tannins. This medium-bodied 1983 has excellent con-
86   centration, and good structure and length. De Fieuzel is a well-
       made, polished, and refined wine that has taken on weight and
       fat in the last 3–4 years. Anticipated maturity: 1992–2001. Last
       tasted, 3/89.

1982—This has always been an attractive as well as deceptively forward
·   wine that is dark ruby, with a rich, chocolate, berry-like aroma, a
86   prominent oakiness, and a toasty, smoky quality. For a de Fieu-
       zal, this is a muscular, more intense style than is usual. The 1982
       should age well for at least a decade. It is reminiscent of the 1989,
       but less concentrated. Anticipated maturity: Now–1998. Last
       tasted, 1/89.

1981—The 1981 has a pleasant herbaceous, berry-like bouquet, good
·   acidity, medium weight, and moderate tannin. It is a polite, re-
80   strained, compact style of wine. Anticipated maturity: Now–
       1995. Last tasted, 1/89.

1978—Deep ruby, with a slightly amber edge, de Fieuzal's 1978 has a
·   surprisingly unevolved, even reticent bouquet, some attractive
82   ripe, smoky fruit, medium body, good depth and length, but also
       plenty of tannin that has yet to melt away. Will the wine's fruit
       fade before the tannins fall off? Anticipated maturity: Now–2000.
       Last tasted, 1/89.

1975—This wine has several of the best and worst characteristics of the
·   1975 vintage. The color is still deep ruby, with only a slight amber
83   edge. The bouquet exhibits dusty, herbaceous, plummy, roasted
       notes that are followed by a relatively hard, yet ripe, medium- to
       full-bodied wine with plenty of grip and tannin. However, a cer-
       tain toughness and coarseness keeps my score conservative. An-
       ticipated maturity: Now–2002. Last tasted, 1/89.

1970—This is a surprisingly strong effort in a period when de Fieuzal
·   had little or no reputation. Deep ruby, with some orange/brown at
86   the edge, the smoky, tobacco, herbaceous, and curranty bouquet
       is textbook Graves. In the mouth, the wine is round and gener-
       ously endowed, with good ripeness, and a lovely, soft, velvety
       finish. I suspect this wine has been fully mature for some time,

but it displays no signs of decline. Drink it over the next 7–8 years. Anticipated maturity: Now–1997. Last tasted, 1/89.

White Wines

1989—Like many 1989 white Graves, de Fieuzal does not quite have the
·   grip and delineation one expects because of the vintage's low
90   acidity. Nevertheless, this has still turned out to be one of the most successful wines of the vintage. It is a rich, honeyed, smoky-scented wine with wonderfully ripe apple and melon-like flavors. Anticipated maturity: Now–1996. Last tasted, 4/91.

1988—This beautiful example of white Graves displayed a full-intensity
·   bouquet of honey, flowers, and smoky new oak. In the mouth,
92   it has an opulence and richness that can only be the result of low yields and/or old vines. This is a wonderfully precise, rich, classic white Graves. Anticipated maturity: Now–1999. Last tasted, 4/91.

1987—Light gold, with a restrained, yet provocative bouquet of figs,
·   melons, smoky new oak, and honey, in the mouth, this wine is
88   less concentrated and full when compared to the 1988, but delicate, with good acidity, complexity, and an entirely satisfying finish. Anticipated maturity: Now–1996. Last tasted, 4/91.

1986—I have never been a great admirer of the 1986 white Graves and
·   this effort from de Fieuzal is more straightforward than usual,
85   without the underlying complexity and precision to its flavors. It is full, but comes across as chunky and foursquare. The wine remains slightly formless. Anticipated maturity: Now–1994. Last tasted, 4/91.

1985—To date, this is my favorite vintage of white de Fieuzal. It also
·   marks the breakthrough when de Fieuzal began making white
93   wines that rivaled the best of the region. Still young in color, the bouquet has that wonderfully intense, honeyed, fig-, melon-, orange-, herb-, and oaky-scented nose. Full bodied, rich, with substantial extract and length, this admirably endowed, beautifully balanced white Graves is quite sensational. Anticipated maturity: Now–1996. Last tasted, 5/91.

DE FRANCE (Unclassified) Pessac-Léognan GOOD

Production: 15,000 cases red; no production to date of white	Grape varieties: Red: Cabernet Sauvignon—60% Merlot—40% White: Sauvignon—50% Semillon—30% Muscadelle—20%
Secondary label: none	
Vineyard size: 74 acres	Proprietor: Bernard Thomassin
Time spent in barrels: 12–15 months	Average age of vines: 20 years
Evaluation of present classification: Since 1986, the quality has improved immensely; it is now one of the obscure, yet better wines of the region	
Plateau of maturity: red: 4–10 years following the vintage; white: not yet in production	

Virtually the entire vineyard of this property, which is a neighbor of the more-renowned Château de Fieuzal, has been replanted since 1971. The proprietor—an industrialist—has spared little expense in renovating the property and building a new winery with state-of-the-art stainless-steel fermentation tanks. The early results were not impressive, but in 1986, proprietor Thomassin began to do two things that have had a significant positive impact on the resulting wines. First, he decided to harvest as late as possible. Second, a severe selection of the finished wine was employed so that only the best vats were sold under the de France name. The results have been wonderfully supple, smoky, elegant wines produced in 1986, 1988, and 1989.

This could well be a property to take more and more seriously as the vineyard comes of age.

LA GARDE (Unclassified) Pessac-Léognan

Production: 20,000 cases red; 3,000 cases white	Grape varieties: Red: Cabernet Sauvignon—62% Merlot—27% Cabernet Franc—9% Petit Verdot—2% White: Sauvignon—100%
Secondary label: none	
Vineyard size: 111 acres	Proprietor: Dourthe
Time spent in barrels: 15–18 months	Average age of vines: 14 years
Evaluation of present classification: The quality equivalent of a Médoc Cru Bourgeois	
Plateau of maturity: red: 2–6 years following the vintage; white: 2–4 years following the vintage	

Despite significant renovations and improvements to the vineyards and winemaking facility, La Garde remains an average-quality wine-producing estate. The white wine is a dry, austere, light-bodied example of a white Graves, and the red is medium bodied, and often excessively tannic. A greater concentration of fruit and charm would be worthwhile goals at this relatively large estate in the commune of Martillac. The huge *négociant*, Dourthe, became the new owner in 1990, an encouraging sign that better things may emerge in the future.

LA GRAVE (Unclassified) Graves

Production: 1,000 cases red; 500 cases white	Grape varieties: Red: Cabernet Sauvignon—50% Merlot—50% White: Semillon—100%
Secondary label: none	
Vineyard size: 15 acres	Proprietor: Peter Vinding-Diers
Time spent in barrels: 20–22 months	Average age of vines: 28 years
Evaluation of present classification: The quality equivalent of a Médoc Cru Bourgeois	
Plateau of maturity: red: 3–8 years following the vintage; white: 2–7 years following the vintage	

I have only had the opportunity to taste a few vintages of the wines of Peter Vinding-Diers, who is widely respected in Bordeaux winemaking circles. I have been more impressed with the oaky white wine made from 100% Semillon than the relatively woody, austere red wine. Nevertheless, there is talent in the cellars and this tiny estate near Portets could emerge as a respectable producer of red and white Graves wines.

HAUT-BAILLY (Cru Classé) Pessac-Léognan   VERY GOOD

Production: 12,000 cases red	Grape varieties: Cabernet Sauvignon—60% Merlot—30% Cabernet Franc—10%
Secondary label: La Parde de Haut-Bailly	
Vineyard size: 62 acres	Proprietor: Jean Sanders
Time spent in barrels: 20–22 months	Average age of vines: 40 years
Evaluation of present classification: The quality equivalent of a Médoc third-growth	
Plateau of maturity: 5–20 years following the vintage	

By Graves standards, Haut-Bailly is a relative newcomer. The history, however, is not uninteresting. A Monsieur Bellot des Minières, who was the second owner of Haut-Bailly in 1872, apparently believed that the wine was greatly improved by the addition of copious quantities of cognac, which was left in the barrels after they were rinsed with this spirit. Today one hears rumors of Burgundy producers who fortify weaker vintages wth *eau-de-vie* or brandy, but Monsieur Bellot de Minières was proud of his wine's "extra" dimension.

The Sanders family became the proprietors in 1955. According to the family, Daniel Sanders—a wine enthusiast from Belgium—was so astounded by the 1945 Haut-Bailly, that after some investigation, he decided to buy the property. His son, Jean, who lives at the nearby estate of Château Courbon (which produces a pleasant, dry, white Graves), has managed the property since his father's death.

Since the early sixties, Haut-Bailly has had an inconsistent track record for quality. The 1961 was fabulous, as was the delicious 1964, but it was not until 1979 that the quality began to bounce back after a prolonged period of mediocrity. The decision to relegate as much as 30% of the crop to a second wine, the increase of new oak to 55%, and a conscious decision to harvest later in order to obtain riper grapes have all resulted in increasingly better wines for Haut-Bailly during the eighties.

When young, this is not the easiest wine to evaluate. I am not sure why, but it often comes across as a bit skinny and light, yet seems to take on weight and depth in the bottle. When I asked Jean Sanders about this, he said he was not the least bit interested in making a wine to impress writers, particularly before it is bottled. He believes the extremely old age of his vineyard, and his traditional winemaking style with absolutely no filtration (rare in modern-day Bordeaux) result in a wine that requires some time to reveal all of its charm and character. Haut-Bailly will never have the size or power of its nearby neighbor de Fieuzal, but it does exhibit exceptional elegance in the top vintages.

VINTAGES

1989—With the 1989, Haut-Bailly has made its best wine since 1979.
· Normally a very light, delicate wine, the 1989 is made in a more
90 forceful style. Deep ruby/purple, with a jammy nose of ripe blackberries and new oak, this medium-bodied, alcoholic wine has low acidity, but very high tannins in the finish. The overall impression is one of bigness and strength, without heaviness. This should prove to be an uncommonly long-lived Haut-Bailly. Anticipated maturity: 1994–2012. Last tasted, 4/91.

1988—This is a typical example of how Haut-Bailly can change so dra-
· matically after bottling. Tasted from cask numerous times, the
89 wine seemed agreeably fruity, light, and pleasant, but not exciting. After bottling, the wine appears much fuller and richer, with that profound mineral, spicy, sweet oak, curranty aroma, gentle, yet full-bodied, creamy-textured flavors, and a long, smooth, marvelous finish. This wine may well turn out to be outstanding with another 3–4 years in the bottle. Anticipated maturity: 1992–2003. Last tasted, 4/91.

1986—Considering the strong, tannic personality of the vintage, the 1986
· is a soft wine that can be drunk at a very early age. The full-
85 intensity bouquet of sweet, smoky oak and ripe, plummy fruit is very attractive. On the palate, the wine is long, rich in fruit, and supple, and finishes surprisingly smoothly. Anticipated maturity: Now–2001. Last tasted, 3/90.

1985—The 1985 will no doubt live longer than I envision. However, I
· find it hard to ignore the precocious, charming, berry fruitiness
87 backed up with sweet toasty oak. It is medium bodied, with very soft tannins and moderate length. Anticipated maturity: Now–1998. Last tasted, 3/90.

1984—This wine provided inconsistent results in my tastings, ranging
· from light and watery to something with adequate sweet, ripe,
78 herbaceous fruit in a delicate, understated style. Recent tastings

have suggested that Haut-Bailly's 1984 is moderately successful. Anticipated maturity: Now–1994. Last tasted, 3/88.

1983—A typical Haut-Bailly, the 1983 is dark ruby in color, with a rich,
·   voluptuous, ripe, blackcurrant bouquet, and some attractive va-
87   nillin oaky aromas. On the palate, the wine is forward, with lush, silky, ripe, round tannins evident. Medium-bodied, with a Pomerol-like, silky, fat texture, this wine is already fully mature. Anticipated maturity: Now–1996. Last tasted, 1/91.

1982—All my notes on the 1982 Haut-Bailly tasted since bottling have
·   shown tremendous inconsistency and bottle variation. I have had
69–   thin, relatively light-colored, somewhat insipid, diluted wines,
87?   as well as those showing wonderfully charming, supple, rich fruit. In two separate tastings in 1991 the wine again displayed its Dr. Jekyll/Mr. Hyde personality. One bottle was light in color, exhibiting some brown and amber at the edge, thin in flavor, and faded in the finish. From the other bottle, the wine was totally ready to drink, richly fruity, with a wonderful toasty, smoky, vanillin aroma, and gobs of soft, velvety, berry fruit. If you own any, this is a wine to try on your own. My last tasting of this wine was positive, but I remain perplexed by the bottle variation. Anticipated maturity: Now–1997? Last tasted, 5/91.

1981—The 1981 Haut-Bailly is neither profound nor intensely concen-
·   trated, but perfumed, elegant, spicy, soft, fruity, and remarkably
84   easy to drink. It does not have the punch and depth of the 1982, 1983, or 1979, but is agreeable and pleasant in a lighter style. Anticipated maturity: Now–1993. Last tasted, 12/87.

1979—Consistently one of the most delicious wines of this somewhat
·   overlooked vintage, the 1979 Haut-Bailly has excellent deep ruby
87   color, a rich, moderately intense, smoky, oaky, ripe-fruit bouquet, soft, silky, fat, plump, fruity flavors, light tannins, and a velvety finish. It is harmonious and lovely. Anticipated maturity: Now–1995. Last tasted, 3/88.

1978—For whatever reason, the now-mature 1978, while fruity, quite
·   charming, and soft, never quite had the depth and dimension of
81   the 1979. Now taking on some amber/orange color, this wine has a herbaceous, oaky fragrance, soft, loosely knit flavors, and a smooth finish. Anticipated maturity: Now–1995. Last tasted, 1/91.

1976—Haut-Bailly is not a success in 1976. The intense heat prior to the
·   harvest caused the grapes to become overripe. The wine is now
62   mature, even old looking, with a loosely knit structure, very low acidity, and diluted flavors. Last tasted, 9/79.

1975—Another problem vintage for Haut-Bailly, the 1975 is light in color,
· with some brown at the edge. The herbaceous, spicy, washed-out
67 bouquet exhibits none of the expected ripeness that is present in
the best 1975s. It is a thin, meager, and skinny wine, with very
little charm or personality. Anticipated maturity: Now–1995. Last
tasted, 7/88.

1973—This wine has totally collapsed, exhibiting washed-out, vegetal,
· thin aromas, shallow, sweet, light flavors, and no grip, concentra-
55 tion, or length. It is educational in that it is a Bordeaux in complete decline. Last tasted, 9/88.

1971—Charming, but a little light and flabby, the 1971 Haut-Bailly is
· now in decline, taking on an even deeper and pronounced brown-
75 ish cast. The velvety, soft, fruity flavors are likable, but fade
quickly in the glass. Anticipated maturity: Now–probably in serious decline. Last tasted, 12/83.

1970—In a 1970 claret tasting held several years ago, Haut-Bailly per-
· formed well, indicating that this is probably the best vintage for
87 the château between 1964 and 1979. It still has that in-your-face,
up-front, smoky, sweet, herbaceous fruit, medium body, soft,
velvety tannins, and a long, smooth, alcoholic finish. Anticipated
maturity: Now–1993. Last tasted, 10/88.

1966—Fully mature, quite fruity, yet a little more reserved and sterner
· than the richer, more opulent 1970, the 1966 reveals some brown-
85 ing at the edge, good concentration, earthy, fruity flavors, and a
soft, round finish. Anticipated maturity: Now–may be in decline.
Last tasted, 4/82.

1964—I had the good fortune to taste this wine in Bordeaux and thought
· it to be excellent, nearly outstanding. The ripe, roasted bouquet
88 of caramel, tobacco, smoke, and black fruits was close to sensational. In the mouth, this plump, generously endowed, velvety-
textured Haut-Bailly probably has been fully mature for at least a
decade, but exhibits no signs of losing fruit. It is heady, soft, and
totally seductive. Anticipated maturity: Now–1996. Last tasted,
3/90.

1961—This wine is splendid, undoubtedly the finest Haut-Bailly I have
· ever tasted. It is even better than when I first tasted it nearly 6
93 years ago. The huge bouquet of earthy, smoky tobacco and ripe
berry fruit soars from the glass. The opulent, nearly unctuous
flavors are awesomely concentrated, thick, rich, and powerful.
There is not a bit of astringency and harshness left, but, rather,
relatively high alcohol, and that splendidly intense, long, explosively rich finish. How long will the 1961 last? I thought it would
be in decline by now, but this wine has the potential to keep for

another decade or more. Anticipated maturity: Now–2001. Last tasted, 3/90.

HAUT-BERGEY (Unclassified) Pessac-Léognan   AVERAGE

Production: 6,500 cases red	Grape varieties: Cabernet Sauvignon—70% Merlot—30%
Secondary label: Ponteilh	
Vineyard size: 32 acres	Proprietor: Jacques Deschamps
Time spent in barrels: 15–18 months	Average age of vines: 22 years
Evaluation of present classification: The quality equivalent of a Médoc Cru Bourgeois	
Plateau of maturity: 4–8 years following the vintage	

This property has a certain following in France, but I must confess I have never seen examples of the wine that merited much interest. Reports continue to circulate that Michel Rolland, the highly talented Libourn oenologist, was brought in as a consultant in the late eighties to upgrade the quality of the wine. Neither the 1988 nor the 1989 was an impressive wine. No white wine is produced at this estate.

HAUT-BRION (First-Growth) Pessac-Léognan   OUTSTANDING

Production: 12,000–18,000 cases red; 800 cases white	Grape varieties: Red: Cabernet Sauvignon—55% Merlot—25% Cabernet Franc—20% White: Sauvignon—50% Semillon—50%
Secondary label: Bahans-Haut-Brion	
Vineyard size: 113.6 acres	Proprietors: Duc and Duchesse de Mouchy, Domaine Clarence Dillon Administrator: Jean Delmas
Time spent in barrels: 24–30 months	Average age of vines: 30 years
Evaluation of present classification: Should be maintained	
Plateau of maturity: red: 6–25 years following the vintage; white: 5–25 years following the vintage	

Haut-Brion is the only non-Médoc estate to be included in the famous 1855 Classification of the Wines of the Gironde. In the seventeenth century, it was Bordeaux's first internationally acclaimed winemaking estate.

Located in the bustling commercial suburb of Pessac, Haut-Brion is also the only first-growth to be American owned. The Dillon family purchased Haut-Brion in 1935 in a very poor condition, and invested considerable sums of money in the vineyards and wine cellars. This lovely property is now one of the showpiece estates of Graves.

The winemaking at Haut-Brion is managed by the articulate and handsome Jean Delmas, who fervently believes in a hot, short fermentation. As Bordeaux wines go, Haut-Brion is kept a long time (up to 30 months) in new oak barrels. It is often the last château to bottle its wine.

The style of wine at Haut-Brion has changed over the years. The magnificently rich, earthy, almost sweet wines of the fifties and early sixties gave way in the period 1966–1974 to a lighter, leaner, easygoing, somewhat simplistic style of claret that lacked the richness and depth one expects from a first-growth. Whether this was intentional or just a period in which Haut-Brion was in a bit of a slump remains a mystery. The staff at Haut-Brion is quick tempered and sensitive about such a charge. Starting with the 1975 vintage, the wines have again taken on more of the customary earthy richness and concentration that existed during the pre-1966 era. Haut-Brion today is undoubtedly making wine that merits its first-growth status. In fact, the wines from 1978 onward have consistently proven to be among the finest wines produced in the region.

Coincidence or not, the quality of Haut-Brion began to rebound from the 1966–1974 era when Douglas Dillon's daughter, Joan, became president of the company in 1975. After the death of her first husband, Prince Charles of Luxembourg, she married the Duc de Mouchy in 1978. It was at this same time that the quantity of the crop relegated to Bahans-Haut-Brion was increased, a practice that has irrefutably improved the quality of Haut-Brion. Moreover, it appears that Jean Delmas has been given total responsibility for running the estate, and, as almost everyone in Bordeaux will acknowledge, he is one of the most talented and knowledgeable winemakers in France. His extraordinary state-of-the-art research with clonal selections is unsurpassed in France. With the advent of the superabundant crops during the decade of the eighties, Delmas began, much like his counterpart in Pomerol, Christian Moueix of Château Pétrus, to crop-thin by cutting off grape bunches. This has no doubt accounted for the even greater concentration, as well as the extraordinary quality, of the 1989, which at this early stage would appear to be the greatest Haut-Brion made since the 1959 and 1961.

It is interesting to note that in blind tastings Haut-Brion often comes across as the most forward and lightest of all the first-growths. In truth, the wine is not light, but just different from the big, oaky, fleshy wines of the Médoc, and the softer, Merlot-dominated wines from the right bank. Despite the precociousness, it has the cunning ability to age for 20 or more years in top vintages, giving it a greater window of drinkability than any other first-growth.

Accompanying the increased level of quality in Haut-Brion since 1978 has been the increased quality of the second label, Bahans-Haut-Brion. This is now one of the best second wines of Bordeaux, surpassed in certain vintages only by the renowned second wine of Château Latour, Les Forts de Latour. The 1988 and 1989 were both extremely successful vintages for Bahans.

With respect to the white wine made at Haut-Brion, most observers rate it the best white wine of the Graves region. However, at the request of the proprietors it has never been classified because the production is so tiny (less than 1,000 cases). Nevertheless, under Jean Delmas, who has sought to make a white Graves with the opulent texture of a great Montrachet, the white wine has gone from strength to strength during the eighties. The two most recent great vintages have been the 1985 and 1989.

On a personal note, I should also add that after more than 25 years of intensely tasting as many Bordeaux wines as I can, the only general change I have noticed in my taste has been a greater and greater affection for Haut-Brion. The smoky, mineral, intense Graves character of this wine has increasingly appealed to me as I have gotten older, and as Jean Delmas would undoubtedly state, wiser as well.

VINTAGES

Red Wines

1989—Jean Delmas, the proud and handsome manager of Haut-Brion,
·   has apparently grown tired of hearing all the superlatives doled
99   out by the wine press to such Médoc first-growths as Margaux
       and Mouton-Rothschild. In 1989 he acted boldly, and in July, 60%
       of Haut-Brion's crop was pruned from the vines. During the first
       week of September he harvested the grapes. (Actually he started
       harvesting some Merlot the last few days of August.) The result
       of these decisive actions is one of the most profound Haut-Brions
       I have ever tasted. While most producers made significantly more
       wine in 1989 than in 1988, Delmas made 30% *less*. His daring
       strategy has paid off, as the 1989 Haut-Brion should excite the

wine press and wealthy amateurs alike. Significantly more concentrated than the great 1986 and 1982, this is a monumental wine that Delmas says is reminiscent of, but even superior to, the heroic 1959. Deep ruby/purple, with a roasted tobacco, cassis, smoky aroma, the 1989 has enormous depth, an opulent texture suggestive of the 1982, but greater length as well as higher alcohol. Charged with fruit and tannin, it seems destined to drink sublimely for 20–30 years. Anticipated maturity: 1996–2015. Last tasted, 4/91.

1988—The 1988 is no weak sibling. Built along the lines of the 1966, but
  ·   better made and more concentrated, it will easily last as long as
 90   the 1989, according to Delmas, but never provide the level of complexity or pleasure of that wine. Medium bodied, rich, and very tannic, it will have to be cellared until the end of this century. Anticipated maturity: 2000–2025. Last tasted, 4/91.

1987—The bold and dramatic Haut-Brion bouquet is apparent in this
  ·   wine, which exhibits a strong smell of tobacco, minerals, and
 87   black plums. Medium bodied, round, and generous, with some weediness lurking under the surface, this intensely scented wine has a surprisingly long finish. Anticipated maturity: Now–1998. Last tasted, 4/91.

1986—The 1986 may not please those people who do not find the smoky,
  ·   tobacco-scented character of Graves to their liking. This wine is
 92   a remarkably concentrated, powerful Haut-Brion that should prove to be extremely long-lived. Very deep in color, with a staggering wealth of fruit and flavor, the huge, smoky, tobacco-and-mineral-scented bouquet seems to fill the room. Explosively rich, full bodied, and with gobs of tannin, this classic wine is one of the superstars of the 1986 vintage. Anticipated maturity: 1995–2015. Last tasted, 12/90.

1985—The 1985 Haut-Brion, along with the flamboyant Mouton-Roth-
  ·   schild, is one of the finest first-growths of the vintage. The epit-
 91   ome of elegance and finesse, the 1985 is a deep ruby-colored wine and has a full-intensity bouquet of jammy fruit, spices, and tobacco. On the palate, it exhibits a soft, very generous texture, super concentration, exquisite balance, and a long, impressive
  ·   finish. While it does not have the power of the 1989 or 1986, it is a gorgeously elegant wine. Interestingly, Delmas prefers the 1985 to his 1986. Anticipated maturity: 1993–2010. Last tasted, 12/90.

1984—Attractively perfumed with mineral scents, tobacco, and ripe
  ·   fruit, the medium-bodied 1984 Haut-Brion has surprisingly good
 84   depth and length. It is not at all a big wine, but is soft, creamy,

and ideal for drinking young. Anticipated maturity: Now–1995. Last tasted, 4/88.

1983—Haut-Brion's 1983 is a very good wine that has fine depth, rich,
·   soft, fat, lush fruit, and a good measure of soft tannins in the
87   finish. The overall impression is of a forward, ripe, and voluptuous wine. It is successful, but by Haut-Brion's recent standards,
the wine lacks excitement and has reached full maturity at an
alarmingly fast pace. Anticipated maturity: Now–2001. Last
tasted, 7/91.

1982—The 1982 appears to be one of the best Haut-Brions made since
·   the 1961. The 1982 has excellent deep ruby/purple color, as well
93   as an emerging bouquet of minerals, tobacco, and ripe plums.
Elegant, medium to full bodied, rich, and concentrated, with
plenty of tannins still to be resolved, this is a lusty wine with a
great deal of glycerin that can be drunk now, but promises to
reach full maturity in another 3–4 years, and last for at least 15
years. Anticipated maturity: 1993–2015. Last tasted, 5/91.

1981—My early notes on this wine were inconsistent, but two tastings of
·   the 1981 in the late eighties revealed a flattering, gentle, medium-
85   bodied wine with a smoky, vanillin oakiness, round, ripe flavors,
and a soft, luscious finish. It lacks some guts and richness by the
standards of most Haut-Brion vintages since 1978, but, nevertheless, it is a charming, lighter-weight, forward wine that has
reached its plateau of maturity. Anticipated maturity: Now–2000.
Last tasted, 1/91.

1979—One of the very best wines of the vintage, the 1979 Haut-Brion
·   continues to develop splendidly in the bottle, although it remains
93   5–6 years away from maturity. It is very dark in color, with a
closed, but very complex bouquet of ripe fruit, tobacco, and mineral, earthy scents. Rich, ripe, medium to full bodied, and extremely well-structured, this is a wine that seems to balance
power and elegance, richness and harmony, perfectly. The finest
wine of the vintage from Bordeaux's left bank? Anticipated maturity: 1992–2005. Last tasted, 1/91.

1978—The 1978 is a seductively rich, very fruity, well-colored Haut-
·   Brion that is presently much more evolved than the 1979, no doubt
92   due to very ripe fruit and a lower acid level. An exotic and com-   ·
plex bouquet of ripe fruit, hot stones, tar, and oak soars from the
glass. On the palate, the wine is supple, round, and very generous, creating the impression that it is fully mature. However,
there is plenty of tannin in the finish. The wine (from a double
magnum) is drinking splendidly well. Anticipated maturity: Now–
2003. Last tasted, 6/91.

1977—Haut-Brion was clearly outperformed by its neighbor, La Mission-
· Haut-Brion in this poor vintage. Medium ruby, with an aromatic,
74 spicy, somewhat vegetal aroma, and lightish flavors with some
harshness in the finish, this wine is best drunk up over the next 5
years. Anticipated maturity: Now–may be in decline. Last tasted,
9/83.

1976—Medium ruby in color, with some amber creeping in at the edges,
· the 1976 Haut-Brion has been fully mature since the early
86 eighties, yet it is still drinking well. A spicy, earthy, oaky, moderately fruity bouquet offers elegance. On the palate, the wine is
soft, round, medium bodied, and charming. It even seems to have
put on some weight in the late eighties. However, do not push
your luck; drink it over the next 4–5 years. Anticipated maturity:
Now–1996. Last tasted, 1/90.

1975—In 1984, this surprisingly forward and mature-looking 1975 wine
· had a full-blown, burnt wax, tobacco-scented bouquet, round,
90 alcoholic, relatively rich, deep flavors, and a long finish. In 1991,
I had Haut-Brion twice, on both sides of the Atlantic. Terrific in
both tastings, the wine is fully mature wth the characteristic
burnt, mineral, tobacco aromas and flavors. The wine has developed far greater richness and intensity than I ever imagined. A
full-bodied Haut-Brion that fortunately lacks the tannic ferocity
of many 1975s, this interesting wine is at its apogee. Anticipated
maturity: Now–2001. Last tasted, 4/91.

1974—Given the vintage, the Haut-Brion could be considered a modest
· success. Now fully mature and a bit short in fruit, this wine has
76 an open-knit, spicy, earthy bouquet, somewhat angular, medium-
bodied flavors, and a short finish. Anticipated maturity: Now–
may be in decline. Last tasted, 3/79.

1971—For me, the 1971 is the best Haut-Brion produced between 1966
· and 1975. This fully mature 1971 has a sumptuous, sweet, ripe,
88 earthy, richly fruity flavor, medium to full body, a big, full-intensity, spicy bouquet, and a silky, supple texture. Very stylish and
delicious, this wine should be drunk up. Not retasted since 1982,
but I suspect this wine should still be in fine condition. Anticipated maturity: Now–1996. Last tasted, 4/82.

1970—This is a good Haut-Brion, but in the context of the vintage, and
· the fact that so many châteaux in Graves made excellent wine in
84 1970, it is a disappointment. Surprisingly compact, medium
bodied, and not nearly as concentrated or as rich as it should
be, this wine has shed its tannins, but remains a lean, relatively
innocuous Haut-Brion. Anticipated maturity: Now–1993. Last
tasted, 10/88.

1966—At its apogee, the 1966 Haut-Brion has an attractive, earthy, moderately intense, fruity bouquet. In weight and richness, it is me-
86   dium weight and bordering on being too lean and light. It is a
satisfying, lighter-styled Haut-Brion that is quite attractive, but
not really of first-growth proportions. Drink over the next 1–2
years. Anticipated maturity: Now–1994. Last tasted, 11/84.

1964—1964, while a mixed vintage for the wines of the Médoc as a result
of many properties being caught by the heavy rains, was a very
90   good year for the Graves châteaux. Haut-Brion's 1964 is fully
mature as evidenced by the amber edge to its color, and has a
splendidly rich, earthy, tobacco-and-mineral-scented bouquet.
Ripe, deep, supple, voluptuous flavors are present on the palate.
This full-bodied wine should be drunk up as it is living dangerously. Anticipated maturity: Now–1993. Last tasted, 10/88.

1962—Another smashingly delicious wine from Haut-Brion, the 1962 is
fully mature, and is not likely to hold this intensity of rich, earthy,
88   spicy fruit for much longer. However, for the lucky few who own
a bottle of this wine, it is quite soft and round, with an opulent
richness that resembles a Pomerol. Anticipated maturity: Now–
1994. Last tasted, 1/81.

1961—This is a great Haut-Brion, but it is eclipsed in my view by its
predecessor, the 1959, and more recently by the monumental
96   1989. Not as darkly colored as many 1961s, with surprisingly more
amber/brown at the edge, this rich, luxurious wine has an intense,
earthy, ripe, cedary, spicy bouquet crammed with sweet fruit. On
the palate, the wine has fabulous intensity of fruit, a long, rich,
alcoholic finish, and a chewy texture. The 1961 has been fully
mature for the last decade, but does not reveal any signs of decline. This is Haut-Brion at its most sumptuous and hedonistic.
Anticipated maturity: Now–2000. Last tasted, 12/90.

OLDER VINTAGES

There are several vintages of Haut-Brion prior to 1961 that merit almost perfect ratings. The 1959 goes from strength to strength. It has
everything the 1961 has, but even greater concentration, as well as more
grip and structure. It will outlive the 1961 by at least a decade or more.
I had the good fortune to enjoy it several times in the late eighties, and
on each occasion I rated it between 97–99, wondering if I was not too
conservative. It is a magnificently rich Haut-Brion. I have not tasted the
off years of 1957 and 1958 since 1986, but both vintages produced good
Haut-Brions, and I would suspect that larger format bottles would be
worth buying, although I have never rated either vintage higher than 87.

The 1955 is excellent, but considerably overshadowed by the monumental (and may I say perfect?) 1955 La Mission-Haut-Brion. I have seen the 1953 only twice, but both bottles were fully mature, gloriously perfumed with that hot tobacco, herbaceous, sweet fragrance that Haut-Brion exudes in ripe vintages. Both were rated 92–94. Neither tasting note revealed the opulence, power, or fullness of vintages such as 1959 or 1961, but I am convinced that 1953 is a great vintage for Haut-Brion.

In the last 2 years, I have had three occasions to taste the 1949, once Stateside and twice in Bordeaux. In New York I was served a glass in a restaurant by a well-known collector who was sitting at an adjacent table drinking the wine from a magnum. While the collector admired it, I found it totally maderized and undrinkable, but discretion kept me from engaging in discussion of the lack of merits of this particular bottle. Tasted twice in Bordeaux in 1990, the 1949 was indeed a spectacular wine. On one occasion, when it was served blind, I thought it resembled a top vintage of Pétrus, given its thick, muscular, powerful constitution. Both bottles were considerably better than the magnum from New York. Top bottles of this wine would merit a rating between 92–94. I would not place the quality of the 1949 Haut-Brion in the same exalted class as the 1959 and 1961.

Among other older vintages, I have also had the good fortune to taste the 1947. It was tired, but extremely powerful and alcoholic, with that deep, burnt, earthy character so typical of this property's wines. I rated it 88 when drunk in 1987. On the two occasions I have had the 1945 it was a 99- to 100-point wine. Still spectacularly deep ruby/purple, with only some amber at the edge, this exceptionally concentrated, almost essence of wine has plenty of tannin, but not the overbearing, harsh tannin often found in many 1945s. It was fully mature when drunk in both 1987 and 1989, and both tastings revealed that the wine could easily keep for another two decades.

Among the pre-war vintages, the 1929 has consistently tasted tired, but sweet, earthy, and exotic. In April 1991, I rated it 86 and preferred it to Lafite, Margaux, and Latour at a tasting in Bordeaux. I am sure this wine was superb in its day, but now much of the freshness and fruit has dissipated. The 1928, drunk in a blind tasting of wines from the twenties in both 1990 and 1991, was interesting if not bizarre in its overripe, blatant superconcentrated port-like style. I did not detect much Graves character, but the wine is still drinking well, if in an atypical and exaggerated style. I wonder if all the 1928 share such a similar character!

White Wines

1989—Whether this wine ultimately turns out to be better than the great
·   1985 remains to be seen, but there is no doubt that this is the
98   most immense and large-scaled Haut-Brion Blanc I have ever
      tasted. Jean Delmas, administrator of the Dillon properties, felt
      the 1989 fully replicated the fleshy, chewy texture of a great
      Grand Cru white Burgundy. Only 600 cases were made of this
      rich, alcoholic, sumptuous wine. It is amazingly full and long in
      the mouth, with a very distinctive mineral, honeyed character.
      The low acidity would seemingly suggest a shorter life than nor-
      mal, but I am convinced this wine will last 10–15 or more years.
      It is a real show stopper! Anticipated maturity: 1993–2005. Last
      tasted, 6/91.

1988—Tightly knit, with a reticent but light-intensity bouquet of min-
·   erals, lemons, figs, and melons, this tightly structured, relatively
85   high acid Haut-Brion Blanc will no doubt prove to be a long-
      distance runner, but how much pleasure and character will evolve
      remains difficult to assess. Anticipated maturity: 1995–2005. Last
      tasted, 4/91.

1987—This wine continues to evolve beautifully and offers up an elegant,
·   moderately intense bouquet of herbs, creamy minerals, and fig-
88   like fruit. Medium bodied, wonderfully concentrated in a more
      delicate, yet still-flavorful style, this impeccably balanced Haut-
      Brion Blanc should be drunk early on. Anticipated maturity:
      Now–1995. Last tasted, 11/90.

1986—I have tasting notes on this wine from cask and bottle, but it was
      never released by the château as it did not meet their expecta-
      tions.

1985—This has been a head turner since it was made. Unbelievably rich,
·   with a velvety, fat consistency oozing with herb, melon, and fig-
97   like fruit, this voluptuously textured wine exhibits great length,
      richness, and character. It never closed up after bottling and
      remains an exceptionally full-bodied, intensely concentrated, yet
      well-delineated white Graves. If you have the income of a rock
      superstar, this would be worth having to *fête* the turn of the cen-
      tury. Anticipated maturity: 1995–2010. Last tasted, 6/91.

OLDER VINTAGES

I have virtually no tasting notes on older vintages of Haut-Brion Blanc.
I did like, and gave a good rating (between 86–89) for, the 1983, 1982,
and 1981, and I remember once having an extremely powerful, full-

bodied 1976. Other than that, this is a wine one rarely ever sees because of the tiny production.

HAUT-GARDÈRE (Unclassified) Pessac-Léognan GOOD

Production: 10,000 cases red; 1,200 cases white	Grape varieties: Red: Cabernet Sauvignon—58% Merlot—35% Cabernet Franc—7% White: Sauvignon—63% Semillon—37%
Secondary label: none Vineyard size: 51.8 acres	Proprietor: Bernadette Lesineau
Time spent in barrels: 14–18 months	Average age of vines: 10 years
Evaluation of present classification: The quality equivalent of a Médoc Cru Bourgeois	
Plateau of maturity: red: 2–6 years following the vintage; white: 2–6 years following the vintage	

This property is extremely well run. In spite of the youth of the vines, the last several vintages have produced generously rich, tobacco-scented, flavorful red wines and stylish white wines. The vineyard sits on a very fine outcropping of gravelly soil in the Léognan area and is impeccably run by Bernadette Lesineau. Prices are remarkably low, largely because word has not circulated about how good these wines can be. Before World War II Haut-Gardère had such a high reputation it sold for the same price as Domaine de Chevalier, de Fieuzal, and Malartic-Lagravière.

Since the late eighties, this property has made great strides in quality, and as the young vineyard becomes mature, I fully anticipate that this will become a name to remember in the Léognan area.

L'HOSPITAL (Unclassified) Graves

Production: 3,000 cases red; 300 cases white	Grape varieties: Red: Cabernet Sauvignon—30% Merlot—30% Cabernet Franc—30% Malbec—10% White: Sauvignon—100%
Secondary label: none	
Vineyard size: 15 acres	Proprietor: Madame A. de Lacaussade
Time spent in barrels: 15–24 months	Average age of vines: 32 years
Evaluation of present classification: The quality equivalent of a Médoc Cru Bourgeois	
Plateau of maturity: red: 5–10 years following the vintage; white: 3–8 years following the vintage	

Lamentably, I have never been impressed with the wines from this property, whose château is classified as an historic monument under French law. The red wines tend to be stubbornly hard, austere, dusty, and not always the cleanest examples of winemaking. The miniscule quantity of white wine is flinty, smoky, sometimes overwhelmingly earthy and austere. They would seemingly benefit from a small quantity of Semillon to give the wines more fat, flesh, and charm. The wines of l'Hospital are seen in some marketplaces, but are generally overpriced.

LARRIVET-HAUT-BRION
(Unclassified) Pessac-Léognan   AVERAGE

Production: 7,500 cases red; 450 cases white	Grape varieties: Red: Cabernet Sauvignon—55% Merlot—40% Petit Verdot—5% White: Sauvignon—60% Semillon—40%
Secondary label: none Vineyard size: 39.5 acres	Proprietor: Société Civile Administrator: Philippe Gerverson
Time spent in barrels: 14–20 months	Average age of vines: 20 years

Evaluation of present classification: The quality equivalent of a Médoc Cru Bourgeois

Plateau of maturity: 3–10 years following the vintage

Larrivet-Haut-Brion is well known in European wine circles, but is rarely seen in America. The vineyard, located in the southern section of Graves near Léognan, is adjacent to that of the much more famous Haut-Bailly. It recently changed hands, and rumors abound in Bordeaux about a renaissance in quality. I have rarely seen the white wine, but the 1988 and 1989 tasted in April 1991 appeared to be well-made, oaky, rich examples of both vintages.

VINTAGES

Red Wines

1989—The 1989 has a suspiciously light color and is medium bodied, but
·   the tart green tannins are astringent and excessive. Frankly, there
77   is not much to this wine. Last tasted, 4/91.

1988—The 1988 is a much finer wine, exhibiting a good ruby color, an
·   earthy, fruity nose, round, ripe, charming flavors, and soft tannins
85   in the finish. Anticipated maturity: Now–1997. Last tasted, 4/91.

1986—The 1986 seems surprisingly light and somewhat diluted. This
·   medium ruby-colored wine, with its soft, strawberry and cherry
78   fruitiness, should be drunk over the next 4–5 years. Anticipated
         maturity: Now–1994. Last tasted, 3/90.

1985—The 1985 has merit in the sense that the bouquet of tobacco and
·   ripe fruit is textbook Graves. On the palate, one would have liked
84   to see more flesh and substance. Anticipated maturity: Now–
       1994. Last tasted, 3/89.

1984—Soft and light, but for uncritical quaffing, there is enough tobacco-
·   scented fruit in this wine to hold one's interest for 1–2 years.
80   Anticipated maturity: Now–may be in decline. Last tasted, 11/89.

LAVILLE-HAUT-BRION
(Cru Classé) Graves-Pessac   OUTSTANDING

Production: 2,000 cases white	Grape varieties: Semillon—60% Sauvignon—40%
Secondary label: none Vineyard size: 14.8 acres	Proprietor: Domaine Clarence Dillon Administrators: Duc and Duchesse de Mouchy and Jean Delmas
Time spent in barrels: 12 months	Average age of vines: 20 years
Evaluation of present classification: Consistently one of the three best white wines of Graves	
Plateau of maturity: 5–25 or more years following the vintage	

This tiny vineyard produces one of the most remarkably long-lived white
wines of France. The soil is less gravelly and heavier than the vineyard
of La Mission-Haut-Brion. The production is tiny, adding to the rarity
value of this white wine. Fermented and aged in new oak casks, Laville-
Haut-Brion takes on a waxy richness with aging. It is marvelous to taste
from cask, but after bottling it completely closes up, not to reopen in
some instances for 5–10 years. Reputation and a consistent high level of
quality insure that it sells for a frighteningly high price. Perhaps that
explains why 95% of the production is exported.

VINTAGES

1989—This utterly mind-blowing effort from Laville-Haut-Brion, with its
·   decadent bouquet of honeyed, superripe melons, figs, and toasty
96   new oak is a real turn on. In the mouth, the wine is stunningly
       rich, concentrated, and intense, with a texture more akin to a
       Grand Cru white Burgundy than an austere white Graves. Acidity
       is low and the alcohol level is high, suggesting this wine will have
       to be drunk in its first 10–15 years. For pure power, as well as a

sumptuous texture, this may well be the most dramatic Laville-Haut-Brion ever produced. Production was tiny; only 900 cases were made. Anticipated maturity: 1997–2020. Last tasted, 4/91.

1988—While lacking the personality of the blockbuster 1989, the 1988 is
·
87   a beautifully made, waxy, melon-scented wine with a touch of herbs and smoky oak. It has better acidity and a more delineated personality than the 1989, but not the latter vintage's flamboyant character. Nevertheless, this should turn out to be an extremely long-lived Laville, and while it may not hit the heights of hedonism that the 1989 will, it still offers plenty of flavor in a more polite and civilized fashion. Anticipated maturity: 1995–2008. Last tasted, 4/91.

1987—As I have said many times, the 1987 turned out to be a very good
·
86   vintage for the white wines of Graves. This is a lighter-weight Laville-Haut-Brion, but its wonderfully precise herb, melon, and fig-like flavors are offered in a medium-bodied format with a great deal of charm and character. There is enough acidity to give the wine some lift, and add focus to its medium-bodied flavors. Drink this charmer over the next decade. Anticipated maturity: Now–2001. Last tasted, 1/90.

1986—A Laville-Haut-Brion was made in 1986, but before it was officially released, the château, disappointed with the way it was tasting, declassified it.

1985—This is a sumptuous, rich, honeyed Laville-Haut-Brion that
·
93   should drink beautifully for the next two decades. It is among the more powerful and richer wines produced by the château, yet it has the requisite acid to give it balance and freshness. Not quite as superripe and alcoholic as the 1989, it is perhaps more typical of Laville-Haut-Brion at its richest and fullest. Anticipated maturity: 1992–2008. Last tasted, 12/90.

OLDER VINTAGES

I have not seen the 1984 since it was in cask, but the 1983 Laville-Haut-Brion (rated 90) is an elegant, classy, textbook Laville, whereas the 1982 (87) is a chunky, foursquare, heavyweight Laville that lacks the finesse and elegance of the 1983. Older vintages I have tasted include a powerhouse, now fully mature 1976 (91), a classic, long-lived, tightly knit, well-structured 1975 (90), and a glorious 1966 (92) and 1962 (88). In 1990 I finally had a chance to taste the Laville-Haut-Brion that Michael Broadbent dubbed spectacular, the 1945 "Crème de Tête." In a blind tasting against the regular *cuvée* of the 1945 Laville-Haut-Brion there was indeed a difference. The wines were stunning efforts that resembled an old, powerful Sauternes more than a white Graves. Both were massive, rich, honeyed wines that were quite dry, but because of their richness and fullness, they had overwhelming impact on the palate. The Crème de Tête clearly was richer and fuller. I rated it a 93.

LA LOUVIÈRE (Unclassified) Pessac-Léognan   VERY GOOD

Production: 18,000 cases red; 5,000 cases white	Grape varieties: Red: Cabernet Sauvignon—70% Merlot—20% Cabernet Franc—10% White: Sauvignon—70% Semillon—30%
Secondary labels: L de Louvière, Coucheray, and Clos du Roi	
Vineyard size: 116 acres	Proprietor: André Lurton
Time spent in barrels: 18–20 months	Average age of vines: 22 years
Evaluation of present classification: The quality equivalent of a Médoc fourth-growth	
Plateau of maturity: red: 3–12 years following the vintage; white: 2–6 years following the vintage	

While unclassified, La Louvière in Léognan is now making wines superior to many of the Crus Classés of Graves. In particular, recent vintages since 1981 have been on a quality level with a Médoc fourth-growth. The proprietor, André Lurton, acquired the property in 1965 and has thoroughly rejuvenated the estate, which has its vineyards impressively situated between Haut-Bailly and Carbonnieux.

The emphasis is on producing wines of immediate drinkability, but also wines that are concentrated, fresh, and pure. Lurton has achieved all of that. While it used to be true that the red wines could not match the brilliance of the whites, that has changed since the mid-1980s as both wines are now excellent. Moreover, La Louvière remains notoriously undervalued, so consumers still have an opportunity to stock up on some delicious high-quality wines that compete with many of the best Graves properties.

VINTAGES

Red Wines

1989—I doubt the 1989 will be one of this estate's star performers. It is
· a good wine, medium bodied, attractively fruity, soft, and alco-
85 holic, with a silky finish. Anticipated maturity: Now–1998. Last
tasted, 4/91.

1988—The 1988 is the finest La Louvière I have tasted. It is a concen-
· trated well-balanced wine that possesses a delectable smoky, cassis
89 fruitiness that expands on the palate. Impressively concentrated,
with an opulent texture, it is a complete wine from start to finish.
Given the velvety tannins, it should provide delicious drinking
over the next decade. Anticipated maturity: 1992–2002. Last
tasted, 4/91.

1986—The red wine from La Louvière is made in a style that is meant to
· be drunk young, and the 1986 is no exception. It is a soft wine,
85 but rich in flavor, with a weedy, tobacco, spicy fruitiness, deep
color, and fleshy, sweet, concentrated flavors. Anticipated maturity: Now–1996. Last tasted, 3/89.

1985—The 1985 displays more structure than usual (somewhat surpris-
· ing in view of the loose-knit character of the vintage), but it has
85 generous portions of ripe, plummy tobacco-scented and -flavored
fruit in a medium-bodied format. Anticipated maturity: Now–
1994. Last tasted, 3/89.

1984—Too light and frail, without much grip and flavor, the 1984 is soft,
· fruity, and fresh, but shallow. Anticipated maturity: Now–1993.
74 Last tasted, 3/89.

1983—A notable success in 1983, La Louvière had one of the darkest
· colors of all the wines in a tasting of major Graves wines put on
87 for me by the Union des Grands Crus. This medium- to full-bodied
wine has shed the tannins and now exhibits wonderful ripeness,
excellent balance, deep, concentrated flavors, and a sweet,
earthy, tobacco fragrance. Anticipated maturity: Now–2000. Last
tasted, 1/88.

1982—This wine has the telltale dark ruby color of this vintage, and a very
· expressive bouquet suggesting ripe fruit, and toasty, vanillin oak.
86 On the palate, the wine is full bodied, silky, and velvety, with
layers of fruit. The ripe, round tannins in the sumptuous finish have
melted away. Anticipated maturity: Now–1998. Last tasted, 1/90.

1981—The least successful of the La Louvière vintages of the early
· 1980s, the 1981 is lean, a trifle austere, medium bodied, and
75 relatively compact and bland in taste. Anticipated maturity:
Now–1992. Last tasted, 6/84.

1978—Fully mature, the 1978 La Louvière is charmingly fruity, soft,
·   round, and supple, with a pleasing, ripe berry, tobacco-scented
83   character. Medium to full bodied, with little tannins present, this
     precocious, easy-to-drink wine should be drunk up. Anticipated
     maturity: Now–may be in decline. Last tasted, 12/84.

White Wines

1989—This is a relatively fat, open-knit, richly fruity La Louvière that
·   lacks some grip and delineation. There is no denying the four-
86   square, chunky fruitiness and easygoing texture. It will not be
     long-lived. Anticipated maturity: Now–1995. Last tasted, 4/91.
1988—This is a textbook example of just how delicious the white La
·   Louvière can be. It has just enough acidity to give it definition,
87   and the general impression is one of abundantly rich, honeyed,
     melony, fig-like fruit. There is a nice touch of toasty oak, and
     even some flintiness in the wine's finish. It is a lovely, extremely
     well made white Graves for drinking over the next 4–5 years.
     Anticipated maturity: Now–1995. Last tasted, 4/91.
1987—1987 is a terribly underrated vintage for white Graves. La Lou-
·   vière produced a tasty, honeyed, melony and fig-like wine with
85   medium body, a touch of oak, good acidity, and a crisp, long
     finish. Anticipated maturity: Now–1994. Last tasted, 11/90.

MALARTIC-LAGRAVIÈRE
(Cru Classé) Pessac-Léognan   AVERAGE

Production: 7,000 cases red; 1,000 cases white	Grape varieties: Red: Cabernet Sauvignon—50% Cabernet Franc—25% Merlot—25% White: Sauvignon—100%
Secondary label: none	Proprietor: Laurent-Perrier
Vineyard size: 50 acres	Administrator: Bruno Marly
Time spent in barrels: 18–20 months	Average age of vines: 20 years
Evaluation of present classification: An average-quality Graves estate equivalent to a Médoc Cru Bourgeois	
Plateau of maturity: red: 5–12 years following the vintage; white: 3–10 years following the vintage	

One of the numerous estates in the southern Graves region of Léognan, Malartic-Lagravière is a property that makes much better white wine than red wine. The production per hectare at this estate is high as the former proprietor, Jacques Marly, holds the minority point of view that young vines and high yields produce a better wine than low yields and old vines.

In stylistic terms, the red wine of Malartic-Lagravière is light, stern, tannic, and generally lacking richness and depth. Since it is unappealing when young, one would hope that age would fill it out and enhance its development. That has not been the case. Whether the recent retention of Bordeaux's famous oenologist, Emile Peynaud and the 1990 sale of the estate to the huge Champagne firm of Laurent-Pierrier, will change what has been a history of mediocrity for the red wine will have to be answered in the future.

VINTAGES

Red Wines

1989—The 1989 is extremely subtle, light to medium bodied, forward,
· yet structured enough to last until the end of the century. Antici-
82 pated maturity: 1992–2007. Last tasted, 4/91.

1988—The 1988 is lean, austere, light bodied, and too polite. A little
· excess would have been appreciated. I remain unsure of whether
77 I am fully capable of either appreciating or evaluating this excessively introverted, shy style of winemaking. Anticipated maturity:
1992–2000. Last tasted, 4/91.

1986—Medium ruby in color, the 1986 is pleasant, but undistinguished,
· and appears to have suffered somewhat from the huge rainstorms
82 that hit the Graves area just prior to the harvest. Anticipated
maturity: Now–1998. Last tasted, 11/90.

1985—Ripe, modestly fruity, with a healthy dosage of new oak, the 1985
· is a very pleasant wine, but it has little length or grip. Anticipated
84 maturity: Now–1995. Last tasted, 3/90.

1984—Malartic-Lagravière seems to always produce a very delicate,
· lighter-styled yet flavorful, cherry-and-oak-scented wine. The
78 1984 is a modest success—soft, fruity, and ready to drink. Anticipated maturity: Now–1993. Last tasted, 3/89.

1983—A decent effort from this property, the 1983 is a light- to medium-
· weight Graves, with a dry, tannic finish, an attractive spicy,
80 cherry-like bouquet, and moderately intense flavors. Anticipated
maturity: Now–1995. Last tasted, 5/87.

1982—The nicely colored 1982 has more flesh and fruit than one nor-
  ·   mally finds from this property. On the palate, the wine has stiff,
82   hard tannins, good fruit, and medium body. Anticipated maturity:
      Now–1995. Last tasted, 6/84.

1979—Medium ruby in color, with some amber, the 1979 has an open-
  ·   knit bouquet of light, berry fruit as well as some herbaceous
74   elements. In the mouth, the wine is light, too tannic for the pau-
      city of fruit, but pleasant in a rather tough, austere way. Antici-
      pated maturity: Now. Last tasted, 2/82.

1978—The bouquet is quite herbaceous and overly oaky. This medium-
  ·   bodied wine is very hard, closed, and not very attractive as
62   a result of severe, mouth-puckering tannins that obscure any
      hint of ripe fruit. It is quite a disappointing effort. Last tasted,
      2/82.

1975—Typically backward, stiff, unyielding, and seemingly incapable of
  ·   ever developing well, this medium ruby wine is a very tannic,
70   high-strung, skinny wine without much flesh or fruit. Anticipated
      maturity: Now–1993. Last tasted, 2/82.

1970—This is the best Malartic-Lagravière of the seventies I have
  ·   tasted. Hardly inspirational, but fruity, with a good color, a one-
78   dimensional bouquet of black cherries and oak, and not too
      tannic, the 1970 should be drunk up. Anticipated maturity: Now–
      1993. Last tasted, 2/82.

White Wines

1989—The decision to use 100% Sauvignon Blanc, ferment the wine in
  ·   stainless steel, and then age the wine for 7–8 months in vat is
82   something I find curious. I say that because this property often
      produces a white wine with a shrill character that comes across
      as too lemony and tart. No doubt, given the high acidity, the wine
      will hold up. But if the question is the degree of pleasure it is
      capable of providing, Malartic-Lagravière fails. The 1989 is too
      tart, seemingly more akin to a Muscadet than a serious white
      Graves. It is light straw/green in color and reserved, and has an
      unimpressive finish. Anticipated maturity: Now–1995. Last
      tasted, 4/91.

1988—This is one of the best white wines I have ever tasted from this
  ·   property. However, I should warn potential tasters that the com-
87   pelling bouquet of minerals, green peas, and freshly mowed grass
      may be too intense for those who like their wines shy. In the
      mouth, this wine exhibits a crisp, melony richness, but finishes

with an austere lightness and slightly high acidity. Anticipated maturity: Now–1997. Last tasted, 4/91.

1986—A bit dilute and light, yet crisp, tart, and refreshing in a low-
· keyed way, this pleasant, straw-colored wine has medium body,
81 and should be drunk over the next 7–8 years. Anticipated maturity: Now–1996. Last tasted, 3/89.

1985—This is an attractive Malartic-Lagravière with pronounced scents
· of mowed grass and green peas. Light straw in color with plenty
85 of fruit (for a change), this medium-bodied, crisp, austere wine
displays no signs of age. Anticipated maturity: Now–2000. Last
tasted, 3/89.

OLDER VINTAGES

If this wine never becomes profound or compelling, it certainly stands the test of time as evidenced by examples of the 1971, 1975, 1978, and 1979 I tasted in 1988. None of these wines was over the hill, and many had a moderately attractive, herbaceous, slightly honeyed, melon-like character. Nevertheless, there was also an impression of austerity and meagerness in the finish. This distinctive style of white wine has ad-mirers, but I must confess, I am not one of them.

LA MISSION-HAUT-BRION
(Cru Classé) Pessac-Léognan   OUTSTANDING

Production: 8,000 cases red	Grape varieties: Cabernet Sauvignon—50% Merlot—40% Cabernet Franc—10%
Secondary label: none	
Vineyard size: 49.4 acres	Proprietors: Duc and Duchesse de Mouchy, Domaine Clarence Dillon
Time spent in barrels: 24–26 months	Administrator: Jean Delmas Average age of vines: 35 years
Evaluation of present classification: The quality equivalent of a Médoc first-growth	
Plateau of maturity: 8–30 or more years following the vintage	

La Mission-Haut-Brion in Talence produces one of the greatest wines in the entire Bordeaux region. This estate sits across the road (RN 250) confronting its long-time rival, Haut-Brion, and has a record of virtually unmatched brilliance that predates the scope of this book by a good 40 years.

The Woltner family acquired La Mission in 1919. It was they—particularly the late Frederic and his son Henri—who were responsible for the ascendancy of La Mission-Haut-Brion's wine quality to a level that matched and frequently surpassed the first-growths of the Médoc and neighboring Haut-Brion.

Woltner's genius was widely recognized in Bordeaux. He was known as a gifted taster and oenologist, and pioneered the installation of easy-to-clean, metal, glass-lined fermentation tanks in 1926. Many observers attributed the dense, rich, powerful, fruity character of La Mission to these short, squat vats that, because of their shape, tended to increase the grape-skin-to-juice contact during the fermentation.

La Mission-Haut-Brion's style of wine has always been that of intense richness, full body, great color and extract, and plenty of tannin. I have had the pleasure of tasting all of the best vintages of La Mission back to 1921, and it is a wine that can easily last 30 or 40 years in the bottle. It has always been a much richer and more powerful wine than that of arch rival Haut-Brion. For this reason, as well as remarkable consistency in poor and mediocre vintages (along with Latour in Pauillac, it has had the finest record in Bordeaux for good wines in poor vintages), La Mission has over the years become a more popular wine than Haut-Brion.

Henri Woltner passed away in 1974, and until the sale of La Mission-Haut-Brion to the present owners of Haut-Brion in 1983, La Mission was managed by Françoise and Francis Dewavrin-Woltner. Internal family bickering over the administration of this property ultimately led to the sale of La Mission and two sister properties, La Tour-Haut-Brion and the white wine–producing estate of Laville-Haut-Brion.

Since 1983, Jean Delmas has moved quickly to stamp his winemaking philosophy on the wines of this estate. After the property was sold in 1983, the winemaking staff was promptly dismissed and Delmas began to augment the percentage of new oak that had deteriorated due to the financial difficulties experienced by the Woltner regime. Now La Mission, like Haut-Brion, is aged in 100% new oak. In addition, the percentage of Merlot has been increased to 40% with both the Cabernet Sauvignon and Cabernet Franc lowered.

The first vintages under Delmas were very good, but lacked the power and extraordinary richness seen in La Mission in previous top years. They were technically correct wines, but something seemed to be missing. With the installation of a state-of-the-art winemaking facility at the estate in time for the 1987 vintage, the quality of the wine appears to have returned to that of its glory years. The wine is cleaner, and flaws such as elevated levels of volatile acidity that appeared in certain older vintages of La Mission are unlikely to ever rear their unpleasant heads under the management of Delmas. Nevertheless, after a transitional period between 1983 and 1986, La Mission-Haut-Brion returned in the late eighties to produce one of the very best wines of the vintage in 1987, a star in 1988, the glorious 1989, undoubtedly the finest La Mission of the decade, and a 1990 that from the cask appeared superior to Haut-Brion.

It is unlikely that the newer style of La Mission will age as long as older vintages, but neither will it be as unapproachable and tannic in its youth. Yet I am happy to say that La Mission-Haut-Brion remains a wine of first-growth quality

VINTAGES

1989—The 1989 La Mission-Haut-Brion is irrefutably the finest wine
·   made at this château since the perfect 1975. It is a thick, muscu-
99   lar, sensationally concentrated wine that is even bigger than that
       of nearby sibling Haut-Brion. Once past the roasted cassis and
       smoky nose, the wine is superbly extracted with plum and tar-
       like flavors framed with generous quantities of new oak (100%, in
       fact). While there is a tendency to compare the 1989 to the volup-
       tuous, unctuous 1982, the 1989 is much more concentrated and
       has greater structure and grip. Nevertheless, it should drink well
       given the heady alcohol content and soft tannins. It is clearly a
       La Mission that will last for at least several decades. Anticipated
       maturity: 1995–2015. Last tasted, 4/91.

1988—The 1988 La Mission displayed ferociously hard tannins from
·   cask, but after bottling it has improved significantly. Perhaps the
89   high quality of Merlot (45% in this vintage's blend) has helped
       provide the wine with opulence and depth of fruit. The 1988
       has turned out to be a beautifully made, deep, full-bodied, con-
       centrated, rich, well-structured wine that will last for 15–20
       years. It is a bigger, deeper, yet softer, more concentrated wine
       than Haut-Brion. Anticipated maturity: 1994–2012. Last tasted,
       4/91.

1987—This is one of the most perfumed and seductive wines of the
·   vintage. It exhibits the smoky, tobacco, exotic character of a
87   good Graves, and is remarkably smooth and tasty on the palate.
       I am tempted to say that it should be drunk over the next
       4–5 years given the low acidity and absence of any real tannin.
       However, I would not be surprised to see it last for up to a
       decade. In any event, prudence is best, so plan on drinking this
       wine in its youth. Anticipated maturity: Now–2000. Last tasted,
       5/91.

1986—This La Mission-Haut-Brion is dark ruby in color, with a spicy,
·   mineral-and-tobacco-scented bouquet, hard tannins, medium to
90   full body, and excellent potential for extended cellaring. Interestingly, it has neither the size nor opulence and depth of the extraordinary 1986 Haut-Brion. Nevertheless, it is one of the
outstanding wines of this vintage. Anticipated maturity: 1996–
2010. Last tasted, 11/90.

1985—The 1985 La Mission is a rich, ripe, smooth, and flavorful wine
·   with oodles of berry fruit, toasty new oak, and a full-bodied,
87   loosely knit, fleshy, somewhat fluid texture. It is already drinking
well. Anticipated maturity: Now–2000. Last tasted, 1/90.

1984—A successful wine for the vintage, La Mission's 1984 has a mod-
·   erately dark color and is round, herbaceous, fruity, and easy to
82   drink. Anticipated maturity: Now–1996. Last tasted, 3/89.

1983—The first La Mission-Haut-Brion produced under Jean Delmas
·   and his staff, the 1983 represents a change in style from pre-
89   vious wines of La Mission. Dark colored, spicy, with predominate scents of vanilla and minerals, this medium-bodied wine
has evolved quickly. It has a more austere structure than usual,
and a good, solid finish. It is a very good, potentially excellent
La Mission. Anticipated maturity: 1993–2007. Last tasted, 7/91.

1982—Among the La Mission-Haut-Brions of the last 25 years, the 1982
·   is certainly the most opulent and fleshiest of all the vintages.
95   Deep, dark ruby/purple with a ripe bouquet of cassis fruit, the
1982 has yet to develop any nuances to its bouquet. On the palate,
the wine is crammed with rich, unctuous, berry fruit, is showing
a great deal more tannin than it did several years ago, and is very
full bodied and concentrated. At this stage, it looks to be in need
of 5–6 more years of bottle age, but should last for at least 20–30
years. Anticipated maturity: 1993–2010. Last tasted, 4/91.

1981—No doubt this vintage of La Mission-Haut-Brion was probably
·   overlooked once the highly publicized 1982 vintage was con-
90   ceived, but this wine has always been, in my opinion, one of the
stars of the vintage. It showed extremely well with a big, rich,
berry, smoky-scented bouquet, medium-bodied, alcoholic, deep
flavors, huge fruit, and a long finish. It has shed much tannin, and
seems to be nearing its plateau of maturity, where I would expect
it to last for 10–15 years. Anticipated maturity: Now–2005. Last
tasted, 2/91.

1980—I had felt this wine would show a bit better than it did in this
·   tasting, but it came across as extremely light, with a delicate,
72   restrained, almost watery bouquet, innocuous, medium-bodied
flavors, and a short, rather diluted finish. It should be drunk up

before it fades any further. Anticipated maturity: Now–1993. Last tasted, 1/89.

1979— The 1979 is one of the few vintages in the seventies in which I
· find La Mission to be less successful than its neighbor, Château
91 Haut-Brion. Nevertheless, in this bountiful year, La Mission made a wonderfully elegant, surprisingly concentrated wine that stylistically resembles the 1971. While it lacks the extraordinary depth and complexity that La Mission is capable of achieving in great years such as 1982 or 1978, the 1979 is still a very fine wine, with a life expectancy of 15 years. Anticipated maturity: Now–2005. Last tasted, 2/91.

1978— The 1978 La Mission-Haut-Brion is a strong candidate, like the
· 1975, for the wine of the vintage. It is much more backward than
94 Haut-Brion (which, by the way, is drinking beautifully now), and in a vertical tasting it displayed a supple, smooth, velvety texture, and well-developed, rich, cassis, gravel, and smoky scents and flavors. Very full bodied, rich, and supple, this wine clearly can be drunk now, but promises to be even better with additional bottle age. It will not be one of the longest-lived La Missions, but should certainly last 10–15 years. Anticipated maturity: Now–2005. Last tasted, 6/91.

1977— While this wine tasted highly chaptalized and extremely herba-
· ceous, I was somewhat surprised that it was still palatable and,
74 in its own way, easy to drink. There is no question that the wine is slightly too vegetal, but it is soft and fully mature, and for those who have any cellared, it should be consumed. Anticipated maturity: Now–1992. Last tasted, 1/89.

1976— I never found the 1976 La Mission to be a very good wine, as it
· began to show age and take on an amber/brown color when only
76 4 years old. However, it seems to have changed little since I last tasted it. It is an alcoholic, loosely knit, rather flabby La Mission, with somewhat of a stewed, roasted character. Yet, the wine does have ripe fruit, a good bit of alcohol, and very low acidity. Anticipated maturity: Now–1993. Last tasted, 1/89.

1975— This wine continues to demonstrate that it is one of the most
· extraordinary wines made at La Mission-Haut-Brion in the post–
100 World War II era. It has a fabulous perfume of cassis fruit, minerals, spicy oak, and I thought I even detected a trace of violets. Unbelievably concentrated, full bodied, with no sign of age in the very dark ruby color, this massive La Mission is still extremely tannic and nowhere near maturity. The finish must be experienced to be believed, as it must last 90 seconds or more. This is one of the most concentrated and highly extracted La Missions

made in the last 20 years, and I can't see it ever being ready to drink before the year 2000. It is a monumental effort and certainly the wine of the vintage. In terms of aging potential, it may be the wine of the decade. Anticipated maturity: 2005–2050. Last tasted, 12/90.

1974 — When I did my original tastings of the 1974s, the three wines that stood out in that mediocre vintage were Latour, Trotanoy, and La Mission-Haut-Brion. The 1974 is still very alive, and has at least another 7–10 years of aging potential. It remains a tougher, more sinewy style of La Mission-Haut-Brion, but exhibits an excellent deep, dark garnet color, a big, mineral-scented, smoky, earthy, spicy bouquet, medium to full body, very hard tannins, and very good flavor depth, particularly for a 1974. No doubt the deep günzian gravel and subsoil of La Mission's vineyard resulted in this wine's turning out to be one of the successes of this rain-soaked vintage. Anticipated maturity: Now–1993. Last tasted, 3/91.

·

86

1973 — The spicy, somewhat watery bouquet fades after 30 or 40 seconds in the glass. On the palate, the wine is thin and hard. Last tasted, 1/89.

·

58

1972 — This vintage clearly demonstrates how well La Mission-Haut-Brion can do in an off year. The year 1972 was certainly the worst vintage of the decade, yet this wine displays a wonderfully fragrant, spicy, cedary, slightly herbaceous, berry-scented bouquet, ripe, round, spicy flavors, medium body, and an attractively lush finish. Delicious, this wine should be drunk up over the next 2–3 years. It is an amazing success for this vintage. Anticipated maturity: Now–1993. Last tasted, 1/89.

·

86

1971 — 1971 is a delicious La Mission that has been fully mature for the last 5–6 years. This rustic wine has a big, earthy, cigar-box, mineral-scented bouquet, generous yet coarse flavors, and a powerful, dusty finish. I would expect it to continue to drink well for at least a decade. Anticipated maturity: Now–2000. Last tasted, 10/90.

·

87

1970 — Much has been made about certain lots of the 1970 La Mission-Haut-Brion having excessive levels of volatile acidity. I have had this wine at least a dozen times, and I do have notes of certain bottles that seemed to have the smell of vinegar in their bouquet. However, whether it is good fortune or not, the last five times I have had the 1970 have all been from sound, totally healthy bottles. At its best, the wine can be super, with a big, rich, cedary, cigar-box, ripe, cassis-scented bouquet. It is a very full-bodied,

·

94

concentrated wine, with plenty of alcohol, and still-noticeable tannin. The wine is much more developed than the 1975, and can now be drunk with a great deal of pleasure. It is a superb La Mission-Haut-Brion that should last for another 20–25 years. Anticipated maturity: Now–2010. Last tasted, 1/89.

1969—A dull, hard, almost neutral bouquet reminded me of some of our
·   modern-day California Cabernets that are sterile filtered. On the
67   palate, the wine is hollow with hard, rough, coarse tannins that have obliterated what fruit may have once been present. While 1963 and 1968 were certainly much worse years for most châteaux, I continue to believe that 1969 may have turned out Bordeaux's least attractive wines in the last 30 years. Last tasted, 1/89.

1968—In the fifties, sixties, and seventies, La Mission-Haut-Brion and
·   Latour were the two châteaux that were considered to be one's
82   best gambles in the terrible vintages. With the 1968, La Mission clearly proved its ability to turn out good wines in disastrous years. No vintage had worse climatic conditions than 1968. Yet this 1968 proved to be one of the surprises, even though it's hardly a great wine. A soft, warm, generously fruity, leather-scented bouquet is followed by a wine that is round, alcoholic (no doubt the wine was chaptalized quite a bit), with a velvety, oaky, sweet finish. The wine lacks complexity, but still has fruit, and the high alcohol gives it a generous, warm, pleasant character. For those who might have any, it should be consumed, as it fades in the glass after 3–4 minutes. Anticipated maturity: Now–1993. Last tasted, 1/89.

1967—In the early seventies the 1967 La Mission-Haut-Brion was one of
·   the top eight or ten wines of this vintage from the Médoc and
84   Graves. It has begun to lose its fruit, and has a coarse, chewy texture with some tough tannins that seem to be taking over the personality of the wine. There is still some fruit, and the wine has appeal, but I would suggest drinking it up immediately. Anticipated maturity: Now–1993. Last tasted, 1/89.

1966—The 1966 La Mission-Haut-Brion, never quite as rich and deep as
·   the 1964, is still a beautifully made, elegant La Mission, with a
89   very cedary and leather-scented, fruity bouquet, medium to full body, and a long, supple, velvety finish. I would advise those who have it in their wine collections to consume it over the next 4–5 years. It does not appear capable of getting any better, and may, in fact, be just starting to lose the fruit. Anticipated maturity: Now–1995. Last tasted, 1/89.

1964—The year 1964 is one of those vintages that turned out to be great
  ·   for Pomerol, St.-Emilion, and Graves, but most of the Médoc
 91   properties got caught with their Cabernet Sauvignon unpicked
        when the heavy rains began to fall. La Mission-Haut-Brion has
        always been one of the great successes of the vintage, but it has
        just turned the corner and is beginning a slow decline. I say that
        having cellared quite a few bottles of this vintage, which allows
        me to taste it frequently. It displays a dark ruby color that is just
        beginning to show a trace of amber and orange. The bouquet is
        classic La Mission with scents of cedar, leather, smoke, and even
        a trace of truffles in this vintage. It is still an expansively flavored
        wine with a lovely, sweet ripeness to its fruit, and a heady, alco-
        holic finish. Those who have it cellared should contemplate drink-
        ing it. Anticipated maturity: Now–1997. Last tasted, 6/91.

1963—For a vintage that many considered to be one of the two worst in
  ·   the post–World War II era, La Mission-Haut-Brion certainly
 72   turned out to be a pleasant wine. There is nothing vegetal or
        diluted about the cedary, spicy, smoky, fruity, yet somewhat
        chaptalized bouquet. On the palate, the wine exhibits surprising
        body and vibrant fruit, but has a hot, alcoholic finish. After sev-
        eral minutes in the glass, it fades completely. For the vintage,
        one would have to consider this a major success. Anticipated
        maturity: Now–probably in serious decline. Last tasted, 1/89.

1962—I have never thought the 1962 to be a great success. It is an
  ·   elegant, medium-bodied wine without a great deal of complexity
 84   or depth, but it exhibits a pleasant supple, cedary, smoky, cigar-
        box character. There is also some pleasant plummy fruit and a
        soft finish. Still vibrant and alive, those who have it cellared
        should have no problem keeping it for another 2–7 years. Antici-
        pated maturity: Now–1997. Last tasted, 1/89.

1961—I have been fortunate enough to have this wine three times in the
  ·   last year. It is a sensational La Mission-Haut-Brion, with that
 99   incredibly fabulous, full bouquet of spices, tobacco, cedar,
        smoke, and sweet black fruits. Full bodied, with a viscous, rich,
        opulent texture, this lavishly endowed wine has aged slightly
        faster than the 1959, but remains immense, even by the standards
        of this great vintage. It has a sumptuous finish that must be ex-
        perienced to be believed. It is extraordinary, and should continue
        to drink well for at least another decade. Anticipated maturity:
        Now–2005. Last tasted, 1/91.

OLDER VINTAGES

La Mission-Haut-Brion's record since 1945 is unequaled by any other château during this half century. The 1945 (rated 94 in 1/89) has fabulous concentration, but also a tough, hard texture, with as much tannin as one would ever want in a great wine. Even the underrated 1946 (rated 90 in 1/89) has an intense bouquet of coffee, cedar, tar, and ground beef. In the mouth, it is extremely massive, hot, dense, and highly extracted with a considerable amount of tannin. Amazingly, it is more youthful than some of the more recent vintages. I have had the 1947, my birth year (rated consistently between 94 and 97), on at least a half-dozen occasions. Its port-like bouquet of chocolate, cedar, and earthy, plummy fruit is profound. It is probably the most alcoholic and sweet-tasting La Mission I have ever had. I am sure the level of volatile acidity is too high for purists, but it is an extraordinary wine.

Just as good is the 1948 (rated 93 in 1/89), which offers up a powerful, roasted, rich bouquet of tobacco, ripe curranty fruit, and smoky chestnuts. Again, it is a massive wine that, like the 1947 and 1945, can last another two decades. The 1949 (rated 97 in 1/89) is my favorite vintage of the late forties, although it, too, has some volatile acidity. However, who can resist the fabulously plummy, cedary, smoky, leather-scented bouquet that overwhelms the olfactory senses? A wine of staggering depth and richness, it is clearly one of the greatest post–World War II La Mission-Haut-Brions.

In the fifties, La Mission made a superb 1950 (90), a decent 1951 (81), a great 1952 (93), a stunningly explosive, fragrant 1953 (93), and a perfect 1955 (rated 100 twice and 99 once in my three most recent tastings). The 1955, which still has an opaque, deep, dark ruby/purple color, with only a hint of amber, offers up an irresistible bouquet of minerals, cedar, smokey, cassis fruit, and exotic spices. A wine of overwhelming richness and depth, it is one of the greatest wines made during the fifties. Amazingly, it still seems to be improving, and may have 25–30 additional years of longevity! Lovers of off years should seek out auctions for the 1957 (rated 93) and the 1958 (rated 94). Both are fabulous wines that are fully mature, but are faithful to the style of the château and extremely concentrated and rich. Another perfect wine was produced by La Mission-Haut-Brion in 1959 (rated 100 three times and 99 once in my last four tastings). The 1959 has a deeper, more opaque ruby/purple color than the 1961, and probably greater potential for extended longevity. It is a profound and extraordinary wine with a degree of flavor dimension and complexity that defies articulation. It has not yet reached its plateau of maturity, and I would not be surprised to see this wine last another 30 or more years!

I know of no château in the post—World War II era that has a quality track record that comes close to matching that of La Mission-Haut-Brion.

OLIVIER (Cru Classé) Pessac-Léognan   AVERAGE

Production: 12,500 cases red; 10,000 cases white	Grape varieties: Red: Cabernet Sauvignon—65% Merlot—35% White: Semillon—70% Sauvignon—25% Muscadelle—5%
Secondary label: Mineur J.J. de Bethmann	
Vineyard size: 84 acres	Proprietor: Jean-Jacques de Bethmann
Time spent in barrels: red: 18 months; white: 2–4 months	Average age of vines: 12 years
Evaluation of present classification: Should be downgraded; the quality equivalent of a Médoc Cru Bourgeois	
Plateau of maturity: red: 2–8 years following the vintage; white: 2–4 years following the vintage	

This estate is one of the oldest in the entire Bordeaux region, tracing back to the twelfth century. One of its most famous visitors in the fourteenth century was the Black Prince (son of King Edward III of England), the Bordeaux commander who led many of England's greatest knights in their battles against the French for control of the Aquitaine province. Since the end of World War II, a family of German origin, the de Bethmanns, have been the proprietors. It has not been a management that has resulted in profound wines. Both the white and red wines vinified at Olivier have been mediocre in quality, and unusually simple, light, and innocuous for a Cru Classé with vineyards so well placed in the Léognan region. Insiders in Bordeaux argue that the exclusivity the Bethmanns gave to the large *négociant* firm of Eschenauer often prevented the wine from being shown in comparative tastings, where its weaknesses would have been obvious. However, that exclusivity ended in the mid-1980s and now the wine can easily be compared with that of its neighbors. Despite reports that improvements have been made, all my recent tastings, through the 1989 vintage, continue to demonstrate that this is a property in need of a wake-up call.

The white wines from Olivier in both 1988 and 1989 were eviscerated, flavorless wines that were, in short, reprehensible for a Cru Classé. My notes do indicate that the quality of the red wines improved, with a lusciously fruity, seductive, generally well-balanced, fragrant, easy-to-drink 1988, and a light, but adequate, 1989. Hopefully, these two vintages signal a slight increase in the quality of Olivier, which remains one of Bordeaux's most conspicuous underachievers.

PAPE-CLÉMENT (Cru Classé) Pessac-Léognan   EXCELLENT

Production: 11,000 cases red; 1,500 cases white	Grape varieties: Red: Cabernet Sauvignon—60% Merlot—40% White: Semillon—50% Sauvignon—50%
Secondary label: Le Clémentin du Pape-Clément	
Vineyard size: 86.4 acres	Proprietor: Leo Montagne Administrator: Bernard Pujol
Time spent in barrels: 24 months	Average age of vines: 30 years
Evaluation of present classification: Since 1986 the quality equivalent of a Médoc second-growth	
Plateau of maturity: red: 5–20 years following the vintage; white: 3–8 years following the vintage	

Pape-Clément is located in the suburban sprawl of Pessac several miles from the famed Château Haut-Brion. Historically, Pape-Clément is among the most significant estates of the Bordeaux region. One of the original owners, Bertrand de Goth, purchased this country estate in 1300, and 6 years later became Pope Clement V. He was admired by the French for his bold decision to move the papacy to the sun-drenched, hallowed Provençal city of Avignon, where the historical period of the papacy became known as the Babylonian Captivity, and the wine produced by Clement at his country estate outside Avignon became known as Châteauneuf du Pape. While Pope Clement V remained in Avignon, he turned over the vineyards of Pape-Clément to the church, where they remained undisturbed until divested during the French Revolution.

The vineyard is now controlled by the heirs of the late French poet, Paul Montagne. While no one doubted the quality of Pape-Clément's wines in the fifties, sixties, and early seventies, lack of attention to detail, and little investment in winemaking equipment or barrels resulted in a significant deterioration of quality at Pape-Clément after 1975. For the next decade, the wines produced at the château were often musty, lacked freshness, and in short, were poorly made. The succession of poor-to-mediocre results ended in 1985 subsequent to the hiring of the young, enthusiastic Bernard Pujol. Pujol was given total responsibility for res-urrecting the quality of Pape-Clément, and the result, first evidenced with a profound 1986, has been a succession of wines that now come close to rivaling the great Haut-Brion and La Mission-Haut-Brion.

Pape-Clément, which sits on extremely light, gravelly soil, produces a wine that at its best has a fascinating and compelling bouquet offering up gobs of black fruits intermingled with strong smells of tobacco and minerals. Because of the relatively high percentage of Merlot, it is a wine that can be drunk extremely young, yet ages easily for several decades in the best vintages. In the last half of the decade of the eighties, Pape-Clément became one of the stars of Bordeaux, producing profound wines in 1990, 1988, and 1986.

The new commitment to quality has also been evidenced by an in-crease in the vineyard area for their rare white wines. Previously, the microscopic production, usually less than 100 cases, was reserved for exclusive use by the château. The property hopes to produce nearly 1,500 cases by 1991, when the vineyard is mature enough to make quality wine.

VINTAGES

Red Wines

1989—Pape-Clément produced a charming, medium-bodied wine in
  ·   1989, but it suffers in comparison with their exquisite 1990 and
  88   1988 as well as the 1986. For the record, the 1989 was made from
         grapes harvested between September 11 and 26. Production was
         higher than in 1986 or 1988, no doubt contributing to the lighter
         style. It is a wine with plenty of charm, good color, medium body,
         soft tannins, and an alluring blackcurrant fruitiness. Anticipated
         maturity: 1994–2003. Last tasted, 4/91.

1988—Since 1985 it has been apparent that the dreadful era of Pape-
  ·   Clément's insipid performances (1976–1984) is ancient history—
  92   witness the delicious 1985, brilliant 1986, and the 1988—the fin-
         est Pape-Clément made since 1961. It possesses good weight,
         power, and flavor extraction as well as the quintessential Graves
         elegance and perfume. It is impressively deep in color for a
         Graves, with a big, fragrant nose of roasted chestnuts, tobacco,
         currants, and earthy stones that is thrilling. On the palate, one
         notices that this is an atypically backward, full Pape-Clément,
         but there is wonderful ripeness, and while the tannin level is high,

they are velvety tannins. The finish is all smoky-scented black cherries. This is a wine that I suspect is marginally superior to the five other potentially outstanding Graves wines of the 1988 vintage (La Mission-Haut-Brion, Haut-Brion, Haut-Bailly, Domaine de Chevalier, and La Louvière). Anticipated maturity: 1993–2008. Last tasted, 4/91.

1987—Similar to La Mission-Haut-Brion in the soft, seductive, velvety
 · texture and easygoing flavors, this wine is a notable success for
85 the vintage. It is charming and fruity. Anticipated maturity: Now–
 1995. Last tasted, 11/90.

1986—The 1986 is a remarkable wine, which is amazing given the fact
 · that this vineyard was inundated during the severe rainstorms
91 prior to the harvest. No doubt a very strict selection resulted in
 only the later-picked grapes going into the 1986. It has a stylish
 blackcurrant-and-mineral-scented bouquet backed up nicely by
 spicy new oak. Deep ruby/purple in color, medium bodied, with
 excellent ripeness and richness, this wine is not a blockbuster,
 but it does have a beautifully crafted, graceful texture, and a long,
 stylish finish. It is undoubtedly the finest wine produced at this
 beautiful estate in Pessac between 1961 and 1988. Anticipated
 maturity: 1994–2008. Last tasted, 2/91.

1985—The 1985, the best Pape-Clément since the 1975, is a fragrant,
 · supple, tasty wine with a great deal of finesse and charm. It is
87 deeply concentrated, medium bodied, long, and complex. Anticipated maturity: Now–2000. Last tasted, 3/89.

1983—This is an adequate Pape-Clément. The wine is medium ruby,
 · with an attractive, herb-like, spicy, ripe fruity nose somewhat
78 dominated by vanillin oak and tight, compact, rustic flavors. Anticipated maturity: Now–1996. Last tasted, 3/89.

1982—This wine continues to deteriorate as it evolves in the bottle.
 · Despite some early notes that indicated the wine had decent fruit,
59 it has taken on an increasingly dirty, musty, vegetal aroma, and
 washed-out, disjointed, disappointing flavors. It appears irrefutable that this wine was brought up in unsanitary conditions. It is
 now almost undrinkable. Last tasted, 3/89.

1981—This wine has held up better than the 1982, but does display
 · relatively weak, diluted, frail flavors, an earthy, dirty-barrel,
65 barnyard smell, and soft, fading flavors. Anticipated maturity:
 Now–1993. Last tasted, 1/89.

1979—Medium bodied and one-dimensional, with only a hint of the
 · famed tobacco, mineral-like bouquet, this is a light-bodied, aus-
75 tere, attenuated Pape-Clément. Anticipated maturity: Now–
 1993. Last tasted, 1/89.

1978—This wine has dropped most of its fruit, taking on an earthy, stale
·   mushroom-like quality. The medium ruby color exhibits a great
72   deal of amber and brown. The finish is marked by excessive acid-
       ity and a slight dirtiness. There is still some underlying fruit, but
       this wine seems to be collapsing quickly. Last tasted, 1/89.

1976—All the fruit has now faded from what was never a good example
·   of this vintage. Last tasted, 7/88.
62

1975—The best Pape-Clément of the seventies. A complex smoky,
·   roasted-chestnut, earthy bouquet is intense and top class. On the
87   palate, the wine is medium bodied and lighter than many 1975s,
       but has good concentration, a surprising suppleness, and a fine,
       spicy, mineral-flavored finish. Anticipated maturity: Now–1996.
       Last tasted, 1/91.

1971—Fully mature and beginning to show the telltale sign of old age (a
·   significant brown color), the 1971 still remains an elegant, cedary,
80   spicy, soft, fruity wine that should be drunk up immediately.
       Anticipated maturity: Now–may be in decline. Last tasted, 12/84.

1970—While the 1970 was impressive when young, like many vintages
·   of Pape-Clément made during the seventies it has not stood the
84   test of time. Now becoming loosely knit and losing some fruit,
       this medium-bodied, very soft and supple wine has a classy,
       earthy, cedary, spicy bouquet, and good flavors, but both fade
       quickly in the glass. Anticipated maturity: Now–probably in se-
       rious decline. Last tasted, 12/84.

1966—This wine has been fully mature since the early seventies, and
·   has always represented one of the best examples of this estate's
85   style. Consistently elegant, with Pape-Clément's telltale bouquet
       of smoky tobacco and earthy, cedary, currant fruit, since the late
       seventies, the 1966 has ever-so-slowly begun to lose some inten-
       sity and take on more amber color. The wine is still very good,
       but the acidity and tannins are more noticeable in the finish, and
       the fruit is less intense. This was once a beautiful, elegant wine
       that is now beginning to decline. Anticipated maturity: Now–
       1995. Last tasted, 11/87.

1964—I purchased a half case of this wine and had five marvelous bot-
·   tles, but the last bottle, tasted in 1979, had faded badly. However,
88   in the late-1980s, two bottles tasted in Bordeaux were excellent,
       nearly outstanding examples of what was always considered a top
       vintage for Pape-Clément. If this wine has been well stored it
       should still reveal a big, smoky, roasted, truffle-and-berry-
       scented bouquet, relatively fat, alcoholic flavors, and a long, lush
       finish. Look for this wine in larger formats at auctions because it

is clearly one of the sleepers of the vintage. Anticipated maturity: Now–1996. Last tasted, 3/88.

1961—Tasted three times since the last edition of this book, the 1961
· Pape-Clément was remarkable in each tasting. Obviously bottle
93 variation and storage account for everything, but my last three looks at this wine have revealed what must be the best Pape-Clément ever made. Extremely rich and full bodied, with an opulent, almost roasted chestnut fruitiness, layer upon layer of richness, and a long, silky, heady finish, this is almost the essence of the mineral, tobacco, Graves-like style that most people associate with Haut-Brion. Given how superb this wine tasted, it should be drunk over the next 5–8 years. Anticipated maturity: Now–1998. Last tasted, 12/90.

PICQUE-CAILLOU (Unclassified) Pessac-Léognan   GOOD

Production: 8,000 cases red	Grape varieties:
	Cabernet Sauvignon—35%
	Cabernet Franc—35%
	Merlot—30%
Secondary label: none	
Vineyard size: 42 acres	Proprietor: The Denis family
Time spent in barrels: 16–20 months	Average age of vines: 25 years
Evaluation of present classification: At its best, the quality equivalent of a Médoc fifth-growth	
Plateau of maturity: 3–12 years following the vintage	

Picque-Caillou is the last surviving vineyard of the commune of Merignac, which is now better known as the location of Bordeaux's ever-expanding international airport. The light, gravelly, stony soil, plus the high percentage of Cabernet Franc and Merlot in the blend, produce a wonderfully aromatic, fruity wine that can be undeniably seductive when drunk young. The soil is not unlike the terrain of the famous Pessac châteaux of Haut-Brion and Pape-Clément. The quality of the winemaking is excellent, largely because of the Denis family, who has owned this property since 1920. No white wine is made.

VINTAGES

1989—Given the high quality of Picque-Caillou's wines during the
· eighties, this is a disappointment. The wine is overripe, with a
76 cooked, smoked component. Anticipated maturity: Now–1995. Last tasted, 4/91.

1988—The 1988 is, along with the 1985, their wine of the decade. Deep
  ·   ruby, with a pronounced earthy, curranty aroma, this fleshy, even
86   opulent wine is loaded with fruit. Anticipated maturity: Now–
         1998. Last tasted, 4/91.

1986—This vineyard tends to produce very fragrant, supple, deliciously
  ·   fruity wines that display the tobacco/mineral character of Graves,
86   and a seductive, forward fruitiness. The 1986 exhibits an in-
         creased usage of new oak barrels, has opulent, ripe fruitiness,
         soft tannins, and low acidity. Anticipated maturity: Now–1996.
         Last tasted, 11/90.

1985—The 1985 is seductive as a result of its juicy cherry fruit, medium
  ·   body, pleasing ripeness, and creamy, lush texture. Anticipated
86   maturity: Now–1994. Last tasted, 3/90.

1984—This reliable little estate made a good 1984 that is filled with the
  ·   aromas of raspberry fruit, is soft and fully mature. Anticipated
82   maturity: Now–1992. Last tasted, 3/88.

PIRON (Unclassified) Graves   AVERAGE

Production: 2,000 cases red; 7,000 cases white	Grape varieties: Red: Cabernet Sauvignon—50% Merlot—50% White: Sauvignon—50% Semillon—50%
Secondary label: none	
Vineyard size: 47 acres	Proprietor: G.F.A. du Piron
Time spent in barrels: 15–18 months	Average age of vines: 20 years
Evaluation of present classification: The quality equivalent of a Médoc Cru Bourgeois	
Plateau of maturity: red: 2–6 years following the vintage; white: 2–6 years following the vintage	

I rarely see this wine outside of France, but this estate, located in the
commune of St.-Morillon, is much more famous for its stylish, crisp
white wine than for the red. If the wines are never inspirational, they are
certainly well made, satisfying, consistently enjoyable, as well as reasonably priced.

PONTAC-MONPLAISIR (Unclassified) Pessac-Léognan   GOOD

Production: 1,800 cases red; 2,700 cases white	Grape varieties: Red: Cabernet Sauvignon—60% Merlot—40% White: Sauvignon—70% Semillon—30%
Secondary label: none	
Vineyard size: 34 acres	Proprietor: Jean Maufras
Time spent in barrels: 12–15 months	Average age of vines: 15 years
Evaluation of present classification: The quality equivalent of a Médoc Cru Bourgeois	
Plateau of maturity: red: 3–6 years following the vintage; white: 1–4 years following the vintage	

The vineyard of Pontac-Monplaisir sits on very sandy, light gravelly soil near Château Baret, which is administrated by the famous Bordeaux *négociant* firm of Borie-Manoux. The white wine from this estate is a textbook white Graves with a pronounced intense, herbaceous, mineral character, medium body, and gobs of fruit. Some people find it almost too herbaceously scented. It is not a wine to lay away in the cellar, but rather to be drunk in its first 2–3 years. The red wine is of less interest —soft, straightforward, relatively light, but tasty and correctly made.

RAHOUL (Unclassified) Graves   GOOD

Production: 6,000 cases red; 1,000 cases white	Grape varieties: Red: Merlot—70% Cabernet Sauvignon—30% White: Semillon—100%
Secondary label: Petit Rahoul	
Vineyard size: 34.6 acres	Proprietor: Alain Thiènot
Time spent in barrels: 18–20 months	Average age of vines: 12 years
Evaluation of present classification: The quality equivalent of a Médoc Cru Bourgeois	
Plateau of maturity: red: 5–12 years following the vintage; white: 3–8 years following the vintage	

This property near the village of Portets is highly regarded in some circles, but to date I have found the wines almost overwhelmingly oaky, as well as slightly out of balance. There is no doubt that Château Rahoul, which has been totally rejuvenated by the syndicate that purchased this vineyard in 1978, has had high aspirations. Until 1989, the wine has been made by the highly respected Danish oenologist, Peter Vinding-Diers, but from the beginning I have questioned the high percentage of new oak used for both the red and white wines. The vineyard is still young, and perhaps when mature the concentration of fruit in the wines will be sufficient to stand up to the wood. Certainly those readers who prefer more oaky-styled wines would rate these wines more highly. In 1989 Rahoul was sold to Alain Thiènot, a wealthy property owner from Champagne.

The best recent vintage I have had of the red wine is the 1989. It had a big, smoky, black cherry aroma, medium body, and a soft, even exotic finish, although the alcohol was extremely noticeable and the acids suspiciously low.

I have not been impressed with the overwhelming amount of oak in the white wines. It is a detriment to both charm and finesse. Nevertheless, the 1988 tasted more balanced than many of the other vintages.

ROCHEMORIN (Unclassified) Pessac-Léognan　　　GOOD

Production: 9,000 cases red; 2,500 cases white	Grape varieties: Red: Cabernet Sauvignon—60% Merlot—40% White: Sauvignon—80% Semillon—20%
Secondary label: none Vineyard size: 104 acres Time spent in barrels: 15–18 months	Proprietor: André Lurton Average age of vines: 12 years
Evaluation of present classification: The quality equivalent of a Médoc Cru Bourgeois	
Plateau of maturity: red: 3–8 years following the vintage; white: 2–5 years following the vintage	

This is an up-and-coming estate in the commune of Martillac whose name is believed to have been taken from the Moorish expression for a fortified château. Many Graves observers feel the vineyard is one of the best placed of the appellation, sitting on high ground with superb drainage. The vineyard, however, remains relatively young as André Lurton, the dynamic empire builder in the Léognan area of Graves and Entre-Deux-Mers, only acquired the property in 1973. Lurton has replanted the vineyard, which had become covered with large trees.

Among recent vintages, I have been impressed with the tobacco, mineral, spicy, richly fruity character of all the red wines since 1985, made in the straightforward, commercial style that Lurton prefers. The white wines have been wonderfully delicate and light, extremely dry and aromatic, but still classic expressions of a white Graves in a more austere, flinty style. This should be a property to search out when looking for impeccably made wines at reasonable prices.

SMITH-HAUT-LAFITTE (Cru Classé) Pessac-Léognan AVERAGE

Production: 22,000 cases red; 3,000 cases white	Grape varieties: Red: Cabernet Sauvignon—70% Merlot—20% Cabernet Franc—10% White: Sauvignon—100%
Secondary label: Les Hauts-de-Smith-Haut-Lafitte	
Vineyard size: 126 acres	Proprietor: Louis Eschenauer
Time spent in barrels: 15 months	Average age of vines: 21 years
Evaluation of present classification: Should be downgraded; the quality equivalent of a Médoc Cru Bourgeois	
Plateau of maturity: red: 5–10 years following the vintage; white: 2–5 years following the vintage	

When tasting the wines of Smith-Haut-Lafitte I am always perplexed by why these wines are not better. The property was acquired by the large Bordeaux house of Eschenauer in 1958, and a major renovation and replanting of the vineyards was instituted. This was completed in the mid-1970s, and the beautiful eighteenth-century château now has one of the most user-friendly cellars in all of Bordeaux. Spacious and air-conditioned, it seems perfect for turning out high-quality wine. Nevertheless, despite the enormous progress made at the other Eschenauer estate of Rausan-Ségla in Margaux, Smith-Haut-Lafitte continues to stumble along. I should note that colleagues of mine in France claim that significant improvements have been made, but that has not been borne out in my tasting notes.

The white wines are certainly a better gamble than the relatively simple, straightforward, emaciated red wines. This remains an overrated and overpriced wine that could be improved immensely. At the time of writing, there werre unconfirmed reports of an imminent sale of this estate.

LA TOUR-HAUT-BRION (Cru Classé) Pessac-Léognan   GOOD

Production: 2,000 cases red	Grape varieties:
	Cabernet Sauvignon—85%
	Merlot—15%
Secondary label: none	
Vineyard size: 14.8 acres	Proprietors: Duc and Duchesse
	de Mouchy, Domaine
	Clarence Dillon
	Administrator: Jean Delmas
Time spent in barrels: 24 months	Average age of vines: 15 years

Evaluation of present classification: Since 1983, the quality equivalent of a Médoc fifth-growth; prior to 1983, the quality equivalent of a Médoc second-growth

Plateau of maturity: Since 1983, 5–10 years following the vintage; before 1983, 8–35 years following the vintage

La Tour-Haut-Brion was, until 1983, owned by the Woltner family, also the proprietors of La Mission-Haut-Brion. In 1983, these two properties, plus the white wine–producing Woltner property—Laville-Haut-Brion— were sold to the American owners of Haut-Brion.

The wines of La Tour-Haut-Brion up to 1983 were vinified at La Mission-Haut-Brion and handled identically. After both wines were completely finished with the secondary (or malolactic) fermentation, a selection process commenced in which the most promising barrels were chosen for the wine of La Mission-Haut-Brion, and the others reserved for La Tour-Haut-Brion. In vintages such as 1982 and 1975, the difference in quality between these two wines was negligible. To give La Tour-Haut-Brion a unique personality, the wine had more of the black/purple-colored, very tannic, press wine added to it than La Mission-Haut-Brion. The result was a wine with more size, tannin, color, and grip than even La Mission-Haut-Brion.

The addition of press wine caused most vintages of La Tour-Haut-Brion to evolve slowly. In a few vintages—notably 1973 and 1976—the wine turned out better than those of the more famous sibling.

Since the Dillon family and Jean Delmas assumed control of the wine-making, the style of La Tour-Haut-Brion has changed considerably. It is no longer the second wine of La Mission-Haut-Brion. Delmas has chosen to make La Tour-Haut-Brion in a lighter style from the property's own vineyards, which are now planted with relatively young vines. The result has been a less imposing, more supple wine that is significantly inferior to not only La Mission, but even to the second wine of Haut-Brion, Bahans-Haut-Brion. For admirers of the old beefy, muscular, brawny style of La Tour-Haut-Brion made before 1983, the new style must be not only disappointing, but a tragic loss. Nevertheless, it is drinkable at an earlier age, and therein, I suppose, lies the modern-day rationale.

VINTAGES

1989—The 1989 La Tour-Haut-Brion is the finest wine made during the
·   Delmas/Dillon era of ownership. Primarily a Cabernet Sauvi-
86   gnon–based wine (85% Cabernet, 15% Merlot), it exhibits plenty
      of ripeness, medium to full body, and a big, alcoholic, low-acid
      finish. Anticipated maturity: 1992–2000. Last tasted, 4/91.

1988—The 1988 has the telltale aggressive, hard tannins so prominent
·   in this vintage, good body, and persistence on the palate. Not
82   charming, but austere and forceful. Anticipated maturity: 1995–
      2003. Last tasted, 4/91.

1986—The 1986 has turned out to be a soft, supple, commercial wine
·   that lacks depth, dimension, and complexity. Anticipated matu-
82   rity: Now–1998. Last tasted, 11/90.

1985—The 1985 is good, but a little short, a trifle too tannic for the
·   amount of fruit present, and lacking length and excitement. An-
84   ticipated maturity: 1992–1998. Last tasted, 3/89.

1984—Relatively light for this property, the 1984 La Tour-Haut-Brion is
·   a straightforward, pleasant, fruity wine with some Graves char-
82   acter. It should be drunk up. Anticipated maturity: Now–1995.
      Last tasted, 3/88.

1983—A potentially good La Tour-Haut-Brion. However, it is lighter and
·   more supple in texture than previous vintages of this wine. The
84   1983 is a product of the different approach to winemaking em-
      ployed by the staff at Haut-Brion who controlled the vinification
      for the first time in this vintage. Good medium-to-dark ruby color,
      spicy, soft, supple, and very approachable, this wine should ma-
      ture fairly quickly. Anticipated maturity: Now–1996. Last tasted,
      3/89.

1982—Deep ruby/black in color, with a very intense blackcurrant, tarry,
·   earthy bouquet, the 1982 La Tour-Haut-Brion is a great success.
94   Rather massive on the palate, with great depth and concentration,
      full body, significant tannin content, and exceptional length, grip,
      and richness, this is a bigger, more tannic wine than its more
      famous sibling, La Mission-Haut-Brion. It is a great success

in this vintage. Anticipated maturity: 1993–2010. Last tasted, 1/91.

1981—The 1981 La Tour-Haut-Brion is a robust, aggressive, rather
   ·   tannic wine, with plenty of power and guts, but lacking finesse.
  85   The color is impressively dark, the weight of fruit and body on
         the palate considerable, but this is not a wine for Bordeaux enthu-
         siasts who want immediate gratification. Anticipated maturity:
         1993–2005. Last tasted, 3/88.

1980—Rather light, slightly bitter, and underendowed, the 1980 La Tour-
   ·   Haut-Brion has a smoky, earthy, interesting bouquet and straight-
  75   forward flavors. Anticipated maturity: Now–may be in decline.
         Last tasted, 4/83.

1979—Somewhat similar in style to the 1981, only less tannic, more open
   ·   knit and fruity, yet darkly colored, the 1979 La Tour-Haut-Brion
  85   has a spicy bouquet, and good weight, richness, medium to full
         body, and length on the palate. The bouquet is beginning to ma-
         ture, revealing earthy, Graves, smoky, mineral scents. This is an
         attractively forward La Tour-Haut-Brion which can be drunk now.
         Anticipated maturity: Now–1997. Last tasted, 10/84.

1978—After the great 1975 La Tour-Haut-Brion, the 1978 is certainly the
   ·   best wine from this property in the seventies. It is still dark ruby,
  93   with a rich, ripe blackcurrant, earthy, spicy, truffle-scented bou-
         quet of excellent intensity and penetration. On the palate, the
         wine is full bodied, still aggressively tannic, and rich, with
         an explosively long, concentrated finish. It is just beginning to
         open up and develop. This long-distance runner is one of the
         stars of the vintage. Anticipated maturity: 1993–2010. Last tasted,
         2/91.

1976—Clearly better than the diffuse and diluted La Mission-Haut-
   ·   Brion, yet really not very deep or complex for La Tour-Haut-
  80   Brion, this fully mature wine has an open-knit, smoky, earthy
         bouquet, soft, rather diffuse flavors, medium to full body, and a
         short, rather coarse finish. Anticipated maturity: Now–1992. Last
         tasted, 10/80.

1975—Along with the 1947, 1959, and 1961, this is the greatest La Tour-
   ·   Haut-Brion I have ever tasted. This magnificent wine has a bou-
  98   quet of great penetration, revealing intense, spicy, chocolate,
         earthy, tobacco, and truffle aromas. In the mouth, this big, ripe,
         rich wine explodes with layer upon layer of fruit. Massive in body
         and extract levels, with enormous potential, this is a monumental
         wine that will not be fully mature until 1995 or later. Anticipated
         maturity: 1995–2030. Last tasted, 2/91.

1974— Like the wine from sister château La Mission, La Tour-Haut-
· Brion is an unqualified success for the vintage. This is a robust,
83 somewhat rustic, unpolished, rich, hefty wine that lacks finesse,
 but delivers plenty of punch and taste. It is medium to full bodied,
 with good concentration. Anticipated maturity: Now—may be in
 decline. Last tasted, 7/82.

1971— More firm and tough than La Mission, with perhaps a little too
· much tannin and acidity for its own good, the 1971 La Tour-Haut-
84 Brion has now been mature for several years. A textbook mineral-
 scented, burnt-tobacco bouquet offers some interest. On the
 palate, the wine is medium to full bodied, a trifle austere and
 hard, but big and robust. Anticipated maturity: Now–1994. Last
 tasted, 2/83.

1970— Still impenetrably closed, broodingly dark in color, with little sign
· of maturity, this big, robust, hefty wine has tremendous power
87 and weight, but borders on being excessively tannic. Certainly,
 fanciers of massive, tannic wines will want to have some of this
 wine in their collection. Will it ever develop any finesse or charm?
 Anticipated maturity: 1995–2020. Last tasted, 2/91.

1966— Fully mature, with the telltale dark ruby, dense color of La Tour-
· Haut-Brion, punctuated only slightly by amber, this big, rich,
88 spicy wine has a voluptuous bouquet of rich fruit, and earthy,
 tobacco aromas. On the palate, it is less massive than some La
 Tour-Haut-Brions, and has more finesse and overall balance. It is
 a very attractive Graves. Anticipated maturity: Now–1993. Last
 tasted, 3/81.

1961— Only tasted once, the 1961 La Tour-Haut-Brion exhibited remark-
· able concentration and richness, and seemed to have a full 20
95 years of life ahead of it. Very dark in color, with just a touch of
 amber, this big, chewy, viscous wine had an opulent and exotic
 bouquet of ripe currants, cinnamon, tobacco, and truffles. Massively proportioned, with layers of fruit, and oodles of tannin still
 present, the 1961 La Tour-Haut-Brion was a gustatory tour de
 force. Anticipated maturity: Now–2030. Last tasted, 3/79.

OLDER VINTAGES

I would love to have come across more examples of old vintages of La
Tour-Haut-Brion, as those that I have tasted were extraordinary in quality. The 1947 (rated 95 in 1990) was magnificently rich, but the volatile
acidity may put off purists. It possessed huge quantities of fruit, as well
as a chewy, even viscous texture. It is a great wine that should continue
to drink well for another decade. The other two great vintages of La

Tour-Haut-Brion I have had an opportunity to taste include a massive, still backward and frightfully young 1959. I last had this wine at the restaurant Clavel in 1988, and the wine was still black/purple in color and at least a decade away from maturity. I rated it 92, but I am sure that when this wine has reached its apogee, it will merit a higher score. Lastly, the 1955 (rated 94 in 1990), while not having quite the blockbuster bouquet of its sibling—the 1955 La Mission—is still an enormously concentrated, chewy, old-style Graves that should continue to last for a minimum of two more decades. It is a shame that La Tour-Haut-Brion is no longer made in this style, but shrewd buyers at auctions are well advised to seek out top vintages of old La Tour-Haut-Brion that may show up from time to time.

LA TOUR-MARTILLAC (Cru Classé) Pessac-Léognan   GOOD

Production: 10,000 cases red; 3,000 cases white	Grape varieties: Red: Cabernet Sauvignon—60% Merlot—25% Cabernet Franc—6% Malbec—5% Petit Verdot—4% White: Semillon—60% Sauvignon—30% Mixed—10%
Secondary label: La Grave-Martillac	
Vineyard size: 62 acres	Proprietor: Jean Kressmann
Time spent in barrels: 12–16 months	Average age of vines: 30 years
Evaluation of present classification: The red wine is the quality equivalent of a Médoc Cru Bourgeois; the white wine, since 1987, is excellent and merits its status as a Graves Cru Classé	
Plateau of maturity: red: 5–10 years following the vintage; white: 3–7 years following the vintage	

By the standards of other Graves properties, La Tour-Martillac is not an old estate, as the history of the vineyard traces only to the mid-nineteenth century. However, it has been owned by one of Bordeaux's most famous families, the Kressmanns, since 1930, and is now managed by Jean Kressmann.

The white wine has exhibited remarkable improvement since the 1987 vintage, and now has become one of the most profound white Graves. Unfortunately, the same cannot be said for the red wine. It continues to represent a straightforward, mediocre wine that usually has some correct cherry fruit. Even in opulent vintages such as 1982 and 1989, it has a compact, simple, undistinguished character. I know of no recent red wine vintages that did not require consumption within the first 7–8 years of their life.

VINTAGES

White Wines

1989— While the 1989 is not so concentrated as the 1987 or 1988, it still
·   possesses an immensely attractive lemony, grassy, oaky nose,
88   medium-bodied, soft, richly fruity flavors, and good length. It will not have extended aging potential given the low acidity, but it already provides great enjoyment. Anticipated maturity: Now– 1995. Last tasted, 4/91.

1988— This is an authoritative example of how delicious and complex a
·   fine white Graves can be. The honeysuckle, spicy, melony, fig-
90   like nose exhibits just enough oak to provide definition and complexity. In the mouth, the wine is medium bodied, long, and rich, with excellent focus, and a surprisingly fresh, yet full-bodied, intense finish. Anticipated maturity: Now–1998. Last tasted, 2/91.

1987— As I have said so many times, 1987 was an excellent year for
·   white Graves, although many observers dismissed the vintage,
88   preferring to see things in black-and-white terms. This honeyed, herbaceous, smoky-scented white Graves has wonderfully precise, rich flavors, medium body, and a lush, long, zesty finish. Anticipated maturity: Now–1995. Last tasted, 1/91.

THE WINES OF POMEROL

The smallest of the great red wine districts of Bordeaux, Pomerol produces some of the most expensive, exhilarating, and glamorous wines in the world. Yet Pomerol, whose wines are in such demand that they must be severely allocated, remains the only major appellation of Bordeaux

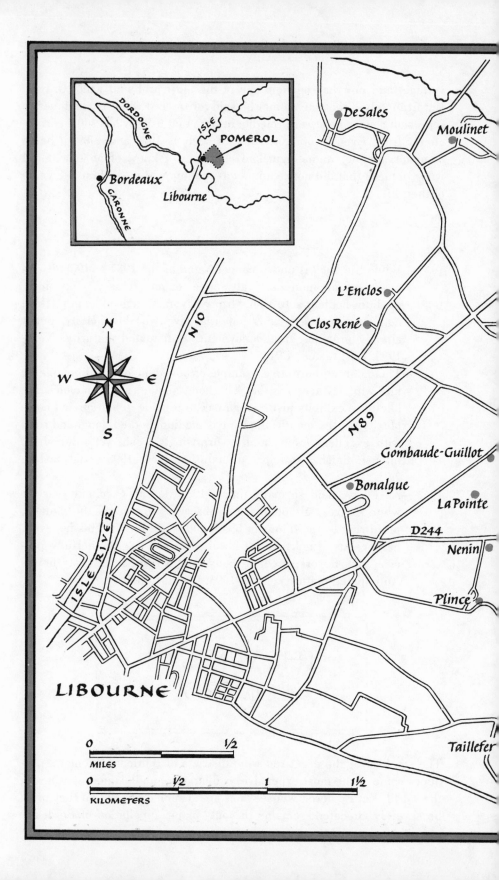

DORDOGNE

ISLE

POMEROL

CARONNE

Bordeaux

Libourne

De Sales

Moulinet

L'Enclos

Clos René

N10

N89

Gombaude-Guillot

Bonalgue

La Pointe

D244

Nenin

Plince

N
W E
S

ISLE RIVER

LIBOURNE

Taillefer

0   ½
MILES

0   ½   1   1½
KILOMETERS

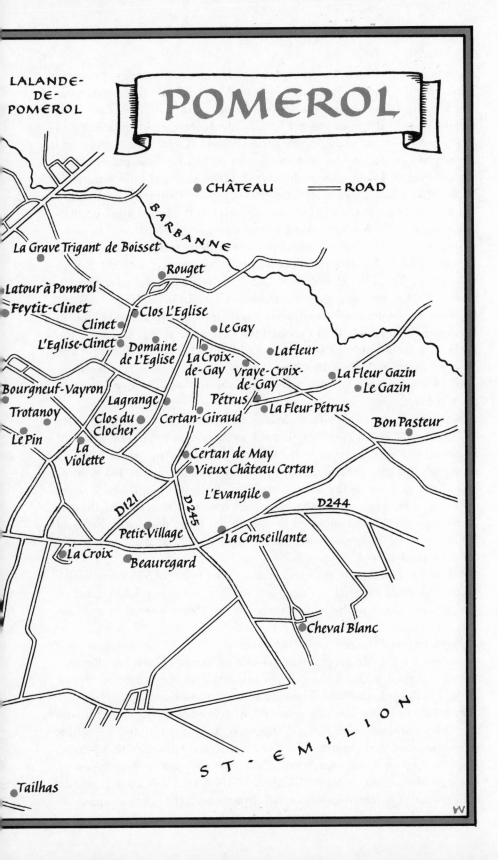

never to have had its wines formally placed in a rigid hierarchy of quality. When members of the Bordeaux wine trade established the now-famous and historic 1855 Classification of the Wines of the Gironde, they completely ignored Pomerol and St.-Emilion, both some eighteen miles east of Bordeaux on the right bank of the Gironde River. These areas had developed reputations for high-quality wine, but because travel across the Gironde to Libourne was difficult (bridges were not built until after 1820), St.-Emilion and Pomerol developed most of their trade with northern France, Belgium, and Holland. In contrast, the larger wine-producing estates in the Médoc worked through brokers in Bordeaux. In many cases, these firms, called *négociants*, were run by transplanted English, as well as Irish, families that relied on existing contacts with the British wine trade. The 1855 classification was, in essence, a short list of well-known Médoc estates, plus the famous Haut-Brion in Graves. Why? Because these chateaux traditionally sold most of their production to Bordeaux brokers who then exported the wine to England. And since the brokers, who did little or no business with the châteaux of Pomerol and St.-Emilion until the late 1860s, were responsible for the 1855 classification, they were ignorant—or worse, self-serving—when they classified the top five-dozen or so châteaux of the Bordeaux region.

Since 1855, the wines of St.-Emilion have been classified three times —first in 1954, with revisions in 1969 and again in 1985. The wines of Pomerol, however, have never been classified. This is surprising because they began to gain great popularity and notoriety in the late 1940s, after being highly touted by the well-known English wine buyer, Harry Waugh, who was then working for the respected house of Harvey's in Bristol. Their reputation has continued to soar to the point that many Pomerol wines are now in greater demand than some of the most celebrated Médocs and Graves.

While St.-Emilion covers an enormous area (with 12,350 acres under vine), Pomerol, its northern neighbor, is tiny, with only 1,830 acres of vineyards—less than the total acreage for the Médoc's smallest appellation, St.-Julien.

To understand the success of the wines of Pomerol, one must take into consideration the Merlot grape (the dominant varietal of the appellation), the changing drinking habits of consumers, and the influence of and empire built by Jean-Pierre Moueix and his son, Christian.

First, there is the Merlot grape, which, according to the INAO (Institute National des Appellations d'Origines), accounts for 70–75% of the grapes planted in Pomerol. The Cabernet Franc follows with 20–25%, and the Cabernet Sauvignon with 5%. No other major appellation of Bordeaux has as much Merlot planted. Merlot-based wines are generally softer, more opulently and obviously fruity and lush, lower in apparent tannin, and higher in alcohol than wines based primarily on the Cabernet Sauvignon grape.

Second, many modern-day consumers (and restaurants, too) seek wines that can be drunk at a younger age, so the wines of Pomerol have a ready-and-waiting audience. Most Pomerols tend to be ready to drink within 4–6 years of the vintage. Yet despite the early maturation of these Pomerols, the top wines retain their fruit and evolve extremely well, frequently lasting 15–25 years.

Third, no other wine region in France owes its success to a single individual more than Pomerol does to Jean-Pierre Moueix. In 1930, when he was in his early twenties, Jean-Pierre Moueix arrived in Libourne from France's Corrèze region, a desolate section of the Massif Central. He was regarded as an outcast by the aristocratic blue bloods who traded in Médoc château wines on the famous riverfront street called the Quai de Chartrons. Moueix turned east to the viticultural areas the Bordeaux brokers considered an afterthought—Pomerol and St.-Emilion. His timing and luck were bad, however, for in the early thirties the world was in the midst of a depression, not to fully emerge until after World War II. Yet, prior to the war, the young Moueix was smart enough to realize that the historic market for top Bordeaux—England—was off limits to him. That trade was dominated by the brokers of the Quai des Chartrons, but no one there paid much attention to the wines of Pomerol. Moueix began by setting up a small merchant business and traveling regularly to northern Europe—Brittany, Belgium, and Holland—where he found enthusiastic buyers for his Pomerols. By 1937 he had established a *négociant* business in Libourne, the commercial town that today serves as Pomerol's port of entry. In the post–World War II years he purchased three properties in Pomerol—Trotanoy, Lagrange, and La Fleur Pétrus—and where he was unable to buy a property, he arranged to be the exclusive selling agent for that estate's wine.

In 1964 Moueix finally realized his dream and purchased a 50% interest in a vineyard he'd long coveted. The vineyard was called Pétrus. Moueix believed it was producing as great a wine as any of the first-growths in Bordeaux. In spite of Moueix's enthusiasm, Pétrus was not yet well known in established wine circles. That would soon change.

Throughout the fifties and sixties, Moueix was a tireless crusader (some would say an inexhaustible promoter) for the wines of Pomerol. His spectacular rise to a leadership position in Pomerol and his achievement of great wealth was, in short, accomplished by working extremely hard and producing exceptional wines, particularly at his two flagship châteaux, Pétrus and Trotanoy. In the sixties and early seventies these two wines often surpassed the first-growths of the Médoc in qualitative terms.

The extraordinary rise to prominence of both Moueix and his wines brought Pomerol attention and prestige that did not go unnoticed by other producers in this bucolic appellation. As a result, other properties began to upgrade the quality of their wines. Today, while no one can challenge the domination that Jean-Pierre Moueix's firm enjoys over the sale of the wines of Pomerol, there is an increasing number of challengers to the previously uncontested superiority of Pétrus.

The most celebrated Pomerol châteaux are located on the plateau of Pomerol. Pétrus sits on the highest elevation, and most of its 28.4 acres benefit from a soil base that is largely clay; the surrounding prestigious neighbors have much more gravel. To the south of Pétrus are La Fleur Pétrus, Certan de May, Vieux Château Certan, La Conseillante, and L'Evangile. Immediately to the west are Lafleur, L'Eglise-Clinet, and La Croix de Gay. Yet while these vineyards' deep, gravelly soils (which also contain some clay) are excellent for both the Merlot and Cabernet Franc grapes, only Pétrus is planted with 95% Merlot and 5% Cabernet Franc. Other Pomerol properties, recognizing the fact that Cabernet grape varieties, especially Cabernet Franc, are well suited for this soil, plant somewhat higher percentages of Cabernet Franc.

Heading west, toward the end of the plateau of Pomerol, where Trotanoy and Le Pin are located, the soils become even more full of gravel. Properties in this locale often excel in wet vintages because of the superb drainage provided by these deep beds. Farther west, in the direction of Route National N89 (connecting Libourne and Bordeaux), the soil changes to a mixture of gravel and sand, then to a light sandy, flint-based soil. These areas cannot support the production of great wine, but many soft, fruity, extremely pleasant and supple Pomerols are made here. However, even the best of these wines will never have the strength, aging potential, or richness of the Pomerols from the gravel and gravel/clay/iron–based soils of the plateau.

For those familiar with the Médoc and Graves regions of Bordeaux, Pomerol—with its limited acreage and modest farmhouse "châteaux"—must come as a surprise. Pétrus itself is a remarkably humble building that truly stretches the definition of "château" to the limit. The appellation's largest estate, de Sales, is 117 acres in size, and is the only Pomerol property to have a building that could be said to resemble a great Médoc château. The other three sizable vineyards of Pomerol are Nenin and Taillefer (both 61.75 acres), and La Pointe (49.4 acres). Not one of these three estates, however, could be accused of being in the top league of quality. Most of the best Pomerol vineyards encompass between 22.4 acres and 34 acres, but many are much smaller. For example three current Pomerol superstars are true micro-estates. Lafleur (11.5

acres), Certan de May (12.3 acres), and L'Eglise-Clinet (14.8 acres) could sell their entire production within the Bordeaux city limits if they desired.

What are the telltale characteristic traits of Pomerol wines? The ruby color. The intense, plummy, sometimes truffle-and-mocha-scented but always ripe, fruity bouquet. A lush, voluptuous, almost unctuous texture. All are a result of the Merlot grape.

As for the styles of wine produced in Pomerol, generally these are Bordeaux's most gentle, smooth, silky, lush, and richly fruity wines. However, that does not explain the diversity of styles that can be found; the individual producers do. The overall quality of winemaking in Pomerol is extremely high. Only in the Médoc appellation of St.-Julien is there as brilliant an overall level of talented winemakers.

Pétrus is frequently this appellation's greatest wine, as well as the most massively concentrated, rich, and long-lived. The heavy clay soil that the vineyard of Pétrus sits on results in a powerful wine. Yet until the early eighties Trotanoy was often indistinguishable from Pétrus in blind tastings and was clearly the most complete and demanded Pomerol after Pétrus. Not surprisingly, Pétrus is made from 95% Merlot and Trotanoy 90%, and they are treated identically by the same winemaking team. The other Pomerol that has always rivaled, and in many vintages eclipsed, Pétrus, but is terribly obscure, is the tiny estate of Lafleur. Interestingly, Lafleur's vineyard sits adjacent to that of Pétrus on the plateau, and it, too, has extremely old vines that render small quantities of very concentrated, exotically flavored, highly structured grape juice.

If Pétrus, Trotanoy, and Lafleur have traditionally made Pomerol's richest, deepest-colored, most-massive wines, L'Evangile, La Conseillante, Petit-Village, La Fleur Pétrus, and L'Eglise-Clinet produce this appellation's most graceful, smooth, elegant, burgundian-like wine. None of these properties can lay claim to making as massive or as rich a wine as Pétrus, Trotanoy, or Lafleur, but no Pomerol enthusiast would dare pass up the opportunity to lay away a few bottles or cases of any of these wines.

L'Evangile and La Conseillante have two of Pomerol's greatest reputations, but have been irregular performers. La Conseillante was a notorious underachiever during much of the sixties and seventies, but came on strong in the eighties, making some of the greatest wines in its famed history. The 1981, 1982, 1983, 1985, 1989, and 1990 are decadently hedonistic wines. L'Evangile has also been inconsistent. But when it makes great wines, they rival the best that can be produced by Pétrus, Trotanoy, or Lafleur. L'Evangile made spectacular wines in 1975, 1982, 1983, 1985, 1989, and 1990. Given the fact that a major interest in

L'Evangile was acquired by the Rothschild family (of Lafite-Rothschild) in 1989, this property could soon challenge Pétrus, both in quality and price; the dreamy 1990 is a case in point.

La Fleur Pétrus has the right name for fame, yet it rarely seems to produce wines at a level its name suggests it could. It is a very good rather than superb Pomerol, velvety, quick to mature, yet elegant and graceful.

Petit-Village, until recently, lacked the meticulous care and concern that comes from a committed proprietor. This potentially great vineyard began to make great wines in the late 1970s under the guidance of Bruno Prats. Prats then sold the property in the late eighties, and Petit-Village has now continued to soar in quality, with superb vintages in 1982, 1985, 1988, and 1989.

Since the release of their great 1985, L'Eglise-Clinet has been a more recent rising superstar of the appellation. Possessed with some of Pomerol's oldest vines, this traditionally run property produces an explosively fruity, densely colored Pomerol that always seems to taste like the essence of black fruits and minerals. Significantly, it is one of the few tiny Pomerol estates to employ a second wine for vats considered not rich enough for the grand vin.

A third style of Pomerol wine might also be called the "Médoc" style. Two Pomerol estates, Vieux Château Certan and Clos L'Eglise, do indeed make a wine with a high percentage of Cabernet Sauvignon and Cabernet Franc (rather than Merlot), and their wines often have more Médoc-like characteristics than other Pomerols. Vieux Château Certan has the greater reputation of the two and in the nineteenth century and first half of the twentieth century was considered the greatest Pomerol of all. However, this property's wines passed through an uninspired period in the sixties and seventies that resulted in a decline in their reputation. That has all been reversed since the 1982 vintage.

A fourth school of Pomerols produces wines that are light, supple, and offer immediate drinking. These wines rarely last more than a decade, but they do provide considerable value in an appellation whose wines are fetching higher and higher prices. Most of these Pomerols are located in the western part of the area on light, sandy soils. None of them have great reputations, but several of these estates, particularly L'Enclos, Clos René, and de Sales, make complete wines that satisfy the palate, the purse, and the impatient.

There are numerous other Pomerols, and perhaps the greatest story of the eighties was the emergence of such potential superstar estates as Certan de May, Clinet, La Fleur de Gay, and Le Pin.

La Fleur de Gay was inaugurated in the 1982 vintage by Dr. Alain

Raynaud, the proprietor of the well-known Pomerol château, La Croix de Gay. It is very unusual in Bordeaux to see a proprietor take a parcel of his very best vines (in this case a plot of 100% Merlot located near Pétrus and Lafleur) and make a separate wine from it. However, La Fleur de Gay, aged in 100% new oak casks, is a wine of astonishing richness and exotic superripeness. One sip of the 1989, 1988, 1987, 1986, 1985, or 1983 will make anyone a believer. Only 1,000 cases are produced, but this is a wine that rivals Pétrus.

Clinet was another perennial underachiever until 1985, when the son-in-law of the proprietor, Jean-Michel Arcaute, assumed management of the property. In a remarkably short time, Clinet shed a cloak of mediocrity and started to produce wines that are among the most complex and profoundly concentrated of the appellation. This would now appear to be one of the titans of Pomerol, capable of challenging the very best. At the time of writing (June 1991) Clinet was sold to a large French corporation, raising speculation about its future.

The other superstar to emerge during the last decade is the micro-estate of Le Pin. This wine, made from a tiny vineyard that is nearly 100% Merlot, is perhaps the most extraordinarily perfumed, hedonistic, kinky wine in all of Bordeaux. The proprietors, the Thienpont family, have clearly decided to make a wine in the image of Pétrus, even more exotic. The only question concerning Le Pin is how well it will age.

Other top-flight Pomerols include Latour à Pomerol, which has made some legendary wines (1947 and 1961), and Bon Pasteur, an estate run by one of the most gifted oenologists in Bordeaux, Michel Rolland.

All things considered, Pomerol has fewer underachievers today than it did a decade ago. Nevertheless, there is no question that some of the larger properties, such as Nenin, Taillefer, and La Pointe, could make better wines. It is a shame they don't, since they are large vineyards by Pomerol standards and could provide a good introduction to the rich, fleshy, hedonistic wines of this appellation.

A CONSUMER'S CLASSIFICATION OF THE CHÂTEAUX OF POMEROL

OUTSTANDING

La Conseillante
Lafleur
La Fleur de Gay
Pétrus
Le Pin

Certan de May
Clinet
L'Eglise-Clinet
L'Evangile
Latour à Pomerol
Petit-Village
Trotanoy
Vieux-Château-Certan

VERY GOOD

Bon Pasteur, Certan-Giraud, La Croix de Gay, Domaine de L'Eglise,
L'Enclos, La Fleur Pétrus, Le Gay, Gombaude-Guillot, La Grave
Trigant de Boisset

GOOD

Bellegrave, Bonalgue, Clos du Clocher, Clos René, La Croix, La Croix
du Casse, Gazin, Haut-Maillet, Rouget, de Sales, La Violette,
Vraye-Croix-de-Gay

OTHER NOTABLE POMEROL PROPERTIES

Beauregard, Bourgneuf-Vayron, La Cabanne, Clos L'Eglise, Feytit-
Clinet, La Fleur Gazin, Lafleur du Roy, Lagrange, Mazeyres, Moulinet,
Nenin, Nouvelle Eglise, Plince, La Pointe, Prieurs de la Commanderie,
Tailhas, Taillefer

BEAUREGARD (Unclassified)   AVERAGE

Production: 5,500 cases	Grape varieties:
	Merlot—48%
	Cabernet Franc—44%
	Cabernet Sauvignon—6%
	Malbec—2%
Secondary label: Domaine des Douves	Proprietor: Crédit Foncier de France
Vineyard size: 32.1 acres	Administrator: The Clauzel family
Time spent in barrels: 18–20 months	Average age of vines: 20 years
Evaluation of present classification: The quality equivalent of a Médoc Cru Bourgeois	
Plateau of maturity: 3–12 years following the vintage	

As one leaves the tiny village of Catusseau, the vineyards of Beauregard are situated on the southern perimeter of the plateau of Pomerol. This is one of the few properties in the appellation that actually has a building grand enough to be called a château. The vineyard has significant potential. Most Pomerol observers consider the deep, gravelly soil to be ideal for producing high-quality wine. Until the mid-1980s, most of the vintages produced quick-to-age, rustic wines. Since then, administrator Paul Clauzel has been making finer wine, with better color and more ripeness and concentration. Moreover, greater attention is also being paid to sanitary conditions in the cellar. Despite the improvements, the quality of Beauregard's wines still places it well behind the top Pomerols. The Clauzel family sold the property in 1991 to Crédit Foncier de France.

BELLEGRAVE (Unclassified) GOOD

Production: 3,000 cases	Grape varieties:
	Merlot—55%
	Cabernet Franc—30%
	Cabernet Sauvignon—10%
	Malbec—5%
Secondary label: none	
Vineyard size: 14.8 acres	Proprietor: Jean Bouldy
Time spent in barrels: 18–20 months	Average age of vines: 22 years
Evaluation of present classification: The quality equivalent of a Médoc Cru Bourgeois	
Plateau of maturity: 3–8 years following the vintage	

The Bellegrave vineyard, located west of RN 89, on light, sandy, gravelly soil, produces soft, easy-to-drink, and easy-to-understand wines that must be consumed in their youth. It would appear that the proprietor, Jean Bouldy, has a sensible view of what he is able to achieve in one of the less-promising soil types of Pomerol. The results are cleanly made, fresh, fruity wines with mass appeal.

VINTAGES

1989—The 1989 Bellegrave is exceptionally low in acidity and very alcoholic. For those who like their wines fat, ripe, plummy, and
84 obvious, this straightforward, chunky, yet well-endowed Pomerol will provide delicious drinking early on. Anticipated maturity: Now–1997. Last tasted, 11/90.

1988—The 1988 is lighter styled, but manifests the same emphasis on
·   straightforward, ripe, tasty fruit in a medium-bodied, easy-to-
82   appreciate style. Anticipated maturity: Now–1995. Last tasted,
    11/90.

1985—I found the 1985 Bellegrave attractively sweet, plummy, soft,
·   medium bodied, and ideal for current drinking. Anticipated
83   maturity: Now–1994. Last tasted, 3/90.

BON PASTEUR (Unclassified)   VERY GOOD

Production: 3,500 cases	Grape varieties: Merlot—90% Cabernet Franc—10%
Secondary label: none	
Vineyard size: 17.3 acres	Proprietor: Michel Rolland
Time spent in barrels: 18–20 months	Average age of vines: 40 years
Evaluation of present classification: The quality equivalent of a Médoc fourth- or fifth-growth	
Plateau of maturity: 5–14 years following the vintage	

Bon Pasteur is the property of one of Bordeaux's most gifted oenologists,
Michel Rolland. Rolland, along with his highly talented wife, Dany—who
is also an oenologist—has a laboratory in Libourne. Additionally, he
boasts a list of clients that reads like a Who's Who of Pomerol, St.-
Emilion, and the other major appellations of Bordeaux, and he has been
directly responsible for the turnaround in quality of many estates.

Michel Rolland's success, as well as the formation of an association of
Pomerol estates called the Circle of Prestige of Pomerol, has given rise
to two prevailing schools of thought about harvest dates and winemaking
philosophies. One school—represented by the firm of Jean-Pierre
Moueix and its two leading spokespeople, Christian Moueix and their
oenologist, Jean-Claude Berrouet—believes that the Merlot grape should
not be picked too late. Their argument is that early harvesting is essential
to preserve the wine's acidity. Furthermore, Moueix and Berrouet believe in shorter maceration periods to give the wines more elegance.

In contrast, Michel Rolland and his colleagues believe in harvesting as
late as possible in order to obtain fruit that has an element of *sur-maturité*
(over-ripeness). Rolland also believes in extended macerations to produce wines of profound color, richness, and aging potential.

There is no doubt that Rolland's philosophy has caught the fancy of
some of France's leading writers, particularly the outspoken Parisian,

Michel Bettane, probably Europe's finest taster and wine critic. He is a solid defender of Rolland, who he believes possesses the philosophy necessary to produce extraordinary wines. Interestingly, two of Rolland's clients, Clinet and La Fleur de Gay, are now turning out wines that compete with Pétrus.

The Bon Pasteur vineyard is not one of the best situated in Pomerol. The 17-plus acres are spread out in northeast Pomerol, near the village of Maillet. There are essentially two soil types, a gravel and clay-based one, as well as lighter, deep gravel beds. Because of the extremely old vines, late picking, long maceration, and the use of 50% new oak, Rolland gets as much out of his vineyard as is possible. He made extraordinary wines in vintages such as 1982 and 1988. It is important to remember that Bon Pasteur's wines have only been estate-bottled since 1978.

VINTAGES

1989—The brilliant Libourne oenologist, Michel Rolland, fervently be-
·   lieves his 1989 is this estate's finest wine since 1982. In the first
88   6–8 months after the vintage, I thought it to be in a very awkward,
clumsy period, revealing very little bouquet, plenty of size, power, and alcohol, but a flat, roasted character. Fortunately, it picked up structure in late 1990 and now appears to be a fine, potentially outstanding Bon Pasteur. Very rich, opulent, and intense, with a huge, smoky, plum-like bouquet, this full-bodied, soft, and seductive wine should be drunk young. Anticipated maturity: Now–2001. Last tasted, 4/91.

1988—The 1988 is a sure bet. Deep, opaque dark ruby (darker than the
·   1989), with a huge bouquet of chocolate, plums, currants, and
89   herbs, this full-bodied, admirably extracted wine should prove to
have considerable longevity. Anticipated maturity: 1994–2010. Last tasted, 4/91.

1986—The 1986 Bon Pasteur is excellent. Proprietor Rolland is one of
·   the few producers with a significant percentage of Merlot planted
87   in his vineyard (90%) who was able to achieve a better wine in
1986 than in 1985. The 1986 has a deep ruby color, a forceful, big, rich, toasty, plummy bouquet, and luscious medium- to full-bodied flavors backed up by some sizable tannins. It should be ready to drink relatively soon, but last for well over a decade. Anticipated maturity: 1992–2000. Last tasted, 3/90.

1985—The 1985 is ready to drink, soft, fruity, medium bodied, but lack-
·   ing the concentration and structure of the top years. Anticipated
84   maturity: Now–1995. Last tasted, 3/90.

1984—Quite acceptable, the 1984 Bon Pasteur is one of the better Pom-
·   erols of the vintage. Moderately deep in color and extract, this
80   plummy wine displays what brilliant winemaker Michel Rolland
       can do in a terrible vintage. Anticipated maturity: Now–1997.
       Last tasted, 3/90.

1983—The 1983 Bon Pasteur is a richly fruity wine, with a lovely per-
·   fumed bouquet of blackcurrants. Supple, lush, and precocious,
85   this medium-bodied wine is drinking well. Anticipated maturity:
       Now–1996. Last tasted, 3/90.

1982—In retrospect, the 1982 Bon Pasteur was a turning point for the
·   career of Michel Rolland, now recognized as one of Libourne's
94   legitimate superstars because of his exceptional palate and re-
       markable oenological skills. It was in this vintage that he made
       one of the great wines of Pomerol. As a result, it brought attention
       not only to Rolland, but to those properties for which he consults
       in Pomerol and St.-Emilion. The 1982 Bon Pasteur possesses an
       absolutely remarkable concentration of ripe, plummy, chocola-
       tey, fleshy fruit, an immense bouquet of ripe berries and toffee,
       and dazzling length. Although many good Bon Pasteurs have been
       made, there has been nothing to compare with this remarkable
       1982, when this property clearly achieved something well beyond
       what observers consider its finest potential. Amazingly, the wine
       has changed little from cask, seeming only to become richer and
       more complex from an aromatic point of view. Anticipated matu-
       rity: Now–2005. Last tasted, 1/91.

1981—Supple, richly fruity, elegant, spicy, and soft, this medium-bodied
·   wine has a jammy, mocha-flavored blackcurrant fruitiness, a har-
85   monious, lush texture, and immediate accessibility. It is fully
       mature. Anticipated maturity: Now–1994. Last tasted, 12/90.

1980—Very well made in this difficult vintage, the 1980 Bon Pasteur is a
·   soft, medium-weight wine with good ripeness, and a savory, mel-
82   low personality. Anticipated maturity: Now–may be in decline.
       Last tasted, 6/84.

1979—The 1979 Bon Pasteur has always lacked the generous, ripe,
·   richly fruity character I enjoy and associate so much with the
78   wine from this estate. While well made, it remains austere and a
       little lean. Anticipated maturity: Now–1992. Last tasted, 6/84.

1978—A successful 1978, the Bon Pasteur has a caramel, toasty, herb,
·   and coffee-scented bouquet. The wine is amply endowed, rich,
86   and concentrated, with layers of ripe Merlot fruit, and a long
       alcoholic, lush finish. It is one of the top Pomerols of this vintage.
       Anticipated maturity: Now–1993. Last tasted, 1/90.

BONALGUE (Unclassified)   GOOD

Production: 2,000 cases	Grape varieties:
	Merlot—65%
	Cabernet Franc—30%
	Malbec—5%
Secondary label: Burgrave	
Vineyard size: 12.5 acres	Proprietor: Pierre Bourotte
Time spent in barrels: 16–22 months	Average age of vines: 20 years
Evaluation of present classification: The quality equivalent of a Médoc Cru Bourgeois	
Plateau of maturity: 4–10 years following the vintage	

Bonalgue remains a relatively obscure Pomerol, but the quality is consistently sound, and in top vintages, very good. The vineyard, situated on a mixture of gravelly and sandy soil, just at the entrance of Libourne, behind the racetrack on RN 89, turns out deeply colored, chunky, fleshy wines that lack complexity, but not character, fruit, or mouth-filling pleasure.

VINTAGES

1989—The 1989 is not far behind the 1982. Deep ruby/purple, with an
·   obvious yet enticing bouquet of sweet, plump blackberries, this
85   lush, deceptively easy, generously endowed wine goes down the
      throat far too easily for its 13+% alcohol content. It will not be
      long-lived. Anticipated maturity: Now–1996. Last tasted, 4/91.

1988—The 1988 has more tannin than the 1989, is spicy and harder in
·   style, but has still managed to retain Bonalgue's rich black fruit
83   character. It is a medium-bodied wine that should be at its best
      between 1992 and 1998. Anticipated maturity: 1992–1998. Last
      tasted, 4/91.

1986—The 1986 is a bit light and less impressive than I had hoped but
·   offers straightforward, plummy fruit that displays decent extract
82   and a soft, smooth finish. Drink this wine over the next 3–4 years.
      Anticipated maturity: Now–1996. Last tasted, 3/90.

1985—The 1985 displays a healthy dosage of toasty new oak and has
·   lush, medium-bodied flavors that are packed with berry fruit, and
85   soft tannins in the finish. Anticipated maturity: Now–1995. Last
      tasted, 3/89.

1984—Quite spicy and robust, but a little coarse and charmless, the
·   1984 Bonalgue should drink decently for 2–4 more years. Antici-
78   pated maturity: Now–1993. Last tasted, 3/88.

BOURGNEUF-VAYRON (Unclassified)   AVERAGE

Production: 6,500 cases	Grape varieties: Merlot—85% Cabernet Franc—15%
Secondary label: none	
Vineyard size: 25 acres	Proprietors: Charles and Xavier Vayron
Time spent in barrels: 18–24 months	Average age of vines: 22 years
Evaluation of present classification: The quality equivalent of a Médoc Cru Bourgeois	
Plateau of maturity: 5–10 years following the vintage	

Given the well-situated position of Bourgneuf's vineyard in the center of the appellation, on the plateau just to the west of Trotanoy, it has always puzzled me why higher-quality wines do not emerge from this estate. The production yields are reasonable, and when talking to the proprietors, it is clear that they pay a great deal of respect to a traditional vinification. All of this is perplexing, because what I continue to taste are monolithic, one-dimensional wines, with a great deal of body and tannin, but an absence of underlying elegance, finesse, and what is subjectively called "breed." This is an ancient estate, and while there remains vast potential for exquisite wine, the quality level is, lamentably, mediocre.

VINTAGES

1989—Bourgneuf's 1989 is a chunky, ripe, foursquare style of wine that
·   has abundant quantities of fruit, good body, and soft tannins in
84   its alcoholic finish. Anticipated maturity: 1992–1998. Last tasted,
     4/91.

1988—The 1988 lacks the fruit and heady qualities of the 1989, but is a
·   respectable, straightforward, medium-bodied Pomerol. Antici-
82   pated maturity: Now–1997. Last tasted, 4/91.

1986—The 1986 Bourgneuf displays a judicious use of spicy, toasty oak,
·   a lovely supple, fleshy fruitiness, and good length. This is a
84   straightforward-styled wine. Anticipated maturity: Now–1995.
     Last tasted, 3/90.

1985—The 1985 is typical of this estate. It is thick, plummy, foursquare,
·   but essentially simple and grapey. Anticipated maturity: Now–
82   1995. Last tasted, 3/89.

LA CABANNE (Unclassified) AVERAGE

Production: 5,000 cases	Grape varieties: Merlot—80% Cabernet Franc—20%
Secondary label: Compostelle	
Vineyard size: 25 acres	Proprietor: Jean-Pierre Estager
Time spent in barrels: 18–22 months	Average age of vines: 22 years
Evaluation of present classification: The quality equivalent of a Médoc Cru Bourgeois	
Plateau of maturity: 5–12 years following the vintage	

La Cabanne is run by one of the great gentlemen of Pomerol, Jean-Pierre Estager. In addition to owning Château La Cabanne, he also owns property in Montagne-St.-Emilion (Château La Papeterie), and leases another estate in Pomerol (Château Haut-Maillet). La Cabanne, whose sizable production is distributed internationally, represents a solidly made, plump Pomerol that offers rustic aromas of dusty, cedary, plummy fruit, followed by a generous, yet often coarse texture that can lack finesse and be overcharged with tannin. Nevertheless, if never dazzling, it is a reliably made wine that can stand the test of time. The vineyard is highly morsellated, but the château itself is situated in the heart of Pomerol, not far from the famed Château Trotanoy.

VINTAGES

1989—La Cabanne tends to produce ready-to-drink, easygoing, lighter-
· styled Pomerols. The 1989, because of the vintage, carries more
84 fruit, alcohol, and tannin than usual. Exhibiting some toasty new
oak scents, and a good dark ruby color, this generously fruity,
soft, medium-bodied Pomerol should drink well young. Anticipated maturity: Now–1997. Last tasted, 4/91.

1988—The 1988 is a lighter wine, more oaky, with a sound, unexciting
· character. Anticipated maturity: Now–1996. Last tasted, 4/91.
82

1986—The 1986 is extremely light, with watery, diluted flavors that point
· out the overabundant size of the Merlot crop in this vintage. Drink
73 this lightweight, medium-bodied wine over the next 3–4 years.
Anticipated maturity: Now–1994. Last tasted, 3/90.

1985—The 1985 has a light-intensity bouquet of cherry fruit and simple,
· pleasant, somewhat boring flavors. Last tasted, 3/89.
74

1984—A trifle austere, but certainly above average, the 1984 La Ca-
·   banne displays decent ripeness and fruit. Anticipated maturity:
80   Now–1992. Last tasted, 3/88.

CERTAN-GIRAUD (Unclassified) VERY GOOD

Production: 3,500 cases	Grape varieties:
	Merlot—70%
	Cabernet Franc—30%
Secondary label: Clos du Roy	
Vineyard size: 17.3 acres	Proprietor: The Société Civile
	des Domaines Giraud
Time spent in barrels: 22–24	Average age of vines: 33 years
months	
Evaluation of present classification: The quality equivalent of a	
Médoc fifth-growth	
Plateau of maturity: 3–10 years following the vintage	

Given its immediate neighbors—Pétrus, Certan de May, and Vieux-Château-Certan—one would not be foolish to assume that the wines of Certan-Giraud have something special to offer. The vineyard, which is
sandwiched between these much more famous properties on Pomerol's
famed plateau, does indeed produce high-quality, typically rich, plump,
fruity, Pomerol wine.

The wines of Certan-Giraud were steadily moving upward in quality
until an unexplained slump began in 1983. Fortunately, 1988 and 1989
suggest a return to the ripe, round, savory style that has made Certan-
Giraud a popular wine both in France and abroad.

This property produces the least-expensive Pomerol from the prestigious plateau section of the appellation. The vineyard's deep gravelly
soils make for one of the most superbly located domains in Pomerol.
Would the utilization of a higher percentage of new oak and a longer
maceration period result in even greater wines? Some observers have
claimed the Giraud family has allowed yields to soar out of control, which
explained the indifferent quality of the wines after 1982. Nevertheless,
this is an estate to take seriously. The owners also make the fine St.-
Emilion, Château Corbin.

VINTAGES

1989—This fine estate tends to harvest very late, thus producing very
·   jammy, alcoholic wines that have been somewhat diluted (be-
87   cause of excessive yields) since 1983. The 1989 looks to be a

return to the style of the 1982. A black/ruby-colored wine, with an intoxicatingly intense nose of cassis, this velvety, large-scaled, rich, alcoholic wine has low acidity, but high tannins—a telltale sign of the 1989 vintage. Anticipated maturity: Now–2001. Last tasted, 4/91.

1988—The 1988 is a good wine, more herbaceous in aroma, and not
·   nearly as concentrated or as alcoholic as the 1989. It is a firmer
85   wine than the 1989 because of a drier, more noticeable tannin level. Anticipated maturity: 1992–1999. Last tasted, 4/91.

1986—The 1986 Certan-Giraud is watery, one-dimensional, and, given
·   the lovely wines made at this property over the last decade, dis-
78   appointing. This wine could have used a higher percentage of new oak, as well as a stricter selection, or any selection process at all. Anticipated maturity: Now–1994. Last tasted, 3/90.

1985—The 1985 is loaded with fruit and very low in acidity, so take
·   advantage of its creamy-textured style and drink it. Anticipated
84   maturity: Now–1995. Last tasted, 3/90.

1984—Decent ruby color, spicy, soft, slightly metallic, this light-bodied
·   wine should be drunk up. Anticipated maturity: Now–1992. Last
78   tasted, 3/88.

1983—One of the very top Pomerols of this vintage, Certan-Giraud is a
·   dark ruby-colored wine, with a big, ripe black cherry bouquet,
87   interlaced with the scent of fresh garden herbs and overripe to-matoes. Dense, unctuous, full bodied, and moderately tannic, this is a rich, fat, deeply concentrated wine that offers considerable pleasure. Anticipated maturity: Now–1994. Last tasted, 12/90.

1982—The 1982 Certan-Giraud is an excellent, fully mature wine. It is
·   dark ruby/garnet, with a dense, ripe, rich, plummy, truffle-
89   scented bouquet, full body, excellent concentration, and a lush, voluptuous, smooth-as-silk finish. The 1982 is a precociously styled wine that will captivate tasters with its dazzling fruitiness for at least the next decade. Anticipated maturity: Now–1995. Last tasted, 12/90.

1981—Not quite up to the quality of the 1982 and 1983, but still attrac-
·   tive, fruity, and delicious, the 1981 Certan-Giraud is forward and
84   ready to drink. Dark ruby, with a moderately intense, plummy bouquet, this medium- to full-bodied wine has very light tannins, and a round, lush finish. Anticipated maturity: Now–may be in decline. Last tasted, 6/84.

CERTAN DE MAY (Unclassified)   EXCELLENT

Production: 2,000 cases	Grape varieties: Merlot—65% Cabernet Franc—25% Cabernet Sauvignon—10%
Secondary label: none	
Vineyard size: 12.35 acres	Proprietor: Madame Barreau- Badar
Time spent in barrels: 24–26 months	Average age of vines: 35 years
Evaluation of present classification: The quality equivalent of a Médoc second-growth, particularly since 1979	
Plateau of maturity: 6–20 or more years following the vintage	

This tiny gem of a vineyard has become a superstar in the Pomerol firmament. Certan de May's vineyard is superbly located on the highest ground of Pomerol, right between Vieux Château Certan and Pétrus. For years the wine was made by another château, but since 1974 the present proprietors, Madame Odette Barreau-Badar and her son, Jean-Luc, have been responsible for every detail. The result has been a series of remarkably rich, concentrated Pomerols that make Certan de May one of this appellation's stars.

There are a number of reasons why Certan de May has, since 1976, emerged as one of Pomerol's greatest wines. In 1976 the old wooden fermentation vats were replaced with stainless steel. Additionally, the increasing responsibilities given to Jean-Luc have resulted in several decisions that no doubt account for the greater quality of Certan de May. This estate believes in harvesting as late as possible, and in vintages since the mid-1970s, it has generally harvested 5–10 days later than Pétrus. Also, the extremely long maceration—nearly one month—insures that the wines are superextracted, opaque black/purple-colored, and loaded with tannin for a long evolution. The use of one-third to one-half new oak casks seems to result in the perfect marriage between new oak and the ripe, concentrated fruit obtained by Certan de May.

However, this is not a Pomerol that can be drunk young. Most top vintages since the mid-1970s have needed at least 7–10 years of bottle age before they have exhibited a great deal of development. Prices for Certan de May have gone up, but given the wine's quality, they are still among the most reasonable of the appellation.

VINTAGES

1989—The 1989 is excellent, more loosely knit than usual, with a her-
·   baceous, cassis, smoky, roasted bouquet. The wine exhibits
89   plenty of extraction, but falls short of the quality of this property's
      wines in years such as 1982, 1985, 1986, and 1988. It has put on
      weight in the cask, and may ultimately prove to be outstanding.
      Certainly, it is one of the most alcoholic wines I have ever tasted
      from this estate. Anticipated maturity: 1994–2006. Last tasted,
      4/91.

1988—This wine has consistently performed as a superstar in all my
·   tastings of the 1988 clarets. It dwarfs the very good 1989 Certan
93   de May, which is not so much an indication that the 1989 is not
      up to snuff, but rather, just how profound the 1988 has turned
      out. Its dark ruby/purple color is thick and opaque (contrast that
      to the relatively translucent 1989). What first overwhelms the
      taster is the spectacular spicy, cedary, toasty, black-raspberry
      fragrance that roars from the glass. While commercialized by the
      firm of Jean-Pierre Moueix, Certan de May is not vinified and
      looked after by them. Madame Barreau consistently chooses new
      oak barrels that have a much heavier toast aroma inside, and
      consequently, the wine has that exotic, kinky, irresistible grilled-
      or smoked-meat character in the nose. However, it is not just the
      new barrels, because this wine is crammed with black fruits that
      exhibit a subtle herbaceous quality. The 1988 has superb extrac-
      tion of fruit, is full bodied, and is a rich, classic Pomerol that,
      while much more forward than Pétrus, does have at least 20 or
      more years of aging potential. Keen observers of geographical
      detail may find it interesting that the adjacent vineyards of Certan
      de May and Vieux Château Certan both produced finer 1988s than
      1989s. Anticipated maturity: 1994–2010. Last tasted, 4/91.

1987—The 1987 Certan de May is one of the broadest-shouldered, most
·   alcoholic, massive wines of the vintage. It might deserve a higher
87   rating, but there is no denying the appeal, with a moderately
      intense, smoky, roasted, berry fruit aroma, and long alcoholic,
      concentrated, yet lush, herbaceous, fruity flavors. Drink this
      sumptuously styled 1987 in its youth. Anticipated maturity: Now–
      1997. Last tasted, 3/90.

1986—The 1986 is less flattering and seductive than the 1985, but it is
·   awesomely proportioned, with a deep black/ruby color and gobs
92   of extract, tannin, and body, and is at least 7–8 years away from
      maturity. All things considered, it should be among the top four
      or five wines made in Pomerol in 1986. The price may seem steep,

but when one considers the impeccably high quality and minuscule production (half that of Pétrus), this is a gem to seek out. Anticipated maturity: 1995–2015. Last tasted, 3/90.

1985—The voluptuous 1985, with its staggering bouquet of cedar, plums,
  ·   toasty oak, and herbs, and a wealth of opulent fruit, is a real head
 94   turner. Very deep and concentrated, with a finish that just goes on and on, this wine will provide splendid drinking over the next 10–15 years. Anticipated maturity: Now–2003. Last tasted, 3/90.

1983—Perhaps too tannic, oaky, and astringent for its own good, the
  ·   1983 Certan de May is a brawny, very powerful wine with a tough
 86   texture, excellent concentration, but a coarse taste in the finish. The wine will take a long, long time to shed the tannins. Anticipated maturity: 1998–2010. Last tasted, 3/85.

1982—Since the late seventies, Certan de May has emerged as one of
  ·   the top half-dozen wines made in the tiny appellation of Pomerol.
 98   It is unfortunate so little of this wine is produced, because there have been fabulous wines made in 1979, 1981, 1982, 1985, 1986, and 1988. The best of them, however, is the 1982, which is turning out to be a strong candidate for the Pomerol of the vintage. In two broad tastings of the 1982s, I rated it the best of the Pomerols, and in one of them I was positive it was Pétrus. The wine is extremely backward and not nearly ready to drink. It displays the sort of extraction, richness, and length that one only sees in the top wines in vintages such as 1982, 1961, 1959, 1947, and 1945. Exceptionally concentrated, splendidly exotic, loaded with glycerin, body, and tannin, it is a good 5–7 years away from maturity. My original notes on this wine seem still right on target, as it reminded me of some of the colossal Pomerols of the 1947 vintage. Anticipated maturity: 1997–2015. Last tasted, 1/91.

1981—A wine for the student and connoisseur of Bordeaux, this authen-
  ·   tic *vin de garde* is deep and dark, with a big, spicy, blackcurrant
 90   bouquet, medium body, a powerful, rich, concentrated fruity texture, and excellent length. The tannins have melted away to reveal a rich, as well as elegant, wine. Anticipated maturity: Now–2005. Last tasted, 3/91.

1979—The 1979 Certan de May produced a wonderfully rich, brawny,
  ·   broad wine with layers of ripe fruit, a top-rank bouquet of oak,
 92   herbs, Asian spices, and caramel scents. This well-crafted wine is full bodied, impeccably balanced, and rich, and has a finish that lingers and lingers on the palate. It is one of the great wines of the vintage. Anticipated maturity: Now–2005. Last tasted, 5/91.

1978—Unusually spicy, slightly peppery and herbaceous, but rich,
·   dusty, ripe, and full bodied, the 1978 Certan de May has dark
85   ruby color, very good extract, but rather pungent Rhône-like flavors. Anticipated maturity: Now–1995. Last tasted, 11/89.

1976—The 1976 Certan de May is an opulent, very ripe, rich, dense,
·   full-bodied, alcoholic wine that has much more structure and
84   richness than many wines of this vintage. Drinkable and fully
mature since 1980, the wine still shows no signs of losing its fruit.
This big, corpulent wine is a delight to drink now and should hold
for another 4–5 years. Anticipated maturity: Now–1994. Last
tasted, 7/90.

CLINET (Unclassified)   EXCELLENT

Production: 3,000 cases	Grape varieties: Merlot—75% Cabernet Sauvignon—15% Cabernet Franc—10%
Secondary label: none Vineyard size: 22.2 acres	Proprietor: George Audy* Administrator: Jean-Michel Arcaute
Time spent in barrels: 20–24 months	Average age of vines: 22 years
Evaluation of present classification: Since 1986, the quality equivalent of a Médoc second-growth	
Plateau of maturity: 7–18 years following the vintage	

One of the appealing arguments often offered for the quality of a wine is
the notion of *terroir*, that magical sense of a vineyard's soil giving a wine
a particular character. However, Clinet, which does indeed possess a
magnificent *terroir* at the summit of the plateau of Pomerol (not more
than one-half mile from such superstars as Lafleur and Pétrus) is an
example where a dedicated young man proved that the human commitment to quality can have greater influence than just relying on the vineyard's soil to turn out high-quality wine.

I am speaking of Jean-Michel Arcaute, who married the daughter of
the proprietor, George Audy. In 1986 Arcaute assumed control of Clinet
and in less than 4 years he has taken this perennial underachiever to the
very top of the Pomerol hierarchy. How did he do it? First, the famed

*The estate was sold in June 1991 to a French insurance company.

oenologist Michel Rolland was given full responsibility to call the shots regarding picking dates and style of vinification and *élevage*. This meant that Clinet would be harvested as late as possible. In fact, since 1987, the vineyards of Clinet have been harvested 2 full weeks after those of Pétrus. Moreover, the use of mechanical harvesters, utilized first with the 1982 vintage, was discontinued. The results have been a 1987 that is probably not only the wine of the appellation, but may well be one of the two best wines produced in the vintage (the other being Mouton-Rothschild), a glorious 1988, and another great wine in 1989. Arcaute macerates Clinet for up to a month, and simultaneously has reduced the onetime high percentage of Cabernet Sauvignon to just under 15%.

I may have been conservative with my placement of Clinet in the excellent category. If vintages since 1987 are indicative of what we can expect in the future, this is now an outstanding producer of great wine. Clinet has become one of the most exciting new wines not only of Pomerol, but of all Bordeaux, and is worth every effort to find.

VINTAGES

1989—Neither the talented Michel Rolland—who directs the wine-
 ·   making and upbringing—nor the administrator, Jean-Michel Ar-
94   caute—who is committed to doing whatever he has to in order to
      resurrect the image of Clinet—could have asked for a better vin-
      tage to showcase the philosophy of late picking and long macera-
      tion periods that Rolland counsels. Here is a black/purple–
      colored wine that is one of the few blockbusters of the vintage.
      The bouquet has closed down since I first tasted the wine in the
      spring of 1990, when it was gushing with aromas of black raspber-
      ries, licorice, chocolate, and minerals. In the mouth, the weight,
      concentration, and highly extracted style have resulted in a mas-
      sive wine with extraordinary tannin levels, and a whopping finish.
      Again, critics will no doubt say it is a bit heavy-handed, too pow-
      erful, and too rich, but were not the greatest 1945s, 1947s, 1949s,
      1959s, 1961s, and 1982s this concentrated as well? Anticipated
      maturity: 1995–2015. Last tasted, 4/91.

1988—The 1988 is a dazzling example of Clinet. However, it is more
 ·   closed and will require more patience than the opulent 1989. The
90   color is a deep black/purple, and the bouquet exhibits the classic
      Pomerol scents of truffles, plums, subtle herbs, and new oak. In
      the mouth, the wine makes a huge impression, with extraordinary
      extraction of fruit, and a full-bodied, tannic finish. This is an
      atypically powerful, backward 1988 that may, when mature, merit
      a score several points higher. Patience, however, will most defi-

nitely be required. Anticipated maturity: 1997–2010. Last tasted, 4/91.

1987— Dark ruby, with an emerging bouquet of licorice, blackcurrants,
·   herbs, and toasty new oak, this surprisingly powerful, medium-
90   to full-bodied, concentrated wine is an extraordinary success.
        Amazing! Anticipated maturity: Now–2000. Last tasted, 1/91.

1986— The 1986, while not so enticing a wine as the 1985, is certainly an
·   excellent success for the vintage. Medium dark ruby, with a pro-
88   nounced spicy, oaky bouquet, impressive flavor depth and length,
        and some hard tannin in the finish, this big wine should be drunk
        over the next decade. Anticipated maturity: 1992–2002. Last
        tasted, 3/89.

1985— The 1985 represents the return of Clinet from the throes of medi-
·   ocrity. Packed and concentrated with jammy berry fruit encased
87   in a veil of toasty oak, this lusty, kinky, enticing fleshpot of a wine
        has broad, creamy flavors, and is an absolute joy to drink, al-
        though its low acidity and overripe style suggest that it will be
        short-lived. Anticipated maturity: Now–1997. Last tasted, 4/91.

1984— Aromas of tea and spicy fruit fill the nose. On the palate, the wine
·   is disjointed, soft, sweet, and adequate. Drink it up. Anticipated
78   maturity: Now–may be in decline. Last tasted, 3/88.

CLOS DU CLOCHER (Unclassified)   GOOD

Production: 3,000 cases	Grape varieties: Merlot—80% Cabernet Franc—20%
Secondary label: none	
Vineyard size: 14.82 acres	Proprietor: Jean Audy
Time spent in barrels: 20–22 months	Average age of vines: 20 years
Evaluation of present classification: The quality equivalent of a Médoc Cru Bourgeois	
Plateau of maturity: 5–12 years following the vintage	

A terribly underpublicized property situated just south of the large church that dominates the landscape of Pomerol's vineyards, Clos du Clocher's 3,000-case production rarely makes its way outside Europe. The vineyard, planted with 80% Merlot and 20% Cabernet Franc, produces a generously flavored, full-bodied wine that lacks some polish and finesse, but is quite attractive. Clos du Clocher consistently produces very burgundian-styled wines with a silky, supple texture that offer considerable charm and fruit.

All things considered, this is a slightly underrated Pomerol that in top vintages can produce excellent wines. Prices, however, have never been inexpensive because the tiny production is eagerly gobbled up by the enthusiastic fans of Clos du Clocher, whose traditional market has been in the Benelux countries.

VINTAGES

1989—The 1989 Clos du Clocher may prove to be the positive exception
  ·   to the "always good, rarely dazzling" rule. Potentially the finest
  89   example of this property's wines I have tasted, the 1989 is deep
        purple/ruby, with a penetrating blackberry and vanillin fragrance.
        Highly extracted fruit is buttressed by good supporting tannins,
        yet the acidity is low. This massive, superconcentrated wine will
        provide impressive drinking early, but should have the potential
        to last for 10–12 years. Anticipated maturity: Now–2001. Last
        tasted, 4/91.

1988—The 1988 is also a ripe, fleshy, chewy wine that is currently dis-
  ·   playing an oaky character. It has more obvious and aggressive
  85   tannins than the 1989, but not the sheer flavor drama. Anticipated
        maturity: 1992–1999. Last tasted, 4/91.

1986—The 1986 is a more muscular, tannic wine than the 1985, with less
  ·   charm and up-front fruit, but for those who prefer a Médoc-like
  84   structure to their Pomerols, it may seem better than my rating
        indicates. Anticipated maturity: 1992–1999. Last tasted, 3/90.

1985—The 1985 has vivid cherry fruit, a fragrant, enticing bouquet,
  ·   medium body, an elegant feel in the mouth, and considerable
  85   charm. This is a wine that is more satisfying to drink than my
        score might indicate. Anticipated maturity: Now–1995. Last
        tasted, 3/88.

1984—The 1984 Clos du Clocher, a fragile wine, is light, sweet, spicy,
  ·   but fully mature. Anticipated maturity: Now–may be in decline.
  79   Last tasted, 3/88.

1982—Until the advent of the 1989, this was my favorite vintage of Clos
  ·   du Clocher. The wine has reached full maturity, yet should con-
  87   tinue to drink well until 1997. Dark ruby/garnet, with only slight
        amber at the edge, this extroverted wine offers up a bouquet filled
        with scents of roasted chestnuts, ripe plums, and licorice. In the
        mouth, the wine is opulent, generously endowed, with low acidity,
        and a lush, heady finish. It makes for a seductive tasting experi-
        ence. Anticipated maturity: Now–1997. Last tasted, 11/90.

CLOS L'EGLISE (Unclassified)   AVERAGE

Production: 2,500 cases	Grape varieties: Merlot—55% Cabernet Sauvignon—25% Cabernet Franc—20%
Secondary label: none	
Vineyard size: 14.8 acres	Proprietor: The Moreau family
Time spent in barrels: 18–24 months	Average age of vines: 28 years
Evaluation of present classification: The quality equivalent of a Médoc Cru Bourgeois	
Plateau of maturity: 5–12 years following the vintage	

The vineyard of Clos L'Eglise, one of the numerous châteaux in Pomerol with the word *église* in its name (because so many of the vineyards abut the large church that sits amongst the vines), is well situated on the plateau adjacent to that of Château Clinet. While I have tasted some good vintages from Clos L'Eglise (1964 is a favorite), the relatively high percentage of Cabernet Sauvignon and Cabernet Franc used in the blend tends to give the wine a Médoc-like austerity. In fact, it is this lack of richness and opulence in top vintages that causes it to come across as anorexic. In years where the Cabernet does not fully ripen, Clos L'Eglise can be herbaceous to the point of being vegetal. The use of a mechanical harvester also seems at odds with a high commitment to quality.

The proprietors—the Moreau family—also own the neighboring estate of Château Plince, which, I think, produces a more interesting wine.

VINTAGES

1989—The 1989 is very light, intensely herbaceous, and short on the
·   palate. It has some alcohol, body, and the potential to last for up
76   to a decade. Anticipated maturity: Now–1999. Last tasted, 4/91.

1988—The 1988 is similar to the 1989, but with less alcohol and body. It
·   should be consumed over the next 5–6 years. Uninspiring. Antic-
72   ipated maturity: Now–1996. Last tasted, 4/91.

1986—Because of the vintage, the 1986 demonstrates more class and
·   richness than the watery, lightweight 1985. Perhaps the late-
81   picked Cabernet Sauvignon has given the wine more depth, but it
       still comes up short in comparison with other Pomerols. There is
       an attractive oakiness, but overall, this is a lightweight wine that
       could use more flesh and muscle. Anticipated maturity: Now–
       1996. Last tasted, 3/90.

1985—I found the 1985 to be light, medium bodied, and elegant, but a
· little short on substance and length. Anticipated maturity: Now–
78 1996. Last tasted, 3/90.

1984—Surprisingly deep in color, with a spicy, herbaceous nose, this
· wine's austere, undernourished palate delivers enough fruit to
82 provide decent drinking. Anticipated maturity: Now–1995. Last
tasted, 3/88.

1983—Fully mature, with a moderately intense, herbaceous bouquet,
· this soft, medium-bodied wine has shed its light tannins, and now
83 offers a spicy, straightforward style of wine. Anticipated maturity: Now–1993. Last tasted, 1/89.

1982—This skinny, weedy, muddled wine lacks acidity, comes across as
· malnourished, and finishes with a compact, attenuated taste. It
79 also appears to be losing its fruit. Last tasted, 1/89.

CLOS RENÉ (Unclassified)   GOOD

Production: 6,800 cases	Grape varieties:
	Merlot—60%
	Cabernet Franc—30%
	Malbec—10%
Secondary label: Moulinet- Lasserre	
Vineyard size: 27 acres	Proprietor: Pierre Lasserre
Time spent in barrels: 22–24 months	Average age of vines: 30 years
Evaluation of present classification: The quality equivalent of a Médoc fifth-growth	
Plateau of maturity: 5–15 years following the vintage	

Clos René sits well to the west of the major châteaux of Pomerol, in an
area that is just south of the appellation of Lalande de Pomerol. The
wines made in this area tend to be open knit in style, quite fruity, supple,
and easy to drink. While the style of Clos René is no exception to this
rule, I have noticed a perceptible change—starting with the 1981—to a
wine that is a bit bigger framed, darker colored, and a little more substantial and concentrated. Perhaps the counseling of Michel Rolland, the
highly respected Libourne oenologist and proprietor of Bon Pasteur, has
made the difference between a good, round, fruity Pomerol, and a very
fine, more serious wine. Whatever the reason, there is no doubt that the
vintages of the eighties have produced the best wines from Clos René in
recent memory. Not one of the best-known Pomerols, Clos René remains
reasonably priced.

VINTAGES

1989—Clos René's 1989 has an alluring bouquet of superripe, almost
· sweet, jammy, cassis fruit. In the mouth, the initial pleasant
85 impression is dampened slightly by a wine that is a bit light,
showing evidence of too high a crop yield. It is alcoholic, soft, and
fruity. Anticipated maturity: Now–1996. Last tasted, 4/91.

1988—The 1988 has more tannin than the 1989, as well as more struc-
· ture. It will last longer than the 1989, but I am not sure it has the
83 underlying fruit and character to provide as much pleasure as its
successor. Anticipated maturity: Now–1997. Last tasted, 4/91.

1986—The 1986 has good tannins, but the overall impression is one of
· softness and supple, silky fruit. I prefer the 1985, but the 1986
84 merits attention if you admire a lighter-weight Pomerol that requires drinking over the next 5–6 years. Anticipated maturity:
Now–1996. Last tasted, 3/90.

1985—The 1985 has broad, ripe, rich, plummy fruit, long, lush, medium-
· to full-bodied flavors, a silky, lengthy finish, and impressive con-
87 centration. Anticipated maturity: Now–1996. Last tasted, 3/90.

1983—Quite successful, the 1983 Clos René is atypically dense, full
· bodied, ripe, corpulent, and loaded with layers of fruit. Rather
86 viscous and jammy, but intensely perfumed and decadently
fruity, with soft tannins in the finish, this wine presents a hedonistic mouthful. Anticipated maturity: Now–1996. Last tasted,
3/90.

1982—Lush, rich, and fruity, but surprisingly not as deep or as big as
· the 1983, the 1982 Clos René is a heady, supple, delicious wine,
86 with some round, nonaggressive tannins in the finish. Anticipated
maturity: Now–1994. Last tasted, 1/85.

1981—Supple, spicy, intensely fruity, with plenty of blackcurrant fla-
· vors, the 1981 Clos René is a lovely, richly textured wine, with
84 medium to full body, and light to moderate tannin. Anticipated
maturity: Now–1992. Last tasted, 6/84.

1979—The 1979 Clos René is rather bland and straightforward, with
· average intensity, ripe berryish flavors, light body, and little tan-
74 nin. Anticipated maturity: Now–may be in decline. Last tasted,
6/83.

1978—The 1978 is a nicely concentrated, round, fruity wine that lacks
· grip and complexity. However, it does offer ripe, fruity flavors in
83 a medium-bodied format. Anticipated maturity: Now–1994. Last
tasted, 4/84.

1976—Diffuse, overripe, loosely knit, and quite fragile, the 1976 Clos
· René is a medium ruby-colored wine with some amber at the
73 edges. It has a sweet, candied flavor, and overly soft, disjointed

flavors. It was more attractive several years ago, and now is beginning to fade. Anticipated maturity: Now–probably in serious decline. Last tasted, 12/84.

1975—This is a typical 1975, tannic, still youthfully hard and closed,
  ·   though somewhat less weighty, concentrated, and authoritative
  80   than other wines from this vintage. The wine is moderately dark
        in color, with the hard 1975-style tannins still quite assertive.
        Anticipated maturity: Now–1995. Last tasted, 5/84.

LA CONSEILLANTE (Unclassified)   OUTSTANDING

Production: 5,000 cases	Grape varieties: Merlot—45% Cabernet Franc—45% Malbec—10%
Secondary label: none	
Vineyard size: 32 acres	Proprietor: The Nicolas family
Time spent in barrels: 22–24 months	Average age of vines: 40 years
Evaluation of present classification: The quality equivalent of a Médoc second-growth	
Plateau of maturity: 5–20 years following the vintage	

A very highly regarded Pomerol estate, La Conseillante produces some of this appellation's most elegant, lush, and delicious wines. On the negative side, many of the vintages during the seventies had a tendency to turn out diluted and they matured at an overly rapid rate. This was especially noticeable between 1971 and 1980. La Conseillante, owned by the Nicolas family, has been brilliant in most vintages of the eighties, with the 1981, 1985, 1989, and 1990 among the top-dozen wines produced in all of Bordeaux. The vineyard is superbly situated in eastern Pomerol next to L'Evangile, Petit-Village, and Vieux-Château-Certan, right on the boundary of the St.-Emilion/Pomerol appellations. In fact, the deep, gravelly soils intermixed with clay and iron deposits in this area are common not only to La Conseillante and neighbor, L'Evangile, but also to the two great St.-Emilion estates across the road, Figeac and Cheval Blanc.

La Conseillante is a meticulously made wine. It is vinified in stainless-steel tanks and aged in oak barrels of which 50% are new each year. In both 1989 and 1990, 100% new oak was employed. The wine is not so powerful in style as Pétrus, Trotanoy, Lafleur, or Certan de May, but always more supple and ready to drink sooner. Because La Conseillante never seems to show as well early on as it does after several years in the bottle, I have consistently underrated it, only to find myself revising my ratings upwardly. Perhaps it is the elevated percentage of Cabernet Franc (45%) that makes the wine look lighter in its infancy than it ultimately turns out to be. Recent vintages have, as a general rule, reached full maturity within 6–8 years. Being highly prized, as well as occasionally profound, La Conseillante is an expensive wine, normally selling at a price well above most Médoc second-growths.

VINTAGES

1989—The 1989 is the wine to buy. Tasted seven different times, it is
· this property's greatest effort since their 1949. An awesome bou-
97 quet of plums, exotic spices, and vanillin is followed by a wine that has brilliant definition, remarkable power, but also grace and elegance. Fabulously long, pure, sweet, and expansive, with an explosive finish, this wine should be at its best between 1993 and 2015. It was aged in 100% new oak because of its richness. How much fun millionaires will have debating the virtues of the 1989 versus the 1990 La Conseillante. I should also note that several of Bordeaux's most trusted tasters consider this the wine of the vintage. Anticipated maturity: 1994–2010. Last tasted, 4/91.

1988—The 1988 suffers in comparison to the 1989, but it is a light,
· charming, supple, medium-bodied wine for drinking over the next
85 7–8 years. It is tasty, but where is the grip and depth? Anticipated maturity: Now–1997. Last tasted, 4/91.

1987—Better than the 1988, this expansive, burgundian-styled, deli-
· ciously fruity, soft, charming wine makes for a seductive, succu-
86 lent drink. No hard edges are present given the absence of tannin and the low acidity. The ripe Merlot fruit is well displayed in a medium-bodied format. Anticipated maturity: Now–1996. Last tasted, 4/91.

1986—The 1986 is forward and extremely precocious for the vintage, but
· it does display La Conseillante's characteristically fragrant, full-
89 intensity bouquet of ripe raspberries, plums, sweet oak, and vi-olets. On the palate, the velvety, supple fruit oozes from the glass. This wine is total hedonistic pleasure. Anticipated maturity: Now–2005. Last tasted, 4/91.

1985—The 1985 La Conseillante is the type of Pomerol that wins many
· friends. The big, rich, expansive perfume of sweet raspberry
93 fruit, coffee, chocolate, and smoky new oak will steal just about anyone's heart. In the mouth, a purist might quibble over a lack of grip, but this wine is crammed with supple, velvety, superripe

fruit. It is irrefutably one of the superstars of the vintage. Drinkable now, this wine promises to evolve gracefully. Anticipated maturity: Now–2005. Last tasted, 4/91.

1984— A success for the vintage, the 1984 La Conseillante has a fragrant
·   bouquet of jammy raspberry fruit and spicy oak. On the palate, it
84   is smooth, ripe, and medium bodied. Anticipated maturity: Now–
     1993. Last tasted, 4/91.

1983— The third straight top-notch success for La Conseillante, the 1983
·   has excellent ripeness and big, creamy, velvety, concentrated
88   flavors nicely complemented by a toasty oakiness. There is moderate tannin present, but the overall impression created by this wine is one of voluptuousness and decadently ripe fruit. The big, smoky, raspberry nose is a knock-out. Anticipated maturity: Now–2000. Last tasted, 4/91.

1982— I love the style of La Conseillante because it is so different from
·   any of the other Pomerols. It is perhaps the most elegant and
91   stylish of the wines of Pomerol, with a burgundian-like complexity, and sweet, expansive, fruit flavors. When one adds the smoky, toasty, oakiness to the creamy, velvety texture of this wine, the potential for mass appeal is obvious. La Conseillante always shows extremely well (some might say too well) when young, and one frequently wonders how it will ultimately age. Given the vintage, one might have hoped the 1982 would be better, but it is still an outstanding wine, displaying a very perfumed bouquet of cassis and raspberry fruit along with its telltale smoky, toasty, vanillin oak scents. On the palate, it is medium bodied and not nearly as powerful and concentrated as many 1982 Pomerols, but what it lacks in muscle and power it makes up for in finesse and elegance. The wine has matured a bit faster than I would have thought and seems 1–2 years away from full maturity. Anticipated maturity: 1992–2003. Last tasted, 4/91.

1981— A great success for La Conseillante, this wine does not have the
·   weight, power, and authority of Pétrus or Certan de May, but it
91   is a remarkably elegant, balanced wine with layers of gorgeous, plummy, sweet, spicy, ripe fruit. The right touch of new oak adds complexity without overwhelming the rich, savory, supple, lush fruitiness. The intense bouquet of plums, minerals, and smoke is to die for. Anticipated maturity: Now–2000. Last tasted, 4/91.

1979— Rather light and insubstantial, the 1979 La Conseillante is ready
·   to drink, has little tannin, not much body, and rather soft, some-
78   what diluted flavors, but it is attractive and pleasant. Anticipated maturity: Now–1992. Last tasted, 4/83.

1978—The 1978 is not terribly different from the 1979, and suffers from
·   the same ills—lack of depth, grip, and body. Medium ruby with
75   some amber at the edge, this medium-bodied wine tastes soft,
ripe, a trifle diffuse and unstructured, and short and bland in the
finish. Drink up! Anticipated maturity: Now—may be in decline.
Last tasted, 6/87.

1976—The 1976 is very brown and on the verge of complete collapse. If
·   one rushes to drink the 1976 La Conseillante there is still enough
72   overripe, jammy, soft fruit and velvety texture to produce enjoyment, but please hurry. Anticipated maturity: Now—probably in
serious decline. Last tasted, 6/84.

1975—The 1975 La Conseillante, which had such impressive credentials
·   when young, has not developed. Now fully mature, as the telltale
83   brownish cast to the color indicates, this is a very evolved 1975.
The weedy, spicy, disjointed nose lacks direction and focus. In
the mouth, it is a ripe, open knit, elegantly wrought wine that
inexplicably lacks the depth and richness of the top Pomerols of
this year. It needs drinking up. Anticipated maturity: Now—1995.
Last tasted, 12/90.

1971—Quite charming, fruity, and seductively easy to drink in 1976, the
·   1971 La Conseillante has now begun to fade, taking on more and
80   more brown color and losing its fruit. It still offers a supple, round
mouthful, but the prime of its life is but a fleeting memory. Anticipated maturity: Now—probably in serious decline. Last tasted,
6/82.

1970—The 1970 is a magnificent La Conseillante that has been fully
·   mature for 5–6 years. Still dark ruby in color with a hint of amber,
92   the wine has a sensational bouquet of ripe blackcherries and violets. Lush and deep, with powerfully concentrated flavors that
are firm and admirably balanced, this is an intense, big, very rich
style of La Conseillante. Anticipated maturity: Now—1996. Last
tasted, 12/90.

1966—Almost Médoc-like with a cedary, tobacco-scented bouquet, the
·   1966 La Conseillante has reached its apogee. However, it is un-
85   likely to decline for several years because of the firmness and
structure. Medium ruby with some amber color, this is a rather
restrained La Conseillante, yet it is complex and interesting. Anticipated maturity: Now—1994. Last tasted, 5/84.

1964—I had an excellent bottle of the1964 La Conseillante in the late
·   eighties that proved to be better than I indicated in my tasting
88   notes in the first edition of this book. Medium ruby, with some
amber at the edge, this wine has a sensational nose of smoky,

almost buttery, nutty, superripe, plummy fruit and herbs. In the mouth, it is round, generous, even opulent, with a great deal of concentration, and a long, alcoholic finish. By the standards of the château, this is a larger-framed, more muscular wine than usual. Anticipated maturity: Now–1994. Last tasted, 11/89.

1961—I have only tasted this wine once, and although I enjoyed it, it did
·   not strike me as an exciting example of this great vintage. Me-
85   dium ruby/amber, with a spicy, ripe, attractive nose, on the pal-
        ate, the wine exhibited a loosely knit structure. Ripe, but not in
        the least concentrated, as one might suspect given the vintage's
        reputation, this is a fully mature 1961 that requires consumption.
        Anticipated maturity: Now–1996. Last tasted, 9/88.

OLDER VINTAGES

The three best older vintages of La Conseillante that I have had the opportunity to taste included the 1949 (rated between 94 and 96 on multiple occasions during the decade of the eighties). This is the finest mature La Conseillante I have ever tasted. I have high hopes that the 1989 will match its splendor. The other two fine examples I have tasted were a light but deliciously fruity, fragrant, altogether captivating 1953 (rated 90 in 1987), and a typically port-like, fat, alcoholic, slightly volatile, but impressive 1947 (rated 91 in 1987). I do not have any notes on La Conseillante from the pre–World War II period.

LA CROIX (Unclassified)   GOOD

Production: 5,000 cases	Grape varieties:
	Merlot—60%
	Cabernet Franc—20%
	Cabernet Sauvignon—20%
Secondary label: Le Gabachot	
Vineyard size: 25 acres	Proprietor: The Janoueix family
Time spent in barrels: 20–24 months	Average age of vines: 35 years
Evaluation of present classification: The quality equivalent of a Médoc Cru Bourgeois	
Plateau of maturity: 4–12 years following the vintage	

La Croix, located on the outskirts of Libourne, just off route D24, has a soil composition of gravel and sand. No wine made in this area ranks in the top dozen or so estates of Pomerol. Nevertheless, La Croix is a reputable property, producing big, dark-colored, tannic, full-bodied wines that can be criticized only for their lack of refinement and finesse. The best examples offer a mouth-filling, plump, rustic, simple pleasure, and also repay 6–12 years of cellaring. I have noticed in some vintages that a musty quality does intrude, suggesting that the cellar's sanitary conditions could be improved. Fortunately, this happens infrequently. The château never receives a great deal of press, and given the fact that La Croix can turn out wines that are representative of the appellation, it remains a somewhat undervalued estate.

VINTAGES

1989—This rich, unctuous, highly extracted wine has layer upon layer
·   of fruit, and a long, alcoholic finish. The wine lacks grip and
85   structure, but there is no doubting the overwhelmingly big, intense flavors. A full-throttle, almost blockbuster style may overwhelm some tasters. Anticipated maturity: 1993–2005. Last tasted, 4/91.

1988—The 1988 has a stale as well as fecal aroma, as if it came out of
·   badly tainted barrels. I cannot imagine that this property could
?   produce a wine with such obvious defects, so I am reserving judgment. Last tasted, 4/91.

1986—With an earthy bouquet filled with weedy scents of tobacco and
·   cassis, the 1986 La Croix is quite attractive, and already devel-
84   oped. In the mouth, the wine is alcoholic, ripe, somewhat fat, but with a tough, hard finish. Anticipated maturity: 1992–2000. Last tasted, 3/90.

1985—The 1985 is an exuberantly plump, fruit-filled wine with full body,
·   and a sweet, round, generous texture that offers a mouthful of
84   clean, opulent, berry fruit. Anticipated maturity: Now–1995. Last tasted, 3/90.

1983—La Croix produced a very powerful wine in 1983, with nearly
·   14.8% alcohol. Deep ruby/garnet, with a dense, plummy, viscous,
86   powerful presence on the palate, this full-bodied wine is chewy and thick. What it lacks in finesse and elegance, it compensates for with power. Anticipated maturity: Now–1997. Last tasted, 3/89.

1982—Another very successful wine, the 1982 La Croix is slightly less
·   alcoholic than the big, massive 1983, but dark ruby, with layers
86   of ripe, rich fruit, soft tannins, and an impressively long, spicy finish. Anticipated maturity: Now–2000. Last tasted, 1/91.

1981—The 1981 La Croix has been an inconsistent performer. Some
·   bottles have shown a deficiency in color, whereas others have a
84   rich, ripe cherry flavor, with full body, and hefty weight. The

score reflects the better bottlings. Anticipated maturity: Now–
1993. Last tasted, 11/84.

LA CROIX DU CASSE (Unclassified)　　　GOOD

Production: 5,000 cases	Grape varieties: Merlot—50% Cabernet Franc—40% Cabernet Sauvignon—10%
Secondary label: none	
Vineyard size: 22 acres	Proprietor: George Audy Administrator: Jean-Michel 　　Arcaute
Time spent in barrels: 18–22 　months	Average age of vines: 22 years
Evaluation of present classification: Since 1986, the quality 　equivalent of a Médoc Cru Bourgeois	
Plateau of maturity: 4–10 years following the vintage	

Jean-Michel Arcaute, the manager who has taken Château Clinet from
mediocrity to superstardom in less than 5 years, administers this property and is also responsible for resurrecting the quality. Located south of
the village of Catusseau, on a terrace of sandy and gravel-based soils,
this tiny Pomerol estate is not as renowned or as well placed as that of
Clinet. However, it would appear that in both the 1988 and 1989 vintages
Arcaute has extracted as much quality and character as is possible from
the vineyard.

VINTAGES

1989—The 1989 is a black/ruby/purple color, with a big, rich, expansive
·　　　bouquet filled with aromas of ripe plums, chocolate, cedar, and
87　　toasty new oak. In the mouth, it offers splendid concentration,
　　　full-bodied flavors, and plenty of alcohol and soft tannins in the
　　　finish. It should provide delicious drinking over its first decade of
　　　life. This is potentially a sleeper of the vintage in Pomerol. Antic-
　　　ipated maturity: Now–1996. Last tasted, 4/91.

1988—The 1988 also exhibits deep, well-endowed, full-bodied, admira-
·　　　bly extracted flavors with good tannins, better acidity than the
86　　1989, as well as a very satisfying, moderately long finish. Antici-
　　　pated maturity: 1992–2000. Last tasted, 4/91.

1984—Not bad, this wine is spicy, has adequate fruit, and some intrusive
·　　　alcohol. Anticipated maturity: Now–1993. Last tasted, 3/88.
77

LA CROIX DE GAY (Unclassified)   VERY GOOD

Production: 6,000 cases	Grape varieties: Merlot—80% Cabernet Sauvignon—10% Cabernet Franc—10%

Secondary label: none, but a
  luxury *cuvée*, La Fleur de Gay, is
  produced	

Vineyard size: 29.6 acres	Proprietor: The Raynaud family
Time spent in barrels: 18–23 months	Average age of vines: 25 years
Evaluation of present classification: Since 1985, the quality equivalent of a Médoc fifth-growth	
Plateau of maturity: 4–12 years following the vintage	

La Croix de Gay, one of the greatest discoveries of Englishman Harry Waugh in the late forties, proved to be an inconsistent, even inadequate, performer in the seventies and early eighties. However, the proprietor, the handsome Dr. Raynaud, has increasingly upgraded the quality, and now produces one of the most attractive and easy-to-drink Pomerols. In 1982 Dr. Raynaud launched his luxury *cuvée* of La Croix de Gay—called La Fleur de Gay—from a 5-acre parcel of very old vines of Merlot planted between Pétrus and Lafleur. This luxury *cuvée* of old vines (profiled separately, see page 605) is very rare in Bordeaux, but it is one of the most magnificent wines of the appellation, rivaling even the great Pétrus in complexity and intensity. Some skeptics have argued that Dr. Raynaud's decision to make a special *cuvée* robs the primary wine, La Croix de Gay, of its best source of richness and backbone. Despite the addition of a luxury *cuvée*, one cannot ignore the fact that La Croix de Gay has improved immensely.

The vineyards of La Croix de Gay sit at the very northern section of Pomerol's plateau, immediately behind a cemetery and the tiny road called D245 that traverses the appellation. The soil in this area is gravel intermixed with sand.

VINTAGES

1989—The 1989 La Croix de Gay appears to be the best wine made at
  ·   this estate since 1964. While it has nowhere near the richness and
  88   compelling character of the 1989 La Fleur de Gay, it is unusually
       deep, concentrated, and full bodied, with excellent tannin and

extract levels. The acidity is low, but the high tannins and the elevated alcohol level should allow this wine to age well for 6–15 years. It is the most impressive young La Croix de Gay I have tasted, reflecting this estate's increasing attention to detail and commitment to excellence. Anticipated maturity: 1995–2007. Last tasted, 4/91.

1988—The 1988 exhibits a great deal of new oak, has good concentra-
·   tion, but is a bit compact and straightforward, particularly in
86   comparison to the generously flavored 1989. Anticipated matu-
        rity: 1992–1998. Last tasted, 11/90.

1986—The 1986 displays a healthy use of new oak, a deep ruby color,
·   medium body, an attractive sweet, pure, plummy fruitiness, good
85   length, and moderate tannin in the finish. It will be ready to drink
        within several years. Anticipated maturity: 1992–2000. Last
        tasted, 3/90.

1985—The 1985 is a success for La Croix de Gay, with a moderately
·   intense, elegant, ripe, spicy bouquet, attractive flavors wrapped
85   gently in new oak, medium body, and a velvety finish. Anticipated
        maturity: Now–1994. Last tasted, 3/89.

1984—The 1984 is light, but fruity, soft, round, and a delight to drink
·   over the next 2–3 years. Anticipated maturity: Now–1992. Last
80   tasted, 3/89.

1983—Medium ruby, with some garnet at the edge, the 1983 La Croix
·   de Gay has a weedy, herbaceous, plum-scented bouquet, round,
80   somewhat disjointed, flabby, alcoholic flavors, and a hot, soft,
        unstructured finish. Fully mature, it should be drunk up. Antici-
        pated maturity: Now–1993. Last tasted, 11/90.

1982—Medium ruby, with some brown at the edge, the 1982 La Croix de
·   Gay has a monolithic, ripe bouquet of no great distinction, me-
77   dium-bodied, slightly watery, low-acid flavors, and a flabby, fully
        mature finish. Anticipated maturity: Now–1994. Last tasted,
        3/89.

OLDER VINTAGES

I have never had the privilege of tasting the 1947 La Croix de Gay, the wine Harry Waugh made legendary with his glowing accolades. The best older vintage I have tasted is the 1964 (rated 90 in 1990). Like so many Pomerols in what is clearly a great vintage for the appellation, this full-bodied, rich, alcoholic wine is loaded with fruit, and has a sumptuous, opulent texture. It should continue to drink well until about 1996.

DOMAINE DE L'EGLISE (Unclassified) VERY GOOD

Production: 3,000 cases	Grape varieties: Merlot—90% Cabernet Franc—10%
Secondary label: none	
Vineyard size: 17.3 acres	Proprietors: The Philippe Castèja and Preben-Hansen families
Time spent in barrels: 20–22 months	Average age of vines: 30 years
Evaluation of present classification: Since 1986, the quality equivalent of a Médoc fifth-growth	
Plateau of maturity: 5–15 years following the vintage	

This beautifully situated vineyard is adjacent to the cemetery of Pomerol on the high plateau and has a gravelly soil intermixed with some sand. The château and vineyard are believed to be the oldest of Pomerol. The property was run as a winemaking estate by the Hospitaliers de Saint-Jean de Jerusalem who managed a hospital in Pomerol for lepers long before the French Revolution and was known as the domain Porte Rouge. As with many church-run properties, the revolution resulted in divestiture and placement in private hands where it has remained. It was acquired by the *négociant* firm of Borie-Manoux in 1973.

Solid and reliable wines were made in the seventies and early eighties, but since the late eighties the quality has even increased. Domaine de L'Eglise was particularly damaged during the 1956 freeze and the vineyard has been totally replanted since. The lighter, more commercial style of wines produced in the seventies and early eighties gave way in the late eighties to a richer, more profound and compelling product.

VINTAGES

1989—The firm of Borie-Manoux has become deadly serious about the
· quality of its top wines. There is no better evidence of this than
90 in the splendidly rich, highly extracted, immensely impressive 1989 Domaine de L'Eglise. It is irrefutably the finest wine I have ever tasted from this property, and should be on any serious Pomerol consumer's shopping list. Given the fact that it is not so well known as many of the more prestigious names in Pomerol, it promises to be one of the better values from this vintage. Black/ruby in color, with fabulous, highly extracted flavors, gobs of tannin as well as alcohol, yet decent acidity for the vintage, this

rich, broad-shouldered Pomerol is the most massive wine I have
yet tasted from the Domaine de L'Eglise. Anticipated maturity:
1995–2015. Last tasted, 4/91.

L'EGLISE-CLINET (Unclassified)   EXCELLENT

Production: 2,500 cases	Grape varieties:
	Merlot—80%
	Cabernet Franc—20%
Secondary label: La Petite	
L'Eglise	
Vineyard size: 14.8 acres	Proprietor: Denis Durantou
Time spent in barrels: 18–22	Average age of vines: 50 years
months	
Evaluation of present classification: Since 1985, the quality	
equivalent of a Médoc third-growth	
Plateau of maturity: 5–15 years following the vintage	

One of the least known Pomerol estates, L'Eglise-Clinet often produces
a typically fat, succulent, juicy, richly fruity style of Pomerol. The wine
is admirably and traditionally made, but because of the tiny production,
it is not well known. The vineyard is well situated on the plateau of
Pomerol behind the church where the soils are deep gravel beds intermingled with sand, clay, and iron.

L'Eglise-Clinet is one of the few Pomerol vineyards that was not replanted after the 1956 killing freeze, and consequently it has very old
vines, a few of which exceed 100 years in age.

Until 1983, Pierre Lasserre, the owner of the bigger and better-known
Pomerol property of Clos René, farmed this vineyard under the *métayage*
system (a type of vineyard rental agreement), and turned out a wine that
was rich, well balanced, supple, firm, and always well vinified. Since
then, the winery has been run by the young, extremely dedicated Denis
Durantou, who is trying to take this tiny 14.8-acre vineyard to the very
top of the unofficial Pomerol hierarchy. The secret here is not only Durantou's remarkable commitment to quality, but vines that average 50
years in age, plus the fact that in vintages such as 1986 nearly one-third
of the crop was relegated to the launching of a new second wine called
La Petite L'Eglise. Given the miniscule quantities of wine produced,
such a decision is virtually unparalleled in Bordeaux. One cannot ap-
plaud the efforts of Denis Durantou enough.

The price for a bottle of L'Eglise-Clinet is high, as European connoisseurs recognize that this is one of the top dozen wines of the appellation.

VINTAGES

1989—The 1989 is a rich, velvety, alcoholic wine that is disarmingly
·   seductive and smooth. It has a good tannin level when analyzed,
90   but the high alcohol and low acidity give it a precocious character.
         Gloriously fruity, this sumptuous, velvety-textured wine will pro-
         vide immense satisfaction. Anticipated maturity: Now–2000. Last
         tasted, 4/91.

1988—The 1988 is a more typical (or classic as some may say), more
·   tannic style of wine. Medium bodied, admirably concentrated,
88   with a nose of smoky oak and plums, the 1988 L'Eglise-Clinet is
         a stylish yet authoritative tasting Pomerol. Anticipated maturity:
         1993–2002. Last tasted, 4/91.

1986—The extraordinary 1986 is black in color, with huge, ripe, dense
·   fruit, stunning length, and wonderfully opulent, intense, ex-
92   tremely rich, mouth-filling flavors. This is a blockbuster Pomerol.
         Anticipated maturity: 1992–2005. Last tasted, 12/90.

1985—The 1985 L'Eglise-Clinet is fabulous, with the exceptional rich-
·   ness and depth of a very great wine. Dark ruby, with a full-
95   intensity bouquet of crushed berries and toasty oak, the wine is
         explosively rich and has layers of extract and a super, well-delin-
         eated finish. It has firmed up considerably in the bottle. Proprie-
         tor Durantou considers this the finest wine he has made during
         the eighties. Anticipated maturity: 1994–2005. Last tasted, 4/91.

1984—Except for the hardness at the finish, this well-colored, decently
·   made wine has good fruit and displays impeccable winemaking.
81   Give it 2–3 years of cellaring. Anticipated maturity: 1992–1997.
         Last tasted, 3/89.

1983—A success in 1983, L'Eglise-Clinet is dark ruby, with some amber
·   at the edge. It exhibits a dense, ripe, fat, black-cherry bouquet,
86   chewy, dense, ripe flavors, full body, low acidity, and soft tan-
         nins. This big wine has matured quickly. Anticipated maturity:
         Now–1995. Last tasted, 3/89.

1982—The 1982 is dark in color, with an emerging bouquet of black
·   cherries and truffles. On the palate, the wine exhibits excellent
86   concentration, full body, a vivid blackberry, plummy fruitiness,
         and velvety tannins. It is a plump, round, easygoing wine that is
         immensely enjoyable. Anticipated maturity: Now–1998. Last
         tasted, 1/91.

1981—Less powerful and rich than the 1982 and 1983, the 1981 L'Eglise-
·   Clinet is a light, yet still very fruity, supple, spicy wine, with
84   medium to full body, moderate tannin, and a good finish. Antici-
         pated maturity: Now–1992. Last tasted, 6/84.

1978—The 1978 is fully mature, with a chocolatey, somewhat smoky,
·   fruity bouquet. It is a soft, round, moderately concentrated wine
82   that is pleasant, but lacks a little weight and richness. Anticipated
      maturity: Now–1993. Last tasted, 1/85.

OLDER VINTAGES

Older vintages of L'Eglise-Clinet are difficult to find because of the tiny production and the fact that much of it was sold to the château's traditional clients in Belgium. Single tastings of bottles from 1962 and 1961 revealed good rather than inspiring wines. Both vintages still had their fruit, with the 1961 maintaining more density and opulence. Neither displayed the extract levels or concentration of the vintages produced at the château since 1985. The best older vintage I have tasted was the 1959 (rated 87 in 1988). It was fuller, richer, and more interesting than either the 1961 or 1962.

L'ENCLOS (Unclassified)   VERY GOOD

Production: 5,000 cases	Grape varieties:
	Merlot—80%
	Cabernet Franc—19%
	Malbec—1%
Secondary label: none	
Vineyard size: 26.5 acres	Proprietor: Madame Carteau
Time spent in barrels: 20 months	Average age of vines: 30 years
in barrels and vats	
Evaluation of present classification: The quality equivalent of a	
Médoc fifth-growth	
Plateau of maturity: 3–15 years following the vintage	

Located on sandy, gravelly, and flinty soil in the most western portion of the Pomerol appellation, L'Enclos is an unheralded property that produces very fine wine. Perhaps I have been lucky and only seen the best vintages of L'Enclos, but I have been impressed with this wine for the consistently smooth, velvety, rich, supple, nicely concentrated, pure blackberry fruitiness, and for an overall harmony. In most vintages, L'Enclos only needs 3–4 years of bottle age to reveal the opulent, rich, silky fruitiness, yet the wines hold up well in the bottle.

Most consumers think of Pomerols as expensive, which they are, because of the tiny vineyards and worldwide demand for these Merlot-based wines. However, L'Enclos represents one of the best quality/price rapport wines of any estate in the appellation.

VINTAGES

1989—This vineyard is capable of turning out some wonderful wines.
· Those who remember the 1975, 1979, and 1982 should plan on
88 taking a serious look at the 1989. It may be the best L'Enclos
produced since the great 1947. The style here is to produce wines
that are rich, fleshy, opulent, and easy to drink in their first 10–
12 years of life. However, they have surprising holding power, as
this 1989 will ultimately demonstrate. At present, it offers a hedonistic mouthful of superconcentrated blackberry-and-violet-
scented fruit. Full-bodied and silky smooth, the masses of rich
fruit nearly obscure some sizable tannins in the finish. This beautifully made, intensely perfumed wine should prove to be one of
the sleepers of the vintage, and ultimately to be as good as, and
probably better than, the 1982. Anticipated maturity: 1992–2002.
Last tasted, 4/91.

1988—The 1988 L'Enclos is a straightforward, fruity, soft-textured wine,
· with adequate concentration, an attractive, spicy, plummy bou-
83 quet, decent concentration, and a moderately long finish. It is
already drinking well and can be expected to evolve pleasantly.
Anticipated maturity: Now–1996. Last tasted, 11/90.

1986—The 1986 is not quite as good as the 1975, 1979, or 1982, but it
· shares with them the personality of L'Enclos. The style is one
84 that produces a very precocious, soft, fruity wine redolent of
plums and blackcurrants, with a silky, smooth texture. Drink it
over the next 4–5 years for its charm, not its great depth or
complexity. Anticipated maturity: Now–1995. Last tasted, 11/90.

1985—The 1985 is delectably rich, long, expansive, velvety, and already
· a complete pleasure to drink. Medium bodied, with oodles of
85 caramel and berry fruit, this Pomerol gives an impression not
unlike biting into candy. Anticipated maturity: Now–1996. Last
tasted, 3/90.

1983—The 1983 L'Enclos is a succulent, fat, juicy wine, with a very
· forward, exuberant, grapey appeal, round, ripe, lush flavors, and
86 a velvety finish. Anticipated maturity: Now–1994. Last tasted,
3/89.

1982—More concentrated than the 1983, but equally forward and
· precociously styled, the 1982 has a medium to dark ruby color, a
87 full-blown, ripe blackberry bouquet intermingled with scents of
minerals, a wonderfully lush, deep, unctuous texture, and a
sweet, velvety finish. Seemingly drinkable since its release, this
wine has changed little during the last 6 years. A crowd pleaser,
it should continue to provide pleasure for at least a decade. Anticipated maturity: Now–2000. Last tasted, 1/91.

1979—Deliciously fruity with a lovely perfumed quality suggesting black-
·　　　currants, this medium-bodied wine has a silky, velvety texture,
85　　light tannins, and a round, generous finish. An extremely enjoy-
　　　able style of wine, it has continued to drink well and shows no
　　　signs of imminent decline. Anticipated maturity: Now–1996. Last
　　　tasted, 1/91.

1975—This is an outstandingly sweet, ripe, round, gentle, smooth wine,
·　　　with oodles of blackberry fruitiness, a complex berry, truffle-
89　　scented bouquet, and a velvety finish. The 1975 L'Enclos is me-
　　　dium to full bodied and is drinking well now, but this beautifully
　　　made wine can support additional cellaring. It is a sleeper of the
　　　vintage. Anticipated maturity: Now–2001. Last tasted, 1/85.

1970—The 1970 L'Enclos is very similarly styled to the 1975 and 1982.
·　　　Perhaps more tannic, but nevertheless velvety, ripe, smooth, and
86　　polished, this dark ruby wine is loaded with fruit, and has a finish
　　　that caresses the palate. Anticipated maturity: Now–1994. Last
　　　tasted, 1/85.

L'EVANGILE (Unclassified)　　　　　　　　　　　EXCELLENT

Production: 4,500 cases	Grape varieties: Merlot—71% Cabernet Franc—29%
Secondary label: none Vineyard size: 34.6 acres	Proprietors: Domaines Lafite- Rothschild and Madame Ducasse
Time spent in barrels: 20–24 months	Average age of vines: 37 years
Evaluation of present classification: The quality equivalent of a Médoc second-growth	
Plateau of maturity: 6–25 years following the vintage	

Anyone who has tasted the 1947, 1975, 1982, 1985, 1989, or 1990 L'Evangile knows full well that this property can make wines of majestic richness and compelling character. Bordered on the north by the vineyards
of La Conseillante, Vieux-Château-Certan, and Pétrus, and on the south
by the great St.-Emilion, Cheval Blanc, the 35-acre vineyard is brilliantly
situated on deep, gravelly soil mixed with both clay and sand. With these
advantages, I believe that L'Evangile (never a model of consistency
under the management of the Ducasse family) could, with more meticulous attention to detail, produce wines that rival Pétrus and Lafleur.

That may well happen during the nineties, because in 1990 the Roth-schild family (of Lafite-Rothschild) purchased a controlling interest. They are fully aware of the unlimited potential of this estate, and L'Evangile may soon be challenging Pétrus and Lafleur in both quality, and, lamentably, price. The 1990, tasted from cask in spring, 1991, was the first wine made under the Rothschild management and it looked to be one of the few superstars of that vintage—encouraging news!

Certainly the late Louis Ducasse must have realized the distinctive-ness of his vineyard because he often browbeat visiting wine critics with his observation that L'Evangile was every bit as good as, and even more complex than, neighboring Pétrus. However, 1947 was the only vintage where L'Evangile had the body and power of Pétrus. There were some top successes, though, as the following tasting notes reveal. But in truth, L'Evangile has been a schizophrenic performer over the last four de-cades.

If the Rothschild winemaking team continues the late harvesting that produces such rich, concentrated grapes, and additionally lowers the yields to under 45 hectoliters per hectare, as well as increases the new oak to 50% or more, I predict L'Evangile will become one of the bright shining stars of Pomerol, not just in great vintages, but in less glamorous years as well.

VINTAGES

1989—Deep ruby/purple, with a superripe, port-like nose of licorice,
· black fruits, and spring flowers, this gorgeously rich, opulent wine
90 makes a massive impact on the palate. Low in acidity, alcoholic, and rich, this big, beefy wine will require drinking in its first 12–15 years. If more structure and grip emerge, my rating may prove conservative. Anticipated maturity: 1994–2005. Last tasted, 4/91.

1988—The 1988 reminds me of the beautiful, elegant, always drinkable
· 1979. Medium dark ruby, with this château's characteristic black-
87 berry, plum-like nose, the 1988 has considerable grace and charm, as well as depth and harmony. It is very precocious and should continue to drink well for 10–12 years. Anticipated matu-rity: Now–2002. Last tasted, 4/91.

1986—The 1986 has an intense tea, coffee, chocolatey, plummy bouquet
· that is fully evolved and intense. On the palate, the wine is ex-
87 tremely soft, with a flattering, open-knit, ripe fruitiness. Given the low acidity and its delicious forward appeal, I would opt for drinking this wine over the near term, rather than cellaring it. Anticipated maturity: Now–1996. Last tasted, 3/90.

1985—For sheer class, complexity, and a magnificent perfume, L'Evan-
· gile may be the top wine of Pomerol in 1985. It does not have the
95 power, aging potential, and massive texture of Lafleur, or the
exceptional finesse of L'Eglise-Clinet. However, the dark ruby
color, the hugely complex, multidimensional bouquet of blackcurrants, raspberries, exotic spices, and oak is unbelievably exciting.
Rich, medium to full bodied, concentrated, well balanced, and
moderately tannic, this wine has evolved slowly. Along with the
splendid 1975, 1982, and 1990 L'Evangile, this is the finest wine
made at this estate in over three decades. Anticipated maturity:
1994–2010. Last tasted, 5/91.

1984—Soft, herbal-tea-like aromas fill the olfactory senses. In the
· mouth, the wine is light, soft, and fruity, but falls off and has a
76 watery finish. Drink it up. Anticipated maturity: Now–1993. Last
tasted, 3/89.

1983—Destined to be recognized as one of the top Pomerols, maybe one
· of the two best of this vintage (the other is La Fleur), L'Evangile's
92 1983 is dark ruby in color with an intense bouquet of oriental
spices, minerals, and ripe, crushed blackberries. Medium-bodied, dense, lush, very concentrated flavors lack some acidity, but
exhibit excellent richness and soft, even velvety tannins. This is
a deep, unctuous, exotic L'Evangile that has turned out to be one
of the finest Pomerols of the vintage. Anticipated maturity: Now–
2005. Last tasted, 1/91.

1982—The bouquet of the 1982 displays intense, pure aromas of cassis
· intermixed with scents of saddle leather and ground beef. I am
96 sure the California technocrats would find some brettanomyces (a
yeast) in this wine, and therefore consider it defective and undrinkable. The wine still has considerable tannin, but the tannins
have always been ripe, round, and buried beneath the cascade of
unctuous, lavishly rich fruit. I doubt that this wine will be the
longest-lived Pomerol of the vintage, but for drinking now and
over the next 15 years, this is an exceptional bottle of wine. The
only other vintage of L'Evangile it resembles is the property's
extraordinary 1947. Anticipated maturity: 1992–2005. Last
tasted, 5/91.

1981—Unexpectedly light, diffuse, and inadequately concentrated, the
· 1981 is well below the standard for this excellent estate. It is
73 medium ruby and just too bland without much concentration to
it. Drink up! Anticipated maturity: Now–1993. Last tasted, 4/84.

1979—This wine has been fully mature since the mid-1980s. The 1979
· L'Evangile is a seductive, sensual wine with a soft, raspberry,
88 blackcurrant fruitiness, a wonderful bouquet of violets, minerals,

and spice, medium body, and a smooth, velvety finish. It is almost reminiscent of a Grand Cru from Chambolle-Musigny. Anticipated maturity: Now–1995. Last tasted, 1/91.

1978— Attractively plump, spicy, and solid, but for whatever reason, not
· terribly complex, the 1978 L'Evangile has always struck me as a
84 good, straightforward, nicely concentrated wine, but nothing special. Anticipated maturity: Now–1994. Last tasted, 4/84.

1975— This wine has become even more exciting as it has evolved in the
· bottle. Still opaque ruby/purple, with only a hint of amber, this
95 gorgeously opulent, concentrated wine has a bouquet of minerals, flowers, grilled nuts, and abundant quantities of rich, blackberry fruit. Fabulously rich and exotic, with multidimensional flavors, the 1975 L'Evangile has none of the hard tannins of this vintage, but rather, a lush, rich, savory texture, and a superb finish. This full-bodied, perfectly balanced wine can be drunk now and over the next 10–20 years. Superb! Anticipated maturity: Now–2008. Last tasted, 11/90.

1971— Beginning to decline, the 1971 L'Evangile is displaying an in-
· creasingly brown color and its bouquet has begun to suggest de-
70 caying vegetation. The wine is also a trifle unstable on the palate. Medium ruby/brown with a spicy, minty, somewhat burnt aroma and short, medicinal flavors. Anticipated maturity: Now–probably in serious decline. Last tasted, 3/80.

1970— Fully mature, quite round, fruity, soft, elegant, and charming with
· L'Evangile's telltale violet, raspberry-like bouquet, this medium-
84 bodied, velvety wine should be drunk up. Anticipated maturity: Now–1993. Last tasted, 3/81.

1966— Fully mature, yet seemingly longer-lived than the 1970, the 1966
· has more body and tannin, a vividly brilliant dark ruby color with
85 just a touch of amber, and a long, satisfying, rich, plummy finish. It is a harmonious, supple, very fruity wine. Anticipated maturity: Now–1993. Last tasted, 3/79.

1964— Quite full bodied and robust for L'Evangile, this fleshy, meaty
· wine is ready to drink and has a big, rich, toasty, spicy, blackcur-
84 rant bouquet and soft, fat, slightly rough-edged, big flavors. Anticipated maturity: Now–1993. Last tasted, 1/80.

OLDER VINTAGES

In 1990 I gave a perfect rating to the 1947 L'Evangile, which must be one of the least-known great wines produced in the post–World War II era. Drinking it was a mind-boggling experience, and it still had a decade, perhaps even two decades, of life left to it. I have never tasted a L'Evangile that spectacular. As thrilling as the 1975, 1982, 1985, and

1990 promise to be, I doubt if they will ever attain the greatness of this monumental wine. I have good rather than great tasting notes for the 1955 (rated 88 in 1987), and one outstanding tasting note for the 1959 (rated 90 in 1989). I am told by friends in Bordeaux that the latter wine is a stronger effort from L'Evangile than their 1961, a vintage I have never had the good fortune to taste.

FEYTIT-CLINET (Unclassified) AVERAGE

Production: 3,000 cases	Grape varieties: Merlot—80% Cabernet Franc—20%
Secondary label: none	
Vineyard size: 17.3 acres	Proprietor: The Tane-Domergue family Administrator: La Maison Jean-Pierre Moueix
Time spent in barrels: 18–22 months	Average age of vines: 25 years
Evaluation of present classification: The quality equivalent of a Médoc Cru Bourgeois	
Plateau of maturity: 5–12 years following the vintage	

Feytit-Clinet, despite the fact that the vineyard has been farmed under what is called a *métayage* agreement by the renowned firm of Jean-Pierre Moueix since 1967, tends to produce relatively straightforward, simple wines of no great distinction. The vineyard, situated on the western section of the Pomerol plateau (next to Latour à Pomerol), should produce more interesting wine. Perhaps the yields are too high, but there is no firm in all of Bordeaux with more concern for crop management than that of Jean-Pierre Moueix. Most vintages of Feytit-Clinet are drinkable upon release. They can be cellared for 7–10 years.

VINTAGES

1989—This is one château in Pomerol that may have produced a slightly better wine in 1988 than in 1989. The 1989 exhibits a moderately
84   intense, ripe, spicy, straightforward bouquet, medium to full body, lots of extract, and high, surprisingly hard tannins. Anticipated maturity: 1993–2002. Last tasted, 4/91.

1988—The 1988 is not so alcoholic as the 1989, and displays better overall balance and fresh acidity, which give the flavors more
85   precision and clarity. It also possesses an elegant, plummy bou-

quet, and a long, lush, spicy finish. Not a big Pomerol when measured against the heavyweights of the appellation, it is nevertheless a charming, stylish wine. Anticipated maturity: 1993–2001. Last tasted, 4/91.

1985—The 1985 has an intense bouquet of Bing cherries and toasty oak,
 ·   good richness, firm tannins, and some elegance. Anticipated ma-
84   turity: Now–1996. Last tasted, 3/89.

LA FLEUR DE GAY (Unclassified) OUTSTANDING

Production: 1,000–1,500 cases	Grape varieties: Merlot—100%
Secondary label: none	
Vineyard size: 5 acres	Proprietor: Dr. Alain Raynaud
Time spent in barrels: 24 months	Average age of vines: 35 years
Evaluation of present classification: The quality equivalent of a Médoc first-growth	
Plateau of maturity: 5–15 or more years following the vintage	

La Fleur de Gay, the luxury *cuvée* of La Croix de Gay, was launched by Dr. Alain Raynaud in 1982 (see page 593). The wine comes from a small parcel of very old vines situated between Pétrus and Vieux-Château-Certan that is part of Dr. Raynaud's better-known estate called La Croix de Gay. Aged in 100% new oak, it is a wine that is characterized by a compelling opulence and sweetness, as well as exceptional purity of fruit. Michel Rolland oversees the vinification and upbringing of this luxuriously flavored, intense, full-bodied wine. Vintages to date give every indication of possessing 10–15 years of aging potential.

VINTAGES

1989—The story here is almost identical to that of Clinet, although the
 ·   proprietor has sought the same goal via a different route. Dr.
95   Alain Raynaud has, since 1982, vastly upgraded the quality of La
     Croix de Gay, but felt that by limiting production to one parcel of
     vines, located near Vieux Château Certan, Pétrus, and Lafleur,
     he had the potential to render a wine of sublime quality. He was
     right. Interestingly, Dr. Raynaud considers the 1988 to be the
     best wine he has made of this luxury *cuvée* produced from old
     Merlot vines. However, the 1989 offers a veritable smorgasbord
     of heavenly delights. The dark ruby/purple color is opaque, sug-
     gesting low yields and super concentration. In the mouth, there

is only one word to describe the texture and intensity, and that is *explosive*. It is amazingly concentrated, and much more structured and tannic than I remembered. In spite of the low acidity, the tannins tend to keep the level of enjoyment down. Nevertheless, it is so crammed with ripe fruit that I suspect many will find it irresistible when young. The problem with this wine, much like many of the finest Pomerols, is that the production is miniscule (1,500 cases). The Guigal La Mouline of Pomerol? Anticipated maturity: 1995–2008. Last tasted, 4/91.

1988— This is another riveting example of a great 1988 that is, lamenta-
·   bly, available only in limited quantities (1,000 cases). It is, how-
93   ever, worth whatever arm twisting, retailer browbeating one must
         do to latch onto a few bottles. Proprietor Dr. Raynaud prefers this
         vintage to his 1989 (I tend to disagree, but I see his point), be-
         cause it is probably the first La Fleur de Gay he has made that
         has the potential to last 20–25 years. Its black/ruby/purple color
         makes it perhaps the darkest-colored wine of the vintage. The
         bouquet is more restrained, particularly when compared to the
         terrific fragrance and opulence it displayed from cask. However,
         it takes no great talent to detect scents of smoky, toasty oak,
         black plums, allspice, and oriental spices, as well as gobs of
         superripe fruit. Extremely concentrated on the palate, but very
         structured, with considerable tannin, this massive, full-bodied,
         more aggressive La Fleur de Gay will not have the sumptuous
         appeal of many Pomerols, but give it 4–5 years to mellow, and it
         will provide a dazzling glass of decadent Pomerol. Anticipated
         maturity: 1994–2010. Last tasted, 4/91.

1987— The 1987 La Fleur de Gay is fat, seductive, and lush, with expan-
·   sive blackberry flavors, low acidity, and light tannins. Its lush,
90   gloriously rich, admirably extracted flavors are nicely framed by
         the use of 100% new oak. This exotic crowd-pleaser will have to
         be drunk over the next 5–7 years, but who cares? This is one of
         the few great wines of the 1987 vintage. Anticipated maturity:
         Now–2002. Last tasted, 4/91.

1986— The 1986 has good structure, and displays the intense, deep, rich
·   fruit and sexy new oak used for this wine. It is a big, powerful,
90   fleshy wine with considerable complexity and appeal. One of the
         superstars of the vintage, only 1,000 cases were produced. Antic-
         ipated maturity: 1992–2003. Last tasted, 1/91.

1985— The 1985 exhibits superrichness, a stunningly intense bouquet,
·   luxurious flavors, full body, and melted tannins giving it a satiny
89   texture. Given the softness, I hesitate to advise long-term cellar-

ing, but drunk young, this treasure should provide memorable drinking. Anticipated maturity: Now–1998. Last tasted, 1/91.

1983—This wine has reached its plateau of maturity. The color is still
· wonderfully dark ruby/purple, and the bouquet is beginning to
90 take on intriguing scents of coffee, mocha, chocolate, and blackberries in addition to its intense, smoky, spicy oak. This fleshy,
full-bodied wine has excellent concentration, and is clearly one of
the top Pomerols of the vintage. Anticipated maturity: Now–1998.
Last tasted, 4/91.

1982—The debut vintage of La Fleur de Gay was not a particularly
· auspicious effort. Loosely knit, unstructured, too alcoholic, and
83 lacking acidity and concentration, this wine has matured quickly.
Anticipated maturity: Now–1993. Last tasted, 11/90.

LA FLEUR GAZIN (Unclassified)   AVERAGE

Production: 2,500 cases	Grape varieties: Merlot—75% Cabernet Franc—25%
Secondary label: none Vineyard size: 17.3 acres	Proprietor: Maurice Borderie Administrator: La Maison Jean-Pierre Moueix
Time spent in barrels: 18–22 months	Average age of vines: 20 years
Evaluation of present classification: The quality equivalent of a Médoc Cru Bourgeois	
Plateau of maturity: 5–10 years following the vintage	

La Fleur Gazin is situated between the two estates of Gazin and Lafleur. The wine is produced by the firm of Jean-Pierre Moueix, which farms this property under a lease arrangement. The wine is supple, round, and straightforward in style. Given the vineyard's location, it remains perplexing that the wines are so simple and light.

VINTAGES

1989—The performance of the 1989 La Fleur Gazin suggests that per-
· haps the vineyard was harvested too early, given attenuated,
78 higher-than-normal acidity levels, and green, hard, unripe tannins. However, the wine does possess noticeable alcohol, and is
otherwise well made, though lacking the generosity, concentration, ripeness, and interest of many of the other 1989 Pomerols.

It should keep for 5–10 years given the greenness and hardness of the tannins, but it will never merit a great deal of interest. Anticipated maturity: 1992–2000. Last tasted, 4/91.

1988—The 1988 is even more tannic, austere, and lean, lacking both
  ·   fruit and character. Again, it will keep well, but never provide
74   much pleasure. Anticipated maturity: 1993–2001. Last tasted, 4/91.

LA FLEUR PÉTRUS (Unclassified)   VERY GOOD

Production: 3,500 cases	Grape varieties:
	Merlot—80%
	Cabernet Franc—20%
Secondary label: none	
Vineyard size: 19.8 acres	Proprietor: Jean-Pierre Moueix
Time spent in barrels: 20–24 months	Average age of vines: 30 years
Evaluation of present classification: The quality equivalent of a Médoc third-growth	
Plateau of maturity: 5–15 years following the vintage	

Located on the eastern side of the plateau of Pomerol between Lafleur and Pétrus (hence the name) where so many of the best estates are found, La Fleur Pétrus should be one of the most exquisite Pomerols. The famous firm of Jean-Pierre Moueix purchased the estate in 1952 and the vineyard was entirely replanted after 1956, when it was virtually destroyed by the winter freeze. The wine at La Fleur Pétrus is lighter in weight and texture than other Moueix Pomerols such as Pétrus, Trotanoy, and Latour à Pomerol, but connoisseurs prize it for elegance and a supple, smooth, silky texture. It usually matures quickly and can be drunk as soon as 5 or 6 years after the vintage. Recent vintages have produced very fine wines, but I cannot help thinking that the quality could and should be higher. The local cognoscenti claim the Moueix firm consistently harvests this vineyard too early. Perhaps 1989 is an indication that La Fleur Pétrus is ready to challenge the top-dozen Pomerol estates.

La Fleur Pétrus, because of its name, quality, and small production, tends to be expensive.

VINTAGES

1989—This property's name has always evoked an image of a wine that
  ·   was far more sublime than that which appeared in the bottle—at
92   least that has been my impression for the last three decades. In

1989, 50% of the grapes were cut off to reduce the crop size and to augment the wine's intensity. The results are what must be the finest La Fleur Pétrus since the 1947. In fact, it is so exceptional that it surpasses both Trotanoy and Certan de May in 1989. Dark opaque ruby, with an expressive bouquet of exotic spices and deep, superripe black cherry fruit, this full-bodied wine has an inner core of remarkable depth and length. The great intensity of flavor is backed up by a formidable degree of alcohol and considerable tannins. This is a majestic wine that clearly merits its name in 1989. Anticipated maturity: 1994–2009. Last tasted, 4/91.

1988 —The 1988 is a tasty, attractive, ripe, agreeable wine with good
·   depth, medium body, and enough length and tannin to warrant
86   drinking over the next decade. The only sin is that it precedes the 1989. Anticipated maturity: 1992–2000. Last tasted, 4/91

1987 —In 10 years' time, this wine will probably not rival Pétrus, but for
·   the next 5–6 years, there is no doubt that it is a more supple,
87   more richly fruity, concentrated wine. In fact, this is one of the better examples from this château in recent years. Displaying a surprisingly dark ruby/purple color, plenty of rich, ripe, plummy fruit, and a lush, alcoholic finish, it should be drunk young. A sleeper of the vintage. Anticipated maturity: Now–1997. Last tasted, 11/90.

1986 —I would have liked to taste a bit more flesh and depth in the
·   insubstantial yet still pleasant 1986. It is somewhat forward,
83   slightly compact and attenuated, and quite evolved, with some light tannins in the finish. One wonders why it is not more concentrated given the winemaking team that produced it. Anticipated maturity: 1992–1998. Last tasted, 3/90.

1985 —The 1985 La Fleur Pétrus is fruity, stylish, suave, and tasty. It
·   exhibits good ripeness, medium body, an aromatic bouquet, and
85   a soft, velvety finish. Anticipated maturity: Now–1997. Last tasted, 3/90.

1983 —Rather light and fruity, but nevertheless charming, with medium
·   body, an open-knit, fruity, plummy, spicy, somewhat oaky bou-
81   quet, this is an indifferent effort from La Fleur Pétrus. It is ready to drink. Anticipated maturity: Now–1995. Last tasted, 3/85.

1982 —I have been overwhelmed by the quality of the 1982 La Fleur
·   Pétrus because it is not a wine I own and I had not seen it since
92   my first tastings of the 1982 vintage out of bottle in the spring of 1985. In several tastings I thought it to be Trotanoy because it was so concentrated and impressive. Very dark ruby with no sign of age, this wine has a beautifully complex, rich bouquet of berry

fruit and spicy new oak as well as a chocolatey, coffee smell. Full bodied, and atypically powerful and rich, this beautifully made wine needs another 3–4 years to reach full maturity. It should keep for at least 10–15 years thereafter. Except for the 1947 and 1989, I have never tasted a La Fleur Pétrus this intense and broad-shouldered. Usually it tends to be among the lighter, more elegant Pomerols made. Anticipated maturity: 1992–2000. Last tasted, 1/89.

1981 — Very soft, a trifle jammy, and too supple, the 1981 La Fleur Pétrus
·   is still a deliciously fruity, savory, medium-bodied wine that is
84   ideal for drinking over the next 5–6 years. Anticipated maturity: Now. Last tasted, 10/84.

1979 — The 1979 is an elegant, supple, very fruity wine, with the smell of
·   ripe plums and spicy, vanillin oak very prominently displayed.
85   Medium bodied, with medium to dark ruby color and a lush, nicely concentrated texture, this is not a big, hefty, rich Pomerol, but rather a suave, delicate, yet fruity, interesting wine. Anticipated maturity: Now–1994. Last tasted, 2/83.

1978 — Quite similar to the 1979, yet showing a more perceptible amber/
·   brown edge to it, the 1978 La Fleur Pétrus has a supple, rich, fat,
84   ripe Merlot fruitiness, medium to full body, and light, round tannins. Anticipated maturity: Now–1993. Last tasted, 2/85.

1977 — In this poor vintage, La Fleur Pétrus produced a decent, soft,
·   fruity wine with medium body, not too much annoying vegetal
73   stalkiness, and a pleasant, clean bouquet. Anticipated maturity: Now–probably in serious decline. Last tasted, 4/82.

1976 — The 1976 La Fleur Pétrus is quite mature, with some browning at
·   the edges. It is a charming, open knit, very soft, round wine, with
83   considerable appeal, but like the great majority of 1976 Bordeaux, it is a trifle diluted and flabby, with low acidity. Anticipated maturity: Now–probably in serious decline. Last tasted, 1/80.

1975 — An impressive wine that has just begun to open up and become
·   drinkable, the 1975 La Fleur Pétrus is a concentrated, rich wine,
90   with ripe plummy fruit, full body, plenty of tannin, and unusual power for this Pomerol. Just now approaching its apogee, this wine should continue to evolve. Anticipated maturity: Now–2005. Last tasted, 1/91.

1970 — A top-notch success for the vintage, the 1970 La Fleur Pétrus is
·   now at its apogee. It is very round and richly fruity, with medium
87   body, a lush, velvety texture, and a long finish. The predominant impression is one of rich, roasted black cherries and spices. Anticipated maturity: Now–1997. Last tasted, 1/91.

1966—Fully mature, the 1966 Le Fleur Pétrus has a bouquet of oak,
· truffles, and soft, ripe Merlot fruit. Medium bodied and amber at
84 the edge, this is a wine that can be kept, but is best drunk up.
Anticipated maturity: Now–may be in decline. Last tasted, 1/80.

1964—1964 was a wonderful vintage for the wines of Pomerol, and for
· the properties of the firm of Jean-Pierre Moueix. Chunky and a
85 trifle rustic for La Fleur Pétrus, this is a corpulent, jammy, ripe
wine, full and flavorful, with good body, but a touch of coarseness
does come through on the palate. Anticipated maturity: Now–
1994. Last tasted, 4/78.

OLDER VINTAGES

I have only seen some older vintages of La Fleur Pétrus, the best of
which was a magnificent bottle of the 1947 (rated 96 in 1990). Two other
outstanding wines were the 1950 (rated 95 in 1989) and the 1952 (rated
91 in 1989). All three of these wines have lots of life left in them.

LE GAY (Unclassified)   VERY GOOD

Production: 3,000 cases	Grape varieties:
	Merlot—70%
	Cabernet Franc—30%
Secondary label: none	
Vineyard size: 22 acres	Proprietor: Madamoiselle
	Marie Robin
Time spent in barrels: 18–24	Average age of vines: 40 years
months	
Evaluation of present classification: The quality equivalent of a	
Médoc fourth-growth	
Plateau of maturity: 10–25 years following the vintage	

Just to the north of the Pomerol plateau is the run-down property of Le
Gay, with its unkempt and rather poorly lit wine cellar. Since the death
of her sister, Therese, several years ago, Marie Robin, and her niece and
nephew, Sylvie and Jacques Guinaudeau, own Le Gay and the adjacent
vineyard of Lafleur. The Libourne firm of Jean-Pierre Moueix controls
Le Gay's commercialization throughout the world.

Le Gay is a vineyard of enormous potential, with old vines and miniscule yields of 15–20 hectoliters per hectare, but historically it has been
inconsistent. Great raw materials from the vineyard are often translated
into mediocre wine as a result of old and sometimes dirty barrels. Until

1982, the ancient barrels that housed the wine at Le Gay had to share space with flocks of chickens and ducks.

The style of winemaking at Le Gay results in powerful, rich, tannic, sometimes massive and impenetrable wines. In some years, Le Gay can turn out to be coarse and overbearing, whereas in other vintages the power of Le Gay is in harmony and well balanced against ripe fruit, firm acidity, and tannin. Le Gay is almost always the least flattering Pomerol to taste at a young age, often needing 8–10 years of cellaring to shed its cloak of tannin. For those who prefer their claret soft and easy to drink, Le Gay is an intimidating sort of wine.

VINTAGES

1989—Have you been longing for the post–World War II style of heavy-
·   weight, thick, mouth-coating wine that modern-day winemakers
92   eschew? The 1989 Le Gay will give you a déjà vu of the late
       forties. This Herculean-sized wine (from old vines and yields that
       were one-fourth those of other Pomerols) is fascinating in all re-
       spects. The opaque purple/black color, the savage, animal,
       roasted blackcurrant-scented nose, the spectacular depth, the
       thick, concentrated flavors, and the mouth-shattering tannins are
       the stuff legends were made of . . . in the last century. Patience
       will be required, but I can assure you a case of this wine is going
       in my cellar. Anticipated maturity: 2005–2030. Last tasted, 4/91.

1988—The 1988 is also hugely tannic, but tastes reasonably civilized
·   next to the 1989. Rich, full bodied, deep, and oaky, this wine
86   should reach maturity, optimistically, by the turn of the century,
       and last for two decades thereafter. Anticipated maturity: 1997–
       2020. Last tasted, 4/91.

1986—The 1986 Le Gay will appeal primarily to those with nineteenth-
·   century tastes for big, beefy, bulky wines that assault the senses
87   and palate with layer upon layer of tannin. It remains a closed
       and dense wine that only stubbornly offers up the ripe fruit that
       the deep color and weight of the wine suggest it possesses. It is a
       wine that will require a significant amount of time to pull itself
       together and smooth out. How many consumers will have the
       patience to wait? Anticipated maturity: 1998–2010. Last tasted,
       3/90.

1985—I have never enjoyed tasting Le Gay when young. With age, the
·   finesse and breed come through, but at the moment, the 1985 is
86   mean, moody, and murky, as well as terribly tannic. It is full
       bodied and deep, and exhibits good richness, but how long is one
       expected to wait? The rating may turn out to be conservative if

this wine pulls itself together and smooths out. Anticipated maturity: 1995–2008. Last tasted, 3/89.

1983— The 1983 is a good Le Gay—alcoholic, tannic, a little clumsy and
·   awkward, but powerful and ripe. Low acidity may prevent a long,
83   graceful evolution, but this wine will please many buyers for a
        direct, full-bodied, rich, aggressive style. Anticipated maturity:
        Now–2000. Last tasted, 9/87.

1982— I have experienced considerable bottle variation with the 1982 Le
·   Gay, but the best bottles are extremely powerful, rich, and con-
88?   centrated, with a big, deep, blackberry, earthy, almost peppery,
        Rhône-like bouquet. The color remains dense, almost opaque,
        and the wine has great depth, full body, mouth-gripping tannin,
        and excellent potential for long-term cellaring. Other bottles have
        exhibited an annoying locker-room, sweaty-socks aroma. Antici-
        pated maturity: 1995–2015. Last tasted, 12/90.

1981— The deliciously fruity, supple, deep, cask samples of the 1981 Le
·   Gay were impressive, but in the bottle it has shown a remarkable
?   degree of variation. Some bottles have dirty, flawed bouquets,
        while others are rich, fruity, and clean. It is impossible to tell
        which bottle is the clean one, so this wine is best avoided. Re-
        tasted twice in 1988 with similar results. Last tasted, 4/88.

1979— A success for Le Gay, the 1979 is richly fruity with the smell of
·   blackcurrants and violets, and earthy, truffle-scented aromas.
84   This medium- to full-bodied wine has light to moderate tannins
        and a good finish. Anticipated maturity: Now–1994. Last tasted,
        6/82.

1975— An outstanding effort from Le Gay, the 1975 is a rich, powerful,
·   concentrated, tannic, deeply scented wine (aromas of minerals,
90   licorice, and blackcurrants are pervasive). The wine has a long
        evolution ahead. Still dark ruby, with full-throttle flavors that give
        this muscular wine a huge, massive, nearly thick feel in the
        mouth, this is a blockbuster wine! Anticipated maturity: 1993–
        2010. Last tasted, 12/90.

1966— Mature and fully ready to drink, the 1966 Le Gay has an amber,
·   moderately dark ruby color, an earthy, austere Médoc-like, re-
83   strained bouquet, medium body, and a solid, somewhat rustic
        finish. Anticipated maturity: Now–may be in decline. Last tasted,
        9/82.

1962— Still firm, but mature, Le Gay's 1962 has a moderately intense
·   bouquet of ripe plums and mineral scents. On the palate, the wine
85   is concentrated, surprisingly well balanced, and interesting. An-
        ticipated maturity: Now–may be in decline. Last tasted, 11/79.

1961—A disappointment in this great vintage, Le Gay has a bizarre,
·   medicinal bouquet and a loosely knit structure, harsh fruity fla-
68   vors, and little balance. Anticipated maturity: Now–probably in
        serious decline. Last tasted, 11/79.

GAZIN (Unclassified)   GOOD

Production: 10,000 cases	Grape varieties:
	Merlot—80%
	Cabernet Franc—15%
	Cabernet Sauvignon—5%
Secondary label: none	
Vineyard size: 49.4 acres	Proprietor: Etienne de
	Bailliencourt
Time spent in barrels: 24 months	Average age of vines: 30 years
Evaluation of present classification: Since 1988, the quality	
equivalent of a Médoc fifth-growth	
Plateau of maturity: 5–15 years following the vintage	

Most commentators on Bordeaux have generally held Gazin in high regard, no doubt because the vineyard is ideally situated behind Pétrus in
the northeast corner of the appellation. In fact, Gazin sold 12.5 acres of
its vineyard to Pétrus in 1969. However, the track record for Gazin, one
of the largest vineyards of Pomerol, has been one of mediocrity throughout the sixties and seventies, and through the mid-eighties. The wine is
vinified very traditionally, but far too many good years—1961, 1970,
1975, 1978, 1979, 1981, 1982, 1983, 1985, and 1986—have produced dull,
light, and one-dimensional wines. Most vintages have matured quickly,
normally within 5–7 years.

Strangely enough Gazin is an expensive wine. A historic reputation
and the strategic placement on the Pomerol plateau next to Pétrus and
L'Evangile have served it well. The optimistic signs that 1988 and 1989
mark a new period of higher-quality wines from Gazin should be enthusiastically greeted by consumers wanting a tasty, plump, succulent Pomerol.

VINTAGES

1989—The 1989 Gazin possesses an intense bouquet of toasty new oak
·   intertwined with aromas of rich, jammy, plump fruit, and flowers.
88   In the mouth, a chewy texture suggests opulence, even unctuous-
        ness. The finish, with its elevated alcohol level and low acidity,
        should provide immense gratification for those who prefer sensual
        over intellectual wines. This is the best Gazin in decades. Antici-
        pated maturity: 1994–2005. Last tasted, 4/91.

1988—After years of mediocrity, has Gazin finally changed direction?
· The turnaround started with the 1988, which is a wonderfully
87 seductive, rich, sweet, broad-flavored, hedonistic wine, with light
tannins, a rich, savory texture, and a satiny, alcoholic finish. It
will be a real charmer early on, but has the potential to last at
least through the end of the century. Anticipated maturity: Now–
2003. Last tasted, 4/91.

1986—The 1986, with a lightly vegetal, spicy, plum-like bouquet, seems
· to slip off the palate, revealing only a trace of tannin and alcohol.
79 Anticipated maturity: Now–1997. Last tasted, 3/90.

1985—The 1985 has adequate ripeness, but is somewhat dull, medium
· bodied, and overall a mediocre, one-dimensional wine. Antici-
76 pated maturity: Now–1994. Last tasted, 3/89.

1984—A very marginal wine, the 1984 Gazin is watery, light, and diffuse,
· and should be avoided. Last tasted, 3/88.
64

GOMBAUDE-GUILLOT (Unclassified) VERY GOOD

Production: 3,000 cases	Grape varieties: Merlot—50% Cabernet Franc—42% Malbec—8%
Secondary label: none, but a luxury "Cuvée Speciale" that is aged in 100% new oak is produced in certain vintages	
Vineyard size: 16.7 acres	Proprietor: The Laval family
Time spent in barrels: 24 months	Average age of vines: 30 years
Evaluation of present classification: The quality equivalent of a Médoc fifth-growth	
Plateau of maturity: 5–15 years following the vintage	

This has become an intriguing property to follow. I remember tasting the
wine in the early eighties and being unimpressed with the range of vintages I saw from the seventies, but a recent vertical tasting back through
1982 left me with the conclusion that in certain years Gombaude-Guillot
can produce a Pomerol of spectacular quality.

The vineyard is comprised of three parcels made up of totally different
types of soil. The only parcel from the plateau consists of a heavier, clay-
and-gravel-dominated parcel with a great deal of iron in it. A second
parcel is primarily sandy soil intermixed with some gravel, and a third
parcel consists largely of gravel.

The old vines and relatively low yields that are 30% below many of the more prestigious names often result in strikingly rich, concentrated wines. Interestingly, in 1985 Gombaude-Guillot launched a Cuvée Speciale from a selection of wine that represented some of the best lots from their vineyards, and aged it in 100% new oak. It was such an enormously successful wine that the château repeated this experiment in 1988 and 1989.

As the following tasting notes evidence, this is not a consistent wine, but when Gombaude-Guillot does everything right, it ranks as one of the top-dozen Pomerols of the appellation.

VINTAGES

1989—According to the Laval family, there would be a Cuvée Spéciale
 · in 1989. Unfortunately, I was unable to taste it. The regular *cuvée*
90 is an impressive black/purple–colored wine, with a huge aroma of roasted black plums and cassis. In the mouth, it is intensely concentrated and full bodied, with a luxurious richness and opulence seen only in the best examples from this vintage. Long, somewhat low in acidity, with moderate tannins, this is a sumptuous Pomerol. Anticipated maturity: 1994–2005. Last tasted, 4/ 91.

1988—Medium ruby, with a spicy bouquet and medium-bodied, ade
 · quately concentrated flavors, the finish has some sharp tannins.
84 The overall impression is that of a wine with adequate rather than great depth. Anticipated maturity: 1992–2001. Last tasted, 4/91.

1988—Cuvée Spéciale—This luxury *cuvée*, aged in 100% new oak, sur
 · prisingly does not exhibit as much of a smoky, vanillin character
89 in the nose as one might suspect. It is, however, rich and full bodied, and may merit an outstanding rating in another 3–4 years. Quite concentrated, with intense aromas and flavors of blackcurrants, plums, and minerals, this beauty should have a graceful evolution. Anticipated maturity: 1993–2003. Last tasted, 11/90.

1987—This is a light, relatively soft, somewhat diluted, soundly made,
 · but uninteresting Pomerol. Anticipated maturity: Now–1994.
78 Last tasted, 11/90.

1985—Deep ruby/purple in color, with an intense bouquet of cassis and
 · other black fruits, and rich, with an unctuous texture and gobs of
88 sweet, superripe fruit, this expansive, generously endowed wine is already delicious to drink. Anticipated maturity: Now–2001. Last tasted, 4/91.

1985—Cuvée Spéciale—Make no mistake about it, the 1985 Cuvée Spe
 · ciale rivals the great Pomerols such as Lafleur, L'Evangile,
93 L'Eglise-Clinet, and Pétrus. It is still a very young wine, as the

opaque, purple/black color suggests. The huge bouquet of minerals, superripe cassis, and smoky new oak is enthralling. In the mouth, the wine is powerful, exceptionally concentrated, and well balanced, with a finish that must last for well over a minute. There are plenty of tannins, but they are soft. Although this wine can be drunk now, it is still undeveloped and needs a good 4–5 years of cellaring. Anticipated maturity: 1995–2008. Last tasted, 1/91.

1982—This big, round, generously endowed, chewy-textured wine has
·   reached full maturity, as the amber at the edge suggests. The big
87   nose of grilled nuts, smoke, and superripe plums is followed by opulent, alcoholic, heady flavors. This hedonistic wine is ideal for current consumption. Anticipated maturity: Now–1994. Last tasted, 12/90.

LA GRAVE TRIGANT DE BOISSET (Unclassified)   VERY GOOD

Production: 3,500 cases	Grape varieties: Merlot—90% Cabernet Franc—10%
Secondary label: none	
Vineyard size: 19.8 acres	Proprietor: Christian Moueix
Time spent in barrels: 18–22 months	Average age of vines: 30 years
Evaluation of present classification: The quality equivalent of a Médoc fifth-growth	
Plateau of maturity: 3–12 years following the vintage	

La Grave is another of the relatively obscure Pomerol estates that is making better and better wine. Since 1971, the château has been owned by the meticulous and introspective Christian Moueix who directs the business affairs of his father's firm in Libourne.

La Grave is located just to the east of Route Nationale 89 in the direction of France's truffle capital, Périgueux. It is adjacent to the border of Lalande-de-Pomerol, and situated on unusually gravelly, sandy soil, which results in wines that are a little lighter and less powerful than those from the Pomerol plateau.

All the vintages from 1980 on have been successful, with the 1989 and 1982 being classics. Normally La Grave is a wine to drink after 5–6 years of bottle age, although in some vintages it can be cellared for 12–15 years. While not one of the most expensive Pomerols, neither is it one of the bargains of this appellation. However, given the increasing quality exhibited by this wine in recent vintages, this is a property to take more and more seriously.

VINTAGES

1989—The best vintage of La Grave in the eighties has been the 1982,
· but the 1989 promises to rival that vintage. It is more concen-
87 trated, alcoholic, and structured than the 1982. The excellent
bouquet of spicy, toasty oak, black cherries, and plums is followed by a medium-bodied wine, with a heady alcohol content,
plenty of tannin, and very good concentration. Anticipated maturity: 1992–2002. Last tasted, 4/91.

1988—The 1988 boasts an intense, new-oak-dominated bouquet, some
· spicy, medium-bodied, ripe fruit, moderate tannins, more acidity,
85 and less alcohol in the finish. It does not have the ampleness of
the 1989, but those who like a more restrained, polite style of
Pomerol may prefer the 1988. Anticipated maturity: Now–2001.
Last tasted, 4/91.

1986—The 1986 displays more tannin than is usual, but the overall
· impression is one of lightness and delicate, understated fruit and
81 light to medium body. Anticipated maturity: Now–1996. Last
tasted, 3/90.

1985—As usual, La Grave Trigant de Boisset's 1985 is an elegant, soft,
· fruity wine. Anticipated maturity: Now–1995. Last tasted, 3/90.
84

1984—The 1984 La Grave is light, herbaceous, but spicy, soft, fruity,
· and cleanly made. It is ready to drink. Anticipated maturity:
78 Now–1993. Last tasted, 3/88.

1983—A rather big, richly fruity wine for La Grave, the 1983 has a ruby/
· garnet color, surprisingly sound acidity for a 1983 Pomerol, a ripe,
85 toasty, plummy fruitiness, and medium body. Anticipated maturity: Now–1996. Last tasted, 1/89.

1982—A gorgeously ripe, richly scented Pomerol, the 1982 does not have
· the huge power and richness of some top Pomerols, but it does
87 offer considerable elegance and grace. Moderately rich and concentrated, this is a sensual, lush Pomerol that will provide rewarding drinking over the next 4–6 years. Anticipated maturity:
Now–1996. Last tasted, 2/91.

1981—The 1981 La Grave has elegant, herbaceous, ripe berry fruit,
· medium body, light tannins, and a short, compact finish. Antici-
81 pated maturity: Now–1994. Last tasted, 6/88.

1976—One of the most successful 1976 Pomerols, La Grave, which is
· fully mature, has a toasty, ripe fruity bouquet, soft, round, nicely
84 concentrated flavors, and no noticeable tannins remaining. Anticipated maturity: Now–may be in decline. Last tasted, 4/83.

HAUT-MAILLET (Unclassified)   GOOD

Production: 2,500 cases	Grape varieties: Merlot—60% Cabernet Franc—40%
Secondary label: none	
Vineyard size: 12.5 acres	Proprietor: Jean-Pierre Estager
Time spent in barrels: 20 months	Average age of vines: 25 years

Evaluation of present classification: The quality equivalent of a
 Médoc Cru Bourgeois
Plateau of maturity: 4–10 years following the vintage

Jean-Pierre Estager, the well-known proprietor of La Cabanne, owns this tiny vineyard situated on the outskirts of Pomerol, adjacent to Bon Pasteur. Very little of their wine is ever exported since the estate consists of only 12.5 acres. My experience is limited to the following two vintages.

VINTAGES

1989—Aged in 50% new oak casks, the 1989 possesses an attractive
·   bouquet of vanillin and black cherry and plummy fruit. In the
84   mouth, there is adequate extraction of fruit, full body, plenty of
       alcohol, and low acidity. Anticipated maturity: 1992–1997. Last
       tasted, 4/91.

1988—The 1988 is very light, is medium bodied, and has a short finish.
·   Anticipated maturity: Now–1994. Last tasted, 4/91.
76

LAFLEUR (Unclassified)   OUTSTANDING

Production: 1,000 cases	Grape varieties: Merlot—50% Cabernet Franc—50%
Secondary label: Les Pensées de Lafleur	
Vineyard size: 11.1 acres	Proprietor: Mademoiselle Marie Robin Administrators: Sylvie and Jacques Guinaudeau
Time spent in barrels: 20–24 months	Average age of vines: 33 years

Evaluation of present classification: The quality equivalent of a
 Médoc first-growth
Plateau of maturity: 8–30 years following the vintage

I have always had a personal attachment to this tiny Pomerol vineyard. In the mid-1970s, when I first started tasting the wines of Lafleur, I could find nothing written about them. Yet in my small tasting group, we frequently found the wine to be every bit as compelling as Pétrus. I made my first visit to Lafleur in 1978, speaking very little French, and found the two elderly proprietors, the late Therese Robin and her sister, Marie, decrepit, but utterly charming. The Lafleur château was, and remains today, more of a barn than a winery. Despite the advanced age of these two spinsters, they would ride their bikes out to Le Gay, the official reception center for both Lafleur and Le Gay. They were no doubt amused by my size, referring to me as Monsieur Le Taureau (bull). I probably did look a bit oversized walking in the tiny *chai*, where the barrels, as well as a bevy of ducks, chickens, and rabbits, were housed. It always amazed me how wines of such great extraction and utterly mind-blowing character could be produced in such filthy conditions.

Only one Robin sister, Marie, remains alive, and she has given over the reins of running Lafleur to her niece and nephew, Sylvie and Jacques Guinaudeau. They took responsibility starting with the 1985 vintage, and not only declassified the entire crop of 1987 Lafleur, but at the same time introduced a second wine, Les Pensées de Lafleur. This is rather remarkable given the tiny production of this micro-estate. The cellars remain the same, but they are now devoid of the ducks, chickens, and rabbits, as well as the dung they left behind. Additionally, Lafleur now benefits from 50–66% new oak casks for each vintage.

Is the wine any better? Certainly Lafleur remains the only wine of the Pomerol appellation that is consistently capable of challenging, and in some cases surpassing, Pétrus. Even Jean-Pierre Moueix once admitted this to me, and I have been fortunate to have had Lafleur and Pétrus side by side enough times to know the former is a wine every bit as extraordinary as Pétrus. In many vintages, from an aromatic point of view, it is more complex than Pétrus, no doubt because of the Cabernet Franc.

Much of the greatness of Lafleur lies in the soil, which is a deep, gravelly bed enriched with iron and some sand, but also characterized by extremely important deposits of phosphorus and potassium. Over the years, the yields have been tiny, reflecting the motto of the Robin sisters' father, who often said that at Lafleur, "quality surpasses quantity."

Old vintages of Lafleur are legendary, but the history of the property has not been without mixed results. I have never had a great bottle of the 1961, although friends of mine in Bordeaux tell me examples do exist. Furthermore, the 1971 should be better, and more recently, the 1981 is flawed by the presence of fecal aromas. However, the wine is now being looked over by an oenologist, and even though the incredibly old vines (there was no replanting at Lafleur after the freeze of 1956) are having to be grubbed up, the average age is still impressive. Since 1982 (the 1982 and 1983 were made by Christian Moueix and Jean-Claude Berrouet), Lafleur has become less exotic, and perhaps more influenced by modern-day oenologists with their obsession with wines that fall within certain technical parameters. Nevertheless, Lafleur, measured by the highest standards of Bordeaux, while now made within proper technical parameters, still remains one of the most distinctive, exotic, and greatest wines of the entire region.

VINTAGES

1989 —Lafleur is one of the greatest wines of Bordeaux, as anyone who has followed the quality of this property over the last several
·
96 decades can attest, and it is one of the most difficult to find. The problem is there are only 1,000 cases for the world, a big chunk of which is purchased by the Belgians who have long known about its extraordinary quality (often rivaling, sometimes even surpassing, Pétrus). The 1989 is marginally superior to the 1988, but compared to the big, exotic, dense, kinky style that Lafleur has exhibited in vintages such as 1975, 1979, 1982, and 1983, this is a refined, more gentleman-like wine. It is dark ruby/purple in color, concentrated, and very closed, with a great deal of tannin and alcohol in the finish. This is a wine to be drinking between the turn of the century and the first two and a half decades of the next millennium. Anticipated maturity: 2000–2030. Last tasted, 4/91.

1988 —The 1988 is a legitimate superstar of the vintage. Very deeply colored (even more opaque than the 1989), with a powerful, for-
·
94 midable mouth feel, this wine represents the essence of old vines and low yields (under 20 hectoliters per hectare). Along with Lafite-Rothschild, Lafleur should prove to be among the longest-lived and most fulfilling wines of the 1988 vintage. Anticipated maturity: 2005–2030. Last tasted, 4/91.

1986 —The 1986 is an enormously powerful, exceptionally deep, full-bodied wine. It offers a formidable presence on the palate, tre-
·
95 mendous tannins, a colossal framework, and immense structure. More than one sophisticated taster has told me that this wine reminded him of some of the vintages from the late forties, with its intense, concentrated, old-style power and richness. One then might wonder when the 1986 Lafleur can be drunk. No earlier than the turn of the century would seemingly make any sense, so you will do a lot of waiting before imbibing this giant of a wine. Anticipated maturity: 2000–2030. Last tasted, 12/90.

1985—The 1985 Lafleur is a much larger-scaled wine than the 1985
·   Pétrus. It possesses a very special bouquet suggesting ripe plums,
96   minerals, violets, and an intensity that comes only from old vines.
        Deep ruby/purple, with an exceptional richness and depth of fruit,
        full body, and a powerful, long finish, this wine ranks with the
        mammoth-sized vintages of Lafleur—1989, 1988, 1986, 1982,
        1979, 1975, and 1964. Anticipated maturity: 1995–2015. Last
        tasted, 1/91.

1984—Certainly a success for the vintage, the 1984 Lafleur has a sweet,
·   ripe nose and is obviously much lighter on the palate than usual,
84   but I must admit I was surprised by the depth of fruit and length.
        Anticipated maturity: Now–1994. Last tasted, 2/89.

1983—The 1983 is a powerful, rich, alcoholic (over 14%) wine with tre-
·   mendous presence, richness, and power on the palate. The huge
94   bouquet of sweet plums, licorice, minerals, and exotic spices is
        sensational. Typically Lafleur, it is a brawny, ripe, intense, kinky
        wine with considerable concentration and soft tannins. Antici-
        pated maturity: 1993–2010. Last tasted, 12/90.

1982—According to the firm of Jean-Pierre Moueix, the 1982 is the great-
·   est Lafleur ever made, even better than the majestic 1975 and
96   legendary 1947. I do not believe this wine has the sheer weight,
        concentration, or power of these two previous vintages. Neverthe-
        less, this is no wine wimp. Consistently impressive from the cask
        and bottle, this is a titan of a wine. Still dense ruby/purple in
        color, with an amazing concentration of rich, layered plummy,
        blackcurrant fruit and an enormous bouquet of oriental spices
        and plums, this is a voluptuous, satiny-textured, unctuous bottle
        of wine. Anticipated maturity: 1994–2010. Last tasted, 2/91.

1981—Considerable bottle variation seems to be the culprit with the 1981
·   Lafleur. The good examples exhibit a savory, supple, chewy,
?   spicy, velvety, concentrated fruitiness, medium body, and light
        tannins. The others display an annoying musty, fecal aroma that
        refuses to dissipate with aeration. Are you a gambler? Last
        tasted, 3/87.

1979—The wine of the vintage! Lafleur's power and richness are readily
·   apparent. Still dark ruby, almost opaque, Lafleur's bouquet is
96   tight and unyielding but reluctantly renders aromas of black
        fruits, mineral scents, herbs, and exotic spices. On the palate,
        the wine is full bodied, still very tannic, extremely concentrated,
        and long in the finish. This wine is an atypical 1979 because of its
        backwardness and mammoth size. In fact, it tastes more like the
        1975 than any other recent vintage of Lafleur. Anticipated matu-
        rity: 1996–2015. Last tasted, 1/91.

1978—This wine has improved immensely since I first tasted it. I have
·   always been astonished that the elderly, frail, small-framed Robin
90   sisters could produce such robust, intense, powerful wine. The
  1978 lacks the huge weight and awesome extract of the 1979, but
  it remains a big, rich, full-bodied, atypically powerful 1978 Pomerol. Will this wine develop along the lines of the superb 1966?
  Anticipated maturity: 1993–2008. Last tasted, 2/91.

1976—Like many Pomerols of this vintage (which was marked by the
·   intense heat and drought of that year's summer), Lafleur's 1976
78   exhibits an overripe character. Diffuse in structure, with a flabby,
  soft texture, the flavors of the 1976 Lafleur are pleasingly plump
  and ripe, but the acidity is quite low, and the tannin is quickly
  fading. Anticipated maturity: Now–probably in serious decline.
  Last tasted, 9/82.

1975—This legendary effort recalls some of the old-style, heavyweight,
·   right-bank wines from vintages such as 1945, 1947, and 1949.
100   Very dark with an unbelievable bouquet of ripe fruit, spices, tobacco, and leather, this huge, full-bodied, tannic, opulent, viscous wine lingers and lingers on the palate. It has hardly evolved
  since the first edition of this book; a monumental wine that begs
  for prolonged cellaring. Anticipated maturity: 2001–2035. Last
  tasted, 12/90.

1971—Fully mature, this wine has an opulent, savory, cedary, spicy,
·   slightly jammy, herbal bouquet. Soft, supple, broad flavors dis-
83   play a lot of ripe fruit and little tannin. Anticipated maturity:
  Now–probably in serious decline. Last tasted, 2/84.

1970—Brawny, beefy, full bodied, and still rustic and tannic, the 1970
·   Lafleur has, I believe, reached its apogee. The bouquet exhibits
87   good ripe fruit, an earthy, mineral-and-leather-scented bouquet
  intermingled with the smell of roasted chestnuts and tea-smoked
  duck. On the palate, the wine is rich, well structured, and long.
  It is a solid, robust wine that could use more finesse. Anticipated
  maturity: Now–2010. Last tasted, 1/91.

1966—This may be one of the three best wines of the vintage. The huge
·   bouquet of minerals, cedar, licorice, and oriental spices is pro-
94   found. Full bodied, with a fascinating display of superripe flavors
  and brilliant balance, this wine is still remarkably fresh and vigorous. Anticipated maturity: Now–2005. Last tasted, 5/91.

1964—Still dark colored with just a slight rim of amber, the 1964 Lafleur
·   is a big, rich, full-bodied, intense wine with oodles of extract and
89   body. Still tannic, but beginning to open up, this old-style, chewy,
  powerful wine lacks a little in complexity, but delivers quite a
  mouthful. Anticipated maturity: Now–1996. Last tasted, 6/84.

1962 —One of the three best Pomerols of the vintage, Lafleur lacks the
· complexity and elegance of the 1962 Trotanoy, but is a more
87 substantial wine than the Pétrus. Surprisingly dark in color, with
a full-intensity, waxy, ripe black cherry bouquet, this wine is
much tougher and more tannic than most 1962s. It is still in
excellent condition. Anticipated maturity: Now–2000. Last
tasted, 12/88.

1961 —For whatever reason, this wine has never been impressive in the
· three tastings of it I have had. The wine is dark in color with some
70 browning, the bouquet has a hot, charred aroma, and the flavors
are astringent and out of balance. There is fruit present, but it is
buried behind a wall of bitterness. Last tasted, 3/88.

OLDER VINTAGES

The 1959 (rated 88 in 12/87) is a ruggedly built, muscular, tough-
textured wine that is impressive for its size and weight. But much like
the 1964 and 1970, it lacks charm and finesse. It should continue to age
well for another 10–15 years. I have always preferred the 1955 (rated 92
in 12/87). It possesses that exotic, mineral, black fruit character so typical of Lafleur, massive weight, an unctuous texture, and plenty of hard
tannin still left in the finish. Perhaps the greatest single bottle of red
wine I have ever tasted was the 1947 Lafleur (rated 100 in 3/87). I have
had this wine on four occasions, but three of them were from a Belgium
bottling where the wine merited a score in the high eighties. They were
good, but the château bottling I drank with Christian Moueix in 1987 was
the only wine that ever brought tears to my eyes. I was depressed upon
finishing the wine—it was that spectacular! I do not know how many
bottles of this wine are left, but for those readers who have had a chance
to taste pristine bottles of the 1947 Pétrus or 1947 Cheval Blanc, the 1947
Lafleur was even more concentrated and unctuous than those two legends. I would be remiss in not mentioning the nearly perfect, profound
1950 Lafleur (rated 99–100 in 3/88). It is as concentrated as the 1961
Pétrus!

LAFLEUR DU ROY (Unclassified) AVERAGE

Production: 2,000 cases	Grape varieties: Merlot—75% Cabernet Franc—15% Cabernet Sauvignon—10%
Secondary label: none	
Vineyard size: 10 acres	Proprietor: Yvon Dubost
Time spent in barrels: 15–20 months	Average age of vines: 27 years
Evaluation of present classification: The quality equivalent of a Médoc Cru Bourgeois	
Plateau of maturity: 4–10 years following the vintage	

I rarely see the wines of Lafleur du Roy, whose vineyard is located in the southwestern section of the Pomerol appellation on sandy, gravelly soil, between Château Plince and Château Nenin. Most of the production is sold in Belgium and Denmark. Monsieur Dubost is also the proprietor of the St.-Emilion Grand Cru, Vieux-Château-Carré.

VINTAGES

1989—Despite some ripe cassis fruit, this wine is excessively woody, with high tannin and gobs of oak flavor obscuring much of the fruit and charm. That's sad, because the quality of the fruit seemed attractive. Anticipated maturity: 1993–2003. Last tasted, 4/91.

· 70

LAGRANGE (Unclassified) AVERAGE

Production: 3,500 cases	Grape varieties: Merlot—90% Cabernet Franc—10%
Secondary label: none	
Vineyard size: 22.2 acres	Proprietor: Jean-Pierre Moueix
Time spent in barrels: 22 months	Average age of vines: 20 years
Evaluation of present classification: The quality equivalent of a Médoc Cru Bourgeois	
Plateau of maturity: 5–12 years following the vintage	

One rarely sees the wine of Lagrange, another of the properties owned and managed by the firm of Jean-Pierre Moueix. Lagrange is well situated near the plateau of Pomerol, but the vineyard has been recently replanted significantly with the composition being changed to 90% Merlot and 10% Cabernet Franc. The wine tends to be a rather brawny, densely colored Pomerol with significant power and tannins, but not much complexity. Older vintages such as 1970, 1975, and 1978 have all proven to be stubbornly big, brooding, coarse wines that have been slow to develop. This is not a style of wine that I find attractive.

VINTAGES

1989—This property seems to produce a hard, tough, frequently charmless style of Pomerol. The 1989 is typically rough edged, lean,
·   austere, and too tannic for graceful aging. Anticipated maturity:
82   1992–2000. Last tasted, 4/91.

1988—The 1988 is shallow, insipid, and undistinguished. Given the vineyard's location, as well as the winemaking team at this estate,
·   this is a disappointment. Anticipated maturity: 1993–2000. Last
76   tasted, 4/91.

1986—This wine has consistently displayed a dull, one-dimensional character with barely adequate fruit, as well as a mouthful of
·   tannin in the finish. Perhaps I have missed something along the
73   way, but I would opt for drinking it over the near term because its balance is slightly suspect. Anticipated maturity: Now–1996. Last tasted, 3/90.

1985—The 1985 is an easygoing, fruity, supple wine that offers immediate gratification. Anticipated maturity: Now–1996. Last tasted,
·
83   3/89.

LATOUR À POMEROL (Unclassified)   EXCELLENT

Production: 3,500 cases	Grape varieties: Merlot—90% Cabernet Franc—10%
Secondary label: none	

Vineyard size: 19.76 acres	Proprietor: Madame Lily Paul
	  Lacoste
	Administrator: Jean-Pierre
	  Moueix

Time spent in barrels: 24 months	Average age of vines: 32 years
Evaluation of present classification: The quality equivalent of a Médoc second-growth	
Plateau of maturity: 6–20 years following the vintage	

Latour à Pomerol produces splendidly dark colored wine that usually represents a powerful, opulent, fleshy style of Pomerol. The vineyard is comprised of two parcels. One is located near the church of Pomerol on a deep, gravelly bed. The second, and smaller parcel, is located further west near RN 89 on sandier, lighter soil. The second parcel is closest to the vineyard owned by Christian Moueix called La Grave Trigant de Boisset.

Latour à Pomerol can be a majestic wine and can often be one of the two or three greatest wines of the appellation in certain vintages. The 1947, 1961, and 1970 offer persuasive evidence that this estate can rival the greatest wines of Bordeaux. While some observers have claimed that Latour à Pomerol comes closest in weight and structure to Pétrus, that would not appear to be the case. This is a wine that, while rich and full, tends to have more in common with other Moueix-controlled properties such as La Fleur Pétrus or Trotanoy than with the great Pétrus itself.

Latour à Pomerol is usually about one-fifth the price of Pétrus and about one-half the price of Trotanoy and Lafleur. For a limited-production Pomerol of such high quality, it remains a relative bargain.

VINTAGES

1989—For the first time since 1982, Latour à Pomerol is of star quality.
· In fact, the 1989 resembles the 1982, being slightly less concen-
90 trated, but more tannic and alcoholic. Deep opaque ruby/purple with a full-intensity bouquet of spices, new wood, plums, and cassis, this expansively flavored, seemingly sweet (because of the fruit's ripeness), full-flavored wine has considerable tannin in the finish, giving rise to the perplexing question as to when it will be at its best. Anticipated maturity: 1995–2015. Last tasted, 4/91.

1988—The 1988 is much lighter and soft, fruity, and well made, but
· hardly of the quality level one expects from this château. Antici-
85 pated maturity: Now–1999. Last tasted, 4/91.

1986—The 1986 is more burly and tannic than usual, with an excellent
· deep color, full body, and a cedary, tea, and plum-like bouquet
87 admirably backed up by new oak. Given its tannic clout and power, I would want to cellar this wine for at least 3–5 years. Anticipated maturity: 1993–2002. Last tasted, 3/90.

1985—I continue to see a resemblance in the rich, full-bodied, concen-
· trated, ripe, and sexy 1985 to the brilliant wine made at this estate
88 in 1970. Full, long, and powerful, this expansively flavored wine has considerable length and plenty of tannin, and will require some cellaring prior to consumption. Anticipated maturity: 1992–2005. Last tasted, 3/89.

1984—This is a firm, tough, unyielding sort of wine that seems to have
· fruit lurking beneath the tannins. Anticipated maturity: Now–
82 1994. Last tasted, 3/89.

1983—A top success for the vintage, the 1983 Latour à Pomerol is among
·   the richest, most powerfully constructed, broodingly opaque, and
88   enormous Pomerols from the 1983 vintage. It has remained big,
        brawny, ripe, and muscular, although the tannins have melted
        away. The bouquet, filled with scents of mocha, chocolate, and
        plums, is a delight. Anticipated maturity: Now–2005. Last tasted,
        5/91.

1982—The 1982 needs another 5–6 years to reach full maturity, but
·   is a super wine with fabulous power, richness, opulence, con-
93   centration, and length. It is the fullest-bodied, and most con-
        centrated Latour à Pomerol since the 1961, although it will
        never quite approach that monumental wine in richness and
        aging potential. Anticipated maturity: 1997–2015. Last tasted,
        12/90.

1981—The 1981 is a fine example of Latour à Pomerol. However, it has
·   subsequently been eclipsed by both the 1982 and 1983 wines.
85   Moderately dark in color for a 1981, with a dense, ripe, rich,
        medium-bodied texture on the palate, this well-balanced wine
        offers a velvety mouthful of wine, but it is less impressive than I
        originally thought. Anticipated maturity: Now–1997. Last tasted,
        3/89.

1979—Precociously fat, supple, and easy to drink, this vintage of Latour
·   à Pomerol seems to have produced an amply endowed, charming,
85   silky wine without much tannin. It is medium bodied, dark ruby
        in color, and quite forward. Anticipated maturity: Now–1993.
        Last tasted, 10/84.

1978—Jammy, soft, ripe, and round, the 1978 Latour à Pomerol is ready
·   to drink. Like many Pomerols of this vintage, I detect a degree of
83   overripeness and shortness in the finish, but nevertheless, this is
        a pleasant, fruity wine. Anticipated maturity: Now–may be in
        decline. Last tasted, 2/83.

1976—In 1976, this estate managed to produce a rich, flavorful, spicy,
·   concentrated wine while avoiding the overripe character that af-
86   flicted so many Pomerol estates. Lush, silky, creamy, fat, and
        fruity, this medium-bodied wine is complemented nicely by spicy
        oak. It has been fully mature for a decade, and there are no
        discernible tannins remaining. Anticipated maturity: Now–1994.
        Last tasted, 1/89.

1975—In a vintage where a number of Pomerols are superb, the 1975
·   Latour à Pomerol is inexplicably disappointing. Severe, tannic,
67   hollow, and totally charmless, this wine lacks fruit, substance,
        and color. Last tasted, 11/88.

1971—Beginning to fade ever so slightly, this lovely wine peaked in the
· middle seventies. With some brown at the edges, the 1971 is soft,
82 round, and medium bodied, with no tannins left. The classy bouquet still exhibits some cedary, spicy fruit, but fades in the glass.
Anticipated maturity: Now–probably in decline. Last tasted,
10/82.

1970—This is the most successful vintage for Latour à Pomerol between
· 1961 and 1982. The wine has always been impressive, even from
90 the earliest days. It remains dark ruby (only a hint of amber), with
a huge bouquet of sweet, ripe fruit, spicy, vanillin oak, and grilled
chestnuts. In the mouth, the wine has gobs of glycerine, and is
ripe, expansive, velvety, long, and concentrated. All the tannins
have melted away and the wine is fully mature. Anticipated maturity: Now–1996. Last tasted, 1/90.

1966—The 1966 is an atypically ripe, rich, dense wine that, in style,
· seems an anomaly in this vintage that produced lean, elegant,
87 restrained wines. Still quite dark in color with an orange rim, the
wine has a bouquet of ripe, deep fruit and oak, as well as a tarry,
truffle-scented aroma. Powerful, full bodied, and rich, this wine
should be drunk up. Anticipated maturity: Now–1994. Last
tasted, 4/81.

1961—A compelling wine of extraordinary flavor dimension and depth,
· the 1961 Latour à Pomerol resembles a great vintage port. A
100 sensational bouquet of rich, blackcurrant fruit, exotic spices, licorice, and tar inundates the nose. Viscous, ripe, and incredibly
concentrated, this sweet, succulent, velvet-textured wine has a
staggering level of extract, as well as amazing length. It is even
more concentrated than Pétrus, and appears to be maturing less
quickly. Anticipated maturity: Now–2002. Last tasted, 12/88.

OLDER VINTAGES

Two remarkable older vintages of Latour à Pomerol that have stood
out in my tasting notes include the 1959 (rated 92 in 3/89) and the 1947
(rated 99 in 4/90). The 1959 is, surprisingly, not far off the pace of the
monumental 1961. It is, again, a very port-like, rich, powerful, unctuous
wine of great flavor dimension and concentration. Still remarkably
young, it can easily last another 10–15 years. The 1947 may turn out to
be a perfect wine. I have only tasted it once and it was awesomely
concentrated with a profound bouquet of sweet fruit (plums, cedar, exotic spices), that opulent, thick, port-like texture that suggests tiny yields
and super-maturity of the grapes, and a smashing finish with what must

be at least 14% alcohol. The bottle I tasted was in pristine condition. If it typified the 1947, this wine could last for another 20 years!

MAZEYRES (Unclassified)   AVERAGE

Production: 5,000 cases	Grape varieties: Merlot—70% Cabernet Franc—30%
Secondary label: none	
Vineyard size: 22 acres	Proprietor: Michel Querre
Time spent in barrels: 14–16 months	Average age of vines: 20 years
Evaluation of present classification: The quality equivalent of a Médoc Cru Bourgeois	
Plateau of maturity: 3–8 years following the vintage	

I rarely see the wines from this property, located on primarily sandy soil with some gravel. Those vintages I have seen—1981, 1982, and 1983— were straightforward, soft, somewhat commercially oriented wines of no great distinction or character.

MOULINET (Unclassified)   AVERAGE

Production: 7,500 cases	Grape varieties: Merlot—60% Cabernet Sauvignon—30% Cabernet Franc—10%
Secondary label: none	
Vineyard size: 44.5 acres	Proprietor: Armand Moueix
Time spent in barrels: 16–22 months	Average age of vines: 22 years
Evaluation of present classification: The quality equivalent of a Médoc Cru Bourgeois	
Plateau of maturity: 3–8 years following the vintage	

One of Pomerol's largest estates, Moulinet is located in the northwest section of the Pomerol appellation near the large estate of de Sales. The soil in this area renders lighter-style Pomerols, and Moulinet is certainly one of the lightest. Unusually light in color and faintly perfumed, Mouli-net is made in a very commercial style by the owners, the Armand Moueix family. At best, in vintages such as 1989 and 1982, it can be round, fruity, and elegant, but frequently the wine is bland and innocuous, although clean and consistently made.

VINTAGES

1989—The 1989 is about as good a wine as Moulinet is capable of pro-
·   ducing. It is a big, jammy, ripe, hedonistic wine lacking complex-
85   ity, but offering straightforward, chunky, luscious fruit, medium
     body, with a soft texture and alcoholic finish. Anticipated matu-
     rity: Now–1997. Last tasted, 4/91.

1988—The 1988 will last longer than the 1989, but will never provide as
·   much pleasure given the undernourished, lean, compact, short
79   flavors. It has a good amount of tannin, and I would expect it to
     last for up to a decade. Anticipated maturity: Now–2001. Last
     tasted, 4/91.

1986—The 1986 is austere and lean for a Pomerol. It should be drunk
·   over the next 5–6 years given its weight and character. Antici-
78   pated maturity: Now–1996. Last tasted, 3/90.

1985—The 1985 is an above-average-quality wine with a soft, somewhat
·   obvious commercial fruitiness, and medium body, but agreeable,
82   ripe, easy-to-appreciate, and easy-to-understand flavors. Antici-
     pated maturity: Now–1993. Last tasted, 3/90.

NENIN (Unclassified)   AVERAGE

Production: 12,000 cases	Grape varieties:
	Merlot—50%
	Cabernet Franc—30%
	Cabernet Sauvignon—20%
Secondary label: none	
Vineyard size: 69.2 acres	Proprietor: François Despujol
Time spent in barrels: 22–24 months	Average age of vines: 25 years
Evaluation of present classification: The quality equivalent of a Médoc Cru Bourgeois	
Plateau of maturity: 5–15 years following the vintage	

This is a historic estate of Pomerol, owned by the Despujol family since 1847. Nenin has a loyal following of wine enthusiasts, but I have never been able to quite figure out why. I was certainly taken by a bottle of their 1947 I tasted in 1983, but aside from that splendid wine, as well as an excellent 1975, I have always found Nenin to be good, but unfortunately somewhat coarse and rustic.

Traditionally, Nenin tends to be a firm, hard, chewy wine. Since 1976, the property has not performed well, turning out wines that have lacked intensity, character, and complexity. Are the yields too high? Did the decision to employ a mechanical harvester starting in 1982 negatively affect quality? To their credit, a serious effort has been made to bring Nenin out of their slump. The estate had the wisdom to bring in the brilliant Libourne oenologist, Michel Rolland, who insisted that more new oak be used, and that the sanitary conditions be improved. Yet Nenin continues to be machine harvested, and despite the presence of Rolland, recent vintages have been uninspiring.

VINTAGES

1989—The 1989 is frightfully light and simple for the vintage, resembling
·　　a generic Bordeaux rather than one of the better-known estates of
78　　Pomerol. It possesses soft tannins, a meager fruitiness, and an innocuous character. Anticipated maturity: Now–1996. Last tasted, 4/91.

1988—The 1988 is similar to the 1989, only more herbaceous, with an
·　　intrusive mustiness that is cause for concern. Anticipated matu-
76　　rity: 1993–2000. Last tasted, 4/91.

1986—The 1986 is lighter than the 1985, with more tannin, but it is still
·　　a loosely knit Pomerol for near-term drinking. Anticipated matu-
83　　rity: Now–1996. Last tasted, 3/90.

1985—The 1985 displays good fruit, richness, and fine winemaking. It is
·　　not a blockbuster Pomerol, but rather, a charming, supple, fruity,
84　　medium-bodied wine with an attractive, open-knit personality. Anticipated maturity: Now–1995. Last tasted, 3/89.

1984—Medium ruby, with a sugary, chaptalized nose, this wine is soft,
·　　light, but agreeable. Anticipated maturity: Now–1992. Last
75　　tasted, 3/88.

NOUVELLE EGLISE (Unclassified)　　　　　AVERAGE

Production: 1,200 cases	Grape varieties:
	Merlot—50%
	Cabernet Franc—50%
Secondary label: none	
Vineyard size: 6.9 acres	Proprietor: Servant-Dumas
Time spent in barrels: 18–24 months	Average age of vines: 25 years
Evaluation of present classification: The quality equivalent of a Médoc Cru Bourgeois	
Plateau of maturity: 4–8 years following the vintage	

This tiny estate, with its vineyard located near the church of Pomerol, produces straightforward, fruity wines that require consumption within their first decade of life. Recent vintages I have tasted include an attractive, but straightforward 1985, and a more compact 1988.

PETIT-VILLAGE (Unclassified)   EXCELLENT

Production: 5,000 cases	Grape varieties:
	Merlot—70%
	Cabernet Sauvignon—18%
	Cabernet Franc—12%
Secondary label: none	
Vineyard size: 27 acres	Proprietor: AXA Insurance Group
	Administrator: Jean-Michel Cazes
Time spent in barrels: 18–22 months	Average age of vines: 30 years
Evaluation of present classification: The quality equivalent of a Médoc third-growth	
Plateau of maturity: 5–15 years following the vintage	

Petit-Village is a Pomerol estate on the move. In 1971, when Bruno Prats, also the dynamic owner of the famous Médoc estate of Cos d'Estournel, took over responsibility for the making of the wine, the quality increased dramatically. Petit-Village had the benefit of significant capital investment, the care of a dedicated owner, and the state-of-the-art technology necessary for producing wine. The result was a succession of wines that ranged in quality from good to exceptional. In the late eighties, Prats sold Petit-Village to an insurance conglomerate that installed Jean-Michel Cazes and his brilliant winemaking team, led by Daniel Llose, from Lynch-Bages as administrators.

The style of Petit-Village emphasizes the toasty, smoky character of new oak barrels, a fat, supple, blackcurrant fruitiness, and impeccably clean winemaking and handling. Recent vintages have the ability to age for 10–15 years, although they are fully ready to drink by age 5 or 6. Older vintages (prior to 1982) have generally proven to be a disappointment, so wine enthusiasts are well advised to restrict their purchases to vintages since 1978.

It can be argued strongly that Petit-Village has joined the top hierarchy of Pomerol estates and now ranks as one of the top-dozen wines of the appellation. Certainly the vineyard is superbly situated. Bordered by Vieux-Château-Certan and Certan de May on the north, La Conseillante on the east, and Beauregard on the south, the vineyard has plenty of gravel, as well as an iron-rich subsoil intermixed with deposits of clay. The high percentage of Merlot insures a rich, voluptuous wine in years when the Merlot reaches full maturity and yields are reasonable.

Petit-Village is a Pomerol to buy as the price has not kept pace with its rejuvenated quality level.

VINTAGES

1989 — Critics might take exception to this sweet, round, in-your-face
· 　　style of wine that is obvious, but oh, so delicious. Its huge, choc-
90 　　olate, plum, and sweet-oak-scented bouquet roars from the glass.
　　　In the mouth, there are expansive, fat, hedonistic flavors that coat
　　　the palate with gobs of sweet, ripe fruit. There is a glaring lack of
　　　acidity and structure, but there is no doubt this generous wine
　　　will offer loads of pleasure over the next 5–7 years. Its only limi-
　　　tation is that it must be drunk early for its youthful, gutsy, volup-
　　　tuous character. Anticipated maturity: Now–1996. Last tasted,
　　　4/91.

1988 — Let me say immediately that this will not be a long-lived 1988.
· 　　Prospective purchasers should consider the fact that the 1988
92 　　Petit-Village will probably have to be drunk within its first de-
　　　cade. But, oh what pleasure it will provide! The 1982 (which is
　　　decadently exotic and delicious at the moment) is the modern-day
　　　reference point for Petit-Village, but there is no denying the
　　　sumptuous, seductive character of this superconcentrated yet
　　　velvety 1988. I had this wine in a tasting, but subsequently was
　　　fortunate enough to see it on a restaurant wine list, so I proceeded
　　　to down a bottle in record time. The dark ruby/purple color sug-
　　　gests ripeness and extract. The huge aroma of exotic spices,
　　　bacon fat, jammy plums, and smoky, toasty new oak is a complete
　　　turn-on. In the mouth, this heady, concentrated, splendidly ex-
　　　tracted Pomerol is all velvet and suppleness. This is a wine that
　　　most Bordeaux enthusiasts would consider to be a textbook ex-
　　　ample of the lushness and opulence that a top-notch Pomerol can
　　　provide. It is also a wine worth buying by the case—as long as
　　　you plan to drink it over the next decade. Anticipated maturity:
　　　Now–2000. Last tasted, 4/91.

1987 — Oh, how delicious the 1987 Pomerols turned out to be. Given all
· 　　of the negative press concerning this vintage and the relatively
85 　　low prices when compared with more recent years, consumers
　　　and restaurants looking for immediately drinkable Pomerols
　　　would be well advised to reconsider the best 1987s. This soft,

spicy, oaky, plum-scented wine has surprisingly good concentration, a round, satiny-smooth texture, and a heady, alcoholic, toasty finish. Drink it over the next 4–6 years. Anticipated maturity: Now–1997. Last tasted, 2/91.

1986—Intense aromas of smoky new oak, herbs, and black fruits are
· immediately enthralling. In the mouth, the wine is medium bod-
87 ied and moderately concentrated, with soft tannins and perhaps more structure than other recent vintages of Petit-Village. Anticipated maturity: 1992–2000. Last tasted, 3/90.

1985—This opulent, fully mature, fragrant, deliciously rich, soft wine
· lacks backbone and grip, but offers gobs of spicy, fat fruit that
89 seduces the taster. There is a wonderful, even explosive finish to this wine without a rough edge to be found. Anticipated maturity: Now–1997. Last tasted, 3/90.

1983—Quite supple, fat, and richly fruity, this full-bodied, dark ruby/
· garnet–colored wine is redolent of blackberries and toasty oak.
87 On the palate, the wine is precocious, sweet, ripe, fleshy, and delicious. Anticipated maturity: Now–2000. Last tasted, 7/88.

1982—I have come to learn that no matter how wonderful, seductive,
· and precocious Petit-Village tastes when young, it actually firms
93 up in the bottle and has much greater potential for longevity than one might originally expect. I had thought the 1982 would be approaching full maturity by 1990, but it is not. Certainly the 1982 was among the most seductive and easiest to drink of any of the top wines of the 1982 vintage when first released. It has not only expanded in flavor, but also firmed up in structure. Fortunately, it has not shed any of its wonderful fat, lush, smoky, exotic, berry and Asian spice scents and flavors. Anticipated maturity: Now–2002. Last tasted, 5/91.

1981—Definitely lighter and less concentrated than the powerful 1982
· and deeply fruity 1983, the 1981 Petit-Village does manifest a
85 precocious, soft, ripe, fat, Merlot fruitiness, ripe, round tannins, and a long, voluptuous finish. Anticipated maturity: Now–1995. Last tasted, 3/87.

1979—The 1979 Petit-Village does not have the concentration of the
· 1981, 1982, and 1983, but offers a ripe, moderately intense fruiti-
84 ness, medium body, a spicy, smoky bouquet, and a pleasant finish. Anticipated maturity: Now–1993. Last tasted, 2/83.

1978—Medium ruby, with a great deal of amber/brown at the edge, this
· wine has a spicy, slightly herbaceous, oaky bouquet. The 1978
83 Petit-Village exhibits supple, moderately concentrated, fruity, berry-like, herbaceous flavors, light tannins, and a soft, round finish. Anticipated maturity: Now–1996. Last tasted, 2/89.

PÉTRUS (Unclassified)   OUTSTANDING

Production: 4,000–4,500 cases	Grape varieties: Merlot—95% Cabernet Franc—5%
Secondary label: none	
Vineyard size: 28.4 acres	Proprietors: Madame Lily Paul Lacoste and Jean-Pierre Moueix Administrator: Christian Moueix
Time spent in barrels: 24–26 months	Average age of vines: 35 years
Evaluation of present classification: The quality equivalent of a Médoc first-growth	
Plateau of maturity: 10–30 years following the vintage	

The most celebrated wine of Pomerol, Pétrus has, during the last decade, become Bordeaux's most expensive red wine. Situated on a button-
hole of clay in the middle of Pomerol's plateau, the tiny 28.4-acre vineyard renders wines that are treated as well and as carefully as any wines
produced on earth. After proprietors Jean-Pierre Moueix and Madame
Lily Paul Lacoste make their selection, most vintages of Pétrus turn out
to be 100% pure Merlot.

There have been a tremendous number of legendary Pétrus vintages,
which no doubt has caused prices to soar into the stratosphere. The 1945,
1947, 1948, 1950, 1961, 1964, 1970, 1971, 1975, 1982, and 1989 are among
the most monumental wines I have ever tasted. Yet as Pétrus has become deified by much of the world's wine press, one must ask, particularly in view of this property's track record from 1976 on, "Is Pétrus as
great today as it once was?" There is no doubt that the 1989 should turn
out to be one of the top two or three wines of the vintage, and that the
1982 is a legend in the making. But there have been other vintages, such
as 1986, 1983, 1981, 1979, 1978, and 1976, that are not even among the
top four or five wines of Pomerol. And what about the decision to bottle
Pétrus in years such as 1977?

There are also growing comments from the Pomerol cognoscenti that
the Moueixs have become too conservative and no longer take the risks
that produced the great Pétrus vintages of old. For one thing, Christian
Moueix and his oenologist, Jean-Claude Berrouet, decided to begin filtering Pétrus with the 1976 vintage. While downplayed by both men as
having no effect whatsoever on Pétrus, this does indeed seem at odds

with the public image that Pétrus is a wine made with no compromises. Excessive fining and filtration are indeed compromises.

Additionally, the vineyard of Pétrus, once the last harvested in Pomerol, is now one of the first. Many other châteaux, most notably Le Pin, La Fleur de Gay, Lafleur, Clinet, Certan de May, and L'Evangile are usually harvested 1 to 2 weeks after Pétrus. Observers argue that the Moueix simply do not want to take the risk of having Pétrus spoiled by late harvest rains.

There is another unsettling issue regarding Pétrus. One of France's leading wine writers claims that while Pétrus is so spectacular from cask, it rarely ever tastes as impressive from bottle. Is, in fact, an aggressive fining and filtration robbing Pétrus of some of the potential richness? Or is it the fact that Pétrus needs at least 10–12 years after the vintage to return to form? I remember a spectacular 1979, 1981, and 1985, as well as a perfect 1982 from cask samples I saw. As great as the 1982 has turned out to be, it is not as majestic as it appeared from cask. Moreover, the 1985, 1981, and 1979 do not appear as spectacular as they promised in their prebottling stages. Do they merely need 15–20 years to reveal their true character?

Nevertheless, Pétrus remains the longest-lived and potentially greatest wine of Pomerol. The immense talent of oenologist Jean-Claude Berrouet and the brilliance of Christian Moueix are unquestionable. But have they become too obsessed and influenced by new-world technology and specific, "correct" winemaking parameters?

Perhaps the real problem is that when consumers are spending $200–$400 or more for a bottle of Pétrus, the expectations are, to say the least, difficult to fulfill. The remarkable thing about the great vintages of Pétrus prior to 1975 was that it was irrefutably the most incredibly concentrated, opulent wine made in Bordeaux. That can no longer be said, as the style today seems more polite, more restrained, and no longer the blockbuster it was in the past.

VINTAGES

1989—If the image of Pétrus needed any resurrection after its excellent
·   but less-than-dazzling performances in 1979, 1981, 1983, 1985,
98   1986, and 1987, the 1989 is this property's showcase vintage.
      Christian Moueix has responded to the challenge from a half-
      dozen or so other Pomerols that have been making noises about
      dethroning the unofficial King of Pomerol. By cutting off nearly
      half the crop in July and August, by deciding to pick early (Sep-
      tember 5 and 6, and the balance on September 14), and by elimi-

nating anything less than perfect from the final blend. In 1989
Moueix authoritatively demonstrated that only Pétrus can out-
Pétrus itself. This is a compelling wine, resembling the 1982 in
many aspects. But it is even more concentrated, as hard as that
may be to believe. Moueix thinks it is the finest Pétrus since
the 1947, and he will get few rebuttals from those who have a
chance to taste it. Black/purple, with the intense, dramatic
bouquet of superconcentrated blackcurrants and plums, this
wine makes a palate impression that is unforgettable. A number of respected Bordelais tasters I know claim they have never
tasted a wine like the 1989 Pétrus. Though this remark could
be construed in several ways, it is intended to be positive. I
thought the 1982, at least when it was in barrel, would be difficult to surpass, but the 1989 may possess even greater extraction of fruit, a dense, huge, massive texture, and a fabulous
black fruit nose that is gently touched by aromas of new oak and
spice. Almost thick, this wine is also extremely tannic. My
guess is that despite its high alcohol and low acidity, it will
need at least 10 years after bottling to fully reveal its considerable potential. If you have not realized it by now, Pétrus is
making a wine to drink later and last longer than any of the first-
growths in the Médoc. Anticipated maturity: 2000–2035. Last
tasted, 4/91.

1988—The 1988 Pétrus is more impressive than I had originally believed.
·   It rivals the 1982 and 1985 in terms of density and power, but
94   tastes more tannic and backward than either of those two vin-
       tages. I cannot emphasize enough how difficult this wine is to
       taste young. Despite the nearly 100% Merlot content, the propri-
       etors aim is to produce a wine that will outlive anything in the
       Médoc. That may not sit well with those who desire a sumptuous
       Pétrus to drink in the first 10–15 years of life. The 1988 is the
       most concentrated wine in what is a very good vintage for Pom-
       erol. It is dark ruby/purple, with a thickness to the color that
       suggests a high glycerin content. The nose is muted, no doubt
       because of the recent bottling, but it does offer intense smells of
       jammy black fruits intermingled with aromas of coconut, tea,
       superripe oranges, and some vanillin oakiness. In the mouth,
       this firmly structured, full-bodied, massive Pétrus is super-
       charged with both extract and tannin. It will need at least 8–10
       years of cellaring. Christian Moueix continues to rate it the third-
       best Pétrus of the decade, preferring it to all except 1989 and
       1982. Anticipated maturity: 2002–2030. Last tasted, 4/91.

1987—Given the past performance of Pétrus in vintages such as 1980
  ·   and 1984, I would not be surprised to see the rating of the 1987
  87   go up three or four points in 5–6 years. This is one of the most
       backward and full-bodied wines of the vintage, with a tremendous
       amount of tannic clout, yet excellent underlying power and body.
       The problem is that it is impossibly closed, almost impenetrable,
       suggesting that my score may be entirely too conservative. If you
       are a millionaire who wants to buy wine for a child born in 1987,
       this wine will still be in reasonable condition by the time he or
       she turns 21. Anticipated maturity: 1996–2010. Last tasted,
       11/90.

1986—The 1986 Pétrus was more tannic than either the 1982 or 1985
  ·   from cask. Once in the bottle, it displayed a hulking, monolithic
  88   character, and a huge, dense, powerful structure to go along with
       the abundant amounts of tannin. It is admirably concentrated and
       medium to full bodied. Anticipated maturity: 1996–2010. Last
       tasted, 5/91.

1985—From cask, the 1985 Pétrus was splendid, close in quality to
  ·   rivaling the 1982. Early tastings after bottling suggested that the
  89   wine was significantly lighter, more herbaceous, and not nearly
       so profound as cask tastings indicated. The wine is just beginning
       to throw off its postbottling shock, but still does not appear to
       be nearly as concentrated as the cask tastings suggested. Never-
       theless, the wine has medium dark ruby color with a hint of
       amber at the edge, an interesting coffee, creamy, chocolate,
       and black fruit–scented bouquet, deep, full-bodied, concen-
       trated flavors, and a long, moderately tannic, admirably con-
       centrated finish. Anticipated maturity: 1995–2015. Last tasted,
       5/91.

1984—The 1984 Pétrus has turned out to be amazingly good. Deep in
  ·   color, with an intense, jammy, herbaceous bouquet, medium to
  87   full body, fine length, and plenty of tannin, this wine needs 2–3
       years to mature, but will keep for 10–12 years. It is very impres-
       sive for the vintage. Anticipated maturity: Now–1996. Last
       tasted, 11/90.

1983—The 1983 Pétrus, while quite excellent, is a very big, jammy,
  ·   densely colored wine that has considerable power and authority
  89   on the palate, but is lacking a bit in finesse and balance. Quite
       full bodied, viscous, and chewy, with outstanding ripeness and
       plenty of tannin, this is a rather gawky Pétrus that needs time to
       completely pull itself together. Anticipated maturity: 1993–2015.
       Last tasted, 11/90.

1982—The most backward, tannic, and possibly densest wine of Pomerol
·   in 1982 is indeed Pétrus. This wine was absolutely celestial from
98   cask, which led me to give it a perfect rating in March 1985. Since
          that time, it has continually grown and expanded in the bottle,
          but it has not yet reached the prebottled form. It is massive,
          concentrated, and the richest and deepest Pétrus since the 1975
          and 1961. Whether it will attain the perfection I predicted for it
          remains to be seen, but for those who own it, I do not believe this
          wine will reach maturity until the turn of the century. After that,
          it should last for 30 or more years. It is an extraordinary Pétrus,
          and certainly nothing from this legendary vineyard since (except
          for the 1989) has been as compellingly intense and complex.
          Opaque dark ruby/purple with absolutely no trace of amber or
          orange, the wine is extremely closed, tannic, very powerful, deep,
          and unctuous yet hard to penetrate. As I have said many times
          before, those who think Pétrus, because of the unique 100% Mer-
          lot content, is a soft, forward wine, have either not tasted or
          understood Pétrus. In this property's great years, it will live as
          long as any of the Médoc first-growths, and often take longer to
          throw off the postbottling awkwardness. Anticipated maturity:
          1999–2025. Last tasted, 5/91.

1981—This is another example of a Pétrus that tasted absolutely pro-
·   found from cask, yet appears significantly lighter and less impres-
87   sive from the bottle. Christian Moueix compares it to the 1971,
          but at 10 years of age, it does not appear to have nearly the
          opulence or concentration of that vintage. The color is medium
          ruby, with a slight amber edge. The bouquet, which was explosive
          before bottling, is just emerging, offering up aromas of herbs, tea,
          vanillin oak, grilled nuts, and caramel. In the mouth, the wine is
          medium bodied, with good concentration, moderate tannins, and
          a long, heady finish. Comparing my early notes on this wine to all
          the notes since bottling leaves me perplexed. Nevertheless, this
          is still an excellent rather than dazzling Pétrus. It does not appear
          to be as good as I predicted it would be. Anticipated maturity:
          1995–2010. Last tasted, 5/91.

1980—This vintage is an example of why Pétrus is such a difficult wine
·   to judge. Somewhat light and herbaceous after bottling, the wine
86   has continued to put on weight and is now displaying considerably
          more depth, concentration, and complexity than I ever thought
          possible. Medium dark ruby, with an intense bouquet of herbs,
          oriental spices, sweet black fruits, and toasty new oak, this
          medium-bodied, generously endowed, supple effort has turned

out to be one of the two best wines of the vintage. Anticipated maturity: Now–2000. Last tasted, 11/90.

1979— I thought Pétrus to be one of the very top wines of the 1979
· vintage, but at age 12, the wine, while solid and concentrated,
89 seems to lack the extra flavor dimension and complexity I had hoped would develop. It is medium deep ruby, with a tight but emerging bouquet of chestnuts, cocoa, vanillin, and ripe red fruits. In the mouth, the wine is medium bodied, with very good concentration, and flavors of cassis, caramel, and oak. The acidity is relatively high for Pétrus, and the tannins still have a tough edge to them. I recommend cellaring this wine for several more years. Anticipated maturity: 1993–2015. Last tasted, 2/91.

1978— I have never found the 1978 Pétrus to be typical of this estate's
· wines. Although it enjoys a good reputation and sells at strato-
88? spheric prices, it has (except for one profound example tasted in 1989) tasted loosely knit and a trifle flabby and overripe, and has a distinctively vegetal and herbaceous scent. Still rather soft with round, ripe, moderate tannins, this is a Pétrus that has put on some weight and richness, but it is by no means a great wine. Anticipated maturity: Now–2005. Last tasted, 3/91.

1977— In retrospect, I would imagine that if Christian Moueix and his
· father had it to do over again, they would not have released the
69 1977 Pétrus. Not that it is unpalatable, but it is a disappointing wine, stalky and vegetal tasting with ungenerous, thinnish flavors. Anticipated maturity: Now–may be in decline. Last tasted, 1/83.

1976— A good but not special Pétrus, this wine is now fully mature with
· a full-blown bouquet of herbaceous, tobacco aromas, spicy oak,
87 and overripe fruit. Somewhat loosely knit and unstructured, and lacking the firmness of the best vintages, this is a big, alcoholic, immensely enjoyable wine to drink. Anticipated maturity: Now–1996. Last tasted, 1/91.

1975— One of the best wines of the vintage as well as the most concen-
· trated and tannic Pétrus of the seventies, the 1975 is a blockbus-
98 ter wine, opulently rich, still broodingly dark in color, and massive. This wine has layers of sweet, ripe blackcurrant fruit, awesome extract, huge tannins, and an explosive finish that suggest decades of life. It is a monumental Pétrus that will keep for 50 plus years. Anticipated maturity: 2000–2050. Last tasted, 12/90.

1973— The wine of the vintage, this is the best Pétrus for immediate
· consumption from those wines produced in the seventies. Given
87 the prolific yield in 1973 and diluted quality of many wines, the

Pétrus is sensationally concentrated, rich, supple, fat, and so, so flavorful. Friends tell me that it is still a delicious wine. Anticipated maturity: Now–1993. Last tasted, 12/84.

1971—This is a sensational Pétrus that has drunk well since the mid-
•   1970s. The chocolate, mocha, sweet, fruit-scented bouquet is fol-
95   lowed by a rich, velvety, full-bodied wine with layers of silky fruit. The 1971 must surely be the wine of the vintage. Light to moderate tannins and high alcohol will continue to preserve this plump, unctuous wine for another decade. This is Pétrus at its most seductive. Anticipated maturity: Now–2000. Last tasted, 1/91.

1970—Here is another example of a Pétrus that has taken 20 years to
•   reveal an extraordinary character. I have always preferred the
97   1971, and acknowledge that the latter vintage is much more mature than the 1970. However, over the last several years I have had numerous occasions to taste the 1970 and it has been magnificent. I appear to have underrated it when it was younger. It is still an opaque, impressive, dark ruby color. The huge bouquet of exotic spices and jammy, highly extracted, sweet fruit is followed by a massively extracted, full-bodied, old-style Pétrus that is crammed with concentration and has a finish that must last several minutes. This spectacular, still amazingly youthful Pétrus should last for at least another 20–30 years. I cannot imagine vintages of the late seventies and early eighties, except for the 1982 and 1989, ever approaching the quality of this vintage. Anticipated maturity: 1994–2020. Last tasted, 11/90.

1967—In this vintage that produced so many lightweight wines, only the
•   stablemate of Pétrus, Trotanoy, can compete with the great Pé-
92   trus. Fully mature, with good dark ruby color and minimal browning, this chunky, fleshy, warm, and generous wine has plenty of ripe Merlot fruit, a viscous, weighty texture, and fast-fading tannin. A lovely Pétrus, it is best drunk over the next decade. Anticipated maturity: Now–2000. Last tasted, 1/90 (from a magnum).

1966—Excellent, but even more highly regarded elsewhere than by me,
•   the 1966 Pétrus has a cedar, herbaceous, sweet, fruity bouquet
89   and is full bodied, with very good viscous, ripe, berry flavors. A big, dense, somewhat coarse wine that seems just a trifle out of synch, the 1966 Pétrus has plenty of tannin, alcohol, and flavor, but they have never fully meshed. Anticipated maturity: Now–2002. Last tasted, 6/91.

1964—A massive, even mammoth wine, the 1964 has extraordinary con-
•   centration and weight. The bouquet gushes from the glass carry-
97   ing with it intense aromas of ripe fruit, caramel, framboise, and vanillin oak. Incredibly dense, powerful, and viscous, this multi-

dimensional wine is 5 years away from maturity. Anticipated maturity: 1995–2010. Last tasted, 12/90.

1962—This is a very good Pétrus, yet I have never found it to have the
   ·   great richness and individual personality so prevalent in other
  87   vintages of this great wine. Quite fruity, but straightforward and
         lacking direction, this plump, chunky wine has some attraction,
         but tastes short in the finish for Pétrus. Anticipated maturity:
         Now–1996. Last tasted, 10/83.

1961—I have been fortunate enough to have the 1961 Pétrus on seven
   ·   different occasions, all from a regular-size bottle. On only two
 100   occasions did I rate the wine below 100, giving it a 98 and a 97.
         This is indeed a legendary effort from this property, but I think
         the wine is fully mature and needs to be drunk over the next
         decade. The unforgettable bouquet of sweet, ripe cassis, herbs,
         caramel, exotic spices, smoke, and grilled nuts is mind-boggling.
         In the mouth, the wine is massively proportioned, yet so perfectly
         balanced as to be unbelievable given its astonishingly concen-
         trated, expansive, opulent flavors, and almost port-like viscosity.
         This massive, powerful, riveting example of Pétrus is the reason
         why people are willing to pay over $1,000 a bottle for a wine. Last
         tasted, 12/89.

OLDER VINTAGES

The decade of the fifties was not a great period for Pétrus. I have had a number of the vintages from then and have never been overwhelmed by the 1959 (rated 88), 1955 (rated 87–89), or the 1953 (rated consistently in the mid-eighties). I have once given an outstanding rating to the 1952 (rated 93 in 10/87), but on other occasions I thought it to be only good. The great vintage for Pétrus in the fifties is the 1950 (rated 98 and 99 on the two occasions I have drunk it). I know this vintage receives little press, but I have no doubt this is one of the greatest vintages of Pétrus in the last 40 years. The second time I had the wine I gave it a 98, but I tasted it side-by-side with Jean-Pierre Moueix next to the 1950 Lafleur (which I rated 99–100). The year 1950 must have been a spectacular vintage in Pomerol, but where does one find these wines today? Anyone coming across bottles of the 1950 Pétrus would be well advised to snatch them up. They should, in all likelihood, be priced below some of the more glamorous vintages. The 1949 (rated 87–92) has never quite lived up to its great reputation, although the best bottles have been superb, and are still amazingly youthful. The most underrated vintage of Pétrus in the forties is the 1948 (consistently rated 95–98 in three separate tastings in the late eighties). Of course, the 1947 (consistently rated between 97 and 100) is, to me, a greater wine than even Cheval Blanc, although it was eclipsed by the otherworldly 1947 Lafleur. Nevertheless, for pure, port-like opulence, power, and extract, few dry red table wines in the world have ever been more concentrated than the 1947 Pétrus. One that comes close is the 1945 Pétrus (rated 97 and 99). Amazingly, it is still backward, and probably will last another 20–30 years. Whether or not it fully resolves its tannins remains to be seen, but there is no doubt that it is practically the essence of Merlot.

LE PIN (Unclassified)　　　　　　　　　　　　　OUTSTANDING

Production: 500 cases	Grape varieties: Merlot—88% Cabernet Franc—12%
Secondary label: none	
Vineyard size: 2.96 acres	Proprietor: The Thienpont family
Time spent in barrels: 18–24 months	Average age of vines: 25 years
Evaluation of present classification: The quality equivalent of a Médoc first-growth	
Plateau of maturity: 4–12 years following the vintage	

The Thienpont family, who owns the neighboring and very well known estate, Vieux Château Certan, acquired the miniature Le Pin vineyard, located in the heart of the Pomerol plateau, in 1979. Previously it had been owned by Madame Laubie, whose family acquired Le Pin in 1924. By their own admission, they are trying to make a Pétrus-like wine of great richness and majesty. The first vintages had Pomerol enthusiasts jumping with glee, as this looks to be a splendidly rich, but noticeably oaky, big-styled Pomerol. It is not too early to say that Le Pin is one of the great wines of Pomerol, as the first ten vintages have been smashing successes.

Much of the exotic character of Le Pin is probably explained by the fact that it is one of only a handful of Bordeaux estates to actually conduct the primary, or alcoholic fermentation of the wine in new oak casks. The only other estate I know that does this is one of the up-and-coming stars of St.-Emilion, Château L'Angélus. This is a dangerous and labor-intensive procedure, and can only be done by estates that have relatively small productions where the wine can be constantly monitored. However, I believe it is this technique that gives Le Pin its huge, smoky, and exotically scented bouquet. Whatever the secret, no doubt the iron-enriched, gravelly soil on this part of the Pomerol plateau (which I have been told has the highest elevation of any vineyard) has helped to create a cult following for the microscopic quantities of Le Pin.

If Le Pin is to be criticized at all, it is because the wine may not fare well with extended cellaring. I have my reservations about its aging potential, but there is no denying that for sumptuous, complex drinking within the first 10–12 years of the vintage, there is no wine made in Pomerol, or even in Bordeaux—except for perhaps the decadently styled Haut-Marbuzet from St.-Estèphe—that rivals Le Pin for pure joy and hedonistic appeal.

VINTAGES

1989—Pomerol and Bordeaux's most exotic and flamboyant wine ap-
·   pears less stunning than I thought. The 1989 is already remark-
90   ably drinkable, which surely raises doubts about its longevity.
      The 1989 offers a gloriously hedonistic mouthful of wine, but it is
      not nearly as concentrated as previous efforts (i.e., 1982, 1983,
      1985, and 1986). With very low acidity, as well as masses of new
      oak and fruit, this wine tries to redefine the word decadent. Sim-
      ilar to the 1985, but less rich. Anticipated maturity: Now–2000.
      Last tasted, 4/91.

1988—The 1988 is more subdued than the 1989, very oaky, but concen-
·   trated and rich, with a deep inner core of black fruit that lingers
89   on the palate. It has more aggressive tannins than the 1989. An-
      ticipated maturity: 1992–2003. Last tasted, 4/91.

1987—A big, exotic, perfumed, smoky, oaky bouquet is at first forceful
·   and unrestrained. However, as the wine sits in the glass, the ripe,
88   red fruit character emerges and is followed by a wonderfully lush,
      flattering, precocious wine that should be drunk over the next
      4–5 years. It is absolutely delicious—another notable success for
      the 1987 vintage in Pomerol. Anticipated maturity: Now–1997.
      Last tasted, 11/90.

1986—The 1986 Le Pin is a less flattering and opulent wine than the
·   unctuous, lavishly rich, fleshpot of a wine produced in 1985, but
91   it is no ugly duckling. Its extraordinary nose of smoky oak and
      plummy fruit is followed by a wine that is very concentrated and
      powerful with the highest level of tannins produced by this vine-
      yard since the first vintage was conceived a decade ago. It will
      not provide the up-front, precocious charm that the 1985, 1983,
      and 1982 have done, but for those with patience, the 1986 is sure
      to be an attention getter in any tasting. Anticipated maturity:
      1993–2008. Last tasted, 11/90.

1985—The 1985 is more forward than the 1986, with a deep ruby color
·   and a full-throttle bouquet of sweet, ripe berry fruit, herbs, toffee,
90   mocha, and toasty oak. On the palate, the wine has a lavish
       texture, unctuous flavors, and a ripe, velvety, fleshy finish. Antic-
       ipated maturity: Now–1998. Last tasted, 2/91.

1984—This must be one of the finest examples of the 1984 vintage. The
·   sweet, oaky, herb, coffee, chocolatey aroma is a real turn-on. In
87   the mouth, this round, opulent, shockingly ripe (particularly for
       the vintage) wine is loaded with fruit, and finishes with a velvety,
       spicy taste. Anticipated maturity: Now–1994. Last tasted, 11/90.

1983—If it were not for the 1982, most people would probably think the
·   1983 would be about as great a wine as one could taste. It has all
94   the same characteristics as the 1982, but does not have near the
       depth or the incredible expansiveness and intensity in the bou-
       quet. Nevertheless, it is still a wonderfully lush, lavish, perfumed,
       hedonistic, stunningly rich and concentrated wine that will please
       the most demanding taster. Anticipated maturity: Now–1997.
       Last tasted, 2/91.

1982—If one wanted a simple lesson in the immense seductive power of
·   the Merlot grape as well as the awesome potential for extraordi-
97   nary wines from Pomerol, then he should taste the 1982 Le Pin.
       It is a wine that has gone from one strength to another since it
       was bottled. I never dreamed it would turn out to be this mind-
       blowing in quality. There have been amazing wines made at Le
       Pin. Certainly the 1985, 1986, 1987, 1988, and 1989 are all great
       wines, but none is better than the extraordinary 1982. It is black
       ruby in color with a compelling bouquet of smoky, toasty oak,
       plums, exotic spices, and vanillin-scented new oak. In the mouth,
       the wine is explosively rich, and when I say it is a fleshpot be-
       cause of a lavish, unctuous, opulent texture, I mean just that. I
       cannot think of any 1982, with perhaps the exception of Pichon
       Lalande in Pauillac, that is any more extraordinary to drink at
       this moment than the 1982 Le Pin. Anticipated maturity: Now–
       1998. Last tasted, 2/91.

1981—This is an opulent 1981, with a pronounced spicy, oaky, penetrat-
·   ing bouquet interlaced with the scent of melted toffee and ripe
88   blackcurrants. On the palate, the wine is voluptuous, powerful,
       and rich. Fully mature, this impressive wine has turned out to be
       one of the leading Pomerols of the vintage. Anticipated maturity:
       Now–1995. Last tasted, 11/90.

PLINCE (Unclassified) AVERAGE

Production: 4,000 cases	Grape varieties: Merlot—75% Cabernet Franc—20% Cabernet Sauvignon—5%
Secondary label: none	
Vineyard size: 20.5 acres	Proprietor: The Moreau family
Time spent in barrels: 18–24 months	Average age of vines: 25 years
Evaluation of present classification: The quality equivalent of a Médoc Cru Bourgeois	
Plateau of maturity: 5–10 years following the vintage	

Plince is a solid Pomerol, fairly rich, hefty, spicy, and deep, rarely complex, but usually very satisfying. The Moreau family, also owners of Clos L'Eglise, own this property, but the commercialization is controlled by the Libourne firm of Jean-Pierre Moueix.

I have found Plince to be a consistently sound, well-made wine. Though it may never have the potential to be great, it seems to make the best of its situation. It is a well-vinified wine in a big, chunky style that seems capable of aging for 8–10 years.

VINTAGES

1989 • 85—The 1989 reveals the opulent, superripe, plum and black fruit character of the vintage. In the mouth, it is a deep and surprisingly intense and extracted wine, with a good amount of tannin in the finish, and an alcohol level of 13–13.5%. It is one of the most impressive wines from this vineyard that I have tasted. Anticipated maturity: 1993–2000. Last tasted, 4/91.

1988 • 80—The 1988 has less tannin, but it is tougher and harder, giving the wine an overall impression of leanness and austerity. The concentration is adequate, but next to the fuller, richer, more complete 1989, the 1988 comes across as sinewy and charmless. However, it will age decently. Anticipated maturity: Now–2002. Last tasted, 4/91.

1986 • 82—The 1986 Plince is surprisingly forward for the vintage, with a medium-bodied, ripe, plummy fruitiness, adequate complexity, and a pleasant, yet unspectacular finish. Anticipated maturity: Now–1997. Last tasted, 3/90.

1985 • 84—The 1985 is a very ripe, succulent, plump wine with a fat, full-bodied texture, low acidity, low tannins, and a tasty finish. Anticipated maturity: Now–1995. Last tasted, 3/89.

LA POINTE (Unclassified)   AVERAGE

Production: 9,500 cases	Grape varieties:
	Merlot—80%
	Cabernet Franc—15%
	Malbec—5%
Secondary label: none	
Vineyard size: 61.7 acres	Proprietor: Bernard d'Arfeuille
Time spent in barrels: 20–22 months	Average age of vines: 25 years
Evaluation of present classification: The quality equivalent of a Médoc Cru Bourgeois	
Plateau of maturity: 3–10 years following the vintage	

La Pointe has been an irregular performer. The wines can be round, fruity, simple, and generous, as in 1970, but far too frequently they are boringly light and unsubstantial. Older vintages, such as 1975, 1976, 1978, and 1979, were all uncommonly deficient in the rich, chewy, supple, zesty fruit that one finds so typical of a good Pomerol. The large production ensures that the wine is widely promoted. The owners have increased the percentage of Merlot significantly since the early seventies. All things considered, this is a mediocre Pomerol.

VINTAGES

1989—The light-bodied, watery, simple, fruity, alcoholic 1989 leaves a
·   great deal to be desired. It should be drunk early in its life.
74   Anticipated maturity: Now–1996. Last tasted, 4/91.

1988—The 1988 is somewhat more interesting, but, again, light, medium
·   bodied, and one-dimensional. Anticipated maturity: Now–1996.
76   Last tasted, 4/91.

1986—The 1986 could well be among the better wines. Displaying some
·   spicy new oak, an attractive plummy fruitiness, medium body,
84   and a good finish, it clearly is meant to be drunk over the next
         5–6 years. While Pomerols tend to be expensive because of their
         small production, this wine is not unfairly priced when one considers its quality. Anticipated maturity: Now–1997. Last tasted,
         3/90.

1985—The 1985 La Pointe is quite light, but well balanced, richly fruity,
·   and medium bodied; it is an agreeable luncheon or picnic wine.
83   Anticipated maturity: Now–1992. Last tasted, 3/89.

PRIEURS DE LA COMMANDERIE (Unclassified)   AVERAGE

Production: 1,800 cases	Grape varieties: Merlot—70% Cabernet Franc—30%
Secondary label: none	
Vineyard size: 7.5 acres	Proprietor: The Fayat family
Time spent in barrels: 18–22 months	Average age of vines: 25 years
Evaluation of present classification: The quality equivalent of a Médoc Cru Bourgeois	
Plateau of maturity: 3–8 years following the vintage	

This vineyard, situated in the very western part of the appellation, used to be called Château Saint-André. It is now owned by Monsieur Fayat, the proprietor of the renowned St.-Emilion estate called La Dominique. I have only tasted a few vintages of Prieurs de la Commanderie, and the wines were sound if uninspiring. The sandy, mineral-enriched soil of this area is known for producing a lighter style of Pomerol that is meant to be drunk early on.

VINTAGES

1989—The 1989 lacks acid and tannin, has flabby, unstructured flavors,
· and finishes with entirely too much alcohol and oak taste. Antici-
83 pated maturity: 1992–1996. Last tasted, 4/91.

1988—The 1988 is diluted and excessively oaky, as well as having a color
· that seems extremely advanced for the vintage. Anticipated ma-
76 turity: Now–1993. Last tasted, 4/91.

ROUGET (Unclassified)   GOOD

Production: 6,500 cases	Grape varieties: Merlot—90% Cabernet Franc—10%
Secondary label: none	
Vineyard size: 39.5 acres	Proprietor: François-Jean Brochet
Time spent in barrels: 24–30 months	Average age of vines: 20 years
Evaluation of present classification: The quality equivalent of a Médoc Cru Bourgeois	
Plateau of maturity: 5–15 years following the vintage	

Historically, Rouget is one of Pomerol's most illustrious estates. In one of the early editions of Cocks et Féret's, *Bordeaux et ses Vins,* the vine-

yard was ranked fourth among all the Pomerols. At present, their reputation has been surpassed by numerous properties, but there is no question that Rouget can be a very rich, very interesting wine. For example,
both the 1945 and 1947 vintages were dazzling wines that were both still
drinking superbly in the late eighties.

Since 1974, François-Jean Brochet has run this old, yet beautiful estate
that sits in the northernmost part of the Pomerol appellation on very
sandy soil, with a lovely view of the Barbanne River visible through the
trees. The wine is traditionally made by Brochet. He is unique in Pomerol
in that he maintains an immense stock of old vintages.

The style of Rouget is one that makes no concessions to consumers
who want to drink their wine young. It is a darkly colored, rich, full-
bodied, often very tannic wine that usually is in need of a minimum of
8–10 years of cellaring. It is sometimes too coarse and rustic, but almost
always a delicious, rich, ripe, spicy wine. The vintages of the eighties
have tasted more supple and less concentrated, giving rise to questions
about a change in style. I should also note that recent vintages have
tasted far better from cask than from bottle.

Rouget is a good value among the wines of Pomerol, with even the old
vintages being very fairly priced.

VINTAGES

1989—If the proprietor of Château Rouget would invest in more new oak
· barrels and pay a bit more attention to the wine's upbringing in
86 the cellar, I am convinced that this property—which has old vines
and tends to produce impressively rich, full-bodied, tannic wines
—would receive greater acceptance in export markets. Often the
promising raw materials are negated by indifferent cellar practices. The 1989 Rouget should be this estate's best wine since the
large-scaled, tannic 1982. It does not have the size of the 1982,
but is an abundantly rich, full-bodied wine, with dusty tannins,
plenty of alcohol, excellent ripeness, and a long, hard, tannic
finish. It will never achieve a great deal of elegance, but for a
more rough-and-tumble style of Pomerol, it should provide interesting drinking. Anticipated maturity: 1992–2006. Last tasted,
4/91.

1988—The 1988 is a success for the vintage. More obviously tannic than
· the 1989, it has excellent rich black cherry fruit partially hidden
85 behind the tannin, medium body, and a blossoming bouquet of
earthy fruit intertwined with the scents of minerals and herbs.
Anticipated maturity: 1994–2006. Last tasted, 4/91.

1986—For whatever reason, the 1986 Rouget seems to be made in a very
·   forward, precocious, commercial style that I hope does not signal
82   a new style for the future. It is soft and fruity, but it is also quite
       simple, and that is not what Rouget could strive to achieve. Antic-
       ipated maturity: Now–1994. Last tasted, 3/90.

1985—The 1985 showed considerably better from the cask, but after
·   bottling the wine has gone into a shell. It has a good ruby color,
84   but the charm and depth are concealed, maybe submerged, be-
       hind a wall of rustic tannins. By the standards of the vintage, it is
       tough and backward. Anticipated maturity: 1993–2005. Last
       tasted, 3/89.

1983—Richly fruity, spicy, fat, and quite concentrated, the 1983 Rouget
·   is a big, full-bodied, moderately tannic wine that is drinking well
82   now. Anticipated maturity: Now–2000. Last tasted, 2/88.

1982—It appears that I overrated the quality of the 1982 Rouget in my
·   earlier assessment of this wine. It is still relatively closed and
85   hard, but I did not find the rich, ripe, intense fruit that existed
       in the prebottling cask samples I tasted. Nevertheless, this is
       certainly a good wine, but those who own it may want to wait
       another 3–4 years before drinking it as this property tends to
       produce wines that need a good decade of cellaring to reveal
       their full potential. Anticipated maturity: 1992–2000. Last tasted,
       1/91.

1981—Rouget's 1981 is good, but seems to suffer in comparison with the
·   more powerful 1982, and grapey, fat, succulent 1983. Neverthe-
80   less, it has good fruit, rather hard, aggressive tannin, and an
       adequate, but uninspiring finish. Anticipated maturity: Now–
       1994. Last tasted, 6/83.

1978—A chunky, spicy, fruity, medium- to full-bodied wine, the 1978
·   Rouget is attractive, but a trifle awkward and clumsy on the pal-
82   ate. Moderate tannin is present, so perhaps the wine will pull
       itself completely together. Anticipated maturity: Now–1994. Last
       tasted, 6/83.

1971—Fully mature, the 1971 Rouget has a dusty texture, a spicy,
·   earthy, cedary bouquet, nicely concentrated flavors, but a some-
80   what coarse texture. This medium amber, ruby-colored wine
       should be drunk up. Anticipated maturity: Now–may be in de-
       cline. Last tasted, 6/84.

1970—A big, rather fat, well-endowed wine, with full body and a cedary,
·   rich blackcurrant fruitiness, the 1970 Rouget has roughly textured
84   flavors, and moderate, aggressive tannin still very much in evi-
       dence. Anticipated maturity: Now–1995. Last tasted, 6/84.

1964—The 1964 is a total success for Rouget. The predilection to wines
· with a rough, big, tannic structure has—in this vintage—resulted
87 in a wine with more balance and harmony. Very deeply fruity,
with earthy, blackcurrant flavors in abundance, this full-bodied
wine has power, symmetry, and surprising length. Rouget is one
of the better Pomerols in this vintage. Anticipated maturity:
Now–1996. Last tasted, 1/85.

DE SALES (Unclassified) GOOD

Production: 20,000 cases	Grape varieties: Merlot—70% Cabernet Franc—15% Cabernet Sauvignon—15%
Secondary label: Chantalouette	
Vineyard size: 117.3 acres	Proprietor: Bruno de Lambert
Time spent in barrels: 18–22 months	Average age of vines: 30 years
Evaluation of present classification: The quality equivalent of a Médoc Cru Bourgeois	
Plateau of maturity: 3–10 years following the vintage	

De Sales is the largest vineyard in Pomerol, and boasts the appellation's
only grand château. The property is located in the northwestern corner
of Pomerol with a vineyard planted primarily on sandy soil intermixed
with gravel. The owners and managers are the de Lambert family. The
wines are increasingly among the most enjoyable of the Pomerols. They
are prized for their sheer, supple, glossy, round, generous, ripe fruitiness, and lush, silky personalities. De Sales has always made good wine,
but the recent vintages have been particularly strong. It is never a powerful, aggressive, oaky, or big wine, and always offers immediate drinkability. In spite of a precocious style, it has a cunning ability to age well
for 10–12 years.

While consistently good, de Sales will never be a great Pomerol, but it
has rarely ever disappointed me. Its price remains modest, making it a
good value.

VINTAGES

1989—The 1989 promises to be one of the biggest wines made by this
· château. It not only compares favorably to their excellent 1982
86 (which is now drinking extremely well), but may ultimately prove
to be superior. It is surprisingly full bodied for de Sales, with a

deep, intense, black cherry–scented bouquet intertwined with the scents of vanillin and toast. In the mouth, the wine displays the exceptional ripeness that is typical of so many wines from this vintage, full body, a heady alcohol content, and a long, tannic, rich finish. Most wines from de Sales are drinkable upon release, and no doubt the 1989 will also have its admirers, but it might be one de Sales that is capable of lasting beyond a decade. Anticipated maturity: 1993–2003. Last tasted, 4/91.

1988—The 1988 is a smaller-scaled wine, with less alcohol, tannin, con-
· centration, and complexity. Nevertheless, if you are looking for a
83 lighter-styled, perhaps more typical wine from de Sales than the more bullish 1989, the 1988 will provide attractive if less exciting drinking. Anticipated maturity: Now–1996. Last tasted, 4/91.

1986—The 1986 is light, but does offer charm and appeal in a very light-
· to medium-bodied format. Anticipated maturity: Now–1996. Last
80 tasted, 4/91.

1985—The 1985 is a very soft, easygoing, supple, fruity wine meant to
· be drunk young. It could use more grip and length, but for uncom-
83 plicated quaffing at a decent price, it is hard to beat. Anticipated maturity: Now–1994. Last tasted, 4/91.

1984—An open-knit, engaging, soft, fruity character displays no vegetal
· or unripe components. Light to medium bodied, this wine should
78 be drunk up. Anticipated maturity: Now–1993. Last tasted, 4/91.

1983—Perhaps a little atypical for de Sales, the 1983 is a fat, jammy,
· alcoholic wine, with an opulent fruitiness, a ripe bouquet of black
85 cherries and peaches, and a soft, viscous texture. Low acidity seems to suggest that this wine should be consumed quickly. Anticipated maturity: Now–1994. Last tasted, 4/91.

1982—The 1982 de Sales has been fully mature for several years and
· exhibits no sign of declining. It has a round, ripe, creamy, spicy,
86 berry-scented bouquet with medium body, good, ripe, concentrated fruit, and a soft, moderately long finish. I see no reason to postpone gratification. Anticipated maturity: Now–1995. Last tasted, 4/91.

1981—The 1981 de Sales is a notable success for the vintage. Quite lush
· and concentrated, with ripe, rich fruit, some spicy oak, medium
86 body, and a long finish, this is a graceful, savory wine. Anticipated maturity: Now–1992. Last tasted, 11/84.

TAILHAS (Unclassified)   AVERAGE

Production: 5,000 cases	Grape varieties: Merlot—80% Cabernet Sauvignon—10% Cabernet Franc—10%
Secondary label: none	
Vineyard size: 25 acres	Proprietor: Daniel Nebout
Time spent in barrels: 15–22 months	Average age of vines: 25 years
Evaluation of present classification: The quality equivalent of a Médoc Cru Bourgeois	
Plateau of maturity: 3–10 years following the vintage	

Tailhas is well situated on the St.-Emilion border, adjacent to the famed Château Figeac. Tailhas usually produces a medium-bodied, robustly styled Pomerol with good richness and weight. However, it has had a tendency to be bland and monolithic in some vintages. The 1979 and 1981 are disappointing, but the 1982 is very good, a dense, ripe, fat, chewy Pomerol that will provide enjoyment through the mid-1990s. The 1983 is less interesting, but fruity, supple, concentrated, and precocious. The best recent vintage appears to be the jammy, ripe, opulent, yet simple 1989. Much of the production of Tailhas is sold in Europe, but it is beginning to receive an audience in America for its rich, chewy, fruity, and fairly priced wines.

TAILLEFER (Unclassified)   AVERAGE

Production: 10,000 cases	Grape varieties: Merlot—55% Cabernet Franc—30% Cabernet Sauvignon—15%
Secondary label: none	
Vineyard size: 49.4 acres	Proprietor: Armand Moueix
Time spent in barrels: 18–23 months	Average age of vines: 25 years
Evaluation of present classification: The quality equivalent of a Médoc Cru Bourgeois	
Plateau of maturity: 3–10 years following the vintage	

Taillefer is a straightforward, fruity, medium-bodied wine without a great deal of complexity, but generally soundly made, round, and capable of evolving for 7–10 years before losing its fruit. Recent vintages have rendered consistently sound, attractive, cleanly made wines that are uninspirational, but correct. The vineyard, which is comprised of a number of parcels surrounding the château, is situated to the extreme south of the appellation, along the frontier with St.-Emilion.

VINTAGES

1989— The 1989 Taillefer is less weighty and powerful than many Pom-
·   erols in this vintage, but does possess richly fruity, velvety flavors
85   in a medium-bodied texture, with a good deal of alcohol, and some
surprisingly tough tannins in the finish. Despite the roughness of the tannins, this wine will require drinking early. Anticipated maturity: Now–1998. Last tasted, 4/91.

1988— The 1988 is straightforward and light bodied, with a hint of ripe
·   fruit and toasty vanillin oak. There is not much of a finish. Antic-
82   ipated maturity: Now–1995. Last tasted, 4/91.

1986— The 1986 is soft, lacks depth, and gives the impression of being
·   an undernourished wine made from an excessive production from
73   this vineyard. Anticipated maturity: Now–1994. Last tasted,
3/90.

1985— The 1985 Taillefer does not offer much to get excited about. It
·   lacks depth of color, has an undernourished feel, and tastes light
76   and commercial. Anticipated maturity: Now–1992. Last tasted,
3/89.

TROTANOY (Unclassified)   EXCELLENT

Production: 3,500 cases	Grape varieties: Merlot—90% Cabernet Franc—10%
Secondary label: none	
Vineyard size: 21 acres	Proprietor: Jean-Pierre Moueix
Time spent in barrels: 20–24 months	Average age of vines: 28 years
Evaluation of present classification: The quality equivalent of a Médoc second-growth	
Plateau of maturity: 7–20 or more years following the vintage	

Trotanoy has historically been one of the great wines of both Pomerol and all of Bordeaux. Since 1976, Trotanoy has been the quality equivalent of a second-growth. In vintages prior to 1976, Trotanoy was often as profound as a first-growth.

Since 1953, Trotanoy has been owned by the firm of Jean-Pierre Moueix. The château is unmarked (it is the residence of Jean-Jacques Moueix). The vineyards of this modest estate, which lie a kilometer to the west of Pétrus between the church of Pomerol and the village of Catusseau, are situated on soil of clay and gravel. The wine is vinified and handled in exactly the same way as Pétrus, except only 33–50% new oak barrels are used each year.

Until the late seventies, Trotanoy was an opulently rich, intense, full-bodied wine that usually needed a full decade of cellaring to reach its zenith. In some vintages, the power, intensity, and concentration came remarkably close to matching that of Pétrus. It had an enviable track record of producing good, sometimes brilliant, wines in poor Bordeaux vintages. The 1967, 1972, and 1974 are three examples of vintages where Trotanoy was among the best two or three wines of the entire Bordeaux region.

In the late seventies, the style became lighter, although Trotanoy appeared to return to full form with the extraordinarily opulent, rich, decadent 1982. Since then, however, there has been a succession of good rather than thrilling wines. There is no question that there has been some major replanting of the micro-sized vineyard of Trotanoy, and that the production from these younger vines is being blended in, but one also wonders if the wine is not having something stripped out of it by perhaps an excessive fining or filtration. (It is interesting to note that the Moueix firm began to filter all of their wines with the 1976 vintage.) Whatever the case might be, Trotanoy no longer seems to be one of the top three or four wines of Pomerol, and has been surpassed in the eighties (with the exception of the 1982 vintage) by such châteaux as Clinet, L'Eglise Clinet, Vieux-Château-Certan, Certan de May, Le Pin, Lafleur, Lafleur de Gay, L'Evangile, La Conseillante, and even Bon Pasteur in specific vintages. Given the competitiveness and talent of Christian Moueix and his staff, I would think this is a situation they would desire to change.

Trotanoy is an expensive wine because it is highly regarded by connoisseurs the world over. Yet it rarely sells for more than half the price of Pétrus—a fact worth remembering since it does (in certain vintages) have more than just a casual resemblance to the great Pétrus itself.

VINTAGES

1989—Does the 1989 suggest the beginning of the resurrection of Trotanoy? The 1989 is the finest Trotanoy since the heroic 1982.
90   Opaque ruby/purple, with a promising aroma of ripe cassis fruit gently kissed by oak, this broad-shouldered Trotanoy should go a long way toward reassuring fans of this property's wines following

the indifferent results in 1983, 1984, and 1986. More alcoholic and tannic than the 1982, but also less concentrated and lower in acidity, I suspect the 1989 Trotanoy will drink extremely well young in spite of the high tannin level. Anticipated maturity: 1994–2010. Last tasted, 4/91.

1988—The 1988 is an excellent wine, as well as the third-best Trotanoy
· of the decade (following the 1982 and 1989). A big plum and
88 vanillin nose is seductively full. Luscious on the palate, with good, firm tannins in the finish, as well as less alcohol than the 1989, look for the 1988 to be at its peak of maturity between 1993 and 2005. Anticipated maturity: 1994–2005. Last tasted, 4/91.

1986—The 1986 has good color and a reticent, tight bouquet of herbal
· tea, plums, and spicy oak. On the palate, the wine tastes light
84 and insubstantial, but it does have a good finish and some weight. Anticipated maturity: 1992–2005. Last tasted, 4/91.

1985—In my initial tastings, I appear to have seriously overrated the
· 1985 Trotanoy. It now looks to be very good, but more in line with
86 the 1981 or 1979 than any other vintage. Light by the standards of this estate, this vintage of Trotanoy is elegant and medium bodied, with good color, yet I keep wondering where the richness and length have gone. Anticipated maturity: Now–2000. Last tasted, 4/91.

1984—Considering the difficulties posed by this vintage, this wine has
· turned out well. It is a ripe, tannic, firmly structured wine with
84 depth and length. Anticipated maturity: Now–1996. Last tasted, 3/89.

1983—The 1983 Trotanoy is a disappointment, and is the first of a
· succession of vintages for this famous property that produced
81 wines of lesser quality than one might expect. The 1983 is a bit dull and light, and seems slightly out of balance, with an excess of tannin for the meager fruitiness. My rating may well turn out to be overly generous as this wine continues to evolve, since it seems to be losing fruit rather than filling out as I had hoped it might. Anticipated maturity: Now–1996. Last tasted, 1/89.

1982—Trotanoy's 1982 has turned out to be even more fascinating and
· dazzling than I initially thought. Recent tastings confirmed that it
97 is the finest wine made at this estate since the 1961. Still black ruby/purple in color, the wine has a profound bouquet of rich berry fruit, licorice, coffee, minerals, and spicy oak. Massive and huge on the palate, with superb balance and phenomenal concentration and richness, it is much more evolved and forward than Pétrus. From cask there is no doubt that Pétrus was the deeper and richer of the two wines, so I suspect Pétrus is simply still

closed and impenetrable, and just needs another decade of aging. This is not to suggest that Trotanoy is ready to drink, but I do feel that for those who have more than a handful of bottles, it is simply too good not to try at least one of them over the next several years. The 1982 should reach full maturity by the mid-1990s and last for another 15 years thereafter. It is a monumental wine, even for this great estate. Anticipated maturity: 1994–2008. Last tasted, 1/91.

1981 — The 1981 Trotanoy is an elegantly wrought, yet authoritative, moderately rich wine with good, deep, ripe fruit, a spicy, oaky,
·
85 leathery bouquet, medium body, decent concentration, and light tannins in the finish. Anticipated maturity: Now–2000. Last tasted, 12/90.

1979 — Surprisingly precocious and charmingly supple and fruity, the 1979 Trotanoy continues to develop well in the bottle. Quite
·
86 drinkable now, this is not a big or massive Trotanoy, but rather a round, ample, elegant wine with good overall balance. Anticipated maturity: Now–1995. Last tasted, 12/90.

1978 — The 1978 Trotanoy has matured rapidly. Ready to drink now, it has a full-blown bouquet suggestive of herbs, fresh tomatoes, and
·
84 blackcurrants. On the palate, the wine is medium bodied, soft, and velvety, without the depth of fruit normally found in this wine. Little tannin remains in this loosely knit, herbaceous, somewhat austere Trotanoy. Anticipated maturity: Now–1993. Last tasted, 12/90.

1976 — Generally very highly regarded by other critics, I have enjoyed the 1976 Trotanoy, but it is now fully mature and showing signs
·
84 of overripeness and a jammy, low acid character. Quite plummy, fat, even peppery, with a lovely lush structure, this is an exotic style of Trotanoy that is delicious, but lacks backbone and structure. Anticipated maturity: Now–may be in decline. Last tasted, 10/83.

1975 — The 1975 Trotanoy is a great success. It is very concentrated with broad, deep, rich, long, ripe fruity flavors, and a bouquet that
·
94 combines scents of tobacco, toffee, leather, and mulberries to reveal sensationally complex aromas. Fleshy, full bodied, and velvety, this is an excellent Trotanoy for drinking over the next decade. Anticipated maturity: Now–2005. Last tasted, 5/91.

1974 — One of the best wines of the vintage (clearly the best Pomerol), Trotanoy's 1974 is now fully mature and should be drunk over the
·
86 next 2–3 years. Uncommonly concentrated and surprisingly ripe and fruity, this medium- to full-bodied wine has a smooth, mocha,

coffee, chocolate-tasting finish. Anticipated maturity: Now–1993. Last tasted, 2/91.

1971—I remember this wine being absolutely delicious in the mid-
· 1970s, and every time I go back to it, it seems to improve in the
93 bottle. It is still superb, with gobs of velvety, ripe, decadent Merlot fruit, an opulent texture, and a long, full-bodied, heady finish.
This must be the second-best wine of the vintage (eclipsed only
by Pétrus). Given how long it has been able to rest at its apogee,
I may be wrong in saying it should be consumed over the next
3–4 years. Will it still be as rich and flavorful in 10 years? I say
yes! Perhaps. Anticipated maturity: Now–2000. Last tasted, 2/91.

1970—In contrast to the 1971, which has provided over 15 years of
· sumptuous drinking pleasure, the 1970 remains a broodingly
90 dark, powerful, closed Trotanoy that is still not ready to drink. It
is extremely full bodied, concentrated, amazingly deep in color,
and loaded with extract. There is vast potential for the 1970, but
it is still a wine for those who have a great deal of patience. I am
beginning to lose mine. Anticipated maturity: 1993–2010. Last
tasted, 12/90.

1967—This is spectacular for the vintage. I would have thought it would
· be losing its fruit by now, but when last tasted the wine was still
91 exuberantly rich, crammed with fruit, and a total joy to drink.
Full bodied and remarkably concentrated, this multidimensional
wine offers amazing opulence and richness for the vintage. A
smashing success! Anticipated maturity: Now–1995. Last tasted,
12/90.

1966—I am beginning to wonder when this still-tannic, tough, and
· closed-in wine, which remains impressively colored and concen-
85 trated, will open up. It is a big, brawny Trotanoy that may very
well lose its fruit before its tannin. Anticipated maturity: Now–
1998. Last tasted, 1/87.

1964—This is an impressively big, deep, darkly colored Trotanoy with
· only a trace of amber at the edge. The wine has outstanding
90 ripeness and concentration, with an almost port-like viscosity to
its texture. The slight bitterness that I mentioned in the first
edition of this book has not been a problem the last two times I
tasted this wine. It is clearly an outstanding effort from Trotanoy
in 1964. Fully mature, given its size and concentration, it should
continue to drink well for at least another decade. Anticipated
maturity: Now–2002. Last tasted, 11/90.

1962—The top Pomerol of the vintage, Trotanoy is still delicious with a
· big, spicy, cedary, tobacco-scented bouquet, and soft, generous,
88 round flavors that linger on the palate. Harmonious and attrac-

tive, this wine should be drunk up. Anticipated maturity: Now–1995. Last tasted, 1/83.

1961—I last tasted this wine from a magnum in November 1990 and it
·   was hard to keep my hands away from my glass. Dark ruby/
98   purple/garnet, with a magnificent bouquet of sweet, ripe, exotic
    fruit, this port-like, fabulously concentrated, full-bodied, unc-
    tuously textured wine is explosive on the palate, and has a finish
    that lasts for over two minutes. It is a magnificent example of
    Trotanoy, and the best wine I have ever tasted from this property.
    It should continue to drink well for at least another 10–15 years.
    Anticipated maturity: Now–2005. Last tasted, 11/90.

OLDER VINTAGES

The greatest vintage I have tasted of older Trotanoys was the 1945 (rated 96 in 1990), which was a massive, powerful wine with at least 20–25 years of life left to it! In fact, it seemed shockingly young, but there was no denying the awesome extract, and huge, opaque, black/purple color. The only bottle of the 1947 I have tasted was a bit attenuated, volatile, and probably not a good example, since so many Pomerols were fabulous in that vintage. The 1959 (rated 92 in 1989) is another top-notch Trotanoy that is probably better than the 1964, but not so profound as the 1961. It is full bodied, with a roasted tobacco, leather, fruitcake-scented bouquet, and huge, rich, chocolatey, powerful flavors that still have considerable tannin to shed. A massive example of Trotanoy, it should continue to drink well until at least the turn of the century.

VIEUX-CHÂTEAU-CERTAN (Unclassified)   EXCELLENT

Production: 6,500 cases	Grape varieties: Merlot—50% Cabernet Franc—25% Cabernet Sauvignon—20% Malbec—5%
Secondary label: Clos de la Gravette	
Vineyard size: 33.6 acres	Proprietor: The Thienpont family
Time spent in barrels: 20–24 months	Average age of vines: 30 years
Evaluation of present classification: The quality equivalent of a Médoc second-growth	
Plateau of maturity: 5–20 or more years following the vintage	

One of the most famous names in Pomerol is the pride and joy of the Thienpont family, the owners of Vieux-Château-Certan. In the nineteenth century, as well as the early part of the twentieth century, Vieux-Château-Certan was considered to produce the finest wine of Pomerol. However, following World War II, this distinction was surpassed by Pétrus. The two wines could not be more different. Vieux-Château-Certan bases its style and complexity on a high percentage of Cabernet Franc and Cabernet Sauvignon, whereas Pétrus is nearly 100% Merlot. The vineyard, located in the heart of the plateau, surrounded by much of the reigning aristocracy of the appellation, Certan de May, La Conseillante, L'Evangile, Petit-Village, and Pétrus, has a gravelly soil with a subsoil of iron-enriched clay. The wine that emerges from the vineyard never has the strength of a Pétrus, or other Merlot-dominated wines of the plateau, but it often has a perfume and elegance that recalls a top wine from the Médoc.

A visit to the *chai* of Vieux-Château-Certan reveals a healthy respect for tradition. The fermentation still takes place in old wooden vats, and the château refuses to use more than 33% new oak for each vintage. The wine rests in vats for up to 2 years, and according to the château, they do no filtration at bottling. For most of the post–World War II era, Vieux-Château-Certan was made by Léon Thienpont, but since his death in 1985 the property has been managed by his son, Alexandre, who apprenticed as the *régisseur* at the St.-Emilion château of La Gaffelière. When the young, shy Thienpont took over the estate, old-timers scoffed at his lack of experience, but he asserted himself immediately, introducing crop-thinning techniques practiced by his neighbor Christian Moueix at Château Pétrus.

Because of its historic reputation for excellence, Vieux-Château-Certan is an expensive wine.

VINTAGES

1989—This vintage of Vieux-Château-Certan is highly revered in many
·   circles, but I felt the wine was too lacking in concentration to be
89   considered profound. It also did not appear to have the depth,
      grip, or focus of the 1988. Nevertheless, it is still a very good
      wine, with dark ruby/purple color, a big, spicy, herb-and-cassis-
      scented bouquet, medium body, and a long, relatively opulent
      finish. Anticipated maturity: 1994–2005. Last tasted, 4/91.

1988—For the life of me I cannot agree with the handful of people who
·   suggest that the 1989 Vieux-Château-Certan is superior, or even
92   comparable, to the 1988. It is just not so. If the 1989 is a trifle
      short, there is no such problem with the beautifully made, ele-

gant, yet highly extracted, rich 1988. This is a classic Vieux-Château-Certan. Among all the Pomerols, this property has much more Cabernet Sauvignon planted, and, therefore, the wine often is a bit less obvious and somewhat lighter, and always has a more Médoc orientation to its personality. The huge bouquet of cassis, herbs, and new oak is followed by a wine that is medium to full bodied and has deep, black cherry flavors wrapped intelligently in toasty oak. Extracted, deep, yet impeccably well balanced, this beautifully pure, yet delineated Pomerol not only rivals the fine 1982 and 1986, but may well turn out to be the best wine made at Vieux-Château-Certan since the 1964. Anticipated maturity: 1994–2010. Last tasted, 4/91.

1987 —The intense herbaceousness exhibited by this wine from the cask
  ·   has now calmed down. The result is a flattering, cedary, black-
 85   currant-and-herb-scented wine, with good depth, some light tan-
        nins, and a plump, satisfying finish. Anticipated maturity: Now–
        1997. Last tasted, 4/91.

1986 —The 1986 is a very deeply colored wine, with a profound and
  ·   complex bouquet of exotic spices, herbs, blackcurrants, and spicy
 93   oak. On the palate, the wine is impeccably balanced, with great
        concentration, superb length, and at least 5–25 years of aging
        potential. Yes, the 1982 is more hedonistic, but I think the 1986
        appears to be the finest wine made at this historic estate since the
        extraordinary 1959, 1961, and 1964. I would further suggest it is
        one of the best wines of the vintage for Pomerol. Anticipated
        maturity: 1994–2010. Last tasted, 12/90.

1985 —The 1985 is richly fruity as are most wines from this vintage. It is
  ·   long, deep, complex, medium to full bodied, light in tannins, but
 88   delicious and seductive. Anticipated maturity: Now–2000. Last
        tasted, 3/89.

1984 —This is a lean wine, but there is an attractive spicy character,
  ·   adequate fruit, and 3–5 years of drinkability. Anticipated matu-
 78   rity: Now–1993. Last tasted, 3/89.

1983 —Vieux-Château-Certan is quite successful in this vintage. The
  ·   wine is dark ruby, with a rich, berry-like, slightly minty, oaky
 88   bouquet, plump, round, fat flavors, good, round, tannin content,
        and medium to full body. Like most Pomerols of 1983, it is slightly
        deficient in acidity, but it is round, generously flavored, and pre-
        cocious. Anticipated maturity: Now–1997. Last tasted, 1/89.

1982 —There was a time when I thought the 1983 was the better of these
  ·   two wines, but that would be impossible to think when tasting the
 91   1982 and 1983 side by side today. While I do not believe either

vintage has turned out to be as successful as the great 1986 made at this property, the 1982 has, on occasion, performed better than the above score. However, on other occasions it has scored lower. It has begun to display some muscle, richness, and length, but what gives it away in a tasting of Pomerols is its somewhat Médoc-like, herbaceous, cedary character. It also possesses less fat and flesh than most other 1982 Pomerols. However, it is an outstanding wine by anyone's standards, with an extremely complex bouquet, which in 1982 reminds me of Figeac, the great St.-Emilion. Anticipated maturity: Now–2005. Last tasted, 5/91.

1981— The 1981 is extremely good, richly fruity, with a blackcurrant,
· cedary bouquet interlaced with subtle, herbaceous scents. Rather
87 Medoc-like in its firm, well-structured feel, with medium body and tough tannins, this wine is well made and surprisingly generous for the vintage. Anticipated maturity: Now–2005. Last tasted, 7/91.

1979— Rather light for a wine of its reputation, the 1979 Vieux-Château-
· Certan is medium ruby, with a moderately intense, cherryish,
78 oaky bouquet, medium body, soft, light tannins, and an adequate finish. Anticipated maturity: Now–1994. Last tasted, 7/83.

1978— The 1978 Vieux-Château-Certan has much more color than
· the 1979, with better concentration, a relatively rich, supple,
82 medium-bodied texture, light tannins, and a round, attractive finish. Anticipated maturity: Now–1994. Last tasted, 7/83.

1976— Quite one-dimensional, with soft, ripe plummy fruit, and some
· oaky aromas, the 1976 has average concentration, no noticeable
75 tannin, and a pleasant, yet uninteresting finish. Anticipated maturity: Now—may be in decline. Last tasted, 7/83.

1975— The best Vieux-Château-Certan of the seventies, the 1975 has
· excellent power and richness as well as complexity and balance.
90 Medium to dark ruby, with a fragrant, ripe, rich, plummy, cedary, spicy bouquet, full body, big, concentrated flavors, and moderate tannin, the wine is just beginning to reach its apogee. Anticipated maturity: Now–2000. Last tasted, 12/88.

1971— The 1971 is a little wine, pleasant enough, but lacking concentra-
· tion, richness, character, and length. It has been ready to drink
74 for some time, and now seems to be losing its fruit. Anticipated maturity: Now—may be in decline. Last tasted, 9/79.

1970— A burgundian aroma of cherry fruit and earthy, oaky, spicy com-
· ponents is satisfactory enough. On the palate, the 1970 Vieux-
80 Château-Certan is moderately concentrated, light, fruity, and

charming. However, it has little of the power, richness, and depth expected. Anticipated maturity: Now–1994. Last tasted, 4/80.

1966—The 1966 Vieux-Château-Certan is browning badly, but is still
·   solid and showing moderately ripe fruit, medium body, a rather
74   severe, unyielding texture, and a short finish. Some astringent
        tannin still remains. This wine is very Médoc-like in character,
        but not very impressive. Last tasted, 2/82.

1964—A lovely wine that is round, generous, velvety, and deeply fruity,
·   the 1964 has a very sweet, ripe bouquet of fruit, oak, and truffles,
90   soft, amply endowed flavors, medium to full body, and a long,
        silky finish. It remains a sumptuously rich, intensely flavored
        wine (from a magnum). Anticipated maturity: Now–1996. Last
        tasted, 3/91.

1961—This wine has gotten mixed reviews in my notes. Several years
·   ago it was big and powerful, but coarse, dumb, and totally lacking
86   in finesse. At a vertical tasting of Vieux-Château-Certan, it was
        still a little rough around the edges, but displayed rich, deep,
        youthfully scented fruit, full body, plenty of weight and power,
        and impressive length. The score reflects the better effort. Antic-
        ipated maturity: Now–1995. Last tasted, 5/83.

OLDER VINTAGES

Three older vintages of Vieux-Château-Certan stand out for their exemplary quality. The 1959 (rated 93 in 1988) is a greater wine than the
1961. It possesses a huge, coffee, chocolatey, herb, and cassis-scented
bouquet, followed by rich, full-bodied, opulent flavors. The bottle I saw
was in fabulous condition, and could easily last for another 10–15 years.
The two best examples I have ever tasted of Vieux-Château-Certan included a 1950 (rated 96) and a 1947 (rated 94) I tasted from magnum. The
1950 offered more persuasive evidence that Pomerol had a great vintage
that year, but because the wine world was obsessed with the Médoc at
that time, no one other than Pomerol enthusiasts were apparently aware
of the quality of this vintage. Amazingly young, with a port-like viscosity
and richness that one only sees in great vintages, this spectacular wine
can easily last for another 10 years. The 1947 was fully mature, with a
huge, roasted bouquet, port-like flavors, and at least 14% alcohol in its
taste and finish. In spite of its size, power, and age, there were gobs of
decadently rich fruit remaining.

LA VIOLETTE (Unclassified) GOOD

Production: 2,000 cases	Grape varieties: Merlot—80% Cabernet Franc—20%
Secondary label: none	
Vineyard size: 10 acres	Proprietor: The Servant- Dumas family
Time spent in barrels: 24 months	Average age of vines: 35 years
Evaluation of present classification: The quality equivalent of a Médoc Cru Bourgeois	
Plateau of maturity: 5–15 years following the vintage	

This obscure Pomerol estate produces 2,000 cases of wine from a well-placed vineyard near the church of Pomerol. While La Violette can be inconsistent, it can also produce splendidly rich wine. While I have only tasted these vintages once, the 1962, 1967, and 1982 all merited outstanding ratings for their intensity, extract levels, complexity, and character. However, other vintages exhibit a loosely knit, sometimes musty, old-barrel smell, and all too frequently come across as rustic and disjointed. Nevertheless, this is not a property to arbitrarily dismiss.

VRAYE-CROIX-DE-GAY (Unclassified) GOOD

Production: 2,000 cases	Grape varieties: Merlot—80% Cabernet Franc—15% Cabernet Sauvignon—5%
Secondary label: none	
Vineyard size: 9.1 acres	Proprietor: Baronne Guichard
Time spent in barrels: 18–22 months	Average age of vines: 25 years
Evaluation of present classification: The quality equivalent of a Médoc Cru Bourgeois	
Plateau of Maturity: 5–12 years following the vintage	

This tiny vineyard, beautifully situated on deep gravelly soils surrounded by high-quality Pomerol vineyards such as Lafleur, Le Gay, Certan-Giraud, and La Fleur Pétrus, should be a source of excellent, perhaps even profound, wine. The problem to date has been that the proprietor will not crop thin and yields are far too excessive to obtain a great deal of extract. Nevertheless, Vraye-Croix-de-Gay remains a vineyard with immense potential, if the owners ever decide that quality, not quantity, is their priority.

The proprietor, Baronne Guichard, also owns two other estates, Château Siaurac in Lalande de Pomerol and Château Le Prieuré in St.-Emilion.

ST.-EMILION

St.-Emilion is Bordeaux's most aesthetically pleasing tourist attraction. Some will even argue that the walled, medieval village of St.-Emilion, which is perched on several hills amid a sea of vines, is France's most beautiful wine town.

The wine community of St.-Emilion is a very closely knit fraternity who maintain a fierce belief that their wines are the best in Bordeaux. They have always been sensitive and have felt slighted because the region was entirely omitted from the 1855 Classification of the Wines of the Gironde. This is the largest serious red wine appellation of Bordeaux, encompassing over 12,800 acres.

St.-Emilion is only a forty-minute drive from Bordeaux. Pomerol sits to the north and the obscure satellite appellations of Montagne, Lussac, Puisseguin, and St.-Georges St.-Emilion, as well as the Côtes de Francs and Côtes de Castillon, border it on the east and south. The top vineyards are centered in distinctive and geographically different parts of St.-Emilion. For simplicity, St.-Emilion's best vineyards tend to all be planted on the limestone plateau, the limestone hillsides (the *côtes*), and the gravel terraces adjacent to Pomerol. A handful of good estates are located on another band of soil frequently referred to as the plain of St.-Emilion. The vineyards called "*côtes* St.-Emilions" cover the limestone hillsides around the town of St.-Emilion. There are even a few vineyards located in the town. Most of St.-Emilion's best and most famous wines—Ausone, Belair, Canon, Magdelaine, L'Arrosée, Curé-Bon-La-Madeleine, and Pavie—are located along these hillsides. Of the official eleven Premier Grand Cru properties of St.-Emilion, eight have at least part of their vineyards on these limestone hillsides. The wines from the *côtes* vineyards are all unique and distinctive, but they share a firm, restrained, more austere character in their youth. However, with proper aging as a general rule the youthful toughness gives way to wines of richness, power, and complexity.

Certainly Ausone, with its impressive wine cellars carved out of the rocky hillside and steep vineyard filled with very old, gnarled vines, is the most famous wine of the St.-Emilion *côtes*. This property was considered capable of making one of Bordeaux's best wines in the nineteenth century, but the wine of Ausone was surprisingly undistinguished until 1976 when a new winemaking team was installed. Ausone tends to be different from the other *côtes* St.-Emilions. Tougher, more tannic, with an exotic, sweet bouquet, it has more of a Médoc austerity on the palate than many of its neighbors. Since 1976, Ausone has been impeccably vinified. In 1982, 1983, 1989, and 1990, the château produced great wines.

The only other *côtes* vineyards capable of achieving the complexity and sheer class of Ausone are Canon and Magdelaine. Much of Canon's vineyard, like that of Ausone, sits on the limestone hillside. Canon has always had an excellent reputation, but has attained new heights under the leadership of Eric Fournier, who took over management of Canon in 1972. Canon is one of the most powerful and richest wines made from the *côtes* St.-Emilions. However, despite the excellent aging potential, it is a wine that matures more quickly than Ausone (which can remain backward and impenetrable for 30 or more years).

Magdelaine should be a worthy challenger to Ausone. The vineyard, like those of Ausone and Canon, sits on the limestone hillside to the south of St.-Emilion. However, whereas Ausone and Canon use approximately 50% Cabernet Franc and 50% Merlot in their formula for making great wine, Magdelaine uses up to 90% Merlot. For that reason, Magdelaine tends to be a fleshier, rounder, creamier wine than either Ausone or Canon. However, its general quality during the seventies and eighties has been only good rather than inspirational.

Of the other top *côtes* vineyards in St.-Emilion, L'Arrosée, not a Premier Grand Cru, but Grand Cru Classé, has been making splendid wine since the early sixties and can often be counted on to produce one of the half-dozen best wines of St.-Emilion. L'Arrosée's wine lasts well, and it has a richness and highly aromatic bouquet that lead some to call it the most burgundy-like St.-Emilion of the *côtes* section.

Pavie and its sister château that sits further up the hillside, Pavie-Decesse, are both owned by one of the friendliest and kindest men in St.-Emilion, Jean Paul Valette. Pavie is the Premier Grand Cru Classé, Pavie-Decesse the Grand Cru Classé, and both have always been good,

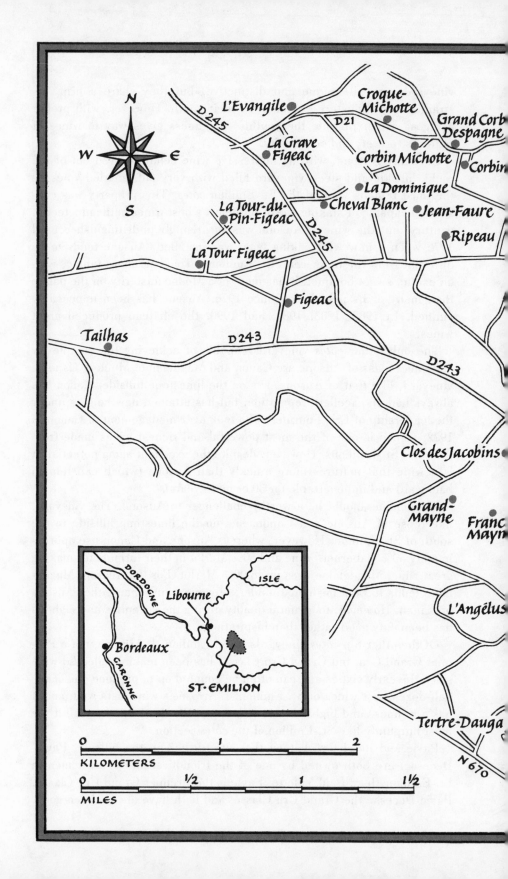

N
W · E
S

L'Evangile

D 245

D 21

Croque-
Michotte

Grand Corb
Despagne

La Grave
Figeac

Corbin Michotte

Corbin

La Dominique

La Tour-du-
Pin-Figeac

Cheval Blanc

Jean-Faure

D 245

Ripeau

La Tour Figeac

Figeac

Tailhas

D 243

D 243

Clos des Jacobins

Grand-
Mayne

Franc
Mayn

DORDOGNE

ISLE

Libourne

L'Angélus

Bordeaux

GARONNE

ST·EMILION

Tertre-Dauga

N 670

0   1   2
KILOMETERS

0   ½   1   1½
MILES

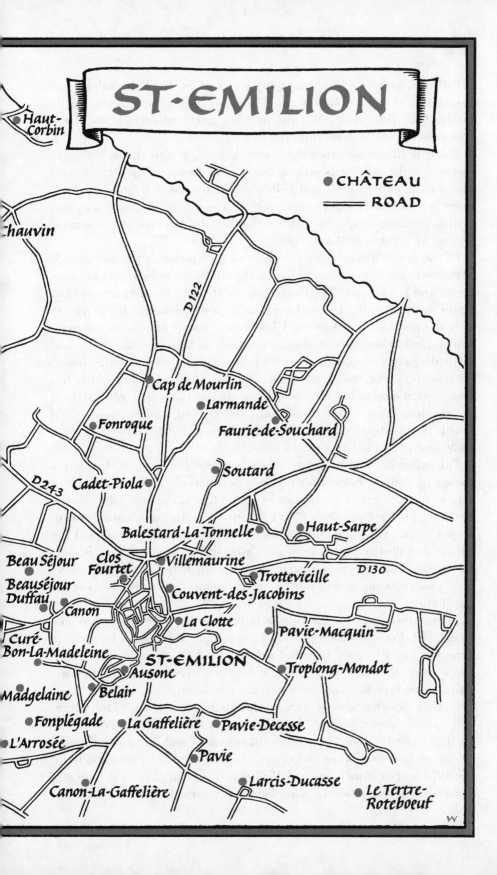

ST·EMILION

● CHÂTEAU
═══ ROAD

Haut-Corbin

Chauvin

D122

Cap de Mourlin

Larmande

Fonroque

Faurie-de-Souchard

Soutard

D243 Cadet-Piola

Haut-Sarpe

Balestard-La-Tonnelle

D130

Beau Séjour

Clos Fourtet

Villemaurine

Trottevieille

Beauséjour Duffau

Couvent-des-Jacobins

Canon

La Clotte

Pavie-Macquin

Curé-Bon-La-Madeleine

ST·EMILION

Ausone

Troplong-Mondot

Madgelaine

Belair

Fonplégade

La Gaffelière

Pavie-Decesse

L'Arrosée

Pavie

Canon-La-Gaffelière

Larcis-Ducasse

Le Tertre-Roteboeuf

W

yet lighter, more elegant, easygoing styles of St.-Emilion. Valette has been trying to make richer, bigger wines, and during the eighties, particularly 1982, 1986, and 1989, and in 1990, produced some of the finest wines ever made at these two estates.

Belair is the immediate neighbor of Ausone. It also shares the same owner and the same winemaking team. Like Ausone, Belair rarely produced memorable wines until 1976 when its renaissance begin. Lighter, more delicate, and earlier to mature than Ausone, Belair can be a classy, stylish, medium-weight St.-Emilion that has the potential to reach great heights as it did in 1983 and 1989.

Of the other famous *côtes* vineyards of St.-Emilion, a number of poor performers have just recently begun to turn things around and produce better and better wine. The Beauséjour estate of Duffau-Lagarrosse, and Clos Fourtet of André Lurton have both improved considerably in quality over the last half-dozen years. Clos Fourtet's style of wine is the more commercial of the two, having abandoned its hard, tannic, stern, and unyielding style of *côtes* St.-Emilion in favor of a modern, supple, fruity, very easy to like and drink wine. Not so for Beauséjour, which has improved in quality but continues to emphasize the classic *côtes* style of St.-Emilion: tannic, firm, reasonably well colored, and age worthy. Of note is the fact that this estate turned in three superlative efforts in 1988, 1989, and 1990, the latter wine a true blockbuster.

The other Beauséjour estate on the western slopes of St.-Emilion is owned by Michel Bécot (Beau Séjour-Bécot) and the demotion of this estate from a Premier Grand Cru to Grand Cru in the new 1985 classification of St.-Emilion wines didn't surprise me. This is a publicity-conscious estate, yet the quality of winemaking had been suspect and the wines often disappointing. Ironically, after the demotion of Beau Séjour-Bécot, the estate began to produce significantly better wine and by 1991 most observers considered it to be one of the most improved wines of the appellation.

Three other *côtes* St.-Emilions estates have the potential to produce some of St.-Emilion's most profound wines, but until recently have rarely done so. The Premiers Grands Crus Classés La Gaffelière and Trottevieille, and the Grand Cru Classé L'Angélus, have superb vineyard expositions and the soil necessary to make wonderful wine.

La Gaffelière has always been a perplexing wine, and one of the perennial underachievers among the Premiers Grands Crus Classés of St.-Emilion. The location of the vineyard is superb and, in tasting through the wines from the sixties and seventies, one is struck by how wonderful the 1970 is. But it was not until 1982 that the quality began to improve. Since the early eighties La Gaffelière has returned to form. While this

will never be a blockbuster St.-Emilion, it is perhaps the most quintessentially elegant and finesse-styled St.-Emilion of all the Premiers
Grands Crus Classés.

Trottevieille used to be another disappointing property, but under the
inspired leadership of Philippe Castéja, the progress in the late eighties
has been spectacular. The 1987, 1988, and 1989 are all remarkable for
their richness, intensity, and underlying complexity and character.

The other property that remains a Grand Cru Classé but should be
elevated to a Premier Grand Cru Classé, if it were not for politics, is
L'Angélus. This property, which went through a dreadfully mediocre
period during the sixties and seventies, began to make good wines in the
early eighties, but has, since 1986, made remarkably intense, rich, even
outstanding, wines that are among the greatest wines of not only St.-
Emilion, but of all Bordeaux.

These are not the only up-and-coming estates that are either situated
on the limestone plateau or the hillside sections of St.-Emilion. One of
the newest superstars of St.-Emilion is Canon-La-Gaffelière, which actually is one of the châteaux often referred to as being located on the
"pieds de côtes," meaning that its vineyard is situated at the foot of the
hillsides. This property has made profound wines in the late eighties and
should be one of the stars of the nineties.

Other properties to keep an eye on in this part of St.-Emilion include
Troplong-Mondot and Pavie-Decesse. The exciting quality of recent vin-
tages of Troplong-Mondot has begun to be noticed outside St.-Emilion.
The wine, produced by one of the leading ladies of Bordeaux, Christine
Fabre, has all of the earmarks for becoming one of the great classics of
St.-Emilion. Pavie-Decesse is run by the amiable Jean Paul Valette.
While the wine is rated below the more famous Premier Grand Cru
Classé, Pavie, I think Pavie-Decesse may in fact be the better wine. This
undervalued wine has been especially brilliant during the eighties.

Another Pavie worth considering seriously is Pavie-Macquin. This
property, much like L'Angélus, Troplong-Mondot, Canon-La-Gaffelière,
and Trottevieille, produced wines of mediocre quality during the decade
of the seventies and into the early eighties. However, Pavie-Macquin
finished the eighties with superb wines in 1988, 1989, and 1990. It appears this is another up-and-coming star of the appellation. The vineyard
is beautifully located on the plateau above the limestone hillside referred
to as the Côte Pavie.

Another property, which I had no knowledge of when I wrote the first
edition of this book, is Le Tertre-Roteboeuf, a tiny gem of a château
located on the hillside sections of St.-Emilion near its more famous
neighbor, Larcis-Ducasse. Le Tertre-Roteboeuf has made monumental

wines since the early eighties under the compulsive/obsessive eyes and hands of proprietor François Mitjavile. This property is the single greatest discovery I have ever made in the Bordeaux region. No compromises are made in producing the wine, and the result is the only St.-Emilion that can truly be called the Pétrus of St.-Emilion—it is that rich and compelling. Le Tertre-Roteboeuf should be promoted to a Premier Grand Cru Classé.

Another section where St.-Emilion's best wines can be found is called the *"graves terraces,"* often referred to as *"graves et sables anciens"* (or stones and ancient sand). Only 4 kilometers from the town of St.-Emilion, the soil in this area is, as the name implies, a gravelly bed intermixed with some clay and sand. The top properties here, Cheval Blanc, Figeac, La Dominique, Corbin, and Corbin-Michotte, produce a lush, more velvety, voluptuous wine that shows quite well when young. Yet in the top vintages these wines have excellent aging potential. These properties sit right on the southeastern border of Pomerol and often exhibit the same lush, supple fruitiness as the two closest Pomerol estates of L'Evangile and La Conseillante.

Of these *graves* St.-Emilions, none is greater than Cheval Blanc. Even with the renaissance at Ausone, Cheval Blanc remains the quintessential St.-Emilion, opulent, decadently rich, exotic, surprisingly easy to drink when young, but capable of lasting 30–40 years in the great vintages. Cheval Blanc and Figeac are the only two Premiers Grands Crus from the *graves* section of St.-Emilion. An objective analysis of the top estates of this region would reveal that La Dominique merits inclusion as well.

Cheval Blanc's vineyard is situated on deep gravelly soil with certain parts clay and sand as well as iron. Perhaps the most unique aspect of this wine is that nowhere else in Bordeaux does the Cabernet Franc grape reach such heights. Cheval Blanc can be almost overpoweringly rich, deep, and fruity in vintages such as 1947, 1948, 1949, 1953, 1961, 1964, 1982, and 1983, and this fact, no doubt, explains why much of this wine is drunk before it ever achieves maturity. Figeac, the immediate neighbor of Cheval Blanc, is often compared to Cheval Blanc; however, Figeac is a very different style of wine. With a high percentage of Cabernet Sauvignon (35%) for a St.-Emilion and much sandier soil than Cheval Blanc, Figeac tends to be a more herbaceous-scented, lighter wine. However, Figeac in great vintages is a very fruity, soft, charming, concentrated wine that can be drunk when it is only 4–5 years old. Lamentably, only a handful of recent vintages—1964, 1970, 1975, 1982, and 1990— have exhibited the stuffing to suggest they can stand the test of time.

La Dominique, an impressive wine and up-and-coming estate, sits just to the north of Cheval Blanc. La Dominique produces excellent wine with lush richness, a deep fruitiness, plenty of body, and aging potential of 10–20 years. It is a wine that merits elevation to a Premier Grand Cru Classé. In some vintages—1955, 1970, 1971, 1982, and 1989—this property can produce wine rivaling the best in St.-Emilion.

It would be an oversimplification to think that the only fine wines of St.-Emilion come from the *graves* plateau and the hillside or limestone plateau sectors of this appellation. There are other portions of St.-Emilion that have slightly different soils and several properties in these sections of the appellation are capable of producing excellent wines.

On the sand-covered slopes, often called the plains of St.-Emilion, properties like Larmande, Cap de Mourlin, and Cadet-Piola are making excellent wine. The plateau that fans out to the east of St.-Emilion has predominantly clay and sand soil with a limestone base. Soutard is the outstanding estate in this area. Two other perennial overachievers are La Clotte and Balestard-La-Tonnelle; both are capable of producing excellent wines.

Lastly, one property that is in none of the above geographic areas of St.-Emilion but makes excellent wine is Clos des Jacobins, a property located a kilometer northwest of St.-Emilion.

St.-Emilion developed its own classification of wine quality in 1954. On paper, the system developed by St.-Emilion should be the best of all the Bordeaux wine classifications. The classification is based on reputation, soil analysis, and tasting. Unlike the 1855 classification, which has been infinitely rigid and inflexible (except for the elevation of Mouton-Rothschild in 1973), the St.-Emilion classification is supposed to be revised every 10 years, so that in theory top vineyards can be promoted and poorly run vineyards demoted. However, the first major revision in 1969 changed very little. The 1969 classification established a four-tiered hierarchy. The hierarchy that was in effect until 1985 established at the top level twelve Premiers Grands Crus Classés of which two were given recognition as the best. These were called Premiers Grands Crus Classés "A," and the remaining ten Premiers Grands Crus Classés "B." The second rung of this ladder of quality was the Grands Crus Classés, of which there were seventy-two. The third level of quality was for wines entitled to the status Grand Cru. The bottom level of St.-Emilion's quality hierarchy was for the wines that are only entitled to the appellation of St.-Emilion. Most of these wines are made by the large cooperatives.

What has this progressive system of quality classification meant for the wine consumer? Well, there is no doubt that this system has encouraged proprietors to produce higher-quality wine in the hope that a better product will result in a promotion to a higher rank. On the negative side, the commission that issued the new 1985 classification was unwilling to promote several ambitious properties making fine wine, and they have refused to demote several properties that have been notorious underachievers, given their reputation. For example, among the top twelve Premiers Grands Crus Classés in the 1969 classification, Beau Séjour-Bécot, Trottevieille, and La Gaffelière have, for much of the last two decades, consistently produced mediocre wine in most vintages. In the new classification of 1985, only Beau Séjour-Bécot was dropped down. However, the new 1985 classification (see pages 928–929) does simplify the St.-Emilion quality hierarchy a great deal. The new classification has only three levels of wine quality. At the top, there are eleven Premiers Grands Crus Classés after the demotion of Beau Séjour-Bécot. At the next level, which is now called Grand Cru Classé, there are sixty-four estates instead of seventy-two. The third and last level is the generic St.-Emilions. Two excellently run properties, Soutard and L'Angélus, had applied for consideration for promotion from Grand Cru Classé to Premier Grand Cru Classé. Unfortunately, neither of these two wines was promoted in the new 1985 classification, yet both merited elevation.

St.-Emilion produces wines that have enormous crowd appeal. Fleshy, quick maturing, round, and generous, they are easy to like, easy to drink, and easy to understand. While the Premiers Grands Crus Classés are expensive, many of the Grands Crus Classés are significantly undervalued and can represent excellent bargains.

Since quality of the soils, the winemaking, and the combination of grape varietals planted in the vineyards are so diverse in St.-Emilion, it is exceedingly difficult to generalize about vintages in this vast appellation. Certainly the great vintages for St.-Emilion have been 1990, 1983, and 1982 (probably the three best vintages for this region in the post–World War II era), 1989, 1986, 1970, 1964, and of course 1961. The key to any excellent or great vintage for St.-Emilion is the healthy flowering and ripening to full maturity of the Merlot and Cabernet Franc grapes, the two most important grapes for this region.

Since this area has an enormous number of wine-producing estates, I have emphasized in my tastings and in this chapter the Premiers Grands Crus Classés and Grands Crus Classés. It may be arbitrary and capricious, but given the sheer number of St.-Emilions that merit coverage from the two aforementioned categories, I have generally disregarded the generic St.-Emilion, except where their level of quality merits interest. Some of these wines can, in fact, be good, but they never have the consistency of the top estates.

A CONSUMER'S CLASSIFICATION OF THE CHÂTEAUX OF ST.-EMILION

OUTSTANDING
Ausone, Cheval Blanc

EXCELLENT
L'Angélus, L'Arrosée, Canon, Canon-La-Gaffelière, La Dominique, Figeac, Larmande, Soutard, Le Tertre-Roteboeuf, Troplong-Mondot, Trottevieille

VERY GOOD
Balestard-La-Tonnelle, Belair, Cadet-Piola, Clos des Jacobins, Couvent-des-Jacobins, Croque-Michotte, Curé-Bon-La-Madeleine, La Gaffelière, Grand-Mayne, Magdelaine, Mauvezin, Pavie, Pavie-Decesse, Pavie-Macquin, La Tour du Guetteur, La Tour-du-Pin-Figeac-Moueix

GOOD
Béard, Beau Séjour-Bécot, Beauséjour (Duffau-Lagarrosse), Bergat, Cap de Mourlin, Chante-Alouette-Cormeil, Clos Fourtet, Clos la Madeleine, Clos Saint-Martin, La Clotte, Corbin, Corbin-Michotte, Dassault, Destieux, Faurie-de-Souchard, de Ferrand, Fleur-Cardinale, La Fleur Pourret, Fonplégade, Fonroque, Franc-Mayne, Godeau, Grand-Pontet, Haut Brisson, Haut-Corbin, Haut-Sarpe, Le Jurat, Jean-Faure, Larcis-Ducasse, Laroze, Petit-Faurie-de-Soutard, Pindefleurs, Ripeau, Rocher-Bellevue-Figeac, Rolland-Maillet, St.-Georges-Côte Pavie, Tertre-Daugay, La Tour-Figeac

OTHER NOTABLE ST.-EMILION PROPERTIES
Bellefont-Belcier, Bellevue, Berliquet, Cadet-Bon, Chauvin, Clos de L'Oratoire, La Clusière, Cormeil-Figeac, La Couspade, La Fleur, Fombrauge, Grand-Barrail Lamarzelle-Figeac, Grand-Corbin, Grand-Corbin-Despagne, La Grave-Figeac, Guadet St.-Julien, Laniote, Laroque, Matras, Monbousquet, Moulin du Cadet, Pavillon-Cadet, Le Prieuré, Prieuré-Lescours, Puy-Blanquet, Sansonnet, La Serre, Tauzinat L'Hermitage, La Tour-du-Pin-Figeac-Giraud-Bélivier, Trimoulet, Vieux-Château-Carré, Villemaurine, Yon-Figeac

L'ANGÉLUS (Grand Cru Classé)   EXCELLENT

Production: 15,000 cases	Grape varieties: Cabernet Franc—50% Merlot—45% Cabernet Sauvignon—5%
Secondary label: Carillon de L'Angélus	
Vineyard size: 61.75 acres	Proprietor: Hubert de Boüard de Laforest
Time spent in barrels: 18–22 months	Average age of vines: 25 years
Evaluation of present classification: Should be upgraded to a Premier Grand Cru Classé; the quality equivalent of a Médoc third-growth	
Plateau of maturity: 4–12 years following the vintage	

L'Angélus has always been a St.-Emilion with great popular appeal. With a large production, much of it exported, a lovely label, and a charming, supple style of wine, L'Angélus has been able to build a strong following among enthusiasts of the wines of St.-Emilion. L'Angélus is located in the Mazerat Valley, with vineyards planted on calcareous clay loam and clay/sandy soil on the lower slopes. The entire vineyard enjoys a perfect southern exposure.

In the sixties and seventies L'Angélus produced a wine that started life with a charming fruity intensity, then proceeded to disintegrate in a matter of a few short years. This all changed in the eighties. The well-known Bordeaux oenologist, Pascal Ribereau Gayon, was brought in to provide consultation, and he insisted that the property age the wine in oak casks, of which two-thirds should be new each vintage. Previously, the wine had been aged in vats and saw no oak aging at all. The idea of fermenting the wine in small oak casks (much like the Pomerol, Le Pin) tends to add an extraordinary amount of complexity and intensity to the wine. This can only be done by small estates, or by those committed to spending huge sums of money on labor because it is a time-consuming, back-breaking process.

The results have been stunning. No doubt the young proprietor, Hubert de Bouard de Laforest, is also making a much stricter selection of only the best lots for the final wine. L'Angélus applied for elevation to Premier Grand Cru status in the new 1985 classification of the wines of St.-Emilion. This was denied—a mistake in my opinion. Based on vintages of the eighties, L'Angélus has increased its quality significantly.

The style of the *new* L'Angélus is one that still emphasizes early drinkability, with intense, rich, supple, fat fruitiness. However, the wine is now much deeper colored and more concentrated and has more supportive tannins to help it age better. Certainly the finest wines of the last three or four decades are the profound 1988, 1989 and 1990. Older vintages, prior to 1986, must be approached with extreme caution, as many of these wines have fallen completely apart.

VINTAGES

1989—I do not think anyone can doubt that L'Angélus is one of the
  ·   up-and-coming superstars, not only in St.-Emilion, but in all of
92   Bordeaux. The 1989 is opaque black/ruby/purple, with a huge bouquet of smoky vanillin oak, olives, cassis, and grilled nuts. In the mouth, it has sensational extract, full body, superb balance, and a fascinating long finish that must last for at least one minute. This is a great wine that will be put in the bottle with little manipulation, as proprietor Hubert de Boüard de Laforest has said he does not want to either fine or filter it. Anticipated maturity: 1993–2008. Last tasted, 4/91.

1988—The 1988 is a rich, almost lusty St.-Emilion, with a full-throttle
  ·   bouquet of licorice, spicy new oak, cassis, olives, and minerals.
91   In the mouth, it is full bodied, deep, and concentrated, with excellent extract, and a long, heady, moderately tannic finish. Anticipated maturity: 1992–2006. Last tasted, 4/91.

1986—The 1986 has a dark ruby color, a broad, expansive, forward
  ·   bouquet of ripe plums, spicy, smoky, new oak, and subtle herbs.
89   On the palate, the wine displays exceptional richness, fine length, and ripeness. While drinkable young, it has the potential to last another 10–15 years. Anticipated maturity: 1992–2006. Last tasted, 3/90.

1985—The 1985 is a seductively smooth, supple, broadly flavored wine
  ·   with aromas and flavors of berry fruit and herbs. Full bodied,
87   concentrated, but forward and delicious, this is a luscious wine. Anticipated maturity: Now–1997. Last tasted, 3/90.

1984—Light in color, with an almost burgundy-like bouquet of woodsy,
  ·   cherry, mushroom-like fruit, the 1984 is soft and fully mature. It
72   requires drinking. Anticipated maturity: Now–may be in decline. Last tasted, 3/89.

1983—Much like the 1982, this wine has matured all too quickly. Of
  ·   course, it was made during a period when the raw materials were
83   excellent, but the proprietor was excessively fining and filtering the wine. (Both procedures were eliminated in the late eighties.) The 1983 is medium ruby with some amber at the edge, a weedy,

cassis, oaky nose, and soft, loosely knit, nearly flabby flavors. The tannins have melted away, and this wine requires immediate consumption. Anticipated maturity: Now–may be in decline. Last tasted, 1/89.

1982—This was an excellent wine from cask, but a heavy-handed fining
  ·   and filtration eviscerated the wine at bottling. Additionally, the
  77   wine has aged at an alarmingly fast pace. Now medium ruby with an orange/amber edge and a woodsy, herbal, and curranty bouquet, this soft-textured wine has little grip and finishes with noticeable alcohol. It has lost its fruit at a shocking pace and should be drunk immediately. Anticipated maturity: Now–1993. Last tasted, 1/91.

1981—The 1981 has not fallen off the table quite as fast as either the
  ·   1982 or 1983, but it has lost much of its glossy, up-front fruit and
  76   taken on a more compact, straightforward, even attenuated character. Anticipated maturity: Now–may be in decline. Last tasted, 3/89.

1979—The 1979 has a vegetal, very herbaceous bouquet that is a trifle
  ·   unusual not to mention unpleasant. On the palate, this wine is
  72   very light, diffuse, medium bodied, and quite shallow and feeble. Anticipated maturity: Now–probably in serious decline. Last tasted, 2/81.

1978—A typical pre-1981 L'Angélus, the 1978 is light, fully mature, and
  ·   beginning to exhibit plenty of brown in the color and lose its fruit.
  75   Pleasant and charming in a light, picnic sort of style. Anticipated maturity: Now–probably in serious decline. Last tasted, 3/83.

1976—The 1976 L'Angélus is a total disaster—light, pale, no fruit, no
  ·   character, no charm, just alcohol and distant flavors of fruit. Last
  55   tasted, 6/80.

1975—The 1975 is a very poor wine, brown in color with an old, decaying
  ·   leafy, vegetal aroma, and hardly any ripe fruity intensity. This
  50   wine is unacceptably poor in what was an excellent if somewhat irregular vintage for the wines of Bordeaux. Last tasted, 3/86.

L'ARROSÉE (Grand Cru Classé)

Production: 5,000 cases	Grape varieties:
	Merlot—45%
	Cabernet Sauvignon—35%
	Cabernet Franc—20%
Secondary label: Les Côteaux du Château L'Arrosée	
Vineyard size: 39.5 acres	Proprietor: François Rodhain
Time spent in barrels: 22–24 months	Average age of vines: 32 years
Evaluation of present classification: Should be upgraded to a Premier Grand Cru Classé; the quality equivalent of a Médoc third-growth	
Plateau of maturity: 5–20 years following the vintage	

One of the least known and publicized wines of St.-Emilion, L'Arrosée, which sits on the slopes or *côtes* of St.-Emilion, is destined to become more famous as the high quality of its wine becomes better known.

The estate was purchased by the Rodhain family in 1911 and since 1956 has been managed by François Rodhain. The production was, unfortunately, sold off in bulk to the local St.-Emilion cooperative for over three decades because the property had no winemaking facilities. Now the entire production is made and bottled at the château.

The style of L'Arrosée's wine is unique. Fleshy, yet firm and powerful, fragrant, as well as rich and full, it is a wine with plenty of character and has a style that seems at times to recall a southern Médoc property such as La Lagune. At other times—for example in 1985 and 1986—the wine resembles a rich, lusty burgundy. In fact, the 1985 continues to remind me of a Henri Jayer Richebourg! L'Arrosée is a great wine that the renowned Dutch author Hubrecht Duijker called "the finest wine of the appellation."

The increasing fame of L'Arrosée, slightly tarnished by lackluster performances in both 1988 and 1989, appears to have been resurrected with a blockbuster wine in 1990.

VINTAGES

1989—After a succession of wonderful vintages (1982, 1983, 1985, and 1986), L'Arrosée has lost the magic touch. I wonder what has
85 happened? The 1989 is a tasty, amply endowed wine, but it is terribly low in acidity as well as diffuse and muddled. Also, where is the great extract and long finish of several years ago? The wine is tasty, but given past efforts, somewhat uninspired. Are the

yields now too high? Anticipated maturity: 1992–1999. Last tasted, 4/91.

1988— The 1988 is also not up to previous standards. Medium bodied,
· spicy, and fruity, with good depth, but not much length, this wine
83 lacks complexity and intensity. It saddens me to see this property, whose wines I adore, fall off the pace set by its recent past performances. Anticipated maturity: 1992–2000. Last tasted, 4/91.

1986— This great wine has profound richness, an extraordinarily complex bouquet of plums, herbs, blackcurrants, and spicy oak, dazzling length and intensity on the palate, and soft tannins in its finish. It will drink well by the mid-1990s, but last for at least 20–25 years. A clone of the 1961? Anticipated maturity: 1993–2012. Last tasted, 1/91.
·
93

1985— Every time I taste the 1985 I am more impressed. It is staggeringly exotic, fleshy, aromatic, and flashy. The awesome bouquet most recently seemed to suggest the exquisite Richebourg of Henri Jayer. Aside from the intense perfume of raspberries and new oak, the texture of the 1985 is one of an extravagant richness of fruit, full body, great depth and length, and remarkable complexity. I suspect this beauty will age well for another decade. Anticipated maturity: Now–2004. Last tasted, 5/91.
·
94

1984— The best wine of St.-Emilion in 1984? There is no question that M. Rodhain is one of those perfectionist owners who harvests very late in order to attain superripeness. He also began using almost 100% new oak in this vintage. The 1984 is a revelation. Broad, smooth, oaky, black cherry flavors seem to suggest a Clos Vougeot more than a St.-Emilion. This is a ripe, fruity wine with surprising depth. Anticipated maturity: Now–1995. Last tasted, 3/89.
·
86

1983— A powerful, concentrated, yet still elegant wine, the 1983 L'Arrosée has a big, rich bouquet of ripe black cherries, oak, and spice. Medium bodied, high in alcohol, and velvety textured, this lush wine exhibits the great ripeness this vineyard attained in 1983. Anticipated maturity: Now–2003. Last tasted, 1/91.
·
88

1982— Not much has changed with respect to the quality level or potential development of this wonderful wine. While I would rate both the 1985 and 1986 wines of L'Arrosée better than the 1982, it is still a magnificent bottle of wine with perhaps the most concentration of any L'Arrosée made in the last 20 years. It is not as complex or as structured as the 1986, nor does it have the upfront, seductive, burgundian-like appeal and sweetness of the 1985, but it is a very powerful, rich, tannic, spicy, herbaceous,
·
90

blackberry-scented wine with a great deal of length and power. I thought it would be fully mature by now, but it seems to need another 2–3 years to reach that plateau. Anticipated maturity: 1992–2004. Last tasted, 1/91.

1981— A classically proportioned wine of power and balance, the 1981
    · L'Arrosée is one of the better wines of St.-Emilion. Medium dark
   85 ruby, with an intense perfume of ripe black cherries and spicy oak, this medium-bodied wine has surprising power for the vintage, good tannin, and a moderately long finish. Anticipated maturity: Now–1997. Last tasted, 3/90.

1978— This is one of the very best St.-Emilions of this vintage. Many
    · wines became too ripe in the very late harvest of 1978, but L'Ar-
   87 rosée is extremely well structured and vinified. Dark ruby, with some amber at the edge, this wine has a deep, rich, ripe fruity, oaky bouquet that suggests a Médoc more than a St.-Emilion. On the palate, the wine is full bodied, concentrated, beefy, and long in the finish. It is a big, substantial wine. Anticipated maturity: Now–1992. Last tasted, 1/85.

1970— This big, full-bodied wine has a dark ruby color, with some amber
    · at the edge, a spicy, oaky, black cherry bouquet, medium body,
   85 rich, rustic, spicy, long flavors, and a long but slightly astringent finish. Are the tannins too excessive? Anticipated maturity: Now– 1999. Last tasted, 3/89.

1964— Now fully mature, but in no danger of declining, this wonderfully
    · fragrant wine has a big, rich, deep bouquet that develops in the
   87 glass. The wine is quite fleshy, concentrated, and rich, with a chewy texture, substantial weight, and a surprising amount of alcohol. Anticipated maturity: Now–1995. Last tasted, 6/84.

1961— I hope more recent vintages, such as 1982, 1985, and 1986, will
    · ultimately rival this great wine. It challenges the finest St.-Emi-
   94 lions in this legendary vintage. Medium ruby/garnet, with a huge, spicy, jammy, fruitcake sort of bouquet crammed with intensity, the lush, expansive, generously endowed flavors are smooth as silk. The wine has an opulent texture and a long, smoky, alcoholic finish. It has been fully mature for 5–6 years. Anticipated maturity: Now–1996. Last tasted, 12/90.

AUSONE (Premier Grand Cru Classé) OUTSTANDING

Production: 2,200 cases	Grape varieties: Merlot—50% Cabernet Franc—50%
Secondary label: none Vineyard size: 19.76 acres	Proprietors: Madame Dubois- Challon and the Vauthier family
Time spent in barrels: 20–24 months	Average age of vines: 50 years

Evaluation of present classification: Since 1976, it has merited its status as a Premier Grand Cru Classé and is the quality equivalent of a Médoc first-growth

Plateau of maturity: 15–50 years following the vintage

If the first-time visitor to Bordeaux had just one château and vineyard to visit, it should be the tiny Ausone property, perched on one of the hillsides outside the medieval walls of St.-Emilion.

Ausone has a spectacular location, made all the more startling because of its tiny vineyard of very old vines and the extensive limestone caves that house the property's wine cellar.

Ausone is named after the Roman poet Ausonius, who lived between 320 A.D. and 395 A.D. He was also known to have had a vineyard in the area (closer apparently to Bordeaux than St.-Emilion), and while there are Roman ruins at Ausone, it is highly doubtful that Ausonius himself had anything to do with Ausone's vineyard.

Ausone is now owned jointly by the Dubois-Challon and Vauthier families who can trace their families' ownership of Ausone back to the late eighteenth century.

Despite the great historical significance of Ausone and the fact that it has one of the most privileged locations for making wine in all of Bordeaux, the record of wine quality was mediocre—even poor—during the sixties and seventies. The turnabout in quality came in 1976 when the owners hired a new régisseur, Pascal Delbeck. While Ausone produced many dry, tired, and feebly colored wines in the forties, fifties, and sixties, Delbeck turned out one excellent wine after another, starting with the outstanding 1976, which is one of the two best wines of Bordeaux in that vintage.

The miniscule production of Ausone makes it a wine that is almost impossible to find commercially. Even more rare than the famous Pomerol estate of Pétrus, yet considerably less expensive, Ausone has a style that is totally different from St.-Emilion's other famous estate, Cheval Blanc.

From 1976 onward, the wines of Ausone have been characterized by a ruby color, a bouquet of ripe fruit, oriental spices, strong mineral scents, and spicy oak, and a firm, solidly tannic texture. No doubt the addition of 5% to 20% stems to the fermenting wine produces a powerfully tannic wine that is meant to be cellared a long time. In fact, the two most prominent features of Ausone in blind tastings of younger wines are the unmistakably backward, almost severe style and its lightish color. Purchasers of Ausone should generally be prepared to wait 10–15 years for Ausone to shed its considerable tannin. If patience is not your virtue, buying Ausone makes little sense.

VINTAGES

1989—In 1989, Ausone harvested their splendidly situated micro-vine-
·   yard between September 7 and 19. Their first *cuvée* of Merlot
92   reached 14.6% alcohol naturally, the highest anyone at the châ-
      teau could ever remember. They also cut off 50% of the grape
      bunches in an effort to avoid overproduction and the diluted taste
      that plagued their 1985 and 1986. The result is a wine with re-
      markable strength, yet stunning balance because of an extremely
      high tannin content. It is the tannin that gives focus and definition
      to the wine's intense core of exotic black fruits. This is a medium-
      to full-bodied, backward 1989, possessing a haunting underlying
      mineral character that seems to be a characteristic of this prop-
      erty's greatest vintages. On potential this is certainly the finest
      Ausone since the 1982 (which remains impossibly impenetrable
      and closed). Those readers who possess a millionaire's income
      and cozy trade connections necessary to buy Ausone should be
      prepared to wait a good 25 years minimum for this wine to reach
      its apogee. Anticipated maturity: 2015–2035. Last tasted, 4/91.

1988—The 1988 may need 20 years to reach its peak, as the wine is
·   probably the most tannic, young Ausone I have ever tasted. The
90   tannins are extremely hard—even astringent—but unlike a num-
      ber of 1988s where the balance between tannins and fruit favors
      the tannin (always a troubling sign), here is plenty of juicy red and
      black fruit extract in a medium-bodied, superbly concentrated,
      very intense and powerful wine. Anticipated maturity: 2008–
      2040. Last tasted, 4/91.

1987—This is a successful vintage for Ausone, which produced a wine
·   with nearly 13% natural alcohol. Surprisingly ripe, with the ex-
87   otic, mineral-scented character so typical of this property, the
      1987 Ausone is a medium-bodied, ripe, richly fruity, classy wine

that should drink beautifully for another 12–20 years. If it continues to firm up and gain weight in the bottle, it may turn out to be as good as their wonderful 1976, as well as have 20 or more years of aging potential. A sleeper! Anticipated maturity: 1994–2010. Last tasted, 12/90.

1986— The 1986 is a deeper and fuller wine than the 1985, but every time
·   I have it I wonder if it could not have been better. The bouquet is
86   extremely reserved, but does offer up mineral scents, some herbaceous, spicy elements, and hints of ripe fruit. On the palate, the wine is extremely hard, with medium body, and a lot of tannin in the finish. I would not want to open a bottle for consumption prior to the late nineties. From both my cask and bottle tastings, this wine has consistently been ungenerous and tough textured. Anticipated maturity: 1997–2020. Last tasted, 3/90.

1985— The 1985 Ausone appears light, supple, pleasant, and attractive,
·   but somewhat one-dimensional by the standards of this splendid
85   estate. Will it put on weight? Anticipated maturity: 1993–2005. Last tasted, 3/90.

1983— This wine is a great success for the vintage. Ausone's 1983 is a
·   powerful, rich, full-bodied wine with a higher alcohol content than
93   normal. Medium ruby, rich, and jammy, with low acidity but great concentration as well as that glorious perfume of minerals and oriental spices, this wine should last 15–20 years, but provide fine drinking early on—a rarity for Ausone. Anticipated maturity: 1993–2010. Last tasted, 1/91.

1982— In the early cask tastings of the 1982s, there was no wine with a
·   greater reputation among the courtiers and the *négociants* of Bor-
94?   deaux than the 1982 Ausone. Many people not only thought it was the wine of the vintage, but perhaps one of the greatest wines made this century. A visit to the cellars seemed to confirm this. The *maître de chai*, Pascal Delbeck, literally let you pick any cask or casks in the cellar you wanted to taste, and the results were all the same—an incredibly exotic, rich, fabulous wine that left nothing to be desired. At present, one must wonder why, from the bottle, this wine shows such a lean, austere, tough texture, not much bouquet, and not nearly the depth or concentration that would suggest either a great wine or a great vintage. Believe it or not, the highest rating I have given the 1982 Ausone in blind tastings has been an 84, and yet my confidence in this wine is not shaken. I think that Ausone is simply one of the most tricky wines to evaluate, and I do indeed believe that the 1982 is going to blossom and emerge in 10–15 years' time to reveal the quality

and exotic richness it so consistently displayed earlier. Although this was clearly a monumental wine from cask, it has not performed close to that level of quality out of the bottle. So for now, let's call it judgment reserved, with another tasting of this wine in the late nineties to decide whether it indeed compares favorably with some of the legendary vintages produced by Ausone earlier in this century. Anticipated maturity: 2000–2030. Last tasted, 12/90.

1981— This medium ruby wine remains closed, but exhibits adequate
·   ripeness of fruit. However, the hard tannins are cause for con-
82   cern. A medium-weight wine, the 1981 Ausone has good concen-
       tration, but will, I believe, always be an austere, tough-textured,
       charmless wine. It still needs 10 years to soften and develop.
       Anticipated maturity: 1996–2010. Last tasted, 1/90.

1980— A lightweight wine from a lightweight vintage, the 1980 Ausone
·   has medium ruby color, a minor, straightforward bouquet of
75   plums and herbs, medium body, and average-intensity flavors.
       Anticipated maturity: Now–1992. Last tasted, 6/84.

1979— From the cask, I preferred the 1979 to the highly heralded 1978,
·   but now the wine has closed up, and seems unyielding and dumb.
87   Light to medium ruby, with a spicy, tight bouquet with hints of
       oak, ripe black cherries, spices, and charred earth, this medium-
       bodied wine continues to taste surprisingly backward and austere.
       Will the marvelous fruit it exhibited when young reappear and
       outlive the tannins? Anticipated maturity: 1996–2010. Last
       tasted, 2/91.

1978— A classic Ausone, still backward and remarkably youthful, the
·   1978 has a dark ruby color, an aroma of ripe fruit, as well as
88   scents of minerals and spicy oak. Medium bodied with high tan-
       nins and a long finish, this wine is austere, stubbornly slow to
       evolve, and obviously made for long-term cellaring. Will the fruit
       hold up? Anticipated maturity: 1998–2015. Last tasted, 3/91.

1976— The finest Ausone of the seventies, and along with Lafite-Roth-
·   schild of Pauillac, one of the two outstandingly great wines of this
93   vintage, the 1976 Ausone is indeed a profound wine. Surprisingly
       dark colored for the vintage, with a voluptuous, intense, complex
       bouquet of minerals, licorice, truffles, and ripe, spicy blackcur-
       rant fruit, this full-bodied, powerful, large-scaled Ausone has re-
       markable size given the year. Amazingly, it is a bigger wine than
       more recent Ausone such as the 1978, 1979, 1985, and 1986. It
       is a winemaking triumph for this difficult vintage. Anticipated
       maturity: 1992–2010. Last tasted, 12/90.

1975—Rather pale colored for a 1975, with a bouquet of fading fruit,
·   damp vegetation, and musty cardboard, the 1975 Ausone has
76   power and average concentration of fruit, but appears to be prematurely drying out. Some British authorities have rated it highly,
claiming it to be on par with the 1976. Is bottle variation a factor?
Anticipated maturity: Now–2000. Last tasted, 12/88.

1971—Light to medium ruby with a rust-colored edge, this pleasant, yet
·   insubstantial wine has a light perfume of spicy oak as well as
78   scents of minerals and decaying leafy vegetation. Not terribly well
concentrated, but adequately fruity in a savory, satisfying manner, the 1971 is a nice wine for drinking immediately. A magnum
drunk at the château in 1988 merited a more enthusiastic review
(86 points), but it was far from profound. Anticipated maturity:
Now–1998. Last tasted, 3/88.

1970—The 1970 Ausone is very light, with a bouquet that suggests old,
·   faded flowers and dusty fruit. Brown at the edges, and beginning
69   to dry out, this medium-bodied wine is the poorest of the "Big
Eight" of Bordeaux in this excellent vintage. Very disappointing.
Last tasted, 1/87.

1967—A diluted, insipid bouquet is followed by a wine with bland,
·   washed-out flavors, and significant browning to the color. Al-
65   though not a complete failure, it is extremely disappointing. Last
tasted, 9/83.

OLDER VINTAGES

The kindest thing that can be said about many of the older vintages of
Ausone, particularly those in the post–World War II era, is that they
have survived. It is hard to find a vintage of Ausone from the forties or
fifties that is not at least drinkable. In spite of the fact that Ausone often
proves this potential for longevity, the question remains as to how much
pleasure these wines ultimately provide. Top vintages such as 1945,
1947, 1952, 1955, 1959, and 1961, while still alive, all represent the
austere, undernourished, and somewhat charmless style of Ausone. Why
more richness and depth were not forthcoming escapes me, but there is
no denying the high level of dry, astringent tannins in so many of these
wines. My favorite older vintage of Ausone is the 1955, but even that
wine is far from meriting an outstanding rating. Before World War II,
particularly in the twenties, Ausone apparently made a number of great
wines, but I have never had the opportunity to taste the 1929, or the
legendary 1900, but certainly the 1928 acquitted itself well (rated 91)
when drunk in the late eighties.

BALESTARD-LA-TONNELLE (Grand Cru Classé) VERY GOOD

Production: 5,000 cases	Grape varieties: Merlot—65% Cabernet Franc—20% Cabernet Sauvignon—10% Malbec—5%
Secondary label: Les Tourelles de Balestard	
Vineyard size: 26 acres	Proprietor: G.F.A. Capdemourlin
Time spent in barrels: 16–22 months	Average age of vines: 30 years
Evaluation of present classification: The quality equivalent of a Médoc fifth-growth	
Plateau of maturity: 5–14 years following the vintage	

I have always regarded Balestard-La-Tonnelle as the Lynch-Bages of St.-Emilion. This property, owned by Jacques Capdemourlin, like Lynch-Bages in Pauillac, produces a densely colored, big, deep, rich, and chewy style of wine. It can sometimes be too big and alcoholic for its own good, but this is an immensely enjoyable style of St.-Emilion that can normally be drunk after 5 or 6 years of bottle age, yet also evolve gracefully for 10 or more years.

The property takes its name from the writings of the fifteenth-century poet François Villon, who wrote about "drinking this divine nectar which carries the name of Balestard." The vineyard, enclosed by tall cypress (look for the windmill that sits on the knoll), is located on a limestone plateau adjacent to Château Soutard, to the east of the town of St.-Emilion. Balestard has been especially successful since 1970. Given the realistic prices Jacques Capdemourlin charges for his wines, this is one of St.-Emilion's great bargains.

VINTAGES

1989—The 1989 is a jammy, raspberry-and-blackberry-scented wine that
·   is fat, lacks acidity, but has high alcohol, and a chunky, fleshy,
86   mouth-filling feel. If drunk young, this wine will provide a great
       deal of pleasure over the first 7–9 years of life. Given the resem-
       blance to the 1982—a wine that has continued to develop more
       grip and structure over the last decade—this wine may well have
       greater longevity than I am predicting. It typifies the "house
       style" of Balestard. Anticipated maturity: 1992–2005. Last
       tasted, 4/91.

1988—The 1988 is a narrowly constructed, compact, austere wine that
·   should be consumed over the next 5–10 years. It certainly will
83   last, but again, the problem is the lack of balance between the
excessive tannins and the amount of fruit present. Anticipated
maturity: 1993–2000. Last tasted, 4/91.

1986—This full-throttle, powerhouse offers explosive levels of macho
·   fruit and body along with a chewy texture. It is never a delicate
85   or particularly charming wine, but rather one that tends to grab
the taster's attention with intensity and muscle more than anything else. The 1986 is typical of this estate, but has a bit more
tannin in the finish to go along with its ponderous, robust style.
Anticipated maturity: Now–2001. Last tasted, 3/89.

1985—The 1985 is a hefty, fat, rich, but not ponderous wine, with plenty
·   of gutsy, meaty fruit and body. Anticipated maturity: Now–1996.
86   Last tasted, 3/89.

1984—For a St.-Emilion from this vintage, the 1984 Balestard is a suc-
·   cess. It is fruity, soft, clean, and surprisingly fleshy and solid.
77   Anticipated maturity: Now–1993. Last tasted, 3/88.

1983—A huge wine that may be too big for some tasters, the 1983
·   Balestard has a black/ruby color and a ripe, full-blown bouquet of
86   plums and tarry, truffle scents. On the palate, the wine is powerful, dense, and alcoholic. This is a mammoth-styled anachronistic
wine that is sure to provoke controversy in tasting circles. Anticipated maturity: Now–1997. Last tasted, 1/89.

1982—Always one of the most chewy and fleshy St.-Emilions, the 1982
·   Balestard-La-Tonnelle is a hulky, beefy, in-your-face type of St.-
87   Emilion with impressive color, a big, jammy, concentrated feel
on the palate, and a toasty, tarry, plummy bouquet. Power rather
than finesse is the rule here. I should note that the wine, while
delicious, has developed structure in the bottle. Anticipated maturity: Now–2000. Last tasted, 1/90.

1981—I have always liked the uncomplicated fleshy texture and rich
·   fruitiness of Balestard. The 1981 has begun to lose its powerful,
84   fruity gusto. Straightforward, generous and full bodied, but beginning to tire, this wine requires consumption. Anticipated maturity: Now–may be in decline. Last tasted, 3/87.

1978—Fully mature when last tasted, the 1978 Balestard is a richly
·   fruity, soft, generously flavored, full-bodied wine with plenty of
84   appeal. Anticipated maturity: Now–may be in decline. Last
tasted, 2/83.

1976—Not as concentrated or as powerful as Balestard normally is, the
·   1976 is a trifle flabby and diffuse. Nevertheless, at last tasting it
78   was a soft, foursquare, one-dimensional wine with plenty of

punch. Anticipated maturity: Now–probably in serious decline. Last tasted, 9/80.

1975—This is one of the best Balestards I have ever tasted. Concen-
· trated and powerful, yet better balanced and less alcoholic than
87 the big jammy 1982 and 1983 wines, the 1975 has a complex bouquet of ripe plums, herbs, leather, and spicy oak. It is full bodied and rich, with soft tannins. Anticipated maturity: Now–1993. Last tasted, 3/89.

1971—Beginning to display a generous amount of browning at the edges,
· this plump, fat, slightly sweet wine has always exhibited good
82 ripeness and a rich, open-knit, plummy fruitiness. Anticipated maturity: Now–probably in serious decline. Last tasted, 5/83.

1970—A very good wine from Balestard, the 1970 is full bodied, dark
· ruby colored, fragrant, chewy, and rich on the palate, and has a
84 long, somewhat alcoholic finish. This is a big, rich, succulent, fully mature St.-Emilion. Anticipated maturity: Now–probably in serious decline. Last tasted, 8/82.

BÉARD (Grand Cru Classé) GOOD

Production: 3,000 cases	Grape varieties: Merlot—65% Cabernet Franc—35%
Secondary label: none Vineyard size: 19.8 acres	Proprietor: The Goudichaud family
Time spent in barrels: 16–20 months	Average age of vines: 30 years
Evaluation of present classification: The quality equivalent of a Médoc Cru Bourgeois	
Plateau of maturity: 3–8 years following the vintage	

Unfortunately, I have not had enough experience with Béard to form a strong opinion about their wines. However, the vintages I have tasted—1985, 1986, 1988, and 1989—were competently made wines that had good, pure fruit, and a chunky, robust character. The domain, which can trace its existence to 1858, is now run by Veronique Goudichaud. The vineyard is situated in the commune of Saint-Laurent-des-Combes, and Madame Goudichaud believes in hand harvesting, no herbicides, and a traditional vinification and *élevage*. While this estate is not in the top rung of St.-Emilions, it would appear to offer a reliable, reasonably priced alternative.

BEAU SÉJOUR-BÉCOT (Grand Cru Classé) GOOD

Production: 7,000 cases	Grape varieties: Merlot—70% Cabernet Franc—24% Cabernet Sauvignon—6%
Secondary label: Tournelle des Moines	
Vineyard size: 47 acres	Proprietors: Gérard and Dominique Bécot
Time spent in barrels: 18–22 months	Average age of vines: 30 years
Evaluation of present classification: The quality equivalent of a Médoc Cru Bourgeois	
Plateau of maturity: 5–12 years following the vintage	

There used to be two Beauséjour Premiers Grands Crus in St.-Emilion. As of 1985, there is only one, since this property was, not surprisingly, demoted in the new classification of wines that was issued in 1985. Whether it was that demotion or not, there is no doubt that the quality of Beau Séjour-Bécot since the mid-1980s has improved significantly. Many observers remain skeptical as to the reason why Beau Séjour-Bécot was singled out for reclassification. Certainly other estates making mediocre wine were not changed in the new classification. One reason may have been that when Beau Séjour-Bécot annexed the vineyards of the two adjacent châteaux, La Carte and Des Trois Moulins, it increased in size by 85%. Many people believed that this type of aggrandizement of Grand Cru vineyards to a Premier Grand Cru Classé could not be permitted and that the proprietors should be punished.

The vineyard, situated on a limestone plateau, has, since 1985, produced wines that are richer, fuller, and more obviously marked by new oak (90–100% new oak casks are employed). It is ironic that now that Beau Séjour-Bécot is entitled to only Grand Cru Classé status, the wines are significantly better than when it was entitled to Premier Grand Cru Classé status.

VINTAGES

1989—Over the last several vintages, this wine has had a tendency to be
· overwhelmingly oaky in youth. In fact, if there is any criticism, it
87 would be that the proprietors may be using too much new wood.
However, a high percentage of new oak tends to work well in a
vintage such as 1989 where the underlying concentration and

jammy, low-acid fruit character need the structure of oak to give the wine definition and focus. The 1989 has a dizzyingly high alcohol level, luscious, concentrated, rich, jammy, black cherry fruit, an opulent texture, and plenty of soft tannins in the finish. It should provide delicious drinking early in its life. Anticipated maturity: 1992–2002. Last tasted, 4/91.

1988—The 1988 is similar to the 1989 with its aggressive oak-scented
· bouquet. However, with airing, the oak seems to step back and
85 the ripe, curranty fruit emerges. The tannins are more aggressive than in the 1989, and the wine appears to have good to very good concentration of fruit as well as length. In all likelihood, the 1988 will outlive the 1989, but will it provide as much pleasure? Anticipated maturity: 1992–2004. Last tasted, 4/91.

1986—Along with the 1989, the 1986 is the finest wine I have ever tasted
· from this property. It has an amazing level of smoky oak and
87 dazzling quantities of fruit. A very powerful, full-bodied, rich wine, with an impressive black/ruby color, it has an undeniably seductive, even sexy, bouquet, and a lush, opulent texture. Anticipated maturity: Now–2005. Last tasted, 3/90.

1985—The 1985 is a rich, ripe, relatively alcoholic wine possessing a
· charming, precocious personality, medium to full body, low acid-
85 ity, but plenty of flesh and fruit. Anticipated maturity: Now–1995. Last tasted, 3/90.

1983—The 1983 exhibits surprisingly good color, a ripe raspberry, oaky
· bouquet, lush, concentrated, soft flavors, and medium to full
86 body. Given the usually mediocre performance of this property, the 1983 is an encouraging effort. Anticipated maturity: Now–1995. Last tasted, 1/89.

1982—In the context of the vintage, this is hardly an inspiring wine, but
· for Beau Séjour it is a minor success, and undoubtedly an im-
78 provement over some of the distressingly mediocre wines of the last several decades. Straightforwardly fruity, one-dimensional, and medium bodied, this is an enjoyable, moderately intense wine that should be consumed. Anticipated maturity: Now–1993. Last tasted, 1/87.

1981—Suspiciously light in color, with an innocuous, barely discernible
· bouquet of fruit, the 1981 Beau Séjour seems to be overly oaky,
70 as well as hollow and lean. Quite disappointing. Anticipated maturity: Now–probably in serious decline. Last tasted, 9/84.

1979—For its class and obviously for the price, this skinny little wine
· leaves a lot to be desired. Medium ruby, with a simple, oaky,
72 light-intensity, cherry bouquet, medium body, and tannic, short

flavors that tail off in the mouth, this wine is palatable, but outclassed by numerous generic St.-Emilions made by the town's cooperative. Anticipated maturity: Now–probably in serious decline. Last tasted, 11/82.

1978—A respectable effort from Beau Séjour, the 1978, which is fully
· 　　mature, is fruity, plummy, soft, adequately concentrated, and
78　　medium bodied. There is no bitterness in the finish, and the wine
　　　has decent balance. Anticipated maturity: Now–probably in serious decline. Last tasted, 10/82.

1976—Now totally faded and dried out, the 1976 has a vegetal, barnyard
· 　　aroma, soft, diluted flavors, medium body, and a very short finish.
62　　Last tasted, 10/83.

1975—An acceptable wine was produced by Beau Séjour in 1975. Me-
· 　　dium ruby, with an emerging bouquet of cherries and oak, this
75　　wine has tight, hard, tannic flavors, medium body, and a good
　　　finish. Anticipated maturity: Now–1993. Last tasted, 5/84.

1971—Probably the best wine from this estate in the 1970s, this vintage
· 　　has resulted in a soundly made wine, with an open-knit, plummy,
80　　oaky bouquet, soft, spicy, medium-bodied flavors that exhibit
　　　good ripeness, and light tannins present in the finish. Anticipated
　　　maturity: Now–may be in decline. Last tasted, 12/84.

1970—Tired and too tannic for its meager intensity of fruit, this lean,
· 　　compact wine will only deteriorate further. Last tasted, 5/84.
65

BEAUSÉJOUR (DUFFAU-LAGARROSSE)
(Premier Grand Cru Classé)　　　　　　　　　　　　　　GOOD

Production: 3,000 cases	Grape varieties: Merlot—55% Cabernet Franc—25% Cabernet Sauvignon—20%
Secondary label: La Croix de Mazerat	
Vineyard size: 17.3 acres	Proprietor: The Duffau-Lagarrosse family
Time spent in barrels: 20–22 months	Average age of vines: 30 years
Evaluation of present classification: Should be downgraded to a Grand Cru Classé; the quality equivalent of a Médoc Cru Bourgeois	
Plateau of maturity: 5–15 years following the vintage	

There are two Beauséjour estates in St.-Emilion. Both are located on the *côtes* of St.-Emilion. Both were among the crème de la crème of St.-Emilion's hierarchy—that of Premiers Grands Crus. The other, Beau Séjour-Bécot, was demoted in the 1985 classification of the wines of St.-Emilion, but the status of this Beauséjour has remained unchanged. Both estates have produced terribly overrated wines and have been living off their reputations for too long.

Beauséjour, owned by the Duffau-Lagarrosse family, is the better of the two and has offered hints at turning things around since the 1982 vintage. The irrefutable success of both the 1988 and 1989 as well as the blockbuster 1990 may mark the renaissance of this estate.

The tiny vineyard, owned by the same family for over 150 years, is planted in a mixture of calcareous clay and limestone soil. The higher quality of recent years may be a result of a lower percentage of Cabernet Sauvignon, as well as much later harvesting, thus accounting for the wine's greater depth and ripeness.

VINTAGES

1989—While the 1989 has a promising, understated bouquet of black
·   cherry fruit, minerals, and spicy oak, it is surprisingly restrained
88   for a 1989. Nevertheless, the ruby/purple color, the velvety, ex-
      tracted, almost sweet, alcoholic flavors, and good tannins in the
      finish are clearly reminiscent of a vintage where tremendous ripe-
      ness was attained. It is not a blockbuster, but rather an extremely
      well-balanced, concentrated, impressive effort that still has some
      baby fat to shed. Anticipated maturity: 1993–2007. Last tasted,
      4/91.

1988—I believe the 1988 is slightly superior to the 1989, and one of the
·   best examples from this famous estate in the last several decades.
89   On the palate, the wine has even more depth and fullness than
      the 1989, and possesses a more focused bouquet that is filled with
      aromas of licorice, plums, spices, new oak, and subtle herbs.
      Exceptionally concentrated, with better acidity and less alcohol
      than the 1989, this beautifully made, complex wine should attain
      maturity by the mid-1990s and last through the first decade of the
      next century. Anticipated maturity: 1995–2010. Last tasted, 4/91.

1986—From both cask and bottle, the 1986 has never seemed to be
·   anything more than a lightweight, shallowly constructed, one-
83   dimensional wine, with a lot of wood and tannin in the finish.
      Some fruit and charm has developed, but this is not one of the
      leaders in 1986. Anticipated maturity: 1992–1997. Last tasted,
      3/89.

1985—The 1985 did not exhibit as much depth as I would have expected.
· It is lightweight and medium bodied, with a good spicy fruitiness,
84 soft texture, and pleasant length. However, for its class, it is an
uninspiring effort. Anticipated maturity: Now–1997. Last tasted,
3/89.

1983—This has turned out to be a very good example of Beauséjour.
· Medium dark ruby, with some amber at the edge, the wine's
86 bouquet offers up moderately intense aromas of black fruits,
smoke, licorice, and minerals. In the mouth, the wine is medium
bodied, and has some firm tannins to shed, but there appears to
be very good extract. Almost fully mature, it should continue to
evolve gracefully for at least another decade. Anticipated maturity: 1992–2001. Last tasted, 1/89.

1982—Along with the 1988 and 1990, this is one of the three best exam-
· ples I have ever tasted from Beauséjour. Medium dark ruby, with
87 an expansive bouquet of sweet, toasty oak, black fruits, and
herbs, this lush, sweet, supple, superripe wine flows across the
palate with a velvety texture. The finish is surprisingly long for
Beauséjour, normally an understated, almost excessively polite
wine. Anticipated maturity: Now–2000. Last tasted, 1/89.

1981—Medium ruby with a firm, astringent, tough personality, I admire
· the wine's tight structure, but only wish that there were a little
82 more fruit and depth. Anticipated maturity: Now–1996. Last
tasted, 11/84.

1979—Inexcusably light, feeble, frail, and lacking the richness and con-
· centration one expects from wines of this class, Beauséjour's 1979
74 has no tannin, so it is best consumed now. Last tasted, 7/83.

1978—A bigger, richer, more substantial wine than the pale 1979, the
· 1978, despite more flesh and weight, is flawed by a very metallic,
61 bizarre bouquet that seems atypical and foreign. If you can
get past the smell, the wine exhibits good structure and fruit.
Anticipated maturity: Now–may be in decline. Last tasted,
7/83.

1976—A satisfactory effort from Beauséjour, the 1976 has some ripe
· concentrated fruit, medium body, a little structure, and a charm-
70 ing, fruity bouquet. Not a big wine, but cleanly made and pleasant. Anticipated maturity: Now–may be in decline. Last tasted,
7/83.

1970—Extremely thin, hard, acidic flavors display none of the character
· of the 1970 vintage. Shockingly diluted and hollow, one cannot
60 possibly speculate what could have gone wrong with this wine.
Last tasted, 7/83.

1964—In a year in which many St.-Emilions excelled, Beauséjour pro-
· duced an insipid, dull, weakly colored, fruitless wine without
62 charm or appeal. Quite disappointing. Last tasted, 7/83.

BELAIR (Premier Grand Cru Classé)   VERY GOOD

Production: 4,500 cases	Grape varieties: Merlot—60% Cabernet Franc—40%
Secondary label: Roc-Blanquant (a nonvintage wine)	
Vineyard size: 32.1 acres	Proprietor: Madame Dubois-Challon
Time spent in barrels: 20–22 months	Average age of vines: 35 years
Evaluation of present classification: The quality equivalent of a Médoc fifth-growth, particularly since 1979	
Plateau of maturity: 5–15 years following the vintage	

Belair, like so many other properties in Bordeaux, has emerged from a
prolonged period of mediocrity. This property had a great reputation in
the nineteenth century and its history can be traced back as far as the
fourteenth. Bernard Ginestet, the leading French writer on the wines of
Bordeaux, boldly calls Belair, "the Lafite-Rothschild among the hillsides
of St.-Emilion." That may be overstating the case. The tiny vineyard of
Belair is owned by the Dubois-Challon family, who are also coproprietors
of Ausone, Belair's next-door neighbor. The level of wine quality at Belair has followed that of Ausone. The rehabilitation and renaissance of
Ausone started with the 1976 vintage, and it was also during this time
that higher-quality wines from Belair began to be produced. The same
team that makes Ausone—Pascal Delbeck/Marcel Lanau/Jean-Claude
Berrouet—is also the main brain trust at Belair, and as the tasting notes
that follow demonstrate, this wine has improved. In style, one would
assume that because of the vineyard's location on the *côtes* next to Ausone, in addition to having the same winemakers, Belair would resemble
Ausone. It does not. While part of the vineyard does lie on the hillside,
another part is squarely on the plateau. The wine can be as concentrated
as Ausone, but it is also softer and earlier to mature. It is also significantly less expensive.

VINTAGES

1989—The 1989 Belair is the finest wine I have ever tasted from this
·   famous Premier Grand Cru Classé of St.-Emilion. The huge,
90   smoky, roasted, exotic bouquet of plums and oriental spices is
       decadent as well as thrilling. In the mouth, the wine exhibits
       surprisingly good acidity and plentiful but soft tannins. There is
       also a formidable level of alcohol and sensationally extracted,
       multidimensional fruit flavors. It is a brilliant effort. Anticipated
       maturity: 1995–2010. Last tasted, 4/91.

1988—The 1988 is a good rather than exceptional effort. Given the vin-
·   tage, no one should be surprised that it is a leaner, more austere
85   wine. But it does have a good inner core of curranty fruit, fine
       tannins, and a general sense of elegance and grace. Anticipated
       maturity: 1995–2010. Last tasted, 4/91.

1987—This elegant, ripe, supple, deliciously fruity, complex wine is,
·   amazingly, better and paradoxically cheaper than the more highly
86   touted 1988, 1986, and 1985. There is plenty of extract, and the
       wine exhibits a long, ripe, seductive finish. A top success for a
       1987 St.-Emilion, it should be drunk early in its life. Anticipated
       maturity: Now–1996. Last tasted, 3/90.

1986—This is a disappointing effort from Belair. The medium ruby color
·   appears slightly washed out, and the bouquet is closed, but does
76   offer up some dusty, herbaceous, red-fruit scents. In the mouth,
       the wine is astringent, too tannic, and very austere, and finishes
       without any charm or concentration. Its future is suspect. Antic-
       ipated maturity: 1992–2000. Last tasted, 3/90.

1985—I am perplexed by the 1985 Belair, as it seems somewhat light,
·   and lacking grip and intensity. Have I misinterpreted this wine
77   from both cask and bottle? Anticipated maturity: 1992–1997. Last
       tasted, 3/89.

1983—Surprisingly powerful and rich for Belair, with excellent color and
·   a deep, ripe, tannic, full-bodied texture, this is a big-styled wine
88   that should prove to be the longest-lived Belair in over 20 years.
       Quite impressive. Anticipated maturity: 1993–2005. Last tasted,
       2/89.

1982—As good as Belair is in 1982, it will have to take a back seat to the
·   lovely, rich 1983, as well as the 1989. Nevertheless, the 1982 has
87   dark ruby color, with an attractive, plummy, leafy, ripe, fruity,
       almost truffle-like aroma. Medium bodied, with good concentra-
       tion, moderate tannins, and a long but hard finish, this wine has
       lost its early charm and entered a closed, tough, awkward stage
       —much like its sibling, Ausone. Anticipated maturity: 1994–
       2006. Last tasted, 11/89.

1981—The 1981 is, as some Bordelais would enthusiastically say, "a
·   finesse wine with plenty of elegance." Light, fruity, and soft, this
74   medium ruby-colored wine has a pleasing texture and some hard
tannins in the finish, but it seems unlikely to gain flavor or depth.
Anticipated maturity: Now–1994. Last tasted, 3/87.

1979—The first attractive Belair in nearly 20 years, the 1979 has a per-
·   fume of ripe blackcurrant fruit, some spicy oak, and violets. On
85   the palate, the wine is medium bodied, with a lush, precocious
fruitiness and light tannins. This is a deliciously soft, fruity, very
elegant wine. Anticipated maturity: Now–1994. Last tasted, 1/87.

1978—This wine is a trifle too light and fleeting on the palate, but it does
·   offer soft, pleasant, easygoing, fruity flavors, and it also finishes
80   well. Anticipated maturity: Now–1993. Last tasted, 2/86.

1976—The 1976 is respectable, but perhaps it could have been better
·   given the excellence of Ausone in this vintage. Rather light, soft,
75   fruity, and sweet, displaying the obvious overripe quality of the
vintage, the 1976 Belair has no discernible tannin. It was fully
mature in the early eighties. Anticipated maturity: Now–may be
in decline. Last tasted, 6/82

1975—I have found this wine to be hollow and lacking fruit, with an
·   excess of tannin present. Medium ruby with some brown at the
70   edges, this medium-bodied wine has a dusty, sparse texture, a
leathery, hard bouquet, and a short, harsh finish. It appears to be
one of the 1975s where the tannin content significantly outweighs
the fruit. Last tasted, 5/84.

1971—Quite meagerly endowed, without much bouquet, this wine has a
·   brownish color, dry, astringent, hard flavors, and no charm. One
65   rarely sees top properties today producing wines at this level of
quality. Last tasted, 9/78.

1970—Adequately colored with just a shade of brown, the 1970 Belair is
·   hard and spicy, and finishes with a coarseness and bitterness. It
68   is an atypical 1970. Last tasted, 7/81.

1967—Extremely poor, the 1967 Belair, from a vintage that was generally
·   better for St.-Emilion and Pomerol than the Médoc, is brown in
55   color, with pale, coarse, diluted flavors. Last tasted, 4/80.

1966—Thin, sharp, acidic flavors dominate the palate. The fruit is fad-
·   ing, and the wine only has wood and alcohol in the finish. Belair
60   is a major disappointment in this vintage. Last tasted, 4/80.

BELLEFONT-BELCIER (Grand Cru) AVERAGE

Production: 8,000 cases	Grape varieties: Merlot—70% Cabernet Franc—20% Cabernet Sauvignon—10%
Secondary label: none	
Vineyard size: 32.1 acres	Proprietor: Société Civile Administrator: Jean Labusquière
Time spent in barrels: 16–20 months	Average age of vines: 25 years
Evaluation of present classification: The quality equivalent of a Médoc Cru Bourgeois	
Plateau of maturity: 3–8 years following the vintage	

This vineyard, located in the commune of Saint-Laurent-des-Combes, produces straightforward, soft, easy-to-drink wines that lack distinction, but offer satisfyingly straightforward, monolithic flavors, and limited aging potential.

BELLEVUE (Grand Cru Classé) AVERAGE

Production: 3,500 cases	Grape varieties: Merlot—60% Cabernet Franc—30% Cabernet Sauvignon—10%
Secondary label: none	
Vineyard size: 15 acres	Proprietor: René de Coninck
Time spent in barrels: 16–20 months	Average age of vines: 20 years
Evaluation of present classification: The quality equivalent of a Médoc Cru Bourgeois	
Plateau of maturity: 3–8 years following the vintage	

Bellevue is an attractive château, located west of Beauséjour, whose wines tend to be made in a relatively robust, straightforward style. If they are deficient, it is because of an excess of tannin and a certain rustic quality. Nevertheless, they can be counted on to last for up to a decade in top vintages such as 1983 and 1989.

BERGAT (Grand Cru Classé) GOOD

Production: 1,500 cases	Grape varieties: Merlot—60% Cabernet Franc—25% Cabernet Sauvignon—15%
Secondary label: none	
Vineyard size: 8.64 acres	Proprietor: Madame Clausse- Bertin Administrator: Philippe Castéja
Time spent in barrels: 20 months	Average age of vines: 20 years
Evaluation of present classification: The quality equivalent of a Médoc Cru Bourgeois	
Plateau of maturity: 3–10 years following the vintage	

This tiny, obscure domain, situated at the edge of the St.-Emilion plateau, is commercialized by the Bordeaux *négociant* firm of Borie-Manoux. I have only tasted two vintages, the 1985 and 1989, and both were chunky, robust St.-Emilions with a great deal of fruit and character. Given the great strides in quality all of the Borie-Manoux estates have made in the late eighties, this could well be a château worth searching out during the nineties.

BERLIQUET (Grand Cru Classé) AVERAGE

Production: 4,000 cases	Grape varieties: Merlot—75% Cabernet Franc—15% Cabernet Sauvignon—10%
Secondary label: none	
Vineyard size: 21.5 acres	Proprietors: The Vicomte and Vicomtesse Patrick de Lesquen
Time spent in barrels: 20 months	Average age of vines: 25 years
Evaluation of present classification: The quality equivalent of a Médoc Cru Bourgeois	
Plateau of maturity: 4–12 years following the vintage	

This is a beautifully situated property with splendid underground caves and a superb exposition just outside the village of St.-Emilion. In fact, one could not ask for a better position on the limestone plateau of St.-

Emilion, adjoining Canon, Magdelaine, and Tertre-Daugay. In 1985 Berliquet became the only château to be promoted to a Grand Cru Classé. Its fame, however, must have been far greater in the eighteenth century. In 1794, a well-known Libourne courtier wrote about the excellent quality of wine in St.-Emilion called Berliquet.

Berliquet was content to stay in the background, as all of its wine, until the 1978 vintage, was made and produced by the huge cooperative in St.-Emilion. Although the staff at the cooperative oversees the production of Berliquet, since 1978 the wine has been made, matured, and bottled at the attractive château.

VINTAGES

1989—Medium ruby, with a spicy, earthy, ripe berry-scented bouquet,
·   this medium-bodied wine has surprisingly good acidity and grip
82   for the vintage, but it lacks the concentration and depth of the
       best wines of the appellation. It possesses some moderately astringent tannins. Anticipated maturity: 1992–1998. Last tasted, 4/91.

1988—This compact, relatively attenuated St.-Emilion could use more
·   fat, depth, and charm. It is spicy, but lean and anorexic. The
80   finish is also surprisingly short, but moderately tannic. Anticipated maturity: Now–1995. Last tasted, 4/91.

1986—I was certainly not overwhelmed by the rather hard, tannic, lean
·   style of the 1986, which simply seemed to lack depth and charm.
78   Anticipated maturity: Now–1996. Last tasted, 3/89.

1985—The 1985 Berliquet has an open-knit character, a moderately intense, ripe cherry-scented bouquet, medium body, and soft tannins. Anticipated maturity: Now–1996. Last tasted, 3/89.
·
81

CADET-BON (Grand Cru)   AVERAGE

Production: 2,000 cases	Grape varieties: Merlot—60% Cabernet Franc—40%
Secondary label: none	
Vineyard size: 10 acres	Proprietor: François Gratadour
Time spent in barrels: 22–24 months	Average age of vines: 25 years
Evaluation of present classification: The quality equivalent of a Médoc Cru Bourgeois	
Plateau of maturity: 5–15 years following the vintage	

This tiny property, located on both the limestone hillside and the plateau of St.-Emilion, consistently produces rustic, full-bodied, robust wines that lack charm and finesse. They often come across as excessively charged with tannin for the amount of fruit. Nevertheless, they have their admirers, particularly in the Benelux countries where consumers like this muscular style of wine. The best recent vintages have been 1982, 1983, and 1989.

CADET-PIOLA (Grand Cru Classé)   VERY GOOD

Production: 3,000 cases	Grape varieties:
	Merlot—51%
	Cabernet Sauvignon—28%
	Cabernet Franc—18%
	Malbec—3%
Secondary label: Chevaliers de Malta	
Vineyard size: 16.79 acres	Proprietor: The Jabiol family
Time spent in barrels: 20–22 months	Average age of vines: 25 years
Evaluation of present classification: Should be upgraded to a St.-Emilion Premier Grand Cru Classé; the quality equivalent of a Médoc fourth-growth	
Plateau of maturity: 6–17 years following the vintage	

It must be the small production of Cadet-Piola that has kept this wine's quality relatively secret for so long a time. Cadet-Piola, which is neither a *côtes* St.-Emilion nor a *graves* St.-Emilion, is just one-half kilometer north of the town. The château—with a splendid view overlooking St.-Emilion—is located on a rocky outcropping with a clay and limestone base; it is used only for making wine and not as a residence. The proprietors claim the micro-climate is warmer than elsewhere in the appellation.

The owners, the Jabiol family (who are also the proprietors of the St.-Emilion estate of Faurie-de-Souchard), are conservative winemakers who produce a black/ruby–colored, rich and intense, full-bodied wine that over the last decade has outperformed many of the more famous and more expensive Premiers Grands Crus. Cadet-Piola is a great value, and hopefully consumer demand will result in more of this estate's wine being imported to America.

VINTAGES

1989—The 1989 is probably a finer wine than my score suggests. This
·   wine has thick black/ruby color, and is impressive, but the nose
87   is closed. On the palate, the wine is an overwhelmingly muscular,
        hard, tough-textured, tannic behemoth that needs at least 7–10
        years of cellaring, but should last several decades. The muscular,
        backward style is typical of Cadet-Piola. Anticipated maturity:
        1996–2010. Last tasted, 4/91.

1988—The 1988 possesses a tremendous tannin level, but the big, rich,
·   black cherry flavors intertwined with new oak, scents of choco-
87   late, and Provençal herbs gives me some basis for saying that
        perhaps there is more there, and that it is well balanced. It is
        medium to full bodied, displaying excellent ripeness, and high
        tannin levels. Anticipated maturity: 1995–2010. Last tasted, 4/91.

1986—The 1986 is an exceptionally backward, tannic, black-colored St.-
·   Emilion. In fact, I was a bit worried about the level of tannin,
85   except for the gobs of rich, long, chewy fruit one can easily sense
        when tasting it. The only question that remains is when will
        enough of the excruciatingly high tannin content fall away to
        make this wine round and seductive. Will the fruit hold? Antici-
        pated maturity: 1998–2010. Last tasted, 11/90.

1985—The 1985 Cadet-Piola is a tannic, well-built wine for the vintage.
·   Deep ruby, with a spicy, plummy, intense bouquet, this is a full-
86   bodied, dense, chewy wine with plenty of character. It can be
        drunk now. Anticipated maturity: Now–1998. Last tasted, 3/90.

1984—The medium ruby, soft, fruity, one-dimensional 1984 is totally
·   ready to drink. Anticipated maturity: Now–1993. Last tasted,
76   3/89.

1983—Although not the success of the wonderful 1982, the 1983 Cadet-
·   Piola is still a darkly colored, ripe, full-bodied, admirably con-
85   structed St.-Emilion with plenty of concentration, muscle, and
        power. Anticipated maturity: 1992–1998. Last tasted, 1/89.

1982—A sleeper of the vintage, this wine has excellent structure. Some
·   spicy new oak in the bouquet complements nicely the oodles of
87   ripe black cherry and chocolate aromas that emerge with airing.
        Full bodied, concentrated, tannic, and deep, this large-scaled,
        structured wine is well made, but has aged very slowly. Antici-
        pated maturity: 1994–2005. Last tasted, 1/89.

1981—While 1981 was a good vintage for Bordeaux, I have found the
·   St.-Emilions to be rather spotty, with too many unacceptably me-
85   diocre wines. Certainly, the 1981 Cadet-Piola is a success for this
        appellation. Impressively colored, with a moderately intense bou-

quet of blackberries and cedary, herbaceous notes, this medium-bodied, concentrated wine still has firm tannin. Anticipated maturity: 1992–2000. Last tasted, 3/89.

1979—Another excellent success, the 1979 Cadet-Piola has a dark ruby
   ·   color, and rich, spicy, deep, velvety flavors, soft, round tannins,
  86   medium to full body, and good length. The 1979 is a surprisingly meaty, fleshy wine that is worth seeking out. Anticipated maturity: Now–1993. Last tasted, 2/84.

1978—Like many St.-Emilions of this vintage, the 1978 is loosely knit,
   ·   overly ripe, and alcoholic. However, Cadet-Piola has come out
  82   better than many. Medium ruby color with some amber at the edge, this wine is not as concentrated as the 1979, more open knit, and round, soft, and ready to drink. Anticipated maturity: Now. Last tasted, 1/85.

1976—The only sub-par wine I have tasted from Cadet-Piola, the 1976
   ·   lacked color, grip, and direction. It also tasted overly soft and
  72   diffuse. Anticipated maturity: Now–probably in serious decline. Last tasted, 7/82.

1975—A match for the exquisite wine made at Cadet-Piola in 1982, the
   ·   1975, a more powerful and aggressively tannic wine, is beginning
  87   to shed tannins and display a lovely, rich blackcurrant fruitiness, as well as deep concentration of fruit. Quite plump, big, and full bodied, this wine is just entering its mature plateau. Anticipated maturity: Now–2000. Last tasted, 1/85.

CANON (Premier Grand Cru Classé)   EXCELLENT

Production: 8,000 cases	Grape varieties: Merlot—55% Cabernet Franc—45%
Secondary label: Clos J. Kanon	
Vineyard size: 44.5 acres	Proprietor: Eric Fournier
Time spent in barrels: 22–24 months	Average age of vines: 35 years
Evaluation of present classification: Since 1982, the quality equivalent of a Médoc second-growth; prior to 1982, the quality was generally mediocre	
Plateau of maturity: 7–25 years following the vintage	

One of the *côtes* St.-Emilions, Canon has a splendid location on the southwestern slopes of the town of St.-Emilion, where its vineyard is sandwiched between Premiers Grands Crus Classés vineyards such as Belair, Magdelaine, Clos Fourtet, and Beauséjour. This vineyard, which lies partly on the hillside and partly on the plateau, has several different soil types, ranging from limestone and clay to sandy soils on a limestone base.

Canon has been the property of the Fournier family since 1919. The name, however, comes from the eighteenth-century owner, Jacques Kanon. Young, articulate Eric Fournier runs the property today. He produces a wine without compromise. A very traditional, long, hot fermentation in oak vats suggests that the property pays little heed to consumers who want to drink supple Bordeaux wines. This is a tannic, powerful wine, built to last and last. It is marked by a pronounced oakiness that can, in lighter vintages, obliterate the fruit. This overzealous, yet expensive use of new oak (a minimum of 50% is used in every vintage) is my only criticism of Canon. I adore this wine in vintages such as 1982, 1983, 1985, 1986, 1988, and 1989. In the eighties, under the leadership of Eric Fournier and his brilliant *maître de chai*, Paul Cazenave, Canon has attained a quality that has often equaled, sometimes even surpassed, that of the St.-Emilion super growths Cheval Blanc and Ausone.

Canon is a splendidly rich, deep, and concentrated wine, muscular and full bodied, and when mature, richly fruity, cedary, and often magnificent. It remains a mystery why this wine is not better known, because Canon has certainly been one of the top three or four St.-Emilions during the decade of the eighties.

VINTAGES

1989—The 1989 Canon will not approach the 1982 in terms of concentration and complexity, yet it does resemble a synthesis in style
·
92   between the 1985 and 1986. Deep ruby/purple in color, with a rich, spicy, new oak, blackcurrant bouquet of moderate intensity, this full-bodied, rather burgundian-textured wine is tannic and deeply endowed. The flavor extraction as well as purity of taste is impressive. Anticipated maturity: 1993–2008. Last tasted, 4/91.

1988—The 1988's deep ruby/purple color exhibits more opaqueness and depth than the 1989. The spicy, mineral-, cassis-, and tar-scented
·
89   bouquet has excellent focus and dimension. In the mouth, there is an elevated level of tannins in keeping with the style of the 1988 vintage, but unlike many 1988s, this wine possesses impressive concentration, plenty of length, and a sense that the yields were kept conservative, as there is an inner strength and depth that suggests this wine will ultimately outlive the 1989. Anticipated maturity: 1996–2012. Last tasted, 4/91.

1987—Canon made a lovely wine in this sometimes underrated vintage.
·   Medium ruby, with a fragrant bouquet of black fruits and spicy
85   oak, this is a supple, easygoing, graciously endowed Canon. Anticipated maturity: Now–1996. Last tasted, 3/90.

1986—The 1986 Canon has the potential to live as long as the great
·   Canons made in 1982, 1985, and 1989. The wine displays an ex-
91   traordinary perfume of toasty, smoky, new oak and blackcurrants
and has great extract, as well as a wonderful purity of currant
fruit that reminded me of the classic Cabernets made by the tiny
Napa Valley winery of Spottswoode. Anticipated maturity: 1997–
2015. Last tasted, 3/90.

1985—This wine has the deepest color of all the St.-Emilions except for
·   Le Tertre-Roteboeuf in this vintage. The intense fragrance of oak
90   combines with aromas of ripe plums and cherries. On the palate,
the wine is rich, full bodied, deep, alcoholic, and for Canon, surprisingly supple. If not quite the 1982 in stature, the 1985 is not
far behind. Anticipated maturity: 1993–2007. Last tasted, 3/90.

1983—The 1983 is not aging as well as I might have hoped from early
·   tastings. It is very alcoholic but has nowhere near the depth,
89   richness, and power of the 1982, and seems to be slightly lower
in acidity. It is an impressive Canon, but I would rank it behind
the 1985, 1986, 1989, and, of course, well behind the monumental
1982. Anticipated maturity: 1992–2001. Last tasted, 1/91.

1982—The 1982 Canon is the finest wine I have ever tasted from this
·   impeccably run property. It is still deep, dark ruby/purple in
93   color, with a fabulous bouquet that seems to explode upward from
the glass. The wine tastes essentially unchanged from the early
days in cask. It is very concentrated with the aroma of pure
blackcurrants, toasty vanillin oak, and licorice. On the palate, the
1982 is massive, extremely rich, still tannic, and in need of another 5–6 years to reach its plateau of maturity, where it no doubt
will remain for another 15 or 20 years. Anyone who has cellared
this beauty should feel fortunate as it, like most 1982s, sold at a
bargain price as a wine future. Anticipated maturity: 1996–2015.
Last tasted, 1/91.

1981—While Canon produced a good wine in 1978 and 1979, and a great,
·   perhaps legendary, wine in 1982, and excelled in 1985, 1986,
75   1988, and 1989, the 1981 falls way short of my expectations. The
château's obsession with new oak barrels has rendered a wine
that from its birth was too light and fragile to absorb the full
impact of the tannin and vanillin from new barrels. The wine is
overly tannic, lean, and out of balance. Time may help, but don't
count on it. Anticipated maturity: Now–2000. Last tasted, 2/88.

1980—In this vintage I have found the 1980 Canon to have good fruit and
·   average color, but excessive oak in its bouquet. One could call
72   this a modest success for the vintage, yet I would like to see less
        of the annoying vegetal character and more of the pleasant, sup-
        ple, blackcurrant fruitiness. Anticipated maturity: Now–1992.
        Last tasted, 7/87.

1979—One of the best St.-Emilions in this vintage, this Canon is impres-
·   sively dark ruby in color without any amber, and has tannic and
86   youthful flavors. It exhibits good concentration, depth, and body,
        but the tannins are still foreboding. Canon's 1979 is a young,
        muscular wine with potential, but will the fruit hold up? Antici-
        pated maturity: 1993–2003. Last tasted, 1/91.

1978—Similar to the 1979, but leaner and more austere, the 1978 Canon
·   still needs time to develop. Dark ruby with some amber, this
85   relatively big, tannic wine has evolved much slower than I ex-
        pected. It is a harder, less charming style of Canon than usual.
        Anticipated maturity: 1992–2005. Last tasted, 1/91.

1976—Not one of my favorite Canons, the 1976 is diffuse, and lacks both
·   depth and structure. Browning, and overly tannic and oaky with-
70   out supporting fruit for balance, this wine will only continue to
        get more awkward. It should be drunk soon, if ever. Last tasted,
        10/82.

1975—The 1975 Canon is not evolving well. Still ferociously tannic, with
·   the fruit beginning to fade, this wine clearly lacks the extract and
68   concentration necessary to stand up to its astringent, hard person-
        ality. The color has changed from medium ruby to a strong amber/
        orange at the edge. The dusty tannins obliterate what fruit is left.
        The wine's future is dubious. Last tasted, 1/89.

1971—Disappointingly thin, attenuated, and lacking fruit and charm,
·   this wine has become dried out, with a bitter, harsh finish. Caveat
65   emptor! Last tasted, 1/89.

1970—This is a good Canon, yet not nearly up to the quality that the
·   young Eric Fournier, who took over direct management in 1972,
84   has produced in the period 1978 to the present. Fully mature,
        somewhat lighter, and less concentrated than expected, but fra-
        grant and spicy, with a plummy, roasted character, there is little
        tannin remaining, so this lightweight Canon should be consumed.
        Anticipated maturity: Now–may be in decline. Last tasted, 2/85.

1966—One of Canon's top efforts, this rich, intense, deeply concentrated
·   wine is still in top-notch shape, with a big, full-intensity bouquet
86   of ripe fruit and melted toffee. On the palate, the wine is in
        complete harmony, soft, rich, velvety, full bodied, and fleshy.

Retasted from a half bottle in 1987, the fruit appeared to be fading. Anticipated maturity: Now–1993. Last tasted, 6/87.

1964—One of the finest wines made at Canon during the sixties, this
·   full-bodied, rich, still vigorous, and opulent wine has a roasted,
88   spicy, tar, and plummy bouquet, heady, alcoholic flavors, and considerable length. There's more muscle than finesse to this vintage of Canon. Anticipated maturity: Now–1996. Last tasted, 4/91.

1961—An excellent wine, deep, ripe, with a bouquet suggesting smoky,
·   ripe fruit and grilled chestnuts, the 1961 Canon is medium bodied,
88   with an amber-edged, deep garnet color. Somewhat austere for a 1961, the wine is still impressively extracted, deliciously full, and long. While fully mature, it has the potential to last for another 4–8 years. Anticipated maturity: Now–1995. Last tasted, 1/90.

CANON-LA-GAFFELIÈRE (Grand Cru Classé)   EXCELLENT

Production: 8,000 cases	Grape varieties: Merlot—55% Cabernet Franc—40% Cabernet Sauvignon—5%
Secondary label: Côte Migon- La-Gaffelière	
Vineyard size: 48.16 acres	Proprietor: Stephan Von Neipperg
Time spent in barrels: 18–23 months	Average age of vines: 25 years
Evaluation of present classification: Since 1985, the quality equivalent of a Médoc third-growth; should be elevated to a St.-Emilion Premier Grand Cru Classé	
Plateau of maturity: 3–14 years following the vintage	

Another of the *côtes* St.-Emilions, Canon-La-Gaffelière actually has most of its vineyard on flat, sandy soil at the foot of the hills. For over two decades, Canon-La-Gaffelière was widely promoted, offering light, bland, mediocre wines at surprisingly high prices. That has changed dramatically since the young, brilliant Stephan Von Neipperg assumed responsibility. In fact, there is probably no St.-Emilion Grand Cru Classé that has exhibited greater improvement than Canon-La-Gaffelière.

Changes that have led to the recent successes at this property include late harvesting to ensure maximum maturity of the grapes, the introduction of a second wine for weaker vats, and a longer maceration to extract more color and intensity. The percentage of new oak utilized has also been increased. The results of all these changes are some of the most opulent and flattering wines of St.-Emilion. This is clearly one of the up-and-coming stars of the appellation, as the 1986, 1988, 1989, and 1990 so admirably attest. Prices can only rise.

VINTAGES

1989—The 1989 is an aggressively powerful, extremely alcoholic, rich,
· broadly flavored, soft, oaky wine that will probably need to be
89 drunk within its first 10–12 years of life. Its high alcohol, high tannins, yet extremely low acidity give it a seductive, precocious feel in the mouth now, but the tannins and heady alcohol content should allow it to age reasonably well. My guess is that this wine will be drinkable when released, but should last at least a decade. It is a real crowd pleaser! Anticipated maturity: Now–2002. Last tasted, 4/91.

1988—The 1988 has everything the 1989 possesses, in addition to defi-
· nition, structure, and greater depth and concentration. This
90 splendidly perfumed wine offers up a veritable smorgasbord of aromas, ranging from smoky, toasty, new oak, to jammy black-currants and Asian spices. In the mouth, it is full bodied, seduc-tively round, and expansively flavored, with a luscious and velvety, long, heady finish. This is a gorgeously made, rich, won-derfully pure, highly extracted wine that should drink well for the next 10–12 years. Smart consumers will be buying cases of this sumptuous St.-Emilion. Anticipated maturity: Now–2004. Last tasted, 4/91.

1986—Except for the 1988 and 1989, the 1986 is the finest wine made at
· this property in over three decades, and is certainly one of the
87 sleepers of the vintage. It may eventually merit an even higher score. The use of 65% new oak, an extended maceration, and careful attention to detail have resulted in a wine that is black/ruby in color and has exceptional concentration and length, with a wonderful opulence and fatness in the mid-range that makes for exciting drinking. I do not believe it will be the longest-lived St.-Emilion in 1986, but it does have more precocious appeal than many wines, and therein lies its value. Anticipated maturity: 1992–2005. Last tasted, 3/90.

1985—The 1985 Canon-La-Gaffelière is a good, supple, richly fruity,
· tasty, expansively flavored wine. It requires drinking. Anticipated
85 maturity: Now–1997. Last tasted, 3/89.

1984—The 1984 is cleanly made, correct, simple, fruity, and mature.
· Anticipated maturity: Now–may be in decline. Last tasted, 7/89.
73

1983—Light, supple, fruity, spicy, and ready to drink, the 1983 Canon-
· La-Gaffelière displays a medium-bodied, spicy, easygoing charm
82 and light tannins. Anticipated maturity: Now–may be in decline.
Last tasted, 3/85.

1982—Soft, ripe, round, generous, fruity flavors, medium body, and light
· tannins suggest drinking this wine immediately before it loses its
83 exuberance. Anticipated maturity: Now–may be in decline. Last
tasted, 1/85.

1981—A rather hollow wine, without adequate fruit to balance out the
· oak and tannins, the 1981 Canon-La-Gaffelière should be drunk
72 over the next several years before it becomes more unbalanced.
Anticipated maturity: Now–probably in serious decline. Last
tasted, 2/83.

1979—Ready to drink, the 1979 Canon-La-Gaffelière is soft, slightly her-
· baceous, medium bodied, pleasantly fruity, but undistinguished.
75 Anticipated maturity: Now–probably in serious decline. Last
tasted, 2/84.

1978—The 1978 is fully mature, and given this wine's inclination to
· behave like a burgundy and die quickly, it is best drunk up. Light
75 ruby with some browning, this round, soft, fruity wine is one-
dimensional and light, but cleanly made. Anticipated maturity:
Now–probably in serious decline. Last tasted, 2/84.

1976—Premature senility afflicted this wine in 1979. Even then it was
· brown, stalky, diluted, and astonishingly unpleasant. Now it must
50 be completely shot. Last tasted, 12/79.

1971—When last tasted in 1978, this wine was thin, decrepit, too her-
· baceous and watery, and totally unrepresentative of a St.-Emilion
50 in a vintage that produced a considerable number of flavorful
wines. Last tasted, 1/78.

CAP DE MOURLIN (Grand Cru Classé)　　　GOOD

Production: 6,000 cases	Grape varieties: Merlot—60% Cabernet Franc—25% Cabernet Sauvignon—12% Malbec—3%
Secondary label: none	
Vineyard size: 34.6 acres	Proprietor: Jacques Capdemourlin
Time spent in barrels: 18–22 months	Average age of vines: 25 years
Evaluation of present classification: The quality equivalent of a fine Médoc Cru Bourgeois	
Plateau of maturity: 3–10 years following the vintage	

The Capdemourlin family have been property owners in St.-Emilion for over five centuries. They also own the well-known St.-Emilion Grand Cru Classé, Balestard-La-Tonnelle, as well as Petit-Faurie-de-Soutard, and the excellent Montagne St.-Emilion, Château Roudier.

Until 1983, there were two Grand Cru St.-Emilions with the name Cap de Mourlin, one owned by Jean Capdemourlin and one by Jacques Capdemourlin. These two estates have been united since 1983, and the confusion consumers have encountered in the past between these two different wines has ceased to exist.

Cap de Mourlin produces typically robust, rich, full-bodied St.-Emilions with a great deal of fruit and muscle. They sometimes fall short with respect to finesse, but they are consistently mouth-filling, satisfying wines. The vineyard is located on the flat, sandy, rocky soil of what is often called the *"pieds de côtes."*

VINTAGES

1989—The 1989 exhibits plenty of toasty, smoky, new oak and is full
· bodied, with high alcohol, low acidity, and a rich, jammy, long
86 finish. There are plenty of tannins, but they are soft. Anticipated maturity: 1992–2006. Last tasted, 4/91.

1988—The 1988 has a more typical Bordelais feel to its lean, under-
· stated, more toughly knit texture. The tannins are high, but the
85 wine is concentrated, and this is one case where the fruit seems proportional to the amount of tannin. Anticipated maturity: 1993–2004. Last tasted, 4/91.

1986—This estate produces wines that are extremely dense in color, with
·   fat, unctuous textures, and powerful, ripe, sometimes port-like
85   bouquets that come from letting the grapes achieve a superripeness. If the wine lacks complication and complexity, it makes up
for it with a macho-sized, brawny intensity and texture. Anticipated maturity: Now–1996. Last tasted, 3/90.

1985—The 1985 is a typical Cap de Mourlin—a full-throttle, rich, pow-
·   erful, ruby/purple–colored wine that lacks elegance, but not fla-
86   vor. The dense color, fat, unctuous texture, powerful, very ripe,
port-like bouquet from *sur-maturité*, and full body are all telltale
traits of Cap de Mourlin. This is a winter-weight wine to consume
with stews, cassoulets, and the like. Anticipated maturity: Now–
1995. Last tasted, 3/90.

1984—This is a disjointed, soupy, very soft, flat wine that lacks back-
·   bone. Last tasted, 3/89.
74

1983—The first vintage produced from the combined estates under the
·   management of Jacques Capdemourlin, the 1983 is an uncom-
85   monly powerful, dense, black-colored wine that is reminiscent of
some of the huge mountain-styled California Cabernet Sauvignons of the mid-1970s. Massive on the palate, with an unbelievable density of viscous fruit, this huge, full-bodied, very tannic
wine is a trifle too high in alcohol and low in acidity to get higher
marks, but it is quite a corpulent mouthful of wine. Anticipated
maturity: Now–1995. Last tasted, 1/85.

CHANTE-ALOUETTE-CORMEIL (Grand Cru)   GOOD

Production: 3,500 cases	Grape varieties:
	Merlot—60%
	Cabernet Franc—20%
	Cabernet Sauvignon—20%
Secondary label: none	
Vineyard size: 20 acres	Proprietor: Yves Delol
Time spent in barrels: 20–24 months	Average age of vines: 20 years
Evaluation of present classification: The quality equivalent of a good Médoc Cru Bourgeois	
Plateau of maturity: 3–10 years following the vintage	

I have had surprisingly well made wines from this property in both 1982
and 1985. Other vintages, such as the 1983, 1986, and 1988, while not

quite up to the quality of the two former vintages, were still fleshy, rustic, concentrated St.-Emilions that exhibited a great deal of character. The property has been owned for over a century by the Delol family, and much of the wine is sold to private consumers in northern Europe. Prices are reasonable, so this is a property that offers satisfaction to both the purse and the palate.

CHAUVIN (Grand Cru Classé)   AVERAGE

Production: 6,000 cases	Grape varieties: Merlot—60% Cabernet Franc—30% Cabernet Sauvignon—10%
Secondary label: Chauvin Variation	
Vineyard size: 33 acres	Proprietor: The Ondet family
Time spent in barrels: 18–22 months	Average age of vines: 20 years
Evaluation of present classification: Since 1989, the quality equivalent of a Médoc Cru Bourgeois	
Plateau of maturity: 3–8 years following the vintage	

This property, a neighbor of Cheval Blanc, has made remarkable progress in the last several vintages, particularly the 1989. The decision to harvest later, as well as to institute a stricter selection with a second wine, has resulted in major improvements to the quality of the wines at this estate. And yes, the omnipresent Michel Rolland is the oenologist in charge. Chauvin may be an emerging star in St.-Emilion.

VINTAGES

1989— The ubiquitous Libourne oenologist, Michel Rolland, had for the
·   first time full charge of overseeing the winemaking at Chauvin in
86   1989. The result is a broad-flavored, hedonistic, concentrated, deeply extracted, luscious wine. Anticipated maturity: Now– 1996. Last tasted, 4/91.

1988— Medium dark ruby, with a spicy, subtle plum-and-herb-scented
·   bouquet, this medium-bodied wine has good extraction flavor, a
84   nice, spicy, vanillin oakiness, and medium-bodied, tightly knit flavors. It may outlive the 1989, but I do not see it ever providing the same degree of pleasure. Anticipated maturity: 1993–2002. Last tasted, 4/91.

1986—This is a straightforward, ripe, fruity, cleanly made wine that
·　　seems to lack the extra dimension of complexity and flavor that
77　　the top wines of St.-Emilion have in this vintage. Anticipated
　　　maturity: Now–1994. Last tasted, 3/90.
1985—The 1985 Chauvin is one-dimensional, with a simple ripe fruiti-
·　　ness, medium body, and a soft, undistinguished finish. Antici-
76　　pated maturity: Now–1993. Last tasted, 3/89.

CHEVAL BLANC (Premier Grand Cru Classé)　　OUTSTANDING

Production: 12,000 cases	Grape varieties: Cabernet Franc—66% Merlot—33% Malbec—1%
Secondary label: Le Petit Cheval	
Vineyard size: 88.9 acres	Proprietor: The Fourcaud-Laussac family
Time spent in barrels: 16–20 months	Average age of vines: 34 years
Evaluation of present classification: The quality equivalent of a Médoc first-growth	
Plateau of maturity: 5–20 or more years following the vintage	

Cheval Blanc is undoubtedly one of Bordeaux's greatest and most unique wines. For most of this century it has sat alone at the top of St.-Emilion's hierarchy, representing the finest wine this appellation can produce. Since the renaissance began at Ausone in the mid-1970s, Cheval Blanc has had to share the limelight. Cheval Blanc is a remarkably distinctive wine. Sitting right on the Pomerol border, in the St.-Emilion *graves* sector, with only a ditch separating its vineyards from those of L'Evangile and La Conseillante, it has for years been accused of making a wine that is as much a Pomerol as it is a St.-Emilion.

Among the "Big Eight" of Bordeaux, Cheval Blanc probably has the broadest window of drinkability. It is usually delicious when first bottled, and yet has the ability in the top years to last and last. None of the Médoc first-growths, or Pétrus in Pomerol, can claim to have such flexibility. Only Haut-Brion comes closest to matching Cheval Blanc's early drinkability and precociousness, as well as the stuffing and overall balance and intensity to age for 20–30 years.

For me, Cheval Blanc is Cheval Blanc—it is like no Pomerol or no other St.-Emilion I have ever tasted. The distinctive choice of grape varieties used at Cheval Blanc, two-thirds Cabernet Franc and one-third Merlot, with a tiny parcel of old vines of Malbec, is highly unusual. No other major château uses this much Cabernet Franc. Yet curiously this grape reaches its zenith in Cheval Blanc's gravelly, sandy, and clay soil that is underpinned by a bed of iron rock, producing an extremely rich, ripe, intense, viscous wine.

Cheval Blanc is also unique in that the property has been in the same family's hands since 1852. Until 1989, the Fourcaud-Laussac family's live-in owner was the towering Jacques Hébrard, who was obsessed with taking Cheval Blanc's reputation to even greater heights. Following Hébrard, Bernard Grandchamp was brought in to run the estate but resigned his position in 1990, fueling rumors of family in-fighting about the future of Cheval Blanc.

The style of wine produced at Cheval Blanc has no doubt contributed to its immense popularity. Dark ruby in color, in the very good vintages it is an opulently rich and fruity wine, full bodied, voluptuous, and lush, and deceptively easy to drink when young. The bouquet is especially distinctive. At its best, Cheval Blanc is an even more fragrant wine than Margaux. Scents of minerals, menthol, exotic spices, tobacco, and intense, as well as superripe, black fruits can overwhelm the taster. Many tasters, fooled by its cunning show of precocious charm, falsely assume that it will not age well. In the big, rich vintages, Cheval Blanc evolves exceptionally well, although one suspects that far too much of this wine is consumed long before its real majesty begins to emerge.

As the tasting notes demonstrate, Cheval Blanc can produce a decadently exotic wine of unbelievable depth and richness. However, in some vintages, it has been one of the most disappointing wines of the top "Big Eight" châteaux of Bordeaux. Cheval Blanc was not a strong performer during the decades of the sixties and seventies. However, with the increasing attention to quality and detail provided by administrator Jacques Hébrard, the quality of this wine during the eighties became more consistent. The three consecutive vintages of the early eighties— 1981, 1982, and 1983—were the finest Cheval Blanc trilogy since the splendid wines of 1947, 1948, and 1949.

Cheval Blanc, along with Haut-Brion, remains one of the two least expensive members of Bordeaux's "Big Eight."

VINTAGES

1989—The 1989 is an excellent wine, but I had expected more power, depth, and intensity than the wine currently reveals. The big,
89   very precocious, forward bouquet displays aromas of herbs, tobacco, sweet blackcurrants, and the telltale smoky, exotic character that often sets Cheval Blanc apart. In the mouth, the wine

tastes like candy, given the expansive, sweet palate impression. There is excellent depth, but when compared to the 1983 and 1982 (the two best vintages of the eighties), the 1989 does not possess the concentration of those two top vintages. If the 1989 Cheval Blanc does indeed broaden out and take on an extra dimension of flavor and character, my rating will look ungenerous. Anticipated maturity: 1992–2005. Last tasted, 4/91.

1988—The 1988 is more structured, less alcoholic and intense than the
· 1989. It exhibits fine ripeness, and a cool, almost menthol,
87 plummy bouquet intertwined with aromas of smoke and new oak. In the mouth, there are some aggressive tannins, but it does not possess the sheer drama of the 1989. It is a very good Cheval Blanc, but having tasted it numerous times in cask and bottle, I had expected it to be more impressive than it appears to be. Anticipated maturity: 1994–2005. Last tasted, 4/91.

1987—The 1987 Cheval Blanc is a successful wine for the vintage. The
· spicy, herbaceous, sweet nose is followed by a precocious, round,
85 fat, fruity wine without much grip or structure. It does possess delicious, weedy, curranty fruit buttressed by gobs of sweet, smoky oak. It is a seductive wine. Anticipated maturity: Now– 1996. Last tasted, 3/90.

1986—The compelling 1986 is the best wine made at Cheval Blanc since
· the 1983. Perhaps it is the unusually high percentage of Cabernet
93 Franc (66%) that accounts for the wine's complexity and hedonistic appeal. It has more depth and dimension than the 1988 and 1985, as well as a bouquet that seems to jump from the glass, with a combination of exotic, herbaceous, curranty scents intermingled with sweet, vanilla-scented new oak. On the palate, the wine is splendidly rich and lush, and seems quite forward and evolved, but I suspect in 3–4 years its tannins will become much more noticeable. Anticipated maturity: 1993–2008. Last tasted, 3/91.

1985—The 1985, while not a big or boldly concentrated wine, is quite
· delicious, ripe, and a total joy to drink. It is very aromatic, soft,
90 and medium bodied, and should turn out to resemble the 1976 or perhaps the 1981, only better. Anticipated maturity: Now–1998. Last tasted, 3/91.

1983—I have had a tendency to consistently underrate the 1983 Cheval
· Blanc when tasted from cask, only to be surprised at how much
94 weight and character the wine develops in the bottle. Perhaps this is a telltale characteristic of wines with a high percentage of Cabernet Franc. In any event, the 1983 continues to broaden and deepen and is now, in my opinion, the third-best Cheval Blanc of the last 25 years. Very dark ruby, with an intense bouquet of ripe,

currany fruit, smoke, subtle herbs, minerals, and exotic spices, this medium- to full-bodied, rich, voluptuous Cheval Blanc is only a notch behind the perfection of the 1982. Given the fact that the 1983's price is less than half that of the 1982, this is one Cheval Blanc to take stock of. Anticipated maturity: 1993–2008. Last tasted, 4/91.

1982 — The 1982 Cheval Blanc is the greatest wine made at this famous
·   property since their legendary 1947. It was phenomenal from both
100   cask and bottle, and has not only deepened in color and gotten richer as it has aged in the bottle, but at the same time has taken on more structure and focus. It is an extraordinary wine that in a recent tasting of 1982s was the group's preference as the wine of the vintage. Perhaps that will change in 10 or 15 years, and I would still argue that from a purely hedonistic standpoint the 1982 Pichon Lalande and 1982 Le Pin would get higher marks on the pleasure meter, but there is no doubt that the 1982 Cheval Blanc is pure perfection in wine. From the penetrating and fascinating bouquet that offers up gobs of rich berry fruit, subtle herbs, toasty, smoky oak, minerals, and perhaps even a flower or two, to its extraordinary depth, concentration, balance, and length, this is the quintessential Cheval Blanc of our generation. It is the only wine from this estate that has the opulence and almost port-like viscosity of the 1947, yet it manages to pull off that kind of extract and intensity without the wine's tasting heavy or overly alcoholic. This wine is remarkably drinkable now; however, it should be even better with another 2–3 years in the bottle, and will evolve well for at least another 15 years thereafter. Anticipated maturity: 1993–2010. Last tasted, 3/91.

1981 — I had this wine several times from the barrel, and also twice in
·   comparative tastings prior to bottling. I never gave it more than
90   average marks. Tasted numerous times after bottling, it is a different wine, relatively rich, spicy, plummy, with soft, silky, layered flavors, good concentration, and moderate tannin. It continues to drink well, yet it has the potential to last for 5–7 more years. Not a blockbuster in the mold of the 1982 and 1983, it is delicious and fully mature. Anticipated maturity: Now–2000. Last tasted, 10/90.

1980 — The 1980 Cheval Blanc is a relative success for this mediocre
·   vintage. Medium ruby, with a moderately intense bouquet of
80   herbal, cedary, fruity scents, this wine has medium body, adequate concentration, and a supple, soft finish. Anticipated maturity: Now–1994. Last tasted, 10/90.

1979—The 1979 Cheval Blanc is a charming, elegant wine that lacks
·   some depth and richness (no doubt because of the prolific yields),
84   but it displays moderately intense, ripe plummy fruit, a cedary,
      herbaceous aroma, and soft, very forward, easygoing, round
      flavors. This is a lightweight but well-made Cheval Blanc that
      will age quickly. Anticipated maturity: Now–1993. Last tasted,
      3/89.

1978—This is a firmly built, concentrated Cheval Blanc that, curiously,
·   has not displayed the precocious, fleshy, charming fruit in its
87   early life that most vintages of Cheval Blanc exhibit. The wine is
      still dark ruby, with a relatively stubborn and backward bouquet
      suggestive of rich, ripe blackcurrants, mineral scents, herbs, and
      grilled nuts. On the palate, the wine is tannic, medium bodied,
      and admirably concentrated. It resembles the stylish, austere
      1966, but appears more concentrated. Anticipated maturity:
      1994–2008. Last tasted, 10/90.

1977—Cheval Blanc had a disastrous year in 1977 with over 75% of the
·   crop lost because of the poor weather. The resulting wine should
68   have been declassified. It is light in color, with a sweet vegetable
      aroma and shallow flavor, and has a nasty, harsh, astringent fin-
      ish. Last tasted, 10/90.

1976—In this vintage marked by extreme drought, heat, and hope-crush-
·   ing rains at harvest time, Cheval Blanc has produced an open-
82   knit, superripe, roasted style of wine that is now fully mature. It
      has put on weight, and while there is some browning at the edge,
      the 1976 Cheval Blanc has a full-blown bouquet of ripe fruit,
      minerals, nuts, and toasty oak. On the palate, the wine is opulent,
      even fat, with generous, savory, fleshy, plummy, fruity flavors.
      Low in acidity and very soft, the 1976 Cheval Blanc has been
      drinkable since its release, yet it continues to expand and de-
      velop. I initially underestimated this wine. Anticipated maturity:
      Now–1995. Last tasted, 10/90.

1975—The best Cheval Blanc of the seventies, the 1975, cunningly and
·   deceptively drinkable when young, has also continued to put on
90   weight and richness. It now looks like one of the best Cheval
      Blancs in the last 30 years. Dark ruby/garnet, with a rich bouquet
      of roasted fruit, oak, cedar, herbs, and mineral scents, this big,
      full-bodied wine has considerable strength and weight to comple-
      ment its tannic clout. A big, virile, large-scaled Cheval Blanc,
      it should continue to age gracefully, although it is close
      to full maturity. Anticipated maturity: Now–2015. Last tasted,
      10/90.

1973—The 1973 Cheval Blanc has totally faded, and is now just a pale,
·   washed-out wine, with a thin, diluted finish. Last tasted, 3/91.
55

1971—Somewhat of a disappointment, the 1971, while very good, has,
·   in the last several years, begun to brown badly. Nevertheless, the
84   wine still has plenty of sweet fruit, a burnt, roasted character to
           its bouquet, and medium body. The 1971 is a pleasant, lowbrow
           Cheval Blanc that should be drunk over the next 2–3 years. An-
           ticipated maturity: Now–1994. Last tasted, 10/90.

1970—A better wine than the 1971, the 1970 has been fully mature for
·   over a decade. Medium ruby/garnet with some browning, this
85   wine has a cedary, sweet, tobacco-scented aroma, plump, ripe,
           round flavors that exhibit decent concentration, and soft tannins.
           The wine is medium bodied, very soft, yet lacks the focus and
           concentration a Premier Grand Cru Classé should possess. It
           should be drunk up. Anticipated maturity: Now–1994. Last
           tasted, 10/90.

1967—Now in decline, the 1967 Cheval Blanc drank well for the first
·   decade of life, but has begun to take on a decaying, leafy compo-
77   nent in an otherwise tobacco-scented, plummy bouquet. In the
           mouth, the wine is soft and round, but fades quickly. Anticipated
           maturity: Now–probably in serious decline. Last tasted, 4/90.

1966—A good rather than great effort from Cheval Blanc, the 1966 is
·   now fully mature. Medium ruby with an amber edge, this is a
85   restrained version of Cheval Blanc, with a stylish, reserved bou-
           quet of mineral scents, blackcurrants, and spicy oak. On the
           palate, the wine is medium bodied, moderately fleshy, but not so
           voluptuous or as concentrated as one expects Cheval Blanc to be
           in this highly regarded vintage. Anticipated maturity: Now–1996.
           Last tasted, 10/90.

1964—In the Libournais, only Pétrus is better than Cheval Blanc in this
·   vintage that has proven to be very good to outstanding for many
95   wines of Pomerol, Graves, and St.-Emilion, but disappointing (be-
           cause of late rains) for the wines of the Médoc. Wonderfully rich,
           thick, powerful, and concentrated, this is the most authoritative
           Cheval Blanc produced since the monumental wines made by this
           château in 1947 and 1949. Opaque dark ruby, with only some
           amber, and a powerful, yet restrained bouquet of roasted ripe
           fruit, cedar, herbs, and gravelly, mineral scents, the wine re-
           mains amazingly young and tannic, with layer upon layer of ripe
           fruit. This is a heavyweight, old-style Cheval Blanc that should
           be pure nectar for at least another 10–15 years. It continues to

evolve at a snail's pace. Anticipated maturity: Now–2010. Last tasted, 10/90.

1962—Compact, small sized, and disappointing, the 1962 Cheval Blanc
·   has never been one of my favorite wines from this underrated
76 vintage. Now in decline, losing its fruit and drying out, the 1962 is a light, pretty wine, with some charm, and round, gentle fruitiness. It is best drunk from large-format bottles as I suspect the regular-size bottles are well past their prime. Friends of mine tell me they have tasted good examples of this vintage. Last tasted, 10/90.

1961—I have consistently mistaken this wine for a great Graves in tastings where it has appeared. Opaque dark ruby/garnet with a rust-
·
93 colored edge, this wine has a big, full-blown bouquet of burnt tobacco, and earthy, gravelly scents. On the palate, it is sweet, ripe, full bodied, extremely soft and supple, and clearly at its apogee. I have noticed above-normal bottle variation with the 1961 Cheval Blanc, but the best bottles of this wine are marvelously rich, lush wines. Anticipated maturity: Now–1997. Last tasted, 10/90.

OLDER VINTAGES

In October 1990, a well-known New York collector assembled virtually every vintage of Cheval Blanc back through the teens. The bottles were in exceptional condition, and it gave those in attendance a rare opportunity to look at the general performance of this extraordinary estate.

In the fifties, the greatest vintage is the 1953 (rated 96 as recently as 2/91). I am sure this wine has been fully mature for at least 15–20 years. Nevertheless, it has held its magic for that considerable period, and is still the most fragrant, and from an aromatic perspective, the most compelling Cheval Blanc I have ever tasted. Perhaps the 1982 will turn out to be this profoundly perfumed. It is not a blockbuster, but is incredibly seductive, and so soft and silky. Another vintage of note during the fifties is the 1959 (rated 92), a denser, more structured wine than the 1961, although I am not sure it will ever hit the heights the 1961 has already achieved. However, it certainly appears to have the stuffing and muscle to outlive the 1961. The 1955 (rated 90) is a tougher-textured, fuller-bodied, less seductive style of Cheval Blanc. Nevertheless, it is immensely impressive, rich, and capable of another 5–10 years of evolution. It has been nearly a decade since I tasted it, but I loved the smooth-as-silk 1950, another top example from that underestimated vintage.

There is probably no château that made four greater wines than Cheval

Blanc did in the post–World War II era. Most recently, I had all four of these vintages in October 1990, and have consistently rated them between 95 and 100. It has been a toss-up as to whether I prefer the 1949 or 1947, but both of these wines can, depending on the condition of the bottle, be as perfect a wine as I have ever tasted. The 1947 is more port-like and thick, with a viscosity and unctuosity to its texture that I have only seen in several other 1947s, all from the appellation of Pomerol. The 1949 does not have the size and thickness of the 1947, but is extraordinarily rich, complex, and at its best, a perfect wine. It is one of the great winemaking efforts of this century. The 1948 (rated in the mid-nineties) is a stunning example of Cheval Blanc that has largely gone unrecognized because of all the publicity surrounding the 1945, 1947, and 1949. As for the 1945 (rated 91), it is still powerful, rich, and intense, but it is my least favorite of these four great vintages.

During the twenties and thirties, all the vintages of Cheval Blanc I tasted were still generally drinkable, but had passed their prime. The legendary 1921, considered to be one of the greatest Cheval Blancs ever made, was faded and dried out when I last had it in 3/91.

CLOS FOURTET (Premier Grand Cru Classé)   GOOD

Production: 7,000 cases	Grape varieties: Merlot—70% Cabernet Franc—20% Cabernet Sauvignon—10%
Secondary label: Domaine de Martialis	
Vineyard size: 44.5 acres	Proprietor: The Lurton family
Time spent in barrels: 18–22 months	Average age of vines: 30 years
Evaluation of present classification: Should be downgraded to a Grand Cru Classé; the quality equivalent of a Médoc Cru Bourgeois	
Plateau of maturity: 3–12 years following the vintage	

It is unfortunate that the most interesting thing about the estate of Clos Fourtet is the vast underground wine cellars, which are among the finest in the Bordeaux region. This winery, like a number of highly respected, yet overrated St.-Emilion Premiers Grands Crus Classés, has been making wine over the last two decades that is good, but not up to the standards of its classification. The wines have been plagued by a bland, dull, chunky, dry, astringent fruitiness, and a curious habit of getting older without getting better. In short, they have not developed well in the bottle.

This property is on the *côtes* of St.-Emilion, almost at the entrance to St.-Emilion, opposite the Place de L'Eglise and Hôtel Plaisance. Over the last few years, the ubiquitous Lurton family (owners of numerous châteaux throughout Bordeaux) has made significant renovations at the winery, and has retained the services of Emile Peynaud, the famed oenologist, to get things just right. The results have been better, but hardly spectacular, wines. Certainly, the new style of Clos Fourtet, which commenced with the 1978 vintage, is a supple, overtly fruity, less tannic, and easier wine to comprehend and enjoy. However, there are hundreds of Bordeaux châteaux that make wine such as this from far less prestigiously situated vineyards. Clos Fourtet needs a wake-up call.

VINTAGES

1989—The style chosen by the proprietor of Clos Fourtet during the
·   eighties frequently produces a big, jammy, overtly fruity, heady
86   wine for drinking in its first 10–12 years of life. The 1989 (obviously because of the vintage) admirably fulfills this formula. It is an alcoholic, exuberantly styled wine that seems too easy to drink, and lacks grip, definition, and tannin. More length would also have been appreciated. Anticipated maturity: 1992–1998. Last tasted, 4/91.

1988—The 1988 has not fared well in comparative tastings. The fruit has
·   faded, and the tannins have become hard, lean, and noticeably
79   aggressive. In fact, I would argue that the 1988 is overburdened with tannins to the detriment of its concentration and fruit. Caveat emptor. Last tasted, 4/91.

1986—The 1986 is one-dimensional and lacks grip and depth. Antici-
·   pated maturity: Now–1995. Last tasted, 3/90.
78

1985—The 1985 Clos Fourtet is the lightest of all the Premier Grand Cru
·   Classé wines. Medium ruby, with a supple, monolithic, fruity
84   taste, and soft tannins, it has an easy, agreeable finish. Anticipated maturity: Now–1994. Last tasted, 3/90.

1983—This is a one-dimensional, soft, light-bodied wine with hardly any
·   tannin, as well as a short finish. It is one of the disappointments
78   of the 1983 St.-Emilion vintage. Anticipated maturity: Now–1993. Last tasted, 3/89.

1982—This St.-Emilion estate that has long been in the throes of medi-
·   ocrity produced a satisfying wine in 1982. Medium ruby, with an
84   attractive bouquet of vanillin oakiness and ripe, herb-scented, berry fruit, this medium-bodied wine has a forward, precocious, rich, supple fruitiness that caresses the palate. It is fully mature. Anticipated maturity: Now–1996. Last tasted, 3/89.

1981—Another medium-weight 1981 St.-Emilion, the Clos Fourtet has
    · above-average fruit intensity, but the wood flavors dominate the
 78 frail composition of the wine. A nice ripe cherry component indi-
    cates good ripeness of the grapes, but the wood tannins are en-
    tirely too pronounced. Anticipated maturity: Now–1992. Last
    tasted, 2/87.

1979—The 1979 provides some indication that Clos Fourtet's wines are
    · on an upswing in quality. The 1979 is dark in color, with attrac-
 82 tive, ripe fruit, medium to full body, and a good, clean finish.
    The wine's bouquet has opened, and this precocious wine has
    reached full maturity. Anticipated maturity: Now–1992. Last
    tasted, 6/84.

1978—The first wine in a line of good rather than superb Clos Fourtet's,
    · the 1978 has settled down nicely in the bottle and reveals alluring
 84 scents of blackcurrants, an open-knit, soft, ripe fruity texture,
    medium body, and a good finish with moderate tannins present.
    Anticipated maturity: Now–may be in decline. Last tasted, 5/83.

1975—This wine seems to have lost its fruit and dried out, revealing an
    · excess of tannins, and a charmless, hollow structure. Last tasted,
 70 5/84.

1971—Well colored for a 1971, this wine has very little bouquet, a dull,
    · tough, bland fruitiness, and very astringent tannin in the finish.
 70 There is just not enough fruit to balance the tannin. Anticipated
    maturity: Now–probably in serious decline. Last tasted, 2/79.

1970—The 1970 has the same personality traits as the 1971. Even though
    · it is a bigger, riper wine, it is one-dimensional, slightly coarse,
 72 and tannic, and just tastes boring. Anticipated maturity: Now–
    probably in serious decline. Last tasted, 8/78.

CLOS DES JACOBINS (Grand Cru Classé) VERY GOOD

Production: 5,000 cases	Grape varieties:
	Merlot—60%
	Cabernet Franc—25%
	Cabernet Sauvignon—15%
Secondary label: none	
Vineyard size: 18.5 acres	Proprietor: Domaines Cordier
Time spent in barrels: 18–22 months	Average age of vines: 30 years
Evaluation of present classification: The quality equivalent of a Médoc fifth-growth	
Plateau of maturity: 3–12 years following the vintage	

The large *négociant* firm of Cordier acquired this lovely ivy-covered châ-teau located just outside the gates of St.-Emilion in 1964. Unlike the firm's famous Médoc properties, Talbot and Gruaud-Larose, Clos des Jacobins, despite increasingly high quality wines, receives little public-ity, and is undoubtedly Cordier's least-known fine wine. It has been remarkably consistent over the last decade, producing a wine that is deeply colored, rich, round, creamy, and plummy, often with an opu-lence of ripe fruit. There is an absence of astringent, aggressive tannins, making Clos des Jacobins a wine that requires consumption within its first 10–12 years.

VINTAGES

1989—The 1989 may be one of the finest offerings this property has ever
·
88   made. It is a highly extracted, voluptuous, almost decadently rich wine, with a bouquet filled with aromas of smoky herbs, black fruits, and toasty new oak. In the mouth, the smooth, lush texture is evident, but in the finish, one sees potential greatness given the length and the intense fruit that lingers on the palate. Because of the high alcohol and low acidity, this wine should be drinkable young. Anticipated maturity: 1992–2002. Last tasted, 4/91.

1988—The 1988 is also a successful wine, but of a totally different style.
·
87   More austere, more tannic, and therefore, more typical of what one sees in good to very good Bordeaux vintages, this deep ruby-colored wine has a bouquet of spring flowers, blackcurrants, and licorice. In the mouth, there is plenty of rich, concentrated fruit, hard tannins, and fine length. Anticipated maturity: 1993–2003. Last tasted, 4/91.

1986—Clos des Jacobins can often resemble the poor person's Figeac.
·
86   Its cedary, herbaceous, blackcurrant-scented bouquet seems to resemble that of the more famous Figeac in blind tastings. The 1986 is a fairly muscular, alcoholic wine with a good deal of soft tannin in the finish. The wine can be drunk now or cellared for up to a decade. Anticipated maturity: Now–2000. Last tasted, 3/90.

1985—The 1985 is very soft, fruity, medium bodied, pleasant, and ideal
·
84   for drinking over the next 3–4 years. It lacks the extract levels of more recent vintages. Anticipated maturity: Now–1995. Last tasted, 3/89.

1984—The 1984 Clos des Jacobins is a surprisingly good wine. Deep in
·
81   color, spicy, ripe, fruity, and round. Anticipated maturity: Now–1994. Last tasted, 3/89.

1983—One of the top successes of the appellation in this very good, yet
·
87   very irregular vintage, the 1983 Clos des Jacobins is dark ruby, with an intense, supple, blackberry fruitiness, a lush, ripe,

creamy, fat texture, moderate tannins, plenty of alcoholic punch, and a long finish. It has matured quickly. Anticipated maturity: Now–1994. Last tasted, 3/85.

1982—Probably the finest Clos des Jacobins I have ever tasted, the 1982 has a herbaceous, ripe, jammy bouquet that is filled with black-
•
89   berry fruit. On the palate, the wine is full bodied, sweet, and ripe, with layers of satiny-textured fruit. This is a soft, decadently fruity, succulent, and delicious wine. In blind tastings, I have consistently mistaken it for Figeac. Anticipated maturity: Now–1998. Last tasted, 2/91.

1981—The 1981 is a success for the vintage. However, this vintage of Clos des Jacobins gets overwhelmed in the company of the re-
•
85   markable 1982 and big-styled 1983 wines. The 1981 is preco-ciously soft and intensely fruity, with a complex cedary, herbaceous bouquet, medium body, and lush, nicely concentrated flavors. Anticipated maturity: Now–1993. Last tasted, 11/90.

1979—Fully mature, this wine lacks the great concentration of the vin-tages of the eighties, but is fat, juicy, and spicy, with a smooth,
•
84   graceful, lush fruitiness, medium body, and light tannins. It re-quires drinking. Anticipated maturity: Now–1993. Last tasted, 2/82.

1978—Another top-notch success for the vintage and the appellation, the 1978 Clos des Jacobins has a fine dark color, a rich blackberry
•
86   bouquet, medium to full body, a beefy, weighty feel on the palate, and round, ripe, moderate tannins. Very appealing when young, this Clos des Jacobins has also aged well. Anticipated maturity: Now–1993. Last tasted, 3/82.

1976—This is a notably good wine from a vintage that has provided quite a few disappointments. Fully mature, this fleshy, open-knit style
•
83   of St.-Emilion has good concentration for the vintage, a very sup-ple, smooth texture, and no tannins in the soft finish. Anticipated maturity: Now–may be in decline. Last tasted, 9/80.

1975—Now entering its mature period where it should remain for 5–8 years, the 1975 Clos des Jacobins, despite a higher level of tan-
•
87   nins than usual for this estate, still displays the rich, glossy, fat fruitiness that makes this wine so appealing. Full bodied, succu-lent, and exhibiting good depth, this is one of the few major 1975s that can be drunk early. Anticipated maturity: Now–1997. Last tasted, 3/86.

CLOS LA MADELEINE (Grand Cru Classé)   GOOD

Production: 825 cases	Grape varieties: Merlot—50% Cabernet Franc—50%
Secondary label: none	
Vineyard size: 5 acres	Proprietor: Hubert Pistouley
Time spent in barrels: 18–26 months	Average age of vines: 20 years
Evaluation of present classification: The quality equivalent of a Médoc fifth-growth	
Plateau of maturity: 4–15 years following the vintage	

This tiny gem of a property, situated on the famous hillside between such illustrious châteaux as Belair and Magdelaine, was never considered for Premier Grand Cru Classé status, despite the fact that all the vineyards in the area are Premiers Grands Crus Classés. Was it because of the tiny production of under 1,000 cases and the micro-sized vineyard that Clos la Madeleine was excluded from consideration? Nevertheless, this is a seriously run property. Based on the half-dozen or so vintages I have tasted, it is one of St.-Emilion's most interesting wines, both from a rarity and quality perspective.

If the wines are to be criticized at all, it is because their softness and easy drinkability suggest they will not have a long evolution in the bottle. A tasting done in 1990 revealed totally mature bottles of the 1979, 1981, 1982, and 1983. Among recent vintages, only the 1988 would appear to have more than a decade's longevity.

CLOS DE L'ORATOIRE (Grand Cru Classé)   AVERAGE

Production: 4,500 cases	Grape varieties: Merlot—75% Cabernet Franc—25%
Secondary label: Château Peyreau	
Vineyard size: 25 acres	Proprietor: Société Civile Administrator: Michel Boutet
Time spent in barrels: 16–18 months	Average age of vines: 22 years
Evaluation of present classification: The quality equivalent of a Médoc Cru Bourgeois	
Plateau of maturity: 3–8 years following the vintage	

I have had some good experiences with this chunky, robust, fleshy St.-Emilion that lacks finesse, but offers juicy, succulent flavors. The 1982,

1983, and 1985, if one-dimensional, were still pleasurable because of their juicy, crunchy fruit. Nevertheless, this is a wine that requires consumption in youth.

The Clos de L'Oratoire vineyard is not as well situated as many in St.-Emilion, located northeast of St.-Emilion on very light, less well-drained, sandy soils. The administrator, Michel Boutet, also runs another St.-Emilion property called Château Peyreau, which serves as the secondary label for Clos de L'Oratoire.

CLOS SAINT-MARTIN (Grand Cru Classé) GOOD

Production: 800 cases	Grape varieties: Merlot—60% Cabernet Franc—40%
Secondary label: none	
Vineyard size: 3.2 acres	Proprietor: The Reiffers family
Time spent in barrels: 18–20 months	Average age of vines: 25 years
Evaluation of present classification: The quality equivalent of a good Médoc Cru Bourgeois	
Plateau of maturity: 5–10 or more years following the vintage	

Colleagues of mine in France have long extolled the quality of the wines from this tiny St.-Emilion estate (the smallest Grand Cru Classé of the appellation) located on clay and limestone soil behind the church of Saint-Martin, hence the name. Production is very tiny. The two vintages I have tasted included a firmly structured, concentrated, full-bodied 1988, and a potential sleeper of the vintage in 1989. The latter vintage represented a splendidly concentrated, rich, full-bodied, highly extracted style of wine that should age up to 15 years. If the 1989 typifies the quality and style of wine produced at Clos Saint-Martin, this property merits a more generous rating than I have given it. Libourne's famous Michel Rolland is the property's oenologist.

VINTAGES

1989—The 1989 from this estate is a potential sleeper of the vintage, given the splendidly concentrated, rich, full-bodied, highly extracted style. There are enough ripe tannins to warrant aging for up to 15 years, but considering this wine's harmony and luscious, lavish richness on the palate, most readers will probably prefer to drink it in its first decade of life. Anticipated maturity: 1992–2002. Last tasted, 4/91.

·

88

LA CLOTTE (Grand Cru Classé)   GOOD

Production: 1,600 cases	Grape varieties: Merlot—80% Cabernet Franc—20%
Secondary label: none	
Vineyard size: 9.4 acres	Proprietor: The Chailleau family
Time spent in barrels: 18–20 months	Average age of vines: 25 years
Evaluation of present classification: The quality equivalent of a Médoc Cru Bourgeois, sometimes even a Médoc fifth-growth	
Plateau of maturity: 3–12 or more years following the vintage	

The tiny vineyard of La Clotte is owned by the Chailleau family, who are probably better known as the owners of the immensely popular restaurant snuggled in a back alley of St.-Emilion, Logis de la Cadène. They have hired the firm of Jean-Pierre Moueix to manage the vineyard, and in return the Moueix firm receives three-fourths of the crop for selling on an exclusive basis throughout the world. The rest of La Clotte's production is sold in the restaurant.

I have often enjoyed this wine and found it very typical of a plump, fleshy, well-made St.-Emilion. Drinkable when released, it holds its fruit and develops for 10–12 years. The best recent vintages have included fine wines in 1975, 1982, 1983, 1985, 1986, 1988, and 1989.

The vineyard is well situated on the edge of the limestone plateau, just outside the ancient town walls of St.-Emilion.

LA CLUSIÈRE (Grand Cru Classé)   AVERAGE

Production: 800 cases	Grape varieties: Merlot—70% Cabernet Franc—20% Cabernet Sauvignon—10%
Secondary label: none	
Vineyard size: 8.64 acres	Proprietor: The Valette family
Time spent in barrels: 20–24 months	Average age of vines: 30 years
Evaluation of present classification: The quality equivalent of a Médoc Cru Bourgeois	
Plateau of maturity: 6–15 years following the vintage	

Anyone who has visited Château Pavie has probably been taken by the affable owner, Jean Paul Valette, up the slope of Pavie to the underground cellars at the top of the hill. On this high ridge are the tiny vineyard and cellars of La Clusière. The wine that emerges from this vineyard tends to be surprisingly tough textured, with hard tannins and an ungenerous personality. One would suspect that moderate cellaring would soften the wine, but that has not been my experience. I have tasted too many wines that get older, but not better, and therein lies the problem I have with La Clusière. If you like sinewy, muscular, austere, even harsh clarets, you will enjoy this St.-Emilion more than I do.

VINTAGES

1989—Neither the 1989 nor the 1988 performed well in my tastings.
·   Given the excellent showing of the other wines from the family of
77?   Jean Paul Valette, I was surprised by their apparent mediocrity. The 1989 appears to have been picked too early. Its alcohol level is very high, and the green, harsh, unripe tannins suggest that the grapes may have been analytically but not physiologically mature. It is a sinewy, charmless wine. Anticipated maturity: 1992–1998. Last tasted, 4/91.

1988—The 1988 is slightly better than the 1989, but it is still overwhelm-
·   ingly tannic and mean spirited, with an aggression to its tannins
81   that seems to obliterate any charm that could have been present. Anticipated maturity: 1994–1998. Last tasted, 4/91.

CORBIN (Grand Cru Classé)   GOOD

Production: 6,500 cases	Grape varieties:
	Merlot—65%
	Cabernet Sauvignon—20%
	Cabernet Franc—15%
Secondary label: none	
Vineyard size: 32.1 acres	Proprietor: Domaines Giraud, Société Civile
	Administrator: Madame Blanchard-Giraud
Time spent in barrels: 20 months	Average age of vines: 25 years
Evaluation of present classification: From time to time Corbin produces wines of a Premier Grand Cru Classé status, but in general, this is the quality equivalent of a good Médoc Cru Bourgeois	
Plateau of maturity: 3–12 years following the vintage	

Corbin is clearly a property capable of making rich, deeply fruity, luscious wines. My first experience with this wine was at a dinner party where the 1970 was served blind. It was an immensely enjoyable, round, full-bodied, concentrated, delicious wine with plenty of fruit. Since then I have made it a point to follow this estate closely. In the great vintages, for instance, 1970, 1975, 1982, and 1989, this wine can rival the best St.-Emilions. Its problem has been inconsistency.

Corbin sits on the *graves* plateau near the Pomerol border. Bordeaux's famed Professor Enjalbert argues that Corbin's vineyard is situated on a band of soil that is contiguous with that of Cheval Blanc. The current administrator is Madame Blanchard-Giraud, who also manages the excellent, but inconsistent Pomerol estate of Certan-Giraud. The style of wine produced at Corbin reaches heights in hot, sunny, drought years when the wine is dark in color, fat, ripe, full bodied, and admirably concentrated. Unfortunately, Corbin is a moderately expensive wine as it has long been popular in the Benelux countries and Great Britain.

VINTAGES

1989—After 1982, this property's wines took a nosedive and it appeared
· the management was unwilling to reduce their yields. The results
88 were wines that were simply too diluted. The 1989 should prove
to be the finest Corbin made since the 1982. It is not a wine for
everyone, because of the philosophy of picking extremely late and
turning out wines marked by the overripe smells of peaches, apricots, and jammy black fruit. The 1989 has extremely low acidity
and very soft tannins, but the overall impression is one of great
power, an opulent, even unctuous texture, and precocious drinkability. Assuming you like this big, new-world, Australian style of
wine, and intend to drink it within its first decade of life, this wine
will undoubtedly provide a level of exhilaration that will be hard
to beat for its price. Anticipated maturity: Now–1977. Last
tasted, 4/91.

1988—The 1988 is light and diluted, with a weedy, indifferent character.
· Last tasted, 4/91.
74

1986—The 1986 is too loosely knit and too soft, and seems entirely
· unfocused, as well as overcropped. It is a fruity, soft, pleasant
75 wine that is easy to drink, but a bit more structure and concentration would be welcome. Anticipated maturity: Now–1993. Last
tasted, 3/90.

1985—The 1985 exhibits the overripe character I find common in Corbin,
· a soft, exuberantly fruity, agreeable constitution, and a finish that
83 is a trifle short and too alcoholic. Anticipated maturity: Now–
1995. Last tasted, 3/90.

1984—Sweet and obviously chaptalized, this plump, simple wine re-
·　　quires drinking up. Anticipated maturity: Now—may be in de-
72　　cline. Last tasted, 3/88.

1983—This jammy, fat, alcoholic effort offers a seductive mouthful of
·　　wine. Dark ruby with some amber, the 1983 Corbin is a chewy,
86　　corpulent mouthful of St.-Emilion. It lacks finesse, but for fleshy
　　　fruitiness, it is a delight. Anticipated maturity: Now—1995. Last
　　　tasted, 3/89.

1982—In top vintages, Corbin can be excellent. The 1982 promises to be
·　　as good as the lovely 1970. Still dark ruby, with a full-blown, ripe
87　　blackcurrant, herbal-scented, toasty bouquet, this full-bodied
　　　wine has excellent concentration, silky tannins, and exceptional
　　　balance and length. Jammy and slightly disjointed, this robust
　　　wine should be drunk up. Anticipated maturity: Now—1997. Last
　　　tasted, 2/91.

1978—Now mature, the 1978 is a big, juicy, fat, ripe, richly fruity wine,
·　　with plenty of soft, velvety fruit, full body, and an alcoholic, yet
84　　long finish. Anticipated maturity: Now—1993. Last tasted, 2/84.

1975—Not quite the size and dimension of the two big wines Corbin
·　　produced in 1982 and 1989, the 1975 remains a richly fruity,
86　　spicy, muscular wine that still possesses moderate tannins. The
　　　wine is fully mature, and if the fruit holds up, it should remain at
　　　this plateau for 3–5 years. Anticipated maturity: Now—1995. Last
　　　tasted, 11/88.

1970—A wonderfully fragrant, round, generous, richly fruity wine, the
·　　1970 Corbin is a textbook example of what a well-vinified St.-
87　　Emilion is all about. This wine has been fully mature for over 15
　　　years. Anticipated maturity: Now—1994. Last tasted, 10/87.

CORBIN-MICHOTTE (Grand Cru Classé)　　　　GOOD

Production: 3,000 cases	Grape varieties:
	Merlot—65%
	Cabernet Franc—30%
	Cabernet Sauvignon—5%
Secondary label: Les Abeilles	
Vineyard size: 18.8 acres	Proprietor: Jean-Noel Boidron
Time spent in barrels: 22 months	Average age of vines: 35 years
Evaluation of present classification: From time to time this property	
produces wines of Premier Grand Cru Classé quality, but in	
general, the quality is equivalent to a good Médoc Cru Bourgeois	
Plateau of maturity: 3–12 years following the vintage	

Corbin-Michotte is one of five châteaux that sit along the Pomerol border with the word Corbin in their name. This property has the potential to be one of the best of the area. It is a small estate with relatively old vines that are planted on a sandy, loam soil intermixed with fine gravel, and what the French call *"crasse de fer,"* meaning a ferruginous iron-rich subsoil. The vineyard is also laden with minerals, which the proprietor claims gives the wine's bouquet its extra dimension.

I have not had enough vintages of Corbin-Michotte to make a definitive judgment on the overall quality, but those wines I have tasted have greatly impressed me. Unfortunately for American consumers, much of Corbin-Michotte is sold directly to European clients and in Switzerland, which remains the strongest market for this property. Vintages I have tasted have reminded me more of a Pomerol than a St.-Emilion. They have been deeply colored wines, with a very pronounced black fruit, plummy character, and a luscious, opulent texture.

VINTAGES

1989—The 1989 appears to be one of the sleepers of the vintage. It is a
·   black/purple–colored wine, oozing with extract. Full bodied,
89   richly perfumed, with the scent of superripe plums and minerals,
        this staggeringly rich wine has an alcohol level of nearly 14%,
        relatively low acidity, but high tannins. It is a decadently rich
        blockbuster for the vintage. Anticipated maturity: 1993–2002.
        Last tasted, 4/91.

1988—The 1988 is a medium-bodied, pleasant, correct wine, with decent
·   acidity and length. It should be drunk over the next 5–7 years.
83   Anticipated maturity: Now–1998. Last tasted, 4/91.

1985—Now fully mature, the 1985 Corbin-Michotte has a dark ruby
·   color, with a spicy, blackcurrant, plum-scented nose, lush, round,
86   generously endowed flavors, and a soft, silky texture. Anticipated
        maturity: Now–1997. Last tasted, 11/90.

1982—This stunning example of Corbin-Michotte has matured rapidly
·   and should be consumed. It offers a roasted, plummy, mineral-
87   scented bouquet, rich, heady, alcoholic, fleshy, chewy flavors,
        considerable body, and abundant glycerin and alcohol in its soft
        finish. It makes for a hedonistic mouthful of delicious St.-Emilion,
        but aging it any longer would be foolish. Anticipated maturity:
        Now–1994. Last tasted, 3/90.

CORMEIL-FIGEAC (Grand Cru Classé)   AVERAGE

Production: 4,000 cases	Grape varieties: Merlot—70% Cabernet Franc—30%
Secondary label: none Vineyard size: 25 acres	Proprietor: The Moreaud family
Time spent in barrels: 18–22 months	Average age of vines: 25 years
Evaluation of present classification: The quality equivalent of a Médoc Cru Bourgeois	
Plateau of maturity: 3–8 years following the vintage	

This is a vineyard with a great deal of potential given the location adjacent to the famed Château Figeac. However, its soils are more sandy than those of Figeac, and one wonders what could be obtained if the selection were a bit stricter, and the proprietor used more new oak casks. From time to time there is an underlying mustiness that is off-putting. Otherwise, the wines are supple, fleshy, and generally well endowed.

VINTAGES

1989—Fleshy, superripe aromas of jammy plums and herbs emerge from
  ·   the glass. On the palate, the wine is medium to full bodied, cor-
 85   pulent, and generously endowed, with low acidity and some firm
       tannins in the finish. If this wine develops more harmony and
       bouquet, the rating may look conservative. Anticipated maturity:
       1992–2001. Last tasted, 4/91.

1988—The 1988 is medium deep ruby, with a spicy, herbaceous bouquet
  ·   and cedary, round flavors that exhibit moderate tannins, medium
 81   body, and adequate ripeness. The finish is a bit short. Anticipated
       maturity: Now–1995. Last tasted, 3/90.

1986—The 1986 Cormeil-Figeac is a one-dimensional, yet muscular, me-
  ·   dium- to full-bodied wine with a good deal of fruit, but lacking
 83   charm and complexity. Hefty tannins in the finish suggest it needs
       to be cellared for at least 3–4 years. Anticipated maturity: Now–
       2000. Last tasted, 4/91.

1985—The 1985 has medium to full body, a deep ruby color, an open-
  ·   knit texture, a ripe, plummy bouquet, and a generous suppleness.
 85   It is quite tasty. Anticipated maturity: Now–1994. Last tasted,
       3/89.

LA COUSPADE (Grand Cru)   AVERAGE

Production: 4,500 cases	Grape varieties: Merlot—60% Cabernet Franc—40%
Secondary label: none	
Vineyard size: 17.3 acres	Proprietor: The Aubert family
Time spent in barrels: 18 months	Average age of vines: 23 years
Evaluation of present classification: The quality equivalent of a Médoc Cru Bourgeois	
Plateau of maturity: 2–8 years following the vintage	

This moderately sized vineyard located on the limestone plateau east of St.-Emilion was downgraded in the 1985 classification of the wines of St.-Emilion, presumably because the wines were not bottled at the château. I have only tasted four vintages of La Couspade, the most impressive of which was the 1989. It exhibited a rich, concentrated, chunky texture and plenty of length, with a corpulent, ripe fruitiness. Neither the 1986 nor the 1988 was a distinguished wine.

COUVENT-DES-JACOBINS (Grand Cru Classé)   VERY GOOD

Production: 3,800 cases	Grape varieties: Merlot—60% Cabernet Sauvignon—30% Cabernet Franc—10%
Secondary label: Beau-Mayne	
Vineyard size: 24 acres	Proprietors: Madame Joinaud- Borde and the Borde family
Time spent in barrels: 18–22 months	Average age of vines: 40 years
Evaluation of present classification: The quality equivalent of a Médoc fourth-growth	
Plateau of maturity: 4–14 years following the vintage	

Couvent-des-Jacobins, named after the thirteenth-century Dominican monastery that was built on this site, is an up-and-coming estate, meticulously run by the Joinaud-Borde family, who have owned the property since 1902.

The vineyards are immediately situated adjacent to the town of St.-Emilion, on a sandy, clay soil of the *côtes* that produces darkly colored, rich, fairly alcoholic wines of substance and character. During the eighties, the quality of Couvent-des-Jacobins improved, largely because the owners introduced a second label for vats not considered superb enough for the grand vin. They also increased the use of new oak casks to 33% or more for each vintage.

Couvent-des-Jacobins, located immediately to the left-hand side of the main entrance to the town, has one of the most remarkable underground cellars of the region. It is a showpiece property that would make for an interesting visit even if the wines were not so distinguished.

VINTAGES

1989—The 1989 has a remarkable resemblance to the wonderful 1982. It
·   is a deeply colored, intensely perfumed, full-bodied wine with
86   layers of extract, an unctuous, plummy fatness, high alcohol, and
        very low acidity. Anticipated maturity: Now–1997. Last tasted,
        4/91.

1986—The 1986 should prove to be one of the longest-lived wines from
·   this property in over two decades. Deep ruby/purple in color, with
87   a pronounced spicy, oaky, curranty bouquet intermingled with
        the scent of herbs, this wine displays a superripeness, medium
        body, and an excellent finish, with plenty of soft tannins. Antici-
        pated maturity: 1992–1998. Last tasted, 3/90.

1985—The 1985 is a textbook St.-Emilion—supple, generous, easy to
·   appreciate, with gobs of blackcurrant fruit interlaced with a touch
86   of toasty oak. This medium- to full-bodied wine offers both com-
        plexity and a mouth-filling plumpness. Anticipated maturity:
        Now–1994. Last tasted, 3/90.

1983—Nearly as concentrated and as deep as the 1982, the 1983
·   Couvent-des-Jacobins is a soft, supple, fruity, medium-bodied,
85   well-colored wine that is fully mature. Anticipated maturity:
        Now–1993. Last tasted, 11/89.

1982—The 1982 Couvent still has impressive dark ruby color, and a
·   complex, berry bouquet of cedar, herbs, chocolate, and licorice.
87   On the palate, this fleshy wine is deep, rich, and full bodied, with
        a seductive, silky texture. It has attained full maturity. Antici-
        pated maturity: Now–1994. Last tasted, 1/91.

1981—The 1981 represents a rustic effort from Couvent-des-Jacobins. I
·   have found this wine a trifle austere and hard, with an unexciting
76   bouquet of herbs, oak, and plummy fruit. It has never blossomed,
        remaining hard and tannic. Anticipated maturity: Now–1994.
        Last tasted, 11/90.

CROQUE-MICHOTTE (Grand Cru Classé)   VERY GOOD

Production: 6,500 cases	Grape varieties: Merlot—75% Cabernet Franc—20% Cabernet Sauvignon—5%
Secondary label: none Vineyard size: 37 acres	Proprietor: Madame Helene Rigal-Geoffrion
Time spent in barrels: 18–20 months	Average age of vines: 35 years
Evaluation of present classification: The quality equivalent of a Médoc fifth-growth	
Plateau of maturity: 4–12 years following the vintage	

The vineyard of Croque-Michotte is well situated in the *graves* section of the St.-Emilion appellation adjacent to the Pomerol border, close to the better-known estates of Cheval Blanc and La Dominique. The wine produced here is usually ready to drink within the first 5 or 6 years of a vintage and it rarely improves beyond a decade. Nevertheless, especially among those who lack patience, this fleshy, sumptuous style of wine has many admirers.

VINTAGES

1989 · 87 —This deep ruby/purple–colored wine has an intense bouquet of jammy cassis, herbs, new oak, and minerals. In the mouth, it is explosively fruity, lush, and medium to full bodied, with a great deal of glycerin, and an almost thick texture. It is a hedonistic St.-Emilion for drinking over the next 7–8 years. I would not age it longer given its low acidity and high alcohol. Anticipated maturity: Now–1998. Last tasted, 4/91.

1988 · 85 —More compact and linear than the 1989, the 1988 has an attractive, spicy, cedary, berry-scented bouquet touched up judiciously by toasty, vanillin oak. In the mouth, the wine is medium bodied, with better acidity, more tannin, and a compact, less generous personality than the 1989. It will probably last longer, but will never provide the pure hedonistic appeal that the 1989 will. Anticipated maturity: 1992–2000. Last tasted, 4/91.

1986 · 86 —The 1986 is unabashedly fruity, supple, and a total joy to drink. In fact, I question my rating, given how much satisfaction I actually derived from drinking the wine. It is not the most complex style of Bordeaux; however, for pure, gushy fruitiness, it is hard to beat. Anticipated maturity: Now–1996. Last tasted, 3/90.

1985—The 1985 offers plenty of hedonistic, rich fruit, a succulent tex-
· 　　ture, a long, heady finish, and an intoxicating, intense bouquet.
87　　While not a keeper, it has oodles of berry fruit, a gorgeous silky
　　　texture, and a smooth finish. Anticipated maturity: Now–1995.
　　　Last tasted, 3/89.

1984—Very light and spicy, with soft, watery, fruity flavors, the 1984
· 　　requires immediate consumption. Anticipated maturity: Now–
72　　may be in decline. Last tasted, 3/89.

1983—This fat, jammy, viscous, alcoholic wine has exhibited consider-
· 　　able concentration and weight, but lacks acidity and finishes with
80　　an alcoholic hotness. It appears to be a big, rather clumsy wine.
　　　Anticipated maturity: Now–1993. Last tasted, 1/85.

1982—The 1982 Croque-Michotte is full bodied, very flavorful and
· 　　fleshy, cleanly made, ripe, savory, and ready to drink. In many
85　　ways, this is a textbook, full-bodied St.-Emilion that now should
　　　be drunk. Anticipated maturity: Now–1992. Last tasted, 11/88.

1978—Starting to fade and lose freshness and grip, this mellow wine has
· 　　a soft, medium-bodied texture, average concentration, and a
75　　pleasant, yet tiring alcoholic finish. Anticipated maturity: Now–
　　　may be in decline. Last tasted, 2/84.

CURÉ-BON-LA-MADELEINE (Grand Cru Classé)　　VERY GOOD

Production: 2,000 cases	Grape varieties:
	Merlot—90%
	Cabernet Sauvignon—5%
	Malbec—5%
Secondary label: none	
Vineyard size: 12.5 acres	Proprietor: Maurice Landé
Time spent in barrels: 20–24 months	Average age of vines: 30 years
Evaluation of present classification: The quality equivalent of a Médoc fourth-growth	
Plateau of maturity: 5–15 years following the vintage	

This tiny estate has a splendid location on the *côtes* St.-Emilion, sandwiched between the famous vineyards of Canon, Belair, and Ausone. It
is a wine with a very good reputation, but one that is rarely seen in export
channels. My experience with Curé-Bon-La-Madeleine is very limited,
but the wines I have seen have been generally powerful, intense, muscular, surprisingly tannic and firmly structured St.-Emilions that can
support considerable cellaring.

VINTAGES

1985—An intense, cedary, herbaceous bouquet is followed by a wine
· with relatively dusty, muscular flavors, surprising firmness and
86 tannin for a 1985, but good concentration and noticeable astringence in its finish. If the wine softens and becomes more harmonious, the rating may look conservative. Anticipated maturity:
1993–2001. Last tasted, 11/90.

1983—A big, cedary, herbaceous, curranty bouquet is followed by a
· relatively alcoholic wine, with a lot of glycerin, fatness, and ripe-
85 ness. It has matured quickly. Ready to drink, with an expansive
palate and lush texture, this chunky, robust St.-Emilion is fully
mature. Anticipated maturity: Now–1995. Last tasted, 11/90.

1982—This is probably the best Curé-Bon-La-Madeleine that I have
· tasted, although it—like the 1983—has reached full maturity.
88 Medium dark ruby with some amber at the edge, this full-flavored, intense, spicy, cedary wine has plenty of guts, and a rich,
chewy texture, with soft tannins and a great deal of glycerin. The
finish is smooth as silk, but there is noticeable alcohol to be dealt
with. Anticipated maturity: Now–1994. Last tasted, 11/90.

1981—With the exception of Cheval Blanc, there are not that many 1981
· St.-Emilions that I have found particularly exciting, but Curé-
84 Bon, if not compelling, is a full-bodied, chewy, darkly colored
wine with a robust personality, moderate tannins, and a good
finish. Although not complex, it is quite attractive. Anticipated
maturity: Now–1994. Last tasted, 3/83.

1979—Very ripe, soft, fat, and sweet, this wine has an expansive bou-
· quet of ripe Merlot fruit, spicy oak, and broad, rich, viscous,
85 somewhat alcoholic flavors. Dark ruby, and still moderately
tannic, this wine should be drunk now. Anticipated maturity:
Now–may be in decline. Last tasted, 1/85.

1978—One of the most successful St.-Emilions, the 1978 Curé-Bon is
· just beginning to shed its tannic cloak and reveal spicy, plummy,
86 ripe Merlot scents and aromas. On the palate, the wine displays
good power and concentration, and more firmness than most
wines of St.-Emilion do in this vintage. Anticipated maturity:
Now–1994. Last tasted, 1/85.

1976—The 1976 is a very successful effort from Curé-Bon. Dark ruby
· with just a trace of brown, this well-made wine has a rich,
84 plummy, cedary, leather-scented bouquet, broad, velvety, rich
and supple flavors, and light tannins. Fully mature, it has held up
much better than many wines of this vintage. Anticipated maturity: Now–may be in decline. Last tasted, 1/85.

DASSAULT (Grand Cru Classé)   GOOD

Production: 9,500 cases	Grape varieties: Merlot—65% Cabernet Franc—20% Cabernet Sauvignon—15%
Secondary label: none	
Vineyard size: 56.8 acres	Proprietor: SARL Château Dassault
Time spent in barrels: 14–18 months	Average age of vines: 27 years
Evaluation of present classification: The quality equivalent of a good Médoc Cru Bourgeois	
Plateau of maturity: 3–9 years following the vintage	

Dassault consistently produces smooth textured, fruity, supple, straight-forward wines that are meant to be drunk in their youth. They are very cleanly made and perhaps too commercial in orientation, but there is no denying their attractive, uncomplicated style. The only caveat here is that aging rarely results in a better wine. As long as one is prepared to drink this wine at a relatively early age, it is unlikely that Dassault will be disappointing. The perfect restaurant St.-Emilion?

VINTAGES

1989—The 1989 is a loosely structured, grapey, expansively flavored,
·   very soft and alcoholic wine that lacks structure and precision.
84   However, it will offer a deliciously smooth glass of wine if drunk
       young. Anticipated maturity: Now–1996. Last tasted, 4/91.

1988—The 1988 is more concentrated than the 1989, with a deeper ruby
·   color. In the mouth, it has the ripe, sweet, plummy fruit character
85   of the 1982, but greater concentration, more focus to its flavors,
       as well as more acidity and less alcohol. It has a soft finish, but
       there is enough tannin to ensure longevity of 6–8 years. This wine
       would make an excellent choice for restaurants, as well as con-
       sumers needing a classy St.-Emilion for early drinking. Antici-
       pated maturity: Now–1996. Last tasted, 4/91.

1986—This is not a complicated or terribly compelling wine, but it deliv-
·   ers an exuberant blackberry and plummy fruitiness married
82   nicely with some spicy oak, finishing with a silky, smooth, heady
       taste. It is hard not to like a wine with this character, even though
       one should drink it over the near term. Anticipated maturity:
       Now–1994. Last tasted, 3/89.

1985—The 1985 is light, ripe, and effusively fruity, but lacks grip and
· focus. It should be drunk up. Anticipated maturity: Now–1992.
83   Last tasted, 3/89.

DESTIEUX (Grand Cru)   GOOD

Production: 3,800 cases	Grape varieties: Merlot—65% Cabernet Franc—25% Cabernet Sauvignon—10%
Secondary label: none	
Vineyard size: 19.8 acres	Proprietor: The Dauriac family
Time spent in barrels: 18–22 months	Average age of vines: 25 years
Evaluation of present classification: The quality equivalent of a good Médoc Cru Bourgeois	
Plateau of maturity: 5–15 years following the vintage	

Located in the satellite commune of St.-Hippolyte, on clay and limestone
soils, in a particularly torrid St.-Emilion micro-climate, Destieux makes
an especially attractive, plummy, fleshy, tough-textured wine, with good
concentration and plenty of alcohol.

The force behind the recent string of successes is both the owner, M.
Dauriac, and his talented consulting oenologist, Michel Rolland. The
wines of Destieux are among the deepest colored and most powerful and
dense of the appellation. If bulk and muscle were criteria for greatness,
Destieux would be near the top.

VINTAGES

1989—For much of the eighties I have been enthusiastic about the efforts
· of the proprietor of Destieux, Monsieur Dauriac, who tends to
85   produce powerful, dense, tannic wines with the potential to last
for 10–15 years. At first unfocused and lacking definition, the
1989 has developed into a rich, highly extracted, powerful, dense
wine that may be too charged with tannin. Anticipated maturity:
1996–2005. Last tasted, 4/91.

1988—The 1988 has a tremendously impressive ruby/purple color, but
· no charm or finesse, as the overbearing tannins are so astringent
77   and excessive that this wine has little possibility of ever coming
together and aging gracefully. Last tasted, 4/91.

1986—The 1986 Destieux is a powerful, dense, tannic wine, with tremen-
· dous depth of fruit, full body, and gobs of extract and tannin in
86   the finish. It should prove to be the longest-lived Destieux made

in the last several decades. This Destieux has the fruit necessary to hold up to the tannin. Anticipated maturity: 1994–2005. Last tasted, 3/90.

1985—The 1985 is another broodingly dense wine. Full flavored, it has a
·   sumptuous amount of ripe fruit, a voluptuous texture, and mod-
87   erate aging potential. Anticipated maturity: Now–1997. Last tasted, 3/90.

LA DOMINIQUE (Grand Cru Classé)   EXCELLENT

Production: 6,000 cases	Grape varieties: Merlot—75% Cabernet Franc—15% Cabernet Sauvignon—5% Malbec—5%
Secondary label: Saint-Paul de la Dominique	
Vineyard size: 44.5 acres	Proprietor: Clément Fayat
Time spent in barrels: 18–22 months	Average age of vines: 30 years
Evaluation of present classification: The quality equivalent of a Médoc third growth; should be upgraded to a St.-Emilion Premier Grand Cru Classé	
Plateau of maturity: 5–20 years following the vintage	

Except for a handful of bad vintages in the 1970s, there has only been one unsuccessful vintage (the 1985) of La Dominique since Clément Fayat became the proprietor in 1969. This superbly situated estate, located near the border of Pomerol, close to Cheval Blanc, has a soil base composed of limestone gravel and sandy clay. An intensive system of drain tiles installed in the mid-nineteenth century has greatly enhanced this property's ability to produce fine wines in wet years. The truly great wines made at La Dominique—1970, 1971, 1982, 1983, 1986, 1989, and 1990—should easily qualify La Dominique for elevation to a Premier Grand Cru Classé in any future St.-Emilion classification. However, the property continues to lack the glamour and reputation of many of the other Premiers Grands Crus Classés, a fact that can be put to advantage by consumers looking for reasonably priced St.-Emilions.

Proprietor Fayat, who purchased the Cru Bourgeois Château Clement-Pichon in the Médoc in 1978, utilizes the services of the highly respected Libourne oenologist Michel Rolland to oversee the vinification and *élevage* of La Dominique. The resulting wine is richly colored, intense, superripe, opulent, and full bodied. It benefits immensely from the 33–45% new oak barrels utilized each vintage. The decision to make a second wine for less successful vats and young vines has increased the quality even further.

La Dominique's wines continue to be undervalued.

VINTAGES

1989—The 1989 is the most massive wine I tasted from this vintage in
· St.-Emilion. They harvested very late, producing Merlot and Cab-
92 ernet Franc grapes that reached 14% alcohol naturally. The frightening thing is that despite an alcohol level that would make a grower in Châteauneuf-du-Pape jump with joy, there is not a trace of hotness in the wine's nose, flavors, or finish, largely because of the extraordinary intensity and concentration. In 1989, the wine was stored in 100% new oak, and that, plus its stupendous levels of extract, make for one of the most dramatic and flamboyant wines of St.-Emilion. This is an example of a winemaker taking the ultimate risk and pulling it off with a breathtaking wine of great flavor dimension, complexity, and aging potential. This awesome effort from La Dominique may ultimately surpass even their 1982 and 1971. Anticipated maturity: 1993–2008. Last tasted, 4/91.

1988—In some ways, it is a shame that the 1989 is such a show-stopping
· effort, because it eclipses the 1988, which deserves a great deal
87 of recognition. It is a more typical (or as the Bordelais would have you believe, "more classic") effort, with an alluring and precocious, big bouquet of plummy fruit and sweet vanillin-scented oak. In the mouth, there is not a hard edge to be found. This wine offers exuberantly rich, fruity, opulent flavors, medium to full body, and a long, satiny finish. Anticipated maturity: Now–2001. Last tasted, 4/91.

1986—The 1986 has deep ruby color, an exceptional bouquet of toasty
· new oak, rich, plummy fruit, and minerals. This is followed by a
90 wine that is full bodied and intense, with gobs of extract, and tremendous power and persistence in its finish. It does not have the opulence or precocious appeal of the 1982, but for those with some patience, it will provide exceptional drinking for at least two decades. Anticipated maturity: 1993–2005. Last tasted, 3/90.

1985—The 1985 La Dominique is a disappointment, tasting of green sap
· from improperly cured barrels and too large a crop. Its evolution
74 in the bottle has not been of benefit. Avoid it. Last tasted, 12/88.

1983 —The third consecutive successful wine in this wonderful trilogy
  ·   for La Dominique, the 1983, while not a match for the heavenly
  87   1982, is still a well structured, flavorful, medium-bodied wine,
         with plenty of class. Slightly more rustic and alcoholic than usual,
         this fleshy wine has plenty of rich, supple fruit, as well as a long,
         smooth finish. Anticipated maturity: Now–2000. Last tasted,
         12/89.

1982 —One of the best wines I have ever tasted from this property is the
  ·   1982 La Dominique. Perhaps only the 1970, 1971, or 1989 equal
  91   it in potential. It is very tasty, and no one would regret opening a
         bottle today, but the wine still needs several more years to reach
         its plateau of maturity and to resolve all the tannins. The bouquet
         reveals a generous use of smoky, toasty, new oak and has a vivid
         scent of herbs, and oodles of plummy, rich, blackcurrant fruit. It
         is a powerful, broad flavored, muscular wine that should age well
         for another 10–15 years. Anticipated maturity: 1993–2008. Last
         tasted, 7/91.

1981 —La Dominique's 1981 is a complex, medium-weight, nicely bal-
  ·   anced wine, with a tight, but promising bouquet of new oak, ripe
  84   fruit, and herbal scents. Well made, this medium-bodied wine
         has reached full maturity, but should hold nicely in the bottle for
         4–6 years. Anticipated maturity: Now–1995. Last tasted, 2/89.

1980 —A success given the vintage in 1980, La Dominique produced a
  ·   supple, fruity wine, with a slightly herbaceous, vegetal quality to
  78   its bouquet. On the palate, the wine displays good fruit, medium
         body, and a soft, pleasant finish. Anticipated maturity: Now–may
         be in decline. Last tasted, 6/84.

1979 —I have never been a great admirer of this wine. Consistently lean,
  ·   austere, and lacking generosity, it is an acceptable wine, with an
  75   attractive bouquet, but for La Dominique, a disappointment.
         Time may yield some hidden fruit, but I would not gamble on it.
         Anticipated maturity: Now–1993. Last tasted, 11/88.

1978 —Fully mature, this lovely, ripe, fleshy, fruity La Dominique has a
  ·   cedary, spicy, herb-and-oak-scented bouquet, medium body,
  85   light tannins, and a soft, supple, spicy finish. This is a well-
         rendered wine that will keep and continue to drink well for an-
         other decade. Anticipated maturity: Now–2000. Last tasted,
         1/91.

1976 —A trifle loosely knit (as most 1976s are), but La Dominique has
  ·   managed to produce a wine that avoids the soupy softness and
  83   unstructured feel of many wines of this vintage. A ripe, cedary,
         oaky, spicy bouquet is fully developed. On the palate, the wine is
         soft, nicely concentrated, and expansive. This is a delightful

medium-weight wine. Anticipated maturity: Now–may be in decline. Last tasted, 2/84.

1975—A typical 1975, hard, astringent, promising, but obnoxiously
·   backward and tannic, this wine has remained closed and slightly
79   dumb, but exhibits very good color, a hint of ripe, cedary, plummy fruit in its nose, and adequate weight and length in the finish. The fruit continues to take a back seat to the tannins. Anticipated maturity: Now–1998. Last tasted, 3/88.

1971—One sip of the 1971 can turn a skeptic into an instant devotee of
·   La Dominique. A sensational wine for La Dominique, the 1971 is
90   not only the best St.-Emilion, but one of the top wines of the vintage. Medium garnet, with a concentrated, jammy, rich bouquet of herbs, cedar, oriental spices, and ripe berry fruit, this wine is lush and silky, with layer upon layer of ripe fruit, and a lush, alcoholic finish. This is certainly one of the sleepers of the vintage. The wine has held at its plateau for over a decade, but why push your luck? Drink it up. Anticipated maturity: Now–1995. Last tasted, 1/90.

1970—The 1970 is a very attractive, mature St.-Emilion that is in no
·   danger of falling apart, but it is best drunk up over the next
88   several years. Medium ruby with some amber, this wine is soft, fragrant, ripe, and admirably concentrated, with a velvety finish. The wine has actually put on weight in the last several years. Drink it over the next 2–4 years. Anticipated maturity: Now–1995. Last tasted, 1/91.

FAURIE-DE-SOUCHARD (Grand Cru Classé)   GOOD

Production: 4,000 cases	Grape varieties: Merlot—65% Cabernet Franc—26% Cabernet Sauvignon—9%
Secondary label: none	
Vineyard size: 25.9 acres	Proprietor: The Jabiol family
Time spent in barrels: 18–24 months	Average age of vines: 27 years
Evaluation of present classification: The quality equivalent of a good Médoc Cru Bourgeois	
Plateau of maturity: 5–15 years following the vintage	

Faurie-de-Souchard, one of the oldest properties in St.-Emilion, has been owned by the Jabiol family since 1933. The vineyard, located on both a limestone plateau as well as chalky clay and sandy soil, tends to produce relatively full-bodied, tannic, intense wines that require some patience in the bottle. Unlike many St.-Emilions that are made to be drunk within their first 5–6 years, most vintages of Faurie-de-Souchard can last up to 10–15 years. If the wines are to be criticized at all, it is because their tannins often exceed the extraction levels of fruit.

The best recent vintages have been 1989, 1988, 1986, and perhaps the finest wine I have ever tasted from this property, the 1982.

DE FERRAND (Grand Cru)   GOOD

Production: 12,500 cases	Grape varieties:
	Merlot—68%
	Cabernet Sauvignon—18%
	Cabernet Franc—14%
Secondary label: none	
Vineyard size: 69.2 acres	Proprietor: Baron Bich
Time spent in barrels: 20–24 months	Average age of vines: 25 years
Evaluation of present classification: The quality equivalent of a good Médoc Cru Bourgeois; in vintages such as 1982 and 1985 de Ferrand can compete with the best	
Plateau of maturity: 4–12 years following the vintage	

The Baron Bich, celebrated for his "Bic" pens, purchased de Ferrand in 1978, and has significantly increased the quality of the wine.

The vineyard itself is located in the commune of St.-Hippolyte on a plateau of limestone. The key to the success of many de Ferrand vintages has been an unusually late harvest and the use of a significant percentage of new oak, ranging from 50% to nearly 100%. De Ferrand makes wines with the potential for a moderately long evolution in the bottle.

VINTAGES

1989—The 1989 appears to have the structure and concentration neces-
  ·   sary to support its tannic ferocity. It is a dark ruby/purple–
 85   colored wine, closed for a 1989, but still easy to recognize as big
        and muscular, yet lacking charm. This impressively sized speci-
        men will need plenty of time in the cellar. Anticipated maturity:
        1996–2008. Last tasted, 4/91.

1988—The 1988 suffers from what will ultimately be the undoing of many
  ·   of this vintage's wines. The tannins are green and excessively
 83   hard and dry, and tend to overwhelm the wine's concentration.

There is some decent black cherry fruit, but it will undoubtedly lose the battle in its struggle against the tannin. Anticipated maturity: 1992–2002. Last tasted, 4/91.

1986—The 1986 is not far behind the 1982 and 1985, although it lacks
· the splendid opulence of the 1985, and is more tannic and reti-
85 cent. Deep ruby in color, with a closed yet burgeoning bouquet of spicy oak, flowers, and mineral-scented fruit, this medium-bodied, elegantly wrought wine needs to be cellared for several years before it will be ready to drink. Anticipated maturity: 1993–2001. Last tasted, 3/89.

1985—The 1985 is the finest de Ferrand I have tasted. Deep ruby, with
· a forward, classic bouquet of blackcurrants and toasty oak, this
89 medium- to full-bodied, rich yet well-balanced, elegant wine has quite a bit of staying power in the mouth. Anticipated maturity: Now–2000. Last tasted, 10/90.

1984—Spicy, light, compact, and short on the palate, this wine requires
· drinking. Anticipated maturity: Now–1993. Last tasted, 3/89.
72

1983—This is an atypically austere, dry, extremely tannic wine, with
· plenty of structure, but it lacks the ampleness, fruit, and charm
82 that most St.-Emilion enthusiasts have come to expect. I am skeptical about its future. Anticipated maturity: Now–1994. Last tasted, 11/88.

1982—This beautiful de Ferrand was the first vintage that made me
· aware of the potential of this vineyard. The wine has now reached
88 full maturity, and should have no difficulty lasting at this plateau for another 7–8 years. Dark, dense, deep ruby/garnet, with a roasted bouquet of coffee, grilled nuts, chocolate, and prunes, this full-bodied, velvety, abundantly endowed wine is delicious to drink. It is a wine of Premier Grand Cru Classé quality. Anticipated maturity: Now–1998. Last tasted, 1/90.

FIGEAC (Premier Grand Cru Classé) EXCELLENT

Production: 11,500 cases	Grape varieties: Cabernet Sauvignon—35% Cabernet Franc—35% Merlot—30%
Secondary label: Grangeneuve	
Vineyard size: 98.8 acres	Proprietor: Thierry Manoncourt
Time spent in barrels: 20 months	Average age of vines: 35 years
Evaluation of present classification: The quality equivalent of a Médoc second-growth	
Plateau of maturity: 3–15 years following the vintage	

This moderately large property of just over 98 acres sits on the gravel plateau diagonally across the road from Cheval Blanc. (It once was even larger, including land holdings that are now part of Cheval Blanc.) Many observers have long felt Figeac produced St.-Emilion's second-best wine. Its proprietor, Thierry Manoncourt, believes it to be the finest wine of the appellation, and unashamedly shares these feelings with all visitors. The fact that the wine from what is now Cheval Blanc's vineyard used to be sold as Vin de Figeac only seems to strengthen his case. Since the emergence of Ausone with the 1976 vintage and the heightened consumer awareness of the excellence of other St.-Emilions, Figeac has had to contend with increased competition.

The aristocratic-looking, yet amiable Thierry Manoncourt makes Figeac in a very popular style. In top vintages the wine is much closer in style and quality to its fabulously expensive neighbor, Cheval Blanc, than the price difference would seemingly suggest. Usually ruby colored, richly fruity, with a distinctive perfume of menthol, herbs, cedar, and black fruits, the precociously supple and charming Figeac tends to show well young and mature quickly, despite the fact that it has the highest percentage of tannic and astringent Cabernet Sauvignon used in any major St.-Emilion. Most recent vintages (even those admirably concentrated) have tended to be fully ready for imbibing by the time they were 5 or 6 years old. Only the finest years of Figeac have had the cunning ability to last well in the bottle for 15 or more years. This shortcoming has not gone unnoticed.

Figeac's critics claim the wine could be profound, perhaps the greatest wine of the appellation, if the vineyard were harvested later and the maceration period extended beyond its surprisingly short 7 days. One of Libourne's most talented oenologists once told me that if he were making the wine, Figeac could be superior to Cheval Blanc.

Figeac has had a good record in off vintages. The 1977, 1974, and 1968, while hardly inspirational wines, were considerably better than most of their peers. I often have difficulty judging Figeac when it is less than a year old. At this infant stage the wine frequently tastes thin, stalky, and overtly vegetal, only to fill out and put on weight in its second year in the cask. Perhaps the high percentages of Cabernet Sauvignon and Cabernet Franc from the vineyard's gravel-based soil account for this peculiar characteristic.

Figeac is generally priced at the high level of the best Médoc second-growths, but the price seems fair and realistic given the quality of wines produced.

Visitors to St.-Emilion would be remiss in not making an appointment to visit Monsieur Manoncourt at his château. Be prepared for a beautiful country estate with enormous, tastefully done underground cellars, and a proprietor who fervently believes that Figeac should be spoken of not in the same breath as Cheval Blanc and Ausone, but before them! I did not taste it from the bottle but I would be remiss in not sharing with readers my enthusiasm for the 1990 Figeac; a profound wine that in time should rival the 1982 and 1964.

VINTAGES

1989—The first time I tasted the 1989 I rated it exceptional, and con-
·   cluded it was the best wine produced at this estate since the 1982.
86   It was a big, alcoholic, wonderfully concentrated, lavishly rich,
        intense sample. However, further tastings seemed to negate the
        early showing, with the wine merely performing in the good to
        very good category. In each instance, the wine displayed a lack
        of richness and revealed a slightly diluted finish, which suggest
        that the high crop yields and too short vatting time may have
        produced a wine that is no better than the third- or fourth-best
        Figeac of the decade. My experience has taught me that Figeac is
        among the most perplexing wines to evaluate young, and often
        can do a 180 degree turnabout in quality. With that in mind, these
        notes may prove to be conservative yet. Subsequent tastings have
        shown this to be a very good, rather than great, Figeac. Seductive
        and forward it may be, but some additional stuffing and extract
        could have resulted in a sublime wine. The 1990, tasted from cask
        in April 1990, blows the 1989 away. Anticipated maturity: 1992–
        2002. Last tasted, 4/91.

1988—The 1988 falls short of one's expectations for this property's
·   wines. It has a moderately deep ruby color, extremely high tan-
83   nins, and a tart, lean, austere, even overtly herbaceous character

that is followed by a light, surprisingly short finish. Anticipated maturity: Now–1997. Last tasted, 4/91.

1986—The 1986 is the best wine made at this estate since the 1982, and

·

90
is a much more powerful and interesting wine than the soft, fruity, charming 1985. It is typical of a great Figeac, with a mineral and herbaceous bouquet, intermingled with scents of smoky new oak and blackcurrants. On the palate, the wine displays fine extract, outstanding elegance and complexity, and a long, smooth finish, with soft, rather than aggressive, tannins. As is the case with virtually every vintage of Figeac, this wine shows surprisingly well young, but one can expect it to continue to fill out and evolve for at least another 10 years. Anticipated maturity: Now–2005. Last tasted, 3/90.

1985—The 1985 Figeac, while neither so deep nor so powerful as the

·

86
1982 or 1986, is still an exceptionally elegant, smoky, cedary-scented wine with a healthy dosage of new oak. On the palate, the wine is smooth, velvety, very forward, and seemingly ready to drink, but I am sure it will age well for 10–12 years. Anticipated maturity: Now–2002. Last tasted, 3/89.

1984—Figeac produced one of the best wines of St.-Emilion in 1984. The

·

85
high percentage of Cabernet Sauvignon and Cabernet Franc planted in the vineyards accounts for the wine's success in this difficult vintage. The 1984, which is fully ready to drink, is a smoky, cedary, herbaceous-scented wine, velvety on the palate and surprisingly fruity and deep. Anticipated maturity: Now–1994. Last tasted, 3/89.

1983—The 1983 is a very good bottle of Figeac, displaying soft, rich, ripe

·

87
fruit, medium body, soft tannins, and a smooth, velvety finish. It is surprisingly opulent and ready to drink. Anticipated maturity: Now–1997. Last tasted, 2/91.

1982—The 1982 appears to get fuller and fuller each time I go back to

·

92
it. I have already said I have had a tendency to underestimate Figeac young, when it seemed to lack concentration and structure. I have frequently regretted those early low marks, as the wine has an uncanny ability to fill out and display more richness and structure than it initially suggests. The 1982 is turning out to be the best Figeac made at this property since their glorious 1964. It reveals gobs of Cabernet fruit in its herbaceous, cedary, olive-like bouquet, but there is plenty of berry fruit behind it to balance out the herbaceousness. On the palate, the wine is dense and rich, has great extract and length, and is supple and precocious, but as I have already indicated, the wine has increasingly become

more and more structured as it has aged. It is a great bottle of
Figeac. Anticipated maturity: Now–2010. Last tasted, 2/91.

1981 —Not terribly impressive, either from the cask or in the bottle, the
·   1981 Figeac tastes like a rather dull, commercial sort of wine. It
82   is herbaceous, very soft, velvety, and medium bodied, with light
        tannins, and a low acidity that points to a rapid maturation. Antic-
        ipated maturity: Now–1994. Last tasted, 3/88.

1980 —A successful wine in this mediocre vintage, the 1980 Figeac, al-
·   ready fully mature, has a pleasant, light-intensity, cedary, spicy,
78   fruity aroma, soft, easy, round flavors that are marked by a slight
        vegetal element, and a surprisingly adequate finish. Anticipated
        maturity: Now–may be in decline. Last tasted, 3/84.

1979 —Now mature and fully ready to drink, the 1979 Figeac has a mod-
·   erately intense bouquet of soft, spicy, cedary fruit, adequate but
83   unexceptional richness and concentration, medium body, and a
        soft finish, with no tannins present. Certainly good, but for Fi-
        geac's class and price, a bit disappointing. Anticipated maturity:
        Now–may be in decline. Last tasted, 2/84.

1978 —Early in its life, the 1978 Figeac seemed very fruity, soft, rather
·   straightforward, and destined to be drunk young. The evolution
85   in the bottle has been marked by a deepening of flavor and a more
        pronounced richness, and the emergence of more body. At pres-
        ent, this wine is more impressive, but still a lightweight, fully-
        mature wine that lacks concentration. Anticipated maturity:
        Now–1995. Last tasted, 3/91.

1977 —One of the few successes in this poor vintage, somehow Figeac
·   has managed to produce a fruity, soft, and velvety wine, with
75   good body and adequate length. Anticipated maturity: Now–prob-
        ably in serious decline. Last tasted, 10/84.

1976 —One of the top successes of the vintage, the 1976 Figeac was
·   consistently impressive in tastings. A big, deep, cedary, ripe
86   fruity bouquet shows good complexity. On the palate, this lush,
        rich, full-bodied wine avoids the soupy softness and diluted char-
        acter of many wines produced in 1976. Round, concentrated, gen-
        erous, and fully mature, this was a lovely wine from the 1976
        vintage. Anticipated maturity: Now–probably in serious decline.
        Last tasted, 6/83.

1975 —This vintage typifies how Figeac behaves. In one of the most
·   tannic and hard vintages of Bordeaux in the last two decades,
89   Figeac was drinkable upon release, and has continued to evolve
        graciously in the bottle, displaying rich, velvety, weedy, black-
        currant fruit, and a long, lush, opulent finish. I remember think-

ing in the late seventies that the wine would probably not last this long, but in 1991 it is still at its peak, and exhibiting no signs of decline. There is some amber at the edge, but the overall impression is of a rich, full-bodied, concentrated, smoky, and herb-flavored Figeac that is probably the best wine made at this property between 1964 and 1982. Anticipated maturity: Now–2000. Last tasted, 1/91.

1974—Always a little stalky and too herbaceous, the 1974 Figeac was a
  ·   good wine from this generally poor vintage. Nicely colored, this
  75   medium-bodied wine has adequate fruit and a decent finish. Anticipated maturity: Now–probably in serious decline. Last tasted, 3/79.

1971—I had always thought this wine was lacking richness and depth,
  ·   and therefore was disappointing in a vintage that was generally
  84   quite good for the right-bank communes of St.-Emilion and Pomerol. But in 1984 I saw two examples of the 1971 Figeac that were ripe, roasted, deep, and deliciously fruity, making me wonder about the abnormal degree of bottle variation. Anticipated maturity: Now–probably in serious decline. Last tasted, 12/84.

1970—This wine has been fully mature for at least a decade, but it
  ·   continues to exhibit an herb-, mineral-, and plum-scented bou-
  90   quet, with ripe, lush, expansive flavors that appear to have put on a bit of weight and intensity since the mid-1980s. The tannins have completely melted away, and the overall impression is one of a round, generously endowed, silky-textured wine. I would opt for drinking it over the next 3–5 years, but I have been wrong so many times in the past about the aging potential of Figeac, this wine may last longer. Anticipated maturity: Now–1996. Last tasted, 1/91.

1966—A respectable effort from Figeac, nicely made, fruity, fragrant,
  ·   with scents of ripe fruit and cedarwood, this wine was fully ma-
  85   ture when last tasted, yet has the stuffing and balance to age well. Not as big or as full bodied as either the 1964 or 1970, the 1966 is elegant and attractive. Anticipated maturity: Now–1992. Last tasted, 1/82.

1964—After having gone through numerous regular-sized bottles and a
  ·   case of magnums, I can unequivocally say this is one of the two
  92   or three greatest Figeacs I have ever tasted. It has drunk fabulously well since the early seventies and is the type of wine that offers persuasive evidence that Figeac has one of the broadest windows of drinkability of any Bordeaux wine. The wine is still a great example of the 1964 vintage—opulent, with an intense, deep, rich, fruitiness, a velvety texture, and a sensational bouquet

of cedar, chestnuts, plums, herbs, and smoke. Extremely smooth
and ripe, it continues to defy the laws of aging. Anticipated maturity: Now–1995. Last tasted, 1/91.

1962—Still enjoyable, but beginning to lose its fruit and to brown signif-
  ·   icantly, the 1962 Figeac, a rather lightweight wine from this es-
80   tate, should be drunk up. Anticipated maturity: Now–probably in
       serious decline. Last tasted, 7/80.

1961—At one time I thought this wine to be the rival of Cheval Blanc,
  ·   but it is now beginning to lose some of its fruit, take on a slight
89   coarseness, and reveal its high alcohol in the finish. Nevertheless,
       there is still plenty of exotic, cedary, spicy, intense fruit, and the
       velvety texture is hard to resist. However, I have enjoyed this
       wine more in the past, and now believe it is ever so slowly crack-
       ing up. Anticipated maturity: Now–1995. Last tasted, 1/91.

OLDER VINTAGES

I have never had the good fortune to taste that many truly ancient
vintages of Figeac. The two best examples of Figeac I have had are the
1953 (rated 93 in 1988) and the 1959 (rated 91 in 1990). I have no idea
what the 1959 tasted like when it was young, but it has certainly outlived
the 1961 and has another 5–8 years of longevity—at least. It is a powerful, rich, roasted style of Figeac that typifies the hot 1959 vintage. As for
the 1953, it is a gloriously fragrant, super wine with a remarkable resemblance in this vintage to Cheval Blanc. It has no doubt been drinkable
for more than 30 years, but it exhibits no signs of imminent collapse.

LA FLEUR (Grand Cru)   AVERAGE

Production: 3,000 cases	Grape varieties: Merlot—75% Cabernet Franc—25%
Secondary label: none	
Vineyard size: 16 acres	Proprietor: Lily Lacoste
Time spent in barrels: 18–20 months	Average age of vines: 20 years
Evaluation of present classification: The quality equivalent of a Médoc Cru Bourgeois	
Plateau of maturity: 2–6 years following the vintage	

Lily Lacoste, the coproprietor of Château Pétrus and owner of Latour à
Pomerol, also runs this small estate in St.-Emilion. For whatever reason,
the wines have never exhibited a great deal of character, but rather, a
straightforward, soft, light, easygoing style. The wines are vinified and

distributed by the firm of Jean-Pierre Moueix. As a general rule, most vintages of La Fleur should be drunk in the first 7–8 years after the vintage as the wines rarely have exhibited the stuffing necessary for extended cellaring.

VINTAGES

1989 —This has never been one of my favorite wines of St.-Emilion, but
·   I have to admit that the 1989 is a jump up in quality. The tannins
83   are a little unripe and hard, but in the mouth the wine exhibits an
       attractive fruitiness, medium body, and some heady alcohol in
       the finish. It is straightforward and one-dimensional. Anticipated
       maturity: Now–1996. Last tasted, 4/91.
1988 —The 1988 is light in color, with insipid, monolithic, diluted flavors,
·   and a short, undistinguished finish. Last tasted, 4/91.
76

FLEUR-CARDINALE (Grand Cru)   GOOD

Production: 4,500 cases	Grape varieties: Merlot—70% Cabernet Franc—15% Cabernet Sauvignon—15%
Secondary label: none	
Vineyard size: 22.9 acres	Proprietor: Madame Claude Asséo
Time spent in barrels: 16 months	Average age of vines: 30 years
Evaluation of present classification: The quality equivalent of a Médoc Cru Bourgeois	
Plateau of maturity: 3–8 years following the vintage	

Fleur-Cardinale is made in a very satisfying, round, generous style that offers immediate satisfaction. The wine is rarely complex, but rather, solid and robust. The vineyard, located in the commune of Saint-Etienne de Lisse, is not well placed, but with a serious owner and the excellent counsel of the famed oenologist Michel Rolland, the quality of Fleur-Cardinale is consistent. The best recent vintages have included a fleshy, chunky 1985, a lighter, more tannic 1986, a fine 1988, and a soft, somewhat alcoholic, but seductive 1989.

LA FLEUR POURRET (Grand Cru)   GOOD

Production: 2,500 cases	Grape varieties:
	Merlot—50%
	Cabernet Sauvignon—50%
Secondary label: none	
Vineyard size: 16 acres	Proprietor: AXA Insurance
	Group
Time spent in barrels: 18 months	Average age of vines: 25 years
Evaluation of present classification: Should be considered for elevation to Grand Cru Classé status	
Plateau of maturity: 3–10 years following the vintage	

I have been immensely impressed on the rare occasions when I have been permitted to taste this wine produced just outside the walls of St.-Emilion. The gravelly soil in this area is reputed to produce richly fruity, deeply colored, fleshy wines of surprising distinction and flavor extraction. The vintages I have tasted—1982, 1985, and 1986—were all fleshy, well-endowed, satiny-smooth St.-Emilions for drinking in their first 7–8 years of life. I wish more of this wine would show up in the marketplace.

FOMBRAUGE (Grand Cru)   AVERAGE

Production: 27,000 cases	Grape varieties:
	Merlot—60%
	Cabernet Franc—30%
	Cabernet Sauvignon—10%
Secondary label: none	
Vineyard size: 125 acres	Proprietor: G.F.A. de
	Fombrauge
	Administrator: Charles Bygodt
Time spent in barrels: 16–18 months	Average age of vines: 25 years
Evaluation of present classification: The quality equivalent of a Médoc Cru Bourgeois	
Plateau of maturity: 3–12 years following the vintage	

This is another reliable, solidly made St.-Emilion that rarely ever hits great heights in quality. The vineyard, located in Saint-Christophe des Bardes, sits primarily on a limestone soil base, with a northerly exposition. Perhaps that explains why ripening in cold years is a problem at this property. Improvements have been made at Fombrauge, but yields are still too high, as the wines often lack grip and stuffing. Nevertheless, if you are looking for a cleanly made, straightforward, fruity, softer style of St.-Emilion, this is a property worthy of consideration. Prices are realistic, even surprisingly fair, for the quality of the wine. The only caveat when buying Fombrauge is that vintages since the early eighties should be consumed in their first decade of life.

FONPLÉGADE (Grand Cru Classé)   GOOD

Production: 9,000 cases	Grape varieties: Merlot—60% Cabernet Franc—35% Cabernet Sauvignon—5%
Secondary label: Château Côtes Trois Moulins	
Vineyard size: 44.5 acres	Proprietor: The Armand Moueix family
Time spent in barrels: 18 months	Average age of vines: 25 years
Evaluation of present classification: The quality equivalent of a Médoc Cru Bourgeois, although certain vintages are the quality equivalent of a Médoc fifth-growth	
Plateau of maturity: 3–12 years following the vintage	

Fonplégade merits greater renown than it has received. The vineyard is beautifully situated on the southerly slopes of St.-Emilion, not far from the famous estate of Magdelaine. The château, built in the late nineteenth century by the proprietor—a *négociant* by the name of Boisard—is one of the more attractive of the appellation. Since 1953, the property has been owned by the Armand Moueix family.

The style of wine produced at Fonplégade has not changed over the years. One of the best wines from the Armand Moueix portfolio, it is usually darkly colored, with a great deal of rich, plummy, black cherry fruit, a dash of smoky, toasty, new oak, and a soft, luscious texture. It is a wine that can be drunk young, but most vintages have the potential to last for 10 or more years. In the St.-Emilion hierarchy, Fonplégade remains an underrated wine.

VINTAGES

1989—The 1989 is an amply endowed, generously fruity, alcoholic wine
·   that should last for up to a decade. But it lacks the extra dimen-
85   sion of concentration and complexity the top wines of the appel-
          lation achieved in this vintage. Nevertheless, there is still plenty

to like. The wine is round, supple, and already a delight to drink. Anticipated maturity: Now–1997. Last tasted, 4/91.

1988—The 1988 does not possess the ripeness and fruit necessary to
· stand up to its lean, sinewy, attenuated character. The astringent,
80 dry tannins in the finish also suggest that the balance between fruit and tannin is suspect. Anticipated maturity: 1992–1996. Last tasted, 4/91.

1986—For whatever reason, the 1986 did not show well from cask, and
· out of bottle it remains a hard, extremely tannic, stern wine that
78 lacks charm and seems short in the finish. Perhaps it will blossom with further aging, but it appears to be a gamble at present. Last tasted, 3/90.

1985—The 1985 Fonplégade is a typical yet very good example of the
· 1985 vintage. Richly fruity, plump, tasty, fat, this wine is medium
85 to full bodied. Anticipated maturity: Now–1997. Last tasted, 3/90.

1982—Reminiscent of this estate's lovely 1970 and 1975 wines, the 1982
· has good dark ruby color and a moderately intense bouquet of
86 roasted chestnuts and ripe fruit. On the palate, the wine is medium to full bodied, exhibits good, ripe tannin, fine length, and aging potential of 8–12 years. Anticipated maturity: Now–2000. Last tasted, 1/90.

1981—The 1981 is not as robust as some of this château's previous
· efforts, but displays good color, a spicy, almond-like, plummy
78 bouquet, and soft, nicely textured flavors. Anticipated maturity: Now–1993. Last tasted, 3/88.

1976—Starting to show the telltale sign of old age—a brown color—the
· 1976 Fonplégade is still drinking well, with a rich, ripe berryish
76 bouquet, soft, creamy, pleasant, round flavors, and no tannins in the finish. Anticipated maturity: Now–probably in serious decline. Last tasted, 6/87.

1975—Fully mature, but holding nicely, the 1975 Fonplégade is a fat,
· plummy, very fruity wine that has good body, a fleshy texture,
83 and an alcoholic, soft finish. Anticipated maturity: Now–1994. Last tasted, 3/83.

1970—This is a typical Fonplégade—fat, very fruity, succulent, and
· immensely satisfying rather than cerebral or complex. While it
84 still continues to offer a mouthful of corpulent St.-Emilion, it is now beginning to lose its fruit. Anticipated maturity: Now–maybe in decline. Last tasted, 12/82.

1961—Still alive and well, the 1961 Fonplégade has no discernible tan-
· nins left, but plenty of viscous, ripe, savory, supple fruit, full
87 body, and a long, silky, velvety finish. Anticipated maturity: Now–1997. Last tasted from a magnum, 11/89.

FONROQUE (Grand Cru Classé)   GOOD

Production: 8,000 cases	Grape varieties: Merlot—85% Cabernet Franc—15%
Secondary label: none	
Vineyard size: 44.5 acres	Proprietor: Jean-Pierre Moueix Administrator: Jean-Jacques Moueix
Time spent in barrels: 18–20 months	Average age of vines: 30 years
Evaluation of present classification: The quality equivalent of a Médoc Cru Bourgeois	
Plateau of maturity: 4–12 years following the vintage	

Fonroque is situated in an isolated location north and west of St.-Emilion. The vineyard is owned by the highly respected Libourne firm of Jean-Pierre Moueix and run by Jean-Jacques Moueix. While the Moueix name is more commonly identified with such famous estates of St.-Emilion and Pomerol as Pétrus, Trotanoy, and Magdelaine, the wine of Fonroque usually represents an excellent value, as well as being an interesting and distinctive style that is always vinified properly.

In style it tends to be of the robust, rich, tannic, medium-bodied school of St.-Emilions. It can take aging quite well, and in good vintages actually needs cellaring of at least 2–3 years before being consumed.

VINTAGES

1989—The 1989 is excellent, exhibiting the size, richness, and heady
·   alcohol content of the vintage, as well as an opulent, fleshy tex-
86   ture. This larger-scaled Fonroque should make delicious drinking
       for the next 5–9 years. Anticipated maturity: Now–2000. Last
       tasted, 4/91.

1988—The 1988 displays underlying ripe fruit, spicy new oak, good acid-
·   ity, and some aggressive tannins in the finish. It is a pleasant but
83   an essentially undistinguished effort. Anticipated maturity: 1992–
       2000. Last tasted, 4/91.

1983—A typical Fonroque, broodingly dark with a high (but soft) tannin
·   content, this wine has layers of ripe fruit, is medium bodied, and
85   should have a fine future. Anticipated maturity: Now–1998. Last
       tasted, 3/88.

1982—The 1982 Fonroque is made in an open-knit style, with an in-
·   tensely fruity, spicy, plummy fruitiness. This full-bodied wine has
85   dark ruby color with some amber, a velvety texture, and a soft,

generous finish. It is big, plump, and decadently fruity with plenty
of ripe tannins. It should be drunk over the next several years.
Anticipated maturity: Now–1995. Last tasted, 1/90.

1981—A chunky sort of wine, the 1981 Fonroque has an open-knit,
   ·   fruity, oaky, earthy bouquet, a rustic, rich, full-bodied texture,
  84   and good length. Anticipated maturity: Now–may be in decline.
        Last tasted, 6/84.

1979—A precociously styled Fonroque, easy to drink, soft, not as pow-
   ·   erful or as concentrated as usual, but pleasant and fully mature.
  74   Anticipated maturity: Now–may be in decline. Last tasted, 4/83.

1978—A trifle clumsy and awkward when young, this full-bodied, nicely
   ·   concentrated wine has developed well in the bottle. It possesses
  83   a spicy, ripe plummy bouquet, soft, fat, chewy flavors, and some
        light tannin in the finish. Anticipated maturity: Now–1992. Last
        tasted, 3/86.

FRANC-MAYNE (Grand Cru Classé)   GOOD

Production: 3,500 cases	Grape varieties: Merlot—70% Cabernet Franc—15% Cabernet Sauvignon—15%
Secondary label: none Vineyard size: 19 acres	Proprietor: AXA Insurance Group Administrator: Jean-Michel Cazes
Time spent in barrels: 18 months	Average age of vines: 20 years
Evaluation of present classification: The quality equivalent of a Médoc Cru Bourgeois	
Plateau of maturity: 3–8 years following the vintage	

The huge insurance company AXA acquired Franc-Mayne in 1987. They
very wisely hired the proprietor of Château Lynch-Bages, Jean-Michel
Cazes, and his talented winemaker, Daniel Llose, to oversee the renovation of the estate and the making of the wine.

Franc-Mayne is by far the best known of the St.-Emilion châteaux with
the word *Franc* in their name. There are seventeen other châteaux with
Franc as part of their name, although none produce wines of the quality
level of Franc-Mayne. The vineyard is located in the northwest section
of the St.-Emilion appellation, on the same hillside that runs into the
appellation called the Côtes de Francs. (Before 1987, the property was
controlled by the Libourne *négociant* Theillasoubre.)

This has never been one of my favorite St.-Emilions, although better things are expected under the Cazes management. Nevertheless, this is a wine that requires consumption within the first 7–8 years of life.

VINTAGES

1989—This is the darkest-colored wine I have ever seen from Franc-
·　　Mayne. Still with a great deal of purple in its color, this spicy,
85　　slightly musty-scented wine has plenty of ripe cassis fruit, a soft
　　　texture, low acidity, and some alcohol in the finish. It should be
　　　drunk in its first 5–6 years of life. Anticipated maturity: Now–
　　　1995. Last tasted, 4/91.

1988—An attractive, spicy, intensely herbaceous nose is followed by a
·　　wine that is relatively hollow, attenuated, and short in the finish.
79　　The color is sound, but the overall impression is uninspiring.
　　　Anticipated maturity: 1992–1998. Last tasted, 4/91.

1986—The 1986 Franc-Mayne is a fruity, tasty, plummy St.-Emilion with
·　　an absence of complexity, yet satisfying flavors and immediate
79　　appeal. Anticipated maturity: Now–1994. Last tasted, 3/89.

LA GAFFELIÈRE (Premier Grand Cru Classé)　　　VERY GOOD

Production: 7,000 cases	Grape varieties: Merlot—60% Cabernet Franc—30% Cabernet Sauvignon—10%
Secondary labels: Clos la Gaffelière and Château de Roquefort	
Vineyard size: 53.3 acres	Proprietor: The de Malet-Roquefort family
Time spent in barrels: 20–22 months	Average age of vines: 40 years
Evaluation of present classification: Since 1985, La Gaffelière has merited its Premier Grand Cru Classé status; prior to 1985, the wine was inconsistent	
Plateau of maturity: 5–15 years following the vintage	

The impressive four-story château and cellars of La Gaffelière sit opposite each other just outside the walls of St.-Emilion. Historically, this is one of the most distinguished properties in all of Bordeaux because the de Malet-Roquefort family has owned the property for over four centuries. The current proprietor, Comte Léo de Malet-Roquefort, is both an experienced rider and hunter; not surprising, given that members of his family—descendants of the Normans—were honored by William the Conqueror for their heroism and fighting skills at the battle of Hastings.

La Gaffelière, however, has been a perplexing wine to evaluate. The wine was well made during the sixties, and the 1970 was impressive. However, after 1970 it took 12 years for another top-notch vintage of La Gaffelière to emerge from the cellars. I am not sure why this happened, because the vineyard is well situated on limestone/clay soils, and on every one of my visits I have been impressed by the cleanliness of the winemaking facilities, and the dedication of the Count and his staff. Nevertheless, there were far too few wines to get excited about prior to the mid-1980s. Since then, La Gaffelière has been making wines befitting its status as one of St.-Emilion's elite Premiers Grands Crus Classés.

The style aimed for at this estate is one of elegance and tenderness. This will never be a large-scaled, tannic monster of a wine, but when the wine is at its best, it will have a degree of finesse generally unmatched by other St.-Emilions.

Comte de Malet-Roquefort is also the proprietor of the up-and-coming St.-Emilion property, Tertre-Daugay.

VINTAGES

1989 · 89 —Not since 1970 has La Gaffeliére made so promising a wine as the 1989. The vines of this well-placed vineyard never produce block-buster wines, but can, when well made, turn out stylish, graceful, yet still concentrated wines that balance power and finesse. The 1989 is such an effort. The bouquet of black cherries, spring flowers, minerals, and toasty new oak is enthralling. In the mouth, the wine is medium to full bodied and shows good acidity for the vintage, relatively high yet soft tannins, and a long, velvety, rich finish. This is a very stylish yet authoritative La Gaffelière. Antic-ipated maturity: 1996–2010. Last tasted, 4/91.

1988 · 87 —The 1988 is well made, less impressively sized if compared to the 1989, but still an elegant, understated, charming wine that has avoided the excesses of tannin so prevalent in many 1988s. Antic-ipated maturity: 1992–2000. Last tasted, 4/91.

1986 · 87 —The 1986 La Gaffelière has the potential to be one of the proper-ty's best wines. It is a rich, elegantly rendered wine with a bou-quet of spicy new oak, cedar, and blackcurrants. Medium to full bodied, with wonderful focus and grip, this stylish, graceful wine should drink well for the next 12–15 years. Anticipated maturity: Now–2006. Last tasted, 3/91.

1985—The 1985 has a full-intensity, spicy, herbaceous, richly fruity bou-
· quet, medium body, soft tannins, and a supple finish. Anticipated
86 maturity: Now–1997. Last tasted, 3/91.

1984—Very light in color, with a faint perfume of candied, berry fruit
· and new oak, the 1984 is smooth and has decent ripeness. Antic-
76 ipated maturity: Now–1992. Last tasted, 3/89.

1983—In early tastings, this was certainly not one of the stars of the
· vintage, but is a good wine, clearly better than many of the below-
84 par efforts from this property in the seventies. Medium dark ruby
with a fine bouquet of crushed berry fruit, this is a medium-
bodied, elegant, moderately tannic wine. Anticipated maturity:
Now–1995. Last tasted, 1/89.

1982—Early in its life, this wine was consistently inconsistent, but it has
· settled down in the bottle to reveal a rich, medium- to full-bodied,
87 relatively opulent style of wine with the best concentration of any
La Gaffelière I have tasted—save for the 1989. The early bottle
variation seems to be a thing of the past. This delicious, fully
mature wine should continue to provide excellent drinking for at
least another decade. Anticipated maturity: Now–2000. Last
tasted, 11/90.

1981—This wine has lost what little fruit it once possessed and now
· comes across as unacceptably lean, attenuated, compact, and
72 lacking charm and fruit. Its future is suspect. Last tasted, 11/90.

1979—Fully mature, this relatively shallow-looking La Gaffelière has a
· moderately intense, berry, vanilla, herbaceous-scented bouquet,
76 round, pleasant, light-bodied flavors, and a soft, clean finish. It is
unlikely to get any better. Last tasted, 11/90.

1978—Extremely herbaceous to the point of being vegetal, with soft,
· muddled, inadequately concentrated flavors, this wine is begin-
67 ning its decline and should be consumed now if at all. Last tasted,
11/90.

1975—This wine has turned out far better than I initially thought it
· would. It has none of the hard tannins so typical of the 1975
79 vintage, but rather, a soft, elegant, medium-bodied, ripe, fruity
nose and flavors, complemented nicely by some vanillin-scented
new oak. The wine displays some amber at the edge, and given
its lightness and softness, it should be consumed. Anticipated
maturity: Now–1994. Last tasted, 11/90.

1971—In the first edition of this book I indicated that this wine was on
· the verge of cracking up. It is now in full decline, as the decaying,
68 mushroom-like, woody, slightly oxidized bouquet suggests. In the
mouth, the wine is feeble, lacks concentration, and finishes with

noticeable alcohol and acidity. It is past its prime. Last tasted, 11/90.

1970—This has always been one of the best La Gaffelières produced during the sixties and seventies. The wine is still relatively rich
·
86   and elegant, with a bouquet of smoky, plummy fruit. In the mouth, the wine is round, with a silky texture, and a lush, medium-bodied finish. It has been fully mature for well over a decade, but has lost none of its fruit or charm. Anticipated maturity: Now–1995. Last tasted, 11/90.

1966—A straightforward sort of wine, La Gaffelière's 1966 is lean, austere, with some elegance and charm, but compact and rather one-
·
78   dimensional. It is fully mature. Anticipated maturity: Now–may be in decline. Last tasted, 10/78.

1964—Diffuse, shallow, awkward flavors seem to struggle with each other. The medicinal, bizarre bouquet suggests something went
·
60   afoul during the making of this wine. Last tasted, 4/80.

1961—When I last wrote about this wine, I commented that the wine required drinking up, but a bottle I tasted in France in 1990 had
·
85   more depth and freshness. It could easily have held up for another 7–8 years. Medium ruby with some amber/rust color at the edge, the bouquet exhibits the vintage's telltale intensity and opulence. In the mouth, the wine is ripe and full, with an underlying spicy, mineral-like fruitiness. The finish is long and alcoholic. It should be drunk up, but based on the most recent bottle I tasted, it could hold up to another 4–5 years of cellaring. Anticipated maturity: Now–1995. Last tasted, 11/90.

OLDER VINTAGES

The two finest vintages I have seen of La Gaffelière included a deliciously elegant, round, very perfumed 1953 (rated 89 in 1988), and a rich, fat, surprisingly intense, full-bodied 1947 (rated 88 and drunk when I celebrated my 40th birthday in 1987).

GODEAU (Grand Cru)   GOOD

Production: 2,000 cases	Grape varieties: Merlot—60% Cabernet Sauvignon—35% Cabernet Franc—5%
Secondary label: none	
Vineyard size: 10 acres	Proprietor: Georges Litvine
Time spent in barrels: 18–22 months	Average age of vines: 25 years
Evaluation of present classification: The quality equivalent of a good Médoc Cru Bourgeois, perhaps superior	
Plateau of maturity: 5–15 years following the vintage	

Since the Belgian industrialist Georges Litvine took over this property in 1978, there have been major renovations to the cellars, as well as an undeniable commitment to higher quality. Much of the wine is sold directly to consumers who visit the property.

Vintages I have tasted, 1988 and 1989, exhibited a great deal of intensity, plenty of muscular tannin and body, and glycerin. This may well be a property to keep an eye on during the nineties.

GRAND-BARRAIL LAMARZELLE-FIGEAC
(Grand Cru Classé)   AVERAGE

Production: 8,500 cases	Grape varieties: Merlot—75% Cabernet Franc—15% Cabernet Sauvignon—10%
Secondary label: Lamarzelle-Figeac	
Vineyard size: 50 acres	Proprietor: Association Carrère
Time spent in barrels: 18–20 months in both vats and small barrels	Average age of vines: 25 years
Evaluation of present classification: The quality equivalent of a Médoc Cru Bourgeois	
Plateau of maturity: 3–8 years following the vintage	

This well-situated property, with its lovely château set amidst numerous huge trees, was part of the vast Figeac estate during the nineteenth century. The vineyards are located south of Figeac on light, sandy soil. My experience with the wine is limited, but those vintages I have tasted suggest this is a very early-maturing, soft, fruity, relatively undistinguished wine. Given its tongue-twisting name and uninspiring quality, it is not an estate that is likely to be remembered in export markets.

GRAND-CORBIN (Grand Cru Classé) AVERAGE

Production: 6,000 cases	Grape varieties: Merlot—65% Cabernet Sauvignon—30% Cabernet Franc—5%
Secondary label: Tour du Pin Franc	
Vineyard size: 32.1 acres	Proprietor: G.F.A. Giraud
Time spent in barrels: 12–18 months	Average age of vines: 25 years
Evaluation of present classification: The quality equivalent of a Médoc Cru Bourgeois	
Plateau of maturity: 3–8 years following the vintage	

Grand-Corbin, a well-situated property on the Pomerol/St.-Emilion border, consistently produces round, chunky, generally well-colored St.-Emilions that require drinking in their first decade. The Girauds, an ancient family originally from Pomerol, own Grand-Corbin and, like their nearby neighbor, Figeac, employ a relatively high percentage of Cabernet Sauvignon in the blend. This works well when the Cabernet ripens fully, but in years that it does not, there is a tendency for Grand-Corbin to come across as too herbaceous, even vegetal. The best recent vintages I have tasted included an excellent 1985, followed by a soft, alcoholic, fleshy 1989 that will not make old bones, but will certainly provide delicious drinking in the first 7–8 years of life.

GRAND-CORBIN-DESPAGNE (Grand Cru Classé)   AVERAGE

Production: 10,000 cases	Grape varieties:
	Merlot—70%
	Cabernet Franc—25%
	Cabernet Sauvignon—5%
Secondary label: Laporte	
Vineyard size: 64 acres	Proprietor: The Despagne family
Time spent in barrels: 18–20 months	Average age of vines: 55 years
Evaluation of present classification: The quality equivalent of a good Médoc Cru Bourgeois	
Plateau of maturity: 5–12 years following the vintage	

Despite the fact that the renowned oenologist Michel Rolland oversees the vinification and upbringing of this wine, I have always found Grand-Corbin-Despagne to be a wine highly charged in tannins and too rustic for its own good. Nevertheless, if you like your claret on the big, beefy, macho side, this wine will appeal to you. There is no questioning its aging potential; even light, soft vintages such as 1979 and 1985 are capable of lasting for at least a decade. The vineyard is situated near the Grand-Corbin (owned by the Giraud family) and adjacent to the appellation of Pomerol. With perhaps a less robustly styled wine, this estate could be a candidate for promotion in the St.-Emilion hierarchy.

GRAND-MAYNE (Grand Cru Classé)   VERY GOOD

Production: 10,000 cases	Grape varieties:
	Merlot—75%
	Cabernet Franc—20%
	Cabernet Sauvignon—5%
Secondary label: Les Plantes du Mayne	
Vineyard size: 47 acres	Proprietor: Jean-Pierre Nony
Time spent in barrels: 18–22 months	Average age of vines: 25 years
Evaluation of present classification: While inconsistent, when Grand-Mayne does everything right, it can easily compete with the better of the Premiers Grands Crus Classés of St.-Emilion; a serious candidate for elevation in any new classification of the wines of St.-Emilion; the quality equivalent of a Médoc fifth-growth	
Plateau of maturity: 3–12 years following the vintage	

The famed authority on the soils of Pomerol and St.-Emilion, Professor Enjalbert, has made it very clear in his lectures and other works that Grand-Mayne possesses one of the most privileged sites in all of St.-Emilion. The exceptionally high altitude—55 meters above sea level—and soil base, consisting primarily of clay and limestone intermixed with iron deposits, make this vineyard potentially one of the best of the entire appellation. Aesthetically, the magnificent vanilla ice cream–colored château has been totally renovated and is a striking sight to behold on a bright, blue-skied day.

The wines have gone from one strength to another during the eighties, with the brilliant Libourne oenologist Michel Rolland asserting his wine-making philosophy. The results are some of the more opulent and richer wines now being made in St.-Emilion. This is a wine that can be exceptionally full bodied, with gobs of glycerin because of the superb vineyard soil and great exposition the vineyard enjoys. Since 1975, Grand-Mayne has been fermented in temperature-controlled stainless-steel tanks. In the mid-1980s the percentage of new oak was increased to 70%, which —to me—seems like a perfect marriage to balance out the rich, intense fruit character of this wine.

Grand-Mayne is one of the up-and-coming stars of the appellation, yet prices have remained very reasonable, a fact that should be put to good use by wine consumers.

If my enthusiasm for Grand-Mayne seems excessive, consider the fact that the late Baron Philippe de Rothschild, after tasting the 1955 Grand-Mayne at a restaurant in Belgium, immediately placed an order for several cases, offering to replace the Grand-Mayne with a similar number of bottles of the 1955 Mouton-Rothschild!

VINTAGES

1989—It is unfortunate this property is not better known, as this is a wine of hedonism at a most decadent level. The 1989 has an
90   almost overwhelming bouquet of sweet, jammy black fruits and spices intertwined with the toasty scent of new oak barrels. In fact, the bouquet seemed to resemble a great vintage of the highly fashionable, seductive Cru Bourgeois from St.-Estèphe, Haut-Marbuzet. In the mouth, this wine's exuberance and opulence are nicely framed by plenty of toasty new oak, which gives the wine structure as well as definition. Quite a flamboyant, intensely flavored, rich, full-bodied wine, look for the 1989 Grand-Mayne to provide thrilling drinking over the next decade. No, it will not make old bones, but if you consider wine to be a beverage of pleasure rather than a museum piece, then you should be search-

ing out a case of this thrill-a-sip wine. Anticipated maturity: 1993–2005. Last tasted, 4/91.

1988 —The 1988 is nearly as dramatic a show-stopper as the 1989. It is a big, alcoholic, obvious wine displaying tremendously intense, new
87 oaky, black plum-like fruitiness, and fleshy, chewy flavors. The proprietor has managed to keep the aggressive tannin levels of the 1988 vintage in check, and the result is a meaty, chewy wine that should drink beautifully for a decade or more. Anticipated maturity: 1992–2003. Last tasted, 4/91.

1987 —Grand-Mayne made one of the most successful wines of this unfairly maligned vintage. Suprisingly dark ruby with a pronounced,
85 rich cassis bouquet and soft, generously endowed flavors, soft tannins, and low acidity, this is a wine to drink over the near term. Anticipated maturity: Now–1996. Last tasted, 4/91.

1986 —The 1986 Grand-Mayne has performed extremely well, with a full-intensity bouquet of cedary, ripe fruit and spicy oak that is fol-
87 lowed on the palate by excellent depth, plenty of extract, and a long, tannic, powerful, and impressive finish. Anticipated maturity: 1993–2002. Last tasted, 3/90.

1985 —The 1985 has very good color, a moderately intense bouquet of spicy oak and ripe fruit, medium body, well-focused, expansive
86 flavors, and an overall elegant feel to it. Anticipated maturity: Now–1994. Last tasted, 3/89.

GRAND-PONTET (Grand Cru Classé)   GOOD

Production: 7,000 cases	Grape varieties: Merlot—75% Cabernet Franc—15% Cabernet Sauvignon—10%
Secondary label: none	
Vineyard size: 37 acres	Proprietor: The Bécot family
Time spent in barrels: 22 months	Average age of vines: 50 years
Evaluation of present classification: For decades this was a perennial underachiever, but since 1988 the quality has significantly improved	
Plateau of maturity: Before 1988, 3–7 years following the vintage; since 1988, 6–15 years following the vintage	

Grand-Pontet, owned by St.-Emilion's Bécot family, is situated next door to their more renowned property, Château Beau Séjour. The vineyard sits in the highly regarded western limestone plateau of St.-Emilion. For years, many of St.-Emilion's cognoscenti have suggested that this is a property that, with improvements and a more strict selection, could emerge as a potential candidate for elevation to Premier Grand Cru Classé status. Improvements have indeed been made, and the 1988 and 1989 are two of the best efforts to emerge from this estate in decades.

It is unlikely, in my opinion, that this property would merit elevation to Premier Grand Cru Classé status, but there is no doubt that the quality has risen, and Grand-Pontet is now a property to watch.

VINTAGES

1989—Grand-Pontet tends to produce an overt and obvious style of St.-
·   Emilion that packs a great deal of toasty new oak in its moderately
86   endowed, fleshy flavors. The 1989 is lighter than many other
       wines in this vintage, displaying some dilution in the mid-palate.
       Otherwise, it is an alcoholic, chunky, softly styled St.-Emilion.
       Anticipated maturity: Now–1997. Last tasted, 4/91.

1988—The 1988 has an indifferent bouquet of new oak and some vague
·   spicy, ripe fruit. On the palate, it is soft, nicely concentrated, but
81   somewhat one-dimensional and simple. Anticipated maturity:
       Now–1996. Last tasted, 4/91.

1986—The 1986 Grand-Pontet is an obvious St.-Emilion with soft,
·   plummy fruit, a heady, alcoholic finish, and immediate appeal.
83   Anticipated maturity: Now–1997. Last tasted, 3/90.

1985—The 1985 is a light, simple, fruity wine without a great deal of
·   body, but with good, straightforward appeal. Anticipated matu-
77   rity: Now–1994. Last tasted, 3/89.

LA GRAVE-FIGEAC (Grand Cru)   AVERAGE

Production: 2,500 cases	Grape varieties:
	Merlot—75%
	Cabernet Franc—25%
Secondary label: none	
Vineyard size: 10 acres	Proprietor: Georges Meunier
Time spent in barrels: 18 months	Average age of vines: 30 years

Evaluation of present classification: Until 1985, this was a perennial overachiever in the appellation; since 1985, the quality equivalent of a Médoc Cru Bourgeois

Plateau of maturity: 3–8 years following the vintage

This property proved to be quite a discovery when I first tasted the 1982 and 1983—both of which were still drinking beautifully in 1991. However, after 1983, the production soared and the wines became more loosely structured and lacked the concentration and character of the previous vintages. The vineyard is extremely well located on the Pomerol border near the great estates of Figeac and Cheval Blanc.

VINTAGES

1986—As with the 1985, the proprietor made entirely too much wine
· from his vineyard, and the resulting dilution has shown up in the
74 final product. The 1986 is soft and shallow, without a finish, and with little aging potential. *Quel dommage!* Last tasted, 3/88.

1985—The quality of La Grave-Figeac slipped in 1985 due to too much
· wine being produced. The 1985 lacks depth, structure, and com-
80 plexity, but it does offer a straightforward appeal. Anticipated maturity: Now–1994. Last tasted, 3/88.

1983—This big, rich, concentrated, medium-bodied wine could easily be
· confused with one of the better Premiers Grands Crus Classés of
87 St.-Emilion. Fruity, still black/ruby in color, with oodles of ripe blackberry fruit, soft tannins, and a spicy, long finish, this is a delicious wine that has been fully mature for at least 3–4 years. It requires drinking. Anticipated maturity: Now–1995. Last tasted, 3/91.

1982—Sitting opposite Cheval Blanc, this estate has produced a very
· lush, rich, full-bodied, deeply concentrated St.-Emilion. Dark
87 colored, with a rich blackcurrant-and-herb-scented bouquet, as well as a velvety texture, this wine is one of the great values of the vintage. Anticipated maturity: Now–1994. Last tasted, 3/91.

1981—This is a delicious St.-Emilion, big, concentrated, fleshy, richly
· fruity, savory, and spicy. Full bodied, with light to medium tan-
84 nins, this wine was a lovely mouthful of claret in the mid-1980s. Anticipated maturity: Now–may be in decline. Last tasted, 11/84.

GUADET ST.-JULIEN (Grand Cru Classé)   AVERAGE

Production: 2,000 cases	Grape varieties:
	Merlot—75%
	Cabernet Franc—25%
Secondary label: none	
Vineyard size: 13.5 acres	Proprietor: Robert Lignac
Time spent in barrels: 18–20 months	Average age of vines: 25 years
Evaluation of present classification: The quality equivalent of a Médoc Cru Bourgeois	
Plateau of maturity: 3–9 years following the vintage	

This property's vineyard is located north of the town of St.-Emilion on the limestone plateau, but the cellars and winemaking facility are in St.-Emilion. The style of wine produced is soft, round, somewhat monolithic and straightforward, but pleasant and attractive in top vintages. Buyers are advised to drink the wine when it is young.

VINTAGES

1989—The 1989 lacks fruits and is extremely hard, hollow, and astrin-
·   gent. Last tasted, 4/91.
72

1988—The 1988 is lean and compact. It has a bit more weight, but the
·   overbearing tannin levels makes for a stark, austere, forbiddingly
73   severe-styled wine. Last tasted, 4/91

HAUT BRISSON (Grand Cru)   GOOD

Production: 7,000 cases	Grape varieties:
	Merlot—60%
	Cabernet Sauvignon—30%
	Cabernet Franc—10%
Secondary label: none	
Vineyard size: 32 acres	Proprietor: Yves Blanc
Time spent in barrels: 18–20 months	Average age of vines: 22 years
Evaluation of present classification: The quality equivalent of a good Médoc Cru Bourgeois	
Plateau of maturity: 3–10 years following the vintage	

For decades the wines of Haut Brisson were vinified by the big coopera-tive in St.-Emilion. However, since 1974, they have been made by the proprietor and are now estate-bottled. Nearly the entire production is sold in export markets, particularly in northern Europe, England, and the United States. It is one of the tastier St.-Emilion Grands Crus, and in my estimation, based on vintages such as 1982, 1983, 1985, and 1988, it deserves to be elevated to a Grand Cru Classé. Prices for Haut Brisson remain among the most realistic of the entire St.-Emilion appellation.

HAUT-CORBIN (Grand Cru Classé)   GOOD

Production: 3,500 cases	Grape varieties: Merlot—70% Cabernet Sauvignon—20% Cabernet Franc—10%
Secondary label: none	
Vineyard size: 15 acres	Proprietor: SMABPT Administrator: Domaines Cordier
Time spent in barrels: 18–20 months	Average age of vines: 20 years
Evaluation of present classification: The quality equivalent of a good Médoc Cru Bourgeois	
Plateau of maturity: 3–8 years following the vintage	

Haut-Corbin, with a vineyard situated on relatively light, sandy soil, near the border of the appellation of Montagne-St.-Emilion, has completely changed the style of its winemaking since its acquisition in 1986 by the huge conglomerate called SMABPT. This syndicate wisely installed the Cordier firm to make and commercialize the wine, and the results have been increasingly better and more interesting products. The percentage of new oak has been increased to one-third, and under the brilliant leadership of Cordier's oenologist, Georges Pauli, the wines of Haut-Corbin have taken on richer, more intense flavors.

This property, always an obscure St.-Emilion, is now considered to make one of the better wines among the St.-Emilion Grands Crus Classés.

VINTAGES

1989—The 1989 is a chewy, intense, full-bodied wine with considerable
·   power. The overwhelming character offers a huge amount of ripe
87   black fruit, nicely buttressed by toasty new oak and the scent and
        taste of herbs. There is plenty of alcohol in the finish. This long,
        rich, spicy, intensely flavored wine should continue to drink well
        for at least another decade. Anticipated maturity: 1992–2001.
        Last tasted, 4/91.

1988—While the 1988 does not have the size or alcohol levels of the
·   1989, it is perhaps a more classic example, with deep ruby/purple
86   color, a big, spicy, licorice, herbaceous, cassis-scented bouquet,
        medium body, and plenty of tannin in the relatively long finish.
        Anticipated maturity: 1993–2001. Last tasted, 4/91.

HAUT-SARPE (Grand Cru Classé)   GOOD

Production: 6,000 cases	Grape varieties: Merlot—70% Cabernet Franc—30%
Secondary label: none	
Vineyard size: 30 acres	Proprietor: Joseph Janoueix
Time spent in barrels: 20–22 months	Average age of vines: 30 years
Evaluation of present classification: The quality equivalent of a good Médoc Cru Bourgeois	
Plateau of maturity: 5–12 years following the vintage	

Haut-Sarpe is a reliable St.-Emilion owned by the Libourne *négociant* firm of J. Janoueix. The château, which is one of the most beautiful of the region, sits to the northeast of St.-Emilion next to the highly regarded estate of Balestard-La-Tonnelle. The style of wine produced here is darkly colored, rustic, generously flavored, and usually firmly tannic. In good vintages, the wine should be cellared for at least 5–6 years.

VINTAGES

1989—The 1989 is compact, lacks dimension and flavor breadth, has
·   very good color, but seems to have been made from grapes that
81   were picked a bit too green and unripe. Anticipated maturity:
       1992-2000. Last tasted, 4/91.

1988—The 1988 exhibits a little more fruit in the nose, displays some
·   attractive ripeness on the palate, but finishes with some mean-
82   spirited, aggressive tannins, which suggest that this wine should
       be consumed early on for its exuberance rather than overall bal-
       ance. Anticipated maturity: Now–2000. Last tasted, 4/91.

1982—A darkly colored wine, with a tight, but promising bouquet of ripe
·   blackberry fruit and some spicy oak, the 1982 Haut-Sarpe is a
85   muscular, moderately big wine, with very good concentration,
       medium tannin, and quite good balance. Anticipated maturity:
       Now–2000. Last tasted, 3/89.

1981—This wine displays a good concentration of ripe fruit, soft tannins,
·   medium body, and a long finish. Quite well made, this wine from
83   the impeccably run estate of Haut-Sarpe should be drunk up.
       Anticipated maturity: Now–may be in decline. Last tasted, 7/86.

1978—Ready to drink, Haut-Sarpe's 1978 is a straightforwardly fruity,
·   well-colored wine with medium body and an earthy, plummy bou-
82   quet. Anticipated maturity: Now–1994. Last tasted, 6/83.

LE JURAT (Grand Cru) GOOD

Production: 3,500 cases	Grape varieties:
	Merlot—60%
	Cabernet Franc—40%
Secondary label: none	
Vineyard size: 17.5 acres	Proprietor: SMABPT
	Administrator: Domaines
	Cordier
Time spent in barrels: 18 months	Average age of vines: 25 years

Evaluation of present classification: The quality equivalent of a good
  Médoc Cru Bourgeois
Plateau of maturity: 3–10 years following the vintage

Le Jurat, a relatively obscure vineyard located on the northern slopes of
the appellation near the Pomerol border in a mixture of clay and limestone soils, was acquired by the huge syndicate SMABPT in 1986. Just
as with their other St.-Emilion acquisition, Haut-Corbin, they installed
the Domaines Cordier to look after the winemaking and commercialization. Under the Cordier management, the results have been especially
impressive wines. Starting with the 1988 vintage, the use of 25% new
oak and an extended maceration have resulted in deeper colored, more
concentrated wines.

VINTAGES

1989—The Cordier firm has been making intense efforts to upgrade the
·   quality of this estate in St.-Emilion. The 1989 should prove to be
86   the finest wine in living memory produced at Le Jurat. Black/ruby
       in color, with a huge bouquet of smoky, ripe, superrich fruit, this
       intensely concentrated, alcoholic, large-scaled wine has a supple,
       lush texture, plenty of soft tannins in the finish, and surprising
       length. It is undoubtedly a sleeper in this vintage. Anticipated
       maturity: 1993–2005. Last tasted, 4/91.

1988—The 1988 is also successful, exhibiting soft tannins, as well as
·   sufficient herb-scented, black cherry fruit. Medium to full bodied,
85   with very good color, this is a wine to drink until the end of the
       decade. Anticipated maturity: 1992–2000. Last tasted, 4/91.

1986—The 1986 has a deep ruby color, a moderately intense bouquet of
·   toasty oak and herbaceous-scented blackcurrant fruit, and a long,
85   lush, supple texture. It is drinkable now. Anticipated maturity:
       Now–1996. Last tasted, 3/90.

1985—The 1985 Le Jurat is a pleasant, medium-bodied, supple, agree-
·   able, but not very distinguished wine. It should be drunk up.
81   Anticipated maturity: Now–1993. Last tasted, 3/89.

JEAN-FAURE (Grand Cru)   GOOD

Production: 8,000 cases	Grape varieties:
	Cabernet Franc—60%
	Merlot—30%
	Malbec—10%
Secondary label: none	
Vineyard size: 42 acres	Proprietor: Michel Amart
Time spent in barrels: 18–22 months	Average age of vines: 30 years
Evaluation of present classification: The quality equivalent of a Médoc Cru Bourgeois	
Plateau of maturity: 3–12 years following the vintage	

This is often a perplexing wine to evaluate given the extremely high
percentage of Cabernet Franc used in the blend. However, the proprietor
has long argued that the sandy soils of Jean-Faure's vineyard near both
Cheval Blanc and Figeac are perfect for this much Cabernet Franc.
Interestingly, in the most recent St.-Emilion classification in 1985, Château Jean-Faure was declassified—a rare as well as shocking demotion.

The vintages I have seen—1981, 1982, 1983, and 1985—were all relatively austere, meagerly endowed wines. However, I have been told that
this is a property where the wines need 5–6 years in the bottle to reveal
their charm.

Of all the oenologists in Bordeaux, perhaps the famed Emile Peynaud
has been the greatest defender of this property. I have been less impressed, but it appears that later harvesting and lower yields might result
in more intensely concentrated wines from Jean-Faure. But this is one
wine that tends to evoke strong emotions, both positive and negative.

LANIOTE (Grand Cru Classé)   AVERAGE

Production: 2,500 cases	Grape varieties: Merlot—70% Cabernet Franc—20% Cabernet Sauvignon—10%
Secondary label: none	
Vineyard size: 12.5 acres	Proprietor: The Freymond-Rouja family
Time spent in barrels: 16–18 months	Average age of vines: 25 years
Evaluation of present classification: The quality equivalent of a Médoc Cru Bourgeois	
Plateau of maturity: 3–9 years following the vintage	

I have had very limited experience with the wines from the tiny vineyard of Laniote. The property, located northwest of the town of St.-Emilion on rich clay, limestone and iron-enriched soils, has been controlled by the same family for over seven generations. The best wine I have tasted was the 1982, which was opulent and soft, but fully mature by 1990. The 1981, 1983, and 1985 were above average in quality, but unexciting.

LARCIS-DUCASSE (Grand Cru Classé)   GOOD

Production: 5,000 cases	Grape varieties: Merlot—65% Cabernet Franc—25% Cabernet Sauvignon—10%
Secondary label: none	
Vineyard size: 25 acres	Proprietors: Madame Gratiot-Alphandéry and her children
Time spent in barrels: 22–28 months	Average age of vines: 30 years
Evaluation of present classification: The quality equivalent of a Médoc fifth-growth	
Plateau of maturity: 8–20 years following the vintage	

Larcis-Ducasse sits on the *côtes* of St.-Emilion, southeast of the town with its vineyard abutting that of Pavie. The vines, planted on calcareous clay slopes, enjoy a full southerly exposure. This wine enjoys an excellent reputation, but until the early eighties the quality was unimpressive. Prior to 1982, too many wines consistently displayed a lean, austere, skinny taste and structure, although I have fond memories of a profound 1945. Since 1982, the quality of Larcis-Ducasse has dramatically improved.

VINTAGES

1989—The 1989, while filled with tannin and structured for aging up to
·   30 years, did not seem to have quite the inner core of fruit, depth,
86   and intensity that the 1988 possessed. Full and tannic, it will not
        be at its best until midway through the first decade of the next
        century. This is an imposingly backward style of wine that may
        ultimately merit a higher score—provided the fruit does not dry
        out before the tannin fades. Anticipated maturity: 1998–2010.
        Last tasted, 4/91.

1988—The 1988 is an excellent wine, full-bodied, exceptionally rich, and
·   exhibiting great ripeness and length, and at least 25 years of
89   potential evolution. This is an admirable, old-styled wine that will
        appeal to those who have patience. Anticipated maturity: 1996–
        2010. Last tasted, 4/91.

1986—The 1986 displays fine ripeness, long, rich, cedary, plummy fla-
·   vors, medium to full body, and a concentrated, supple, alcoholic
85   finish, with some serious tannins present. Anticipated maturity:
        1992–2002. Last tasted, 3/90.

1985—The 1985 is overproduced, lacking focus, depth, and definition. It
·   should be drunk up over the next 4–5 years. Excessive crop yields
79   have left their mark on this wine. Anticipated maturity: Now–
        1997. Last tasted, 3/89.

1983—When I tasted this wine after bottling it never performed well.
·   But more recently, the wine has thrown off the bottle shock and
86   appears much richer and fuller than I would have ever imagined.
        Medium dark ruby with a slight trace of amber at the edge, with
        a big, spicy, cedary, herb– and red fruit–scented bouquet, this
        wine offers both complexity and character. In the mouth, the wine
        is classically structured, with medium body, plenty of tannin, and
        very good extract. While drinkable now, it should continue to
        evolve for at least another 7–10 years. Anticipated maturity:
        Now–2001. Last tasted, 3/90.

1982—Here is another example of Larcis-Ducasse that I vastly under-
·   rated when it was younger, making me wonder whether I consis-
88   tently fail to comprehend this wine's character in its youth. The
        lightness and lack of depth the wine exhibited when younger has
        disappeared as the 1982 continues to put on weight and complex-
        ity. Now the wine is loaded with glycerin in a full-bodied, more

opulent style than one normally expects from Larcis-Ducasse. The deep ruby color is saturated with only a slight amber edge. The finish is long, alcoholic, and intense. The tannins are soft, so the wine can be drunk now, but there is no denying that this wine has the size and requisite depth to last for another 10–12 years. Anticipated maturity: Now–2002. Last tasted, 3/90.

1981—The 1981 is too angular, and lacks flesh, generosity, and fruit.
·　　This is another so-so wine for near-term drinking, from an estate
75　　with a good reputation. Anticipated maturity: Now–may be in decline. Last tasted, 6/84.

1979—Medium ruby, with a spicy, fruity aroma of moderate intensity,
·　　this Larcis-Ducasse has average- to above-average-intensity fla-
78　　vors that are plainer scaled than other St.-Emilions. The wine does have some underlying firmness and texture. Anticipated maturity: Now–may be in decline. Last tasted, 11/83.

1978—Quite mediocre, this pale-colored, lightweight wine has a bouquet
·　　suggestive of strawberry and cherry fruit. On the palate, there is
72　　not much to find but short, shallow, watery flavors, with some tannin and dry oaky flavors in the finish. Anticipated maturity: Now–may be in decline. Last tasted, 9/82.

LARMANDE (Grand Cru Classé)　　　　　EXCELLENT

Production: 8,000 cases	Grape varieties: Merlot—65% Cabernet Franc—30% Cabernet Sauvignon—5%
Secondary label: Château des Templiers	
Vineyard size: 54.3 acres	Proprietor: Société Civile Administrator: Philippe Mèneret
Time spent in barrels: 18–20 months	Average age of vines: 35 years
Evaluation of present classification: The quality equivalent of a Médoc third-growth	
Plateau of maturity: 4–15 years following the vintage	

I remember when I first visited Larmande in the mid-1970s at the request of the late Martin Bamford, one of Bordeaux's most knowledgeable observers. He had told me that this would be one of the best wines made in St.-Emilion because of the commitment to quality evidenced by the Mèneret family. Larmande, situated in the northern area of St.-Emilion, is named after the historic *lieux-dit* (place name) of the vineyard. It is one of the oldest vineyards in St.-Emilion, with a wine-producing history going back to the thirteenth century. For most of this century, however, the property was owned by the Mèneret-Capdemourlin family, and run with great enthusiasm by Philippe and Dominique Mèneret. In 1991 the Mènerets sold the property to a large French firm, and at the time of this writing it was uncertain whether the Mènerets would be retained as consultants.

In the mid-1970s the entire *chai* was renovated with the introduction of temperature-controlled stainless-steel tanks. The percentage of new oak utilized was also increased to nearly 50% in top vintages.

The key to Larmande's quality is late harvesting, a strict selection (the production of a second wine was introduced during the decade of the eighties), and relatively low yields. As a consequence, Larmande's track record since the mid-1970s has been impeccable. There are few Premiers Grands Crus Classés that can boast such consistently fine wines. As the decade of the eighties closed, I felt Larmande produced the two finest wines it had yet made, the 1988 and 1989.

Prices, however, have remained remarkably reasonable, but will that change under the new corporate ownership? Larmande can be found just to the northeast of the town of St.-Emilion, near the two more famous estates of Cadet-Piola and Soutard.

VINTAGES

1989—The 1989 Larmande is a flattering wine. It is perhaps not so
  ·   structured or so concentrated a wine as this excellent property
  88   usually produces, but if you like wonderfully round, hedonistic,
        soft, alcoholic, luscious St.-Emilions, this superripe, heady, and
        voluptuously textured wine will offer many thrills. Anticipated
        maturity: Now–2001. Last tasted, 4/91.

1988—For most of the decade, I have been bullish on this consistent
  ·   overachiever. However, I never thought the 1988 would turn out
  90   to be this thrilling. Larmande has made some wonderful wines
        during the eighties; the 1982, 1983, 1985, 1988, and 1989 are all
        show-stoppers. However, it is the 1988 that looks to be Lar-
        mande's wine of the decade. Black/ruby/purple in color, with a
        super bouquet of plums, minerals, and spicy new oak, this rich,
        highly extracted, lusciously put together St.-Emilion has the kind
        of extract levels that many Premiers Grands Crus Classés wish
        they had. Deep, full bodied, impeccably pure, and well balanced,
        it should drink well for the next 10–15 years. While former pro-
        prietor Philippe Mèneret continues to feel that 1982 is his best

vintage of the eighties, I would have to give my nod to the classic 1988. Furthermore, thrifty consumers looking for spectacular quality at moderate prices should be stockpiling the 1988 Larmande. Anticipated maturity: Now–2002. Last tasted, 4/91.

1986—The 1986 should prove to be one of the longest-lived vintages of
  ·   Larmande yet made. While it does not have the opulence of the
 86   1989, 1982, or 1983, it does have much more structure, and every
        bit the concentration of those three successful vintages. There is
        even the deceiving impression that this wine will come around
        earlier because of the lush, intense, blackberry fruit. However,
        the color is opaque, there is great extraction of fruit, and in the
        finish, one senses an elevated level of ripe tannins. This is a
        brawny, big-styled Larmande that should age for almost two de-
        cades. Anticipated maturity: 1993–2008. Last tasted, 3/90.

1985—The 1985 competes favorably with the 1982 and 1983. A deep
  ·   color, an intense bouquet of Bing cherries, and a ripe, fat, con-
 87   centrated texture give the deceiving impression of early matura-
        tion, but there is a lot of tannin in the finish. Anticipated maturity:
        Now–2000. Last tasted, 3/89.

1984—Light ruby, with a spicy, oaky, light-intensity bouquet, the 1984
  ·   Larmande is correct and agreeable. Anticipated maturity: Now–
 80   1992. Last tasted, 3/88.

1983—The 1983 Larmande is big, rich, full bodied, and luscious. This
  ·   deeply colored, powerfully built Larmande has shed its tannins
 87   and should continue to drink well for another 5–6 years. Antici-
        pated maturity: Now–1997. Last tasted, 1/89.

1982—This wine, drinkable when released, has continued to perform
  ·   well in nearly every tasting I have had. It has actually put on
 87   weight and gained structure in the bottle. Still dark, nearly
        opaque ruby/purple with only a slight tinge of amber at the edge,
        the 1982 Larmande has a huge, herbaceous, spicy, cassis-scented
        nose, rich, full-bodied, unctuous flavors, low acidity, and plenty
        of grip from silky tannins and the positive effects of aging in small
        oak casks. Delicious since the mid-1980s, the wine exhibits no
        signs of decline. I fully expect this bigger-styled Larmande to
        continue to drink well until the turn of the century. Anticipated
        maturity: Now–2000. Last tasted, 12/90.

1981—The lightest and most elegant of the three good vintages of the
  ·   early eighties, Larmande's 1981 has medium ruby color, a ripe,
 83   moderately intense, plummy, slightly herbaceous bouquet, me-
        dium body, good concentration, and a fine crisp, clean finish.
        Anticipated maturity: Now–may be in decline. Last tasted, 6/84.

1980—A success given the trying vintage conditions, Larmande's 1980
    · is fairly light and supple, but exhibits a fragrant, light-intensity
    75 bouquet of herbs, oak, and cherry fruit, medium body, and soft,
       pleasant flavors. Anticipated maturity: Now—may be in decline.
       Last tasted, 6/84.
1978—Fully mature, the 1978 Larmande is a very stylish, elegant, fruity
    · wine, with medium body, a fine cedary, herbaceous, plummy
    82 bouquet of moderate intensity, and nicely balanced, medium-
       bodied flavors. Anticipated maturity: Now—may be in decline.
       Last tasted, 6/84.

LAROQUE (Grand Cru)   AVERAGE

Production: 22,000 cases	Grape varieties: Merlot—65% Cabernet Franc—20% Cabernet Sauvignon—15%
Secondary label: none Vineyard size: 111 acres	Proprietor: S.C.A. Château Laroque
Time spent in barrels: 12–18 months	Average age of vines: 25 years
Evaluation of present classification: The quality equivalent of a Médoc Cru Bourgeois	
Plateau of maturity: 3–8 years following the vintage	

The impressive château at Laroque, which almost resembles a miniature
Château Versailles, was built in the Middle Ages and reconstructed during the eighteenth century in the style of Louis XIV. It remains one of
the most impressive buildings in the entire Bordeaux region. The same
cannot be said for the wine. The wine's production is controlled by the
huge *négociant* firm, Alex Lichine et Cie. Perhaps because it does not
have to compete in comparative tastings there is little incentive to increase the quality. I have found the wine, even in top vintages such as
1982, 1988, and 1989, to be light, extremely commercial in style, and
lacking grip and depth.

LAROZE (Grand Cru Classé)   GOOD

Production: 11,000 cases	Grape varieties: Merlot—50% Cabernet Franc—47% Cabernet Sauvignon—3%
Secondary label: Clos Yon-Figeac	
Vineyard size: 62 acres	Proprietor: Georges Meslin-Gurchy
Time spent in barrels: 15–18 months	Average age of vines: 20 years
Evaluation of present classification: The quality equivalent of a good Médoc Cru Bourgeois	
Plateau of maturity: 4–8 years following the vintage	

While I have never considered the wines of Laroze to be that profound, there is something to be said for a style of wine that is fragrant, soft, fruity, and easy to drink. These are wines that require consumption within their first 5–7 years of life (both the 1982 and 1983 are already drying out and losing their fruit), but if consumers keep that fact in mind, there is plenty of charm to be found with the wines of Laroze.

The vineyards are planted in light, sandy soil, and the wines are vinified in a modern, up-to-date facility.

MAGDELAINE (Premier Grand Cru Classé)   VERY GOOD

Production: 5,000 cases	Grape varieties: Merlot—90% Cabernet Franc—10%
Secondary label: none	
Vineyard size: 27 acres	Proprietor: Jean-Pierre Moueix
Time spent in barrels: 22–24 months	Average age of vines: 35 years
Evaluation of present classification: The quality equivalent of a Médoc third-growth	
Plateau of maturity: 7–20 years following the vintage	

Magdelaine, one of the *côtes* St.-Emilions, with its vineyard beautifully situated on a limestone plateau overlooking the Dordogne Valley, has been one of the very best St.-Emilions since the early sixties. Since 1952, the famous Libourne firm of Jean-Pierre Moueix has been the sole proprietor of this property. Magdelaine has the highest percentage of Merlot (90%) of any of the renowned châteaux located on the St.-Emilion limestone plateau.

Most experts have considered this property to have the best potential of any of the plateau properties, but in the late seventies and during the decade of the eighties, the quality of Magdelaine has been surpassed by its neighbor, Canon. It may also be eclipsed by the up-and-coming Château Trottevieille.

Nevertheless, Magdelaine remains a very distinctive St.-Emilion, largely because of this high proportion of Merlot. One would assume that the wine is soft, fleshy, and forward. It is not. Because of the relatively long fermentation, early harvesting, and the use of a small percentage of stems, Magdelaine is an extremely tannic, slow-to-evolve wine. It normally requires 5–7 years after bottling to reveal its character.

Given the small production and its historic reputation, as well as its ownership by the Moueix firm, Magdelaine has always been an expensive wine, selling at prices comparable to a top Médoc second-growth.

VINTAGES

1989—The 1989 is the finest young Magdelaine I have ever tasted. Deep
· ruby/purple in color, with an intense, chocolatey, super-extracted
93 bouquet of plummy fruit, this wine has an extra dimension to its flavors and awesome length, yet has retained a balance that is remarkable for its size. There is a great deal of tannin in the finish, but the alcohol seems less exaggerated than in many St.-Emilions, and the acidity is sound, although not high. This should prove to be a great Magdelaine, but I would not want to drink it before the turn of the century. Anticipated maturity: 2000–2025. Last tasted, 4/91.

1988—The 1988 is an understated, relatively lean, highly sculptured
· wine with good fruit, medium body, and firm tannins. However,
85 it lacks the fabulous concentration and length of the 1989. Anticipated maturity: 1995–2005. Last tasted, 4/91.

1986—The 1986 is so tannic and unyielding that it is simply impossible
· to judge how much depth of fruit is there. Perhaps within 6–8
80? years its true potential will emerge, but for now, this wine represents a distinct gamble, as the balance among its components does not appear to be in harmony. Last tasted, 3/89.

1985—Moderately deep ruby with medium body, the 1985 is a ripe,
· stylish, fruity wine with good rather than great depth. It is stylish,
82 but underwhelming. Lacking extract and relatively light and shal-

low, the 1985 Magdelaine is a disappointment. Anticipated maturity: Now–2000. Last tasted, 3/89.

1983—Brutally tannic, backward, and aggressive, the 1983 Magdelaine
·   has excellent color, full body, and plenty of rich, ripe fruit and
85   weight, but the ferocious tannins make it reminiscent of the 1975.
       Anticipated maturity: 1996–2010. Last tasted, 1/90.

1982—Is it possible that the 1989 will be even more compelling? This
·   beautifully made wine is full bodied and still dark in color, with a
90   powerful, rich, deeply concentrated, opulent personality, fine
       structure, and a sensationally long, richly fruity finish. Magde-
       laine has produced a superrich wine with the potential to be one
       of the finest wines made at the estate in several decades, yet it is
       evolving at a snail's pace. Anticipated maturity: 1994–2015. Last
       tasted, 3/91.

1981—Here is an example of a wine that had a lovely, perfumed, soft,
·   berry bouquet, and moderately intense flavors, yet because of
80   extensive oak aging, now tastes hard, astringent, tannic, and de-
       ficient in fruit. The color is very sound, the bouquet suggests
       vanillin, woodsy aromas, but on the palate, the wine is unyielding
       and ungenerous. Perhaps time will unleash the fruit. Anticipated
       maturity: Now–2000. Last tasted, 3/87.

1979—Here is an example of a Magdelaine that behaves as if it were
·   made with 90% Merlot. Quite accessible, with round, gentle, for-
84   ward, silky flavors, this medium-bodied wine displays good con-
       centration and light tannins. It is ready to drink. Anticipated
       maturity: Now–1995. Last tasted, 5/82.

1978—A very ripe wine, Magdelaine's 1978 is jammy and intensely
·   fruity, with a round, generous, nicely concentrated texture. Per-
86   haps a little low in acidity, but generally well balanced, with a
       spicy, vanillin oakiness, this is a forward-styled Magdelaine. An-
       ticipated maturity: Now–1993. Last tasted, 3/86.

1975—This wine, like so many 1975s, has evolved at an incredibly slow
·   pace. Still painfully backward, yet so promising, this big, dense,
87   tannic wine has a ruby/garnet color, a powerful, ripe plum and
       oak-dominated bouquet, and rich, somewhat coarse, but highly
       extracted flavors. It is just about ready to drink. Anticipated ma-
       turity: 1992–2006. Last tasted, 10/90.

1970—Now beginning to reach its apogee, the 1970 Magdelaine is dark
·   ruby with some amber, has a stylistic resemblance to the 1975 in
88   power and tannic ferocity, but seems to have just a little more
       flesh and fruit. Quite full bodied, big, rich, oaky, and spicy, this
       wine can be drunk now, but promises to be even better in several
       years. Anticipated maturity: 1992–2005. Last tasted, 3/86.

1967—Always one of the best examples of the 1967 vintage, Magdelaine
·   has begun to fade, but still offers an interesting chocolatey, ce-
82   dary, minty bouquet and soft, rich, surprisingly deep flavors
       marred by a slight astringence. Anticipated maturity: Now–1994.
       Last tasted, 2/85.
1962—A lovely success for the vintage, the 1962 Magdelaine has been
·   mature for quite some time, but seems to be holding its fruit. A
85   full-blown bouquet of cedary, herbal, spicy, ripe fruit is altogether
       impressive. Round, generous flavors exhibit good body and no
       tannins, and despite the brown color at the edges, this wine still
       has plenty of life. Anticipated maturity: Now–1994. Last tasted,
       1/81.
1961—The plague of severe bottle variation among old vintages is ex-
·   emplified well with this wine. Two bottles tasted in the mid-1970s
91   seemed tired and close to senility. Another bottle proved sensa-
       tionally rich, exotic, and intense, with layers of ripe fruit, and a
       superb bouquet. The score reflects the well-preserved bottle. An-
       ticipated maturity: Now–1995. Last tasted, 3/86.

OLDER VINTAGES

Both the 1959 and 1955 were somewhat mediocre. I did taste one very
good example of the 1953 (rated 87) in 1989. It was an opulent, fragrant,
softly styled, fully mature Magdelaine. I also have enjoyed the 1952
(rated 88 in 12/91).

MATRAS (Grand Cru Classé)   AVERAGE

Production: 5,000 cases	Grape varieties: Merlot—35% Cabernet Sauvignon—30% Cabernet Franc—30% Malbec—5%
Secondary label: Hermitage de Mazeret	
Vineyard size: 34.5 acres	Proprietor: G.F.A. du Château Matras
Time spent in barrels: 16 months	Average age of vines: 20 years
Evaluation of present classification: The quality equivalent of a Médoc Cru Bourgeois	
Plateau of maturity: 3–10 years following the vintage	

Proprietor Jean-Bernard Lefebre has made significant improvements to
this property, which was in lamentable condition in the early sixties. No

doubt the vineyard has potential. It sits on the southern slopes of the St.-Emilion hills, bordering the excellent properties of L'Angélus, Tertre-Daugay, and the great Premier Grand Cru Classé, Canon. This sheltered location has soils that vary from clay and limestone to mostly limestone intermixed with what the French call *crasse de fer*, or iron-enriched soil.

Several vintages I tasted in the seventies were disappointing, and even the 1981 and 1982 lacked character and did not fare well in comparative tastings against their peers. I was more impressed with the 1985 and cask samples of the 1988, so perhaps the quality is improving.

MAUVEZIN (Grand Cru Classé) VERY GOOD

Production: 1,200 cases	Grape varieties: Cabernet Franc—55% Merlot—35% Cabernet Sauvignon—10%
Secondary label: none	
Vineyard size: 8.6 acres	Proprietor: G.F.A. Cassat
Time spent in barrels: 18–20 months	Average age of vines: 18 years
Evaluation of present classification: The quality equivalent of a good Médoc Cru Bourgeois	
Plateau of maturity: 3–10 years following the vintage	

Take a look at this interesting property. The tiny vineyard, located on the limestone plateau near Balestard-La-Tonnelle and Haut-Sarpe, has been completely replanted since 1969 when proprietor Pierre Cassat arrived. Mauvezin is a distinctive wine because the entire production is aged in 100% new oak casks. Additionally, such a high percentage of Cabernet Franc is rarely seen in this part of the St.-Emilion appellation. In years of great ripeness, such as 1982, 1983, 1985, and 1989, the results are relatively rich yet delicate wines, with superb fragrance and suppleness. In cooler years where the Cabernet Franc does not fully ripen, Mauvezin tends to produce relatively herbaceous-scented wines lacking concentration. Virtually the entire production is sold directly from the château to private customers. I have never seen a bottle available in the export markets. Visitors to the region might take note of this.

MONBOUSQUET (Grand Cru)   AVERAGE

Production: 14,000–15,000 cases	Grape varieties: Merlot—50% Cabernet Franc—40% Cabernet Sauvignon—10%
Secondary label: none	
Vineyard size: 74 acres	Proprietor: Daniel Querre
Time spent in barrels: 14–18 months	Average age of vines: 25 years
Evaluation of present classification: The quality equivalent of a Médoc Cru Bourgeois	
Plateau of maturity: 3–8 years following the vintage	

This large estate is the pride and joy of the Querre family, who produce a deliciously fruity, supple style of St.-Emilion that has broad commercial appeal and is always fairly priced.

The wine tends to be ready to drink when released, and while it rarely improves after 5 or 6 years of bottle age, some vintages (1970, 1975) of Monbousquet have proven they can live for over a decade. Nevertheless, this is a wine to drink very young.

MOULIN DU CADET (Grand Cru Classé)   AVERAGE

Production: 2,500 cases	Grape varieties: Merlot—85% Cabernet Franc—15%
Secondary label: none	
Vineyard size: 12.5 acres	Proprietor: The Mouliérac family
	Administrator: Jean-Pierre Moueix
Time spent in barrels: 16–20 months	Average age of vines: 25 years
Evaluation of present classification: The quality equivalent of a Médoc Cru Bourgeois	
Plateau of maturity: 3–8 years following the vintage	

Moulin du Cadet is a micro-estate of 12 acres located on the plateau north of St.-Emilion. It tends to produce rather fragrant, lighter-styled wines lacking depth, but displaying attractive bouquets. With the famous firm of Jean-Pierre Moueix attending to the estate's winemaking, one can expect to see more richness and depth. For example, the 1989 exhibited significant improvement over previous vintages.

VINTAGES

1989—A significant difference in quality exists between the 1989 and
·   1988 from Moulin du Cadet. The 1989 possesses rich, sweet,
85   expansive flavors, and exhibits good concentration and length.
      Anticipated maturity: Now–1996. Last tasted, 4/91.

1988—The 1988 is a hard, austere, malnourished, skinny wine that lacks
·   charm and character. Avoid it. Last tasted, 4/91.
75

1986—The 1986 is light, elegant, and ready to drink, but not terribly
·   deep or profound. Anticipated maturity: Now–1994. Last tasted,
74   3/90.

1985—The 1985 Moulin du Cadet is dull and uninteresting. Last tasted,
·   3/89.
78

PAVIE (Premier Grand Cru Classé)   VERY GOOD

Production: 15,000 cases	Grape varieties: Merlot—55% Cabernet Franc—25% Cabernet Sauvignon—20%
Secondary label: none	
Vineyard size: 92.6 acres	Proprietor: The Valette family
Time spent in barrels: 20–24 months	Average age of vines: 40 years
Evaluation of present classification: The quality equivalent of a Médoc fourth- or fifth-growth	
Plateau of maturity: 7–20 years following the vintage	

Pavie has the largest vineyard of all the St.-Emilion Premiers Grands Crus Classés. With a production seven times the size of one of its neighbors, Ausone, and twice that of the adjacent vineyard, La Gaffelière, Pavie's wines are widely known throughout the world.

The vineyard is superbly situated just to the southeast of St.-Emilion (a five-minute drive), on the eastern section of the hillsides of the town. Therefore, it is one of the *côtes* St.-Emilions.

Pavie is now owned and run by Jean Paul Valette, who has been at Pavie since 1967 after giving up ranching in Chile. He is one of St.-

Emilion's friendliest proprietors, and his hospitality, combined with the fact that Pavie has some of the region's most interesting limestone caves for storing wine, makes this a must stop for tourists to the area.

Pavie, despite the large production and popularity, has not been a top performer among the St.-Emilion first-growths. In many vintages the wine has been too light and feebly colored, with a tendency to brown and mature at an accelerated pace. Valette was well aware of these problems, and there was a strong movement to a more densely concentrated, deeper-colored, fuller-bodied Pavie with the vintages of 1979 onward. This is not to suggest that all of the wines of Pavie produced before 1979 were insipid and weak; but far too many vintages, for example 1976, 1975, 1974, and 1966, were well below acceptable standards. Fortunately, this period of inconsistency is past history. The famous oenologist Pascal Ribereau-Gayon is now taking an active interest in the fermentation of Pavie and recent vintages have gone from one strength to another. However, this is not a St.-Emilion to drink young; most vintages, particularly in the eighties, have been stubbornly hard at their outset and a minimum of 7–10 years of bottle age is required for mellowing.

Pavie is fairly priced for a Premier Grand Cru Classé St.-Emilion. The large production has guaranteed that the price to date has remained realistic.

VINTAGES

1989— The 1989 is a deep, dark ruby-colored wine with excellent ripeness, a firm, fleshy texture, and an attractively long, intense yet
· alcoholic finish. This wine has gobs of extract and is among the
89 most powerful wines produced at Pavie in the last two decades. Anticipated maturity: 1996–2009. Last tasted, 4/91.

1988— The 1988 is perhaps a more typical Pavie in that it offers a more structured, tannic overlay, balanced nicely by elegant, ripe, to-
· bacco- and black cherry–scented fruit, good acidity, and a long,
87 spicy, tannic finish. Anticipated maturity: 1994–2005. Last tasted, 4/91.

1986— Excluding the 1982, the 1986 is the finest Pavie made in the last three decades. It is a full-bodied, deep, tannic, highly extracted
· wine, with a bouquet that displays a great deal of sweet, toasty
90 oak, and a finish that goes on and on. There are noticeable tannins in the wine, so expect to defer your gratification for some time while waiting for this wine to mature. Quite impressive, Pavie is clearly one of the stars of the St.-Emilion appellation in 1986. Anticipated maturity: 1996–2010. Last tasted, 3/90.

1985—The 1985 is firm, tannic, and unyielding, particularly for a wine
·   from this vintage. Deep in color, ripe, medium bodied, but need-
86   ing time, this wine will provide graceful drinking if cellared. An-
       ticipated maturity: 1993–2005. Last tasted, 3/90.

1983—Now reaching full maturity, the 1983 Pavie has an attractive bou-
·   quet of rich raspberry and plummy fruit intermingled with the
88   scents of new oak and herbs. The color is still medium dark ruby,
       but some amber has crept in at the edge. On the palate, the wine
       is crammed with rich, opulent, expansive, red fruit flavors, but
       has enough acidity and tannin to give it grip and focus. This is a
       surprisingly drinkable, exuberantly styled Pavie that should con-
       tinue to evolve for at least another 10–15 years. Anticipated ma-
       turity: Now–2005. Last tasted, 3/91.

1982—This is the finest Pavie I have ever tasted. Still very dark in color,
·   with a closed but emerging bouquet of grilled nuts, fruitcake, and
92   superconcentrated red and black fruits, this full-bodied, muscular
       Pavie still has plenty of tannin to shed. There is great structure,
       superb extraction and flavor, and a long, heady finish. This is a
       Pavie for drinking over the next 20–25 years. Anticipated matu-
       rity: 1993–2010. Last tasted, 3/91.

1981—This vintage of Pavie has developed fast. A classy and complex
·   bouquet of spicy, vanillin oak and ripe cherries is attractive. In
85   the mouth, the wine is medium bodied and flavorful, with a sweet,
       oaky component that has blended in well with the wine's fruit. In
       short, Pavie's 1981 is a very good, elegant, medium-weight wine.
       Anticipated maturity: Now–1994. Last tasted, 11/90.

1979—This is an attractive Pavie that is nearing maturity. The 1979 has
·   surprisingly dark ruby color with only a trace of amber, with a
85   toasty, smoky, herb-and-berry-scented bouquet, medium body,
       good power and weight, and moderate tannins. It is a tasty but
       compact wine. Anticipated maturity: Now–2000. Last tasted,
       3/91.

1978—A loose, open-knit style of wine, the 1978 Pavie lacks concentra-
·   tion, structure, and firmness, but offers a sweet, ripe (possibly
78   overripe) Merlot fruitiness, and one-dimensional charm. I also
       detected a vegetal quality to the bouquet. Anticipated maturity:
       Now–1993. Last tasted, 4/82.

1976—Quite disappointing, the 1976 Pavie is an insipid, dull, diluted
·   wine, with marginal flavor interest, a vegetal, overly spicy, woody
56   aroma, and pale, shallow flavors. Last tasted, 9/80.

1975—A minor wine in this vintage, the 1975 Pavie exhibits sweet, ripe,
·   lightly concentrated, fruity flavors, medium body, and surpris-
72   ingly little tannin. A compact little wine, the 1975 Pavie should

be drunk up. Anticipated maturity: Now–probably in serious decline. Last tasted, 5/84.

1971— The 1971 Pavie is a graceful, well-balanced, fruity, soft, elegant
· wine that always impressed me as being among the most re-
81 strained and subdued of the 1971 St.-Emilions. Now beginning to lose its fruit, this medium-bodied wine still has charm and finesse, but is displayed in an understated way. Anticipated maturity: Now–may be in decline. Last tasted, 3/86.

1970— Produced in a period when Pavie was obviously in a performance
· slump, the 1970 Pavie is still a modest success for the vineyard.
83 Not terribly complex, but chunky, straightforward, and "foursquare" (as I suspect Michael Broadbent would say), this wine has a roasted, ripe cherry bouquet, and full, oaky, yet one-dimensional flavors. It is a good effort. Anticipated maturity: Now–1994. Last tasted from a magnum, 3/88.

1967— Not retasted in a long time, I have always enjoyed the 1967 Pavie
· and thought it to be one of the underrated wines of this vintage.
82 Probably past its peak, this wine has a wonderfully smooth, graceful, supple texture, with no hard edges, and an enjoyable, oaky, ripe bouquet. Anticipated maturity: Now–may be in decline. Last tasted, 3/76.

1966— Consistently inferior, and rather disturbingly light-colored and
· shallow, this wine has been fully mature for over a decade, and is
64 no doubt now close to total senility. Pavie is a major disappointment of the vintage. Last tasted, 11/78.

1961— The first few times I tasted this wine I was unimpressed, but in
· 1988 at a blind tasting, the wine revealed a huge, spicy, cedary,
90 black plum–scented nose, rich, concentrated, opulent flavors, amazing youthfulness, and plenty of tannin and alcohol in the finish. I was shocked when I learned it was the 1961 Pavie. The bottle I saw could easily last for another 10–15 years. It bore no resemblance to the relatively tired examples I had tasted previously. Will the real 1961 Pavie please come forward? Anticipated maturity: Now–2005. Last tasted, 2/88.

PAVIE-DECESSE (Grand Cru Classé)   VERY GOOD

Production: 4,000 cases	Grape varieties: Merlot—60% Cabernet Franc—25% Cabernet Sauvignon—15%
Secondary label: none	
Vineyard size: 25 acres	Proprietor: The Valette family
Time spent in barrels: 20–24 months	Average age of vines: 40 years
Evaluation of present classification: The quality equivalent of a Médoc fifth-growth	
Plateau of maturity: 5–15 years following the vintage	

Since 1971, this small estate has been owned by Jean Paul Valette, the proprietor of the Premier Grand Cru Classé, Pavie, which sits several hundred feet further down the hill below Pavie-Decesse. This is a *côtes* St.-Emilion, with a vineyard situated on chalky, clay, and limestone soils. The quality at this estate has followed that of its bigger, more famous sibling, Pavie. Consequently, after some mediocre wines in the seventies, the vintages from 1979 onward have promised much higher quality.

Because Pavie and Pavie-Decesse are adjacent vineyards and have the same winemaker, there is an inclination to believe that the wines are similar. They are not. Pavie-Decesse is a less fleshy, more tannic, and a significantly more austere wine than Pavie.

For visitors to the area, I highly recommend a visit not only to Pavie, but also to Pavie-Decesse. It is reached by a long and winding road further up the hill from Pavie. The view of the vineyards from Pavie-Decesse is breathtaking.

VINTAGES

1989—The 1989 Pavie-Decesse is a tannic, full-bodied, rich, yet surprisingly backward wine for the vintage, with gobs of tannin, an herbaceous, mineral-scented, black cherry fruitiness, full body, and good acidity. Anticipated maturity: 1995–2010. Last tasted, 4/91.

· 88

1988—The 1988 is, I believe, marginally superior to the 1989. It has all the concentration of the 1989, but greater length, a more compelling bouquet of earthy, mineral, exotic fruit character, tremendous weight and tannin in the finish, and the potential to last for up to 20 years. Very tightly knit, it needs some coaxing from the glass. Anticipated maturity: 1997–2009. Last tasted, 4/91.

· 89

1986—An extremely impressive wine that is very tannic and powerful,
· the 1986 will require long-term cellaring. It is almost opaque in
89 color, and very reserved and backward in terms of development,
but with the requisite patience to wait at least a decade, it should
prove to be one of the sleepers of the vintage. Anticipated maturity: 1999–2010. Last tasted, 4/91.

1985—The 1985 Pavie-Decesse has turned out to be even better than
· Pavie. Very deep in color, with an intense aroma of blackcurrant
88 fruit, toasty oak, and tar-like scents, this rich, long, very big and
structured wine has loads of fruit that is tightly bound in a full-
bodied format. It should be a very long-lived 1985. Anticipated
maturity: 1993–2005. Last tasted, 3/90.

1983—This looks to be a very good Pavie-Decesse, provided one is will-
· ing to invest the time necessary for it to mature. Quite tannic,
86 with plenty of ripe, concentrated fruit, as well as high alcohol,
this big, virile, tough, and brawny wine is quite aggressive, yet
also very, very promising. Anticipated maturity: 1993–2000. Last
tasted, 3/88.

1982—Pavie-Decesse has turned in a fine performance in 1982. Big, rich
· aromas of ripe fruit and toasty oak jump from the glass. On the
86 palate, the wine is medium bodied and still tannic, with excellent
concentration. The wine has still not reached its apogee. Anticipated maturity: 1992–2005. Last tasted, 2/91.

1981—This is a very elegant, medium-weight wine, with a spicy, oaky,
· soft fruity bouquet and round, supple flavors. Anticipated matu-
81 rity: Now–1993. Last tasted, 6/84.

PAVIE-MACQUIN (Grand Cru Classé)   VERY GOOD

Production: 4,000 cases	Grape varieties: Merlot—80% Cabernet Franc—15% Cabernet Sauvignon—5%
Secondary label: none Vineyard size: 34.6 acres	Proprietor: The Corre- Macquin family
Time spent in barrels: 18–20 months	Average age of vines: 25 years
Evaluation of present classification: Since 1988, the quality equivalent of a Médoc fifth-growth	
Plateau of maturity: 3–12 years following the vintage	

Pavie-Macquin takes its name from Albert Macquin, who was the leading specialist of his time in grafting European vines onto American root stocks, a practice that became essential after the phylloxera louse destroyed most of the vineyards of Bordeaux in the late nineteenth century.

The vineyard is well situated on what is frequently referred to as the Côte Pavie, adjacent to the more renowned vineyards of Troplong-Mondot and Pavie. The wines of Pavie-Macquin, which were frequently disappointing in the seventies and eighties, made a significant leap in quality with the 1988, 1989, and 1990 vintages, largely because the Corre family hired the brilliant services of Maryse Barre to work in the vineyards. His contributions to the viticultural aspects, along with the retention of the great Libourne oenologist Michel Rolland to look after the vinification and *élevage*, have completely turned around the fortunes of this well-placed St.-Emilion. This could well become one of the underpriced stars of the nineties.

VINTAGES

1989—Which St.-Emilion tastes like a Grand Cru red burgundy—let's
·   say Musigny? The 1989 Pavie-Macquin, which is one of the great
90   sleepers of the vintage. The opaque, deep, black/purple color
         suggests very old vines and sensational extract. The implications
         drawn from the wine's color are fulfilled in the mouth. Fabulously
         concentrated, with wonderful purity of raspberry flavor, and great
         balance, this massive, highly extracted, full-bodied wine should
         last for up to 20 years. It is a real blockbuster. Since the property
         is largely unknown, it could well provide a great value. Antici-
         pated maturity: 1993–2015. Last tasted, 4/91.

1988—While there is no doubt that the 1988 Pavie-Macquin is less gen-
·   erous than the gloriously opulent, seductive 1989, it is an excel-
87   lent wine that is better than many of the Premiers Grands Crus
         Classés. Deep in color, with a big, spicy, black fruit–scented
         bouquet caressed gently by sweet vanillin oak, this medium-bod-
         ied, concentrated, classy wine offers considerable generosity, as
         well as great finesse and length. Anticipated maturity: Now–2001.
         Last tasted, 4/91.

PAVILLON-CADET (Grand Cru Classé)   AVERAGE

Production: 1,300 cases	Grape varieties:
	Merlot—60%
	Cabernet Franc—40%
Secondary label: none	
Vineyard size: 6.2 acres	Proprietor: Madame Llammas
Time spent in barrels: 14–22 months	Average age of vines: 25 years
Evaluation of present classification: The quality equivalent of a good Médoc Cru Bourgeois	
Plateau of maturity: 5–14 years following the vintage	

The information that I have assembled with respect to Pavillon-Cadet is based on interviews with several people in St.-Emilion who regularly taste this wine. Virtually all of it is sold to private clients in France and Europe. I have never tasted any of Pavillon-Cadet's wine, but the vineyard is well situated just to the north of St.-Emilion on what is referred to as the hill of Cadet. The wine is kept in small oak casks, of which 25% are new each year.

PETIT-FAURIE-DE-SOUTARD (Grand Cru Classé)   GOOD

Production: 3,500 cases	Grape varieties:
	Merlot—60%
	Cabernet Franc—30%
	Cabernet Sauvignon—10%
Secondary label: under consideration	
Vineyard size: 20 acres	Proprietor: Madame Françoise Capdemourlin
	Administrator: Jacques Capdemourlin
Time spent in barrels: 18–22 months	Average age of vines: 25 years
Evaluation of present classification: The quality equivalent of a good Médoc Cru Bourgeois	
Plateau of maturity: 5–12 years following this vintage	

This is an underrated St.-Emilion property with a relatively small production. The administrator, Jacques Capdemourlin, often promotes his wines from Balestard-La-Tonnelle more than those from Petit-Faurie-de-

Soutard. Nevertheless, this vineyard, once part of the famous Soutard domain, is well situated on the limestone plateau. The wines tend to have a great deal of fat and richness of fruit, much like Balestard, but also perhaps more structure and grip because of higher tannin levels. The best recent vintages have been 1982, 1983, and 1985. Unlike Balestard-La-Tonnelle, this is a wine that needs 3–4 years in the bottle to shed the tannins; it can last for more than a decade.

PINDEFLEURS (Grand Cru) GOOD

Production: 2,200 cases	Grape varieties: Merlot—53% Cabernet Franc—47%
Secondary label: none Vineyard size: 19.7 acres	Proprietor: Madame Dior Administrator: Roger Toulon
Time spent in barrels: 18–22 months	Average age of vines: 22 years
Evaluation of present classification: Should be elevated to a St.-Emilion Grand Cru Classé; the quality equivalent of a very good Médoc Cru Bourgeois	
Plateau of maturity: 3–14 years following the vintage	

Perhaps the most difficult wine to find in all of St.-Emilion is that made by the modestly sized estate of Château Pindefleurs, and this is a wine one wishes to see more often. Owned by a cousin of the famous clothing designer Christian Dior, this well-run property would appear to make consistently rich, fragrant, elegant wines with a great deal of character and complexity that have largely gone unnoticed in the St.-Emilion hierarchy. Much of it is sold to private customers in Europe. I have never seen a bottle offered by a *négociant*, which is a shame, because this property—at least based on the quality of the 1982, 1983, and 1985—produces wines that merit significantly more interest than they have received.

LE PRIEURÉ (Grand Cru Classé) AVERAGE

Production: 2,000 cases	Grape varieties: Merlot—60% Cabernet Franc—30% Cabernet Sauvignon—10%
Secondary label: Château L'Olivier	
Vineyard size: 11 acres	Proprietor: Olivier Guichard
Time spent in barrels: 18–20 months	Average age of vines: 23 years
Evaluation of present classification: The quality equivalent of a Médoc Cru Bourgeois	
Plateau of maturity: 3–8 years following the vintage	

I have always been at a loss as to why the wines of Le Prieuré do not turn out better. The vineyard—beautifully situated across from Ausone near Troplong-Mondot and Trottevieille—could not have a better location. However, too often the wines have turned out relatively light and undistinguished. Everything else seems to be in order: the weaker vats are relegated to a second wine, and a small percentage (20–25%) of new oak is used each year. Nevertheless, much like the situation involving the owner's superbly situated estate in Pomerol, Vraye-Croix-de-Gay, the problem may be that the yields are entirely too high to produce top-quality wine. That is a shame, because like Vraye-Croix-de-Gay in Pomerol, Le Prieuré has a splendid situation within the St.-Emilion appellation.

VINTAGES

1989—Le Prieuré's 1989 is a soft, commercial wine with round, agree-
· able, currant fruit flavors and some endearing fatness and
83 charm, but it is just too easy to drink. Anticipated maturity: Now–
1996. Last tasted, 4/91.

1988—The 1988 is a straightforward, extremely light, medium-bodied
· wine lacking concentration and finish. Anticipated maturity:
79 Now–1996. Last tasted, 4/91.

PRIEURÉ-LESCOURS (Grand Cru)   AVERAGE

Production: 2,000 cases	Grape varieties: Merlot—75% Cabernet Franc—20% Malbec—5%
Secondary label: none	
Vineyard size: 10 acres	Proprietor: The Sinsout family
Time spent in barrels: 12–14 months	Average age of vines: 30 years
Evaluation of present classification: The quality equivalent of a Médoc Cru Bourgeois	
Plateau of maturity: 3–8 years following the vintage	

This property has been in the same family for over 150 years. While the quality is undistinguished, the wine tends to be robust and well colored, but straightforward and somewhat monolithic. Perhaps the location of the vineyard in the commune of Saint-Sulpice-de-Faleyrens (less well drained soils and a mediocre exposition) explains the lack of complexity and finesse that are so frequently characteristics of Prieuré-Lescours.

PUY-BLANQUET (Grand Cru)   AVERAGE

Production: 12,000 cases	Grape varieties: Merlot—75% Cabernet Sauvignon—20% Cabernet Franc—5%
Secondary label: none	
Vineyard size: 56.8 acres	Proprietor: Roger Jacquet
Time spent in barrels: 16–20 months	Average age of vines: 24 years
Evaluation of present classification: The quality equivalent of a Médoc Cru Bourgeois	
Plateau of maturity: 3–8 years following the vintage	

I have consistently found this wine ranging from mediocre to disappointing on nearly every occasion I have tasted it. It lacks generosity, has yet to be complex, and comes across as attenuated and compact. As the following tasting notes indicate, this is one of St.-Emilion's perennial mediocrities.

VINTAGES

1989—The 1989 Puy-Blanquet has a streak of greenness that suggests
· the grapes were picked before they were fully ripe. In the mouth,
73 the hardness and toughness of the tannins seem to be struggling
   with the wine's moderately endowed fruitiness. This should turn
   out to be a lightweight, stern, hard-edged wine. Anticipated maturity: 1992–2003. Last tasted, 4/91.

1988—The 1988 exhibits more ripeness, richness, and length on the
· palate in a medium-bodied, more charming and graceful style.
81 Anticipated maturity: 1992–2002. Last tasted, 4/91.

1986—Puy-Blanquet is not an estate making terribly seductive Bor-
· deaux. Their wines tend to have a leanness and hardness despite
74 the high-quality winemaking. The 1986 is no exception, and just
   seems to be short in charm and fruit. Anticipated maturity: Now–
   1995. Last tasted, 3/89.

1985—The 1985 tasted awkward and not quite right. Judgment reserved.
· Last tasted, 3/89.
?

RIPEAU (Grand Cru Classé)   GOOD

Production: 6,000 cases	Grape varieties: Merlot—60% Cabernet Franc—40%
Secondary label: none	
Vineyard size: 38.2 acres	Proprietor: Madame de Wilde- Janoueix
Time spent in barrels: 18–20 months	Average age of vines: 20 years
Evaluation of present classification: The quality equivalent of a good Médoc Cru Bourgeois	
Plateau of maturity: 3–12 years following the vintage	

Ripeau is one of the older estates of St.-Emilion, taking its name from
the parcel of land on which the vineyard and château are situated. The
soil is primarily sand intermixed with some gravel. Ripeau's vineyard
sits near Cheval Blanc and La Dominique, but is less well placed than
either. The new owners acquired the property in 1976 and major renovations have taken place. This has always been a relatively chunky,
fruity wine that lacked consistency, but when it was good it could be
counted on to drink well for at least a decade. Until recently, Ripeau was
one of only a handful of vineyards to be planted by the old, extremely
dense system of more than 10,000 vines per hectare.

I have not seen any vintages of Ripeau from the late eighties, but the 1981, 1982, and 1983 were all competently made, robust St.-Emilions that should have been consumed by 1990.

ROCHER-BELLEVUE-FIGEAC (Unclassified) GOOD

Production: 2,000 cases	Grape varieties: Merlot—85% Cabernet Franc—15%
Secondary label: none	
Vineyard size: 10 acres	Administrator: Domaines Cordier
Time spent in barrels: 18 months	Average age of vines: 30 years
Evaluation of present classification: The quality equivalent of a good Médoc Cru Bourgeois	
Plateau of maturity: 3–8 years following the vintage	

The Domaines Cordier has been overseeing the vinification and commercialization of this wine since the mid-1980s. The wines have definitely benefited from the attention of Cordier's brilliant oenologist, Georges Pauli. However, this is not one of St.-Emilion's long-lived wines. Why? No doubt because the vineyard, situated on the plateau near both Figeac and the border of Pomerol, is planted with an extremely high percentage of Merlot. The result is a juicy, almost succulently fruity, round wine that makes for delicious drinking early, and is best consumed by 7–8 years of age. I would be cautious about buying anything older.

VINTAGES

1989—From the cask, the 1989 looked a bit diluted and unstructured,
· but it has firmed up considerably in the bottle. It offers dark ruby
84 color and fat, forward, generously endowed flavors, with a great
deal of glycerin and alcohol. There is low acidity and plenty of
soft tannin. A juicy, jammy mouthful of Merlot. Anticipated maturity: Now–1996. Last tasted, 4/91.

1988—The 1988 is a more classic wine, superior in all aspects to the
· 1989. Deep ruby/purple, structured, and intense, in a medium- to
86 full-bodied format, this is a rich, nicely concentrated, complex
wine. Anticipated maturity: 1992–1998. Last tasted, 4/91.

1985—This wine is clearly one of the sleepers of the vintage. Deep ruby/
· purple in color, this lush, voluptuous, full-bodied wine has an
88 intense bouquet of ripe plums, blackberries, and oak. Exceptionally concentrated, rich, supple, and velvety, this excellent wine

should age gracefully. Anticipated maturity: Now–1997. Last
tasted, 4/91.

ROLLAND-MAILLET (Grand Cru)   GOOD

Production: 2,000 cases	Grape varieties:
	Merlot—75%
	Cabernet Franc—25%
Secondary label: none	
Vineyard size: 10 acres	Proprietor: Michel Rolland
Time spent in barrels: 18 months	Average age of vines: 25 years
Evaluation of present classification: A solidly made St.-Emilion that is consistently good to very good	
Plateau of maturity: 3–9 years following the vintage	

Bordeaux insiders often look for this well-made St.-Emilion owned and
vinified by the famous Libourne oenologist Michel Rolland. It tends to
be a chunky, robust, deeply concentrated, as well as opaquely colored
St.-Emilion that can age for up to a decade. What it lacks in finesse and
elegance, it often makes up for with pure power and robustness. The
best recent vintages include very fine wines in 1982, 1983, 1986, 1988,
1989, and 1990.

ST.-GEORGES-CÔTE PAVIE (Grand Cru Classé)   GOOD

Production: 2,200 cases	Grape varieties:
	Merlot—60%
	Cabernet Sauvignon—40%
Secondary label: none	
Vineyard size: 15 acres	Proprietor: Jacques Masson
Time spent in barrels: 18–22 months	Average age of vines: 30 years
Evaluation of present classification: The quality equivalent of a Médoc Cru Bourgeois	
Plateau of maturity: 3–12 years following the vintage	

This is another tiny St.-Emilion vineyard that is extremely well placed
on the hillside known as the Côte de Pavie. In fact, the vineyards of
Pavie sit on one side of this property, with those of La Gaffelière on the
other.

The only vintages I have tasted, 1988, 1989, and 1990, were round,
generously endowed, easy-to-like St.-Emilions that lacked complexity,

but offered copious amounts of straightforward, chunky, black fruit married nicely with the scent of new oak and herbaceous aromas. My best guess is that they will last for 8–10 or more years. This could be a property to take seriously. An unusually high percentage of Cabernet Sauvignon is used in the blend.

SANSONNET (Grand Cru Classé)   AVERAGE

Production: 4,000 cases	Grape varieties:
	Merlot—60%
	Cabernet Franc—20 %
	Cabernet Sauvignon—20%
Secondary label: Domaine de la Salle	
Vineyard size: 17.5 acres	Proprietor: Francis Robin
Time spent in barrels: 16–20 months	Average age of vines: 25 years
Evaluation of present classification: The quality equivalent of a Médoc Cru Bourgeois	
Plateau of maturity: 4–14 years following the vintage	

This property, which has been in the Robin family for four generations, is located east of the town of St.-Emilion on well-placed hillsides composed of a limestone and clay soil base, with a very rocky subsoil. The wine is aged in small oak barrels, yet seems to turn out relatively austere and rough-edged wines if what I tasted of the 1978, 1979, 1982, 1983, and 1985 were representative of Sansonnet's style. This wine may have greater appeal for consumers who prefer more rustic-styled St.-Emilions.

LA SERRE (Grand Cru Classé)   AVERAGE

Production: 3,000 cases	Grape varieties:
	Merlot—80%
	Cabernet Sauvignon—20%
Secondary label: none	
Vineyard size: 17.5 acres	Proprietor: The d'Arfeuille family
Time spent in barrels: 18 months	Average age of vines: 35 years
Evaluation of present classification: The quality equivalent of a Médoc Cru Bourgeois	
Plateau of maturity: 3–8 years following the vintage	

This property, well situated between the more renowned vineyards of Villemaurine and Trottevieille, has a clay and gravel soil base. The relatively high percentage of Merlot results in wines that are round, with a great deal of glycerin and fat. While I have had several very fine examples of La Serre (1982, 1985, and 1989), other vintages have lacked concentration and come across as too diluted and simple. It is a property to take seriously in certain vintages, but it has been characterized by inconsistency.

SOUTARD (Grand Cru Classé)   EXCELLENT

Production: 10,000 cases	Grape varieties: Merlot—60% Cabernet Franc—40%
Secondary label: Clos de la Tonnelle	
Vineyard size: 55.3 acres	Proprietor: The Ligneris family
Time spent in barrels: 22–28 months	Average age of vines: 30 years
Evaluation of present classification: Should be upgraded to a St.-Emilion Premier Grand Cru Classé; the quality equivalent of a Médoc third- or fourth-growth	
Plateau of maturity: 10–25 or more years following the vintage	

This is one of the oldest St.-Emilion estates and has been owned by the same family since 1785. Situated in the northern part of the appellation, the vineyard is located on a soil base composed primarily of limestone.

Soutard is highly prized in the Benelux countries, but the wine has largely been ignored outside Europe. That is a shame, because this is one of the most traditionally made and longest-lived wines in St.-Emilion, rivaled only by Ausone and a handful of other St.-Emilions in terms of potential longevity. Most vintages can easily last for 25 or more years, and are often unapproachable for a decade.

The property employs at least one-third new oak for bringing up the wine, and often bottles it much later than other St.-Emilion châteaux. Soutard is usually an opaque dark ruby color (there is no fining or filtration), and possesses a powerful, tannic ferocity that can be off-putting when the wine is young. Nevertheless, this is one of St.-Emilion's best-kept secrets. For consumers looking for wines capable of lasting 20 or more years, Soutard should be seriously considered.

VINTAGES

1989—As one might expect, Soutard's 1989 is one of the most backward
· wines of the vintage. Impressively opaque ruby/purple, with a
90 spicy, vanillin-scented, plum and licorice bouquet, this full-bodied, muscular, densely concentrated wine needs at least 7–10
years of bottle aging. It may well merit an outstanding rating by
the turn of the century. Look for it to last at least 20 or more
years. One of the most impressive wines of the vintage, it may
well be the longest-lived St.-Emilion produced in 1989. Anticipated maturity: 2000–2020. Last tasted, 4/91.

1988—Backward, dense, concentrated, and unforthcoming, this rela-
· tively powerful, more herbaceous-scented Soutard has plenty of
87 extract, but it is now buried beneath considerable quantities of
tannin. The tannins are sharper and more aggressive than in the
1989. Nevertheless, this is a worthy candidate for 20 or more
years of cellaring. Anticipated maturity: 1998–2020. Last tasted,
4/91.

1986—Soutard remains one of the longest-lived wines in the appellation
· of St.-Emilion. There is no doubt that the proprietors intentionally
86 pack this wine with gobs of extract and mouth-seering tannins,
making it a sure bet to last 20 years, but not approachable before
10. The 1986 is a very backward, unyielding wine, with tremendous tannin levels, but also rich, highly extracted, concentrated
fruit. Anticipated maturity: 1996–2015. Last tasted, 3/90.

1985—The 1985 Soutard is a sensationally rich, tannic, deep, multidi-
· mensional wine that balances muscle and grace. It is more supple
90 than usual, but still capable of 20 or more years of longevity.
Anticipated maturity: 1996–2010. Last tasted, 3/90.

1982—The 1982 is an old-style St.-Emilion made to last and last. It
· belongs with enthusiasts who have the patience to lay it away for
87 a decade or more. The 1982 is typically huge, backward, almost
abrasively tannic. However, this wine—which is now quite closed
—has a broodingly dark color and excellent richness, ripeness,
and weight on the palate, and will no doubt receive a higher score
circa 2000, but it is brutally tannic now. Anticipated maturity:
2000–2025. Last tasted, 3/89.

1981—The 1981 is closed in, but exhibits ripe, spicy, plummy fruit, a
· tight, firm structure, and plenty of weight and richness. Soutard
84 has made an impressive wine in 1981, but once again one needs
patience. Anticipated maturity: 1995–2005. Last tasted, 6/84.

1979—A very successful 1979, but unlike most wines from this vintage,
· Soutard is backward and tannic, with a deep ruby color, and a
84 big-framed structure. It is still raw, undeveloped, and tastes like

a barrel sample rather than a 5-year-old wine. Anticipated maturity: Now–2005. Last tasted, 6/84.

1978—Totally different in style from the 1979, the 1978 Soutard tastes
·　　much softer and riper, and has more mid-range fruit, full body,
84　　relatively low acidity, and a good, lush, moderately tannic finish. For Soutard, this wine will develop much more quickly than normal. Anticipated maturity: Now–1998. Last tasted, 6/84.

1975—A very impressive wine, the 1975 Soutard is still youthfully dark
·　　ruby, with rich, savory, ripe, full-bodied flavors, plenty of mouth-
87　　coating tannins, and a long finish. This is a big, typical Soutard that will continue to evolve very slowly. Anticipated maturity: Now–2005. Last tasted, 10/84.

1966—Not so big or so intense as one might expect, the 1966 Soutard is
·　　fully mature and has a dark color with some brown at the edge, a
82　　ripe, harmonious, sweet palate impression, and some light tannins in the finish. This vintage of Soutard is surprisingly elegant and lighter than expected. Anticipated maturity: Now–may be in decline. Last tasted, 6/81.

1964—This is one of the few great Soutards that can be said to have
·　　reached full maturity. The huge bouquet of roasted cassis, grilled
90　　nuts, and smoky oak also has a touch of volatile acidity that adds rather than detracts from its appeal. In the mouth, it has a voluptuous, full-bodied, opulent texture, gobs of fruit, and plenty of alcohol in its heady finish. This is a dense, old-styled, superbly concentrated wine that should continue to drink well for another 10–15 or more years. Anticipated maturity: Now–2000. Last tasted, 3/90.

OLDER VINTAGES

The only old Soutard I had the privilege of tasting was the 1955 (rated 88 in 1989). I am sure at one time it was an unbearably rustic wine, but the tannins have largely melted away, even though the wine is still relatively firm. The result is a rich, full-bodied, mineral-scented wine offering gobs of black fruits (plums) in its taste. Along with Ausone, could it be that Soutard is the longest-lived wine of St.-Emilion?

TAUZINAT L'HERMITAGE (Unclassified) AVERAGE

Production: 4,000 cases	Grape varieties:
	Merlot—70%
	Cabernet Franc—30%
Secondary label: none	
Vineyard size: 21 acres	Proprietor: Armand Moueix
Time spent in barrels: 12–18 months	Average age of vines: 25 years

Evaluation of present classification: An indifferently made, mediocre St.-Emilion

Plateau of maturity: 3–7 years following the vintage

Based on the half-dozen or so vintages I have tasted from this property located in the commune of Saint-Christophe des Bardes, the quality of the wine is disappointing. Watery and thin, it is of little interest. Clearly improvements are warranted.

TERTRE-DAUGAY (Grand Cru Classé) GOOD

Production: 5,000 cases	Grape varieties:
	Merlot—60%
	Cabernet Franc—30%
	Cabernet Sauvignon—10%
Secondary label: Château de Roquefort	
Vineyard size: 40 acres	Proprietor: Comte Léo de Malet-Roquefort
Time spent in barrels: 18–22 months	Average age of vines: 25 years

Evaluation of present classification: The quality equivalent of a good Médoc Cru Bourgeois

Plateau of maturity: 5–15 years following the vintage

This was a property that, because of sloppy winemaking and the lack of effective management, lost complete credibility during the sixties and seventies. In 1978, the proprietor of La Gaffelière, Comte Léo de Malet-Roquefort, purchased the property and has made significant improvements both to the vineyards and to the wine cellar. It has taken some time for the vineyard to totally rebound, but both the 1988 and 1989 look promising, particularly after such a prolonged period of mediocrity.

Historically, Tertre-Daugay is one of the most ancient properties in

St.-Emilion. It is located on the hillside near most of the Premiers Grands Crus Classés. The actual name is derived from the Gascon term, Daugay, which means "look-out hill." The excellent exposure enjoyed by the vineyard of Tertre-Daugay ensures maximum ripening of the grapes. The soil, a combination of clay and limestone with significant iron deposits in the subsoil, is claimed to give the wines great body and concentration. Tertre-Daugay is a property to keep an eye on in the nineties.

VINTAGES

1989—After extensive replanting, this longtime underachiever is finally
      · beginning to resurrect its image for quality. The 1989 is the best
   88   wine produced at the property in the last 30 years. Concentrated, full bodied, with a heady alcohol content, this lavish, richly fruity, broad-shouldered wine should be drunk in its first decade of life. Anticipated maturity: 1992–2005. Last tasted, 4/91.

1988—The attractive aroma of dried herbs and black fruits is integrated
      · nicely with the smell of toasty new oak. In the mouth, the wine is
   86   medium bodied and spicy, with better acidity and more aggressive tannins than in the opulent 1989. This is a well-made, amply endowed St.-Emilion that needs some time to round out and shed the tannin. Anticipated maturity: 1992–2001. Last tasted, 4/91.

1985—The 1985 offers up succulent fruit, plenty of toasty oak, a meaty,
      · chewy texture, and a long, velvety finish. Anticipated maturity:
   85   Now–1996. Last tasted, 3/90.

LE TERTRE-ROTEBOEUF (Grand Cru)   EXCELLENT

Production: 2,000 cases	Grape varieties: Merlot—80% Cabernet Franc—20%
Secondary label: none	
Vineyard size: 11 acres	Proprietor: François Mitjavile
Time spent in barrels: 18–22 months	Average age of vines: 24 years
Evaluation of present classification: Should be elevated to a St.-Emilion Premier Grand Cru Classé; the quality equivalent of a Médoc second-growth	
Plateau of maturity: 3–15 years following the vintage	

It is unfortunate, but, I suppose, given the commercial world in which we live, totally understandable that there are just so few people in the wine world like François Mitjavile. While many famous producers push yields to such preposterous levels that they risk destroying any concept of *terroir* of the vineyard, or even muting the character of a vintage, here is one man whose talent and obsession for producing the finest possible wines are refreshing. I do not mean to suggest there are not individuals like Mitjavile in other countries. There are Angelo Gaja, Luciano Sandrone, and Elio Altare in Piedmont, and California's Josh Jensen to name a few, but quite honestly, there are just too few in the wine world like Mitjavile.

Le Tertre-Roteboeuf's micro-sized vineyard now receives worldwide attention. It is no doubt justified, but one hopes nothing changes at this estate, which is run with single-minded determination by Monsieur Mitjavile. He makes no compromises. What Mitjavile has in mind is to make a wine from this splendidly situated vineyard that has the extract and intensity of wines such as Lafleur, Pétrus, and Certan de May in Pomerol. To do so, Mitjavile is one of the last to harvest, keeps his yields small, and since 1985, utilizes 100% new oak to harness the power of his wine. There is no doubt that recent vintages have had dazzling levels of fruit, and a flashy flamboyance that have drawn numerous rave reviews from the European wine press.

The steep, sheltered vineyard (near Larcis-Ducasse) is named after the oxen that are necessary to cultivate the soil. When translated, the name means "the hill of the belching beef." Le Tertre-Roteboeuf is irrefutably one of Bordeaux's new superstars.

VINTAGES

1989—The 1989 Le Tertre-Roteboeuf is the most concentrated wine of
·   the vintage. That tells you something about proprietor Mitjavile
94   and his refusal to let yields soar to limits that many of his famous
        neighbors are permitting with great regularity. The wine is
        opaque black/purple in color, with a splendid aroma of roasted
        chestnuts, black fruits, exotic spices, and minerals. In the mouth,
        it is so rich and concentrated one thinks of the opulence and
        richness of a Pétrus or a Guigal La Mouline rather than a St.-
        Emilion. Of course, when anyone has low yields and picks this
        late, there is always the danger that the wine can become flabby
        and overripe. Somehow, Mitjavile avoids that, and now that he is
        using a very high percentage of new oak, the wood frames this
        awesomely structured and massively concentrated wine. The re-
        sults reveal winemaking genius. Anticipated maturity: 1993–
        2010. Last tasted, 4/91.

1988—Mitjavile's 1988 is extraordinary, and, once again, supercon-
·   centrated, with a dazzling level of extract, and a powerful, full-
91   bodied, concentrated finish. It is less flashy and unctuous than

the 1989, and those who like their Bordeaux a bit more linear and obviously tannic may prefer the 1988. It is a spectacular, riveting wine from one of the most driven winemakers in the world. I know the wine has now become hard to find, but producers like this deserve consumers' support, even allegiance. Anticipated maturity: 1995–2010. Last tasted, 4/91.

1986—The 1986 is a prodigious wine, aged in 100% new oak, with fabu-
  ·   lous ripeness and richness, as well as an amazingly long, opulent,
  91   fleshy finish. The wine is immensely seductive and full bodied, and despite its precocious appeal, should age well for at least a decade. Anticipated maturity: 1992–2002. Last tasted, 3/91.

1985—The 1985 Le Tertre-Roteboeuf has an astonishing level of rich-
  ·   ness, a perfume of a wine costing three to four times as much,
  90   full body, an opulent texture that recalls a great 1982, and a penetrating fragrance and taste that are top class. Anticipated maturity: Now–2000. Last tasted, 3/91.

1984—A successful 1984, this wine is meaty, cleanly made, soft, and
  ·   well colored. Anticipated maturity: Now–1994. Last tasted, 3/91.
  81

1983—This wine has reached full maturity and has taken on a slightly
  ·   amber edge to its deep ruby color. The big, spicy, ripe nose offers
  87   up gobs of mineral scents and superripe black fruit. In the mouth, this fleshy, chewy, full-bodied wine has excellent extract, a velvety texture, and a long, heady, alcoholic finish. Anticipated maturity: Now–2000. Last tasted, 3/90.

1982—Deep ruby, with some orange/amber at the edge, this full-bodied,
  ·   dramatically styled St.-Emilion has reached full maturity. Expan-
  87   sively flavored, with sweet, ripe fruit intermixed with smells and flavors of smoky almonds, cedar, and herbs, this rich wine was made at a time when Mitjavile could not afford to use new oak. Consequently, the wine was aged in older barrels. Given the raw materials, one suspects that if this wine had been put in new oak, it would have merited at least five more points. Nevertheless, this is a deliciously succulent, generously endowed wine. Anticipated maturity: Now–1996. Last tasted, 3/91.

LA TOUR DU GUETTEUR (Unclassified)

Production: 100 cases	Grape varieties: Merlot—50% Cabernet Franc—50%
Secondary label: none	
Vineyard size: .8 acre	Proprietor: Antoinette Andrieux
Time spent in barrels: 24 months	Average age of vines: 55 years
Evaluation of present classification: Should be elevated to a St.-Emilion Premier Grand Cru Classé	
Plateau of maturity: 8–30 or more years following the vintage	

This is one of the two smallest vineyards in St.-Emilion, and that is probably the reason why it has never been considered for classification. That is a shame, because the wine, represented in America by Hand-Picked Selections in Warrenton, Virginia, can last for 30 or more years as vintages from the late fifties evidenced. The tiny vineyard is located within the walls of St.-Emilion. The average age of the vines is extremely old, which results in amazingly low yields. The huge concentration of flavor and full-bodied texture are the result of low yields and the wine-making philosophy of this château's oenologist, Michel Rolland.

I have not seen any recent vintages of La Tour du Guetteur, but I have fond memories of the 1959 and 1964. The best way of obtaining a bottle is by calling the château directly. Their telephone number is 57.84.38.52.

LA TOUR-FIGEAC (Grand Cru Classé)

Production: 6,000 cases	Grape varieties: Merlot—60% Cabernet Franc—40%
Secondary label: none	
Vineyard size: 33.3 acres	Proprietor: Michel Boutet
Time spent in barrels: 15–22 months	Average age of vines: 35 years
Evaluation of present classification: The quality equivalent of a good Médoc Cru Bourgeois	
Plateau of maturity: 3–10 years following the vintage	

This property, like so many St.-Emilion estates with the name Figeac, was once part of the huge domain of Figeac until it was partitioned in

1879. The vineyard, which is easy to spot because of the tower that sits in the middle of the vineyards, and from which the château takes part of its name, is bordered on one side by Cheval Blanc and on the south by Figeac. To the west is the appellation of Pomerol.

The winemaking has been consistently very good at La Tour-Figeac. The vinification takes place in stainless-steel vats and there is a lengthy maceration of almost 3 weeks. One-third new oak casks are used, and, depending on the vintage, the wine is generally aged for up to 18 months in small oak.

Unfortunately, I have not seen a vintage of La Tour-Figeac after 1983.

VINTAGES

1983—This is an uncomplicated style of St.-Emilion, yet few can deny
    ·   its charm and appeal. Dark ruby, with an open-knit bouquet of
   84   black cherry fruit, this medium- to full-bodied wine has soft, vel-
          vety, fat, fruity flavors, a long, smooth finish, and a heady alcohol
          content. Anticipated maturity: Now–1993. Last tasted, 1/85.

1982—This wine has been delicious since its release and still evidences
    ·   no signs of decline. It has always been characterized by a big,
   86   jammy, blackcurrant, spicy, cedary nose, a lush, medium-bodied,
          silky texture, and soft tannins in an alcoholic finish. It is a very
          satisfying, fleshy style of St.-Emilion that has consistently pro-
          vided me with great enjoyment. Anticipated maturity: Now–1999.
          Last tasted, 1/91.

1981—A shade lighter and less concentrated than either the 1982 or
    ·   1983, the 1981 La Tour-Figeac has a ripe berryish, lovely bou-
   84   quet, supple, soft, fruity flavors, medium body, and no tannins.
          Anticipated maturity: Now–may be in decline. Last tasted, 1/85.

1978—Still very darkly colored, this wine appears fully mature, with an
    ·   open-knit, crushed blackberry bouquet, jammy, rich, yet soft fla-
   85   vors, medium body, and plenty of alcoholic kick in the finish.
          Anticipated maturity: Now–may be in decline. Last tasted, 1/85.

LA TOUR-DU-PIN-FIGEAC-GIRAUD-BÉLIVIER
(Grand Cru Classé)

AVERAGE

Production: 5,000 cases	Grape varieties: Merlot—75% Cabernet Franc—25%
Secondary label: none Vineyard size: 26.5 acres	Proprietor: The Giraud- Bélivier family
Time spent in barrels: 20–22 months	Average age of vines: 40 years
Evaluation of present classification: The quality equivalent of a Médoc Cru Bourgeois	
Plateau of maturity: 3–9 years following the vintage	

This property was separated from the other La Tour-du-Pin-Figeac in 1882 and was purchased by the Giraud family in 1972. I had some disappointing experiences with this wine in the early eighties and have not seen a vintage since 1983. The wine's reputation among Bordeaux brokers is one of mediocrity. That is a shame as many believe their vineyards, adjacent to Cheval Blanc, are among the best in this portion of the St.-Emilion appellation.

LA TOUR-DU-PIN-FIGEAC-MOUEIX
(Grand Cru Classé)

VERY GOOD

Production: 4,000 cases	Grape varieties: Merlot—60% Cabernet Franc—30% Malbec—10%
Secondary label: none Vineyard size: 22 acres	Proprietor: Armand Moueix
Time spent in barrels: 16–22 months	Average age of vines: 20 years
Evaluation of present classification: Since 1982, the quality equivalent of a Médoc fifth-growth	
Plateau of maturity: 3–12 or more years following the vintage	

There are two estates called La Tour-du-Pin-Figeac. One is owned by the Giraud family (described above) and that property makes mediocre wine. The other estate, owned by the Armand Moueix family, makes much better wine and that estate is described here. La Tour-du-Pin-

Figeac-Moueix is situated on a sandy, clay, gravelly soil base on the Pomerol border between Cheval Blanc and La Tour-Figeac.

The wine of La Tour-du-Pin-Figeac-Moueix is made in a straightforward, fleshy, fruity style, with good body, and an aging potential of 6–12 years. Few vintages of this wine will improve beyond their 12th birthday. I have, I believe, detected much higher quality since 1982.

VINTAGES

1989—The 1989 is one of the sleepers of the vintage. It is a concentrated,
·   powerful, full-bodied wine, with gobs of extract, and a penetrating
88   bouquet of black fruits, new oak, and subtle herbs. A powerhouse
      of a wine, it is well balanced, with decent acidity for the vintage,
      and a super finish. Anticipated maturity: 1994–2003. Last tasted,
      4/91.

1988—The 1988 is a worthy competitor to the 1989, with excellent ex-
·   tract, more elegance but less power, and a rich, toasty, plummy
87   bouquet intertwined with scents of licorice, toast, and spring flow-
      ers. It is full bodied and intense for a 1988. Anticipated maturity:
      1992–2004. Last tasted, 4/91.

1986—The 1986 is packed with oodles of berry fruit, is full bodied, and
·   has significant tannins in the finish. While it lacks the charm of
87   the excellent 1985, it should last for at least two decades. Antici-
      pated maturity: 1993–2005. Last tasted, 3/90.

1985—The 1985 is an impressive St.-Emilion, with grip and very fine
·   balance. Powerful, concentrated, rich, opaque in color, full bod-
87   ied, and soft enough to drink now, this boldly flavored wine will
      keep well for another decade. Anticipated maturity: Now–2000.
      Last tasted, 3/89.

1982—One of the best efforts in years from this property, the 1982 is
·   dark ruby, with an attractive ripe berryish, spicy bouquet. On the
85   palate, the wine is silky, velvety, and medium to full bodied, with
      light to moderate tannins, and a good, lush finish. Anticipated
      maturity: Now–1993. Last tasted, 1/85.

1981—Soft and fleshy, with a moderately intense, perfumed bouquet,
·   the 1981 La Tour-du-Pin-Figeac-Moueix is tasting quite preco-
82   cious, with good solid fruit, plenty of body, and moderate tannin.
      Not complex, but very agreeable. This wine may now be tiring.
      Anticipated maturity: Now. Last tasted, 6/83.

1979—Approaching maturity, this medium ruby wine has a spicy, ripe
·   berryish bouquet, round, moderately concentrated flavors, and
82   light tannin in the finish. Anticipated maturity: Now. Last tasted,
      1/83.

1976—Beginning to fade and lose its fruit, the 1976 La Tour-du-Pin-·
·   Figeac-Moueix displays a lot of brown in the color, washed-out,
67   dull fruity flavors, and a short finish. Last tasted, 11/82.

TRIMOULET (Grand Cru Classé)   AVERAGE

Production: 10,000 cases	Grape varieties: Merlot—60% Cabernet Franc—25% Cabernet Sauvignon—10% Malbec—5%
Secondary label: Cadet de Trimoulet	
Vineyard size: 50 acres	Proprietor: Michel Jean
Time spent in barrels: 16–18 months	Average age of vines: 40 years
Evaluation of present classification: The quality equivalent of a Médoc Cru Bourgeois	
Plateau of maturity: 3–7 years following the vintage	

At one time this property had an excellent reputation for the aging potential of its wines. Something must have changed, because the vintages in
the eighties have been soft, straightforward wines of relatively indifferent
quality. The vineyard, situated in the northeast section of the appellation
near the boundary of the satellite appellation of St.-Georges, possesses
soils of clay and sand, with beds of iron-enriched subsoil. Amazingly for
such light wines, 100% new oak casks are claimed to be used, which is
surprising in view of the lack of grip and vanillin character I have detected in recent years.

    Nevertheless, in years such as 1982, 1985, and 1988, this is a soft,
straightforward, competent, and correct St.-Emilion that most tasters
would find uninspiring.

TROPLONG-MONDOT (Grand Cru Classé)   EXCELLENT

Production: 10,000 cases	Grape varieties: Merlot—65% Cabernet Sauvignon—15% Cabernet Franc—10% Malbec—10%
Secondary label: Mondot	
Vineyard size: 75 acres	Proprietor: Claude Valette Administrator: Christine Fabre-Valette
Time spent in barrels: 20 months	Average age of vines: 40 years

Evaluation of present classification: Since 1985, should be elevated
to a St.-Emilion Premier Grand Cru Classé; the quality equivalent
of a Médoc third-growth

Plateau of maturity: 5–15 or more years following the vintage

This lovely château, with a magnificent view overlooking the town and vineyards of St.-Emilion, sits on a slope facing the Côte de Pavie. There are numerous old vines, with some plantings of Malbec nearly 100 years in age. Since Michel Rolland was brought in as the oenologist, and Christine Fabre began assuming more control, the quality of the vintages since the mid-1980s has soared. There is an extended maceration in stainless-steel vats and aging of the wine for at least 18 months in oak casks, of which one-third are new. Although the wine is fined, it is never filtered.

I should also note that the introduction of a secondary label has resulted in weaker vats being relegated to that wine, which has only served to strengthen the wine that appears under the label Troplong-Mondot.

All the conditions seem to be present to allow Troplong-Mondot to become one of the stars of the St.-Emilion appellation in this decade. St.-Emilion and Pomerol have had their share of famous, even legendary, female proprietors. There was Madame Fournier at Château Canon, and of course, the well-known Madame Loubat of Pétrus. Now the appellation boasts Christine Fabre, whose extraordinary commitment to quality is especially evident in great wines produced at Troplong-Mondot in the 1988, 1989, and 1990 vintages.

VINTAGES

1989—The 1989 has a full-bodied, enormously rich, powerful, concen-
·   trated feel on the palate, with highly extracted flavors of plums
91   and cassis. Quite tannic, yet voluptuous because of its low acid-

ity, this is a stunning, intensely fragrant, and compelling wine. I suspect Christine Fabré probably prefers the more restrained and elegant 1988 to her 1989. Anticipated maturity: 1994–2008. Last tasted, 4/91.

1988— The 1988 is a beautifully made wine with a deep ruby/purple
   ·   color, a fascinating bouquet of plums, spicy new oak, and min-
  90   erals, rich, multidimensional flavors, better acidity and lower al-
cohol than the 1989, but good tannins, and an endearing lushness and intensity to its long finish. Again, this is an example of a young proprietor committed to making a strict selection, taking the risk and waiting to pick the vineyard late, and introducing a second label for the vats not impressive enough for the grand vin. Anticipated maturity: 1993–2007. Last tasted, 4/91.

1986— The 1986 is a more structured version of the elegant, complex
   ·   1985. There is a good lashing of toasty new oak, medium body, a
  89   moderately intense bouquet of cedary, blackcurrant fruit, excel-
lent length, and complete harmony among the wine's elements. Anticipated maturity: 1992–2005. Last tasted, 3/90.

1985— The 1985, with a deep ruby color and a complex bouquet of spicy
   ·   oak and ripe currants, offers extremely well-balanced and well-
  87   delineated flavors, medium body, excellent depth, and firm, but
soft tannins. Anticipated maturity: Now–1998. Last tasted, 3/90.

1984— Very light, dilute, short on the palate, but drinkable, the 1984
   ·   Troplong should be drunk up. Anticipated maturity: Now–may be
  73   in decline. Last tasted, 3/87.

1982— Refreshingly fruity, forthright, and attractive, this medium-bod-
   ·   ied wine is surprisingly light for the vintage, has some tannins
  81   and a soft, supple, berryish fruitiness, and finishes slightly sweet.
Anticipated maturity: Now–1994. Last tasted, 11/90.

1981— Not much different from the 1982, the 1981 is perhaps less fleshy,
   ·   ripe, and concentrated, but it has a light- to medium-bodied feel
  79   on the palate, soft, fruity flavors, and some light tannins in the
finish. Anticipated maturity: Now–may be in decline. Last tasted, 1/85.

1979— The 1979 is an attractively fruity, soft, ripe, moderately rich wine,
   ·   with good body and concentration, a supple, round, easygoing
  82   texture, and a warm, soft finish. Anticipated maturity: Now–may
be in decline. Last tasted, 3/83.

1978— Ready to drink, this wine is soft, supple, and medium bodied,
   ·   with a loose-knit structure, moderately intense, jammy fruit, light
  75   tannins, and some alcohol showing through in the finish. Anticipated maturity: Now–may be in decline. Last tasted, 1/82.

1976—Disturbingly brown in color, the 1976 Troplong-Mondot lacks con-
·   centration and fruit, and since it seems to be cracking up at the
65   seams, it is best drunk up as soon as possible. Last tasted, 2/83.

TROTTEVIEILLE (Premier Grand Cru Classé)   EXCELLENT

Production: 3,500 cases	Grape varieties: Merlot—50% Cabernet Franc—45% Cabernet Sauvignon—5%
Secondary label: none Vineyard size: 25 acres	Proprietor: Emile Castéja Administrator: Philippe Castéja
Time spent in barrels: 18–24 months	Average age of vines: 40 years
Evaluation of present classification: Since 1986, the wines justify Trottevieille's rating as a Premier Grand Cru Classé; previously the wine was the quality equivalent of a Médoc Cru Bourgeois	
Plateau of maturity: 5–20 years following the vintage	

One of the celebrated Premiers Grands Crus Classés of St.-Emilion, Trottevieille's vineyard is located east of St.-Emilion in a relatively iso-lated spot on clay and limestone soil. Since 1949, it has been the property of the well-known firm of Bordeaux *négociants*, Borie-Manoux. This firm also owns Batailley, the fifth-growth Pauillac, and Domaine de L'Eglise, an up-and-coming Pomerol, as well as a bevy of lesser-known Bordeaux châteaux.

Trottevieille is a wine with which I have had many disappointing ex-periences. Until the mid-1980s, the property produced wines that were among the most mediocre of St.-Emilion. Prior to 1985, Trottevieille too frequently lacked concentration and character, and was often disturb-ingly light and dull; in some vintages it was also poorly vinified.

Since the mid-1980s, the indifferent winemaking at Trottevieille has come to a halt. I suspect the young and dedicated Philippe Castéja is largely responsible for the remarkable turnaround in the quality of this estate's wines. The stricter selection process, the use of 100% new oak, as well as the decision to harvest later and extend the maceration, has resulted in a relatively profound wine that now appears capable of chal-lenging the best of the appellation.

VINTAGES

1989
·
90
—The 1989 is an immensely impressive wine, exhibiting an opaque black color, and a sensational bouquet of licorice, chocolate, and superripe plums. In the mouth, the wine displays immense size, enormous concentration, a tremendous level of tannins, and an intense, alcoholic, long, opulent finish. Given the size of this wine, the acidity seems sound, and the fact that it is now aged in 100% new oak suggests that the wine will have the proper marriage of toasty oak for balancing out its awesomely concentrated fruit flavors. The 1989 could well turn out to be the finest Trottevieille made in the last three or four decades. Anticipated maturity: 1996–2015. Last tasted, 4/91.

1988
·
86
—This is a very good, but exceptionally tannic, backward style of wine that needs a good 5–6 years in the bottle to shed its toughness. There is plenty of ripe, extracted fruit, the color is dark ruby, and there is a feeling of weight and length, but the tannins dominate the wine at present. Anticipated maturity: 1996–2008. Last tasted, 4/91.

1987
·
85
—One of the better efforts for a well-known St.-Emilion estate, the 1987 has an herbaceous, spicy, blackberry-scented nose, soft, oaky, ripe flavors, and a smooth texture with some surprising power. Anticipated maturity: Now–1995. Last tasted, 4/91.

1986
·
87
—The 1986 Trottevieille has a deep ruby color, and a relatively well-developed and forward, big, plummy, herbaceous bouquet that displays a considerable measure of smoky oak. On the palate, the wine is tannic, oaky, full bodied, and concentrated. One might ask for a bit more complexity from one of the very top vineyards in St.-Emilion. Anticipated maturity: 1994–2008. Last tasted, 3/90.

1985
·
86
—The 1985 displays very ripe berry aromas, some evidence of new oak, a sweet, supple, round, and generous texture, medium to full body, and soft tannins in the finish. Anticipated maturity: Now–1996. Last tasted, 3/90.

1983
·
75
—In comparative tastings against the other St.-Emilion Premiers Grands Crus Classés, Trottevieille came off as one of the weaker wines of the vintage. Decently colored, but a stewed, bizarre bouquet and diffuse, awkward flavors exhibited little promise of anything exciting. Anticipated maturity: Now–1992. Last tasted, 2/87.

1982
·
79
—Fully mature, the 1982 is a bit diffuse and lacks focus and grip. It does offer straightforward, chunky, fleshy, velvety smooth, cassis fruit, and plenty of alcohol in the finish. I see no point in holding

on to the wine any longer. Anticipated maturity: Now–1994. Last tasted, 1/90.

1981—Lacking color, fruit, body, and uncommonly bizarre to smell, this
·   is a feeble, lightweight wine without any substance to it. Disap-
70   pointing. Last tasted, 4/84.

1979—A reasonably good effort from Trottevieille, the 1979 displays
·   adequate color, a medium- to full-bodied, nicely concentrated feel
84   on the palate, moderate tannin, and good ripeness. This is a rare
      success for this estate. Anticipated maturity: Now–1993. Last
      tasted, 2/84.

1978—Quite frail, beginning to brown, and seemingly on the edge of
·   cracking up, this loosely knit, shallow, lean wine has little to
64   offer. Last tasted, 2/84.

1976—A failure, the 1976 Trottevieille was apparently picked when the
·   grapes were overripe and waterlogged. Unstructure, with a wa-
55   tery, jammy quality, and an unusually harsh finish, this is a most
      unattractive wine. Last tasted, 9/80.

1975—There is certainly not much to get excited about here—light,
·   underendowed, medium bodied, and tannic, or, as several En-
70   glish wine writers would say, "not enough flesh to cover the
      bones." Last tasted, 5/84.

1971—Completely dead, this brown-colored wine has lost its fruit, and
·   offers only tart acidity, alcohol, and old, oaky scents and flavors.
55   Last tasted, 2/78.

UNION DE PRODUCTEURS DE ST.-EMILION

> Production: 575,000 cases
> President: Claude Tribaudeau
> Director: Jacques Baugier
> Principal *cuvées:* Royal St.-Emilion, Côtes Rocheuses, Haut-
> Quercus, and Cuvée Gallus

The Union de Producteurs de St.-Emilion is the largest cooperative in the Bordeaux region. It was founded in 1931, largely inspired because of the difficulties encountered by the growers in selling their wine during the great international economic depression of the early thirties.

There are over 380 members (membership entails owning vineyards within the appellation of St.-Emilion), and the cooperative manages nearly 2,600 acres of vines. They account for over 25% of the total production of St.-Emilion. There have been major improvements to the facility in the eighties, and when I toured the cooperative in 1988 I was impressed by the overall level of quality for a cooperative wine. Many of the estate wines are bottled by the cooperative, which is indicated by the expression "Mis en Bouteille par l'Union de Producteurs-St.-Emilion." However, the labels will principally feature the name of the estate.

Some of the best of these wines include (in alphabetical order) Château d'Arche, Château Barail du Blanc, Château du Basque, Château Bel-Air Ouÿ, Château Billerond, Château La Boisserie, Château La Bonnelle, Château Cazenave, Château Côte de Tauzinat, Château Destieux-Berger, Château Franc Jaugue Blanc, Château Franc Lartigue, Château Franc le Maine, Château Grangey, Château Les Graves d'Armens, Château Haut-Bruly, Château Haut-Montil, Château Haut-Moureaux, Château Haute-Nauve, Château Hautes-Versannes, Château Juguet, Château Lavignère, Château Le Loup, Château La Martre, Château Mauvinon, Château Mondou Nerignean, Château Paran-Justice, Château Piney, Château Queyron Patarabet, Château Rastouillet Lescure, Château La Rouchonne, Château Vieux Garouilh, Château Vieux Labarthe, and Château Viramière.

Additionally, there are the commercial brands that are produced and bottled by the cooperative, such as Royal St.-Emilion, Côtes Rocheuses, Haut-Quercus, and Cuvée Gallus. The Royal St.-Emilion, first marketed in 1945, is made from blends of grapes from estates located on the St.-Emilion plateau. According to the cooperative, it is a *cuvée* designed to be more opulent and open knit, with a certain rusticity. The *cuvée* called Côtes Rocheuses is produced from those vineyards located at the foot of the St.-Emilion hillsides. It is a more tannic, sterner wine, with a bit more power and potential longevity than the Royal St.-Emilion. In 1978, the cooperative, at the request of its clients, created the *cuvée* Haut-Quercus. This wine is aged entirely in small oak casks, of which a high percentage are new. Only a tiny quantity, usually under 3,000 cases, is produced, and all the bottles are numbered. After tasting a number of vintages of Haut-Quercus, this is a wine with surprising flavor, and aging potential of up to 7–8 years. For a cooperative wine, it is made to very high standards.

The most recent creation of the cooperative is its Cuvée Gallus. This selection, created in 1982, is meant to represent the best *cuvée* of the cooperative. Aged entirely in new oak casks, all of the wine of the Cuvée Gallus comes from selected hillside vineyards that are planted on the limestone plateau.

While many readers no doubt turn up their noses at the mention of a cooperative wine, the individual estate wines bottled by this cooperative as well as the four commercial brands are often as good as, if not better than, many of the lower-level estate-bottled St.-Emilions. In most vintages, the Cuvée Royal St.-Emilion will consist of 70% Merlot, 20%

Cabernet Franc, and 10% Cabernet Sauvignon, and constitute a production of 20,000 cases. The Côtes Rocheuses normally is made from a blend
of 60% Merlot, 25% Cabernet Franc, and 15% Cabernet Sauvignon. The
cooperative tries to limit its production to 20,000 cases as well. The
Cuvée Gallus is made from a blend of 60% Merlot, 30% Cabernet Franc,
and 10% Cabernet Sauvignon. The production is usually between 5,500–
6,000 cases. As for the very limited selection Haut-Quercus (which is
bottled with a very colorful, artistic label), production is limited to 2,500
cases and the wine is made from a blend of 60% Merlot and 40% Cabernet Franc.

VIEUX-CHÂTEAU-CARRÉ (Grand Cru)　　　　　　AVERAGE

Production: 1,500 cases	Grape varieties: Merlot—60% Cabernet Franc—20% Cabernet Sauvignon—20%
Secondary label: none	
Vineyard size: 7.5 acres	Proprietor: Yvon Dubost
Time spent in barrels: 14–20 months	Average age of vines: 20 years
Evaluation of present classification: The quality equivalent of a Médoc Cru Bourgeois	
Plateau of maturity: 3–7 years following the vintage	

This solidly made if uninspiring St.-Emilion Grand Cru is made by the
same individual who is the proprietor of the Pomerol estate called Lafleur
du Roi. The wine is generally medium bodied, well colored, lacking in
finesse and charm, but solid and robust in a monolithic sort of way. Most
vintages should be consumed earlier rather than later.

VILLEMAURINE (Grand Cru Classé)　　　　　　AVERAGE

Production: 4,000 cases	Grape varieties: Merlot—70% Cabernet Sauvignon—30%
Secondary label: none	
Vineyard size: 17.5 acres	Proprietor: Robert Giraud
Time spent in barrels: 18–20 months	Average age of vines: 40 years
Evaluation of present classification: The quality equivalent of a Médoc Cru Bourgeois	
Plateau of maturity: 3–10 years following the vintage	

Villemaurine is one of St.-Emilion's most interesting vineyards. The property gets its name from an eighth-century army of invading Moors who supposedly set up camp on this site, which was called 'Ville Maure the City of Moors by the French. In addition, Villemaurine has enormous underground cellars that merit considerable tourist interest. As for the wine, it is considerably less interesting. In good, abundant years, close to 4,000 cases of wine are made from a blend of 70% Merlot and 30% Cabernet Sauvignon. Despite increasing promotional efforts by the proprietor, Robert Giraud, also a major *négociant*, claiming that Villemaurine's quality is improving, I have found the wines to lack richness and concentration, to be rather diffuse, hard and lean, and to have little character.

VINTAGES

1989—The 1989 is a black/purple color, but it is virtually impenetrable
·   because of an astonishingly high tannin content. It is a big,
80   chewy, dense wine that is impressively long and concentrated.
    But the high level of tannins and high alcohol make precise judgment nearly impossible. If this wine develops more balance as opposed to power and density, it could ultimately merit a much higher rating. Anticipated maturity: 1995–2003. Last tasted, 4/91.

1988—The 1988 exhibits abundant quantities of high tannin, a large,
·   oaky, yet simple, ripe, plummy bouquet, and plenty of alcohol
78   and size in the finish. Anticipated maturity: 1993–2002. Last tasted, 4/91.

YON-FIGEAC (Grand Cru Classé)   AVERAGE

Production: 10,000 cases	Grape varieties: Merlot—80% Cabernet Franc—20%
Secondary label: none	
Vineyard size: 54.3 acres	Proprietor: G.F.A. Château Yon-Figeac
	Administrator: Bernard Germain
Time spent in barrels: 18 months	Average age of vines: 25 years
Evaluation of present classification: The quality equivalent of a Médoc Cru Bourgeois	
Plateau of maturity: 3–10 years following the vintage	

Yon-Figeac is a beautifully turreted château, with vineyards located northwest of the town of St.-Emilion on shallow, sandy soil. The style of wine produced tends to be round and silky, with a great deal of red and black fruit character. It is not a wine that would seemingly last long, although I have had no experience with vintages older than 7 years. Those years that I have tasted—1982, 1983, 1985, and 1986—were all ready to drink upon release. The property has begun to emphasize more grip and concentration in the wines and is now using one-third new oak casks. The old practice of aging the wine in both small barrel and vat has been discontinued in favor of all the wine being brought up in small barrels.

THE WINES OF BARSAC AND SAUTERNES

The Barsac and Sauternes wine-producing regions are located a short forty minute drive south from downtown Bordeaux. They are the dinosaurs of Bordeaux. Labor intensive and expensive to produce, the sweet wines of Barsac and Sauternes have long had huge climatic and manpower problems to overcome almost every year. Additionally, for most of this century, the producers have had to confront a dwindling demand for these luscious, sweet, sometimes decadently rich and exotic wines because of the consumer's growing demand for drier wines. Given the fact that it is rare for a particular decade to produce more than three excellent vintages for these wines, the producers in this charming and rural viticultural region have become increasingly pessimistic that their time has passed. Château owners have changed at a number of properties, more and more vineyards are also producing a dry white wine to help ease cash-flow problems, and at one classified-growth property—Château de Myrat—the owner simply gave up after the 1975 vintage and tore out all his vines, saying it was no longer profitable to produce this type of wine.

Yet surprisingly, many growers continue. They know they make one of the most remarkable wines in the world, and they hope that Mother Nature, good luck, and an increasing consumer awareness of their products will result in accelerated demand and appreciation of these white wines, which until recently were France's most undervalued and underappreciated great wines.

Perhaps their persistence has finally paid off. The second half of the

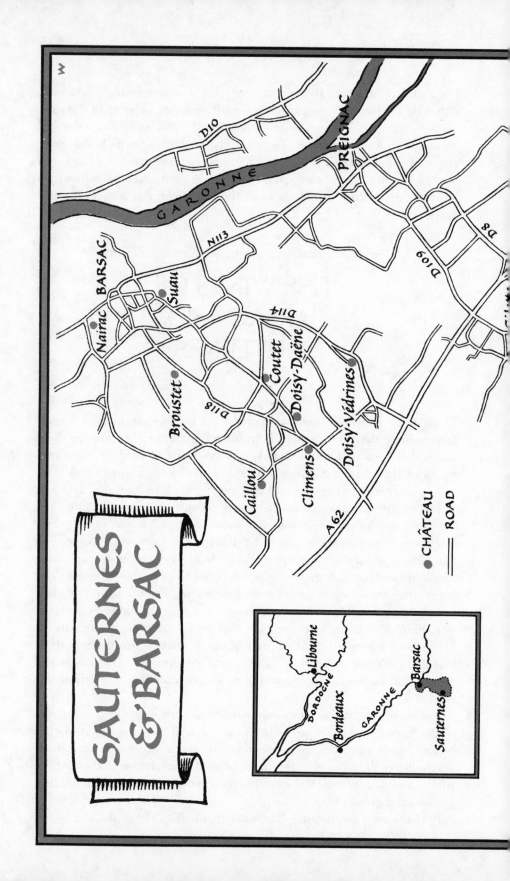

SAUTERNES & BARSAC

W

GARONNE

PRÉIGNAC

D10

N113

D8

D109

BARSAC

Nairac

Suau

D114

Coutet

Doisy-Daëne

D118

Broustet

Doisy-Védrines

Caillou

Climens

A62

● CHÂTEAU

—— ROAD

Libourne

DORDOGNE

Bordeaux

GARONNE

Barsac

Sauternes

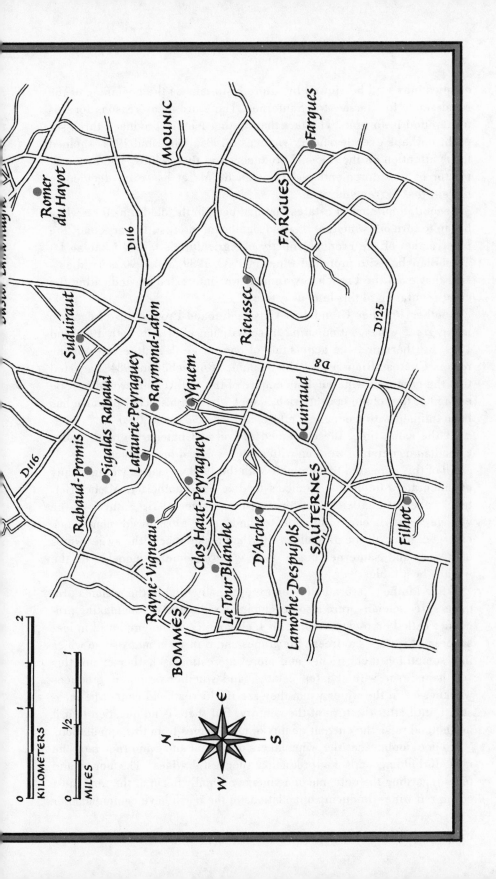

eighties may well be viewed by future historians as the beginning of the renaissance for Barsac and Sauternes. There are many reasons for this turnaround in fortune. The fact that Mother Nature produced three superb, perhaps even legendary vintages—1986, 1988, and 1989—helped focus attention on the regions' producers and their wines. The new proprietor of the aforementioned Château de Myrat has even decided to replant that barren vineyard.

Second, a number of estates that had been in the doldrums for a while began to turn out wine that merited significant interest. In particular, the resurrection of the French Ministry of Agriculture's famed Château La Tour Blanche, with profound wines in 1988, 1989, and 1990, served as a sign that even the French government was interested in vindicating the great reputation of this famous estate.

Another Premier Grand Cru Classé, Rabaud-Promis, also began to make great wines, culminating in sensational efforts in both 1988 and 1989. Furthermore, the acquisition of one of the flagship estates of the region, Château Rieussec, by the Domaines Rothschild in 1984 suggested that the great red wine–making empire of the Rothschilds would now be expanded to include lavishly rich, sweet white wines. That promise has been fulfilled with compelling efforts in 1988, 1989, and 1990.

At the same time, the continued revival of Château Guiraud, under Canadian ownership, went on with a succession of fine vintages.

All of this appeared to culminate with the 1988 vintage, a vintage many commentators (including France's leading wine authority, Michel Bettane) called the greatest Sauternes vintage since 1937. Futures of the vintage have become difficult to find, and a renewed confidence emerged: after all the difficulties they had experienced, the sweet wines of Barsac and Sauternes might once again become fashionable on the world's best tables.

While Mother Nature had been exceptionally kind to the region's producers, technicians were also developing a radical new winemaking procedure called cryo-extraction. This technique could be employed in less successful vintages to freeze the grapes and transform many so-so wines into something much richer and more interesting. Whether or not this will gain favor with the top estates, and whether or not it produces weaknesses in the wines when they are 10–15 years old cannot be measured until after the turn of the century. But there is no question that it has helped raise the current quality of many wines from this appellation.

No one doubts that the winemakers of Barsac and Sauternes face the most forbidding odds for producing successful wines. The hopes and fears regarding the outcome of a vintage normally begin at the time most of the red wine–producing appellations to the north have commenced or even finished their harvests. During the latter half of September Mother Nature begins to unfold the climatic conditions that will be important for the vintages of this region. The climate in Barsac and Sauternes is normally misty, mild, and humid at this time of year. The foggy, damp mornings (created by the Ciron River that runs through the heart of Sauternes) and sunny, dry afternoons encourage the growth of a mold called *Botrytis cinerea*. This mold—commonly called "noble rot"—attacks each ripe, mature grape individually, devouring the grape skin and causing the grape to die and become dehydrated. Of course, only grapes that are undamaged and have been attacked by the noble botrytis rot are selected. Botrytis causes a profound change particularly in the Semillon grape. It shrivels the skin, consumes up to 50% of the sugar content, forms glycerol, and decomposes the tartaric acids. The result is a grape capable of rendering only one-fourth of its volume of juice prior to the botrytis attack—an unctuous, concentrated, aromatic, sweet nectar. Curiously, the reaction causes a superconcentration of the grape's juice, which becomes considerably higher in sugar than normal. This happens without any loss of acidity.

This process is erratic and time-consuming. It can often take as long as 1 or 2 months for a significant portion of the white grapes to become infected by the botrytis mold. In some years (for example, 1978, 1979, and 1985) very little botrytis develops and the wines lack flavor dimension and complexity. When the noble rot does form, its growth is painfully slow and uneven. Therefore, the great wines of this region can only be made by an arduous, time-consuming, labor-intensive process of sending teams of pickers into the vineyard to pick the afflicted grapes one at a time rather than bunch by bunch. The best estates have their pickers descend on the vineyard up to half a dozen times over this period, which usually occurs throughout October and November. The famous Château d'Yquem often sends pickers through the vineyard ten separate times. As expensive and time consuming as picking is, the most hazardous risk of all is the weather. Heavy rains, hailstorms, or frost, all common meteorological developments for Bordeaux in late fall, can instantly transform a promising vintage into a disaster.

Since the conditions for making great wine are so different for Barsac and Sauternes, it is not surprising that what can be a great vintage for the red wines of Bordeaux can be mediocre for the sweet white wines from this area. The years 1982 and 1961 are two vintages in point. Both are undeniably great years for the red wines, but for the sweet wines of Barsac and Sauternes, the vintages are at best average. In contrast, 1988, 1980, 1967, and 1962 are four vintages for Barsac and Sauternes that most observers would consider very fine to superb. With the exception of 1988 and 1962, these vintages were less successful for most of the red wines of Bordeaux.

Like the red wines of the Médoc, the wines of Barsac and Sauternes were considered important enough to be classified into quality groupings in 1855. The hierarchy (see page 926) established Yquem as the best of the region, and it was called a "Premier Grand Cru Classé." Following Yquem were "Premiers Crus Classés" (now eleven as a result of several vineyards' being partitioned), and fourteen "Deuxièmes Crus Classés" (now twelve because one has ceased to exist and two others have merged).

From a consumer's perspective, three unclassified Cru Bourgeois estates, Raymond-Lafon, de Fargues, and Gilette, are making exquisite wines that rival all of the best estates' wines except for Yquem. However, they were not included in the 1855 classification. Additionally, there are a number of first-growths and second-growths that simply cannot afford to make wine the traditional way—using numerous crews of pickers working sporadically over a 4- to 8-week period. Several do not merit their current status, and have been downgraded in my evaluations of the châteaux of these regions.

As for Château d'Yquem, it towers (both literally and figuratively) above the other estates here, producing a splendidly rich, distinctive, unique wine. In my opinion, it is Bordeaux's single greatest wine. The official first-growths of the Médoc have worthy challengers every year who produce wine often as impressive, and the right-bank trio of Cheval Blanc, Ausone, and Pétrus can in some vintages not only be matched, but surpassed by the brilliance of other estates in their respective appellations. Yquem, however, never has a challenger (except perhaps the rarely seen microscopic luxury *cuvées* of Coutet and Suduiraut called Cuvée Madame). This is not because top Barsac and Sauternes properties such as Climens, Rieussec, or Suduiraut cannot produce superlative wine, but rather that Yquem produces a wine at such an extravagantly expensive level of quality that it is commercial madness for any other property to even attempt to emulate it.

When I wrote the first edition of *Bordeaux* in 1984, I was skeptical about the potential of all but a handful of the Barsac/Sauternes estates. In 1991, a mere 7 years later, the entire region has been transformed by the great success of the vintages from the mid-1980s on. Most producers are now enjoying a degree of financial prosperity (perhaps even security) that they had only dreamed of in the early eighties. These wines, even with such revolutionary techniques as cryo-extraction, will always be the most difficult wines in the world to produce, and a few bad vintages in a row or overreliance on new technology would no doubt dampen much of the appellation's enthusiasm, but for now, optimism reigns supreme in what once was one of the most distressingly sad regions of Bordeaux.

A CONSUMER'S CLASSIFICATION OF THE CHÂTEAUX OF BARSAC AND SAUTERNES

OUTSTANDING

Climens, Coutet-Cuvée Madame, Gilette, Rieussec, Suduiraut-Cuvée Madame, Yquem*

EXCELLENT

de Fargues, Guiraud, Lafaurie-Peyraguey, Raymond-Lafon, Suduiraut, La Tour Blanche

VERY GOOD

Coutet, Doisy-Dubroca, Doisy-Védrines, Haut-Claverie, Rabaud-Promis, Sigalas Rabaud

GOOD

d'Arche, Bastor-Lamontagne, Broustet, Doisy-Daëne, Les Justices, Lamothe-Guignard, Liot, de Malle, Nairac, Piada, Rayne-Vigneau, Romer du Hayot, Roumieu-Lacoste

OTHER NOTABLE PROPERTIES OF SAUTERNES AND BARSAC

Caillou, Clos Haut-Peyraguey, Filhot, Lamothe-Despujols, Lamourette, de Rolland, Saint-Marc, Suau

D'ARCHE (Deuxième Cru Classé)   GOOD

Production: 4,000 cases	Grape varieties: Semillon—90% Sauvignon Blanc—10%
Secondary label: d'Arche-Lafaurie	
Vineyard size: 74 acres	Administrator: Pierre Perromat
Dry white wine: none	
Time spent in barrels: 24 months	Average age of vines: 25 years
Evaluation of present classification: Should be maintained	
Plateau of maturity: 5–15 or more years following the vintage	

* Yquem, despite the existence of other outstanding estates, rarely has any competition and must be considered to be the only Bordeaux wine in a class by itself.

Château d'Arche is another Sauternes that began producing better and better wine during the eighties. Given the quality of the wines, their prices are among the most reasonable of the appellation. The style of wine produced at d'Arche offers very unctuous, rich fruit, no doubt because of the high percentage of Semillon, but also because of the late harvesting and the proprietor's serious commitment (there are normally seven to ten passes through the vineyard to pick only those grapes affected by the *Botrytis cinerea*).

VINTAGES

1989—This wine has consistently tasted muddled, out of focus, too low
· in acidity, and excessively alcoholic and heavy-handed. Wines
? such as this sometimes turn around and develop more structure.
   But after tasting this wine four different times, I am at a loss to
   understand its lack of definition. Judgment reserved. Last tasted,
   4/91.

1988—This is a beautifully made, intense wine with a gorgeous nose of
· honeyed pineapple fruit. In the mouth, it is unctuous and full
88 bodied, with great sweetness and presence, and a long, rich,
   nearly viscous finish. It is very forward for the vintage. Anticipated maturity: 1993–2005. Last tasted, 4/91.

1986—This is another highly successful vintage for d'Arche. Not so rich
· or thick as the 1988, but more classy from an aromatic point of
88 view, this full-bodied, concentrated wine exhibits telltale flavors
   of honeyed oranges and pineapples, and even the smell of coconut. The finish is long and crisp with a great deal of botrytis in
   evidence. Anticipated maturity: 1992–2006. Last tasted, 3/90.

OLDER VINTAGES

D'Arche made a very good 1983, and a less interesting 1982 and 1981. I also have notes on a surprisingly good 1969. I think it can be safely said that the efforts of proprietor Pierre Perromat, who took over the running of the property in 1981, have resulted in far greater wines in the eighties than in previous decades.

BASTOR-LAMONTAGNE (Cru Bourgeois)   GOOD

Production: 9,000–10,000 cases	Grape varieties: Semillon—77% Sauvignon Blanc—18% Muscadelle—5%
Secondary label: Les Remparts du Bastor	
Vineyard size: 98.8 acres	Proprietor: Crédit Foncier de France
Dry white wine: none	
Time spent in barrels: 18–24 months	Average age of vines: 20 years
Evaluation of present classification: Should be upgraded to a Deuxième Cru Classé	
Plateau of maturity: 3–15 years following the vintage	

Bastor-Lamontagne has always been a personal favorite of mine, particularly when I am looking for a reasonably priced Sauternes to buy as an alternative to some of the more glamorous (as well as more expensive) names. The property, located in Preignac, near the great estate of Suduiraut, has, to my knowledge, never made bad wines. Everything I have tasted from the mid-1970s onward has been made in an intelligent, ripe, rich, velvety style filled with opulent, pure fruit. These are not woody Sauternes since very little new oak (only 20%) is used. Rather they are luscious, amply endowed, sweet wines for drinking in their first 10–15 years of life.

As the following tasting notes attest, Bastor-Lamontagne, while never outstanding, is consistently very fine. In fact, the great value is the realistic price and steady quality from vintage to vintage.

VINTAGES

1989—Very typical of the vintage, the 1989 Bastor-Lamontagne is ex-
·   tremely low in acidity, and ripe, with surprisingly evolved me-
85   dium gold color, and a great deal of fruit and coarseness that I
     have rarely seen in other vintages of this wine. It will no doubt
     have to be drunk quite early. Anticipated maturity: Now–1995.
     Last tasted, 4/91.

1988—This is an excellent wine with abundant quantities of botrytis, as
·   evidenced by its honeyed pineapple-and-orange-scented nose. In
87   the mouth, it is full, wonderfully pure, focused, and long, with
     moderate sweetness. This Sauternes could actually serve as a

good apéritif as well as a dessert wine. Anticipated maturity: Now–2000. Last tasted, 4/91.

1986—Another excellent example of Bastor-Lamontagne, the nose of
· caramel, oranges, and spices intermixed with scents of flowers is
86 enthralling. Full bodied and luscious, with a lot of alcohol and glycerin, as well as evidence of botrytis, this honeyed wine is already drinking beautifully. Anticipated maturity: Now–1996. Last tasted, 3/89.

1983—A voluptuous, luscious wine with oodles of ripe, botrytised pine-
· apple fruit, medium- to full-bodied texture, and a long, rich, silky
87 finish all combine to titillate the palate. This Bastor-Lamontagne is precocious, but so tasty. Anticipated maturity: Now–1995. Last tasted, 3/88.

1982—Bastor-Lamontagne has made a shockingly good wine in 1982. It
· is a lovely, richly fruity, moderately sweet, well-balanced Sau-
85 ternes with plenty of character. The wine is forward and ready. Anticipated maturity: Now–1995. Last tasted, 1/85.

1980—The aromas of ripe pineapples and fresh melons are quite appar-
· ent in this medium-weight wine with a lush, nicely concentrated
82 personality. Not as good as the 1982 or 1983, this is still a notable effort from what is Sauternes's best-priced estate-bottled wine. Anticipated maturity: Now–1993. Last tasted, 1/84.

1976—Bastor-Lamontagne is a success in this very fine vintage for the
· wines of Barsac and Sauternes. Fully mature, but capable of hold-
85 ing, this unctuous, ripe, orange-and-apricot-scented and -flavored wine has plenty of body to go along with its excellent flavor. Anticipated maturity: Now–1994. Last tasted, 3/86.

1975—A lemony, buttery, tropical fruit–scented bouquet, ripe, medium-
· to full-bodied flavors, and good crisp acidity all complement each
85 other in this moderately sweet, well-structured wine. Anticipated maturity: Now–1996. Last tasted, 2/83.

BROUSTET (Deuxième Cru Classé) GOOD

Production: 2,000 cases	Grape varieties:
	Semillon—63%
	Sauvignon Blanc—25%
	Muscadelle—12%
Secondary label: Château de Ségur	
Vineyard size: 39.5 acres	Proprietor: The Fournier family
Dry white wine: Vin Sec de Château Broustet	
Time spent in barrels: 24 months	Average age of vines: 28 years
Evaluation of present classification: Should be maintained	
Plateau of maturity: 5–20 or more years following the vintage	

Broustet is one of the rarely encountered and least-known Barsacs, largely because the production is so small. The property has been in the Fournier family since 1885 and is now run by Eric Fournier, the handsome and highly dedicated proprietor of the famous St.-Emilion, Château Canon.

Many improvements have been made at Broustet since the mid-1980s. While the wine is still fermented in stainless-steel tanks, the percentage of new oak barrels has been increased to 50%, and the château has introduced a second wine for weaker vats. They have also added a dry white wine to their portfolio.

VINTAGES

1989—The 1989 should be consumed in its first decade of life because it
·   already offers a big, fat, plump, juicy mouthful of wine. Surpris-
86   ingly elegant for a 1989, but still extremely alcoholic and not that
         complex, it is a sweeter wine than the 1988, but lacks the flavor
         dimension and character of the previous vintage. Anticipated ma-
         turity: Now–2002. Last tasted, 4/91.

1988—The 1988 has the advantage of having more acidity, additional
·   complexity, and an uplifting bouquet of honeyed apricot/peach
88   fruit, which, along with its vibrancy, gives its powerful, rich,
         intense flavors a sense of balance and focus. It is the best Broustet
         I have ever tasted. Anticipated maturity: 1992–2008. Last tasted,
         4/91.

1980—A successful vintage for Broustet, the 1980 is chunky, and dis-
·   plays good botrytis, creamy pineapple fruitiness, and a soft, ripe,
82   generous finish. Anticipated maturity: Now–1995. Last tasted, 1/85.

1978—Quite aggressively oaky, the 1978 Broustet has clean, crisp, ripe
　·　　fruity flavors behind a wall of oak. On the palate, the wine is
　80　relatively full bodied but seems a little hollow and less succulent
　　　and sweet than it should be. It's big and oaky, but a little more
　　　fleshy ripe fruit would have made a big difference. Anticipated
　　　maturity: Now–1992. Last tasted, 2/84.

1975—One of the better Broustets I have tasted, the 1975 is a rather
　·　　powerful wine with a luscious pineapple, peachy, appley sweet
　85　fruitiness, medium to full body, and a medium-bodied feel on the
　　　palate. The long, lively finish is surprisingly crisp. Anticipated
　　　maturity: Now–1993. Last tasted, 4/82.

1971—Beginning to fade and lose its freshness and vigor, the 1971 Brous-
　·　　tet is spicy, a touch too oaky, but medium to full bodied with good
　78　concentration and slightly sweet flavors. Anticipated maturity:
　　　Now–may be in decline. Last tasted, 4/78.

CAILLOU (Deuxième Cru Classé)　　　　　AVERAGE

Production: 4,500 cases	Grape varieties: Semillon—90% Sauvignon Blanc—10%
Secondary label: Petit-Mayne	
Vineyard size: 32.1 acres	Proprietor: Jean-Bernard 　Bravo
Dry white wine: Vin Sec de 　Château Caillou	
Time spent in barrels: 20–24 　months	Average age of vines: 25 years
Evaluation of present classification: Should be maintained, although readers should take note of the fact that the quality has increased since the mid-1980s	
Plateau of maturity: 5–10 years following the vintage	

This is a relatively obscure Barsac property located on route D118 to the
east of Barsac. The vineyard's soil is limestone and clay. The château's
twin towers dominate the modest two-and-a-half-story building and are
easily seen from the road.

　The reputation of Caillou's wines has been mixed, although many
critics have claimed Caillou has been largely ignored as a competent
producer of lighter-styled Barsacs. Fermentation takes place in temperature-controlled, stainless-steel tanks, after which the wine is filtered
before it goes into small barrels, of which 20% are new each year. I have

never been that impressed with the wines of Caillou, although a 1947 I tasted in 1987 was in good shape. Recently, there does appear to have been significant improvement, as the 1988, 1989, and 1990 (tasted from cask) all tasted more serious and complex than their predecessors.

VINTAGES

1989—This is an excellent wine, with a lot of sweetness, much more
·   fruit (decadent amounts of pineapples), body, and glycerin than
87   one normally finds in Caillou, in an opulent, almost lavishly rich
        style. As is typical in this vintage, the acidity is low. The wine
        should probably be consumed early in its life. Anticipated maturity: Now–2005. Last tasted, 4/91.

1988—A totally different style from the 1989, this is a more elegant,
·   crisper, more focused style of Barsac, with lovely waxy, pineapple-like fruitiness, medium body, good grip, and an overall zesty,
87   lively feel to it. It cannot match the 1989 in terms of weight and
        alcohol, but it is every bit as good. Anticipated maturity: Now–2006. Last tasted, 4/91.

1986—This is an unexciting, even insipid wine that lacks depth and
·   finishes with a short, attenuated feel. It is hard to understand
77   what went wrong in this excellent vintage. Anticipated maturity:
        Now. Last tasted, 3/90.

1985—Light-intensity flavors of pineapples and oranges are attractive in
·   a low-key way. In the mouth, the wine is off dry, medium bodied,
82   and relatively light, with no evidence of botrytis. Anticipated maturity: Now–1995. Last tasted, 3/90.

CLIMENS (Premier Cru Classé)   OUTSTANDING

Production: 6,000 cases	Grape varieties: Semillon—98% Sauvignon Blanc—2%
Secondary label: Les Cyprès de Climens	
Vineyard size: 86.7 acres	Proprietor: Lucien Lurton
Dry white wine: none	
Time spent in barrels: 24–26 months	Average age of vines: 38 years
Evaluation of present classification: One of the greatest sweet wines produced in the world ·	
Plateau of maturity: 7–25 or more years following the vintage	

The most famous estate of the Barsac/Sauternes region is, without question, Château d'Yquem, which makes the most concentrated and expensive sweet white wine in France. But the wine I find most companionable with food, and most complex and compelling to drink, is that of Château Climens in Barsac. Climens has been owned since 1971 by Lucien Lurton, who presides over a considerable empire of Bordeaux estates, including the famous Margaux properties of Châteaux Brane-Cantenac, Durfort-Vivens, and Desmirail, as well as the reputable Graves estate of Château Bouscaut. All of these properties produce very good wine, but none of them has quite the standing in its respective commune that Château Climens has in Barsac.

For much of the last two centuries, Climens has been considered one of the two leading estates in the commune of Barsac. The 61.7-acre vineyard and modest one-story château (the only physical distinctions are two slate-roofed towers at each end) is located just north of the tiny village of La Pinesse, sitting on the highest plateau of the Barsac region, a full 70 feet above sea level. Most observers claim that this elevation has contributed to the vineyard's excellent drainage, giving Climens a distinct advantage over lower-lying properties in wet years.

While the names of most châteaux here can be traced back to former owners, no one is quite sure how Climens acquired its name. For most of the nineteenth century the château was owned by the Lacoste family, who produced a wine they called Château Climenz-Lacoste. At that time the vineyard's 70 acres achieved an annual production of 6,000 cases, but the devastating effects of phylloxera in the late nineteenth century destroyed most of the vineyards in Bordeaux, including those of Climens. In 1871, Climens was sold to Alfred Ribet, the owner of another estate called Château Pexoto, which was subsequently absorbed into what is today known as Château Sigalas Rabaud.

In 1885, Ribet sold the property to Henri Gounouilhou, whose family managed Climens until the current proprietor, the dynamic Lucien Lurton, purchased it in 1971. It was Henri Gounouilhou, director of Bordeaux's most famous daily newspaper, *Sud-Ouest,* and his successors who raised not only the level of quality at Climens, but also the public's awareness of this great estate. The legendary vintages of 1929, 1937, and 1947 enabled Climens to surpass the reputation of its larger neighbor, Château Coutet, and rival even that of the great Château d'Yquem.

Lurton has merely enhanced the extraordinary reputation of this outstanding property. His only change has been the removal of the small quantities of Muscadelle planted in the gravel, red sand, and clay-like soil of the vineyard. The current plantings, which he believes produce the best wine from the *terroir* of Château Climens, are a blend of 98%

Semillon and 2% Sauvignon Blanc. Lurton eschews a larger proportion of Sauvignon in the blend because it has a tendency to lose its aroma after several years. The average age of the vines is maintained at an impressive 35–38 years, as Lurton believes in replanting only 3–4% of his vineyard per year. In addition, his yield of 12 hectoliters per hectare remains one of the smallest of all the estates in the Sauternes/Barsac region. (Today, when most major wine-producing estates are doubling the yields from their vineyards, Climens commendably maintains an average annual production of only 6,000 cases, from a vineyard area 17 acres larger than it was in the mid-nineteenth century.) No doubt this statistic alone accounts for the exceptional concentration and quality of the wine produced.

Lurton is aided by his daughter Brigette in the operation of Château Climens, and also, in no small measure, by the Janin family, who have looked after this estate as *régisseurs* for nearly a century. Once this brain trust has determined the proper picking date—usually not before mid-October—the vines of Climens are harvested on four, five, or even six separate occasions. The wine is fermented in cask and aged for 2 years in 55-gallon barrels before being bottled. In most vintages, 45–50% new oak is used; this is believed to develop the proper marriage of honeyed, pineapple-and-apricot-flavored fruit with the vanillin toastiness of new oak barrels. The wines are fined with egg whites and filtered lightly through cellulose pads prior to bottling.

What makes Climens so precious is that it produces the region's most compellingly elegant wine. There is no doubt that for sheer power, viscosity, and opulence Climens will never rival Château d'Yquem, nor even Château Rieussec, Château Suduiraut, and the luxurious, rare "Cuvée Madame" of Château Coutet. However, if one measures the greatness of a wine by its extraordinary balance and finesse, Climens not only has no peers, but deserves the reputation as the most quintessentially graceful wine of the region. Many Sauternes can border on the cloying, but in the top vintages Climens seems to combine a rich, luscious, exotic character of honeyed pineapple fruit with a remarkable inner core of lemony acidity—giving the wine zestiness, precision to its flavors, and a profound, hauntingly pleasurable bouquet.

VINTAGES

1989—For whatever reason, the 1989 is merely outstanding rather than
  ·   dazzling. While it lacks the complexity of the 1988, it is a plump,
  90   muscular, rich, intense, full-bodied, sweeter wine than usual. For
        a 1989, it even possesses good acidity. If more complexity and

grip develops, my rating will look stingy. Anticipated maturity: 1995–2010. Last tasted, 4/91.

1988—Climens made such a spectacular 1986 it is hard to believe the 1988 may ultimately turn out to be superior. I am not sure it will,
96   but, nevertheless, they certainly turned in another superstar performance in 1988. What makes Climens so stunning is the penetrating acidity, combined with the fabulous richness and complexity this estate seems to routinely obtain. The 1988 has layer upon layer of honeyed pineapple-and-orange-scented and -flavored fruit, vibrant acidity, high levels of botrytis, and a fabulously long yet well-focused finish. It is a great wine, but don't bet the farm that it will turn out to be better than the profound 1986. Anticipated maturity: 1998–2015. Last tasted, 7/91.

1986—A totally compelling Climens and every bit as good as the 1988. It is probably the best Climens made since their spectacular 1971.
96   Still light gold in color, it has an expansive bouquet of new oak, oranges, pineapples, and other tropical fruits. In the mouth, there is great richness that seems all the more impressive because of the wine's remarkable clarity and definition. There is as much botrytis in the 1986 as in the 1988. Despite the intensity and extract levels, this sweet wine comes across as crisp and relatively light. The 1986 is a stunning example of Climens at its very best. Anticipated maturity: 1994–2010. Last tasted, 1/91.

1985—The problem with virtually all the wines from the 1985 vintage in the Barsac/Sauternes region is that there was very little botrytis.
85   Nevertheless, Climens has made an attractive, fruity, floral, honey-styled wine without a great deal of complexity. It does offer rich, forward, tasty flavors in a medium- to full-bodied format. Anticipated maturity: Now–2003. Last tasted, 11/90.

1983—The 1983 has consistently improved since bottling and is a far greater wine than I ever imagined after tasting it from cask. It
92   exhibits the classic honeyed pineapple and spicy oakiness that makes Climens so profound. In the mouth, this wine is opulent, extremely rich, with gobs of glycerin, yet enough acidity to give it plenty of definition and crispness. It is a beautifully made, even stunning Barsac that is eclipsed by the great 1986 and 1988. Anticipated maturity: 1993–2009. Last tasted, 11/90.

1982—Only tasted twice, but on each occasion Climens did not display the crisp acidity and structure that one has come to expect from
80   this property. Somewhat diffuse, sweet, and flabby, without enough counterbalancing acidity, this is a wine that will no doubt

mature quite quickly. Anticipated maturity: Now–1993. Last tasted, 3/86.

1980 · 90 —1980 is a wonderful vintage of Climens, which has produced an outstanding Barsac. An exotic bouquet of tropical fruit, pineapples, and melons is really top class. On the palate, the wine is rich, yet never heavy or cloyingly sweet, with crisp, rich, medium-bodied, lush, velvety, ripe fruity flavors. This is a superb effort from Climens, and one of the best sweet wines of the vintage. Anticipated maturity: Now–2000. Last tasted, 12/90.

1979 · 85 —A success for Climens, this pale golden-colored wine with a greenish tint is less concentrated and affected by botrytis than the 1980. Lighter and drier, but still relatively rich, this stylish and graceful wine has great flexibility as a Barsac in that it can be matched with a dessert or served to open a meal. Anticipated maturity: Now–2000. Last tasted, 3/88.

1978 · 86 —The 1978 Climens is slightly more concentrated than the 1979, but like the 1979, it lacks the extra dimension that botrytis gives these wines. Because of the weather conditions, little botrytis formed in this vintage. The 1978 is a plump wine, with a fat, fruity concentration, moderate sweetness, full body, and a top-class bouquet of grilled nuts, flowers, and candied apples. This is an elegant wine. Anticipated maturity: Now–1996. Last tasted, 2/85.

1977 · 80 —Climens produced a very respectable wine from this poor vintage. Light golden with a green tint, the wine lacks richness and depth, but offers surprisingly crisp, fresh tropical fruit flavors. good elegance, and a style not unlike a good dry Graves. Anticipated maturity: Now–may be in decline. Last tasted, 3/84.

1976 · 87 —Quite fat and advanced in evolution for Climens, the 1976 is drinking gorgeously now. Charmingly fruity, with an expansive bouquet of ripe fruit, fresh honey, a vanillin oakiness, and some subtle herbal notes, this medium-bodied wine has average acidity, and a plump, soft texture. Anticipated maturity: Now–1998. Last tasted, 3/88.

1975 · 89 —Still remarkably youthful and closed, the 1975 Climens has a light golden color and a tight bouquet of coconut, flowers, and ripe fruit. On the palate, it is impeccably balanced, displaying crisp acidity, excellent richness, and an alcoholic, rich, very, very long finish. Full bodied and powerful for Climens, as well as still remarkably backward and unevolved, this will surely be a long-distance runner. Anticipated maturity: 1996–2020. Last tasted, 3/90.

1973—One of the top successes in this vintage that produced such light-
    ·   weight wines, the 1973 Climens should be drunk now before its
    84   freshness and crisp, lively, fruity intensity disappear. Rather dry
           for a Barsac, and medium bodied, this wine has good acidity and
           enough flavor to merit interest. Anticipated maturity: Now–1993.
           Last tasted, 3/84.

1972—I was shocked at how good this wine was when I first tasted it.
    ·   The year 1972 was dreadful but Climens managed to produce a
    80   wine with good ripeness, some hints of botrytis, a fleshy texture,
           and sound balance. Anticipated maturity: Now–may be in de-
           cline. Last tasted, 3/84.

1971—I have had some of the fabled mature vintages of Climens (the
    ·   1947 and 1949 come to mind immediately), but the 1971 remains
    94   my favorite mature vintage of this wine. It is a classic Climens,
           powerful yet restrained, rich and opulent, yet also delicate. This
           wine has superb balance, a long, lively, crisp finish, and moderate
           sweetness kept light and delightful by excellent acidity. It is one
           of the finest Barsacs I have ever tasted. The honeyed pineapple
           character, so much a personality trait of this wine, is abundantly
           displayed. Anticipated maturity: Now–2001. Last tasted, 2/91.

1970—The 1970 is only an adequate Climens as it is dull, a little clumsy,
    ·   and heavy. Its pale gold color is nice enough, but this lighter-
    70   styled Climens lacks grip and, as the English say, "attack." It
           seems to be an uninspired winemaking effort. Last tasted, 5/82.

1967—Perhaps I have been unlucky and never seen a top-flight bottle of
    ·   the 1967, but I have generally found this wine to be powerful and
    83   richly concentrated, yet not the best-balanced example of Cli-
           mens. Nevertheless, it is full and mouth-filling, and if the finish
           is a little coarse and unpolished the wine is still quite satisfying.
           Anticipated maturity: Now–1994. Last tasted, 12/79.

1962—Beginning to deepen in color and take on an amber/golden color,
    ·   the 1962 Climens must certainly be the best Climens of the six-
    89   ties. A fragrant, roasted bouquet of melted caramel and brown
           sugar sautéed in butter is captivating. On the palate, the wine has
           rich, luscious, unctuous flavors that have remained crisp and
           lively because of good acidity. It is a worthy challenger to the
           Yquem in 1962. Anticipated maturity: Now–1996. Last tasted,
           1/85.

OLDER VINTAGES

Notwithstanding the legendary vintages of 1929 and 1937 (both rated 92 and 90, respectively, when tasted alongside each other in 11/88); the 1947 (I have experienced several disappointing bottles of that wine—the result of poor storage; however, one bottle justified its phenomenal reputation, rated 94 in 11/90); and the 1949 (rated 94 in 4/91), it seems to me that Climens has never been stronger in terms of both greatness and consistency than it is now, some two decades after Lucien Lurton assumed control. Of the fifties vintages, only the 1959 (rated 90 in 1/89) stands out as memorable. Climens did not begin to produce its greatest wines until the seventies.

CLOS HAUT-PEYRAGUEY (Premier Cru Classé)   AVERAGE

Production: 5,000 cases	Grape varieties: Semillon—83% Sauvignon Blanc—15% Muscadelle—2%
Secondary label: Haut-Bommes Vineyard size: 37 acres	Proprietor: G.F.A. du Clos Haut-Peyraguey Administrator: Jacques Pauly
Dry white wine: Domaine de Menaut Larrouquey	
Time spent in barrels: 24 months	Average age of vines: 25 years
Evaluation of present classification: Should be downgraded to a Cru Bourgeois	
Plateau of maturity: 5–12 years following the vintage	

In the 1855 classification there was only one Premier Cru Classé, Château Peyraguey, but in 1879 the property was divided. The smaller parcel became known as Clos Haut-Peyraguey. For much of the sixties, seventies, and early eighties, the quality of the wines was indifferent. However, improvements have been made in the late eighties.

Fermentation takes place in stainless-steel vats and there is a filtration before the wine goes into small casks, of which 20% are new each year. The wine spends 2 years in oak before it is bottled.

The problem with most of the wines of Clos Haut-Peyraguey is that they are relatively light. Many have bordered on being insipid. Fortunately several recent vintages have suggested that higher-quality wines may be forthcoming. I thought the 1990, tasted from cask in spring, 1991, was the finest example I have tasted from this property.

VINTAGES

1989—This thick, cloying, excessively sweet wine lacks acidity, and
·   comes across as muted, fat, unfocused, and just a bit heavy and
82   too obvious. There is plenty of fruit, but it lacks complexity.
       Anticipated maturity: Now–1995. Last tasted, 4/91.

1988—The 1988 is a much more graceful style of wine than the 1989,
·   with an attractive vanillin, apricot-scented bouquet, medium
86   body, good acidity, and plenty of delineation to its plump, round,
       attractive flavors. Anticipated maturity: Now–1997. Last tasted,
       4/91.

1986—While much lighter than most 1986s, this is still an attractive, and
·   fruity, medium-bodied wine with good length and balance, and
85   some evidence of botrytis in its peach/apricot flavors. Anticipated
       maturity: Now–1996. Last tasted, 3/89.

1985—One-dimensional, straightforward, simple honeyed flavors offer
·   little complexity or grip. I could not detect any evidence of botry-
75   tis. Anticipated maturity: Now–1993. Last tasted, 6/87.

COUTET (Premier Cru Classé) VERY GOOD

Production: 7,000 cases	Grape varieties: Semillon—75% Sauvignon Blanc—23% Muscadelle—2%
Secondary label: none, but a luxury *cuvée* called Cuvée Madame is produced in very great years	
Vineyard size: 95.1 acres	Proprietor: Marcel Baly
Dry white wine: Vin Sec de Château Coutet	
Time spent in barrels: 24 months	Average age of vines: 29 years
Evaluation of present classification: Should be maintained, but the Cuvée Madame is the only wine of the Barsac/Sauternes region that is the quality equivalent of Château d'Yquem	
Plateau of maturity: 5–25 years following the vintage	

Coutet has always been one of the leading as well as one of the largest estates of Barsac. Famous for an elegant, less sweet, and less powerful wine, Coutet is usually well made, stylish, and probably a more flexible wine to serve with a variety of food dishes than many of the intense, superconcentrated, lavishly oaked wines that this region produces in abundance.

Coutet does produce a tiny amount of incredibly rich, unctuous wine that is rarely ever seen commercially, but is worth mentioning because it is one of this region's two finest wines (the other of course being Yquem). In certain vintages, Coutet produces a special *cuvée* called Cuvée Madame. Produced from the oldest vines and most botrytised grapes, it is one of the most powerful and decadently intense wines produced anywhere. Between 1943 and 1989 it was only produced in 1943, 1949, 1950, 1959, 1971, 1975, 1981, 1986, 1988, and 1989. Approximately 1,200 bottles—or just four barrels—of this wine are made, and should you ever see any, do not hesitate to try it because the Cuvée Madame of Coutet is pure nectar. The 1971, 1981, 1986, 1988, and 1989 vintages of Cuvée Madame, along with the 1921 Yquem, represent the greatest sweet wines from this region that I have ever tasted.

As for the regular *cuvée* of Coutet, the vintages produced immediately after Marcel Baly purchased the property in 1977 appeared light and indifferent; but since 1983, Coutet has been making top-notch wines nearly every vintage. In fact, this appears to be a property that is deadly serious about challenging Climens's historical role as the top estate in the Barsac region.

Coutet also produces a dry wine that is very fresh, attractively priced, and best drunk when it is 4–5 years old.

VINTAGES

1989—The 1989 Coutet has more finesse and acidity than many wines
· from this vintage. It exhibits plenty of new oak, but also plenty of
90 opulent, unctuous fruit. The bouquet is not as compelling as the 1988, but there is plenty of honeyed, nearly chewy richness and intensity. It is a relatively powerful wine for Coutet, and probably 1–2% higher in alcohol than the 1988. It will probably have to be drunk within its first 20 years of life. Anticipated maturity: 1995–2015. Last tasted, 4/91.

1989—Cuvée Madame—Probably the richest and fullest Cuvée Madame
· I have ever tasted, this medium-light-gold-colored wine has a
95 huge bouquet of coconuts, mocha, peaches, and vanillin. Unctuous and crammed with fruit, this gloriously extracted wine has less grip and focus than the nearly perfect 1988, but the concentration is akin to the essence of Coutet. The finish is spectacular in this sweet, decadent wine. Anticipated maturity: 1996–2015. Last tasted, 4/91.

1988—Coutet seems to be on a hot streak at the moment, having pro-
· duced four super wines in the last two vintages. Even the 1988
93 regular *cuvée* is a deliciously full, huge wine for Coutet, with gobs of botrytis, a full-bodied, opulent texture, zesty acidity, and spec-

tacular length. It is the finest regular *cuvée* of Coutet I have ever tasted. A classic! Anticipated maturity: 1996–2012. Last tasted, 4/91.

1988—Cuvée Madame—As wonderful as the 1988 regular *cuvée* is, it

·

98   pales in comparison to the limited-production, luxury *cuvée*, Cuvée Madame. This wine has a mind-blowing richness, a fabulous bouquet that seems to soar from the glass, astonishing intensity, impeccable balance, and a remarkable finish. This is true nectar! Anticipated maturity: 1997–2020. Last tasted, 4/91.

1986—This is a fine example of Coutet, quite precocious, with an

·

87   evolved bouquet of tropical fruit, honey, and spring flowers. It is full bodied, and rich, with crisp acidity, and plenty of evidence of botrytis in its apricot-, peach-like flavors. The finish is heady and long, with just enough acidity for balance. Anticipated maturity: 1992–2005. Last tasted, 3/91.

1986—Cuvée Madame—This unbelievably decadent, unctuous wine has

·

96   the type of extract (but without the overlay of heavy, toasty oak) that one normally finds only in a great vintage of Yquem. The wine is much less evolved than the regular *cuvée* of Coutet. At the moment, it is crammed with honeyed tropical fruit that comes across in a powerful format. This is an enormously rich, almost overwhelmingly intense Barsac that needs another decade to begin to reveal its subtleties and complexities. It is mind-blowing! Anticipated maturity: 1997–2015. Last tasted, 12/90.

1985—The problem with so many 1985 Barsac/Sauternes is that they

·

84   come across as monolithic and one-dimensional, particularly when compared with years where there is a great deal more botrytis, such as 1986 and 1988. Nevertheless, for those readers who like to drink these wines as an apéritif, 1985 is the type of vintage where the wines can be drunk early in the meal. The 1985 is fresh, with plenty of fruit, but lacking the complexity one normally associates with this château. Anticipated maturity: Now–2000. Last tasted, 3/90.

1983—Not the biggest, most concentrated, or most luscious Coutet, this

·

87   wine gets high marks because of undeniable elegance, breed, class, and a fresh, lively feel on the palate. The flavors reveal excellent ripeness, and the wine's refreshing crispness makes this an exceptionally enjoyable, noncloying Barsac. Anticipated maturity: Now–2000. Last tasted, 3/89.

1981—Surprisingly mature and ready to drink, the 1981 Coutet is an

·

78   agreeable wine, but lacks richness and complexity. What it does offer is straightforward, fruity, lemony, melon aromas, and mod-

erately sweet, somewhat short flavors. Drink up. Anticipated maturity: Now–1993. Last tasted, 6/84.

1981—Cuvée Madame—This is a medium-golden wine with a huge
· honeyed aroma filled with the scents of oranges, toast, coconuts,
96 and other tropical fruits. Thick, unctuous flavors coat the palate. There is just enough acidity to provide lift and focus. This is a colossal wine. Anticipated maturity: Now–2008. Last tasted, 12/90.

1980—A good but rather uninspired effort from Coutet, the 1980 lacks
· richness and depth, even for the lighter-scaled wines of Coutet.
80 Nevertheless, the wine is perfect as an apéritif Barsac, and can do double duty with lighter, not-too-sweet desserts. Anticipated maturity: Now–1995. Last tasted, 3/86.

1979—The 1979 is one of the better efforts from Coutet in this period
· when the property may have been slightly off its normally top
83 form. Light golden, with a spicy, lemony, floral, fruity bouquet, this wine is elegant, has medium weight, and is clean and crisp in the mouth. Anticipated maturity: Now–1994. Last tasted, 7/82.

1978—Quite light, and a little insubstantial, this medium-bodied, mod-
· erately sweet Coutet is fruity and pleasant but reveals little evi-
75 dence of botrytis and seems to tail off in the mouth. Anticipated maturity: Now. Last tasted, 5/82.

1976—One of the best Coutets of the seventies, the 1976 is a relatively
· big Coutet, with a surprising amount of alcohol (15%), a ripe
86 apricot, spicy, floral, lemon-scented bouquet, full body, fat, succulent flavors, and Coutet's trademark—crisp, fresh acidity. Anticipated maturity: Now–1998. Last tasted, 3/86.

1975—Every bit as good as the more open-knit and expressive 1976, the
· 1975 is lighter and more typically Coutet in its proportions, with
86 a graceful, fresh taste, very good concentration, and years of evolution ahead. Anticipated maturity: Now–2002. Last tasted, 3/86.

1971—The 1971 is a gorgeous example of a Barsac that is not that pow-
· erful, but has an authoritative presence in the mouth and wonder-
87 ful, fresh, crisp acidity that admirably balances the apricot, honeyed flavors. Anticipated maturity: Now–1994. Last tasted, 3/86.

1971—Cuvée Madame—Wines such as this are almost impossible to
· describe effectively. Spectacular from the first time I tasted it in
98 the mid-1970s, I have been fortunate enough to have had this wine three more times and each bottle has been better than the last, suggesting that perhaps more magical things may emerge.

There is an extraordinary fragrance of spring flowers, honeyed fruits, herbs, and vanillin, and a strong scent of *crème brûlée*. In the mouth, there is remarkable richness and super acidity that give the wines clarity and lift. Gobs of botrytis are obvious and the richness and extract levels are amazing. The color has changed little since I first tasted it. I would predict at least another 10–20 years of longevity. This is one wine to go out of your way to taste. Anticipated maturity: Now–2005. Last tasted, 3/88.

1970—Rather undistinguished, the 1970 Coutet seems diluted, with a
·   bizarre, tarry, vegetal aroma, and little depth. Last tasted, 2/79.
72

1967—In this very fine vintage for the wines of Barsac and Sauternes,
·   Coutet is a disappointment. Extremely light and a little herba-
70   ceous, this is more akin to a dry Graves than a sweet wine. Last
        tasted, 12/80.

DOISY-DAËNE (Deuxième Cru Classé)   GOOD

Production: 4,200 cases	Grape varieties: Semillon—70% Sauvignon Blanc—20% Muscadelle—10%
Secondary label: none	
Vineyard size: 34.6 acres	Proprietor: Pierre Dubourdieu
Dry white wine: Vin Sec de Doisy-Daëne	
Time spent in barrels: 12 months	Average age of vines: 30 years
Evaluation of present classification: Should be maintained	
Plateau of maturity: 3–12 years following the vintage	

One of the most ambitiously and innovatively run estates in Bordeaux, Doisy-Daëne produces a very fine Barsac that seems to be undervalued in the scheme of Barsac/Sauternes realities. While I would not rate it a Premier Cru Classé, it is certainly one of the leaders among the Deuxièmes Crus Classés. The proprietor of Doisy-Daëne, Pierre Dubourdieu, also produces one of the finest dry wines of the region, Doisy-Daëne Sec. Five thousand cases of this full and refreshing, vibrant, fruity, and—best of all—very inexpensive wine are produced each year. Pierre's son, Denis, a professor at the Institute of Oenology in Bordeaux, more than anyone else, has totally revolutionized white wine–making in the Bordeaux region with his classic *macération pelliculaire* (skin contact and very cool fermentation temperatures). The objective is to produce wines that retain their remarkable fruit and freshness, and to reduce the amount of sulphur used in the winemaking process to negligible quantities. The 1990 Sec de Doisy-Daëne could easily be confused with a serious white Graves!

Doisy-Daëne's sweet wine is surprisingly enjoyable when young, causing many tasters to think that it will not last. Although the style today is certainly different from when the 1924 and 1959 were made, I remember drinking both of those wines in 1984 when they were still fresh, lively, and full of fruit. Doisy-Daëne remains one of the more fairly priced sweet wines of the Barsac/Sauternes region. For those who want to drink their sweet wines on the younger side, this is a property of which to take note.

VINTAGES

1989—The 1989 is a surprisingly restrained, elegant example of the vin-
·   tage. It does not possess the depth of the 1988, but there are
86   abundant ripe, obvious, honeyed fruit flavors, and decent acidity.
         This is an admirable example of balancing power and finesse.
         Anticipated maturity: 1992–2007. Last tasted, 4/91.

1988—The 1988 Doisy-Daëne is a medium-weight wine, exhibiting a
·   great deal of botrytis in a lemony, pineapple-and- apricot-scented
88   nose. In the mouth, it is crisp, with brilliant focus to the compo-
         nent parts, a wonderful sweetness buoyed by fresh acidity, and a
         long, harmonious finish. Anticipated maturity: Now–2005. Last
         tasted, 4/91.

1986—While less viscous and chewy than the 1983, this is still an admi-
·   rably rich, husky, intense Barsac with vividly pure, well-focused
88   fruit, full body, and a long, honeyed finish. Anticipated maturity:
         Now–2000. Last tasted, 3/90.

1985—I could find no evidence of botrytis in this wine that comes across
·   as relatively fat, uncomplex, and straightforward. Anticipated
82   maturity: Now–1994. Last tasted, 3/90.

1983—Doisy-Daëne finished its harvest 1 month after Yquem, and has
·   possibly produced this property's finest wine in over two decades.
90   A big, ripe bouquet of pineapples, peaches, and spring flowers is
         very attractive. On the palate, the wine is concentrated, full bod-
         ied, and unctuous, without being too heavy or alcoholic. Excellent
         acidity suggests a long, eventful evolution. Anticipated maturity:
         Now–2010. Last tasted, 3/90.

1982—One of the better 1982s, ripe and fruity, with the taste of fresh
·   oranges, this medium-bodied Doisy-Daëne has good length, a
82   fresh, lemony acidity, moderate sweetness, and a solid finish.
         Anticipated maturity: Now–1995. Last tasted, 3/87.

1981—Somewhat light, and perhaps dominated by oak to an extreme,
　·　　this fruity, soft, moderately concentrated wine has little botrytis,
　78　　and a short finish. Anticipated maturity: Now–1995. Last tasted,
　　　　1/85.

1980—Surprisingly advanced on the nose, the 1980 Doisy-Daëne has a
　·　　light golden color, an aromatic floral-and-pineapple-scented bou-
　82　　quet, soft, moderately sweet, fat, plump flavors, and just enough
　　　　acidity to keep the wine from feeling heavy. Anticipated maturity:
　　　　Now–1995. Last tasted, 6/84.

1979—A tightly knit, restrained rendition of Doisy-Daëne, the 1979 ex-
　·　　hibits very good ripeness, a rich, full-bodied texture, plenty of
　84　　vanillin, oaky aromas, and good acidity. Anticipated maturity:
　　　　Now–2000. Last tasted, 11/85.

1978—Not a terribly impressive vintage, this wine made from grapes
　·　　picked very late in November displays less intensity than the
　83　　1979, but has an elegant, fruity, spicy nose, firm, sweet flavors,
　　　　and good, firm acidity. Anticipated maturity: Now–1993. Last
　　　　tasted, 6/84.

1975—Some disturbing sulphur aromas in the bouquet seem to con-
　·　　stantly appear in bottles of this wine. On the palate, the wine is
　78　　rich and creamy, with a honeyed, pineapple fruitiness, and a
　　　　succulent, sweet finish. The taste is considerably better than the
　　　　bouquet. Anticipated maturity: Now–1994. Last tasted, 11/82.

DOISY-DUBROCA (Deuxième Cru Classé)　　　　　VERY GOOD

Production: 2,000 cases	Grape varieties: Semillon—100%
Secondary label: none	
Vineyard size: 10 acres	Proprietor: Lucien Lurton
Dry white wine: none	
Time spent in barrels: 30 months	Average age of vines: 30 years
Evaluation of present classification: I have too little experience with this wine to be certain, but this could well justify elevation to Premier Cru Classé status	
Plateau of maturity: 7–20 years following the vintage	

While I have only tasted a handful of recent vintages of Doisy-Dubroca,
this wine has an uncanny resemblance to the great Barsac estate of
Climens. In fact, for years the vinification and aging of the wines has
been controlled by the same team that makes the wine at Climens. The
wine, however, has been commercialized through an exclusive arrangement with the Bordeaux *négociant* firm of De Rivoyre.

As great as this wine has tasted in vintages such as 1986, 1988, and 1989, it has remained a fabulous value because few consumers know anything of this château, and fewer still have access to the wine. It remains very much an insider's wine to buy.

VINTAGES

1989—A gorgeous lemony, pineapple, waxy nose is followed by unc-
·   tuous, rich flavors that exhibit more acidity and definition than I
89   found in many 1989s. Full bodied, round, and generous, with
        excellent concentration, this beauty should continue to drink well
        for another 15–20 years. Anticipated maturity: Now–2008. Last
        tasted, 4/91.

1988—This could easily be confused with the great 1988 Climens. The
·   stylish yet authoritative bouquet of pineapples, spring flowers,
92   and underlying citrusy, mineral scents is provocative. In the
        mouth, the wine exhibits great concentration, remarkable deline-
        ation and focus (because of good acidity), and a smashingly long,
        zesty, crisp finish. This is a brilliant marriage of power and fi-
        nesse. Anticipated maturity: 1993–2010. Last tasted, 4/91.

1986—Gorgeously opulent, roasted pineapple fruit and new oak are fol-
·   lowed by a rich, full-bodied wine exhibiting a great deal of the
90   apricot, peachy, botrytis flavors. Full, rich, and long, this wine is
        just now reaching full maturity. Anticipated maturity: Now–2005.
        Last tasted, 4/91.

DOISY-VÉDRINES (Deuxième Cru Classé)   VERY GOOD

Production: 2,500 cases	Grape varieties: Semillon—80% Sauvignon Blanc—20%
Secondary label: La Tour-Védrines	
Vineyard size: 50 acres	Proprietor: Pierre Castéja
Dry white wine: Chevalier de Védrines	
Time spent in barrels: 24 months	Average age of vines: 29 years
Evaluation of present classification: Should be maintained	
Plateau of maturity: 4–16 years following the vintage	

This Barsac estate is well placed just to the southeast of the two most famous Barsacs, Climens and Coutet. Unfortunately, the tiny production of sweet Doisy-Védrines prevents many wine enthusiasts from ever discovering how good this wine can be. Most wine drinkers probably know the dry white and red table wine produced at this estate much better. It is called Chevalier de Védrines and is a delightful commercial wine that is equally good in either white or red. As for the sweet wine, Doisy-Védrines is a much fatter, richer, more intense wine than the wine of next-door neighbor Doisy-Daëne. Doisy-Védrines is a wine that is usually at its best 5–7 years after the vintage, but will age considerably longer, particularly in the top vintages.

The estate is run by the well-known Pierre Castéja whose family controls the *négociant* firm Roger Joanne. Doisy-Védrines has been in the Castéja family since 1840. Castéja is one of the few Barsac producers who is quick to declassify any vintage he deems to be of unsatisfactory quality. For example, no wine was produced under the Doisy-Védrines label in 1974, 1968, 1965, 1964, or 1963.

VINTAGES

1989—The 1989 is an unctuous and viscous wine, with a chewy, heavy-
  ·   weight style, low acidity, mammoth size, and splendidly concen-
  90   trated fruit suggestive of superripe, honeyed pineapples. Perhaps
        it comes down to personal taste, but in this case the 1989 seems
        to have even more complexity and botrytis than the excellent
        1988. Anticipated maturity: 1993–2010. Last tasted, 4/91.

1988—The 1988 is a beautifully poised wine, with great richness, full-
  ·   ness, and an underlying sweetness. Superb high acidity brings
  88   everything into focus. Endowed with plenty of botrytis, the wine
        has a deep, long, alcoholic finish. Anticipated maturity: 1992–
        2006. Last tasted, 4/91.

1986—Doisy-Védrines made a superb wine in 1986. It is powerful, com-
  ·   plex, and nearly as mouth-filling as their great 1989. It does have
  90   crisper acidity, and for the moment, a more complex, floral,
        honeyed bouquet. There is no denying the unctuous, huge, tropi-
        cal fruit flavors. Anticipated maturity: 1992–2005. Last tasted,
        11/90.

1985—This wine strikes me as surprisingly mediocre, even in a vintage
  ·   where there was too little botrytis to give the wines that honeyed,
  75   unctuous quality. It is straightforward and crisp, and comes
        across as uncomplicated, short, and compact. Anticipated matu-
        rity: Now–1994. Last tasted, 11/90.

1983—1983 has reached its apogee. It comes across on the palate as a
  ·   plump, round, tasty wine with a great deal of fruit, sweetness,
  87   and surprising unctuousness. However, it lacks acidity for grip
        and focus. Nevertheless, there is a great deal to admire about this
        chunky, lush, very sweet Barsac. Anticipated maturity: Now–
        1996. Last tasted, 11/90.

1980—A fat, spicy, apricot-and-coconut-scented bouquet is quite capti-
·   vating. On the palate the wine is ripe, very sweet, almost jammy
84   and marmalade-like, with a good, sweet, alcoholic finish. It lacks
      a little finesse, but the 1980 Doisy-Védrines exhibits plenty of fruit
      and a chewy texture. Anticipated maturity: Now–1993. Last
      tasted, 2/85.

1978—Charming but considerably lighter in style than normal, the 1978
·   lacks botrytis, but has a fresh, clean, lemony, pineapple fruitiness
80   and a decent finish. It may now be tiring. Anticipated maturity:
      Now. Last tasted, 2/82.

1976—In many respects a typically chunky, fat, corpulent Doisy-Véd-
·   rines, the 1976 reveals plenty of ripe, viscous, honeyed fruit, good
84   botrytis, full body, and enough acidity to keep the wine from
      tasting cloyingly sweet or heavy. Anticipated maturity: Now. Last
      tasted, 9/82.

1975—A tight, reticent bouquet needs coaxing from the glass. In the
·   mouth, there is no doubt this is an intense, full-bodied, ripe, very
86   fruity Doisy-Védrines. Unctuous, luscious flavors of apricots and
      melons are admirably balanced by spicy oak and good acidity.
      Anticipated maturity: Now–2003. Last tasted, 3/89.

DE FARGUES (Cru Bourgeois)   EXCELLENT

Production: 850–1,000 cases	Grape varieties: Semillon—80% Sauvignon Blanc—20%
Secondary label: none Vineyard size: 29.6 acres	Proprietor: Comte Alexandre de Lur Saluces
Dry white wine: none Time spent in barrels: 36 months	Average age of vines: 25 years
Evaluation of present classification: Should be elevated to a Premier Cru Classé	
Plateau of maturity: 8–25 or more years following the vintage	

In 1472, 300 years before the Lur Saluces family acquired the famous
Château d'Yquem, they owned Château de Fargues. While de Fargues
has never been classified, the quality of the wine produced is brilliant.
Still owned by the Lur Saluces family, it receives virtually the identical
winemaking care that Yquem does. In some vintages, de Fargues has
often been the second-best wine produced in the Sauternes region, and
when it is tasted blind, many tasters, including most experts, usually

judge it to be Yquem. In all fairness, the wine lacks the aging potential of Yquem, but when young, the resemblance can be extraordinary.

Interestingly, the vineyard of de Fargues is located well to the east of Yquem's, and the harvest occurs on an average of 10 days later. Additionally, the yield is less than at Yquem, causing some to say that if Yquem's tiny yield per vine equals only one glass of wine, the yield of a vine at de Fargues must equal only two-thirds of a glass of wine.

De Fargues's similarity to Yquem is uncanny and given the price charged for de Fargues—approximately one-third that paid for a bottle of Yquem—it is irrefutably a bargain. Unfortunately, the production of de Fargues is tiny, thereby reducing the opportunity for many wine enthusiasts to taste this wine, which some by the way, jokingly call Yquem, Jr.

VINTAGES

1986—This is the finest young vintage of de Fargues I have had the
·　　　privilege of tasting. That should not come as a surprise given how
93　　extraordinary Yquem turned out in this vintage. The toasty,
　　　honeyed, rich bouquet is redolent of pineapples, coconut, *crème
　　　brûlée*, and coffee. In the mouth, this fabulously rich, full-bodied
　　　wine offers plenty of the botrytised, pineapple and other tropical-
　　　fruit flavors, a lavish, unctuous texture, enough acidity to provide
　　　freshness and focus, and a heady, spicy, truly intoxicating finish.
　　　Anticipated maturity: 1995–2010. Last tasted, 3/90.

1985—This is a big, corpulent, chunky wine without much botrytis, but
·　　　plenty of flesh and a muscular, heady alcohol content. The wine
87　　drinks beautifully now because of the forward, lush fruit married
　　　with copious amounts of smoky, toasty new oak. The good acidity
　　　gives the wine freshness. While I am sure this wine will evolve
　　　nicely, I do not expect to ever encounter a great deal of complex-
　　　ity. Anticipated maturity: Now–2002. Last tasted, 3/90.

1983—While no match for the extraordinary wine produced at Yquem in
·　　　this vintage, the 1983 de Fargues (aged 3 years in 100% new oak
92　　casks) is, nevertheless, a sensational example of a Sauternes with
　　　an amazing resemblance to Yquem. A big, buttery, caramel,
　　　smoky, *crème brûlée* and honeyed pineapple nose is enthralling.
　　　In the mouth, the wine is powerful, very sweet, rich, extremely
　　　full, and framed beautifully by toasty new oak. Quite full bodied
　　　and intense, this large-scaled wine should have a great future.
　　　Anticipated maturity: 1993–2008. Last tasted, 3/90.

1981—This wine has improved significantly and actually tastes better
·　　　than the 1981 Yquem—as hard as that may be to believe. Spec-
90　　tacularly rich, very sweet, and alcoholic, it has taken on a me-

dium gold color. There is plenty of evidence of botrytis, but the low acidity and unctuous, thick, viscous feel on the palate suggest this is a wine that is probably best drunk over the next decade. Anticipated maturity: Now–2000. Last tasted, 3/90.

1980— A great vintage for de Fargues, the 1980 from this estate is very
· powerful, opulent, and exotic. The bouquet of coconuts, apricots,
91 grilled almonds, and spicy oak is sensational. In the mouth, the wine is decadently rich, full bodied, and remarkably similar in taste, texture, and viscosity to Yquem. Retasted twice in 1989 with equally enthusiastic notes. Anticipated maturity: Now–2000. Last tasted, 3/89.

1979— Less powerful and rich than normal, the 1979 de Fargues is light
· golden, with a toasty, lemony, fruity, oaky bouquet, medium to
85 full body, some botrytis, good acidity, and a clean, spicy, rich, alcoholic finish. Anticipated maturity: Now–1997. Last tasted, 3/86.

1976— A full-blown *crème brûlée* aroma intermingled with scents of car-
· amel and apricots is penetrating. Full bodied, with viscous,
90 sweet, ripe flavors of tropical fruit and smoked nuts, this big, robust, yet surprisingly mature wine remains fully mature, but displays no signs of declining. Anticipated maturity: Now–2005. Last tasted, 2/91.

1975— The 1975 is one of the finest de Fargues ever produced. It has the
· Yquem-like bouquet of coconuts, grilled nuts, ripe exotic fruit,
91 and spicy oak. On the palate, the 1975 is much tighter structured and less evolved than the 1976. It has a lighter golden color and more acidity, but every bit as much concentration and richness. Anticipated maturity: Now–2010. Last tasted, 2/91.

1971— Incredibly rich, unctuous, fat, spicy, and chewy, this huge wine
· offers oodles of coconut, apricot, and almond flavors, yet viscous
90 fruitiness, huge body, and a head-spinning alcohol content. Fully mature, this is a big, old-style, intense Sauternes. Anticipated maturity: Now–1998. Last tasted, 12/80.

FILHOT (Deuxième Cru Classé) AVERAGE

Production: 10,000 cases	Grape varieties: Semillon—60% Sauvignon Blanc—35% Muscadelle—5%
Secondary label: none	
Vineyard size: 148.2 acres	Proprietor: G.F.A. du Château Filhot
	Administrator: Comte Henri de Vaucelles
Dry white wine: Château Pineau du Rey	
Time spent in barrels: None; the wine is matured entirely in fiberglass vats	Average age of vines: 25 years
Evaluation of present classification: Should be downgraded to a Cru Bourgeois	
Plateau of maturity: 4–12 years following the vintage	

Filhot, one of the most magnificent estates in the entire Sauternes region, possesses an eighteenth-century manor home beautifully situated among ancient trees that has the look of an ivy-league college campus. This property has the potential to produce extraordinary wines, particularly given this superb location just to the north of the village of Sauternes on gravelly hillside beds with a southwest orientation. However, it has only been since the mid-1980s that Filhot has begun to produce wines that merit its Deuxième Cru Classé status.

Because of the relatively high percentage of Sauvignon and the refusal of the proprietors not to use any new oak, Filhot tastes fruitier, more aromatic, and lighter than some of the larger-scaled Sauternes wines. That fact does not, however, account for the lack of consistency and the numerous indifferent and mediocre efforts that were turned out by Filhot during the sixties, seventies, and early eighties.

VINTAGES

1989—This wine appears to be taking on a very mature look at an alarm-
  ·   ingly fast pace. The color is already medium gold and the wine,
86   while exhibiting very low acidity, is extremely sweet, with a big,
      pineapple-scented bouquet. There is an attractive purity, but soft-
      ness and lack of grip suggest this is a wine that needs to be
      consumed in its first decade of life. Anticipated maturity: Now–
      2000. Last tasted, 4/91.

1988—This example of Filhot typifies not only the style of the château,
  ·   but also the shortcomings that are so frequent in this vintage.
 84   There is a very obvious, fruity, ripe, attractive bouquet without
         much complexity. In the mouth, this off-dry, slightly sweet, mono-
         lithically styled, soft, fruity, round, foursquare wine is pleasant,
         but it lacks any real distinction, focus, or character. Anticipated
         maturity: Now–1996. Last tasted, 4/91.

1986—The 1986 is the best Filhot in my memory. The light golden color
  ·   is followed by a wine with a floral, pineapple, and tropical fruit–
 87   scented bouquet, medium body, as well as lovely, elegant, and
         brilliantly pure, botrytised, lively flavors. Just medium sweet, this
         wine could be served as an apéritif wine. Anticipated maturity:
         Now–1998. Last tasted, 3/90.

1985—Extremely sweet to the point of being cloying, with unstructured,
  ·   flabby, fat flavors, this is a straightforward, indifferent style of
 78   Sauternes that lacks a centerpoint and focus. Anticipated matu-
         rity: Now. Last tasted, 3/90.

1983—This is an attractive, lighter-weight Sauternes without any evi-
  ·   dence of serious botrytis. The wine possesses straightforward,
 83   flowery, ripe quasi-viscous flavors presented in a medium-bodied
         format. There is an overall lack of focus and complexity. Antici-
         pated maturity: Now. Last tasted, 4/86.

GILETTE (Cru Bourgeois)   OUTSTANDING

Production: 500–1,000 cases	Grape varieties: Semillon—94% Sauvignon Blanc—4% Muscadelle—2%
Secondary label: none Vineyard size: 11 acres	Proprietor: Christian Médeville
Dry white wine: none	

Time spent in barrels: None; aged
  in small concrete vats for a
  minimum of 20 years
	Average age of vines: 32 years

Evaluation of present classification: Should be upgraded to a Premier Cru Classé	
Plateau of maturity: 20–40 years following the vintage	

Gilette is one of the most unusually run properties in the Sauternes
region. It is one of the finest made wines in Sauternes despite the fact
that Gilette was not classified. The vineyard, situated several miles north
of Yquem, adjacent to route D109, is planted on sandy soil with a subsoil

of rock and clay. However, what is bizarre and unbelievable in today's harsh world of commercial realities, is that Gilette's proprietor, Christian Médeville, holds his sweet wines for over 20 years in concrete vats prior to bottling them. For example, he bottled the 1955 in 1984, 29 years after the vintage. The fact that his wines are excellent and have a honeyed maturity has caused some of France's leading restauranteurs (like Pierre Troisgros) to beat a path to his door to purchase his old vintages of Sauternes.

Giletteis late-released wines, called "Crème de Tête," are extremely well-balanced, remarkably well-preserved wines, with plenty of viscous, fruity flavors, and deep amber/golden colors. After being held in vats for decades, the wines often taste much younger when they are released than their vintage date would suggest. If my instincts are correct, most vintages of Gilette can benefit from another 15–25 years of cellaring after being released. The following are some of the vintages of Gilette that have been released for sale by M. Médeville over the last decade.

VINTAGES

1970—Crème de Tête—The 1970 has a deep, rich golden color and a
　　　big, spicy bouquet of buttery apricot-scented fruit, is full bodied
　88　and amazingly fresh and youthful for its age, and will probably
　　　keep another 15–25 years. It lacks the complexity of the great
　　　vintages of Gilette, but, nevertheless, is an impressively full,
　　　complex wine. Anticipated maturity: Now–2005. Last tasted,
　　　3/90.

1967—Crème de Tête—Everyone agrees that no greater wine was made
　　　in 1967 than Château d'Yquem, but I would love to have the
　96　opportunity to taste Gilette's 1967 Crème de Tête alongside
　　　Yquem. This fabulously rich wine has an awesomely intense bou-
　　　quet of caramel and buttery hazelnuts, combined with intense
　　　aromas of honeyed fruit such as pineapples, oranges, and apri-
　　　cots. Decadently rich, with an unctuous, chewy texture, yet with
　　　enough acidity to provide great delineation and balance, this is a
　　　magnificent wine that has miraculously retained an amazing
　　　freshness for its 23 years of age. It should continue to evolve and
　　　improve for another 30, perhaps even 40, years. This is an outra-
　　　geous thrill-a-sip Sauternes! Anticipated maturity: Now–2025.
　　　Last tasted, 3/90.

1962—Crème de Tête—The 1962 offers a very complex, honeyed nose
　　　filled with decadent apricot and peach scents that can come from
　90　heavily botrytised fruit. Very full bodied, with good acidity and
　　　opulent, rich crème brûlée flavors, this luscious, full-throttle Sau-

ternes should continue to drink well for at least another 15–20 years. Anticipated maturity: Now–2015. Last tasted, 3/90.

1961—Crème de Tête—I have never tasted a great 1961 Sauternes,
 · although I am sure this region's wines benefited immensely from
87 the great reputation of the reds in this vintage. However, the white wines were nowhere near the quality of either the 1962s or 1959s. Most have turned out to be very good, relatively dry, old white wines with a great deal of alcohol, but not much charm or fat. Gilette's 1961 is very fine, although significantly less rich and opulent than the 1962. It is almost dry. It could be the perfect partner with a rich dish that contained foie gras as one of the primary ingredients. Anticipated maturity: Now–2001. Last tasted, 3/90.

1959—Crème de Tête—This is a decadent, honey-pot of a wine. It is
 · medium deep golden, with a huge bouquet of smoked nuts, cof-
94 fee, mocha, coconut, and decadently jammy apricot and peach-like fruit. In the mouth, the wine has astonishing richness, super glycerin content, a great deal of body, and a long, alcoholic, smashingly intense, heady finish. Seemingly fully mature, yet still remarkably fresh and young, this wine can easily last for another 20 or more years. Anticipated maturity: Now–2010. Last tasted, 3/90.

1955—Crème de Tête—Fully mature, but still astonishingly fresh and
 · alive, the 1955 Gilette is deep golden in color, with a rich,
87 honeyed bouquet, full body, and a ripe, long finish. It can proba-bly last another 10–15 years. Anticipated maturity: Now–2005. Last tasted, 11/90.

1953—Crème de Tête—Slightly less rich and fat than the 1955, the 1953
 · is spicy and oaky, with a bouquet suggesting melted caramel and
86 ripe pineapples. Full bodied, still fresh and lively, this unctuous, rich wine is quite impressive. Anticipated maturity: Now–2001. Last tasted, 11/90.

1950—Quite fat and sweet, with excellent ripeness, full body, and a long,
 · deep, velvety finish, this wine is a revelation given its age. This is
89 a big, heavyweight Sauternes that will last for 15–20 more years. Anticipated maturity: Now–2005. Last tasted, 1/85.

GUIRAUD (Premier Cru Classé)　　　　　　　EXCELLENT

Production: 8,500 cases	Grape varieties: Semillon—65% Sauvignon Blanc—35%
Secondary label: Le Dauphin	Proprietor: S.C.A. du Château Guiraud
Vineyard size: 210 acres	Administrator: Xavier Planty
Dry white wine: "G" de Guiraud	
Time spent in barrels: 26–30 months	Average age of vines: 30 years
Evaluation of present classification: Should be maintained	
Plateau of maturity: 5–20 or more years following the vintage	

Guiraud is one of the largest estates of the Sauternes district, covering almost 300 acres, of which 210 are planted with vines. Curiously, the estate produces a red wine with the Bordeaux Supérieur appellation, and a dry white wine called "G."

The sweet wine of Guiraud has undergone a metamorphosis. In 1981 an ambitious Canadian, Hamilton Narby, purchased the estate and made bold promises that Yquem-like techniques of individual grape picking, barrel fermentation, and long aging in new oak barrels would be employed at Guiraud. Consequently, Bordeaux wine enthusiasts, particularly the nectar lovers, have taken great interest in the goings-on at Guiraud in the hopes that his administrator, Xavier Planty, has the talent to bring Narby's dreams to fruition.

The most surprising thing about Guiraud is that the wine is so rich given the high percentage of Sauvignon Blanc used in the blend. No doubt the use of new oak, late picking, and numerous passes through the vineyard ensure that only the ripest Sauvignon Blanc is harvested. But I am still perplexed as to why this wine is so intense despite that Sauvignon Blanc.

Vintages since 1983 have been especially strong, and Guiraud is often one of the top half-dozen wines now being made in the Barsac/Sauternes region.

VINTAGES

1989—Huge as well as penetrating aromas of vanillin-scented, smoky new oak and superripe pineapple soar from the glass. In the
90　　mouth, this is a terrific, rich, full-bodied, in-your-face style of Sauternes that goes right to the edge of being almost too massive and overbearing. Fortunately, there is enough acidity to give grip

and focus. It will have to be monitored as the wine evolves, given this precarious balance, but there is no denying the sumptuous appeal of this very sweet, alcoholic, honeyed wine. Anticipated maturity: 1993–2006. Last tasted, 4/91.

1988—The 1988 marks Guiraud's finest effort to date. An extraordinarily
·
91 rich, concentrated wine, it is full bodied, fabulously long, but ever so precise and clear. The huge bouquet of toasty vanillin-scented new oak, pineapples, coconuts, and buttery oranges is a joy to experience. In the mouth, there is very little with which to find fault. Spectacularly concentrated, potentially long-lived, Guiraud is another dazzling star of the vintage. Anticipated maturity: 1996–2025. Last tasted, 4/91.

1986—Wealthy collectors will have a great deal of fun comparing the
·
92 1986, 1988, and 1989 as they evolve over the years. The 1986 was the finest Guiraud made up to that point. I believe it to be a worthy rival of the great 1988, although I suspect the 1988 will last longer and have higher acidity and better overall balance. However, the 1986 is a super concentrated, aromatic wine with gobs of botrytis, and creamy, unctuous, peach, pineapple, and apricot flavors. There is plenty of new oak to frame the wine, although the overall acidity is less than in the 1988. The finish is exceptionally long and well balanced. This is a massive, concentrated wine that should easily develop over several decades. Anticipated maturity: 1996–2009. Last tasted, 3/90.

1985—Guiraud has turned out a well-made 1985, with a great deal of
·
85 sweetness, plenty of ripeness, and obvious aromas of toasty, smoky new oak. There is no botrytis in evidence and the wine exhibits less finesse and complexity than vintages such as 1983 and 1986. Nevertheless, this straightforward style of Sauternes will have its admirers, particularly among those who like to drink these wines as an apéritif. Anticipated maturity: Now–1998. Last tasted, 3/90.

1983—Light golden, with a ripe, intense bouquet of apricots and pine-
·
88 apples, as well as the vanillin scents from having been aged in cask, this full-bodied, lush, rich wine has excellent concentration, superb balance, and a zesty, long, alcoholic finish. Anticipated maturity: Now–2005. Last tasted, 3/90.

1982—Big and ponderous on the palate, with a sticky, viscous fruitiness
·
78 that comes too close to being ponderous and heavy, and lacking finesse and sufficient acidity to give the wine crispness, this effort from Guiraud has plenty of richness, but is tiring to drink. Antic-ipated maturity: Now–1996. Last tasted, 6/84.

1981—An attractively fruity bouquet displays aromas of new oak, some
 ·   spice, an herbal element, and some pineapple fruit. On the pal-
 80   ate, the wine is fruity and medium to full bodied, but lacks com-
       plexity and dimension. Anticipated maturity: Now. Last tasted,
       6/84.
1980—Surprisingly dull, and too aggressively oaky, the 1980 Guiraud
 ·   tastes fruity, but flat. Anticipated maturity: Now. Last tasted,
 75   6/84.
1979—Firm with a reticent bouquet of fresh oranges and vanillin spices,
 ·   this medium- to full-bodied wine has good acidity, and good con-
 84   centration and length. Anticipated maturity: Now. Last tasted,
       3/84.
1976—Dark amber/gold in color, this wine has a roasted, ripe fruity
 ·   bouquet suggestive of sautéed oranges and almonds. On the pal-
 87   ate, the wine is full bodied, sweet, and rich, with a heady alco-
       holic finish. The wine has reached its plateau of maturity.
       Anticipated maturity: Now–2009. Last tasted, 3/84.
1975—Significantly lighter in color than the 1976, the 1975 Guiraud has
 ·   a honeyed bouquet of peach and orange-like scents, intermingled
 86   with the scent of new oak. On the palate, the wine is fat, and full-
       bodied, with hints of almonds, butter, and caramel. This is a rich,
       impressive Guiraud. Anticipated maturity: Now–1996. Last
       tasted, 3/87.

HAUT-CLAVERIE (Cru Bourgeois)   VERY GOOD

Production: 3,000 cases	Grape varieties: Semillon—85% Sauvignon Blanc—10% Muscadelle—5%
Secondary label: none	
Vineyard size: 35 acres	Proprietor: The Sendrey family
Dry white wine: none	
Time spent in barrels: 15–20 months	Average age of vines: 30 years
Evaluation of present classification: Should be elevated to a Deuxième Cru Classé	
Plateau of maturity: 5–15 years following the vintage	

This obscure yet excellent property is located just south of the village of
Fargues. In a number of blind tastings held in France Haut-Claverie
consistently has come out near the top. The wine continues to sell at
bargain-basement prices. The secret here is not only an excellent micro-

climate, but late harvesting, several passes through the vineyard, and one of the most conscientious owners in the entire appellation. This could well be one of the up-and-coming stars from the Barsac/Sauternes region in the nineties. Consumers might want to act quickly, and be sure to try the excellent 1989, outstanding 1988, and delicious, compelling 1986.

LES JUSTICES (Cru Bourgeois)   GOOD

Production: 2,000 cases	Grape varieties: Semillon—88% Sauvignon Blanc—8% Muscadelle—4%
Secondary label: none	
Vineyard size: 20 acres	Proprietor: Christian Médeville
Dry white wine: none	
Time spent in barrels: aged 18 months in both barrels and vats	Average age of vines: 25 years
Evaluation of present classification: Should be elevated to a Deuxième Cru Classé	
Plateau of maturity: 3–15 years following the vintage	

The vineyards of Les Justices, located to the west of the Gironde River just to the north of the town of Preignac, produces plump, rich, generally intensely concentrated wines. While lacking complexity and finesse, they make up for that deficiency with a pure display of power. This estate is a perennial overachiever, and vintages such as 1983, 1986, and 1988 have been prized for their excellent quality/price ratio. If the wine has a shortcoming, it is that it must be drunk within 10–15 years of the vintage.

The proprietor, Christian Médeville, is also responsible for the wines at the great Château Gilette.

LAFAURIE-PEYRAGUEY (Premier Cru Classé)   EXCELLENT

Production: 5,000 cases	Grape varieties: Semillon—93% Sauvignon Blanc—5% Muscadelle—2%
Secondary label: none	
Vineyard size: 74 acres	Proprietor: Domaines Cordier
Dry white wine: Brut de Lafaurie	
Time spent in barrels: 24 months	Average age of vines: 32 years
Evaluation of present classification: Should be maintained	
Plateau of maturity: 5–25 years following the vintage	

Long in the doldrums, Lafaurie-Peyraguey has emerged in the eighties as one of the great producers of decadently rich, complex, and compelling Sauternes wines. The Cordiers' decisions to reduce the percentage of Sauvignon in the wine, to increase the amount of new oak, and to institute a stricter selection began to result in a string of highly successful Sauternes starting with 1981, and culminating with the great wines produced in 1983, 1986, 1988, and 1989.

The château, one of the most extraordinary in the Sauternes region, was built in the thirteenth century as a fortification overlooking the surrounding countryside. The property was acquired by the Cordiers in 1913. At present, based on the performance of Lafaurie-Peyraguey during the last decade, this is one of the top half-dozen Sauternes, combining an unctuous richness with great finesse and a profound fragrance of honeyed fruit.

In the late eighties, a dry white wine called Brut de Lafaurie was introduced. While I am not a great admirer of many of the relatively heavy, dry white wines made in the Sauternes region, this is the best I have tasted from the appellation. Produced from 40% Sauvignon Blanc, 40% Semillon, and 20% Muscadelle, it is a wonderfully delicious, perfumed wine with surprising richness yet it is totally dry and crisp. Unfortunately, only 5,000 bottles were produced in both 1988 and 1989.

VINTAGES

1989—This wine started off life relatively heavy, fat, and perhaps too
·   alcoholic and low in acidity. It has taken on much more structure,
92   and is clearly one of the top wines of the vintage. An explosive
     nose of honeyed apricot/orange fruit is followed by viscous, thick,
     rich, huge, mouth-filling flavors that coat the palate. There is
     barely enough acidity to give the wine a certain grip and focus.
     This heavyweight, old-style Sauternes will no doubt last because
     of the hefty alcohol content. But it will be drinkable very young
     and its aging will have to be monitored carefully. Anticipated
     maturity: 1994–2005. Last tasted, 4/91.

1988—The 1988 is probably the greatest wine this estate has ever pro-
·   duced. The level of botrytis is stunning, as is the extract level.
95   The 1988 is a massively rich, concentrated effort, yet never tastes
     heavy or thick. The length is mind-boggling, as is the splendid
     combination of power and elegance. It is a superlative effort, and
     belongs in any serious Sauternes lover's cellar. Anticipated ma-
     turity: 1995–2015. Last tasted, 4/91.

1986—A wonderful bouquet of pineapples, smoky nuts, honeysuckle,
·   and other flowers soars from the glass. In the mouth, the wine is
92   rich, with the essence of apricots, pineapples, and other tropical

fruits. The acidity is crisp, giving the wine great definition and clarity. The finish is sweet, honeyed, and long. This beautifully made Sauternes is one of my favorites from the 1986 vintage. Anticipated maturity: 1993–2010. Last tasted, 3/91.

1985—Because of the lack of botrytis, the 1985 is a relatively straightfor-
·   ward, fruity, fat yet fresh-tasting Sauternes that would be ideal
86   as an apéritif rather than served as a dessert wine. It will last for 10–15 years, but is best drunk within the next decade. Antici-pated maturity: Now–2000. Last tasted, 3/91.

1983—The staff at Cordier have every right to be happy with this splen-
·   didly concentrated, complex, fully mature wine. Tremendous in-
92   tensity, viscous, ripe, and layered with honeyed, apricot-flavored fruit, this unctuous wine is not tiring or heavy to drink, but lively and effusively fruity. Anticipated maturity: Now–2000. Last tasted, 3/91.

1982—Much lighter than the 1983, with little botrytis evident, the 1982
·   is quite fresh and fruity, with aromas of melons and flowers pres-
84   ent. On the palate, the wine is medium bodied, moderately sweet, spicy, and cleanly made. Anticipated maturity: Now–1996. Last tasted, 3/87.

1981—Quite exceptional, the 1981 Lafaurie-Peyraguey exhibits ripe
·   apricot aromas, a rich, chewy, viscous texture, good acidity, and
88   a long, sweet, fat finish. This wine displays considerable botrytis, and is clearly one of the top efforts in this vintage. Anticipated maturity: Now–1997. Last tasted, 6/84.

1980—Not quite up to the top-quality wines produced in 1983 and 1981,
·   the Lafaurie-Peyraguey is still well turned out. Medium in weight
84   for a Sauternes, with a good, ripe pineapple, spicy fruitiness, this wine has average acidity. Anticipated maturity: Now–1992. Last tasted, 3/83.

1979—The 1979 is the first in a line of successful Lafaurie-Peyraguey
·   wines that seem to have taken on greater richness as the Cordier
85   firm has moved to upgrade the quality. A lovely spicy-scented pineapple bouquet is attractive. The wine displays good botrytis, good acidity, moderate sweetness, and a crisp, clean finish. An-ticipated maturity: Now–1993. Last tasted, 3/82.

1976—There is really nothing wrong with this wine, but it seems one-
·   dimensional and innocuous and clearly lacks character and
75   depth. It is a minor Sauternes. Anticipated maturity: Now. Last tasted, 11/82.

1975—A very atypical Sauternes, the 1975 has an olive-like, earthy
·   aroma that seems slightly unclean and unripe. On the palate, the
67   wine is light, and surprisingly thin, and finishes poorly. Something

clearly went wrong in 1975 for Lafaurie-Peyraguey. Last tasted, 12/80.

1970—The 1970 is pleasant and agreeable, but very short on the palate,
·　　and not very sweet or concentrated. It is disappointing for a Sau-
74　　ternes of this class. Last tasted, 12/80.

LAMOTHE-DESPUJOLS (Deuxième Cru Classé)　　AVERAGE

Production: 1,700 cases	Grape varieties: Semillon—70% Sauvignon Blanc—15% Muscadelle—15%
Secondary label: none	
Vineyard size: 18.5 acres	Proprietor: Jean Despujols
Dry white wine: none	
Time spent in barrels: 20–24 　months in both barrels and vats	Average age of vines: 20 years
Evaluation of present classification: Too inconsistent to merit its 　rank; should be downgraded to a Cru Bourgeois	
Plateau of maturity: 3–12 years following the vintage	

This property was known in the nineteenth century as Lamothe-d'As-sault, but the property was partitioned and there are now two Lamothe estates, both carrying the suffix of the current owner's family name. Lamothe-Despujols tends to make relatively light wines, but they are worth tasting since there have been some surprises (as in 1986). With the high percentage of Muscadelle in the blend, the style is one of fragrance and soft, forward fruit.

VINTAGES

1989—Very thick, heavy, excessively alcoholic, with no grip, focus, or
·　　delineation to the flavors, this cloyingly sweet, chunky, overdone
84　　style of wine is akin to being hit on the head with a sledgehammer.
　　　Anticipated maturity: Now–1999. Last tasted, 4/91.

1988—It is hard to understand what could have happened at Lamothe-
·　　Despujols in such a superb vintage as 1988. This wine is dull,
72　　muted, and lacking fruit, freshness, and character. It performed
　　　this way in three separate tastings. Anticipated maturity: Now.
　　　Last tasted, 4/91.

1986—For as inconsistent and indifferent as Lamothe-Despujols can be,
·　　the 1986 is irrefutably a sleeper of the vintage. A wonderful
88　　honeyed nose with a whiff of toasty oak is followed by an opulent,

intense, rich, glycerin-filled, full-bodied, beautifully balanced Sauternes that should drink well for another 10–15 years. It is undoubtedly the best example I have ever tasted from this property. Anticipated maturity: Now–2005. Last tasted, 3/90.

1985—This big, fat, surprisingly rich and intense wine exhibits a great
·   deal more weight and character than many other properties in
85   this vintage. There is very little evidence of botrytis, but there are gobs of fruit in a relatively straightforward, chunky style. Anticipated maturity: Now–1996. Last tasted, 3/90.

LAMOTHE-GUIGNARD (Deuxième Cru Classé)   GOOD

Production: 2,900 cases	Grape varieties:
	Semillon—90%
	Sauvignon Blanc—5%
	Muscadelle—5%
Secondary label: none	
Vineyard size: 37 acres	Proprietors: Philippe and
	Jacques Guignard
Dry white wine: none	
Time spent in barrels: 24 months	Average age of vines: 27 years
Evaluation of present classification: Should be maintained	
Plateau of maturity: 5–15 years following the vintage	

The proprietors of Lamothe-Guignard, Philippe and Jacques Guignard, purchased this property in 1981 and have set about in an aggressive manner to resurrect the image of Lamothe-Guignard. This could be a property to keep a close eye on in the nineties, as the quality of the wines since the mid-1980s has been promising.

The vineyard is well located several miles to the south of Yquem, just off route D125. Among the Premiers Crus Classés, it is closest to Guiraud, La Tour Blanche, and Lafaurie-Peyraguey. The proprietors have increased the percentage of new oak, and have begun making more passes through the vineyard to harvest only fully botrytised grapes. The results have been impressive and somewhat undervalued wines.

VINTAGES

1989—There is a remarkable contrast in styles between the 1988 and
·   1989 vintages of Lamothe-Guignard. The 1989 is a blockbuster in
88   the heavy, brawny, outrageously alcoholic, unctuous style that is impressive at first, but that may become tiring. It is an extremely powerful, intense wine, but it comes across as a bully when com-

pared to the charm of the 1988. Nevertheless, this wine has many admirers. Anticipated maturity: 1993–2002. Last tasted, 4/91.

1988—The 1988 is all finesse, with a wonderfully intense bouquet of
·   pineapples, bananas, mangos, honey, and toasty oak. In the
89   mouth, the wine displays splendid concentration, medium body, and vivid clarity and precision to its flavors because of excellent acidity. It should drink beautifully for 10–15 years. It does not have the weight of the 1989, but oh what charm! Anticipated maturity: 1993–2008. Last tasted, 4/91.

1986—The 1986 Lamothe-Guignard has a lovely moderately intense,
·   pineapple fruitiness, rich, velvety flavors, plenty of botrytis, and
87   a long, silky finish. While it will not be one of the longest-lived 1986s, it certainly is capable of providing immense satisfaction for another 5–7 years. Anticipated maturity: Now–1999. Last tasted, 3/90.

1985—Once again, the shortcomings of the 1985 Barsac/Sauternes vin-
·   tage are obvious in this straightforward, relatively fat, but unin-
84   teresting and monolithically styled Sauternes. It is sweet, rich, full, and heavy, but there is a lack of grip as well as complexity. Anticipated maturity: Now–1993. Last tasted, 3/90.

LAMOURETTE (Cru Bourgeois)   AVERAGE

Production: 2,000 cases	Grape varieties: Semillon—90% Sauvignon Blanc—5% Muscadelle—5%
Secondary label: none	
Vineyard size: 18.5 acres	Proprietor: Ann-Marie Leglise
Dry white wine: none	
Time spent in barrels: None; aging takes place in vats	Average age of vines: 25 years
Evaluation of present classification: Should be maintained	
Plateau of maturity: 3–8 years following the vintage	

This is a straightforward, fruity, soft style of Sauternes that is meant to be consumed upon release. The best vintage I have tasted was a stylish 1986.

LIOT (Cru Bourgeois) GOOD

Production: 6,000 cases	Grape varieties: Semillon—80% Sauvignon Blanc—10% Muscadelle—10%
Secondary label: none	
Vineyard size: 50 acres	Proprietor: The David family
Dry white wine: Saint-Jean (white Graves)	
Time spent in barrels: 18–22 months	Average age of vines: 20 years
Evaluation of present classification: Should be maintained	
Plateau of maturity: 3–10 years following the vintage	

This relatively obscure yet competently run vineyard sits on the limestone/clay plateau of the Haut-Barsac hills. The wines I have tasted—1983, 1985, and 1986—were rich, fruity, round, straightforward examples that were cleanly made and pure, if not terribly sweet. This is a vineyard area with plenty of potential because it adjoins the great estate of Château Climens. Based on the handful of vintages I have tasted, this is a wine that must be consumed when young.

DE MALLE (Deuxième Cru Classé) GOOD

Production: 1,300 cases	Grape varieties: Semillon—75% Sauvignon Blanc—23% Muscadelle—2%
Secondary label: Château de Sainte-Hélène	
Vineyard size: 62 acres	Proprietor: Comtesse de Bournazel
Dry white wine: Chevalier de Malle	
Time spent in barrels: 24 months	Average age of vines: 25 years
Evaluation of present classification: Should be maintained	
Plateau of maturity: 5–15 years following the vintage	

This magnificent estate, with its extraordinary seventeenth-century château, was at one time owned by a member of the Lur Saluces family (the proprietors of Yquem and de Fargues). However, that ownership ended in 1785. Since then the property has been in the de Bournazel family. De

Malle is a vast estate, with over half its acreage in Graves. In fact, there are only 62 acres in Sauternes, with 75 acres located in Graves. Those readers who have tasted the excellent white Graves made by Château de Malle, the M. de Malle, or their red wine, Château Cardaillan, know how serious those wines can be. I also recommend that visitors to the Barsac/ Sauternes region go out of their way to get an appointment to visit Château de Malle, which was classified as a historic monument by the French government in 1949.

Even if you have no interest in architecture, the wines are worth tasting as they are among the most elegant of the appellation. At times they can have a tendency to turn out light, but recent vintages (from the more restrained and refined school of Sauternes) have been extremely well made. I should note that the 1990 de Malle is the finest young wine I have tasted from the property, a sentiment shared by many of the region's cognoscenti.

VINTAGES

1989—The lovely, moderately intense bouquet of vanillin spices and
  ·   pineapples is followed by a wine with excellent acidity for a 1989,
  86   good grip and definition, and a medium-bodied, crisp finish. This
         will be a Sauternes to drink early in life, but it should last well.
         Anticipated maturity: 1993–2003. Last tasted, 4/91.

1988—Forgetting the 1990, the 1988 is the best example I have ever
  ·   tasted of a sweet wine from Château de Malle. The wonderfully
  88   perfumed bouquet of pineapples and honeyed, buttery, apple fruit
         is intense and persistent. In the mouth, the wine has the precision
         that is so much a characteristic of the 1988 vintage, and an attrac-
         tive hint of toasty new oak that frames the rich, concentrated,
         highly extracted, moderately sweet, honeyed flavors. This well-
         balanced wine should drink beautifully for the next 10–15 years.
         Anticipated maturity: Now–2005. Last tasted, 4/91.

1986—The 1986 is a medium-bodied, deliciously fruity wine that is rela-
  ·   tively light, but offers a considerable display of fruit salad–like
  84   flavors. There is plenty of freshness, but not as much botrytis as
         I would have expected given the vintage. Anticipated maturity:
         Now–1997. Last tasted, 3/90.

1985—I have always found this wine to be one-dimensional and innocu-
  ·   ous, with straightforward, slightly sweet, monochromatic flavors.
  79   Anticipated maturity: Now–1994. Last tasted, 3/90.

NAIRAC (Deuxième Cru Classé)   GOOD

Production: 2,000 cases	Grape varieties: Semillon—90% Sauvignon Blanc—6% Muscadelle—4%
Secondary label: none	
Vineyard size: 40 acres	Proprietor: Madame Nicole Tari
Dry white wine: none	
Time spent in barrels: 36 months	Average age of vines: 28 years
Evaluation of present classification: Should be maintained	
Plateau of maturity: 5–15 years following the vintage	

Nairac is one of the most meticulously and passionately operated Barsac estates. In 1971, the property was purchased by American-born Tom Heeter and Nicole Tari. Heeter apprenticed at the red wine–producing property, Giscours, in the Margaux appellation where he met his wife (they are now divorced), a member of the Tari winemaking family. The celebrated Emile Peynaud was brought in to provide oenological advice, and Nairac began to produce some of the best wines of Barsac.

Nairac is a relatively big-styled, oaky, ripe, concentrated wine for a Barsac. To say that it is impeccably made is an understatement. No compromises are made, and this is clearly demonstrated by the fact that no Nairac was made in 1977 and 1978, and in 1979, 60% of the crop was deemed unworthy to be sold under the Nairac label.

Nairac represents a good value, and should be sought out by consumers looking for a very good Barsac at a reasonable price.

VINTAGES

1989—When I first tasted the 1989 Nairac from cask, it appeared to be
·   excessively oaky, as well as a bit too fat and alcoholic. However,
87   it has evolved gracefully in the cask and now exhibits plenty of
       toasty vanillin-scented new oak, an opulently rich nose and tex-
       ture, long, heady, unctuous flavors, and enough acidity for grip
       and focus. It will evolve quickly as the color is already a deep
       medium golden. Anticipated maturity: 1992–2003. Last tasted,
       4/91.

1988—This wine has consistently tasted dull and muted, with its fruit
·   suppressed. It was like that from cask and has repeatedly per-
?   formed in a similar manner from bottle. It is hard to understand
       why this wine tastes so backward and unexpressive. Judgment
       reserved. Last tasted, 4/91.

1986—This is one of the finest Nairacs I have ever tasted. It is an
·   especially rich, powerful, concentrated wine with gobs of glyc-
89   erin-injected pineapple fruit, full body, and a long, luscious,
smooth finish. There is plenty of acidity and evidence of botrytis,
so I would expect a relatively long evolution for this top-class
wine. Anticipated maturity: 1993–2010. Last tasted, 3/90.

1985—The 1985 lacks botrytis, a problem that is typical of most wines
·   of the 1985 vintage. Other than that, there is straightforward or-
81   ange and pineapple fruit, heavily dosed with generous quantities
of toasty new oak. Anticipated maturity: Now–1997. Last tasted,
2/87.

1983—Extremely aromatic, the 1983 Nairac has a flowery, tropical fruit–
·   scented bouquet, big, rich, fruit salad–like flavors, full body, and
86   a luscious, honeyed finish. Anticipated maturity: Now–2002. Last
tasted, 3/90.

1982—Probably the most successful Barsac of the vintage, Nairac's 1982
·   exhibits a light golden color, a spicy pineapple and vanillin oaky
85   bouquet, medium to full body, and surprisingly good concentration and length. It is a nice, medium-weight Barsac. Anticipated
maturity: Now–1995. Last tasted, 3/89.

1981—Certainly good, but like many 1981s, Nairac's wine lacks the
·   botrytis that gives the great vintages of this region so much char-
83   acter. Perhaps a little too plump, and with a tendency toward
dullness, this medium- to full-bodied wine has average acidity.
Anticipated maturity: Now–1996. Last tasted, 11/84.

1980—Nairac's 1980 is a well-balanced, light golden–colored wine that
·   displays a good level of botrytis, a spicy, tropical fruit, oaky
84   bouquet, medium body, soft acidity, and a fat, tasty finish. It
is fully mature. Anticipated maturity: Now–1995. Last tasted,
11/84.

1979—A good Barsac, rather light for Nairac, but elegant, adequately
·   concentrated, with a crisp, clean, moderately sweet finish. Antic-
83   ipated maturity: Now. Last tasted, 11/84.

1976—One of the best Nairacs, the 1976 has a powerful, oaky, ripe fruity
·   bouquet and strong vanillin, spicy, oaky notes. On the palate, the
86   wine is full bodied, long, lush, and quite concentrated, and has a
high level of botrytis. Anticipated maturity: Now–1995. Last
tasted, 11/84.

1975—Lighter in style than the 1976, with less power and obvious ap-
·   peal, the 1975 Nairac has a quiet, introverted charm, with a fresh,
84   lively fruitiness, good acidity and presence on the palate, and a
long, moderately sweet finish. It is quite well made. Anticipated
maturity: Now–1996. Last tasted, 11/84.

PIADA (Cru Bourgeois) GOOD

Production: 2,000 cases	Grape varieties: Sauvignon—95% Sauvignon Blanc—5%
Secondary label: none	
Vineyard size: 35 acres	Proprietor: Jean Lalande
Dry white wine: Clos du Roy	
Time spent in barrels: 18 months	Average age of vines: 25 years
Evaluation of present classification: One of the best of the Cru Bourgeois, this property would get serious consideration for elevation to a Deuxième Cru Classé	
Plateau of maturity: 3–12 years following the vintage	

This is one of the oldest estates of the Barsac region. Amazingly, it can trace its history as a wine-producing estate to the late thirteenth century. The wines tend to be richly fruity, round, and honeyed, which is not surprising given the fact that half the crop is aged in stainless-steel *cuves* and the other half in oak casks.

While the aging potential of Piada is suspect, it can be a delicious wine to drink in its first 5–10 years. The best recent vintages include 1988 and 1986.

RABAUD-PROMIS (Premier Cru Classé) VERY GOOD

Production: 5,000 cases	Grape varieties: Semillon—80% Sauvignon Blanc—18% Muscadelle—2%
Secondary label: Domaine de l'Estremade	
Vineyard size: 82 acres	Proprietor: G. F. A. du Château Rabaud-Promis Administrator: Philippe Dejean
Dry white wine: none	
Time spent in barrels: 24–30 months	Average age of vines: 35–40 years
Evaluation of present classification: Since 1986, the wines have merited their classification; previously, the wines ranged from mediocre to disappointing	
Plateau of maturity: 5–20 or more years following the vintage	

Rabaud-Promis was once part of a huge ancient domain called Rabaud. In 1903 Rabaud was divided into Rabaud-Promis and the more well-known Sigalas Rabaud. Curiously, the properties were reunited 26 years later, but then partitioned again in 1952.

Until 1986, Rabaud-Promis may have been the most disappointing wine among the Premiers Crus Classés. However, no estate has made more progress in such a short period of time. Not only has a second wine been introduced, but the top wine now goes into small oak barrels, of which a healthy percentage is new each year. In the past, there was no selection and the entire crop was matured in cement vats.

Shrewd connoisseurs of the sweet wines of Barsac/Sauternes should put such information to use as it will probably take several years before the price catches up to the quality level now being exhibited. If the excellent examples of Rabaud-Promis that have emerged from the 1986, 1988, 1989, and 1990 vintages are typical of the new direction of this property, it will be one of the fuller-bodied, more luscious and intense Sauternes on the market. Virtually all of the credit for this positive change must go to Michelle Lanneluc and her husband, Philippe Dejean.

VINTAGES

1989—The 1989 is opulent, with superb intensity, but the alcohol is high
·   in the finish; the wine comes across as large scaled, very oaky,
89   and rich. A little more acidity would have improved the focus, and could have made this wine sublime. Those who like their Sauternes lusty and obvious will drool over this wine. Anticipated maturity: 1995–2012. Last tasted, 4/91.

1988—What a turnaround this famous old estate has made. The 1986
·   was the best Rabaud-Promis in decades, and the 1988 promises
93   to be superior. It is a full-bodied, splendidly rich, chewy, unctuous, well-delineated wine with excellent acidity. The spectacularly heady, long, concentrated finish is a showstopper. The 1988 Rabaud-Promis promises to be one of the sweetest and most powerful wines of the vintage. Magnificent! Anticipated maturity: 1996–2020. Last tasted, 4/91.

1986—1986 marked the first in a succession of vintages manifesting the
·   return of Rabaud-Promis to its status as a Premier Cru Classé.
89   Full bodied, with an intense bouquet of caramel, pineapples, and apricots, this wine has gobs of glycerin, adequate acidity for balance, and a full-bodied, oaky, rich finish. Its evolution should continue to be graceful and long. Anticipated maturity: 1993–2010. Last tasted, 3/90.

1985—An attractive nose of flowers, pineapples, and coffee is followed
·   by a straightforward, relatively powerful wine with a great deal of
83   fruit, but it is lacking the complexity and focus that is essential

for these large-scaled sweet wines. Anticipated maturity: Now–
1996. Last tasted, 3/90.

1983—This wine has turned out slightly better than I initially believed it
· would. It is fat, round, and full bodied, with gobs of fruit, but it
84 comes across as a bit cloying and heavy-handed, without sufficient botrytis or acidity. It was made at a time when Rabaud-
Promis was aging its wine in vats rather than small oak casks,
which probably explains the wine's lack of delineation. Anticipated maturity: Now–1996. Last tasted, 3/90.

RAYMOND-LAFON (Cru Bourgeois)   EXCELLENT

Production: 1,000–1,500 cases	Grape varieties: Semillon—80% Sauvignon Blanc—20%
Secondary label: none	
Vineyard size: 37 acres	Proprietor: Pierre Meslier
Dry white wine: none	
Time spent in barrels: 36–48 months	Average age of vines: 22 years
Evaluation of present classification: Should be upgraded to a Premier Cru Classé	
Plateau of maturity: 8–25 or more years following the vintage	

Raymond-Lafon is a name to watch in the Sauternes district, particularly
if one is looking for a wine that is close to the brilliance and majestic
richness of Yquem for less than one-third the price.

This small estate abuts Yquem's vineyard and has had an excellent
reputation. The 1921 Raymond-Lafon was considered even better than
Yquem's wine in that great vintage. I have never tasted the 1921 Raymond-Lafon, but the single greatest Sauternes I have ever drunk was the
Yquem of that vintage. However, the estate of Raymond-Lafon fell into
neglect, and it was not until 1972 that Pierre Meslier, the manager of
Yquem, purchased this vineyard and began to slowly rebuild this wine's
once-fabulous reputation.

With a tiny yield of 9 hectoliters per hectare (even less than Yquem's),
with the same grape blend and winemaking techniques employed as
Yquem, and with the same ruthless selection procedure (normally 20–
80% of a harvest is declassified), Raymond-Lafon has already produced
a succession of splendid Sauternes beginning with a great 1975 and just
recently concluding with a monumental 1990.

Raymond-Lafon looks to be well on the road to becoming one of the great classic wines of Sauternes. Unfortunately, the wine is extremely difficult to find because of the tiny production and the fact that proprietor Pierre Meslier sells much of it to private clients in Europe. One must wonder why this vineyard, situated next to Yquem and surrounded by all the Premiers Crus Classés of Sauternes, was overlooked in the 1855 classification.

VINTAGES

1989—In several blind tastings against Premiers Crus Classés held in
·   France, this wine came out first. It is a remarkably rich, exotic,
96   unctuously styled wine with sensational extract, a very sweet, concentrated palate, and a long, heady finish. Its predominate character at the moment is that of honeyed pineapples, interwoven with scents of spring flowers and new oak. It is a great 1989 with the acidity to provide the necessary delineation. Anticipated maturity: 1995–2020. Last tasted, 4/91.

1988—This beautifully proportioned, surprisingly massive wine for the
·   vintage is impressive from all perspectives. The honeyed, floral
94   bouquet offers a great deal of botrytis and ripeness. In the mouth, the wine does not have the size of the 1989, but it is more elegant, with wonderfully precise, botrytised flavors. Full bodied, rich, and intense, this gorgeous wine should provide stunning drinking for at least two decades. Anticipated maturity: 1993–2010. Last tasted, 5/91.

1987—Very light, with straightforward, fruity, slightly sweet flavors, this
·   would make an attractive, but lowbrow apéritif wine. It does not
84   have the requisite weight, sweetness, or complexity to stand by itself as a dessert wine. Anticipated maturity: Now–1995. Last tasted, 4/91.

1986—It is hard to believe this wine will eclipse the great 1983, but the
·   differences in the two wines are negligible. I do not believe the
92   1986 makes quite the impact on the palate that the huge, massive 1983 does, but there is a great deal of botrytis, and a profound, penetrating fragrance of sautéed pineapple, vanillin, toast, and honeyed peaches. In the mouth, the wine is more streamlined than the 1983, but lusciously rich and full bodied, with very good acidity and a creamy, intense finish. It will be interesting to compare the 1983 and 1986 as they evolve. My guess is that the 1986 will age faster. Anticipated maturity: 1993–2012. Last tasted, 3/90.

1985—This is one of the best 1985s I have tasted from Sauternes. It is
·   rich and full, and although there is a general absence of any
87   botrytis, the quality of the fruit is impeccably high. There is

plenty of citrusy, pear-, peach-, and apricot-scented fruit backed up by some vague notes of roasted almonds. This is a delicious 1985 that should evolve gracefully. Anticipated maturity: Now–2002. Last tasted, 3/90.

1983—This is a magnificent wine. Light golden, with a wonderfully pure
· tropical fruit aroma of ripe pineapples and melons, this deca-
93 dently rich, full-bodied wine has layers of viscous, sweet fruit, an astonishing finish, and excellent balancing acidity. The wine remains stubbornly slow to evolve. Anticipated maturity: 1996–2020. Last tasted, 11/90.

1982—In this rain-plagued harvest, Raymond-Lafon only bottled 33% of
· its production, and all of that from grapes picked prior to the rain.
86 The wine is fat, very fruity, sweet, and rich, with good botrytis, a full-bodied, rich, velvety texture, and low to moderate acidity. This vintage of Raymond-Lafon should develop fairly quickly. Anticipated maturity: Now–1997. Last tasted, 3/87.

1981—Because of low acidity, I predict a rapid evolution for the 1981
· Raymond-Lafon. A glorious bouquet of spicy, vanillin oak, lem-
87 ony, honeyed, pineapple fruit, and floral scents is intense and expansive. On the palate, the wine is quite fat, succulent, rich, and sweet, with high alcohol, and a soft, supple, long, clean finish. Anticipated maturity: Now–1996. Last tasted, 3/87.

1980—1980 was a great vintage for Raymond-Lafon, as it also was for
· Yquem and de Fargues, two other properties that proprietor
90 Pierre Meslier looks after. A full-intensity bouquet of ripe tropical fruit and spicy oak is followed by an unctuous, powerful, very rich, full-bodied wine, with layers of fruit, refreshingly high, crisp acidity, and a decade of evolution ahead. Anticipated maturity: Now–2005. Last tasted, 3/87.

1978—This was a good, but hardly special vintage for the wines of Sau-
· ternes. However, the 1978 Raymond-Lafon gets my nod as the
89 best sweet wine of this vintage. It lacks the high level of botrytis found in vintages such as 1975 and 1980, but exhibits beautifully textured, viscous, velvety flavors, full body, a refreshing lemony acidity, and a clean, crisp finish. This is not the biggest Raymond-Lafon, but it is certainly one of the most graceful. Anticipated maturity: Now–2000. Last tasted, 1/85.

1975—Like many Sauternes from this vintage, Raymond-Lafon has been
· slow to develop. Light golden with a green tint, this luscious, rich,
90 creamy wine has a tight, yet expansive bouquet of very ripe fruit. Full bodied, rich, and sweet, yet tightly knit because of good acidity, this big, rich wine has enormous potential. Anticipated maturity: Now–2005. Last tasted, 3/86.

RAYNE-VIGNEAU (Premier Cru Classé)　　　GOOD

Production: 7,500 cases	Grape varieties: Semillon—80% Sauvignon Blanc—20%
Secondary label: none	
Vineyard size: 180 acres	Proprietor: Société Civile du 　Château Rayne-Vigneau Administrator: Jean-Pierre de 　la Beaumelle
Dry white wine: Le Sec de Rayne- 　Vigneau	
Time spent in barrels: 30–36 　months	Average age of vines: 30 years

Evaluation of present classification: Until the mid-1980s, a strong argument could be made that this property should be downgraded; since 1986, however, the quality has improved immensely

Plateau of maturity: 5–20 years following the vintage

During the nineteenth century, Rayne-Vigneau had a reputation second only to that of Yquem. Certainly no other estate in the region is as superbly located as Rayne-Vigneau. However, because of neglect and indifferent winemaking the twentieth century has not been kind to the reputation of Rayne-Vigneau. Since 1971, the estate has been managed and the wines commercialized by Mestrezat, a well-run *négociant* firm. They are also the proprietors of the classified-growth Pauillac, Grand-Puy-Ducasse. They appear to have become deadly serious about the quality of their wines since the early eighties. Rayne-Vigneau has improved immensely since 1985, with the 1986, 1988, and 1990 being the best wines I have tasted from this estate.

The wine now spends nearly 24 months in oak barrels, of which 50% are new each year. In the past, the percentage of new oak utilized was minimal and one always suspected there was a lack of strict selection.

VINTAGES

1989—This wine has consistently tasted muted and uninteresting with a
· 　　lack of richness and concentration. There is an almost artificially
79　　sweet, flabby, unstructured character to the wine. Could this be
　　　a case of where cryo-extraction went afoul? Anticipated maturity:
　　　Now–1996. Last tasted, 4/91.

1988—As disappointing as the 1989, both in the context of the vintage
· 　　and the increasing quality of the wines now emerging from Rayne-
91　　Vigneau, the 1988 is the best example I have tasted from this
　　　property. An intense, honeyed, pear, flower, and apricot fra-

grance is reminiscent of Muscat de Beaumes de Venise. In the mouth, there is exceptional richness, super focus because of fine acidity, a wonderful touch of toasty new oak, and an elegant, very positive, crisp finish. This is a beautifully made, authoritative tasting, and impeccably well-balanced Sauternes. Anticipated maturity: 1992–2006. Last tasted, 3/90.

1987— This straightforward, soft, fat, richly fruity wine comes across as
· sweet and disjointed, but pleasant in a low-key way. It lacks
82 focus, botrytis, and acidity, but for drinking as an apéritif it has a place. Anticipated maturity: Now–1995. Last tasted, 11/90.

1986— This is the first reassuring example of Rayne-Vigneau in years,
· exhibiting a deft touch of new oak, an elegant, yet concentrated,
90 flavorful style, and a great deal of finesse. The overwhelming impression is one of pears, pineapples, and great balance and character. Anticipated maturity: Now–2001. Last tasted, 11/90.

1985— This is a ripe pineapple-scented and -flavored wine with just
· enough new oak and relatively thick, monolithic flavors, but it
85 lacks acidity and comes across as monochromatic. It is tasty and juicy, but a bit simple. Anticipated maturity: Now–1996. Last tasted, 11/90.

1983— Light aromas of pineapples and some faint botrytis emerge with
· breathing from this simply proportioned Sauternes. In the mouth,
82 the wine reveals good ripeness, a pleasant, velvety, creamy texture, medium sweetness, and crisp acidity. In the context of the vintage, this is an uninspiring wine, but for Rayne-Vigneau, a good effort. Anticipated maturity: Now–1996. Last tasted, 11/90.

1982— One-dimensional, fruity, sweet flavors offer little complexity, but
· do exhibit pleasing ripeness and adequate balancing acidity. An-
75 ticipated maturity: Now–may be in decline. Last tasted, 1/85.

1981— Soft, fruity, moderately sweet flavors exhibit average concentra-
· tion and some alluring scents of grilled almonds and pineapples,
75 but this wine has a diluted finish, and just not enough stuffing and concentration to warrant much interest. Anticipated maturity: Now–may be in decline. Last tasted, 2/85.

1979— A straightforward, fruity, rather sweet wine, without much botry-
· tis, but displaying solid, underripe flavors of peaches and mint.
74 Typically light, and lacking muscle and concentration, the 1979 Rayne-Vigneau should be drunk up. Anticipated maturity: Now. Last tasted, 6/83.

1976— For a 1976, this is a lightweight wine, but it does have a good,
· ripe apricot fruitiness, medium body, and a decent, moderately
78 sweet finish. I am tempted to say that this is a nice picnic Sauternes. Anticipated maturity: Now–1994. Last tasted, 2/84.

1975—A disappointing effort, the 1975 has excessively high acidity, a
·   lean, austere, ungenerous texture, and light, vegetal, washed-out
65   flavors. One wonders what could have gone afoul in this excellent
       vintage. Last tasted, 6/84.
1971—Hot alcohol tends to intrude on this wine's soft, delicate pineapple
·   fruitiness and medium-bodied texture. It will only become more
75   imbalanced. Anticipated maturity: Now–1993. Last tasted, 2/80.

RIEUSSEC (Premier Cru Classé)   OUTSTANDING

Production: 7,000 cases	Grape varieties: Semillon—80% Sauvignon Blanc—18% Muscadelle—2%
Secondary label: Clos Labère	
Vineyard size: 165 acres	Proprietor: Domaines Barons de Rothschild
Dry white wine: "R" de Rieussec	
Time spent in barrels: 26–32 months	Average age of vines: 29 years

Evaluation of present classification: Since the acquisition by the
Domaines Rothschild in 1984, the quality of Rieussec has soared to
even greater heights; it is now one of the four-best wines of the
region

Plateau of maturity: 6–25 or more years following the vintage

As one approaches the heart of the Sauternes appellation, Château
Rieussec and its prominent lookout tower can be spotted on one of the
highest hillsides. The Rieussec vineyard, spread across the hillsides of
Fargues and Sauternes overlooking the left bank of the Garonne, has the
highest altitude after that of Yquem. Quite surprising for a Bordeaux
property, the entire vineyard is one single unit.

Rieussec has always had an outstanding reputation, but after its acquisition by Albert Vuillier in 1971, the quality improved even more,
largely because of the increase in new oak and more frequent passes
through the vineyard to harvest only heavily botrytised grapes. In fact,
some critics of Rieussec claimed that Vuillier's wines took on too deep a
color as they aged (i.e., the 1976). Vuillier remains chairman, but sold a
majority interest in 1984 to the Domaines Barons de Rothschild, who
have spared no expense nor permitted any compromising in the making
of Rieussec. The results since 1986 have been truly profound wines that
are now routinely among the top three or four wines of the appellation.

Wealthy collectors will no doubt argue for decades whether the 1988, 1989, or 1990 produced the most profound Rieussec.

Under the Rothschild ownership, it is unlikely that Rieussec's style— one of power and almost roasted richness—will change. The wine is usually deeply colored and generally alcoholic, with excellent viscosity. Rieussec, like several other estates in Barsac and Sauternes, produces a tiny amount of decadently rich, intensely concentrated wine under a "Crème de Tête" label. Should you ever come across this rare, unctuous nectar, don't hesitate to give it a try. Rieussec also produces a dry white wine called "R." Such wines help ease cash-flow problems considerably, and "R" is one of the most popular and best of the dry Sauternes.

VINTAGES

1989—The 1989 Rieussec is one of the stars of the vintage. It is a fat,
·   rich, very broad-shouldered wine, with great depth and richness,
94   and considerably more alcohol than the 1988. I did not detect as
       much botrytis as I would have hoped. Nevertheless, it is a block-
       buster, massive wine. Its evolution should be fascinating to fol-
       low. Anticipated maturity: 1998–2015. Last tasted, 4/91.

1988—The 1988 is another great Rieussec. After tasting all the 1988 and
·   1989 Barsac/Sauternes blind, it gets top marks for both vintages.
95   It is an utterly mind-blowing performance for the château, with a
       hauntingly perfect bouquet of great precision and persistence. In
       the mouth, the wine has remarkable clarity, stunning power and
       depth, and a finish that must last several minutes. It is a wine-
       making tour de force, and one of the greatest young Sauternes I
       have had the pleasure of tasting. This is a wine to rush to buy, as
       the price can only get higher and higher. Anticipated maturity:
       1998–2015. Last tasted, 4/91.

1986—This is a stunningly complex and elegant wine, but it is less mus-
·   cular as well as less fat than either the 1983 or 1989. There are
91   plenty of smoky almonds, peaches, and honeyed apricot fruit in
       the nose and flavors. In the mouth, the wine has a certain ele-
       gance, and perhaps not quite the punch one normally expects
       from Rieussec. Nevertheless, it is still a compelling Sauternes
       that should age magnificently. Anticipated maturity: 1994–2010.
       Last tasted, 11/90.

1985—This is a very good Sauternes for the vintage—rich, round, open
·   knit, with a great deal of juicy, sweet, candied fruit—but the
86   absence of botrytis results in a wine lacking in complexity and
       coming across as plump and succulent, but not terribly interest-
       ing. Anticipated maturity: Now–1998. Last tasted, 11/90.

1983—Light golden with just the slightest tint of green, the 1983 Rieus-
  ·   sec, from an excellent year for Sauternes, is certainly one of this
  92   property's greatest wines. Well structured with excellent acidity,
         and a deep, long, rich, full-bodied, viscous texture, this wine,
         despite the richness and power, is neither heavy nor cloying. It
         has gorgeous balance and a very long, lingering, spectacular fin-
         ish. One of the great successes of the vintage. Anticipated matu-
         rity: Now–2005. Last tasted, 3/88.

1982—A maligned vintage for the sweet white wines of Bordeaux, Rieus-
  ·   sec has, through a very strict selection process, turned out a
  82   lovely, fruity, spicy, lighter-styled wine with medium body and
         delicate tropical fruit flavors. Anticipated maturity: Now–1996.
         Last tasted, 3/86.

1981—One of the top 1981s, Rieussec must certainly be among the best
  ·   Sauternes of this vintage. A very fragrant, spicy, richly fruity
  86   bouquet intermingled with scents of apricots and melted butter is
         top class. On the palate, the wine is well balanced, fairly big and
         rich, and already showing well. Anticipated maturity: Now–1995.
         Last tasted, 3/86.

1980—Somewhat dull and a trifle heavy, Rieussec's 1980 is a good,
  ·   relatively rich, spicy, full-bodied wine revealing high acidity,
  80   some botrytis, and adequate flavor intensity. However, it is not
         one of the leaders in this vintage. Anticipated maturity: Now–
         may be in decline. Last tasted, 3/84.

1979—A lightweight Rieussec that does not have the intensity and rich-
  ·   ness of vintages such as 1981 or 1983, it does offer an elegant,
  84   well-made, less powerful wine that is light enough to be served as
         an apéritif. Anticipated maturity: Now–1993. Last tasted, 3/84.

1978—The 1978 Rieussec just missed the mark. While quite good, it is
  ·   not special. Too alcoholic, and a trifle too heavy and overblown,
  82   this wine has a nice honeyed character and rich, unctuous flavors,
         but evidences little botrytis. Anticipated maturity: Now–1994.
         Last tasted, 6/84.

1976—This is one of the most controversial vintages of Rieussec. Very
  ·   dark gold in color, some observers have said it is oxidized and is
  90   falling apart. Despite the dark color, the remarkable taste seems
         to suggest that this wine has a way to go. The huge nose of toasted
         almonds, caramel, chocolate, and brown sugar does exhibit a
         trace of volatile acidity, so technocrats are likely to be turned off.
         Incredibly rich and full bodied, with a honeyed, luscious texture
         and extremely intense flavors, this exotic, hugely proportioned
         wine (15% alcohol) can *only* be served as a dessert. The yield at

Rieussec in 1976 was 2.5 hectoliters per hectare, which is approximately one-third of a glass of wine per vine. This is a bold, rather overblown style of Sauternes, but I love it. Anticipated maturity: Now–2005. Last tasted, 12/90.

1975—Still remarkably youthful looking, and slow to evolve, this is a
·   powerful, concentrated, and rich Sauternes, with decades of life
90   ahead of it. Lemon, tropical fruit, and vanillin oaky aromas titillate the olfactory glands. Tight, yet rich, full-bodied flavors reveal marvelous balance and richness. It is aging at a snail's pace. Anticipated maturity: 1995–2025. Last tasted, 12/90.

1971—Now fully mature, the 1971 Rieussec has a light-intensity,
·   honeyed, ripe apricot, oaky nose, a ripe, sweet, full-bodied feel
85   on the palate, and a crisp, spicy finish. Anticipated maturity: Now–1995. Last tasted, 10/80.

1970—A little heavier to taste and a bit less elegant than the 1971, the
·   1970 is a corpulent, rich, sweet mouthful of viscous, chewy Sau-
82   ternes. The moderately amber/gold color is a sign of approaching maturity, but this wine has the acidity and overall balance to drink nicely for at least another decade. Anticipated maturity: Now–1995. Last tasted, 6/83.

1967—Rieussec made a very fine 1967. Not having tasted it for some
·   time, I suspect this wine has been fully mature since the mid-
84   1970s. It is lighter in style and body than some of the more recent vintages of Rieussec, but richly fruity and spicy, with a roasted, grilled-nut aroma. Anticipated maturity: Now–1996. Last tasted, 9/79.

DE ROLLAND (Cru Bourgeois)   AVERAGE

Production: 4,000 cases	Grape varieties: Semillon—60% Sauvignon Blanc—20% Muscadelle—20%
Secondary label: none	
Vineyard size: 50 acres	Proprietor: Jean Guignard
Dry white wine: none	
Time spent in barrels: 18 months	Average age of vines: 25 years
Evaluation of present classification: Should be maintained	
Plateau of maturity: 3–10 years following the vintage	

I have tasted only two vintages (1985 and 1986) of this Barsac property. I liked the wines, although I deemed them uninspiring. Nevertheless, the Barsac cognoscenti consider the potential of Château de Rolland's vineyard to be very high, as it sits in an area where the micro-climate is superb for making sweet wine. The property is located just to the west of RN 113, with a view overlooking the Ciron River.

ROMER DU HAYOT (Deuxième Cru Classé)　　　　　　GOOD

Production: 4,200 cases	Grape varieties:
	Semillon—70%
	Sauvignon Blanc—25%
Secondary label: none	Muscadelle—5%
Vineyard size: 40 acres	
Dry white wine: none	Proprietor: The du-Hayot family
Time spent in barrels: 16–20 months in both barrels and vats	Average age of vines: 25 years
Evaluation of present classification: Should be maintained	
Plateau of maturity: 3–15 years following the vintage	

I have generally enjoyed the wines of Romer du Hayot, a small Sauternes estate located near the beautiful Château de Malle. The style of wine produced emphasizes a fresh fruity character, medium body, and moderate sweetness. The wine sees limited aging in barrels, so its exuberant fruitiness is not masked by spicy, oaky aromas and flavors.

While it is a lighter-styled Sauternes, it has plenty of interest and generally ages well for 4–7 years. The 1983, 1979, 1976, and 1975 were all successful vintages for Romer du Hayot. Fortunately, the price asked for the wines from this little-known property is reasonable.

VINTAGES

1989—The 1989 is too alcoholic, very sweet, and cloying, but fat and
·　　deep, with a lack of acidity creating a certain diffusiveness among
86　　its component parts. Nevertheless, among those who love lusty,
　　　slightly out-of-balance, thick Sauternes, this wine will have its
　　　admirers. Anticipated maturity: Now–1997. Last tasted, 4/91.

1988—The 1988 Romer du Hayot has a beautifully rich, concentrated
·　　bouquet filled with evidence of botrytis, and fully mature fruit. In
85　　the mouth, it is medium to full bodied, with good acidity, and
　　　plenty of length and concentration. Ideally, it should be drunk
　　　over the next 10–12 years. I should note that several samples of
　　　this wine had an inexcusable fecal aroma. Anticipated maturity:
　　　Now–1998. Last tasted, 4/91.

1986—Fully mature, this tasty, complex wine exhibits fine richness and
·   length as well as evidence of botrytis in its honeyed peach, pear,
86   and apricot flavors. Anticipated maturity: Now–1996. Last tasted,
    3/90.

1985—Sweet, round, and aromatic, but one-dimensional, with mono-
·   chromatic flavors, this medium-bodied, chunky Sauternes pro-
78   vides unexciting drinking. Anticipated maturity: Now–1993. Last
    tasted, 3/89.

ROUMIEU-LACOSTE (Cru Bourgeois)   GOOD

Production: 2,700 cases	Grape varieties:
	Semillon—80%
	Sauvignon Blanc—10%
	Muscadelle—10%
Secondary label: none	
Vineyard size: 30 acres	Proprietor: Hervé Dubourdieu
Dry white wine: Graville-Lacoste (Graves)	
Time spent in barrels: 18–24 months	Average age of vines: 25 years
Evaluation of present classification: Should be elevated to a Deuxième Cru Classé	
Plateau of maturity: 5–12 years following the vintage	

The quality of the wines at Roumieu-Lacoste should not be surprising
given the fact that this vineyard is adjacent to the famed Climens in
Barsac. The old vines and impeccable winemaking practices of the Dubourdieu family result in consistently high-quality wines. The style, as
befitting a Barsac, is relatively light, but there is plenty of complexity,
rich pineapple fruit, and just a touch of toasty new oak. The best recent
vintages have included a fine 1986 and 1983. I first came across this wine
when it was served with dessert following a luncheon at Château Latour.
This would appear to be a wine that is best consumed within 10–12 years
of the vintage.

SAINT-MARC (Cru Bourgeois)   AVERAGE

Production: 4,000 cases	Grape varieties: Semillon—80% Sauvignon Blanc—20%
Secondary label: none	
Vineyard size: 40 acres	Proprietor: Didier Laulan
Dry white wine: Le Lion	
Time spent in barrels: 18–20 months in both barrels and vats	Average age of vines: 25 years
Evaluation of present classification: Should be maintained	
Plateau of maturity: 3–10 years following the vintage	

I have a competent tasting note for the 1983. The vineyard, completely replanted following World War II, is reputed to turn out light, elegant, very flowery-styled wines from the Barsac region. Their aging potential is considered to be limited.

A small amount of dry white wine called Le Lion is produced. The proprietor also has a small estate in Graves called Château Brochon.

SIGALAS RABAUD (Premier Cru Classé)   VERY GOOD

Production: 2,500 cases	Grape varieties: Semillon—90% Sauvignon Blanc—10%
Secondary label: none	
Vineyard size: 35 acres	Proprietor: The family of the Marquise de Lambert des Granges
Dry white wine: none	
Time spent in barrels: At least 20 months in vats	Average age of vines: 28 years
Evaluation of present classification: Since the early eighties, it has merited its Premier Cru Classé status	
Plateau of maturity: 5–15 years following the vintage	

This has always been a perplexing wine to evaluate. There is no question that the ideal positioning of the south-facing vineyard on the hillsides of Haut-Bommes, with gravelly clay soil, should produce exceptionally ripe grapes. However, when tasting the wines of Sigalas Rabaud, I have always sensed a certain laissez-faire attitude. Perhaps that has changed, since the mid-1980s because the wines have significantly improved.

The style of wine produced at Sigalas Rabaud is much lighter, and at its best, more elegant and graceful than several of its overblown, rich, and alcoholic peers. Interestingly, aging in oak barrels is not utilized at this estate because the proprietors prefer cement and stainless-steel vats. For that reason, I always find Sigalas Rabaud to have one of the most exuberantly fruity bouquets and tastes, which would no doubt please more wine enthusiasts than some of the aggressively alcoholic, thick, viscous, oaky giants elsewhere in Sauternes.

Sigalas Rabaud is most definitely a wine to drink young, before it attains the age of 7 or 8 years. Since it is lighter and less alcoholic, it is a more flexible Sauternes with food than many others.

VINTAGES

1989—Not surprisingly, the 1989 is sweeter and more alcoholic than the
· 1988, with a candied fruit-salad character. It is a bit monolithic
89 when compared with the 1988, but, nevertheless, it is impressive, if only because of its size and weight, which are atypically considerable for Sigalas Rabaud. Anticipated maturity: 1994–2005. Last tasted, 4/91.

1988—The 1988 is the richest Sigalas Rabaud I have yet to taste, with
· unctuous, fleshy, highly extracted flavors, great length, and a
91 stunningly perfumed, fragrant bouquet of honey, melons, and oranges. It also possesses a big, rich, vibrant finish. A top success, it is one of the finest wines from this château in years. Anticipated maturity: 1994–2007. Last tasted, 4/91.

1986—Sigalas Rabaud made a complex, elegant, botrytis-filled 1986.
· The honeyed, flowery, spicy aromas leap from the glass in this
90 beautifully proportioned wine. In the mouth, there is fine acidity, some rich, honeyed, pear- and pineapple-like fruit, and a soft, yet adequately delineated, long, alcoholic finish. Anticipated maturity: Now–2002. Last tasted, 11/90.

1985—Elegant, stylish, medium bodied, but essentially one-dimensional
· given the lack of botrytis, this wine is already offering pleasant,
84 satisfying drinking. Anticipated maturity: Now–1995. Last tasted, 11/90.

1983—The 1983 has an intensely fruity bouquet suggestive of pineap-
· ples, fine depth and concentration, an unctuous quality, and
86 crisp, fresh acidity. It is a very fruity, moderately sweet, well-knit Sauternes. Anticipated maturity: Now–1997. Last tasted, 1/85.

1982—The 1982 is a middle-of-the-road Sauternes, with good fruit, me-
· dium body, and a pleasant finish, but like so many 1982s, it has
75 no complexity. Anticipated maturity: Now. Last tasted, 1/85.

1981—Light but charming, with a fragrant, fruity, herbaceous, almost
·   flowery bouquet, the 1981 seems to be a typically proportioned,
80   medium-weight wine from Sigalas Rabaud. Anticipated maturity:
       Now. Last tasted, 6/84.

1980—Rather one-dimensional and dull, the 1980 is light, not very con-
·   centrated, and missing the usual fruity intensity and charm that
75   this wine frequently offers. Anticipated maturity: Now–may be in
       decline. Last tasted, 2/84.

1979—Quite appealing in a lighter, more refreshing manner, the 1979
·   Sigalas Rabaud has a moderately intense, fruity, minty, spicy
78   bouquet, medium body, not much botrytis, but crisp acidity, and
       some sweetness. It is a charming Sauternes. Anticipated matu-
       rity: Now. Last tasted, 9/83.

1976—Light, fruity, and typically Sigalas Rabaud, this medium-bodied
·   wine has a light perfume of pineapple fruit, good acidity, and
80   moderately sweet, nicely balanced flavors. It is fully mature. An-
       ticipated maturity: Now–may be in decline. Last tasted, 7/80.

1975—Highly touted by the château, this wine has more in common with
·   a German Auslese from the Mosel than a Sauternes. Flowery,
?   rather simple and compact, this lean, atypical Sigalas Rabaud is
       also suffering from an intrusive amount of sulfur dioxide. Last
       tasted, 3/86.

1971—This is another lightweight effort from Sigalas Rabaud, but it is
·   graceful and fruity, with a honeyed, fruity bouquet that is clean
82   and fresh. Medium body, moderately sweet flavors, and crisp
       acidity are admirably balanced. Anticipated maturity: Now–1994.
       Last tasted, 3/81.

1967—Just beginning to lose its fruit and freshness, this has always been
·   one of my favorite vintages of Sigalas Rabaud. The antithesis of a
85   powerhouse, oaky, viscous Sauternes, the 1967 is moderately
       sweet and has a honeyed bouquet of pineapples. Medium bodied
       and concentrated, but surprisingly light, this is a textbook exam-
       ple of Sigalas Rabaud that requires consumption. Anticipated
       maturity: Now–1994. Last tasted, 3/87.

SUAU (Deuxième Cru Classé) AVERAGE

Production: 1,500 cases	Grape varieties: Semillon—85% Sauvignon Blanc—15%
Secondary label: none	
Vineyard size: 20 acres	Proprietor: Roger Biarnès
Dry white wine: none	
Time spent in barrels: 18–22 months	Average age of vines: 25 years
Evaluation of present classification: Should be downgraded to a Cru Bourgeois	
Plateau of maturity: 3–10 years following the vintage	

The tiny estate of Suau tucked away on a back road of Barsac is largely unknown. Much of the production is sold directly to consumers. The quality is uninspiring. In general, this is a wine to consume within its first decade of life.

VINTAGES

1989—The 1989 is sweet, alcoholic, clumsy, and heavy. Anticipated
·   maturity: Now–1997. Last tasted, 4/91.
83

1988—The 1988 Suau is a light, relatively shallow wine, with good acid-
·   ity. It should be consumed over the next 4–5 years. Anticipated
79   maturity: Now–1996. Last tasted, 4/91.

1986—Among the recent vintages, this is the best example of this Barsac
·   I have tasted. An interesting bouquet of oranges and pineapples
85   makes for a fine initial impression. In the mouth, the wine is soft,
       unctuous, and very precocious. Anticipated maturity: Now–1994.
       Last tasted, 11/90.

1985—This one-dimensional, chunky, muscular, relatively fat-styled
·   wine with little complexity or character should be drunk over the
79   next 2–3 years. Anticipated maturity: Now–1994. Last tasted,
       11/90.

SUDUIRAUT (Premier Cru Classé)   EXCELLENT

Production: 8,500 cases	Grape varieties: Semillon—80% Sauvignon Blanc—20%
Secondary label: none, but in certain years (i.e., 1982 and 1989) a luxury *cuvée* called Cuvée Madame is produced	
Vineyard size: 187 acres	Proprietor: The Fonquernie family
Dry white wine: none	
Time spent in barrels: 30 months in small casks and 12 months in vats	Average age of vines: 25 years
Evaluation of present classification: Should be maintained	
Plateau of maturity: 5–25 or more years following the vintage	

Just down the road from Yquem, abutting Yquem's vineyards on the north, is the large, beautiful estate of Suduiraut. Suduiraut can be one of the great wines of Sauternes. For example, the 1959, 1967, 1976, 1982, 1988, 1989, and 1990 are staggering examples of Suduiraut's potential. At its best, Suduiraut turns out very rich, luscious wines that in blind tastings can be confused with Yquem. However, I have always been perplexed by the shocking inconsistency in quality of the wines from this estate. In the first half of the seventies, Suduiraut produced several wines well below acceptable standards. Apparently some of the criticism caught up with the Paris-based owners, the Fonquernie family, who put their best foot forward with the fantastic 1976, and hired a new *maître de chai*, Pierre Pascaud, in 1978. Now, all things at Suduiraut seem to be in good order as the wines have been consistently successful.

When Suduiraut is good, it is very, very good. In great vintages, the wine needs a decade to be at its best, but will keep easily for 25 years. Richly colored, quite perfumed, and decadently rich, even massive in the top years, Suduiraut, while less consistent than properties like Climens and Rieussec, appears to now be back on track.

In 1982 and 1989 the château produced a sumptuous, super quality, rare and expensive Crème de Tête—Cuvée Madame. This *cuvée*, much like the limited edition Cuvée Madame of Château Coutet, is capable of rivaling Yquem, but the production is miniscule—less than 1,000 cases.

VINTAGES

1989—The 1989 regular *cuvée* is a blockbuster, heavyweight, oily, almost
·   overdone version of Sauternes. There is no denying its opulence,
90   high alcohol, and almost cloying sweetness. It is undoubtedly the
        most massive wine I have ever tasted from Suduiraut. Is it an-
        other 1959 in the making? Anticipated maturity: 2000–2020. Last
        tasted, 4/91.

1989—Cuvée Madame—This is an extraordinary Sauternes. Fabulously
·   concentrated, with an unctuous texture, and what must be nearly
96   14–15% natural alcohol, this mammoth-sized Sauternes should
        prove to be one of the monumental efforts of the vintage. For
        those who prefer power and finesse, the 1988 may take prefer-
        ence; for those who want pure brute strength and unbelievable
        size, the 1989 Cuvée Madame is without equal. Anticipated ma-
        turity: 2000–2025. Last tasted, 4/91.

1988—I suspect arguments are going to rage over which is the better
·   vintage for Suduiraut—1988 or 1989. The 1988 has greater bal-
92   ance, but at present, the explosive power and richness seem well
        harnessed by the wine's superb balance and good acidity. The
        nose is suppressed at the moment, but on the palate, the formi-
        dable power and extraordinary concentration are easily observed.
        It is one of the most backward wines of the vintage, as the fabu-
        lous length attests. Anticipated maturity: 2000–2030. Last tasted,
        4/91.

1986—I would have expected Suduiraut to be outstanding in 1986, but it
·   is not. It is very good, but this wine should have been a classic.
87   Plump, rich, honeyed, pineapple, coconut, and buttery fruit fla-
        vors abound in this full-bodied, rich wine that falls just short of
        being profound. It is muscular and rich, but it is missing an ele-
        ment of complexity that I found in many other 1986s. Also, is it
        possible that the 1986 Suduiraut has less botrytis than the other
        top examples from this vintage? Anticipated maturity: Now–2003.
        Last tasted, 3/90.

1985—Shockingly light, with straightforward, bland, even innocuous fla-
·   vors, this fruity yet one-dimensional Suduiraut is disappointing
79   given the reputation of the château. Anticipated maturity: Now–
        1995. Last tasted, 3/90.

1983—This looks to be a good Suduiraut. A medium golden color, with
·   a very honeyed, rich, floral bouquet, this full-bodied wine is not
87   as profound as the other 1983s. Sweet, with fine honeyed flavors,
        this is an elegant, graceful Suduiraut with plenty of character.
        However, given the vintage, I had expected even more. Antici-
        pated maturity: Now–2005. Last tasted, 3/90.

1982—Cuvée Madame—The 1982 vintage, while great for Bordeaux's
·   red wines, is not special for the sweet wines. However, the 1982
90   Suduiraut Cuvée Madame is a smashing success. *Régisseur*
       Pierre Pascaud thinks it is the best wine made at the property
       since the great 1967 and 1959. Only the grapes harvested before
       the rains fell were used, and the result is a very concentrated,
       deep, luscious, honeyed wine, with great length, the buttery, vis-
       cous richness that Suduiraut is famous for, and superb balance.
       If it had just a trifle more botrytis character it would be perfect.
       Anticipated maturity: Now–2010. Last tasted, 3/90.

1981—A very attractive, elegant Suduiraut, the 1981 does not have the
·   richness of the 1982 or 1983, but is agreeably forward, spicy, and
84   ripe, with less power and concentration than normal. It is clearly
       well made and moderately sweet. Anticipated maturity: Now–
       1997. Last tasted, 3/84.

1979—One of the top 1979s, Suduiraut has produced an uncommonly
·   rich, deep, powerful wine for this vintage. The wine is medium
86   golden, with a ripe, toasty, caramel-and-apricot-scented bouquet,
       full body, plenty of viscous fruit, and a long finish. Anticipated
       maturity: Now–1998. Last tasted, 3/84.

1978—A down-scaled version of the 1979, the 1978 is elegant, less sweet,
·   and significantly less rich, with medium body, fairly light texture
83   for a Suduiraut, and good acidity. Anticipated maturity: Now–
       1998. Last tasted, 3/86.

1976—For me, the 1976 is the greatest Suduiraut of the seventies, and
·   the only wine other than the 1989 that resembles the magnificent
92   1959 this property produced. Medium to dark amber/gold, this
       full-bodied, massive wine has a very intense bouquet of vanillin
       oak, ripe pineapples, and melted caramel. Very deep and viscous,
       this is a decadently opulent Suduiraut with enormous presence in
       the mouth. Anticipated maturity: Now–2010. Last tasted, 3/90.

1975—Produced when Suduiraut was in a slump, this wine, from an
·   excellent vintage, has good ripeness, but is shockingly light and
78   is a little too simple and one-dimensional for a top-rated estate.
       The finish also leaves a lot to be desired. Anticipated maturity:
       Now–1996. Last tasted, 6/82.

1971—Pleasant, but light and rather meagerly endowed, the 1971 Sudui-
·   raut while agreeable and quite palatable is a disappointment for a
75   wine from this estate. I have not tasted it recently, but this wine
       is probably in decline. Last tasted, 2/78.

1970—A good Suduiraut, but despite the concentration and depth, it
·   tastes flabby, overly alcoholic, and just too one-dimensional. An-
80   ticipated maturity: Now–may be in decline. Last tasted, 8/81.

1969—Surprisingly rich, fruity, and mouth-filling, the 1969 Suduiraut is
· one of a number of 1969 Sauternes that turned out considerably
78 better than their red wine siblings. Anticipated maturity: Now—
may be in decline. Last tasted, 6/77.

1967—A classic vintage for Suduiraut, this rich, full-bodied, expansive,
· viscous, fully mature wine has a wonderful honeyed, almond,
89 caramel-scented bouquet, rich, sweet, deep, succulent flavors,
full body, and a muscular, aggressive finish. The 1967 is perhaps
not a match for the 1959 or 1976, but it is certainly the best wine
produced at this château between these two vintages. Anticipated
maturity: Now–2000. Last tasted, 3/88.

OLDER VINTAGES

In the tasting notes I alluded to the great 1959 Suduiraut produced. I
have consistently rated this wine between 92 and 94 on the occasions I
have tasted it (most recently 12/89). Among the other vintages for which
I have notes, I have given excellent ratings to the 1945 (rated 90 in 11/
86) and the 1947 (rated 93 in 7/87). I have never seen a pre–World War
II vintage but the 1928 and 1899 are considered legendary years for this
estate. The other years I have tasted, 1949 and 1955, left me unmoved.

LA TOUR BLANCHE (Premier Cru Classé)   EXCELLENT

Production: 4,000 cases	Grape varieties: Semillon—78% Sauvignon Blanc—20% Muscadelle—2%
Secondary label: Mademoiselle de Saint-Marc	
Vineyard size: 84 acres	Proprietor: The Ministry of Agriculture Administrator: Jean-Pierre Jausserand
Dry white wines: Osiris and Le Sec de la Tour Blanche	
Time spent in barrels: 22–26 months	Average age of vines: 30 years
Evaluation of present classification: Since 1986, the quality of La Tour Blanche has increased dramatically with truly compelling wines being made in 1988, 1989, and 1990; the château now merits its classification	
Plateau of maturity: 5–30 years following the vintage	

La Tour Blanche was ranked in the top of its class right behind Yquem in the 1855 classification of the wines of the Sauternes region. Since 1910, the Ministry of Agriculture has run La Tour Blanche, and until the mid-1980s seemed content to produce wines that at best could be called mediocre. That has changed significantly with the employment of 100% new oak beginning in 1988, followed by a complete fermentation of the 1989 in new oak barrels. The cellars are completely air-conditioned and the yields have been reduced to a meager 25–35 hectoliters per hectare. All things considered, La Tour Blanche looks to be one of the up-and-coming superstars of the appellation of Sauternes during the nineties. Fortunately, prices have not yet caught up with La Tour Blanche's new quality.

There are also small quantities of a second wine made from weaker vats, as well as two different dry Bordeaux Blancs.

VINTAGES

1989—The 1989 stood out in my tastings as one of the best Sauternes of
·   the vintage. Explosive, with a fabulous bouquet of oranges, man-
92   goes, and coconut, this decadently rich, full-bodied, monstrous-
       sized Sauternes has enough acidity for balance. It is one of the
       greatest wines of the 1989 Barsac/Sauternes vintage. Anticipated
       maturity: 1996–2030. Last tasted, 4/91.

1988—Perhaps the most remarkable story in Barsac/Sauternes is the
·   tremendous progression in quality made by La Tour Blanche.
91   This property has always been capable of turning out good wine,
       but never in recent history have they produced such enthralling
       wines as the 1988 and 1989. It is one example where the 1989 is
       actually greater than the 1988. The 1988 is astonishingly rich and
       deep, with a pervasively intense nose of botrytis. In the mouth, it
       is extremely full bodied and powerful, with great persistence and
       intensity of flavor, as well as a fascinating balance between acid-
       ity and power. Anticipated maturity: 1996–2015. Last tasted,
       4/91.

1986—When I tasted this wine from cask I thought it would be better.
·   But it has turned out to be a relatively straightforward, compact,
82   monolithic-styled Sauternes, with good fruit, but without the great
       underlying depth and evidence of botrytis one normally sees in
       this vintage. It should provide good but uninspired drinking for
       another decade or more. Anticipated maturity: Now–2003. Last
       tasted, 3/90.

1985—Normally the 1985 Sauternes are less impressive than the 1986s,
·   but La Tour Blanche's 1985 comes across as more concentrated,
84   with greater intensity and length than the 1986. Nevertheless,

there is still a glaring lack of complexity and botrytis. Anticipated maturity: Now–2001. Last tasted, 3/90.

OLDER VINTAGES

The finest older vintage of La Tour Blanche I have had the privilege of tasting was a very fine example of the 1975 (rated 87 in 1990). It was still youthful when tasted at age 15.

YQUEM (Premier Grand Cru Classé)   OUTSTANDING *

Production: 5,000–6,000 cases	Grape varieties: Semillon—80% Sauvignon Blanc—20%
Secondary label: none	
Vineyard size: 255 acres	Proprietor: Comte Alexandre de Lur Saluces
Dry white wine: Y d'Yquem	
Time spent in barrels: 42 months	Average age of vines: 25 years

* Evaluation of present classification: Probably the only Bordeaux wine that truly can be said to be in a class by itself

Plateau of maturity: 10–70 years or more following the vintage; top vintages can actually last for over 100 years

Yquem, located in the heart of the Sauternes region, sits magnificently atop a small hill overlooking the surrounding vineyards of many of the Premiers Crus Classés.

Since 1785, this estate has been in the hands of just one family. Comte Alexandre de Lur Saluces is the most recent member of this family to have responsibility for managing this vast estate, having taken over for his uncle in 1968.

Yquem's greatness and uniqueness are certainly a result of a number of factors. First, it has a perfect location that is said to have its own micro-climate. Second, the Lur Saluces family installed an elaborate drainage system with over 60 miles of pipes. Third, there is a fanatical obsession at Yquem to produce only the finest wines regardless of financial loss or trouble. It is this last factor that is the biggest reason why Yquem is so superior to its neighbors.

At Yquem, they proudly boast that only one glass of wine per vine is produced. The grapes are picked at perfect maturity one by one by a group of 150 pickers who frequently spend 6–8 weeks at Yquem, and go through the vineyard a minimum of four separate times. In 1964, they canvassed the vineyard thirteen separate times, only to have harvested grapes that were deemed unsuitable, leaving Yquem with no production whatsoever in that vintage. Few winemaking estates are willing or financially able to declassify the entire crop. However, no wine has been produced at Yquem in 1964, 1972, or 1974.

Yquem has unbelievable aging possibilities. Because it is so rich, opulent, and sweet, much is drunk before it ever reaches its tenth birthday. However, Yquem almost always needs 15–20 years to show best, and the great vintages will be fresh and decadently rich for as long as 50 or more years. The greatest Yquem I ever drank was the 1921, served in November 1983. It was remarkably fresh and alive, with a luxuriousness and richness I shall never forget.

This passionate commitment to quality does not stop in the vineyard. The wine is aged for over 3 years in new oak casks, at a loss of 20% of the total crop volume due to evaporation. Even when the Comte Lur Saluces deems the wine ready for bottling, a severe selection of only the best casks is made. In excellent years, such as 1975, 1976, and 1980, 20% of the barrels were eliminated. In difficult years, such as 1979, 60% of the wine was declassified, and in the troublesome vintage of 1978, 85% of the wine was declared unworthy of being sold as Yquem. To my knowledge, no other property has such a ruthless selection process. Yquem is never filtered for fear of removing some of the richness.

Yquem also produces a dry wine called "Y." It is a distinctive wine, with a bouquet not unlike that of Yquem, but oaky and dry to taste and usually very full bodied and noticeably alcoholic. It is a powerful wine and, to my palate, best served with a rich food such as foie gras.

Yquem, unlike other famous Bordeaux wines, is not sold *"en primeur,"* or as a wine future. The wine is usually released 4 years after the vintage at a very high price, but given the labor involved, the risk, and the brutal selection process, it is one of the few luxury-priced wines that merits a stratospheric price tag.

VINTAGES

1986—There is no other wine in the world like it, and there is no other
luxury wine that can possibly justify its price as much as Yquem.
98   The remarkable amount of painstaking labor necessary to produce the nectar known as Yquem is almost impossible to comprehend. This is another fascinating effort. With greater evidence of botrytis than the colossal 1983, but less power and alcohol, the 1986 Yquem tastes reminiscent of the 1975, only more precocious, as well as more concentrated. Several highly respected Bordeaux *négociants* who are Yquem enthusiasts claim the 1986 Yquem is the greatest wine produced at the property since the

legendary 1937. Its enthralling bouquet of pineapples, sautéed hazelnuts, vanillin, and ripe apricots is breathtaking. Compellingly concentrated, the breadth as well as depth of flavor seemingly know no limits. This full-bodied, powerful, yet impeccably balanced Yquem should provide memorable drinking for 40–55 more years. Like the 1983, this is another winemaking tour de force. Anticipated maturity: 2000–2040. Last tasted, 4/91.

1985—The 1985 Yquem is a very powerful, rich, exceptionally concentrated wine. Yet because of the lack of botrytis in the vineyards
· during this hot, dry vintage, the wine does not have the complex-
89 ity so frequently encountered. Nevertheless, this massive, unctuous, light-golden-colored Yquem makes quite a mouthful of wine given the honeyed flavors. It is hard to know when a wine such as this will be fully mature, but I have no hesitation saying that the wine will certainly last for 25–30 or more years. But I do not see it ever being among the great Yquems. Anticipated maturity: 1995–2025. Last tasted, 3/90.

1984—This is a surprisingly good wine made under very trying conditions. Yquem began to harvest on October 15 and made the last
· pass through the vineyards on November 13. Seventy-five percent
87 of the crop was retained for Yquem. The wine at present exhibits a great deal of toasty oak in the bouquet, which is also filled with scents of smoked almonds, glazed pineapples, and honey and caramel. In the mouth, the wine is less flamboyant, with less glycerin and power than usual, but it is still a rich, full-bodied Yquem with a great deal of personality and character. It will not have the great aging potential of the top vintages, but I fully expect it to last at least another 20 years. Anticipated maturity: 1995–2008. Last tasted, 3/90.

1983—Arguments will no doubt rage as to which Yquem is greater—
· 1986 or 1983. Lord only knows how profound the 1988 and 1989
96 may be, but those wines will not be released until 1992 and 1993. Personally I like the 1986 because the botrytis is more evident, whereas in the 1983, the emphasis tends to be more on pure power given the huge, massive mouthful of wine Yquem offers. The 1983 is among the most concentrated wines from this property over the last 20 years, with a staggering display of extract and a mind-boggling amount of glycerin. The vintage commenced early for Yquem, beginning on September 29 and finishing on November 18. Most observers feel the 1983 will mature more slowly than the 1986, and will last for almost 100 years. Given Yquem's unbelievable aging potential, such comments do not seem far fetched. At

present, the 1983 is enormous, with huge, honeyed, pineapple, coconut, and caramel flavors, massive extract, and an unctuous quality barely framed by acidity and new oak. I do not feel the wine has changed since bottling, and I would not want to start drinking it for at least another 10–15 years. Anticipated maturity: 2005–2050. Last tasted, 12/90.

1982—This vintage, seriously maligned because of the rains that plagued the harvest in Sauternes, was actually an outstanding vintage for
·
92   both Yquem and its nearby neighbor, Château Suduiraut, which brought in much of their crops before the rains did any damage. Yquem then waited until the vineyards dried out, bringing in their last grapes on November 7. The 1982 is a very forward style of Yquem, plump, succulent, with honeyed pineapple, peach, and apricot flavors, exhibiting some, but not a great deal of botrytis. In the mouth, it is massive, thick, and almost as impressive as the 1983, but one does not sense the same degree of length or potential complexity. Nevertheless, this is still a great Yquem that has been somewhat overlooked because of the attention lavished on the 1983 and 1986. Anticipated maturity: 1997–2020. Last tasted, 12/90.

1981—The 1981 is certainly an outstanding Yquem, but it will not be considered one of this property's greatest efforts. Light golden,
·
90   with a moderately intense bouquet of spicy, vanillin oak, fresh melons, and tropical fruit, this full-bodied Yquem has average acidity and a plump, viscous, somewhat precocious feel on the palate. Remarkably long and clean in the finish, it will develop relatively rapidly. Anticipated maturity: 1995–2015. Last tasted, 3/87.

1980—This year is a perfect example of a vintage that was much better for the sweet wines of Barsac and Sauternes than it was for the
·
93   red wines. Yquem produced its greatest wine since the twin titans of 1975 and 1976. Medium golden, with a big, opulent, honeyed, oaky, flowery, tropical-fruit bouquet, this wine is rich and concentrated, has very good acidity, a lot of botrytis, and a stunning finish. It is a great success, and it continues to evolve at a snail's pace. Anticipated maturity: 1998–2035. Last tasted, 12/90.

1979—This is an immensely attractive Yquem, yet it seems to be missing something. Light golden, with Yquem's typically oaky, spicy, but-
·
88   tery, ripe bouquet, it is only slightly more reserved than usual. On the palate, this full-bodied wine is intense and well balanced, but falls just a trifle short in the finish. The 1979 Yquem is not as powerful or as rich as this wine can be in the top vintages. Only

40% of the crop was retained, Anticipated maturity: 1995–2020. Last tasted, 12/90.

1978—1978 was an extremely difficult year for the wine producers in
· Barsac and Sauternes. Unlike the red wine producers who had a
87 late, yet excellent harvest, the weather was not humid enough for the formation of the noble rot. While the wines are rich, full bodied, and viscous, they lack character and often taste dull. Yquem's 1978 is the best wine produced in the appellation. It is rich and honeyed, with excellent concentration and plenty of alcohol and body. Unfortunately, it does not have the majestic bouquet and complex flavors and aromas that can only result from rampant botrytis-infected grapes. Only 15% of the crop went into Yquem. Anticipated maturity: Now–2008. Last tasted, 12/90.

1977—In what was a miserable vintage, Yquem managed to produce a
· toasty, ripe, pineapple, buttery-scented wine with a predominate
85 oaky character. Seventy percent of the crop was eliminated in 1977, and the result is a wine that may well turn out to be almost as good as the underrated 1973. Anticipated maturity: Now–2000. Last tasted, 2/84.

1976—The 1976 Yquem continues to go from strength to strength. Who
· can ignore the awesome bouquet of spices, honeyed fruit, pine-
96 apples, bananas, coconuts, and overripe melons? This full-bodied, viscous, luscious wine has been absolutely delicious since bottling, given its relatively low acidity and precocious personality. It is one of the few true great vintages of Yquem that can actually be drunk with tremendous pleasure at such a young age. Eighty percent of the harvest made it into the final wine. Anticipated maturity: Now–2025. Last tasted, 12/90.

1975—The 1975 may turn out to be the greatest of the modern-day
· Yquems. When fully mature in another 25–30 years, it may rival
99 the extraordinary 1937 and 1921. This wine continues to evolve at a stubbornly slow pace. It is far more backward than recent vintages such as 1983 and 1986. Nevertheless, it is awesomely concentrated, has perfect balance, and displays the telltale Yquem aromas of vanillin oak, tropical fruit, pineapples, honeyed peaches, and grilled almonds. There is exceptionally crisp acidity that pulls all of the massive extract into precise focus. This is a wine of astonishing power and finesse, with a finish that must be tasted to be believed. It is a monumental effort that may well justify a perfect score in another decade. Anticipated maturity: 2005–2060. Last tasted, 1/91.

1973—Surprisingly successful in what was a mediocre vintage for the
· wines of this region, the 1973 Yquem is overtly oaky and too
86 spicy, but has very good concentration, less sweetness and botrytis than in vintages like 1975 and 1976, and is well balanced, fat,
and long on the palate (only 12% of the crop was used for Yquem).
Anticipated maturity: Now. Last tasted, 3/84.

1971—This is an outstanding Yquem, but I have been plagued by bad
· bottles in tastings, which I hope is only attributable to poor stor-
92 age and handling. The top bottles exhibit plenty of ripe, concentrated tropical fruit and botrytis. Full bodied, deep golden in
color, with a spicy, caramel, toasted *rôti*, fat flavor, this big, rich
wine is developing quickly for an Yquem. Although irrefutably
outstanding, this may be a slightly overrated vintage for Yquem.
Anticipated maturity: Now–2010. Last tasted, 12/90.

1970—Somewhat less evolved than the 1971, and for me always a shade
· less interesting and complex, the 1970 Yquem is a large-scaled,
90 rich, full-bodied, fairly alcoholic Yquem with significant flavor
interest as well as crisp acidity. Unlike the 1971, which is close
to peak maturity, this wine has a long way to go and is impressive,
but not yet revealing all of its potential. Anticipated maturity:
1992–2025. Last tasted, 11/84.

1967—Based solely on the strength of what is unquestionably a great
· Yquem, many have concluded that 1967 was a superb vintage
96 for Sauternes. The truth is that 1967 was a very good but irregular vintage. As for Yquem, it is close to perfection. Medium
amber/golden with a full-intensity bouquet of vanillin spice,
honey, ripe pineapples, and coconut, this intense, very ripe, unctuous Yquem has layers of sweet, opulent fruit, excellent balance,
and a hefty, powerful finish. Almost too big and rich to be served
with food, this wine should be drunk alone as a dessert. From the
point of view of this wine's evolution, it has hardly budged in the
last six years. Anticipated maturity: Now–2035. Last tasted, 12/
90.

1966—The 1966 is a very good wine, but for Yquem it is mediocre. Not
· nearly as rich and intense as one would expect, this wine is still
85 big, a trifle clumsy, and too oaky, but enjoyable. Anticipated
maturity: Now–2000. Last tasted, 1/82.

1962—This is an excellent, even outstanding Yquem, but I must admit
· to being less impressed with it than others who have ecstatically
90 called it one of the greatest Yquems produced. It is rich and
honeyed, with a spicy, oaky, tropical-fruit aroma, rich butter-
scotch, toasted fruit, and caramel flavors, and an astringent, dry,

slightly coarse finish that, for me, keeps it from getting higher marks. Anticipated maturity: Now–2025. Last tasted, 11/82.

1961—The year 1961 was only a mediocre vintage for Barsac and Sau-
 ·   ternes; however, the sales of these wines have long been helped
84   by the greatness of this vintage for the red wines of Bordeaux. I
        have consistently found Yquem's 1961 to be a muscular, out-of-
        balance wine, with a burnt character to the bouquet, and overly
        oaky, aggressive flavors that lack this estate's ripeness and great
        richness. The wine is now beginning to dry out and become more
        awkward. Drink it up. Anticipated maturity: Now–1998. Last
        tasted, 4/82.

OLDER VINTAGES

There is no doubt that the two most profound mature Yquems I have ever tasted were the 1921 (rated 100 on two separate occasions) and the 1937 (rated between 96 and 99 on three separate occasions in the late 1980s). After those two vintages, there are a number of superb Yquems that I have had the good fortune to taste, but frankly, none have matched the 1921 and 1937. My favorites in order of preference are 1945 (rated 98 in 3/88), 1928 (rated 97 in 4/91), 1929 (rated 97 in 3/90), and 1959 (rated between 94 and 96 on three occasions in the late 1980s). Although I have only tasted the 1947 once (that is my birth year), I was surprised by how dry the wine tasted, without the fat and sweetness one finds in the great vintages of Yquem.

THE SATELLITE APPELLATIONS OF BORDEAUX

There are very large quantities of wine produced in a bevy of other lesser-known appellations of Bordeaux. Most of these wines are widely commercialized in France, but have met with little success in America because of this country's obsession with luxury names and prestigious appellations. For the true connoisseur, the wines of Bordeaux's satellite appellations can in fact represent outstanding bargains, particularly in

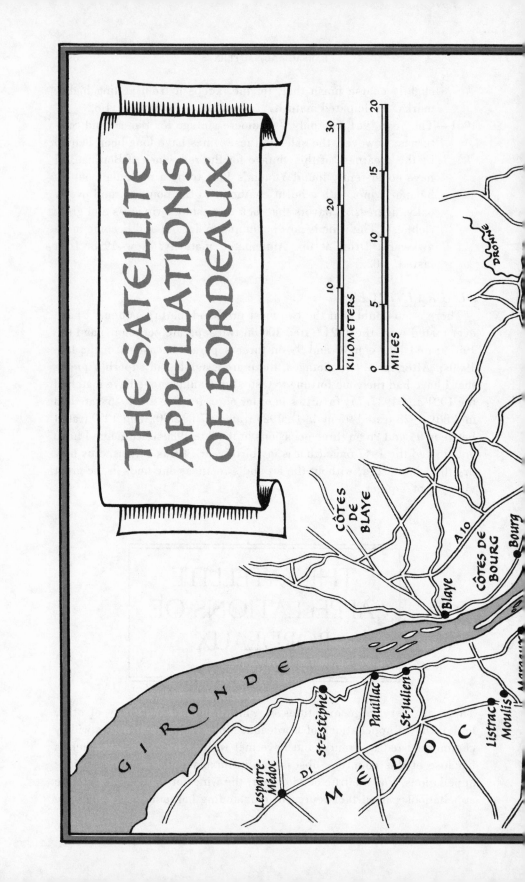

THE SATELLITE
APPELLATIONS
OF BORDEAUX

KILOMETERS
0   10   20   30

MILES
0   5   10   15   20

DRONNE

CÔTES DE BLAYE

Blaye

A10

CÔTES DE BOURG

Bourg

GIRONDE

Lesparre-Médoc

DI   St-Estèphe

Pauillac

St-Julien

MÉDOC

Listrac

Moulis

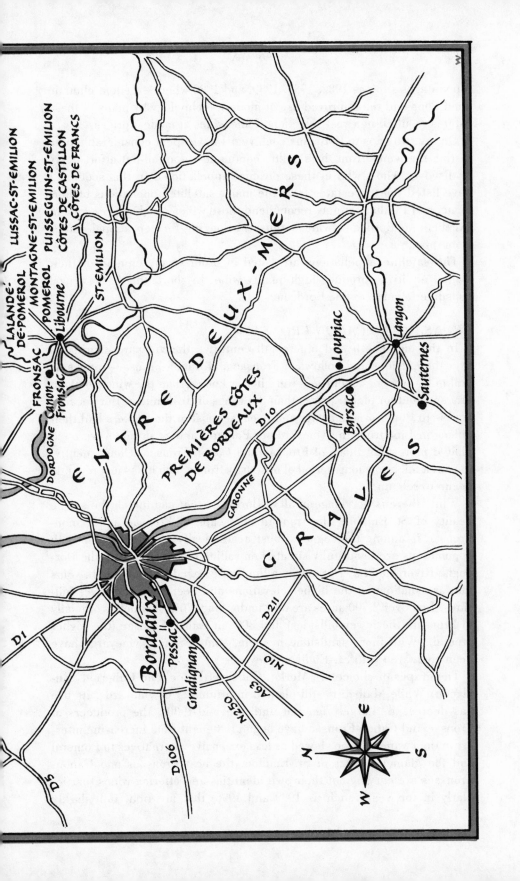

LUSSAC-ST-ÉMILION
MONTAGNE-ST-ÉMILION
PUISSEGUIN-ST-ÉMILION
CÔTES DE CASTILLON
CÔTES DE FRANCS

LALANDE-DE-POMEROL
FRONSAC
POMEROL

Libourne

Canon-Fronsac
Dordogne

ST-ÉMILION

E N T R E - D E U X - M E R S

Langon

Loupiac

Barsac

Sauternes

PREMIÈRES CÔTES
DE BORDEAUX

D10

GARONNE

Bordeaux

Pessac

Gradignan

G R A V E S

D1

D5

D106

N250

A63

N10

D211

top vintages such as 1982, 1985, 1989, and 1990 where excellent climatic conditions and the improved use of modern technology by many of these estates resulted in a vast selection of fine wines at modest prices.

On my two trips to Bordeaux each year I have spent considerable time tasting the wines from the satellite communes in an all-out effort to try to discover who's who in these obscure appellations. In this section, I have listed the top estates from the major satellite appellations of Bordeaux and I unhesitatingly recommend those wines rated as very good or excellent to Bordeaux wine enthusiasts looking for sensational values from this area.

The satellite appellations are listed in order of my opinion of their overall ability to produce high-quality wine. In short, this is the frugal consumer's guide to fine Bordeaux.

FRONSAC AND CANON-FRONSAC

In the eighteenth and nineteenth centuries the vineyards sprinkled over the hillsides and hollows of Fronsac and Canon-Fronsac—only several miles west of Libourne—were better known than the wines of Pomerol and sold for higher prices than the wines of St.-Emilion. But because access to Pomerol was easier and because most of the brokers had their offices in Libourne, the vineyards of Pomerol and St.-Emilion were exploited more than those of Fronsac and Canon-Fronsac. Consequently, this area fell into a long period of obscurity from which it has just recently begun to rebound.

While there is no village in all of Bordeaux that can match the scenic beauty of St.-Emilion, the tranquil landscape of Fronsac and Canon-Fronsac is among the region's most aesthetically pleasing areas. Both appellations are beautifully situated on rolling hills overlooking the Dordogne River, and have primarily a limestone-based soil running in veins that are shallow on the higher elevations and deeper on the lower hillsides. Just over 2,700 acres are now under vine, 70% of which is officially in Fronsac (the lower hillsides) and 30% in Canon-Fronsac (the higher ground). With more sandstone in them, some Fronsac vineyards have been compared with St.-Emilion vineyards.

The grapes of choice are Merlot, Cabernet Franc, and Cabernet Sauvignon. While Malbec is still planted in a number of vineyards, its use has decreased. Largely ignored until the mid-1980s, the producers of Fronsac and Canon-Fronsac have begun to benefit from increasing interest in their wines. Once viewed as less expensive alternatives to Pomerol and the glamour wines of St.-Emilion, the best Fronsacs and Canon-Fronsacs are carving out their own identities and offering wines (particularly in top years such as 1989 and 1990) that are rich, full, darkly colored, relatively large-scaled efforts with considerable aging potential. The toughness and hardness, so much a problem with older-styled Fronsacs and Canon-Fronsacs, has been less of a concern in vintages such as 1985, 1989, and 1990. Additionally, the fertile soils of many Fronsac vineyards, which can result in overproduction, are more carefully and conservatively managed. Oddly enough, far greater attention is paid to yields in these appellations than in many of the more famous Bordeaux winemaking regions.

Even the famous firm of Jean-Pierre Moueix has taken an active interest in these appellations, buying up properties such as La Dauphine, Canon de Brem, and Canon (Moueix), as well as controlling the distribution and marketing of other estates such as Mazeris and de Carles. Other Bordeaux *négociants*, principally Vintex and Europvin, have augmented their selections of wines from this region, recognizing the excellent potential for high-quality wines.

I have been routinely tasting these wines at least once a year, and I have visited most of the major estates in the region. There has been increasing quality in almost every vintage. The years 1989 and 1990 were the two best back-to-back vintages these appellations have ever enjoyed. The classification that follows is based on the performance of these estates during the decade of the eighties. All of the estates rated very good or excellent produced wines in vintages such as 1985, 1989, and 1990 that have the capacity to last for 10–12 years. I suspect many will last even longer. I remember a dinner at Château Dalem, where the proprietor of another Fronsac, Jean-Noel Hervé, brought a bottle of 1928 Moulin-Haut-Laroque. It was quite stunning at age 60. I am not suggesting these wines will routinely have that kind of aging potential, but they are wines with a great deal of firmness and richness that tend to possess a Médoc-like austerity and structure to them. Even though the vineyards are in close proximity to Pomerol, the wines seem, for the most part, very un-Pomerol-like.

A CONSUMER'S CLASSIFICATION OF THE CHÂTEAUX OF CANON-FRONSAC

EXCELLENT
Fontenil, Moulin-Haut-Laroque, La Vieille-Cure

VERY GOOD
Dalem, La Dauphine

GOOD
Cardeneau, de Carles, Clos du Roy, La Grave, Jeandeman,
Meyney, La Rivière, Rouet, Villars

AVERAGE
La Croix, Magondeau, Mayne-Vieil, Plain-Point, Puyguilhem,
Richelieu, Rousselle, Trois-Croix

A CONSUMER'S CLASSIFICATION OF THE CHÂTEAUX OF FRONSAC

EXCELLENT
Canon de Brem, Cassagne-Haut-Canon-La-Truffière,
Moulin-Pey-Labrie

VERY GOOD
Canon, Canon (Moueix), Mazeris, Pez-Labrie

GOOD
Bodet, La Fleur-Cailleau, Grand-Renouil, Mazeris-Bellevue,
du Pavillon, Vray-Canon-Boyer

AVERAGE
Coustolle, Gaby-Mausse, Junayme, La Riveau, Toumalin,
Vincent, Vrai-Canon-Bouché

PROFILES—THE TOP CHÂTEAUX

Canon (Canon-Fronsac)

Proprietor: Mademoiselle
 Henriette Horeau
Vineyard size: 25 acres
Production: 4,000 cases
Plateau of maturity: 5–15 years

Grape varieties:
Merlot—95%
Cabernet Franc—5%

Canon de Brem (Canon-Fronsac)

Proprietor: The firm of Jean-
  Pierre Moueix
Vineyard size: 50 acres
Production: 8,000 cases
Plateau of maturity: 5–15 years

Grape varieties:
Merlot—66%
Cabernet Franc—34%

Canon (Moueix) (Canon-Fronsac)

Proprietor: Christian Moueix
Vineyard size: 2.7 acres
Production: 500 cases
Plateau of maturity: 5–15 years

Grape varieties:
Merlot—80%
Cabernet Franc—20%

Cassagne-Haut-Canon-La-Truffière (Canon-Fronsac)

Proprietor: The Dubois family
Vineyard size: 29.6 acres
Production: 4,500 cases, of which
  2,000 cases of the luxury *cuvée*
  La Truffière is produced
Plateau of maturity: 3–10 years

Grape varieties:
Merlot—70%
Cabernet Franc—20%
Cabernet Sauvignon—10%

Dalem (Fronsac)

Proprietor: Michel Rullier
Vineyard size: 29.6 acres
Production: 6,500 cases
Plateau of maturity: 4–12 years

Grape varieties:
Merlot—70%
Cabernet Franc—20%
Cabernet Sauvignon—10%

La Dauphine (Fronsac)

Proprietor: The firm of Jean-
  Pierre Moueix
Vineyard size: 25 acres
Production: 4,500 cases
Plateau of maturity: 4–10 years

Grape varieties:
Merlot—60%
Cabernet Franc—40%

Fontenil (Fronsac)

Proprietor: Michel Rolland
Vineyard size: 17.3 acres
Production: 3,500 cases
Plateau of maturity: 4–14 years

Grape varieties:
Merlot—85%
Cabernet Sauvignon—15%

Mazeris (Canon-Fronsac)

Proprietor: Christian de
  Cournaud
Vineyard size: 35 acres
Production: 4,500 cases
Plateau of maturity: 5–15 years

Grape varieties:
Merlot—75%
Malbec—25%

Moulin-Haut-Laroque (Fronsac)

Proprietor: Jean-Noel Hervé
Vineyard size: 34.6 acres
Production: 6,000 cases
Plateau of maturity: 5–20 years

Grape varieties:
Merlot—65%
Cabernet Franc—20%
Cabernet Sauvignon—10%
Malbec—5%

Moulin-Pey-Labrie (Canon-Fronsac)

Proprietor: Gregoire Hubau
Vineyard size: 20 acres
Production: 4,000 cases
Plateau of maturity: 5–15 years

Grape varieties:
Merlot—75%
Cabernet Sauvignon—15%
Cabernet Franc—5%
Malbec—5%

Pez-Labrie (Canon-Fronsac)

Proprietor: Société Civile
Vineyard size: 14 acres
Production: 2,000 cases
Plateau of maturity: 4–12 years

Grape varieties:
Merlot—70%
Cabernet Sauvignon—20%
Cabernet Franc—10%

La Vieille-Cure (Fronsac)

Proprietor: S.N.C., an American
 syndicate
Vineyard size: 50 acres
Production: 8,200 cases
Plateau of maturity: 4–12 years

Grape varieties:
Merlot—75%
Cabernet Franc—15%
Cabernet Sauvignon—10%

LALANDE-DE-POMEROL

Lalande-de-Pomerol is a satellite commune of nearly 2,250 acres of vineyards located just to the north of Pomerol. It includes the two communes of Lalande-de-Pomerol and Néac. The vineyards, which produce only red wine, are planted on relatively light, gravelly, sandy soils with the meandering river, Barbanne, as the appellation's northern boundary. The very top level of good Lalande-de-Pomerol is easily the equivalent of a mid-level Pomerol, with certain wines, such as Belles-Graves, La Croix-St.-André, and du Chapelain, very good, even by Pomerol's standards.

The top vintages for this satellite appellation have been 1982 (all of which are fully mature and should have already been consumed) and 1989, a vintage that resembles the 1982s in style, but the wines are less concentrated.

Prices for these wines have risen, but the top efforts still represent reasonably good values for wines that are essentially dominated by their Merlot content.

A CONSUMER'S CLASSIFICATION
OF THE CHÂTEAUX OF LALANDE-DE-POMEROL

EXCELLENT
Belles-Graves, du Chapelain, La Croix-St.-André

VERY GOOD
Bel-Air, Bertineau-St.-Vincent, Grand-Ormeau, Siaurac, Tournefeuille

GOOD
des Annereaux, Clos des Templiers, Garraud, Haut-Chatain, Haut-Surget, Les Hauts-Conseillants, Laborde, Moncets

AVERAGE
La Borderie-Mondesir, Bourseau, Brouard, Chevrol-Bel-Air, La Croix-Chenevelle, des Moines, Montviel, Perron, Teysson

PROFILES—THE TOP CHÂTEAUX

Bel-Air
Proprietor: The Musset family
Vineyard size: 30 acres
Production: 5,000 cases
Plateau of maturity: 3–12 years

Grape varieties:
Merlot—60%
Cabernet Franc—15%
Pressac—15%
Cabernet Sauvignon—10%

Belles-Graves
Proprietor: Madame Theallet
Vineyard size: 28.4 acres
Production: 5,500 cases
Plateau of maturity: 3–10 years

Grape varieties:
Merlot—60%
Cabernet Franc—40%

Bertineau-St.-Vincent
Proprietor: Michel Rolland
Vineyard size: 10 acres
Production: 2,000 cases
Plateau of maturity: 3–10 years

Grape varieties:
Merlot—80%
Cabernet Franc—20%

du Chapelain
Proprietor: Madame Xann Marc
Vineyard size: 2.5 acres
Production: 350 cases
Plateau of maturity: 5–10 years

Grape varieties:
Merlot—90%
Cabernet Franc—10%

La Croix-St.-André

Proprietor: Francis Carayon
Vineyard size: 37 acres
Production: 6,500 cases
Plateau of maturity: 4–12 years

Grape varieties:
Merlot—70%
Cabernet Franc—30%

Grand-Ormeau

Proprietor: Jean-Paul Garde
Vineyard size: 40 acres
Production: 8,000 cases
Plateau of maturity: 4–10 years

Grape varieties:
Merlot—75%
Cabernet Franc—25%

Siaurac

Proprietor: Baronne Guichard
Vineyard size: 62 acres
Production: 7,500 cases
Plateau of maturity: 3–10 years

Grape varieties:
Merlot—75%
Cabernet Franc—25%

Tournefeuille

Proprietor: G.F.A. Sautarel
Vineyard size: 45 acres
Production: 6,500 cases
Plateau of maturity: 5–12 years

Grape varieties:
Merlot—70%
Cabernet Franc—15%
Cabernet Sauvignon—15%

CÔTES DE BOURG

The Côtes de Bourg, a surprisingly vast appellation of nearly 10,000 acres, is located on the right bank of the Gironde River, just a five-minute boat ride from the more famous appellation of Margaux. The vineyards here are actually older than those in the Médoc, as this attractively hilly area was once the center of the strategic forts built during the Plantagenet period of France's history. The views from those hillside vineyards adjacent to the river are magnificent. The local chamber of commerce has attempted to draw the public's attention to this area by calling Bourg "the Switzerland of the Gironde." They should instead stress the appeal of the best wines from the Côtes de Bourg, which are made in an uncomplicated, but fruity, round, appealing style, and the lovely port village of the area, the ancient hillside town of Bourg-Sur-Gironde.

The Bourg appellation, located north of Fronsac and south of the Côtes de Blaye, has variable soils. They are primarily limestone-based, with different proportions of clay, gravel, and sand. The soils exhibit a far greater degree of fertility than in the Médoc, and consequently, the problem facing many producers is to keep their yields reasonable in order to obtain a degree of concentration in their wines. The dominant grape is Merlot, followed by Cabernet Franc, Cabernet Sauvignon, Malbec, and to a very small extent, Petit Verdot.

In March 1991, I spent several days tasting the 1988s, 1989s, and 1990s of all the leading estates of the Côtes de Bourg. Most of the wines of the Côtes de Bourg are average to below average in quality, lack concentration (because of excessive yields), and often have tannins that are too green and high (because of the tendency to harvest too early). However, there are at least seven or eight estates that consistently make good wines, and several whose wines can easily age for 10–15 or more years. This could be an increasingly important appellation in the future because the increased demand for wines from the prestigious appellations of Bordeaux has caused prices to soar. Most Côtes de Bourg wines are reasonably priced. However, with the exception of Tayac, Roc des Cambes, and Guerry, they must be consumed within their first 4–6 years of life.

A CONSUMER'S CLASSIFICATION OF THE CHÂTEAUX OF THE CÔTES DE BOURG

EXCELLENT

Roc des Cambes, Tayac—Cuvée Prestige

VERY GOOD

de Barbe, Brûlesécaille, Guerry, Haut-Maco, Mercier,
Tayac—Cuvée Réservé

GOOD

Clos La Barette, Croûte Courpon, Falfas, La Grolet, Gros Moulin, Les Heaumes, Moulin des Graves, Moulin Vieux, Nodoz, Rousselle, Rousset, Soulignac de Robert, Tayac, La Tour-Séguy

AVERAGE

Begot, Belair-Coubet, Le Breuil, Bujan, Caruel, Clos du Notaire, Colbert, Conilh, Coubet, Dumezil, Fougas, Gazin, Genibon, La Grave, Gravettes-Samonac, de Grissac, Haut-Canterane, Haut-Casenet, Haut-Guiraud, Haut-Mevret, Haut-Rousset, L'Hospital, Laroche, de Lucas, Macay, Montaigut, Peychaud, Peyrolan, Les Rocques

PROFILES—THE TOP CHÂTEAUX

de Barbe

Proprietor: Savary de Beauregard   Grape varieties:
Vineyard size: 138 acres   Merlot—70%
Production: 35,000 cases   Cabernet Sauvignon—25%
Plateau of maturity: 3–8 years   Malbec—5%

Brûlesécaille

Proprietor: Jacques Rodet
Vineyard size: 50 acres
Production: 6,500 cases
Plateau of maturity: 3–8 years

Grape varieties:
Merlot—50%
Cabernet Franc—50%

Guerry

Proprietor: Bertrand de Rivoyre
Vineyard size: 54 acres
Production: 8,500 cases
Plateau of maturity: 4–12 years

Grape varieties:
Malbec—34%
Cabernet Sauvignon—33%
Merlot—33%

Haut-Maco

Proprietors: The Mallet brothers
Vineyard size: 86 acres
Production: 12,000 cases
Plateau of maturity: 3–7 years

Grape varieties:
Cabernet Franc—70%
Merlot—30%

Mercier

Proprietor: Philippe Chéty
Vineyard size: 74 acres
Production: 6,000 cases
Plateau of maturity: 3–10 years

Grape varieties:
Merlot—55%
Cabernet Sauvignon—25%
Cabernet Franc—15%
Malbec—5%

Roc des Cambes

Proprietor: François Mitjavile
Vineyard size: 23 acres
Production: 3,000 cases
Plateau of maturity: 3–10 years

Grape varieties:
Merlot—35%
Malbec—25%
Cabernet Franc—25%
Cabernet Sauvignon—15%

Tayac—Cuvée Prestige

Proprietor: Pierre Saturny
Vineyard size: 50 acres
Production: 1,000–2,000 cases
Plateau of maturity: 5–15 years

Grape varieties:
This luxury *cuvée* usually consists of 80% Cabernet Sauvignon and 20% Merlot from very old vines. Only made in great years such as 1982, 1985, 1986, 1988, and 1989.

BLAYE

There are just over 6,700 acres of vines in the Blaye region, located directly north of Bourg. The best vineyard areas are entitled to the appellation called Premières Côtes de Blaye. While there are quantities of white wine produced in the Blaye region, most of the Premières Côtes de Blaye are dedicated to the production of red wine, which is very similar to the red wine of Bourg. At its best, it is forward, round, richly fruity, soft, and immensely satisfying in a low-key manner.

Blaye, like Bourg, is a much older wine-producing region than the more renowned Médoc. Its origins date back to Roman times when the area served as a defensive front line against invaders intent on attacking the city of Bordeaux. Today, the tourist route from Bourg to Blaye is one of the more charming in the Bordeaux region. In Blaye itself is a perfectly preserved seventeenth-century military fortress (the citadel) that is classified as an historical monument by the French government. Additionally, gourmets may be surprised to note that if the French government ever permits extensive sturgeon fishing and caviar preparation, Blaye would probably be the center for this industry because of the growing population of sturgeon that make the nearby Gironde River their habitat.

Most of the Blaye vineyards sit on steeply sloping hills with a southerly exposure overlooking the Gironde. The soil tends to be dominated by limestone, with outbreaks of clay and, from time to time, gravel. It is a very fertile soil that must be cultivated conservatively if the yields are to be kept under control. The grape varieties are essentially the same as in Bourg, with Merlot dominating the blend, followed by Cabernet Franc, Cabernet Sauvignon, and Malbec. The best red wines from the Côtes de Blaye are extremely well made, and richly fruity, and are best drunk within their first 5–6 years of life. There is an interesting group of white varietals planted in the appellation including Semillon, Sauvignon Blanc, Muscadelle, Merlot Blanc, Folle Blanche, Colombard, Chenin Blanc, and Ugni Blanc.

A CONSUMER'S CLASSIFICATION
OF THE CHÂTEAUX OF BLAYE

EXCELLENT
Bertinerie, La Tonnelle

VERY GOOD
Haut-Sociando, Les Jonqueyres, Pérenne, Peyraud

GOOD
Bellevue, La Bretonnière, Peraud, Petits-Arnauds, Segonzac

AVERAGE
Barbé, Chante-Alouette-la-Roseraie, Clairac, Le Cone-Taillasson-de-Lagarcie, L'Escarde, La Grange, Loumede, Magveleine-Bouhou, Mayne-Boyer-Chaumet, Les Moines, Pardaillan, Peybonhomme, Peymelon, Ricaud, Sociando, Les Videaux

PROFILES—THE TOP CHÂTEAUX

Bertinerie

Proprietor: Daniel Bantegnies
Vineyard size: 75 acres
Production: 7,000 cases
Plateau of maturity: 3–10 years

Grape varieties:
Cabernet Sauvignon—40%
Cabernet Franc—30%
Merlot—30%

Note: This is the only estate in the Blaye appellation producing an
  excellent white wine made from Sauvignon Blanc.

Haut-Sociando

Proprietor: Louis Martinaud
Vineyard size: 35 acres
Production: 6,000 cases
Plateau of maturity: 2–3 years

Grape varieties:
Merlot—65%
Cabernet Franc—35%

Les Jonqueyres

Proprietor: Pascal Montaut
Vineyard size: 35 acres
Production: 5,000 cases
Plateau of maturity: 2–7 years

Grape varieties:
Merlot—75%
Cabernet Franc—25%

Pérenne

Proprietor: A syndicate of Danish
  bankers
Vineyard size: 227 acres
Production: 32,000 cases
Plateau of maturity: 2–5 years

Grape varieties:
Merlot—50%
Cabernet Sauvignon—44%
Cabernet Franc—4%
Malbec—2%

Peyraud

Proprietor: The Rey family
Vineyard size: 25 acres
Production: 4,500 cases
Plateau of maturity: 3–6 years

Grape varieties:
Merlot—50%
Cabernet Sauvignon—30%
Cabernet Franc—15%
Malbec—5%

La Tonnelle

Proprietor: Eve Rouchi
Vineyard size: 25 acres
Production: 5,000 cases
Plateau of maturity: 2–5 years

Grape varieties:
Merlot—75%
Cabernet Franc—25%

PUISSEGUIN-ST.-EMILION

Puisseguin-St.-Emilion, the easternmost of the satellite appellations,
has been growing in size. The vineyard area now encompasses over 1,650
acres. The name is of Celtic origin, meaning "the hill with the powerful
wine." Over one-half of the appellation's production is dominated by the

local cooperative under the label "Roc de Puisseguin," but most of the estates that bottle their wines produce noteworthy wines that require drinking within 5–6 years of the vintage. They are considerably less expensive than most St.-Emilions.

Vintages in Puisseguin tend to follow those of the Libournais, with top years, such as 1982, 1989, and 1990, the best for bargain hunters in this appellation.

A CONSUMER'S CLASSIFICATION
OF THE CHÂTEAUX OF PUISSEGUIN-ST.-EMILION

GOOD
Durand Laplagne, de Roques, Vieux-Château-Guibeau

AVERAGE
Beauséjour, Cassat, La Croix-de-Mouchet, Fayan, Gontet-Robin, de Mole, Moulin, Rigaud, Roc de Boissac, Soleil, Teyssier, La Tour Guillotin

PROFILES—THE TOP CHÂTEAUX

Durand Laplagne
Proprietor: The Consorts Bessou
Vineyard size: 32 acres
Production: 6,000 cases
Plateau of maturity: 3–7 years

Grape varieties:
Merlot—70%
Cabernet Franc—15%
Cabernet Sauvignon—15%

de Roques
Proprietor: Société Civile
Vineyard size: 62 acres
Production: 12,000 cases
Plateau of maturity: 3–10 years

Grape varieties:
Merlot—60%
Cabernet Franc—40%

Vieux-Château-Guibeau
Proprietor: Société Civile
Vineyard size: 100 acres
Production: 25,000 cases
Plateau of maturity: 2–7 years

Grape varieties:
Merlot—66%
Cabernet Franc—17%
Cabernet Sauvignon—17%

LUSSAC-ST.-EMILION
Lussac, located in the northeastern portion of the viticultural region of St.-Emilion, encompasses more than 2,725 acres. Over one-half of the vineyard area is controlled by the local cooperative, but there are a

number of fine estates making smooth, delicious, round, fruity wine that must be consumed in the first 5–6 years of life.

The vineyards generally consist of limestone-dominated *terroirs*, with a handful on more sandy soils. As with the other satellite appellations in St.-Emilion, Lussac is a veritable treasure trove for bargains.

A CONSUMER'S CLASSIFICATION OF THE CHÂTEAUX OF LUSSAC-ST.-EMILION

GOOD
Bel-Air, Bellevue, Cap de Merle, Carteyron, Courlat, Lyonnat, Villadière

AVERAGE
de Barbe-Blanche, de Bellevue, Lucas, de Tabuteau, La Tour de Grenet, La Tour de Ségur, des Vieux Chênes

PROFILES—THE TOP CHÂTEAUX

Bel-Air
Proprietor: Jean-Noel Roi
Vineyard size: 50 acres
Production: 10,000 cases
Plateau of maturity: 3–7 years

Grape varieties:
Merlot—70%
Cabernet Franc—20%
Cabernet Sauvignon—10%

Bellevue
Proprietor: Charles Chatenoud
Vineyard size: 26 acres
Production: 4,000 cases
Plateau of maturity: 3–10 years

Grape varieties:
Merlot—70%
Cabernet Franc—30%

Cap de Merle
Proprietor: Jacques Bessou
Vineyard size: 20 acres
Production: 3,000 cases
Plateau of maturity: 2–7 years

Grape varieties:
Merlot—75%
Cabernet Franc—25%

Courlat
Proprietor: Pierre Bourotte
Vineyard size: 33 acres
Production: 8,000 cases
Plateau of maturity: 2–6 years

Grape varieties:
Merlot—60%
Cabernet Franc—20%
Cabernet Sauvignon—20%

du Lyonnat

Proprietor: Jean Milhade
Vineyard size: 111 acres
Production: 25,000 cases
Plateau of maturity: 5–12 years

Grape varieties:
Merlot—75%
Cabernet Franc—12.5%
Cabernet Sauvignon—12.5%

MONTAGNE-ST.-EMILION

Not far from the Graves sector of northern St.-Emilion and Pomerol is the satellite commune of Montagne-St.-Emilion. There are just over 3,700 acres in vine. The hillside soils of this area consist of a clay/limestone blend, and the plateaus are primarily limestone-based soils intermixed with hard outbreaks of rock.

The best wines of Montagne almost always emerge from the hilly terrain along the southern border with a splendid view of the Barbanne River that runs through Lalande-de-Pomerol and Pomerol. Among all the satellite communes, some of the deepest, richest wines consistently come from Montagne. The top wines can represent excellent bargains since they are the qualitative equivalent of a good Grand Cru St.-Emilion.

A CONSUMER'S CLASSIFICATION OF THE CHÂTEAUX OF MONTAGNE-ST.-EMILION

EXCELLENT
Roudier

VERY GOOD
Calon, Croix-Beauséjour, Maison Blanche, Tour-Musset, des Tours

AVERAGE
Barraud, Beauséjour, Bonneau, Chevalier St.-Georges, Corbin, Coucy, La Croix-de-Mouchet, Gachon, Gilet, Grand-Baril, Guadet-Plaisance, de Maison Neuve, Montaiguillon, Négrit, La Papeterie, Petit-Clos-du-Roy, Rouchet-Gardet

PROFILES—THE TOP CHÂTEAUX

Calon

Proprietor: Jean-Noel Boidron
Vineyard size: 100 acres
Production: 14,000 cases
Plateau of maturity: 5–15 years

Grape varieties:
Merlot—70%
Cabernet Franc—15%
Cabernet Sauvignon—15%

Croix-Beauséjour

Proprietor: Olivier Laporte

Vineyard size: 19 acres

Production: 3,000 cases

Plateau of maturity: 5–12 years

Grape varieties:

Merlot—70%

Cabernet Franc—15%

Malbec—15%

Maison Blanche

Proprietors: Françoise and
  Gerard Despagne-Rapin

Vineyard size: 80 acres

Production: 15,000 cases

Plateau of maturity: 4–12 years

Grape varieties:

Merlot—60%

Cabernet Franc—20%

Cabernet Sauvignon—20%

Roudier

Proprietor: Jacques
  Capdemourlin

Vineyard size: 75 acres

Production: 14,000 cases

Plateau of maturity: 5–12 years

Grape varieties:

Merlot—60%

Cabernet Franc—25%

Cabernet Sauvignon—15%

Tour-Musset

Proprietor: Henri Guiter

Vineyard size: 62 acres

Production: 12,000 cases

Plateau of maturity: 2–7 years

Grape varieties:

Merlot—50%

Cabernet Sauvignon—50%

des Tours

Proprietor: G.F.A. Louis Yerles

Vineyard size: 175 acres

Production: 55,000 cases

Plateau of maturity: 2–5 years

Grape varieties:

Merlot—34%

Cabernet Franc—34%

Malbec—32%

ST.-GEORGES ST.-EMILION

Beginning in 1972, the proprietors in the tiny commune of St.-Georges St.-Emilion were permitted to label their wines with the Montagne-St.-Emilion appellation. However, a number of them continued to seek their own identity with their appellation listed as St.-Georges St.-Emilion.

There are several serious estates in St.-Georges, including Château St.-Georges, and the much smaller Château Saint-André Corbin.

A CONSUMER'S CLASSIFICATION
OF THE CHÂTEAUX OF ST.-GEORGES ST.-EMILION

VERY GOOD
Saint-André Corbin, St.-Georges

AVERAGE
Macquin-St. Georges, Belair-Montaiguillon,
Tour-du-Pas-St. Georges

PROFILES—THE TOP CHÂTEAUX

Saint-André Corbin

Proprietors: Jean-Claude
  Berrouet and Robert Carré
Vineyard size: 42 acres
Production: 8,000 cases
Plateau of maturity: 4–12 years

Grape varieties:
Merlot—75%
Cabernet Franc—25%

St.-Georges

Proprietor: Desbois-Pétrus
Vineyard size: 125 acres
Production: 25,000 cases
Plateau of maturity: 4–15 years

Grape varieties:
Merlot—50%
Cabernet Sauvignon—30%
Cabernet Franc—10%
Malbec—10%

THE CÔTES DE CASTILLON

The Côtes de Castillon is located east of Puisseguin-St.-Emilion, approximately twenty five miles from Bordeaux. The appellation is named after the commune called Castillon-la-Bataille, which commemorates the Battle of Castillon. This 1453 battle marked the conclusion of the Hundred Years' War when the English commander, Talbot, died during the defeat of his army.

As one of the older winemaking regions in the area, viticultural practices can be traced to Roman times. The soils, which range from extremely fertile, gravelly, and sandy soils, become mixed with more gravel and clay moving up the hillsides. On the highest areas, the soils are limestone mixed with clay, marl, and sandstone. The entire viticultural area encompasses over 6,200 acres of vineyards. According to the syndicate, 65% of the area's production is controlled by the large Cooperative de Castillon. Appellation status was awarded in 1955 and there has been significantly more interest expressed in the wines as a lower-priced alternative to the wines of St.-Emilion.

If the Côtes de Castillon is never a source of superb wines, there are several properties making round, supple, deliciously fruity, occasionally complex wines that can be found at bargain prices.

A CONSUMER'S CLASSIFICATION OF THE CHÂTEAUX OF THE CÔTES DE CASTILLON

VERY GOOD
de Pitray

GOOD
de Belcier, Puycarpin, La Terrasse

AVERAGE
d'Aiguilhe, Beynat, Blanzac, du Bois, Les Desmoiselles, Faugères, Fontbaude, La Fourquerie, Haut-Tuquet, Lartigue, Maisières-Aubert, Moulin-Neuf, Moulin Rouge, Palanquey, Robin, Rocher-Bellevue, Roqueville, Tarreyro, Terasson

PROFILES—THE TOP CHÂTEAU

de Pitry

Proprietor: Vicomte Louis de Pitry
Vineyard Size: 62 acres
Production: 8,500 cases
Plateau of maturity: 2–8 years

Grape varieties:
Merlot—75%
Cabernet Franc—25%

THE CÔTES DE FRANCS

The Côtes de Francs is one of the newer appellations in the environs of St.-Emilion. Although the area traces wine-producing origins to the eleventh century, it received appellation status only in 1976. There are 1,480 acres of vines, of which 20% is planted in white wine varietals, such as Semillon, Sauvignon Blanc, and Muscadelle.

The highest potential would appear to be for red wines as the Côtes de Francs is a natural extension to the east of Puisseguin-St.-Emilion and Lussac-St.-Emilion. The soils are ideal, with the lower slopes and valley floors containing a lot of clay, and the hillsides clay and limestone mixtures with outbreaks of marl and chalk. The grapes of choice are Cabernet Sauvignon, Cabernet Franc, Malbec, and Merlot. The Côtes de Francs does have the distinction of having one of Bordeaux's only east-facing vineyard areas.

A CONSUMER'S CLASSIFICATION OF THE CHÂTEAUX OF THE CÔTES DE FRANCS

VERY GOOD
Château de Francs, Puygueraud

GOOD
Godard

AVERAGE
Chene-Vert, Clotte, Lamour, Puylandry, Strabourg

PROFILES—THE TOP CHÂTEAUX

Château de Francs

Proprietor: Hébrard and Bouard
Vineyard size: 25 acres
Production: 4,500 cases
Plateau of maturity: 3–10 years

Grape varieties:
Merlot—60%
Cabernet Franc—40%

Puygueraud

Proprietor: The Thienpont family
Vineyard size: 50 acres
Production: 10,000 cases
Plateau of maturity: 3–10 years

Grape varieties:
Merlot—40%
Cabernet Franc—30%
Cabernet Sauvignon—30%

LOUPIAC AND STE.-CROIX-DU-MONT

With the wine prices of Barsac and Sauternes soaring, I predict a more important role for the producers of the sweet white wines of Loupiac and

Ste.-Croix-du-Mont. These two appellations, twenty-four miles south of Bordeaux on the right bank of the Garonne, facing Barsac and Sauternes across the river, have an ideal southern exposure. These areas received appellation status in 1930, and many observers believe the excellent exposition of the top vineyards and the clay/limestone soil base is favorable for producing sweet wines, particularly in view of the fact that the morning mists—so essential for the formation of the noble rot, *Botrytis cinerea*—are a common occurrence in this area. The entire appellation of Loupiac consists of 1,359 acres. Although the sweet wines are receiving increasing attention from wine lovers, dry white wines, as well as a moderate quantity of dry red wines, are also produced.

A CONSUMER'S CLASSIFICATION OF THE CHÂTEAUX OF LOUPIAC AND STE.-CROIX-DU-MONT

Sweet Wines

VERY GOOD
Bourdon-Loupiac, Clos Jean, du Cros, Loupiac-Gaudiet, Ricaud, de Tastes

AVERAGE
Les Courtines, Domaine du Noble, Grand-Peyruchet, Loubens, Mazarin, Portail-Rouge, La Raine, Rondillon, Le Tarey, Terrefort, Vieux-Moulin

PROFILES—THE TOP CHÂTEAUX

Clos Jean

Proprietor: Lionel Bord
Vineyard size: 27 acres
Production: 4,000 cases
Plateau of maturity: 4–15 years
  for the sweet wine; 1–3 years for
  the dry wine

Grape varieties:
Semillon—90%
Sauvignon Blanc—10%

Note: This property also makes an excellent Graves-like dry white wine.

du Cros

Proprietor: Michel Boyer

Vineyard size: 222 acres

Production: 17,000 cases

Plateau of maturity: 3–10 years
 for the sweet wine; 1–3 years for
 the dry wine

Grape varieties:

Semillon—80%

Sauvignon Blanc—20%

Note: This property also makes one of the finest dry white wines of the
 region.

Loupiac-Gaudiet

Proprietor: Marc Ducau

Vineyard size: 50 acres

Production: 7,500 cases

Plateau of maturity: 3–12 years

Grape varieties:

Semillon—75%

Sauvignon Blanc—25%

Ricaud

Proprietor: Société Civile/
 Garreau-Ricard

Vineyard size: 27 acres

Production: 6,000 cases

Plateau of maturity: 5–15 years

Grape varieties:

Semillon—75%

Sauvignon Blanc—20%

Muscadelle—5%

Note: This estate's sweet wine, in vintages such as 1986 and 1988, can
 compete with some of the better estates of Barsac/Sauternes.

de Tastes

Proprietor: Bruno Prats

Vineyard size: 2.47 acres

Production: 450 cases

Plateau of maturity: 8–15 years

Grape varieties:

Sauvignon Blanc—100%

OTHER APPELLATIONS

While so much of the world of wine connoisseurship focuses on the great
names and renowned appellations, there are a number of perennial
overachievers operating in lowly regarded appellations.

I make it a habit to taste through the so-called *petits vins* of Bordeaux
each time I visit. The following dry white and red wines represent the
crème de la crème of my tastings from such appellations as Entre-Deux-
Mers, Premières Côtes de Bordeaux, and generic Bordeaux. These wines
are very fine, are, for the most part, humbly priced, and are made by
highly motivated, sometimes compulsive/obsessive proprietors. I enthusiastically recommend that readers search them out. Even allowing for
wide fluctuations in the value of the dollar, these wines rarely retail for
more than $10 a bottle, yet frequently compete with wines selling for two
to three times as much.

RECOMMENDED PRODUCERS
FROM THE APPELLATIONS OF
ENTRE-DEUX-MERS, BORDEAUX, BORDEAUX SUPÉRIEUR,
AND PREMIÈRES CÔTES DE BORDEAUX

White Wines

VERY GOOD

Bauduc-Les Trois-Hectares (Bordeaux)
Bonnet-Cuvée Reservée (Entre-Deux-Mers)
Carpia (Bordeaux)
Cayla-Le Grand-Vent (Bordeaux)
Fondarzac (Entre-Deux-Mers)
Fongrave (Entre-Deux-Mers)
Launay (Entre-Deux-Mers)
Moulin-de-Launay (Entre-Deux-Mers)
Reynon-Vieilles Vignes (Bordeaux)
Roquefort (Entre-Deux-Mers)
Thieuley-Cuvée Francis Courselle (Bordeaux)
La Tour Mirambeau (Entre-Deux-Mers)
Turcaud (Entre-Deux-Mers)

GOOD

Alpha (Bordeaux)
Bonnet (Entre-Deux-Mers)
Cayla (Bordeaux)
La Closière (Bordeaux)
Numero 1-Dourthe (Bordeaux)
Thieuley (Bordeaux)
Toulet (Bordeaux)

Red Wines

VERY GOOD

La Croix de Roche (Bordeaux Supérieur)
Fussignac (Bordeaux Supérieur)
La Grande-Chapelle (Bordeaux Supérieur)
Jonqueyrès (Bordeaux Supérieur)
Latour (Bordeaux Supérieur)
La Marechale (Bordeaux Supérieur)
Parenchère (Bordeaux Supérieur)
Recougne (Bordeaux Supérieur)

GOOD

Bon Jouan (Bordeaux Supérieur)

Bouilh (Bordeaux Supérieur)

de Bru (Bordeaux)

Cablanc (Bordeaux)

Cazalis (Bordeaux)

de Chastelet (Premières Côtes de Bordeaux)

La Cour d'Argent (Bordeaux Supérieur)

Courteillac (Bordeaux)

Fontenille (Bordeaux Supérieur)

Le Grand-Verdus (Bordeaux Supérieur)

Haut-Frère (Bordeaux)

La Joye (Bordeaux Supérieur)

Laroche-Bel-Air (Premières Côtes de Bordeaux)

Pintey (Bordeaux Supérieur)

Plaisance-Cuvée Tradition (Bordeaux)

de Plassan (Bordeaux)

Prieuré-Ste.-Anne (Premières Côtes de Bordeaux)

Puyfromage (Bordeaux Supérieur)

Reynon (Premières Côtes de Bordeaux)

La Terasse (Bordeaux Supérieur)

Terreford-Quancard (Bordeaux Supérieur)

Terres d'Agnes (Bordeaux Supérieur)

Thieuley (Bordeaux)

Tour de l'Espérance (Bordeaux Supérieur)

La Tuilerie de Puy (Bordeaux Supérieur)

Vacques (Bordeaux Supérieur)

5: THE BORDEAUX WINE CLASSIFICATIONS

Bordeaux wines, in the minds of the wine trade and the wine consumer, are only as good as their official placement in one of the many classifications of wine quality. These classifications of wine quality have operated both for and against the consumer. Those few châteaux fortunate enough to "make the grade" have had guaranteed to them various degrees of celebrity status and respect. They have been able to set their price according to what their peers charged, and have largely been the only châteaux to be written about by wine writers. As this book demonstrates, these top châteaux have not always produced wine becoming of their status in the official French wine hierarchy. As for the other châteaux, many have produced excellent wine for years, but because they were not considered of classified-growth quality in 1855, or 1955, or 1959 (the dates at which the major classifications of wine quality occurred), they have received significantly less money for their wines, and significantly less attention, particularly from writers. Yet it is the excellent wine produced from some of these lesser-known châteaux that represents potential gustatory windfalls for the wine consumer.

THE 1855 CLASSIFICATION OF THE WINES OF THE GIRONDE

Of all the classifications of wine quality in Bordeaux, it is the 1855 Classification of the Wines of the Gironde that is by far the most important of these historical categorizations of Bordeaux wine quality. Among the thousands of châteaux in the Bordeaux region, 61 châteaux and wine-making estates in the Médoc and one in the Graves region were selected on the basis of their selling price and vineyard condition. Since 1855, only one change has occurred to the classification. In 1973, Château Mouton-Rothschild was elevated to first-growth status. The 1855 classification,* which established a five-tiered pyramid with originally 4 (now 5 as the result of the elevation of Mouton-Rothschild) First-Growths, 15 Second-Growths, 14 Third-Growths, 10 Fourth-Growths, and 18 Fifth-Growths, while being a good general guide to the quality of some of the best Bordeaux wines, has numerous deficiencies that are chronicled in detail throughout this book.

While the classification of the wines of the Gironde dealt with red wine–producing estates, there was also a classification in 1855 of the estates in the Sauternes/Barsac region south of the city of Bordeaux that produce sweet, white wines.** One estate, Château d'Yquem, was rated first, followed by 23 other châteaux divided equally into two groupings, "Premiers Crus" and "Deuxièmes Crus."

The other classifications of Bordeaux wine quality are much more modern-day creations, yet are no more accurate or reliable than the 1855

* See page 924: Bordeaux Wine: The Official Classification of 1855.

** See page 926: Sauternes-Barsac: The Official Classification of 1855.

classification. In 1959, the wines of the Graves region immediately south of the city of Bordeaux were classified.* Thirteen châteaux that produced red wine were given classified or "Cru Classé" status. Eight châteaux that produced white wine were classified. In 1955 the wines of St.-Emilion were classified into two categories, "Premiers Grands Crus Classés," or first great growths, and "Grands Crus Classés." This was followed by some corrections to the 1955 classification in 1959 and a revised classification in 1969.** The 1985 revision appears on pages 928–929.

Pomerol, the smallest of the major Bordeaux wine districts, just north-west of St.-Emilion, has never had a classification of the wine quality of its châteaux. The lack of any categorization of Pomerol's wines has certainly not deterred quality. The most expensive and sought-after wine of all Bordeaux is Pétrus, and it is a Pomerol. In addition to Pétrus, there are at least another dozen châteaux in this district that fetch prices for their wines that are equivalent to any one of the Médoc's famous second-growths.

There is still another classification of Bordeaux wines that merits significant attention. It is the classification of the so-called Crus Bourgeois of the Médoc. Pejoratively called *"petits châteaux"* by many, these numerous, small, moderate, and large-sized properties have never had the prestige or glory of the famous classified growths. Regardless of how high the quality of winemaking was, or how carefully the vineyards were managed and cared for, the Crus Bourgeois have for years been considered minor wines. In fact, many of them are, but there are increasing numbers of these châteaux that make wine on a very high level of excellence, comparable to at least a Médoc classified growth. Furthermore, they represent outstanding value and quality to knowledgeable wine consumers.

There were several unsuccessful attempts in the early half of the century to get an effective organization to promote the virtues of the Médoc's hundreds of lesser-known châteaux. A classification was accomplished in 1932 that listed 444 Cru Bourgeois châteaux, broken down into three categories. There are 6 "Crus Bourgeois Supérieurs Exceptionnels," 99 "Crus Bourgeois Supérieurs," and 339 "Crus Bourgeois."

Over the following decades many of these vineyards were absorbed by adjacent properties or went out of the winemaking business. In an effort to update this classification, new rankings were issued in 1966 by an organization of the Bourgeois châteaux called the Syndicat des Crus

* See page 926: Graves: 1959 Official Classification.
** See page 927: St.-Emilion: 1955 Official Classification.

Bourgeois. The most recent result has been an updated list of 128 châteaux issued in 1978.* Eighteen châteaux were given "Crus Grands Bourgeois Exceptionnels" status, 41 are entitled to the title "Crus Grands Bourgeois," and 68 are designated as "Crus Bourgeois."

The selection process utilized by the Syndicat left open a number of questions regarding the overall validity of the 1978 classification. First, only members of the Syndicat were entitled to be recognized in the classification. For example, highly respected Cru Bourgeois châteaux such as de Pez in St.-Estèphe and Gloria in St.-Julien refused to join the Syndicat and are therefore excluded from its official rankings. In short, there is no question that while the current classification of the Crus Bourgeois is of some benefit, the exclusion of at least 10 well-known Crus Bourgeois producing top-quality wine, merely on the grounds that they refused to become members of the Syndicat, leaves a lot to be desired.

While Bordeaux has an elaborate "ranking" system for its multitude of wine-producing châteaux, it is true that many of the châteaux clearly merit their placement, but many don't. In addition, there are quite a few châteaux that have not been officially recognized at all but make very fine wine year in and year out.

These historic classifications of wine quality were employed both to promote Bordeaux wines and establish well-delineated quality benchmarks. The classification system was based on the vineyard's soil base and reputation. However, owners and winemakers change, and whereas some famous Bordeaux estates consistently make the best wine possible given the year's climatic conditions, others, because of negligence, incompetence, or just greed, produce mediocre and poor wine that hardly reflects its official pedigree.

The Bordeaux classifications are looked at in this book only from a consumer's or buyer's perspective. The quality of wine produced by a vineyard over the period 1961–1990 has been thoroughly examined. A qualitative analysis rather than historical analysis of each major and many serious lesser-known estates has been conducted, focusing on (1) the style and overall quality of the wine, (2) the wine's relative quality and record of quality over the period 1961–1990, and (3) its relative value.

The judgments, the commentaries, and the evaluations of the wines in this book are mine. They have been made on the basis of my extensive comparative tastings and numerous trips to Bordeaux since 1970. While no one will argue with the premise that the enjoyment of wine is strictly a personal and subjective matter, it is important to note that critical wine tasting at either the amateur or professional level without prejudice usu-

* See page 929: The Crus Bourgeois of the Médoc: The 1978 Syndicat's Classification.

ally results in general agreement as to the greatest and worst wines. There are indeed quality benchmarks for Bordeaux wines, as there are for all the world's finest wines, and this book is intended to be a guide to those Bordeaux vineyards that establish the benchmarks not only for quality, but also value.

BORDEAUX WINE: THE OFFICIAL CLASSIFICATION OF 1855

FIRST-GROWTHS

Château Lafite-Rothschild	*Pauillac*
Château Latour	*Pauillac*
Château Margaux	*Margaux*
Château Haut-Brion *	*Pessac, Graves*

SECOND-GROWTHS *(Deuxièmes Crus)*

Château Mouton-Rothschild **	*Pauillac*
Château Rausan-Ségla	*Margaux*
Château Rauzan-Gassies	*Margaux*
Château Léoville-Las Cases	*Saint-Julien*
Château Léoville-Poyferré	*Saint-Julien*
Château Léoville-Barton	*Saint-Julien*
Château Durfort-Vivens	*Margaux*
Château Lascombes	*Margaux*
Château Gruaud-Larose	*Saint-Julien*
Château Brane-Cantenac	*Cantenac-Margaux*
Château Pichon-Longueville Baron	*Pauillac*
Château Pichon Lalande	*Pauillac*
Château Ducru-Beaucaillou	*Saint-Julien*
Château Cos d'Estournel	*Saint-Estèphe*
Château Montrose	*Saint-Estèphe*

THIRD-GROWTHS *(Troisièmes Crus)*

Château Giscours	*Labarde-Margaux*
Château Kirwan	*Cantenac-Margaux*
Château d'Issan	*Cantenac-Margaux*
Château Lagrange	*Saint-Julien*
Château Langoa-Barton	*Saint-Julien*
Château Malescot St.-Exupéry	*Margaux*

* This wine, although a Graves, was universally recognized and classified as one of the four First-Growths.
** This wine was decreed a First-Growth in 1973.

Château Cantenac-Brown	*Cantenac-Margaux*
Château Palmer	*Cantenac-Margaux*
Château La Lagune	*Ludon-Haut-Médoc*
Château Desmirail	*Margaux*
Château Calon-Ségur	*Saint-Estèphe*
Château Ferrière	*Margaux*
Château Marquis d'Alesme-Becker	*Margaux*
Château Boyd-Cantenac	*Cantenac-Margaux*

FOURTH-GROWTHS *(Quatrièmes Crus)*

Château St.-Pierre	*Saint-Julien*
Château Branaire	*Saint-Julien*
Château Talbot	*Saint-Julien*
Château Duhart-Milon	*Pauillac*
Château Pouget	*Cantenac-Margaux*
Château La Tour-Carnet	*Saint-Laurent-Haut-Médoc*
Château Lafon-Rochet	*Saint-Estèphe*
Château Beychevelle	*Saint-Julien*
Château Prieuré-Lichine	*Cantenac-Margaux*
Château Marquis-de-Terme	*Margaux*

FIFTH-GROWTHS *(Cinquièmes Crus)*

Château Pontet-Canet	*Pauillac*
Château Batailley	*Pauillac*
Château Grand-Puy-Lacoste	*Pauillac*
Château Grand-Puy-Ducasse	*Pauillac*
Château Haut-Batailley	*Pauillac*
Château Lynch-Bages	*Pauillac*
Château Lynch-Moussas	*Pauillac*
Château Dauzac	*Labarde-Margaux*
Château Mouton-Baronne-Philippe (now D'Armhailac)	*Pauillac*
Château du Tertre	*Arsac-Margaux*
Château Haut-Bages-Libéral	*Pauillac*
Château Pédesclaux	*Pauillac*
Château Belgrave	*Saint-Laurent-Haut-Médoc*
Château de Camensac	*Saint-Laurent-Haut-Médoc*
Château Cos Labory	*Saint-Estèphe*
Château Clerc-Milon-Rothschild	*Pauillac*
Château Croizet-Bages	*Pauillac*
Château Cantemerle	*Macau-Haut-Médoc*

SAUTERNES-BARSAC: THE OFFICIAL CLASSIFICATION OF 1855

FIRST GREAT GROWTH
Château d'Yquem

FIRST-GROWTHS

Château Guiraud

Château La Tour Blanche

Château Lafaurie-Peyraguey

Château de Rayne-Vigneau

Château Sigalas-Rabaud

Château Rabaud-Promis

Clos Haut-Peyraguey

Château Coutet

Château Climens

Château Suduiraut

Château Rieussec

SECOND-GROWTHS

Château d'Arche

Château Filhot

Château Lamothe

Château de Myrat *

Château Doisy-Védrines

Château Doisy-Daëne

Château Suau

Château Broustet

Château Caillou

Château Nairac

Château de Malle

Château Romer

GRAVES: 1959 OFFICIAL CLASSIFICATION

CLASSIFIED RED WINES OF GRAVES

Château Haut-Brion	*Pessac*
Château Bouscaut	*Cadaujac*
Château Carbonnieux	*Léognan*
Domaine de Chevalier	*Léognan*
Château de Fieuzal	*Léognan*
Château Haut-Bailly	*Léognan*
Château La Mission-Haut-Brion	*Pessac*
Château La Tour-Haut-Brion	*Talence*
Château La Tour-Martillac	*Martillac*
Château Malartic-Lagravière	*Léognan*
Château Olivier	*Léognan*
Château Pape-Clément	*Pessac*
Château Smith-Haut-Lafitte	*Martillac*

* No longer in existence, but now in the process of being replanted.

CLASSIFIED WHITE WINES OF GRAVES

Château Bouscaut	*Cadaujac*
Château Carbonnieux	*Léognan*
Domaine de Chevalier	*Léognan*
Château Couhins	*Villenave-d'Ornon*
Château La Tour-Martillac	*Martillac*
Château Laville-Haut-Brion	*Talence*
Château Malartic-Lagravière	*Léognan*
Château Olivier	*Léognan*

ST.-EMILION: 1955 OFFICIAL CLASSIFICATION

FIRST GREAT GROWTHS *(Saint-Emilion—Premiers Grands Crus Classés)*

(A) Château Ausone	Château Figeac
Château Cheval Blanc	Clos Fourtet
(B) Château Beau Séjour-Bécot	Château La Gaffelière
Château Beauséjour	Château Magdelaine
(Duffau-Lagarrosse)	Château Pavie
Château Belair	Château Trottevieille
Château Canon	

GREAT GROWTHS *(Saint-Emilion—Grands Crus Classés)*

Château L'Angélus	Château Fonplégade
Château L'Arrosée	Château Fonroque
Château Baleau	Château Franc-Mayne
Château Balestard-La-Tonnelle	Château Grand-Barrail-
Château Bellevue	Lamarzelle-Figeac
Château Bergat	Château Grand-Corbin
Château Cadet-Bon	Château Grand-Corbin-Despagne
Château Cadet-Piola	Château Grand-Mayne
Château Canon-La-Gaffelière	Château Grand-Pontet
Château Cap de Mourlin	Château Grandes-Murailles
Château Chapelle Madeleine	Château Guadet-Saint-Julien
Château Le Châtelet	Château Haut-Corbin
Château Chauvin	Clos des Jacobins
Château Corbin-Michotte	Château Jean Faure
Château Coutet	Château La Carte
Château Couvent-des-Jacobins	Château La Clotte
Château Croque-Michotte	Château La Clusière
Château Curé-Bon	Château La Couspaude
Château Dassault	Château La Dominique
Château Faurie-de-Souchard	Clos La Madeleine

Château La Marzelle
Château La Tour-Figeac
Château La Tour-du-Pin-Figeac
  (Giraud-Bélivier)
Château La Tour-du-Pin-Figeac
  (Moueix)
Château Laniotte, Château
  Chapelle-de-la-Trinité
Château Larcis-Ducasse
Château Larmande
Château Laroze
Château Lasserre
Château Le Couvent
Château Le Prieuré
Château Matras
Château Mauvezin
Château Moulin du Cadet
Château L'Oratoire

Château Pavie-Decesse
Château Pavie-Macquin
Château Pavillon-Cadet
Château Petit-Faurie-
  de-Soutard
Château Ripeau
Château St.-Georges-Côte-
  Pavie
Clos St.-Martin
Château Sansonnet
Château Soutard
Château Tertre-Daugay
Château Trimoulet
Château Trois-Moulins
Château Troplong-Mondot
Château Villemaurine
Château Yon-Figeac

ST.-EMILION: 1985 OFFICIAL CLASSIFICATION

PREMIERS GRANDS CRUS CLASSÉS

Ausone
Cheval Blanc
Beauséjour (Duffau-Lagarrosse)
Belair
Canon
Clos Fourtet

Figeac
La Gaffelière
Magdelaine
Pavie
Trottevieille

GRANDS CRUS CLASSÉS

L'Angélus
L'Arrosée
Balestard-La-Tonnelle
Beau Séjour-Bécot
Bellevue
Bergat
Berliquet
Cadet-Piola
Canon-La-Gaffelière
Cap de Mourlin
Le Chatelet
Chauvin

Clos des Jacobins
Clos La Madeleine
Clos St.-Martin
La Clotte
La Clusière
Corbin
Corbin-Michotte
Couvent-des-Jacobins
Croque-Michotte
Curé-Bon
Dassault
La Dominique

Faurie-de-Souchard
Fonplégade
Fonroque
Franc-Mayne
Grand Barrail Lamarzelle Figeac
Grand-Corbin-Despagne
Grand Corbin
Grand Mayne
Grand Pontet
Guadet-St.-Julien
Haut-Corbin
Haut-Sarpe
Laniote
Larcis-Ducasse
Lamarzelle
Larmande
Laroze
Matras
Mauvezin

Moulin-du-Cadet
L'Oratoire
Pavie-Decesse
Pavie-Macquin
Pavillon-Cadet
Petit-Faurie-de-Soutard
Le Prieuré
Ripeau
Sansonnet
St.-Georges-Côte-Pavie
La Serre
Soutard
Tertre-Daugay
La Tour-du-Pin-Figeac
La Tour-Figeac
Trimoulet
Troplong-Mondot
Villemaurine
Yon-Figeac

THE CRUS BOURGEOIS OF THE MÉDOC: THE 1978 SYNDICAT'S CLASSIFICATION

CRUS GRANDS BOURGEOIS EXCEPTIONNELS

d'Agassac (Ludon)
Andron-Blanquet (Saint-Estèphe)
Beau-Site (Saint-Estèphe)
Capbern Gasqueton (Saint-Estèphe)
Caronne-St.-Gemme (Saint-Laurent)
Chasse-Spleen (Moulis)
Cissac (Cissac)
Citran (Avensan)
Le Crock (Saint-Estèphe)

Dutruch-Grand Poujeaux (Moulis)
Fourcas-Dupré (Listrac)
Fourcas-Hosten (Listrac)
du Glana (Saint-Julien)
Haut-Marbuzet (Saint-Estèphe)
de Marbuzet (Saint-Estèphe)
Meyney (Saint-Estèphe)
Phélan-Ségur (Saint-Estèphe)
Poujeaux (Moulis)

CRUS GRANDS BOURGEOIS

Beaumont (Cussac)
Bel-Orme (Saint-Seurin-de-Cadourne)
Brillette (Moulis)
La Cardonne (Blaignan)
Colombier-Monpelou (Pauillac)

Coufran (Saint-Seurin-de-Cadourne)
Coutelin-Merville (Saint-Estèphe)
Duplessis-Hauchecorne (Moulis)
La Fleur Milon (Pauillac)
Fontesteau (Saint-Sauveur)

Greysac (Bégadan)

Hanteillan (Cissac)

Lafon (Listrac)

de Lamarque (Lamarque)

Lamothe-Cissac (Cissac)

Larose-Trintaudon (Saint-Laurent)

Laujac (Bégadan)

Liversan (Saint-Sauveur)

Loudenne (Saint-Yzans-de-Médoc)

MacCarthy (Saint-Estèphe)

de Malleret (Le Pian)

Martinens (Margaux)

Morin (Saint-Estèphe)

Moulin à Vent (Moulis)

Le Meynieu (Vertheuil)

Les-Ormes-de-Pez (Saint-Estèphe)

Les Ormes-Sorbet (Couquèques)

Patache d'Aux (Bégadan)

Paveil de Luze (Soussans)

Peyrabon (Saint-Sauveur)

Pontoise-Cabarrus (Saint-Seurin-de-Cadourne)

Potensac (Potensac)

Reysson (Vertheuil)

Ségur (Parempuyre)

Sigognac (Saint-Yzans-de-Médoc)

Sociando-Mallet (Saint-Seurin-de-Cadourne)

du Taillan (Le Taillan)

La Tour de By (Bégandan)

La Tour du Haut-Moulin (Cussac)

Tronquoy-Lalande (Saint-Estèphe)

Verdignan (Saint-Seurin-de-Cadourne)

CRUS BOURGEOIS

Aney (Cussac)

Balac (Saint-Laurent)

La Bécade (Listrac)

Bellerive (Valeyrac)

Bellerose (Pauillac)

Les Bertins (Valeyrac)

Bonneau (Saint-Seurin-de-Cadourne)

Le Bosq (Saint-Christoly)

du Breuilh (Cissac)

La Bridane (Saint-Julien)

de By (Bégadan)

Cailloux de By (Bégadan)

Cap Léon Veyrin (Listrac)

Carcanieux (Queyrac)

Castera (Cissac)

Chambert (Saint-Estèphe)

La Clare (Saint-Estèphe)

Clarke (Listrac)

La Closerie (Moulis)

de Conques (Saint-Christoly)

Duplessis-Fabre (Moulis)

Fonpiqueyre (Saint-Sauveur)

Fonréaud (Listrac)

Fort Vauban (Cussac)

La France (Blaignan)

Gallais-Bellevue (Potensac)

Grand-Duroc-Milon (Pauillac)

Grand-Moulin (Saint-Seurin-de-Cadourne)

Haut-Bages-Monpelou (Pauillac)

Haut-Canteloup (Couquèques)

Haut-Garin (Bégadan)

Haut-Padargnac (Pauillac)

Houbanon (Prignac)

Hourton-Ducasse (Saint-Sauveur)

De Labat (Saint-Laurent)

Lamothe-Bergeron (Cussac)

Le Landat (Cissac)

Landon (Bégadan)

Larivière (Blaignan)

Lartigue de Brochon (Saint-Seurin-de-Cadourne)

Lassalle (Potensac)

Lavalière (Saint-Christoly)

Lestage (Listrac)

Mac-Carthy-Moula (Saint-Estèphe)

Monthil (Bégadan)

Moulin de la Roque (Bégadan)

Moulin Rouge (Cussac)

Panigon (Civrac)

Pibran (Pauillac)

Plantey de la Croix (Saint-Seurin-de-Cadourne)

Pontet (Blaignan)

Ramage La Batisse (Saint-Sauveur)

Romefort (Cussac)

La Roque de By (Bégadan)

de la Rose Maréchale (Saint-Seurin-de-Cadourne)

St.-Bonnet (Saint-Christoly)

St.-Roch (Saint-Estèphe)

Saransot (Listrac)

Soudars (Avensac)

Tayac (Soussans)

La Tour Blanche (Saint-Christoly)

La Tour du Haut-Caussan (Blaignan)

La Tour du Mirail (Cissac)

La Tour Saint-Bonnet (Saint-Christoly)

La Tour Saint-Joseph (Cissac)

des Tourelles (Blaignan)

Vernous (Lesparre)

Vieux-Robin (Bégadan)

WHO'S ON FIRST?

The 1855 Classification of the Wines of the Gironde and the subsequent classifications of the wines of Graves and St.-Emilion created a rigid hierarchy that, to this day, dictates how much a consumer must spend for a bottle of classified-growth Bordeaux. Ironically, these historic classifications, which were created in an attempt to classify the quality of Bordeaux wine, are of little relevance with respect to determining the quality of wine produced by a specific château. At most, these classifications should be regarded by both the wine connoisseur and novice as informational items of historical significance only.

The following is my classification of the top 153 wines of Bordeaux divided into the same five-tiered hierarchy that was used in 1855. It is based on the performance of these châteaux from 1961–1990. More weight has been given to the direction the property is heading and the quality of wine produced from 1982–1990 than what the property may have done in the 1961–1981 period. This is done simply because today is the golden age of Bordeaux. Bordeaux is prosperous, and more properties are making better wine with better facilities and advice than ever before.

There are 153 properties in my classification. Since I have included the wines of all the major appellations of Bordeaux, particularly St.-Emilion, Pomerol, Graves, Fronsac, and Canon-Fronsac, that were excluded (except for Haut-Brion), the number of top classified growths is larger than the 61 that made the grade in 1855.

This classification is, of course, my own, but I can say that I have tasted all of these producers' wines from all of the significant vintages, not once, but numerous times. In addition, I have visited the great majority of these properties, and have studied their placement in this classification intensely. Nothing I have stated is arbitrary, but it is a personal judgment based on years of tasting and years of visiting Bordeaux. Furthermore, I think I can say it was done with no bias. Some of the proprietors with whom I have had some very difficult times over the years are included as first-growths. Some of the owners who I personally like and respect have not done well. That is the risk, but in the end, I hope this consumer's look at the top estates in Bordeaux serves a constructive purpose for those properties who feel unfairly demoted, while I hope those that have won acclaim and recognition here will continue to do what it takes to make the best wine.

MY CLASSIFICATION OF THE TOP CHÂTEAUX OF BORDEAUX (as of 1991)

FIRST-GROWTHS (18)

Ausone (St.-Emilion)
Cheval Blanc (St.-Emilion)
Cos d'Estournel (St.-Estèphe)
Ducru-Beaucaillou (St.-Julien)
La Fleur de Gay (Pomerol)
Gruaud-Larose (St.-Julien)
Haut-Brion (Graves)
Lafite-Rothschild (Pauillac)
Lafleur (Pomerol)

Latour (Pauillac)
Léoville-Las Cases (St.-Julien)
Margaux (Margaux)
La Mission-Haut-Brion (Graves)
Mouton-Rothschild (Pauillac)
Palmer (Margaux)
Pétrus (Pomerol)
Pichon-Lalande (Pauillac)
Le Pin (Pomerol)

SECOND-GROWTHS (19)

Canon (St.-Emilion)
Certan de May (Pomerol)
Clinet (Pomerol)
Domaine de Chevalier (Graves)
La Conseillante (Pomerol)
L'Evangile (Pomerol)
Figeac (St.-Emilion)
La Lagune (Ludon)
Latour à Pomerol (Pomerol)
Léoville-Barton (St.-Julien)

Lynch-Bages (Pauillac)
Montrose (St.-Estèphe)
Pape-Clément (Graves)
Pichon-Longueville Baron
   (Pauillac)
Rausan-Ségla (Margaux)
Talbot (St.-Julien)
Le Tertre-Roteboeuf (St.-Emilion)
Trotanoy (Pomerol)
Vieux Château Certain (Pomerol)

THIRD-GROWTHS (25)

L'Angélus (St.-Emilion)
L'Arrosée (St.-Emilion)
Beychevelle (St.-Julien)
Branaire-Ducru (St.-Julien)
Calon-Ségur (St.-Estèphe)
Canon-La-Gaffelière (St.-Emilion)
Cantemerle (Macau)
Chasse-Spleen (Moulis)
La Dominique (St.-Emilion)
Duhart-Milon (Pauillac)
L'Eglise-Clinet (Pomerol)
de Fieuzal (Graves)
Giscours (Margaux)

Grand-Puy-Lacoste (Pauillac)
Haut-Bailly (Graves)
Haut-Marbuzet (St.-Estèphe)
La Fleur Pétrus (Pomerol)
Lagrange (St.-Julien)
Langoa-Barton (St.-Julien)
Larmande (St.-Emilion)
Magdelaine (St.-Emilion)
Meyney (St.-Estèphe)
Monbrison (Margaux)
Petit-Village (Pomerol)
Troplong-Mondot (St.-Emilion)

FOURTH-GROWTHS (18)

Cadet-Piola (St.-Emilion)
Les Carmes Haut-Brion (Graves)
Couvent-des-Jacobins
   (St.-Emilion)
Curé-Bon-La-Madeleine
   (St.-Emilion)
Les Forts de Latour (Pauillac)
Le Gay (Pomerol)
Gloria (St.-Julien)
Lafon-Rochet (St.-Estèphe)

Lascombes (Margaux)
Léoville-Poyferré (St.-Julien)
La Louvière (Graves)
Marquis de Terme (Margaux)
Pavie (St.-Emilion)
Prieuré-Lichine (Margaux)
St.-Pierre (St.-Julien)
Sociando-Mallet (Médoc)
Soutard (St.-Emilion)
Trottevieille (St.-Emilion)

FIFTH-GROWTHS (73)

d'Angludet (Margaux)
Bahans-Haut-Brion (Graves)

Balestard-La-Tonnelle
   (St.-Emilion)

Batailley (Pauillac)

Beauséjour-Duffau (St.-Emilion)

Belair (St.-Emilion)

Bon Pasteur (Pomerol)

Brane-Cantenac (Margaux)

Canon-de-Brem (Canon-Fronsac)

Canon-Moueix (Canon-Fronsac)

Cantenac-Brown (Margaux)

Cassagne-Haut-Canon-
   La Truffière (Canon-Fronsac)

Certan-Giraud (Pomerol)

Chambert-Marbuzet (St.-Estèphe)

Citran (Médoc)

Clerc-Milon (Pauillac)

Clos des Jacobins (St.-Emilion)

Clos la Madeleine (St.-Emilion)

Clos René (Pomerol)

La Croix de Gay (Pomerol)

Croque-Michotte (St.-Emilion)

Dalem (Fronsac)

La Dauphine (Fronsac)

Durfort-Vivens (Margaux)

Domaine L'Eglise (Pomerol)

L'Enclos (Pomerol)

Fonbadet (Pauillac)

Fontenil (Fronsac)

Fourcas-Loubaney (Listrac)

La Gaffelière (St.-Emilion)

Gazin (Pomerol)

Gombaude-Guillot (Pomerol)

Grand-Mayne (St.-Emilion)

Grand-Puy-Ducasse (Pauillac)

La Grave Trigant de Boisset
   (Pomerol)

Gressier Grand-Poujeaux (Moulis)

La Gurgue (Margaux)

Haut-Bages-Libéral (Pauillac)

Haut-Batailley (Pauillac)

d'Issan (Margaux)

Kirwan (Margaux)

Labegorcé-Zédé (Margaux)

Lanessan (Haut-Médoc)

Larcis-Ducasse (St.-Emilion)

Larruau (Margaux)

Malescot St.-Exupéry (Margaux)

Maucaillou (Moulis)

Moulin-Haut-Laroque (Fronsac)

Mouton-Baronne-Phillipe
   (D'Armailhac)
   (Pauillac)

Les-Ormes-de-Pez (St.-Estèphe)

Pavie-Decesse (St.-Emilion)

Pavie-Macquin (St.-Emilion)

Pavillon Rouge de Margaux
   (Margaux)

de Pez (St.-Estèphe)

Moulin-Pey-Labrie (Canon-Fronsac)

Picque-Caillou (Graves)

Pitray (Côtes de Castillon)

Pontet-Canet (Pauillac)

Potensac (Médoc)

Pouget (Margaux)

Poujeaux (Moulis)

Roc des Cambes (Côtes de Bourg)

Rouget (Pomerol)

de Sales (Pomerol)

Siran (Margaux)

Tayac-Cuvée Prestige
   (Côtes de Bourg)

Du Tertre (Margaux)

La Tour-Haut-Brion (Graves)

Tour Haut-Caussan (Médoc)

Tour du Haut-Moulin
   (Haut-Médoc)

La Tour-du-Pin-Figeac-Moueix
   (St.-Emilion)

La Vieille-Cure (Fronsac)

6: THE ELEMENTS FOR MAKING GREAT BORDEAUX WINE

Traditionalists often wax poetic about "the good ol' days" and that "they just don't make Bordeaux the way they used to." In fact, for Bordeaux wines, times have never been better, both climatically and financially. Moreover, the quality of winemaking in Bordeaux has never been higher. The greatest wines ever made in Bordeaux are those that are produced today.

The most prominent factor about the best red and white wines of Bordeaux is their remarkable longevity. In great years, the aging potential of these wines is unequalled by any other table wines produced in the world. Even in lesser vintages, the wines often need a good 5–8 years to develop fully. The reasons? In order of importance: the grape varieties, the soil, the climate, and the methods of winemaking that are discussed in the sections that follow.

BORDEAUX GRAPES FOR RED WINES

For red wines there are three major grape varieties planted and two minor varieties that have largely now fallen out of favor. The choice of grape varieties used for making Bordeaux has a profound influence on the style of wine that is ultimately produced. Hundreds of years of practice have allowed specific winemaking châteaux to select only the grape varieties that perform best in their soil.

For red wines in the Médoc, if one were to give an average formula for a percentage of grapes planted at a majority of the Médoc châteaux, it would be 60%–65% Cabernet Sauvignon, 10%–15% Cabernet Franc, 20%–25% Merlot, and Petit Verdot, 3%–8%. Each château has its own best formula for planting its vineyards; some prefer to use more Merlot, some, more Cabernet Sauvignon or Cabernet Franc, and some, more Petit Verdot. As a general rule, the very light, highly drained, gravel soils tend to support Cabernet Sauvignon better than Merlot. For that reason, one finds very high percentages of Cabernet Sauvignon in the appellation of Margaux. In contrast, in the heavier, more clay-dominated soils of St.-Estèphe, Merlot tends to fare better. Consequently, a higher percentage of Merlot is found in St.-Estèphe. Of course, there are exceptions. In the Margaux appellation, Château Palmer uses a significant portion of Merlot in their final blend, as does Château Pichon-Longueville–Comtesse de Lalande in Pauillac. However, the two most important grapes for a highly successful vintage in the Médoc are Cabernet Sauvignon and Merlot. The Cabernet is more widely planted in the Médoc simply because it ripens well and flourishes in the gravelly, well-drained soil that exists in the top vineyards there. The Merlot is popular because, when blended with the tannic, tough, deeply colored Cabernet Sauvignon, it offers softness, flesh, and suppleness to balance out the sterner texture of the Cabernet Sauvignon.

If a château uses a high percentage of Cabernet Sauvignon in its blend, in all likelihood the wine will be densely colored, big, full bodied, tannic, and very ageworthy. On the other hand, if a high percentage of Merlot is used in the blend, then in most cases suppleness and precocious charm are the preferred personality traits.

In the Médoc, Cabernet Franc is also used in small percentages. Cabernet Franc lacks the color of Cabernet Sauvignon and Merlot, but does offer complex, aromatic components (particularly aromas of mint, herbs, and spices) that the Bordelais call finesse. The Petit Verdot is planted in very small percentages because it ripens very late and in most vintages rarely achieves full maturity. It is, however, often used by those châteaux who employ a high percentage of Merlot. The Petit Verdot provides the hard tannic backbone to those wines that would otherwise be soft as a result of a high concentration of Merlot.

Each of these four major red grape varieties ripens at a different time. The Merlot is always the first grape to blossom and to become fully mature. Cabernet Franc is second, followed by Cabernet Sauvignon and then Petit Verdot. Few wine consumers realize that spring frost and varying weather patterns at different times during the growing season can seriously affect some of these grape varieties, while sparing others. The production from the Merlot grape, because of its early flowering characteristic, is frequently curtailed by spring frost. In addition, Merlot is the grape most susceptible to rot from moist or damp weather conditions because its skin is less tough and less resistant to disease than that of the Cabernet Sauvignon or Petit Verdot.

This fact alone can be critical for the success of châteaux with extensive Merlot plantations. Late-season rains have on more than one occasion washed out the late-picking properties with vineyards dominated by Cabernet Sauvignon, while the vineyards of Merlot plantings have already been harvested under optimum conditions. When one asks why the Merlot-based wines, such as Pétrus and Trotanoy, were so successful in 1964 as compared to the disappointing Cabernet Sauvignon–based wines, such as Mouton-Rothschild and Lafite-Rothschild, the answer is that the Merlot crop was harvested in perfect weather conditions long before the Cabernet crop, which was drenched and diluted by late occurring torrential rains.

On the right bank of the Gironde River are the two principal appellations of St.-Emilion and Pomerol. Here, significantly higher percentages of the Merlot and Cabernet Franc grapes are planted. Much of the soil of these two appellations is less well drained and frequently heavier because of a significant clay content. The Cabernet Sauvignon is not fond of such soils and accordingly smaller amounts of it are planted, unless the vineyard is situated on a particularly well-drained, gravelly soil base, as a few are in these appellations. The Merlot, however, takes well to this type of heavier soil and surprisingly so does the Cabernet Franc. There are many exceptions, but in St.-Emilion the standard formula for grape varieties is close to 50% Merlot and 50% Cabernet Franc with Cabernet Sauvignon mixed in various percentages. In Pomerol,

Merlot is clearly the key. Except for a handful of estates, such as Clos L'Eglise and Vieux-Château-Certan, little Cabernet Sauvignon is planted. The average vineyard's composition in Pomerol would be 70%–80% Merlot and the balance, Cabernet Franc. Consequently, it is not surprising to find wines from these two regions maturing faster and being generally fruitier, more supple, and lusher than wines from the Médoc.

In the Graves region, the soil is extremely gravelly as the name implies, thereby affording excellent drainage. As in the Médoc, the Cabernet Sauvignon is favored, but there is more Cabernet Franc and Merlot in Graves, with wines that are usually lighter as a result. However, in rainy years, the Graves wines frequently turn out better than others simply because of the outstanding drainage the vineyards enjoy in this region. The 1987 vintage is a classic case in point.

The advantage of knowing the percentage of grape varieties planted at a particular château is that one can predict with some degree of certainty which areas may have performed better than others even before the critics begin issuing their tasting judgments. This can be done by knowing the climatic conditions leading up to and during the harvest and matching those conditions against how the different grape varieties perform under such conditions.

Rarely does Bordeaux have a perfect vintage for all four red wine grape varieties. Over recent vintages, the Merlot crop was devastated in 1984 by a poor flowering, but the Cabernet Sauvignon crop ripened decently and was harvested under healthy conditions. Not surprisingly, 1984 is considered a Médoc year. In 1989, 1985, and 1982, all the grape varieties ripened superbly, although everyone agrees that Merlot and Petit Verdot were virtually perfect. These three years were profoundly influenced by the opulence and ripeness of the Merlot grape, and consequently, the wines are higher in alcohol, are fleshier and softer than in years that favor the Cabernet Sauvignon. A classic example of a top Cabernet Sauvignon year is 1986. The Merlot overproduced and many wines that contain a large percentage of Merlot were fluid and lacking structure. Those Médocs with a high percentage of Cabernet Sauvignon produced superb wines that were very much influenced by their fully ripe Cabernet Sauvignon grapes.

CABERNET SAUVIGNON—A grape that is highly pigmented, very astringent, and tannic that provides the framework, strength, dark color, character, and longevity for the wines in a majority of the vineyards in the Médoc. It ripens late, is resistant to rot because of its thick skin, and has a pronounced blackcurrant aroma that is sometimes intermingled with subtle herbaceous scents that take on the smell of cedarwood with aging.

Virtually all Bordeaux châteaux blend Cabernet Sauvignon with other red grape varieties. In the Médoc, the average percentage of Cabernet Sauvignon in the blend ranges from 40%–85%, in Graves, 40%–60%, in St.-Emilion, 10%–50%, and in Pomerol, 0%–20%.

Examples of wines with very high percentages of Cabernet Sauvignon: Latour (Pauillac) (80%), Haut-Bages-Libéral (Pauillac) (70%), Mouton-Rothschild (Pauillac) (76%), du Tertre (Margaux) (80%), and d'Issan (Margaux) (75%).

MERLOT—Utilized by virtually every château in Bordeaux because of its ability to provide a round, generous, fleshy, supple, alcoholic wine, Merlot ripens, on an average, 1–2 weeks earlier than Cabernet Sauvignon. In the Médoc, this grape reaches its zenith in several châteaux that use high percentages of it (Palmer and Pichon Lalande), but its fame is in the wines it renders in Pomerol where it is used profusely. In the Médoc, the average percentage of Merlot in the blend ranges from 5%–45%. In Graves, it ranges from 20%–40%, in St.-Emilion, 25%–60%, and in Pomerol, 35%–98%. Merlot produces wines lower in acidity and tannin than Cabernet Sauvignon, and as a general rule, wines with a higher percentage of Merlot mature faster than wines with a higher percentage of Cabernet Sauvignon.

Examples of wines with a very high percentage of Merlot are Pétrus (Pomerol) (95%), Trotanoy (Pomerol) (90%), Latour à Pomerol (Pomerol) (90%), L'Enclos (Pomerol) (80%), and Coufran (Médoc) (85%).

CABERNET FRANC—A relative of Cabernet Sauvignon that ripens slightly earlier, Cabernet Franc (called Bouchet in St.-Emilion and Pomerol), is used in small to modest proportions to add complexity and bouquet to a wine. Cabernet Franc has a pungent, often very spicy, minty, sometimes weedy, olive-like aroma. It does not have the fleshy, supple character of Merlot, nor the astringence, power, and color of Cabernet Sauvignon. In the Médoc, an average percentage of Cabernet Franc used in the blend is 0%–30%, in Graves, 5%–25%, in St.-Emilion, 25%–66%, in Pomerol, 5%–50%.

Examples of wines with a very high percentage of Cabernet Franc are Cheval Blanc (St.-Emilion) (66%), Lafleur (Pomerol) (50%), La Conseillante (Pomerol) (45%), and Ausone (St.-Emilion) (50%).

PETIT VERDOT—A useful, but generally difficult red grape because of its very late ripening characteristics, Petit Verdot provides intense color, mouth-gripping tannins, and high sugar, and thus high alcohol when it ripens fully, as it did in 1982 and 1989 in Bordeaux. When unripe, it provides a nasty, sharp, acidic character. In the Médoc, few châteaux use more than 5% in the blend. In Graves, St.-Emilion, and Pomerol, very little Petit Verdot now exists.

Examples of wines with a very high percentage of Petit Verdot are Pichon-Longueville–Comtesse de Lalande (Pauillac) (8%), and Marquis d'Alesme-Becker (Margaux) (10%).

MALBEC—The least-utilized red grape (also called Pressac in St.-Emilion and Pomerol) of the major varietals, Malbec has fallen into disfavor and in most vineyards has now been replanted with one of the more favored grapes. Its future in Bordeaux's best vineyards seems doubtful.

An example of a wine with a high percentage of Malbec is La Tour-Martillac (Graves) (5%).

BORDEAUX GRAPES FOR WHITE WINES

Bordeaux produces both dry and sweet white wine. There are usually only three grape varieties used, Sauvignon Blanc and Semillon for both dry and sweet wine, and Muscadelle, which is used sparingly for the sweet wines.

SAUVIGNON BLANC—Used for making both the dry white wines of Graves and the sweet white wines of the Barsac/Sauternes region, Sauvignon Blanc renders a very distinctive wine with a pungent, somewhat herbaceous aroma, and crisp, austere flavors. Among the dry white Graves, a few châteaux employ 100% Sauvignon Blanc, but most blend it with Semillon. Less Sauvignon Blanc is used in the winemaking blends in the Sauternes region than in Graves.

Examples of dry Graves with a high percentage of Sauvignon Blanc are Smith-Haut-Lafitte (100%), Malartic-Lagravière (100%), La Louvière (70%), Domaine de Chevalier (70%), and Couhins-Lurton (100%).

Examples of sweet Sauternes with a high percentage of Sauvignon Blanc are Guirard (35%), Filhot (35%), and Romer du Hayot (30%).

SEMILLON—Very susceptible to the famous noble rot called botrytis, which is essential to the production of excellent, sweet wines, Semillon is used to provide a rich, creamy, intense texture to both the dry wines of Graves and the rich, sweet wines of Sauternes. Semillon is quite fruity when young, and wines with a high percentage of Semillon seem to take on weight and viscosity as they age. For these reasons, higher percentages of Semillon are used in making the sweet wines of the Sauternes/Barsac region than in producing the white wines of Graves.

Examples of dry Graves wines with a high percentage of Semillon are Laville-Haut-Brion (60%), de Fieuzal (40%), Haut-Brion (50%), and Olivier (70%).

Examples of sweet Sauternes wines with a high percentage of Semillon are Doisy-Dubroca (100%), Doisy-Daëne (70%), Nairac (90%), Suduiraut (80%), Lafaurie-Peyraguey (93%), Yquem (80%), and Climens (98%).

MUSCADELLE—The least planted of the white wine grapes in Bordeaux, Muscadelle is a very fragile grape that is quite susceptible to disease, but when healthy and mature, it produces a wine with an intense flowery, perfumed character. It is used only in tiny proportions by châteaux in the Sauternes/Barsac region. It is used sparingly by the white wine producers of Graves.

Examples of sweet Sauternes wines with a high percentage of Muscadelle include Broustet (12%), Lamothe-Despujols (15%), and de Rolland (20%).

SOIL

It is not unusual to hear Bordeaux's best winemakers say that the "wine is made in the vineyard," not the winery. It is interesting to compare the traditional attitude in California where the primary considerations for making quality wine have been the region's climatic profile, the expertise of the winemaker, and the availability of high technology to sculpture the wine. While a growing number of California wineries are beginning to pay greater attention to soil, few Bordelais will argue with the premise that the greatness of their wine is a result of the soil, or *terroir*, and not the winemaker or vinification equipment.

The famous Médoc area of Bordeaux is a triangular land mass, bordered on the west by the Atlantic Ocean, on the east by the wide Gironde River, and on the south by the city of Bordeaux. The top vineyards of the Médoc stretch out on the eastern half of this generally flat land on slightly elevated slopes facing the Gironde River. The soil is largely unfit for any type of agriculture other than grape growing. It is extremely gravelly and sandy, and the subsoil of the Médoc ranges from heavy clay soil (producing heavier, less fine wines), to lighter chalk and gravels (producing finer, lighter wines).

The very gravelly soil that is the predominate geological characteristic of the Bordeaux vineyards operates as an excellent drainage system, as well as being permeable enough for the vines' roots to penetrate deep into the subsoil for nutrients, water, and minerals.

In the Graves region south of the city of Bordeaux, the name of the region reflects the very rocky soil, which is even more deeply embedded with gravel than in the Médoc. This contributes to the unique flavor that some commentators have suggested is a mineral-like, earthy taste in the wines of this region. The regions of St.-Emilion and Pomerol are situated 20 miles to the east of the city of Bordeaux. St.-Emilion has various soil bases. Around the charming medieval city of St.-Emilion are the châteaux that are said to sit on the *côtes*, or hillsides. These hillsides were once the sides of a river valley, and the soil is primarily chalk, clay, and limestone. Some of the famous châteaux that sit on the *côtes* of St.-Emilion include Ausone, Canon, Pavie, and Belair.

Several miles to the northwest of St.-Emilion is the *graves* section of St.-Emilion, a gravelly, sandy outcropping bordering the Pomerol appellation. The St.-Emilion châteaux located in this *graves* area produce a different style of wine—more fleshy, more fruity, more accessible than the austere, tannic, and reserved wines produced from vineyards on the limestone, chalk, and clay hillsides of the town of St.-Emilion. Two of the best-known châteaux in this area of St.-Emilion are Cheval Blanc and Figeac. Of course, exceptions in style within each subregion exist, but in broad terms, there are two major types of St.-Emilion wines, a *graves* style and a *côtes* style, and the style is a direct result of the soil base in which the vines are planted.

In Pomerol, which borders the *graves* section of St.-Emilion, the soil composition is quite similar, yet variations exist. Pomerol's most famous estate—Pétrus—sits on an elevated plateau that has a unique, rather heavy clay soil unlike any other vineyard in Pomerol.

The subtle differences in soil composition and their effect on the style and personality of the wine are best exemplified by three examples of adjoining vineyards. On the border of the Médoc communes of Pauillac and St.-Julien, three highly respected properties—the first-growth Latour, the second-growth St.-Julien, Léoville-Las Cases, and the second-growth Pauillac, Pichon-Longueville Baron—sit together with each one's vineyard contiguous to the other. The yield from the vineyards, the percentage of each vine planted, the method of making the wine, the average age of the vines, the types of grape varieties, and finally, the time the wine spends aging in the cask are not dramatically different for all three châteaux. However, all three wines differ substantially in taste, style, texture, and in their evolution. All three have totally different soil bases.

In Pomerol, one has only to compare the vineyard of that appellation's most famous wine, Pétrus—which is planted in heavy clay soil rich in iron—with the soil of its immediate neighbor, La Fleur Pétrus—which has little clay, but much more sand and gravel. Both wines could not, despite almost exactly the same vinifications by the same people, be more different.

Soil is undoubtedly a very important factor in the character and diverse style of Bordeaux wines. It is not, as the Bordelais would have one believe, the only element necessary to make a great wine. The importance of a hospitable climate, conservative viticultural practices whereby the use of fertilizers is kept to a minimum, aggressive pruning procedures, and of course, the careful vinification and handling of the wine are all significant factors in the making of great wine. Even with the finest technology, a great winemaking team, and the best, well-drained, gravelly soil, great wine can not be made without optimal climatic conditions that produces fully mature ripe grapes.

CLIMATE

The great vintages of Bordeaux have always been characterized by growing seasons that have been abnormally hot, dry, and sunny. The excellent to great vintages of Bordeaux such as 1900, 1921, 1929, 1945, 1947, 1949, 1959, 1961, 1970, 1982, and 1989 have all shared several distinctive climatic characteristics—heat, sunshine, and drought-like conditions.

Several prominent Bordeaux château proprietors, who have recently claimed that disastrous vintages such as 1968, 1965, and 1963 will never occur again because of the technological winemaking advances, seem to forget that good wine cannot be made from unripe, vegetal-tasting grapes. Bordeaux, like any major viticultural area, must have plenty of sunshine, dry weather, and heat in order to produce excellent wine.

When the Bordeaux châteaux have to wait until October to harvest their grapes rather than September, it is usually a sign that the growing season has been abnormally cool and even worse, wet. A review of the finest vintages in Bordeaux reveals that the commencement date of the harvest almost always occurs in September.

1870—September 10	1959—September 20
1893—August 18	1961—September 22
1899—September 24	1970—September 27
1900—September 24	1975—September 22
1921—September 15	1978—October 7
1929—September 23	1982—September 13
1945—September 13	1985—September 29
1947—September 15	1986—September 23
1949—September 27	1989—August 31
1953—September 28	1990—September 12

In comparison, here are the commencement dates of the harvests for some of Bordeaux's most notoriously bad vintages.

1951—October 9	1968—September 20
1954—October 10	1969—October 6
1956—October 14	1972—October 7
1957—October 4	1977—October 3
1963—October 7	1984—October 5
1965—October 2	

The pattern would appear to be obvious. Great years are characterized by plentiful amounts of sunshine, heat, and dry weather. Under such conditions the grapes ripen steadily and quickly, and the harvests begin early. Poor years result from inadequate supplies of these precious natural commodities. The grapes never ripen fully and are picked in either an unripe or a rain-diluted condition.

There are few exceptions to the climatic patterns for excellent and poor vintages. For example, 1979 (picked October 3) was a late-October harvest year that produced very good wines. In recent years there has been a growing tendency by producers to attempt to obtain what they call *sur-maturité*. The old rule that governed the harvest in Bordeaux was the so-called 100-day rule, which dictated harvesting the grapes 100 days after the flowering. Now, in an effort to make wines full-bodied, richer, and lower in acidity, the 100-day custom has grown to 110 or even 120 days. This new trend in Bordeaux may well result in many more excellent October harvests, such as 1979, than in the past when an October harvest often meant poorer quality.

The climatic patterns leading to excellent vintages for red wines in Bordeaux do not apply to the production of the sweet white wines made in the Sauternes/Barsac region. Great vintages in this region require a combination of misty, humid mornings and dry, sunny afternoons. This daily pattern of climatic events enable the noble rot (botrytis) to begin to develop on the grapes. It is interesting that each grape succumbs to the botrytis infection on a different timetable. Some grapes quickly become totally infected, others not until weeks later. The key to forming the great, luscious, sweet wines in this area is an extended period of alternating humidity and dry heat that permits the botrytis infections to take place. During this period, the château must harvest the infected grapes by hand numerous times if the highest quality is to be achieved, for it is the botrytis infection that causes the remaining grape juice to be intensely concentrated, and imparts to it the distinctive smell and flavor of a late-harvest, decadently rich, sweet wine. Of course, the harvest for the sweet wines of Barsac/Sauternes almost always takes place long after the red wine grapes have been picked and made into wine in the Médoc, Graves, St.-Emilion, and Pomerol. It also occurs when Bordeaux's weather becomes the most risky—late October and November.

A week or more of a deluge can destroy the chances for a successful crop in Sauternes and Barsac. More often than not, the grape crop is damaged by late season rains that wash the noble rot from the grapes, and also cause other grapes to swell, thus diminishing their intensity. In the last twenty years, only 1971, 1975, 1976, 1983, 1986, 1988, and 1989 have been uniformly excellent growing seasons for the sweet wine producers of this region.

THE VINIFICATION AND *ÉLEVAGE* OF BORDEAUX WINES

The production of red wine begins when the freshly harvested grapes are crushed. The steps are as follows: (1) picking, (2) destemming and crushing, (3) pumping into fermentation tanks, (4) fermenting of grape sugar into alcohol, (5) macerating, or keeping the grape skins and pips in contact with the grape juice for additional extract and color, (6) racking, or transferring the wine to small 55-gallon barrels or large tanks for the secondary or malolactic fermentation to be completed, (7) putting the wine in oak barrels for aging, and (8) bottling the wine.

In Bordeaux, the average harvest takes three weeks or more to complete for the dry white and red wines. For the sweet wines, the harvest can take as long as two months to complete. The white wine grapes used for making the dry wines ripen earliest and are picked first. This is followed by the red grape Merlot, and then the other red grape varieties, Cabernet Franc, Cabernet Sauvignon, and lastly, Petit Verdot. The fact that the Merlot ripens earliest makes it an interesting sequence to monitor. In 1964, 1967, and 1987, the châteaux that had extensive plantings of Merlot, primarily those in St.-Emilion and Pomerol, harvested early and their vineyards produced much better wines than the châteaux in the Médoc who had to wait for their Cabernet to ripen and were caught by fall rains. In such a year when significant rains damage the overall crop quality, the early pickers, normally the right-bank communes of St.-Emilion and Pomerol, will have completed most of their harvest. As vintages such as 1964, 1967, and 1987 attest, they may have succeeded brilliantly whereas their counterparts in the Médoc have had to deal with bloated, rain-swollen Cabernet Sauvignon grapes and, therefore, mediocre- or poorer-quality wine.

MAKING
THE RED WINE

When the grapes arrive from the vineyards, few châteaux today still employ the traditional and laborious method of hand sorting them before they go to the destemmer-crusher machine. One major château that continues to adhere to this procedure is Palmer, a third-growth Margaux. Palmer feels hand sorting is mandatory if top-quality wines are to be made.

Most châteaux claim to get the best results by instructing their pickers to remove and discard damaged or unhealthy grape bunches in the vineyard. Certainly the need for careful picking of grapes exists every year, but in vintages where there has been extensive rot in the vineyards, the most reputable châteaux have the pickers make a very severe selection —called a *triage*—in which the damaged berries are removed from each bunch at the time of picking.

The first decision the winemaker must make is whether the grapes are to be partially destemmed or totally destemmed. Today the great majority of the châteaux destem completely. This policy is in keeping with Bordeaux's current passion to make rich, supple wines that can be drunk young, but will age well. Several notable châteaux continue to throw a percentage of stems into the fermentation tank with the crushed grapes. Both Pétrus, which uses between 10% and 30% stems, and Ausone, which uses 20% stems, believe that adding them produces a tougher wine that will age better and longer.

The opponents of adding the stems argue that they add a vegetal coarseness to a wine, soak up some of the color-giving material, and can add too much tannin to the wine.

Once the grapes have been destemmed by an apparatus the French call a *fouloir égrappoir*, the partially crushed berries are pumped into tanks for the commencement of the fermentation.

Today, the trend in Bordeaux is to replace the large, old, oak and cement fermentation vats with stainless-steel, temperature-controlled tanks. They are easy to clean and make it easy to control the temperature, an element that is especially important when the grapes are harvested in torridly hot conditions as in 1982. Despite the increasing numbers of properties that have converted to stainless-steel tanks, the traditional large oak *cuves* and concrete *cuves* are still the most widely used.

Of the most famous Bordeaux properties, Latour, Haut-Brion, and Ausone use stainless steel, Lafite, Mouton, and Margaux use oak, and Cheval Blanc and Pétrus use cement. While stainless steel may be easier to use, great vineyards managed by meticulous winemakers have proven that great wine can be made in oak, cement, or steel fermentation tanks.

Once the grapes have been put into the vat, the wild yeasts that inhabit the vineyard, and in many cases additional cultured yeasts, begin the process called fermentation—the conversion of the grape sugars into alcohol. At this critical point, the temperature of the fermenting juice must be monitored with extreme care, and how hot or how cold the fermentation is affects the resulting style of the wine.

Most Bordeaux winemakers ferment a red wine at 25 to 30 degrees centigrade. Few châteaux allow the temperature to exceed 30 degrees centigrade. Several of those that do include Pétrus, Mouton-Rothschild, Domaine de Chevalier, and Haut-Brion. These properties allow the fermentation to go up to 32 to 33 degrees centigrade. The higher temperatures are aimed at extracting as much color and tannins as possible from the grape skins. The risk of a temperature in excess of 35 degrees centigrade is that acetic bacteria will grow and flourish. It is these acetic bacteria that cause a wine to take on a flawed, vinegary smell. An additional danger of fermentation temperatures in excess of 35 degrees centigrade is that the natural yeasts will be destroyed by the heat, and the fermentation will stop completely, causing what is referred to as a "stuck fermentation." As a general rule, the châteaux that ferment at high temperatures are normally aiming for high-extract, rich, and tannic wines. Those châteaux that ferment at cooler temperatures of 25 degrees centigrade or less usually are trying to achieve a lighter, fruitier, less tannic style of wine. However, for châteaux that ferment at high temperatures, constant vigilance is mandatory.

Fermentation tanks must be watched 24 hours a day, and if a dangerously high temperature is reached, the grape juice must be cooled immediately. With stainless-steel tanks, this can be done rather simply by running cool water over the outside of the tanks. For concrete and wooden tanks, the wine must be siphoned off and run through cooling tubes.

During the vinification, a cap or *chapeau* is formed, as a result of the solid materials, grape skins, stems, and pips rising to the top of the fermentation tank. Winemakers must be careful to keep the cap moist, even submerged in some cases, to encourage additional extractive material to be removed from the color- and tannin-giving skins. Additionally, the cap must be kept wet so as to prevent bacterial growth. The pumping of the fermented wine juice over the cap is called the *remontage* in French and "pumping over the cap" in English.

When the fermentation begins, the winemaker must make another critical decision that will influence the style of the wine: to chaptalize or not. Chaptalization is the addition of sugar to increase the alcohol content. It is employed widely in Bordeaux because this region only occassionally has a vintage where perfect grape ripeness and maturity are obtained. In most years, the grapes do not have sufficient natural sugar content to produce wines with 12% alcohol. Therefore, the Bordeaux châteaux aim to increase the alcohol content by 1–2 degrees. Only in years such as 1961, 1982, 1983, 1985, 1989, and 1990 has little or no chaptalization been necessary because of the superb ripeness achieved by these grapes in those years.

After the total grape sugar (and added sugar if necessary) has been converted to alcohol, the primary or alcoholic fermentation is completed. It is at this stage that another important winemaking decision must be made. The winemaker must decide how long to macerate the grape skins with the wine. The length of the maceration period has a direct bearing on whether the wine will be rich, well colored, tannic, and long lived, or supple, precocious, and ready to drink earlier. At most major Bordeaux châteaux the maceration period is 7–14 days, making the average total time the wine spends in contact with the skins about 21 days. This period is called the *cuvaison*.

Well-known châteaux that adhere to a particularly long *cuvaison* of more than 20–21 days include Pétrus, Trotanoy, Cos d'Estournel, Montrose, Latour, Lafite-Rothschild, Léoville-Barton, and Palmer.

Well-known châteaux that adhere to a particularly short *cuvaison* of less than 15 days include Figeac, Rauzan-Gassies, and Prieuré-Lichine.

Following the *cuvaison*, the infant wine is transferred off its *lees*, which are composed of the grape skins and pips—called the *marc*,—into clean tanks or wood barrels. This free-run juice is called the *vin de goutte*. The skins are then pressed and the resulting press wine, or *vin de presse*, is a heavily pigmented, tannic, chewy, coarse wine that will, in many instances, be eventually blended back into the free-run wine juice. Some winemakers, not wanting a firm, tannic wine, refuse to use any press wine in the blend. Others, who want to add a little muscle and firmness to their wines, will add 10–20%. Some winemakers desirous of a robustly styled, intense wine will blend it all back in with the free-run *vin de goutte*. In most cases, the decision to utilize the press wine is conditioned on the type of wine the vintage produced. In a year such as 1975 or 1982, the addition of press wine would, in most cases, make the wine too tannic and robust. In light vintages where the quality of the free-run juice lacks strength, firmness, and color, for example 1973 and 1980, more of the highly pigmented, tannic press wine will be used.

The secondary fermentation, or malolactic fermentation, in which the tart malic acidity is converted into softer, creamier, lactic acidity, is a gentle step in the evolution of the young red wine. In some châteaux, the malolactic fermentation occurs simultaneously with the alcoholic fermentation, but at most properties the malolactic fermentation takes place over a period of months, usually October following the harvest through the end of January. In certain years, the malolactic fermentation may continue through spring and summer following the vintage, but this is quite unusual. Malolactic fermentation is especially critical for red wines because it adds roundness and character.

The use of new versus old oak barrels for wine aging has been hotly debated in winemaking circles. In Bordeaux, the famous first-growths, —Lafite-Rothschild, Mouton-Rothschild, Latour, Margaux, and Haut-Brion, and the famous trio from the right-bank communes of St.-Emilion and Pomerol, Cheval Blanc, Ausone, and Pétrus—use 100% new oak barrels for virtually every vintage. For the other well-run châteaux, 33%–60% new oak barrels per vintage seems to produce a comfortable marriage of fruit, tannin, and oak. Unquestionably, the higher the percentage of new oak barrels used, the richer the wine must be so as not to be overwhelmed by the oaky, vanillin aromas and flavors. For example, many of the wines from the 1973 and 1980 vintages, which produced light yet fruity wines, were simply not big enough or rich enough wines to handle aging in the new oak barrels they received. New barrels impart a significant tannin content, as well as vanillin oakiness to a wine, and therefore, they must be used judiciously.

One of the side effects of Bordeaux's modern-day prosperity from the success of recent vintages is the tremendous investment in new winery equipment, and, in particular, new barrels. Abuse of new oak can obliterate the fruit of a wine, and while the huge massive fruit and concentration of wines from a vintage like 1982 can easily handle exposure to ample amounts of new oak, my tastings of the more delicate, less intense and concentrated 1981s, and even some 1989s, has frequently left me wondering whether too much new oak cooperage was doing more harm than good. It seems that with many of the estates below the first-growth level now routinely using 50%–75% new oak there is a danger that too many Bordeaux wines are becoming excessively woody. While the use of new oak is recommended and avoids the potential sanitation problems posed by the usage of older barrels, the extremely high yields witnessed in Bordeaux since the mid-1980s and lack of extract in many wines is not fully masked by the gobs of new oak aromas often found in recent Bordeaux vintages.

One of the remarkable aspects of a red Bordeaux wine is its long sojourn in small oak barrels. In most vintages, this period of aging will take from 12 months to as long as 24–30 months. This period of barrel aging has been shortened noticeably over the last several decades. For example, the rich, powerful 1989 vintage may go into the record book for a lot of reasons. It was the earliest vintage since 1893 and the largest crop harvested during the decade of the eighties. However, more interesting is the decision by every château's proprietor, except Philippe Gasqueton of Calon-Ségur and Jean-Michel Arcaute of Clinet, to bottle their wines after only 12–15 months in oak barrels. Is the rush to get the wine in the bottle and to the marketplace becoming an obsession? Bordeaux winemakers have tried to capture more fruit and freshness in their wines, and to reduce the risk of oxidation or overly woody, dry, tannic wines from too much exposure to wood. The great majority of Bordeaux châteaux now bottle their wine in late spring and early summer of the second year after the harvest. For example, the 1980 and 1981 Bordeaux wines were bottled from May through July in 1982 and 1983 respectively. It is rare for a châteaux to bottle in late fall or the following winter, as was the practice 20 years ago. Several prominent châteaux that do bottle later than the others include Lafite-Rothschild, Haut-Brion, Latour, Pétrus, and Calon-Ségur, all of whom rarely bottle (1989 being the exception) unless the wine has had at least 24 months in small oak casks.

The period of cask aging will be shorter in vintages like 1981, 1979, or 1976 where the wines lack great concentration and depth of character, and will be longer in years such as 1975, 1982, 1983, and 1986, where the wines are very full, rich, highly pigmented, and concentrated. The principle is simple: lighter, frailer wines can easily be overwhelmed by oak aging, whereas robust, virile, rich wines need and can take significantly more exposure to oak casks. However, there is no question that the practical and commercial realities of the Bordeaux wine business now dictate that the wine will be bottled within two years of the harvest in all but the most unusual circumstances.

During the aging period in oak barrels, the new wine is racked four times the first year. Racking is an essential step necessary for clarifying the wine. This process involves transferring the clear wine off its deposit or *lees* that have precipitated to the bottom of the barrel. If racking is not done promptly or carefully, the wine will take on a smell of rotten eggs as a result of hydrogen sulfide emissions that come off the *lees*. The rackings are an intensely laborious process, but the French theory is that it is these *lees*, which float in the wines and which eventually fall to the bottom of the barrel, that are the substance and material that give Bordeaux wines their remarkable aromatic and flavor complexity.

One of the most significant new technological developments in this area—and one used now by major Bordeaux châteaux such as Cos d'Estournel, Lynch-Bages, Pichon-Longueville Baron, Cantenac-Brown, Petit-Village, and de Fieuzal—is the filtration of the new wine prior to its placement in barrels. This process, employed widely in California, removes the solids from the wine and results in a clearer wine that needs to be racked significantly less—only one time the first year. The proponents of this process such as Cos d'Estournel's proprietor, Bruno Prats, and Jean-Michel Cazes, proprietor of Lynch-Bages, argue that they get a cleaner, purer wine that does not have to be handled as much, and therefore is less prone to oxidation. They also can get their wine into new oak barrels by the end of October, giving it a 3- to 4-month head start on its neighbors' wines when the critics arrive in April to do their tastings. Wines such as Lynch-Bages and Pichon-Longueville Baron always taste more evolved and flattering. Opponents of such a procedure argue that the process strips the wine of its solids and therefore deprives the wine of the important elements necessary for it to achieve complex aromas and flavors. The critics claim that it is only a labor-saving, cunning procedure designed to make the wine show well at an early stage. Since both Cos d'Estournel and Lynch-Bages make superb wine, the effectiveness of the procedure will be left to determine in due time.

While the red wine rests in barrels, all châteaux carry out another procedure designed to ensure that the wine is brilliant, clean, and free of hazy, suspended colloidal matter when bottled. It is called fining. Fining has traditionally been done with egg whites that function to attract and trap suspended solids in the barrel of wine. They are then dropped to the bottom of the barrel with the other solids that have been precipitated. Wines that are overly fined lose body, length, concentration, and character. Today, fining is often done immediately prior to bottling, in large tanks. Additionally, many châteaux have abandoned the traditional egg whites in favor of more efficacious substances like bentonite and gelatin. In Bordeaux, rarely is a wine fined more than twice for fear of removing too much flavor at the expense of absolute clarity. There is no doubt that too many wines in Bordeaux are excessively fined and stripped of flavor and body.

In addition to the careful vinification and handling of the young red wine, one of the common characteristics at the best-run châteaux in Bordeaux is an extremely rigid selection process for determining which wine will be bottled under the château's name, and which wine will be bottled under a secondary label, or sold in bulk to a cooperative or broker in Bordeaux. The best châteaux make their first selection in the vineyard. For example, the wine from young vines (normally those under 7–8 years old) is vinified separately from the wine from older vines. The difference to even a neophyte taster between wine produced from 25-year-old vines and a wine from 5-year-old vines is remarkable. Young vines may produce a well-colored wine, but the wine rarely has the depth or rich, concentrated character of a wine from older vines. For that reason, the top châteaux never blend in wine from the younger section of the vineyard with the wine from the older vines.

There are a number of châteaux that refuse to discriminate between old and new vines, and the quality of their wines frequently suffers as a result.

In addition to the selection process in the vineyard, the best châteaux also make a strict selection of the finished wine, normally in January or February following the vintage. At this time, the winemaking staff, together with the consulting oenologist, and in many cases the owner, will taste all the different lots of wine produced in the vintage, and then decide which lots or *cuvées* will go into the château's wine, and which lots will be bottled under a secondary label, or sold off in bulk. This procedure is also accompanied by the *assemblage*, wherein the best lots of wine are blended together, including the blending of the different red grape varieties, Merlot, Cabernet Sauvignon, Cabernet Franc, and Petit Verdot. It is no coincidence that the châteaux that make the most severe selections frequently produce the best wines of Bordeaux. Virtually all châteaux make their assemblage in December or January following the vintage.

Unless there is something unusual that occurs in the barrel (a dirty barrel that causes bacterial spoilage is the most common problem) during the aging process, called *élevage*, the wine will be transferred from the barrel to the fermentation tanks, given its last fining, and then bottled at the château.

The idea of exclusively bottling the wine at the château (it is designated on the label with the words *mise en bouteille au château*) is a rather recent development. Until the late sixties, many of the Bordeaux châteaux routinely sent barrels of their wine to brokers in Bordeaux, and merchants in Belgium or England where the wine would be bottled. Such a practice was fraught with the potential not only for fraud, but for sloppy handling of the wine as a result of poor, unsanitary bottling facilities.

Now the châteaux all have modern bottling facilities, and all the classified growths, as well as the great majority of Crus Bourgeois, bottle their own wine. The bottling of the château's entire production in a given vintage can take from one month to almost three months at the largest properties. Yet one of the distinctive characteristics of Bordeaux wine is that each château's production for a given year is bottled within this time frame. This guarantees to the consumer that, given the same treatment and cellar storage, the wine should be relatively consistent from bottle to bottle.

At the time of the bottling operation, the winemaker has one last decision to make that will influence the style (and perhaps the quality) of the wine. More and more châteaux have begun to purchase German-made, sophisticated micropore filter machines to remove any solids or other colloidal particles that may have escaped the various racking procedures and finings. Fortunately, most châteaux continue to filter only by passing the wine through a coarse cellulose filter pad. I know of no serious property that sterile filters their wines. Some châteaux believe that filtration is essential for a healthy, clean bottle of wine, whereas others claim that it is totally unnecessary, and robs and strips the wine of body, flavor, and potential life.

Who is right? There is ample authority to support both sides in the filtration versus nonfiltration argument. Certainly, the current fear on the part of retailers, restaurateurs, wholesalers, importers, and the wine producers themselves that wine consumers think that sediment in a wine is a sign of a flawed wine has tragically caused many châteaux to over-react and run their wines through very fine, tight filters that undoubtedly eviscerate the wine. Fortunately, the major châteaux have been content to do just a slight, coarse polishing filtration, aimed at removing large colloidal suspensions, or have simply refused to filter the wine at all, hoping the fickle consumer will learn one day that a sediment, or *dépôt* as the French say, is in reality one of the healthiest signs in an older bottle of Bordeaux.

Prominent châteaux that adamantly refuse to conduct any type of filtration on their wine include Palmer, Margaux, Latour, Pichon-Longueville–Comtesse de Lalande, Mouton-Rothschild, Montrose, Ducru-Beaucaillou, Grand-Puy-Lacoste, La Conseillante, Clinet, Bon Pasteur, and Léoville-Barton.

Prominent châteaux that now run the wine through a filtration machine prior to bottling include Pétrus, Trotanoy, Ausone, Lynch-Bages, Haut-Brion, Domaine de Chevalier, Cos d'Estournel, Lafite-Rothschild, Gruaud-Larose, Talbot, Branaire, Cheval Blanc, Figeac, Giscours, Brane-Cantenac, Léoville-Poyferré, and Trottevieille.

Since filtration of wine is a relatively recent trend (it came of age in the mid-1970s) in oenology, and since most of the châteaux in both groupings above make excellent wine, only time in the bottle will tell whether filtration robs a wine of richness, complexity, and life as its opponents argue. For the record, if the wine is biologically stable and clear, as are most Bordeaux wines, excessive fining and filtration seems unnecessary. I have done enough blind tastings of filtered versus unfiltered *cuvées* to remain adamantly against the entire process. Anyone who says that filtration removes nothing from an otherwise stable wine is either a fool or a liar.

Once the wine is bottled, the châteaux usually refuse to release the wine for shipment until it has rested for 2–4 months. The theory is that the bottling operation churns up the wine so much that it is shocked, and requires at least several months to recover. My tastings of immediately bottled Bordeaux have often corroborated this fact.

MAKING THE WHITE WINE

The most important consideration when producing the dry white wines of Bordeaux is to retain an element of crispness and freshness in the wines. Otherwise they would taste stale or heavy. No one in Bordeaux has made more progress with white wine vinification than Denis Dubourdieu. It was Dubourdieu, the great white winemaking guru of Bordeaux, who pioneered the use of cold fermentation temperatures (15–17 degrees centigrade) and extended skin contact called *maceration peliculaire*. Because the skins impart the wine's aroma and flavor, this process extracts considerably more fragrance and flavor intensity. These techniques have resulted in a plethora of interesting, tasty, character-filled, dry white wines not only from the prestigious Graves region of Bordeaux, but also from such appellations as the Premières Côtes de Bordeaux and Entre-Deux-Mers.

The style of the wine is also affected by whether it is either vinified and/or aged in stainless-steel tanks or oak barrels. In either case, the winemaker must be careful to guard against oxidation. This is easily done by treating the wine with sulphur dioxide, an anti-oxidant. Most of the high-class white wines, such as Domaine de Chevalier, Haut-Brion-Blanc, Laville-Haut-Brion, and de Fieuzal, clarify the young, grapy white wine by a process known as *debourbage*. More commercially-oriented producers use a centrifuge, or intensely filter the wine after the vinification to clarify it. The more traditional *debourbage*, in my opinion, produces a more complex and interesting wine.

Another of the most crucial decisions made regarding the ultimate style of white Bordeaux is whether or not the wine is allowed to go through a malolactic fermentation. Malolactic fermentation can be encouraged by heating the vats. This process converts higher, sharper malic acids into the softer, creamier malo acids. While most burgundies are put through a malolactic fermentation, Bordeaux wines usually have their malolactic blocked by the addition of sulphur. The numerous low-acid vintages of the eighties have dictated that malolactic be eschewed.

If the wine is stable, most of the dry white wines of Bordeaux tend to be bottled within 3–6 months of the vintage in order to emphasize their freshness and crispness. Those white wines that are meant to be longer-lived and more ageworthy are often kept in new oak casks from one month to as long as 16–18 months (as in the case of the great white wine made at Domaine de Chevalier). All dry white Bordeaux wine is routinely fined and filtered at bottling. Yet producers of wines such as de Fieuzal, Laville-Haut-Brion, Haut-Brion-Blanc, and Domaine de Chevalier process them as minimally as possible for fear of stripping the wines of their aromatic complexity and flavor dimension.

The production of the sweet white wines of Barsac and Sauternes is an even more labor-intensive and risky procedure. The best wines are almost always the result of numerous passes through the vineyard to select only those grapes that have been attacked by the noble rot, *botrytis cinerea* (see page 989). The yields from such selective harvesting (done grape by grape rather than bunch by bunch) are not permitted to exceed 25 hectoliters per hectare, which is well below two tons per acre. Compared to the 80–100 hectoliters per hectare that many of the neighboring red wine producers routinely obtain, the difficult economics of producing a Barsac/Sauternes wine are obvious. Once the botrytized grapes are harvested, the grapes are crushed. The fermentation is allowed to continue until the sugar is converted into a 14–15% alcohol level in the wines. This still leaves unfermented sugar in the wine. The combination of the heady alcohol character with the sweetness of the wine, as well as the distinctive aromas and lavishly rich texture created in part by the botrytis, results in sweet wines that are among the most riveting in the world.

One of the interesting techniques developed in Barsac/Sauternes was the introduction in the late eighties of a procedure called cryo-extraction. This controversial process involves chilling the incoming grapes in order to turn their water into ice particles before pressing, leaving the water behind and increasing the concentration of richness in the grape must.

It has been practiced at such celebrated châteaux as Rayne-Vigneau, Rieussec, and Rabaud-Promis. A cryo-extraction machine even exists at Château Yquem. This procedure, while still in an experimental stage, has yielded impressive early results. Critics who claim that it is simply a labor-saving gimmick may be proven wrong. With cryo-extraction, the botrytis-affected grapes are processed without any potential for dilution because the frozen water is left behind, concentrating the extracted juice to just the essence of the grapes.

After the fermentation, the sweet white wines of the top estates are usually aged in cask, of which a significant percentage is new. At Yquem, the wine is always aged in 100% new oak for at least 3 years. At other top estates, such as Climens and Suduiraut, the percentage of new oak varies from 50–100%. There remain a handful of estates, most notably Gilette, that abhor new oak, yet also produce great wine.

At bottling, most of the sweet wines are fined and lightly filtered, although Yquem, along with neighboring de Fargues and Gilette, continue to bottle their wines after an assemblage without any filtration.

7: A USER'S GUIDE
TO BORDEAUX

CELLARING

Bordeaux, like any fine wine, has to be stored properly if it is to be served in a healthy condition when mature. All wine enthusiasts know that subterranean wine cellars that are vibration free, dark, damp, and kept at a constant 55 degrees Fahrenheit are considered perfect for wine.

However, few of us have our own castle with such accommodations for our beloved wines. While such conditions are the ideal, Bordeaux wines will thrive and develop well in other environments as well. I have tasted many old Bordeaux wines from closet and basement cellars that reach 65 degrees Fahrenheit in the summer, and the wines have been perfect. When cellaring Bordeaux, keep the following rules in mind and you are not likely to be disappointed by a wine that has gone prematurely over the hill.

RULE 1

Do try to guarantee that the wine is kept as cool as possible. The upper safe limit for long-term cellaring of 10 years or more is 65 degrees Fahrenheit, but no higher. Wines kept at such temperatures will age a bit faster but they will not age badly. If you can somehow get the temperature down to 65 degrees or below, you will never have to worry about the condition of your wines. At 55 degrees Fahrenheit—the ideal temperature—the wines actually evolve so slowly that your grandchildren will probably benefit from the wines more than you do. As for temperature, constancy is highly prized and any changes in temperature should occur slowly. As for white wines, they are much more sensitive to less-than-ideal cellar temperatures. Therefore, while the dry white wines of Bordeaux should be kept at temperatures as close to 55 degrees as possible, the bigger, more alcoholic, sweet white wines of Barsac and Sauternes can age quite well at cellar temperatures up to 65 degrees Fahrenheit.

RULE 2

Be sure the storage area is odor free, vibration free, and dark. A humidity level of 50%–80% is ideal. Above 80% is fine for the wine, but the labels will become moldy and deteriorate. A humidity level below 50% can cause the corks to become drier than desired.

RULE 3

Bordeaux wines from vintages that produced powerful, rich, concentrated, full-bodied wines travel and age significantly better than wines from vintages that produced lightweight wines. For example, the oceanic voyage for Bordeaux can be traumatic for wines from vintages such as 1971, 1977, 1976, and 1980. The wines from these vintages—less concentrated, less tannic, and more fragile—often suffer considerably more from travel to this country than big, rich, tannic, full-bodied wines such as 1970, 1975, 1978, 1982, 1983, 1985, 1986, 1988, and 1989. When you decide which Bordeaux wines to cellar, keep in mind that the fragile wines will develop much faster—even under ideal storage conditions.

RULE 4

When buying new vintages of Bordeaux to cellar, I personally recommend buying the wine as soon as it appears on the market, assuming of
course you have tasted the wine and like it. The reason for this is that
few American wine merchants, importers, wholesalers, or distributors
care about how wine is stored. This attitude—that wine is just another
spirit that like whiskey or beer can be left standing upright and exposed
to dramatic extremes of temperature, as well as damaging light—is fortunately changing as more knowledgeable wine people assume positions
of control in major wine shops. However, far too many fine wines are
damaged early in their life by terrible storage conditions, so the only way
a wine enthusiast can prevent such tragedies from happening is to assume custody and control over the wine as early in its life as possible.
This means acting promptly to secure your wines.

SERVING

There are no secrets concerning the formalities of serving Bordeaux. All
one needs is a good corkscrew, a clean, odor-free decanter, and a sense
of order as to how Bordeaux wines should be served and whether the
wine should breathe.

Bordeaux wines do throw a sediment, particularly after they have attained 6 or 7 years of age. This mandates decantation—the procedure
where the wine is poured into a clean decanter to separate the brilliant
wine from the dusty particles that have precipitated to the bottom of the
bottle. First, older bottles of Bordeaux should be removed carefully from
storage so as not to disturb them and make the wine cloudy. Decanting
can be an elaborate procedure, but all one needs is a clean, soap- and
odor-free decanter and a steady hand. If you lack a steady hand, consider
buying a decanting machine, which is a wonderful, albeit an expensive
invention for making decanting fun and easier. Most important of all, be
sure to rinse the decanter with unchlorinated well or mineral water regardless of how clean you think it is. A decanter or a wine glass left
sitting in a china closet or cupboard acts as a wonderful trap for room
and kitchen odors that are invisible, but rear their off-putting smell when

the wine is poured into the decanter or glass. In addition, many glasses have an invisible soapy residue left in them from less-than-perfect dish-washer rinses. I can't begin to tell you how many dinner parties I have attended where the wonderful cedary, blackcurrant bouquet of a 15- or 20-year-old Pauillac was flawed by the smell of dishwasher detergents or some stale kitchen smell that accumulated in the glass between uses.

Assuming that you have poured the wine into a clean decanter, you should also consider the optimal temperature at which the wine should be served, whether you should allow the wine to breathe, and if you are serving several Bordeaux wines, the order of presentment.

The breathing or airing of a Bordeaux wine is rather controversial. Some connoisseurs adamantly claim that breathing is essential, while others claim it is simply all nonsense. Who is right? I have done numer-ous comparisons with wines to see if breathing works or doesn't. I still don't know the answers, if in fact they indeed exist, but here are my observations. The art of decanting a Bordeaux wine is probably all the preserving breathing most wines need. I have found that when serving young, muscular, rich, tannic vintages of Bordeaux, 20–90 minutes of breathing can sometimes result in a softer wine. However, the immediate gush of intense fruitiness that often spills forth when the wine is opened and decanted does subside a bit. So for the big, rich wines of Bordeaux, breathing is often a trade off—you get some softening of the wine, but you also lose some of the wine's fruity aroma.

With lighter-weight, less-tannic Bordeaux wines I have found extended breathing to be detrimental to their enjoyment. Such wines are more fragile and often less endowed, and prolonged breathing tends to cause them to fade. With respect to older vintages of Bordeaux, 15–20 minutes after decantation is usually all that is necessary. With lightweight, older vintages and very, very old vintages, I recommend opening the wine, decanting it, and serving it immediately. Once an old wine begins to fade it can never be resuscitated.

There are always exceptions to such rules and I can easily think of 1945s and even a few 1961s that seemed at their peak 4–5 hours after decantation rather than the 20–25 minutes that I have suggested here. However, it is always better to err on the side of needing more time to breathe and let the guest swirl and aerate the wine in the glass, than to wait too long and then serve a wine that, while magnificently scented when opened and decanted, has lapsed into a dumb comatose state by the time it is served. I have noticed that the more massive 1982s have benefitted from 12–14 hours of airing, but that is probably because of their size and density.

The serving temperature of wine is another critical aspect of presenting Bordeaux. I am always surprised at how many times I am given a great Bordeaux wine that is too warm. Every wine book talks about serving fine red wines at room temperature. In America's overly warm and generously heated dining rooms, room temperature is often 70–75 degrees Fahrenheit, a temperature that no fine red Bordeaux cares for. A Bordeaux served at such a temperature will often taste flat and flabby, and its bouquet will be diffuse and unfocused. The alcohol content will also seem higher than it should. The ideal temperature for red Bordeaux is 65 to 67 degrees Fahrenheit, and for a white Bordeaux 55–60 degrees. If your best wines cannot be served at this temperature, then you are doing them a great injustice. If a red Bordeaux must be put in an ice bucket for ten minutes to lower its temperature, then do it. I have often requested on a hot summer day in Bordeaux or the Rhône Valley to have my Pomerol or Châteauneuf du Pape "iced" for ten minutes rather than drink it at a temperature of 80 degrees Fahrenheit.

Lastly, the effective presentation of Bordeaux wines at a dinner party will necessitate a sense of order. The rules here are easy to follow. Lighter-weight Bordeaux wines or wines from light vintages should always precede richer, fuller wines from great vintages. If such an order is not followed, the lighter, more delicate wines will taste pale after a rich, full-bodied wine has been served. For example, to serve a delicate 1979 Margaux like d'Issan after a 1975 Lafleur would be patently unfair to the d'Issan. Another guideline is to sequence the wines from youngest to oldest. This should not be blindly applied, but younger, more astringent wines should precede older, more mellow, mature wines.

BORDEAUX WITH FOOD

The art of serving the right bottle of Bordeaux with a specific course or type of food has become one of the most overly legislated areas, all to the detriment of the enjoyment of both wine and food. Newspaper and magazine articles, and even books, are filled with precise rules that practically make it a sin not to choose the perfect wine for a particular meal. Thus, instead of enjoying their dinner party, most hosts and hostesses fret, usually needlessly, over choosing the wine. They would be better off to remember the wise advice from a noted French restaurateur, Henri Berau, who stated it best: "The first conditions of a pleasant meal depend, essentially, upon the proper choice of guests."

The basics of the Bordeaux/food matchup game are not difficult to master. These are the tried-and-true, allegedly cardinal principles, such as young wines before old, dry before sweet, white before red, red with meat, and white with fish. However, times have changed, and many of the old shibboleths have disappeared. Today one would not be surprised to hear that a certain variety of edible flower, nasturtiums for example, should be served with a flowery white Graves.

The question one should pose is, does the food offer simple or complex flavors? Two of the favorite grapes of American wine drinkers are Merlot and Cabernet Sauvignon, both of which are able to produce majestic wines of exceptional complexity and depth of flavor. However, as food wines, they are remarkably one-dimensional. As complex and rewarding as they can be, they work well only with dishes that contain relatively simple flavors. Both marry beautifully with basic meat and potato dishes: filet mignon, lamb filets, steaks that are sautéed or grilled. Furthermore, as Cabernet Sauvignon and Merlot-based wines get older and more complex they require increasingly simpler dishes to complement yet not overwhelm their complex flavors. This principle is applied almost across the board in restaurants and dining rooms in Bordeaux. The main courses chosen to show off red wines are usually a simple lamb or beef dish. Thus the principle is: simple wines with complex dishes, complex wines with simple dishes. Richard Olney made this same observation in his classic treatise on food, *The French Menu Cookbook*.

Another question to be posed is, What is the style of wine produced in the vintage that you have chosen? Several of France's greatest chefs have told me they prefer off years of Bordeaux to great years, and have instructed their sommeliers to buy the wines for the restaurant accordingly. Can this be true? From the chef's perspective, the food, not the wine, should be the focal point of the meal. Many chefs feel that a great vintage of Bordeaux, with wines that are exceptionally rich, powerful, alcoholic, and concentrated, not only takes attention away from their cuisine, but makes matching a wine with the food much more troublesome. Thus, chefs prefer a 1987 or 1980 Bordeaux rather than a super-concentrated 1986 or 1982. Curiously, the richest vintages, while being marvelous wines, are not always the best years to choose when considering a food matchup. Lighter-weight yet tasty wines from unexceptional years can complement delicate and understated cuisine considerably better than the great vintages, which should be reserved for very simple food.

THE FRUGAL CONSUMER'S WINE CELLAR (HOW TO PUT TOGETHER AN IMPECCABLE COLLECTION WITHOUT SPENDING MORE THAN $20 A BOTTLE)

The following Bordeaux wines represent what I consider to be the best values in the marketplace. Few cost more than $20 a bottle, based on spring 1991 prices with a dollar that traded for 5.8 francs.

BORDEAUX'S BEST WINE VALUES

ST.-ESTÈPHE—Marbuzet, Meyney, Les-Ormes-de-Pez, Phélan-Ségur, Tronquoy-Lalande

PAUILLAC—Fonbadet, Grand-Puy-Ducasse, Pibran

ST.-JULIEN—Clos du Marquis, Gloria, Hortevie

MARGAUX AND THE SOUTHERN MÉDOC—D'Angludet, La Gurgue, Labegorcé-Zédé

GRAVES—Bahans-Haut-Brion, La Louvière, Picque-Caillou

MOULIS AND LISTRAC—Fourcas-Loubaney, Gressier-Grand-Poujeaux, Maucaillou, Poujeaux

MÉDOC AND HAUT-MÉDOC—Beaumont, Le Boscq, Lanessan, Latour St.-Bonnet, Moulin-Rouge, Potensac, Sociando-Mallet, La Tour de By, Tour Haut-Caussan, Tour du Haut-Moulin, Vieux-Robin

POMEROL—Bonalgue, L'Enclos

ST.-EMILION—Grand-Mayne, Grand-Pontet, Haut-Corbin, Pavie-Macquin

FRONSAC AND CANON-FRONSAC—Canon-de-Brem, Canon (Moueix) de Carles, Cassagne-Haut-Canon-La-Truffière, Dalem, La Dauphine, Fontenil, La Grave, Mazeris, Moulin-Haut-Laroque, Moulin-Pey-Labrie, Du Pavillon, Pez-Labrie, Rouet, La Vieille-Cure

LALANDE DE POMEROL—Bel Air, Bertineau-St.-Vincent, Domaine de Chapelain, Les Hauts-Conseillants, Le Grand-Ormeau, Siaurac

CÔTES DE BOURG—Brûléscailles, Guerry, Haut-Macao, Mercier, Roc des Cambes, Tayac-Cuvée Prestige

CÔTES DE BLAYE—Bertinèrie, Pérenne, La Rose-Bellevue, La Tonnelle

BORDEAUX PREMIÈRES CÔTES AND SUPÉRIEURS—Dudon-Cuvée Jean-Baptiste, La Croix-de-Roche, Fontenille, Haux Frère, Jonquerès, Plaisance, de Plassan, Prieuré-Ste.-Anne, Recougne, Reynon

CÔTES DE CASTILLON—Pitray

BARSAC/SAUTERNES—Bastor-Lamontagne, Doisy-Dubroca, Haut-Claverie, de Malle

LOUPIAC—Bourdon-Loupiac, Clos-Jean, Loupiac-Gaudiet, Ricaud

ENTRE-DEUX-MERS (dry white wines)—Bonnet, Bonnet-Cuvée Réserve, Tertre-Launay, Turcaud

BORDEAUX PREMIÈRES CÔTES AND GENERIC BORDEAUX (dry white wines)—Alpha, Bauduc-Les-Trois-Hectares, Blanc de Lynch-Bages, Caillou Blanc de Talbot, Cayla-Le Grand Vent, Clos-Jean, De la Cloisère du Carpia, Numero 1-Dourthe, Reynon-Vieilles Vignes, Roquefort-Cuvée Speciale, Sec de Doisy-Daëne, Thieuley

BUYING BORDEAUX WINE FUTURES: THE PITFALLS AND PLEASURES

The purchase of wine, already fraught with abundant pitfalls for consumers, becomes immensely more complex and risky when one enters the wine futures' sweepstakes.

On the surface, buying wine futures is nothing more than investing money in a case or cases of wine at a predetermined "future price" long before the wine is bottled and shipped to this country. You invest your money in wine futures on the assumption that the wine will appreciate significantly in price between the time you purchase the future and the time the wine has been bottled and imported to America. Purchasing the right wine, from the right vintage, in the right international financial climate, can represent significant savings. On the other hand, it can be quite disappointing to invest heavily in a wine future only to witness the wine's arrival 12–18 months later at a price equal to or below the future price and to discover the wine to be inferior in quality as well.

For years, future offerings have been largely limited to Bordeaux wines, although they are seen occasionally from other regions. In Bordeaux, during the spring following the harvest, the estates or châteaux offer for sale a portion of their crops. The first offering, or *première tranche*, usually provides a good indication of the trade's enthusiasm for the new wine, the prevailing market conditions, and the ultimate price the public will have to pay.

Those brokers and *négociants* who take an early position on a vintage frequently offer portions of their purchases to importers/wholesalers/retailers to make available publicly as a "wine future." These offerings are usually made to the retail shopper during the first spring after the vintage. For example, the 1990 Bordeaux vintage was being offered for sale as a "wine future" in April 1991. Purchasing wine at this time is not without numerous risks. While 90% of the quality of the wine and the style of the vintage can be ascertained by professionals tasting the wine in its infancy, the increased interest in buying Bordeaux wine futures has led to a soaring number of journalists—some qualified, some not—to judge young Bordeaux wines. The results have been predictable. Many writers serve no purpose other than to hype the vintage as great, and have written more glowing accounts of a vintage than the publicity firms doing promotion for the Bordeaux wine industry.

Consumers should read numerous points of view from trusted professionals and ask the following questions: (1) Is the professional taster experienced in tasting young, as well as old Bordeaux vintages? (2) How much time does the taster actually spend tasting Bordeaux during the year, visiting the properties, and studying the vintage? (3) Does the professional taster express his viewpoint in an independent, unbiased form, free of trade advertising? (4) Has the professional looked deeply at the weather conditions, harvesting conditions, grape variety ripening profiles, and soil types that respond differently depending on the weather scenario?

When wine futures are offered for sale there is generally a great deal of enthusiasm for the newest vintage from both the proprietors and the wine trade. The saying in France that "the greatest wines ever made are the ones that are available for sale" are the words many wine producers and merchants live by. The business of the wine trade is to sell wine, and consumers should be aware that they will no doubt be inundated with claims of "great wines from a great vintage at great prices." This has been used time and time again for good vintages and, in essence, has undermined the credibility of many otherwise responsible retailers, as well as a number of journalists. In contrast, those writers who fail to admit or recognize greatness where warranted are no less inept and irresponsible.

In short, there are only four valid reasons to buy Bordeaux wine futures.

(1) *Are you buying top-quality, preferably superb wine, from an excellent —or better yet, great—vintage?*

No vintage can be reviewed in black-and-white terms. Even in the greatest vintages there are disappointing appellations, as well as mediocre wines. At the same time, vintages that are merely good to very good can produce some superb wines. Knowing who are the underachievers and overachievers is paramount to making an intelligent buying decision. Certainly, when looking at the last twenty years, the only irrefutably great vintages have been 1982 for Pomerol, St.-Emilion, St.-Julien, Pauillac, and St.-Estèphe; 1983 for selected St.-Emilions and Pomerols, as well as the wines from Margaux; 1985 for the wines of Graves; 1986 for the northern Médocs from St.-Julien, Pauillac, St.-Estèphe, and the sweet wines from Barsac/Sauternes; 1989 for selected Pomerols, St.-

Emilions, St.-Juliens, Pauillacs, and St.-Estèphes; and 1990 for the first-growths and a handful of Pomerols and St.-Emilions. There is no reason to buy wines as futures except for the top performers in a given vintage because prices generally will not appreciate in the period between the release of the future prices and when the wines are bottled. The exceptions are always the same—top wines and great vintages. If the financial climate is such that the wine will not be at least 25–30% more expensive when it arrives in the marketplace, then most purchasers are better off investing their money elsewhere.

Recent history of the 1975 and 1978 Bordeaux future offerings provides a revealing prospectus to "futures" buyers. Purchasers of 1975 futures did extremely well. When offered in 1977, the 1975 future prices included $140–$160 per case for such illustrious wines as Lafite-Rothschild and Latour, and $64–$80 for second-growths, including such proven thoroughbreds as Léoville-Las Cases, La Lagune, and Ducru-Beaucaillou. By the time these wines had arrived on the market in 1978, the vintage's outstanding and potentially classic quality was an accepted fact, and the first-growths were retailing for $325–$375 per case; the lesser growths, $112–$150 per case. Buyers of 1975 futures have continued to prosper, as this vintage is now very scarce and its prices have continued to escalate to $900–$1,200 a case for first-growths, and $350–$550 for second- through fifth-growths. In 1991, the 1975 prices have come to a standstill because of doubts about how gracefully many of the wines are evolving. I would not be surprised to see some prices even drop—another pitfall that must always be considered.

The 1978 Bordeaux futures, offered in 1980, present a different picture: 1978 was another very good vintage year, with wines similar in style but less intense than the excellent 1970 vintage. Opening prices for the 1978 Bordeaux were very high, and were inflated because of a weak dollar abroad and an excessive demand for the finest French wines. Prices for first-growths were offered at $429–$499, prices for second-through fifth-growths at $165–$230. Consumers who invested heavily in Bordeaux have purchased good wine, but when the wines arrived on the market in spring 1981, the retail prices for these wines were virtually the same as future price offerings. Thus consumers who purchased 1978 futures and invested their money to the tune of 100% of the case price could have easily obtained a better return by simply investing in any interest-bearing account.

With respect to the vintages 1979, 1980, 1981, 1982, 1983, and 1985, the only year that has represented a great buy from a "futures" perspective was 1982. The 1980 was not offered to the consumer as a wine future because it was of mediocre quality. As for the 1979 and 1981, the enthusiast who purchased these wines on a future basis no doubt was able, within two years after putting his or her money up, to buy the wines when they arrived in America at approximately the same price. While this was not true for some of the highly rated 1981s, it was true for the 1979s. As for the 1982s, they have jumped in price at an unbelievable pace, outdistancing any vintage in the last twenty years. The first-growths of 1982 were offered to consumers in late spring 1983 at prices of $350–$450 for wines like Lafite-Rothschild, Latour, Mouton-Rothschild, Haut-Brion, and Cheval Blanc. By March 1985, the Cheval Blanc had jumped to $650–$800, the Mouton to $800–$1,000, and the rest to $700. Today, prices for first-growths range from a low of $1,200 a case for Haut-Brion, to $1,800–$2,000 a case for any of the three Pauillac first-growths. This is a significant price increase for wines so young, but it reflects the insatiable worldwide demand for a great vintage. Rare, limited-production wines, for instance the Pomerols, have also skyrocketed in price. Pétrus has clearly been the top performer in terms of escalating prices; it jumped from an April 1983 future price of $600 to a 1991 price of $5,000. This seems absurd given the fact that the wines will not be close to maturity for a decade. Other top 1982 Pomerols such as Trotanoy, Certan de May, and L'Evangile have doubled and tripled in price. Trotanoy, originally available for $280, now sells (when you can find it) for at least $1,000. Certan de May has jumped from $180–$750, as has L'Evangile.

The huge demand for 1982 Bordeaux futures and tremendous publicity surrounding this vintage have led many to assume that subsequent years would similarly escalate in price. That has not happened, largely because Bordeaux has had too many high-quality, abundant vintages in the decade of the eighties. The only exceptions have been the 1986 first-growths that continue to accelerate because they are great, long-lived, so-called classic vintage wines.

(2) *Do the prices you must pay look good enough that you will ultimately save money by paying less for the wine as a future than for the wine when it is released in 2–3 years?*

Many factors must be taken into consideration to make this determination. In certain years, Bordeaux may release wines at lower prices than it did the previous year (the most recent examples are 1986 and 1990). There is also the question of the international marketplace. In 1991 the American dollar is beginning to rebound but is still generally weak, not to mention the fact that our country is still mired in a recession. Other significant Bordeaux buying countries, such as England, have unsettled and troublesome financial problems as well. Even France is beginning to enter a recession, at least according to all the financial experts. Newer marketplaces, such as Japan, are experiencing financial apprehension and increasing banking problems. Even Germany, which has become such a major Bordeaux player, has experienced an economic downspin because of the financial ramifications of trying to revitalize the moribund economy of East Germany. Consequently, the saturated marketplace is a matter of fact. The only three countries that appear to have sound economies and are in healthy enough economic positions to afford top-class Bordeaux are Belgium, Denmark, and Switzerland. These factors change, but the international marketplace, the perceived reputation of a given vintage, and the rarity of a particular estate all must be considered before deciding whether the wine will become much more expensive when released than its price when offered as a wine future.

(3) *Do you want to be guaranteed of getting top, hard-to-find wine from a producer with a great reputation who makes only small quantities of wine?*

Even if the vintage is not irrefutably great, or you cannot be assured that prices will increase, there are always a handful of small estates, particularly in Pomerol and St.-Emilion, that produce such limited quantities of wine, and who have worldwide followers, that their wines warrant buying as futures if only to reserve a case from an estate whose wines have pleased you in the past. In Pomerol, limited-production wines such as Le Pin, Clinet, La Conseillante, L'Evangile, Le Fleur de Gay, Lafleur, Gombaude-Guillot, and Bon Pasteur have produced many popular wines during the decade of the eighties, yet are very hard to find in the marketplace. In St.-Emilion, some of the less-renowned, yet modestly sized estates such as L'Angélus, L'Arrosée, Canon, Grand-Mayne, Pavie-Macquin, La Dominique, Le Tertre-Roteboeuf, and Troplong-Mondot produce wines that are not easy to find after bottling. Consequently, their admirers throughout the world frequently reserve and pay for these wines as futures. Limited-production wines from high-quality estates merit buying futures even in good to very good years.

(4) *Do you want to buy wine in half bottles, magnums, double magnums, jeroboams, or imperials?*

Frequently overlooked as one of the advantages of buying wine futures is that you can request that your merchant have the wines bottled to your specifications. There is always a surcharge for such bottlings, but if you have children born in a certain year, or you want the luxury of buying half bottles (a size that makes sense for daily drinking), the only time to do this is when buying the wine as a future.

Lastly, should you decide to enter the futures market, be sure you know the other risks involved. The merchant you deal with could go bankrupt, and your unsecured sales slip would make you one of probably hundreds of unsecured creditors of the bankrupt wine merchant hoping for a few cents on your investment. Another risk is that the supplier the merchant deals with could go bankrupt or be fraudulent. You may get a refund from the wine merchant, but you will not get your wine. Therefore, be sure to deal only with a wine merchant who has dealt in selling wine futures before and one who is financially solvent. And finally, buy wine futures only from a wine merchant who has received confirmed commitments as to the quantities of wine he or she will receive. Some merchants sell Bordeaux futures to consumers before they have received commitments from suppliers. Be sure to ask for proof of the merchant's allocations. If you do not, then the words *caveat emptor* could have special significance for you.

For many Bordeaux wine enthusiasts, buying wine futures of the right wine, in the right vintage, at the right time guarantees that they have liquid gems worth four or five times the price they paid for the wine. However, as history has proven, only a handful of vintages over the last twenty years have appreciated that significantly in their first two or three years. The situation in 1991, with a highly saturated marketplace and a bevy of top vintages in the pipeline, has lessened the need to buy wine futures, unless, of course, you desire one of the limited-production wines, or want to take advantage of buying wines in half bottles, magnums, or larger formats.

8: A VISITOR'S GUIDE TO BORDEAUX

HOTELS AND RESTAURANTS

MÉDOC

Pauillac—**L'Hotel France et Angleterre** (30 miles from downtown Bordeaux)

3 Quai Albert Pichon; Tel.—56.59.01.20; Fax—56.59.01.89

Twenty rooms for about $60 a person. Ask for a room in the annex, which is more quiet. The restaurant is surprisingly good with a competent wine list.

Pauillac—**Château Cordeillan Bages** (adjacent to Lynch-Bages on the south side of Pauillac next to D2)

Tel.—56.59.24.24; Fax—56.59.01.89

The deluxe restaurant, hotel, and wine school of Jean Michel Cazes, the proprietor of Lynch-Bages. The excellent restaurant boasts a stupendous wine list and the hotel is quiet and spacious. This is the place to stay and eat when visiting châteaux in St.-Julien, Pauillac, and St.-Estèphe. Expect to pay $125–$150 per night for lodging and approximately the same for dinner for two.

Margaux—**Relais de Margaux** (14 miles from downtown Bordeaux)

Tel.—56.88.38.30; Fax—56.88.31.73

A luxury hotel with 28 rooms for $150–$175 that has had ups and downs since opening in the mid-eighties. Rooms are splendid, the cooking overpriced, contrived, and inconsistent. The wine selection is good, but the mark-ups of 200%–400% are appalling.

Arcins—**Lion d'Or** (in the village next to D2)

Tel.—56.58.96.79

Jean-Paul Barbier's roadside restaurant in Arcins (several miles north of the village of Margaux) has become one of the hottest eating spots in the Médoc. Barbier, an enthusiastic chef of some talent, encourages clients to bring their own bottles to complement his rustic, country cooking. Portions are generous, the restaurant noisy, and if you bring a good bottle or you are with a well-known proprietor, chances are Barbier will be at your side most of the night. This is a fun place with surprisingly good food, but if you are looking for a quiet, relaxing evening, Lion d'Or is not the place. Who can resist the idea of doing your own comparative tasting with such local specialties as shad in cream sauce and the famous lamb from Pauillac? Prices are moderate.

Gaillan-en-Médoc—**Château Layauga** (2 miles from Lesparre)

Tel.—56.41.26.83; Fax—56.41.19.52

This charming restaurant (there are also 7 attached rooms), which was coming on strong in the late eighties, earned its first star from the Guide Michelin in 1991. The cooking is excellent, featuring many wonderful fish courses, as well as local specialties such as the lamb of Pauillac and the famed *lamproie* Bordelais (eels cooked in their own blood). As reprehensible as that may sound, I find this dish superb, and one of the few fish courses that works sensationally well with a big, rich bottle of red Bordeaux.

BORDEAUX

Hotel Burdigala, 115 Rue Georges Bonnac; Tel.—56.90.16.16; Fax—56.93.15.06

This is one of Bordeaux's newest hotels and the "in" spot for many business travelers. There are 71 rooms and 7 suites, an excellent restaurant, and the location in the center of the city, not far from the Place Gambetta, is ideal. Prices are $125–$150 a night.

Hotel Normandie, 7 Cours 30 Juillet; Tel.—56.52.16.80; Fax—56.51.68.91

Located several blocks from the opera and Maison du Vin in the center of the city, the Hotel Normandie has always been the top spot for visiting wine writers because of its ideal location just off the Allées de Tourny. The three leading Bordeaux wine shops are within a three-minute walk. The rooms are spacious but clearly not as modernly equipped as the newer hotels. There is a certain charm about the Hotel Normandie, but if you have a car, parking in this area is often troublesome. Rates ($50–$80 a night) for one of the 100 rooms at the Normandie make it one of the best values in Bordeaux.

Hotel Sainte-Catherine, 27 Rue Parlement Ste.-Catherine; Tel.—56.81.95.12

Not as well known as many others, this lovely, moderately sized hotel with rooms that cost about $100 a night is located in the middle of the city. For those looking for privacy and anonymity, this discrete hotel is a good choice.

Le Chapon Fin, 5 Rue Montesqieu; Tel.—56.79.10.10; (Chef Garcia)

One of the finest restaurants in France, it has always puzzled me as to why Chef Garcia has not received a second star in Guide Michelin. Admittedly, I am unable to eat here anonymously, and perhaps see better service than a stranger off the street. I have enjoyed extraordinary food from Garcia everywhere he has been. He was the force that resurrected the reputation of the Pessac restaurant/hotel La Reserve before he moved across from Bordeaux's train station and opened Clavel. He is now in the famous turn-of-the-century grotto-like restaurant, Le Chapon Fin just off the Place des Grands Hommes. The ambiance is superb, the wine list excellent, and the cooking outstanding. Garcia is a generous chef and I have never left his restaurant without a feeling of total satisfaction. Prices are high, but not unreasonable. Le Chapon Fin is closed on Sunday and Monday.

La Chamade, 20 Rue Piliers de Tutelle; Tel.—56.48.13.74 (Chef Carrère)

This basement restaurant in the old section of Bordeaux, just a few minutes' walk from the Place de la Bourse, consistently turns out fine cooking. It is one of my favorite places to eat on Sunday evening, when just about every other restaurant in the city has shut down. If you visit La Chamade, do not miss the superb first-course called "Salade de Chamade." La Chamade's prices are moderately expensive.

Le Rouzic, 34 Cours Chapeau Rouge; Tel.—56.44.39.11 (Chef Gautier)
Reservations are essential at this excellent restaurant as it accommodates less than 40 people. The cooking is a blend of traditional Bordeaux classics and imaginative newer-styled juxtapositions. Do not miss anything that involves Chef Gautier's specialties—lobster, sweetbreads, and lamb. Prices are moderately expensive; two dinners plus a bottle of wine will cost between $100–$150.

Jean Ramet, 7 Place J. Jaurès; Tel.—56.44.12.51 (Chef Ramet)
Jean Ramet's tiny restaurant located just down the street from the Grand Theater, near the Gironde, just past the Place J. Jaurès, should not be missed. The cooking merits two, perhaps even three stars, but Ramet will never receive them because of the miniscule size of the restaurant, which seats only 27 people. Ramet and his wife run the restaurant with a staff of nine—one for every three clients. Ramet, who apprenticed under such great chefs as Pierre Troigros and Michel Guerard, is a wizard. I cannot recommend this moderately expensive restaurant enough. The Jean Ramet restaurant is closed Saturday and Sunday.

La Tupina, 6 Rue Porte de la Monnaire; Tel.—56.91.56.37 (Chef Xiradakis)
This moderately priced restaurant in the old city is run by one of Bordeaux's great characters, Jean-Pierre Xiradakis. He is unquestionably a wine enthusiast, but his first love is his restaurant, which features the cooking of southwestern France. Consequently, expect to eat rich, heavy, abundant quantities of food such as duck and foie gras. The wine list focuses on high-quality, little-known producers and there is also a selection of rare Armagnacs. The restaurant, which is difficult to find, is located near the Cathedral of Ste.-Croix, between the Rue Sauvageau and the riverside Quai de la Monnaie.

Le Pavillon des Boulevards, 120 Rue Croix de Seguey; Tel.—56.81.51.02 (Chef Franc)
This relative newcomer burst on the scene in the late eighties and has become one of the Bordeaux's hottest new restaurants. The cooking tends to reflect an oriental influence and those who have

tired of nouvelle cuisine will find Pavillon des Boulevards a bit too precious. But the undeniable talent of Chef Franc is evident in every dish served. Prices are moderately expensive.

Le Mably, 12 Rue Mably; Tel.—56.44.30.10

This old-fashioned, pink-enameled, wood-paneled bistro in the center of town offers hearty portions of grilled meats and fowl. There is little ambiance, but hearty, straightforward cooking is available at surprisingly low prices.

Chez Philippe, 1 Place des Parlement; Tel.—56.81.83.15 (Chef Philippe)

If you are in the mood for seafood, Chez Philippe is a good choice. Some may complain about the high prices, but there is no doubt that when it comes to fish—particularly the local specialties that include the abundant oysters from Arcachon, lamproie, the baby eels called *Les piballes*, daurade, sardines, or just superb filet of sole—this charming restaurant, outfitted like the interior of a boat —is not to be missed.

Clement-Dubern, 42 Allées Tourny; Tel.—56.48.03.44 (Chef Clement)

I have always had mixed feelings about this restaurant located on one of the most fashionable streets of Bordeaux. There is, no doubt, considerable talent in the kitchen, but there has always been an unevenness and inconsistency that I find perplexing. I have had excellent, as well as disappointing meals at Clement-Dubern. Prices are moderately high.

THE SUBURBS OF BORDEAUX

Bordeaux Le Lac—(10 minutes from the city center)

Hotel Sofitel Aquitania, Tel.—56.50.83.80; Fax—56.39.73.75
Hotel Novotel, Tel.—56.50.99.70; Fax—56.43.00.66

I have spent a considerable amount of my lifetime at the Hotel Sofitel Aquitania and Hotel Novotel. Bordeaux Le Lac, an ambiance-free commercial center just north of Bordeaux, is an ideal lodging spot, particularly if you have a car. The hotels offer antiseptic rooms with hot running water, telephones, and fax machines that work. Sofitel Aquitania is more expensive, costing $100–$125 a night, whereas the Novotel is about $90–$100 a night. Both have similar rooms, although the Sofitel does offer mini-bars. Both have hassle-free parking, which I consider to be of considerable importance. They also are good choices as the Médoc, Pomerol, and St.-Emilion are only 20 minutes away.

Bouliac—(a 20-minute drive from Bordeaux)

Le St.-James, Place C. Holstein; Tel.—56.20.52.19; Fax—56.20.92.58 (Chef Amat)

For the last decade, Le St.-James, run by the idiosyncratic Chef Amat, has been considered the best restaurant in the Bordeaux region. It is the only Bordeaux restaurant to have two stars in the Guide Michelin and the inspired, eccentric cooking of Amat wins rave reviews also from the Gault-Millau Guide. I have had some remarkable courses, but having eaten there over a dozen times over the last decade, I have also had disappointing courses, as well as listless, unenthusiastic service. Frankly, I find the restaurant overrated, too expensive, and I am still not used to the sommelier drinking at least three or four ounces of one's bottle of wine to "test it." Nevertheless, there is immense talent in the kitchen. If Amat's mental attitude is correct, then one can be tantalized by some of his courses. A luxury hotel has recently been opened nearby. Prices are extremely high. For infrequent visitors to Bordeaux, the best way to get to Bouliac is to take one of the bridges across the Garonne, immediately picking up D113 south. Within 4 or 5 miles, signs for Bouliac and Le St.-James restaurant should be visible on your left.

Pessac—(a 10-minute drive from the city center)

Hotel La Reserve, Ave., Bourgailh; Tel.—56.07.13.28; Fax—56.07.13.28

When Chef Garcia was at La Reserve it was the finest restaurant in the region. However, he left and its reputation fell because of inattention to detail, and for much of the decade of the eighties La Reserve has been trying to regain its standing. The tranquil setting in the woods makes it an ideal place to stay if you are visiting the nearby Château Haut-Brion or La Mission-Haut-Brion. It is also a good location if you want to be close to the city of Bordeaux and have immediate access to the region of Barsac/Sauternes, or the other Graves estates. Rooms average $125–$150 per night. Although there are signs that the restaurant is coming back, it is still far behind the other top Bordeaux restaurants. La Reserve is reached by taking exit 13 off the beltway that encircles the northern, western, and southern sides of Bordeaux. The hotel is well marked once you leave the beltway.

Langon—(30 miles south of Bordeaux)

Claude Darroze, 95 Cours General Leclerc; Tel.—56.63.00.48; Fax.—56.63.41.15; (Chef Darroze)

Some of the finest meals I have eaten in France have been at the superb restaurant, Claude Darroze, located in the center of Langon. Langon is a good place to stop if you are visiting the châteaux of Barsac/Sauternes. Of primary importance is the superb quality of Darroze's cooking, and there are also 16 rooms, reasonably priced at about \$60–\$75 a night. Darroze's cooking emphasizes foie gras, truffles in season, and excellent lamb and fish. It is a rich, highly imaginative style of cooking that clearly merits the two stars it has earned from the Guide Michelin. The wine list is also super, as well as reasonably priced. Should you be an Armagnac lover, the finest Bas-Armagnacs from Darroze's brother, Francis Darroze, are available, going back to the beginning of this century. Prices are a steal given the quality of these rare items. If you are driving from Bordeaux, the best way to get to Claude Darroze is to take the autoroute (A62), exit at Langon, and follow the signs for "Centre Ville." You cannot miss Darroze's restaurant/hotel once you are in the center of the city.

Langoiran—(25 minutes from downtown Bordeaux)

Restaurant Saint-Martin, (located directly on the Garonne River) Tel.—56.67.02.67

If you are looking for a tiny, charming restaurant/hotel in an historic village that few people other than the locals know about, consider eating and staying at the Restaurant Saint-Martin. Located on the Garonne, the food is country French, but imaginative, well pre-pared, and moderately priced. The wine list is excellent. To reach Langoiran, take autoroute A62, exit at Labrede, and follow the signs and Route 113 to Portets and then turn left, following the signs for Langoiran. This charming, quiet village is reached by a frightfully ancient bridge over the Garonne. Rooms are bargain priced at \$45–\$60 a night.

St.-Emilion—(24 miles east of Bordeaux)

Hotel Plaisance, Place Clocher; Tel.—57.24.72.32; Fax—57.74.41.11

This is the leading hotel in the fascinating walled town of St.-Emilion, which gets my vote as the most interesting and charming area in the entire Bordeaux region. The hotel is situated on the Place Clocher, overlooking the hilly town. The comfortable rooms are priced between \$100–\$150. The restaurant serves fine food and of course the wine list is chock full of St.-Emilions. My only objec-tion to Hotel Plaisance is the relatively chilly greeting one receives from the proprietors.

St.-Emilion—**Logis des Remparts,** Rue Guadet; Tel—57.24.70.43

There is no restaurant, but this is a fine hotel if you cannot get into the Hotel Plaisance. There are 15 rooms that range in price from \$50–\$80.

St.-Emilion—**Logis de la Cadène,** Place Marché au Bois; Tel.—57.24.71.40

Run with great enthusiasm by the Chailleau family, this is my favorite restaurant in the city of St.-Emilion. Situated just down the hill from the Hotel Plaisance, Logis de la Cadène serves up copious quantities of robust bistro food. The wine list is interesting, but the real gems here are the numerous vintages of Château La Clotte, the Grand Cru Classé St.-Emilion that is owned by the restaurant owners. One of the better St.-Emilions, it is rarely seen in the export market because so much of the production is consumed on the premises of this eating establishment. Prices are moderate.

Bourg-Blaye—**Hotel La Citadelle;** Tel.—57.42.17.10; Fax—57.42.10.34 Monsieur Chaboz runs this superbly situated hotel with an unsurpassed view of the Gironde. The hotel is in the historic citadelle of Blaye. The restaurant serves up well-prepared, reasonably priced local specialties. The 21 rooms are a bargain (how many foreigners pass through Blaye?) at $50–$60 a night. There is also a tennis court and a swimming pool.

ROMANTIC AND HEDONISTIC EXCURSIONS

Brantome—(about 60 miles northeast of Bordeaux)
Moulin de L'Abbaye; Tel.—53.05.80.22; Fax—53.05.75.27
Take plenty of money to this splendidly situated old mill located along the side of an easy-flowing river in the beautiful town of Brantome in the heart of the Dordogne. Brantome is a good two hours from Bordeaux, but it is a beautiful scenic drive when you cross over the Garonne and take N89 through Libourne, past the vineyards of Pomerol and Lalande-de-Pomerol in the direction of Perigeux. Once in Perigeux, Brantome is only 15 minutes away. There are only nine rooms (costing about $175 a night) and three apartments in the gorgeous Moulin de L'Abbaye. The food is excellent, occasionally superb. My main objection is that the wine list is absurdly expensive.

Champagnac de Belair—(two hours from Bordeaux)

Moulin du Roc; Tel.—53.54.80.36; Fax—53.54.21.31

Three miles northeast of Brantome, off of D78, is the quaint village of Champagnac de Belair and another ancient mill that is built over a meandering river. This is the most romantic hotel and restaurant in the region. For those special occasions, or just a sublime night away, ask for one of the four apartments in the Moulin du Roc. It will cost you close to $200 a night, but it is a magnificent setting and the charm and tranquility of this establishment, run with perfection by Madame Gardillou, is unsurpassed. The food is superb, though extremely expensive. Only the wine list leaves me less than excited because of its outrageously high prices. Nevertheless, even that can be overlooked when eating and sleeping in paradise.

Eugénie Les Bains—(a 2 hour drive south of Bordeaux)

Les Prés d'Eugénie; Tel.—58.05.06.07; Fax—58.51.13.59 (Chef Guérard)

If I had one last meal to eat, I would be hard pressed not to have it at this magnificent establishment located several hours south of Bordeaux. The nearest town is Mont-de-Marsan, which is approximately 18 miles to the north. Michel Guérard is an internationally famous chef, and his restaurant has long been one of the renowned three-star eating establishments in France. There are many three-star restaurants that I would downgrade to two stars, and there are others that are so superb one wonders why the Guide Michelin does not create a four-star category. The latter is the case at Les Prés d'Eugénie where innovation, originality, and quality all come together with the formidable talents of Michel Guérard to create what are some of the most remarkable dishes my wife and I have ever eaten. Huge quantities of money are necessary to enjoy the food, but the 28-room hotel has surprisingly fair prices, averaging $200–$225 a night. Should you want to splurge, there are apartments that cost $350–$400 a night. If you have the time, money, and appetite, try to have at least two meals from this genius.

Arcachon—(36 miles west of Bordeaux)

Arc Hotel sur Mer; Tel.—56.83.06.85; Fax—56.83.53.72

Le Nautique, 20 Bord de la Plage; Tel.—56.83.01.48; Fax—56.83.04.67

Thirty-six miles west of Bordeaux is the seaside resort town of Arcachon. The easiest way to get there is by taking the autoroute A63 south from Bordeaux and then picking up A66 directly into Arcachon. Another route is RN250 that runs directly from Bordeaux to Arcachon. The two hotels above have excellent locations on the beach, modern accommodations, and reasonable prices of $70–$90 a night. I do not know the restaurants in Arcachon to the extent that I do those in the vineyard areas and Bordeaux itself, but I have enjoyed fine meals at **Chez Yvette**, 59 General Leclerc, Tel. —56.83.05.11. This is a place to order fish and the superb oysters that come from the nearby oyster beds.

OTHER DIVERSIONS

WINE SHOPS

Bordeaux—**L'Intendant,** 2 Allées de Tourny; Tel.—56.48.01.29

Buying Bordeaux either from the châteaux or in the city itself is usually far more expensive than buying the same wines in the United States. However, it is always interesting to see the wine selection in shops in another country. Bordeaux boasts L'Intendant, the most architecturally stunning wine shop I have ever seen. Furthermore, its selection of Bordeaux wines is exceptional. Located on the luxury shopping street, Allées de Tourny (just across from the Grand Theatre), it offers an extraordinary number of wines as well as many old vintages. Just visiting the shop is a must because of its fabulous design and spiral staircase. Bordeaux wine enthusiasts will require at least an hour to view the incredible selection. It is one of the greatest wine shops, not only in France, but in the world—exclusively for Bordeaux.

Bordeaux—**Badie,** 62 Allés de Tourny; Tel.—56.52.23.72

Badie, situated several blocks away from L'Intendant, has the same owners, but the selection is not so comprehensive. But it is still a fine shop that is renowned for its values and knowledgeable staff.

Bordeaux—**La Vinotheque,** 8 Cours du 30 Juillet; Tel.—56.52.32.05

La Vinotheque offers relatively high prices for decent wines, as well as a plethora of wine accessories, but it is overshadowed by L'Intendant, Badie, and Bordeaux Magnum.

Bordeaux—**Bordeaux Magnum,** 3 rue Godineau; Tel.—56.48.00.06
Bordeaux Magnum does not specialize so much in larger-format bottlings such as magnums, but in high-class Bordeaux wines.

BOOK SHOPS, ETC.

Bordeaux—**Librairie Mollat,** 15 Rue Vital-Carles; Tel.—56.56.40.40
One of the greatest book shops in France, the Librairie Mollat is located in the old city on one of the walking streets. Its collection of wine books is extraordinary. Just about anything you could ever want in terms of literature is available at Mollat. The collection of English books is limited.

Bordeaux—**Virgin Megastore,** Place Gambetta; Tel.—56.56.05.70
This high-tech, state-of-the-art shop is a must for those looking for that rare compact disk or wine book. The Bordelais, who are proud to have the second Virgin shop (the first is on the Champs L'Eysées in Paris), make this one of the most heavily trafficked spots in all of Bordeaux. The shop includes a small cafeteria that serves surprisingly good food and great coffee.

VISITING BORDEAUX CHATEAUX

When visiting Bordeaux, I recommend that someone in your party be able to speak a little French. Most of the big-name Bordeaux châteaux now have someone working there who speaks English, but do not count on many châteaux other than first-growths or super seconds having anyone who speaks much English.

For getting the maximum out of your visit, you should write directly for an appointment or ask your local wine merchant to have an importer set up an appointment for you.

If planning a program for visiting the Bordeaux châteaux, you should remember that four full visits a day are probably the maximum. Unless you and your travel mates are true aficionados, four a day is probably too many. In deciding which châteaux to visit, you should always arrange visits at châteaux that are close to each other. For example, if you want to visit Château Margaux at 9:30 A.M., you should allow 45–60 minutes for a visit, as well as a 30- to 35-minute car drive from downtown Bordeaux. It is also advisable to schedule only one other visit that morning, preferably in the commune of Margaux. If you schedule an appointment in Pauillac or St.-Estèphe for 11:00 A.M., the 30- to 40-minute drive north from Margaux to either of these two appellations would probably make you late for your appointment. Remember, the French are far more respectful of appointment hours than most Americans tend to be and it is an insult not to arrive on time.

The following are several recommended itineraries that include visits to the most interesting properties and allow sufficient time to do so. You can expect to taste the two youngest vintages on your visit, but do not hesitate to ask to sample a recent vintage that has been bottled. Unless you are a Hollywood superstar, it is unlikely that anything older than 4–5 years will be opened. A visit generally involves a tour of the château, a tour of the cellars, and then a short tasting. Spitting the wine out is not only permissible, but is expected. Normally you spit in small buckets filled with sawdust. In some of the state-of-the-art tasting rooms that have been constructed at the châteaux, huge, modern tasting spitoons are available.

Must visits in the Médoc are Mouton-Rothschild with its splendid museum, Prieuré-Lichine, the home of the late Alexis Lichine and the only château open seven days a week, and of course, any property of which you have numerous vintages squirreled away in your cellar.

Some important things to remember are that Bordeaux, as elsewhere in France, takes a two-hour lunch between 12:00 and 2:00 P.M., which means you will not be able to see any properties during that time. Secondly, very few châteaux receive visitors during the harvest. During the decade of the eighties the harvests have tended to be relatively early because of the hot summers. In general harvests can be expected to occur between mid-September and mid-October.

RECOMMENDED ITINERARIES

Itinerary I (Margaux)

8:45 A.M.—Leave Bordeaux
9:30 A.M.—Château Giscours
10:30 A.M.—Château Margaux
2:00 P.M.—Château Palmer
3:30 P.M.—Prieuré-Lichine
Note: Have lunch at the Lion d'Or
    in Arcins, a tiny village several
    miles north of Margaux.

Itinerary II (Pauillac)

8:15 A.M.—Leave Bordeaux
9:30 A.M.—Château Latour
11:00 A.M.—Château Pichon-
    Longueville–Comtesse de
    Lalande
2:00 P.M.—Château Lynch-Bages
3:30 P.M.—Château Pichon-
    Longueville Baron
5:00 P.M.—Château Mouton-
    Rothschild
Note: Take your lunch at the
    restaurant Cordeillan-Bages,
    just south of the town of
    Pauillac and only 5 minutes
    from any of these châteaux.

Itinerary III (St.-Julien)

8:30 A.M.—Leave Bordeaux
9:30 A.M.—Château Beychevelle
11:00 A.M.—Château Ducru-
    Beaucaillou
2:00 P.M.—Château Talbot
3:30 P.M.—Château Léoville-Las
    Cases
Note: Lunch at Cordeillan-Bages.

Itinerary IV (St.-Estèphe and Pauillac)

8:15 A.M.—Leave Bordeaux
9:30 A.M.—Château Lafite-
    Rothschild
11:00 A.M.—Château Cos
    d'Estournel
2:00 P.M.—Château Montrose
3:30 P.M.—Château Calon-Ségur
Note: It is preferable to stay at
    Cordeillan-Bages in Pauillac
    when visiting St.-Estèphe, St.-
    Julien, and Pauillac.

Itinerary V (Graves)
8:30 A.M.—Leave Bordeaux
9:30 A.M.—Châteaux Haut-Brion
and La Mission-Haut-Brion
11:00 A.M.—Château Pape-
Clément
2:30 P.M.—Domaine de
Chevalier
4:00 P.M.—Haut-Bailly
Note: Have lunch at La Reserve
in Pessac, which can also be
utilized as your hotel if you
want to save 15–20 minutes of
travel time from Bordeaux.

Itinerary VII (St.-Emilion)
8:30 A.M.—Leave Bordeaux
9:30 A.M.—Château Cheval
Blanc
11:00 A.M.—Château Couvent des
Jacobins
2:00 P.M.—Château Ausone and
Belair
3:00 P.M.—Château Pavie
Note: Have lunch at either the
Hotel de Plaisance or Logis de
la Cadène. If you stay at a hotel
in St.-Emilion, the time to reach
any St.-Emilion or Pomerol
estate is less than 10 minutes.

Itinerary VI (Barsac/Sauternes)
8:30 A.M.—Leave Bordeaux
9:30 A.M.—Château Yquem
11:00 A.M.—Château Suduiraut
2:00 P.M.—Château Rieussec
3:00 P.M.—Château Climens
Note: Have lunch at the great
restaurant Claude Darroze in
Langon. If you decide to lodge
at Darroze's restaurant/hotel,
travel time to any of the
Sauternes properties is less
than 15 minutes.

Itinerary VIII (Pomerol)
8:30 A.M.—Leave Bordeaux
9:30 A.M.—Château Pétrus
11:00 A.M.—Vieux-Château-
Certan
2:00 P.M.—Château de Sales
3:30 P.M.—Château La
Conseillante
Note: Lunch in St.-Emilion at La
Plaisance or Logis de la
Cadène. If you stay in St.-
Emilion, travel time to Pétrus,
or any of the Pomerol estates, is
less than 10 minutes.

When arriving in Bordeaux, the Maison du Vin, 1 Cours 30 Juillet, tel. —56.52.82.82, in downtown central Bordeaux is a good place to pick up information on Bordeaux wine regions in addition to some decent maps.

If you want to write directly to the châteaux to make an appointment, you can use a format similar to the following letters, one in French and one in English. To address the letter, just put the name of the château, its commune, and zip code. The major châteaux zip codes are as follows:

for châteaux in St.-Estèphe   —33250 Saint-Estèphe, France
for châteaux in Pauillac   —33250 Pauillac, France
for châteaux in St.-Julien   —Saint-Julien-Beychevelle
    33250 Pauillac, France

for châteaux in Margaux	—33460 Margaux, France
for châteaux in Graves (Pessac)	—33602 Pessac, France
for châteaux in Graves (Léognan)	—33850 Léognan, France
for châteaux in Sauternes	—33210 Langon, France
for châteaux in Barsac	—Barsac 33720 Podensac, France
for châteaux in St.-Emilion	—33330 Saint-Emilion, France
for châteaux in Pomerol	—33500 Pomerol, France

These zip codes will cover a great majority of the châteaux, but some of the major properties are controlled by *négociants* or brokers, and it is better to write directly to the *négociant* to request an appointment at one of their château. The following are the addresses for the top *négociants* that own some of the major Bordeaux châteaux.

The Cordier firm—for visiting Talbot, Gruaud-Larose, Meyney, Cantemerle, Lafaurie-Peyraguey, and Clos des Jacobins, send a letter to: La Maison Cordier, 10 Quai de Paludate, 33800 Bordeaux, France.

The Moueix firm—For visiting Pétrus, Trotanoy, Magdelaine, La Fleur Pétrus, Latour à Pomerol, and la Grave Trigant de Boisset, send a letter to: La Maison Jean-Pierre Moueix, 34 Quai du Priourat, 33500 Libourne, France.

RECOMMENDED FORM LETTER
(ENGLISH VERSION)

To: Château Margaux
   33460 Margaux, France
re: Visit

To Whom It May Concern:

I would like to visit Château Margaux on Monday, March 14, 1992, to see the winemaking facilities and receive a tour of the château. If possible, I would like to be able to taste several recent vintages of Château Margaux. if this is agreeable, I will arrive at the château at 9:30 A.M. on Monday, March 14.

I realize that you are busy, but I am an admirer of your wine and it would be a great pleasure to visit the property. I look forward to hearing from you.

Sincerely,

Cher Monsieur ou Chère Madame,

Je suis un très grand admirateur de vos vins et je serais très reconnaissant si vous me permettriez de visiter Château XYZ

lundi	le _____	janvier	, 1992.
mardi		fevrier	
mercredi		mars	
jeudi		avril	
vendredi		mai	
		juin	
		juillet	
		août	
		septembre	
		octobre	
		novembre	
		décembre	

Si possible, je voudrais bien aussi faire une dégustation des derniers 2 millésimes de votre vin.

Merci en avance, en attendant votre réponse et avec mes meilleurs sentiments.

Your signature

9: A GLOSSARY OF WINE TERMS

acetic—Wines, no matter how well made, contain quantities of acetic acid. If there is an excessive amount of acetic acid, the wine will have a vinegary smell.

acidic—Wines need natural acidity to taste fresh and lively, but an excess of acidity results in an acidic wine that is tart and sour.

acidity—The acidity level in a wine is critical to its enjoyment and livelihood. The natural acids that appear in wine are citric, tartaric, malic, and lactic. Wines from hot years tend to be lower in acidity, whereas wines from cool, rainy years tend to be high in acidity. Acidity in a wine preserves the wine's freshness and keeps the wine lively.

aftertaste—As the term suggests, the taste left in the mouth after one swallows is the aftertaste. This word is a synonym for length or finish. The longer the aftertaste lingers in the mouth (assuming it is a pleasant taste), the finer the quality of the wine.

aggressive—Aggressive is usually applied to wines that are either high in acidity or harsh tannins, or both.

angular—Angular wines are wines that lack roundness, generosity, and depth. Wine from poor vintages or wines that are too acidic are often described as being angular.

aroma—Aroma is the smell of a young wine before it has had sufficient time to develop nuances of smell that are then called its bouquet. The word aroma is commonly used to mean the smell of a relatively young, unevolved wine.

astringent—Wines that are astringent are not necessarily bad or good wines. Astringent wines are harsh and coarse to taste, either because they are too young and tannic and just need time to develop or because they are not well made. The level of tannin in a wine contributes to its degree of astringence.

austere—Wines that are austere are generally not terribly pleasant wines to drink. An austere wine is a hard, rather dry wine that lacks richness and generosity. However, young, promising Bordeaux can often express itself as austere, and aging of such wine will reveal a wine with considerably more generosity than its youthful austerity suggested.

balance—One of the most desired traits in a wine is good balance, where the concentration of fruit, level of tannin, and acidity are in total harmony. Well-balanced wines are symmetrical and tend to age gracefully.

barnyard—An unclean, farmyard, fecal aroma that is imparted to a wine because of unclean barrels or generally unsanitary winemaking facilities.

berrylike—As this descriptive term implies, wines, particularly Bordeaux wines that are young and not overly oaked, have an intense berry fruit character that can suggest blackberries, raspberries, black cherries, mulberries, or even strawberries and cranberries.

big—A big wine is a large-framed, full-bodied wine with an intense and concentrated feel on the palate. Bordeaux wines in general are not big wines in the same sense that Rhône wines are, but the top vintages of Bordeaux produce very rich, concentrated, deep wines.

blackcurrant—A pronounced smell of the blackcurrant fruit is commonly associated with red Bordeaux wines. It can vary in intensity from faint to very deep and rich.

body—Body is the weight and fullness of a wine that can be sensed as it crosses the palate. Full-bodied wines tend to have a lot of alcohol, concentration, and glycerine.

Botrytis cinerea—The fungus that attacks the grape skins under specific climatic conditions (usually interchanging periods of moisture and sunny weather). It causes the grape to become superconcentrated because it causes a natural dehydration. Botrytis cinerea is essential for the great sweet white wines of Barsac and Sauternes.

bouquet—As a wine's aroma becomes more developed from bottle aging the aroma is transformed into a bouquet, which is hopefully more than just the smell of the grape.

brawny—A hefty, muscular, full-bodied wine with plenty of weight and flavor, although not always the most elegant or refined sort of wine.

briary—I usually think of California Zinfandel rather than Bordeaux when the term briary comes into play. Briary denotes that the wine is aggressive and rather spicy.

brilliant—Brilliant relates to the color of the wine. A brilliant wine is one that is clear, with no haze or cloudiness.

browning—As red wines age, their color changes from ruby/purple, to dark ruby, to medium ruby, to ruby with an amber edge, to ruby with a brown edge. When a wine is browning it is usually fully mature and is not likely to get better.

cedar—Bordeaux reds often have a bouquet that suggests either faintly or overtly the smell of cedarwood. It is a complex aspect of the bouquet.

chewy—If a wine has a rather dense, viscous texture from a high glycerine content it is often referred to as being chewy. High-extract wines from great vintages can often be chewy.

closed—The term closed is used to denote that the wine is not showing its potential, which remains locked in because it is too young. Young Bordeaux often close up about 12–18 months after bottling, and depending on the vintage and storage conditions, remain in such a state for several years to more than a decade.

complex—One of the most subjective descriptive terms used, a complex wine is a wine that the taster never gets bored with and finds interesting to drink. Complex wines tend to have a variety of subtle scents and flavors that hold one's interest in the wine.

concentrated—Fine wines, whether they are light, medium or full bodied, should have concentrated flavors. Concentrated denotes that the wine has a depth and richness of fruit that gives it appeal and interest. Deep is a synonym of concentrated.

corked—A "corked" wine is a flawed wine that has taken on the smell of cork as a result of an unclean or faulty cork. It is perceptible in a bouquet that shows no fruit, only the smell of a musty cork or damp cardboard.

decadent—If you are an ice cream and chocolate lover, you know the feeling of eating a huge sundae lavished with hot fudge, real whipped cream, and rich vanilla ice cream. If you are a wine enthusiast, a wine loaded with opulent, even unctuous layers of fruit, with a huge bouquet, and a plump, luxurious texture can be said to be decadent.

deep—Essentially the same as concentrated, the word deep expresses the fact that the wine is rich, full of extract, and mouth filling.

delicate—As this word implies, delicate wines are light, subtle, understated wines that are prized for their shyness rather than extroverted robust character. White wines are usually more delicate than red wines.

diffuse—Wines that smell and taste unstructured and unfocused are said to be diffuse. Often when red wines are served at too warm a temperature they become diffuse.

dumb—A dumb wine is also a closed wine, but the term dumb is used in a more pejorative sense. Closed wines may only need time to reveal their richness and intensity. Dumb wines may never become any better.

earthy—This term may be used in both a negative and a positive sense; however, I prefer to use earthy to denote a positive aroma of fresh, rich, clean soil. Earthy is a more intense smell than woodsy or truffle scents.

elegant—Although more white wines than red are described as being elegant, lighter-styled, graceful, well-balanced Bordeaux wines can be elegant.

exuberant—Like extroverted, somewhat hyper people, wines too can be gushing with fruit, and seem nervous and intensely vigorous.

fat—When Bordeaux gets a very hot year for its crop, and the wines attain a super sort of maturity, they are often quite rich and concentrated with low to average acidity. Often such wines are said to be fat, which is a prized commodity. If they become too fat, that is a flaw and they are then called flabby.

flabby—A wine that is too fat or obese is a flabby wine. Flabby wines lack structure and are heavy to taste.

fleshy—Fleshy is a synonym for chewy, meaty, or beefy. It denotes that the wine has a lot of body, alcohol, and extract, and usually a high glycerine content. Pomerols and St.-Emilions tend to be fleshier wines than Médocs.

floral—With the exception of some Sauternes, I rarely think of Bordeaux wines as having a floral or flowery aspect to their bouquets or aromas. However, wines like Riesling or Muscat do have a flowery component.

focused—Both a fine wine's bouquet and flavor should be focused. Focused simply means that the scents, aromas, and flavors are precise and clearly delineated. If they are not, the wine is like an out-of-focus picture: diffuse, hazy, and problematic.

forward—A wine is said to be forward when its charm and character are fully revealed. While it may not be fully mature yet, a forward wine is generally quite enjoyable and drinkable. Forward is the opposite of backward.

fresh—Freshness in both young and old wines is a welcome and pleasing component. A wine is said to be fresh when it is lively and cleanly made. The opposite of fresh is stale.

fruity—A very good wine should have enough concentration of fruit so that it can be said to be fruity. Fortunately, the best Bordeaux wines will have more than just a fruity personality.

full-bodied—Wines rich in extract, alcohol, and glycerine are full-bodied wines.

green—Green wines are wines made from underripe grapes, and lack richness and generosity as well as having a vegetal character. Green wines were often made in Bordeaux in poor vintages such as 1972 and 1977.

hard—Wines with abrasive, astringent tannins or high acidity are said to be hard. Young vintages of Bordeaux can be hard, but they should never be harsh.

harsh—If a wine is too hard it is said to be harsh. Harshness in a wine, young or old, is a flaw.

hedonistic—Certain styles of wine are meant to be inspected and are more introspective and intellectual wines. Others are designed to provide sheer delight, joy, and euphoria. Hedonistic wines can be criticized because in one sense they provide so much ecstasy they can be called obvious, but in essence, they are totally gratifying wines meant to fascinate and enthrall—pleasure at its best.

herbaceous—Many wines have a distinctive herbal smell that is generally said to be herbaceous. Specific herbal smells can be of thyme, lavender, rosemary, oregano, fennel, or basil.

hollow—A synonym for shallow; hollow wines are diluted and lack depth and concentration.

honeyed—A common personality trait of sweet Barsacs and Sauternes, a honeyed wine is one that has the smell and taste of bees' honey.

hot—Rather than mean that the temperature of the wine is too warm to drink, hot denotes that the wine is too high in alcohol and therefore leaves a burning sensation in the back of the throat when swallowed. Wines with alcohol levels in excess of 14.5% are often hot.

jammy—When Bordeaux wines have a great intensity of fruit from excellent ripeness they can be jammy, which is a very concentrated, flavorful wine with superb extract. In great vintages such as 1961 and 1982, some of the wines are so concentrated that they are said to be jammy.

leafy—A leafy character in a wine is similar to a herbaceous character only in that it refers to the smell of leaves rather than herbs. A wine that is too leafy is a vegetal or green wine.

lean—Lean wines are slim, rather streamlined wines that lack generosity and fatness but can still be enjoyable and pleasant.

lively—A synonym for fresh or exuberant, a lively wine is usually a young wine with good acidity and a thirst-quenching personality.

long—A very desirable trait in a fine Bordeaux is that it be long in the mouth. Long (or length) relates to a wine's finish, meaning that after you swallow the wine, you sense its presence for a long time. (Thirty seconds to several minutes is great length.)

lush—Lush wines are velvety, soft, richly fruity wines that are both concentrated and fat. A lush wine can never be an astringent or hard wine.

massive—In great vintages where there is a high degree of ripeness and superb concentration, some wines can turn out to be so big, full-bodied, and rich that they are called massive. Great wines, such as the 1961 Latour and Pétrus and the 1982 Pétrus, are textbook examples of massive wines.

meaty—A chewy, fleshy wine is also said to be meaty.

mouth-filling—Big, rich, concentrated wines that are filled with fruit extract and are high in alcohol and glycerine are wines that tend to texturally fill the mouth. A mouth-filling wine is also a chewy, fleshy, fat wine.

nose—The general smell and aroma of a wine as sensed through one's nose and olfactory senses is often called the wine's nose.

oaky—Most top Bordeaux wines are aged from 12 months to 30 months in small oak barrels. At the very best properties, a percentage of the oak barrels are new, and these barrels impart a toasty, vanillin flavor and smell to the wine. If the wine is not rich and concentrated, the barrels can overwhelm the wine, making it taste overly oaky. However, when the wine is rich and concentrated and the winemaker has made a judicious use of new oak barrels, the results are a wonderful marriage of fruit and oak.

off—If a wine is not showing its true character, or is flawed or spoiled in some way, it is said to be "off."

overripe—An undesirable characteristic; grapes left too long on the vine become too ripe, lose their acidity, and produce wines that are heavy and imbalanced. This happens much more frequently in hot viticultural areas than in Bordeaux.

oxidized—If a wine has been excessively exposed to air during either its making or aging, the wine loses freshness and takes on a stale, old smell and taste. Such a wine is said to be oxidized.

peppery—A peppery quality to a wine is usually noticeable in many Rhône wines, which have an aroma of black pepper and a pungent flavor. It occasionally appears in some Bordeaux wines.

perfumed—This term usually is more applicable to fragrant, aromatic white wines than to red Bordeaux wines. However, some of the dry white wines and sweet white wines can have a strong perfumed smell.

plummy—Rich, concentrated wines can often have the smell and taste of ripe plums. When they do, the term plummy is applicable.

ponderous—Ponderous is often used as a synonym for massive, but in my usage a massive wine is simply a big, rich, very concentrated wine with balance, whereas a ponderous wine is a wine that has become heavy and tiring to drink.

precocious—Wines that mature quickly—as well as those wines that may last and evolve gracefully over a long period of time, but taste as if they are aging quickly because of their tastiness and soft, early charms—are said to be precocious.

pruney—Wines produced from grapes that are overripe take on the character of prunes. Pruney wines are flawed wines.

raisiny—Late-harvest wines that are meant to be drunk at the end of a meal can often be slightly raisiny, which in some ports and sherries is desirable. However, in dry Bordeaux wines a raisiny quality is a major flaw.

rich—Wines high in extract, flavor, and intensity of fruit are described as being rich.

ripe—A wine is ripe when its grapes have reached the optimum level of maturity. Less than fully mature grapes produce wines that are underripe, and overly mature grapes produce wines that are overripe.

round—A very desirable character of wines, roundness occurs in fully mature Bordeaux that have lost their youthful, astringent tannins, and also in young Bordeaux that are low in tannin and acidity and are meant to be consumed young.

savory—A general descriptive term that denotes that the wine is round, flavorful, and interesting to drink.

shallow—A weak, feeble, watery or diluted wine lacking concentration is said to be shallow.

sharp—An undesirable trait; sharp wines are bitter and unpleasant with hard, pointed edges.

silky—A synonym for velvety or lush; silky wines are soft, sometimes fat, but never hard or angular.

smoky—Some wines, either because of the soil or because of the barrels used to age the wine, have a distinctive smoky character. In Bordeaux, some of the Graves wines occasionally are smoky.

soft—A soft wine is one that is round and fruity, low in acidity, and has an absence of aggressive, hard tannins.

spicy—Wines often smell quite spicy with aromas of pepper, cinnamon, and other well-known spices. These pungent aromas are usually lumped together and called spicy. Scents and flavors of Oriental spices refer to wines that have aromas and/or flavors of soy sauce, ginger, hoisin sauce, and sesame oil.

stale—Dull, heavy wines that are oxidized or lack balancing acidity for freshness are called stale.

stalky—A synonym for vegetal, but used more frequently to denote that the wine has probably had too much contact with the stems and the result is a green, vegetal, or stalky character to the wine.

supple—A supple wine is one that is soft, lush, velvety, and very attractively round and tasty. It is a highly desirable characteristic as it suggests that the wine is harmonious.

tannic—The tannins of a wine, which are extracted from the grape skins and stems, are, along with a wine's acidity and alcohol, its lifeline. Tannins give a wine firmness and some roughness when young, but gradually fall away and dissipate. A tannic wine is one that is young and unready to drink.

tart—Sharp, acidic, lean, unripe wines are called tart. In general, a red Bordeaux that is tart is not pleasurable.

thick—Rich, ripe, concentrated wines that are low in acidity are often said to be thick.

thin—A synonym for shallow, a thin wine is an undesirable characteristic meaning that the wine is watery, lacking in body, and just diluted.

tightly knit—Young wines that have good acidity levels, good tannin levels, and are well made are called tightly knit, meaning they have yet to open up and develop.

toasty—A smell of grilled toast can often be found in wines because the barrels the wines are aged in are charred or toasted on the inside.

tobacco—Many red Graves wines have the scent of fresh burning tobacco. It is a distinctive and wonderful smell in wine.

unctuous—Rich, lush, intense wines with layers of concentrated, soft, velvety fruit are said to be unctuous. In particular, the sweet wines of Barsac and Sauternes are unctuous.

vegetal—An undesirable characteristic; wines that smell and taste vegetal are usually made from unripe grapes. In some wines a subtle vegetable garden smell is pleasant and adds complexity, but if it is the predominant characteristic, it is a major flaw.

velvety—A textural description and synonym for lush or silky, a velvety wine is a rich, soft, smooth wine to taste. It is a very desirable characteristic.

viscous—Viscous wines tend to be relatively concentrated, fat, almost thick wines with a great density of fruit extract, plenty of glycerine, and high alcohol content. If they have balancing acidity, they can be tremendously flavorful and exciting wines. If they lack acidity, they are often flabby and heavy.

volatile—A volatile wine is one that smells of vinegar as a result of an excessive amount of acetic bacteria present. It is a seriously flawed wine.

woody—When a wine is overly oaky it is often said to be woody. Oakiness in a wine's bouquet and taste is good up to a point. Once past that point the wine is woody and its fruity qualities are masked by excessive oak aging.

INDEX

Robert Parker gave up a career in law to devote himself full time to evaluating and writing about wine. In 1978 he founded *The Wine Advocate*. He lives with his wife, Pat, daughter, Maia, and various basset hounds in the countryside of northern Maryland.

Much of the material in this book is based upon tastings and research done in conjunction with the publishing of *The Wine Advocate*, an independent consumer's guide to fine wines, which is issued six times a year. A one-year subscription to *The Wine Advocate* costs $35.00, and interested readers may obtain a free sample copy of *The Wine Advocate* or a subscription by writing to *The Wine Advocate*, P.O. Box 311, Parkton, Maryland 21120 or send fax to 301-357-4504.